PENGUIN BOOKS

THE RELIGIONS OF INDIA

Roshen Dalal was born in Mussoorie and studied in various schools across the country. After a BA (Hons) in history from the University of Bombay, she completed an MA and PhD in ancient Indian history from Jawaharlal Nehru University, New Delhi. She has taught at both school and university, and been involved in research in the fields of history, religion and philosophy, and education. Apart from books, she has written numerous articles and book reviews. After working for many years as an editor, she is now a full-time writer, living in Dehradun.

ALSO BY ROSHEN DALAL

The Vedas: An Introduction to Hinduism's Sacred Texts

Hinduism: An Alphabetical Guide

The Illustrated Timeline of the History of the World

The Puffin History of India, Vols 1 and 2

The Puffin History of the World, Vol. 1

THE
RELIGIONS
OF
INDIA

ROSHEN DALAL

A CONCISE GUIDE
TO NINE MAJOR FAITHS

PENGUIN BOOKS

An imprint of Penguin Random House

PENGUIN BOOKS

USA | Canada | UK | Ireland | Australia
New Zealand | India | South Africa | China | Singapore

Penguin Books is part of the Penguin Random House group of companies
whose addresses can be found at global.penguinrandomhouse.com

Published by Penguin Random House India Pvt. Ltd
4th Floor, Capital Tower 1, MG Road,
Gurugram 122 002, Haryana, India

Penguin
Random House
India

First published by Penguin Books India 2006
Revised edition published by Penguin Books India 2010
This edition published 2014

To my Mother Nergis Dalal

ISBN 9780143423164

Typeset in ITC Stone by InoSoft Systems, Noida
Printed at Repro India Limited

www.penguin.co.in

MIX
Paper from
responsible sources
FSC® C047271

This is a legitimate digitally printed version of the book and therefore might not
have certain extra finishing on the cover.

Introduction

Religion is an integral part of life in India, where nine major religions, along with several other beliefs, coexist with the highest and most complex philosophies.

This book is the result of years of reading and study, accompanied by inner reflection and thought. It reflects the ideas of the greatest thinkers and spiritual leaders of India, who saw that all religions are different aspects of One Truth, and that a truly religious person can never be divisive. From the sages of the Upanishads, to the Bhakti saints, the Sufi mystics, and the spiritual gurus of more recent times, they all emphasize the Oneness of life and the sense of universal love that underlies every spiritual experience.

The quotes given below are a few examples of thousands of similar sayings:

'God has no country, dress, form, limit or hue. God is omnipresent, his universal love is everywhere.' (Guru Gobind Singh, *Jap Sahib*)

'In every age and dispensation all Divine Ordinances are changed and transformed according to the requirements of time, except the law of love.' (Bahaullah)

'I have come to light the lamp of Love in your hearts, to see that it shines day by day with added lustre. I have not come on behalf of any religion.' (Sathya Sai Baba, 4 July 1968)

Recognizing that all religions, spirituality and philosophy represent One Truth, each religion, sect and group has equal importance in this book. However, there is no one religion that is the sole representative of Truth, or has all the answers.

'Truth cannot be shut up in a single book, Bible or Veda or Quran, or in a single religion. The Divine Being is eternal and universal and infinite,' says Sri Aurobindo, and adds, 'All religions have some truth in them, but none has the whole truth; all are created in time and finally decline and perish.' (*The Integral Yoga: Selected Letters*, p. 352) This can clearly be seen in India, where so many religious beliefs coalesce, and where religions change over time, and are re-created, emerging in different forms.

There are several different approaches to religion, including the sociological approach, the Marxist approach, the psychoanalytical approach, as well as the anthropological, historical and phenomenological approaches. In a descriptive book of this kind, it is not possible to use any one approach, or to go into extensive analyses. In general, this book explains religion in a historical and social context, and looks at the ways in which religion is practised. It incorporates philosophy, ethics, deities, rituals, beliefs, myths and legends. It examines the expression of religion in material form, as images, and in temples, mosques and other religious monuments. It emphasizes the spiritual essence behind all forms.

The sources for the study of religion are immense. They include artefacts and material remains, discovered through archaeological explorations and excavations; texts of all kinds, beginning with the Rig Veda; coins, seals and inscriptions; sculptures, images, and various extant structures.

The religions

Each of these religions is equally vast but in this book the nine religions and other miscellaneous beliefs dealt with are approximately proportionate to the number of their followers, and their significance and antiquity within India. For worldwide religions such as Christianity, Islam and Judaism, apart from some basic principles, the emphasis is on the specific nature of the religion within India. For Buddhism, which originated in India but then spread to other parts of the world, the focus is on its origin, growth and decline within India, and its re-introduction in the last two centuries.

Hinduism is the most widely prevalent religion, practised in most parts of India. It has a wide variety of beliefs and practices, with some common underlying concepts. In India, even adherents of other religions accept some of its basic principles such as karma and reincarnation. Included within the broad framework of Hinduism are the six ancient philosophies of Nyaya, Vaisheshika, Mimamsa, Yoga, Samkhya and Vedanta.

Jainism has ancient origins, but emerged in its present form in the sixth century BCE. With its emphasis on non-violence and asceticism, and its unique method of philosophical analysis, it has an important role in India.

Buddhism originated in India, and after a period of decline, is reviving. It spread to different parts of the world, and the Buddhism of Tibet has returned to India over the last fifty years. Buddhist concepts of compassion and social equality are important in the India of today, while the visual imagery and esoteric philosophy of Tibetan Buddhism are slowly becoming known.

Islam was known in India from the seventh century, but gained prominence with the advent of Islamic kings and dynasties. Sufis and other saints of Islamic origin are revered by all communities, and the influence of Islam can be seen in some of the sects of medieval days. There were once a number of syncretic cults, particularly in rural areas, where the differences between Islam and Hinduism were blurred, and even today some of these continue to exist.

Sikhism originally arose in the fifteenth century with aspects of both Hinduism and Islam, though it gradually grew closer to Hinduism. The concept of a formless God, and of an active life in the world, rather than an ascetic life of retreat, are among its many contributions.

Christianity is said to have existed in India from the first century CE, but became more widespread after the sixteenth century. Its emphasis on helping and serving disadvantaged groups has had an impact in India, with other religious groups incorporating these principles.

Judaism is thought to have been in India from ancient days. After 1948, most of the Jews in India migrated to Israel. However, new groups are emerging, claiming Jewish ancestry.

Bahais became prominent in the twentieth century. Though official figures do not reflect this, India perhaps has the largest number of Bahais in any country in the world.

Zoroastrianism, despite the small number of its followers, is important for two reasons. Firstly, there are similarities between the *Gathas*, the earliest Zoroastrian text, and the Rig Veda. Secondly, after the migration of Zoroastrians to India in the eighth century and later, India is the country where Zoroastrian beliefs and practices are best preserved.

Tribal religions are many and varied, and only a small sample could be included in this book. They are not so different from the major religions, each believing in a creator god or a creator couple, and incorporating myths and stories on the creation of the world.

Other: There are other systems of belief and philosophies, materialistic schools of thought, ancient sects that no longer exist, and modern philosophers who cannot be placed in any category.

Different aspects

The dictionary looks at several different aspects of these religions. Among them are:

Sacred geography: Sacred geography is a well-known aspect of ancient religions. A place of exceptional beauty, a mountain peak, a waterfall, or any unique natural phenomenon, was once considered sacred all over the world. The gods were thought to dwell in these places and spiritual power was thought to be contained in them. India has preserved these ancient traditions, and mountains, rivers, trees, and other aspects of nature are still invested with sanctity. Some of the sacred rivers, streams, plants and mountain peaks are described in this book.

Animals, birds, snakes, aquatic creatures: All living creatures are considered aspects of the divine, particularly in Hinduism, Buddhism and Jainism, and animals, birds and other creatures are also represented in this book.

Places: In India, there is probably not a single village, town or city without a place of worship. Large cities have monuments representing all religions; other cities usually have Hindu and Jain temples, mosques, gurdwaras and churches, and sometimes Buddhist stupas. Small towns have monuments representing two or three religions, while the smallest village has at least one temple or other religious structure. In addition there are places which are specifically associated with a particular religion, such as Bodh Gaya with Buddhism. Out of these millions of places, a few which have widespread religious significance have been chosen for this book. For some of the places, only the more important religious significance has been mentioned. For instance, Ajmer is primarily associated with the Dargah of the Sufi saint Muinuddin Chisti and Kurukshetra with the Bhagavad Gita.

Religious monuments: There are thousands of religious monuments in India. The territory of Delhi has over 8000 religious structures, whereas a small state like Kerala has more than 10,000 temples. The monuments chosen for this book are therefore those which are specially popular today, or those which are historically or architecturally significant.

Ideas, concepts and terms: This book looks at a number of different ideas and concepts, and explains the ways in which certain terms are used. It includes topics related to philosophy, logic and methods of analysis, as well as cosmic and real time, and great and vast ages.

Deities: Deities in India reflect every aspect of form and belief. All major deities have been described in this book, as well as several others; deities of south India have been given equal importance as those from north India. Local deities are innumerable. Practically every village has its own deity or set of deities, apart from those more widely worshipped, and only a few of these could be included here. Semi-divine beings, yakshas, nagas, asuras, daityas, rakshasas, etc., are also described.

Texts: There are thousands of religious texts in India. These include Sanskrit texts, texts in Pali, in various Prakrits, in Arabic, Persian and Urdu, in regional languages, and in English. New texts are constantly being written. Major texts have separate entries in this book, while several others are mentioned.

Legends and myths: Myths, legends and religious stories are found in all texts, in Sthala Puranas of temples, and in oral tradition. There is no one version of a myth or legend; a different account can be found in each text, and many more in local stories. Those narrated and analysed in this book represent some of the commonly accepted versions.

Festivals: Hundreds of festivals take place in India every year. The main festivals have been described here, as well as some local festivals. At one time there was much syncretic worship and deliberate attempts to tolerate and participate in rituals and festivals of other communities. Such participation still takes place, but has reduced.

Saints and gurus: There are innumerable saints and gurus in India, both in the past and in the present. Saints of any kind are revered by people of all religions. It is impossible to include them all, and the choice has to be selective. Choosing from gurus of present times is particularly difficult; a few of those who are known worldwide have been selected.

Dates: Dates of texts, saintly figures and founders of philosophies in ancient days are usually controversial. In this book dates accepted by reputed scholars have been used. In spiritual traditions, some of the saints and religious leaders are placed thousands of years earlier. For instance the philosopher Shankara, who is believed to have lived in the eighth and ninth centuries CE, is placed in some traditions in 2500 BCE.

In Islam, dates are calculated from the Hijrah era, using a lunar calendar. Different methods of converting these to CE can lead to marginally different dates.

Using this book

Lists are provided of the entries pertaining to each religion. Some topics may occur in more than one list.

Cross references to entries are indicated through words in small capitals. The main religions, Hinduism, Buddhism etc. are not cross-referenced, as entries relating to each religion appear in the lists.

Quotes

For quotes used in the text, the name of the translator is given wherever known, with the full reference in the Bibliography.

Spellings

For Sanskrit and languages derived from it, a standard system of spelling has been used, based on Monier-Williams' *Sanskrit–English Dictionary*, though without diacritical marks. Spellings for Arabic, Persian and Urdu names and terms are based on the pronunciation used in India. Thus, for example, we have Nizamuddin, rather than Nizam al-Din, and Ramzan rather than Ramadan. In general, for all languages, a simplified system is used, closest to the approximate sound, without using diacritical marks. Variant spellings are given in many cases. In all cases, there is some divergence based on popular usage, as for instance, Swami, not the more correct Svami. Spellings of place names and names of gods may vary, e.g. 'Badrinath' is the modern name of the place, while 'Badrinatha' is the name of the deity; old and new spellings of places may be used depending on the context, e.g. Vrindavana or Vrindavan. Where the name has changed, the old name is given in brackets, e.g. Mumbai (Bombay). For identification purposes, a place may be located in a district or state; modern names are used here.

CE, BCE: The use of CE (Common Era) and BCE (Before Common Era) in place of AD and BC, is now quite usual. They have specially been chosen for this book which represents all religions, as they have no religious connotation.

Acknowledgement

I would like to thank Udayan Mitra of Penguin India for suggesting this book, and Archana Shankar for editing it. I would also like to thank my family and friends for their encouragement, and for the many discussions over the years which have contributed to this book.

List of Entries by Religion

Bahai

Abdul Baha
Bab
Bahai
Bahai administration
Bahai Lotus Temple
Bahais in India
Bahaullah
Nau Ruz
Ridvan
Shoghi Effendi

Buddhism

abhidhamma/abhidharma
Abhidhamma Pitaka
Abhidharma Pitaka
Abhidharmakosha
Abhidharma-Samuchchaya
abhijna
Abhinishkramana Sutra
Adi Buddha
Agamas
ahimsa
Ajanta Caves
Ajatashatru
Akhnur
Akshobhya
Alara Kalama
Alchi Temples
Amaravati
Amaravati Stupa
Ambedkar, B.R.
Amitabha
Amoghasiddhi
Anagarika Dharmapala
Ananda
Anathapindaka
anatman/anatta
Angas, Buddhist
Angkor
Anguttara Nikaya
animals in religion
anitya
Anuttarayoga Tantra
Apadana
arama

arhat/arhant/arihant
arya satya
Aryadeva
Asanga
Ashoka
Ashokan Pillars
ashtangika marga
Ashtasahasrika Prajnaparamita Sutra
Ashvaghosha
asrava, in Buddhism
Atisha
Atman
Avalokiteshvara
Avatamsaka Sutra
avatara
Ayodhya
Bagh Caves
Bardo Thodol
Basgo
Bedsa
Bhaishajyaguru Buddha
Bhaja
Bharatrihari
Bharhut Stupa
bhavana
Bhavanakrama
Bhavaviveka
bhikkhu
Bimbisara
Bka-gdams-pa
Bka-gyur
Bka-rgyd-pa
Bodh Gaya
Bodhi Tree
Bodhicharyavatara/Bodhisattvacharyavatara
bodhichitta
Bodhidharma
Bodhiruchi
Bodhisattva
Bodhisattvabhumi Sutra
Bodhisattva-yana
Borobudur
Bstangyur
Buddha
Buddha Charita
Buddha Jayanti/Buddha Purnima

Shantirakshita
Shariputra
shila
Shravasti
Shrivatsa
shunyata
siddha
siddhi
skandha
Soka Gakkai
Sthaviravada
stupa
Sumtsek Temple
sutra
sutta
Sutta Pitaka
Suttanipata
Svatantrika
Tabo Monastery
Taglung Kagyu
Tangyur/Tanjur
Tantras
Tantric
Tantrism, Buddhist
Tara
Taranatha
tar-chok
Tathagata
Tathagata-garbha
tathata
thangkas
Theragatha
Theravada
Therigatha
Tibetan Buddhism
Tilopa
Tipitaka (Tripitaka)
trapa
trikaya
Triratna, of Buddhism
triskandhaka
Tsong Khapa
Tsuglagkhang Temple
tulku
Udana
Upali
Uruvela
Vaibhashika
Vairochana
Vaishali
vajra
Vajrachchhedika-prajnaparamita-sutra
Vajrayana Buddhism
Vasubandhu
Vasumitra
Vatsiputriya
Vibhjyavada
Vibhanga

vihara
Vijnanavada
Vikramashila
Vimanavatthu
Vinaya Pitaka
Vipassana (Vipashyana)
Xuanzang
Yab-Yum
yakshas and yakshis
Yamaka
Yashodhara
Yellow Hats
yidam
Yogachara

Christianity

Afghan Church
Agra
Allahabad
Alphonsa, Sister
Amalorpavadoss, Father D.S.
angels
Anglican Church
Anglicans
Apostles
Aquaviva, Father Rudolfo
Armenians
Assyrian Church of the East
Azariah, Vedanayagam Samuel
baptism
Baptist Church
Beschi, Constanzo
Bible, Christian
Bom Jesus Basilica
Brethren Assembly
Canai Thoma
Carey, William
Catholic
Chaldean Syrian Church of the East
Christian festivals and sacred days
Christian saints
Christianity
Christianity in India
Christmas
Church
Church of God (Full Gospel)
Church of North India
Church of South India
Church organization
Communion of Churches of India
congregational
Coonen Kurisu, revolt of
Diamper, Synod of
Duff, Alexander
Easter
ecumenical movement
episcopal
eucharist

Hinduism

Lakshmi-Narayana Temple
Lakulisha
Laleshvari (Lal Ded)
Lalita
Lanka
Lava
linga
Linga Purana
Lingaraja Temple
Lingayats
Lohri
loka
Lokacharya
Lokapalas
lotus
Ma (Maa)
Madana
Madhava Kandali
Madhavacharya
Madhavi
Madhu-Kaitabha
Madhva
Madri
Madurai
Magadha
Magha Mela
Mahabali
Mahabalipuram
Mahabharata
Mahadeva
Mahadeva Temple
Mahadevi
Mahadeviyakka
Mahakala
Mahakuta
Mahalakshmi
Mahamaha/Mahamakha
mahant
Mahanubhava
mahapralaya
Mahashveta
mahasiddha
Mahatala
mahatma
mahatmya
Mahavidyas
mahayuga
Mahesh Yogi, Maharishi
Maheshvara
Maheshvara Sutra
Mahishasura
Mahuli
Mainaka
makara
Makara Sankranti
Makara Vilakku
makaras
mala

Mallikarjuna
Mamalapuram
Manasa
Manasarovara
mandala
Mandana Mishra
mandapa
Mandara
Mandukya Upanishad
Mangala
Mangala-Kavya
Manibhadra
Manikkavachakar
Manimekhalai
Maninaga
Manipura Chakra
Manmatha
mantra
Mantra Yoga
Manu
Manu Smriti
Manu Vaivasvata
manvantara
Manyu
Mariamma
Marichi
Markandeya
Markandeya Purana
Markandeyeshvara Temple
Martand Surya Temple
Martanda
Maruts
Matangi
Matarishvan
matha (math, muth)
Mathura
Matrikas
Matsya
Matsya Purana
Matsyendranatha
Maudgalya Purana
Maya
maya (maayaa)
Mayon
Mena, Menaka
Meos
Meru, Mount
Meykanta Shastras
Mimamsa
Minakshi
Minakshi Temple
Minjar festival
Mira Bai
Mitakshara
Mithila
mithuna
Mitra
Mittani inscription

Modhera Surya Temple
Mohini
moksha
Moreshvara Temple
mother goddess
mountains, sacred
mudra
Muktananda, Swami
Mukteshvara Temple
Muladhara
Mumbai
muni
murti
Murugan
Naba Barsha
nada
nadis
naga deities
Naga sadhus
Nagapanchami
Nagara
Nagari
Nageshvara Temple
nagi/nagini
Naigamesha
naivedya
nakshatra
Nakula
Naladiyar
Nalayira Divya Prabandham
Namadeva
Nambi Andar Nambi
Nambudiri, Cherusseri
Nammalvar
Nanda
Nanda Devi
Nandana
Nandi
Nandini
Nannaya
Narada
Naradiya Purana
Narahari Tirtha
naraka
Narakasura
Nara-Narayana
Narasimha
Narasimha Mehta
Narayan Guru
Narayana
Narmada river
Nasatyas
Nashik
Nataraja
Nataraja Temple
Natha yogis
Nathamuni
Nathdwara Shrinathji Temple

Natya Shastra
Navagraha
Navagraha Temple, Guwahati
Navagraha Temples, Tamil Nadu
Navaratra
Nayanars/Nayanmars
Nilakantha
Nilamata Purana
Nimbarka
niranjana
nirankara/nirakara
nirguna
Nirmala Devi
Nirmala Jhara temples
Nirriti
Nirukta
nirvana
Nisargadatta Maharaja
Nityananda, Swami or Bhagwan
Nivedita, Sister
niyama
nyasa
Nyaya
Om
Omkareshvara
Onam
Oraon, religion of
Oshadhipati
padartha
Padinenkilkanakku
Padma
Padma Purana
Padmanabha Temple
Padmavati
Paila
Pampa
pancha-makara
Pancharatra
Panchashikha
Panchatantra
panchayatana
Pandava Rathas
Pandavas
Pandharpur
pandit
Pandu
Panini
Papanatha Temple
Paramahansa Yogananda
Parashurama
Parashurameshvara
Parida, Sidheswar
parijata
Parjanya
Parthasarthy Temple
Parvati
Pashupata
Pashupati

Patala
Patanjali
pathashala
Pattadakal
Pattupattu
Pavaka
Periya Puranam
Perumal
Phalakaksha
Phul Walon ki Sair
pinda
Pingala
Pingala Nadi
Pippalada
pishachas
Pitamaha
Pitra Paksh
pitris
Pongal
Pooram
Potana
Prabhas Patan
Prabhupada, Swami
Pradyumna
Prahlada
Prajapati
Prajapatis
Prakriti
pralaya
pramana
prana
Pranami Panth
pranayama
Prarthana Samaj
prasada
Prashna Upanishad
Pratishakhyas
Pratyabhijna
Prayaga
prema
preta
Prithvi
puja
Pulastya
Puranas
Purandaradasa
Puri
purohita
Puru
Pururavas
Purusha
Purva Mimamsa
Pushan
Pushkar
Pushpaka
Pushtimarga
Puttaparthi
Radha

Radhasoami/Radhaswami sect
raga
Raghava
Raghu
RagniyaTemple
Rahu
Raidas
Rajagriha
rajarishi
rajasuya
Raka
Raksha Bandhan
rakshasas
Rama
Rama Gita
Rama Lila
Rama Setu
Rama Tirtha, Swami
Ramachandra Temple
Ramacharitamanasa
Ramadas
Ramakrishna Mission
Ramakrishna Paramahansa
Ramana Maharshi, Sri
Ramananda
Ramananda Tirtha, Swami
Ramanathaswamy Temple
Ramanavami
Ramanuja
Ramappa Temple
Ramayana
Rameshvara Temple, Nashik
Rameshvaram
Ramtek
Ranganatha
Ranganatha Temple
Rasatala
Rati
Ratri
Ravana
Ravi
Ravi Shankar, Sri Sri
Ravidas
Renuka
Revanta
Revati
Rewalsar Lake
Ribhu
Ribhus
Riddhi
Rig Veda
rishi
Rishyashringa
rivers, sacred
Rodasi
Rudra
Rudras
Rukmangadacharita

urs
uwaisi
Wahdat al-Shuhud
Wahdat al-Wujud
Wahhabi
Wajihuddin Ahmad, Shaikh
Waliullah, Shah
Waris Shah
Zain ul Abidin
zakat
Zanjiri Mosque
zikr

Jainism

Abhayadeva Suri
Abu, Mt
Acharanga Sutra
adharma
Adi Purana, Jain
Adinatha
Agamas
ahimsa
Ajatashatru
ajiva
Ajmer
Akalanka
akasha
Ambika, Jain
Amtagadadasao (Antakriddasah)
anekantavada
Angas, Jain
animals in religion
Anuogadara
Anuttarovavaiyadasao (Anutaraupapatikadasah)
ara
Ardha-Magadhi
arhat/arhant/arihant
Arishtaneminatha
asrava, in Jainism
astikayas
Atman
avasarpini
avashyakas
Avassaya Sutta
ayagapattas
Ayaramga Sutta
Ayodhya
Badami
Bahubali
Banarsidasa
Bhadrabahu I
Bhadrabahu II
Bhagavati Sutra
Bhagavati Viyaha-pannati (Vyakhya-Prajnapti)
Bharata
Bharatavarsha
Bhattaparinna
bhattaraka

bhavana
Bikaner Jain temples
Bisapantha
Chandragupta Maurya
Cheya-Suttas (Cheda Sutras)
Churnis
Dasaveyaliya Sutta
Dashavaikalika Sutra
dharma
Digambara
Dilwara Temples
Ditthivaya (Drishtivada)
dravya
elephants in religion
Ellora
gachchha
gana, Jain
ganadhara
Girnar
Gommateshvara Image, Shravana Belagola
Goyama Indabhuti (Skt:Gautama Indrabhuti)
Gumanapantha
Gunabhadra
Gunadhara
Haribhadra Suri
Harivamsha Purana
Hemachandra Suri
Hira Vijaya Suri
Hastinapura
Jain art and architecture
Jain ascetics
Jain Councils
Jain deities
Jain festivals
Jain texts
Jainism
Jina
Jinachandra Suri
Jinadasagani
Jinasena
jiva, in Jainism
Jivandhara
jnana
Kalakacharya
kalpa
Kalpa Sutra
Kalyanaka
Kanchipuram
Kanjipantha
karma
Karmaprabhrita
Kashayaprabhrita
Kaushambi
Kavipantha
kayotsarga
Kevali/Kevala-jnani
Khajuraho
Khandagiri

Judaism

Aleph/Alef
Andhra Jews
angels
Ashkenazim
Baghdadi Jews
Bar Mitzvah
Bene Israel
Bible, Jewish
Bnei Menashe
Chabad Lubovitch
Chanukah/Hanukah
Cochin Jews
Dead Sea Scrolls
Israel, Lost Tribes of
Jewish Calendar and Festivals
Jews in India
Judaism
Kabbalah
Kerala Jews
Marrano Jews
Merkabah
messiah, in Judaism
midrash
Mishnah
mitzvah
Passover
Persian-speaking Jews
Rosh Hashanah
Sabbath/Shabbat
Shabuoth
shekhinah
Sukkoth
synagogue
Talmud
Tanakh
Torah

Sikhism

Achal Sahib
Adi Granth
Akal Purakh
Akal Takht
Akali
Akali Movement
Akhand Path
Amar Das, Guru
amrit
Amritsar
Anandpur Sahib
Angad, Guru
Ardas
Arjan Dev, Guru
Atal Rai
Baba Atal Gurdwara
Baba Bakala Gurdwara
Badshahi Bagh Gurdwara
Bahadurgarh Gurdwara

Baisakhi
Bala
Bala Sahib Gurdwara
Banda Bahadur Gurdwara
Banda Singh Bahadur
Bandichhor Gurdwara
Bangla Sahib Gurdwara
bani
Baoli Sahib, Goindwal
Barchha Sahib Gurdwara
Bari Sangat Gurdwara
Bhagel Singh, Sardar
Bhajan, Yogi
Bhangani Sahib Gurdwara
Bhatha Sahib Gurdwara
Budha, Baba
Chamkaur
Chaubara Sahib Gurdwara
Chhevin Padshahi Gurdwara
Damdama Sahib Gurdwara, Delhi
Damdama Sahib Gurdwara, Dhubri
Daroli Bhai Gurdwara
Dasam Granth
Dera Baba Nanak
dharma
Dip Singh, Baba
Dukh Niwaran Sahib Gurdwara
Gangsar Gurdwara
Ghat Sahib Gurdwara
Gobind Singh, Guru
Gobindpura Gurdwara
Golden Temple
Granth Sahib
granthi
Gurdas, Bhai
gurdwara
Gurdwara Reform Movement
gurmukh
Gurmukhi
Guru Granth Sahib
Guru Ka Bagh Gurdwara
Guruparb
Har Krishan, Guru
Har Mandir Sahib, Sri
Har Rai, Guru
Harbhajan Singh, Yogi
Hargobind, Guru
Hargobindpur
Hazur Sahib Gurdwara
Hemkunt Sahib Gurdwara
Hola Mohalla
hukam-nama
Jaitu
Janam Sakhis
Jap Sahib
Japji
Kandh Sahib Gurdwara
Kapal Mochan

Zoroastrianism

A The first letter of the alphabet in Sanskrit and other Indian languages. It is a sacred letter, forming the first syllable of the word OM. In addition it is a name of the Hindu god VISHNU, or in some texts of BRAHMA or SHIVA. The corresponding letters in several languages, for instance ALIF in Arabic and ALEPH in Hebrew, are also considered sacred.

abdal An Arabic term in Islam which literally means 'substitutes'. They are people whom God has sent to sustain the world. According to some accounts, there are seventy abdals, forty of whom reside in Syria and thirty elsewhere, while others state there are forty major abdals and 150 lesser ones. When one dies, God appoints another in his place. No one except God knows who they are, but one of the signs of the last day of the world, is that the abdal will come from Syria. They are mentioned in the MISHKATUL-MASABIH, a SUNNI work popular in India, as well as in other texts. This mystical theme has some similarity with the concept of KALKI, the Hindu AVATARA yet to come, and with the Theosophical theory of perfected beings who exist in the world but do not reveal themselves. According to some texts, abdals form part of a hierarchy of hidden ISLAMIC SAINTS.

Abdul Baha The eldest son of BAHAULLAH, the founder of the BAHAI religion. Born in 1844, his name was Abbas Effendi, but he took the title Abdul Baha or 'servant of Baha' on his father's death in 1891. His father Bahaullah had appointed him as the head of the faith and the only authorized interpreter of the religion, after him. Abdul Baha died in 1921 and passed on the leadership to his eldest grandson, SHOGHI EFFENDI.

Abdul Haqq, Shaikh A SUFI saint who lived from 1551 to 1642, whose full name was Abdul Haqq Muhaddis Dihlawi. He was initiated into the QADIRI order, but differed from other Qadiriyas in some respects and attempted to reconcile the Sufi path with the laws of the SHARIA. Though his teacher, Shaikh Musa, was favourably inclined towards the liberal policies of the Mughal emperor AKBAR, Abdul Haqq was against them, and attempted to convince the emperor Jahangir to return to the path of the Sharia. He wrote a number of books, among them *Akhbarul-Akhyar*, a biographical dictionary of Sufis in India,

and *Madarijun Nubuwwah*, in which he tried to find a middle path between mysticism and rationality. He said that a Sufi should also follow Sharia laws, and that scholarship and study are essential before attempting to attain mystical states, or else Sufism would become an excuse for misconduct and licentious behaviour. His disciples included Sufis and ULAMA.

Abdul Latif, Shah A SUFI poet who lived from 1689 to 1752 and composed verses in Sindhi. His collection of poems is called *Rasalo* (Message).

Born near Hyderabad, Sind, now in Pakistan, he studied Arabic and Persian and later became a wandering ascetic. He visited Hindu and Muslim shrines in Sind, Baluchistan and Gujarat. He then settled near his home town, where he lived a life of prayer and meditation and composed verses on his search for God. He attracted both Hindu and Muslim disciples.

Abdul Quddus Gangohi, Shaikh A SUFI saint of the SABIRI branch of the CHISTI order, who lived from 1456 to 1537. He wrote the *Anwar ul-Uyun* on the teachings of the Sabiri order and popularized the DARGAH of Shaikh Alauddin Sabir, the founder of the order, at Kalyar. He also compiled the *Rushd-Nama*, which includes verses in Hindi written by himself and his gurus. He was influenced by the teachings of GORAKHNATHA and believed in the Sufi doctrine of WAHDAT AL-WUJUD, which sees all religions and approaches as forms of the one reality or Absolute. Reflecting these beliefs, in a letter to one of his disciples, he wrote:

Why this meaningless talk about the believer,
The kafir, the obedient, the sinner,
The rightly guided, the misdirected, the Muslim;
The pious, the infidel, the fire-worshipper
All are like beads in a rosary.

Abdul Wahid, Mir A SUFI saint who was born in 1510 and lived at Bilgram near Lucknow. He wrote *Haqaiq-i Hindi*, explaining the reasons for using Hindu terms in Sufi poetry. He suggested that KRISHNA, RADHA, GANGA, YAMUNA and other names of VAISHNAVISM had Islamic equivalents. For instance, Krishna symbolized the Prophet MUHAMMAD in some passages, and in others represented any person, in contrast to the abstract reality of Oneness. The GOPIS represented angels, Braj and GOKUL were the Sufi concept of the world (*alam*), and the rivers Ganga and Yamuna were the sea of unity (*Wahdat*). In other contexts, the same terms had different symbolic meanings. He died in 1608.

Abdur Rahim Chisti A seventeenth-century SUFI saint who was initiated into several Sufi orders before joining the SABIRI-CHISTI order. He believed he was an UWAISI, that is, directly initiated by Shaikh MUINUDDIN CHISTI, and lived for some time in AGRA before settling in his village of Dhaniti where he died in 1683. He wrote a number of books including the *Mirat-i Madari*, *Miratul-asrar*, and *Mirat-i Masudi*. In the *MIRATUL-MAKHLUQAT (Mirror of the Creatures)* he translated and commented on a Hindu text, explaining Hindu legends. He also translated the BHAGAVAD GITA into Persian as *Miratul-Haqaiq (Mirror of Realities)*.

Abdur Rahim Khan-i Khanan A noble in the court of the Mughal emperor AKBAR in the sixteenth century, who was also a poet known by the name RAHIM. His verses on religious themes are still popular today.

abhanga A verse form, which literally means 'absolute' or 'eternal'. The medieval Hindu BHAKTI saints JNANESHVARA, NAMADEVA, EKNATHA and TUKARAM composed abhangas to God in Marathi, the language of Maharashtra. A typical abhanga consists of four lines, each with three to eight syllables. Most abhangas were addressed to the god VITTHALA, a form of the Hindu god VISHNU.

Abhasvaras A class or GANA of divine beings mentioned in Hindu texts. Literally the word means 'shining ones'. They consist of sixty-four deities said to preside over all forms of enlightenment. They are personifications of mental qualities and the twelve main Abhasvaras are: Atma, the soul; Jnata, the knower; Dama, restraint; Danta, patience; Shanti, peace; Jnana, knowledge; Sama, tranquility; Tapas, penance; Kama, desire; Krodha, anger; Mada, intoxication; Moha, delusion.

Abhayadeva Suri A Jain scholar of the eleventh century who wrote commentaries on nine ANGAS, the basic texts of the SHVETAMBARA sect.

abhidhamma/abhidharma A term in Buddhism which means 'higher DHARMA' or 'the higher subtleties of dharma'. There are a number of abhidhamma (PALI) or abhidharma (Sanskrit) texts, which explore Buddhist doctrines in depth.

Abhidhamma Pitaka HINAYANA Buddhist texts, which form part of the PALI CANON and were composed between the second and first centuries BCE. The texts contain mainly classifications, definitions and explanations of Buddhist doctrines in the NIKAYAS. The seven texts are: *DHAMMASANGANI; VIBHANGA; DHATUKATHA; PUGGALAPANATI; KATHAVATTHU; YAMAKA; PATTHANA*.

The *Abhidhamma Pitaka* form the texts of the THERAVADA school of Hinayana Buddhism. Not all Hinayana schools accept this series of texts. The SAUTRANTIKAS dispute its authority, while the SARVASTIVADA have an entirely different *ABHIDHARMA PITAKA* in Sanskrit. However, in the Theravada sect the *Abhidhamma* is highly revered and is still studied today. Over the centuries, numerous commentaries have been written on its texts. Among the commentators were BUDDHAGHOSHA, BUDDHADATTA, Dhammapala and Upasena. An important later commentary, composed in the twelfth century, is the *Abhidhammatthasangaha* of Anuruddha, which summarizes Theravada ideas.

Abhidharma Pitaka HINAYANA Buddhist texts used by the SARVASTIVADA sect. The seven texts here are entirely different from the Pali *ABHIDHAMMA PITAKA* and were initially composed in Sanskrit, though they are preserved mainly in Chinese and Tibetan translations. They were probably compiled around the same time as the Pali *Abhidhamma*, during the second and first centuries BCE. The texts are: *Jnana-Prasthana; Prakarana; Vijnana-Kaya; Dharmaskandha; Prajnapti-Shastra; Dhatu-Kaya; Sangiti-Paryaya*.

The *Jnana-Prasthana* is the most important of the texts, referred to as the 'body' while the others form the 'feet' (pada).

Among the commentaries written on the *Abhidharma Pitaka* is the *Abhidharma Mahavibhasha* of the second century. This is a very long text. Shorter commentaries were composed in the third and fourth centuries, including the *Abhidharma-hridaya*, *Abhidharma-hridaya Sutra* and *Samyukta-Abhidharma-hridaya*. A fifth-century commentary was the *ABHIDHARMAKOSHA* written by VASUBANDHU.

Abhidharmakosha A Buddhist text written by VASUBANDHU in the fourth or fifth century. Vasubandhu initially belonged to the Hinayana SARVASTIVADA school but had some SAUTRANTIKA ideas. His text presents the ideas of Sarvastivada, particularly of the *Abhidharma Mahavibhasha*, a commentary on the *ABHIDHARMA PITAKA*. At the same time he criticizes these concepts from the Sautrantika point of view. As his text is rather difficult there are several commentaries on it, including some in Chinese.

Abhidharma-Samuchchaya A MAHAYANA Buddhist text written by ASANGA. It deals with understanding and analyzing various DHARMAS and is an important text of the YOGACHARA school.

abhijna A term used in Buddhism for six extraordinary powers which exist in BUDDHAS, BODHISATTVAS and ARHANTS. These are: hearing with the inner ear; entering the minds of others; seeing with the inner eye, i.e., beyond time and space; gaining the memory of former lives; and extinguishing all impurities.

Abhinavagupta A philosopher who lived from c. 950–1015 (alternative dates 975–1025, or 960–1050) and belonged to the monistic school of the Hindu sect of SHAIVISM prevalent in Kashmir. His teachers included Lakshmanagupta, who had been a student of UTPALADEVA, another notable exponent of this school.

Abhinavagupta had an encyclopedic knowledge, having studied Buddhism, Jainism and Shaivism as well as KAULA TANTRISM. Apart from describing TRIKA SHASTRA, he explained the related PRATYABHIJNA philosophy, and provided practical methods of meditation for attaining Pratyabhijna or recognition of the world as a manifestation of the god SHIVA. He wrote a number of texts on Trika and Pratyabhijna, aesthetics and aspects of Tantrism, as well as commentaries on Utpaladeva's works. Among his books are the *Malini-Vijaya-Vartika*, the *Paratrimsika-Vivarana*, the *Tantraloka* and the *Tantrasara*.

Abhinishkramana Sutra   A biography of the BUDDHA popular in China, written in about the second century.

Abu (Bu) Ali Shah   A SUFI saint whose DARGAH or shrine is located at Panipat in Haryana. A number of Sufis lived in Panipat, of whom Ali Shah is the most renowned, revered by people of all religions. Born in 1209, when Qutbuddin Aibak was ruling at Delhi, Ali Shah lived through the reigns of many kings, and finally died in 1324 during the reign of Ghiyasuddin Tughlaq. He was once a religious scholar, but after an experience of divine ecstacy he became a QALANDAR, a wandering ascetic. Sultan Alauddin Khalji is said to have visited him frequently to seek his blessings, and so did AMIR KHUSRAU. After his death, Ghiyasuddin had a decorated marble tomb constructed for him on the outskirts of Panipat. Renovations and additions were made later, and in the time of AURANGZEB (1659–1707), a verandah and marble screen were added.

Pilgrims still visit the dargah, particularly on the occasion of the annual URS. Free food is served at this time and on every Thursday.

Abu Rehan al-Biruni   A Persian scholar who came to India in the eleventh century. Abu Rehan Muhammad-ibn Ahmad al-Biruni was born in Khwarizm (now in Turkmenistan) in 973. He was one of the most learned men of his time, with a knowledge of Turkish, Persian, Sanskrit, Hebrew and Syriac, as well as Arabic. He was first at the court of the Khwarizm Shahs, but later joined the court of Mahmud of Ghazni (in Afghanistan) and came to India with him around 1017. After studying India's culture he returned to Ghazni and wrote *Kitab fi Tarikh al-Hind*, an analysis and description of India. In this he described Hinduism and commented on several Sanskrit texts. He differentiated between the religion of the common people and that of the educated. The latter always tried to formulate general principles and understand abstract ideas, no matter to which religion they belonged. He also described the caste system, the villages, towns and occupations of the people. He was the first outsider to write in such depth and detail on India and her customs.

Al-Biruni wrote a number of other books, including *Kitab al-Athar al-Bakiyah* (Chronology of Ancient Nations), *At-Tafhim* (Elements of Astrology), *Al-Kanun al-Masudi* (The Canon of Masudi), a book on astronomy dedicated to Sultan Masud of Ghazni, and *Kitab as-Saydalah*, a treatise on medicine. He died in 1048 at Ghazni.

Abu, Mt   A hill town in Rajasthan, known for its Jain DILWARA temples. More Jain temples are located at the nearby site of Achalgarh. Mt Abu is also the headquarters of the BRAHMA KUMARIS.

Abul Fazl Allami, Shaikh   A philosopher and scholar at the court of the Mughal emperor AKBAR. Born in 1551, he was the son of Shaikh Mubarak, a learned and liberal scholar. His brother FAIZI was a poet. Abul Fazl was very close to Akbar, and his influence on the emperor was resented by Akbar's son Prince Salim (later the emperor Jahangir). In 1602, Salim caused him to be murdered.

Abul Fazl was a SUFI, known for his liberal views and for his chronicle of Akbar, his life and times in the *Akbar Namah* which included the *Ain-i Akbari*. His collected letters are included in the *Maktubat-i Allami*, also called the *Inshayi Abul Fazl*. Among his other works is the *Iyar-i Danish*, a new version of the *Kalila wa Dimna*, the Arabic *Panchatantra*. He wrote in Persian, but also knew Arabic.

Though a Muslim, he transcended sectarian religious beliefs, as is clear in this verse written by him:

Sometimes I frequent the Christian cloister and sometimes the mosque,
But it is Thou whom I seek from temple to temple.
The elect have no dealings with either heresy or orthodoxy;
For neither of them stands behind the screen of Thy truth.
Heresy to the heretic, and religion to the orthodox,
But the dust of the rose petal
Belongs to the heart of the perfume-seller.

Abul Hasan al-Hujwiri   A SUFI saint of the eleventh century, whose full name was Abul Hasan Ali bin Usman al-Hujwiri and who was popularly known as Data Ganj Baksh, meaning 'the distributor of unlimited treasure'. He came to Lahore in 1035 and lived there until his death in 1089. He wrote the KASHFUL-MAHJUB in Persian, an account of Sufi saints and practices from the time of the Prophet MUHAMMAD onwards. His work influenced the development of SUFISM in India.

Achal Sahib   A GURDWARA or Sikh shrine located in Gurdaspur district of Punjab. According to the story associated with this shrine, it was once a centre of NATHA yogis, where a prominent yogi, Bhangar Natha lived. When Guru NANAK, the first Sikh guru and founder of Sikhism, visited the place, the yogi tried to impress him with his SIDDHIS or powers, but lost them in his presence. Guru Nanak then explained that the blessings of God were more important than miraculous powers. The Achal Sahib Gurdwara was later constructed at this spot. Guru Nanak's dialogue with the siddhas or yogis, which possibly took place here, is recorded in the SIDDHA GOSHT of the GURU GRANTH SAHIB.

Achala One of the names of the Hindu god VISHNU and of the god KARTTIKEYA. Achala is also the name of several others, including a bull, an attendant or Parshada of Skanda or Karttikeya, and of one of the women who assisted Karttikeya in his battle against the asura TARAKA. The name means 'the immovable'.

Acharanga Sutra The Sanskrit name of a Jain text, the *AYARAMGA SUTTA*.

acharya A teacher or guru. A Sanskrit word, it literally means one who teaches or knows the acharas or rules. In ancient days it referred mainly to those who taught the VEDAS and other aspects of the sacred texts. In Hinduism, SHANKARACHARYAS are leaders of large MATHAS or religious establishments. VAISHNAVA teachers of medieval days and some Jain religious leaders are also known as acharyas. The term was used particularly for Jain DIGAMBARA leaders between the first and eighth centuries. Today the title is bestowed on religious leaders and on any saintly or learned person.

Achyuta One of the names of the Hindu god VISHNU or of KRISHNA. Literally, it means 'not fallen', but is interpreted as 'imperishable'.

Adam's Bridge The name of a line of rocks and islets, with a length of about 30 km, connecting the southern tip of India with Sri Lanka. According to legend, first narrated in Gnostic sources (see GNOSTICISM) and later given in Islamic texts, when Adam was expelled from paradise, he crossed this bridge, and then stood in penance on one foot on a mountain further south in Sri Lanka. After one thousand years of standing on Adam's Peak (also known by different names and sacred to Hindus, Buddhists, Muslims and Christians), he was reunited with Eve.

In the Indian tradition, Adam's Bridge is connected with the story of the RAMAYANA, and is known as RAMA SETU, or Rama's Bridge, constructed by HANUMAN and his army to enable RAMA to cross to LANKA and rescue SITA.

Usually dry, the 'bridge' is covered by about 1.2 m of water at high tide.

Aderbad bin Mahrespand The high priest and prime minister at the time of Shapur II (309–79) of the Sasanian dynasty of Iran. At this time Christianity was spreading in Iran and Aderbad was responsible for reviving the Zoroastrian religion. To demonstrate the superiority of the Zoroastrian faith, he performed miracles and went through an ordeal in which molten metal was poured on his chest, but he emerged unharmed. He called himself Raenidar, a PAHLAVI

word, meaning spiritual leader or saviour, and held debates with other religious leaders to prove the supremacy of Zoroastrianism. A number of prayers used by Zoroastrians in India today are said to have been composed by him, including the Patet (prayer of repentance) and the Afrin (blessings), and he is revered by PARSIS.

adharma A Sanskrit term, used in different ways. Generally, it means that which is not right, the opposite of DHARMA. Adharma is also a term for a category or quality. In NYAYA philosophy, dharma and adharma are two of twenty-four qualities which respectively cause pleasure and pain. In Jainism, it is one of the ASTIKAYAS or five categories of knowledge, as well as one of the DRAVYAS or substances comprising the world. In this context adharma is the principle of rest, as opposed to movement.

adhvaryu One of the four main priests who officiated at Vedic sacrifices. The others were the HOTR, UDGATR and BRAHMAN. The adhvaryu measured the ground, built the altar, and prepared the sacrificial vessels, apart from performing other rites. While doing this, he recited verses from the YAJUR VEDA.

Adhyatma Ramayana A Sanskrit text sacred to Hindus. It is considered a part of the BRAHMANDA PURANA but is also used separately. The *Adhyatma Ramayana* promotes BHAKTI or devotion to the god RAMA, and in addition, contains aspects of ADVAITA, as Rama, identified with VISHNU, is considered the supreme soul. The *RAMA GITA* and *Ramahridaya*, which form part of the text, are often memorized by devotees of Rama. The text is fairly late, possibly of the fifteenth century.

Adi Buddha The first or primordial BUDDHA. This concept existed in early Buddhism, but was fully developed in the VAJRAYANA system. The Adi Buddha has been identified at different times with SAMANTABHADRA, Vajradhara or VAIROCHANA, and is at the centre of the Buddhist pantheon. He is the origin and the first of all BUDDHAS. Other Buddhas, who head families of BUDDHIST DEITIES, emanate from him.

Adi Granth The principal sacred text of the Sikhs, also known as the GURU GRANTH SAHIB. It is the main object of worship in GURDWARAS or Sikh shrines.

Adi Purana The 'first Purana', a name sometimes used for the BRAHMA PURANA in Hinduism.

Adi Purana, Jain A Jain text, the first part of the *TRISHASHTILAKSHANA MAHAPURANA*. The *Adi Purana* contains the story of Adinatha or RISHABHA, the first TIRTHANKARA, and of Bharata, the first Chakravartin or ruler of the world. The text is important for DIGAMBARA Jains, and has forty-seven chapters, forty-two of which were written by JINASENA of the ninth century, and five by his pupil GUNABHADRA. The *Adi Purana* also discusses various rituals or Samskaras to be observed from birth to death, similar to the Hindu SAMSKARAS.

A later version of the *Adi Purana*, focusing on the life of Rishabha, was written by the Kannada poet PAMPA who lived in the tenth century. It is one of the first great poems written in Kannada.

Adi Shankaracharya The first SHANKARACHARYA, a term used to refer to the ninth-century philosopher SHANKARA, who set up four or, according to some sources, five MATHAS or religious institutes in India.

Adina Mosque A mosque located at Pandua (also known as Firuzabad) in West Bengal, constructed in 1373 by Sultan Sikandar Shah (1357–93) of the Ilyas Shahi dynasty. One of the largest mosques in India, it measures 155 m by 87 m and is enclosed within a large courtyard. There are cloisters on three sides, as well as a number of pillars and archways, designed to form squares, each covered by a small dome. Altogether, there were 378 domes on the mosque. One part of the mosque has two stories, and is known as the Badshah-ka-Takht, or royal enclosure, probably reserved for the sultan and his family. While other large mosques in Bengal have regional characteristics, this was built in traditional or orthodox style.

The mosque was extensively decorated with abstract, geometric and vegetal designs. These were symmetrically placed and designed, but each was different in its details.

Sikandar Shah stated that he was the 'most perfect of the sultans of Arabia and Persia', and this mosque rivals contemporary structures in other parts of the world. It is now in disrepair.

Adinatha The first of the twenty-four Jain TIRTHANKARAS, who was also known as RISHABHA. Adinatha literally means 'the first lord' and he is said to have existed thousands, or even millions, of years before MAHAVIRA, the twenty-fourth Tirthankara, who lived in the sixth century BCE.

Adinatha is also a name of the Hindu god SHIVA.

Aditi A Hindu deity, the mother of the gods, she is first mentioned in the RIG VEDA. She is the mother of the ADITYAS, a group of gods, and is said to nourish and sustain all existence. In the MAHABHARATA, she is the mother of the thirty-three DEVAS or gods, including twelve ADITYAS, eight VASUS and eleven RUDRAS. DEVAKI, mother of KRISHNA, is said to be Aditi reborn. According to the PURANAS, Aditi, one of the daughters of DAKSHA, married the rishi KASHYAPA and was the mother of all the gods. After doing penance for one thousand years, she gave birth to VISHNU, who was born to her as VAMANA.

Adityas A group of Hindu gods. In the RIG VEDA they are said to be seven or eight, and their names include MITRA, ARYAMAN, BHAGA, VARUNA, DAKSHA and AMSHA. They protect the universe, see the good and evil actions of people and punish the wicked. They are bright, golden and unwinking and provide long lives, good health and offspring to their worshippers. Some scholars feel they are similar to the AMESHA SPENTAS of Zoroastrianism, whereas others reject this theory. In the MAHABHARATA and some later texts, twelve Adityas are listed, among them being VISHNU. Other texts provide different lists of Adityas. In the VISHNU PURANA, the Adityas are Vishnu, Shakra, Aryaman, Dhuti, TVASHTR, PUSHAN, VIVASVAT, SAVITR, Mitra, Varuna, Amsha and Bhaga.They are celestial gods, and are sons of ADITI.

Advaita The philosophy of Oneness or non-duality, which forms one of the main schools of VEDANTA. Its ideas were first expressed in the UPANISHADS and later explained in the *Vedanta Sutra* or BRAHMA SUTRA. GAUDAPADA, a philosopher who lived in the seventh century, and SHANKARA in the ninth century, were the greatest exponents of this philosophy in ancient days. In the nineteenth century, VIVEKANANDA as well as various reform groups used the principles of Advaita in their attempts to revive and reform Hinduism. In the twentieth century, several scholars and gurus have explained Shankara's ideas, notable among them being Swami CHINMAYANANDA and his disciples. Its main concepts are that there is only One Reality, known as BRAHMAN or the Absolute. Brahman always existed and always will exist. Beyond time and space, it never changes, grows or diminishes. The true Self, the ATMAN or individual soul within, is identical with this, while the world and identification with the ego or the individual personality, is unreal, an illusion. This unreality is known as MAYA. Realizing the Self as Brahman brings bliss, joy and freedom. JNANA or wisdom is the direct route for such realization. This philosophical system is considered the most influential in Indian society even today.

Afghan Church A church constructed by the British in MUMBAI (Bombay) in 1865 to commemorate the death of soldiers and officers in the campaigns in Sind and Afghanistan between 1835 and 1843. The church is constructed in Neo-Gothic style with a tapering spire. The font within has an intricate metal screen, and on the walls are carved the names of those who died in the campaign.

Aga Khan The spiritual leader of the Islamic NIZARI Ismaili sect. Aga Khan, meaning 'chief commander', was a title first granted by the Shah of Iran to Hasan Ali Shah, the governor of the Persian province of Kerman in 1818. Hasan Ali traced his descent from the Prophet MUHAMMAD through his daughter Fatimah.

Despite this honour, Hasan led a revolt against the Shah and escaped to India after his defeat. There he sided with the British in the Afghan War of 1839–42 and in the conquest of Sind, and in return was granted a pension by the British. He lived in MUMBAI (Bombay), and soon after his death in 1881, his eldest son Ali Shah became the second Aga Khan.

Ali Shah or Muhammad Ali Khan died in 1885 and was succeeded by his only son Muhammad Shah, then only eight years old. Sultan Sir Muhammad Shah gradually became a leader of Muslims in India. In 1906 he led a deputation to Lord Minto, the British viceroy, to gain concessions for Muslims. Between 1930 and 1932, he attended the Round Table Conferences in London, where several representatives from India joined in discussions with the British on more participation by Indians in government, and plans for self-government. He was India's representative at the World Disarmament Conference in Geneva in 1932 and led the Indian delegation to the League of Nations in 1932, and again from 1934 to 1937. In 1937, he became president of the General Assembly of the League.

During the Second World War he gave up active politics and went to live in Switzerland, where he died at Versoix in 1957. His grandson, Karim Al-Hussain Shah, who was born on 13 December 1936 in Geneva, took over as Aga Khan IV. He provided a new direction to the Nizari Ismaili sect and asked them to become citizens of the countries in which they lived. Karim Aga Khan still directs the community of Nizari Ismailis in a number of countries, including India and Pakistan. In India his followers include the KHOJAS.

Agamas A class of texts. Agama is literally 'that which has come down'. In Hinduism Agamas refer to non-Vedic texts which were accessible to all, unlike the VEDAS, which were meant only for the three higher castes. Most commonly, they are used for Shaivite Tantric texts, and traditionally, there are twenty-eight SHAIVA AGAMAS. Apart from these, other works, including some VAISHNAVA and Shakta texts, are referred to as Agamas.

In Jainism, the sacred texts of the SHVETAMBARAS are known as Agamas.

In Buddhism, Agamas are texts of the *Sutra Pitaka* (Pali: SUTTA PITAKA) written in Sanskrit. The four main Buddhist Agamas include the *Dirgha Agama, Madhyama Agama, Samyukta Agama* and *Ekottara Agama,* corresponding to the DIGHA NIKAYA, MAJJHIMA NIKAYA, SAMYUTTA NIKAYA, and ANGUTTARA NIKAYA of the PALI CANON.

Agastya A sage or RISHI who is said to have lived in ancient days. There are several legends and stories concerning him in the RAMAYANA, MAHABHARATA, and other ancient texts.

Agastya was rather short and has been described as 'dwarfish'. However, he was very learned, well versed in the VEDAS and in the use of various magical weapons. Though he was an ascetic, he finally married because he was told that only those with sons who could perform their ancestral rites would enter heaven. Out of the essence of all living beings, he created a beautiful girl named Lopamudra and gave her as a daughter to the king of Vidarbha. It was this Lopamudra whom he later married. They had a son named Dridhasyu, also called Idmavaha, who chanted the Vedas at birth.

An important legend recounts how Agastya subdued the Vindhya mountains and went to south India. The Vindhyas decided to teach a lesson to Mount MERU, who had become too proud. They wanted to show Meru that they could be taller than it, and so they grew higher and higher, so that even the sun and moon could not pass over them. Agastya went to the Vindhyas and told them he was going to the south. He requested them to remain low until he returned. The Vindhyas agreed, but Agastya, building his ashram at Malayachala or Agastyakuta in south India, never returned to the north. Agastya is still worshipped in some temples, particularly in the south. He is the traditional author of various texts, including the *Agastya Gita,* which forms part of the VARAHA PURANA; the *Agastya Samhita* in the SKANDA PURANA; and the *Dvaidha-Nirnaya Tantra.* The THEOSOPHICAL SOCIETY OF INDIA included him in their mystical hierarchy and believe he exists and takes care of India even today. For historians, the myth of his journey across the Vindhyas is associated with the spread of Vedic and Brahmanical ideas in the south.

Aghora A name of the Hindu god SHIVA, and also of a TANTRIC Shaivite sect. Aghora means 'the non-fearful'.

Aghoreshvara Temple A temple of the Hindu god SHIVA, dating back to the sixteenth and seventeenth centuries, located at Ikkeri in District Shimoga, Karnataka. Constructed at the time of the Keladi Nayakas, the architecture of the temple revives some Hoysala forms. The inner shrine leads to a spacious hall or MANDAPA, surrounded by a passageway. The inner walls of the mandapa have carved friezes. Above is a pyramidal tower, surmounted by a domed roof. Subsidiary shrines include a NANDI pavilion. Ikkeri was the Nayaka capital, and the temple was a royal monument.

agiary A Gujarati term used by PARSIS for a Zoroastrian fire temple in India. It refers to the second or third grade of ZOROASTRIAN TEMPLES, also known as Atash Adaran, Dar-e Meher, Atash Kadeh or Atash Dadgah.

Agni A Hindu deity, the personification of the sacrificial fire. He is the second most important god in the RIG VEDA (the first being INDRA) to whom over 200 hymns are dedicated, while he is mentioned in many more. Adjectives used to describe him are related to sacrificial ceremonies in which offerings of butter and ghi are made. Thus he is described as butter-backed, butter-faced or butter-haired. He has sharp or burning jaws, golden or shining teeth and resembles gold. Wood or ghi (clarified butter) is his food and melted butter is his drink. He is brilliant and shines like the sun. His chariot is of lightning, luminous and golden, and his steeds are tawny and ruddy, but the path he makes in his journey is black. Agni has a threefold nature, born of heaven, men and the waters, a precursor of the later trinity of BRAHMA, VISHNU and

SHIVA. He protects his worshippers behind a hundred iron walls, preserves them from calamities and is the deliverer and friend of those who worship him. He bestows every kind of boon, particularly in the sphere of domestic welfare, offspring, and property.

Agni takes on many forms, just as fire does. He exists wherever there is fire on earth or lightning in the heavens. He is the god of fire sacrifices and the god of the domestic hearth.

Numerous legends are narrated about Agni in the MAHABHARATA, RAMAYANA and later texts. In the Mahabharata he is said to have seven faces, seven red tongues, and a chariot drawn by seven horses, with the wind for its wheels. In the HARIVAMSHA, Agni is said to have four arms and to wear black clothes. Smoke is his banner, and he holds a fiery spear. The seven winds form the wheels of his chariot, and he is accompanied by a goat or ram (AJA).

In later times Agni lost the importance given to him in the VEDAS and became one of the eight DIKAPALAS, or guardians of the world. His description as lord of the south-east quarter is given in the VISHNU-DHARMOTTARA PURANA. He is bearded with four arms, four tusks and three eyes. His chariot is drawn by four parrots and driven by the wind, and his consort SVAHA sits on his lap. He holds flames, a trident and rosary.

In the PURANAS he is the son of Brahma, or of the Virat-Purusha. On earth he was born from Vasubharya and DHARMA. He had three sons, who in turn had forty-five sons. Along with Agni, these are the 'forty-nine fires'.

In iconography Agni is often depicted with a goat or ram, holding a mala or rosary and a water-vessel. He usually has a beard, and flames surround him.

Though Agni is only a Dikapala today, he is still an important deity as he is invoked in every sacrificial fire.

Agni Purana A Sanskrit text, one of the eighteen major PURANAS of Hinduism. The god AGNI is said to have narrated this text to the rishi VASISHTHA. It is an encyclopedic work, which is classified as a SHAIVITE Purana, though it begins with a section on VISHNU, and has several other topics. TANTRIC rites are described, as well as the mystic cult of the LINGA and the worship of the goddess DURGA. There are GANESHA rituals, methods of making and consecrating images, sections on death, transmigration and YOGA. It has a summary of the BHAGAVAD GITA and of the *Yama Gita*, relating to the god YAMA. In addition it deals with politics, the art of war, law, medicine, literature, grammar, poetry, drama, architecture, astronomy and geography, apart from the usual sections on cosmology and genealogy. In its present form it has 12,000 verses and probably dates from the ninth century.

agnikulas The 'fire families', a term used for four Rajput clans. There are several legends about their origin. According to one version, long ago, all the KSHATRIYAS or warriors of the earth were destroyed by PARASHURAMA, a BRAHMANA who was one of the

incarnations of the Hindu god VISHNU, and there was no one left to defend the land. Some brahmanas therefore conducted a sacrifice at Mt ABU (present-day Rajasthan) and out of the fire pit (agni kunda) of the sacrifice arose four strong warriors. These were the ancestors of the four warrior Rajput clans, the Paramaras, Pratiharas, Chahamanas and Solankis. The Rajputs, who ruled over much of the area of Rajasthan from the seventh century onwards, are said to have been a mixture of Indian and foreign groups. This story therefore has been taken to suggest that certain purificatory sacrifices were conducted to give them a higher status, and indicates how outsiders were integrated into the CASTE system.

agnishtoma A fire sacrifice in Hinduism, lasting five days. It is performed at the request of a BRAHMANA householder for religious merit.

Agnishvattah A pitri gana, or class of PITRIS or ancestors mentioned in Hindu texts. They were the ancestors of the DEVAS or gods.

Agra A city located on the river Yamuna in western Uttar Pradesh, best known for its famous Mughal monument, the TAJ MAHAL. Agra was occupied from ancient days but the foundations of the present city were laid by Sultan Sikandar Lodi, who made it his capital city in 1505. It was also one of the capitals of the Mughal emperor AKBAR, and continued to be an important Mughal city up to the middle of the eighteenth century. Agra was taken over by the British in 1803 and remained under British control till 1947.

Apart from the Taj Mahal, Agra has several other religious monuments. Among these are the JAMA MASJID, the MOTI MASJID, the DARGAH and mosque of the SUFI saint Shah Vilayat (d. 1540) and of Jalal-ud-din Bukhari (d. 1647), as well as the Fatehpuri Masjid of the seventeenth century. There is also a Chhatri of Raja Jaswant Singh of Jodhpur, built at the time of the Mughal emperor AURANGZEB, in addition to other old monuments and historic tombs. The ANGLICAN Church of St. George, the first Anglican church constructed in India, was built here in 1826. The city has an ARMENIAN chapel and graveyard dating from the seventeenth century. Agra is also important as one of the main centres of the RADHASOAMI sect. Fatehpur Sikri nearby has the tomb of the renowned Sufi saint, Shaikh SALIM CHISTI.

agricultural rites Early agrarian societies all over the world had rituals associated with agriculture, with the acts of ploughing, sowing and harvesting the crop, and with fertility in general. There were also prayers and sacrifices for rain and special deities associated with agriculture. In India, too, fertility rites and deities associated with agriculture existed from the earliest days. MOTHER GODDESS figurines, presumed to be associated with the concept of fertility, date back to 7000 BCE. A seal of the INDUS VALLEY CIVILIZATION

(2500–1800 BCE) depicts a woman, possibly a deity, with a plant growing from between her legs. In Vedic texts INDRA, PARJANYA, and others were gods associated with rain. The ATHARVA VEDA has chants and spells to bring rain. In the RAMAYANA, SITA, who was born in a furrow, is connected with agriculture. In later times, the goddess DURGA as SHAKAMBHARI was worshipped as a goddess of vegetation. Several NAGA or snake deities are worshipped when sowing the fields. SHAKTI and TANTRIC cults, with their emphasis on the union of male and female, are also indirectly associated with agrarian fertility. These are only some of the innumerable agrarian rituals and deities, many of which remain popular today. Harvest festivals such as BAISAKHI, BIHU and others continue to be celebrated and YAJNAS (sacrifices) and other rites are still performed during times of drought.

Ahi Budhnya/Ahirbudhnya A Hindu deity. In the RIG VEDA he is the serpent of the deep, or of the atmospheric ocean, invoked as a divine being. Later, it becomes the name of RUDRA or SHIVA. In the MAHABHARATA, Ahi Budhnya is one of the eleven RUDRAS, born to Sthanudeva, the son of BRAHMA. He is also mentioned as one of the MARUTS. According to the VISHNU PURANA, Ahi Budhnya was a son of VISHVAKARMA, the divine architect.

ahimsa The principle of non-violence, which is an important element in Hindu, Buddhist and Jain thought. Ahimsa is important in Hinduism in general, and is elaborated on in the system of YOGA where it is the first of the YAMAS, or basic ethical principles. Ahimsa, at one level, means non-injury to any living being. In the later Vedic period (beginning approximately 1000 BCE), sacrifices in which animals were killed became common. Later, there was an aversion to this and BHAGAVATISM or VAISHNAVISM arose, which did away with such sacrifices. Buddhism and Jainism were also against sacrifices and emphasized non-violence. In MAHAYANA Buddhism, ahimsa was raised to the level of loving compassion and sacrifice of oneself for the welfare of every living being. Ahimsa is the essence of Jainism and the killing of any creature, including insects, is forbidden. Several kings passed laws for the welfare of living beings. Among them was ASHOKA, the Mauryan emperor (ruled 269–232 BCE), who reduced the killing of animals for his royal kitchen and provided a list of animals and creatures (including the queen ant) who were not to be killed at any time. The Western Gangas, a dynasty of southern India who ruled between the fifth and tenth centuries, were influenced by Jainism, and the later kings had strict laws against killing animals. AKBAR, the Mughal emperor (ruled 1556–1605), was also against eating meat or killing animals. There are other such instances in India's history.

However, ahimsa implies far more than non-injury. Passages in the PURANAS and other ancient texts explain its implications. For instance, according to the DEVI BHAGAVATA PURANA, 'Ahimsa (non-injury) is what is most righteous. Even those who come to kill you should not be harmed.' The MANU SMRITI states that whoever does not injure any living being, but desires the good of all, obtains endless bliss.

In modern times, Mahatma GANDHI summed up the higher meaning of the ancient tradition of non-violence when he said that ahimsa meant a love for all, even for those who injured one. Applying the concept both to his personal life and to the freedom movement against the British, he frequently stopped or withdrew political movements when his followers became violent. However, ahimsa was not an excuse for cowardice, and those who practised it must have the strength to resist all wrong. Gandhi said: 'Literally speaking, ahimsa means non-violence. But to me it has a much higher, infinitely higher meaning. It means that you may not offend anybody; you may not harbour uncharitable thoughts even in connection with those who consider themselves your enemies. To one who follows this doctrine, there are no enemies . . . If you express your love, ahimsa, in such a manner that it impresses itself indelibly upon your so-called enemy, he must return that love.'

Ahl-e-Hadis/Ahl-i-Hadith An Islamic group that started in India in the second half of the nineteenth century and was an offshoot of the Tariqa-i Muhammadiya, founded by Sayyed AHMAD BARELVI. It uses only the HADIS for interpreting the QURAN and SHARIA, and denies the authority of the schools of law (FIQH). The life of the Prophet MUHAMMAD is the model for followers of this path. They are also against the cult of saints and PIRS. Among former leaders of this group, one of the most outstanding was Maulana Syed Nazir Husain (d. 1902), who founded an institute for instruction in Hadis in Delhi. The group developed its own form of NAMAZ and came in conflict with the DEOBAND SCHOOL, leading to the setting up of separate mosques. They were called WAHHABIS by their opponents because of their rejection of the HANAFI school of law.

Ahl-e-Hadis are still present in India. The largest and oldest Ahl-e-Hadis madrasa in India, is the Jamia Salafia at Varanasi. Other madrasas of the sect were affiliated to it in 2004. In Pakistan, there are several different Ahl-e-Hadis groups.

Ahl-i-Quran An Islamic group founded in India in the nineteenth century. It emphasized direct recourse to the QURAN, rather than to traditions (HADIS) or Islamic law. Maulana Abdullah Chakralwi was one of its main leaders. The group still exists in India.

Ahmad Barelvi, Sayyed A soldier and mystic who started an Islamic movement. Born in 1786, he joined the army of an Afghan, Amir Khan, who was made the nawab of Tonk in 1818. Ahmad Barelvi returned to Delhi and started the Tariqa-i Muhammadiya, a movement to purify Islam. He was helped by two of his disciples, Muhammad Ismail Shahid (1781–1831), and Abdul Hayy (d. 1828). They compiled his teachings into two books in Persian, *Sirat al-Mustaqim* and *Radd al-Ishraq*. Part of the second was translated into Urdu and known as *Taqwiyat al-Iman*. Barelvi condemned the worship of PIRS or saints, and some SUFI practices, though he was not entirely against Sufism. He preached his ideas in DELHI and on tours into the rural areas of the Gangetic plains, asking people to practice pure Islam, give up worshipping saints, DARGAHS, and objects such as TAZIYAS. In 1822–23 he went to Mecca, and there made a vow to undertake JIHAD against unbelievers. Returning to India in 1826, he started a war against the Sikhs of the north-west, and for a short time founded an Islamic state, which he ruled, calling himself Amir al-Muminin. He faced hostility not only from Sikhs, but from Muslim Afghan tribes in the area, and was defeated and killed in a battle against a Sikh army in 1831. His tomb is located at Balakot. Though one of his aims was to eliminate the worship of saints, he himself is considered a saint, and ironically his dargah is still worshipped.

British writers and his opponents in India called him a WAHHABI, claiming that he derived his inspiration from the Arabian Wahhabis, though recent scholars feel his ideas were developed independently. There is, nevertheless, a similarity with Wahhabi ideas.

Ahmad Khan, Syed A Muslim leader and reformer. Born in 1817, he began his career as a clerk in the East India Company in 1837, but his two main interests were religion and education. His writings on religion include *Essays on the Life of Muhammad*, as well as commentaries on the BIBLE and several volumes on the QURAN. In his writings on Islam he tried to correlate modern scientific concepts with Islamic beliefs. He established schools which were open to all, and initially worked for Hindu-Muslim unity. Later, however, he felt the two communities could not be united, and aimed at improving the position of Muslims through educational and social reforms. He started a journal called *Tahzib al-Akhlaq* (Social Reform), and in 1875 established a Muslim school at Aligarh, which was converted into the Anglo-Oriental College and later developed into Aligarh Muslim University. In 1886 he organized the All-India Muhammadan Educational Conference, which met annually and discussed ways to promote education among Muslims, as well as other issues concerning the community. The educational and social reform begun by him is known as the ALIGARH MOVEMENT.

Ahmad Sirhindi, Shaikh A SUFI saint of the NAQSHBANDI order, who claimed to be the MUJADDID or renewer of Islam, and was known as Mujaddid Alf-i Sani.

Born at Sirhind in 1564, he was initiated by his father Shaikh Abdul Ahad into the CHISTI and QADIRI orders.

When he visited Fatehpur Sikri, for some time the capital of the Mughal emperor AKBAR, he found the atmosphere at the court too rational and philosophical. He wanted to emphasize the importance of prophets and miracles, and wrote short books on this theme, among which was *Isbat al-Nubuwwa*. After his father's death in 1599 he decided to visit Mecca. On the way he reached DELHI where he met Khwaja Baqi Billah, leader of the Naqshbandi order, who initiated him into the sect. Though Sirhindi had first followed WAHDAT AL-WUJUD beliefs, he now became an expert in WAHDAT AL-SHUHUD and wrote the *Mabda-wa-maad* on this system. After Akbar's death, he appealed to the emperor Jahangir to reimpose the JIZYA and do away with Akbar's liberal policies. He was also against the SHIAS, and his work *Radd-i Rawafiz* criticizes them. He was equally critical of worldly ULAMA and materialistic SUFIS. He said he was the renewer (mujaddid) of Islam and had been sent by God to restore its purity. He stated that he had had several mystical experiences, and even described his ascent to heaven. As he could not substantiate his mystical claims, he was imprisoned by Jahangir for twelve months and on his release he was allowed to live either at Sirhind or in the imperial camp. He lived at the camp for three years, preaching to all who were there and writing letters to his sons and disciples. He claimed to be the disciple of God, as well as 'God's desire', and seemed to consider himself a prophet. There was considerable opposition to this, but he continued with his claims. He died in 1624, and his sons Muhammad Masum and Khwaja Muhammad Said carried on his mission.

Ahmadiya An Islamic sect, founded in 1889 by Mirza GHULAM AHMAD, who lived from 1839 to 1908 and was based at Qadian in Punjab. Ahmad claimed that he was the MAHDI and the messiah and suggested that he was the reincarnation of the Prophet MUHAMMAD, inbued with the spirit of JESUS and of KRISHNA.

In a time when India was changing and the ARYA SAMAJ was gaining ground in Punjab, Ghulam Ahmad aimed to revive and spread Islam. He wrote a four-volume work, *Proofs of the Ahmadiya*, to explain the QURAN in a rational, logical and systematic way. He preached that JIHAD involved a non-violent method of convincing unbelievers. He also spoke against the Arya Samaj and Hindu revivalism. He began to accept *bayah*, or an oath of allegiance, and Ahmadiyas gradually became a distinct sect, discouraged from marrying outside it or praying behind a non-Ahmadiya IMAM. The Ahmadiyas thus came in conflict with SUNNIS and other Muslim groups. After Ghulam Ahmad's death in 1908, he was succeeded by Mawlawi Nuruddin. On the latter's death in 1914, the Ahmadiya sect split into two factions, the Qadiani and Lahori. The Qadiani believed their's was the only true religion and recognized Ahmad as the Prophet, while the Lahori felt Ahmad was only a MUJADDID who revived and renewed the religion.

Ahmadiyas also started missionary activities and spread the movement to other countries. After 1947, they moved to Pakistan, but faced opposition from the ULAMA and were regarded as heretics. In a case against them in 1953–54, the judge at the court upheld their rights as Muslims, though Sunnis continued to oppose them. In 1974, however, they were declared to be a non-Muslim minority. In the 1980s, the head of the Qadianis, Mirza Tahit Ahmad, moved to London. Ahmadiyas continue to have a missionary zeal and project themselves as modern or forward-looking Muslims. Some Ahmadiyas still live in Pakistan, though they are not recognized as Muslims there and face discrimination.

Ahmadiya is also a name for some SUFI sects, the most important named after Ahmad al Badawi of Egypt (thirteenth century).

Ahobalam   A town in Andhra Pradesh, known for the worship of the Hindu god NARASIMHA, a form of VISHNU. There are a number of Narasimha shrines located here, some dating back to the eleventh century or earlier. It is the only place where nine forms of Narasimha are worshipped. Some of these forms relate to the story of PRAHLADA, such as Prahladavarada Narasimha, or Narasimha blessing Prahlada; Yogananda Narasimha, Narasimha teaching YOGA to Prahlada; Guha Narasimha, where Narasimha conceals himself. Other forms include Kroda Narasimha, the angry form, in which Narasimha is worshipped as a boar; Malola Narasimha, where he sports with his consort LAKSHMI; and Jwala Narasimha, where he emits flames of anger. Ahobalam is mentioned in the hymns of the Vaishnava ALVAR saints and is the centre of a Vaishnava MATHA. It is also considered sacred by the CHENCHU tribe.

Ahriman   The evil spirit in Zoroastrianism, the later PAHLAVI term for ANGRA MAINYU. Ahriman is described at length in the BUNDAHISHN, where he is finally defeated. His defeat is also mentioned in the KHORDEH AVESTA, the book of daily prayers, and in some YASHTS. In later related literature, Ahriman is described in modern terms as 'a shadow of the mind'.

Ahum Bis   A term meaning healer of life, a title of AHURA MAZDA, the name of God in Zoroastrianism, and of his prophet, ZARATHUSHTRA.

Ahuna Vairya   The first and most important prayer in Zoroastrianism, which is also known as the *Yatha Ahu Vairyo*. It states that spiritual teachers in the world have the same power as the supreme lord, through the righteousness (ASHA) that they have practised. The gifts of VOHU MANA, the good mind, and KHSHATHRA, divine strength, descend on those who serve and help others.

This prayer emphasizes the importance Zoroastrianism gives to not merely following the right path inwardly, but performing good actions in the world.

ahura   A term in Zoroastrianism, which indicates a god or deity. It is derived from the root *ahu*, or life. Its equivalent in Sanskrit is ASURA, which in the *RIG VEDA* meant a divine being, though in later Hinduism, asura came to mean a demon. In pre-Zoroastrian Iran, there was a group of deities known as Ahuras, of whom AHURA MAZDA was later chosen as the supreme deity.

Ahura Mazda   The name of God in Zoroastrianism. Literally, the name has been translated as 'the Lord of life and wisdom'. The GATHAS state that Ahura Mazda is the creator of the world, of life and of truth. He is eternal, and through his supreme wisdom he leads a person on the path of truth. He blesses and helps all living beings. He has six powers or aspects, which are truth, the good mind, strength, loving devotion, perfection and immortality. These aspects were personified as the AMESHA SPENTAS. In later PAHLAVI literature, Ahura Mazda was known as Ohrmazd or Hormazd, and was identified with SPENTA MAINYU, the good spirit. This led to the interpretation of the religion as dualistic, with Ahura Mazda and ANGRA MAINYU, the personification of evil, being almost co-existent.

Ahura Mazda is also known from other sources. He is mentioned in an inscription of Darius I (522–486 BCE) of Persia and by later kings. After Alexander's conquest, Ahura Mazda was associated with Zeus in some areas. A god known as Zeus Oromazdes is known from finds of the first century BCE at Commagene in Asia Minor. Oromozdo has also been depicted on Kushana coins of the king Huvishka (first to second century CE). In the early centuries CE a form of Ahura Mazda was worshipped in Sogdiana (Tajikistan/Uzbekistan). His worship in one form or another was thus quite widespread.

Certain scholars and groups of Zoroastrians still interpret the religion as dualistic, with ZURVAN or time being the source of creation, while other Zoroastrians believe the texts show that Ahura Mazda is an all powerful God, the sole creator of all.

Aihole   A small town in District Bijapur, Karnataka, known for its early temples. Once an ancient capital and commercial centre, Aihole has about a hundred temples dating to between the sixth and twelfth centuries, when it was under the Chalukya and Rashtrakuta dynasties. Half the temples are within an old fort, while the others are outside it. The temples include those dedicated to the Hindu deities VISHNU and SHIVA, as well as Buddhist and Jain shrines, and have a diversity of architectural features, including early Buddhist, and northern and southern elements. Among the main temples are the Lad Khan Temple and the DURGA TEMPLE in the central complex, the Chikki Temple and Ravana Phadi Temple to the north-east, and Jain and Buddhist temples to the south. Further north-east is the Huchimalli Temple, as well as a number of temples known as the Mallikarjuna group.

Airavata   A divine elephant, the vehicle of the Hindu god INDRA. Airavata is white with four tusks and is the king of the elephants. There are several stories about the origin of Airavata. According to one version, Airavata emerged at the time of the churning of the ocean for AMRITA. Another story makes him the cause of the DEVAS' misfortunes. It states that when the rishi DURVASA gave Indra a garland, he handed it to Airavata, who threw it down, either because he did not like the smell, or because there were bees in it. Angry at the disrespect shown to his gift, Durvasa cursed the devas who suffered and declined. Their fortunes were only revived after they had drunk the Amrita obtained from the ocean. Airavata is also said to have been created by BRAHMA, as one of the eight male guardian elephants, or ASHTADIGGAJAS.

Airavateshvara Temple A temple of the Hindu god SHIVA located at Darasuram in District Thanjavur, Tamil Nadu. Probably constructed by Rajaraja II (1150–72) of the Chola dynasty, the temple complex has two gateways or GOPURAMS. The main temple is in the centre, with an inner shrine, an ante-chamber and two MANDAPAS. Within the shrine is a LINGA, known as Raja-rajeshvaram-udayar. There are also niches containing different forms of Shiva, DURGA and other deities, as well as depictions of stories from the lives of the Shaiva saints. Some of these have labels in Tamil. The whole temple has exquisite sculptures and carvings. A six-headed KARTTIKEYA, ARDHANARISHVARA, four-armed NAGARAJA, BHAIRAVA, the sage AGASTYA, dance and musical scenes are among the numerous sculptures. The roof is pyramidal, with three diminishing storeys, capped with a dome. This is one of the most important Chola temples.

Aja (1) A name of several Hindu deities including VISHNU, KRISHNA, BRAHMA, SHIVA and SURYA. It means 'unborn' or 'eternal'.

(2) The name of a class of RISHIS or sages, who obtained svarga (heaven) through self-study, as well as the name of one of the sons of the third MANU, Uttama.

(3) Aja also means 'goat' and is a male goat or ram which is the VAHANA or vehicle of some of the Hindu deities. (Ajaa is a female goat). In the RIG VEDA, Aja is associated with PUSHAN. In the HARIVAMSHA, Aja is associated with AGNI. Aja also has a role to play in the ASHVAMEDHA sacrifice, and leads or guides the sacrificial horse to the next world.

Ajamukhi (1) A Hindu deity, a goat-faced goddess. She is a MATRIKA or mother goddess, one of the animal-headed mothers represented in early Indian art.

(2) An ASURA, the daughter of KASHYAPA and Surasa, and the sister of TARAKA. The Hindu god Skanda or KARTTIKEYA was born in order to vanquish Taraka, who had grown too powerful.

Ajanta Caves Buddhist rock-cut caves located near Ajanta village in District Aurangabad of Maharashtra. The caves are excavated along the semi-circular scarp of a cliff-face overhanging a stream. Dating between c. 150 BCE and 650 CE, the caves include CHAITYAS or halls of worship, and VIHARAS or monks' cells. The interiors are decorated with sculptures and paintings for which the caves are world famous. The early caves of the second and first centuries BCE have fragments of paintings, while the second period begins in the fourth to fifth centuries. It is not known who caused the earlier caves to be excavated, but the later caves were made mainly by feudatories of the Vakataka dynasty, and some by the Rashtrakutas. The themes of the paintings are mainly religious, centring around the BUDDHA, BODHISATTVAS and incidents described in the JATAKAS. The depiction of Jataka stories includes representations of daily life, street scenes, king's courts, hermitages, people of all kinds wearing different types of clothes and jewels, warriors and weapons, musicians and their instruments.

The base for the paintings was made with a layer of ferruginous earth, mixed with various substances and coated with lime wash. The colours used include red and yellow ochre, lamp black and lapis lazuli, while the binding medium for the colours seems to have been glue.

The caves are of both the HINAYANA and MAHAYANA schools of Buddhism. The chaityas copy earlier constructions in wood and have barrel-shaped ceilings with stone ribs, galleries, columns and sun-windows. Doorways, windows, capitals and pedestals are richly carved. Within are not merely paintings, but also sculptures.

XUANZANG (Hieun Tsang), the Chinese pilgrim of the seventh century, provided an account of these caves. He said there was a temple here, 31 m high, in which there was a Buddha image of about 22 m.

The caves were made known to the world by a British officer, John Smith, who rediscovered them in the nineteenth century.

Ajatashatru (1) The ruler of the kingdom of MAGADHA between 494 and 460 BCE. He was the son of king BIMBISARA, who was a patron of the BUDDHA. According to Buddhist texts, he conspired with DEVADATTA, the Buddha's cousin, to overthrow his father and at the same time kill the Buddha. The plot did not succeed and Ajatashatru was repentant. Pardoned by his father and the Buddha, he ascended the throne. Later, however, he is said to have imprisoned his father, though he became favourably inclined towards Buddhism. The first BUDDHIST COUNCIL after the death of the Buddha was held during his reign.

Ajatashatru also patronized Jainism and is described in Jain texts.

(2) An early king of KASHI who was also a philosopher.

Ajita Keshakambalin The founder of a non-orthodox sect who lived at the time of the BUDDHA in the sixth century BCE. 'Kesha-kambalin' means hair-blanket, which is evidently what he and his followers wore.

Ajita believed a person consisted of four elements. At the time of death, the earth element returned to earth, the water to water, the fire or heat to fire, and the air to air. The various faculties (*indrayani*), including the five senses and the mind, returned to space (*akasha*). He said that there was no life after death, and no consequence of one's deeds, whether good or evil. Thus there was no point in sacrifices, offerings, or reverence of one's parents. No person had attained any knowledge of the next world.

Some of Ajita's followers were monks, though their type and level of asceticism is not described. Accounts of this sect are found in early Jain and Buddhist texts.

Ajitas A GANA or group of lesser Hindu deities who lived in Maharloka, one of the several LOKAS or worlds. Fourteen Ajitas are listed in some PURANAS, while others list ten.

ajiva One of the two categories of the universe in Jainism. Ajiva signifies non-living beings, the other category being JIVA, or beings with life. Ajiva consists of the following DRAVYAS or substances: PUDGALA or matter, DHARMA, ADHARMA, AKASHA or space, and KALA or time. Ajiva is divided into two categories, those without form or *rupa*, and those with form. Pudgala is in the latter category.

Pudgala can be perceived by the senses. It consists of minute atoms, or *paramanus*, which when combined form SKANDHAS or aggregates. (This is somewhat different from the Buddhist concept of skandhas.) *Paramanus* cannot be perceived by the senses, as they are too small.

Dharma and adharma dravyas indicate the principles of motion and of rest. Dharma dravya does not act, but makes action possible. Adharma enables rest. Dharma and adharma sustain the universe and prevent its disintegration into chaos. Akasha or space is infinite and accomodates the material world. Kala or time is another essential component of the universe, which enables change and evolution to take place.

Ajivika An ancient non-orthodox sect which existed from before the time of the BUDDHA. It was probably founded by Nanda Vachchha who was succeeded by Kisa Samkichcha, but became widespread under Makkhali GOSALA, also known as Gosala Maskariputra, who lived in the sixth century BCE at the time of the Buddha and MAHAVIRA. Gosala was at first a follower of Mahavira, but later founded his own sect. There are no Ajivika texts existing, but records of their practices are found in Buddhist and Jain sources. Ajivikas are also mentioned in inscriptions.

The Jain BHAGAVATI SUTRA states that the Ajivika scriptures consisted of ten Puvvas (PURVAS), while the early Jain texts comprised fourteen Puvvas. The language too was similar to the ARDHA MAGADHI of the Jain texts. Tamil sources mention an Ajivika text called the *Navakadir* (Nine Rays), probably a translation into Tamil from the original.

Gosala believed that living beings had no force or power of their own and were completely controlled by *niyati* or fate. There were six classes (*sangati*) of beings, and their experiences depended on the class to which they belonged, and their inherent nature. There were also five classes of atoms, which are eternal: air, water, fire, earth and life. Of these, only life is endowed with knowledge. A living being passed through 84,00,000 maha or great KALPAS (aeons), followed by twenty-eight lives including seven as a deity, after which the being finally attained bliss. Nothing could be done to speed up the process. No one could attain perfection by his own efforts, nor could anyone help another. Existence was like a ball of yarn, slowly unwinding, the end of the yarn being similar to the end of the series of lives.

Despite this fatalistic attitude, Ajivika monks wandered about nude and practised strict moral observances. They abstained from eating plants with roots, as well as certain types of fruit.

The *Bhagavati Sutra* also states that they worshipped various deities, while according to a Tamil text, they worshipped the Ashoka tree. Gosala was revered as a deity in south India.

The Ajivikas lived in several parts of India. Initially in the north, they moved to the region at the foot of the Vindhyan mountains and to south India. Two caves of the Barabar hills near GAYA have inscriptions recording that they were dedicated by ASHOKA, the Mauryan emperor, and his successor Dasharatha, to Ajivika monks.

Ajmer A city in Rajasthan with several historic monuments, best known for the DARGAH of the SUFI saint Shaikh MUINUDDIN CHISTI.

Ajmer was occupied from ancient days, but the foundations of the present city were probably laid by Ajayadeva, a Rajput ruler of the Chauhan dynasty. The city came under the Delhi sultans, the Mughals and the Marathas, with intermittent periods of Rajput rule. It was finally ceded to the British in 1818 and remained under their control till 1947.

Apart from Shaikh Muinuddin Chisti's dargah which attracts thousands of pilgrims, monuments here include the ARHAI DIN KA JHOPRA MOSQUE, the AKBARI MOSQUE, and a nineteenth-century Jain temple known as Nasiyan, with wooden images of Jain deities.

Ajna Chakra One of the seven main CHAKRAS or invisible energy centres within the body. The Ajna Chakra is located in the centre of the forehead, and represents the so-called third eye. TANTRIC texts state that this chakra is white like the moon, and has two petals, with the Sanskrit letters ha and ksha written on it. Within is the subtle mind, manas, and the inner ATMA or soul, shining with its own light. Within is also the divine word, OM. Meditation on this chakra brings tranquility and manifests higher intelligence (buddhi). The person becomes all-knowing and all-seeing, the creator, destroyer and preserver of the three worlds, and realizes his unity with BRAHMAN, the Absolute.

Akal Purakh 'The eternal One', a name of God in Sikhism. It was used by Guru GOBIND SINGH in his description of God, and is still used today.

Akal Takht 'The Eternal Throne', the symbol of Sikh spiritual authority. The Akal Takht is located opposite the GOLDEN TEMPLE or HAR MANDIR SAHIB in AMRITSAR, and is the place where spiritual decisions are taken and orders given. The concept of a permanent centre of authority was thought of by Guru HARGOBIND, the sixth guru. He began to take decisions seated on an earthen mound on this spot, over which a platform was built in 1606. From here he is said to have issued the first Hukamnama or order to Sikh centres in all parts of the country. A building, known as Akal Banga, was built on the spot. After Guru Hargobind moved to KIRATPUR in 1635, the Akal Takht and other shrines in Amritsar came under the descendants of Prithi Chand, the hostile elder brother of Guru ARJAN DEV, but were regained by Guru GOBIND SINGH in 1699. Between 1762 and 1764, the Akal Takht and the Golden Temple were destroyed by the Afghan invader Ahmad Shah Abdali, but in 1774 the ground floor of the building was reconstructed. Four storeys were added to the structure by Maharaja RANJIT SINGH. By this time spiritual and temporal authority were separated.

In the Akal Takht, the GURU GRANTH SAHIB is located on the first floor, where the Jathedar, or head of the Takht, also sits. There are four other main TAKHTs, the Takht Sri Keshgarh Saheb at ANANDPUR, Punjab, the Takht Sri Harimandir Sahib at Patna, Bihar, the Takht Sri Damdama Sahib at TALWANDI SABO, Punjab, and the Takht Sachkhand Huzur Sahib at Nanded, Maharashtra. The heads of the Takhts are known as Jathedars and are chosen by the SHIROMANI GURDWARA PRABANDHAK COMMITTEE. The Takhts deal with crises affecting the Panth or community, and with enforcing spiritual discipline.

Akalanka A Jain philosopher who wrote a commentary on the TATTVARTHADHIGAMA SUTRA of UMASVAMI, entitled *Tattvartha-rajavarttika*.

Akalanka is considered one of the great DIGAMBARA Jain ACHARYAS of Karnataka. His name is mentioned in an inscription at SHRAVANA BELAGOLA, and according to Jain tradition, he lived around the third or fourth century, while some scholars place him in the eighth century.

His other works include the *Ashtashati*, a commentary on SAMANTABHADRA's *Aptami-mamsa*, and works on Jain logic, the *Nyayavi nishchaya, Laghiyastraya* and *Svarupasambodhana*. Several commentaries were in turn written on his works.

Akalanka's views were opposed by the Brahmana KUMARILA, a philosopher of the eighth century.

Akali A term used to refer to Sikhs, indicating a devotee of AKAL PURAKH or God. In a historical context, it was also used for Sikh warriors who joined Sikh suicide squads during protest movements. The first such group appeared in 1690. The AKALI MOVEMENT started in the twentieth century, the aim being to free the GURDWARAS or Sikh shrines from the hold of corrupt priests. The Shiromani Akali Dal was a political party which began at this time, and though it has gone through several changes and splits, it still exists and is important in Punjab.

Akali Movement A Sikh religious movement which started in the early twentieth century, and gradually acquired a political dimension. At this time the GURDWARAS or Sikh shrines were controlled by mahants (priests), who had lost touch with the Sikh community. Some of them were part of the UDASI sect and had introduced idol worship and other Hindu rituals. The Sikh shrines had huge incomes, both from offerings and from lands attached to them, and some corrupt mahants had appropriated these. The posts had also become hereditary. After the movement started, some mahants voluntarily handed over the shrines, but in 1920 a political component was introduced. India was in turmoil after the Jallianwala Bagh massacre by the British and the beginning of the non-cooperation movement against British rule. In this atmosphere, the British supported the mahants, who preached loyalty to them. The SHIROMANI GURDWARA PRABANDHAK COMMITTEE, an elected committee, and the Shiromani Akali Dal, a political party, were set up to organize and direct the movement. After a long struggle, the Sikh demands were finally conceded and the Gurdwara Act was passed in 1925, giving the reformers control over the gurdwaras. Over 30,000 had been imprisoned, several hundred killed, and thousands wounded during the agitation.

akasha A Sanskrit term which means 'space', atmosphere or 'ether'. In early Indian philosophy it signifies an ethereal substance permeating the world, the vehicle of sound and life. In Jainism, it is one of the DRAVYAS or substances. It can be divided into two categories, the part occupied by the created world, or Lokakasha, and the space beyond it, Alokakasha, which is an empty void.

Akbar A Mughal emperor who ruled in northern India from 1556 to 1605 and is known not only for his conquests and administrative reforms, but also for his liberal policy towards Hindus and his eclectic views on religion. Akbar was the son of Humayun and grandson of Babar, who had first established Mughal rule in India in 1526. Humayun had lost his territory to the Afghan Sher Shah, and regained it only in 1555, one year before his death. Born in 1542, Akbar was thirteen years old when he took over as king. He embarked on a series of conquests until most of north India was under his control. He extended his conquests into Afghanistan and to the Deccan in the south.

His religious views developed over time. Initially, he was an orthodox Muslim, but gradually he changed. Though he was a SUNNI, he is said to have been influenced by his tutors, Bairam Khan and Abdul Latif, who had liberal views.

Akbar abolished the pilgrim tax in 1563 and removed the JIZYA tax, which was levied on non-Muslims, in 1564. He made a number of alliances, particularly with the Rajputs, married Rajput princesses, and appointed Rajputs to high posts. He was influenced by SUFI views and revered Shaikh SALIM CHISTI and Shaikh MUINUDDIN CHISTI. His courtiers ABUL FAZL, FAIZI, and their father Sheikh Mubarak also influenced him.

In 1575 he began discussions at the IBADAT KHANA in Fatehpur Sikri with members of different Islamic sects, and finding conflicting views among them, in 1579 he declared that he himself was the final authority for settling religious disputes. Later, discussions continued with representatives of different religions and sects, including Sufis, Christian fathers, Zoroastrians, Jains and Hindus.

He believed in the concept of SULH-I KUHL, or absolute peace, and became familiar with the doctrine of WAHDAT AL-WUJUD, or universal oneness. He even founded a new religion, or rather a new way of worship, known as the DIN-I ILAHI or Tauhid Ilahi, which included sun worship and the recognition of the emperor as God's representative on earth. For some time he seemed to be against Islam and traditional Islamic methods of worship, and this was used by his son Salim to gather support when he started a revolt against his father.

Akbar celebrated Hindu festivals at court, though this was not unique, as other Muslim rulers followed this practice as well. He was against killing animals for food and prohibited the killing of animals on certain days. He only drank GANGA water, which was despatched from the river in sealed jars.

Apart from his liberal religious views, Akbar was socially progressive and attempted to stop the practice of SATI. He patronized artists, poets and musicians, and sponsored new trends in architecture, representing a fusion of Hindu and Islamic styles. A number of Sanskrit texts were translated into Persian on his orders.

He died in 1605 and was succeeded by his son Salim, who became the emperor Jahangir.

Akbari Mosque A mosque located at AJMER in Rajasthan, near the DARGAH or tomb of the SUFI saint, MUINUDDIN CHISTI. The Mughal emperor AKBAR visited the dargah several times, and built this large mosque in 1571. It was repaired in 1901 by Nawab Ghafoor Ali of Danapur, and one of its wings now houses the Monis Usmani Darul-Uloom, a MADRASA.

Not many mosques were constructed during Akbar's reign, and the erection of the Akbari Mosque here is a mark of his reverence and appreciation of the saint.

Akhand Path A term referring to the non-stop ceremonial recitation of the GURU GRANTH SAHIB, the sacred book of the Sikhs. This recitation continues for two days, that is for forty-eight hours, and is performed at religious festivals and other important functions. A Saptah Path, or reading in seven days, takes place in private homes and temples.

Akhnur The site of the ruins of a Buddhist monastery located in the Jammu region of the state of Jammu and Kashmir, on the banks of the river Chenab. Antiquities found at the site date back to the sixth century, indicating the continued existence of Buddhism in the area, from early days.

akshara A Sanskrit term, which means imperishable, unchanging, or eternal. It designates BRAHMAN or the Absolute. Its other meanings include a letter of the alphabet, a word or sound, a sacrifice or religious austerity.

Akshardham Temple A temple dedicated to Lord SWAMINARAYAN, a Hindu saint who lived from 1781 to 1830 and is considered an incarnation of the god VISHNU. The main temple, located at Gandhinagar in Gujarat, was inaugurated in 1992. The image of Swaminarayan, considered the Supreme God, is installed in the Hari Mandir, a hall on the ground floor of the temple. On either side are images of Gunatitanand Swami, representing Aksharbrahman or god's divine abode, and Gopalanand Swami, representing Aksharmuktas or redeemed souls. On the upper floor the Vibhuti Mandir has some of the sayings of Swaminarayan etched on glass circles edged with gold.

The structure rises to a height of 32.93 m and is 73.15 m long and 39.93 m broad. It is constructed out of 6000 tonnes of pink sandstone, along with some yellow stone, white marble and granite. There are over a hundred carved pillars with sculptures of gods and goddesses, as well as trellised windows and delicate stone screens.

There are several Swaminarayan temples in Gujarat, other parts of India and abroad. The central image in these temples may be of some other form of Swaminarayan or Vishnu, but represents the Supreme Deity. A large Akshardham Temple also exists in Delhi.

Akshobhya A celestial BUDDHA, also referred to as a DHYANI BUDDHA, who heads a group or family of Buddhist deities. Literally, his name means 'immovable', and he is described in both MAHAYANA and VAJRAYANA texts. His direction is the east, and he reigns over Abhirati, the eastern paradise. The *Akshobhya Vyuha*, an early text available in Chinese and Tibetan translations, provides a detailed account of this paradise. According to legend, while Amitabha was a BODHISATTVA, he vowed never to feel anger towards any living being, and thus became a Buddha. Usually he is depicted as dark blue or sometimes golden. He holds a VAJRA (thunderbolt) in his right hand, and touches the earth with his left (bhumisparsha-mudra), and his vehicle is a pair of elephants. The Bodhisattva associated with him is Vajrapani, and his Shakti or consort is Lochana.

Among the gods who emanate from him are HERUKA, HAYAGRIVA, Yamari, Chanda-roshana, Buddhakapala and Vajradaka. Among the goddesses are Mahachina-Tara, Janguli, Ekajata, PRAJNAPARAMITA, Vajracharchika, Mahaman-tranusarini, Mahapratyangira, Dhvaja-grakeyura and Nairatma. In general, all deities who are blue and dwell in the eastern direction belong to this family. In MANDALAS they are in the south-east (Agni) corner.

Alagar/Azhagar A Hindu deity, a name of the god VISHNU in south India.

Alagar Koil A temple of the Hindu deity ALAGAR or VISHNU, located 21 km north-east of MADURAI in Tamil Nadu, at the foot of the Alagar hills. According to the legendary account in the Sthala Purana of the temple, the god YAMA prayed there, and was blessed by NARAYANA (Vishnu). Yama then insisted that Vishnu reside there, and asked VISHVAKARMA, the divine architect, to construct the temple. The temple is mentioned in the *Paripadal*, a Tamil text, and in the hymns of the ALVAR saints. According to another story, Vishnu descended here from VAIKUNTHA, his heaven, to give his sister MINAKSHI in marriage to Sundareshvara (SHIVA). Alagar is also known as Sundararaja (the beautiful), or Kallalagar, as he was worshipped by the Kalla caste. He is depicted in various postures, seated, standing and reclining. The main image is flanked by BHU DEVI and SHRI DEVI. There are several other shrines nearby, including SHAIVITE shrines. The guardian deity of the temple is the local god Karuppan.

This temple and the legends associated with it indicate attempts to bring the Shaivites and Vaishnavites together. The god has an important role in the Chittirai festival of the MINAKSHI TEMPLE at Madurai.

Alai, Shaikh A Muslim saint who lived in the sixteenth century and was a leader of the MAHDAWI movement. Originally from Bengal, his family settled near AGRA. Pious and learned from his youth, he gathered followers around him and claimed to be the MAHDI. For some time he gave up his claims in favour of Shaikh Abdullah Niyazi, a disciple of Mir Sayyid Muhammad of Jaunpur, but later he reasserted himself as a divine leader. He converted several people and as his influence spread, the emperor Islam Shah Sur, the son of Sher Shah, was persuaded by others at the court that Alai was a threat to his power. He ordered his punishment, but Alai, already weak from illness, died. It is said that at the time of his death in 1550, a huge storm arose, and when it abated his body was covered in flowers. People prophesied that now Islam Shah's rule would not last, and indeed it came to an end in 1554. Soon after this, Humayun, the second Mughal emperor, who had been ousted from power by Sher Shah, recaptured DELHI in 1555.

Alakananda The name of the sacred river GANGA, when it flows through Deva Loka, the world of the gods. Alakananda is also a real river, forming a headstream of the Ganga.

Alakshmi A Hindu deity, a form of the goddess LAKSHMI, worshipped primarily in Bengal. Alakshmi is inauspicious and brings misfortune. She is worshipped on the night of DURGA PUJA and rituals are performed to clear the house of Alakshmi, and bring in Lakshmi, the auspicious one, the goddess of wealth and prosperity. Alakshmi is also known as JYESHTHA, and in this form was once popular in south India. She is sometimes identified with DHUMAVATI, one of the MAHAVIDYAS or TANTRIC goddesses.

Alara Kalama An ascetic whom Siddhartha Gautama, later the BUDDHA, came in contact with, in the sixth century BCE, before achieving enlightenment. Alara Kalama had reached the seventh stage of meditation, in which the mind seeks nothing. He taught Siddhartha certain techniques of YOGA, but dissatisfied with these, Siddhartha continued his wanderings and his search.

Alchi Temples Buddhist shrines located at Alchi in LADAKH in the state of Jammu and Kashmir, constructed between the eleventh and thirteenth centuries. There are five shrines in a courtyard, with a path leading to the Dukhang, the main temple. Several CHORTENS, small structures containing holy relics, are in the courtyard. Balconies, doorways and windows are made of wood, and finely carved and painted. The walls are rock, covered with mud, and the flat roofs have stone tiles. Inside, the walls and ceilings are plastered, overlaid with paintings of MANDALAS and Buddhist deities in brilliant colours. The five temples are the SUMTSEK, Dukhang, Lhakang Soma, Lotsawa Lakhang, and Manjushri Lakhang. The Dukhang, the oldest, has a central image of the Buddha VAIROCHANA, while the Sumtsek, just slightly later, is a large temple with three stories.

Aleph/Alef The first letter of the Hebrew alphabet, which is considered sacred. In the mystical KABBALAH of Judaism, it is considered the spiritual root of all letters, including in its essence the whole alphabet, and therefore all that is.

Alif A letter of the Arabic alphabet, considered sacred in Islam, as the word ALLAH begins with it. Alif, the first letter of the alphabet, signifies oneness. According to legend, a SUFI saint, after learning only this letter in school, understood the unity of the universe.

Aligarh Movement An Islamic reform movement in India in the nineteenth century. Led by Syed AHMAD KHAN, it advocated the modernization of education for Muslims. This movement resulted in the foundation of the Anglo-Oriental College at Aligarh in 1875, which became a university in 1920. Known as Aligarh Muslim University, it is today a prominent centre of education with departments in all branches of learning.

alim An Arabic term meaning 'one who has knowledge', used for a person learned in Muslim canonical law. Its plural is ULAMA.

Allah The Arabic name of God in Islam. The QURAN states that there is no God but Allah, and that MUHAMMAD is his prophet. Several passages in the Quran describe the nature of Allah. He is the living and the everlasting. All that is in the heavens and earth belong to him. He is all-hearing, all-knowing, and the protector of believers (2.255–57). He is the light of the heavens and the earth (24.35). There is no God but He, the creator of all; he is to be served, for he is the guardian of everything. The eyes cannot attain Him, but He attains the eyes; He is the All-subtle, the All-aware (6.102–03).

Allah has ninety-nine names, among them being Ar-Rahman, the merciful, and Ar-Rahim, the compassionate.

God in Islam is also known by the Persian word, Khuda. However, in all formal prayers, the word Allah is used.

Allahabad The ancient PRAYAGA, mentioned in texts and inscriptions. At this sacred spot the streams of the GANGA and YAMUNA unite, and according to tradition the SARASVATI river joins them underground, forming the Triveni, or meeting of three streams.

Prayaga was a prosperous place until around the seventh century, after which it declined. AKBAR, the third Mughal emperor, rebuilt the city in the sixteenth century, naming it Allahabad. It came under the British in 1801. There are several historic monuments in the city, including an ASHOKA pillar which was once located at the site of KAUSHAMBI nearby. Religious monuments include mosques, among which is a JAMI MASJID, as well as churches and a cathedral. There are also innumerable temples, though most of them are not very old. Among them are the Adi Madhava temple, Adishesha Bhagvan temple, Bharadvaj temple, HANUMAN temple at Triveni Sangam and Veni Mata temple. Allahabad is one of the four places where the KUMBH MELA is held, once in twelve years.

Allahu Akbar An Arabic phrase in Islam, which means 'God is great'. The AZAN or call to prayer, made five times a day, begins with this phrase.

Allasani Peddana A poet at the court of Krishnadeva Raya, ruler of the Vijayanagara kingdom from 1509 to 1529. Allasani Peddana is best known for his work *Svarochisha-Sambhava* or *Manucharitra*, based on a variant of a story from the MARKANDEYA PURANA. Allasani's story is of an orthodox BRAHMANA, named Pravara, who refuses the love offered to him by Varuthini, an APSARA. A GANDHARVA takes the form of Pravara and lives with Varuthini, and from their union, the second MANU, Svarochisha, was born. (Other PURANAS have different stories on the birth and origin of Svarochisha.) Allasani is known as Andhrakavi-pitamaha, the grandfather of Telugu poetry.

Alphonsa, Sister A Christian nun who was made a saint on 12 October 2008.

Sister Alphonsa was born on 2 August 1910, in Kudumallur, a village in kerala. She lost her mother soon after her birth, and was brought up by her mother's sister. Originally known as Anna Muttathupadathu, she refused to marry, joined the convent in 1925 and was ordained in 1927. She did not live long, and at the time of her death in 1946, she was almost unknown.

However, soon after this, children from a nearby school who knew her used to visit her grave, reported that any prayers they made there were answered. Others began to go there, and soon many miracles of cures and other blessings were reported. She was beatified in 1986, and after investigation of some of the reported miracles, she was declared a saint in 2008.

She is the only woman saint from India.

Alvars/Azhwars VAISHNAVA saints who lived in south India between the sixth and tenth centuries. They composed songs and verses of love and devotion, mainly in Tamil, to the Hindu god VISHNU, which are collected in the *NALAYIRA DIVYA PRABANDHAM* (The Book of Four Thousand Sacred Hymns). Traditionally, there were twelve main saints. The term Alvar means one who has an instinctive knowledge of God, and Alvar was usually added to the names of the saints. The twelve saints are: Poigai, Bhutattalvar, Pey, Tirumazhisai, Kulashekhara, Periya Alvar, Tondaradippodi, Tiruppan, TIRUMANGAI, NAMMALVAR, Madhura Kavi and ANDAL, a woman. These BHAKTI saints have different origins. According to traditional literature, the first three were born in a miraculous way. Tirumazhisai was the son of a rishi. Periya, Tondara and Mathura were BRAHMANAS. Kulashekhara was a KSHATRIYA, Nammalvar, a cultivator, and Tirumangai, a Kalla (lower caste).

The Alvar saints popularized Vaishnavism in the south.

Amalorpavadoss, Father D.S. An Indian Christian priest and theologian. Born in 1932, he founded the National Biblical, Catechital and Liturgical Centre at Bangalore in Karnataka, and later the Anjali Ashram, a Christian ashram, at Mysore. He propagated Indian forms of worship and helped in the liberalization of the CATHOLIC CHURCH in India. He also analyzed the role of Christianity in India and its relationship with other Indian religions, and among his books on this theme are *Gospel and Culture*, and *Integration and Interiorization*. He died in 1990.

Amar Das, Guru The third Sikh guru who succeeded Guru ANGAD. Born on 5 May 1479, he became the guru in 1552, at the age of seventy-three.

Amar Das was originally a VAISHNAVITE Hindu, but after meeting Guru Angad, became his devoted follower. Another disciple of Angad, called Gobind, built a township known as Goindwal on the river Beas for his guru. Amar Das was sent to supervise the construction and then to stay in the completed town. Despite the displeasure of his sons, Angad chose Amar Das as his successor, and he became the next guru after Angad's death in 1552. Simultaneously Angad's son Datu proclaimed himself the guru, but could not acquire a following, and Amar Das was persuaded to continue.

Amar Das expanded the institution of LANGAR, or the free community meal, where people of all castes and religions ate together. He trained a number of people to spread the Sikh religion, and established twenty-two MANJIS, or spiritual divisions. Each Manji consisted of a group of Sikhs under a spiritual leader. This system helped to consolidate and spread Sikhism. Guru Amar Das also constructed a sacred *baoli* (step-well) at Goindwal, which became a centre of pilgrimage, and introduced Sikh rituals for birth and death. He was known to be against SATI and other social evils.

He composed hymns which are included in the GURU GRANTH SAHIB. In the *Anand Sahib*, included in the daily prayers, he describes the joy of discovering god. He says:

The true name, abiding in my heart,
Has given me peace and joy. (Trans. Gopal Singh)

He chose as his successor his son-in-law Jetha, whom he renamed RAM DAS.

He died in 1574, at the age of ninety-five.

Amarakosha A Sanskrit dictionary compiled in the fourth or fifth century CE by Amarasimha. As it gives synonyms of many words and multiple names of each deity, it is a useful text for understanding Hindu gods and goddesses.

Amaravati (1) A divine city of the Hindu god INDRA, located on Mt MERU.

(2) A city in Andhra Pradesh, where the AMARESHVARA TEMPLE and the AMARAVATI STUPA are located.

Amaravati Stupa A Buddhist STUPA, located at AMARAVATI in Andhra Pradesh, constructed between 200 BCE and 250 CE. The whole complex once covered an area of about 600 sq. m. The stupa itself had a height of 35 m and a diameter of 45 m. Around it was a stone railing, with four elaborately carved gateways in the four cardinal directions. At Amaravati, the BUDDHA was depicted in human form and large Buddha images, some more than 2 m high, are preserved in the museum. The railings and cross beams are intricately carved with depictions of JATAKA stories, miniature stupas, foliage and other scenes. The stone used is greenish-white limestone, and the carving is usually in BHARHUT style, though there is some influence of GANDHARA and MATHURA art as well.

The stupa was deserted in the fifth century and rediscovered by a British officer in the late eighteenth century. Several large sculptures were transported to Britain and are still in the British Museum.

Amardad An AMESHA SPENTA or deity in Zoroastrianism, the later name of AMERETAT or immortality.

Amareshvara Temple A temple of the Hindu god SHIVA located on the Krishna river, at AMARAVATI in Guntur District of Andhra Pradesh. Evidence indicates there was once a Buddhist shrine at this spot, as the foundation slabs are characteristically Buddhist. Constructed in the tenth or eleventh century, it is dedicated to Shiva in the form of Amareshvara, the eternal Lord. In the main shrine is a white marble LINGA, about 2.8 m high. Amareshvara's consort, also woshipped in the temple, is the goddess Bala Chamundika. There are other shrines dedicated to minor deities. The sanctity of Amaravati is described in the PURANAS. One legend states that when the DEVAS were being harassed by the RAKSHASAS, they took refuge here, and therefore it was called Amaravati, the place of immortals. The temple is in Dravidian style architecture, with towering GOPURAMS and a VIMANA or tower above the central sanctuary. There are inscriptions of the Kota kings of Dhanyakataka (eleventh to thirteenth centuries), the Reddi kings of Kondavidu and the Vijayanagara rulers. In the late eighteenth century the temple was renovated by a local chief, Raja Sri Vasireddi Venkatadri Nayudu, who also provided for its income and maintenance.

The temple still attracts thousands of pilgrims, the main festivals being at SHIVARATRI, the NAVARATRAs and Kalyana Utsavas. Nearby is the famous AMARAVATI STUPA.

Amarkantak A sacred spot on the Maikala range on the border of Madhya Pradesh/Chhattisgarh, where the river NARMADA originates. Temples dedicated to the Hindu god SHIVA and the river goddess Narmada were constructed to mark this spot in the time of the Marathas in the eighteenth century. The image of Narmada is of black stone, with silver eyes. Opposite is the linga of Amarkanteshvara Shiva, said to be svayambhu, or self-created, near which is an image of Parvati. There are other shrines, of Surya, Vishnu, Gorakhnatha and the eleven Rudras. The source of the river is in the courtyard of the main temple, and is surrounded with marble slabs. To the east is the source of the Sone river, marked by the Sonakshi Shaktipitha Temple. The sanctity of Amarakantak is described in the *Skanda Purana*, *Vishnu Samhita*, and other texts. Amarkantak is a major center of pilgrimage.

Amarnath A natural cave located in the Liddar valley of Kashmir, sacred to the Hindu god SHIVA. At a height of 3962 m, the large cave, 25 m deep, has an ice formation similar to the LINGA of Shiva. It is considered a self-formed (*svayambhu*) linga. According to legend, the cave was first discovered in ancient days when the rishi KASHYAPA drained the Kashmir valley of water. SHANKARA went there in the ninth century, and the site is mentioned in the *NILAMATA PURANA* and *Rajatarangini*, the old chronicles of Kashmir. The king ZAIN UL ABIDIN visited it in the fifteenth century, but after this it was unknown for a few hundred years. In the nineteenth century, it was rediscovered by a Muslim shepherd, Buta Malik, of village Batakoot. According to the story, a sadhu gave Malik a sack of coal, but opening it, he found gold coins. He went to search for the sadhu to thank him, but instead discovered the cave. Until recently a percentage of the donations made here were given to the descendants of Malik, who still act as guides for pilgrims visiting the caves.

In this cave, it is said Shiva told PARVATI the story of creation. A pair of doves overheard it and still live there, reborn endless times. Two more ice lingas in the cave are believed to be of Parvati and GANESHA.

Thousands of pilgrims visit the Amarnath cave every year. The Amarnath Yatra, or journey to the cave, is organized in June/July every year.

amavasya A Sanskrit term, which literally means 'to dwell together'. It refers to the night of the new moon, when the sun and the moon are said to dwell together, or the first day of the first quarter when the moon is invisible. Certain Hindu festivals are celebrated at amavasya, and offerings are made to the PITRIS or ancestors.

Amba A Hindu goddess, a form of DURGA. She is worshipped particularly in Gujarat. A major temple of Amba Mata is located on the Girnar hill near Junagadh in Gujarat. As Amba means 'mother', the word is sometimes used for other goddesses as well. Amba also represents the first syllable of the sacred mantra OM.

In early texts, Amba was one of the daughters of the king of KASHI and her sisters were AMBIKA and Ambalika.

Ambedkar, B.R. A dalit and Buddhist leader. Bhimrao Ramji Ambedkar, popularly known as 'Babasaheb', was a lawyer and jurist, and one of the framers of the Indian Constitution. In addition, he was a leader of backward and lower castes, particularly Scheduled Castes, today known as DALITS. In 1956 he led them in a mass conversion to Buddhism to escape from the oppressive nature of the CASTE system in Hindu society.

Born on 14 April 1891 at Mhow in Madhya Pradesh, he was of the Mahar caste of untouchables. He completed school at Satara and Mumbai (Bombay) and obtained a BA degree from Bombay University, He then went to the USA for further studies on a scholarship offered by the Gaekwad (ruler) of Baroda, where he gained a PhD degree. Later, he went to England where he gained a Dsc degree and also studied law before returning to India. In India he held important positions both before and after Independence.

Despite his unusually privileged position at a time when less than 10 per cent of the population had access to education, Ambedkar never forgot his less fortunate brethren and worked unceasingly to improve their condition. After a lifetime of effort, Ambedkar came to believe that lower castes would never achieve equality within Hinduism. He was attracted by the social equality of Buddhism, and

studied it for several years before deciding to convert to it. The conversion ceremony took place at Nagpur on 14 October 1956, and an estimated 2,00,000 of his followers joined him in this. Not long after this, Ambedkar died on 6 December 1956. However, he had begun a movement of conversion to Buddhism which continues even today. These converts are often known as NEO-BUDDHISTS.

Ambedkar wrote a number of books, including *The Buddha and His Dhamma*, which was published posthumously and later translated into Hindi and Marathi. This book, a reinterpretation of Buddhism to suit the times, is the main text read and studied by Neo Buddhists. It includes sections from texts of the PALI CANON retold by Ambedkar, along with his commentaries and interpretations. Among his other books are *Who were the Shudras?* and *The Untouchables: A Thesis on the origins of Untouchability*.

Ambedkar Jayanti, celebrating his birthday, is an important festival. Dhamma Diksha day, commemorating the first conversion on 14 October, is also celebrated by his followers along with other Buddhist festivals. Ambedkar is revered by dalits and considered their saviour. Statues of him have been set up in several places.

Ambika A Hindu goddess, a form of SHAKTI, PARVATI or DURGA. Ambika is mentioned in the *VAJASENEYI SAMHITA* and the *Taittiriya Brahmana* as the sister of RUDRA. In the *Taittiriya Aranyaka* she is his consort, whereas in later texts she is a form of Parvati or Durga. In other texts, she was one of the daughters of the king of KASHI. There are several temples of Ambika, particularly in western India. An important temple of Ambika, a SHAKTA PITHA, is located at Arasur in the Aravali hills of north Gujarat. Here the deity is represented symbolically by a YANTRA. Another famous Ambika shrine is the Jagat Mata temple at Udaipur, Rajasthan, which has seventeen turrets and a gabled roof. It is a centre of pilgrimage, particularly at the time of the March-April NAVRATRAS, when the GANGAUR festival takes place.

Ambika, Jain A Jain deity, associated with the twenty-second Tirthankara ARISHTANEMINATHA. She is also known as Kushmandini, and her consort is Gomedha. She is usually depicted riding a lion, and has four hands, in which she holds a bunch of mangoes, a noose, a child and an elephant goad. She thus had similarities with the Hindu goddess DURGA, whose names include AMBIKA and Kushmanda.

Ameretat A power of AHURA MAZDA, the name of God in Zoroastrianism. She is personified as an AMESHA SPENTA, representing immortality. aThe word Ameretat is similar to the Sanskrit AMRITA, the nectar of immortality. Ameretat is the twin of HAURVATAT, or perfection. According to the GATHAS, perfection and immortality come to those whose words and actions are in harmony with the Truth. In PAHLAVI texts

Ameretat is known as Amardad. She is said to preside over the vegetable kingdom and her symbol is the white frangipani flower.

Amesha Spentas A term in Zoroastrianism for immortal beings through whom AHURA MAZDA, or God, pervades the cosmos. Created by him, they are his powers, but were later personified and treated as independent deities. They are ASHA or cosmic order, VOHU MANA or the good mind, KHSHATHRA or strength, ARMAITI or loving devotion, HAURVATAT or perfection, and AMERETAT or immortality.

The GATHAS, verses ascribed to ZARATHUSHTRA, mention and describe these powers. The later PAHLAVI term for them is Amshaspand or Amahraspand. The term is often translated as 'bounteous immortals' or 'beneficent immortals'.

The Amesha Spentas are spiritual guides that help people reach perfection. They are also internal powers that dwell within each human being, and as such are similar to the CHAKRAS, or hidden energy centres.

Amir Ali, Syed A Muslim leader who settled in England and wrote on Islam. Born on 6 April 1849 in Cuttack, Orissa, he claimed to be descended from the Prophet MUHAMMAD. He obtained degrees in law from Kolkata (Calcutta) and England and then returned to Kolkata to practise law. He became a judge of the Calcutta High Court in 1890.

In 1877 he founded the National Mohammadan Association to protect Muslim interests. He wrote works on Islam in English, and his books include *The Critical Examination of the Life and Teachings of Mohammad*, and *The Spirit of Islam*.

He moved to England in 1904, and remained there till his death in 1928.

Amir Husain A SUFI saint who lived in the thirteenth century, and was a disciple of Shaikh Sadruddin Arif. He wrote *Zadul Musafirin* and other works on the Sufi doctrine of WAHDAT AL-WUJUD.

Amir Khusrau A poet, musician, historian and SUFI mystic. Amir Khusrau was born in 1253 at Patiali in present district Etah of Uttar Pradesh, and was the court poet of several of the DELHI Sultans. His father Amir Saifuddin Mahmud, was a noble at the court of Sultan Iltutmish, and was descended from the Turkish Hazara clan, while his mother was Indian. Khusrau wrote several romantic and historical works in Persian, Hindi and Urdu and made major contributions to the development of Hindustani music. In 1284 he became a disciple of NIZAMUDDIN AULIYA, a Sufi saint who lived in Delhi, and began to compose poems on mystical themes. In one of his verses he said, ' Though the Hindu is not like me in religion, he believes in the same thing I do'. He said that though Hindus worshipped stones, plants, animals and the sun, they recognized that these were all creations of the one God. He praised Islam compared with Hinduism, but said that even so Hindus were better than materialists, star-worshippers and Christians.

Khusrau was away when Nizamuddin died. When he learnt of the saint's death he became almost mad with grief, and lived only another six months.

Considered the best of the Persian poets in India, he was known as 'Parrot of Hind'. He is said to have written ninety-nine books, or in some sources 199. Around twenty of his works are known today. The Persian works include five diwans or poetry collections, ten masnawis (rhyming verse compositions) and three prose works. Five masnawis are in response to those of the Prsian poet Nizami Ganjavi. These are: *Matla-e-ul-Anwar* (The Rising of the Lights), a mystical work; *Shirin-Khusrau* and *Laila Majnu*, both love poems; *Hasht Bihisht* (The Eight Paradises), on the adventures of Bahram; *Aina-e-Sikandari*, (The Mirror of Alexander) an account of Alexander. Five other masnawis are *Qiran-us-sadain*(The Conjunction of Ten Auspicious Planets), an allegorical work; *Dewal Rani Khizr Khan*,a historical romance; *Nuh Sipihr (The Nine Heavens)*; *Mifta-ul-futuh;* and *Tughlaq Nama*.Three prose works are *Aijaz-e-khusravi; Khazian-ul Fatuh* also known as *Tarikh-i-Alai;* and *Afzal-ul-Fawaid.*

Amir Khusrau developed the qawwali style of singing, as the khayal and tarana. The origin of the sitar and the tabla are traditionally attributed to him. He died in 1325 and is buried near the tomb of the Sufi saint, Nizamuddin Auliya, in Delhi.

Amitabha A celestial BUDDHA, also referred to as a DHYANI BUDDHA. One of the five main Buddhas, he heads a group of BUDDHIST DEITIES. His name means boundless light. He was earlier known as Amitayus, meaning eternal life, and is described in MAHAYANA and VAJRAYANA texts. Amitabha is the Buddha embodying compassion, and worshipping him leads to rebirth in his paradise. His direction is the west, and he rules over the western paradise, Sukhavati. Specific texts describing this paradise are two *Sukhavati Vyuhas*, both different in content, one longer than the other. Another text relating to Amitabha is the *Amitayur Dhyana Sutra*, preserved in its Chinese translation. According to legend, Amitabha was once a monk named Dharmakara who made forty-eight vows, and after perfecting himself in succeeding births, became a Buddha.

In iconography and art, Amitabha is depicted as red in colour and holding a lotus. His vehicle is a pair of peacocks. In TANTRIC texts he is associated with the Bodhisattva Padmapani, also known as AVALOKITESHVARA, and his consort or Shakti is Pandara. Other deities associated with him include Lokeshvara, Mahabala, Saptashatika-Hayagriva, Kurukulla, Bhrikuti, Mahasitavati, Amitaprabha, Bhadrapala, Chandraprabha, Jaliniprabha, Kapalini, Mukunda, Mahodadhi, Maheshvara and Niladanda. In addition to these are all gods and goddesses who are red and associated with the west. In MANDALAS they are assigned to the north-west (Vayu) direction.

Amitabha is also associated with BHAISHAJYAGURU, the healing Buddha.

The concept of Amitabha probably originated in north-west India or Central Asia, but became popular in China, Tibet and Japan. Pure Land schools of Buddhism, still popular in Japan, believe that worshipping Amitabha will enable them to be reborn in his paradise, known as the 'Pure Land'.

amma A term which meams 'mother', used respectfully for women in south India. It is also a generic term for a MOTHER GODDESS, particularly in the south.

Amoghasiddhi A celestial BUDDHA, also known as a DHYANI BUDDHA, whose name means 'unfailing success'. Amoghasiddhi is described in MAHAYANA and VAJRAYANA texts, and is associated with the northern direction. In iconography and art he is depicted as green in colour, holding a *vishvavajra* or double thunderbolt. His VAHANA or vehicle is a pair of GARUDAS. He is one of the five main Buddhas and is associated with the BODHISATTVA Vishvapani. Other Bodhisattvas connected with him are Amitaprabha and Vajragarbha. His consort is TARA. Among the deities emanating from him are Khadirvani Tara, Vashya Tara, Sita Tara, Dhanda Tara, Parnashabari, MAHAMAYURI, Vajrashrinkhala, Amita-prabha, the twelve Dharinis, Gandha-Tara, Gandha-Karmavajri, Mahabala, Muraja, Nritya, Priyadarshana, Rasavajra, Sparshavajra, Vishkambhin, Vighnantaka, Vajrasaumya and Vajraghanta, as well as all deities who are green in colour.

amrit In Sikhism, sweetened water, representing divine nectar. Amrit-sanskar is the term for the initiation ceremony of the KHALSA.

amrita A Sanskrit word meaning immortal or imperishable, it normally refers to the divine drink of immortality. The word is etymologically similar to the Greek ambrotos, the ambrosia of the gods, and also related to the Latin immortalis. In Zoroastrianism, the deity AMERETAT is derived from the same source.

In the *ATHARVA VEDA*, amrita is said to have been created from the cooking of the sacrificial rice-gruel. The most popular story of its origin in the *MAHABHARATA* and the PURANAS, is that it was obtained from the churning of the ocean of milk. This story is told in several texts with some variations. One version of the story states that the rishi DURVASA gave a garland to the god INDRA, who gave it to his elephant AIRAVATA. Airavata threw it on the ground as it attracted bees which troubled him. Angry at the disrespect shown to his gift, Durvasa cursed the DEVAs or gods, and everything declined, withered and grew dull in DEVALOKA, the world of the devas. VISHNU advised the devas on how to restore their glory. He told them to unite with the ASURAS and put all kinds of herbs in the ocean of milk, and then to churn it using Mt MANDARA

as the churning staff and the serpent Vasuki as the rope. Vishnu provided the base, in the form of KURMA, the tortoise. Amrita finally emerged from the ocean, and Vishnu promised he would not allow the asuras to get it. Many wonderful things came out of the ocean as it was churned, including KAMADHENU, the wish-fulfilling cow, the goddess Varuni with dreamy eyes, PARIJATA, the divine tree, a number of beautiful APSARAS, the moon, the divine horse UCCHAISHRAVAS, poison or venom, and finally the sage DHANVANTARI, carrying amrita in a vessel. The asuras first snatched it, but later the devas retrieved it. Drinking it, they regained their former glory.

While the amrita was being carried, drops of it fell on the earth. The four places in India where it fell were HARDWAR, NASHIK, UJJAIN and PRAYAGA. In commemoration of this, the KUMBH MELA is held at these sites.

Amritananda, Mata A world-famous guru popularly known as Amma. The daughter of Sugunandan, a fisherman, Mata Amritanandamayi was born in a village in Kollam district of Kerala. Her fiftieth birthday was celebrated on 27 September 2003, though she states she is uncertain about her age. She has received no formal education, but even as a child she communicated with god and went into spiritual trances.

Amma speaks in Malayalam, the language of Kerala, and her theme is love. She hugs every one of her devotees and disciples, who are attracted by the divine love that radiates from her. She advocates both meditation and studying the scriptures, but the focus of her path is BHAKTI and service. Amma says, 'The beauty and charm of selfless love and service should not die away from the earth . . . Through selfless action we can eradicate the ego that conceals the Self.' She has set up a MATHA at the village of Vallikav in Kollam which receives large donations every year, much of it from foreign disciples. This money has been used to set up schools, colleges, medical and engineering institutes, hospitals, rural clinics, orphanages, old-age homes and other charitable institutions. The educational institutions come under Amrita Vishwa Vidyapeeth, a deemed university.

The matha runs ASHRAMS in more than thirty countries, as well as in various parts of India.

Amritsar A city in Punjab, particularly holy to the Sikhs and linked with their history. The foundations of the present city were laid by the fourth Sikh guru, RAM DAS, in 1577 and hence it was once known as Ramdaspur. The city was destroyed by Ahmad Shah Abdali, the Afghan invader, in 1761–62, but was soon rebuilt. The HAR MANDIR SAHIB, or Golden Temple, the most sacred Sikh shrine, is located here, as well as the AKAL TAKHT, the centre of Sikh religious authority. Among other shrines are temples, mosques and churches.

Amsha   A Vedic deity. In the RIG VEDA, he is one of the ADITYAS, almost synonymous with BHAGA.

amsha-avatara   A partial AVATARA or incarnation of a deity. Several of the characters in the *MAHABHARATA* were amsha-avataras, including the five PANDAVAS, BHISHMA and DURYODHANA. The PURANAS mention a number of other amsha-avataras.

Amtagadadasao (Skt: Antakrid-dasah)   A Jain text, the eighth of the twelve ANGAS. The *Thanamga*, the third ANGA, indicates that its contents were once different, but it now consists of stories of Jain saints. Many of the stories are very briefly stated, with references to their longer form in other texts. Of the longer stories, the most interesting is the story of KRISHNA, which is based on the *MAHABHARATA*, but in this text is a pious Jain.

Amuktamalyada   A poem on a VAISHNAVA saint, written in Telugu by Krishnadeva Raya, a ruler of the Vijayanagara dynasty from 1509 to 1529. The long poem describes the life of Periya ALVAR, also known as Vishnuchitta, and the love between his daughter ANDAL or Goda, who is identified with the goddess Lakshmi or Bhudevi, and the god RANGANATHA. It explains Vaishnava philosophy and simultaneously comments on principles of administration. The text has six cantos and the language is highly Sanskritized.

Anagarika Dharmapala   The name adopted by Don David Hewaviratne (1864–1933), when he became a Buddhist. He was originally a Christian from Sri Lanka, but came to India and founded the MAHABODHI SOCIETY OF INDIA.

Anagra Raochao   A term in Zoroastrianism for the everlasting light in which the God AHURA MAZDA dwells. The later form of the term was Aneran.

Anahata Chakra   One of the seven main CHAKRAS or invisible energy centres of the body. Commonly known as the 'heart chakra' it is located within the body in the centre of the chest. Anahata literally means 'unstruck', and in this centre the unstruck sound, or the divine sound, anahata nada, is heard. According to TANTRIC texts, the chakra has twelve petals, the colour of the bandhuka flower (red), and on its twelve petals are inscribed the Sanskrit letters ka, kha, ga, gha, anga, cha, chha, ja, jha, jna, ta, tha. Within it is smoky grey, with a million flashes of light. Also within is the HAMSA, known as the jivatma or individual soul, which is like the flame of a lamp in a windless place. Meditation on this chakra fulfills all desires and enables one to protect and destroy the worlds.

Ananda Marga   A religious organization started in 1955 by Prabhat Ranjan SARKAR. It was known as the Ananda Marga Pracharak Sangh, and aimed at initiating people into the 'path of bliss' (ananda = bliss, marga = path). Sarkar, later known as Ananda Murti, modified and simplified TANTRIC practices to make them available for all, and was against dogma, superstition and caste. The headquarters of the organization was first at Jamalpur in Bihar, but later shifted to Anand Nagar, in Purulia district of West Bengal. Within a few years it had gained popularity in Bihar and West Bengal, and gradually opened centres in various parts of India and abroad. A structure was given to the organization, with four grades of disciples, the highest being avadhoots, who dedicated their lives to the organization. In 1962, the first monk was initiated by Sarkar and in 1966, the first nun. Apart from engaging in spiritual practices, these devotees also spend time in social and charitable works. Most Ananda Margis, however, are lay followers or sadhaks. The Ananda Marga organizes welfare and relief works, and in 1963 the Education, Relief and Welfare Section was opened, and the first schools run by the Ananda Marga were inaugurated. The Ananda Marga Universal Relief Team was begun in 1965 for relief from natural and man-made calamities. It also set up a political wing, the Proutist Bloc of India.

Despite some initial problems, the organization has branches in 160 countries, and over a million followers.

ananda   A Sanskrit term implying internal happiness or bliss, which can be reached through contact with the higher Self. Each person also has a anandamayi KOSHA or body of bliss, which can be realized through meditative and other practices. Ananda has sometimes been identified with BRAHMAN, the eternal self and underlying reality of the world. According to the UPANISHADS, ananda is the highest state, where the knower, the known, and knowledge, are One.

Ananda   The closest disciple of the BUDDHA, who was also his cousin. He is said to have been born on the same day as the Buddha. There are several descriptions of him and his dialogues with the Buddha are recorded in PALI texts. While women were generally considered inferior, Ananda championed their cause and persuaded the Buddha to admit them into the SANGHA. Monasteries for women were then set up. It was to Ananda that the Buddha gave instructions that after his death there was no need for a leader or teacher for the monks. 'Be a light unto yourselves', said the Buddha.

Ananda was known for his perfect memory. Soon after the Buddha's death, the First BUDDHIST COUNCIL was held at RAJAGRIHA, and Ananda was asked to recite all the sermons of the Buddha. Ananda, however, busy for most of his life in the service of the Buddha, had not gained enlightenment, which was a requirement for all participating monks. The night before the Council was held, he achieved his goal. He recited all the Buddha's sermons, which were collected as the *SUTTA PITAKA*. According to tradition, Ananda lived to the age of 120.

Anandamayi Ma   A mystic and realized soul. Her original name was Nirmala Sundari and she was the daughter of a VAISHNAVA brahmana, Bipin Bihari Bhattacharya. Born in 1896 in East Bengal, now Bangladesh, she began to have visions and trances as a young girl. Married at the age of thirteen, she later went to live with her husband, who became her first disciple. An electric currrent emanating from her was said to prevent any man from approaching her too closely.

In a spontaneous manner without any preparation or deliberate action, she performed various YOGA asanas or postures, and went through other divine experiences. She had healing powers and soon became known as a spiritual person. In 1926 she began to travel, and wherever she went, crowds came to receive her DARSHANA or blessings. She was given the name Anandamayi Ma, and until her death in 1982, she continued to travel, speak and answer questions.

Her early photographs show a young woman of divine beauty, but Anandamayi remained detached from her body. She became so disassociated from it that her disciples had to do everything for her, from feeding to dressing and bathing her. Her talks reveal the Advaitic concept of the One Reality, the Divine Self, and have much in common with those of other mystics and philosophers. She spoke in Bengali and Hindi, and her talks and discussions have been collected and translated into several languages. In a typical statement, she said: 'In this whole universe, in all states of being, in all forms, is He. All names are His Names, all shapes His shapes, all qualities and all modes of existence are truly His.' Anandamayi Ma had founded more than thirty ashrams and still has thousands of followers.

Anandpur Sahib A city in Punjab, sacred to the Sikhs. Its name means 'city of bliss' and it has a number of GURDWARAS. It is closely connected with the tenth guru, GOBIND SINGH.

It is here that Guru Gobind Singh founded the KHALSA on the day of the BAISAKHI festival in 1699. The Takht Sri Keshgarh Sahib, one of the TAKHTS or centres of authority of the Sikhs, is located here. Among the gurdwaras in the city are the Gurdwara Guru ka Mahal, originally the residence of Guru TEGH BAHADUR, the Gurdwara Sisganj, where the head of the martyred Tegh Bahadur was cremated, and the Gurdwaras Keshgarh, Anandgarh and Lohgarh, where fortresses once stood, constructed by Guru Gobind Singh for the defence of the Sikhs.

Ananta (1) A divine serpent, also known as Shesha or Adishesha. He has 1000 heads with 1000 gems that illuminate all the regions. He dwells in PATALA or the nether world and has great powers. The Hindu god VISHNU rests or sleeps on him, between the cycles of creation.

(2) Ananta, meaning 'without end' is also one of the names of several Hindu deities, including SURYA, VISHNU, SHIVA and KRISHNA.

Anathapindaka A wealthy banker who lived at the time of the BUDDHA. He constructed the JETAVANA monastery at SHRAVASTI, where the Buddha lived during the rainy season for the last twenty-five years of his life. He gradually gave away all his wealth to the SANGHA or Buddhist community.

anatman/anatta A Buddhist concept, meaning 'no-self'. It challenged the idea prevalent in the UPANISHADS and other texts that there was a permanent entity, the ATMAN. The Self was rather an impermanent being composed of five SKANDHAS (aggregates). However, rebirth did take place, and KARMA did exist, but what was reborn and how, was a subject of debate in the various schools of Buddhism. One theory was that SAMSKARAS, mental tendencies that existed at the time of death, were transmitted into a new being, another that rebirth was like the flame of a lamp lighting another lamp.

ancient sects, non-orthodox Several sects in ancient India, denied the authority of the VEDAS and were not part of either Jainism or Buddhism. These sects no longer exist but had a following in ancient days. The leaders included religious teachers described by the BUDDHA as heretical (*annatitthiya*), or those who were opposed to the theory of KARMA (*akriyavada* or *akiriyavada*). These included Purana Kassapa, Pakudha Kachchayana, Makkhali GOSALA, AJITA KESHAKAMBALIN, Sanjaya Belatthiputa, and Nigantha Nataputta. Among them Makkhali Gosala's AJIVIKA sect was the most widespread and long-lasting. In addition there was the Barhaspatya or CHARVAKAS, also known as Lokayats.

anda kataha According to Hindu mythology, the shell or covering of the whole universe, also known as BRAHMANDA or the cosmic egg, which contains a number of worlds or LOKAS.

Andal A BHAKTI saint of the Hindu Vaishnava ALVAR group. Like the other members of the group, Andal wrote verses in Tamil. She probably lived in the ninth century.

According to tradition, Vishnuchitta, one of the Alvar saints, also known as Periya Alvar, found a baby girl in a bed of sacred basil he had in his garden. He named this girl Goda, though she was also known as Nachiyar and Andal. Growing up in an atmosphere of reverence to the god KRISHNA, a form of VISHNU, she developed an intense love of the god and wanted to be united with him in marriage. She begged her father to marry her to RANGANATHA (Vishnu), the deity of the temple at SRIRANGAM. Periya Alvar did not know what to do, until he was assured in a dream that the god would accept her in marriage. Finally the marriage took place, and entering the inner shrine of the temple, Andal is said to have merged with the god in a flash, and remained part of him.

Andal is important as a woman poet and her verses form part of the *NALAYIRA DIVYA PRABANDHAM*. Two long poems attributed to her are *Tirumozhi* and *Tiruppavai*. *Tirumozhi* has 143 verses, narrating the different stages of her love for Tirumal (Krishna or Vishnu). She writes,

I rest with the golden garlands
In the garden of Tirumal
Waiting; when will I hear
The sound of the Lord's conch
And the twang of his bow?

Finally she writes of the dream of her marriage, a divine vision.

In the *Tiruppavai*, she uses the form of a ceremony, where girls go to wake each other up for the morning bath. In this poem, the girls go to awaken Krishna from his divine sleep.

Andal is also considered an incarnation of Lakshmi or of BHUDEVI.

Andhra Jews   A group of Jews who live in the state of Andhra Pradesh in southern India. Though they have recently adopted Judaism, they claim that they existed in the region from the ninth or tenth century, but were later converted to Christianity. The leader of the group is Shmuel Yakobi, earlier a DALIT Christian, who on a visit to Israel felt a cultural affinity with the Jewish people. On his return he convinced his family and several neighbours in his village of Kottareddipalli in Guntur District of their Jewish affinity, and they started living as Jews. Others in Ongole, Prakasham District, joined them as well. Led by Yakobi, they learnt Hebrew, built a small one-roomed SYNAGOGUE, and began observing the SABBATH and Jewish ceremonies. Israeli Rabbis visited them in 1994 and Yakobi's son migrated to Israel. According to Yakobi, there are close connections between Hebrew and Telugu, indicating their ancient Jewish ancestry. They have named themselves the Council of Eastern Jewry.

Andu Masjid   A mosque in Bijapur in Karnataka, constructed in 1608 by Itibar Khan, a minister of Ibrahim Adil Shah II, ruler of the kingdom of Bijapur.

It is named after its dome, which is shaped like an egg (*anda*). This small mosque is on the first floor of a double-storeyed building, but is not a double-storeyed mosque, with a hall being located below. The main dome, as well as the domes on the minarets, are egg-shaped.

anekantavada   A concept in Jainism which indicates that everything is relative. No one except an omniscient being, a realized soul, can know the whole truth. There are seven different ways of perception, known as NAYA, and thus there are seven statements that can be made about any one thing. These lead to the related concept of SYADVADA, which deals with the probability of all knowledge.

In practical terms, anekantavada reconciles different and opposing views, and thus leads to tolerance.

Angad, Guru   The second Sikh guru, who succeeded Guru NANAK. Born on 31 March 1504, he was known as Lehna, and was the son of Bhai Pheru, a Hindu trader. Lehna was a devotee of the goddess DURGA, but once, hearing a Sikh reciting the JAPJI, the morning prayer, he was attracted to Sikhism and became a disciple of Guru Nanak. For some time Lehna lived at Khadur, instructing and helping the people there, but then stayed with Guru Nanak at Kartarpur. Nanak appointed him his successor in 1539 and named him Angad, saying he was like his 'ang', his own limb.

Angad popularized the use of the GURMUKHI script, a simple script for writing Punjabi. He had Guru Nanak's hymns transcribed and copied, and a biography of the guru written. He wrote a number of verses himself and sixty-two of his hymns are included in the GURU GRANTH SAHIB.

Guru Angad expanded and organized the practice of LANGAR, or community meals.

Before his death in 1552, Angad chose AMAR DAS as his successor.

Angas, Buddhist   A classification of Buddhist texts into nine, and later twelve, categories. The nine Angas are mentioned in the *SUTTA PITAKA*, and were Sutta (discourses in prose), Geyya (discourses in mixed prose and verse), Veyya-karana (expositions), Gatha (verses), Uddana (sayings), Itivuttaka (quotations), Jataka (birth stories), Abbhutadhamma (mysterious phenomena), and Vedalla (dialectical analysis). Three more categories were added for Sanskrit texts.

Angas, Jain   A series of eleven Jain texts which are the main texts of the SHVETAMBARA sect. The name of a twelfth Anga is known, but the contents are lost. These texts are based on fourteen Puvvas (PURVAS), comprising the original teachings of MAHAVIRA.

According to Shvetambara tradition, their leader BHADRABAHU was the last to know the teachings of MAHAVIRA. On his death, a council was called by STHULABHADRA at PATALIPUTRA, and the Purvas were reconstructed into twelve Angas. Other councils followed, and finally the texts were written down at Valabhi (Gujarat) in the fifth century, along with the UVANGAS and other works. Of these the *Ayaramga* and *Suyagadamga* are thought to record the earliest traditions. The Angas are:

(1) *AYARAMGA SUTTA (ACHARANGA SUTRA)*
(2) *SUYAGADAMGA (Sutrakritanga)*
(3) *THANAMGA (Sthananga)*
(4) *SAMAVAYAMGA*
(5) *BHAGAVATI VIYAHAPANNATI (Vyakhya-Prajnapti)*
(6) *NAYADHAMMAKAHAO (Jnatadhar- mahkatha)*
(7) *UVASAGADASAO (Upasakadasah)*
(8) *AMTAGADADASAO (Antakriddasah)*
(9) *ANUTTAROVAVAIYADASAO (Anutara-upapati-kadasah)*
(10) *PANHAVAGARANAIM (Prashna-Vyakaranani)*
(11) *VIVAGASUYAM (Vipaka-Shrutam)*
(12) *DITTHIVAYA (Drishtivada)* (This text is lost.)

(The above names are in ARDHA-MAGADHI, while those in SANSKRIT are within brackets.)

angels The concept of angels as messengers of God exists in several religions. The word 'angel' comes from the Greek *angelos*, meaning messenger. In Zoroastrianism, the FRAVASHI, or farohar, is something like a guardian angel. Some classify the AMESHA SPENTAS and YAZATAS of Zoroastrianism as angels, though yazatas are actually minor deities.

According to the BIBLE, angels not only served as God's messengers, but watched over people and were at times instruments of God's justice. Judaism accepts the existence of angels and they are described in rabbinical literature, but the MISHNAH and some orthodox Jewish literature does not mention them. They are important in Jewish mysticism, particularly in the MERKABAH.

Angels are a part of Christian tradition, described in the Old and New Testament, and also known through legends and tradition. Three main categories of angels are Seraphim, Cherubim and Archangels. In the sixth century CE angels were classified into nine groups by a theologian who used the name Dionysius the Areopagite (known as the pseudo-Areopagite). The highest of the nine groups are the Seraphim, followed by the Cherubim. Others were Thrones, Dominations, Virtues, Powers, Principalities, Archangels and Angels. His work was used extensively for further discussions and analyses of angels, though many do not agree with his categorization.

The tradition of angels exists in Islam as in Judaism and Christianity. In fact, the QURAN was revealed to the Prophet MUHAMMAD by the Angel Jibril (Gabriel).

Angels are known in Islam by the Arabic word malak, or MALAIKA, similar to the Hebrew word malakh, and in Persian as firishtah. They are said to be created of light and endowed with life, speech and reason.

Angiras A great RISHI or sage, described in the RIG VEDA. He is the first sacrificer, associated with fire rituals, and a teacher of divine knowledge (brahma vidya). In later texts, he is one of the mind-born sons of the Hindu god BRAHMA. He is also said to be one of the sixteen PRAJAPATIS created by Brahma, who then created the universe. His sons include AGNI and BRIHASPATI, while his daughters, SINIVALI, Kuhu, RAKA and ANUMATI, are lunar deities. He also had sons by the wife of a childless KSHATRIYA, who were personifications of light, and are known as ANGIRASAS. In some texts, Angiras is the son of Agni.

Angirasas The descendants of the rishi ANGIRAS, or sometimes of the Hindu god AGNI. They were a class of fire-priests and interpreters of traditional and magical rites.

Angkor The name of a kingdom in Cambodia that existed from around the ninth to the fifteenth centuries. The kingdom was also known as Kambuja. The Khmer dynasty who ruled there claimed descent from India. Their kings had Indian names and their towns and cities were named after Hindu deities. A number of Hindu temples were constructed here from the ninth to the twelfth centuries. Among these were several SHIVA temples including the Preah Ko (sacred bull) Shiva temple of the ninth century, the Bakong Shiva temple and the Lolei Shiva temple, also of the ninth century. The Baphuon Shiva temple was constructed in the middle of the eleventh century. The greatest and best-known monument, however, is the VISHNU temple at Angkor, known as ANGKOR WAT (Wat = temple). After the twelfth century, Buddhism predominated and Buddhist temples were built.

Angkor Wat A temple of the Hindu god VISHNU, located in Cambodia. It was constructed by Surya-varman (1112–52) of the Khmer dynasty. Angkor Wat is the largest of the monuments at Angkor, and is a temple as well as a mausoleum for the king after his death. This huge complex, in Dravidian temple style, covers an area of about 210 hectares, its enclosure wall being surrounded by a moat 200 m wide. The moat is crossed by a bridge which is 250 m long and 12 m wide, and built of sandstone blocks. The entrance is from the west through a large GOPURAM. At the entrance is a large standing image, once of Vishnu, later converted into the BUDDHA. The temple rises to a height of 65 m, with three tiers, and steps leading to successive levels. Each level is progressively smaller. From the third level, five towers rise, capped with domes. Within the temple are columned MANDAPAS and passageways carved with scenes from the RAMAYANA and MAHABHARATA. As the temple was later made a Buddhist monument, there are also Buddhist images. The central shrine, which once had a Vishnu image, is 42 m above the upper level.

Anglican Church An Anglican organization founded in 1964. ANGLICANS existed in India from the time of the British, but the majority joined the CHURCH OF SOUTH INDIA and the CHURCH OF NORTH INDIA. Some of the local converts to Christianity, particularly from Kerala, were not happy with the uniformity imposed by the Church of South India, and re-established the Anglican Church as a separate entity in 1964.

There are thirteen Anglican dioceses in India. Their bishops form the Synod, which governs their activities. Their headquarters are at Kottayam in Kerala.

Anglicans A Christian denomination who are considered PROTESTANTS, though their ideology contains both CATHOLIC and Protestant elements. Its church administration or organization is through bishops, while worship is based mainly on the *Book of Common Prayer* of 1662, and on new prayers introduced after 1965. As the Anglican Church was the official Church of England since the time of the REFORMATION, it had an impact on India with the arrival of the British. The Church Mission Society (CMS) was founded in England in 1799, and its missionaries first reached India in 1814, though there were some Anglican priests in India even in the seventeenth century. The same year the first Anglican See was established, while the first Anglican cathedral, ST. PAUL'S in Kolkata (Calcutta) was constructed in 1847. Anglican churches had been built earlier, from the seventeenth century onwards, notable among them being St. George's Church in Agra (1826) and St. Mary's Church, Chennai (1680). Apart from Kolkata, dioceses were founded in Mumbai (Bombay) and Chennai (Madras). CMS missionaries had reached the Kerala region by 1816, and in 1879 a separate diocese was formed for Travancore–Cochin, the two princely states in that area. In 1928, the Anglican Church of India and adjacent regions became autonomous, and was known as the Church of India, Burma and Ceylon. After Independence and Partition in 1947, it was known as the Church of India, Pakistan, Burma and Ceylon. The same year in south India, it joined together with other churches of Protestant denominations to form the CHURCH OF SOUTH INDIA. Other Anglican groups joined the CHURCH OF NORTH INDIA, formed in 1970. A separate ANGLICAN CHURCH was established in 1964. The Anglicans were associated with the orthodox churches of Kerala, and influenced the founding of the MAR THOMA CHURCH.

Angra Mainyu The name of the evil spirit in Zoroastrianism, known as AHRIMAN in later texts. He is always in opposition to SPENTA MAINYU, the good spirit. The concept of Angra Mainyu or Ahriman changed over time. The GATHAS, the earliest Zoroastrian texts, state that God, known as AHURA MAZDA, created the twin spirits, the good and the bad. They established life (*gaya*) and non-life (*ajyaiti*), so that creation's purpose might be fulfilled. Angra Mainyu chose to perform the worst deeds, while Spenta Mainyu chose the path of good and the way of Ahura Mazda. Similarly, these two aspects are within all people who have a choice between good and bad actions. When people choose rightly, guided by the AMESHA SPENTAS or powers of God, they become Hamkaras, or helpers of God, and help to bring about the perfect existence, or FRASHOKERETI. Later PAHLAVI texts such as the BUNDAHISHN seem to equate Spenta Mainyu with Ahura Mazda, while Ahriman has an independent existence as an evil being. This led Western scholars to interpret Zoroastrianism as a dualistic religion, though even in these texts Ahura Mazda is shown as superior in several ways. In these later texts, Ahriman is finally defeated, after thousands of years of strife.

Anguttara Nikaya A HINAYANA Buddhist text of the PALI CANON, literally 'the collection of suttas or discourses arranged in ascending order'. The *Anguttara Nikaya* forms part of the SUTTA PITAKA and consists of 2308 suttas in eleven sections, each organized around a number. The first section has discourses relating to one, the second to two, etc. For instance section two

has discourses on topics such as two things which must be avoided, two kinds of Buddhas, or two reasons to go to the forest to live; the section on four has suttas on the four things which lead to liberation from existence, four things that lead to heaven, four things that lead to hell, etc. In the course of this, Buddhist ethics and principles are enumerated, including simple topics such as the value of gratitude and respect for parents.

animals in religion Animals are closely associated with deities in Hinduism, Buddhism and Jainism, and are also mentioned in other religions. In Hinduism animals are the VAHANAS or vehicles of various deities and are worshipped in temples. Legends, stories and myths personify animals, who may be wise and cunning, self sacrificing, devotees of god, or incarnations of the divine. In Buddhism, animals play a major role in both HINAYANA and MAHAYANA schools. In the JATAKAS, a text of the PALI CANON, several stories recount the life of BUDDHA in his previous births as an animal. In MAHAYANA Buddhism, BODHISATTVAS dedicate themselves to save all beings, including animals and plants, while in the Buddhist pantheon, animals are associated with various deities. In Jainism, different animals are associated with TIRTHANKARAS and lesser deities. In all three religions, animals also have souls and can reincarnate as humans. Deities and sages can transform themselves into animals for various purposes. Animals at times have symbolic meanings. Some of the more common associations are given below:

Ass: The ass or donkey is associated with the the Vedic deities, the ASHVINS, and with the later Hindu goddess JYESHTHA. Of course, the donkey is also significant in Christianity, for its role in carrying Christ.

Bear: In the RAMAYANA, bears, led by JAMBAVAN, are among those who help RAMA.

Boar: In the RIG VEDA, RUDRA, the MARUTS and VRITRA are figuratively referred to as boars. In the later Vedas, PRAJAPATI, in the form of a boar, raises the earth out of the waters. VARAHA, the boar, is an incarnation of the Hindu god VISHNU, while VARAHI, his consort, is one of the MATRIKAS or mother goddesses.

Buffalo: The buffalo is the mount of the Hindu god YAMA. MAHISHASURA, the buffalo demon, is killed by the goddess DURGA. The buffalo has an important role in the religion of some tribal groups, including the TODAS, and the representation of the buffalo as a demon may be linked with the absorption of tribal cults into Brahmanism.

Cat: The cat is rarely associated with deities in India though it is popular in other parts of the ancient world. Cats are sometimes associated with the goddess Shashthi and with the cat-faced mother-goddess, Bidali.

Deer: The deer is associated with SHIVA in his DAKSHINAMURTI form.

Goat: The goat is known as AJA in Vedic texts, and draws the chariot of the god PUSHAN. Aja Ekapad is a divine being in the Rig Veda, while in later Vedic texts, the goat is associated with AGNI. AJAMUKHI is a goat-faced Hindu goddess, and in Jainism NAIGAMESHA is a goat-faced deity.

Jackal: The jackal is often portrayed in PANCHATANTRA stories as being wily and wise, but is worshipped at the KALADUNGAR TEMPLE associated with DATTATREYA.

Lion: The lion is the mount of the goddess DURGA. One of Vishnu's incarnations is NARASIMHA, half-man, half-lion, and the twenty-fourth Tirthankara, MAHAVIRA, has a lion as his emblem.

Monkey: Monkeys are generally venerated even today, as HANUMAN is the monkey deity who led the monkeys who helped RAMA in the RAMAYANA.

Mouse: The mouse is the vahana or mount of GANESHA, the elephant-headed deity, while rats are worshipped in a temple in Rajasthan.

Tiger: The tiger, first portrayed on seals of the INDUS CIVILIZATION, is also sometimes depicted as the *vahana* or mount of DURGA. The tiger is revered in several tribal religions.

Animals that play a significant role include the BULL, COW, DOG, ELEPHANT and HORSE.

Among reptiles, the iguana is associated with the goddess CHANDI. In the VEDAS, the tortoise, as Kashyapa, is identified with PRAJAPATI, while later KASHYAPA is the progenitor of all the beings in the world. The tortoise, known as KURMA, is an incarnation of the god VISHNU. In the Vedas, frogs are associated with rain and possess magical powers. NAGAS or snakes and snake deities have innumerable cults of their own. A variety of BIRDS, fish and mythical animals also find a place in religion.

Animal SACRIFICES are recorded in ancient texts, and still continue to a limited extent today.

animisha A Sanskrit word, meaning 'unblinking'. In Hindu myths the gods did not blink, and when they took on various forms while attempting to seduce the wives of humans, they could be identified by this trait. Greek myths also refer to this as a characteristic of the gods.

anitya A Buddhist concept meaning 'imperma-nence', i.e., that everything is in a state of change. The BUDDHA preached this in his second sermon.

Anjana Devi A Hindu goddess, the mother of HANUMAN. Anjana is considerd a form of Devi or SHAKTI. There are several temples dedicated to her.

Anjaneya A name of the Hindu god HANUMAN. He was called this because he was the son of Anjana.

Annapurna A Hindu deity, a benevolent form of the goddess DURGA. Her worship in the household ensures plenty of food. There are several temples dedicated to the deity, particularly in hill areas. Her worship is also popular in eastern India.

Anu Gita A Sanskrit text which forms part of the fourteenth parva of the MAHABHARATA. In it, after the great war is over, the Hindu god KRISHNA summarizes the philosophy he had put forward in the BHAGAVAD GITA.

Anumati A Hindu deity. Literally 'the favour of the gods', in two places in the RIG VEDA she is personified as a goddess. In the ATHARVA VEDA she is the goddess of love, presiding over propagation. In later texts she is a lunar deity, the daughter of the rishi ANGIRAS.

Anuogadara (Skt: *Anuyogadvarani*) A Jain text of the SHVETAMBARA canon. It is sometimes listed with the PAINNAS, but is usually not connected to any group of texts. It has an encyclopedic content, similar to the *NANDI SUTTA*, but is arranged in a question-and-answer form.

Anuttarayoga Tantra The fourth and highest class of Buddhist TANTRIC texts. In the Tibetan Canon, it is part of the KAGYUR, and includes twenty-two volumes and over 300 texts. The most important of these are the *GUHYASAMAJA TANTRA* and the *HEVAJRA TANTRA*.

Anuttarovavaiyadasao (Skt: Anuta-raupa-patikadasah) A Jain text, the ninth of the twelve ANGAS. It consists of stories of Jain saints who reached the highest level and practised the rite of starving themselves to death (SALLEKHANA), as prescribed in Jainism.

Apadana A HINAYANA Buddhist text which forms part of the KHUDDAKA NIKAYA of the PALI CANON. It consists of Buddhist stories on ARHATS, a term used to describe an advanced monk or Buddhist saint. Apadana (Sanskrit: Avadana) means heroic deed, or glorious deed. The Apadanas are written in verse and begin with a *Buddhapadana,* on all the BUDDHAS. This is followed by the *Pachchekabuddh-apadana,* on Pachcheka (Sanskrit: *Pratyeka*) or solitary Buddhas, who achieve enlightenment through their own solitary paths. The rest of the text consists of Thera and Theri Apadanas. The *Thera Apadana,* on the great monks, has fifty-five sections (Vaggas) each with ten Apadanas, and the *Theri Apadana,* on the great nuns, has four sections with ten Apadanas each. Mogallana (MAUDGALYANA), ANANDA and RAHULA are among the monks whose lives are described.

Apah Vedic deities. In the RIG VEDA, the term refers to water goddesses. They are mothers and wives, bestow boons and come to the sacrifice. They follow the path of the gods and flow in channels with the sea as their goal. They cleanse and purify worshippers.

Apam Napat A Vedic deity, mentioned in the RIG VEDA. He was the son of the waters, golden in form and appearance, always shining. He is sometimes equated with AGNI. The deity probably dates back to the days of the INDO-IRANIANS, as Apam Napat in the AVESTA is a spirit of the waters.

Aparna A form of the Hindu goddess PARVATI or DURGA. Originally she was probably a tribal goddess, worshipped by the Shabaras and other tribes. According to myths, after practising extreme austerities, she became the consort of the god SHIVA and was known as UMA.

Apostles A term primarily used for the twelve closest disciples of Jesus Christ. Literally, it is derived from a Greek word meaning 'to send out'; they were the disciples Jesus sent to preach his doctrine. The *Acts of the Apostles*, which forms part of the NEW TESTAMENT, provides an account of some of their activities after the death of Jesus. The twelve apostles were: Simon Peter and his brother Andrew, James and his brother John, Philip, Thomas, Bartholomew, Mathew, James, son of Alphaeus, Simon Zealote, Judas, brother of James, usually identified with Thaddaeus, and Judas Iscariot, who later betrayed Jesus. After the betrayal, Judas Iscariot was replaced by Matthias.

Thomas, known as ST. THOMAS, is said to have come to India and died here. According to some accounts Bartholomew also came to India. Some later disciples, such as Paul, also called themselves Apostles.

Appar A BHAKTI saint of the seventh century. He was one of the NAYANARS and worshipped the Hindu god, SHIVA. Born in the Tamil region, he was earlier known as Marulnikkiyar and was a Jain monk of the DIGAMBARA sect, the head of a Jain monastery. Suffering from a stomach ailment for a long time, he was inspired to go to a Shiva temple and sing in praise of the god, and was instantly cured. He then became a devotee of Shiva. He was known as Tirunavukkarasar, but was popularly called Appar or 'father'. He composed verses and songs of devotion to Shiva, which form part of the *Tevaram*, a sacred SHAIVITE text included in the *TIRUMURAI*.

apsaras Divine nymphs mentioned in Hindu texts, who were very beautiful and associated with the GANDHARVAS. In the RIG VEDA they were connected with water, and later with the earth and trees. According to the *Shatapatha Brahmana*, they could assume any form they liked and frequently appeared as aquatic birds. The *MAHABHARATA* states that warriors who died in battle were transported by the apsaras, in brightly coloured chariots, to INDRA's heaven. Apsaras are said to have appeared at the time of the churning of the ocean for AMRITA, or to have emerged from PRAJAPATI. They bewitch and seduce mortals with their beauty. The most famous story about an apsara is that of URVASHI, with whom the mortal Pururavas fell in love. This is first narrated in the RIG VEDA, and later elaborated in several texts. Other apsaras were frequently sent by the gods to seduce RISHIS, so as to prevent them from achieving great powers through their austerities. Among these were Menaka, who seduced the rishi VISHVAMITRA, and many others.

Apsaras are also described in Buddhist texts and appear several times in the JATAKAS.

Aquaviva, Father Rudolfo A Jesuit priest at the court of the Mughal emperor AKBAR (1556–1605).

He was one of the three priests who formed the first mission sent to AKBAR at his request, by the Portuguese in Goa, the others being Father MONSERRATE and Father Henriques. Aquaviva, the son of the Duke of Atri in Italy, was ordained as a priest in 1578 and reached Goa the same year. Though the youngest of the three, he was the head of the delegation. The priests probably reached the court in 1579, and had discussions with the emperor on Christian theology. They stayed for a few years; Aquaviva was the last to leave, in 1583. Returning to Goa and beginning a new missionary programme, Aquaviva and other Jesuits planted a cross outside the village of Cuncolim.

Unfortunately this was at a site where a temple had been destroyed the previous year by other Christian missionaries. Aquaviva and his companions were killed by the villagers, still angry at the earlier desecration. The martyred Jesuits were later beatified.

ara A term in Jainism for a cosmic age. According to Jain cosmology, the wheel of time has twelve aras (literally, spokes)—six ascending (UTSARPINI), and six descending (AVASARPINI)—together making one KALPA.

The kalpas are infinite, when one ends, another begins. The present age belongs to the fifth ara of the avasarpini, which began soon after the NIRVANA of MAHAVIRA. There are twenty-four TIRTHANKARAs in each half-cycle, and the first Tirthankara of this cycle, RISHABHA, lived in the third ara, while the other twenty-three belong to the fourth ara.

Avasarpini (number of years)
1. Sushama-Sushama (4 KKS)
2. Sushama (3 KKS)
3. Sushama-Dushama (2 KKS)
4. Dushama-Sushama (1 KKS–42,000)
5. Dushama (21,000)
6. Dushama-Dushama (21,000)

Utsarpini (number of years)
1. Dushama-Dushama (21,000)
2. Dushama (21,000)
3. Dushama-Sushama (1 KKS–42,000)
4. Sushama-Dushama (2 KKS)
5. Sushama (3 KKS)
6. Sushama-Sushama (4 KKS)

(Sushama = happy; Dushama = unhappy KKS = Koti Koti Sagaropam, a period of time).

Arabic The language of the QURAN, still used in India and elsewhere for prayers and for Islamic studies. It is the language of over 150 million people in Arab countries. Though the Arabic spoken today differs from the classical language, the written language is similar to that used by the Prophet MUHAMMAD.

arama A dwelling place for Buddhist monks in ancient days. At the time of the BUDDHA, monks could not move freely in the rainy season, and *aramas* were set up for them by patrons or devotees. Some of these were temporary structures, while others became permanent monasteries.

Aramati A Vedic deity, literally 'devotion and piety', occasionally personified as a goddesss in the RIG VEDA. She is similar to ARMAITI, who represents loving devotion in Zoroastrianism.

Aranyakas Sanskrit texts which form part of the Vedic literature of Hinduism. These forest texts (aranya = forest) are attached to the VEDIC SAMHITAS and usually form the second part of the BRAHMANAS. They provide instructions for those in the third stage of life who have renounced their householder's life and retired to the forests. Among the Aranyakas available today are the *Brihad, Taittiriya, Aitareya* and *Kaushitaki*. The Aranyakas are closely linked with the UPANISHADS: The *Brihad Aranyaka*, or *Brihadaranyaka Upanishad*, is attached to the *Shatapatha Brahmana*. The *Aitareya Aranyaka* forms part of the *Aitareya Brahmana*. The *Kaushitaki Aranyaka* has three sections, and includes the *Kaushitaki Upanishad*. The *Taittiriya Aranyaka* is a continuation of the *Taittiriya Brahmana*. The Aranyakas discuss philosophical concepts, including the mystical symbolism of sacrifices.

Aranyani A Vedic deity, goddess of the forest, mentioned in the RIG VEDA. She is described only in one hymn, as an elusive spirit of the forest who cannot be seen. Her voice is like that of a man calling his cattle, or of a tree falling. She does not come to the village, but if one stays in the forest in the evening, she can be heard like a voice crying, far away. She is perfumed and fragrant, and the mother of wild things. Aranyani has some parallels with the Roman goddess Diana. She is not known in later times, though there are other goddesses associated with forests. For instance, Aranya Devi, goddess of a temple in Arrah, Bihar, is according to some legends, goddess of the forest.

Arda Viraf, Dastur A Zoroastrian priest or DASTUR who lived in the third century at the time of the Sasanian ruler ARDASHIR BABAGAN. He was chosen by Ardashir for the spiritual exercise of Khalla-e-badan, or the astral projection of the soul into the other world. Arda Viraf entered an ATASH BEHRAM or fire temple and went into a spiritual trance for seven days, during which time he visited heaven (vahisht). His experiences are compiled in the text *Arda Viraf Namah*. While the existing PAHLAVI text is dated to the ninth century, it is probably based on an earlier version. It describes seven heavens (behest *or* vahisht), hell (dazakh) and hamistagan (purgatory). It is based on the morality of the times, but is still a popular text among PARSIS of India, and is said to have inspired Dante's *Divine Comedy*.

Ardas A Sikh prayer. It concludes the prayers recited in a GURDWARA, and is used at other ceremonies as well. The prayer remembers the Sikh gurus and Sikh martyrs, and the founding of the KHALSA. It requests God to accept their prayers and to shelter and protect the Sikh religion and places of worship.

Ardashir I The founder of the Sasanian dynasty in Iran who ruled from 226 to 240. He encouraged the spread of Zoroastrianism, constructed a number of ATASH BEHRAMS or fire temples and had ancient texts recompiled. It was during his reign that ARDA VIRAF is said to have visited the astral world. Ardashir is one of the ancient Zoroastrians still revered today.

Ardha-Magadhi A language in which early Jain literature of the SHVETAMBARA canon was composed, including the twelve ANGAS. Ardha-Magadhi is a dialect of PRAKRIT.

Ardhanarishvara A composite Hindu deity, consisting of SHIVA and PARVATI combined, representing the mystical union of male and female. This form is mentioned in texts and depicted in images as early as the first century CE, though such images were more common later. In Ardhanarishvara images, the right half is usually male, and the left female. Later, myths and legends were created to account for the creation of this deity, and one such relates to the rishi Bhringi. Of all the DEVAS and RISHIS who worshipped Shiva and Parvati on Mt KAILASHA, Bhringi refused to worship Parvati, circumambulating only Shiva. Shiva therefore united his body with that of Parvati. They remained united, while Bhringi, undeterred, took the form of a beetle, and bored a hole through the composite body, still circumambulating Shiva!

Despite this legend, the importance of this deity is its connection with the later Shiva and SHAKTI cults, representing divine union. Ardhanarishvara images can be seen in several Shiva temples. In the BRIHADESHVARA TEMPLE at Thanjavur, of the Chola period, is an Ardhanarishvara image where the deity reclines on NANDI. The right half, representing Shiva, has two arms, one raised in varada mudra (boon-giving pose), and the other holding a TRISHULA. The left half, representing Parvati, has only one hand, which holds a flower.

There are also some temples dedicated exclusively to this deity. Among these is the Ardhanari Temple located at Mandi in Himachal. A modern temple, it has exquisite carvings.

Ardi Behesht An AMESHA SPENTA in Zoroastrianism, the later form of Asha Vahisht, the best ASHA.

Arhai-Din-Ka Jhonpra Mosque A mosque located at AJMER in Rajasthan and constructed between 1199 and 1236 by Qutb-ud-din Aibak (originally a general of Muhammad Ghori, who later ruled as sultan in 1206–10), and Sultan Iltutmish (ruled 1211–36). According to legend, the mosque was constructed in just two-and-a-half days, hence its name (arhai din = two-and-a-half days). The mosque is about 80 m each side, with two minarets above the main archway. The prayer hall has corbelled domes on the roof, and tall, slender pillars within. On the western wall is an intricately carved screen in white marble, while another exquisite screen with seven arches was added by Iltutmish in 1230.

arhat/arhant/arihant (1) In Buddhism, a term for a Buddhist saint, one who was realized and had gained enlightenment. There were several disputes on the nature and characteristics of arhats, and different schools of early Buddhism held varying views on them. To the STHAVIRAVADA, the arhat could not have any imperfections, while other schools disagreed with this. There were also disputes on whether the Arhat could regress having reached this state.

The arhat ideal focused on individual liberation and was important in HINAYANA Buddhism. In MAHAYANA Buddhism, becoming an arhat was not the goal, and the concept of the BODHISATTVA, who worked unceasingly for the liberation of all living beings, was more important.

(2) In Jainism, the term arihant is more commonly used, and refers to a Jain saint.

Arishtanemi The name of several people in ancient Hindu texts, including the following:
(1) In the RIG VEDA, Arishtanemi is a name of the divine horse TARKSHYA. Tarkshya is later a name of GARUDA, as well as the name of a rishi with whom Arishtanemi is identified.
(2) In the MAHABHARATA, Arishtanemi is one of the sons of VINATA, and the brother of the divine bird Garuda, who is the vehicle of the Hindu god VISHNU. Because of his meditation and austerities, Arishtanemi had great powers and could not be killed. Vinata, who in the PURANAS is the wife of KASHYAPA, is here his great-granddaughter.
(3) In the *Mahabharata*, Arishtanemi is also a name of the Hindu god KRISHNA.
(4) In the PURANAS, he is mentioned as a son of the rishi KASHYAPA, and also one of those who married some of DAKSHA's daughters.

Arishtaneminatha The twenty-second Jain TIRTHANKARA, also known as Neminatha. He is said to have lived at the time of the Hindu god KRISHNA, and was his cousin. Some texts state that he lived 84,000 years before the twenty-third Tirthankara. According to Jain sources, Krishna and Arishtanemi were grandsons of Andhaka Vrishni, born from his sons Vasudeva and Samudravijaya respectively. Samudravijaya was the king of Sauripur (or DVARAKA), and Arishtanemi was born there. Before his birth his mother dreamed of a wheel of black jewels (arishta), and therefore he was named Arishtaneminatha, which also means 'the lord whose wheel is unhurt'. Krishna and he were close friends and Krishna arranged his marriage with the beautiful Rajimati, who had been Arishtanemi's wife in previous births. On the day of his marriage a grand feast was being prepared, but hearing the agonized cries of the animals to be slaughtered for the feast, his heart filled with pain, and he had the animals released, and renounced the world. After practising austerities, he became a Tirthankara. Rajimati was filled with sorrow, but after some time also became an ascetic, finally achieving liberation.

The story of Arishtanemi occurs in the ANGAS and in several later texts. Most of these dwell on his act of renunciation and on his relationship with Rajimati. The *Vanhidasao*, one of the UVANGAS, narrates how he converted twelve princes of the Vrishni dynasty to the Jain path. Scholars believe that myths associating Arishtanemi with Krishna, emerged when Krishna worshippers began to be absorbed into Jainism.

Arishtanemi's symbol is the conch shell, and he attained liberation (MOKSHA) at the Girnar hills in Gujarat. He is associated with the deities AMBIKA and Gomedha.

Arjan Dev, Guru The fifth Sikh guru, who succeeded his father Guru RAM DAS and is known for his compilation of the first edition of the GURU GRANTH SAHIB, then known as the Pothi Sahib. Born at Goindwal on 15 April 1563, he was the youngest son of Guru RAM DAS and Mata Bhani. In 1579 he was married to Ganga Devi. In 1581, he became the guru on the death of Ram Das. His elder brother Prithi Chand was extremely jealous of him and tried to prevent him from becoming the guru, and continued to make efforts to obstruct him.

Guru Arjan went to Ramdaspur (AMRITSAR) to complete the work started there by his father. He constructed two tanks of Santoksar and Amritsar and laid the foundation of the HAR MANDIR SAHIB or GOLDEN TEMPLE. He realized the need to compile the hymns of Guru NANAK and other gurus in an authentic version, as various people were composing hymns and attributing them to the gurus. He therefore collected the original verses of the gurus from their sons, and sitting near the Ramsar tank, he began putting together the Guru Granth Sahib, including in it works of other saints whose teachings were consistent with those of the gurus. Simultaneously, he composed hymns himself, of which 2216 are included in the Guru Granth Sahib. The *Sukhmani*, or hymn of peace, is considered one of the most beautiful. In another hymn, he describes the nature of God:

You are the tree,
And the world its branches;
You were unknown,
And you made yourself manifest;
You are the ocean,
You the bubbles, you the foam,
There is nothing that is without you.

His brother Prithi Chand's jealousy continued and he encouraged a complaint to be made to the Mughal emperor AKBAR about the nature of the Granth Sahib, which was said to contain comments derogatory to Muslims. Akbar found nothing objectionable in it, and in fact praised the volume.

In 1605 Akbar was succeeded by his son Jahangir, who was against some of his father's liberal policies. Jahangir's son Khusru had rebelled against his father and was received by Guru Arjan, which further angered the emperor. The guru was summoned to Lahore and was asked to revise the holy book. On his refusal he was tortured for five days. On the sixth day he asked to be permitted to bathe in the river Ravi. He went into the water, prayed, and allowed himself to be swept away by the currents.

His martyrdom changed the nature and course of Sikhism, as after this Sikhs began to organize themselves as a martial group.

Arjuna The third of the PANDAVA brothers whose story is told in the MAHABHARATA. Literally, his name means 'white', 'clear', or 'bright'.

Officially the son of PANDU, who was the son of the rishi VYASA, Arjuna was born by his mother KUNTI invoking the god INDRA, as Pandu could not have children. The guru DRONACHARYA trained him in the art of warfare, and he was better than his brothers and cousins, though Ekalavya posed a challenge in archery. Arjuna married DRAUPADI, daughter of the king of Panchala, after passing various tests, and she became the common wife of the five Pandavas. He travelled to several places, and among the other women he married were Ulupi, daughter of a naga king, Chitrangada of Manipur, and Subhadra, the sister of KRISHNA. Along with his brothers, he was in exile for many years. He had several adventures, lived in Indra's heaven and defeated the DAITYAS near the sea. He fought in the great war, after which he and his brothers occupied the Kuru kingdom including HASTINAPURA, INDRAPRASTHA and adjacent areas. Later, his grandson, Parikshit, became the king of Hastinapura.

Arjuna is famous for his dialogue with the god Krishna in the BHAGAVAD GITA, which took place on the battlefield at the time of the great Mahabharata war.

Stories of Arjuna and his exploits also occur in the PURANAS and other texts.

PANINI, the grammarian of the fourth century BCE, mentions the worship of Arjuna. Some later texts state that he was a secondary incarnation (gauna avatara) of the Hindu god VISHNU. In some temples, he is depicted with the god Krishna, while in others he is with his brothers.

Arjuna's Penance A relief carved on a rock surface at MAMALAPURAM (Mahabalipuram) in Tamil Nadu, said to represent ARJUNA requesting the Hindu god SHIVA for a divine weapon, a story narrated in the *Mahabharata* and PURANAS. The sculpture is on two large boulders with a cleft in between. Flying deities, VIDYADHARAS, elephants and other animals, as well as NAGAS in prayer, are carved along with Arjuna to the left and Shiva to the right. Arjuna stands on one foot, hoping to gain the weapon through his penance. At one time, water flowed over the relief from a tank behind the cleft, which has led to the sculpture alternatively being identified as the descent of the GANGA river.

Armaiti A power of AHURA MAZDA, the name of God in Zoroastrianism. Armaiti is personified as one of the AMESHA SPENTAS, and is similar to the Vedic ARAMATI. She is a feminine power, representing loving devotion, piety and zeal. In the GATHAS she is called the beloved of the wise, and the treasure of the good mind. She is also said to be the daughter of Ahura Mazda. She sustains life and inspires people to perform good deeds. In PAHLAVI texts she is known as Spendarmad. She presides over the earth, and her symbol is the sweet basil flower. The DINKARD states that she is 'perfect thought'. She sits near Ahura Mazda, takes care of paradise, and is the mother of all creatures.

Armenians Armenian Christians came to India as traders, and some of their churches and monuments still exist. Armenia was the first country in the world to officially adopt Christianity in the third century. The first Armenian in India is said to have reached Malabar in Kerala in the eighth century but the majority came in the sixteenth century and after. There were several Armenians at the court of the Mughal emperor AKBAR and according to legend he had an Armenian Christian wife, though there is no historical proof of this. There were also Armenians in the army of the Maratha Scindias of Gwalior.

Trading in spices, precious stones and silk, a number of them became extremely rich and settled in Kolkata, MUMBAI and Chennai, while a few lived in DELHI, Lucknow and Lahore.

The Armenians did not attempt to convert anyone and apart from their residential and other buildings, constructed their own chapels and churches. One of the oldest is the Martyrose Chapel, erected in AGRA in 1611, located in the old Armenian cemetery. There were an Armenian Church in Surat and a chapel in Delhi, which have now crumbled. Some churches are still functioning, however. Among these are the Holy Church of Nazareth, constructed in 1707 in Kolkata; St. Gregory's Chapel (1906) in Kolkata; Chapel of the Holy Trinity (1867), at Thangra, outskirts of Kolkata; Church of John the Baptist (1697) in Chinsura in Bengal; Church of St. Peter (1796) at Mumbai, totally reconstructed in 1957; Church of the Holy Virgin Mary (1772) at Chennai. A few hundred Armenians still live in India, and the Armenian Church Committee of Kolkata manages the churches.

Art of Living An educational and humanitarian organization, founded in 1981 by the guru Sri Sri RAVI SHANKAR to improve health and increase spirituality. It includes a PRANAYAMA or breathing technique, known as the Sudarshan Kriya. The basic Art of Living course is taught over a period of five days, after which more advanced courses are available. The method is taught in most towns and cities of India, and is one of the most popular New Age courses. The Art of Living is also involved in welfare activities.

artha One of the goals of Hindu life, literally meaning profit or prosperity. For the householder,

Artha or economic activities, earning a living and providing for the family, are valid pursuits. The other goals are KAMA, meaning pleasure and desire, and DHARMA, or life lived according to truth and customary laws. Finally, all are subordinate to MOKSHA, or liberation. Followers of a spiritual path should avoid the accumulation of wealth.

arti A ceremony of worship performed with lamps or lights, particularly in Hinduism. Lights or diyas are held in the hand and circled around or near a deity or any sacred object.

Aruna (1) The charioteer of SURYA, the Hindu sun-god, the brother of the divine bird GARUDA, and the son of the rishi KASHYAPA and his wife VINATA. According to the *MAHABHARATA*, the god BRAHMA asked Aruna to become Surya's charioteer, to shield the intense rays of the sun. Aruna married Shyeni, and they had two sons, Sampati and Jatayu. Aruna once assumed a female form, naming herself Arunidevi, to attend a gathering of Devis or goddesses, where no men were permitted. Attracted by her, the god INDRA desired her and a son was born. Another son was born to Arunidevi and Surya. Both sons were entrusted to Ahalyadevi, but were turned into monkeys by her husband Gautama. These were VALI and SUGRIVA of the *RAMAYANA* story, who were adopted by the king of KISHKINDHA.

(2) Aruna was the name of a class of RISHIS who obtained svarga (heaven) through self-study.

(3) Aruna was also the name of several others, including a NAGA, an ASURA, a DANAVA, and a king.

Arunachalam A sacred hill, near the ashram of RAMANA MAHARSHI near TIRUVANNAMALAI in Tamil Nadu. According to legend, when the Hindu god SHIVA appeared as a column of light, his brightness was unbearable, and so he took the form of the hill of Arunachalam. The hill is closely associated with Ramana, and according to him is the 'heart of the earth, the centre of the universe'. For many years Ramana lived in caves on the hillside, while contemplating and meditating on the true Self. He said that while Mt KAILASHA was sacred because Shiva lived there, Arunachalam was more so because it was Shiva himself. Ancient RISHIS and SIDDHAS are said to still inhabit the hill. At the Karttika festival, associated with the ARUNACHALESHVARA TEMPLE, a fire is lit on the hill, representing the divine light of Shiva.

Ramana's ashram is located near the foot of the hill.

Arunachaleshvara Temple A temple of the Hindu god SHIVA, located at TIRUVANNAMALAI in Tamil Nadu. It was constructed at the time of the Chola dynasty in the eleventh century. The Chola kings added to it in the twelfth and thirteenth centuries, Krishnadeva Raya of the Vijayanagara kingdom in the sixteenth century, and the Nayakas in the seventeenth century. The inner shrine is approached through a long ante-chamber and houses a LINGA. A number of images are on the outer walls, including those of Shiva in different forms, as DAKSHINAMURTI, and appearing out of a linga. Corridors surround the shrine, lined with stone lingas and metal images of Shaivite saints.

Another shrine to the north, houses an image of DEVI, in Nayaka style. There are also smaller shrines dedicated to GANESHA and KARTTIKEYA. A major festival takes place here in October/November, known as the Karttika festival. At this time a bonfire is built on the hill, which appears like a beacon of light and can be seen from far.

Arunagirinatha A BHAKTI saint and poet of the Tamil country who worshipped the Hindu god Kumara or KARTTIKEYA. He probably lived in the first half of the fifteenth century and composed verses in Tamil and Sanskrit. He is said to have been a Gauda BRAHMANA, who was born in the village of Mullundrum in the Tamil region, and attained enlightenment at the ARUNACHALESHVARA TEMPLE in TIRUVANNAMALAI. The collection of his verses known as *Tiruppugazh* are the most popular.

Arupattimuvar A term which refers to the NAYANARS, devotees of the Hindu god SHIVA who lived between the seventh and tenth centuries. Traditionally there were sixty-three Nayanars, and Arupattimuvar means 'the sixty-three'.

arya A term used in the VEDAS, meaning 'noble', from which the word ARYAN is derived. Arya also occurs in Zoroastrian texts. In the AVESTA, the aryas or noble ones lived in Airyana Vaeja, the first of the lands created by AHURA MAZDA. It was at the centre of the earth and at its own centre was the mountain Hara-bareza. It was far to the north, and there one year seemed equal to a day. The name 'Iran' is derived from Airyana.

Arya Samaj An organization founded in the nineteenth century with the aim of reforming and revitalizing Hinduism and its practices. The organization is still flourishing today.

Swami DAYANANDA SARASVATI started the Arya Samaj, meaning 'noble society', at MUMBAI (Bombay) in 1875. His aim was not to start a new sect or religion, but to reveal true Hinduism, as it was found in the Vedas. The VEDAS, he believed, contained eternal knowledge. Hindus were converting to other religions because they had forgotten the eternal truths and focused on superstitious practices. Swami Dayananda condemned the caste system, particularly untouchability, unnecessary rituals, child marriage and animal sacrifices. He was in favour of scientific education, the education of women and the remarriage of widows.

He began the Shuddhi Movement or 'purificatory movement', which aimed at bringing untouchable castes into mainstream Hinduism, and reconverting to Hinduism those who had converted to other religions. Swami Dayananda wrote a number of books, of which *Satyartha Prakasha* laid down the basic principles and ideas of the movement.

In 1877 a branch of the Arya Samaj was founded in Lahore, and henceforth Punjab became the centre of the movement. Prominent leaders of the freedom struggle against the British were Arya Samajis, including Lala Lajpat Rai and Swami Shraddhanand.

Education was one of the main activities of the Samaj, and two types of educational institutions were founded. Lala Hansraj, a leader of the Samaj, believed that the best education would combine traditional learning with Western scientific knowledge, and thus founded the Dayananda Anglo-Vedic (DAV) College at Lahore. DAV colleges and schools soon spread all over northern India. A more orthodox group founded a Gurukul or centre of traditional learning at HARDWAR. Initially, this was limited to the study of the Vedas, but it now includes modern subjects as well.

The Arya Samaj, along with both types of educational institutions, is still popular in India. Its motto or primary goal is stated in Sanskrit as *'Krinvanto Vishvam Aryam'*, i.e., 'make the world noble', and it also has followers worldwide, with branches in the US, Canada, the UK and several other countries.

arya satya The term in Sanskrit for the FOUR NOBLE TRUTHS of Buddhism. The PALI term is ariya sachcha.

Aryadeva A Buddhist philosopher of the MADHYAMIKA school of MAHAYANA Buddhism, a disciple of NAGARJUNA. He probably lived in the third century CE and was originally from Sri Lanka. He wrote the *Chatushataka*, which describes the path of the BODHISATTVA, and also explains Madhyamika ideas. Another work of his, the *Shatashastra*, refutes the theories of non-Buddhist schools of thought.

Aryaman A deity mentioned in the VEDAS, where he was one of the ADITYAS, similar to MITRA. He later lost importance. Aryaman is also a YAZATA, a minor deity in Zoroastrianism.

Aryans A term used for the authors of the RIG VEDA and later Vedic texts. The English word Aryan comes from the Sanskrit 'arya' or noble, which the Vedic authors used to describe themselves. There are several controversies about these Aryans and their identity. According to some scholars they were a branch of the INDO-EUROPEANS who spoke a common language and migrated to different parts of the world from an area near the Caspian Sea. One branch entered India after living in Iran, as part of what is called an INDO-IRANIAN group. Among other theories, B.G. Tilak thought their original home was in the Arctic. Several Indian scholars feel they originated in India and spread from India to the rest of the world. Whatever their origin, the texts indicate that they were at first occupants of north-west India (including Pakistan), and later extended their territories across the Gangetic plain and towards the south.

They have been equated with various archaeological cultures, including the Grey Ware and Painted Grey Ware, which together extend from about 1500 BCE to 600 BCE, and alternatively with the much earlier INDUS CIVILIZATION.

Their deities, religious practices and way of life are described in the Rig Veda and the later VEDAS.

arz An Arabic term for the earth. In Islamic mythology, there are seven earths, one below the other, a concept similar to that of the LOKAS in Hindu myths. The earth on which we live is supported by an angel who stands on a rock of ruby. The rock is on a bull, which has 4000 eyes, ears, noses, mouths, tongues and feet. Its name is Kujuta, and it in turn stands on a fish called Bahamut. There are different descriptions of these earths in various texts.

asana A Sanskrit term meaning seat or posture. It specifically refers to physical positions that form part of the system of YOGA, particularly HATHA YOGA. Texts state that there are eighty-four classic asanas, though according to the *Gheranda Samhita* there are 84,00,000, of which 1600 are excellent, and thirty-two the most auspicious. The seated padmasana, or lotus posture, is considered the most basic of all asanas. Certain asanas are described only in TANTRIC texts, for instance mundasana, in which the practitioner is seated on a skull.

Asanas make the body and mind steady, lead to good health and aid clear and correct thought.

Asanga A Buddhist philosopher who founded the YOGACHARA school of MAHAYANA Buddhism and lived from 310 to 390. He was a resident of Purushapura (Peshawar), now in Pakistan, and was originally a monk of the MAHISHASAKA school of HINAYANA Buddhism. According to some accounts, he received a vision of the Bodhisattva MAITREYA, who revealed certain teachings to him that were put together under the name of MAITREYANATHA. Other scholars state that Maitreyanatha, a real person, was his teacher. Asanga composed his own texts which, along with those of Maitreyanatha, formed the basis of the Yogachara school. Asanga's works include the *Mahayanasamgraha*, the *Abhidharma-samuchchaya*, and a commentary on the *Samdhirnirmochana Sutra*. His brother VASUBANDHU also joined this school.

Asha A deity and a power of AHURA MAZDA, the name of God in Zoroastrianism. Asha is personified as an AMESHA SPENTA, or immortal being, representing cosmic order, truth and justice. The term is also translated as righteousness. The concept of Asha is similar to the Vedic rita and the later concept of DHARMA. Asha is praised in several prayers. The GATHAS state that Asha is the way that leads to enlightenment. He is the guardian, the healer of life, the friend. Asha creates life, which is fulfilled through the flame of action and the good mind. The concluding passage of the YASNA states that there is only one path, that of Asha, and all other paths are false. The *Ashem Vohu*, the second most important prayer in Zoroastrianism, is also in praise of Asha.

While in the *Gathas* Asha is the first of the powers, in later texts he takes second place to VOHU MANA, the good mind. In PAHLAVI texts, Asha Vahishta (the highest or best Asha), is known as Ardwahisht, and in Persian as Ardi Behesht. Asha Vahishta is represented by the consecrated fire, and his flower emblem is the sweet marjoram.

Ashariyah (Asharites) A school of Islamic thought, consisting of the followers of Abul Hasan al-Ashari (873–935). Al-Ashari belonged to the Shafi school of law at Baghdad and became part of the MUTAZILA, a 'rationalist' school of thought, but later refuted its doctrines, and stated that revelation was superior to reason. He believed that the QURAN is the word of God and is eternal and uncreated, and that everything happens by the will of God. He said, 'Nothing on earth, whether a fortune or a misfortune, comes to be, save through God's will'. The individul cannot understand or gain the knowledge of good and evil through reason, but must accept all that is revealed. It cannot be asserted that the good will be rewarded and evil punished, as God is the only judge, the only one with knowledge that transcends all human laws. However, moral responsibility could not be denied to man, therefore God has the power to convert desires into action. People may think they are acting according to their own will, but the action is acquired out of the creative power of God, and therefore is known as *kasb* (acquisition).

The Mutazilas denied the eternal attributes of God and explained references to his face, hand and eyes in the Quran as metaphors, while the old believers said these had to be accepted literally. Ashari said that these attributes of God are real, but not to be taken literally, as God knows, sees and speaks through his essence. This essence is different from creation, composed of atoms which unite in different ways. These views contradicted many of the Mutazila concepts.

Other scholars further developed Ashariyah ideas, among them being Al-Baqillani (d. 1013), Al-Juwayni (d. 1085) and Al-Ghazali (d. 1111). Al-Ghazali, who taught at Baghdad, denied the role of reason and logic in religion. Later he accepted SUFI ideas and emphasized the importance of love and devotion to God. As he was a respected scholar, his ideas contributed to the acceptance of Sufism by the ULAMA.

The Ashariyah school of thought has been influential in India and its ideas form part of orthodox SUNNI concepts.

ashavan A term used in Zoroastrianism for the followers of the path of ASHA or Truth, as opposed to the dregvants, or those who follow the false path.

Ashi Vanghui A deity in Zoroastrianism. Ashi, meaning good, represents material and spiritual wealth which comes to those dedicated to AHURA MAZDA who follow the path of ASHA. It has also been translated as 'blessing'. Ashi Vanghui accompanies SRAOSHA, the divine conscience. In later texts, both Ashishvangh, as she came to be known, and Sraosha are also YAZATAS or minor deities. The *Ashishvangh Yasht* is dedicated to Ashi.

Ashkenazim A term for central and east European Jews, first used in the Middle Ages to distinguish them from the Sephardic Jews of Spain and Islamic lands. The Ashkenazim once formed a small group of Jews in India. About 2000 of them came to India as refugees from Nazi Germany in the 1930s and '40s, and lived for some time with other Jewish communities. A few Ashkenazim had settled in India earlier as well. Most Jews in the world today are Ashkenazim, though they account for only about half the population in Israel.

Ashoka An emperor of the Mauryan dynasty who patronized Buddhism. He ruled from 269 to 232 BCE, with his capital at PATALIPUTRA (present-day Patna in Bihar), and his empire extended from Afghanistan to the region of Karnataka in south India. Right across this area, he erected monolithic stone pillars. His edicts, engraved on these pillars, and on rocks, are still preserved. He is also described in Buddhist sources. His Thirteenth Rock Edict tells us of his conquest of Kalinga (Orissa). It states that 'One hundred and fifty thousand were deported, a hundred thousand were killed, and many times that number perished'. Some scholars believe he converted to Buddhism immediately after the Kalinga war, while others feel he was a Buddhist even before this. In any case, moved by the suffering he had caused, Ashoka resolved that his future conquests would be not by war, but by DHAMMA. Though deeply influenced by Buddhism, he reinterpreted Dhamma in his own way. He focused on the welfare of people and of animals, stopped the killing of certain animals, set up hospitals even for animals, and was against unnecessary ceremonies and rituals. In his inscriptions he asks people to respect those of other religions. Thus in the Twelfth Major Rock Edict he states, 'One should honour another man's sect, for by doing so one increases the influence of one's own sect and benefits that of the other . . . Concord is to be commended, so that men may hear one another's principles and obey them.'

One inscription records how he prevented a schism in the Buddhist SANGHA. He also organized the third BUDDHIST COUNCIL at Pataliputra. Ashoka is praised in Buddhist texts, including the *DIPAVAMSHA* and *MAHAVAMSHA*. According to these, his son and daughter went to Sri Lanka and spread Buddhism there.

Ashoka reorganized the administration and personally supervised his vast empire, but it did not hold together after his death. He also caused STUPAS and CHAITYAS to be erected; according to tradition the number of stupas set up by him was 84,000.

Ashokan pillars Monolithic stone pillars erected by the Mauryan emperor ASHOKA in the third century BCE, found from Afghanistan to south India. Ten to seventeen metres high, these polished sandstone pillars weighed about fifty tonnes. At least thirty to fifty such pillars were erected, and possibly more. Each is capped with an animal capital. Ashoka engraved his edicts on these pillars, several of which were erected at sites sacred to Buddhists. Some scholars feel that they had an additional religious significance, representing aspects of the cosmos. John Irwin was one of the scholars who put forward this theory in detail.

ashram/ashrama A Sanskrit term, which in ancient days referred to the hermitage of a RISHI or sage, usually located in serene surroundings and in forests. These ashramas were described as places of peace and harmony, where even wild animals were protected. The term continues to be used today for a residential area where disciples of modern-day gurus live.

ashrama dharma A term referring to the four stages of Hindu life. Traditionally, the males of the higher castes, and particularly BRAHMANAS, were meant to live their lives according to these stages. The first stage was that of BRAHMACHARYA, where the boy studied the Vedas and other texts with his guru. He often lived in his guru's ASHRAM and served him in various ways. This continued till he was in his twenties, when he entered the second stage, that of a householder or Grihastha. At this time he married, had children and took care of his family. When his children had grown up, it was time for the third stage, VANAPRASTHA, when he retired to the forest and pondered on mystical truths. In the fourth stage, he became a homeless wanderer, a SANNYASI. These stages are no longer literally observed today, though some of the ceremonies associated with them still take place.

At a different level, however, the four ashramas are still important, representing stages in a life dedicated to a search for truth.

Ashtachhapa A term which literally means 'eight seals'. It refers to a group of disciples of the sixteenth-century Hindu VAISHNAVA saint VALLABHACHARYA and his son VITTHALANATHA. The saints included poets and singers who were devotees of the god KRISHNA. The most important of these was the blind singer SURDAS. Others included Nanddas, Paramananddas, Krishnadas, Govindswami, Kumbhandas, Chitaswami and Chaturbhujdas.

Ashtadiggajas Eight divine elephants in Hindu mythology. They guard and support the earth, along with their female counterparts and the DIKAPALAS or LOKAPALAS. They are mentioned in the AMARAKOSHA and other texts as AIRAVATA (east), Pundarika (south-east), Vamana (south), Kumuda (south-west), Anjana (west), Pushpadanta (north-west), Sarvabhauma (north), Supratika (north-east). Their female counterparts are the Ashtadikkaranis, known as Abhramu, Kapila, Pingala, Anupama, Tamrakarni, Subhradanti, Angana and Anjanavati. The elephants were created by BRAHMA from two halves of the cosmic egg.

Four more elephants support the earth from below. These are Virupaksha, Mahapadmasama, Saumanasa and Bhadra.

ashtangika marga The Sanskrit term for the EIGHTFOLD PATH to be followed in Buddhism. In PALI the term is atthangika-magga. It is also called the middle way, madhyama-pratipada or majjhima-patipada.

Ashtasahasrika Prajnaparamita Sutra A Buddhist MAHAYANA text, the earliest of the PRAJNAPARAMITA or 'perfection of wisdom' sutras. It probably dates to about 100 BCE. It initially had 8000 lines.

Ashtavakra Gita A Sanskrit text that deals with the Hindu philosophy of ADVAITA Vedanta. While some assign it to the period of the UPANISHADS or the BHAGAVAD GITA, others place it in the ninth century CE or later. The text consists of a dialogue ostensibly between King JANAKA, and Ashtavakra, a learned guru. Ashtavakra is mentioned in the MAHABHARATA and PURANAS. He was named Ashtavakra because he had crooked limbs; the name literally meaning 'eight bends in the body'. Though the text is attributed to Ashtavakra, it is not known who actually wrote it.

In this text, when Janaka asks Ashtavakra the means of attaining knowledge and liberation, he instructs him in words typical of some of the Upanishads. For instance:

You are not a brahmana or kshatriya or of any other caste;
You are not at any stage, nor are you anything that can be seen;
Unattached and formless, you are the witness of all.
(1.5)

Through a series of questions and answers, Janaka finally realizes the truth. He says:

For the one who has transcended all limitations, there is neither initiation nor scripture, neither disciple nor teacher, and no goal to be attained.
There is neither being nor non-being, neither unity nor dualism.
What more is there to say?

(20.13–14)

This profound text was a favourite of Sri RAMAKRISHNA PARAMAHANSA and even today is held in high esteem.

Ashura A term in Arabic, meaning 'the tenth'. It refers to the tenth day of the month of MUHARRAM, observed as a day of fasting by Muslims. It is particularly sacred for SHIAS, and is the only day of Muharram also observed by SUNNIS. It is said to be the day on which God created Adam and Eve, life and death, heaven and hell, the tablet of decrees, and the pen. The Prophet MUHAMMAD is also said to have kept a fast on this day.

Ashvaghosha A Buddhist philosopher, scholar and poet who lived in the first century CE. He wrote a biography of the BUDDHA in Sanskrit verse, called the *BUDDHA CHARITA*. The *Saundarananda Kavya*, another long poem, describes some episodes of the Buddha's life in detail, but focuses on the story of Nanda, the half-brother of the BUDDHA. Nanda loved his wife Sundari but was persuaded by the Buddha to become a monk. For some time he was in sorrow, until he realized the truth of the Buddha's way. A drama, *Shariputra-Prakarana*, deals with the conversion of SHARIPUTRA and MAUDGALYAYANA, chief disciples of the Buddha, to Buddhism. Other works ascribed to Ashvaghosha are the poem *Gandistotra Gatha*, available only in Chinese translation; *Sutralankara*, translated into Chinese in the fifth century; and *Vajrasuchi*. The first was probably his work. Two scholars, Winternitz and Luders, feel the *Sutralankara* was written by Kumaralata, a junior contemporary of Ashvaghosha, while some see it as Ashvaghosha's own work. The complete text is available in Chinese, with only fragments being preserved in Sanskrit. In Sanskrit it was known as *Kalpana-manditaka* and was a collection of Buddhist stories. The author of *Vajrasuchi* is uncertain. The text is a criticism of the caste system, using Brahmanical texts to refute theories of caste.

Ashvaghosha was probably born at Saketa (AYODHYA), though sometimes his birthplace is given as KASHI or PATALIPUTRA. He is said to have converted the Kushana king KANISHKA to Buddhism and to have attended the BUDDHIST COUNCIL held at Purushapura (Peshawar in Pakistan). His story poems are lyrical and beautiful, and he was also a good singer and musician, whose songs were sung in Buddhist monasteries long after his death.

ashvamedha A horse sacrifice, one of the main SACRIFICES in early India, conducted to increase the power of the king. After certain purificatory ceremonies, a horse, marked with the king's name, was set free to roam, accompanied by warriors and nobles. The territory through which it wandered was claimed by the king, and anyone who challenged this had to defeat the accompanying warriors in battle. After a period of time, a year or more, the horse returned to the kingdom and was sacrificed, often along with hundreds of other animals. The sacrificial ritual, involving the priest, the king and the queen, is described in detail in several texts. Some of the flesh of the horse was consecrated to the gods, some eaten by participants in the sacrifice. Before this the queen had to spend one night near the dead horse, during which some rituals were prescribed, including sexual rites.

Inscriptions recording ashvamedhas occur from the second century BCE onwards, though it was practised even earlier. The sacrifice is first mentioned in the RIG VEDA and described in detail in the *RAMAYANA* and other texts. It indicated the power and glory of the king, and important kings performed several ashvamedhas. The Guptas, Chalukyas and Cholas are among the many dynasties whose kings performed the sacrifice, but by the time of the Cholas, the practice was rare, and gradually died out.

In the *BRIHADARANYAKA UPANISHAD* the symbolism of the sacrifice is described, the horse reflecting the cosmos.

Horse sacrifices took place in other ancient cultures as well, including Greece and China. Horse sacrifices in ancient Rome were connected with agriculture and the harvest.

Ashvamedhika Parvan A Sanskrit text said to be part of the *Jaimini Bharata*, a Hindu text. According to tradition, JAIMINI was one of the people to whom the rishi VYASA narrated the *MAHABHARATA*, and he wrote the *Jaimini Mahabharata*, of which only the *Ashvamedhika* is available today. It contains stories and legends from the *Mahabharata* and *RAMAYANA*, as well as stories of the god KRISHNA and of miracles performed by him. Its date is uncertain.

Ashvins Deities prominent in the RIG VEDA. The Ashvins are twins, said to be young but ancient, honey-hued and with a golden brilliance. Their name indicates their connection with horses (ashva = horse). They ride in a three-wheeled golden chariot drawn by horses, or sometimes by deer, birds, buffaloes or a single ass. They are also known as Nasatyas, from 'na-asatya', meaning 'no untruth'. They are helpers in distress, the physicians of the gods, and guardians of immortality. They have been identified with day and night, heaven and earth or twin stars. Some feel they were once real people who were helpful saints, taking care of those in distress. They were married to Surya (Suryaa), daughter of the sun god. In the *MAHABHARATA*, NAKULA and SAHADEVA were their sons, and were therefore known as Ashvineyas. Parallels have been drawn between the Ashvins and the two sons of Zeus, Castor and Pollux in Greek myths.

Asikni (1) The wife of DAKSHA, who was a son of the Hindu god BRAHMA and one of the PRAJAPATIS. She was the daughter of Virana Prajapati and was also known as Virani. From Daksha and Asikni, 5000 sons known as Haryashvas were born, to propagate the human race. However, the rishi NARADA suggested that they should first gain some knowledge and understand the nature and boundaries of the earth. The Haryashvas set off on a tour of the earth, but never returned. When they realized that the Haryashvas were lost, Daksha and Asikni had another 1000 sons, known as Shabalashvas. But they too were persuaded by Narada to explore the earth, and were never found again. Then Daksha and Asikni had sixty daughters, who were married to KASHYAPA, SOMA, ARISHTANEMI and others. All created beings were descended from those married to Kashyapa.

(2) The name of a river mentioned in the RIG VEDA, identified with the Chenab, a tributary of the Indus.

asrava, in Buddhism A term indicating impurity. Three impurities to be eliminated are kamasrava, the impurity of sexual desire; bhavasrava, the impurity of desire for existence; and avidyasrava, the impurity of ignorance.

asrava, in Jainism A term for the inflow of KARMA or karmic matter. To attain enlightenment, the inflow has to be stopped and then eliminated.

Assyrian Church of the East A Christian denomination also known in India as the Chaldean Syrian Church of the East. They trace their origin to the See of Babylon, said to have been founded by ST. THOMAS the Apostle. Historically there is evidence of their existence in the region of Parthia, including Iraq and western Iran, by the second century CE. Their leader has the title of Patriarch. Influenced by NESTORIAN ideas, they were condemned by Rome in the fifth century but continued to exist in Zoroastrian Persia, and spread to China and Mongolia and other areas. After the coming of Islam, the Patriarchate moved to Baghdad, but the Church continued to flourish till the fourteenth century, when many of its followers were killed by Timur.

According to tradition, the Church existed in India from the first century CE. Bishops and priests were sent here from Mesopotamia. The Church used Aramaic in its liturgy and in the sixteenth century, the Portuguese, who were in India at the time, attempted to Latinize it. In 1796, a group of Assyrians were offered land and privileges by the king of Kochi (Cochin) and flourished there. As the Church was weak in other parts of the world, in India they accepted bishops from the Chaldean Church, which has a similar liturgy.

After the British left Iraq in 1933, disputes arose within the church, and gradually, two rival groups emerged. Two groups still exist, but in India they were unified in 1995. The Assyrian Church in India accepts Mar Dinkha IV as Patriarch, with his headquarters in the USA. The Metropolitan, with his headquarters at Thrissur, Kerala, is in charge of the Church in India. The Church has about 30,000 followers in India, based mainly in Kerala.

astika A term used in ancient India for schools of philosophy that were derived from interpretations of Vedic literature. These were the VAISHESHIKA, NYAYA, SAMKHYA, YOGA, MIMAMSA and VEDANTA. Philosophical systems which rejected the VEDAS as the ultimate source of knowledge were known as NASTIKA. According to the grammarian PANINI, astika refers to those systems that believe in a heavenly world.

astikaya In Jainism, a category of five basic realities. These are JIVA, PUDGALA, DHARMA, ADHARMA and AKASHA, that is life, matter, motion, non-motion and space. Astikaya indicates that which exists in space, excluding KALA or time. Along with kala, these five realities constitute the six DRAVYAS or substances. While jiva has life, the others are part of AJIVA, or inanimate beings.

astrology An ancient science, known in India as jyotisha. According to tradition, the science of prediction was developed by the rishi Bhrigu, who wrote the horoscope of every individual of the past, present and future. These were copied on palm-leaves and are said to be still preserved.

Astrology in India was later influenced by Greek and Roman systems, and the *Yavana-Jataka*, possibly of the second century CE, is one of the early astrological texts showing Greek influence. In the fifth or sixth century, VARAHAMIHIRA composed works on astronomy, astrology, the significance of planets, and horoscopy. Some of his works also indicate Greek influence. There were several other works on horoscopy. In the medieval period, Bhattotpala's *Hora Shastra* of the fifteenth century, and the *Tajika* of the thirteenth century are among the important later texts.

Indian astrology uses nine planets (NAVAGRAHA) of which two are 'shadow planets', marking the nodes of the moon. Other aspects are the NAKSHATRAS or lunar mansions, yogas or planetary combinations, and dashas or time periods. Though the signs of the zodiac are adopted from the West, they do not follow the same dates. Nor is Indian astrology uniform, different systems and calendars being used in various parts of the country.

Astrology still plays an important part in everyday life. Astrologers calculate the dates of festivals every year, and of special fasts and ceremonies. Marriages are usually performed only on auspicious days. Many people will not take up employment or move into a new house without consulting an astrologer.

A major branch of astrology is the making of individual horoscopes, and most Indians have their horoscopes cast at birth.

astrology in Islam In orthodox Islam, astrology is not considered lawful. According to the QURAN, God created the stars only for three purposes: as an ornament of the heavens, to stone the devil with, and to direct travellers on their path. The use of stars for any other purpose was unlawful, and thus astrology was not a lawful pursuit. However, the QURAN mentions the constellations (buruj) and other aspects used in astrology, and Muslim astrologers have existed in India from medieval days.

asuras A class of beings in Hindu texts. Originally a divine being, the word asura later came to mean a demon. In the RIG VEDA several deities are referred to as asura, including AGNI, BRIHASPATI, DYAUS, PUSHAN, SAVITR and VARUNA, but by the later Vedic period asuras were always at war with the DEVAS or gods. They were supernatural beings with considerable powers, which the devas recognized. At times the devas temporarily entered into a pact with them, as when churning the ocean of milk for AMRITA or divine nectar. DAITYAS and DANAVAS were types of asuras. The *VISHNU PURANA* states that at the time of the churning of the ocean, the daityas came to be known as asuras because they rejected Varuni, goddess of sura or wine, who emerged from the ocean, while the devas accepted her and were known as suras. Prominent asuras include MAHABALI, still worshipped in Kerala.

In the AVESTA, the Zoroastrian scriptures, asura took the form AHURA, and AHURA MAZDA was the one God, the highest deity, while the DAEVAS were considered demons. The mythical struggle between devas and asuras could therefore reflect a struggle between two groups of the early INDO-IRANIANS, though recent scholars doubt this theory. At a later period it possibly reflects cultural conflicts between the north and the south.

Atal Rai A son of the sixth Sikh guru HARGOBIND. Born at AMRITSAR on 22 December 1619, he had great spiritual power, but was warned by his father not to use it unnecessarily. When he was nine years old, his friend Mohan died, and by his power Atal Rai is said to have restored him to life. Guru Hargobind believed this was not right, and told him no one should intervene in the will of God. The boy acknowledged his words, went to the nearby Kaulsar pool, sat in SAMADHI, and left the world. The BABA ATAL GURDWARA was built at this site.

Atala In Hindu mythology the first of the seven divisions or LOKAS of the netherworld or PATALA. Bala, the son of Maya, reigns here. He has created ninety-six magical arts, capable of fulfilling all one's desires. Three kinds of women emerge from his mouth when he yawns, and they have a charm which entices men, who then live in perfect bliss. In some texts Atala is said to be ruled by Mahamaya.

Atala Masjid A mosque at Jaunpur in Uttar Pradesh constructed during the reign of Ibrahim Shah Sharqi, who ruled in Jaunpur and neighbouring areas from 1401 to 1440. The mosque was completed in 1408.

A temple of Atala Devi was once located here, and fragments of the old temple were used in the mosque, built in a mix of local and Islamic styles. The whole structure covers a square of 78.5 m on each side. There is an open courtyard, with a long, rectangular prayer hall on the west, and double-stored cloisters on the other three sides. The prayer-hall, is exceptional, as it has three large ornamental archways. The enormous central arch reaches a height of 23 m, with a base of 17m, and recessed arches within. There are three gateways, and those on the north and south have domes. The mosque is constructed from grey sandstone and granite, and is quite ornate.

atar/adar/atash A term for fire, which is sacred in Zoroastrianism. It is known as adar in later PAHLAVI and as atash in Persian. In the GATHAS, atar represents the fire of thought and of the mind, through which the true path is chosen. Atar is also a protective power of AHURA MAZDA, and is associated with SPENTA MAINYU, the good spirit, and with ASHA, or righteousness. Fire in the world is a symbol of this inner flame, and is therefore worshipped in ZOROASTRIAN TEMPLES and in homes.

Every Zoroastrian temple, has within it a consecrated fire, which is always kept burning. The consecrated fire in a temple is usually placed in an afarghan, a metal container shaped like an inverted bell. The BOI ceremony takes place five times a day, during which the priest prays and feeds the fire with sandalwood and incense. There are several rules for consecrating a fire, particularly in an ATASH BEHRAM, the highest grade of fire temple. Apart from atar, atash, etc., other fires are mentioned in Zoroastrian texts. Nairyosangha is a personification of the sacred fire; burzin meher was a fire given to King VISHTASPA; it burned without fuel and did not singe the hands of those who held it. Minokirk is the fire of the higher world. The need to keep the fire pure, and methods of doing this, are also discussed in various texts. The *Atash Nyaesh* is a special prayer dedicated to fire.

In the ZOROASTRIAN CALENDAR, the ninth month of the year and the ninth day of every month are named Adar.

Atash Adaran Fire of fires, the fire in an Adaran or second grade of ZOROASTRIAN TEMPLE. The Atash Adaran is consecrated using four types of fire.

Atash Behram Fire of victory, the fire in the first grade of ZOROASTRIAN TEMPLES. Sixteen types of fire are used traditionally in consecrating an Atash Behram, including lightning. Once consecrated, the fire is never allowed to go out. Fire from lightning is the most difficult to acquire, as it has to strike a tree or other object and set it aflame so that it can be collected. It takes at least a year to ceremonially join together the different fires.

There are eight Atash Behrams in India, four in Mumbai, two in Surat, one in NAVSARI, and one in UDVADA. The one at Udvada is considered the most sacred, being the fire that was consecrated when the PARSIS first arrived in India at SANJAN; it was later moved to Udvada. It is also known as Iranshah, the royal fire of Iran.

Atash Dadgah The lowest grade of consecrated fire in Zoroastrianism, installed in homes and in small AGIARYs or temples.

Ate Kaniya A festival celebrated by the tribal GONDS of Mandla. In this festival the Gonds worship the Hindu god KRISHNA and paint scenes of his youth in VRINDAVANA on the walls of their houses. In the drawings, Krishna plays on his flute on the banks of the YAMUNA, roams with his cows and cowherd friends and dallies with the GOPIS, the young women who love him. The story associated with this festival is that such paintings were first made by ARJUNA. Arjuna was depressed because all the women loved Krishna, but no one seemed to love him and so he retired to the forest, painting images of Krishna on the walls of his own hut. Krishna then arranged for Arjuna and Subhàdra, Krishna's sister, to be united in love. (Traditional texts, however, have a somewhat different story of Arjuna and Subhadra).

Atharva Veda One of the four VEDIC SAMHITAS of Hinduism. The *Atharva Veda* or fourth Veda is also known as the *Brahma Veda*. It includes magical chants and MANTRAS, both for protection and for the defeat of enemies. ATHARVAN originally meant 'fire-priest', corresponding with athravan of the AVESTA, therefore this text may have an INDO-IRANIAN origin, though in its present form it is later than the RIG VEDA. The *Atharva Veda* consists of 731 hymns with about 6000 verses divided into twenty books or sections. Some of the Rig Vedic hymns are repeated in the *Atharva*, and Rig Vedic deities are mentioned, but a major part of it consists of songs and spells. Several of these deal with the healing of diseases. Diseases are sometimes personified and hymns are addressed to them, while in other cases there are spells to banish demons considered responsible for ill-health. There are prayers to curative herbs, or to healing waters and fires, chants for health and long life and for harmony within the family. There are spells to win someone's love, and for protection from demons and from people with evil intentions.

Atharva Veda prayers are used at birth, marriage, funeral and other ceremonies, but overall the fourth Veda has never been as popular or held in as high esteem as the other three VEDAS. Parallels between the *Atharva Veda* and Shamanic, Mayan, German Merseburg magic maxims and other magical traditions have been found, and aspects of the *Atharva Veda* later occur in the TANTRAS.

Atharvan An ancient priest. In the RIG VEDA, Atharvan produced AGNI or fire, was the messenger of VIVASVAT and brought order through sacrifices. According to the *ATHARVA VEDA*, Atharvan was a companion of the gods. Atharvan is also used as a generic term for a priest, while Atharvans (plural), are a class of PITRIS or ancestors who live in heaven. In the AVESTA, Athravan is a fire-priest.

Atisha A Buddhist philosopher and scholar, also known as Dipankara, who lived from 982 to 1054 CE. Initially at NALANDA, he was invited to Tibet and went there in 1042, remaining in Tibet till his death. There he helped to reform the SANGHA, insisting on the need for celibacy and discipline. Buddhism had by then taken hold in Tibet and Buddhist texts were being translated into Tibetan. Atisha wrote several texts, including the *Bodhipathapradipa*, or '*Lamp for the Way of Enlightenment*'. He stated that HINAYANA, MAHAYANA and VAJRAYANA were three stages of Buddhism, Vajrayana being the highest. Other scholars went to Tibet, but Atisha is particularly important because his chief Tibetan disciple DROMSTON (1008–64) founded the first distinctive Tibetan monastic order, KADAMPA (Bka-gdams-pa), setting up the monastery of Rwa-sgren. Atisha's work also influenced later Tibetan sects.

Atisha died at Nyethang in Tibet and was interred in the monastery there.

Atman/Atma A Sanskrit term for the Self or soul, which is imperishable, beyond time and eternal. In the RIG VEDA, the term means breath, or vital essence. The concept of the Self is developed in the UPANISHADS. The Atman is not the same as the body, mind or consciousness, but is something beyond, which permeates all these. The Upanishads explore the concept of the Atman from all possible angles, and most later schools of philosophy, base themselves on these texts. In some passages in the Upanishads the Atman is considered identical with BRAHMAN, the underlying reality of the world, and thus there is only one Atman, which permeates all beings. This interpretation is followed by ADVAITA Vedanta. MOKSHA, or liberation, is achieved when the unity of the Atman and Brahman, which already exists, is perceived or realized. In other passages, the jivatma or individual soul is distinguished from the Atman, and is not the same as Brahman, though it can unite with it, or enter a relationship with a personalized deity. In SAMKHYA philosophy there is a plurality of souls. In Jainism, there are many individual souls (JIVAS), and the liberated Jiva, freed from matter, is known as the Atman. Early Buddhist philosophy states that there is no permanent entity, and if only an eternal entity can be known as the Atman, everything is anatta, or ANATMAN, that is, with no Atman or soul.

In Sikhism, Atma is a term for the individual soul, within which a spark of God resides.

Atri An ancient RISHI or sage described in the RIG VEDA and later in the *MAHABHARATA*, PURANAS and other texts. In the Rig Veda, he was one of the ancestors of the human race. In later texts he was one of the sons of the Hindu god BRAHMA and was married to Anasuya. Their sons were the rishi DATTATREYA, an incarnation of VISHNU, DURVASA, an incarnation of SHIVA, and CHANDRA, an incarnation of BRAHMA. There are several stories about Atri and his powers. Once, to help the DEVAS in their battle against the ASURAS, he became both the sun and the moon. The fury of the sun consumed the asuras, while the gentle light of the moon refreshed the devas.

There are some temples dedicated to Atri. Among them is the Atri Rishi Temple at Guru Shikhar in Rajasthan, the highest point of the Aravali hill range.

auliya An Arabic term in Islam, meaning the favourite of God. The term occurs in the QURAN. In India, the SUFI saint Nizamuddin was known as NIZAMUDDIN AULIYA.

Aum A sacred word, also spelt OM, which symbolizes BRAHMAN, the highest state known in Hindu philosophy.

Aurangzeb The sixth Mughal emperor, who ruled from 1659 to 1707 and tried to revive orthodox Islam. He was the son and succesor of the emperor Shah Jahan and brother of the liberal DARA SHIKOH, whom he killed during the struggle for accession to the throne.

Aurangzeb first put down rebellions in the north and consolidated his territories. After 1681 he expanded his empire towards the south, conquered the Deccan states and extracted tribute from kingdoms in the far south. By then, however, the empire had become too large to control effectively. Revolts were frequent, and the Mughals declined after his death. Aurangzeb was pious and orthodox, but is remembered primarily for his bigotry, though historians have pointed out that some of these accounts are exaggerated. Aurangzeb certainly reversed the liberal and tolerant policies of AKBAR, which had been somewhat curtailed by Jahangir and Shah Jahan, the next two rulers, but not totally set aside.

Among Aurangzeb's unpopular acts were the reduction in customs duty for Muslim traders in 1665, and its abolition in 1667 while it was retained for Hindus. In 1669 he issued an order to demolish Hindu temples and centres of learning and a number of temples were destroyed, including the Vishvanatha temple at Varanasi and the Keshav Rai temple at Mathura. In 1679, the JIZYA tax was reimposed on non-Muslims. Employment and stipends were offered to those who converted to Islam. The ninth Sikh guru, TEGH BAHADUR, was executed in 1675 upon his refusal to convert to Islam. Aurangzeb also alienated the Marathas and several of the Rajputs, though some prominent Rajputs remained in his employ.

Aurangzeb was a SUNNI who attempted to live according to Quranic law. He had no personal vices, dressed and ate simply and followed Islamic law in all aspects of his life. His intolerant religious outlook has been attributed not merely to his own personal inclinations, but to compulsions of state, primarily the need to get the support of the ULAMA and nobles. The reimposition of the Jizya was also a means to collect much-needed funds and to provide employment.

Despite these policies he continued to employ Rajputs in high posts, and even gave grants to some temples and Hindu MATHAS as well as to Jains in Gujarat. He visited the DARGAHS of some of the noted SUFI saints, met visiting Sufis, and quoted the *Masnawi* of Rumi, the celebrated Sufi saint, in his correspondence. In his later years he modified some of his policies in an attempt to win over his enemies. He employed a number of Marathas, and in 1704 suspended the Jizya in the Deccan.

After 1681, Aurangzeb never returned to the north and in his absence DELHI regained its eclectic and liberal culture. Shaikh Kalimullah, a CHISTI saint, and Abdul Qadir Bedil, a Sufi and a poet, were among those who enriched the culture of Delhi.

During his reign, the *Fatwa-i Alamgiri* on Islamic law was compiled, while his letters to his sons and grandsons were collected in the *Kalmat-i Taiyyabat*.

Aurangzeb's destruction of temples has reverberations even today, with Hindu groups threatening to destroy the mosques built in their place.

Aurobindo, Sri A noted philosopher of modern India. Sri Aurobindo (Aurobindo Ghose) was born at Kolkata (Calcutta) in India on 15 August 1872, and at the age of seven was sent to England to study. Returning to India as a young man in 1893, he worked for some time in the state of Baroda, but gradually got involved in the Freedom Movement against the British, who ruled most of India at this time. He had already begun certain YOGA practices, and when in prison for his actions in the struggle for freedom (1908), he received a divine revelation. He left British India and moved to the small territory of Puducherry (Pondicherry) in south India, which was then under the French. Here he could not be pursued by British authorities, and, giving up politics, he founded an ASHRAM and developed his own philosophy.

His basic philosophy is what he called Integral Yoga. The aim of this is 'to enter into a higher Truth-Consciousness or Divine Supramental Consciousness in which action and creation are the expression not of ignorance and imperfection, but of the Truth, the Light, the divine Ananda (bliss).' He did not prescribe any fixed method but suggested various ways to make oneself receptive and open to the divine, including surrender and devotion, meditation, and the watching of one's actions.

He believed in the evolution of the human life and mind towards an ultimate spirituality and an increasing universality. The light and power of the spirit, also called by him, the 'Supermind', presiding over human evolution, could transform human consciousness and remould life on earth. He was joined in his ashram in 1920 by 'The MOTHER', a French woman named Mirra Richard. While the Mother ran the ashram, Aurobindo remained in seclusion, reading, studying ancient texts and writing.

His philosophical works include *The Life Divine*, *The Synthesis of Yoga*, *The Integral Yoga*, the epic *Savitri* (a poem with 24,000 lines), and several other works, as well as commentaries on major ancient texts. In these works he questioned many traditional concepts of Indian philosophy, including the commonly accepted views of the world as MAYA or illusion, and of KARMA.

He stated that no religion revealed the whole Truth. He said that 'the Divine Truth is greater than any religion or creed or scripture or idea or philosophy.' Though he had undertaken a deep study of Hindu texts, he ceased to identify with Hinduism as he developed his philosophy. He wrote, 'The Ashram has nothing to do with Hindu religion or culture or any religion or nationality. The Truth of the Divine which is the spiritual reality behind all religions and the descent of the supramental which is not known to any religion, are the sole things which will be the foundation of the work of the future.'

After his death in 1950, the Mother continued to run the ashram and later set up AUROVILLE, an international city near the ashram.

Auroville An 'international city' near Aurobindo Ashram in Puducherry (Pondicherry). Mirra Richard, known as the MOTHER, who was the companion of Sri AUROBINDO, thought of establishing such a city. The idea behind it is expressed in the following words: 'There should be, somewhere upon the earth, a place that no nation could claim as its sole property, a place where all human beings of goodwill, sincere in their aspiration, could live freely as citizens of the world, obeying one single authority, that of the Supreme Truth . . .'

The foundation stone of the city was laid on 28 February 1968. Groups of cottages were set up for residents, with gardens and natural surroundings. Separate pavilions represent different countries. At the centre of Auroville is Matri Mandir, 'the temple of the mother', representing the universal mother. It is a golden sphere surrounded by gardens. Within is an inner chamber, completely white, with white marble walls, and in the centre a crystal globe. Through the apex of the sphere sunlight is electronically guided to fall on the crystal. Here people meditate in silence. Matri Mandir is said to be beyond all religions, a meeting point of silence, in which the spiritual force is revealed.

Auroville, however, is not merely about meditation, but about ways to promote and live a harmonious and constructive life. It has research centres experimenting with local, eco-friendly construction material, with new varieties of crops, the development of natural insecticides, and other products. Fruit trees of various kinds are grown in large orchards. Workshops produce handmade paper, natural oils for aroma therapy, incense, candles and other items. There is an extensive library, a school aligned with Aurobindo's philosophy, and a publishing unit. A medical centre integrates indigenous and Western systems of medicine.

Ava A Hindu deity, a sheep-faced goddess. She is a MATRIKA or mother goddess, one of the animal-headed mothers represented in early Indian art.

Avadhuta Gita A Sanskrit text assigned to the rishi DATTATREYA, though it is not known who wrote it, or when. It is an Advaitic text, by one who has realized the truth. An avadhuta is a liberated soul, one who has renounced the world. Totally beyond all that is, an avadhuta follows no rules, no fixed practices, and has no need to follow conventional norms. In the text, Dattatreya says, 'I am by nature the formless, all-pervasive Self.' He goes on to describe the state of an avadhuta, who lives alone, in solitude, rejoicing in the bliss of BRAHMAN. Such a person has even gone beyond the fourth state of consciousness, TURIYA, and dwells in the state of turiyatita. About this text Swami VIVEKANANDA said, 'Men like the one who wrote this song keep religion alive.'

Avalokiteshvara A celestial BODHISATTVA, the embodiment of compassion. He is associated with the Buddha AMITABHA, and helps all who pray to him. Literally his name means 'the one who looks down'. In art he is variously depicted with many arms and a crown in which Amitabha is seated. He often holds a blue lotus. In Japan and China he turned into a female deity, Kwannon or Kuan Yin, while in Tibet he is known as Chenrezi. The DALAI LAMA is considered an incarnation of Avalokiteshvara.

Avantipur An ancient town in Kashmir with ninth-century Hindu temples. The site is located 28 km by road from Srinagar, the capital of Kashmir. The *Rajatarangini*, a history of Kashmir dating to the twelfth century, states that the town was established at a sacred place earlier known as Vishvaikasara, by Avantivarman, a king of Kashmir. Avantivarman of the Utpala dynasty ruled from 855 to 883 and constructed two temples. The Avantisvamin Temple, dedicated to the god VISHNU, was built before he ascended the throne, and had a two-tier platform approached by a staircase. The inner sanctuary is square, decorated with friezes of elephants, hamsas (swans or geese), lion heads, bells and other motifs, but the main image is missing. Several images found nearby were of a four-headed and four-armed Vishnu, and the main image was probably of the same type. Four smaller shrines are at the corners of the courtyard; two later shrines and sixty-nine small cells on a high basement are arranged around the courtyard with carved pillars in front. The Avantishvara Temple, dedicated to SHIVA, was set up later, while he was the king. This was originally a large temple but is now in ruins. The temple was entered through a gateway and around it was a courtyard surrounded by cells. Carved figures that have been found include those of LAKULISHA, considered an incarnation of Shiva, and of a standing couple, probably the king and queen.

avasarpini A descending cycle of time in Jainism, which consists of six ARAS or ages, and forms part of a KALPA. In a descending cycle, everything deteriorates, including knowledge, the lifespan of an individual, height and stature, and happiness. However, the first three aras of a descending cycle are relatively good. Nature and wish-fulfilling trees (kalpa-vriksha) provide for all. People are simple, peaceful and contented. Water is cold and sweet, the air unpolluted and exhilarating. Even the sand is sweet as sugar. Fruit and grains are nutritious and fulfilling, and a small amount is enough for days. As the third ara of the present time drew to an end, changes occured. With an all-round deterioration in conditions, disputes took place, and there fore people were grouped into kulas (families) headed by a kulkar, to sort out disagreements. It was at this time that RISHABHA, the first TIRTHANKARA, was born, to provide guidance as things deteriorated further.

avashyakas The six essentials, or daily duties, which every Jain should practise. These are listed and explained in a number of texts, both in ARDHA MAGADHI and Sanskrit. Among the early texts dealing with these is the *AVASSAYA SUTTA*. The Sanskrit terms for the six avashyakas are: samayikam, or the practice of equanimity, which can be attained by refraining from evil; chaturvimshatistava, the glorification of the twenty-four TIRTHANKARAS; vandana, or veneration of the guru; pratikramana or confession; kayotsarga or penance by assuming certain body postures; pratyakhyana, renouncing certain pleasures.

Avassaya Sutta A Jain text of the SHVETAMBARA canon, one of the four MULA SUTTAS, known in Sanskrit as the *Avashyaka Sutra*. It has six sections, dealing with the six essential daily duties of a Jain, known as the shad-avashyakam or AVASHYAKAS.

Avatamsaka Sutra A Buddhist MAHAYANA text of uncertain date, translated into Chinese by 420 CE. The whole is available in Chinese, though two major sections, the *Dashabhumika* and the *Gandavyuha*, exist in Sanskrit. The text focuses on the concept of dharma-dhatu, where all phenomena coexist. It states that the dharma-dhatu is the same as SHUNYATA (the void), or TATHAGATA-GARBHA (the underlying Buddha essence). Other aspects deal with the BODHISATTVA ideal and the path to enlightenment. The *GANDAVYUHA SUTRA* and the *DASHABHUMIKA SUTRA* on the ten stages of a BODHISATTVA are used as separate texts.

avatara An incarnation of god on earth. It also means descent, advent or manifestation. In Hinduism, the god VISHNU is most commonly associated with avataras. There are ten main avataras of Vishnu, while up to thirty-nine are mentioned in certain texts. Among Vishnu's avataras, RAMA and KRISHNA are the most popular. The god SHIVA also has avataras, though there are not many temples dedicated to them. Avataras are said to descend to earth from time to time, to guide people on the right path.

In the BHAGAVAD GITA, Krishna states: 'Although I am unborn, everlasting and I am the lord of all, I come to my realm of nature and through my wondrous power I am born. When righteousness is weak and faints and unrighteousness results in pride, then my Spirit arises on earth.' 4.6–7; (trans. Juan Mascaro)

Avataras can also be partial, or AMSHA-AVATARAS, and secondary, or gauna-avataras. A number of saints and heroic figures are included among these. Several gurus of the twentieth century are said to be incarnations of earlier saints. For instance, Satya SAI BABA is thought to be an incarnation of SAI BABA OF SHIRDI, who in turn was considered an avatara of DATTATREYA.

In Buddhism, the DALAI LAMA is said to be an incarnation of the Bodhisattva AVALOKITESHVARA. Each successive Dalai Lama, as well as some other categories of lamas, are incarnations of earlier lamas and saints. The concept also exists in Islam, particularly in the AHMADIYA and MAHDAWI movements, though it is rejected by the orthodox.

In more recent times, various individuals have claimed to be avataras of one deity or the other, or of a prophet, not only in Hinduism, but in other religions as well.

Avesta The collective term for the early religious scriptures of the Zoroastrians. The GATHAS, or songs of the Prophet ZARATHUSHTRA, are among the earliest portions of these scriptures. They are included in the YASNA, or book of worship. In addition there are YASHTS, or hymns to specific deities, and NYAESHES, which with some other prayers form part of the *Khordeh Avesta*, or shorter Avesta, used for personal prayers. Other texts include the *Visperad* and *Videdvat* or VENDIDAD.

The dating of these texts is controversial, but the *Gathas* and some other parts of the *Yasna* probably belong to about 1500 BCE.

Early Zoroastrian literature was said to have been destroyed at the time of Alexander's invasion of Persia in 301 BCE. Existing texts were put together at the time of the Sasanian dynasty, and probably completed by the sixth century CE. According to tradition, they were again destroyed after the Arab invasion of the seventh century. After the Zoroastrians (PARSIS) came to India, some of the texts they brought with them were translated into Sanskrit. Later Zoroastrian texts were composed in PAHLAVI, and as some of these are commentaries on the older texts, they are known as Zand-Avesta or Avesta-e-Zand.

Avesta language A language of ancient Iran, including Gathic or old Avesta, and later Avesta, known as younger Avesta. Gathic Avesta is similar to the language of the RIG VEDA, while younger Avesta is a simplified version of the old language. Avesta was probably in use only till around 400 BCE, but was still known to the priests and thus was used for writing down the texts between the fourth and sixth centuries CE, at the time of the Sasanians. The script used was evolved from PAHLAVI, which had developed from Aramaic.

Avicenna A Muslim philosopher whose name was Abu Ali Al-Husain Ibn Abd-Allah Ibn-Sina. He lived from 980 to 1037. A Persian born near Bukhara, he is believed to have been a genius who had a complete knowledge of the QURAN by the age of ten, and also understood theology and mathematics. He studied medicine, and by the age of sixteen, physicians of the highest eminence are said to have come to learn from him. He was not merely a physician, but also a philosopher. He had absorbed Greek philosophical ideas, which had penetrated some schools of Islam in the ninth century. He went deeply into philosophical concepts and stated that essence (mahiya) was separate from experience or existence (wujud). He also said that creation was the manifestation of God's essence, and that the world was eternal, while orthodox Islam believed that creation took place at a particular point of time. His books include the *Kitabal-Shifa*, or *Book* of Healing, which was a philosophical encyclopaedia, and the *Kanun-fit-tibb*, or *Canon of Medicine*. A later philosophical work was the *Kitab al- Isharat*, in which he described the spiritual journey of a mystic. His philosophy had an impact on Islamic philosophers of India and elsewhere. He was also famous in the West, where he was known as Avicenna.

Awariful Maarif A text on Sufism, written in 1234–35 by Shaikh Shihabudin SUHRAWARDI. It is one of the two main texts on which early SUFI doctrines in India were based, the other being the *KASHFUL MAHJUB*. Both texts emphasized the importance of observing the SHARIA (law), and stated that Sharia, marifah (gnosis) and haqiqa (reality) were three interdependent aspects of the Sufi path. They also deal with Sufi ethics.

ayagapattas A term for Jain tablets of homage, dedicated to TIRTHANKARAS and other Jain saints. A number of ayagapattas have been found at MATHURA, dating from the first century BCE. Early ayagapattas have carvings that depict STUPAS, dharmachakras (wheels of law), ashtamangalas (eight auspicious symbols), and other sacred symbols, while later ones have figures of Tirthankaras or of donors.

Ayaramga Sutta A Jain text, the first of the twelve ANGAS, written in ARDHA MAGADHI, and known in Sanskrit as the *Acharanga Sutra*. The text has two sections and prescribes rules, regulations and the ideal way of life for a Jain monk. The first section, which is earlier than the second, deals mainly with prohibitions, for instance, against killing or injuring a living being. One passage states:

'One may not kill, nor ill-use, nor torment, nor persecute any kind of living being, any kind of creature, any kind of thing having a soul, any kinds of beings. That is the pure, eternal, enduring commandment of religion, which has been proclaimed by the sages who comprehend the world.'

This section also stresses severe asceticism for monks, including methods by which advanced monks can end their lives through starvation. The second part consists of three subdivisions known as chulas (literally, appendices), of which the first two provide rules for the daily life of monks and nuns, how they should wander and beg for food, and what they are permitted to eat. Nothing that destroys the life of any being should be eaten. Monks must speak the truth, but also should not say anything to hurt others. The third chula describes the life of MAHAVIRA, the twenty-fourth TIRTHANKARA of Jainism.

Ayodhya A town in district Faizabad of Uttar Pradesh, sacred to Hindus, Buddhists and Jains. It is considered one of the seven most sacred cities of Hinduism, and according to tradition is the birthplace and capital of RAMA, an incarnation of the god VISHNU. It was also known as Saketa and in ancient days was the capital of the janapada or kingdom of Koshala.

In Jainism, too, it is a sacred site. The first TIRTHANKARA, RISHABHA, was born here. BHARATA, the son of Rishabha, ruled the world with his capital at Ayodhya. Ajitanatha, Abhinandanatha and Anantanatha were the other Tirthankaras born here. One of the earliest Jain images, dating back to the fourth or third century BCE, was found here.

Saketa is mentioned in Buddhist texts, which refer to it as an important city. The BUDDHA lived here for some time. The Chinese pilgrim FA HSIEN passed through here in the fifth century and called it Shachi, while XUANZANG in the seventh century knew it as Vishakha. According to Fa Hsien, there were a number of Buddhist monasteries here.

Archaeology indicates that the place dates back to about the seventh century BCE, but declined in importance after the fourth century CE.

There are several temples located in Ayodhya, as well as sacred sites associated with Rama. The Rama Janma Bhumi site, where the BABRI MASJID stood until 1992, is said to mark the exact birthplace of Rama. Lakshmana Ghat, located near the river, marks the spot where LAKSHMANA ended his life. The Birla Temple is one of the large modern temples constructed in the city. Ayodhya also has mosques and tombs of Muslim saints.

Ayudha Puja The worship of tools, instruments, machines or vehicles. It is commonly performed one day before the Hindu festival of DASHAHARA, particularly in south India. Workmen appreciate that their tools or machines have functioned well throughout the year. They give them a day of rest, adorn them with oil and garlands, and perform a PUJA, or ceremony of worship.

Ayudha Purusha The personified weapon of a deity. Several such weapons are personified in Hinduism, including Vishnu's CHAKRA and Shiva's TRISHULA. Among other cultures, the ancients Celts also personified and worshipped their weapons.

ayyan A term used in south India, which means father, revered person, or a BRAHMANA. It is said to be derived from the Sanskrit word 'ARYA', meaning noble. Ayyan represents the male principle or PURUSHA, while amman represents the female, PRAKRITI, SHAKTI or mother. Ayyan or amman are attached to the names of several deities.

Ayyanar A Hindu deity worshipped mainly in Tamil Nadu. He is the son of SHIVA and of VISHNU, who had assumed a feminine form, Mohini. He is a guardian deity, and is usually depicted as a warrior, either on foot or on a white horse or elephant, holding a sceptre or whip. He is said to ride through the air at night, accompanied by his generals. He is sometimes called 'the king of demons' or else is said to be their master, though he is not one of them. Ayyanar is prayed to for freedom from disease and pests, for a safe journey and for safe childbirth, and in general, for protection. He is the god of the mercantile community, and particularly of potters. Ayyanar temples occur all over

Tamil Nadu. Terracotta horses can be seen outside, usually offerings from devotees, and MATRIKA or mother goddess panels are sometimes found in his temples. The main Ayyanar festival takes place in September/October after NAVARATRI, while there is another festival in May/June. He is a vegetarian god who sometimes has a twin temple with a meat-eating deity, Karuppu or Karuppan. Ayyanar is known as Shivaputra or Harasuta, the son of Shiva, and is considered part of the SHAIVITE pantheon. His origin is the same as that of AYYAPPA, well known in Kerala, and he is sometimes considered another form of that deity.

Ayyappa A Hindu deity popular in Kerala. According to myth, Ayyappa was born as a result of a union between SHIVA and VISHNU in the form of Mohini, the divine enchantress. In the PURANAS, his counterpart is SASTHA or Dharmasastha, which is used as a synonym for this deity. As he is a composite deity, born through the union of Shiva and Vishnu, he is known as Hariharasuta. As the son of Shiva he is called Bhutanatha, and is also known as Manikanta.

There are several myths and stories about the origin of Ayyappa. According to one story, he was found on the banks of the Pampa river by the king of Pandalam. The Pandalam dynasty was an offshoot of the Pandyas. The childless king took the baby back to his palace and reared him with love. The young child showed his great powers when he killed the demon Mahisha. On another occasion, when the queen demanded the milk of a tiger, he brought back a tiger with her cubs from the forest, along with a vessel of its milk.

According to another story, Ayyappa was the son of the king's sister, and was brought up in the forest but later sent to his uncle. Meanwhile, a tribal chief destroyed the shrine of Sastha, located on SABARIMALA hill, which was worshipped by the Pandalam kings. Ayyappa and his Muslim friend Vavar, who became like his brother, defeated those who were against the king. When the idol of Sastha was reinstalled, Ayyappa disappeared into it, and is considered the same as that deity. This took place on the first day of the month of Makara. Thus at Sabarimala, the main centre of worship for Ayyappa, this day is particularly auspicious. There are other Ayyappa temples in Kerala and elsewhere.

Some consider Ayyanar and Ayyappa as two forms of the same deity, as they have the same origin, though they are depicted and worshipped differently.

Azad, Maulana Abul Kalam A nationalist, freedom fighter and minister in independent India, Maulana Azad was also a learned scholar who wrote on Islam.

Born in 1888 in Mecca, he was originally known as Mohiuddin Ahmad. He returned to India with his parents when he was a child. Later he studied at Al Azhar University in Cairo, and back in India he was influenced by Syed AHMAD KHAN and made efforts for the reform of the Muslim community. Apart from his political activities, he tried to promote Hindu-Muslim unity and wrote on various aspects of Islam. His main work is the *Tarjuman al-Quran*, a translation and interpretation of the QURAN, in Urdu. In this he brings out the universal nature of the Supreme Being. He states that god is Rabb-ul-Alamin, the lord of all creation and the sustainer of life, with divine concern for every person, group, community and country, and for every form of existence. He also comments on the need to reinterpret the Quran in modern times. He distinguished between SHARIA (the law), and the Truth, and said that while the former could be modified, the Truth was eternal.

Maulana Azad died in 1958.

azan A term for the Islamic call to NAMAZ or prayer. The MUAZZIN makes the call five times every twenty-four hours, from the MINARET of large mosques or the door of small mosques. The call begins with the Arabic words, 'ALLAHU AKBAR', or 'God is great.'

Azar Kaivan, Dastur A Zoroastrian saint who lived from c. 1530 to 1618. According to various accounts, he was born in Iran and came to India later in life, along with twelve disciples. From childhood he was a saintly person, always engaged in prayers. He was a strict vegetarian who ate very little, and asked his followers to be kind to animals. He first came to Surat in Gujarat, moved to NAVSARI and then to PATNA in Bihar, where he stayed for the rest of his life. The Mughal emperor AKBAR is said to have visited him there. He advocated an ethical and ascetic life and had great spiritual powers. Legends about him recount that he could heal illnesses, walk over water and fire, and appear in two places at the same time. He had a number of disciples who belonged to all religions. He died at Patna at the age of eighty-eight.

Azar Kaivan is revered particularly by followers of the esoteric Zoroastrian ILM-E-KHSHNOOM sect, while some feel his concepts were closer to Sufism and that he was not a Zoroastrian but a SUFI influenced by SUHRAWARDI doctrines

Azariah, Vedanayagam Samuel The first Indian bishop in the ANGLICAN CHURCH. Born in 1874, he was also the secretary of the YMCA between 1895 and 1909, and the founder of the Indian Missionary Society and the National Missionary Society. He took care of the diocese of Dornakal in Andhra Pradesh and converted a number of lower castes and tribals to Christianity. Before his death in 1945, he also worked towards a union of churches, which took place two years later in 1947 with the formation of the CHURCH OF SOUTH INDIA.

Bab A title in Islam used by both SHIAS and SUFIS. In particular it refers to Sayyid Ali Muhammad of Shiraz (1819–50), who called himself 'the Bab' or 'the gateway' to the truth. He believed in the concept of the hidden IMAM, and in 1844 stated that he would reveal the truth. His book *Bayan* (Explanation) was to replace the QURAN. Though he had a large following, his heretical views caused him to be executed at Tabriz in 1850. His two successors, Mirza Yahya and Mirza Husain Ali, founded different groups. The latter called himself BAHAULLAH or 'splendour of God'. His followers are known as BAHAIS and constitute a religion separate from Islam. While the Bahai is a worldwide religion, Mirza Yahya's followers, the Azali, number only a few thousand and live mainly in Iran.

baba A term for a father or revered person. It is often attached to the names of saintly people.

Baba Atal Gurdwara A GURDWARA or Sikh shrine located at AMRITSAR in Punjab, constructed at the spot where ATAL RAI, son of the sixth guru HARGOBIND, was cremated. A small shrine was erected at the site, but later a nine-storeyed gurdwara was built, representing the nine years that the child lived. The first three stories were constructed by 1784, and the rest added by Maharaja Ranjit Singh. Further renovations were made later. Some of the stories have murals on the walls and ceiling, depicting aspects of Sikh history. Near the gurdwara is the Kaulsar tank, made earlier in memory of Kaulan, daughter of the qazi of Lahore. Kaulan was inspired by Guru Hargobind, and leaving her family, came to Amritsar and was given refuge by the guru. The tank was constructed in 1621.

Baba Bakala Gurdwara A GURDWARA or Sikh shrine located at Bakala in District Amritsar, Punjab, associated with the ninth guru, TEGH BAHADUR. Before Guru Hargobind died, he advised Tegh Bahadur, his youngest son, who had become a recluse, to settle in the peaceful village of Bakala. Tegh Bahadur lived here along with his wife Gujri, and mother Bibi Nanaki for twenty years(1644–64).

When the eighth guru, HAR KRISHAN, was on his death-bed in 1664, he is said to have muttered 'Baba Bakala'. This was taken to mean that the next guru would be found at village Bakala. A number of people from Bakala claimed to be the guru and the true succesor of Har Krishan, but it was difficult to verify their claims. Finally, Makhan Khan Lubana, a trader from Bakala, succeeded in doing so. Caught in a storm on a sea-voyage, he prayed to Guru NANAK for help, and vowed to donate 500 dinars to the true guru. He reached Bakala safely and offered two dinars to each of those claiming to be the guru, stating that he was fulfilling a pledge made on the sea-voyage. Tegh Bahadur asked him why, if he had pledged 500, he was offering only two. He added, 'A guru is never in need, but a Sikh is expected to keep his pledge'. Thus Lubana announced that since Tegh Bahadur knew his secret pledge, he must be the true guru.

To commemorate the discovery of the guru, a gurdwara was built at Bakala, at the spot where Guru Tegh Bahadur used to sit in meditation. The gurdwara has become an important centre of pilgrimage, particularly on AMAVAS night, and at the time of the RAKSHA BANDHAN festival, when a fair is held. Two other gurdwaras in Bakala are the Manji Sahib Gurdwara, and Sheesh Mahal Gurdwara. The former was built where the guru was sitting when men sent by his nephew Dhirmal, an aspirant for the guru's post, attempted to kill him. The latter is at the location of the guru's residence.

Babri Masjid A sixteenth-century mosque located at AYODHYA, which was the centre of a controversy between Hindus and Muslims and was demolished in 1992.

The Babri Masjid was probably built at the time of the Mughal emperor Babar (ruled 1526–30). Some Hindu groups claimed that it was located at the spot of an earlier temple that marked the birthplace of the god RAMA. In 1949 an image of Rama was surreptitiously placed inside the mosque, and was said to have arrived there on its own, through divine intervention. Fearing problems between the two communities, the gates of the mosque were shut, and no worship was allowed there by any group. In 1986 the gates were opened, after which there were renewed attempts to construct a temple at the spot. Negotiations failed to bring about a solution and the mosque was demolished by a mob in 1992. It remains a disputed area with a decision on its status still to be given by the courts.

The dispute has been used by various political parties to gain electoral support, and is an example of the misuse of religion in politics.

Badami A town located between two rocky hills in Bijapur district of Karnataka, which is known for its early cave temples, cut into the side of a red sandstone hill. Badami, earlier known as Vatapi, was the capital of the Chalukya dynasty between the sixth and seventh centuries. There are four rock-cut cave temples belonging to this period, of which two are dedicated to the Hindu god VISHNU and one to SHIVA, while the fourth is a Jain temple of PARSHVANATHA. Another natural cave is a Buddhist shrine. There are also several structural temples. Among these is the Jambulinga Temple, dated to 699, with three shrines dedicated to BRAHMA, Vishnu and Shiva, connected to a common MANDAPA. The Yellamma Temple of the eleventh century has a multi-storeyed tower. Images are carved on boulders near the temples, and there are more shrines around the town. The seventh-century Upper Shivalaya Temple on the cliffs to the north has intricate carvings of KRISHNA and NARASIMHA, while the Mallegitti Shivalaya Temple of the same period has panels depicting Vishnu, Shiva and other deities.

Badarayana The author of the *BRAHMA SUTRA*, also known as the *Vedanta Sutra*, who probably lived sometime between 500 BCE and the first century CE. He is identified with the rishi VYASA, a name used for several authors. The *Brahma Sutra* summarizes the UPANISHADS and form the basis for Vedantic thought. They were used by all later writers and exponents of the various schools of VEDANTA.

Badrinath Temple A temple dedicated to the Hindu god VISHNU, located at Badrinath, in Chamoli district of Uttarakhand, at a height of 3133 m above sea-level, in a valley on the right bank of the river ALAKANANDA. Here Vishnu is worshipped as Sri Badrinatha. According to legend, the temple has ancient origins but was re-established by SHANKARA in the ninth century. The temple is 15 m high and is surmounted by a small cupola and spire. The main image of Badrinatha is 1 m high, and there are also images of LAKSHMI, PARVATI, GANESHA and GARUDA. Two thermal springs nearby, known as Tapt Kund, are said to have curative properties. Since the time the temple was re-established, only a Nambudri Brahman from Kerala is allowed to be the priest or rawal. Badrinath is a major centre of pilgrimage and the most important of the Badri temples in the hills of Uttarakhand. The others include Adi Badri, on the route to Ranikhet; Bhavishya Badri at Subain near Tapovan, not far from Joshimath; Bridha Badri also near Joshimath; and Yogdhyan Badri at Pandukeshwar. Badrinath is also the centre of one of the MATHAS established by Shankara.

Badshahi Bagh Gurdwara A GURDWARA or Sikh shrine located at Ambala city in Haryana. It is constructed at a spot where the tenth guru, GOBIND SINGH, stayed, in a garden under a cluster of trees.

Baga A Zoroastrian YAZATA or minor deity, similar to the Rig Vedic BHAGA.

Bagala A Hindu goddess, one of the MAHAVIDYAS or TANTRIC goddesses, a form of PARVATI, the wife of SHIVA. She is depicted with the head of a crane, seated on a throne of jewels, holding a club. Her colour is yellow. Bagala is worshipped mainly in east India. The *Bagala Tantra*, a Tantric text, has several magical rites associated with her worship.

Bagh Caves Buddhist temple caves located in the Bagh Hills in Madhya Pradesh. There are nine caves sculpted in the fifth and sixth centuries CE. Of these, four are similar, with a verandah opening into a large hall, which has small cells on both sides. At the end is a shrine containing a STUPA. Paintings on the walls depict scenes from the life of the BUDDHA, and the windows, doorways and columns are carved.

Baghdadi Jews A group of Jews from Arab countries who reached India in the late eighteenth century. Though collectively known as Baghdadi or Iraqi Jews, they were also from Yemen, Syria and Iran. They came for trade and commerce, as well as to escape religious persecution. Initially most of them settled in Surat on the Gujarat coast, but later moved to MUMBAI (Bombay) and Kolkata (Calcutta). Some of them were extremely rich, and the most well-known among them were the Sassoon family of Mumbai and the Ezras of Kolkata, who not only had business empires, but built hospitals, schools, libraries and SYNAGOGUES in India. Initially most of these were reserved for their own community, not even other Jews being allowed to enter. The Baghdadi Jews at first spoke Arabic, but later adopted English. From the late nineteenth century, many of them began to migrate to England, while others became more Indianized. In the 1940s they numbered about 7000, but now there are less than fifty in India.

Bahadurgarh Gurdwara A GURDWARA or Sikh shrine located at Saifabad, 6 km from Patiala in Punjab. It was built by Maharaja Karan Singh to commemorate the visit of the ninth guru, TEGH BAHADUR, to his friend Nawab Saif Khan. The interior of the gurdwara is decorated with mirror-work, murals and paintings. Thousands of pilgrims visit the gurdwara on BAISAKHI day, when a big festival takes place.

Bahai A religion founded in the mid-nineteenth century by Mirza Husain Ali, who came to be known as BAHAULLAH. Originally an offshoot of Islam, the Bahai religion is gradually gaining ground and spreading through the world. According to official Bahai estimates, there are about five million Bahais in the world, of which over two million are in India.

Bahaullah's followers believe he is a manifestation of the divine and the most recent prophet or messenger of God. His son ABDUL BAHA, followed by SHOGHI EFFENDI, further established and spread the faith.

The Bahai religion believes that there is one God, the creator of the universe. He sends his messengers to guide human beings to develop their spiritual and moral qualities which form their essence. These divine messengers, including Abraham, Moses, ZARATHUSHTRA, BUDDHA, KRISHNA, JESUS, MUHAMMAD, and the BAB, have provided the world with a progressive series of revelations. The final message of God's will for humanity was revealed by Bahaullah. Gradually, traditional barriers of race, caste and creed are breaking down, and the world is ready for something new to take its place. Bahaullah's special message is that the time has come to unify all people of the world and one of the main purposes of the Bahai faith is to enable world unity and peace.

According to the Bahai religion, all people have the free will to choose the right path. There is no force of evil in the world, but not choosing rightly leads to imperfection, which is seen as evil. Bahais believe that true religion is in harmony with reason and science, and that each person has a responsibility to discover the truth.

Apart from world unity, the main goals of the religion include: the abandonment of all forms of prejudice; equality of women; recognition of unity and relativity of religious truth; elimination of extremes of poverty and wealth; universal education; establishment of a global commonwealth of nations.

The Bahai religion has spread to 235 countries and territories across the world, and its adherents come from over 2100 different ethnic groups. It accepts the truth of all religions, and thus explains its beliefs in the context of the beliefs and ideas of each religion.

Bahai administration The BAHAI religion has a special system of administration to co-ordinate its affairs. BAHAULLAH envisaged an administrative order to take care of the Bahai community and expressed his ideas in his *Book of Laws*. His son and successor, ABDUL BAHA, further elaborated on this and appointed SHOGHI EFFENDI as the Guardian of the Faith. He also spoke about the need for an elected legislative assembly of which the Guardian would be the head. Shoghi Effendi further discussed the setting up of this assembly. He said, 'Acting in conjunction with each other these two inseparable institutions administer [the Bahai Faith's] affairs, coordinate its activities, promote its interests, execute its laws and defend its subsidiary institutions.' After Shoghi Effendi's death in 1957, no Guardian was appointed, but Effendi's writings continue to serve as a Guardian or reference point for matters concerning the community. The Universal House of Justice, an elected body set up in 1963, guides the activities of the global community, supervises Spiritual Assemblies, which function at the national and local levels, and legislates on those matters not dealt with in the Bahai sacred texts. Nine members from the worldwide Bahai community are elected to this body every five years.

Bahais in India BAHAIS have been present in India from the time the religion was founded. Five stages of development can be traced: (1) The pre-Bahai or Babi stage, when there were some followers of the BAB in India. In addition, the Afnan clan, relatives of the Bab, were settled in MUMBAI. (2) The initial stages of the Bahai community between 1872 and 1910. At this time, some members of the Afnans in Mumbai who had adopted the Bahai religion, asked BAHAULLAH to send a teacher to India. He sent Sulayman Khan Tunukabani, better known as Jamal Effendi, who stayed in India till 1878. During this time he conveyed the principles of the new religion, mainly through personal visits to high officials and princes, and before his departure delegated some converts to continue his work. In this period, a number of Indian Zoroastrians (PARSIS) became Bahais after a few of the community who had visited Iran came in contact with the new religion there. Leaders of the Bahai community also discussed their principles with the members of the THEOSOPHICAL SOCIETY and the BRAHMO SAMAJ. (3) Between 1910 and 1921 there was an attempt to unify various Bahai groups in India, and it was decided to spread the religion through a national teaching programme. The first All-India Bahai Convention was held in Mumbai in 1921. (4) The next period, between 1921 and 1957, was that of the guardianship of SHOGHI EFFENDI, and saw many changes in the organization of the Bahai community. In 1923 the National Spiritual Assembly of the Bahais of India and Burma was set up. Local spiritual assemblies were established and new teaching plans were adopted. In 1953 an international Bahai convention was held in New Delhi, and a Ten-Year Crusade to spread the teachings was started. (5) Mass teaching, however, only took off after 1957. Within much of rural India, Bahais distanced themselves from their Islamic roots and translated Bahai teachings into local languages. Regional spiritual councils were set up in all states. Bahaullah was called Bhagavan Baha, and equated with KALKI, the tenth incarnation of the Hindu god VISHNU. Rural idioms were used, poems in the BHAKTI tradition were sung in villages, and thousands were persuaded to declare their faith in Bhagavan and his teachings. Doing this was a simple procedure of signing or putting a thumb print on an enrolment card. Converts were not required to give up their original faith or practices, but only to accept Bahaullah and his message of universality and equality.

Thus there is a wide discrepancy between census figures and Bahai claims. According to the 1991 census, Bahais numbered 5575, while Bahai leaders proclaim a figure of more than 2 million. Independent researchers have put the number of those who understand and follow Bahai teachings in India at anywhere between 1,00,000 and 2 million. Conversion is mainly of scheduled castes and tribes, and has not led to any controversies or ill-feeling, as the separateness of the religion is not emphasized.

The Bahais have over 900 local councils in India, and run classes on the religion for adults and children. They have also opened schools and other institutions for social reform.

Bahai Lotus Temple   A BAHAI temple located in New Delhi, which is one of the seven main Bahai centres of worship in the world. The temple, opened in December 1986, is constructed in the shape of a lotus, with three layers of petals, made of reinforced concrete, set in white marble panels. The temple has nine arches and entrances, and nine reflecting pools. The central hall is covered with a dome. The unfolding lotus symbolizes peace and purity, while the nine entrances represent the nine great religions of the world. Nine, the number of perfection, is considered sacred by Bahais, and the nine-pointed star is one of their symbols. According to the Bahais, the Bahai is the ninth religion, and the religion of the Bab is the eighth. The others are Hindusm, Buddhism, Zoroastrianism, Judaism, Christianity, Islam and the religion of the Sabaeans, to which the Bahai believe the Biblical Abraham belonged. Fariborz Sahba, the architect of the temples, was originally from Iran, and is also a devout Bahai. The temple is a centre of pilgrimage for Bahais from all over the world.

Bahauddin Zakariyya, Shaikh   A SUFI saint who is considered the founder of the SUHRAWARDI order in India. Born near Multan (present Pakistan) in 1182 or 1183, he was initiated into the Suhrawardi order at Baghdad, when he was proceeding on a pilgrimage to Mecca. Shaikh Shihabuddin, the founder of the Suhrawardis, made him his khalifa or deputy at Multan. Returning to Multan, Bahauddin set up a large KHANQAH (monastery) and was renowned not only in neighbouring towns but also in Iraq and Iran. He invited Iltutmish, sultan of DELHI, to invade Multan, and Iltutmish established his rule there in 1228. He then appointed Bahauddin, 'Shaikh-ul Islam', or 'leader of the Muslim community'. Though not a political post, this enhanced his standing as a religious leader.

Bahauddin died in 1262.

Bahaullah   The founder of the BAHAI religion, whose original name was Mirza Husain Ali. Born in 1817 in Tehran, Iran, he was the son of a minister in the government, Mirza Buzurq-i-Nuri. He had a princely education, learning swordsmanship and horse-riding, as well as calligraphy and classical poetry. Refusing a government post, he instead devoted himself to philanthropic activities. In 1935 he married Asiyih Khanum and had three children, the eldest of whom, born in 1844, was later known as ABDUL BAHA. The same year Mirza Husain became a disciple of the BAB, and soon became a leader of the Babi movement. After the Bab's execution, Mirza Husain was arrested and placed in prison. He was kept for some months in a black-pit dungeon, and during this time, in 1852, had a divine revelation. He was soon released from prison, but was exiled and spent a short while in Baghdad. He again went to Baghdad which was under the Ottomans, in 1856, but was asked to leave. Before leaving, he and his companions spent twelve days in a garden on the banks of the Tigris river, from 21 April to 2 May 1863. This was later known as the Garden of RIDVAN (paradise). Like John the Baptist, the Bab had predicted that one would come who was greater than him and would reveal God's truth. He would be named Bahaullah. Mirza Husain realized he was this person, and now formally took this name and revealed this truth to his followers. He continued to be persecuted by the Turkish government and was finally exiled to Acre, a penal city in Ottoman Palestine. He arrived there along with his family in August 1868 and spent the rest of his life there. Gradually gaining the respect of the officials and community at Acre, he wrote his most important work at this time, the *Kitab-i-Aqdas* (Most Holy Book).

Altogether he wrote over a hundred works on religious and mystical themes. Bahaullah's basic message, in his own words, was 'The earth is but one country and mankind its citizens'. However, their well-being could not be established until all were united. Bahais thus work for world unity in various ways.

Before his death in 1891, Bahaullah appointed his son, Abdul Baha, as his successor.

Bahinabai   A Maratha BHAKTI saint. Born in 1629, Bahinabai, an orthodox BRAHMANA, was already married when she became a devotee of the saint TUKARAM. Her husband initially was furious with her, as Tukaram was of a low caste and did not have traditional spiritual learning, but later he accepted her devotion and accompanied her to meet Tukaram. Bahinabai kept a journal and wrote devotional verses, which have been translated into English. She died in 1700.

Bahman   An AMESHA SPENTA, a personified power of AHURA MAZDA, in Zoroastrianism. Bahman is the later form of VOHU MANA.

Bahubali   A Jain saint, the son of the first TIRTHANKARA, Adinatha or RISHABHA. His name means 'strong of arm'. According to tradition, Rishabha had one hundred sons, among whom was BHARATA, who ruled at AYODHYA and wanted to extend his sovereignty over his brothers. Bahubali, one of the brothers who ruled at Takshashila, was advised to fight a *dharmayuddha* (righteous war) against his brother. The war was fought and Bahubali won, but seeing the futility of a worldly life, he handed the kingdom over to Bharata. Then he stood meditating for one year in the *pratimayoga* posture, that is, like a statue. He was unattached to the world and all its pleasures, but one thought that still disturbed him was that he was standing on land that belonged to his brother. Bharata came to know of this, and gave the kingdom back to him. Though Bahubali did not accept it, this gesture brought him enlightenment.

This story is narrated in an inscription dated to 1180 at the site of the colossal image of Bahubali, also known as GOMMATESHVARA, located at SHRAVANA BELAGOLA in Karnataka. It also occurs in Jain texts, including the *ADI PURANA* of the Jain poet PAMPA. Bahubali is worshipped in south India but is not popular in the north. The largest image of Bahubali is at Shravana Belagola, and the second largest at Karkala, while others are at MUDABADRI, Yenur and other sites, most of which are in Karnataka.

Baiga religion Baigas, a tribal group of central India, have their own myths and religious practices. Traditionally, Baigas lived in forests and collected forest produce, but now they have varied occupations. They also call themselves Narotrias, Barotrias, Binjhwars and Bhumias.

Accoding to their myths, they are descended from Naga (or sometimes Nanga) Baiga and Naga Baigin, a man and a woman created by Bhagavan or god. They lived in the middle world, where there was water and rock, but no soil. Finally they succeeded in bringing a tiny bit of Dhartia Mata, or fertile soil, from the world below. Naga Baiga and Baigin had two sons and two daughters. They were married to each other and from the elder the Baigas were descended, and from the younger, the Gonds, a related tribal group. Anna Dai is another deity, representing food, or the essence of seeds, while Thakur Deva is a Kshetrapala, or guardian of the fields. These deities are among those worshipped by them, along with forest spirits and some Hindu deities.

Baijnath Temple A temple of the Hindu god SHIVA in his form as Vaidyanatha, located at Baijnath in Himachal Pradesh. First built in the thirteenth century, this stone temple has later structures as well. At the doorway are GANGA and YAMUNA images. The inner shrine contains a LINGA. Adjoining it is a MANDAPA with sculptures on the walls, which include a HARIHARA panel and NATARAJA carved on a column. The pyramidal roof was reconstructed in the eighteenth or early nineteenth century by the Katoch rajas of the region.

Baisakhi A harvest festival now celebrated on 13 April every year. It is most popular in the Punjab, where farmers rejoice over the harvest, dress in traditional costumes, sing songs and perform bhangra dances. Fairs or *melas*, selling various items, are organized. The day is also celebrated in remembrance of the creation of the KHALSA in 1699 by the Sikh guru GOBIND SINGH.

Baitul-Hikmah An Arabic term meaning 'the house of wisdom'. The Abbasid Caliph Al-Mamun (813–33), set up an institution of this name at Baghdad, where Greek philosophical and scientific literature was translated into Arabic. This had an impact on Islamic thought and on the work of Islamic philosophers, which later influenced Islamic scholars in India.

In SUFI sects, the term represents the heart of a sincere seeker of God. A similar term is baitul-quds, the 'house of holiness', when the heart of the true seeker is absorbed in meditation.

Bajreshvari Temple A temple dedicated to the Hindu goddess Bajreshvari, located at Kangra in Himachal. Bajreshvari is a SHAKTA PITHA, one of the sites associated with SATI, the consort of SHIVA. According to legend, at the time of a drought some of the people here prayed to the goddess DURGA, who showed them a place where the breasts of Sati had fallen, and asked for a temple to be built there. Local accounts state that the temple was plundered by the invader Mahmud of Ghazni in 1009, and again by Firuz Shah Tughlaq, sultan of DELHI in the fourteenth century, but was restored by the Mughal emperor AKBAR in the sixteenth century. Thousands visit the temple, particularly at the time of the NAVRATRAS. The Guptganga ghat, about a kilometre away, is also a place of pilgrimage.

Bakr-Id A Muslim festival, also known as Id-ul-Zuha, or Id-ul-Azha which occurs on the tenth day of the month of Zul-hijja, the twelfth month according to the Islamic lunar calendar. This festival is related to the story of Ibrahim (Abraham), which also occurs in the Bible. Asked by God to sacrifice that which was dearest to him, Ibrahim decided to sacrifice his son Ismail (Ishmael), but God replaced the boy with a ram. (In the Bible it is Abraham's other son Isaac, who is offered for sacrifice.)To commemorate this event, goats or sheep are sacrificed on this day. The sacrifice is done after praying and while uttering the name of ALLAH. One-third of the meat of the animal is to be given to beggars or to the poor, while the rest can be consumed by the family of the sacrificer. This is one of the most important Muslim festivals.

Bala According to tradition, one of the two main companions of Guru NANAK, the founder of Sikhism, the other being MARDANA. The *Bhai Bala JANAMSAKHI* is attributed to him, though its real author is unknown. A few other accounts mention Bala, whereas in some sources Mardana is Guru Nanak's only companion. Bala was said to be a Hindu, while Mardana was a Muslim. Some scholars doubt the existence of Bala, but he is popular in Sikh tradition.

Bala Sahib Gurdwara A GURDWARA or Sikh shrine located in DELHI, constructed at a spot where the eighth guru, HAR KRISHAN, was cremated. The river YAMUNA once flowed nearby. A gurdwara was constructed here soon after, and a new building was made in 1957–58. Both the old and new buildings exist side by side. The two wives of Guru GOBIND SINGH, Mata Sundri and Mata Sahib Kaur, were also cremated here. Mata Sahib Kaur's SAMADHI is a small marble structure in the main hall, whereas Mata Sundri's is separate. This is a popular place of pilgrimage, visited by hundreds every day.

Balaji A Hindu god particularly worshipped in south India. Balaji is a popular name of VENKATESHVARA, a form of VISHNU. The most important Balaji or VENKATESHVARA TEMPLE is at TIRUPATI in Andhra Pradesh, but there are several others all over India and abroad.

Balarama A Hindu deity who is the elder brother of the god KRISHNA and an incarnation of VISHNU. He is alternatively said to have been an incarnation of ANANTA Naga, and a deity associated with agriculture. As Krishna's brother, he was the seventh son of DEVAKI and VASUDEVA, the first six having been killed by King Kamsa because of a prophecy that Kamsa would be killed by the son of Vasudeva. At the time of his birth, Devaki and Vasudeva were in Kamsa's prison. To save Balarama after he was conceived, he was placed by divine intervention in the womb of Rohini, another wife of Vasudeva, and thus was born outside prison. He was named Sankarshana or Balarama and was fair, whereas Krishna was dark. Krishna was born later. Balarama accompanied Krishna on many of his adventures. He differed at times with Krishna and tried to bring about a truce between the KAURAVAS and PANDAVAS at the time of the *MAHABHARATA* war. Balarama died while in meditation at DVARAKA.

The *BRIHAT SAMHITA*, an early text, describes how he should be depicted. He holds a plough and stands under a canopy of snakes, sometimes in an inebriated state. He is white like a conch-shell, moon, or white lotus. At one time an important deity, images of him date back to the second century BCE. In later texts, in the list of the ten main incarnations of Vishnu, he is often replaced by the BUDDHA.

Balarama is also known as Halayudha (bearing a plough), and Madhupriya (lover of wine).

Bali (1) A DAITYA, who was the grandson of PRAHLADA, and a good ruler, but was defeated by the Hindu god VISHNU. He was also known as MAHABALI.

(2) An offering or sacrifice made to deities, spirits, animals or even objects. This is common in Hinduism and in tribal religions. It also occurs in Buddhism.

Banarsidasa A DIGAMBARA Jain leader who lived from 1586 to 1643. He was among those who initiated a reform in the community, leading to the founding of the TERAPANTHA sect in north India.

Banda Bahadur Gurdwara A GURDWARA or Sikh shrine located in DELHI, at the spot where the Sikh leader BANDA SINGH BAHADUR was martyred. It is near the DARGAH of the SUFI saint Khwaja QUTBUDDIN BAKHTIYAR KAKI in Mehrauli. Initially a stone pillar marked the site.

Banda Singh Bahadur A Sikh leader who laid the foundations for a Sikh state, but was martyred in 1716. Born in 1670 at Rajouri in Jammu, he was a Rajput Hindu, and his original name was Lachhman. He was always spiritually inclined, and became a VAISHNAVA ascetic, taking the name Madho Das. He spent many years in Hindu MATHAS and ASHRAMS in central India, finally establishing an ashram of his own at Nanded in present-day Maharashtra. After living there for fifteen years he met Guru GOBIND SINGH, and became a Sikh. His new name was Gurbaksh Singh, but he was popularly known as 'Banda' or 'slave' of the guru, whom he served faithfully. When the guru was in the Deccan, he sent Banda to the Punjab to defend the KHALSA and avenge the death of his sons. Soon after this, Guru Gobind Singh was killed in 1708 and Banda became the political leader of the Sikhs. In the Punjab he called on all Sikhs to avenge the murder of the guru's family. He attacked Samana in 1709 and captured Sirhind in 1710. He killed Wazir Khan, the governor of Sirhind, who was responsible for the death of Gobind Singh's two sons, and continued conquering territory in Punjab and up to Saharanpur, issuing coins in the name of Guru NANAK and Guru Gobind Singh. He also converted a number of Muslims to Sikhism, while others joined his army and were free to follow their own faith. In 1713, Farrukhsiyar succeeded Bahadur Shah I as the Mughal emperor, and was determined to destroy Sikh power. His army besieged Banda at a fort in Gurdaspur, and after eight months Banda surrendered and was brought to DELHI. In 1716 he was tortured and killed along with his four-year-old son and his followers. Banda Bahadur is revered as one of the great leaders and martyrs of Sikhism. The renowned mystic Rabindranath TAGORE composed a poem on him entitled *Banda Bir*.

Bandichhor Gurdwara A GURDWARA or Sikh shrine located in Gwalior in Madhya Pradesh, within the fort where the sixth guru, HARGOBIND, was once imprisoned.

The Mughal emperor Jahangir, under whom Hargobind's father Guru ARJAN DEV had been killed, was for some time favourably inclined towards Hargobind. Even so, he was persuaded to imprison Hargobind for the non-payment of a fine imposed on his father. Hargobind was kept in Gwalior fort for a period of forty days, after which he was released along with other political prisoners. Thus he was known as 'Bandi-Chhor' or 'the liberator', and a gurdwara of the same name was later built at the site.

Bangla Sahib Gurdwara A GURDWARA or Sikh shrine located at DELHI, in the former residence of Raja Jai Singh of Amber (Jaipur) and his son Raja Ram Singh, who were officials of the Mughal emperor AURANGZEB. Here the eighth guru HAR KRISHAN stayed when he came to meet the emperor. It was a time of smallpox and cholera epidemics, and after helping countless people Har Krishan died and the meeting did not take place. Water from the well in the compound is said to have healing powers, and people still take small amounts of this home to cure their ailments. A large tank has been constructed nearby. In the basement is a gallery which has paintings depicting events from Sikh history and is named after Sardar BHAGEL SINGH, a Sikh general.

bani A term for Sikh devotional hymns in the GURU GRANTH SAHIB. Hymns composed by revered saints who were not gurus were known as bhagat bani.

Baoli Sahib, Goindwal A GURDWARA or Sikh shrine constructed at Goindwal, 30 km from AMRITSAR in Punjab, near the baoli or step-well made by the third guru, AMAR DAS. Frescoes on the walls depict scenes from Sikh history. The Mughal emperor AKBAR is said to have eaten at the LANGAR or free community meal served here.

baptism A ritual which marks initiation into Christianity and dates back to ancient days. It consists of sprinkling or pouring sacred water on the head, signifying the cleansing of sins and the beginning of a new life with God. Immersion or sprinkling with water, was practised in early Judaism for purificatory ceremonies or the initiation of converts. John, commonly known as John the Baptist, the son of Zachariah and Elizabeth, baptized Jews in the river Jordan, and is even said to have baptized Jesus. In the Gospel of Mathew, Jesus advocates baptism, along with an invocation of the TRINITY, and the ritual gradually become an essential part of Christianity. Baptism is one of the seven SACRAMENTS for ROMAN CATHOLICS, who are baptized soon after birth. Most Protestant denominations also practise baptism, though there are variations in the ritual, including baptism by full immersion and adult baptism. Converts to the religion are also baptized.

Baptist Church A Christian denomination, introduced in India in the late eighteenth century by William CAREY, an English missionary. The Baptist Church was officially founded in England in the early 1600s, but Baptist groups existed earlier in Europe and Scotland. They believed in the sole authority of the BIBLE, salvation by grace, and baptism only for believers. As they did not follow the practice of infant baptism, they were initially called Anabaptists. BAPTISM takes place only at the time of joining the Church, when the candidate is convinced of its principles, and consists of complete immersion in water.

Carey and his associates set up Baptist congregations in Bengal, and later the Baptist Church was introduced into other parts of India, particularly Andhra Pradesh and Karnataka. The Serampore College, a theological college started by Carey, is still functioning. Each local Baptist Church has autonomy and there is no hierarchical authority, but representatives of the churches meet to coordinate their work. There are several councils and groups of Baptist churches. These include: the Council of Baptist Churches of North-East India, the Bengal-Orissa-Bihar Baptist Convention, the Samavesam Telugu Baptist Churches, as well as some others. A group of Baptist Churches have also joined the CHURCH OF NORTH INDIA.

Bar Mitzvah A Jewish term which means 'son of the commandments', and refers to a boy who has reached the age of thirteen, by which time he is considered responsible enough to know and observe the commandments. A ceremony known as Bar Mitzvah takes place to commemorate this.

For a girl the term is Bat Mitzvah or 'daughter of the commandments' which takes place at the age of twelve. Traditionally there was no formal ceremony for the Bat Mitzvah, but now this has been introduced by several Jewish groups.

Bara Gumbad Mosque A mosque located near the Lodi tombs in DELHI, constructed in 1494 by Mughla-Buwa Makhduma-i-Jahan, the widow of Sultan Bahlul Lodi, who ruled at Delhi from 1451 to 1489. It consists of a single hall, and has five bays, the three central ones with hemispherical domed roofs. The mosque has elaborate cut-plaster decoration and gets its name from a domed building named Bara Gumbad, located nearby.

Bara Sona Mosque A mosque located at Gaur in Bengal. It was constructed in 1526 by Sultan Nusrat Shah, who ruled Bengal from 1519 to 1532. It is a large structure, approximately 51 m by 23 m, and is built of brick, with stone facings. The prayer hall is rectangular and has four octagonal towers. The façade has eleven arched entrances on the east, and the interior has three bays, once covered by forty-four domes. The domes were once gilded hence the name sona (gold). The mosque does not have much decoration but is impressive because of its size.

Bara Wafat A Muslim festival, also known as ID-I-MILAD. It is the twelfth (barah) day of the Islamic month of Rabi-ul-Awwal, when the Prophet MUHAMMAD was born.

Barabar caves Rock-cut caves in the Barabar hills in Bihar, excavated in the third century BCE, at the time of ASHOKA, the Mauryan emperor. According to an inscription here, they were dedicated by the emperor for the use of AJIVIKA monks. The caves are cut parallel to the rock face, and the inner surface has a fine, mirror-like polish. Each cave has two small chambers, some with vaulted roofs and sloping sides, recreating a thatched-hut dwelling. The largest is the Lomas Rishi cave, with an elaborately carved doorway, a MANDAPA, and an oval inner chamber. The Sudama cave has a circular vaulted chamber and a rectangular mandapa. Other caves made for Ajivikas by Ashoka and his grandson Dasharatha are at the nearby Nagarjuni and Sitamarhi hills.

Barchha Sahib Gurdwara A GURDWARA or Sikh shrine located at Dhanpur in Assam. Guru NANAK is said to have come here and converted Queen Nur Shah to Sikhism. She was earlier a worshipper of the Hindu goddess KAMAKSHI and believed to be proficient in black magic. She asked Nanak to leave her something to remember him by, and he left his barchha or lance here. He marked a spot with it, where a pond was dug according to his instructions. A gurdwara was later built nearby.

Bardo Thodol A Buddhist text known in English as the *Tibetan Book of the Dead*. It deals with the intermediate states (Bardo) experienced between death and rebirth. The term Bardo is mentioned in the ABHIDHAMMA PITAKA and in VAJRAYANA texts, particularly in the NYINGMA school of Tibetan Buddhism. The *Bardo Thodol*, describes the state of Bardo in detail. The Bardo journey is divided into three stages. In the first stage, that of Chikhai Bardo, the primary clear light can be seen if concentration is maintained. This would enable one to achieve Buddhahood immediately. In case the clear light cannot be seen, the person should meditate on a compassionate BUDDHA in order to pass on to the second stage. In the second stage of Chonyid Bardo, illusions caused by one's own KARMA appear; they may be beautiful or frightening. It is important to stay centred and focus on the pure lights and deities that appear. Even at this time it is possible to attain enlightenment, but if not, the third stage of Sidpa Bardo is entered. Terrifying illusions may arise again, but it is possible to meditate on the true reality and reach Buddhahood. If not, after a period of time, rebirth takes place.

The text is attributed to PADMASAMBHAVA, who lived in the eighth century, though it is probably later.

Barelvi An Islamic sect founded by Maulana Ahmad Riza Khan (1856–1921) in the nineteenth century. He preached the revival of popular Islam and the worship of PIRS or saints. He exalted the Prophet MUHAMMAD and spoke of his light, which emanated from the light of ALLAH, and existed before creation. Thus Muhammad, through his light, was present everywhere. In the late nineteenth and early twentieth centuries, there was considerable hostility between the Barelvis and followers of the DEOBAND SCHOOL, who opposed the worship of pirs, and Muslims in India were divided into two camps. Barelvis also condemned the WAHHABIS. The Barelvi sect still exists in India and in 2005 the Barelvis formed a separate All India Personal Law Board. Barelvi groups have also established themselves in Britain and other countries.

Bari Sangat Gurdwara A GURDWARA or Sikh shrine located at Kolkata in West Bengal. Guru NANAK is said to have stayed at this location, which was known as Bari Sangat, and the gurdwara was built in his memory. Guru TEGH BAHADUR too paid a visit here.

Basant Panchami A festival that takes place in the traditional month of Magha (January-February) on the fifth day (panchami) of Shukla Paksha or the fortnight of the waxing moon. It usually occurs sometime in February. Basant Panchami marks the beginning of spring, and is celebrated by all communities. Sweet rice is cooked, kites are flown, and people dress in yellow, the symbolic colour of spring.

The Hindu goddess SARASVATI, patron of music and learning, is specially worshipped on this day. Books, pens, paint brushes and musical instruments are revered and offered to the deity. Musical functions are held and songs associated with spring are sung.

Basavanna The twelfth century founder of a SHAIVITE sect, which was later known as the LINGAYAT or Virashaiva.

There are several contradictory accounts of Basavanna's life, but he was probably born in 1106 at village Manigavalli in present Karnataka. From a young age he was devoted to the god SHIVA, and at the age of sixteen he decided to dedicate his life to the deity. Though a BRAHMANA, he was opposed to the caste system and to empty rituals. He removed his sacred thread, left his home and went to Kappadisangama, a place where three rivers meet. There he had an experience of Shiva, and worshipped Shiva as Kudalasangamadeva, lord of the meeting rivers. His symbol of worship was the LINGA, and through divine experiences, Shiva became a part of him. In a dream the Lord asked him to go to the court of Bijjala, the king of the Kalachuri dynasty at Kalyana. Basava did so and became Bijjala's prime minister.

Meanwhile he continued to worship Shiva and started a new sect. The linga was its symbol, it was open to all castes, and it advocated the equality of all. Basava also promoted social reforms and was against sacrifices, ceremonies and child marriages, and in favour of widow remarriage and inter-caste marriage. As he gained more followers, traditional society reacted and turned against him. King Bijjala, too, reacted with repression against his reforms. Extremists among Basava's followers advocated changing the government and society by violent means. Basava was against this, but unable to persuade them to follow non-violence, he returned to Kappadisangama, where he died in 1166 or 1168. Some of his extreme followers assassinated King Bijjala, and for some time Lingayats were persecuted and scattered.

Basavanna's sayings and verses, known as vachanas, are collected in the *Vachana Shastra*. One of his famous vachanas states:

The rich will make temples for Shiva
What shall I, a poor man, do?
My legs are pillars, the body the shrine
The head a cupola of gold.

In another he says to his Lord:

Make of my body the beam of a lute
of my head the sounding gourd
of my nerves the strings
of my fingers the plucking rods. (Trans. A.K. Ramanujan)

Basgo The site of a Buddhist monastery with shrines dating from the fifteenth to the seventeenth centuries, located in LADAKH, in the state of Jammu and Kashmir. Basgo village is on a spur of rock overlooking the river Indus, and a royal palace was once also located here. The MAITREYA Temple of the sixteenth century was constructed by a king of the Namgyal dynasty. It has a large image of the Bodhisattva Maitreya, as well as paintings of scenes from BUDDHA's life, and other BUDDHAS and BODHISATTVAS. The Serzang Temple of the seventeenth century has a copy of the Buddhist Canon written in gold, silver and copper letters, which gives it its name (serzang = gold and copper). The walls have murals with figures of Buddhas and Bodhisattvas. There are other small shrines and CHORTENS, while outside the village are MANI stones carved with auspicious symbols.

Bauls Mystics and singers who practise various SADHANAS to reach god, and wander through Bengal singing of the bliss of union with god. The origin of the Bauls is not clear. Some believe they were a branch of the followers of CHAITANYA, the Vaishnava BHAKTI saint, whereas others believe they were similar to the NATHA YOGIS or the SUFIS. Bauls can be either Hindu on Muslim. The word 'baul' means 'mad' or 'crazy', as lost in the ecstacy of divine union, they behaved in unconventional ways. Bauls probably existed at least as far back as the fifteenth century, but their songs were first written down by scholars in the nineteenth and twentieth centuries. The composers of most songs are unknown.

Extracts from two Baul songs are given below:

Scanning the cosmos
you waste your hours:
he is present
in this little vessel.

Another song states:

My soul cries out,
snared by the beauty
of the formless one.
As I cry by myself,
night and day,
beauty amassed before my eyes
surpasses numberless moons and suns.
If I look at the clouds in the sky,
I see his beauty afloat;
And I see him walk on the stars blazing my heart.
(Trans. Deben Bhattacharya, *The Mirror of the Sky: Songs of the Bauls of Bengal*)

Bedsa The site of rock-cut Buddhist CHAITYAS and VIHARAS, dating back to the first century BCE, located along the Western Ghats in Pune District of Maharashtra, not far from the sites of similar caves at BHAJA and KARLE. Among the caves is an apsidal-ended chaitya hall. The front verandah has four large columns, with inverted bell-capitals, surmounted by pairs of animals with riders. Pierced stone windows are on both sides of the main doorway, and the side walls have reliefs with arched windows and railings. Inside, there is a hemispherical STUPA at one end. The vault over the central hall once had timber ribs, which no longer exist.

Begumpuri Masjid A mosque located at Begumpur village in DELHI. It was constructed in the fourteenth century by Khan-i-Jahan, the prime minister of Sultan Firuz Shah Tughlaq, who at that time ruled much of northern India.

Behram A minor Zoroastrian deity or YAZATA. Behram is the later Pahlavi form of VERETHRAGNA, and is the god of victory. According to the *KISSAH-I-SANJAN*, while travelling by ship from Diu to SANJAN, the Zoroastrians prayed to Behram to save them from a storm and promised to erect an ATASH BEHRAM (fire of victory) if they were saved. The *DABISTAN*, a seventeenth-century text, equates Behram with the Angel Gabriel.

Belur A town in Karnataka where there are several temples constructed in the eleventh and twelfth centuries by the Hoysala dynasty. Among them is the CHENNAKESHAVA TEMPLE.

Belur Matha The main centre of the RAMAKRISHNA MISSION, located at Belur near Kolkata. Established in 1899 by Swami VIVEKANANDA, it supervises the activities of the Mission and the training of the monks of the order. A modern temple was built here in 1938 in a syncretic style, incorporating aspects of all religions. There are also other small shrines and residential areas for the monks, while across the river Hughli is the DAKSHINESHVARA TEMPLE, where RAMAKRISHNA attained a vision of the divine.

Bene Israel A community of Jews who, according to tradition, came to India in ancient days. Some scholars believe they were one of the ten lost tribes of Israel, who are said to have left Israel in 721 BCE when the Assyrians conquered their land, and arrived in India before the destruction of the second temple. (*See* Israel, lost tribes of). According to other theories they did not reach India till the seventh century while some doubt their Israeli origin altogether. Legends state that they arrived on the Konkan coast in western India because of a shipwreck. Out of those in the ship, seven couples survived and swam towards land to the village of Navgaon. They settled here and through their descendants a community of Jews was formed. They called themselves Bene Israel, which in Hebrew means 'Children of Israel'.

Though there were already Jews in south India, they did not come in contact with them. Instead, they learnt Marathi and adopted local customs while retaining some Jewish practices. They lived on the western coast, earning their living by extracting oil and were absorbed into the caste structure as telis (oil-pressers). They remained an isolated Jewish community till the eighteenth century, when Ezekiel David Rahabi, a Jew from the community at Kochi (Cochin), discovered them. Shocked by the degree to which they had absorbed local customs, Rahabi organized their re-education, sent them teachers to explain the finer points of Jewish customs, and sought to revive their knowledge of Judaism, emphasizing the use of Hebrew and Jewish prayers. By the late eighteenth and early nineteenth century, a group of the Bene Israel moved to MUMBAI (Bombay), Pune and other cities, practised diverse occupations and established the first SYNAGOGUE there in 1796. However, they were still not accepted by other Jewish groups, particularly those who had come from Baghdad in the early nineteenth century and were known as BAGHDADI JEWS. Even within the Bene Israel, there were two main groups: the Gora (white) and the Kala (black), the first said to be the pure descendants of the original migrants, and the second the products of inter-marriage with locals. The three 'castes' of Gora, Kala and Baghdadi Jews rarely mixed or intermarried.

The Bene Israel follow the Jewish custom of observing the SABBATH on Saturdays, the practice of circumcision, and dietary laws, though these are less strict than those of traditional Jews. Among their unique customs is that they do not eat beef, like their Hindu neighbours. They worship the Biblical Prophet Elijah in two ceremonies. In the Malida ceremony, conducted at home, songs are sung praising God and Elijah, while the men sit around a plate of roasted rice, fruit, flowers and spices. They give thanks to Elijah, who is said to have revived them while they lay unconscious on the beach after the shipwreck. On another occasion, Elijah visited them and left a footprint at Khandala near Alibag in Maharashtra, and this spot was regularly worshipped. A very similar legend of a shipwreck is found among CHITPAVAN BRAHMANAS, indicating a possible connection between the two communities.

By the twentieth century the Bene Israel formed a community of about twenty or thirty thousand, but today most of the community have migrated to Israel, though about four thousand still live in Maharashtra, particularly in Mumbai and the suburb of Thane. In Israel they were initially discriminated against, and for many years were not allowed to marry those from other Jewish groups. It was only in 1964 that they were given equal status with other Jews.

Besant, Annie An Irish- English woman who came to India in 1893 and was a prominent member of the THEOSOPHICAL SOCIETY OF INDIA.

Born in 1847 in London as Annie Wood, she was three-quarters Irish. She married Frank Besant, a minister of the church, and had two children, but left the marriage as her husband could not tolerate her independent views and championing of women's rights. She went through various phases, as a socialist, free-thinker and atheist, and was closely associated with prominent personalities, such as Charles Bradlaugh and Bernard Shaw.

All this changed in 1889, when she first met Madame BLAVATSKY, one of the founders of the Theosophical Society, and came under her spell. Theosophy seemed to provide the answers she had searched for all her life.

In India, initially she supervised the working of the Theosophical Society at Adyar in Chennai (Madras) and later at Varanasi, where she was in charge of its esoteric section. She spoke of the hierarchy of hidden masters, with SANAT KUMARA at the head, and other aspects of esoteric philosophy, and claimed to be in touch with masters in Tibet, who guided the destiny of India. She wrote and spoke on Hinduism, Buddhism and Zoroastrianism, and totally identified herself with India. Helped by Bhagavan Das, she published the Sanatana Dharma series of textbooks on Hinduism. She started a high school and college which developed into Hindu College, and later became Banares Hindu University. J. KRISHNAMURTI was chosen by her and by C.W. Leadbeater, another Theosophist, to be the new Messiah, and though he rejected this destiny, he later became a prominent philosopher.

After some time, according to her, the rishi AGASTYA directed her (from the astral world in which he lived) to focus on helping India achieve independence from the British. Annie Besant started the Home Rule Movement in 1916 and was president of the Indian National Congress Session in 1917, after which her role in the freedom movement declined. She remained involved with the Theosophical Society until her death in 1933, and was its president from 1907.

Apart from books, articles and pamphlets on Theosophy and religion, Annie Besant wrote an autobiography as well as works on education.

Beschi, Constanzo An Italian Jesuit missionary who lived from 1680 to 1747. He came to India in 1707 and was one of the Christian swamis in the tradition of Roberto de NOBILI. He wrote hymns in Tamil praising MARY, mother of JESUS, and a long work *Tembavani* in honour of Joseph, husband of Mary. He also erected an Indian-style statue of Mary in a church at Konankuppam in Tamil Nadu, and converted a number of lower castes to Christianity.

Bhadrabahu I A Jain saint and leader who lived in the fourth century BCE and is said to have died 170 or 162 years after MAHAVIRA. According to tradition, he was the last person who knew the Puvvas (PURVAS), the earliest Jain texts, and all the twelve ANGAS. The SHVETAMBARAS state that he was the sixth Thera (teacher) after Mahavira, and attribute one of their most sacred texts, the *KALPA SUTRA*, to him, as well as some NIJUTTIS (Niryuktis) or commentaries. Sources of the DIGAMBARA sect state that at the time of the emperor CHANDRAGUPTA MAURYA, Bhadrabahu predicted that a severe famine would take place in Ujjayini (according to later tradition in MAGADHA) for a period of twelve years. He, or a Jain known as Prabhachandra, therefore led a group of Jain monks to south India. The emperor, Chandragupta, is said to have gone along with them. Those who remained in the north modified some practices such as the rule of nudity, while those in the south continued with traditional practices. This was the beginning of the two sects that later arose, the Digambaras and Shvetambaras. This tradition is generally accepted, though according to some Shvetambara sources Bhadrabahu went to Nepal at the time of the famine, not to south India.

Bhadrabahu II A Jain saint and leader who is part of the DIGAMBARA tradition. According to their sources, the first BHADRABAHU died 162 years after MAHAVIRA, and the second 515 years later, i.e., in 12 BCE. He was the teacher of KUNDAKUNDA, the Jain scholar and philosopher revered by Digambaras, and the twenty-seventh ACHARYA in the Digambara list. Unlike the first Bhadrabahu, he was an Upangi, i.e. he knew only one ANGA.

Bhadrachalam Ramadas A seventeenth century devotee of the Hindu god RAMA, whose original name was Gopanna. He was an official of the last Qutb Shahi king, known as Taneshah (ruled 1672–87), of the state of Golkonda in the Deccan. In charge of Bhadrachalam district, he built a Rama temple with the revenue he collected, instead of giving it to the king, and was imprisoned for twelve years. During this time, he continuously composed and sang verses in praise of Rama. According to legend, Rama himself then appeared to Taneshah and repaid the money, after which Gopanna was released and reinstated.

Bhadrachalam Temple A temple of the Hindu god RAMA located at Bhadrachalam in Andhra Pradesh, on the river Godavari. According to legend, Rama lived here himself for some time, and a small temple was constructed to mark the sanctity of the spot. The temple was reconstructed by Gopanna (BHADRACHALAM RAMADAS) and has images of Rama, LAKSHMANA and SITA. Because of the tradition of the divine appearance of Rama to Taneshah, the Qutb Shahi ruler, the temple received official patronage and grants, even under the succeeding Asaf Jahi dynasty. It is a major centre of pilgrimage today, particularly at the time of the RAMANAVAMI festival.

Bhaga A Hindu deity, one of the ADITYAS. The name means dispenser or giver and the god is considered the bestower of wealth and divine blessings. In the RIG VEDA, USHA or dawn is his sister. In the *MAHABHARATA*, Bhaga was a member of INDRA's assembly. Baga is a deity in Zoroastrianism, and in INDO-EUROPEAN languages bogu is a term for god.

Bhagamandala A sacred site in Kodagu district in Karnataka, with several temples. At this point the Krishna river unites with its tributaries, the Kannike and Sujoythi. The Bhandeshvar Temple is also located here.

Bhagavad Gita 'The Lord's Song' or 'The Divine Song', an early Sanskrit text, revered as one of the most sacred by Hindus. Though usually published as a separate text, it forms part of the *Bhishma Parva* of the *MAHABHARATA*. Its date is uncertain, but it probably acquired its present form between the second century BCE and the second century CE. It has eighteen chapters with 700 verses, though the number of verses differs in different recensions. The text deals with three main philosophical themes of KARMA Yoga, JNANA Yoga, and BHAKTI Yoga. Most of it is in the form of a dialogue between ARJUNA and KRISHNA, which takes place just before the great Mahabharata war begins.

On the battlefield, where the two armies of the KAURAVAS and PANDAVAS are arrayed against each other, Arjuna's courage fails him as he thinks of fighting against his friends and kinsmen. Surely, he says, it would be better if he left the battlefield and became an ascetic? Krishna encourages him to throw off his weakness and fight, for that is the duty of a KSHATRIYA. In a much-quoted passage, he assures Arjuna that no one ever dies. The Spirit in every living being is immortal and beyond change. After death, the Spirit takes on a new body, just as a person changes his clothes.

Further chapters describe the various paths through which god, either as the formless One, or as Krishna, can be reached. The path of action (Karma Yoga) is described, with particular emphasis on nishkama karma, or work done without focusing on rewards gained through it. Another path is that of Jnana Yoga, the path of knowledge, where union with god is achieved through true knowledge and understanding. A third way is that of bhakti or devotion. The Gita also explains the concepts of PURUSHA and PRAKRITI, which form part of the philosophical system of SAMKHYA, and the nature of the three GUNAS, or characteristics inherent in every person.

Bhagavan A generic name for god in Hinduism, particularly used for KRISHNA and VISHNU.

Bhagavata A Hindu sect that worshipped the god KRISHNA and later developed into VAISHNAVISM. Bhagavatas worshipped god or Bhagavata, also known as Vasudeva Krishna. The term Bhagavata seems to have developed from the concept of the Vedic deity BHAGA, and initially it may have been a monotheistic sect, independent of the Brahmanical pantheon. Krishna was probably identified with VISHNU and incorporated into Brahmanism around 300 BCE.

Buddhism and Jainism were at least partly a reaction against the sacrifices and rituals of the VEDAS. However, the early form of these religions, with their dry pragmatism and absence of deity-worship, did not appeal to everyone. In early Hinduism, new forms of deities developed, and the worship of one primary deity such as Vishnu arose.

Inscriptions recording this worship have been found in MATHURA, Rajasthan, central and south India. A notable inscription of the second century BCE occurs at the ancient site of VIDISHA in Madhya Pradesh. Here, Heliodorus, a Greek ambassador of King Antialcidas, recorded the erection of a Garudadhvaja (a pillar surmounted by an image of GARUDA), in honour of the god Vasudeva, and called himself a Bhagavata. In the *Narayaniya* section of the MAHABHARATA, NARAYANA explains the worship of Vasudeva, the Supreme Soul, which is actually his own essence, and describes the PANCHARATRA philosophy. Perfection could be attained by love and devotion to the god Narayana, which became one of the names of VISHNU.

As the Bhagavata religion developed, it incorporated aspects of VEDANTA, SAMKHYA and YOGA philosophies, while the Pancharatras became a separate sect.

The BHAGAVAD GITA was the main text of the Bhagavatas, with its emphasis on Krishna. Later the *BHAGAVATA PURANA* became one of the principal Vaishnava texts. The *Narada* and *Shandilya Sutras*, the *BRAHMAVAIVARTA PURANA*, and the *VISHNU PURANA* are also Bhagavata texts. In addition there are the devotional hymns of the ALVAR SAINTS, and the twelfth-century theology of RAMANUJA.

By this time Bhagavatism was identical with VAISHNAVISM.

Bhagavata Purana   An early Sanskrit text, one of the eighteen major PURANAS of Hinduism. This Purana is one of the most popular and is particularly sacred to VAISHNAVAS and devotees of the god KRISHNA. It has some similarities with the *VISHNU PURANA*, but is a later work, though with an ancient core. The Purana has 18,000 verses, divided into twelve books or sections. It begins with cosmogonic myths and goes on to describe all the incarnations of VISHNU in great detail. KAPILA, founder of the SAMKHYA philosophy, and the BUDDHA also appear as AVATARAS. Book Ten, which narrates stories of Krishna's childhood and early life, is the most well-known section.

Book Eleven continues with the story, dealing with the end of the YADAVAS and the death of Krishna, while Book Twelve has prophecies concerning the KALI YUGA and the destruction of the world.

Bhagavati   A name of the Hindu goddess DURGA, and also a generic name for a mother goddess.

Bhagavati Sutra   The name by which the Jain text, *BHAGAVATI VIYAHA-PANNATI,* is commonly known.

Bhagavati Viyaha-pannati (*Vyakhya-Prajnapti*)   A Jain text, the fifth of the twelve ANGAS. It provides an account of the life and work of MAHAVIRA, and also of the main principles of Jainism. Part of it is in question-answer form, in which Mahavira answers the questions of his disciple GOYAMA INDABHUTI (Gautama), while the rest of it includes stories, legends and parables. There are passages attributed to Mahavira which are probably authentic and include sections on KARMA, the transmigration of souls, and the evils to be avoided, as well as descriptions of heavens and hells. There is also an account of the AJIVIKA doctrine, whose founder GOSALA Makkhali-putta, was once closely connected with Mahavira.

Bhagel Singh, Sardar   A Sikh general who was in DELHI at the time of the Mughal emperor Shah Alam II and supervised the construction of nine Sikh shrines in the city in 1783. Bhagel Singh, of the Kironsinghia MISL, was one of four Sikh commanders who led a force into Delhi at this time. As they attacked the Red Fort, the Mughal emperor opened negotiations with them, and they agreed to leave Delhi after receiving a sum of money and permission to build GURDWARAS at their sacred sites. While the rest of the army left, Bhagel Singh remained in Delhi to supervise the construction of the gurdwaras. Among the gurdwaras he built were the DAMDAMA SAHIB GURDWARA, SISGANJ GURDWARA, and RAKABGANJ GURDWARA.

Bhagirathi   A name of the river GANGA in ancient texts. The section of the Ganga from its origin at Gaumukh up to Devaprayaga, where it unites with the ALAKANANDA, is still known as the Bhagirathi. In its lower course in West Bengal before it joins the sea, the river is called the Bhagirathi-Hughli. The name is related to various myths about the origin of the Ganga.

Bhai Duj   A Hindu festival that celebrates the bonds between brothers and sisters. It takes place two days after the festival of DIVALI. Brothers and sisters meet on this day, and sisters put a *tika*, or mark of sandalwood paste and vermilion on their brothers' foreheads, along with some rice grains, and offer them sweets. In return, brothers vow to protect and care for them. The origin of this festival is unclear, but a myth of YAMA and YAMI (YAMUNA), who were brother and sister, is associated with this festival and narrated in various texts. According to this myth, the river Yamuna was very depressed on Bhai Duj because her brother had not visited her for twelve years. GANGA then went to Yama and reminded him of the day. He visited his sister and was ecstatically greeted by her. He also granted her a boon, that when a brother and a sister bathed together in her waters on this day, they would never meet an untimely death, or, according to another version, they would never suffer in hell. The festival is important in north India, and specially in MATHURA, where brothers and sisters bathe in the Yamuna on Bhai Duj. In Haryana and Punjab, the festival is more commonly known as Tika.

Another brother–sister festival is RAKSHA BANDHAN.

Bhairava   A form of the Hindu god SHIVA, literally meaning 'the terrible'. The god BRAHMA, it is said, once insulted Shiva, and Bhairava was born out of Shiva's fury. Eight forms of Bhairava are mentioned in the PURANAS: Asitanga or the black-limbed, Ruru, Chanda, Krodha or anger, Unmatta, Kapali or the one who holds a skull, Bhishana and Samhara or destruction. Other variants mentioned in different texts are Kala or black, Tamrachuda or red-crested, and Chandra-chuda or moon-crested. The *AGNI PURANA* describes Bhairava as having five faces, a crescent moon and plaited hair on his head. His ornaments are snakes and his weapons include an arrow, a bow, dagger, sword, and trident. In sculpture he is depicted with a dog. As he is sometimes shown riding on a dog, Bhairava is also known as Shvashva, or 'he whose horse is a dog'.

Bhairavi A Hindu goddess, the consort of BHAIRAVA. She is also one of the MAHAVIDYAS or TANTRIC goddesses. A ferocious goddess, she wears a garland of severed heads. She has four hands and holds a book and a mala or rosary. Her two other hands make the gesture of conferring boons and dispelling fear. There are several Bhairavi temples.

Bhairon A Hindu deity identified with SHIVA. He was originally a village deity associated with agriculture.

Bhaishajyaguru Buddha A celestial BUDDHA in charge of medicine and healing. Worshipping him is said to relieve sickness, hunger, fear and suffering, and to fulfill all desires. The *Bhaishajyaguru Sutra* provides an account of this Buddha and methods of worship. In a previous life, he is said to have made twelve vows necessary to become a healing Buddha or BODHISATTVA. These include offering protection, help and healing to all, and illuminating the world with the rays of one's body. He is often depicted with the Buddha AMITABHA or with SHAKYAMUNI, with his hand in the gesture of protection. Lapis lazuli, symbolizing purity, and yellow myrobalan, a healing herb, are associated with him. Though originating in India, he is more popular in China and Japan, and is also the presiding deity in some schools of REIKI.

Bhaja The site of rock-cut Buddhist CHAITYAS and VIHARAS dating back to 200 BCE, located along the Western Ghats in Pune District of Maharashtra. There are more than twenty caves with viharas and chaityas. Most of the viharas have a verandah and a hall which leads into small cells. There are also chaitya halls and rock-cut STUPAS. Wood was used for beams, though these no longer exist. Images are carved out of the rock and include YAKSHAS or guardian deities, SURYA in a four-horse chariot, and INDRA riding his elephant AIRAVATA. The figures which are in low relief are among the earliest available images. There were several such Buddhist caves along the Ghats including at Bhedsa, KARLE and JUNNAR. These and other caves were located along trade routes and passes, indicating the participation of monasteries in trade.

bhajan A song in praise of god. It is a term normally used for songs praising Hindu deities or concepts. Bhajans are compositions like songs, and may include several RAGAS.

Bhajan, Yogi The popular name of Yogi HARBHAJAN SINGH, who started a Sikh sect in the USA.

bhakti A Sanskrit term implying devotion, faith, and union with god through love. Bhakti includes worship, total surrender and personal love of god in any form. Forgetting everything and everyone else, the devotee yearns for a glimpse of god, and finally for total union. Bhakti probably existed from the earliest days, but began to be expressed in the first few centuries CE.

Bhakti is explained in the BHAGAVAD GITA, as devotion to the Hindu god KRISHNA. Between the seventh and tenth centuries, the NAYANARS and ALVARS popularized it in the south. Bhakti became popular in the region of Maharashtra from around the twelfth century, and later in Gujarat, Bengal and other areas. Bhakti saints usually sang and composed verses to god, many of which are available today. Among the prominent saints were NAMADEVA, EKNATHA, TUKARAM, NARASIMHA MEHTA, CHAITANYA MAHAPRABHU, KABIR, and MIRABAI. There were many more, both known and unknown today, who followed this path. The path of bhakti has no restrictions and no sacrifices, and is open to all. It usually involves singing devotional songs, chanting the name of god, and worshipping an image or visualizing a form of the deity. Both VISHNU and his incarnations as well as SHIVA and other gods are worshipped. Bhakti can also be for god beyond all forms (NIRGUNA).

Some historians have put forward the view that bhakti developed as a response to feudal conditions, and that the reverence and devotion given to god was similar to the reverence of the peasant for the zamindar or landlord. However, this seems too simplistic a view and does not account for the fact that bhakti is still a method of approaching the divine. There are different types of bhakti, and not all are reverential. In his work on Bhakti Yoga, Swami VIVEKANANDA describes five types, which can also be considered stages. The first form is shanta or peaceful, where without any excesses, the worshipper develops a love for god. The second is dasya, where the worshipper is attached to god and considers himself his servant. The third type is sakhya, where god is seen as a beloved friend. The fourth is vatsalaya, loving god as a child so as to eliminate all ideas of power from the concept of god. And the fifth is madhura, in which god is the beloved, the lover. Apart from gods such as KRISHNA and RAMA, gurus too can inspire love and devotion, because they are often considered incarnations or representatives of god.

Bhakti is usually associated with Hinduism but forms a part of other religions as well. Celestial BUDDHAS and BODHISATTVAS are worshipped with loving devotion in MAHAYANA and VAJRAYANA Buddhism.

In Islam, SUFI saints kindle divine love in their hearts. Though they may not use the term bhakti, mystical forms of all religions focus on the love of god.

Bhaktivedanta, Abhay Charanaravinda Another name for Swami PRABHUPADA, who founded the INTERNATIONAL SOCIETY OF KRISHNA CONSCIOUSNESS (ISKCON).

Bhangani Sahib Gurdwara A GURDWARA or Sikh shrine located at Bhangani near Paonta Sahib in Himachal Pradesh. It marks the spot where a battle took place between the Sikhs led by Guru GOBIND SINGH and the Rajput hill rajas Bhim Chand, Fateh Singh and Kesri Singh. The Sikhs, helped by Pir Buddhu Shah and his disciples, were victorious, and a gurdwara was erected to commemorate the win.

Bharadvaja, rishi An ancient RISHI to whom several hymns of the RIG VEDA are attributed. He is also mentioned in the *RAMAYANA, MAHABHARATA,* PURANAS and other Hindu texts. According to the *Ramayana*, his ashram was in the forest around Prayaga, not far from CHITRAKUTA, and at the beginning of their exile RAMA and LAKSHMANA went there to seek his blessings. In the Puranas his love for Vedic study is described. One lifetime was not sufficient, and therefore he obtained a boon from the god INDRA to live for thousands of years in order to continue his study. Bharadvaja was also the name of other RISHIS.

Bharat Mata 'Mother India', a goddess representing the land of India, revered as a divine mother. The concept of Bharat Mata emerged with the nationalistic fervour of the second half of the nineteenth century, when the term began to be used in literary works. Artists soon produced imaginative depictions of the goddess. Early depictions were often of a map of India, superimposed with a goddess, usually a form of Durga or Lakshmi.

In 1936, a Bharat Mata Temple was constructed at Varanasi, and inaugurated by Mahatma GANDHI, who saw the temple as a symbol of unity, transcending religion and caste. Later, other Bharat Mata temples were built. Among these is a temple located at Shanti Kunj near HARDWAR in Uttarakhand. This modern temple was inaugurated by Indira Gandhi in 1983. The main image is of a goddess holding a vessel of milk and sheaves of grain, reflecting India's growth towards prosperity. There are images of several other deities, as well as of religious and political leaders and national heroes, and the temple thus portrays the concept of unity in diversity. Other Bharat Mata temples have been set up in different parts of India.

Bharata The name of several different people described in ancient texts. Among them are: (1) A king in the RIG VEDA from whom the Bharata clan was descended; (2) The son of the king Dushyanta and Shakuntala in the *MAHABHARATA.* (The KAURAVAS and PANDAVAS were descended from him, and hence were also known as Bharatas); (3) The brother of RAMA in the *RAMAYANA,* who acted as regent during Rama's exile; (4) The son of Adinatha or RISHABHA, the first Jain TIRTHANKARA; (5) The author of the *Natya Shastra,* a text on dramatic arts; (6) Several other minor kings and sages.

Bharatavarsha An ancient name for India derived from BHARATA, son of Dushyanta, or, according to other sources, from Bharata, son of RISHABHA. According to the PURANAS, Bharatavarsha was part of Jambudvipa, one of the seven islands or continents that comprise the world. It was also known as Kumara.

Bharati, Gopalakrishna A singer and composer of the nineteenth century, who created musical narratives (*katha kalakshepam*) in Tamil and Sanskrit on Hindu SHAIVA saints and on philosophical themes.

Born in 1810 (or 1800) in Narimanam, a village in Thanjavur District of present-day Tamil Nadu, he was a BRAHMANA, the son of Ramaswami Bharati. After studying Tamil and Sanskrit, he learned classical Hindustani music from Ramdas, who lived at Tiruvidarmarudur. He was also influenced by Ananta Bharati and Ghanam Krishna Aiyar, who composed Tamil songs. At the age of twenty-five he moved to Anandatandavapuram, and composed the *Nandanar Charitram,* his most famous work, on the Shaiva saint Nandanar. This was followed by compositions on other Shaiva saints, as well as devotional and philosophical songs. His works include *Iyarpakai Nayanar Charitram, Tiruneela-kantha Nayanar Charitram* and *Karaikkal Ammaiyar Charitram.* He used at least seventy different RAGAS in his various compositions, along with intricate talas or rhythms. He donated most of what he earned to the CHIDAMBARAM and Mayuram SHIVA temples. He died in 1881 or according to some sources, in 1896.

Bharati, Subramania A poet who wrote in Tamil and English on political, social and religious themes.

Born in 1882 at Ettayapuram in present Tamil Nadu, he was the son of Chinnaswamy Iyer, who owned one of the first textile mills in south India. At a young age, Subramania received the title 'Bharati' from the raja of Ettayapuram when he gave a discourse on education at a contest organized by the raja. In 1904 he settled in Chennai, worked in a Tamil daily, and became involved in politics and the freedom struggle. In 1910 he left British India and settled in Puducherry (Pondicherry) because he was being pursued by the British authorities. Though he is better known for his patriotic poems, his religious compositions are no less significant. He was influenced by Sri AUROBINDO and by early Tamil poetry, including the compositions of the Tamil SIDDHAS and the BHAKTI saints. He wrote several poems in praise of the Hindu god KRISHNA, as well as on nature and the joy of life. He returned to Chennai in 1919, and often went to the PARTHASARTHY TEMPLE there, where he sang his compositions and fed the temple elephant. In 1921, the elephant, in a state of frenzy, attacked and threw him. Subramania did not recover from his injuries and died in September of that year. Among his best works are *Kannan Pattu* (Songs to Krishna), *Panchali Sapatham* (The Vow of Panchali), and *Kuyil Pattu* (Kuyil's Song). The following poem on Krishna celebrates his love of the deity:

I see your complexion, Krishna,
In the crow's dark feathers.
I see the divine green, O Krishna,
In the leaves of all the trees.
Tis thy music, Krishna, that I hear
In all the sounds of the world.
And I thrill with your touch, Krishna,
When my finger feels the flame. (Trans. Prema Nandakumar)

Bharatidasan   A Tamil poet and writer, who wrote against the Hindu CASTE system and the role of BRAHMANAS. His real name was K. Kanaka Subburathnam, but he took the name Bharatidasan because he admired Subramania BHARATI. He was born in Puducherry (Pondicherry) in 1891, and after completing his education he became a school teacher. Before independence he was also engaged in helping revolutionaries who had escaped from British India to Puducherry. He wrote a number of plays, poems and novels. *Sanjivi Parvathathin Saaral*, one of his notable epic poems, is a satire on caste. He died in 1964 and was posthumously awarded the Sahitya Akademi Award in 1969.

Bharavi   A Sanskrit poet who lived at KANCHIPURAM in the time of the Pallava dynasty (sixth century). His best-known work is *Kiratarjuniya*, describing a meeting between the Hindu god SHIVA, in the guise of a Kirata (a member of a forest tribe) and ARJUNA. The work is based on an ancient story.

Bharhut Stupa   A STUPA with Buddhist relics located at Bharhut in Madhya Pradesh, that dates back to the third century BCE. Its construction was begun at the time of the Mauryan emperor ASHOKA, when a brick mound was erected. In the second century BCE, a stone railing with four entrances was added. Further additions came in the first century BCE, when intricately carved gateways (toranas) were made. An inscription records that this was in the time of the Buddhist king Dhanabhuti. The carvings on the railings and gateways include scenes from the JATAKAS, images of YAKSHAS and YAKSHIS, men and women, animals and trees. The BUDDHA himself is not shown, but he is depicted by symbols of footprints or an empty throne.

The stupa was first discovered by Alexander Cunningham of the Archaeological Survey of India in 1873.

Bhartrihari   A philosopher and poet who became a monk and probably lived from 570 to 651. He was of noble birth and was for some time attached to the court of the Maitraka ruler of Valabhi, in the region of Gujarat, but later became an ascetic and lived in a cave in UJJAIN. According to the Chinese traveller I-ching, he made several attempts to become a Buddhist monk and often lapsed, but finally succeeded. *Vakyapadiya* is his major philosophical work written in Sanskrit. It contains Buddhist ideas, along with some concepts similar to VEDANTA. In this text he states that all things create fear in people, and therefore detachment is the only path. The world is imaginary, a vision (*kalpanikam*), and objects in it are soulless (*nairatmya*), but gain an identity through words. BRAHMAN, the underlying reality, has no beginning or end, and is the eternal essence of speech, changed into form as the world evolves.

His poems are somewhat different and describe the dilemma of his desire to become a monk and his inability to give up love and passion. Three books of a hundred verses each, are attributed to him: *Sringara Shataka*, *Niti Shataka* and *Vairagya Shataka*, on love, politics and renunciation, respectively, though some scholars doubt whether all these are really his.

Bhasa   A Sanskrit playwright, probably of the third or fourth century, best known for his play *Svapnavasavadatta* (The Dream of Vasavadatta). He also wrote a number of short plays, mainly based on stories from the RAMAYANA or MAHABHARATA.

Bhaskara   A philosopher who lived around CE 900 and subscribed to the doctrine of BHEDABHEDAVADA, i.e., that both unity and multiplicity are real. He wrote a commentary on the BRAHMA SUTRA called *Bhaskarabhashya*. According to him, BRAHMAN, the underlying reality of the world, is One in its causal state, but has multiplicity in its evolved state. These two aspects coexist and are equally real. The world is not an illusion, but real, yet it is essentially the same as Brahman. The JIVA or individual soul is also of the same essence, but limited by matter. KARMA or right action is the means to knowledge (JNANA) which leads to MOKSHA (liberation).

Bhaskararaya   A scholar of TANTRISM who lived in the eighteenth century. He was originally from the region of Maharashtra, but settled at THANJAVUR. He wrote several works including a text called *Setubandha*, in which he analysed the Shrividya or DEVI tradition in the Tantras.

Bhatha Sahib Gurdwara   A GURDWARA or Sikh shrine located 5 km from Rupnagar in Punjab, associated with the tenth guru, GOBIND SINGH. The guru and his followers stayed here with a Pathan chief, Nihang Khan, who risked his life to shelter them. Here there was a brick kiln (bhatha) and when the guru's horse touched it with his hoof, the red-hot kiln is said to have instantly become cool. A gurdwara was later built to commemorate this incident.

Bhattaparinna   A SHVETAMBARA Jain text, one of the ten PAINNAS (Prakirnas), which deals with the futility of the pleasures of the world, and with the voluntary death by fasting (SALLEKHANA) advocated for a Jain saint. In a typical passage it states, 'Souls which do not renounce the world, and which are lacking in good qualities, plunge into SAMSARA, just as birds with a broken wing and without tail feathers fall into the ocean'. It also contains a number of stories and legends of saints.

bhattaraka   The title of a Jain DIGAMBARA leader who is the head of a MATHA or religious centre. The bhattaraka takes care of the property, estates, temples, schools and libraries of Digambara institutions. Though not the same as a monk, he is usually an ascetic with a vow of celibacy, a learned man and a religious leader of the community, often given the title shankaracharya. Senior Digambara monks, who are bound by the vow of nudity, do not interact much with the outside world and therefore bhattarakas, who wear orange robes, fill that role. Bhattarakas, whose function probably originated in the ninth century, still play important roles among Digambara Jains. The main bhattarakas today are at SHRAVANA BELAGOLA and MUDABADRI, both in Karnataka, and at Kolhapur in Maharashtra.

Bhavabhuti A Sanskrit writer of the eighth century who wrote two plays on the life of the Hindu god RAMA. These are *Mahaviracharita* (The Deeds of the Great Hero) and *Uttara Ramacharita* (The Later Deeds of Rama). His third extant play is *Malti Madhava*, a love story. Bhavabhuti lived at Kannauj in present-day Uttar Pradesh.

bhavana A Sanskrit term that has several meanings, including reflection, contemplation and meditation. In Hinduism, it is one of the terms used for meditation, though the word DHYANA is more common.

In Buddhism, it forms part of Jhana Magga or Dhyana Marga, the path of meditation. Bhavana, or attentive concentration, has two main aspects, samatha (Sanskrit: shamatha) or stillness of mind, and VIPASSANA (Sanskrit: vipashyana) or insight, leading to wisdom and enlightenment. There are several Buddhist texts dealing with bhavana, including those of BUDDHAGHOSHA and ASANGA, Kamalashila's *BHAVANAKRAMA*, as well as texts specific to various schools of Buddhism, which prescribe a number of methods of dhyana and bhavana.

The term is also used in Jainism for meditation or contemplation.

Bhavanakrama A series of MAHAYANA Buddhist texts dealing with meditation. Three texts with the same name were written by KAMALASHILA in the eighth century. The first is theoretical, whereas the second provides practical guidelines. The third deals with shamatha or calming practice.

Bhavani A name of PARVATI, consort of the Hindu god SHIVA.

Bhavaviveka A Buddhist scholar from south India who lived from c. 490 to 570 and founded the SVATANTRIKA sect, a branch of the MADHYAMIKA school of MAHAYANA Buddhism. He wrote several works, including the *Prajnapradipa*, a commentary on NAGARJUNA's *Madhyamika Karika*; the *Karatalaratna*, which refutes YOGACHARA theories and is available only in Chinese; the *Madhyamaka-hridaya*, refuting other philosophies; and a commentary on this, the *Tarkajvala*. His work influenced the later Buddhist scholars SHANTARAKSHITA and KAMALASHILA.

Bhavishya Purana A Sanskrit text, one of the eighteen major PURANAS of Hinduism. The versions available seem to be different from the ancient work as described in other books and have several late additions. The *Bhavishya Purana* starts with a traditional account of creation and describes various KALPAS or ages. Much of it deals with ceremonies to be performed and with the duties of the CASTES. There is a description of the NAGAPANCHAMI festival, as well as of some snake myths. One section is on sun worship in Shakadvipa (the land of the Shakas or Scythians). Here priests named Bhojaka and Maga are mentioned, indicating some connection with Zoroastrianism. Apart from late additions, there are some entirely spurious recensions of this text, composed even in the nineteenth century.

Bhavishyottara Purana A Sanskrit text that forms the last part of the BHAVISHYA PURANA. It contains myths and legends, as well as descriptions of religious ceremonies.

Bhedabhedavada A philosophical doctrine that states that Unity or Oneness and multiplicity are equally real. The Absolute or BRAHMAN is One, but from it multiple forms evolve. One of its main exponents was BHASKARA of the ninth or tenth century, while another was Yadavaprakasha of the eleventh century. Achintya Bhedabheda, or incomprehensible unity in difference, was part of the philosophy of CHAITANYA MAHAPRABHU.

bhikkhu The PALI term for a Buddhist monk, while a bhikkhuni is a nun. In Sanskrit the words are bhiksu and bhikshuni, and are used not only in Buddhism but in other religions as well.

bhikshu A mendicant or monk. In Hinduism, it particularly refers to a BRAHMANA in the fourth ASHRAMA or last stage of life, that of sannyasa, but also to any mendicant or ascetic.

Bhil religion Bhils form the third largest tribe of central India, after the Gonds and SANTHALS and are located mainly in Madhya Pradesh, Gujarat, Maharashtra and Rajasthan. Today they are largely converted to Hinduism but retain some of their tribal practices. One of their origin myths states that a fish warned a washerman sitting on the bank of a river of a great flood. He got into a crate along with his sister and was joined by a cock. They survived the flood, but there was water everywhere, and they did not know what to do. The cock crowed loudly and was heard by the god RAMA. He rescued them and told them to populate the world, because, after being asked four times, the man said the woman with him was not his sister, but his wife. They had seven sons and seven daughters. In the Puranic myth of the flood, MANU too was warned by a fish (MATSYA) of the approaching flood.

Bhils worship Hindu deities as well as legendary heroes and their own gods. Bhilat Dev, who according to their stories was a cowherd proficient in music and magic, is one of the main deities. He caught a huge serpent and took it to the god INDRA, who praised his bravery, presented him with hundreds of cows, and said that Bheru the serpent should henceforth serve him. Bhagavan, or Bholo Ishvar, is another generic deity, usually represented by symbolic stones. Bhils offer terracotta horses at their ancestral shrines on hills and under trees. The sun, moon and stars, as well as other nature deities are worshipped.

Bhima   The second of the five PANDAVA brothers described in the MAHABHARATA. As PANDU, his father, could not have children, KUNTI, his mother, conceived him through the wind god, VAYU. Bhima was extremely strong and fought many battles. He defended and protected DRAUPADI, the joint wife of the Pandava brothers, several times. He married the asura HIDIMBA, and had a son, Ghatotkacha. Another wife of his was Balandhara, princess of Kashi, from whom he had a son named Sarvatraga.

He is worshipped along with his brothers in some temples, while in Nepal he is worshipped as an independent deity. The Bhima temple in Kathmandu, Nepal, is popular among traders and businessmen.

Bhima Bhoi   A blind tribal poet of Orissa who composed beautiful BHAJANS. He died in 1895.

Bhishma   An elder statesman at the court of HASTINAPURA whose life is described in the MAHABHARATA. He was the son of King Shantanu and was earlier known as Devavrata, but after renouncing his succession to the throne and taking a vow of BRAHMACHARYA, he was called Bhishma. He arranged for the rishi VYASA to father DHRITARASHTRA and PANDU from the wives of his brother Vichitravirya. The KAURAVAS and PANDAVAS were their descendants, and thus he was their spiritual grandfather. He was respected and revered by them. In the great Mahabharata War he took the side of the Kauravas. Defeated finally by ARJUNA, his body was embedded with arrows. He lay on this bed of arrows for almost two months, while the war ended, and all the survivors came to pay their respects to him. He then gave a long discourse on spiritual, ethical, political and philosophical aspects of life, which forms the *Shanti Parva*, a section of the *Mahabharata*.

Bhitargaon Temple   A Hindu temple located at Bhitargaon near Kanpur in Uttar Pradesh. It is one of the oldest surviving brick temples of north India, dating back to the fifth century. The square shrine has terracotta panels with sculptures on the outer walls. SHIVA and PARVATI seated together and an eight-armed VISHNU can be identified, most of the rest being damaged. The shrine opens to the east and has a pyramidal tower.

Bhrigu   An ancient RISHI or sage who was one of the PRAJAPATIS. There are references to him in the RIG VEDA, where he is said to have received AGNI (fire) from heaven. In later texts there are several stories relating to Bhrigu. He is said to have been born from the Hindu god BRAHMA's skin, but was killed at DAKSHA's sacrifice by an emanation of the god SHIVA. According to

another account, he was born at the time of VARUNA's sacrifice from Brahma's seed which fell in the fire. He was brought up by Varuna, and thus is also known as Varuna's son. These accounts possibly relate to two different incarnations. His descendants are known as Bhargavas and include PARASHURAMA, the RUDRAS, and several rishis. Bhrigu Tirtha, where he performed penances, was a sacred site. There is a temple dedicated to Bhrigu at Bharuch in Gujarat, the ancient name of which was Bhrigukaccha.

Bhrigus   A class of lesser Hindu deities mentioned in the VEDAS and later texts. They were connected with the Hindu god AGNI and created and nourished fire. They were also makers of chariots.

Bhubaneswar   A city, the capital of Orissa. Bhubaneswar or Bhuvaneshvara, was also known as Ekamrakanana or Ekamrakshetra, Kalinganagari and Harakshetra in the Puranas. The *Brahma Purana* has a long section on Ekamrakshetra, a region sacred to Shiva. The old city nearby was a sacred centre and is the site of at least thirty early temples dating from the eighth to the thirteenth centuries, and once had many more. The most famous among these are the MUKTESHVARA and LINGARAJA temples. Modern temples include a large KRISHNA temple built by ISKCON.

Bhudevi   A Hindu goddess, the mother of the earth, also known as Bhu or Bhumi. There are various stories and legends about her. According to the MAHABHARATA, she is the daughter of BRAHMA, married to VISHNU. The PURANAS state that in the Varaha KALPA, when the asura HIRANYAKSHA oppressed the earth and submerged it under water, Bhu Devi, representing the earth, took the form of a cow and appealed to Vishnu to save the world. He became VARAHA and raised the earth on his tusks. According to the *DEVI BHAGAVATA PURANA*, Bhu Devi then stood up on the water. Seeing her beauty, comparable to the lustre of a million suns, Vishnu fell in love and married her. Their son was MANGALA. She also had a son, an asura known as NARAKASURA, from Hiranyaksha, by the touch of his horns. According to some texts, in one of her births, SITA was the daughter of Bhudevi.

Bhudevi is depicted holding a blue lotus, along with Vishnu and SHRI DEVI or LAKSHMI, and is especially popular in south India.

Bhuiyan religion   Bhuiyans are a tribal group who live in Assam, Bihar, Orissa and West Bengal, in varying stages of development. Pauri Bhuiyans of the hill regions of Orissa retain most of their ancient traditions. According to their myths, Dharam Devata, the sun god, presented them with a jar full of earth. This they considered their wealth, and thus called themselves Bhuiyan (from bhumi, earth). Dharam Devata, also representing the sky, is one of their most important deities, the other being Basumata, the goddess of the earth. Terracotta images of these deities are made and propitiated at all festivals, or before starting any important work, such as ploughing or planting. Dharam Devata and Basumati are benevolent deities, who are husband and wife. They have their counterparts in the Rig Vedic deities of PRITHVI and DYAUS.

bhuta (1) A term for ghosts or spirits. They are attendants of the Hindu god SHIVA, who rules over them, and live in cemeteries or in certain trees. They enter dead bodies, making them seem alive, and attack and devour people. They were created by Shiva in a fit of anger, and according to the *VAYU PURANA*, their mother was KRODHA (anger). According to another story, the RUDRA Nilalohita (Shiva) gave birth to thousands of bhutas through his wife SATI. They were music-haters and wore snakes as their sacred threads. According to the *VAMANA PURANA*, Virabhadra and Nandikeshvara (emanations of Shiva) are two RUDRAS who head the bhutas. SKANDA, Shakha and BHAIRAVA are also said to be their chiefs. The bhutas usually helped Shiva in his battles, but sometimes fought on the side of the ASURAS.

(2) Bhutas are also local deities or ancestral spirits, worshipped particularly in coastal Karnataka. Bhuta rituals are conducted in the Tulu language of the region, and traditional bhuta masked dances are enacted. Over 450 names of bhutas are known in the region. Among them are Angarbhuta, Mayasandaya, Kotichennaya, Junadi, Pilichchhandi, Ullalthi. Similar spirits and rituals exist in Kerala, known as Teyyams. Some of the names common to both groups are Kshetrapalan, Pottan, Bhairavi, Chamundi, Kuttichattan, Mariamma, Muttapan, Alibhuta, Babhiriyan and Panenruli. Special village shrines are dedicated to bhutas, and swords, shields and oil lamps, along with ritualistic objects of silver are kept there, to be used in their performances.

(3) Pancha-bhutas refer to the five elements of earth, fire, water, air and space, and are often personified and worshipped.

Bhuteshvara (1) The lord of all beings, a name applied to VISHNU, BRAHMA, KRISHNA and to other deities.

(2) The Lord of the BHUTAS, who are spirits or goblins, and in this sense applies to SHIVA.

Bhuvaneshvari A Hindu goddess, one of the ten MAHAVIDYAS or TANTRIC goddesses. She nourishes the three worlds, and holds a fruit, a goad and a noose.

Bible, Christian The Christian Bible consists of two parts, the OLD TESTAMENT and the NEW TESTAMENT. The Old Testament, originally written mainly in Hebrew with some Aramaic passages, was probably composed between 1000 BCE and 300 BCE. This was initially the Jewish Bible, and was divided into twenty-four books. These were rearranged into thirty-nine books in the Christian version, along with additional material. The Protestant Bible, which emerged after the Reformation, removed the additional texts, referring to them as the Apocrypha. The thirty-nine main books are: the first five books known as the Pentateuch, followed by twelve historical books, five poetic books and seventeen prophetic books. Catholic and Orthodox churches include additional books. The NEW TESTAMENT, composed in Greek within a little over a hundred years after the death of Jesus Christ, consists of four books describing the life of Jesus—the Gospels of Matthew, Mark, Luke and John. This is followed by the *Acts of the Apostles*, which describes the events soon after the death and resurrection of Jesus. In addition there are twenty-one Epistles, of which thirteen are said to have been written by Paul, and others by James, Peter, John and Jude. In conclusion is the book of *Revelation*, a mystical and symbolical vision of the future.

Several versions and translations of the Bible occur in its history. Early versions include those in Greek, Old Latin, Latin (the fourth century Vulgate), Syriac, Coptic, Aramaic, Armenian, Georgian, Ethiopic, Gothic, German, Dutch and others. The first complete translation into English was in the fourteenth century, following Anglo-Saxon and Anglo-Norman translations. Since then there have been several different English translations. One of the most popular remains the King James Version, first published in 1611, though more colloquial versions in modern English are also widely read. The Bible has by now been translated into innumerable languages in all parts of the world.

In India the Bible is available in over fifty Indian languages and dialects, while sections of it have been translated into about fifty more. Missionaries who came to India in the seventeenth and eighteenth centuries began translating the Bible with the help of Indian scholars. The Gospel of Matthew was first translated into Tamil and printed in Sri Lanka in 1688. In India, the entire New Testament in Tamil was published in 1715, and the full Bible in 1726. Other early translations of the Bible were into Bengali (1801–09), Urdu (1805–43), Marathi (1805–19), Oriya (1809–15), Hindi (1811–18), Punjabi (1815–26) and Assamese (1810–33). Around the same time the New Testament was translated into Telugu, Konkani, Gujarati, Kanarese, Marwari and Nepali.

Bible, Jewish The Jewish Bible, also known as the Hebrew Bible, Tanach, or Mikra, more or less corresponds to the OLD TESTAMENT of the Christian BIBLE, with some differences.

The Hebrew Bible is divided into three parts, Torah, Neviim and Ketuvim, and Tanach or Tenach is an acronym based on the first letters of these parts. Torah, or the Law, is the most important, consisting of the first five books of the Bible, which are Genesis, Exodus, Leviticus, Numbers and Deuteronomy. These are also known as the Pentateuch or the five books of Moses. (TORAH, in a wider sense, includes other Jewish texts as well). Neviim, or the Prophets, contains eight books on the Prophets, while Ketuvim, or the Writings, has eleven books, including the Psalms, Proverbs and the book of Job. Most of these twenty-four books were initially written in Hebrew. A Greek translation, the SEPTUAGINT, was made in the third century BCE.

The Old Testament includes all the books of the Hebrew Bible but is differently arranged and divided, the whole forming thirty-nine books. The Catholic and Orthodox Old Testaments have additional books not included in the Tanach.

Bihu A series of agrarian festivals celebrated in Assam. The main Bihu is a spring festival that usually takes place in April, and is known as Bohag Bihu, or Rangali Bihu. The festival also inaugurates the new year, as Bohag is the first month of the Assamese calendar. Bohag Bihu begins on the last day of Chot, which is the final month of the Assamese year. This day is reserved for cattle, who are bathed and given special food. The next day, the first day of Bohag, is for people. Elders are revered, friends are visited, special food is eaten, and presents are given. On the third day, religious ceremonies are held. The whole festival lasts for seven days and is associated with songs and music, dances and feasts, as well as games and sports. Two other Bihus are celebrated at different times. The Magh Bihu takes place in winter, after the harvesting of crops, and is accompanied by feasts and bonfires. The Kati Bihu is a one-day festival held in October–November, when the crop is yet to ripen, and the granaries are nearly empty. The TULASI plant is worshipped and lamps are lit and placed in the fields and storage rooms for grain. Bihu dances are the state dance of Assam. Bihu songs at Bohag Bihu are romantic and young people are encouraged to seek partners at this time.

Bijli Mahadev Temple A temple of the Hindu god SHIVA located near Kullu in Himachal Pradesh. The temple houses a LINGA that is said to attract lightning (bijli). According to traditional accounts, it is periodically shattered by lightning, and joined together again by the priest with a mixture of parched barley and butter. Above the temple is a white mast, 18 m high. The destruction of the linga is said to signify Shiva's absorption of the negative energy of the atmosphere, and its subsequent purification.

Bikaner Jain temples At least twenty-seven Jain temples are located at Bikaner in Rajasthan, dating to the sixteenth and seventeenth centuries. They are dedicated to various TIRTHANKARAS and are a mix of western and Indian styles with Mughal arches and columns. Among them are the Bhandeshwar and Sandeshwar temples, named after the two merchant brothers who constructed them. These unique temples, dedicated to Parshvanatha, are elaborately decorated with gold-leaf work, floral paintings and frescoes. The Neminatha Temple, constructed in 1536, also stands out because of its high shikhara or tower.

Bimbisara A king of the state of MAGADHA, (Bihar) who ruled from 546 to 494 BCE and was a disciple and patron of the BUDDHA. He made the first gift to the Buddhist SANGHA, of the Venuvana Arama or dwelling place.

birds, sacred A number of birds are considered sacred or associated with deities. In the VEDAS, several deities are compared with birds, including SOMA and AGNI. Agni is called the eagle of the sky, and INDRA once took the form of an eagle. The owl and the pigeon are messengers of YAMA.

In later Hinduism, some sacred birds include: Chanda, a crow associated with the mother-goddess Alambusha, from whom were descended other crows, particularly the wise Bhushunda; GARUDA, the vahana or vehicle of VISHNU; HAMSA, a swan or goose, the vehicle of BRAHMA, Brahmi and VARUNA and the name of a sect of rishis; the parrot, associated with the god KAMA; and the peacock who is the vahana of KARTTIKEYA. In the RAMAYANA, the vulture JATAYU tries to help SITA. Birds are also associated with deities in Buddhism and Jainism. In Islam, birds have a symbolic importance in SUFISM, reflected in *The Conference of the Birds*, a text by the SUFI saint Attar. The hoopoe is considered particularly wise. The QURAN states that birds have a special language of their own, which was taught to King Solomon (xxvii.16). In the Zoroastrian AVESTA, the deity VERETHRAGHNA takes the form of an eagle, while SRAOSHA is associated with a cock, a bird that also occurs in Judaism and Christianity.

Birhor religion Birhors are a tribal group of east-central India. Birhors of Orissa worship Sing Bonga, the sun, and his wife Chandu Bonga, who together created the world. Sing Bonga is extremely powerful and is the creator of the universe. Another important deity is Dharti Mai, who presides over the earth (utaye), and takes care of all natural resources and creatures. A sacrifice of a goat or cock is made to these deities once a year in Pausha-Magha (January–February). Lugu Haram, a male deity who presides over the east, and Birhi Mai, a female deity who presides over the west, are sometimes considered the children of Dharti Mai. They have seven sons, each presiding over a different aspect of creation. Hanuman Bir is the deity of langurs, while Bandra Bir is the god of rhesus monkeys. Bagh Bir is the deity of tigers, and Hunda Bir of bears. Paban Bir or Hoyo Bir is associated with rain and storm, Babsa Bir with thunder and meteors, Nanda Bir with the wind.

Two categories of spirits of the dead are also worshipped, Hapram and Churgin. Haprams are real ancestors, while Churgin are wandering spirits who need to be placated by offerings.

Biruni, Al- See ABU REHAN AL-BIRUNI.

Bisapantha A sub-sect of the DIGAMBARA Jain sect, which originated in north India. The Bisapanthas revere the dharma-gurus or BHATTARAKAS, who are the heads of Jain MATHAS or religious centres. In their temples, they worship not only the TIRTHANKARAS, but other deities such as YAKSHAS and YAKSHIS and

KSHETRAPALAS. The method of worship is similar to that in Hindu temples, with saffron, flowers, fruit and sweets being offered to the deities. PRASAD, or sanctified food is distributed from the offerings. Incense is burnt, and ARTI, or circling of lights over the idol, is performed. Devotees are seated while worshipping the deities.

Between the sixteenth and eighteenth centuries there was a movement against these practices, and the TERAPANTHA sect emerged, which simplified the rituals in temples and attempted to 'purify' Jainism.

Bishnoi   A community that follows the Bishnoi or twenty-nine precepts of their guru and leader Jambeshvara or Jambhoji, who lived in the fifteenth century. These precepts enable Bishnois to live in harmony with nature. They protect trees and wildlife, and do not distinguish between castes and religions.

Members of the Bishnoi community have often sacrificed their lives to save trees and animals. In 1730, in Khejadli village in the state of Jodhpur, they attempted to prevent the cutting of khejadi trees (*Prosopis cineraria*) by clinging to them, and thus were pioneers of the later Chipko movement. At this time 363 people clinging to the trees were killed, including women and children, before the maharaja stopped the massacre. Bishnois continue to live in the region and to defend the trees and wildlife with their lives. Recently, some have died while saving blackbuck from poachers.

Bishnupur   A town in West Bengal with a number of temples of the seventeenth and eighteenth centuries, built by rulers of the Malla dynasty. The Mallas had ruled the area from around the seventh century but became prominent in the time of Bir Hambir, said to have been a wicked king who became noble after his conversion to VAISHNAVISM by Shrinivasa, a follower of CHAITANYA MAHAPRABHU. He introduced the worship of the god Madana-Mohana (KRISHNA), and built the Rasa-Mancha in 1600, a large structure with a pyramidal roof. Here all the gods of neighbouring temples were brought together at a great Rasa festival. Succeeding kings built more temples, of which at least thirty still survive, most of them dedicated to RADHA and Krishna.

Bismillah   A term in Islam that means 'in the name of God'. It is used in two ways: Bismillahi-ar-Rahman-ar-Rahim (in the name of God, the compassionate, the merciful) and Bismillahi-illahi-al-akbar (in the name of God, God the most great). Every Sura of the QURAN, except one, begins with the first statement, which is also used before any activity, such as eating, or any new venture. The second is used when slaughtering animals or fighting a battle.

Bithur   A town located near Kanpur in Uttar Pradesh. In ancient times it was a sacred site for Hindus, and according to one tradition, the *RAMAYANA* of Valmiki was composed here. The god BRAHMA is said to have visited the place, and the mark of his footprint is still worshipped.

Bka-gdams-pa   A school of Tibetan Buddhism, also spelt KADAMPA.

Bka-gyur   A collection of Tibetan Buddhist texts, also spelt KAGYUR or Kanjur.

Bka-rgyud-pa   A school of Tibetan Buddhism, also spelt KAGYU or Kagyupa.

Blavatsky, Helena Petrovna   One of the two founders of the THEOSOPHICAL SOCIETY OF INDIA, the other being Colonel H.S. Olcott. The Theosophical Society is an organization that aims to promote a search for the underlying truths of all religions.

Helena Hahn was born at Ekaterinoslav (now Dnipropetrovsk, Ukraine) in the southern part of the Russian empire in 1831, and even as a child had mystical experiences and an interest in spirituality. At the age of eighteen, she married Nikifor V. Blavatsky, a middle-aged friend of the family, vice-governor of the province of Erivan. The marriage did not last long. Helena soon left Russia and travelled to Egypt, Greece and Eastern Europe before going to London. There she met the Master MORYA, who became her spiritual guide. She then went to the US and later to India and Tibet, where she studied with her Master. She returned to the US in 1873 and came in contact with Col. Olcott and W.Q. Judge, who had similar interests, and together they founded the Theosophical Society in 1875, with its headquarters at New York. An interest in Eastern wisdom led Madame Blavatsky and Olcott to visit India in 1878. Visiting Sri Lanka, they converted to Buddhism and then returned to India, settling there from 1879. In 1882, they bought a large estate, and set up a branch of the Theosophical Society at Adyar near Chennai. In 1884–85 Blavatsky was accused of being a fraud and moved to Germany and then to London, where she continued her work. She died on 8 May 1891.

By this time she had written a number of profound works on philosophy and mysticism, which she claimed revealed the secrets of the Tibetan mystics. She also put forward a hierarchical view of spiritual masters who governed the world but were unknown to most. Her publications include *Isis Unveiled* (1877); *The Secret Doctrine* (1888); *The Key to Theosophy* (1889) and *The Voice of the Silence* (1889). Her collected writings amount to sixteen volumes. Her work is mainly based on a mix of Hindu and Buddhist ideas, and still has considerable influence on spiritualists and New Age mystics in the Western world.

Annie BESANT was inspired by her to join the Theosophical Society and come to India. She played a crucial role in the freedom movement and in popularizing indigenous religions.

Bnei Menashe   A Jewish group in north-east India who claim to be descendants of the Menashe

(Manasseh) tribe of Israel, one of the ten lost tribes. They include tribal groups of Manipur, Mizoram, Assam and Nagaland, extending into Bangladesh and Myanmar. They claim they were enslaved by the Assyrians in the eighth century BCE, and after escaping from them, reached China, from where they later entered north-east India and adjacent areas. They followed tribal practices and were converted to Christianity in the nineteenth century, but later dreams and revelations enabled them to understand their Jewish identity. Around 1951, Tchalah, a local chief, said that God had told him they should return to their original religion and land (Judaism and Israel). Some of the Manipur Jews state that all the original residents of Manipur and Tripura belonged to the Menashe tribe, though there is no historical support for this. DNA tests said to have been conducted on some of the claimants indicate their affinity with Jews of Uzbekistan.

The Bnei Menashe have received instruction from Jewish rabbis and several have converted to Judaism while some have emigrated to Israel. Others have designed their own flag and wish to set up a Jewish state in the north-east.

Bodh Gaya A place in Bihar, that marks the spot where the BUDDHA attained enlightenment under the BODHI TREE. Bodh Gaya is located 9 km from the city of Gaya, and the MAHABODHI TEMPLE here, built in front of the Bodhi Tree, is visited by pilgrims from all over the world. Behind are other shrines recording the events of the seven weeks Buddha spent here. Modern Buddhist temples here include Korean, Thai and Japanese temples. Huge Buddhist statues have been erected, among which are a 25 m Buddha in Japanese style and an even larger statue of the Bodhisattva MAITREYA, on the outskirts of the town.

Bodhi Tree The tree under which the BUDDHA sat in meditation and attained enlightenment. Located at BODH GAYA in Bihar, it has been identified as *Ficus religiosa*, commonly known as the pipal tree. The Mauryan emperor ASHOKA sent a shoot of the tree to be planted in Sri Lanka. Shashanka, ruler of Gauda (in Bengal), destroyed the original tree at Bodh Gaya in the seventh century, but another was planted at the spot from a shoot of the tree in Sri Lanka.

Bodhicharyavatara/Bodhisattvachary-avatara A MAHAYANA Buddhist text composed by SHANTIDEVA who lived in the seventh to eighth centuries. It provides guidance for those on the BODHISATTVA path.

bodhichitta A state of mind referred to in Buddhist texts. It implies cultivating the BUDDHA mind, that is, envisaging the goal of enlightenment as the first step on the BODHISATTVA path. The Bodhisattva aims to become a Buddha in order to help all sentient beings, and by fixing this goal in the mind one realizes the bodhichitta. The *BODHICHARYAVATARA* is among the texts that describes cultivating the bodhichitta as the first step.

Bodhidharma An Indian Buddhist scholar and philosopher who contributed to the spread of Buddhism in China. Bodhidharma probably reached Loyang in northern China between 516 and 526, or even earlier. He is revered in the Chan school of Chinese Buddhism as the founder and first patriarch of this school, though historians question the authenticity of this tradition. He is said to have been a disciple of the scholar Prajnadhara, and to have had a specialized knowledge of the *LANKAVATARA SUTRA*. There are several legends about him in Chinese sources. According to one story, he sat in meditation continuously, without moving for nine years, at a temple in Loyang. Another account states that when asked by Emperor Wu of the Liang dynasty, 'What is the absolute holy truth?', he replied, 'Great emptiness; and there is nothing holy about it.' The word Chan comes from the Sanskrit dhyana, and its equivalent in Japanese is Zen.

Bodhiruchi An Indian Buddhist who reached Loyang in China in 508. He translated a commentary of the *DASHABHUMIKA SUTRA* into Chinese. He also persuaded Tan-Luan, a Chinese Buddhist, to worship the Buddha AMITABHA.

Bodhisattva A Buddhist term implying a Buddha-to-be. The term has different connotations at different times. In HINAYANA Buddhism, it refers to the previous incarnations of the BUDDHA. In MAHAYANA and VAJRAYANA Buddhism, Bodhisattvas are of two types: (1) celestial Bodhisattvas, related to celestial BUDDHAS and worshipped as deities, which include AVALOKITESHVARA, MANJUSHRI, SAMANTABHADRA, MAITREYA and others; (2) individuals who vow to gain enlightenment in order to help all living beings. Any person who follows this path, motivated by compassion for all, is a Bodhisattva.

The path of such a Bodhisattva begins by invoking the BODHICHITTA, the thought of enlightenment. This is followed by a vow (pranidhana), where a person resolves to take on the sorrow and suffering of all, and affirms, 'I resolve to gain supreme wisdom for the sake of all that lives.' A prediction is made regarding his future achievements. The path then followed consists of ten stages or bhumis. The Bodhisattva refuses nirvana or liberation, deliberately takes on rebirth to help others, and shares his merit with all sentient beings. Celestial Bodhisattvas provide a model for those on this path. Several texts describe the stages, vows and practices of a Bodhisattva, including the *BODHICHARYAVATARA*, the *Bodhisattva Pratimoksha*, the *BODHISATTVABHUMI SUTRA* and the *DASHABHUMIKA SUTRA*.

Celestial Bodhisattvas: The corresponding table lists twenty-six celestial Bodhisattvas described in texts, with their colours and emblems, and the celestial BUDDHAS connected with them. There is some variation in the different texts. These Bodhisattvas live in heavenly realms and are worshipped for guidance along the Buddhist path.

Bodhisattva	Meaning	colour	Emblem	Celestial Buddha
1. Akashagarbha	Essence of space	Green	Jewel	
2. Akshayamati	Indestructible mind	Yellow	Sword or vessel	
3. Amitaprabha	Boundless light	Green, white or red	Jar	Amoghasiddhi
4. Amoghadarshin		Yellow	Lotus	
5. Avalokiteshvara	The watchful lord	Red or white	Lotus	Amitabha
6. Bhadrapala		Red or white	Jewel	Amitabha
7. Chandraprabha	Light of the moon	Red or white	Moon on lotus	Amitabha
8. Gaganaganja		Yellow or Red	Kalpataru	Ratnasambhava
9. Gandahasti		Yellow, green or whitish green	Elephant's trunk or conch	Ratnasambhava
10. Jaliniprabha	Light of the sun	Red	Sun-disc	Amitabha
11. Jnanaketu		Yellow or blue	Flag with chintamani jewel	
12. Kshitigarbha	Matrix of the earth	White, yellow or green	Kalpataru (wishing tree)	Vairochana
13. Mahasthama-prapta	One who has obtained great strength	White or yellow	Six lotuses and a sword	
14. Maitreya	The future Buddha	White or golden yellow	Nagakeshara Flower or lotus	Vairochana
15. Manjushri		Golden	Sword or book	All Buddhas
16. Pratibhanakuta		Green, yellow or red	Whip	
17. Ratnapani	Jewel bearer	Yellow or green	Jewel or moon	Ratnasambhava
18. Sagarmati	Ocean mind	White	Sea wave or conch	
19. Samantabhadra	Universal goodness	White, yellow or blue	Jewel	Vairochana
20. Sarvanivaran-avishkambhin	Effacer of all sins	Green, white or blue	Sword or book	Amoghasiddhi
21. Sarvapayanjaha	Recover of all miseries	White	Goad	
22. Sarvashokam-onirghatamati		Whitish yellow, yellow or red	Staff	
23. Surangama		White	Sword	
24. Vajragarbha	Matrix of thunderbolt	Green, blue or bluish white	*Dashabhumika Sutra*	Amoghasiddhi
25. Vajrapani		Blue or white	Vajra	Akshobhya
26. Vishvapani		Green		Amoghasiddhi

Bodhisattvabhumi Sutra A MAHAYANA Buddhist text that forms part of a larger text, the *Yogacharabhumi*, but is also used separately. It is said to have been written by ASANGA, and describes the various stages or *bhumis* on the BODHISATTVA path. The text is divided into three sections. The first describes the basic practices for a Bodhisattva, while the second describes additional practices. The third section deals with the attributes of a Bodhisattva.

This sutra was translated into Chinese by the fifth century, and later into Tibetan.

Bodhisattva-yana Another name for MAHAYANA Buddhism, which focuses on the path of the BODHISATTVA.

Bohras A Muslim group, divided into two sects, Dawoodi, and Sulaimani. Though they live all over India, they are concentrated in Maharashtra and Gujarat. The sect traces its origin to the Prophet MUHAMMAD, and their imams are considered the direct descendants of the prophet's daughter Fatima, and her husband Ali. The imams originally lived in Medina, then established themselves in Tunisia and Egypt and are descended from the Fatimids of Egypt. They are mainly SHIAS and belong to the Mustali sect which originated in Egypt and then moved to Yemen. They migrated to India in the eleventh century, and as most of them were traders and merchants, they were named 'Bohra' from the Gujarati word 'vahaurau', meaning 'to trade'. In 1539, they set up their headquarters at Sidhpur in India. Their leaders are known as DAIS. Dawoodi Bohras believe that the twenty-first imam, Tayyib Abi l-Qasim, who lived in the twelfth century and was in the direct line of Ali, went into seclusion in 1132, concealed himself establishing a dai (Dai al-Mutlaq) as his vice-regent. Al-Malika al-Sayyida, wife of the Fataimid dai of Yemen, was the protector of the child imam, and instituted the office of the dai on his instructions. The first twenty-three dais were in Yemen, after which the headquarters of the dai became India. The first dai in India was Syedna Yusuf Najmuddin in 1539. In the sixteenth century their leader was Dai Dawood Bin Adjab Shah. After his death two groups had a conflict over his successor. One accepted Dai Dawood Burhanuddin ibn Qutb Shah, who was in India, as their leader, while others followed his rival Sulaiman Ibn Hasan, then in Yemen.The dispute was to be decided by the emperor AKBAR, but before that Sulaiman died in Lahore and the two groups came to be known as Dawoodis and Sulaimanis. Most of those in India are Dawoodis, and their dai lives in MUMBAI. Sulaimani Bohras mainly live in Yemen, and their dais are usually from Yemen. Only the forty-sixth Sulaimani dai, who took over in 1936, was an Indian named Gulam Hussan, who was from Mumbai. Muhammad Burhanuddin (b.1915 at Surat) is the fifty-second dai of the Dawoodi Bohras. There are approximately one million Dawoodi Bohras today of whom the majority are in India and Pakistan, Dawoodi Bohras are quite progressive and believe in women's education. They have their own language, Lisanu-i-Dawat, written in Arabic script, consisting of a mix of Urdu, Gujarati and Arabic. The two Bohra groups have similar religious practices, which differ slightly from traditional Islam. For instance, Bohras recite prayers three times a day, and not five. They do not have a sermon (KHUTBA) on Fridays and some aspects of their interpretation of the QURAN are different. In case they are in danger because of their faith, they are permitted to deny their identity (practise of taqiya).

Sunni Bohras followers of the Hannafi school of law. They are often known as Vohras, and have cultural similarities with Dawoodi Bohras

Boi ceremony   A Zoroastrian ritual in the fire temple which traditionally takes place five times a day at the change of a GAH, a time period. In this ceremony the fire is fed with sandalwood and incense by the resident priest. A bell is rung in the temple at the time of the ceremony.

Bom Jesus Basilica   A Roman CATHOLIC church located in GOA, constructed in 1594–95 and consecrated in 1605. The body of the Jesuit saint, ST. FRANCIS XAVIER, who died in 1552, is preserved here, and the church is still an important centre of pilgrimage. It was given the status of a Basilica in 1946 by Pope Pius XII.

'Bom Jesus' means 'good Jesus' or 'infant Jesus'. The large church is built in composite architectural style on a cruciform plan. The church has two chapels, a main altar and sacristy, as well as a choir at the entrance.

St. Xavier's body is kept in a silver casket, once inlaid with precious stones, and placed in a decorated tomb in a separate chapel to the south of the transept, richly decorated with wood carvings and paintings from the life of the saint.

This is one of the most important Catholic churches in India. The sacred relics of St. Xavier are exposed to the public once every ten years. Hundreds of thousands of people throng the church on these occasions, and miracles are said to take place.

Bopadeva   A Sanskrit writer of the thirteenth century. He was a devotee of the Hindu god KRISHNA, and lived at Devagiri, the capital of the Yadava dynasty. Born in a BRAHMANA village called Vedapura, located on the Varada river, he was the son of Kesava and a student of Dhanesa, both of whom were scholars attached to the Yadava court. His main works are the *Harilila* and *Muktaphala*, which contain commentaries and analyses of the BHAGAVATA PURANA. He combined the philosophies of ADVAITA and BHAKTI, and believed in reaching the One through the worship of a personal god. He also wrote works on grammar and medicine.

Borobudur   A Buddhist STUPA constructed in Java in the ninth century by the rulers of the Shailendra dynasty, who were influenced by the Buddhist Pala dynasty of Bengal. Indian cultural influence extended to Southeast Asia at this time, and Borobudur is the best representative of the Indo-Java architectural style. It is the most elaborate stupa ever built and has eight terraces, the first five with images of the five celestial BUDDHAS. On the first four terraces are the Buddhas AKSHOBHYA, RATNASAMBHAVA, AMITABHA and AMOGHASIDDHI in their respective directions, while the fifth terrace has only VAIROCHANA, the ADI BUDDHA or primordial Buddha. All around the stupa are scenes from SHAKYAMUNI's life and from the JATAKAS and MAHAYANA texts. From the base to the top, the stupa represents the journey to NIRVANA. The stupa remains an important centre of pilgrimage for Buddhists from all over the world.

Brahma   A Hindu god, the first of the trinity of three main gods—Brahma, VISHNU and SHIVA. Brahma is the creator, Vishnu the preserver, and Shiva the destroyer, but over the years Brahma declined in importance compared with the other two deities. Brahma is mentioned in the *Shatapatha Brahmana* as the creator of the gods and the source of all. In the VEDIC SAMHITAS many names are given to a creator god, one of which is Brahma. Other names of the creator include VISHVAKARMA, Brahmanaspati, HIRANYAGARBHA and PRAJAPATI. In the *MAHABHARATA*, Brahma is said to be the same as Prajapati. In the *BRIHAT SAMHITA*, he is described as having four faces and seated on a lotus. He holds a kamandalu, or water pot. According to the commentary, he also holds a staff and wears the skin of a black antelope. In the PURANAS, his iconography is fully developed. Here it is stated that he has four hands, holds a mala or rosary, as well as sruk, sruva (sacrificial ladles) and sacred texts, i.e., the VEDAS. He is dressed in white, and his VAHANA or vehicle is the HAMSA, a swan or goose. Sometimes he rides in a chariot drawn by seven swans. His consort, created by him, is SARASVATI, also known as Shatarupa, Brahmi, BRAHMANI, SAVITRI or GAYATRI. Usually, however, Gayatri is considered his second wife, distinct from Sarasvati, while Brahmi or Brahmani is a MATRIKA or mother goddess, depicted differently from Sarasvati. Brahma lives on Mt MERU in the city of BRAHMAPURI or Manovati.

Brahma is associated with creation myths. While Vishnu sleeps on the waters, a lotus springs from his navel and in this, Brahma, the creator, appears. Thus he is also called Nabhija (born from the navel) or Kanjaja (born from a lotus). The cycles of creation and destruction, MAHAYUGAS, KALPAS and MANVANTARAS, are linked with Brahma. He periodically creates and destroys the world, along with everything in it, and finally, after a hundred years of his life, creation, including all the gods, merges back into its essence. This is known as PRALAYA, or dissolution.

Brahma is the source of all knowledge. The four Vedas originated from him and he is connected with other arts, architecture, music and dancing. The four CASTES also emerged from him, and all humans were descended from him. The four Kumaras, SANAT KUMARA and others, were created by him, and according to some texts, remained eternal children. The PRAJAPATIS are his mind-born sons, and Svayambhu MANU was born from him.

The most well-known Brahma temple is at Pushkara in Rajasthan. Among other Brahma temples are those at Dudahi and Khajuraho in Madhya Pradesh, Vasantgarh in Rajasthan, and Unkal in West Bengal. Brahma images also occur in several temples, usually in a secondary position to either Vishnu or Shiva, as well as in Jain and Buddhist temples, as an attendant or worshipper. In most of the later images he is depicted with a beard. There are a number of myths which attempt to explain Brahma's inferior status. One states he was cursed by Shiva, while others indicate his conflict with Vishnu. He is also said to have granted too many boons to DAITYAS and RAKSHASAS, including to HIRANYAKSHA, HIRANYAKASHIPU, TARAKA and RAVANA, thus creating problems for the gods. The real reason for his decline, however, is believed to be the growth of Vaishnavism and Shaivism, and the prominence of Shakti as creative power or engery. The AMARAKOSHA lists a number of names of Brahma, apart from those mentioned above. These include: Atmabhu, the self-born; Pitamaha, grandfather of the Pitris; Dhata, one who holds or bears everything; Vidhata, one who acts; Vedha, one who creates; Hamsavahana, one whose vehicle is a swan.

Brahma Kumaris   A religious sect founded in 1937 by Dada Lekhraj, a diamond merchant, in the region of Sind in present-day Pakistan. In 1951 the headquarters moved to Mt ABU in Rajasthan. The sect is based on Hindu practices but does not accept the authority of the VEDAS, and includes people of all religions. Meditative and YOGA practices are prescribed, as well as vegetarianism and refraining from smoking and alcohol. Family life does not have to be given up, though some take a vow of celibacy. Followers consist of both men and women, but the majority are women and since Dada Lekhraj's death, women head the sect and are its administrators. A Brahma Kumari spiritual university, Prajapita Brahma Kumari Ishwariya Vishva Vidyalaya, is located at Mt Abu, and there are more than 5000 centres in ninety-three countries, with over 7,00,000 followers all over the world (2005 figures).

Brahma Purana   A Sanskrit text, one of the eighteen major PURANAS of Hinduism. It is also called the *Adi Purana*, or first Purana, as it is first in the list of the eighteen Puranas. The introduction states that Lomaharshana narrated this Purana to RISHIS of the Naimisha forest, and it was earlier revealed by the god BRAHMA to DAKSHA. It begins with creation legends, a description of the MANVANTARAS and the history of the solar and lunar dynasties. Much of the remainder consists of MAHATMYAs or descriptions of sacred places, particularly in Utkala (Orissa). The *Gautamimahatmya* glorifies the sacred places on the river Godavari, and is often used as an independent text. The last section deals with sacred places on the river Balaja. The Purana has 25,000 verses and in its present form probably belongs to the thirteenth century.

Brahma Sutra   A Sanskrit text written by BADARAYANA, also known as the *Vedanta Sutra*. It has been assigned to various dates from 500 BCE to the first century CE, and according to tradition, Badarayana is identified with VYASA. The *Sutra* summarizes the main teachings of the UPANISHADS. The text refutes the views of the SAMKHYA and VAISHESHIKA philosophical systems, as well as of Jainism and Buddhism, and explains Vedantic philosophy, and the concept of BRAHMAN. Brahman, the infinite creator, develops into the world, but remains itself, unchanged and pure. It also describes the ATMAN, or individual soul, and its relationship with Brahman.

The short, terse sutras form a base for all the schools of VEDANTA, but have been interpreted differently by each of them.

Brahma Veda   Another name of the ATHARVA VEDA, the fourth of the VEDIC SAMHITAS.

brahmacharya   (1) The first of the four ASHRAMAS or stages of life of higher-caste Hindus, according to tradition. In this stage the student or brahmachari lives with a guru, serves him, and studies the VEDAS and other texts. This practice was common in ancient days, the young boy living with his guru till he reached manhood.

(2) One of the practices of YOGA. It is often taken as a synonym of celibacy, but literally means, 'to walk in the way of god', or 'to be conscious of god'. It is also a principle of Buddhism, Jainism and other Hindu systems.

Brahman   A Sanskrit term used in the UPANISHADS and other texts, signifying the essence of the world from which everything originates. The concept of Brahman has been interpreted in various ways, but is similar to that of the godhead. Brahman is the source of all, the One Truth, the underlying reality of the world. Everything emerges from, and returns to it. It is the creator of all, and permeates creation. Thus the *Taittiriya Upanishad* states: Brahman is 'that from which beings are born, that in which when born they live, and that into which they enter at their death.'

Brahman has no form or shape. It is eternal, infinite and always existed. The *KATHA UPANISHAD* says that, 'Brahman, the immortal, contains all worlds in it, and no one goes beyond it'. Brahman has never been created and can never be destroyed. This view of Brahman is common to most schools of philosophy, with subtle variations. The term is further explained in the context of its relationship with the individual soul and with the world. Thus in ADVAITA, Brahman is the same as the ATMAN or soul in every living being, while in other philosophies, there are different interpretations, corresponding to various concepts of the Atman. Brahman can limit itself and take the form of ISHVARA, or a personal deity. It can also be the cosmic soul, known as HIRANYAGARBHA. In some schools of Buddhism, Brahman is equated with Vijnana, or supreme intelligence.

brahmana   A member of the BRAHMANA CASTE. Most priests officiating at Hindu sacrifices come from this caste. In ancient days, brahman referred to one of the four main priests who performed Vedic sacrifices, the others being the ADHVARYU, HOTR and UDGATR.

brahmana caste   One of the four main CASTES in Hinduism. Brahmanas form the highest caste, their traditional role being one of knowledge of the VEDAS and other sacred texts, the performance of sacrifices or YAJNAS, and of various ceremonies related to birth, marriage and death. Ancient texts prescribe several rules according to which a brahmana must live. Brahmanas are usually vegetarians and follow strict rules regarding food, as well as various rituals to maintain their purity. Originally, they were purohitas or court priests, and advisors to kings. They were also temple priests, gurus and teachers, who interpreted the ancient texts and had a role in formulating customary laws. Today many brahmanas have modernized and entered all professions, but some still retain their traditional customs and roles.

Their privileged position led to some anti-brahmana movements, among which was the DRAVIDIAN MOVEMENT in the south. More recently, reservations for lower castes have also led to a reduction in their privileges.

There are several subsects among brahmanas, and ten major divisions, based originally on their region of origin. These are the Sarasvata, Kannauj, Maithil, Utkal, Gauda, Maharashtra, Karnataka, Andhra, Dravida and Gurjara or Malabar.

Brahmanas   Vedic texts in Sanskrit that were probably composed between 1000 and 600 BCE. They are attached to the VEDIC SAMHITAS, i.e. the *RIG, SAMA, YAJUR* and *ATHARVA VEDAS*, and provide explanations of the VEDAS and guidance for the priests in sacrificial rituals. Among the Brahmanas are: the *Aitareya* and *Kaushitaki* , attached to the Rig Veda; the *Tandya* or *Panchavimsha*, the *Shadvimsha*, which includes *Adbhuta, Jaiminiya* or *Talavakra, Arsheya* and *Vamsha*, attached to the *Sama Veda*; the *Taittiriya*, of the *Black Yajur Veda* or *Taittiriya Samhita*, and the *Shatapatha Brahmana* of the *White Yajur Veda*. The *Shatapatha* has two different recensions, the Kanva and Madhyandina; the *Gopatha Brahmana* is attached to the *Atharva Veda*.

Brahmanaspati   A deity mentioned in the RIG VEDA. It is considered another name of BRIHASPATI.

Brahmanda   A term in Hindu mythology, meaning the egg of the god BRAHMA or the cosmic egg, representing the origin of the universe. According to the PURANAS, the Brahmanda is like the seed of the Kapittha (wood-apple) tree, covered by an egg-shell (anda-kataha). Around this is a shell of water, and over that a shell of fire. Around the fire-shell is a shell of air, and then a shell of space or ether (akasha). Two more shells surround this, of egoism and of intellect. The Brahmanda rests in PRAKRITI, divine nature, which contains several such eggs and permeates them all. At the beginning of the world the egg split and a child emerged, with the radiance of innumerable suns. This was the Virat Purusha, the first person, and from him the universe was born, with fourteen worlds or LOKAS. There are different versions of this myth in various PURANAS, as well as other accounts of creation.

Brahmanda Purana   A Sanskrit text, the last in the list of eighteen major PURANAS of Hinduism. It is said to have been narrated by VAYU. According to the *MATSYA PURANA*, the *Brahmanda Purana* has a description of the cosmic egg (BRAHMANDA) and an account of future KALPAS or ages, but the available text does not have much on this and consists mainly of MAHATMYAS or descriptions of sacred places. The *ADHYATMA RAMAYANA*, also used as a separate text, is considered a part of it.

Brahmani   A Hindu deity, the Shakti or feminine power of the god BRAHMA. She is one of the mother goddesses, or MATRIKAS, and is also known as Brahmi. As the wife of Brahma she is considered a form of SARASAVTI.

Brahmanism   A term which refers to the early stage of Hinduism, a period before the word Hindu became common. In a different context, it refers to the characteristic way of life of the BRAHMANA CASTE.

Brahmapuri The mythological city of the god BRAHMA, said to be located on the summit of Mt MERU. It had an area of 14,000 yojanas, and around it were the eight cities of the guardian deities, the DIKAPALAS. The river GANGA descends here, dividing into four streams: the Sita, ALAKANANDA, Chakshu and Bhadra.

Brahmavaivarta Purana A Sanskrit text, one of the eighteen major PURANAS of Hinduism. It was probably composed in the eighth century, though in its present form it is later. The Purana states that it was narrated by Savarna to NARADA, and has four books, or Kandas. The first deals with creation, where the creator, BRAHMA, is identified with KRISHNA. The second discusses PRAKRITI, the feminine aspect of creation, which is represented here by five goddesses, DURGA, LAKSHMI, SARASVATI, SAVITRI and RADHA. The third has legends of GANESHA, who is also connected with Krishna, whereas the fourth deals with Krishna's life, glorifying his relationship with RADHA.

Brahmo Samaj An organization for social and religious reform. It was founded by Ram Mohan ROY at Kolkata (Calcutta) on 20 August 1828, and since then has gone through several phases.

First phase: The first phase was closely linked with the ideals of its founder. Ram Mohan Roy was a great scholar who had studied the Vedas and Upanishads, as well as the main ideas of Islam and Christianity. He believed that Vedanta was the best philosophy, and was inspired by Christian concepts. The Samaj put forward the idea of one universal God, and the equality of all. Initially, it mainly attracted the upper-caste intellectuals of Bengal, though it was open to people of all castes and religions.

In its religious aspect, the Samaj propagated the ideas of the Vedas and the Upanishads. The Samaj also advocated social reforms, including the abolition of SATI, child marriage and polygamy. It attempted to improve the position of women, and was against CASTE. Ram Mohan Roy promoted these views through several magazines, including the *Samvad Kaumudi*. After his departure for England in 1830, and his death there in 1833, the organization declined, but was revived by Debendranath TAGORE.

Second phase: Debendranath was formally initiated into the Samaj in 1843, though he had been associated with it from 1842. He explained its principles in the *Tattva Bodhini Patrika* and clearly laid out the theological base of the organization. A new system of initiation and membership was started, which gave each Brahmo member a sense of belonging. The concept of the infallibility of the Vedas, which existed earlier, was now dropped after the objection of some rationalist members.

Debendranath formulated the Brahmo creed, and the promises to be made at the time of initiation.

He wrote a book *Brahmo Dharma*, explaining both ethics and theology. Debendranath's work revitalized the Sabha and brought in new members. However, he limited the activity related to social reform, and was opposed by Keshab Chandra SEN and others.

Sen had joined the Sabha in 1857, and initially was very close to Debendranath. In 1864 he visited different parts of India, and spread the message of the Samaj outside Bengal. He aimed at a Brahmo organization which would conduct its own inter-caste and community marriages. Sen also wanted to integrate the true spirit of Christ into the Brahmo movement and was keen on bringing about a social revolution within Hinduism. Debendranath and some other Brahmos could not accept his radical ideas.

Third phase: The organization then split into two groups in November 1866, with the Adi Brahmo Samaj under Debendranath, and the Brahmo Samaj of India under Keshab Chandra Sen. Debendranath retired from active work, and appointed Raj Narain Bose as the president. Later, under the influence of Rabindranath Tagore, this section of the Samaj gained new life. The Brahmo Samaj of India retained many of the original ideas, but began a new programme of spiritual and social reform. The Samaj emphasized women's education and development, and the abolition of all caste. This led to the foundation of the Indian Reform Association in 1870, and the Indian Marriage Act in 1872, which permitted inter-caste marriage. Simultaneously Keshab Chandra was changing the spiritual nature of the organization, incorporating the symbols and ideas of other religions, including Christianity, Islam and Buddhism. Younger members began to have differences with him, and wanted a more democratic constitution for the Samaj. In addition, they opposed the marriage of his young daughter to the prince of Koch Bihar, against the tenets of the Indian Marriage Act and the spirit of social reform.

Fourth phase: In 1878, another split took place in the Brahmo Samaj of India, and the Sadharan Brahmo Samaj emerged under younger leaders.

Keshab Chandra's group was now known as the Nava Vidhan (New Dispensation), and had a missionary zeal with Christian influence. It had a new emblem, incorporating the symbols of Christianity, Islam, Buddhism and Hinduism, and new methods of worship. Missionaries were known as Apostles and members could take special vows, such as the vow of poverty or the vow of self-surrender.

Fifth phase: Later, some attempts at unity were made with the founding of the Brahmo Sammilan Samaj in 1902, so that memebers of the different Samajes could join together for worship and welfare activities. Chittaranjan Das (1870–1925) was one of the key people who organized this. By this time, the Brahmo Samaj and its offshoots had spread from Kolkata to various parts of India. In Mumbai

(Bombay) it inspired a movement known as the PRARTHANA SAMAJ.

The three main branches of the Brahmo still exist. Members of the Brahmo Samaj are liberal and secular, but the movement has a limited role today.

Brahmottara Purana   A supplement or concluding section of the BRAHMA PURANA.

Brethren Assembly   A Christian sect or denomination introduced in India in the nineteenth century, soon after it was initiated in England and Ireland. In the early nineteenth century, there was a move to return to the equality and simplicity of the days of Christ. Groups of people came together to pray regardless of social differences, and were known as the Brethren. They believed there was no need for ordained priests as intermediaries, because St. Peter had said that all who recognize JESUS as their saviour form a 'royal priesthood'. In 1827 four people assembled in Dublin, Ireland, for 'the breaking of the bread' without a priest. This soon became a movement which spread rapidly through the world and was introduced in India in 1835 by Antony Norris Groves, a dentist from England who first went to Baghdad before reaching India. He worked as a missionary in Bihar, Andhra Pradesh and Tamil Nadu. The Brethren also spread to Karnataka and Bengal, and later to Kerala.

In 1848 two groups developed: the Exclusive and the Open Brethren. Those in India mainly belong to the Open Brethren. They believe in the BIBLE as the 'only infallible rule of faith and practice' and Jesus as the sole and sufficient saviour. In these aspects they are EVANGELICAL in their understanding of Christianity. Overall they cultivate an atmosphere of brotherly love, along with spiritual and intellectual freedom, and have no ordained ministers. Each church is autonomous, though there is some coordination of activities. According to estimates there are more than 2000 Brethren churches in India.

Brihad Devata   A Sanskrit text of about the fifth century CE assigned to the rishi Shaunaka. It describes the deities to whom the hymns of the RIG VEDA are addressed, and includes myths and legends pertaining to them.

Brihadaranyaka Upanishad   An UPANISHAD attached to the *Shatapatha Brahmana*, which is ascribed to the rishi YAJNAVALKYA. This is one of the longest and earliest Upanishads, dating to around 600 BCE. It has six chapters, normally divided into three kandas or sections of two chapters each, and is one of the Upanishads with a commentary by SHANKARA. The first section, Madhu Kanda, begins with the symbolism of the ASHVAMEDHA or horse sacrifice, and also deals with other sacrifices, creation, and the knowlegde of the Self. The second section, Yajnavalkya Kanda, or Muni Kanda, describes the teachings of the rishi Yajnavalkya. The third section, Khila Kanda, has miscellaneous items on BRAHMAN or the Absolute,

as well as various meditations. This Upanishad is an important Vedantic text.

Brihaddharma Purana   A Sanskrit text, an Upapurana or minor PURANA of Hinduism. It deals mainly with DHARMA, or duties to both gurus and parents, and of the various CASTES. The AVATARAS of VISHNU are described, and there is a section on the worship of the river GANGA.

Brihadeshvara Temple   A temple of the Hindu god SHIVA located at THANJAVUR in Tamil Nadu. It was constructed in 1010 by the Chola king, Rajaraja I and is also known as the Rajarajeshvara temple. The temple is built in Dravida style and is in the centre of a rectangular court, entered through two gateways on the east. The inner shrine or GARBHA-GRIHA is square, and within it is a large LINGA, 3.66 m high, standing on a circular pedestal. The linga was brought from the river Narmada. Around the shrine, a narrow passageway divided into chambers has SHAIVITE sculptures on the walls. This leads into an ante-chamber and then into a long columned MANDAPA, which opens onto a porch. There are sculptures on the walls of the mandapa, which include Shiva in various forms, as well as paintings in soft, gentle colours. Some of the paintings date to the later Nayaka period, partially hiding the earlier artwork. The VIMANA or tower above the garbha-griha reaches the immense height of 61 m and has a dome made of a single block of stone, weighing 81 tonnes. It has been estimated that to raise it to that height, it had to be dragged up a specially constructed incline, starting 6½ km away. It is constructed so that the shadow of the cupola never falls on the ground. In front of the temple is a monolithic NANDI image, 6 m long, 2.6 m broad and 3.7 m tall, enclosed in a sixteenth-century pavilion. To the north-west is a shrine of Subrahmanya, a name of KARTTIKEYA in south India.

Brihannaradiya Purana   A Sanskrit text, one of the eighteen major PURANAS of Hinduism. It is often called the NARADIYA PURANA, though there is also another minor Purana with that name. As usual, the Purana begins with a discussion of the rishis in the Naimisha forest. A huge gathering of rishis has collected there, to debate and understand dharma, artha and kama, and the attainment of moksha. The rishi Shaunaka suggests they go to Siddhashrama, where Suta, son of Lomaharshana is conducting a sacrifice. They ask Suta to instruct them, and he tells them about a dialogue between the rishi NARADA and SANAT KUMARA. Narada explains the merits of devotion to the god VISHNU.

In the beginning, there was only Mahavishnu, the supreme being beyond form, permeating everything. At the time of creation the three gods Brahma, Vishnu, and Shiva, representing the three gunas of sattva, rajas and tamas, emerged from him. These three gods are said to be equal, and whoever differentiates between them, goes to hell. Shakti, the female energy of Mahavishnu, who is known by many different names, permeates the whole world, and is equally important. Thus Brahma with Sarasvati, creates, Vishnu and Lakshmi preserve creation, and Shiva and Parvati destroy it. The combined Shakti is the same as Prakriti and Mahamaya (illusion).

This Purana has several different aspects, but is primarily a work extolling Vishnu-bhakti. There are passages on the duties of the castes, a description of the manvantaras and yugas, as well as various stories and legends, including that of Markandeya, King Sagara, Mahabali, the birth of Vamana, and others. According to tradition it has 25,000 verses, though available manuscripts have far less.

Brihaspati (1) A Hindu deity first described in the RIG VEDA. Born from great light in the highest heaven, he drove away the darkness with thunder. He was seven-mouthed and seven-rayed, blue-backed, clear-voiced, bright and pure, with a hundred wings. His bow has *rita* or cosmic order as its string, his chariot is drawn by ruddy steeds. In some hymns he is identified with AGNI. He is sometimes called Brahmanaspati. In the BRAHMANAS he is connected with Vedic rituals, but later declined in importance.

(2) In later times, Brihaspati was identified with the planet of the same name, equated with Jupiter. He is thus one of the NAVAGRAHA or nine planets and is represented in temples on Navagraha panels. The AGNI PURANA states that his images should be adorned with a necklace of Rudraksha beads. Brihaspati's chariot is called Nitighosha and is drawn by eight pale horses. In early reliefs, Brihaspati was two-handed, sometimes holding a rosary and a water pot. In modern temples and art, he is depicted dressed in yellow and seated on a lotus, or in his chariot. He has four arms and holds a mace, a rosary and a sphere or water-pot. As Jupiter, Brihaspati is the lord of Brihaspativara, or Thursday. However, myths and legends of him are not the same as those of the Western Jupiter.

(3) Brihaspati is also a RISHI or sage. In the later VEDAS he is known as a *purohita* or priest, who awakens the gods with AGNI or fire. In the MAHABHARATA and the PURANAS, Brihaspati, one of the sons of ANGIRAS, is the teacher of the DEVAS. In some texts he is the son of AGNI. His wife, Tara, was very beautiful, and fell in love with CHANDRA, the moon, and BUDHA (Mercury) was born to them. A war took place over this, and finally Tara returned to Brihaspati. SHUKRA was the teacher of the ASURAS, and Brihaspati once impersonated him and taught the Asuras for ten years. One of Brihaspati's sons was Kacha, with whom Shukra's daughter, Deviyani fell in love.

(4) Brihaspati is said to have founded the materialistic (CHARVAKA) school of philosophy.

Brihaspati is known by other names, including Jiva (the living), and Dhishana (the intelligent).

Brihat Samhita An encyclopedic Sanskrit text written by VARAHAMIHIRA in the sixth century. It includes information on astrology and the effects of the movement of planets, as well as on geography, architecture, the methods for installing images of Hindu deities, their consecration and identifying characteristics, and other miscellaneous topics.

Bstangyur A collection of Tibetan Buddhist texts, also spelt TANGYUR or Tanjur.

Buddha A Sanskrit/Pali word meaning 'one who is enlightened or awakened'. It is used as a title for those who are said to have reached or realized this stage. Though it is primarily used for the historic BUDDHA, GAUTAMA Siddhartha or SHAKYAMUNI, there are several other BUDDHAS within Buddhism. Some Jain texts also refer to MAHAVIRA as a Buddha, and it has been used for others as well.

Buddha, bodies of A concept in Buddhism, which states that a BUDDHA has both physical and non-physical bodies. According to the THERAVADA school, there are two bodies, the rupakaya (physical) and the dharmakaya (body of truth). After passing to NIRVANA, the rupakaya remains in the Buddha's relics, and the dharmakaya in his teachings. The idea was furher developed in MAHAYANA and VAJRAYANA Buddhism, particularly in the YOGACHARA school, and the concept of trikaya (three bodies) emerged. According to the TRIKAYA theory, the Buddha has three bodies revealed in different ways. The initiate sees the NIRMANAKAYA, the physical body in which the BUDDHA appeared on earth. Once on the BODHISATTVA path, the SAMBHOGAKAYA, the enjoyment or bliss body, a glorious form in which BUDDHAS of other worlds appear, can be seen in visions. In the final stage, the DHARMAKAYA, or dharma-body, the true Buddha nature, the origin or source of all, is reached.

Buddha Charita A Buddhist text composed by ASHVAGHOSHA in the first century. Written in Sanskrit verse, it is a biography of the BUDDHA. The whole text is available in Chinese and Tibetan, while the first half is preserved in the original Sanskrit.

Buddha, disciples of The BUDDHA had a number of disciples, but some of them are better known. Among these were: ANANDA, his cousin and beloved disciple; ANATHAPINDIKA, a wealthy banker; Vishakha, a respectable housewife; Amrapali, a courtesan; BIMBISARA, a king; Kaundinya, the first to be admitted to the SANGHA; SHARIPUTRA, master of wisdom; MAUDGALYAYANA; Upali, expert in the monastic code; MAHAPRAJAPATI, the first woman in the Sangha; Yasha, the first householder to receive full initiation.

Buddha, Gautama The founder of the religion later known as Buddhism. He was also known as SHAKYAMUNI. There is some controversy about the date of his birth. Many Western and Indian scholars take the date of his birth as c. 566 BCE, and of his death, 486 BCE. Buddhists in Sri Lanka and Southeast Asia generally follow traditionally accepted dates of 624

BCE for his birth and 564 BCE for his death. Several Japanese scholars take the date of his birth as 448 and of his death as 368 BCE. These various dates are based on chronologies given in different sources.

The story of Gautama Buddha's life as given in Buddhist texts is as follows: His father was Shudhodana, the king of Kapilavastu in present Nepal, a KSHATRIYA of the Shakya clan, and his mother was MAHAMAYA. Ten lunar months after she conceived a child, Mahamaya set off for her parents home in Devadaha. On the way, she passed through the garden of LUMBINI. At night she dreamt that an elephant, white as silver, entered her side, and the next day, a son was born to her in Lumbini. The place of birth was later marked by a pillar set up by the Mauryan emperor ASHOKA, and is today known as Rummindei. Mahamaya's dream was interpreted to mean that the child would either be a great sage or a great emperor, but the sage Asita, King Shudhodana's priest, saw the new-born child and knew he would be a BUDDHA. On the fifth day of the child's birth 108 BRAHMANAS were invited for the name-giving ceremony, and some again predicted that he would either be a king or a Buddha. The child was named Siddhartha. On the seventh day, his mother died. King Shudhodana married Mahamaya's sister, MAHAPRAJAPATI Gautami, who brought up Siddhartha with great love and affection. Thus he came to be known as Gautama or 'Gautamiputra', i.e. the son of Gautami. His father tried to make sure the child had every luxury and remained within the kingdom, so that he might influence him to become a king. In the *ANGUTTARA NIKAYA*, the Buddha is reported to have described his early life: 'I was delicately nurtured . . . I had three palaces, one for winter, one for summer and one for the rainy season . . . in the rainy season . . . entertained only by female musicians, I did not come down from the palace.'

At the age of sixteen Siddhartha was married to his cousin YASHODHARA. He continued to live in protected seclusion, until, at the age of twenty-nine, driving out with his charioteer Channa, he saw four sights on four consecutive days, The first three were an old decrepit man, a sick man and a corpse. Channa explained to him that everyone grew old some day, got sick in various ways, and finally died. Siddhartha was disturbed, but the fourth sight gave him hope: a peaceful and serene ascetic wandering alone, dressed in yellow robes.

That same day a son was born to him, and he named him RAHULA (rope or fetter). However, Siddhartha was determined to leave home to discover the Truth, the reason for suffering, and the way to overcome it. One night he left the palace, cut off his long hair, changed into a mendicant's robes, and began his search. He studied YOGA and meditation from two hermits, but then wandered on. For a while he practised severe asceticism, hardly eating, but realized that weakening his physical and mental faculties would not help. He

began to eat again, and soon understood that the time for his awakening had come. Seating himself beneath the sacred BODHI TREE, where all former BUDDHAS had attained enlightenment, he resolved not to rise till he had reached his goal.

Then MARA, the evil one, came to prevent him. He attacked Siddhartha with thunder, lightening and darkness, and when that did not disturb him, presented him with his three beautiful daughters to tempt him. Mara then told him that his wife, child and father were in danger, but Siddhartha, protected only by his virtue, did not move. Entering successively deeper states of contemplation, he finally gained enlightenment, and became a Buddha.

Initially he did not want to reveal what he had learnt, knowing it was difficult to put his knowledge and understanding into words and thus convey it to others, but he realized it was his duty to try. The Buddha then preached his first sermon at SARNATH, and thus began the 'turning of the wheel of law', DHARMACHAKRA-PRAVARTANA, the teaching of the DHARMA.

For the next forty-five years the Buddha continued to teach, established the SANGHA or community of monks and nuns, and gathered a large number of disciples. In his eightieth year he fell ill, and knew the time had come for him to leave the body. He told ANANDA and others to follow the dharma, the eternal law, and make the Self the refuge. He passed on to NIRVANA at KUSHINAGARA (identified with Kasia in eastern Uttar Pradesh).

Buddha Jayanti/Buddha Purnima A Buddhist festival celebrated in April/May on the full moon day of the month of Vaishakha. The BUDDHA is said to have been born on this day probably in 566 BCE. According to tradition, he also attained enlightenment on this day, and in 486 BCE attained NIRVANA on the same day. Buddhists celebrate this day with prayers and chants, visits to sacred places, gifts of charity to monks and others, as well as by setting free caged birds and saving animals from slaughter. Various countries where Buddhism is practised, celebrate this day with different rituals, but all offer prayers for the welfare of the world. In primarily Buddhist countries, streets, houses and temples are illuminated and decorated and scenes from Jataka stories are depicted.

In India, special celebrations take place at Bodh Gaya, Kushinara and Sarnath. In Sri Lanka and Malaysia the festival is known as Vesak or Wesak, while other countries have other names. It is also celebrated by Buddhists in Sri Lanka, Bhutan, Cambodia, China, Japan, Korea, Mongolia, Myanmar, Nepal, Thailand, Vietnam, and Western countries. The exact date of the festival varies slightly according to the lunar calendar used.

Buddhabhadra A Buddhist monk of the SARVASTIVADA school who lived between 359 and 429. In 409, he travelled from Kashmir to China, where he stayed for several years, translating Buddhist texts into Chinese.

Buddhadatta A Buddhist scholar who lived in the fourth or fifth century. One text states that he was born at Uragapura, a town in south India, and entered a monastery in Sri Lanka. He wrote commentaries on Buddhist texts, and his works include the *Vinaya-vinichchaya* and the *Abhidhamma-vatara*, a commentary on the ABHIDHAMMA PITAKA.

Buddhaghosha A Buddhist scholar who lived in the fourth-fifth century. Not much is known of his life, but he was probably born in India, either at BODH GAYA or in the Andhra region or further south. He went to Anuradhapura (Sri Lanka) and lived in a VIHARA to study the THERAVADA texts that were best preserved there. He then wrote the *Visuddhimagga* (The Path to Purity), an encyclopedic text in PALI bringing together various Pali texts and other sources. His other works include the *Samantapasadika*, a voluminous commentary on the VINAYA PITAKA; the *Kankhavitarani* on the Patimokha portion of the *Vinaya*; the *Sumangavilasini* on the DIGHA NIKAYA; the *Papanchasudani* on the MAJJHIMA NIKAYA; the *Saratthappakasini* on the SAMYUTTA NIKAYA; and the *Manoratha-purani* on the ANGUTTARA NIKAYA. All these, he states, were translations of the commentaries in Sinhala, which were composed by Mahinda, the son of the emperor ASHOKA, who took Buddhism to Sri Lanka in the third century BCE.

He is also said to have written commentaries on all the seven texts of the Pali ABHIDHAMMA PITAKA, though some scholars doubt whether these commentaries were his. Texts attributed to him are the *Atthasalini*, a commentary on the *Dhammsangani*; the *Samohavinodani*, a commentary on the *Vibhanga*; and *Panchappakaranattha-katha* on the rest of the texts of the *Abhidhamma*.

Political turmoil caused him to leave Anuradhapura. Some texts say he returned to India, others that he went to Myanmar.

Buddhapalita A Buddhist philosopher who founded the PRASANGIKA school, a branch of the MADHYAMIKA school of MAHAYANA Buddhism. Born in south India, he lived from c. 470 to 540. He is said to have meditated on the Bodhisattva MANJUSHRI and obtained the highest knowledge. He also attained various SIDDHIS, or supernatural powers.

He wrote commentaries on the works of NAGARJUNA and ARYADEVA. Of these, only one has survived, the *Mulamadhyamakavritti* on the *Mulamadhyamaka-karika* of Nagarjuna.

Buddhas Apart from the historic BUDDHA, there are several other types of Buddhas.

Buddhas of the past and future: The *Mahavadana Sutta*, an early text, refers to six Buddhas before Gautama or SHAKYAMUNI. Each of their life stories was similar to that of the historic Buddha. Buddha Konakamana was his immediate predecessor.

The concept of earlier Buddhas must have been prevalent by the third century BCE, because ASHOKA mentions Konakamana in one of his inscriptions. The BUDDHAVAMSHA, a later text, describes the lives of twenty-four previous Buddhas. Certain principles were stated about when and where Buddhas could be born. These are: (1) There can be only one Buddha in the world at a time; the next arises after the truths he taught have been forgotten. (2) Buddhas are not born at the beginning of a KALPA when people live like gods; there would be no need of them, nor would they then have insight into the nature of suffering and impermanence. (3) Buddhas are born only in Jambudvipa, i.e., the region in which India is located.

Apart from Buddhas of the past, there are future Buddhas too. The Bodhisattva MAITREYA, already existing in another dimension, will be the future Buddha.

Celestial Buddhas: Buddhas are also said to exist in other worlds and can provide help to those who pray to them. Some texts put forward the concept of integrated Buddha pantheons, emanating from primordial Buddhas who are the essence or source of cosmic Buddhas. Primordial Buddhas named in different texts are Vajradhara, ADI BUDDHA and Vairochana. An infinite number of Buddhas can emanate from these, but some are more important. VAIROCHANA, AKSHOBHYA, RATNASAMBHAVA, AMITABHA and AMOGHASIDDHI head families of Buddhist deities. These are also called DHYANI BUDDHAS, though this term is not used in texts.

Living Buddhas: In MAHAYANA and VAJRAYANA Buddhism, Buddhas who gained enlightenment when alive, or who are considered incarnations of celestial Buddhas, are recognized as 'living Buddhas'. Prominent among these are PADMASAMBHAVA, who took Buddhism to Tibet, and Kukai, the founder of Shingon Buddhism in Japan.

Solitary Buddhas: Among other types of Buddhas are Pratyeka Buddhas or 'solitary Buddhas', who gain enlightenment on their own and do not teach others.

Essential similarity of Buddhas: All schools and sects of Buddhism recognize the essential identity of all Buddhas. Reflecting this, a passage in the *MILINDA PANHA* says, 'There is no distinction in form, morality, concentration, wisdom, or freedom . . . among all the Buddhas, because all Buddhas are the same in respect to their nature'.

Buddhavamsha A HINAYANA Buddhist text that forms part of the *KHUDDAKA NIKAYA* of the PALI CANON. It consists of stories of the twenty-four BUDDHAS who are said to have preceded the historic BUDDHA. The narrator is Gautama Buddha, who recalls his past lives in the days of the previous Buddhas. It is one of the late products of Pali literature, in which the Buddha is deified and worshipped.

buddhi A Sanskrit term indicating higher knowledge or intelligence. It is an important term in early philosophical traditions.

Buddhism Buddhism covers a number of diverse ideas which have BUDDHA as the main theme. Out of the vast number of texts and ideas, the basics of Buddhism are found in the PALI CANON, consisting of the early teachings of the historic Buddha. These basic teachings consist of the FOUR NOBLE TRUTHS on suffering and its cause, and the EIGHTFOLD PATH, which is the way to liberation. Other early concepts include the impermanence of everything (anichcha, ANITYA). Not realizing this truth, people are caught in ignorance and sorrow. There is no permanent individual self, this is another delusion. Thus the BUDDHA put forward the concept of anatta (ANATMAN) or non-ego, and of the five aggregates (SKANDHAS) which create human existence. Related to this is the law of dependent origination, or patichcha samutpada (PRATITYA-SAMUTPADA), in which one state of being arises out of the previous state. Understanding these basic concepts, and following the Eightfold Path, enlightenment can be reached. The SANGHA, or community, provided the means to reach the goal. The Buddha accepted certain prevailing beliefs, such as those of KARMA, rebirth and SAMSARA. Early Buddhism, incorporating these basic ideas, is known as HINAYANA BUDDHISM, though within this there were several different schools and variations. A later development was MAHAYANA BUDDHISM, which retained the basic principles and ideas but in addition had certain other aspects. Two key themes were the ideal of the BODHISATTVA and the incorporation of a number of BUDDHIST DEITIES, along with more complex philosophical concepts. Mahayana Buddhism also had different schools of thought. VAJRAYANA BUDDHISM then arose, along with TANTRIC practices. Each of these historical stages is seen as a valid expression of Buddhist ideas.

BUSTON (1290–364) and TARANATHA (1574–1608), two early historians of Buddhism, divided its development into three periods. These were: (1) THERAVADA, the way of the elders, and SARVASTIVADA, which emphasized the idea of no-soul; (2) MADHYAMIKA, the middle way, in which the doctrine of SHUNYATA was important; (3) VIJNANAVADA (consciousness school), which was idealistic. The first period corresponds with the Hinayana, and the second and third with the Mahayana.

Buddhism had a unique path of development in each of the countries where it spread. It had been established in Sri Lanka by the third century BCE and reached China by the early centuries CE. In the sixth century it was in Japan, and in the seventh century began to be established in Tibet. Buddhism spread to Myanmar, Korea, Thailand, Vietnam, Cambodia and elsewhere, and is still a major religion in most of these countries. In Sri Lanka, Thailand, and some other South-east Asian countries, Hinayana systems are popular. Mahayana is prevalent in Vietnam, Korea and Japan, along with some elements of Vajrayana. Mahayana was once prominent in China but declined particularly after the Cultural Revolution, though there has been some revival recently. Tibet, now part of China, is predominantly Vajrayana, mixed with local elements.

In modern times, NEO-BUDDHIST sects have emerged in India, other Asian countries, and the West.

Buddhism in India Buddhism originated in India and spread from here to other parts of the world. Though the BUDDHA was born in what is now Nepal, he lived and preached mainly in present-day Bihar and eastern Uttar Pradesh. He developed his new philosophy against the background of prevailing ideas and philosophical systems. While the UPANISHADS presented concepts of Oneness and liberation, there were at the same time Vedic sacrifices and a CASTE system that was growing increasingly rigid. Around the sixth century BCE, several sects arose among which Jainism and Buddhism developed into major religions. By the time of the BUDDHA'S death around 486 BCE, his teachings already had a large following, and the SANGHA or monastic system was well established. Further developments included the four BUDDHIST COUNCILS, which were held over the next few hundred years. The patronage of ASHOKA, the Mauryan emperor, helped to spread Buddhism. By the first century BCE, there were about thirty different sects and schools within HINAYANA BUDDHISM. Buddhist STUPAS, CHAITYAS and VIHARAS or monasteries were constructed in several parts of India. Many of them were cave temples, cut into the sides of rocky hills.

MAHAYANA BUDDHISM began to emerge from the first century CE, while the origins of VAJRAYANA can be traced to the fourth century. Buddhism continued to develop in India and large monasteries such as that of NALANDA was established, though between the third and seventh centuries, visiting Chinese pilgrims FA-HSIEN, XUAN ZANG and others, recorded some decline. In the sixth century, the Huna invaders destroyed some monasteries, but Buddhism revived under HARSHA in the seventh century. After this the Pala kings of Bihar and Bengal (c. 650–900) were the main patrons of Buddhism and founded the monasteries of VIKRAMSHILA and Odantapura. By around the twelfth century, Buddhist monks and monasteries were few. Some have related this to the advent of Islam, accompanied by a decline in moral standards in the Buddhist viharas. However, more important reasons were the challenge presented by SHANKARA in the ninth century, and the spread of VAISHNAVISM and SHAIVISM through the BHAKTI saints of south India, as well as the development of Shaivism in Kashmir.

After the decline of Buddhism in most of India, there was a revival in some of the Himalayan regions under the influence of Tibet. In the ninth century, Buddhism declined in Tibet, but revived in the eleventh century under Ye-she-od, the lama king of Guge in western

Tibet. He sent RINCHEN ZANGPO to build monasteries and temples and collect and study Buddhist texts, and a number of monasteries in the LAHAUL AND SPITI region of Himachal and in LADAKH were constructed at this time. Some of these still exist. The Tibetan form of Buddhism also existed in Sikkim, Bhutan and Nepal.

In the late nineteenth century, attempts were made to revive Buddhism in India. Madame BLAVATSKY and Col Olcott of the Theosophical Society went to Sri Lanka and converted to Buddhism there. With the founding of the THEOSOPHICAL SOCIETY OF INDIA, Madame Blavatsky and later Annie BESANT promoted indigenous religions. Lama ANAGARIKA DHARMAPALA of Sri Lanka founded the MAHABODHI SOCIETY OF INDIA in 1891 and worked to repair and restore Buddhist sites.

After Independence in 1947, Buddhism began to grow in India for a number of reasons. One was the conversion of AMBEDKAR and his followers to Buddhism in 1956. Such conversions continued over the years, leading to an increase in the number of Buddhists. Another major reason is that, with persecution in Tibet after 1959, TIBETAN BUDDHISM returned to India, and is practised here in its many forms. Tibetan monasteries were refounded in India, and a new impetus was also provided to existing Buddhists in Himachal and Ladakh.

In recent years, without any official conversion, some Buddhist sects from Japan are becoming increasingly popular in India. These include the SOKA GAKKAI, based on the teachings of the thirteenth-century Japanese, Nichiren Daishonin, as well as various systems of Buddhist meditation. Healing systems such as REIKI, which has Buddhist origins, are also proliferating.

The growth of Buddhism can be seen in the census statistics from 1951 onwards: there were 16,70,000 Buddhists in 1951, 32,56,000 in 1961, 38,12,325 in 1971, 47,19,796 in 1981, 63,87,500 in 1991 and 79,55,207 in 2001.

Buddhist art Buddhist art developed gradually over time. After the BUDDHA died, his relics were preserved in funerary mounds around which STUPAS were later constructed. More stupas were built at sacred sites, and ASHOKA, the Mauryan emperor of the third century BCE, had a number of stupas constructed (according to tradition, a total of 84,000). By the seond century BCE, additions were made to the stupas at BHARHUT, SANCHI and elsewhere, in the form of gateways and railings. These were elaborately carved with scenes from the JATAKAS and stories of the life of the Buddha. Trees, people, YAKSHAS and YAKSHIS were shown, but the first visual representations of the Buddha were in the form of a stupa, tree, empty throne or some other symbol. The anthropomorphic stage, with the Buddha depicted in human form begins only in the third century BCE. By this time several Buddhist CHAITYAS, stupas and VIHARAS were cut into rocky hillsides. Caves along the Western Ghats dated between the second century BCE and the second century CE have been found at BEDSA, BHAJA, KARLE, Kondana, KANHERI, JUNNAR and other

sites. Most of these mark passes and routes; possibly Buddhists located them here for the convenience of travellers, or were themselves involved in trade.

In the first century CE, two distinctive schools of Buddhist art, known as the MATHURA and GANDHARA schools, existed. The first was indigenous, while the latter was influenced by Graeco-Roman forms. By the fourth and fifth centuries, Buddhist art had reached its height, its best representation being in the serene and graceful Buddha images at SARNATH and the exquisite paintings in the caves of AJANTA. MAHAYANA Buddhism had emerged, and stone and terracotta images of BUDDHAS, BODHISATTVAS and various BUDDHIST DEITIES were made. After the seventh century, Buddhist art developed under the Pala dynasty in eastern India. In VAJRAYANA Buddhism more complex images were depicted in sculpture and in paintings. Though Buddhism had declined in most of India by the twelfth century, Buddhist art continued to develop in the monasteries of LADAKH in Kashmir, and LAHAUL AND SPITI in Himachal. From the beginning of the twentieth century, attempts were made to reconstruct sacred Buddhist centres. Tibetan Buddhists who came to India after 1959 built new monasteries with Buddhist images of the Vajrayana school. Complex paintings with Buddhist themes, known as THANGKAS, have been made. New stupas and images have been erected, both by Tibetan Buddhists and by Buddhists from other countries, and the rich tradition of Buddhist art continues in monasteries in India. Neo-Buddhists also install images of AMBEDKAR, who is often referred to as a Bodhisattva.

Buddhist councils According to tradition, four Buddhist councils were held to put together the Buddhist scriptures and formulate rules for the SANGHA.

The first council was held at RAJAGRIHA in the kingdom of MAGADHA (present Rajgir in Bihar) soon after the BUDDHA'S death, at the time of King AJATASHATRU. Already there were misinterpretations of the DHAMMA, and the venerable monk Mahakassapa called a council of leading monks. At the council, the Dhamma was recited by ANANDA, and the VINAYA by the monk UPALI.

The second council was held at VAISHALI, one hundred years after the death of the Buddha. By this time several differences had arisen among the monks. The Vajjian monks of Vaishali, known as the Easterners, had started certain practices which were considered unorthodox, such as eating after mid-day, having a second meal, drinking toddy and accepting gold and silver. There were ten such practices, and Yasha, a western monk who visited Vaishali, declared them immoral. The Vajjian monks therefore expelled him from the Sangha. Yasha then invited all the monks of the west and the south to discuss the issue, and a council of 700 monks was held. They declared the conduct of the Vajjian monks wrong, and the Dhamma and Vinaya were again recited. At this council, or soon after, a major schism took place in the order, during which the MAHASANGHIKAS separated from the rest. According to some scholars, there was another, non-canonical council held at PATALIPUTRA at the time of Mahapadma Nanda (ruled from 360 BCE), when the schism took place.

The third council was held at Pataliputra during the reign of ASHOKA. It is not mentioned in the PALI CANON, but in other texts such as the *DIPAVAMSHA* and *MAHAVAMSHA*. By this time there were many different sects. With the conversion of wealthy people, as well as royal patronage, the monasteries had become prosperous. People who had lost their income and honour began to join the Sangha without any belief in the Dhamma. A council of 1,000 learned monks was held to help restore the purity of the teachings. Monks had to declare that they followed the Vibhajyavada (translated as distinctionist, or doctrine of analysis), probably the same as the THERAVADA. After this, Mahinda and Sanghamitta, the son and daughter of Ashoka, went to Sri Lanka to spread the teachings.

The fourth council was held during the reign of KANISHKA, around 100 CE. According to some accounts, it took place in Jalandhara, and according to others in Kashmir or at Purushapura in GANDHARA. Only northern Buddhists were involved in it, and Vibhashashastras, or commentaries on the Pitakas, were said to have been composed. Monks of the SARVASTIVADA school probably dominated the council. Around the same time a new Sarvastivada *Vinaya Pitaka* was written, as well as the *Mahavibhasha* on the *Jnanaprasthana* of the *ABHIDHARMA PITAKA*.

Some scholars doubt the existence of the third and fourth councils, but it is likely that they did take place.

Buddhist deities

The BUDDHA himself did not speak about god. Initially, even the Buddha was revered as an enlightened being and not a god, but gradually he began to be worshipped. Local deities were soon incorporated into Buddhism, and the concept of past and future BUDDHAS emerged. In MAHAYANA BUDDHISM, there are several Buddhist deities, and these became more complex and numerous in VAJRAYANA BUDDHISM. Chief among the deities, are the various types of Buddhas and BODHISATTVAS. In addition there are guardian and personal deities, female deities, and a number of local deities, including YAKSHAS and YAKSHIS. Hindu deities are also represented. In Vajrayana, there is a convenient grouping of deities into five Buddha families, headed by the five main celestial Buddhas emanating from the ADI BUDDHA. In TIBETAN BUDDHISM, there are also CHOEKYONG or protector deities, YIDAM or guardian deities, YAB-YUM or male and female deities together, and famous LAMAS, who are revered and worshipped.

But despite the number of deities, the word 'god' has a different meaning in Buddhism. Many of the Buddhist gods represent aspects present in people; personifying these makes it easier to meditate on or contemplate them. The Bodhisattva AVALOKITESHVARA, for instance, represents compassion, and meditating on him helps to develop this quality. Because of the complexity of human beings, there are innumerable deities representing different aspects of human character. However, this philosophical understanding is reserved for those on the higher stages of the path, whereas the ordinary individual derives comfort from worship and ritual, and views the deity as real.

According to some schools, the real truth of Buddhism is SHUNYATA or emptiness, and deities are only convenient forms that help people realize the truth.

Buddhist literature

The basic literature of Buddhism consists of the PALI CANON, or Tipitaka. However, Buddhist literature is extremely vast and is related to the various schools and sects of Buddhism. Broadly, it can be divided into HINYANA, MAHAYANA, TANTRIC and VAJRAYANA literature. In addition, new ideas were developed and expressed in the literature of different countries.

Buddhist sects and schools

After the death of the BUDDHA, differences in the interpretation of his ideas soon arose. The first schism or split is said to have occurred at the second BUDDHIST COUNCIL at VAISHALI, or soon after, that is, about a hundred years after the death of the Buddha. Buddhist Pali texts state that there were eighteen different schools by the third century BCE, while by the first century CE, using various sources, about thirty can be counted. Later developments of MAHAYANA and VAJRAYANA Buddhism, and the spread of Buddhism to other countries, led to the growth of more sects.

HINAYANA sects include the two main sects of the STHAVIRAVADA and MAHASAMGHIKA. Several other sects emerged out of these over the years.

Among Mahayana sects are the MADHYAMIKA, YOGACHARA and their various branches. Subsects of Vajrayana Buddhism are the SAHAJIYA and KALACHAKRA.

Budha, Baba

A disciple of Guru NANAK, the founder of Sikhism. Baba Budha was pious and much respected, lived a long life and supported and helped succeeding gurus. Born in 1506 in the village of Kathu Nangal, he met Guru Nanak when he was a young boy herding cows in the field. He gave Nanak a drink of milk, and the guru said that though he was young in age he was old (budha) in wisdom. Budha then became his disciple and was much revered. He conducted the guruship ceremony for the next five gurus. Through his blessings Guru ARJAN DEV had a son, who became the sixth guru. Arjan Dev appointed him as the first GRANTHI (custodian) of the sacred GRANTH SAHIB. He was responsible for the early education of HARGOBIND and helped in constructing the AKAL TAKHT. He died in 1631 at Ramdaspur, the earlier name of AMRITSAR.

Budha, planet

In Hindu mythology, Budha is identified with the planet Mercury and is the lord of

Budhavara, or Wednesday. He is the son of Chandra or SOMA, the moon, and of Tara, wife of BRIHASPATI. He is one of the NAVAGRAHA, or nine planets, depicted in early medieval temples. Budha's wife is ILA, who was alternately a man and a woman. From them was born PURURAVAS.

In modern temples, Budha is depicted as light yellow in colour, wearing yellow clothes. He rides a lion and has four arms, carrying a mace, a shield and a sword.

Bulleh Shah A SUFI saint and poet of the seventeenth to eighteenth centuries, who composed verses in Punjabi. His full name was Abdullah Shah, and his father, Sakhi Shah Muhammad Darvesh is also said to have been a noted Sufi. Though there is no agreement about his date or place of birth, most sources state that Bulleh Shah was born in 1680 in village Pandoke in District Lahore in present Pakistan. In other accounts it is said he was born at Lulani near Lahore or in Uch Gilaniyan, Bahawalpur and that his father later moved to Pandoke, or to Sahiwal. Bulleh probably studied first in Pandoke and then in Kasur. One of his teachers, Maulvi Ghulam Murtaza, had a great influence on him. Even as a child, Bulleh used to make spontaneous or 'darveshic' statements. Later he became a wandering ascetic in search of truth, but found no answers either in mosques or temples. He wrote: 'The liars have occupied the mosques, the robbers have occupied the temples'. He searched everywhere for a teacher or murshid, and finally came across Inayat Shah Qadiri, an eminent Sufi of the Qadiri and Shattari traditions, who worked as a gardener, and was known as a learned man. He became his disciple, and learnt mystic practices from Inayat. He also absorbed aspects of Vaishnava and Vedantic traditions, and finally attained an inner realization. Bulleh Shah established his own KHANQAH, where he initiated disciples into various Sufi traditions. He composed a number of mystical poems, which are still popular . Among them is this one, reminiscent of the great Sufi saint, Rumi:

How do I know who I am
Neither a Muslim nor a Hindu
Neither pure nor sinful
I do not dwell in happiness nor in sorrow
I am not of Arabia nor of Lahore
Neither awake, nor asleep
How do I know who I am.

His tomb in the Kasur region of Pakistan is still revered today.

He probably died in 1758–59, though earlier dates of death, including 1729 and 1752, are suggested in some sources.

bulls, sacred A bull cult possibly existed as far back as the INDUS CIVILIZATION, where seals depict humped bulls in front of a stand or altar. In the VEDAS, the bull is an epithet of INDRA, AGNI, and occasionally of other deities. The vehicle or VAHANA of the Hindu god SHIVA is a bull, NANDI, and Shiva was known as Rishabha or bull. The other name of the first Jain TIRTHANKARA, Adinatha, was also RISHABHA. In Zoroastrianism, a bull is associated with the deities VERETHRAGHNA and TISHTRIYA. GAYODAD is a divine bull to whom prayers are offered. Bulls also formed a part of myths of other ancient civilizations.

Bulls remain important today, because of their role in agriculture and form part of several harvest festivals.

Bundahishn A Zoroastrian text describing creation, and the cycles of life. The word also means 'creation'. The Pahlavi text dates to about the tenth century CE, but incorporates earlier material. It begins with a description of Ohrmazd (AHURA MAZDA) and Ahriman (ANGRA MAINYU). Ohrmazd is supreme in omniscience and goodness, and unrivalled in splendour. The region, religion, and time, of Ohrmazd, were and ever will exist, while Ahriman, who lives in darkness, with backward understanding, will not exist. Ahriman, the evil spirit, wished to poison and destroy the creation of Ohrmazd. At first Ohrmazd offered a truce to Ahriman, but seeing it as a sign of weakness, Ahriman refused. Ohrmazd then appointed a period of nine thousand years, for the conflict between them.

These nine thousand years are described in detail.

(1) First three thousand years: Ohrmazd recited the sacred prayer, AHUNA VAIRYA, after which Ahriman retreated.

Creation: Ohrmazd created the divine beings, the AMESHA SPENTAS, followed by the world, starting with the sky, then water, the earth, plants, animals and people. He produced the celestial sphere, the constellation stars, which were divided into twenty-eight divisions, and other stars. All would join in the battle against evil. He asked the consciousness and wisdom of people, as well as their guardian spirits (farohars or FRAVASHIS): 'Which seems to you most advantageous, when I shall present you to the world? That you shall contend in a bodily form with the fiend (druj) and the fiend shall perish, and in the end you will be created again perfect and immortal, . . . or that it will always be necessary to provide you protection from the destroyer?' (2.10) Then the farohars (divine guardian spirits) and Omniscient Wisdom decided that evil could only be defeated for ever, if human beings fought against it in the world.

(2) Next three thousand years: Ahriman began his battle against goodness, beauty, and life. GAYOMARD, the first of the human species, and GAYODAD, the primeval bull died from his assault, but from their essence the world was recreated and the mountains, seas, plants, animals and people came into being again. Evil still affected them, but at the end of this period the prophet ZARATHUSHTRA (Zoroaster) came to save the world. As people listened to him and followed his words, slowly good began to triumph over evil.

(3) Final three thousand years: the struggle between good and evil continues, within each person, but inspired by the words of Zarathushtra, gradually good prevails. Then the renewal of existence, in total perfection (FRASHOKERETI) will take place. Meanwhile the saoshyant (messiah) and his helpers are also in the world to help in the struggle.

This final stage is yet to take place. At this time perfection is achieved. All who have died again come into existence in bodily form. The evil suffer for a period of time, but are finally purified. There is no eternal hell, they recognize their own misdeeds. The world becomes eternal, there is nothing more to be done.

This text is important not merely for its account of creation and description of Ohrmazd, Ahriman and the battle between good and evil, but because it emhasizes the basic principles of Zoroastrianism—to choose rightly, take care of the world, and be a helper of God (hamkar) in preserving and protecting the beauty of creation.

buraq   Literally, 'The Bright One'; a mythical animal in Islam, on which the Prophet MUHAMMAD is said to have made his night journey (MIRAJ) to heaven. It is said to be a white animal, between the size of a mule and an ass, with two wings. The buraq is often depicted in paintings, somewhat like a griffin.

Burhanuddin Gharib, Sayyid   A SUFI saint of the CHISTI order who was a disciple of NIZAMUDDIN AULIYA. Burhanuddin was one of those who introduced the Chisti order in the Deccan. He died in 1340. His DARGAH is at Aurangabad in Maharashtra and many miracles are said to have taken place there.

Buston   A Tibetan Buddhist scholar who lived from 1290 to 1364. He edited Tibetan Buddhist texts and compiled all the texts into two main groups, the KAGYUR and TANGYUR.

calendars There are several calendars used in India. Two calendars are mainly used for official purposes: the Western Gregorian calendar, and the calendar of the Vikrama Samvat, an ancient era which begins in 58–57 BCE. To calculate dates of festivals, fasts or sacred days, each religion follows its own calendar.

The HINDU CALENDAR is not uniform. Several different systems are used, based on lunar and solar months, both for astrological purposes and for calculating the dates of festivals. An attempt has been made to standardize these, and in the standardized calendar, the new year normally begins on 22 March, though other calendars continue to be in use. Jains broadly follow the Hindu system, and begin the new year after DIVALI.

The ISLAMIC CALENDAR is used for calculating the dates of Muslim festivals and has twelve lunar months beginning with the month of MUHARRAM.

The ZOROASTRIAN CALENDAR has twelve lunar months of thirty days each, but there are three different calendars used in India, causing some confusion over festival dates.

Christians follow the solar calendar for certain festivals, for which days are fixed, such as CHRISTMAS, but dates of other festivals such as EASTER shift every year. Festival dates for ORTHODOX Churches, differ slightly. Jews follow a lunar calendar for fixing festival dates, with the new year beginning in September/October. The Buddhist calendar varies in different countries; Bahais have a calendar with nineteen months of nineteen days each, and four extra days or five in a leap year.

Canai Thoma A Christian from Syria, also known as Thomas of Canan, who came to India around 345 CE.

At that time Syria was part of the Persian empire which, under Shapur II of the Sasanian dynasty, was experiencing a Zoroastrian revival, creating problems for Christians there. Canai Thoma and other Christians settled in Kodungallur (Cranganore) in the Kerala region, where they were granted land by the Perumal (title of the king). They were known as SYRIAN CHRISTIANS, and this term was gradually applied to other Christians in the area as well.

Carey, William An Englishman who came to India and started the Baptist Mission at Serampore. Born in England in 1761, Carey was initially an ANGLICAN who converted to the BAPTIST CHURCH in 1783 and became a local preacher and pastor. In 1792 he founded the English Baptist Missionary Society and came to India the following year at the age of thirty-two. At this time the English were not allowing missionary activity, and in 1799 he moved with two other Baptists to Serampore (now Srirampur) near Kolkata, which was under Danish control. He studied Indian languages and translated the BIBLE into Bengali and Sanskrit, organizing and assisting in its translation into several other Indian languages. He also began the conversion of local people to Christianity and became a professor of Bengali and Sanskrit at Fort William College in Kolkata. He founded a college at Serampore that was later given the status of a university by the king of Denmark, and is still a functioning institution, with both secular and religious subjects. He prepared grammars and dictionaries of Indian languages, and, along with Joshua Marshman, translated part of the RAMAYANA into English. He died in India in 1834. His Mission provided an example for other PROTESTANT missionaries in India.

caste Caste, JATI or VARNA, is an important part of the Hindu socio-religious system. Hindu society is divided into four main castes, within which there are more than 3000 castes and 25,000 sub-castes, each with their own rituals, special deities and dietary laws. In olden days, the term Hindu was never used; each person identified themselves by caste, village, region of origin or deity worshipped. To some extent this continues today, despite attempts to link all castes within a common Hindu identity.

The caste system can be traced back to ancient times. The earliest reference to caste is in the RIG VEDA, which in one hymn states that the four main castes emanated from purusha, the primordial man. The BRAHMANA came from his mouth, the rajanaya or KSHATRIYA from his arms, the VAISHYA from his thighs, and the SHUDRA from his feet. The same account occurs in the MANU SAMHITA and the PURANAS, and there was a similar division into occupational groups in ancient Iran. In the ATHARVA VEDA there is a reference to 'varna', literally colour, also used as a synonym for caste. The four varnas are represented by the colours white, red, yellow and black. The Puranas state that caste divisions (varnashrama) did not exist in the golden age, the KRITA YUGA, but were created in the DVAPARA YUGA. The early caste structure was based more on occupation than on birth, and there was interchangeability among castes. Gradually it began to become rigid, and birth and occupation were linked. The brahmana had the priestly duties of conducting sacrifices and studying the VEDAS. Kshatriyas were kings or warriors, vaishyas were merchants or traders, and shudras were peasants or labourers. Gradually a lower group of 'outcastes' came into being, based on occupations considered unclean by the brahmanas, such as working with leather. They were considered 'untouchables' with whom higher castes would have no contact.

The growing rigidity becomes clear by the time of the RAMAYANA of Valmiki. According to the epic poem, things were not going well in RAMA's kingdom. He discovered that the trouble was caused by a shudra, SHAMBUKA, who was practising ascetic penances, which was not permitted for his caste. After Rama cut off his head, order was restored in the kingdom.

The caste system was not uniform. It developed only at a later stage in east and south India, through the influence of the north.

Apart from the challenges posed to it by Buddhism, Jainism and other sects which rejected the Vedas, caste was also challenged from within the system. Both the two main later Hindu groups of VAISHNAVAS and SHAIVAS had sects which went beyond the caste system, while most of the BHAKTI saints totally transcended caste. TANTRISM was also largely beyond the sphere of caste. Nevertheless, the caste system remained a part of Hindu society, with endless sub-groups and sub-castes being formed.

In the nineteenth century there were several reform movements, such as the BRAHMO SAMAJ and ARYA SAMAJ, which attempted to transform Hindu society and the caste system. A more aggressive movement against caste was the twentieth-century DRAVIDIAN MOVEMENT in the south.

Despite modernization and positive legislation in favour of lower castes since independence, the caste system largely remains in place within society. Marriages between people of different castes are rare in rural areas and often have a violent end because of opposition from higher castes. Assertion of rights by lower castes has led to caste wars, particularly in Bihar, while the DALIT movement supports the rights of the untouchables or scheduled castes. However, the link between caste and occupation has changed, and has little impact in urban areas. Politics is linked with caste, with various political parties appealing to particular caste groups.

Tribes were generally outside the caste structure and had their own norms. Today, however, some of them are listed as castes, and there is a move to incorporate them in mainstream Hinduism.

Buddhism, Jainism and Sikhism, the other indigenous religions, initially rejected the caste system, but later Jainism gradually absorbed the caste system from Hinduism, particularly in north India, though it was never as rigid as in Hinduism. Many of the Jain castes are grouped into two broad categories of Visa and Dasa, the former being considered higher, and marriages between the two categories are rare. In north India these two groups are divided into several castes, whereas among the DIGAMBARAS of south India there are only four main castes, the Saitavala (which does not occur in Karnataka), the Chaturtha, Panchama, Bogara or Kasara, and three minor castes. Digambaras of the south usually do not inter-marry with Jains from other parts of the country.

Sikhism was also influenced by the Hindu caste system, and Hindus converted to Sikhism retained their original caste. However, there was more inter-mixing among castes and less rigidity, though dalits were looked down upon.

Converts to other religions, such as Christianity or Islam, usually retain their caste identities, and may be referred to as Brahmana Christians or Dalit Christians.

Catholic A term which means 'universal' or 'general' and is often used in Christianity instead of Roman Catholic. Catholic churches are under the authority of the Pope with his headquarters in Rome. In India these churches include the ROMAN CATHOLIC or LATIN CATHOLIC CHURCH, the SYRO MALABAR CHURCH and the SYRO MALANKARA CHURCH. Each group has its own representative organizations. The Conference of Catholic Bishops of India represents the Latin Churches, the Syro Malabar Bishops Synod, the Syro Malabar Church, and the Syro Malankara Bishops Conference, the Syro Malankara Church. There is also a unified organization, the Catholic Bishops Conference of India (CBCI), which is a forum for all the Catholic churches of India, while the All India Catholic Union represents all Catholic Christians in India.

Chabad Lubovitch A branch of the Jewish Hasidic movement, founded at the end of the eighteenth century by Shneur Zalman of Liadi (1745–1812). It now has thousands of centres around the world, and several in India.Chabad (also spelt Habad) incorporates some aspects of the KABBALAH, and is an acronym of three intellectual processes known in Hebrew as chochma (wisdom), bina (understanding), and da'at (knowledge). Lubavitch comes from Lubavichi, a Russian town, once the headquarters of the movement.

Chabad philosophy gives importance to the mind and control over one's inclinations, rather than to the heart and emotions. It emphasizes Talmudic study, and the need to integrate Torah into daily life. Chabad has more than 3500 emissaries, known as schluchim who run Jewish outreach centres across the world. They have four centres in India (in 2010), at Manali, Himachal Pradesh; Anjuna village, Goa; Bengaluru; and Mumbai, and will be opening more. These centres provide guidance and facilities to Jewish tourists and visiting business persons and to Jewish Indian residents, even if they are non-Chabad Jews. A Chabad House forms the main centre in any location, and is the residence of the shliach (emissary), and the living room is often used as a synagogue.

Chaitanya Goswamis The disciples and followers of the Hindu saint CHAITANYA MAHAPRABHU. The term 'Goswamis' particularly refers to six disciples who lived at VRINDAVANA in the sixteenth century and developed a devotional system and a philosophy of Krishna Bhakti. Scenes from the god KRISHNA's life were recreated and enacted, and BHAKTI, or love and devotion to Krishna, expressed. This could be done in four ways: as a dasa or devoted servant, a vatsalya or parent, a sakhya or friend, and a madhurya, or lover. The two main Goswamis were Rupa Goswami and Sanatana Goswami. Rupa and Sanatana were ministers of the king of Bengal, but left their worldly lives to go to Vrindavana. Their nephew Jiva joined them there and helped to spread the message of Krishna. There they wrote works on bhakti and on the philosophy of the sect, some of which are still preserved. The other Goswamis were Raghunatha Dasa, Raghunatha Bhatta, and Gopala Bhatta. The Mughal emperor AKBAR is said to have visited them, and was impressed by the teachings of Chaitanya. He not only allowed them to build temples, but arranged for special stone to be provided for the purpose, and four Krishna temples were set up at Vrindavana. The Goswamis had several followers themselves, and formalized the worship of RADHA along with that of Krishna. Rupa spread the message of love, while Gopala Bhatta codified the religious practices in his work, *Haribhaktivilasa*. The philosophical basis of the sect was laid down clearly by Jiva and further explained later by Baladeva.

Chaitanya Mahaprabhu A VAISHNAVA saint who is believed to have been an incarnation of the Hindu god KRISHNA. Born in a BRAHMANA family in Navadvipa in Bengal in 1485, his original name was Vishvambara Mishra, though he was also known as Nemai Mishra. He studied the sacred texts and soon became very learned. At the age of twenty-two, he went to GAYA to perform the annual ceremony for his father, who had died some years earlier. At this time he received a divine experience and was filled with an ecstatic love for Krishna.

He became god-intoxicated and wandered to different places, describing the bliss of union with Krishna, which was symbolized for him by RADHA's divine love. He went to DVARAKA, MATHURA, VARANASI and south India, but then settled down in Nilachal near Puri in Orissa. He advocated BHAKTI as a means to reach god, and encouraged singing, dancing and chanting the names of Radha and Krishna, to bring about divine ecstacy. Though born a BRAHMANA, he was

against caste distinctions, and his followers included men and women of all castes and religions. A centre for Krishna worship was set up at VRINDAVANA near Mathura, where later a Krishna temple was built. His disciples were known as CHAITANYA GOSWAMIS, and the Chaitanya sect had a considerable influence both in Bengal and in Mathura.

Chaitanya probably died in 1534.

Chaitanya's sayings were written down by his followers, one of the most important collections being the *Chaitanya-Charitamrita* of Krishna Das Kaviraj, who probably lived from 1517 to 1582.

The Shri Chaitanya Saraswat Matha was set up at Navadvipa in Bengal and still functions as the main centre for the worship of Chaitanya, while in Vrindavana the Goswamis carry on the Chaitanya tradition.

chaitya The term for a Buddhist shrine. Initially the word applied to any sacred Buddhist object worthy of worship, such as a relic or a STUPA. Later it came to refer to the hall or temple built around a stupa or other sacred site, where people gathered for worship and prayer.

chakra A Sanskrit term which literally means 'wheel'. In religion it is used in several different ways and contexts. Some of these are given below: (1) The SUDARSHANA CHAKRA is the wheel or discus of the Hindu god VISHNU; (2) In Buddhism, the dharma chakra refers to the wheel of DHARMA, or of the divine law; (3) CHAKRAS are also mystical energy centres within the body.

Chakradhara The thirteenth-century founder of the MAHANUBHAVA sect. The sect was devoted to the worship of Krishna and DATTATREYA, both incarnations of the Hindu god VISHNU. The founders of the sect were also worshipped.

chakras Mystical energy centres within the human body. Chakras are first mentioned in the UPANISHADS and described in yogic (see YOGA) and TANTRIC texts. There are seven main chakras through which the KUNDALINI, or divine energy, is raised along the spinal cord or SUSHUMNA NADI, through meditative and breathing practices. These are the MULADHARA CHAKRA at the base of the spine (sacral plexus), the SVADHISHTHANA CHAKRA just below the navel, the MANIPURA CHAKRA at the solar plexus, the ANAHATA CHAKRA in the centre of the chest, the VISHUDDHA CHAKRA in the throat, the AJNA CHAKRA in the centre of the forehead, and the SAHASRARA CHAKRA on the crown of the head. In addition there are several other chakras, including chakras in the hands, feet and joints, as well as five higher chakras within the area of the brain.

Chaldean Syrian Church of the East Another name of the ASSYRIAN CHURCH OF THE EAST in India.

Chamkatti Mosque A mosque located at Gaur in Bengal, probably constructed in the fifteenth or sixteenth century. It has a single square brick chamber, with stone facing within, and a verandah on the east. There are four towers on the corners and a curvilinear roof surmounted by a dome. The panels are bordered with glazed tiles, and the mihrab is decorated with floral, chain and bell motifs. This mosque is one of the earliest built in the regional Bengal style, of which the square chamber with a single dome and attached verandadh, are typical. The mosque is thought to get its name from the Chamkatti Muslim community, who lived in the area. They were said to cut themselves in states of religious frenzy, and hence were known as Chamkatti, or skin-cutters.

Chamkaur   A holy site for Sikhs located in Rupnagar district of Punjab. Here there are several GURDWARAS commemorating a battle fought by Guru GOBIND SINGH along with a small Sikh force of forty men, against a large Mughal army. The Sri Chamkaur Sahib Gurdwara is a memorial to those who died fighting. The Garhi Sahib Gurdwara marks the spot where a haveli was converted into a fortress to fight against the Mughals. The Tarhi Sahib Gurdwara is built at the place from where the guru and three surviving followers departed to safety in the middle of the night. Katargarh Sahib Gurdwara commemorates the death of Guru Gobind's two elder sons, Ajit Singh and Jujhar Singh, who died fighting.

Chamunda/Chamundi   A Hindu deity, a form of the goddess DURGA. According to the PURANAS, Durga created her from her forehead in order to defeat the two ASURAS, Chanda and Munda. Chamunda is often depicted along with a corpse and is shown emaciated or with a terrible form. In the *Malti Madhava* of BHAVABHUTI, an eighth century writer, the goddess Chamunda is described as dancing wildly. Her temple is said to be near cremation grounds. She wears a garland of skulls that laugh on their own, and is covered with snakes. Flames shoot out from her eyes and destroy the world. Chamunda thus represents the ferocious or negative aspects of the deity. There are several Chamunda temples, among them the large CHAMUNDA TEMPLE at Mysore. Others include a temple located on a hill near the city of Dewas in Madhya Pradesh, and a temple at Bhubaneswar in Orissa.

Chamunda Temple, Mysore   A temple dedicated to the Hindu deity CHAMUNDA, who is the guardian deity of the Wodeyar dynasty, which once ruled Mysore, and remains the tutelary deity of the Wodeyar family. The temple is located on a granite hill near Mysore in Karnataka. The base of the temple can be dated to the twelfth century, though the main construction is of the seventeenth century, with additions made later. It has two GOPURAMS or gateways, the outer one with a high tower that is a modern construction. The silver-embossed doors have panels with various goddesses. The main shrine housing the goddess is small. The image of the goddess, who is considered the protector of Mysore, is made of gold. The ten-day DASHAHARA festival for which Mysore is famous, begins with a puja (worship) at this temple.

On the road leading to the temple is a 5 m high NANDI image carved out of a single rock, dating to 1569.

Chandi or Chandika Purana   A Shaivite text in Sanskrit that deals with the worship of the goddess CHANDI. It is an UPAPURANA or minor PURANA.

Chandi/Chandika   A Hindu deity, a form of the goddess DURGA. Chandi is mentioned in the *Kadambari*, a work written by Bana in the seventh century. There she is worshipped with animal sacrifices by the Shabaras, a local tribe. Later the goddess became popular in Bengal, where there are medieval texts, known as Mangalakavyas, dealing with her myths, legends and methods of worship. In Bengal she is depicted with four arms, holding a pomegranate, LINGA and trishakha in her hands. At her feet is a godhika (iguana).

In a Puranic story Chandi is described as a protector of animals. Once, it is said, there was a cruel hunter named Kalaketu. The animals appealed to the goddess to protect them from him, and she persuaded Kalaketu to give up his cruel ways. Chandi is also known as Mahamaya (great illusion) or Abhaya (the one without fear). There are numerous temples of Chandi Devi.

Chandidas   A Vaishnava BHAKTI saint of the fourteenth or fifteenth century, who composed verses and songs in praise of KRISHNA and of the divine love between Krishna and RADHA. Not much is known of his life, but his poems are said to have been popular at the time of CHAITANYA MAHAPRABHU, who lived between 1485 and 1534. Two villages in Bengal are associated with Chandidas, Chhatna near Bankura, and Nanur in district Birbhum. According to tradition, he loved a washerwoman known as Tara, Ramatara, or Rami, and compared his love for her with that of Radha's for Krishna. Rami was his companion in parakiya rasa sadhana, or the worship of god through loving a woman who is not one's wife.

Poems of Chandidas are found scattered in VAISHNAVA anthologies, and their uneven quality has led scholars to presume that there were several poets who used the same name. A number of poems deal not only with divine love, but also with his love for Rami. A manuscript discovered in the twentieth century with poems of one Badu Chandidas has also been ascribed to him and published under the title *Sri Krishna Kirtana*.

Poems assigned to Chandidas also form part of TANTRIC worship, and are associated with the SAHAJIYA cult. Some of these, however, probably belong to a later period.

Chandi-Mahatmya/Chandi-patha   Another name of the *DEVI-MAHATMYA*, a Sanskrit text glorifying the goddess DURGA.

Chandra An alternative name of SOMA, or the moon, a Hindu deity. Chandra or Soma is one of the NAVAGRAHA and also a DIKAPALA or guardian of the north-east quarter. He is the father of BUDHA or Mercury.

Chandragupta Maurya The founder of the Mauryan dynasty who ruled from 321 to 297 BCE, with his capital at PATALIPUTRA (modern-day Patna, Bihar). According to Jain tradition, he was a pious Jain who accompanied BHADRABAHU to south India and died at SHRAVANA BELAGOLA through the rite of SALLEKHANA (self-starvation).

Chandrakirti A MAHAYANA Buddhist who lived in the seventh century and belonged to the PRASANGIKA sect of the MADHYAMIKA school. He continued the work of BUDDHAPALITA and wrote the *Prassanapada* and the *Madhyamaka-vatara*.

Chandramoulishvara A name of the Hindu god SHIVA.

Chandravamsha A lineage of kings who claim to be descended from CHANDRA or the moon. According to genealogies given in the PURANAS, BUDHA (Mercury) was descended from Chandra. From him was born PURURAVAS, followed by Ayus and Nahusha. Nahusha had two sons, Ayati and Yayati. Yayati in turn had five sons, three from his wife Sarmishtha (Druhyu, Anudruhyu and PURU) and two from his wife Devayani (YADU and Turvasu). Several dynasties were descended from these, including the Kurus, Yadus and Vrishnis, who all played a part in the great MAHABHARATA war. In later times a number of kings who had no connection with the dynasties described in early texts claimed to belong to Chandravamsha dynasties. Among these were some of the Rajputs. SURYAVAMSHA dynasties, or those tracing their descent from the sun, also existed.

Chanukah/Hanukah A Jewish festival of lights that commemorates the victory of the Jews, led by the Maccabees, over the Greek rulers of Palestine in the second century BCE. During this festival, oil lamps or candles are lit over a period of eight days in memory of a miracle that took place at the time of the victory, when a lamp with oil sufficient for one day remained alight for eight. The festival usually takes place in December and emphasizes the qualities of charity, good deeds, sacrifice and devotion.

charana (1) A group of people following one particular Vedic school. In ancient days there were many different versions of the VEDAS, and a charana consisted of people who adhered to one particular Shakha or recension.

(2) An ascetic who had special powers and was said to be able to fly through the air.

Charanas or Chaaranas A group of minor Hindu deities who live in heaven and are singers and dancers. They sing in praise of heroes.

Charar-e Sharif The shrine of the SUFI saint NURUDDIN (1377–1438), who was also known as Nund Rishi. It was destroyed by militants in 1995 but later partially rebuilt. Popular among both Hindus and Muslims, the shrine in Kashmir is located 32 km from Srinagar and was built in the reign of the Mughal emperor AKBAR. It was elaborately carved, with a tiered roof supported on four pillars of wood, each formed by the trunk of a deodar tree.

Nearby is a mosque constructed by Atta Mohammad Khan, an Afghan governor, who was a devotee of the saint.

Chariya Pitaka A HINAYANA Buddhist text that forms part of the *KHUDDAKA NIKAYA* of the PALI CANON. It consists of a collection of thirty-five Jatakas or stories of the previous births of the BUDDHA, in verse. These express the PARAMITAS (perfections) of the Buddha in his life as a BODHISATTVA. Some of these stories occur in more detail in the JATAKA texts, but the concept of Paramitas is a comparatively late development.

Charminar A monument located in Hyderabad, Andhra Pradesh, constructed in 1591 by Muhammad Quli Qutb Shah (ruled 1580–1612), who founded the city of Hyderabad. It is approximately 57 m high and 30.5 m wide, with minarets surmounted by domes on the four corners. Important announcements were made from here, and there was once a mosque on the first storey. According to legend there was plague spreading through the region and Muhammad Quli promised to build a monument to God if the disease was controlled. He honoured his promise by building the Charminar in the centre of the city. Syncretic legends also relate it to the goddess LAKSHMI, who is said to have visited the monument and been compelled to stay there, thus increasing the prosperity of the region.

Charvaka A materialistic school of thought in ancient India, also known as Lokayata. It was said to have been founded by a philosopher named Charvaka, but Charvaka was also a generic name for materialistic philosophy. In some texts, BRIHASPATI is said to be the founder of the school. Charvaka philosophy is known mainly through Hindu, Jain and Buddhist texts, which are all extremely critical of the Charvakas. The focus of the philosophy is on sense perception and matter. Matter is the only reality, and perception through the senses the only method of gaining knowledge. The four elements of earth, water, fire and air combine in different ways, leading to all forms of life, which end in death. There is no soul or ATMAN, no gods, demons or superior beings, but only the natural world and the forces of nature. Moral rules are created by people, and the aim or goal of life is pleasure. Sorrow is part of the world and has to be accepted for the sake of the joy that is also found.

Materialist philosophers were against the VEDAS, sacrifices and rituals, and probably emerged in reaction to the dominance of BRAHMANAS and the focus on rituals. Scholars believe these ideas existed even before the rise of Buddhism and Jainism.

While materialist ideas can be seen in some texts of ancient India, among later texts that put forth these ideas is the *Tattvopaplavasimha*, written by Jayarashi in the eighth century. Jayarashi criticizes all existing religious systems and attempts to show that they were false.

chaturmasya vrata (1) A four-month period of religious observances practised by Hindus to obtain merit and blessings, beginning at the end of the lunar month of Ashadha (June–July) and observed in Shravana, Bhadrapada and Ashvina, ending in Karttika (October to November). During this time the god VISHNU is said to enter yoga nidra, or a yogic sleep, and the rituals end when he reawakens. Though usually practised by heads of VAISHNAVA monasteries, it is open to all. For its correct practice one should live in solitude, study the scriptures and meditate on the god VISHNU, but modifications are allowed for lay persons.

Each of the four months has particular dietary restrictions. In the first month certain vegetables are avoided; in the second, curd or yoghurt; in the third, milk products; and in the fourth, dicotyledon grains, vegetables with seeds, and tubers. Additional special fasts can also be undertaken during this period.

(2) Chaturmasya also refers to rituals performed at the beginning of each four-monthly season.

Chaubara Sahib Gurdwara A GURDWARA or Sikh shrine located at Goindwal in Punjab, which consists of a three-storeyed structure, with a square plan. Nearby is a *baoli* or well with eighty-four steps, symbolizing the series of 84,00,000 incarnations through which an individual is said to pass. The gurdwara is associated with the lives of three gurus. Guru AMAR DAS lived here, and Guru RAM DAS was bestowed with guruship here in 1574. An annual fair is held here to commemorate this day. Both these gurus died here, while Guru ARJAN DEV was born here.

Chauburji Mosque A mosque located in DELHI, constructed by Sultan Firuz Shah Tughlaq who ruled between 1351 and 58. This double-storeyed mosque has a large central chamber with smaller chambers around it. It once had four towers, now crumbled, from which it gets its name. A short distance away is another double-storeyed structure, also in ruins, part of which was also once used as a mosque. It is known as Pir Ghaib, as a saint (pir) once lived in one of its rooms and one day disappeared (ghaib) mysteriously. Both these structures formed part of Firuz Shah's palace complex.

Chenchu religion Chenchus, a Telugu-speaking tribal group of Andhra Pradesh, live in the hilly forested regions of the state. Traditionally, they collect and sell forest produce, but now their lifestyles are changing. Chenchus have always had a close relationship with Hindusm and worship Hindu deities. They are associated with the sacred sites of AHOBALAM and SRISAILAM, and there are two parallel legends about their connection with the deities here. At Ahobalam, a centre for the worship of VISHNU as NARASIMHA, it is said that the goddess LAKSHMI was once born in the Chenchu tribe, and Narasimha married her. According to the legend at SRISAILAM, the god SHIVA came here on a hunting expedition and fell in love with a beautiful Chenchu woman. All Chenchus are descended from their union. Thus Chenchus call Shiva Chenchu-Malliah or Linga-mayya, while his consort is known as Maisamma or Peddamma. A panel in the Srisailam temple shows Shiva followed by a forest woman, with four dogs. Chenchus are allowed to enter the inner shrine of the temple and have a special role in all temple festivals.

Chennakeshava Temple A temple of the Hindu god VISHNU, dedicated to the deity Vijaya Narayana, located at BELUR in Karnataka. It was constructed in 1117 by Vishnuvardhana, a king of the Hoysala dynasty, in celebration of his victory over the Chola dynasty. Built of grey-green chloritic schist, it has the typical star-shaped ground plan of Hoysala temples. The main shrine is connected with a columned MANDAPA and built on an intricately carved raised basement. There are susidiary shrines on three sides. The whole is enclosed in a courtyard, entered through a GOPURAM on the east, with a soaring tower. Around it are more shrines. Guardian figures, Vishnu images and MAKARAS decorate the doorways. The pillars have mouldings and carved bracket stones, decorated with female figurines.

Cheraman Jumma Mosque A mosque located in Mehala village near Kodungallur in Kerala. The mosque is a double-storeyed structure dating from the sixteenth century, partially reconstructed recently. Once made entirely of wood, its wooden interiors are still intact, and unlike other mosques, it has a large oil lamp in the centre. According to local tradition, King Cheraman Perumal of the seventh century went to Mecca, where he converted to Islam and was renamed Tajuddin. He married the daughter of the king of Jeddah and settled there. Before his death, he appealed to the king to help propagate Islam in Kerala, and the king or his messenger paid a visit to the raja of Kodungallur and with his help converted the Arathali temple into a mosque. This was allegedly the first mosque in India. Another legend is that it was built by a Muslim who arrived there in the seventh century. However, there is no historical evidence supporting these traditions.

Islamic festivals are celebrated at the mosque, and people of other religions also offer oil for the lamp on auspicious occasions.

Cheya Suttas (Cheda Sutras) A series of Jain texts of the SHVETAMBARA canon, composed in ARDHA

MAGADHI. The texts are the *Nisiha (Nishitha); Mahanisiha (Maha-Nishitha); Vavahara (Vyavahara); Ayaradasao (Acharadashah)* or *Dasasuyakkhanda (Dashashru-takandha)*, briefly called *Dasao; Kappa (Brihat-Kalpa); Pamchakappa (Pancha-Kalpa)*. (The Sanskrit equivalents are in brackets.) Some lists contain the *Jiyakappa (Jita-Kalpa)* of Jinabhadra, instead of the *Pamchakappa*. The Cheya Suttas contain the rules for monks and nuns, interspersed with legends, biographies and other aspects of Jainism. The first three texts deal mainly with atonements and penances for the transgression of rules. Of the three, the *Vavahara* is considered the earliest. The fourth text, the *Dasao*, is said to have been written by BHADRABAHU. The eighth section forms the KALPA SUTRA, in itself an extensive text and one of the most important Shvetambara texts. The *Brihat Kalpa Sutra* is earlier than this, and is the basic text of rules for monks and nuns. The *Pancha Kalpa* is no longer in existence. Additional texts are sometimes added to the list of Cheya Suttas.

Chhandogya Upanishad   An UPANISHAD belonging to the SAMA VEDA, consisting of eight out of the ten chapters of the *Chhandogya Brahmana*. It is one of the earliest Upanishads, dating to about 600 BCE. It discusses the nature of BRAHMAN and its identity with the ATMAN. In a famous passage, Uddalaka explains to his son Shvetaketu how Brahman pervades everything. He asks Shvetaketu to break the seed of a banyan tree, and then to tell him what he sees. Shvetaketu responds that he sees nothing, and Uddalaka says: 'What you cannot see is the essence, and in that essence is the mighty banyan tree. In that essence is the Self of all that is.'

Chhath   A Hindu festival in honour of SURYA, the sun god, celebrated mainly in Bihar and eastern Uttar Pradesh. The festival begins soon after DIVALI, with a ceremony inaugurating a three-day fast. The fast ends after worshipping Surya at sunset and sunrise, and bathing in a river or tank. The festival has spread to other states where migrants from Bihar and eastern Uttar Pradesh live.

Chhevin Padshahi Gurdwara   A GURDWARA or Sikh shrine located at Jalandhar in Punjab. It marks the spot where Guru HARGOBIND had a spiritual discussion with a SUFI saint, known as Shaikh Darvesh. An eighteenth century handwritten copy of the GURU GRANTH SAHIB is preserved in this gurdwara.

Chidambaram   A town located in Tamil Nadu, which is a centre of pilgrimage, famous for its SHIVA temples. The NATARAJA TEMPLE here, in which Shiva is worshipped as the lord of dance, is the most famous, and its origin dates back to the sixth century. There are several other temples built in Dravidian style. The Akasha Linga, the ethereal or invisible LINGA of Shiva, is also said to be located here. In ancient days Chidambaram was known for its scholars and as an abode of BHAKTI saints.

Chinmayananda, Swami   A renowned guru and spiritual teacher who spread the teachings of ADVAITA VEDANTA throughout India and the world.

Born in 1916 at Ernakulam, Kerala, his original name was Balakrishna Menon. His mother died when he was five years old and Balan, as he was known, grew up in an extended joint family of aunts, uncles and cousins. He attended an English school and also studied Sanskrit and Malayalam. In 1940 he joined Lucknow University and simultaneously began to participate in the freedom movement. He was arrested and imprisoned but released when, because of illness, he was on the point of death. Nursed back to health by a Christian lady, he completed his education, graduating in English literature and law, and joined the *National Herald* newspaper as a journalist.

Dissatisfied with his life, he read the ancient texts and finally entered the ashram of Swami SIVANANDA, and was ordained as a Swami on 25 February 1949, his new name being Swami Chinmayananda Sarasvati. He studied for eight years with Swami Tapovan in the Himalayas, and then began to teach and explain the truths of the ancient scriptures.

This was the first time that anyone had given lectures on these topics in English, that were open to all, and he met with opposition from traditional swamis. However, his movement soon took off and spread throughout India. He said, 'Vedanta makes you a better Hindu, a better Christian, a better Muslim, as it makes you a better human being'. He also began to teach abroad. After forty-two years of continuous teaching, Swami Chinmayananda died at San Diego, California, on 3 August 1993.

The Chinmaya Mission continues to work for his ideals. Two main ashrams in India are at Siddhbari in the Himalayas and at Mumbai, while there are several more in the USA. The Mission runs schools, hospitals, orphanages and old-age homes, and his disciples continue to teach and spread the message of Vedanta.

Chinnamasta   A Hindu goddess who is widely worshipped. She is one of the ten MAHAVIDYAS or TANTRIC goddesses, and is described as standing on a cremation ground on the bodies of KAMA and RATI, or KRISHNA and RADHA. She has cut off her own head and holds it in one hand, while in the other she holds a sword. Chinnamasta is worshipped to gain SHAKTI or power, as well as in Tantric rites.

Chintamani   A wish-fulfilling gem that could grant all desires. It belonged to the Hindu god BRAHMA, who is also known by this name.

Chintpurni Temple   A temple of the Hindu deity SATI, wife of SHIVA, located in Una District of Himachal Pradesh. It represents a SHAKTA PITHA, a place of divine power, as according to legend, it is one of the places where fragments of Sati's body fell. Her feet are said to have fallen here, and an ancient temple marked the spot. The present temple is said to have been erected by Mai Dasa, a devotee of the goddess DURGA. Thousands of pilgrims visit it, particularly at the time of NAVARATRA. The goddess here is worshipped in the form of a LINGA.

Chinvat Bridge   In Zoroastrianism, the bridge crossed by souls at the time of death. It is called the Chinvato Peretu, the bridge of separation, because it separates the good from the evil. At the bridge the soul is greeted by a symbolic representation of his deeds in life, which takes the form of either a beautiful young woman or an ugly old one. Accoding to the *VENDIDAD*, she is accompanied by dogs who can distinguish between the good and the bad. The good then go to heaven, while the wicked are dragged down. The *Arda Viraf Namah* written by ARDA VIRAF in the third century, has a similar account of the Chinvat, while some stories and legends state that one's own pet dogs appear to guide one safely over the bridge. In Islam, a description of the bridge between the two worlds (Sirat) is thought to be based on Zoroastrian sources. Other early myths too, speak of a bridge to be crossed after death.

Chirag-i Dilli's Dargah   A DARGAH or shrine of a SUFI saint located in DELHI. NASIRUDDIN MAHMUD, who died in 1356, was the successor of NIZAMUDDIN AULIYA, a saint of the CHISTI sect, and was popularly known as Roshan Chiragh-i Dilli ('the illuminated lamp of Delhi'). He was buried in the room in which he lived, along with the articles he treasured, the cloak, staff, cup and prayer carpet given to him by Nizamuddin, as he could not find a worthy successor to whom he could pass these on.

The tomb is in a twelve-pillared square chamber enclosed by perforated screens. A gold cup hangs over the grave. Above the tomb chamber is a red sandstone dome, and there are other mosques and tombs in the enclosure. The settlement around it was named 'Chiragh-Dilli' after the saint. The Dargah remains a holy site and a place of pilgrimage.

chisti   A term in Zoroastrianism for the ray of light that brings divine illumination. In the *GATHAS* it indicates the divine insight that leads to enlightenment. Later Chisti is personified as a YAZATA or minor deity, and is also known as Chista or Razishta Chista.

Chisti Order   An order of SUFI saints. The Chisti order derives its name from Chisti, a village near Herat in present Afghanistan. In India it was founded by Khwaja MUINUDDIN CHISTI who came here from Sijistan (Sistan) in 1191.

Chistis follow the QURAN and SHARIA, but maintain a liberal outlook, accepting that there is only one Truth, but many paths to God, and no difference among the followers of different religions. They preach that God is love, and all creation belongs to the family of God. Most of the Chisti saints lived a life of asceticism and poverty. They attracted many followers in India and are revered by both Hindus and Muslims.

Chisti saints believe in helping and serving others.

Shaikh Muinuddin Chisti said the highest form of devotion to God was 'redressing the misery of those in distress, fulfilling the needs of the helpless, and feeding the hungry'. He urged his disciples to 'develop river-like generosity, sun-like affection and earth-like hospitality'. Chistis also use music and dance to reach the divine.

Most Chisti mystics are followers of WAHDAT AL-WAJUD, a doctrine similar to that of Oneness in the UPANISHADS. In social life this implies treating people of all religions equally, and total freedom from religious prejudices. Chistis are not in favour of conversion to Islam. Shah Muhibbullah of Allahabad, a Chisti saint, told DARA SHIKOH that any discrimination between Hindus and Muslims was against the spirit of Islam. Another saint, Shah Kalimullah of Delhi (d. 1729), told his khalifahs to teach people to remember God (ZIKR) rather than to convert them.

The Chisti order was one of the most popular in India, and spread to Bengal, Malwa, the Deccan and other areas.

Among notable Chisti saints were Muinuddin's disciples Shaikh QUTBUDDIN BAKHTIYAR KAKI and Shaikh HAMIDUDDIN from Nagaur. Shaikh Fariduddin Ganj-i Shakar of Ajodhan, popularly known as Baba FARID, was the chief khalifah (deputy) of Kaki. Three of his disciples founded sub-orders: Shaikh Jamaluddin Hanowi established the Jamaliyah order, which soon died out; Shaikh Alauddin Sabir founded the SABIRI ORDER; Shaikh NIZAMUDDIN AULIYA founded the Nizamiya order, the most widespread in India.

In the Deccan, prominent Chistis were Shaikh BURHANUDDIN GHARIB, Shaikh Muntakhab and Khwaja Hasan. One of the greatest was Mir GESU DARAZ of Gulbarga, who died in 1422. In Malwa, saints included Shaikh Wajihuddin Yusuf (d. c. 1328), Shaikh Kamaluddin Multani Mughisuddin, and in Gujarat, Shaikh Husamuddin Multani (d. c. 1354), Shaikh Barikullah and Syed Hasan. Akhi Siraj, also known as Shaikh Sirajuddin, introduced the Chisti order in Bengal. He died in 1357. His notable successors include Shaikh Alaul Haqq (d. 1398), Shaikh Nur Qutb-i Alam (d.1419), and Shaikh Ashraf Jahangir Simanani (d. 1405). These saints greatly influenced the religious life of Bihar, Bengal and eastern Uttar Pradesh. Sultan Husain Shah of Bengal started the SATYA-PIR movement under their influence and the Bengal sultans had several Hindu texts translated into Bengali. Shah Muhammad Saghir, Zainuddin, Shaikh Kabir and others wove Iranian traditions into Indian legends. Thanesar (in Haryana), Lucknow, Gangoh (east of Delhi), Jaunpur and Burhanpur were among other major Chisti centres.

Chisti saints are still worshipped in India by all communities, and their DARGAHS are popular centres of pilgrimage.

Chitpavan brahmanas   A Hindu BRAHMANA community of Maharashtra. According to legend they were foreigners who were shipwrecked on the western coast. All of them died but were revived by PARASHURAMA, an incarnation of VISHNU. They are said to have originally been Jews or Zoroastrians. This legend probably arose to account for the assimilation of outsiders into the Brahmana community. It is also similar to the legend of the Jewish BENE ISRAEL community, said to have been revived by the Prophet Elijah.

Chitragupta The assistant of the Hindu god YAMA. He lists the good and evil actions of each person after death and judges their worth. He is depicted along with Yama in sculptures.

Chitrakuta A place mentioned in the RAMAYANA. The ashram of the rishi VALMIKI was located here. It is identified with a place of the same name in Chitrakut district in southern Uttar Pradesh. There are several temples and shrines here, and it is a place of pilgrimage. The sacred places of Chitrakuta extend across the border into Madhya Pradesh.

Chitraratha The name of several people in ancient texts, but particularly of the king of the GANDHARVAS. He was the son of the RISHI KASHYAPA and his wife Muni. According to the *MAHABHARATA*, he fought a battle with ARJUNA and was defeated, but later the two became friends.

chitta A Sanskrit term that cannot be defined exactly, but indicates the conscious mind. Manas is another term for the mind, while vritti and BUDDHI indicate different mental states.

choekyong A protector deity in Tibetan Buddhism. Choekyongs were originally Hindu or Bon deities, later incorporated into Buddhism. The Nechung, the oracle who protects the DALAI LAMA, originated as a Bon deity. Mahakala, a popular choekyong, is the embodiment of the Hindu god SHIVA. Hayagriva, a BODHISATTVA, is also considered a choekyong. There are several other choekyongs.

Chokha Mela A BHAKTI saint of the thirteenth or fourteenth century who worshipped the god Vithoba or VITTHALA at PANDHARPUR. Born in a Mahar or low-caste family, he at first lived at Mangalvedhya and later moved to Pandharpur. As he was of a low caste, for a long time the priests would not allow him into the temple. However, he and his wife Sairabai continued to be devoted to the deity and encouraged their relatives too, to live a pious life. According to legend, the god himself once took him into the temple, but he was thrown out by the priests. Later, convinced of the favour the god showed him, he was allowed to enter. Chokha Mela was associated with the saint NAMADEVA and composed devotional ABHANGAS in Marathi, praising Vitthala. He also spoke against the caste system and emphasized the importance of one's own body and soul, which was in itself a temple of god and therefore must be kept pure and clean. Chokha Mela and other workers died when they were buried under the debris of a wall they were building at Pandharpur.

chorten A type of Buddhist shrine, the Tibetan term for a STUPA. The basic structure has a square base with a dome. Steps lead to a parasol, above which are the twin symbols of the sun and moon. Chortens are erected near VIHARAS or sacred places, and usually contain any sacred object.

Chote Hazrat ki Dargah A Muslim shrine located in Hyderabad. It was built in the sixteenth century during the reign of Ibrahim Quli Qutb Shah in honour of Hazrat Ali, son-in-law of the Prophet MUHAMMAD. According to tradition, Yusuf, a eunuch of Ibrahim Quli, climbed a hill and saw a vision of Hazrat Ali. He also found an impression of Hazrat Ali's palm in a rock and installed this in a shrine. Later other structures, including a mosque, were constructed nearby. The shrine is still visited by pilgrims from all over the world, particularly on the eighth and tenth days of MUHARRAM.

Christian festivals and sacred days There are a number of Christian festivals linked with the life of JESUS CHRIST. Some have fixed dates, while the dates of others are variable. The main festivals are: Advent, which begins before Christmas and is a four-week penitential season preparing for the birth of Christ; CHRISTMAS, on 25 December; Epiphany, on 6 January, which commemorates the visit of the MAGI to the baby Jesus (Eastern Christians celebrate this as Theophany, or the baptism of Jesus); Ash Wednesday, which marks the beginning of LENT; Palm Sunday which marks the beginning of Holy Week; and the Sacred Triduum of Holy Thursday (the commemoration of the Last Supper), GOOD FRIDAY (the day of the crucifixion), and Holy Saturday, followed by EASTER Sunday, the day of the resurrection. The Easter season continues for forty days till Ascension Thursday, followed by the Feast of the Pentecost, also known as Whit Sunday, the day when the Holy Spirit descended on the APOSTLES, seven weeks after Easter.

Other festivals include Candlemas, when Jesus was presented to the temple, celebrated on 2 February; the Annunciation, on 25 March; the Transfiguration, on 6 August; and the Assumption of the Blessed Virgin on 15 August. According to some accounts, AKBAR, the Mughal emperor of the sixteenth century, who took an interest in Christianity, celebrated this day.

Eastern and Oriental Orthodox Christians have most of the same festivals, with some variations and additions. They use a different ecclesiastical calendar, therefore several of their festivals fall on days different from those of Western Christians, though Christmas is on the same day.

In India Christmas and Easter are popular festivals, others being observed only by Christians.

Christian saints Christianity recognizes a number of saints who were once Christian leaders, martyrs or missionaries. Very often, some miraculous occurrence is associated with them. Saints of the past include the APOSTLES and a number of others who lived later. New saints continue to be recognized by the Holy See, while Orthodox Churches recognize saints through Synods of bishops. Protestants revere saints but do not declare new ones, though they acknowledge the contribution of some notable Christians. Among saints associated specifically with India, ST. THOMAS and ST. FRANCIS XAVIER are the most important.

In addition, two Indian Christians, Gonzalo GARCIA (1557–97), and Sister Alphonsa (1910–46) were canonized as saints, while three other Indians were beatified (a blessed state less than sainthood). They were Joseph VAZ (1651–1711), Kuriakose Elias Chavara (1805–71), and Mother Mariam Thresia Mankidiyan (1876–1926). The last two belonged to the Syro-Malabar Church. Mother TERESA, a naturalized Indian, was beatified in 2003. The CHURCH OF NORTH INDIA has a list of notable Christians, including Roberto de NOBILI, Samuel AZARIAH and Sadhu SUNDAR SINGH.

Christianity Christianity, a worldwide religion, centres around JESUS CHRIST and his teachings. Its basic text is the NEW TESTAMENT, along with the OLD TESTAMENT, together forming the BIBLE. It has a very rich literature of additional texts written over the centuries.

Early Christians were Jews, but later Christianity and Judaism separated. In 381 Christianity became the religion of the Roman empire, and by this time it had also spread to Persia, India and Ireland. As Christianity spread through the world, it became divided into two groups, the Western, known as Catholic, covering most of western Europe, and the Eastern, known as 'Orthodox', including eastern Europe, Greece, Constantinople, Russia, as well as Africa and Asia. This division had taken place by the eleventh century. The Western Church was under the Pope, while the Orthodox, including the Russian and Greek Orthodox Churches and other national churches, had a symbolic centre in Constantinople (Istanbul). In the sixteenth century the REFORMATION and Counter Reformation split the Western Church into Roman Catholicism and Protestantism. A number of different Protestant sects emerged, while at the same time Western Christianity spread to the USA, Africa, Asia and South America. Christianity now has three broad groups: ROMAN CATHOLICS, PROTESTANTS and ORTHODOX Christians. Some Orthodox Churches are recognized by the Pope and affiliated to the Roman Catholic Church, though they follow their own modes of worship. The number of Christians in the world today is difficult to assess, though it is estimated at between one and two billion, thus forming the largest religion in the world.

Christianity in India Christians consist of 2.3 per cent of the population of India, comprising 2,40,80,016 people (2001 census), forming the third-largest religious group after Hindus and Muslims. A number of Christian denominations are represented, including CATHOLICS, PROTESTANTS, and ORTHODOX Christians.

According to tradition, Christianity was introduced in India in the first century, when ST. THOMAS, an APOSTLE of Christ, came to India. According to Eusebius, a historian of the fourth century, the presence of Christians in India was confirmed by Pantaenus, a Jewish teacher from Alexandria, who visited India in the second century. Pantaenus stated that the Indian community was founded by St. Bartholomew, another of Jesus's Apostles. At the Christian Council of Nicea, held in 325, one of the delegates, John, was described as 'the Bishop of Persia and Great India', indicating the presence of Christians in India. These early Christians were locally known as Nazranis, or followers of the Nazarene.

Around 345, another group of Christians came to India from the Persian empire, led by Thomas of Canan, or CANAI THOMA. They settled at Kodungallur, in Kerala, where they were granted some land by the local king. Along with Thoma came bishops and priests from Syria, which led to the emergence of SYRIAN CHRISTIANS.

Cosmas, an Egyptian merchant known as Indicopleustes because of his frequent voyages to and around India, in the sixth century, recorded the existence of Christian communities in the regions of Malabar (Kerala) and Kalyan, identified either with Kalyan in Maharashtra or in Karnataka.

Christian inscriptions have been found on two seventh or eighth-century crosses from Malabar and Mylapore. In the ninth century, King Alfred of Britain sent gifts to the Christians of India. Other Christians from Syria arrived in the ninth or tenth centuries and settled in Kollam (Kerala). In the thirteenth century, the traveller Marco Polo found communities of Christians in south India. Till then, Indian Christians were associated mainly with West Asia and the ORTHODOX Church. Some Roman Catholic missionaries including Giovanni da MONTECORVINO, reached south India in the thirteenth century, but did not have much influence there.

In the sixteenth century, the Portuguese settled in GOA and brought Catholicism with them. Portuguese priests travelled to north India and Tibet, and were invited to the court of the Mughal emperor AKBAR. They also went to south India, where they attempted to establish ascendancy over the Syrian Christians and block their traditional links with West Asia. They received their authority from the PADROADO, an agreement between the Pope and the king of Portugal. The Synod of DIAMPER (Udayamperur near Kochi in Kerala), held in 1599, brought the Syrians under Portuguese authority. Within Goa, the Portuguese also organized an INQUISITION.

As Portuguese power declined, the Syrians organized a revolt in 1653, known as the Revolt of COONEN

KURISU. After this the Syrian Church was split into different groups.

Meanwhile the ARMENIANS formed another group of Christians in north India, but did not attempt conversion or proselytization.

The seventeenth century saw the British and other European nations establishing their settlements and trading centres in India. With them arrived Christian Protestant missionaries. Danish Lutherans set up missionary centres at Tranquebar in south India and Serampore in Bengal in the early eighteenth century. Initially the British did not allow missionaries, therefore the Englishman William CAREY established his Baptist Mission at Serampore. In 1814, however, the ban was lifted, and Protestant missionaries of all denominations entered India. Conversion to Christianity took place in various parts of India, including the tribal areas of the NORTH-EAST. The Indianization of Christianity was started, notably by Roberto de NOBILI.

From the nineteenth century onwards, Christianity had an effect on several reformist movements in India, as well as on individuals. Its ideals of love, service and compassion influenced many. The BRAHMO SAMAJ, started in 1828, had some Christian concepts and rituals. RAMAKRISHNA PARAMAHANSA had a mystical experience of JESUS, and the RAMAKRISHNA MISSION embodied the Christian ideals of service. Sri AUROBINDO incorporated a passage on Jesus in his epic poem *Savitri*, in which he wrote: 'He who has found his identity with God/Pays with the body's death, the soul's vast light.' Mahatma GANDHI loved the Sermon on the Mount, from the NEW TESTAMENT, and his favourite hymns included *Abide With Me*. PARAMAHANSA YOGANANDA equated the essence of Jesus with that of KRISHNA. Even those who totally rejected Christianity used its ideas while remodelling and reforming Hinduism.

By 1947, there were several Christian denominations in India which asserted their Indian identity. Some of these have formed unions, such as the CHURCH OF SOUTH INDIA and the CHURCH OF NORTH INDIA, apart from associations of CATHOLIC CHURCHES. Among the most notable Christians after Independence was Mother TERESA, who was beatified in 2003. Many of the Christian churches have Indianized and hold their services in local languages. Christian missions continue to work with the underprivileged and to provide relief at the time of calamities. Christian hospitals, hospices, and educational institutions are highly regarded by all classes and communities. However, conversion, which continues particularly among DALITS and tribals, remains a controversial issue.

Christmas A festival that takes place on 25 December every year, celebrating the birth of JESUS CHRIST, the founder of Christianity. Though historically it is doubtful whether Jesus was born on this day, it is the day traditionally associated with his birth. In India it is also a popular festival for other communities, particularly in urban areas. Christians celebrate the day by going to church, exchanging gifts, greeting friends and family members, and eating and serving elaborate meals. Myths and legends are associated with this festival, including those of Father Christmas or Santa Claus, who flies over rooftops in a reindeer sleigh, distributing gifts to houses along the way. The concept of Santa Claus is based on the story of St. Nicholas of Myra (c. 340), reputed for his kindness and help to the poor. A tree, real or artificial, representing the tree of life, is usually decorated and placed inside the house. The gifts are placed under it, and Christmas carols, or hymns celebrating the birth of Christ, are sung.

Church The term is used in Christianity in two ways. It refers both to a place of worship and to a Christian denomination or sect.

Church of God (Full Gospel) An international Christian Pentecostal Church. In India, Robert F. Cook started a Full Gospel Church in 1914. In 1936, J.G. Ingram of the Church of God came to India, and Cook merged the Malankara Full Gospel Church, which had sixty-six churches, with the Church of God. The Church of God spread all over India, and in 1972 its administration was divided into seven autonomous zones. In 1994, the Church of God at Kumbanad separated from the group.

Members of the Church of God follow the King James Version of the BIBLE and believe in unity, simplicity and modesty.

Church of North India A union of six PROTESTANT Churches or denominations, formed on 29 November 1970. The Churches are: United Church of Northern India, Baptist Churches of North India (British Baptists), Churches of the Brethren of India, the Disciples of Christ (Anglican) the Church of India, and the Methodist Church (British and Australian Conference). Negotiations for this union had started as far back as 1929, and meetings and discussions took place regularly. In 1965 a constitution for the Churches was drawn up, known as the 'White Book', and finally the Churches united at Nagpur in 1970. Its administrative body is a Synod that meets once every three years. A moderator elected by it, who should be of the level of a bishop, supervises the day-to-day affairs. Its headquarters are in New Delhi.

Church of South India A union of PROTESTANT Churches in south India, which includes ANGLICAN, PRESBYTERIAN, CONGREGATIONAL and METHODIST (British) Churches.

After twenty-eight years of negotiations, the union took place on 27 September 1947. At this time the groups of Churches which joined were the Madras, Malabar, Madurai, Jaffna, Kannada, Telugu and Travancore Church Councils of the South India United Church (SIUS); the South India province of the Methodist Church, comprising the Madras,

Trichinopoly, Hyderabad and Mysore districts; and the Madras, Dornakal, Tinnevelly, Travancore and Cochin dioceses of the Church of India, Burma and Ceylon. The union then had fourteen dioceses. The North Tamil Church of the SIUS joined in 1950, the Bombay Karnataka Council of the United Basel Mission Church in 1958, and the Anglican Church of Nandyal Diocese in 1975. The union now has twenty-one dioceses, covering south India and Sri Lanka. The Church of South India is autonomous and its ordained ministry includes bishops, presbyters and deacons. A Synod administers the affairs of the church.

Church organization   The ROMAN CATHOLICS, PROTESTANTS and ORTHODOX Christians have different spiritual hierarchies. For Roman Catholics, the Pope is the highest authority, God's representative on earth. He is responsible for the spiritual guidance and welfare of all Roman Catholics. Cardinals, who are appointed by the Pope, are his main advisers. The whole church is divided into dioceses, which are territorial areas, guided by bishops, each of whom is appointed by the Pope. Under the bishops are pastors, who take care of parishes, or smaller areas, within a diocese.

PROTESTANT churches are broadly of three kinds: Episcopal, Congregational and Presbyterian. Episcopal churches are governed by bishops, Congregational by members elected from the congregation, and Presbyterian by elders.

In the ORTHODOX Church, a diocese is called an eparchy and a bishop is known as an eparch. Eparchs are usually given the title Mar (Lord). Some of them are under Patriarchs of West Asia, while others recognize the authority of the Pope.

Churnis   A term for commentaries on SHVETAMBARA Jain texts. A number of Churnis were written between the sixth and ninth centuries.

Chyavana   An ancient sage or RISHI who was the son of the rishi BHRIGU by his wife Puloma. When he was a young man, Chyavana sat in meditation for so long that a mud-hill covered him. One day Sukanya, daughter of the king Sharyati, poked at the mound of earth. Chyavana asked her to stop, but she poked a thorn at two glowing points she saw, which were his eyes, and Chyavana was blinded. He did nothing in response, but as he was an ascetic, Sharyati's whole kingdom began to suffer. When he came to Chyavana to apologize, Chyavana asked for Sukanya's hand in marriage. Sukanya looked after the old and blind sage with great devotion, and finally the ASHVINS, who had healing powers, gave him back his youth and eyesight.

Cochin Jews   An ancient Jewish settlement existed at Cochin (Kochi) in Kerala. See KERALA JEWS.

Communion of Churches of India   A Christian organization formed in 2004, consisting of the CHURCH OF NORTH INDIA, the CHURCH OF SOUTH INDIA, and the MAR THOMA CHURCH. The Communion represents the joint interests of Christians in these Churches.

congregational   A term relating to Church organization. Congregational churches are governed by officers elected by the congregation, or all the members of the church. Initially each congregational church retained its autonomy, though later they joined other church associations.

consciousness   Several states of consciousness are described in Hindu philosophy, both in the UPANISHADS and in later YOGA and TANTRA texts and commentaries. The MANDUKYA UPANISHAD states that the Self has four parts. The first is Vaishvanara or Vishva, who enjoys the world through Jagarita, or the waking state; the second is Taijasa, whose sphere is Svapna, the dreaming state; the third is Prajna, the state of Sushupta or deep sleep; and the fourth is Nanta Prajnam or Turiya, the state of awareness beyond these. The spiritually advanced person remains in the state of Turiya. A fifth state of Turiyatita is also described in some texts, which is beyond all others, as well as three states below normal consciousness. In the highest state the individual consciousness is undivided and whole, identified with BRAHMAN or the Paramatman, or closely related to it.

Coonen Kurisu, revolt of   A revolt of SYRIAN CHRISTIANS against Portuguese control over their Church, which took place in 1653. The Portuguese tried to bring the Syrian Church under their control and to sever its ties with West Asia. These attempts had been going on for some time, but the limit was reached when Mar Atallah, from the Patriarchate of East Syria (Antioch), arrived in Mylapore but was imprisoned and sent back by the Portuguese. Taking an oath in front of the St. Thomas Cross (known as Coonen Kurisu), at Mattancherry, SYRIAN CHRISTIANS vowed never to obey the Jesuits or recognize the Latin Bishops. Instead they acknowledged their local Archdeacon, now known as Mar Thoma, as their leader. After this several groups emerged among Syrian Christians. One recognized the authority of the Pope and of the Archbishop of Goa. The other followed Mar Thoma and came under the West Syrian Church of Antioch, known as the Jacobite Church. There were later developments and factions in both these groups, as well as the emergence of other groups. Thus the Coonen Kurisu revolt marks not merely an assertion of indigenous rights, but an end to the unity of Syrian Christians.

cow, sanctity of   Among several animals considered sacred in Hinduism, the most sacred is the cow. The original reasons may have been partly economic, as the cow provided milk, butter and ghi. She was looked upon as a nourisher and a symbol of motherhood and of the earth. In the RIG VEDA, USHA, the dawn, is the mother of cows, who draw her chariot. The cow is also called a goddess.

The sanctity of the cow probably dates back to the Indo-Iranian period, and in early Zoroastrian texts, GAUSH URVA, the soul of the cow, represents mother earth. Similar associations are made in the PURANAS and the RAMAYANA, where BHUDEVI, the earth goddess, takes the form of a cow to complain to the god VISHNU of the suffering of the earth.

Extraordinary cows wih great powers are mentioned in several texts. One such was KAMADHENU, who could grant all requests. Others were SURABHI or Nandini, often considered the same as Kamadhenu. All other cows were descended from Surabhi.

The cow has a major role in myths and stories of KRISHNA, who was a cowherd. In iconography, Krishna, as a child and as a youth, is often depicted with a cow. Over the years, the sacredness of the cow became an integral part of Hinduism. The banning of cow-slaughter has been advocated in the Directive Principles of the Constitution, and has been implemented in several states.

Dabistan-i Mazahib A seventeenth-century text that describes religious and occult practices prevalent in India. Originally thought to have been written by the Kashmiri scholar Muhsin Fani, later research showed it was written by Mir-Zulfiqar Ardestani (d. 1670), also known as Mulla Moubad or Moubadshah. This authorship is generally accepted, though it has also been attributed to Kekosrow Esfandiar, the son of AZAR KAIVAN. The text contains a lengthy account of Zoroastrianism, which it calls the religion of the Parsian, i.e. of the PARSIS, and describes several Zoroastrian sects. Only two of them conform to Zoroastrianism as it is traditionally known, while the rest entail some aspects of Zoroastrianism along with mystical and esoteric concepts. It also describes Hinduism, Tibetan Buddhism, Judaism, Christianity, and various Islamic sects and philosophers, and includes a brief account of Sikhism. Among its sources is the *DASATIR*, a mystical text of the sixteenth century.

Dadestan-i Denig A Zoroastrian text of the ninth century written in PAHLAVI, consisting of questions and answers on the Zoroastrian religion. Mihro-khurshid, the son of Aturo-mahan, asked these questions to Manushchihar-i-Goshnajaman of Pars and Kerman, Iran. The questions relate to the nature of a righteous man, the life of a soul after death, and similar issues.

Dadhicha An ancient sage or RISHI, often considered the same as DADHYANCH. The *MAHABHARATA* states that he was the son of the rishi BHRIGU. The Hindu god INDRA sent Alambusha, a celestial APSARA, to disturb his penance. Excited by her, his semen fell in the river SARASVATI, who bore him a child named Sarasvat.

Dadhikra A divine horse described in the RIG VEDA, where there are four hymns in praise of him. He is swift, flying through the air like a swooping eagle. He fights against thousands and wins. He was given to the PURUS by the gods MITRA and VARUNA. He is also known as Dadhikravan and is associated with USHA, the dawn. He is said to be symbolic of knowledge, or the morning sun or, alternatively, a real horse who was deified.

Dadhyanch An ancient rishi, first mentioned in the RIG VEDA. He was the son of ATHARVAN and he kindled AGNI or fire. The ASHVINS wanted the secret knowledge of SOMA (Madhuvidya) revealed to him by the god INDRA. They replaced his head with that of a horse, as he had promised not to reveal the knowledge. After the horse's head had told the Ashvins what they wanted to know, his real head was restored. The horse-head fell in a lake on Mt Sharyanavat and remains there, granting boons to men. Indra, with the help of the horse-head, killed ninety-nine Vritras (demons). Here again the horse, or the horse-head, is symbolic of knowledge.

Dadu A saint and teacher who lived from 1544 to 1603. Not much is known of his life, though according to some sources he was born a Muslim. He was a weaver and cotton carder by profession and lived mainly in the area of Rajasthan. He received a divine vision and composed verses to show that Hinduism and Islam were reflections of the same truth. He was against CASTE and unnecessary rituals, and did not believe in worshipping images or wearing sectarian marks. God, the One Essence, was found within oneself. His verses are similar to those of KABIR. His followers are known as Dadupanthis, and belong to Various groups, among them being:Viraktas, who are SANNYASIS and own only a cloth and a water-pot; Nagas, who carry weapons; and Vistar Dharis, who live a householder's life. Naraina in Rajasthan is the main centre of worship for Dadupanthis, where the Khalsas, the main group, are based.

daevas A Zoroastrian term for DEVAS, a term used in Hinduism for deities. In Zoroastrianism, daevas represent false gods, just as in later Hindu texts ASURAS (Zoroastrian AHURA, a term for god) represent demons. According to the GATHAS, the daevas chose wrongly and followed the darkened mind (achista mana), leading them to confusion and wrong acts. In later texts, they are the arrogant dregvants or followers of the false path, dishonoured forever in the seven regions of the world. However, not all references to the daevas are negative, indicating that they were once considered spiritual beings.

The *Gathas* also state that Mazda (God) knows all actions, even those of the Daevas (*Yasna* 29.4). Everyone prays to AHURA MAZDA for bliss, including the daevas (*Yasna* 32.1), and he listens even to their prayers.

The *VENDIDAD* states that those Mazda worshippers who wish to practise the art of healing with a knife should first practice it on the daeva worshippers. If they succeed, they can then practise on Mazda worshippers. Though this places daeva worshippers in a secondary position, it suggests that both groups lived together and that Zoroastrian healers treated both. In the tenth-century *DINKARD*, one of the questions relates to how a man, through his work, can become the equal of yazads (YAZATAS, Zoroastrian deities) and daevas, thus placing both in the same category. There are other such passages in various texts. In addition, several devas of the RIG VEDA have their counterparts in Zoroastrianism and are worshipped as yazatas. According to one theory, devas, devas and asuras are three different categories of beings. Availabe texts, however, do not indicate this.

dai   A term for a leader of BOHRA Muslims.

daityas   A class of ASURAS. They were born from Diti, daughter of DAKSHA, who was married to KASHYAPA, the grandson of the Hindu god BRAHMA and son of Marichi. Among the major daityas were HIRANYAKSHA, HIRANYAKASHIPU, PRAHLADA, and MAHABALI.

dakhma/dokhma   In Zoroastrianism, a tower in which the dead are placed. The practice dates back to ancient Iran, when earth, fire and water were considered sacred and not to be polluted by corpses. The body was therefore exposed on a mountain and later in towers specially built for the purpose. Zoroastrians continued this practice in India, and dakhmas were erected in places where there were a number of PARSIS. After sanctifying the area with prayers and other rituals, a stone tower was constructed, about 9 m high, with steps leading to the top, where there are circular platforms (pavis) with a pit or hollow in the centre. Bodies are placed on the platforms, to be eaten by vultures, while the bones are later dropped into the pit. Many of these towers are still used. As there is currently a shortage of vultures, solar panels are sometimes used to decompose the bodies. Discussions on alternative methods of disposal are opposed by the othodox, who are in favour of breeding vultures to preserve the old traditions. In places where there are fewer Parsis, burial is practised, while some opt for cremation.

dakini   Minor female deities, attendants of the Hindu goddess KALI or of the god SHIVA. They have various powers and can perform miracles and magical feats. In Tantric texts they are said to eat raw flesh. Various dakinis are described in Hindu and Buddhist TANTRAS. Dakini is also a specific deity, a form of SHAKTI, presiding over the MULADHARA CHAKRA.

In TIBETAN BUDDHISM, dakinis are consorts of YIDAMS or guardian deities. They are usually depicted in ferocious form and are widely worshipped.

Daksha   A son of the Hindu god BRAHMA, and one of the PRAJAPATIS, described in ancient texts. He is also listed as one of the ADITYAS. According to the *HARIVAMSHA*, the god VISHNU took the form of Daksha. There are various accounts of Daksha in the PURANAS. In a famous story, Daksha conducted a sacrifice to which he invited all the gods except his own son-in-law, SHIVA, who was married to his daughter, SATI. This is said to reflect the rivalry between SHAIVISM and VAISHNAVISM, as Daksha dedicated the sacrifice to Vishnu. Angry at being excluded from the sacrifice, Shiva created the terrible deities Virabhadra and Bhadrakali, destroyed Daksha's sacrifice, and cut off his head. According to some Puranas, Daksha's head was replaced with that of a goat. Other myths centred around this sacrifice explain the creation of the MAHAVIDYAS, or alternatively, the worship of Sati at SHAKTA PITHAS. The Daksha Mahadeva Temple at Kankhal near Hardwar in Uttarakhand is said to mark the spot of Daksha's sacrifice.

This myth is thought to be related to the absorption of SHIVA, initially possibly a non-Vedic deity, into the Brahmanical pantheon.

Another story connects Daksha with creation. Commanded by Brahma, Daksha, through the power of his mind, created the DEVAS, ASURAS, GANDHARVAS and NAGAS, but they were not multiplying quickly enough, therefore he thought he would create more deities through sexual union. From his wife ASIKNI he created the Haryashvas and later the Shabalashvas, but through a trick of the rishi NARADA, they wandered off and were never seen again. Then he had sixty daughters from his wife Asikni. He gave ten of these in marriage to DHARMA, twenty-seven to SOMA, and thirteen to KASHYAPA. Four were given to ARISHTANEMI, two to Bahuputra, two to ANGIRAS, and two to Krishashva. The twenty-seven married to Soma or the moon, became the NAKSHATRAS or lunar asterisms. From the daughters married to Kashyapa, all beings were descended. Some Puranas state he was married to Prasuti, and the number of his daughters varies from sixteen to sixty.

Some scholars believe these stories are about two different Dakshas, the first who was killed by Shiva being reborn as the second.

dakshina   A gift given to a guru or to BRAHMANAS. In ancient days a cow was often given, while today clothes, money and food are more common.

Dakshina, goddess   Dakshina, the act of giving, is personified as a Hindu goddess and is identified with Shri or LAKSHMI. She represents the sacrifice and protects her worshippers. According to the PURANAS, Dakshina was the daughter of Prajapati Ruchi and Akuti. Her twin brother was YAJNA (sacrifice), whom she married, and twelve sons were born from their union. They formed a class of DEVAS known as Yamas (Yaamas) at the time of the first MANU, Svayambhuva.

According to another Puranic story, Dakshina was reborn as Sushila, a friend of RADHA, the consort of the god KRISHNA. Sushila too loved Krishna, and

RADHA, finding them together, cursed her. Sushila meditated on LAKSHMI and became absorbed in her. But the gods separated them because with Dakshina as part of Lakshmi they could not get the fruits of their sacrifice, as no goddess remained to grant it to them. Dakshina was then given to Yajnapurusha. She became pregnant and after twelve years a child named Phalada (fruits) was born. Phalada provides the rewards of all actions.

Dakshinamurti   A form of the Hindu god SHIVA in which he is the universal teacher. Shiva is said to have taught the RISHIS or sages while facing south, hence the name of this form(dakshina = south). Dakshinamurti has four aspects: Yoga-Dakshinamurti, where he taught the rishis YOGA; Jnana-Dakshinamurti, the teacher of knowledge; Vina-Dakshinamurti, teacher of the vina, a musical instrument; Vyakhyana-Dakshinamurti, explainer of the Sutras or ancient texts. In this form, he is usually depicted seated on a throne, with one hand touching the ground (*bhumisparsha-mudra*) and the other raised. Most of the Dakshinamurti images occur in south India.

Dakshineshvara Temple   A temple in West Bengal dedicated to the Hindu goddess Bhabatarini, a form of KALI. Rani Rasmani, a rich Hindu widow, is said to have had a vision in which she was directed to build a temple here. The construction was completed in 1847, but as Rani was not of the BRAHMANA CASTE, the temple was not appreciated by the orthodox, and it was difficult to find a BRAHMANA priest for it. Finally Gadadhar, later known as RAMAKRISHNA PARAMAHANSA, who was still young then, began serving at the temple, which is now a famous and popular monument. Gadadhar dedicated himself to the deity and through constant worship was transformed into a great saint.

The temple is an impressive structure with nine cupolas. Near it are twelve smaller temples dedicated to the god SHIVA. Across the river Hughli to the south, the BELUR MATHA, headquarters of the RAMAKRISHNA MISSION, was later constructed.

Dalai Lama   The title of a leader of Tibetan Buddhists who belongs to the GELUG sect, and is both the spiritual leader and the head of state. The Gelug school of TIBETAN BUDDHISM was founded in the fourteenth century by TSONG KHAPA, and the third head of the school was given the title Dalai Lama in 1578 by the ruler of Mongolia. It was applied in retrospect to the previous two as well. Literally, it means 'one whose wisdom is as great as the ocean'. The Dalai Lama is considered a reincarnation of Chenrezi, the Tibetan name for the Bodhisattva AVALOKITESHVARA. When one Dalai Lama passes away, the next is chosen through certain signs that point to his reincarnation. Through dreams and visions, high lamas and the State Oracle predict where the Dalai Lama will be reborn. The boy chosen has to identify certain objects belonging to the previous incumbent. The third, fifth and thirteenth are considered the most significant Dalai Lamas, while the sixth is remembered for his poetry. The third (1543–88) revived Buddhism in Mongolia. The fifth (1617–82) unified Tibet and suppressed the rivals of the Gelug sect. The thirteenth (1876–1933) freed Tibet from Chinese rule and attempted to modernize the country. The current Dalai Lama, the fourteenth in line, came to India in 1959 and presides over the Tibetan government in exile.

Dalai Lama, Fourteenth   The head of the Tibetan government in exile, located in India. Tenzing Gyatso, the fourteenth DALAI LAMA, was born in the village of Takster in north-east Tibet on 6 July 1935 in a peasant family. His original name was Lhamo Dhondrub, but he was recognized as the Dalai Lama at the age of two and was renamed Jetsun Jamphel Ngawang Lobsang Yeshe Tenzing Gyatso. He is known respectfully as Yeshe Norbu (the wish-fulfilling gem) or Kundun (the presence), or as Tenzing Gyatso. He began his studies at the age of six and obtained the GESHE Lharampa degree (equivalent to a doctorate) in 1959 at the age of twenty-four. By this time, in 1950, he had become the head of state and government. Meanwhile, the Chinese had invaded Tibet. Efforts to make peace with them did not work, and in 1959 Tenzing Gyatso and his followers took refuge in India. Since 1960 he has lived in DHARAMSALA in Himachal Pradesh, where he set up the Tibetan government in exile, and continues to be the leader of all Tibetans. He attempted to modernize the Tibetan system of government and in 1963, he promulgated a new democratic constitution by which Tibetans elect a parliament, which in turn elects the cabinet.

He was awarded the Nobel Peace Prize in 1989 for his continuous attempts to find a peaceful and non-violent solution to the Tibetan problem. The Dalai Lama is a respected figure in India and abroad and continues his religious studies and practices, and also guides others on the Buddhist path.

dalits   A term used by certain caste groups within the Hindu CASTE SYSTEM. The word dalit, from the Sanskrit root 'dal', means split, broken, destroyed, scattered or torn asunder. The noun 'dala' also has a positive connotation, of something unfolding itself. In the ancient caste structure, some castes remained at the lowest level, discriminated against by upper caste Hindus and called 'untouchables'. These castes, deprived of rights such as eating with other castes, drinking water from the village well, or entering Hindu temples, suffered tremendous oppression. The BHAKTI movement and the various Bhakti saints transcended caste, and there were several gurus who discarded or modified the concept of caste. Later, the equality promoted by Islam and the SUFI saints helped to change the caste system. Christianity, which had an influence in India from the eighteenth century, fostered the growth of reform movements within Hinduism, particularly from the nineteenth century onwards. Mahatma GANDHI called the lowest castes 'Harijans' or 'Children of God', and went on long fasts to end oppression against them. Though all these movements brought about some change, on the whole upper castes continued to avoid contact with them. The British government listed these castes in a Schedule in 1936. This list, included in the new Constitution of India, inaugurated in 1950, led to their official name, 'Scheduled Castes'. The Constitution abolished untouchability, and provided for reservations in government and in educational institutions to help Scheduled Castes reach equality. Another act passed in 1955 made untouchability an offence that could be punished by law. This was revised in 1976 and reframed as the Protection of Civil Rights Act, which imposes stricter penalties on those who discriminate against people on grounds of caste. In spite of all the laws, oppression and discrimination remain.

B.R. AMBEDKAR (1891–1956), one of the composers of the Constitution, was from the Mahar caste and even before Independence worked to improve the status of Scheduled Castes. However, he felt their status would never improve within Hinduism, and in 1956, he led them in a mass conversion to Buddhism. Ambedkar died soon after this, but conversions to Buddhism still continue.

Scheduled Castes gradually found their own identity and chose to call themselves dalits. This word was used even by Ambedkar and earlier by Jyotirao Phule (1827–90), but was used regularly only from the 1970s. Inspired by the Black Panthers of the USA, the Dalit Panthers were formed in 1972, but now only the word dalit is used. Dalit literature began to join the mainstream and by the 1980s several dalit political parties and groups had been formed. Despite all legal protection, oppression continues, and with increasing self-assertion, conflicts with the upper castes have become frequent. Most dalits, particularly in rural areas, still do not enjoy social equality. In some areas dalits still cannot enter temples, use the village well or eat with upper castes. Higher castes do not like them to wear shoes and clean clothes, to ride bicycles, or to ride horses for marriage ceremonies.

Dalits form 15 per cent of the population but are not all united, and conflicts exist among different dalit groups.

dalit deities DALITS who remain within Hinduism worship Hindu deities, but also traditionally have their own deities. The seventh-century SHAIVITE saint Nandanar, who was a Mahar, was asked by his elders not to strive to enter the temples of the higher castes. According to the *PERIYAPURANAM*, a twelfth-century Tamil text, he was told, 'we have our own gods, our own work, temples and celebrations.' The gods mentioned here include Katteri, Munian, Mukkan and Karuppan. Village mother goddesses, such as Pochamma and Kattamaisamma, are also worshipped by DALITS and other non-BRAHMANA castes in south India. Among dalit deities in the north are Saliya, Purbi and Masana. A number of these deities, for instance Karuppan, were later allotted space in the Hindu pantheon.

Damdama Sahib Gurdwara, Delhi A GURDWARA or Sikh shrine located in Delhi near Humayun's tomb, built by Sardar BHAGEL SINGH in 1783. It marks the spot where the tenth guru, GOBIND SINGH met Prince Muazzam, son of the emperor AURANGZEB, and planned his accession to the throne. Prince Muazzam later became the emperor Bahadur Shah I.

The gurdwara was renovated by Maharaja RANJIT SINGH and further expanded in succeeding years. A new building was constructed in 1984. The shrine is a popular place of pilgrimage, particularly at the time of the HOLA MOHALLA festival.

Damdama Sahib Gurdwara, Dhubri A GURDWARA or Sikh shrine located at Dhubri in Assam, at a spot said to have been visited by Guru NANAK. The gurdwara is built in memory of his visit. Dhubri is also associated with Guru TEGH BAHADUR. Raja Ram Singh, leading Mughal forces, asked Tegh Bahadur to accompany him on an expedition against the Ahom king. The guru agreed, but after going there, he brought peace between the two sides. Soldiers of both armies prayed at the shrine of Guru Nanak and built a mound of peace nearby. While he was here, the guru heard about the birth of his son in Patna. This boy later became the tenth guru, GOBIND SINGH.

danavas A class of ASURAS in Hindu mythology, similar to the DAITYAS. They were born from Danu, a daughter of DAKSHA, who was married to KASHYAPA, grandson of the god BRAHMA. Danu had a hundred sons, from whom ten families of danavas were descended. Among the danavas were VRITRA and the king, MAYA. Kalaka and Puloma, two other wives of Kashyapa, gave birth to 60,000 danavas, who were powerful and ferocious. They were called Paulomas and Kalakanjas, or Kalakeyas.

The terms daitya and danava are often used interchangeably.

dance, and religion Dance is often an expression of the divine. Bharata's *Natya Shastra*, dated to about the second century, is one of the earliest texts describing various dance postures. The Hindu god SHIVA, in his form as NATARAJA, is the lord of dance. The classical dances of India, which include Bharatanatyam, Kathakali, Odissi and others, have mainly religious themes, depicting the lives of KRISHNA, RAMA or other deities.

Certain SUFI orders use dance to reach a state of divine ecstacy.

Apart from these, traditional tribal dances are often performed to invoke the deities of the tribe. Dances take place in temples, in honour of the deities. Even harvest dances, are both an expression of joy at a good harvest, and a thanksgiving to god.

Danishmand Khan A noted philosopher in the time of the Mughal emperors Shah Jahan and AURANGZEB. Danishmand was born in Yazd in Iran, but came to the court of Shah Jahan in 1651. Though a Muslim, he was interested in all kinds of philosophy. He studied Hindu philosophy with a Sanskrit scholar and Western philosophy with a French doctor at the court. He was one of the few scholars in India who was familiar with the works of contemporary philosophers such as William Harvey (1578–1657) and Descartes (1596–1650). He died in 1670.

Dara Shikoh The eldest son of the Mughal emperor Shah Jahan, who wrote about the unity of Hinduism and Islam.

Born in 1614 or 1615, he was killed by his brother AURANGZEB in 1659 during the struggle for succession after his father fell ill. Dara Shikoh was deeply interested in religion and spirituality, and studied Islam, SUFI texts, VEDANTA and Christianity. Assisted by Sanskrit pandits, he translated about fifty UPANISHADS into Persian and compiled them in a text known as *Sirr-i Akbar*. In his introduction to it, he stated that the Upanishads represented the 'hidden book' mentioned in the QURAN, and that they revealed the highest truth. He saw in them an explanation of the WAHDAT AL-WUJUD doctrine. It was through Dara Shikoh's Persian Upanishads that these texts first became known in the West after they were translated into French and Latin.

His most important original work is *Majmaul Bahrain*, known in Sanskrit as *Samudra Sangam*, composed in 1654–55, in which he found significant parallels between Hinduism and Islam. He said there were no fundamental differences between the two religions and made detailed comparisons of related concepts. He also composed books on Sufism and verses in Hindi and Persian with mystical themes.

darbha A type of grass used in Vedic SACRIFICES. It is sometimes said to be the same as kusha grass. There are various stories about the origin of darbha grass. According to one account, it grew from a few drops of AMRITA that fell on the ground at the time of the churning of the ocean of milk.

Dar-e Meher A name for a Zoroastrian temple or AGIARY.

dargah A Persian word, literally 'place of a door', used in Iran usually for a royal court or palace. In India, however, it has a special meaning and refers to the shrine of a Muslim saint, often located at his tomb. Pilgrims visit the dargah to worship the saint. Among the most famous dargahs in India is that of Shaikh MUINUDDIN CHISTI, the SUFI saint. The concept of a dargah is similar to that of the SAMADHI of a renowned YOGI.

Daroli Bhai Gurdwara A GURDWARA or Sikh shrine located at Daroli Bhai, a village in district Ferozepur, Punjab. The sixth guru, HARGOBIND, lived here, and

his *chola* or cloak, as well as an iron tava he used for making chapatis, are preserved here. The guru is said to have cooked on this tava for a LANGAR on BAISAKHI day. His eldest son, Baba Gurdita, was born here. The guru's wife Mata Damodri died in this village, and another gurdwara nearby was built in memory of her.

darshana A Sanskrit term meaning 'sight' or 'viewpoint', used in both these ways. As 'sight' darshana usually refers to a divine vision or glimpse of god, or of an image in a temple representing the divine. Through darshana one may see, or be seen, by god.

In its second use, it indicates a school of thought. The shad-darshanas or six darshanas, is a term used for the six early orthodox Indian schools of philosophy, which are: NYAYA, VAISHESHIKA, SAMKHYA, YOGA, MIMAMSA and VEDANTA. Darshana is also used to describe non-orthodox systems, including Jainism, Buddhism and materialism, and in an even wider context, for grammar, alchemy and other forms of knowledge.

dar-ul-harb Literally, 'land of warfare', an Islamic term for a land where Islamic practices could not be observed. This concept was used in India by the WAHHABIS and the FARAIDIS in their struggle against the British. There was much discussion among leading Muslims in India, on whether British presence made the land unholy, and on the concept of dar-ul-harb, which had earlier been expounded by the law-giver Abu Hanifa and others. The main condition for this was that Islam was suppressed in the land and the edicts of unbelievers were propagated. In a dar-ul-harb, it was acceptable to wage war or JIHAD against the infidels. Most Islamic authorities felt that India was not in this category, as the injunctions of Islam were still observed in the land, and therefore warfare against the British was not justified. The mufti of Mecca stated at this time that as long as some Islamic religious practices prevailed in it, India was dar-ul-Islam, a land of Islam.

dar-ul Islam A term that indicates a land or abode of Islam. Right from British days there were conrovesies about whether India was dar-ul Islam, or dar-ul harb, a land against Islam. The interpretation of these terms has always been controversial. Some equate dar-ul kufr, a land ruled by non-Muslims, with dar-ul harb, a land against Islam. According to others, dar-ul Islam refers to any place where Islamic practices are allowed, regardless of by whom it is ruled. The mufti of Mecca stated at that time, that as long as some of the religious practices prevail in it, India was dar-ul-Islam. Several others had the same view. A recent book by Maulana Wahiduddin Khan feels these terms dar ul-Islam, dar-ul-kufr (a non-Muslim land), dar-ul harb themselves should be questioned. The author points out that these three terms were not used by the Prophet, even though he lived under conditions covering all three, and this in itself provides sufficient guidance that there is no reason for their existence. Hence he feels that these terms themselves, created by later scholars, have no relevance.

Dar-ul-Uloom, Deoband A renowned religious and academic centre, the largest institution in India for Islamic learning, located at Deoband in western Uttar Pradesh. It was founded as a small madrasa attached to a mosque on 30 May 1866, at a time when Mughal power had been eclipsed, the British controlled most of north India, and Islamic learning was in disarray. There were no funds available, but the founders, Hazrat Maulana MUHAMMAD QASIM NANAUTAVI and Hazrat Maulana Rasheed Ahmad Gangohi, said that it would be run trusting in ALLAH, with public contributions. The institution began with just one student and one teacher, and an annual expenditure of Rs 68, but soon expanded. It was based on traditional SUNNI interpretations of Islam, the HANAFI school of law, and some SUFI ideals. Thus it was a centre of both SHARIAH and TARIQA. It believed in a purified form of Sufism, and was against the worship of PIRS or saints, but in favour of a close relationship between disciple and teacher.

The Deoband school propagated nationalist ideals and many of its students participated in the freedom movement.

Today it has more than 2000 students, including several from West Asia, as well as over 9000 affiliated institutes. Its large library has books and manuscripts in Urdu, Persian and Arabic. It has several different courses of study, with thirty-three departments. One department, the Darul Ifta, studies the QURAN and HADIS to provide religious decrees (FATWAS) on matters related to dogma. Graduate and postgraduate degrees are provided in Islamic theology, law (FIQH) and literature, as well as in Arabic studies. There are also courses in calligraphy and in crafts such as tailoring, book-binding and other skills.

IMAMS who have graduated from the school are in demand even in other countries.

darvesh A Persian word for a religious mendicant, usually written in English as 'Dervish'. The Arabic word is 'faqir'. Both these words are used for SUFI saints, as well as the term PIR, meaning 'an elder' in Persian.

Dasam Granth A text sacred to Sikhs, attributed to the tenth Sikh guru, GOBIND SINGH, that was compiled by his disciple MANI SINGH. The text is composed in a mix of Punjabi, Persian and Braj Bhasha (a Hindi dialect), and consists of the guru's writings, thoughts and ideas, as well as stories and ethical and philosophical sayings. Some of the stories and myths are borrowed from the PURANAS and other sources.

Parts of the *Dasam Granth* are included in the daily prayers of Sikhs. In the *Savaiye* (quatrains), the guru comments on how all follow some religion or the other, but none love God, or understand the divine:

'The whole world is lost in false ritual, but no one knows the mystery of the One.' The *Dasam Granth* incorporates most of the writings attributed to the guru, including the autobiographical *Bachitra Natak* and the ZAFAR NAMAH, a letter written to AURANGZEB.

Dasatir A text of the sect of AZAR KAIVAN, probably written by Kaivan himself in the sixteenth century. It was composed in a hitherto unknown language, which the author of the DABISTAN called 'the heavenly language', and seems to have a mixture of words derived from AVESTA, Hindi, Arabic, Persian and Sanskrit, as well as invented words. It has sixteen chapters or *namas* (books), each attributed to an ancient Persian prophet or legendary hero. The second part consists of a translation and commentary in Persian, said to be by the sixteenth 'prophet' Sasan V, a contemporary of the Sasanian ruler Khusrau II (ruled 590–628). Later research showed the whole text was of a late date and that the commentary and translation were probably by the author as well. The *Dabistan* indicates that the *Dasatir* was known in India in the seventeenth century, but it was widely publicized only after a copy was brought back from Iran by MULLA FEROZE and his father in 1778. On the basis of its description in the *Dabistan*, the English orientalist Williams Jones felt that the *Dasatir* was a significant sacred text. It was first translated and published in 1818–19. While some refer to this as a Zoroastrian text, others consider it pseudo-Zoroastrian.

Dasauli A folk deity worshipped in Bihar and Jharkhand. The deity is said to live in sal forests or groves, and is worshipped for prosperity and protection. Ritualistic folk dances form part of this worship.

Dasaveyaliya Sutta A Jain text of the SHVETAMBARA canon, one of the four MULA SUTTAS, known in Sanskrit as the *Dashavaikalika Sutra*. Literally, it means 'Ten Evening Recitations', and is to be studied by Shvetambara monks. The first section consists of Jain sayings and rules for monastic life, while the second contains the story of Rajimati, who became an ascetic and rejected the advances of Rathanemi, brother of ARISHTANEMINATHA. The story is also told in the UTTARAJJHAYANA. The *Dasaveyaliya* is said to have been written by Sejjambhava (Sanskrit: Shayyambhava). He was married, but after a vision of a JINA, he gained enlightenment and left home when his wife was pregnant. A son was born to her, whom she named Manaka. When Manaka was eight years old, his mother told him that his father was an ascetic and Manaka went off to seek him. Sejjambhava met his son, who became his disciple. He saw that the child was destined to die in six months and therefore summarized the main principles of Jainism and taught them to Manaka. In deep meditation, Manaka passed to another world and Sejjambhava wrote down what he had taught Manaka in the *Dasaveyalia*. This text thus summarizes the main principles of Jainism, and is one of the most important SHVETAMBARA texts.

Dashabhumika Sutra A MAHAYANA Buddhist text, that describes the ten stages or bhumis on the path of a BODHISATTVA. It was originally a part of the *AVATAMSAKA SUTRA*, but is used as a separate text. It is the most important text for Bodhisattva practices. The ten *bhumis* begin with the Pramudita-bhumi (joyful stage), and go on through the Vimala-bhumi or immaculate stage, to various other stages culminating in the Dharmamegha-bhumi, or stage of DHARMA, here indicating the ultimate.

Dashahara/Dasehra A ten-day Hindu festival celebrated in October. Dashahara literally means ten nights. In north India, the festival is linked with the god RAMA and his triumph over RAVANA, symbolizing the victory of good over evil. For the first nine nights (NAVARATRA), Ram Lilas—dramatic performances of episodes from the *RAMAYANA*—are held in every locality in villages, towns and cities. Some of these performances have grand props and costumes, while others are simple affairs. On the tenth night, huge effigies of Ravana, Meghanada and Kumbhakarna are made. They are usually stuffed with crackers and mounted on poles, and then set alight. In the more elaborate performances, the character acting as Rama shoots flaming arrows to ignite the effigies.

There are several regional variations in the festivities. In Kulu, in Himachal Pradesh, all the local deities are brought to pay homage to Rama, known here as Raghunathji, and to celebrate his victory over Ravana. About 150 to 200 deities arrive in Kulu, some in palkis (palanquins), drawn by carts, or carried by their devotees. When all the deities are gathered together, bands play music and sacrifices are offered.

In some areas of south India, the ten-day celebrations mark the victory of the goddess CHAMUNDA (a form of DURGA) over the demon MAHISHASURA. The traditional celebrations at Mysore, begin with a worship of Chamunda, and culminate in a huge procession of decorated elephants and horses, lights, dances and music.

In Bengal, the festival takes the form of DURGA PUJA, worship of the goddess DURGA. On the tenth day, images of the goddess are immersed in water, usually in a river.

Other deities are also worshipped on these auspicious days. Among them is SARASVATI, goddess of music and learning. Sarasvati Puja or worship of the goddess, is performed for four days. In Maharashtra, the goddess Lalita is worshipped on the fifth day of Dashahara.

In the Bastar region in Chhattisgarh, the local goddess Danteshvari is worshipped. The festival here also commemorates the granting of the title of rathpati (Lord of the Chariot) to their tribal king at the Jagannatha temple in Puri, an event that took place in the fifteenth century.

These are some examples of the different ways Dashahara is celebrated.

AYUDHA PUJA, reverence and thanks given to machines, tools and vehicles, also takes place at this time.

Dasharatha A king described in the *RAMAYANA*. He is the father of RAMA, a popular Hindu deity. Dasharatha ruled at AYODHYA and was of the Ikshvaku dynasty, the son of Aja and Indumati. Under his rule, Ayodhya was rich and prosperous. He had three wives: Kaushalya, Kaikeyi and Sumitra. A daughter named Shanta was born to Kaushalya. Dasharatha gave her to his childless friend Lomapada, king of Anga, and later she was married to RISHYASHRINGA. Dasharatha had no more children for a long time; to have sons, he conducted a great ASHVAMEDHA sacrifice. Rishyashringa assisted at the sacrifice and provided a sacred concoction for the queens to eat. Dasharatha was then blessed with four sons. Kaushalya gave birth to Rama, Kaikeyi to BHARATA, and Sumitra to LAKSHMANA and SHATRUGHNA. Rama was Dasharatha's favourite, but Kaikeyi tricked him into sending Rama into exile. After Rama, his wife SITA, and brother Lakshmana departed for the forest, Dasharatha died of grief.

Dashavaikalika Sutra The Sanskrit name of a Jain text, the *DASAVEYALIYA SUTTA*

Dashavatara Temple A temple of the Hindu god VISHNU constructed in the sixth century, located at Deogarh in district Jhansi, Uttar Pradesh. It is one of the earliest Hindu temples still existing today, though it is only partially preserved. The main shrine is square, built on a moulded basement. A shikhara or tower once rose above it, but no longer exists. The wall panels are beautifully carved and represent the high point of Gupta art. There are sculptures of Vishnu on GARUDA and sleeping on the serpent ANANTA, scenes from the life of KRISHNA and from the *MAHABHARATA* and *RAMAYANA*. Some of the narrative panels have been removed to museums.

Dasnami Ten orders of SHAIVITE ascetics founded by SHANKARA, the Advaitic philosopher, in the ninth century. These orders still exist today and are the following: Aranya, Ashrama, Bharati, Giri, Parvata, Puri, Sarasvati, Sagara, Tirtha, and Vana. Swamis, gurus and ascetics incorporate the name of their order in their names as, for instance, Vedaranya. Each of the orders is attached to one of the four MATHAS founded by Shankara, at BADRINATH, PURI, DVARAKA and SRINGERI.

Dastagir Sahib Dargah A DARGAH or shrine of a SUFI saint located near Srinagar in Kashmir. According to local legend, when the Prophet MUHAMMAD visited heaven, he rode on the lap of Dastagir, and therefore the saint is specially venerated.

The shrine is well-maintained with a graceful white and green exterior, and a colourfully decorated interior. The doorway has brass discs with writings from the Quran, connected with thick chains, and devotees touch these as they enter, to absorb sacred energy.

dastur A term for a Zoroastrian high priest. Lower priests are known as mobeds. Only boys from certain priestly families can become priests and are trained in special schools (madressas). Any male from a priestly family can perform rituals, even if he is not a full-time priest. The priestly caste of ancient Iran, known as athravan, was similar to the BRAHMANAS of India.

Data Ganj Baksh The popular name of the eleventh-century SUFI saint ABUL HASAN AL-HUJWIRI.

Dattatreya An ancient RISHI or sage who is described in the PURANAS and other texts and is considered an incarnation of the Hindu god VISHNU. Dattatreya was born as the son of the rishi ATRI and his wife Anasuya. He was mild, gentle and very learned. He was worshipped by the king Kartavirya, to whom he gave a boon of a thousand arms. The *HARIVAMSHA* states that Vishnu came to the world as Dattatreya to revive the knowledge of the VEDAS. His main characteristic is kshama or mercy. He is also the protector of DHARMA and the teacher of divine knowledge. As a deity, he sometimes represents the three gods BRAHMA, Vishnu and SHIVA together. A Puranic story explains how he came to represent all three deities. Brahma, Vishnu and Shiva, once appeared to Anasuya as BRAHMANAS, and asked her to offer them food after removing all her clothes. Anasuya could not refuse them, but her purity enabled her to turn the gods into babies. Their wives pleaded with her to restore them to their original forms, and in return, she asked for a boon—that they be born to her. Thus Dattatreya was born. (In some stories the three deities are incarnated separately). In his images, the three gods are depicted together, or Vishnu is shown accompanied by the VAHANAS (vehicles) of the other two. Dattatreya images are often accompanied by a cow and four dogs. Some interpret these as representing mother earth and the four Vedas, which came under Dattatreya's protection, though they may also represent his love for animals, for which the sage was known. In several temples Dattatreya is represented only by footprints .

From around the eighth century, Dattatreya the ancient sage, seems to have been appropriated by other sects. According to tradition, he composed the *AVADHUTA GITA*, probably of the ninth century, as well as other texts. This *Gita* describes the liberation of an avadhuta and has Advaitic passages. Dattatreya the ancient sage, and Dattatreya the avadhuta, probably belong to two different traditions. Other accounts in later texts state that he loved songs and musical instruments, and did not bother about caste. He was the creator of the SOMA plant and saved the gods from the asuras. Dattatreya is said to have been adept in TANTRA. The *MARKANDEYA PURANA* indicates that he was involved in Tantric rites and that he stayed at Mahur, a centre of SHAKTI worship. The NATHA YOGIS

take Dattatreya as their guru, and believe he was a great siddha. The MAHANUBHAVA sect of the thirteenth century, also incorporated the worship of Dattatreya. Another aspect of Dattatreya is as a protector from evil influences.

There are Dattatreya temples all over India, particularly in Gujarat and Maharashtra. The worship of Dattatreya is also popular in Andhra Pradesh, Karnataka and Tamil Nadu. At the Dattatreya temple on KALADUNGAR hill in Gujarat, prasad is still offered to jackals, in memory of Dattatreya's kindness to these animals. Among other Dattatreya shrines, one on the Baba Budan Giri hill in Karnataka is interesting. Here Dattatreya is also worshipped as Dada Kalandar, a Muslim saint. Another important shrine is the SUCHINDRAM TEMPLE in Tamil Nadu. Dattatreya is also said to have had eighty-four disciples, who became SIDDHAS, perfected ones. Sacred centres were established by these siddhas, among which is LAKSHMANA SIDDHA. Recently there has been a growth in Tantric sects based on Dattatreya worship. Thus there are many forms and aspects of Dattatreya.

Several saints of the Gujarat–Maharashtra region are considered incarnations of Dattatreya. Among them is SAI BABA OF SHIRDI.

Daud, Mulla A SUFI poet of the fourteenth century who wrote in early Hindi. Mulla Daud was born in Dalmau near Rae Bareli in present Uttar Pradesh, and was a saint of the CHISTI order. He is best known for his work, *Chandayan*, completed in 1379, which is the story of the love of a Rajput princess, Chanda, for Lorik, a man of the Ahir caste, and of their elopement. Sufi ideals are integrated into the story. According to Badauni, a sixteenth-century historian, sections from it were recited by a maulana or religious leader whose name was Taqiuddin, as part of his sermons in a mosque. The maulana believed the text conveyed the divine truth as revealed in the QURAN, despite the Hindu theme and references to BRAHMANAS, RAMA, and SITA.

dawa A term in Islam that means a call or invocation. It can be used in two ways: to invite or call someone to join Islam, that is, as a form of propaganda, or as an invocation, calling on the help of God or his angels. While magic and fortune-telling are forbidden in orthodox Islam, invocations using the name of God are allowed. The *JAWAHIR-I KHAMSAH*, a sixteenth-century text written by Shaikh MUHAMMAD GHAUS, is one of the texts that describes the various methods of dawa. According to Ghaus, dawa or dawat-i asma, could only be learnt from a perfected PIR or MURSHD.

Dayabhaga A Sanskrit text on Hindu laws of inheritance, compiled in the twelfth century. It was written by Jimutavahana and was part of a larger text, the *Dharmaratna*. The *Dayabhaga* includes topics on the division of the father's and grandfather's property, the inheritance of sons after the death of the father, those who should not inherit because of certain disabilities, and those who inherit if a man dies without a son. The MANU SMRITI is often quoted in this text. The *Dayabhaga* has influenced Hindu law.

Dayananda Sarasvati, Swami   The founder of the ARYA SAMAJ. Swami Dayananda Sarasvati was born at Tankara, in Kathiawar, Gujarat, in 1824. His original name was Mulasankar and he was a Hindu BRAHMANA from a well-to-do orthodox family. He studied Sanskrit, the VEDAS and other texts, and was very learned. When he was eighteen years old, his sister died, and soon after, his uncle. Mulasankar began to think deeply about life and death, and left his home in search of answers when he was twenty-one years old. He took sannyasa and was named Dayananda Sarasvati, as he joined the Sarasvati order of ascetics. In 1860, after wandering through different parts of India, meeting gurus and SANNYASIS, he met Guru Virajananda at MATHURA and became his disciple. Virajananada, though blind, was extremely learned, and encouraged him to reveal the true Vedic knowlegde to the world. Dayananda then inaugurated the Arya Samaj at MUMBAI (Bombay) in 1875 to teach people to follow the Vedas and lead a life of nobility (arya = noble). The Samaj headquarters shifted to Lahore and it had a large following. Swami Dayananda tried to stop conversion to other faiths, which led to opposition from Islamic and Christian leaders. Dayananda also tried to bring about reforms in Hindu society, believing that the Vedas represented true Hinduism. He was against the CASTE SYSTEM, child marriage, and the oppression of widows. He wrote several books, including the *Rigvedadi-bhashya-bhumika*, a commentary on the Vedas in nine volumes; *Samskara Vidhi*, the philosophy behind sixteen important Hindu ceremonies; and his most famous work, *Satyartha Prakasha*, which explains the philosophy of the Arya Samaj. Members of his organization opened schools, colleges and orphanages, as well as homes for widows. Several of his followers participated in the freedom movement.

He was respected and revered but died an untimely death at Ajmer in 1883 after visiting the court of the maharaja of Jodhpur. According to a story associated with this, the swami was actually poisoned by a supporter of the maharaja after he rebuked the maharaja for his involvement with a dancing girl. However, the truth of this is not known.

The Arya Samaj is still a popular organization, with thousands of followers in countries all over the world.

Dead Sea Scrolls   A term given to ancient documents found at sites near the Dead Sea, relating to Judaism and Christianity. Most of the documents were found in caves near Qumran, and include texts of the Hebrew Bible with variant readings, Jewish literature known as Intertestemental Literature, and the description of a religious community, led by someone known as the

Teacher of Righteousness. This teacher was initially identified by some with Jesus, but research indicates he lived at least two centuries before Christ. Comparisons have been drawn between the Teacher of Righteousness and some passages in the Zoroastrian *Gathas*.

Delhi   A city with a historic past, with innumerable medieval and modern monuments. In the time of the MAHABHARATA Delhi was known as INDRAPRASTHA, the city of Indra, and excavations at the presumed site of the old city indicate occupation dating back to 1000 BCE or earlier. This and other areas of Delhi were occupied by successive dynasties and kings, including the Rajputs, the sultans and the Mughals. The British made it their capital in 1911, and New Delhi became the seat of the independent Indian government in 1947. Delhi has more than 8000 religious monuments representing all religions.

Among the major temples are the LAKSHMI NARAYAN TEMPLE, the Jhandelwalan Kali Temple, the Yogamaya Temple in Mehrauli, the Kalkaji Temple, the Akshardham Temple, the Chhattarpur Shiva Temple, the Hanuman Temple in Connaught Place, the Shirdi Sai Baba Temple, and the ISKCON Krishna Temple. There are temples of deities from different regions, such as the Ayyappa Temple and the Swami Malai Mandir Temple. Historic mosques include the JAMA MASJID, the JAMALI KAMALI MOSQUE, the QUWWATUL ISLAM MOSQUE and others. Among the most popular DARGAHS of Sufi saints are those of NIZAMUDDIN AULIYA, CHIRAGH DILLI, QUTBUDDIN BAKHTIYAR KAKI and Matka Pir. There are several churches representing most Christian groups and denominations. Some of the earlier churches include ST. JAMES CHURCH, and St. Andrew's Cathedral. Among historic GURDWARAS are the MOTI BAGH GURDWARA, BANGLA SAHIB GURDWARA and SISGANJ GURDWARA. There are Jain temples, of which the most prominent is the Digambara Temple, opposite the Red Fort, to which a charitable bird hospital is attached. Buddhist temples and stupas of Tibetan Buddhism co-exist with those of other Buddhist groups. Other religions are also represented through the BAHAI LOTUS TEMPLE, the Jewish Synagogue and the Zoroastrian Dar-e Meher or AGIARY. There are innumerable other old and new religious shrines.

Deoband School   A popular term for the DAR-UL-ULOOM, a major institute of Islamic theology, located at Deoband in Uttar Pradesh.

Dera Baba Nanak   A sacred place connected with the life of Guru NANAK, the founder of Sikhism, who lived here in the last years of his life. It is located on the river Ravi and is today on the Indo-Pak border. It earlier formed part of KARTARPUR, a township on both sides of the river. Today Kartarpur is on only one side of the river, now in Pakistan. A large GURDWARA was later built at Kartarpur, where the guru had died in 1539 and another, Darbar Sahib, on the Indian side of the river, at Dera Baba Nanak. It was reconstructed in

1827 by Maharaja Ranjit Singh A chola, or cloak of the guru, is preserved here, and it is an important centre of pilgrimage. The gurdwara is a simple structure with a single storey built on a square plan.

According to legend, the guru's body was placed under a sheet, but when the sheet was removed, the body had vanished, leaving only flowers behind.

Dera Sacha Sauda An offshoot of the Radhasoami sect, set up in 1948 in Sirsa, Punjab. Dera Sacha Sauda was founded by Shehanshah Mastanaji Maharaj, a disciple of Baba Sawan Singh of Beas. He was succeeded in 1963 by Shah Satnam Singhji Maharaj, followed in 1990 by Gurmeet Ram Rahim Singh Maharaj. Like other groups with a Radhasoami origin, the sect is open to all religions and communities, and believes in following the true guru, engaging in satsang, and chanting the satnam (true name). It is said to have between 40 lakh and one crore followers in Punjab, Haryana, Rajasthan and other states.

Dev Samaj An organization founded by Shiv Narain Agnihotri on 16 February 1887 in Lahore (now in Pakistan). Shiv Narain, later known as Bhagwan Dev Atma, was born on 20 December 1850 at Akbarpur, district Kanpur, present-day Uttar Pradesh, in a traditional brahmana family. After his early education, he joined an engineering college, and in 1873 became drawing master in Government School, Lahore. Always spiritually inclined, he became a prominent member of the BRAHMO SAMAJ, and later of the Sadharan Brahmo Samaj. In 1882 he changed his name to Satyanand Agnihotri, and became a full time member of the Samaj. He founded his own Samaj in 1887, which was initially considered an offshoot of the Brahmo Samaj, but later diverged. Shiv Narain believed that all living beings and non-living entities had evolved over millions of years, and were not created by God. Each living being has a life-power, often called the soul, which comes into existence with the birth of the being, and ends with death. True salvation of the soul involves shedding all negativity, as well as wrong and selfish ideas and beliefs. Obtaining mastery over one's thoughts and actions, enable one to 'enjoy the bliss of an altruistic and truly religious life'. The different aspects of nature are still not fully known, but true knowledge is not in scriptures, but in learning and understanding the laws of nature. Despite these ideas, he focused on the guru, in the form of himself, as the guide to a higher life. He advocated social reforms such as the education of women, was against caste, other social evils such as child marriage, and laid down strong ethical principles. The Dev Samaj Higher Life Academy, was founded on 15 August 1905 to spread these ideas. Shiv Narain wrote a number of books and articles on the subject. *Dev Shastra*, a four volume work, provides the main ideas of his Vigyan Mulak Dharma or 'Science grounded religion'. Shiv Narain died in 1929.

deva A divine being. All Hindu gods are known as devas or devis. Deva is a Sanskrit word, that stems from the root 'div', which means 'to shine', similar in origin to the Latin 'deus'. In the literature of Zoroastrianism, the word 'daeva', initially a spiritual being, later came to mean a demon.

devadasis A term for girls or women attached to Hindu temples and dedicated to the service of the gods. This practice probably developed in the ninth and tenth centuries, though it originated earlier and was more common in south India. It has, by now, largely been abolished but still exists in some areas. The girls worshipped the deity and sang and danced before it and in processions. They belonged to the temple and in later times were also sometimes used as prostitutes. Early texts classify devadasis into seven categories: datta, who voluntarily dedicates herself; vikrita, who sells herself; bhritya, who gives herself to increase the prosperity of her family; bhakta, who comes to the temple out of devotion to god; hrita, who is presented to the temple after being enticed away from her home; alankara, a well-trained girl given to the temple by a king or noble; gopala, one who is paid wages for her service to the temple.

Many devadasis were dedicated to the temple between the ages of six or eight. They could never marry, as they were considered married to the deity. Though they had a certain status and privileges, with their own customs and laws of inheritance, they often led unhappy lives.

Devadatta A cousin and rival of the BUDDHA. Devadatta became a monk at a young age and was prominent in the SANGHA. He sought more power for himself and conspired with AJATASHATRU, son of BIMBISARA, the ruler of MAGADHA, to overthrow the king and to displace the Buddha. His plot failed, but he succeeded in creating a schism in the sangha. His followers later rejoined the original sangha.

Devaki The mother of the Hindu god, KRISHNA. She is usually said to be the daughter of Devaka, who was the brother of Ugrasena. She was married to VASUDEVA and they lived in the region of MATHURA. The king of Mathura was Kamsa, son of Ugrasena, and thus related to Devaki. According to a prophecy, he would be killed by the eighth son of Devaki. Therefore he imprisoned her and VASUDEVA and killed her first six sons. By divine intervention, her seventh and eighth sons, BALARAMA and Krishna, were born. Devaki and her husband were released by Kamsa when he realized the baby Krishna was no longer with them. In some accounts they were later reimprisoned and remained in prison until Krishna was able to kill Kamsa.

According to Puranic legends, in a previous birth Devaki was Kaikeyi, wife of King DASHARATHA of the RAMAYANA, responsible for sending RAMA into exile. Rama forgave her and promised to be reborn as her son, and thus was born as Krishna. But because of her past sins, Devaki never really had the pleasure of being together with her divine son. Devaki is also revered as a goddess.

Devaloka The LOKA or world of the gods in Hindu mythology.

Devanagari A Sanskrit word meaning 'the divine script'. Devanagari developed from the early Brahmi script used in the third century BCE inscriptions of the emperor ASHOKA, and is the script in which Sanskrit, Hindi and Marathi are written today. Each letter is said to have a specific divine meaning. According to TANTRIC texts, the Devanagari alphabet is arranged in the seven main CHAKRAS, and is recited in special rituals.

devarishis RISHIS or sages who had perfected themselves when on earth and now dwell among the gods. NARADA is one of them.

devata A Sanskrit term meaning god, used as a synonym of DEVA, or for a minor deity.

Devi A generic term for any Hindu goddess, as well as a term for one supreme goddess. In the latter context, she is often referred to as MAHADEVI.

Devi Bhagavata Purana A Sanskrit text, a PURANA dealing with the worship of DEVI or SHAKTI.

Devi-Mahatmya A Sanskrit text which glorifies the Hindu goddess DEVI and forms part of the MARKANDEYA PURANA. It is is used for the worship of DURGA and is recited in Durga temples and at the time of DURGA PUJA. It was probably composed before the sixth century.

Dge-Lugs-pa A school of Tibetan Buddhism, also spelt GELUG or Gelug-pa.

dhamma The Pali term for DHARMA.

Dhammapada A Buddhist text which forms part of the KHUDDAKA NIKAYA of the PALI CANON. Literally the title means 'path of DHAMMA'. The text consists of 423 verses, arranged in twenty-six sections or *vaggas*. It is really an anthology, a collection of Buddhist ideas and principles, and is the best-known Buddhist work, translated into all European languages. More than half the verses can be found in other texts of the Pali Canon, whereas others are original. Some typical examples of verses in the *Dhammapada* are given below:

'What we are today comes from our thoughts of yesterday, and our present thoughts build our life of tomorrow: our life is the creation of our mind. If a man speaks or acts with a pure mind, joy follows him as his own shadow.' (1.2)

'Better than a thousand useless words is one single word that gives peace'. (8.100)

'It is better to go alone on the path of life rather than to have a fool for a companion. With few wishes and few cares, and leaving all sins behind, let a man travel alone, like a great elephant alone in the forest.' (23.330) (Trans. by Juan Mascaro)

Dhammasangani A HINAYANA Buddhist text that forms part of the ABHIDHAMMA PITAKA of the PALI CANON.

It explains the finer points of the DHAMMA and is meant for advanced monks. The philosophy of the NIKAYAS is classified and summarized in this text.

Dhanteras A Hindu festival celebrated two days before DIVALI in October/November, in honour of the deity DHANVANTARI, the divine physician. As Dhanvantari emerged from the ocean of milk carrying a vessel filled with AMRITA or divine nectar, on this day it is traditional to buy some kind of vessel. Dhanteras is also a festival of wealth, and buying other items as well is considered auspicious. The festival is celebrated particularly in north India.

Dhanvantari A Hindu deity considered an incarnation of VISHNU, and the traditional founder of Ayurveda or Indian medicine. Medicine and the science of healing were gifts of the gods, and Dhanvantari was at first the physician of the gods, before bringing the art of healing to the world. At the churning of the ocean for AMRITA, the drink of immortality, Dhanvantari emerged carrying the divine liquid in a vessel. Several Dhanvantaris are mentioned in texts, all of whom were associated with medicine and healing. Divodasa, a legendary king of KASHI, was said to be the incarnation of the first Dhanvantari and to have classified surgery into two branches, apart from developing a scientific methodology for medicine. Another Dhanvantari was associated with the legendary king Vikramaditya. Dhanvantari is worshipped and prayed to for health and healing.

Dharamsala A town in Himachal Pradesh, now the headquarters of the Tibetan Buddhist leader, the DALAI LAMA. The head of the KARMA-KAGYU sect has also made his home there. Dharamsala is located at a height of 4876 m. Apart from other buildings, it has a number of monasteries and a large Tibetan settlement. The Tsuglagkhang complex contains the residence of the Dalai Lama, the Namgyal monastery and the Tsuglagkhang Temple, all located in McLeod Ganj, the upper town. Gangcheng Keyshong, the administrative centre of the Tibetan government in exile, is halfway between the upper and lower towns. Here there is a large library of Tibetan texts and an institute of Tibetan medicine, with the Nechung monastery nearby.

dharana A Sanskrit term that means 'concentration'. Dharana is the sixth step in the system of Raja YOGA, and is also a part of other philosophical systems.

dharma A Sanskrit term from the root 'dhri', that has many different meanings.
(1) It is generally interpreted as duty, right conduct or truth. In Hinduism, the DHARMA SHASTRAS are texts which describe customary laws, though the sources of dharma include all the sacred Hindu texts. The knowledge of texts is usually confined to the learned, but according to tradition, there are four sources of dharma: SHRUTI, that which is revealed; SMRITI, that

which is heard; sadachar, the conduct of good people; and atmatushti, moral reason or conscience. For an ordinary person, dharma or the right way of action is often derived from myths and legends (katha) from the RAMAYANA, MAHABHARATA, PURANAS and other texts, retold with a local flavour. The lives of certain individuals and deities are emphasized to provide examples of lives which embody dharma. Thus SITA and SAVITRI are examples of ideal wives, RAMA, of an ideal man and king. LAKSHMANA is the perfect brother, HANUMAN is known for loyalty and devotion to Rama, and GANESHA for the worship of his parents. Each caste or person has a specific dharma. The dharma of a BRAHMANA is thus to study the VEDAS and perform sacrifices, of a married man to take care of his wife and children, etc.

In Buddhism, dharma (Pali: dhamma) primarily refers to the teachings of the BUDDHA and is part of the TRIRATNA or 'three jewels', and one of the three refuges of all Buddhists. It includes the law, doctrine or ethical precepts, and implies an understanding of the FOUR NOBLE TRUTHS and the EIGHTFOLD PATH. In the third century BCE, the Mauryan emperor ASHOKA laid down his policy of dhamma, a code of conduct to be followed by all his subjects, based on Buddhist principles.

In Jainism, dharma or right conduct involves cultivating the TRIRATNA or three jewels of right belief, right conduct and right knowledge, and following the five vows of AHIMSA (non-violence), satya (truth), asteya (not stealing), aparigraha (non-greed), and BRAHMACHARYA (chaste living). These five, which also form the YAMAS or restraints of the yogic path, are practised at different levels by ascetics and non-ascetics. Jain ascetics follow them strictly, while non-ascetics can marry and acquire what they need, and have fewer restrictions on food.

For Sikhs, dharma refers to a moral way of life, based on god's will or a divine command (hukam), and explained in their scriptures. In Zoroastrianism, the concept of ASHA is similar to that of dharma.

Right conduct is part of all religious systems, though the term dharma may not be used.

(2) Dharma can also be translated as 'religion'.

(3) In Buddhism, Jainism and other early philosophies, dharma is also used in a different context, as an element or substance. In Buddhism the mental and physical world comprise various dharmas, including mental faculties and material elements. In Jainism dharma is one of the six DRAVYAS or basic substances of the world. It pervades the whole world, is continuous and extends through space, but is devoid of any qualities such as smell, sound, colour or taste.

Dharma Deva A Hindu deity. DHARMA, or right conduct, has also been personifed as a deity or person who upholds right action. KUNTI in the MAHABHARATA meditated on Dharma Deva and YUDHISHTHIRA was born to her. When the PANDAVAS started their journey to heaven at the end of their lives, Dharma accompanied them in the form of a dog.

According to the PURANAS, Dharma was the son of BRAHMA and one of the PRAJAPATIS.

DAKSHA gave ten (or in some texts thirteen) of his daughters in marriage to Dharma. Various Puranas have different lists of these, but according to one version, they were: Arundhati, Vasu, Yami, Lamba, Bhanu, Marutvati, Sankalpa, Muhurta, Sadhya and Vishva. Other names include Shraddha, Maitri, Hri and Murti. Among their sons were NARA and NARAYANA.

As Dharmaraja is a name of the god YAMA, Dharma Deva is often identified with Yama, though the two have different origins and myths.

Dharma Shastras Sanskrit texts which deal with the customs, practices, ethical conduct and laws of Hindus. The term Dharma Shastra is sometimes taken to include all texts dealing with Hindu law, but it also refers to a specific set of texts, probably composed from the second century onwards, which expand on the DHARMA SUTRAS. The Dharma Shastras form part of SMRITI or 'remembered' literature, rather than the more sacred SHRUTI or divinely revealed literature, such as the VEDAS. The *Manava Dharma Shastra* (of Manu), also known as the *MANU SMRITI*, is the earliest, while those of YAJNAVALKYA, VISHNU and NARADA are probably from the third to fifth centuries CE. There are several other Dharma Shastras, including those assigned to ATRI, Apastamba, ANGIRAS, BRIHASPATI, DAKSHA, PULASTYA and VYASA, some dating to medieval times. Commentaries on these, such as the *DAYABHAGA* and *MITAKSHARA*, are additional sources for customary Hindu law.

Dharma Sutras Sanskrit texts which form the earliest sources of Hindu law. They were originally composed between the sixth and seventh centuries BCE, with additions made later. The customs and ethics described in these, are written in short aphorisms or sutras and were later expanded and written in verse, forming the DHARMA SHASTRAS. Dharma Sutras are attributed to different authors, among them the sages or RISHIS Apastambha, Baudhayana, Gautama and VASISHTHA. They form part of SMRITI or 'remembered' literature, rather than that directly revealed by the gods.

Dharma Thakur A village deity of Bengal. He is also known as Dharma Raj, or Dharma Rai. Dharma Thakur is worshipped and depicted in different forms, often as a simple stone or mound of earth, as a tortoise, or sometimes in the form of a man with a large moustache. All castes make offerings to him, though the priests are usually from the lower castes. According to one scholar, the deity owes its origin to the Buddhist concept of DHARMA, which was represented as a STUPA, similar to the shape of a tortoise. This is said to account for his worship by lower castes, while other deities were part of Brahmanical Hinduism. His consorts or female counterparts are known as

Dharma Kaminyas and include Kalkali Devi, Kaliburi, Rai Buri, Rai Baghini and others, some of whom have separate temples dedicated to them. The worship of these deities is widespread in rural Bengal, and there are several Bengali texts in praise of Dharma Thakur, known as *Dharma-Mangalas*. Later, Dharma Rai was also absorbed into the Brahmanical pantheon as a form of SHIVA or VISHNU, known as SASTHA or Dharma Sastha. As a guardian deity, he is portrayed seated on a horse. His southern counterpart is AYYANAR.

Dharma Rai is worshipped with sacrificial offerings of goats, pigeons and chickens, as well as with offerings of terracotta elephants and horses.

dharmachakra pravartana Literally, 'the turning of the wheel of law', a term referring to the first teachings of the BUDDHA in the deer park at SARNATH. Here he is said to have revealed the FOUR NOBLE TRUTHS and the EIGHTFOLD PATH, forming the basis of the Buddhist DHARMA or teachings. The dharma chakra in the form of a spoked wheel is an important Buddhist symbol depicted in art. In early art it represents the Buddha and his teachings.

Dharmaguptaka A HINAYANA Buddhist sect, a branch of the VIBHAJYAVADA, which formed a part of the STHAVIRAVADA sect. Literally, the name means 'protectors of the DHARMA'. They have their own versions of the Suttas, *VINAYA* and *ABHIDHAMMA*, and later became popular in Central Asia and China. Their texts describe a number of rituals, as well as rules, not commonly observed by other sects. For instance, there are twenty-six rules regarding correct behaviour at a STUPA. Among their other differences from the various Hinayana sects were their views on gifts given to the SANGHA. They felt gifts should be given to the BUDDHA separately and that gifts to stupas were also meritorious.

dharmakaya A Buddhist concept. In early HINAYANA literature, the BUDDHA is said to have a body 'born of dharma', i.e, a 'dharmakaya'. According to THERAVADA doctrines, the two bodies of the Buddha were the rupakaya (physical) and the dharmakaya (body of truth). After passing to NIRVANA, the rupakaya remained in his relics and the dharmakaya in his teachings.

The concept was further developed in later texts of MAHAYANA and VAJRAYANA. The Buddha is said to have three bodies or states (TRIKAYA), dharmakaya being the third. It represents the Absolute, the state of Buddhahood, that is reached at the final stage on the path.

Dharmakirti A MAHAYANA Buddhist philosopher who lived from c. 600 to 650 and critically assessed the approaches of the YOGACHARA school of Buddhism. His main work is *Pramanavarttika*, which elaborates and comments on the work of DIGNAGA, an earlier Buddhist philosopher. Another of his works is *Nyayabindu*, a text on logic. His writings mark an important stage in the development of Mahayana Buddhist logic and philosophy.

Dharmapala A MAHAYANA Buddhist philosopher who lived in the sixth century and belonged to the YOGACHARA school of Buddhism. He was a disciple of DIGNAGA and took over from him as head of NALANDA University. Dharmapala's best-known text is the *Vijnatamatrata-siddhi*, which was translated into Chinese. It classifies DHARMAS or elements into five categories, including mental dharmas or states of consciousness, mental faculties, material elements, things or situations, and non-created elements. It states that consciousness exists, though other things are unreal. It became the main text of the Fa-hsiang school of Chinese Buddhism.

Dharmaputra A name of YUDHISHTHIRA, one of the five PANDAVAS in the *MAHABHARATA*. He was the son of DHARMA DEVA and is also known as Dharmaraja.

Dharmaraja A Hindu deity, usually a name of YAMA, god of death. Among others referred to as Dharmaraja is YUDHISHTHIRA.

Dhatr A Hindu deity first mentioned in the RIG VEDA. He is said to have created the sun, moon, heaven, earth and air, and to be the lord of the world. In post-Vedic texts, he is the creator and preserver of the world, the equivalent of PRAJAPATI or BRAHMA. He is also one of the Adityas.

Dhatukatha A Buddhist HINAYANA text that forms part of the *ABHIDHAMMA PITAKA* of the PALI CANON. It deals with the dhatus (elements) and their interconnections, and has fourteen short chapters in question and answer form.

Dhishana A deity mentioned in the RIG VEDA. She is the wife of the gods and a goddess of abundance.

Dhritarashtra A king described in the MAHABHARATA who ruled at HASTINAPURA. Born blind, he was the son of the rishi VYASA from Ambika, widow of King Vichitravirya. He was married to GANDHARI and was the father of a hundred sons, collectively known as the KAURAVAS.

Dhruva The pole star. In Hindu myths, he was the son of Uttanapada by his second wife Suniti, and the grandson of MANU Svayambhuva. Though born a KSHATRIYA, he practised austerities and became a RISHI. VISHNU was pleased with him and elevated him to the sky, making him the pole star. In some texts, Dhruva is considered an incarnation of Vishnu.

Dhumavarna A king of the NAGAS. According to the *HARIVAMSHA*, a Sanskrit text, he took YADU, son of YAYATI, to his capital and married his five daughters to him. The YADAVAS were descended from them. This myth probably indicates inter-marriage between different groups.

Dhumavati A Hindu goddess, one of the ten MAHAVIDYAS or TANTRIC goddesses. She is said to be a widow, dressed in dirty clothes, pale, tall, stern and unsmiling. Her hair is dishevelled, she has a crooked nose, a quarrelsome nature, and rides a crow. Dhumavati represents darkness and the negative powers of life. Worshipping her enables transcendence of negativity and leads to inner silence and illumination.

Dhumrorna A Hindu goddess, one of the wives of the god YAMA. She is depicted along with the god in some images, either sitting on his lap or standing nearby. She is said to represent the smoke of the funeral pyre.

Dhurjati A name of the Hindu god RUDRA or SHIVA.

dhyana A Sanskrit term for meditation and contemplation. It is the seventh stage of Raja YOGA, and is also practised in other philosophical systems.

Dhyaneshvara A Maratha BHAKTI saint. His name is also spelt JNANESHVARA.

Dhyani Buddhas A term used for celestial BUDDHAS of the northern Buddhist pantheon. It refers to five Buddhas representing the five SKANDHAS, who head families of BUDDHIST DEITIES. They are popularly called Dhyani Buddhas, as in iconography they are shown in miniature form in the crown or head of the deity which forms part of their family. These Buddhas are described in detail in the *GUHYASAMAJA TANTRA*. Each is assigned a MANTRA, a SHAKTI or female counterpart, a colour, a direction, and a guardian of the gate. The five are VAIROCHANA, RATNASAMBHAVA, AMITABHA, AMOGHASIDDHI and AKSHOBHYA.

Diamond Sutra The popular English name of a MAHAYANA Buddhist text, the *VAJRACHCHHEDIKA-PRAJNAPARAMITA-SUTRA*, one of the many PRAJNAPARAMITA texts.

Diamper, Synod of A Christian council held in 1599 at Udayamperur (Diamper) near Kochi in Kerala. It brought the SYRIAN CHRISTIANS under the Portuguese Catholics in Goa and thus united the Syrian Christians with the ROMAN CATHOLIC Church. After 1653, when the COONEN KURISU revolt took place, the Syrian Church broke up into different groups, one branch remaining Latinized.

Digambara One of the two main sects of Jainism. According to tradition, in the fourth century BCE there was a great famine in north India. A leader of the Jains, probably BHADRABAHU I, went to south India around this time, along with 12,000 followers, and settled at the place now known as SHRAVANA BELAGOLA in Karnataka. CHANDRAGUPTA MAURYA, the emperor of the Mauryan dynasty, also came with them, though according to some accounts he reached Shravana Belagola slightly later.

Those who went south had certain differences with those who remained in the north. The southern Jains came to be known as Digambaras, while the northern were SHVETAMBARAS.

Digambara literally means 'sky-clad', that is, those who do not wear any clothes, while Shvetambaras are those who wear white garments. The initial rule of MAHAVIRA was that Jain monks should discard clothes as part of their asceticism.

The two sects largely follow different JAIN TEXTS, though they have some in common. In the north the Shvetambaras collected the teachings of Mahavira and compiled them into the ANGAS and other texts. These were not accepted as authentic by the Digambaras, who have their own set of texts. Two important texts for Digambaras are the *KARMAPRABHRITA* and *KASHAYA-PRABHRITA*, though there are others as well. Despite this there are not many differences between the ideas and concepts of the two main sects.

Some key differences are: (1) For JAIN ASCETICS, rules are more strict for Digambaras, with nudity practised in advanced stages. Nuns in both groups wear clothes. (2) Digambaras believe a woman cannot attain enlightenment, while Shvetambaras believe both men and women are capable of gaining enlightenment. Digambaras explain this by saying that because of societal pressures, a woman cannot practise the extremes of asceticism required, such as abandoning clothes. (3) Digambaras believe that once a person becomes a TIRTHANKARA, he does not need food, even if he is still in this world; Shvetambaras do not agree. (4) Digambara images of Tirthankaras and deities are plain, with downcast eyes. Images in Shvetambara temples have open eyes and are richly decorated. (5) Digambaras have different versions of the life of Mahavira.

Among the major sub-sects of the Digambaras are the BISAPANTHA, TERAPANTHA and TARANAPANTHA or Samaiyapantha. Other minor sub-sects include the GUMANAPANTHA and TOTAPANTHA. A recent sub-sect is the KANJIPANTHA. The sub-sects differ mainly in the type of rituals performed in temples. The Bisapantha and Terapantha normally do not visit the temples of other sects.

Diggajas Elephants in Hindu mythology. They protect the eight points of the compass and are therefore known as ASHTADIGGAJAS.

Digha Nikaya A HINAYANA Buddhist text of the PALI CANON, literally 'long suttas (sutras) or discourses'. A part of the *SUTTA PITAKA*, the *Digha Nikaya* consists of thirty-four suttas on the teachings of the BUDDHA, each quite long. Some of the suttas are in prose, the others in a mixture of prose and verse. The first sutta, the *Brahmajala Sutta*, criticizes BRAHMANA practices, while the second, *Samana-phala Sutta*, describes non-Buddhist ascetic teachers. These are then contrasted with the Buddhist way. Other interesting suttas inlude the sixteenth, the *MAHAPARINIBBANA SUTTA*, which is an account of the last years of the Buddha's life and his sayings and speeches at this time. The twenty-second, the *Mahasatipatthana Sutta*, discusses the different kinds of mindfulness and the FOUR NOBLE

TRUTHS. While in some suttas the Buddha is treated as a human being, in others, various miracles, powers and divine qualities are ascribed to him. Some suttas have creation stories, as in the PURANAS. On the whole, the *Digha Nikaya* is one of the most valuable texts for the main teachings of Hinayana Buddhism.

Dignaga A MAHAYANA Buddhist philosopher and logician of the YOGACHARA school who lived from c. 480 to 540. He spent many years at NALANDA and is known for two texts, the *Pramanasamuchchaya* and the *Nyayamukha*.

Dikapalas Hindu deities who are guardians of the eight directions. They are also known as Lokapalas and live in the different zones of Brahmaloka, on Mt MERU. Accoding to the *BHAGAVATA PURANA*, they are: in the east, INDRA, in his city of Amravati; in the south-east, AGNI, in his city of Tejovati; in the south, YAMA, in his city of Samyamani; in the south-west, NIRRITI in his city of Krishnanjana; in the west, VARUNA, in his city of Shraddhavati; in the north-west, VAYU in his city of Gandhavati; in the north, KUBERA, in his city of Mahodaya; in the north-east, SHIVA, in his city of Yashovati. BRAHMA sits in the centre in his city called Manovati. Other texts give different lists, including SURYA, SOMA and Ishana among the guardian deities. Each of the guardian deities has a pair of elephants which help in the protection of that quarter. These are known as the ASHTADIGGAJAS and Ashtadikkaranis.

Dilwara Temples A group of Jain temples located at Dilwara at Mt ABU in Rajasthan. The ADINATHA or Vimala Vasahi temple is the earliest, built in 1032, with additions from later periods. The patron of the temple was Vimala, a minister of Bhima I, a king of the Solanki dynasty. Constructed entirely in white marble, the inner shrine has an image of RISHABHA or Adinatha, the first TIRTHANKARA, and is connected to an enclosed MANDAPA with two porches. There are two more mandapas and an enclosing wall lined with small shrines. There are several other Jain images in niches, as well as an image of Vimala on a horse in the front porch. The pillars and side walls are elaborately carved with deities and scenes from their lives, surrounded by delicate scrollwork. On the ceiling are concentric circles with rows of musicians, dancers, soldiers, horses and elephants.

Next to it is the NEMINATHA or Luna Vasahi temple, constructed in 1230 and later, by two merchants, Vastupala and Tejapala. Similar in structure to the Adinatha temple, it is also of white marble and even more elaborately carved.

Another Adinatha temple here dates to the fourteenth century and has a large brass image in the inner shrine. The PARSHVANATHA temple of 1459 is built in grey stone and has a double-storeyed shrine. About 5 km away at Achalgarh fort are two more Jain temples.

Din-i Ilahi A popular term for the religion or system of worship founded by the Mughal emperor AKBAR in 1582, more correctly known as the Tauhid-i Ilahi. The religion is described in the *Ain-i Akbari*, the writings of the contemporary historian Badauni, the *DABISTAN-I MAZAHIB*, and other texts. Akbar established himself as the leader of the religion, which contained a mix of ideas derived mainly from Hindu and Zoroastrian sources. Sun worship formed an important part of it, and Akbar is said to have recited the 1001 names of SURYA, the sun god, in Sanskrit every day. Fire was also revered and a sacred fire was always kept alight. In addition, lamps were lit every day. Followers were urged to give up eating meat and particularly to avoid beef; the slaughter of animals was forbidden on certain days. Disciples also paid obeisance to Akbar, as the guru or head of the religion. The contemporary historian Badauni states that at this time public prayers and the AZAN were prohibited, and mosques and prayer halls were converted into store-rooms, though this is probably not true.

Orthodox Muslims were against these practices, and the Tauhid-i-Ilahi died out after the death of Akbar in 1605. According to some accounts, Akbar himself lost interest in it in his final years, but this has been questioned.

Dinkard A Zoroastrian text of the tenth century that is encyclopedic in nature and consists of an analysis of various aspects of the religion, some of it in question-answer form. It includes a description of the NASKS and of several rituals, and is based on material from earlier texts. The *Dinkard* has nine books, though the first two books and part of the third book no longer exist.

Dinyar, Dastur A Zoroastrian priest who is said to have been a companion of the Prophet MUHAMMAD, though this is not historically confirmed. According to the esoteric school of Zoroastrianism, Dinyar was the same person as Salman-e-Fars, or Salman the Persian, one of the Prophet's companions. This school also believes that Muhammad and his son-in-law Ali, granted freedom of worship to Zoroastrians, a view which goes against traditional PARSI history.

Dip Singh, Baba A Sikh scholar and priest. Born around 1680, he came in touch with Guru GOBIND SINGH in 1700 and became a KHALSA. He, along with Bhai MANI SINGH, transcribed copies of the GURU GRANTH SAHIB for distribution. He fought in the battle of Sirhind and later in other battles, and was the GRANTHI, or head priest of Damdama Sahib. In 1762, after the Afghan invader Ahmad Shah Abdali had desecrated the GOLDEN TEMPLE or Har Mandir Sahib, Dip Singh marched to AMRITSAR with a small force. On the way he was wounded in battle, but he reached the Golden Temple and died near the sacred pool there.

Dipankara A Buddha who existed long before the historic BUDDHA, Shakyamuni. According to the *BUDDHAVAMSHA* and later Buddhist tradition, he was the first of twenty-four BUDDHAS. Long ago he spoke about the path to enlightenment, and among those inspired by him, was a young man known as Sumedha. Sumedha took the vows of the BODHISATTVA, and after countless lives was reborn as Gautama Siddhartha, who became a Buddha, known as Shakyamuni.

Dipavamsha A Buddhist text which deals with the history of Sri Lanka and with the growth and development of Buddhism there. It dates to the fourth century and was probably a composition of several writers.

Diti A deity first mentioned in the RIG VEDA, associated with ADITI. Her children became the MARUTS. In the *MAHABHARATA* and Puranas she was one of the daughters of DAKSHA and was married to KASHYAPA. Apart from the MARUTS, her children were the daityas, HIRANYAKSHA and HIRANYAKASHIPU, and their sister Simhika. Other DAITYAS were descended from them.

Ditthivaya (Drishtivada) A Jain text, the last of the twelve ANGAS. This text no longer exists, but other texts state that it had five divisions and included preparations for the right understanding of the sutras and stories of the TIRTHANKARAS. Two DIGAMBARA texts, the *KARMAPRABHRITA* and the *KASHAYA-PRABHRITA*, are said to be based on the *Ditthivaya*.

Divali One of the most important Hindu festivals. It occurs in October/November on the last day of the dark half of the month of Karttika. It is a festival of lights, celebrated by placing lights outside and within the home, and letting off firecrackers. Several different myths and deities are associated with this festival. Among deities, the most important is the god RAMA. After his exile of fourteen years, Rama is said to have returned to AYODHYA on this day, and the citizens decorated the city with lights to welcome him home. Divali recreates this event. It is also a day associated with LAKSHMI, goddess of wealth, who enters lighted homes and brings prosperity for the rest of the year. Games of chance, particularly dice and cards, are played, symbolizing the role of luck in acquiring and losing wealth. In some areas of south India, the festival marks the victory of the god KRISHNA over NARAKASURA.

Other festivals are associated with Divali and celebrated before or after it. DHANTERAS, when new utensils are bought, occurs two days before. On the day after Divali in rural areas, cattle are worshipped and decorated, and given special food. Two days after Divali is the festival of BHAI DUJ, when sisters honour their brothers.

Jains celebrate Divali as the day when the twenty-fourth Tirthankara, MAHAVIRA, attained nirvana.

Over the years Divali celebrations have changed in nature and character. Once only earthen lamps were used, filled with oil and with home-made wicks, while now candles and electric lights are more common, at least in urban areas. Shops are decorated days in advance of Divali, as it is a festival where gifts are given to friends, relatives and business associates. All communities join in the celebrations.

Divine Light Mission A religious organization founded in the early 1960s, which gained popularity abroad but declined by the 1970s. It was founded by Shri Hans Maharaj ji, originally a member of the Vaishnava VALLABHACHARYA sect. On his death in 1966, his son Prem Pal Singh took the title Guru Maharaj Ji, and spread the movement in the USA, where it had a large following. His followers lived with him and were known as Premis (lovers). After his marriage to an American woman in 1974, the Mission's activities and popularity declined. A successor organization, the Elan Vital, was then founded in 1983, and still attracts followers in the West.

Divine Light Society A social and religious organization founded by Swami SIVANANDA and registered as a trust in 1936. The organization, with its headquarters at Rishikesh, has several branches in India and other parts of the world. It disseminates information on religion and philosophy through publications, lectures and conferences, and runs educational institutions, dispensaries and other charitable organizations. The manifesto of the society states that: 'Anyone devoted to the ideals of truth, non-violence and purity can become a member of the Divine Life Society, which is a non-sectarian institution embodying in its widest perspective the common fundamental principles of all the religions of the world and of spiritual life in general.'

Divyavadana A MAHAYANA Buddhist text in Sanskrit which probably dates to the second or third century. It contains a number of Buddhist legends and stories. The text was translated into Chinese by the year 265.

dog, in religion The dog is a very significant animal in Zoroastrianism, and to some extent in Hinduism.

In Hinduism, dogs are associated with some of the deities. In the RIG VEDA, the god INDRA was helped by a female dog, SARAMA. Sarama is mentioned in later texts as well. In the *MAHABHARATA*, YUDHISHTHIRA refuses to enter heaven without his dog, which finally turns out to be the god DHARMA in disguise. RUDRA is called Shvapati, or lord of dogs, while SHIVA in his form as BHAIRAVA is accompanied by a dog. The god YAMA has two dogs, known as the SARAMEYAS, the descendents of Sarama. The rishi DATTATREYA, an incarnation of VISHNU, is also associated with dogs. In later Hinduism, dogs were condemned by BRAHMANAS as unclean, but certain myths and stories in texts indicate that they were also held in high regard.

In Zoroastrianism, there are several passages in texts that discuss the dog. For instance, the *VENDIDAD* states that the dog is one of the creatures of the good spirit (SPENTA MAINYU), which always serves man and should be cared for. Another passage points out its usefulness: 'The dog, O Spitama Zarathushtra! I, Ahura Mazda have made self-clothed and self-shod, watchful, wakeful and sharp-toothed, born to take his food from man and watch over man's goods . . . Whosoever shall wake at his voice, neither shall the thief nor the wolf steal anything from his house . . .' (xiii.106–07). Part of the *Vendidad* also lists punishments for ill-treating a dog, or not feeding it properly.

A ritual known as the Sagdid ceremony takes place after the death of a person, when a dog is brought to view the dead body.

The dog is also associated with the other world. In the *Arda Viraf Namah*, composed by ARDA VIRAF in the third century, Zerioug Goash is a dog that guards the CHINVAT BRIDGE. Devils quake at his bark, and any soul who on earth has hurt, ill-used or destroyed any of these animals, is prevented from going further.

Dol Purnima   A Hindu festival similar to HOLI, held in March/April in West Bengal. An image of the god KRISHNA is made, decorated with flowers and coloured powder, and worshipped. Then it is placed in a swing and taken out in a procession, accompanied by music and dance. The birthday of CHAITANYA MAHAPRABHU, the BHAKTI saint of the sixteenth century, is celebrated on the same day.

Donyi Polo   A sun and moon cult prevalent among some of the tribal groups of the north-east. The Apatanis and other tribes worship the sun (Donyi) and the moon (Polo) for prosperity, fertility and protection from calamities. Worship includes offering *apong* (rice beer) and rice flour, and animal sacrifices, particularly of a *mithun* (a small variety of bull).

Draupadi   The wife of the PANDAVAS in the MAHABHARATA. Draupadi was the daughter of king Drupada of Panchala. ARJUNA, the third of the Pandavas, excelled all others in his skill with the bow, and thus won her hand at her *svayamvara*. When he took her home he called out to his mother, KUNTI, that he had acquired something good, and without knowing what it was, she asked him to share it with his brothers. Though Kunti tried to retract her words when she saw Draupadi, a mother's words cannot be made false, and so Draupadi became the joint wife of the five brothers. She shared with them their good and bad fortune, and went with them into exile. KRISHNA was her great supporter, and when her husbands failed her, she called on him for protection. BHIMA, the second Pandava, often defended her, though her favourite was Arjuna. Draupadi is usually depicted along with the Pandavas, but also separately. In south India, Draupadi is worshipped as a goddess.

Dravidian Movement   A movement which started before Independence in the region of Tamil Nadu. It opposed BRAHMANAS, superstitious religious practices, and north Indian dominance. One of its main leaders was E.V. Ramaswamy Naicker, who led a protest which included burning copies of the *RAMAYANA*, that he considered a primarily north Indian epic. In 1944, Naicker and C.N. Annadurai founded the Dravida Kazhagam (Federation of Dravida People). Later, two

political parties were founded: the Dravida Munnetra (Progressive) Kazhagam (DMK) in 1949 and the All-India Anna Dravida Munnetra Kazhagam (AIADMK) in 1972. Initially they were against caste and against a number of religious practices, including blind devotion to gods and goddesses. They remain major political parties in the state, but are no longer entirely against religion.

dravya   A Sanskrit term meaning a substance, thing or object. In philosophy it indicates the basic substances that comprise the world. According to NYAYA philosophy, there are nine dravyas, including the five elements, KALA or time, dik or disha (direction space or region), ATMAN (the soul) and manas (mind). In Jainism, there are six dravyas: the five realities or ASTIKAYA, which are JIVA, AKASHA, DHARMA, ADHARMA and PUDGALA, as well as kala. Other philosophies have different categorizations.

Drigung Kagyu   A school of TIBETAN BUDDHISM, a sub-sect of the KAGYU lineage. It was founded by Drigung Kyopa Jigten Gonpo (1143–1217) and has several monasteries in LADAKH. The school is currently (2005) headed by Drigung Kyabgon Che-Tsang, the thirty-seventh successor of the founder.

Drogmi/Drokmi/Brogmi   A Buddhist scholar, the teacher of Khon Konchok Gyalpo, who founded the SAKYA school of TIBETAN BUDDHISM. Born in 992, he was the disciple of Gayadhara, an Indian Buddhist. He studied at VIKRAMASHILA monastery in India for eight years, where he received teachings on the KALACHAKRA and other aspects of VAJRAYANA BUDDHISM. In Tibet, he had a number of disciples, one of whom, Gyalpo, built a monastery known as the Sakya or 'grey earth' monastery, from which this school got its name. Drogmi died in 1074.

Dromston   The founder of the KADAMPA school of TIBETAN BUDDHISM. He lived from 1008 to 1064 and was the disciple of ATISHA. He built a STUPA and monastery housing the relics of Atisha, and based this school on the teachings of Atisha.

Drona/Dronacharya   A teacher of military arts in the MAHABHARATA. He taught both the KAURAVAS and the PANDAVAS, and in the great war sided with the Kauravas.

druj   A term in Zoroastrianism for 'untruth' as opposed to the true path of ASHA or righteousness. In the RIG VEDA, druh is a similar term.

Drugpa Kagyu   A school of TIBETAN BUDDHISM, a sub-sect of the KAGYU lineage. It was founded by Choje Gyare Yeshe Dorje, also known as Ling Repa (1128-89), and is now (2005) headed by the twelfth Drugchen Rinpoche, who has reestablished his monastery in Darjiling.

Duff, Alexander   A Scottish missionary (1806–78) who came to India in the nineteenth century and successfully propagated Christianity. He initiated educational missions which combined traditional Indian and Western concepts, and encouraged intellectual debates on Christianity. He was associated with Ram Mohan ROY and was responsible for converting some prominent citizens of Kolkata (Calcutta) to Christianity.

Dughdova The mother of ZARATHUSHTRA, the founder of the Zoroastrian religion. Born in Rae or Ragha in Media, she was sent away by her father Frahimrava to Arak because her whole body glowed with light and people in her home town were afraid of her. In Arak, Paitaraspa was impressed by her and married her to his son, Pourushaspa. They had five sons, of whom ZARATHUSHTRA was the third.

Dukh Niwaran Sahib Gurdwara A GURDWARA or Sikh shrine located at Patiala in Punjab. It marks the spot visited by the ninth guru, TEGH BAHADUR. Nearby is a sacred tank.

According to the story associated with this shrine, the area was once a village known as Lehal, which is now part of Patiala city. The residents of Lehal were affected by a mysterious illness and one Bhag Ram asked the guru to visit the place, so that his blessings would remove the illness.

Guru Tegh Bahadur visited Lehal in 1672, and sat beneath a banyan tree near a pond. The residents regained their health, and the place where the guru sat was known as Dukh Niwaran, the remover of suffering. The waters of the pond are believed to have developed curative powers, through which both people and animals are healed.

Raja Amar Singh of Patiala (1748–82) had a garden planted in the area around the sacred banyan. The construction of a gurdwara began in 1930 and the gurdwara complex now covers several acres. The main building is double-storeyed, the interior has white and grey marble floors, white marble pillars and a ceiling decorated with floral designs. A large tank has replaced the original pond. Basant Panchami is the main festival here, celebrated as the day of the guru's visit.

Another historic gurdwara in Patiala is the Moti Bagh Gurdwara.

dukhang A term for an assembly hall in a Tibetan Buddhist monastery.

Durga A Hindu goddess who has many forms and roles. Her main role is as a fierce and independent deity, but she also has benign or gentle forms. Though eternal, she incarnates in order to defeat demons and protect her devotees.

Durga is not known in the RIG VEDA. One of her names, AMBIKA, appears in some later Vedic texts and in the *Taittiriya Aranyaka*, Ambika is also called Durga Vairochani, Katyayani and Kanniyakumari. Some other names associated with her, such as Uma Haimavati or KALI, are mentioned in the UPANISHADS. Durga is fully described for the first time in the

MAHABHARATA, but this is a late addition. The PANDAVAS prayed twice to Durga, who granted them boons. Worshipping Durga on the eve of the war, ARJUNA says: 'You are famous as Kumari, Kapila, Kapali, Krishnapingali, Bhadrakali and Mahakali.' The other names he mentions are CHANDI, because of her terrible (prachanda) anger, Katyayani, because of her beauty, and Kali, because of her dreadful form. He also calls her Uma, Shakambhari, Shveta, Krishna, Kaitabhanashini, Hiranyakshi, Virupakshi, and Sudhumrakshi, and the defeater of the asuras Mahisha, Chanda and Munda. Thus the concept of Durga was well-developed at least by around CE 400. Images of Durga also date back to this time.

In the *HARIVAMSHA*, a later appendage of the MAHABHARATA, Durga is associated with various tribes and is said to have been worshipped by the Shabaras, Barbaras and Pulindas. One of her names in the PURANAS is Vindhyavasini, dweller of the Vindhyas, and she may have originated as a tribal goddess in the Vindhyan region. In a later version of the RAMAYANA written by Krittivasa, Durga is worshipped by RAMA. This story occurs in the PURANAS as well.

In the *DEVI BHAGAVATA*, she is said to have emerged in order to defeat an asura known as Durgama. In the *SKANDA PURANA*, PARVATI takes the form of Durga to defeat this demon. Durga is best described in the *DEVI MAHATMYA* of the *MARKANDEYA PURANA*. Here the killing of the asuras is described, and in addition, she is said to represent SHAKTI, MAYA and PRAKRITI. She is often called Mahamaya. Stories about Durga relate that she was very beautiful and had many suitors. She stated that she would only marry someone who could defeat her in battle, but no man could.

Durga is also the mother of the world, known as Jaganmata or Jagadamba. She is also called Bhagavati, MAHADEVI or Devi. She is the giver and protector of weapons.

In early texts she is associated with KRISHNA or VISHNU. In the *Durgastotra* of the *MAHABHARATA*, she is said to have been born in the womb of YASHODA. The goddess EKANAMSHA may represent this early form. Later she is more closely associated with SHIVA, and is considered a form of Parvati. Her worship is important to the Shaktas and she is the main deity of SHAKTI cults, and in her various forms, of Hindu TANTRISM.

In Kashmir, Durga is known as Amba or Bhavani. In Uttar Pradesh, one of her names is Katyayani, and in Mithila she is called Uma. In east India, she is Jagatdhatri, Durga, and KAMAKSHI. In west and central India, Ambika, Hingalaj, Rudrani and Uma are among her names. In south India, Kannaki, Mukamba, Jokulamba and Kamakshi are considered forms of Durga. There are several other forms of Durga; many of the village mother goddesses also represent Durga.

Durga is in addition represented in nine forms, Nava Durgas. Texts have different names for these; in the *Devi Mahatmya* the nine forms are given as: Shailaputri, Brahmacharini, Chandraghanta, Kush-manda, Skandamata, Katyayani, Kalaratri, Mahagauri and Siddhidatri. Another list is: Brahmani, Kalika, Durga, Karttiki, Shiva (Shivaa), Raktadantika, Shokarahita, Chamunda and Lakshmi, and there are other variants as well.

Durga worship takes place in different ways. In some temples there are animal sacrifices. DURGA PUJA, a festival in October, is specially dedicated to the worship of the deity, and here she is also worshipped as a young married woman, visiting her parents' home. Durga is thus a complex and composite deity, indicating feminine power in both its fierce and benevolent aspects.

Durga temples exist all over India under the various names of Durga. Images of the deity are known from about the second century CE, where she is shown with two or more arms as Mahishasuramardini (killing Mahisha). In medieval iconography she has several arms displaying her weapons, which include a trishula (trident), khadga (sword) and chakra (disc). In later images she is seated on a lion, while in earlier images the lion is absent or stands nearby. The Nava Durgas are sometimes represented in panels.

Durga is still a popular deity, depicted in modern temples, as well as in art, with multiple arms, seated on a lion or tiger.

Durga (fort) Temple, Aihole A temple of the Hindu god VISHNU, in AIHOLE, Karnataka, which belongs to the sixth or seventh century, the time of the Chalukya dynasty. It is not a temple primarily of the goddess Durga, but gets its name from the Kannada phrase 'durgadagadi', meaning 'temple near the fort'. The temple is on a high basement, with an apsidal-ended plan like a Buddhist CHAITYA, possibly indicating an earlier date. The inner shrine is semi-circular, with an ambulatory passageway, a MANDAPA and porch. There was once a tower above the shrine, of which only a part remains. The sculptures within the temple are among the best of the Chalukyan period and include NARASIMHA, VARAHA, VISHNU with GARUDA, HARIHARA, DURGA and SHIVA with NANDI. Relief panels depict scenes from the RAMAYANA and MAHA-BHARATA. The columns at the entrance are carved with guardian figures and couples, while the ceiling panels have lotus and NAGA motifs.

Durga Puja A ten-day festival for the worship of the goddess DURGA, celebrated at the same time as DASHAHARA in October. It is most important in West Bengal. Images of the goddess DURGA are set up in houses and temples, as well as in temporary shrines or pavilions, and worshipped for nine days. Songs are sung and verses relating to the goddess are recited, and dances take place before the goddess. The pavilions or pandals also depict contemporary events. On the tenth day the images are taken out in a procession and then immersed in water. The tenth day of Dashahara thus commemorates the victory of the goddess over the demon Mahishasura, representing the victory of good over evil. The festival also has different aspects. Traditionally, DURGA as Shakambhari or the goddess of vegetation is also worshipped at this time. Nine plants (navapatrikas) are placed in an earthen vessel or pot, representing the fertility aspect of the goddess. These are: rambha (plantain), kachu, haridra (turmeric), jayatri (barley), bilva (wood apple), darimba (pomegranate), ashoka, mana and dhanya (rice).

Durga is usually an unmarried and independent deity. However, as Uma or PARVATI, she also represents the young married woman, who visits her parents home, just as other young women visit their parents at the time of Durga Puja. The four days when Durga stays at her parents' home form the main part of the festival. Her arrival is celebrated, and her departure, symbolized by the immersion of the idol, is marked by tears.

Durvasa/Durvasas An ancient RISHI or sage described in the MAHABHARATA and PURANAS, who was the son of the rishi ATRI and his wife Anasuya. Durvasa was known to be both powerful and bad-tempered. According to the VISHNU PURANA, the DEVAS suffered after he cursed INDRA for disrespect to a garland he gave, and their fortunes could only be restored by churning the ocean for AMRITA. In the MAHABHARATA a story is told of how he was angry with KRISHNA, and foretold how Krishna would be killed.

Duryodhana A KAURAVA, the eldest of the hundred sons of King DHRITARASHTRA, whose story and conflicts with his cousins the PANDAVAS, are described in the MAHABHARATA. He was killed on the last day of the great Mahabharata war. Duryodhana was envious of his cousins and wanted to destroy them, which finally led to his downfall. However, he was not without his qualities and could be a loyal friend, as he was to KARNA, who was born to KUNTI before her marriage, and was thus a brother of the PANDAVAS,

Dushyanta A king who is described in the MAHABHARATA. He was the father of BHARATA, a legendary ruler, after whom India is said to have been named Bharatavarsha. The story of Dushyanta and his wife Shakuntala was retold by KALIDASA in the fifth century, in his play *Abhijnanashakuntalam*.

Dvaipayana Another name of the ancient rishi VYASA.

Dvaita A dualistic school of VEDANTA, one of the six classical systems of ancient Indian philosophy. Its main exponent was MADHVA, who lived in the thirteenth century. Basing himself on the BRAHMA SUTRA, UPANISHADS and VEDAS, Madhva challenged SHANKARA's concept of One Reality. He held that there are three distinct entities, god or BRAHMAN, the individual soul, and the world. The latter two cannot exist without God and yet are distinct from it. He saw the highest God as KRISHNA or VISHNU, with his consort LAKSHMI. He advocated BHAKTI and the worship of god in the form of the avataras or incarnations of Vishnu, SHIVA, or the PANCHAYATANAS or five deities. He did not recognize the worship of RADHA. According to his philosophy, knowledge and a moral life lead to the love of God, and salvation is attained by the grace of God. However, even those who have attained liberation remain separate individuals, connected with, but not identical to, God. Madhva differed from RAMANUJA in stating that individual souls are not of the same essence, and not all are eligible for salvation. The texts for this school of philosophy are mainly Madhva's works, particularly his commentaries on the *Brahma Sutra*, Upanishads, BHAGAVAD GITA, *BHAGAVATA PURANA*, and the first forty hymns of the RIG VEDA. His work *Anuvyakhyana* explains his interpretation of the *Brahma Sutra*. *Bharatatatparyanirnaya* is a work on the MAHABHARATA, while his *Prakaranas* expand on some philosophical themes. All these works are collectively known as the *Sarva Mula Grantha*. Commentaries on Madhva's works include those of Jayatirtha and Vyasaraya. Some scholars have suggested the influence of Christianity on his ideas, such as his concept of the individual soul.

Dvaitadvaita One of the schools of VEDANTA, which is one of the six main systems of ancient Indian philosophy. Dvaitadvaita states that both duality and unity or oneness are real. Its major exponent was NIMBARKA, who probably belonged to the twelfth century.His two main works are a commentary on the *BRAHMA SUTRA* called *Vedantaparijata-saurabha*, and a work of ten verses, *Dashashloki*. He believed the soul (JIVA), god (ishvara or BRAHMAN) and the world (jagat) were distinct, yet united. He felt both duality and unity or oneness were real. The soul and the world possess attributes different from Brahman, yet cannot exist independently, being dependent on Brahman, and reflecting a transformation of Brahman. The universe is not an illusion, as it is the manifestation of the nature of god. The pure nature of the soul is clouded by its karma. Through submission to god, as well as devotion or BHAKTI and an ethical life, one can realize god. Nimbarka stressed devotion to a personal god, KRISHNA, along with RADHA.

His philosophy is slightly different from that of RAMANUJA, who placed greater emphasis on unity or identity.

Among other exponents of this school was Keshavakashmirin, who wrote a commentary on the BHAGAVAD GITA called *Tattva-prakashika*.

Dvapara Yuga In Hindu mythology, the third of the four YUGAS or periods of time, which together comprise a MAHAYUGA. The Dvapara Yuga follows the TRETA YUGA, and in it the righteousness that existed in the first yuga is reduced by half. Its primary virtue is sacrifice, and the sacred texts of this age are the PURANAS. Very few follow truth or duty without seeking rewards. Misery, disease and disasters prevail, and the CASTE SYSTEM has come into existence. Human beings live for 2000 years and children are born through sex, which was not the case earlier. A man can have only one wife, and marriage can only take place at the time of the first menstruation of the woman. This yuga lasts for 2400 divine years, which are equal to 8,64,000 human years, and is symbolized by the colour yellow. It is succeeded by the KALI YUGA.

Dvaraka (Dwarka) A sacred town in Gujarat, traditionally associated with the Hindu god KRISHNA. According to the story in the MAHABHARATA, the *HARIVAMSHA* and the PURANAS, Krishna left MATHURA, which was being repeatedly attacked by King Jarasandha of Magadha, and went to Dvaraka on the Saurashtra coast. Along with him went his family and the whole YADAVA clan. Here a magnificent, well-defended city was built. Defeating his enemies, he and his brother BALARAMA ruled the region for thirty-six years. However, at the end of the great Mahabharata War, Krishna was cursed by GANDHARI, mother of the KAURAVAS, for killing all her sons. All that he had built up, she said, would be destroyed.

The curse was fulfilled, when the Yadava clan began to indulge themselves in drink and wild behaviour. Balarama and Krishna banned alcohol, but once allowed them to drink at Prabhas Patan nearby. Intoxicated, the Yadavas fought and killed each other. Krishna and Balarama retired to the forest at Prabhas Patan. Balarama meditated and left his body, while Krishna was accidentally killed by the hunter Jara. Dvaraka was then submerged by the sea.

The present town of Dvaraka (Dwarka) on the sea-coast is full of temples. The most important is the DVARKADHISH TEMPLE. Among other temples is the Rukmini Temple, dedicated to KRISHNA'S chief queen, RUKMINI. The Bhadrakali Temple, dedicated to the goddess KALI, is constructed at a SHAKTA PITHA, or a site associated with SATI, the wife of SHIVA. Nearby lies the Siddheshvara Mahadeva Temple, a Shiva temple with a LINGA said to have been consecrated by the god BRAHMA. The Chakra Narayana Temple is a VISHNU temple, where Vishnu is worshipped as a chakra (disc) on a stone. In the Gomati Temple, the local river Gomati is worshipped as a goddess. She is said to be a form of the river GANGA, who flowed here as the Gomati at the request of some rishis. The Panchanada Tirtha, another sacred site, is associated with the five PANDAVAS. Here there are five sweet-water wells, surrounded by the salty sea. The Samudra Narayana Temple marks the confluence of the Gomati with the sea.

Dvaraka also has one of the four SHANKARACHARYA MATHAS first set up by SHANKARA in the ninth century.

Not all accept that the present town is the site of the ancient city. Marine archaeologists believe they have recovered the remains of a submerged city near the island of Bet Dvaraka, 30 km away, and suggest that this is the real site. Local tradition holds that the island is all that remains of Krishna's ancient city. The island has another Dvarakadhish Temple, with an image of Krishna, as well as several other temples. Several other sites in Gujarat are also identified with Dvaraka.

Dvarakadhish Temple A temple dedicated to the Hindu god KRISHNA, located at DVARAKA in Gujarat. It was constructed in the sixteenth century, though parts of it date back to the twelfth century, and it is said to have been built on the site of an ancient temple. The structure has seven storeys and rests on seventy-two carved pillars. Made of granite and sandstone, it covers a large area of 540 m and rises to a height of 51 m, with a soaring tower and a cluster of smaller towers. The multi-storeyed MANDAPA is decorated on the outside with open balconies. In the GARBA-GRIHA or inner shrine, is an image of the deity, the latest of several images installed in the temple. Earlier images are said to have been of Krishna in warrior form; they were moved to other temples, the last to the Dvarakadhish Temple at Bet Dwarka. The present image is dressed in jewels and silks, placed on a silver throne, and has four arms holding the chakra, mace, conch and lotus. He is known here as Dvarakadhish, the lord of Dvaraka. Krishna is also affectionately called Ranchorji, the 'one who ran away from battle', a reference to his leaving MATHURA to avoid King Jarasandha. The main entrance to the temple is through the Svarga Dvara, or 'heaven's door', which has steps leading up from the river Gomati. JANAMASHTAMI, the celebration of KRISHNA'S birthday, is the biggest festival here.

There are other Dvarkadhish temples at various places, including at Bet Dvaraka and Mathura.

dvarapalas Minor Hindu deities who guard doors or entrances. They are depicted in several temples as large guardian figures, sometimes in the form of YAKSHAS.

Dyaus A deity mentioned in the RIG VEDA. He is the god of the sky or heaven, often associated with PRITHVI, the earth. USHA, the dawn, is said to be his daughter. Other sons or descendants are the Ashvins, Agni, Parjanya, Surya, the Maruts and the Angirasas. By the later Vedic period, Dyaus had lost his importance. His counterpart in Greek mythology is Zeus.

Easter A Christian festival that celebrates the resurrection of JESUS CHRIST, which took place three days after he was crucified. The date of Easter is not fixed but the festival takes place on a Sunday in March or April, according to a lunar calendar. Special church services are held and altars of churches are decorated with white flowers. Easter is one of the earliest CHRISTIAN FESTIVALS to be celebrated, dating back to the second century. The name Easter may be connected with an early Anglo-Saxon spring goddess, Eostra, with the spring festival being absorbed into Christianity. Other scholars feel it comes from the Latin 'in albis', the Christian term for Easter week, which in Old High German became 'eostarum'.

Forty days of LENT precede Easter. The final week, known as Holy Week, has several sacred days. It begins with Palm Sunday, the day when JESUS entered Jerusalem in triumph, his path being strewn with palm leaves and branches; Maundy Thursday commemorates Jesus's Last Supper with his disciples; GOOD FRIDAY is the day of his crucifixion; Easter Saturday marks the transition between crucifixion and resurrection, and the Holy Week concludes with Easter Sunday.

Popular Easter symbols include the rabbit and the Easter egg. Some believe these reflect earlier fertility symbols, while others feel they have a Christian origin. The rabbit is said to have been introduced in Protestant Europe in the seventeenth century, while the egg signifies birth and new life.

Easter is considered the most important Christian festival, as the concept of resurrection leading to eternal life is central to Christianity.

ecumenical movement A worldwide movement in Christianity to promote union and understanding between different types of churches. India is notable for the union of divergent Protestant Churches in the CHURCH OF NORTH INDIA and the CHURCH OF SOUTH INDIA. Among other groups are the NATIONAL COUNCIL OF CHURCHES OF INDIA, the COMMUNION OF CHURCHES OF INDIA, various CATHOLIC groups and the Evangelical Fellowship of India.

eightfold path The path of the right way of living, preached by the BUDDHA and described in Buddhist texts. The Buddha's FOUR NOBLE TRUTHS state that life is full of sorrow, which can be overcome by following the eightfold path. This consists of (1) right views (samyak drishti), which indicates a knowledge and understanding of the four noble truths and other Buddhist concepts; (2) right thought (samyak samkalpa), which is thought that is free from lust, ill-will or cruelty, and leads to a life of benevolence and harmlessness; (3) right speech (samyak vacha), which means speaking the truth and not indulging in idle gossip or slander; (4) right action (samyak karmanta), refraining from killing, stealing and doing wrong, and maintaining control over the senses; (5) right mode of livelihood (samyak ajiva), which implies finding a way of life that is not harmful to living beings, does not involve bloodshed, sale of intoxicants or trafficking in women and slaves; (6) right effort (samyak vyayama), which includes eliminating evil thoughts and replacing them with good ones, and preventing wrong thoughts from arising; (7) right mindfulness (samyak smriti), through which the body, feelings, mind and mental states are viewed correctly, and the right state of mind is established; and (8) right meditation (samyak samadhi), which becomes possible when the five hindrances of covetousness, malevolence, lethargy, restlessness, worry and doubt are eliminated. There are then four successive states of meditation, which finally lead to NIRVANA or liberation.

Ekadanta A name of the Hindu god GANESHA. He is so named because he has only one tusk.

Ekambareshvara temple A temple of the Hindu god SHIVA located at KANCHIPURAM, Tamil Nadu. It was first constructed in the time of the Cholas, but rebuilt in 1509 by the Vijayanagara emperor Krishnadevaraya. In the inner shrine is a Prithvi LINGA, or earth linga. The temple has three GOPURAMS or entrance gateways, one each on the south and west leading into the inner enclosure, while the main gopuram rises to a height of 58.5 m, and can be seen from anywhere in the city. To the front of the east-facing temple is a long MANDAPA or hall, and to the north, a fish-tank.

There are several legends associated with this temple. According to one legend in the Sthala Purana of the temple, when Shiva was concentrating on the universe, his wife PARVATI came and playfully closed his eyes. The universe was in chaos, and the angry Shiva asked Parvati to go down to earth. There she created this linga from earth and maintained and worshipped it with the help of VISHNU, though Shiva put all sorts of obstacles in her way. Finally, when Shiva was pleased with her, they were reunited. This reunion took place under a mango tree, and thus the temple got its name (eka = one, ambra = mango, ishvara = god). The marriage of Shiva and Parvati is celebrated here with great splendour in the month of Phalguna (February–March).

Ekanamsha A Hindu goddess associated with the gods BALARAMA and KRISHNA. She is normally depicted standing between the two gods, holding a lotus or a mirror. The *BRIHAT SAMHITA* says that this goddess can be depicted with two, four or eight arms. The goddess was popular in medieval times in eastern India.

Eknatha A mystic and BHAKTI saint of the sixteenth century. He composed ABHANGAS or verses in Marathi in praise of the god KRISHNA and his form as VITTHALA, and wrote several texts and commentaries. Born in 1540 at ancient Pratishthana (Paithan in present Maharashtra), he studied Sanskrit and became a learned scholar by the age of twelve. He then travelled on his own to sacred places in the north, returning home at the age of twenty-five. He married Girija, who became his companion and support in his ascetic life. He edited *Jnaneshvari*, the work of the Bhakti saint JNANESHVARA, and restored it to its original form, removing later additions and interpolations. He also wrote works on VEDANTA, other philosophical systems and VAISHNAVISM. His best-known works are *Ekanathi Bhagavata*, which is a commentary on the eleventh chapter of the *BHAGAVATA PURANA*; the *Rukmini Svayamvara*, the story of Krishna's marriage with RUKMINI; and the *Bhavartha Ramayana*, a version of the *RAMAYANA*, which he left unfinished and was completed by three other authors. He also translated the rest of the *Bhagavata Purana* into Marathi. He believed in the equality of all castes, and because of this, faced problems in the conventional society of his times.

Elamma A grama devata or village deity. Elamma is a mother goddess, a form of RENUKA in south India. According to myths, Renuka was the mother of PARASHURAMA, an incarnation of the Hindu god, VISHNU. At the request of his father, JAMADAGNI, Parashurama cut off her head because she was once unchaste in thought and desired a GANDHARVA. In most myths, Parashurama then received a boon from his father and restored her to life. But in the story of Elamma, Parashurama mistakenly placed the head of Renuka on the body of an 'untouchable' woman, one of the lowest castes. She was then named Elamma and worshipped by lower castes and outsiders. Elamma-Renuka is still worshipped in village temples in south India. Two images of her are usually made, one in stone and the other in metal, representing the two deities. Near her images are those of Parashurama and Jamadagni. Animal sacrifices are offered to the deity twice a year. The myth of Elamma indicates the absorption of lower castes into the Brahmanical system.

Elephanta Cave Temple A rock-cut temple of the Hindu god SHIVA, located on the island of Elephanta or Gharapuri, about 10 km offshore from MUMBAI in Maharashtra. The temple dates approximately to the sixth century and is carved into the side of a cliff. The inner shrine has a monolithic LINGA set in a pedestal. The north entrance, which is the main doorway today, has a large, triple-headed bust of Shiva, 6 m high, as well as images of LAKULISHA, an incarnation of Shiva, and NATARAJA, a form of Shiva. At the east entrance are Shiva and PARVATI seated on a mountain. They play a game of dice, undisturbed, as RAVANA tries to shake them off their perch. There are several other sculptures of Shiva and Parvati set in panels on the walls. Outside the temple are small courts with shrines of GANESHA, KARTTIKEYA and the MATRIKAS. The temple was named Elephanta by the Portuguese because a huge stone elephant stood at the landing point.

elephants, in religion Elephants form an important part of Hindu, Buddhist and other myths. In Hinduism, the god INDRA rides on the white elephant AIRAVATA, who also represents rain clouds. Eight male elephants, the ASHTADIGGAJAS, along with their female counterparts, are the supporters of the universe. GANESHA, one of the most popular deities, has the head of an elephant, while GAJA-LAKSHMI, another popular deity, has LAKSHMI being bathed by two elephants. GAJENDRA, the king of elephants, was saved by VISHNU when he prayed to him. In the PURANAS elephants are associated with rain and are like rain clouds. There are several stories about them in ancient texts, where they are also known as gaja or naga. According to one story, narrated in the *MAHABHARATA* and other texts, all elephants originally had wings. An elephant is also the symbol of the MULADHARA CHAKRA. Today elephants are kept by certain temples and used in processions. Temple records also have stories of elephants as divine worshippers. For instance, at the KALAHASTI temple, an elephant was one of the first worshippers of the LINGA there.

In Buddhism, a white elephant is considered particularly auspicious and is associated with the birth of the BUDDHA.

In Jainism, dreams of elephants are one of the signs of the birth of a Jain TIRTHANKARA.

In other cultures too, elephants formed part of religious myths.

Ellora The site of several rock-cut temples, dated between the fourth and thirteenth centuries, Ellora is located in Aurangabad district of Maharashtra. There are Hindu, Buddhist and Jain shrines that extend for about 2 km, carved along the side of a basalt cliff. Twelve Buddhist caves are located to the south and can be dated between the seventh and eighth centuries. They belong to the MAHAYANA school of Buddhism, and include both CHAITYAS and VIHARAS. There are images of BUDDHAS and BODHISATTVAS, as well as various Buddhist deities, including TARA, MAHAMAYURI, HARITI and Panchika. To the north are five Jain temples dating to around the ninth century, which depict the TIRTHANKARAS and other Jain images. There are seventeen Hindu temples from between the seventh and ninth centuries. Among the temples are the Dashavatara Temple, which was begun as a Buddhist monastery but was converted into a Hindu temple. It has a free-standing MANDAPA, an inner shrine with a LINGA, and several SHIVA and VISHNU images. The Rameshvara Temple also has a linga shrine with a monolithic NANDI in the front court. Another temple has a DURGA shrine. Though most of the temples are cut into the cliff, the eighth-century KAILASHNATHA TEMPLE is the most extraordinary, as it is a full-size standing temple intricately carved out of rock, each aspect sculpted in great detail.

Eluttachan/Ezhuthachan A writer in Malayalam who lived in the sixteenth century, and composed works on religion. Born about 40 km from Kozhikode in Kerala, his full name was Tunchattu Ramanujan Eluttachan, and he was commonly known as Tunchan. He made a free translation of tha *ADHYATMA RAMAYANA* into Malayalam that became popular throughout Kerala. He incorporated into it aspects of Valmiki's RAMAYANA, the works of KALIDASA, and the earlier *Kannasa Ramayana* in Malayalam. In the month of Karkataka (August–September), the last month of the Malayalam calendar, passages from his Ramayana were traditionally read for twenty-one days. There are several philosophical passages in his free translation, for example when RAMA, explaining to LAKSHMANA why he should not rebel against their father, says that life is transient and the world unreal. He adds, 'We are like travellers resting for a night at a wayside inn. We meet and talk for a while, and depart in the morning.' Eluttachan used a musical verse style known as Kilipattu (parrot song), which makes the oral reading of his *Ramayana* attractive. He also made a free translation of the *MAHABHARATA*, and of the *BHAGAVATA PURANA*.

episcopal A term relating to Christian church organization. Episcopal churches are administered by Bishops, under whom there are priests or presbyters (elders) and deacons. The Orthodox, Roman Catholic and Anglican Churches are episcopal.

Ettutogai Eight anthologies of Tamil verse that form part of the ancient SANGAM LITERATURE, and can

be dated between the third century BCE and the fourth century CE. Most of them contain love poems or verses in praise of kings, but the *Paripadal* includes poems in praise of various gods. Others also have incidental references to religion. For instance, the *Padirrupattu*, which contains verses in praise of kings of the Chera country (Kerala), describes methods of worshipping the god VISHNU. Altogether, there are 2,372 poems in these texts.

eucharist A Christian form of worship, practised in churches in India and elsewhere, which celebrates the life of JESUS CHRIST, and is also known as holy communion. It dates back to the Last Supper that Jesus shared with his disciples before he was betrayed. After giving thanks for the meal, while breaking bread he said, 'This is my body', and while drinking wine, 'This is my blood of the new testament, which is shed for many for the remission of sins'. He asked his disciples to eat bread and drink from the cup in remembrance of him. In churches today a wafer of bread and some wine are consecrated and given to worshippers by the priest. There are many scholarly debates on the real meaning of these words of Jesus and on the significance of this ritual, but for most Christians it represents a close contact with Christ and his spiritual essence, as well as a remembrance of his death and resurrection. The term eucharist comes from the Greek 'eucharista', which means 'thanksgiving'. The ceremony is also an expression of gratitude for Jesus's presence in the world. The eucharist forms part of the celebration of MASS and is often used as a synonym of it.

Evangelical Churches A group of Christian churches. The term 'evangelical' comes from 'evangel', the Greek word for 'gospel', which means 'good tidings' or 'good news', referring to the message of Jesus. It was first used by early PROTESTANT churches, particularly Lutheran Churches that emphasized belief in the BIBLE, divine grace, faith, and conversion through personal conviction. Today there are different types of evangelists, some being modern and liberal, others using a literal interpretation of the Bible and maintaining conservative views. Several evangelical groups are known for their missionary zeal and promote conversion. In India, there are two types of Evangelical churches: the LUTHERAN Churches and the more modern denominations, which include the PENTECOSTAL, BRETHREN, SEVENTH DAY ADVENTISTS, Assemblies of God, MENNONITE Churches, the Hindustan Covenant Church, and others. Many of the latter group are affiliated to the Evangelical Fellowship of India.

Fa Hsien (Faxian) A Chinese Buddhist pilgrim who visited India and Sri Lanka in the fifth century, during the reign of Chandragupta II of the Gupta dynasty. Born in 337, he left China in 399, when he was over sixty years old, arriving in India by an overland route through the Himalayas. In India he studied Sanskrit and travelled to Buddhist sites before going to Sri Lanka. He collected several Buddhist scriptures and left for China in 414 by sea, reaching home after a journey of 200 days, as his ship had been blown off course. He wrote an account of his travels in which he described the places he visited, the kings of India, and the state of Buddhism. The texts he took back to China included the *Vinaya* of the MAHASANGHIKA and of the MAHISHASAKA sect, as well as part of the SARVASTIVADA texts and the *MAHAPARINIRVANA SUTRA*. These were later translated into Chinese and were important for the growth of Buddhism in China.

Fa Hsien died in 422.

Faizi A poet who lived in the sixteenth century at the time of the Mughal emperor AKBAR. He was the brother of ABUL FAZL and the son of Shaikh Mubarak. Born at AGRA, he wrote a number of poetic works and was given the title Malik al-Shuara or 'king of poets' at Akbar's court. His books include *Nal Daman* and a commentary on the QURAN. His poetry was influenced by his SUFI beliefs, and in his last years he changed his name to Fayyazi (super-abundance), saying, 'As I am now chastened by spiritual love, I am the Fayyazi of the Ocean of super-abundance (God's love)'. Another example of his verse is given below:

O Thou who existest from eternity and abidest forever
Sight cannot bear Thy light, praise cannot express Thy perfection.
Thy light melts the understanding, Thy glory baffles wisdom;
To think of Thee destroys reason, Thy essence confounds thought.

Faizi died at the age of forty.

fana Literally, 'extinction', a term used by SUFIS, for the state of ecstacy reached when the soul merges with God.

faqir/fakir The Arabic term for a religious mendicant, also known as a darvesh or PIR in Persian. In India the term came to be used both for SUFIS and for Hindu saints.

Faraizis/Faraidis Followers of a nineteenth century Islamic movement started by Haji Shariatullah of Faridpur. The movement was widespread in east Bengal. The name Faraizi comes from 'farz', meaning obligatory duties laid down by Allah. Haji Shariatullah gave it a broader connotation, interpreting it to include all the religious duties laid down in the QURAN and SUNNAH.

The Faraizis aimed at reforming Islam and removing practices such as the worship of saints, and Hindu deities.

In addition, Shariatullah declared that India had become DAR-UL-HARB, ie. an unholy land, literally, 'a land of warfare', and therefore suspended Friday and Id prayers, and asked his disciples to carry out a struggle against the British. His son Dudu Miyan (1819–60 or 1862) converted it into a wider movement, against the British supported by peasants, as he stated that the earth belonged to God, and no one had the right to own it or levy taxes on it.

The Faraizi Movement declined after Dudu Miyan's death, though it still had some followers. In 1947, most Faraizis were in the newly formed area of East Pakistan (now Bangladesh). Faraizis adhere to the Hanafi school of Islamic law, with some variations.

Farid, Baba A SUFI saint (c. 1175–1265) from Ajodhan in Pak Patan, now in Pakistan. His full name was Faridud-din Ganj-i Shakar, but he was popularly known as Baba Farid. Baba Farid's father was a scholar and his mother was extremely pious, spending long hours in prayer. Influenced by her, Farid became a disciple of QUTBUDDIN BAKHTIYAR KAKI, a Sufi saint of the CHISTI ORDER in DELHI. Farid was revered in Delhi, but constant visitors disturbed his meditations. He moved to Ajodhan, where he set up his KHANQAH with a Jamaat Khana, a thatched hall where everyone lived together, and a separate cell for his meditation. He lived simply, and fasted all day, eating only in the evening. Here too he had many visitors and did not refuse entry to anyone.

One of the most renowned Sufi saints, he died in 1265. His chief disciple was NIZAMUDDIN AULIYA. Some of Baba Farid's verses are included in the GURU GRANTH SAHIB, though scholars feel a few of these could be assigned to his successors.

Faridun A legendary king of ancient Iran revered by Zoroastrians. Faridun was the later name of THRAETONA, described as a sage in Avestan texts. According to the SHAH NAMAH and some Pahlavi texts, helped by Kava, the blacksmith, he defeated the evil tyrant Zohak, who had killed King JAMSHED, and chained Zohak to the Daemavand mountain. This event is celebrated in the Meherangan festival, which occurs on the Meher day of the Meher month, as the triumph of good over evil. Faridun knew a number of NIRANGS (sacred chants) by which he could heal diseases and change his form at will. Some of these Nirangs are still used as prayers today.

farishta A Persian word meaning an angel or angelic being. The term is used in both Islam and Zoroastrianism.

Fatiha, al The first sura or chapter of the QURAN, which is considered particularly sacred. It begins:

Praise be to God, Lord of all the Worlds,
The compassionate, the merciful;
King on the day of judgement.
Thee do we worship, and to Thee do we cry for help!
Guide us on the right path.

The Prophet MUHAMMAD is said to have stated it was the greatest sura of the Quran. It forms part of the daily prayers and is also used when praying for the sick or the souls of the departed.

fatwa A religious or judicial decree pronounced by an Islamic authority, such as an IMAM, MUFTI or QAZI. It is generally written and can relate to some interpretation of Islamic law or may provide advice on a course of action. It is not legally binding. In India there are several collections of fatwas dating from medieval times, that provide both religious and historic material. Among them is the *Fatwa-i Alamgiri*, compiled at the time of the Mughal emperor AURANGZEB in the seventeenth century. This text belongs to the HANAFI school of law. Various Islamic bodies in India, continue to pronounce fatwas on issues pertaining to personal law or general issues. Recently fatwas have been issued against terrorism, stating that it is un-Islamic.

fiqh A term for Islamic law or jurisprudence. The term Fiqh means 'understanding' and included both law and theology, but now refers mainly to law. Fiqh incorporates laws relating to prayers, rituals, social obligations and punishments. There are four main schools of law for SUNNIS. These are the Maliki, HANAFI, Shafi and HANBALI, each based on texts initially compiled by individuals of those names. The Hanafi school is mainly followed by SUNNIS in India, though

some follow the Shafi school. Several compilations of FATWAS provide additional material for the followers of these schools. SHIAS have separate schools of law.

Firdausi A Persian poet of the eleventh century who wrote the SHAH NAMAH or *Book of Kings*, a legendary history of the kings of Iran. His real name was Abul Kasim Mansur.

Firdausi silsila An order of SUFI saints, a branch of the SUHRAWARDI, that gained importance in the fourteenth century. It was established in DELHI by Shaikh Badruddin of Samarqand, a disciple of Shaikh Saifuddin Bakharzi, who in turn was the Khalifa or senior disciple of Shaikh Najmuddin Kubra (d. 1221). Shaikh Ruknuddin Firdausi succeeded Shaikh Badruddin, and hence this branch came to be known as Firdausi. Shaikh Badruddin and his disciples were prominent in Delhi before the CHISTI order reached India. The Firdausi saints did not reject contacts with the sultans and Shaikh Najmuddin Sughra, a saint of this order (sughra = junior), was the minister of religious affairs at the time of Sultan Iltutmish (1211–36). Firdausis were on the whole, pious and austere, and for some time the branch remained confined to Delhi. It then became prominent in Bihar, where Shaikh SHARAFUDDIN YAHYA MUNYARI (d. 1381) was one of the leading saints.

fire Fire is considered sacred in several religions, with various rituals related to it. In Hinduism all ceremonies and sacrifices are performed with fire. AGNI, the god of fire, is important from the time of the RIG VEDA. The three essential fire offerings are mentioned in the VEDAS: the garhaptya or fire of the hearth, dakshina or fire offerings to deities, and ahavaniya or fire used in sacrifices and worship. The Agnihotra or fire sacrifice consists of daily worship of the domestic and sacrificial fires (garhaptya and ahavaniya). In the KATHA UPANISHAD, the boy Nachiketa learnt the fire sacrifice from the god YAMA. According to the VISHNU PURANA, PURURAVAS received instructions for the threefold fire sacrifice, and by performing this was reunited with Urvashi. Forty-nine sacred fires are mentioned in early Sanskrit texts, personified by Agni along with his sons and grandsons.

Celebrations of several festivals, particularly that of Divali, include the lighting of lamps, while ARTI, the circling of flames, is performed in temples and at sacred sites.

In Zoroastrianism, fire is known as ATAR or Atash, and is considered sacred. The sacred flame is kept burning in temples and homes. JASHANS and YASNAS, similar to the Sanskrit YAJNAS, are conducted around the sacred fire on auspicious occasions and at special ceremonies. In Buddhism and Jainism lamps are lit in temples or sacred places.

In Christianity, too, candles are lit in churches, while in Judaism the menorah is a many-branched candlestick used in rituals, and the Ner Tamid, representing eternal light, is kept burning in SYNAGOGUES. CHANUKAH is also a festival of lights. In Islam a flame often burns at the shrine of a PIR or saint.

five pillars of Islam The five basic practices for all Muslims. These are: (1) bearing witness that there is no god but ALLAH; (2) offering NAMAZ (salat in Arabic) or prayers five times a day; (3) ZAKAT, giving the prescribed alms once a year; (4) roza (saum in Arabic) or fasting during the month of RAMZAN; (5) going on a pilgrimage (HAJ) to Mecca at least once in a lifetime.

four noble truths The basis of the philosophy of the BUDDHA, which formed part of his first sermon at the Deer Park in SARNATH. The four truths are: (1) Life is suffering (dukha); (2) Suffering is caused by desire or craving (trishna, literally 'thirst'); (3) Suffering can end through the elimination of desire; (4) Desire can be removed by following the EIGHTFOLD PATH.

The four truths are accepted by all schools of Buddhism, as Part of the basic philosophy of the religion.

frashokereti A concept in Zoroastrianism that signifies the renewal of existence. The idea occurs in the *GATHAS*, where ZARATHUSHTRA says, 'O living One, Ahura, by your power, renew (ferashem) [my] life, and re-create it as you wish' (*Yasna*, 34.15). Another passage in the *GATHAS* (*Yasna* 30.11) states that there will be a long period of suffering for the wicked, while the truth leads to bliss but finally, light prevails

everywhere. The word frashokeriti, however, occurs only in later texts. It implies a perfect world that will ultimately exist as a culmination of the struggle of good against evil. All souls will be purified and live in this world, which is not merely a spiritual state but an actual material existence.

fravashi A term in Zoroastrianism, for a divine spark that exists in every living being, including animals and plants, and functions as a guardian spirit. The fravashi is always pure and perfect and cannot be destroyed or corrupted. Each being has its own fravashi, which provides guidance, persuading the individual to follow the right path. There are some similarities with the concept of the ATMAN or soul, or the JIVA, but the difference is that the fravashi provides active guidance. The fravashi is the ideal, and thus when individual souls reach perfection they unite with their fravashis. The term is not mentioned in the *GATHAS*, though it is implied, but the concept is fully developed in later texts. In the *BUNDAHISHN* the fravashis are given the choice of entering the material world and battling against evil, or remaining in the spiritual world. The fravashis of the righteous are remembered in all prayers and ceremonies, and particularly in the MUKTAD. The *Fravardin Yasht* is a special prayer dedicated to righteous people of the past, present and future, and to their fravashis. The later term used in Pahlavi is fravahr or farohar. In art, the fravashi is depicted as a winged deity.

gachchha A group or subdivision among SHVETAMBARA Jains. Gachchhas were formed by various Jain leaders, usually monks, mainly between the eleventh and thirteenth centuries. According to some accounts there were at one time eighty-four gachchhas, but probably many of these did not last long. Three gachchhas are still important, and most Shvetambaras in western and northern India belong to one of them. They are the Kharatara Gachchha, the Tapa Gachchha and the Anchala Gachchha. Each has its own temples and holy men, but there are no doctrinal differences between them. The Kharatara Gachchha, the most popular today, is mentioned in an inscription of 1090. There are several legends about its formation, one being that it was founded by Jineshvara Suri who, after defeating other monks in a religious debate, was given the title Kharatara (a strong character) by a king of Gujarat. The Tapa Gachchha is said to have been founded by Jagachandra Suri, who practised severe austerities (tapas) and therefore was given the title Tapa by the king of Mewar in the thirteenth century. The *Brihat Kalpa* list of Jain leaders states that these two gachchhas owe their origin to the Jain leaders Vardhamana and Sarvadeva, respectively. The Anchala Gachchha, earlier known as the Vidhipaksha Gachchha, was said to have been formed in the twelfth century, though it occurs in inscriptions only from the fifteenth century.

The Lonka Gachchha, founded by LONKA SHAHA in the fifteenth century, led to the formation of several sub-sects, among which the most important is the STHANAKAVASI. According to some scholars, gachchha is a later term for GANA, but the two words are also used simultaneously.

Gahambars A seasonal festival in Zoroastrianism which occurs six times a year. The term Gahambar means 'full season' and thus the festival occurs in the middle of summer, winter, and other seasons. Each Gahambar is linked with some aspect of creation. The mid-spring Gahambar (maidhyoi-zarema) is asociated with heaven or the sky, and with KHSHATHRA; mid-summer (maidhyoi-shema) with water and HAURVATAT; the harvest (paitishahya) with the earth and ARMAITI; mid-autumn (ayathrima) with vegetation and AMERETAT; mid-winter (maidhyairya) with animals and VOHU MANA; and early spring or the beginning of the year with humans and AHURA MAZDA. This last corresponds to the MUKTAD ceremonies for ancestors, according to the Fasli calendar. Initially, each Gahambar lasted five days, but now is often confined to one day. Prayers, feasts and acts of charity form an essential part of the festivals.

gahs A term in Zoroastrianism for the five periods of the day. In Zoroastrian temples, the BOI ceremony is performed by the priests at the changing of each of the gahs, and special prayers are said. Havan Gah lasts from dawn to noon, Rapithwan Gah from noon to 3 pm, Uziren Gah from 3 pm to sunset, Aiwisuthrem Gah from sunset to midnight, and Ushain Gah from midnight till dawn. The timings of the Boi ceremony almost correspond with NAMAZ timings in Islam, and according to scholars, Zoroastrian customs had an influence on Islam.

Gaja-Lakshmi A form of the Hindu goddess LAKSHMI. In this form, Lakshmi is depicted with an elephant on each side ,who pour water on her from their trunks or from upturned pots. The goddess is seated or standing on a lotus, which usually grows out of a pot, and is surrounded by flowers or plants.

Gaja-Lakshmi, symbol of wealth, is among the earliest deities to be depicted and occurs on coins dating back to the second century BCE. She appears on carvings on the early STUPAS of central India, including SANCHI and BHARHUT, though some have identified this image with that of MAHAMAYA, mother of Buddha, or another Buddhist deity.

The *VISHNUDHARMOTTARA* provides a description of this type of image, stating that she should be depicted with a pair of elephants behind her head, pouring on her the contents of two jars. Variations of Gaja-Lakshmi are seen in several early temples, particularly in Orissa. Gaja-Lakshmi is also depicted in the KAILASHA TEMPLE at Ellora, as well as in some south Indian temples. This form of Lakshmi remains popular even today.

Gajendra The king of elephants in Hindu mythology. According to stories in the PURANAS, when playing in the water with his wives, Gajendra was seized by a *graha*, an aquatic monster. He was unable to free himself and began to pray to VISHNU, who rescued him. In his previous life, Gajendra is said to have been a king named Indradyumna, but he was cursed by the rishi AGASTYA and became an elephant. After his rescue by Vishnu he attained a divine form. This episode is depicted in art and sculpture, and is known as Gajendra-moksha, the liberation of Gajendra.

gana   A Sanskrit term that means a class or group.

(1) In a specific sense, the term refers to the attendants of the god SHIVA. These ganas are described in various texts as fearful and strange. Drawing on earlier material, the sixteenth-century RAMACHARITAMANASA of Tulasidasa provides a graphic description of the ganas who accompanied Shiva in his marriage procession: 'Some had lean and thin bodies, while others were very stout; some looked pure, and some impure. They wore frightful ornaments, carried skulls in their hands, and were all smeared with fresh blood. Their faces looked like those of donkeys and dogs, swine and jackals. Their various forms, which included spirits (pretas, pisachas), and yoginis, were beyond description.'

Ganas are thought to be a collection of non-Aryan deities, assimilated in the worship of Shiva and his sons GANESHA and KARTTIKEYA or Skanda. Ganesha is usually considered their leader. Some Ganas are attendants of the god Skanda and are known as Parshadas. They have faces of animals or birds.

(2) Other groups of minor deities are also referred to as ganas. Among these are: ADITYAS, RUDRAS, VASUS, VISHVADEVAS, TUSHITAS, ABHASVARAS, Anilas, Maharajikas, and SADHYAS. They are mentioned in the VAYU PURANA and other texts.

(3) Ganas also refer to various groups and classes, including clans of RISHIS or sages.

gana, Jain   In Jainism, a group or school headed by a GANADHARA. Ganas were divided into branches known as shakhas and kulas, and often formed part of a SANGHA. There was not much difference between one gana and another. The KALPA SUTRA contains a list of ganas, their shakhas and kulas, and their ganadharas. Some of these are also known from inscriptions. The names of ganas were often derived from their place of origin.

ganadhara   The chief disciples of a Jain TIRTHANKARA or leader, who usually headed a GANA or group of Jains. MAHAVIRA, the twenty-fourth TIRTHANKARA, had eleven ganadharas.

Ganapati   A name of the Hindu god GANESHA, who is also the leader of the GANAS, a group of minor deities.

Ganapatihridaya   A Buddhist mother goddess with an elephant head. When GANESHA was incorporated into Buddhism, several Buddhist deities gained elephant heads.

Ganapatya   A Hindu sect that worships the god GANESHA, also known as GANAPATI. Its practices are described in the GANESHA PURANA, the *Ganapati Upanishad*, and the *Ganesha Gita*. The last is similar

to the BHAGAVAD GITA, except for the insertion of the name of Ganesha instead of KRISHNA. At one time the Ganapatyas had six different sub-sects, worshipping different aspects of the god, known as Maha, Haridra, Svarna, Santana, Navanita, and Unmatta-Uchchhista. These included Tantric sects. Another sect, also Tantric, was the HAIRAMBA or Heramba. The *Prapanchasara Tantra* describes the Tantric worship of Ganesha. Tantric-Ganesha rites were also incorporated into VAJRAYANA Buddhism. The MAUDGALYA PURANA describes various aspects of Ganesha and his worship.

The Ganapatyas never became a major sect like the SHAIVITES or VAISHNAVITES, as Hindus of most sects incorporate the worship of Ganesha in their rituals, invoking the god at the beginning of any venture, and on auspicious occasions.

Gandavyuha Sutra   A MAHAYANA Buddhist text that forms part of the AVATAMSAKA SUTRA, but is used as a separate text. It narrates the story of Sudhana and his search for enlightenment, which he ultimately attained. The Bodhisattva MANJUSHRI inspired him to experience the bodhichitta, or thought of enlightenment. He then journeyed through south India, listening to the teachings of several others, including the Bodhisattva MAITREYA. Finally, after meeting the Bodhisattva SAMANTABHADRA, he attained enlightenment.

Gandhamadana   A mountain in Hindu mythology, where some of the gods live, including INDRA, KUBERA and the YAKSHAS. It is said to be located south of Mt KAILASHA. Fragrant and healing herbs grow on it. The god HANUMAN also lived here and brought a fragment of the mountain to RAMESHVARAM in south India.

Gandhara   A state in north-west India (present Pakistan) which existed at the time of the BUDDHA and later. The SARVASTIVADA, which later developed into the SAUTRANTIKA school of HINAYANA Buddhism, was prominent here. Between the second century BCE and the second century CE, Gandhara was known for a particular style of Buddhist art. The BUDDHA was depicted in human form for the first time, in Graeco-Roman style. Related Buddhist deities were also depicted in this style. The images were realistic, graceful and serene. At the same time, an indigenous artistic style was developing at MATHURA.

Gandhari   The wife of DHRITARASHTRA, the king of HASTINAPURA, described in the MAHABHARATA. As Dhritarashtra was blind, Gandhari too put a blindfold around her eyes. She had a hundred sons, collectively known as the KAURAVAS, born through divine intervention, and one daughter. After the Mahabharata War, Gandhari was filled with sorrow at the death of all her relatives and cursed the god KRISHNA. The later disasters at DVARAKA were the results of this curse.

gandharvas   A class of minor Hindu deities who are divine musicians. In the RIG VEDA, Gandharva is mentioned in the singular, as a deity, like the sun, but as one who generated rain. He knew the secrets of heaven and the divine truths. In the later VEDAS, gandharvas are mentioned as a group, and according to the ATHARVA VEDA, they number 6333. The PURANAS and other texts state that they lived in the sky or atmosphere, and prepared SOMA, the divine drink, for the gods. Their food is the scent of fragrant herbs and the smell of water, and they wear sweet-smelling clothes. They love women and are very handsome. Most commonly, they are known as divine singers, dancers and musicians who live in Indraloka, one of the heavens of the gods. Their king is CHITRARATHA, and they have beautiful cities. They are usually depicted with human bodies and the head of a bird or horse, and a similarity with centaurs has been suggested. Their female counterparts are APSARAS.

Gandhi, Mahatma A leader of the freedom movement in India, who is also considered the soul and conscience of the nation, providing ethical and moral guidelines which are still remembered.

Mohandas Karamchand Gandhi, born on 2 October 1869, was affectionately called 'Mahatma' or 'great soul'. His role in the freedom struggle against the British is well known, but many of his discussions on religion have been forgotten. It was his practice to hold a prayer meeting every evening, when he read out passages from texts of different religions and commented on them. Though he affirmed his identity as a Hindu, he respected all religions. He held that being a Hindu meant serving those of other religions and put his words into practice during the partition riots, being the first to visit areas where Muslims had been attacked. Among his favourite religious texts were the BHAGAVAD GITA and the Sermon on the Mount from the NEW TESTAMENT. The songs that inspired him included Rabindranath Tagore's *Ekla Chalo Re* (Walk Alone), and the Christian hymn *Abide With Me*, still played every year in his memory. He preached the virtues of AHIMSA or non-violence, truth, love, and the forgiveness of all.

Gandhi, who was assassinated on 30 January 1948, is the foremost example of how religion can be integrated into one's daily life for the benefit of all.

Ganesha A Hindu deity, an elephant-headed god, who is one of the most popular deities today, revered by Hindus of all sects. Ganesha is the patron deity of writers, accountants, traders and businessmen, and is worshipped at the start of any new venture. He grants progress, prosperity, wisdom, and the removal of obstacles.

Historically, he was incorporated into the Hindu pantheon somewhat late, around the fourth century, though he existed in different forms earlier. An elephant-headed deity was depicted on some early coins and at AMRAVATI in about the second century. Vinayaka, one of his names, was a term initially used

in texts for several spirits such as Shala, Ushmita and others, who possessed men and women and placed obstacles in their way. In the MAHABHARATA, Ganesha is the scribe who writes the whole epic down. In the *Yajnavalkya Smriti*, Vinayaka is mentioned as the son of AMBIKA.

In a number of myths and stories in the PURANAS he is described as a son of SHIVA and PARVATI, of Parvati alone, or as a deity with an independent origin. According to one story, at one time Shiva and Parvati took the form of elephants, and thus Ganesha was born. The most popular myth recounts that he was created by Parvati. When he was a young, handsome youth, Parvati asked him to guard her door, and Ganesha did his job so well that he would not even let Shiva in. Shiva, therefore, cut off his head, but seeing Parvati's grief, replaced his head with that of an elephant. In another myth, the god KRISHNA was born as Ganesha.

Ganesha is generally depicted seated or standing, with four arms. He has an elephant head, is pot-bellied, and has only one tusk. He normally holds in his hands any four of the following: his own tusk or tooth (svadanta), a wood-apple (kapittha), a sweet (modaka), an elephant-goad (ankusha), a noose (pasha), a snake (naga), a rosary, a lotus, an axe (parashu), or a radish (mulaka). In early images he had only two hands, while in some he has eight or more hands. His VAHANA or vehicle is a mouse (mushaka), and around his waist he ties a snake. Each of these aspects is explained through different stories.

Ganesha is also known as GANAPATI, the leader of the GANAS; Vinayaka or Vighneshvara, the remover of obstacles; Gangeya, because in one story he was nurtured by GANGA; EKADANTA, with one tusk. Other names include Lambodara and Gajanana.

He normally has two wives, called Buddhi (intelligence) and Siddhi (divine powers or success), who represent his attributes. Buddhi is sometimes replaced by Riddhi (prosperity).

Various texts also describe different representations of the deity, including Bija-Ganapati, Bala-Ganapati, Taruna- Ganapati, Lakshmi-Ganesha, Maha-Ganesha, Heramba-Ganapati, Haridra-Ganesha, Nritya-Ganapati, Unmatta- Vinayaka, Shakti-Ganesha, Uchchhishta-Ganapati. Maha-Ganesha refers to Ganesha as the Supreme Lord; Bala-Ganapati depicts Ganesha as a child; Lakshmi and Ganesha are worshipped together for prosperity, particularly at DIVALI; Nritya Ganapati is Ganesha dancing; as Heramba Ganapati he rides a lion. Heramba, Unmatta, Shakti and Uchchhista forms are associated with the TANTRIC worship of Ganesha. There are other forms of Ganesha as well.

The GANAPATYAS are sects specially focused on the worship of Ganesha, and use texts dealing specifically with Ganesha. Ganesha also forms one of the PANCHAYATANA, or five main gods of Hinduism.

While art historians feel his elephant head and pot-belly indicate the absorption of a local YAKSHA cult into

Hinduism, others explain his aspects as symbols of a greater truth. Symbolically, Ganesha's elephant head represents the Unmanifest, the ultimate goal, and the decapitation of his human head indicates the removal of the individual ego. He has a huge belly because it contains the whole universe, his single tusk represents illusion, and the mouse is the Self, hidden within.

Ganesha temples are located all over India, but he is specially worshipped in Maharashtra. Notable among these are the Ashtavinayaka temples, of which the MORESHVARA TEMPLE is the most popular, and the Siddhi Vinayaka Temple in MUMBAI. In recent times he has become very popular in Tamil Nadu, though there are ancient Ganesha temples there too. Ganesha is worshipped in all SHIVA temples, often in a separate shrine. His brother and rival is KARTTIKEYA or SKANDA.

Ganesha is venerated by Buddhists and Jains as well, and in the early medieval period his images occur in Indo-China, Java and elsewhere. Similar elephant-headed deities are known in China, Japan and other parts of South-East Asia.

Ganesha Chaturthi A festival in celebration of the Hindu god GANESHA. It is most popular in Maharashtra, but is also celebrated in other states. The festival lasts for ten days and takes place in August/September. On the first day a clay image is brought into the house, and then worshipped every day, and on the last day it is immersed in water, either a river, the sea, or even a lake. Prosperity, wisdom and freedom from obstacles are said to be achieved by celebrating this festival. Ganesha is venerated by Buddhists and Jains as well.

Ganesha Purana A Sanskrit text, a minor PURANA or UPAPURANA, dealing with the worship of GANESHA as the supreme deity.

Ganga, goddess A Hindu goddess who represents the river GANGA. Through the mythology of the river, she is also the second wife of SHIVA, though at one time she was one of the three wives of VISHNU. YAMUNA, her main tributary, is her sister in myths.

Among other stories about Ganga is that she once came to earth as a beautiful woman. King Shantanu of HASTINAPURA married her and she gave birth to eight sons, who were once the eight VASUS. The first seven were returned to the Ganga (river), the eighth grew up as Devavrata, also known as BHISHMA.

Ganga as a goddess is usually depicted as a beautiful woman, holding a vessel filled with water on her hip, and standing on a *MAKARA*, a mythical creature who dwells in water. Images of the goddess Ganga are placed in front of temple doors, or carved on them. In some sculptures she is depicted with Shiva, along with PARVATI, and in others she is shown in Shiva's hair.

Ganga river The Ganga is the most sacred of all Indian rivers. It starts at Gaumukh in the Himalayas at a height of 4600 m, descends into the plains at HARDWAR, and has a total length of 2525 km before it joins the sea in the Bay of Bengal. Several myths and legends are associated with the river. The Ganga, it is said, first flowed in heaven from the god VISHNU's foot. King Bhagiratha prayed that it descend to earth to revive his ancestors. The god BRAHMA felt the earth could not bear her strong flow, so SHIVA allowed her to flow on his head. She wandered through his matted locks for some time until Bhagiratha prayed again. Then she descended from the hair of Shiva, and finally flowed to GANGA SAGARA, where the ashes of Bhagiratha's ancestors were.

Bathing in the river is said to cleanse one of all sins. In Hindu rituals, a few sips of water are given to those on their deathbed. In earlier times, Ganga water was given to the sick in the belief that it would cure them. According to the *MAHABHARATA*, to chant the name of the Ganga brings purity, to see her assures prosperity, and to bathe in her provides salvation.

The purity of the river was recognized even by the Muslim sultans and the Mughals. The sultan Muhammad bin Tughlaq and the Mughal emperors AKBAR and Jahangir drank only Ganga water. Special officials carried the water over long distances when they were on campaigns. Even some of the kings of Tibet drank Ganga water.

Along the course of the Ganga are innumerable sacred places or tirthas. Among these are GANGOTRI, near its source. It descends into the plains at Hardwar, earlier known as Gangadvara, an extremely sacred site. Rishikesh nearby, also has great sanctity. BITHUR, ALLAHABAD (Prayaga), VARANASI (Kashi) and Sonpur in Bihar are some of the other sacred places, apart from Ganga Sagara, where it joins the sea. The Ganga's tributaries include the YAMUNA, Ramganga, Gomati, Ghaghara, Gandak and Kosi rivers and there are sacred sites located along all these.

Ganga Sagara A sacred place located in West Bengal where the river GANGA joins the Bay of Bengal. Here there are small islands submerged in water after the rains. Around MAKARA SANKRANTI (13–14 January) every year, a festival is held here. Thousands of pilgrims bathe in the confluence of the river and the sea at the time of the festival, and it is a centre of pilgrimage even at other times.

In Hindu myths, Ganga Sagara is connected with a story of the descent of the Ganga to earth. In ancient times there was a famous king named Sagara who had two wives, Keshini and Sumati, but no children. He prayed for sons to the god SHIVA, who granted his wish, and had one son from Keshini and a lump of flesh from Sumati, which grew into 60,000 sons. In gratitude, Sagara decided to perform the ASHVAMEDHA or horse sacrifice, where a horse is set free to roam and later sacrificed. The god INDRA stole the horse, afraid of the king's growing might, and tied it underground, where the rishi KAPILA was meditating. The 60,000 sons searched for it, and locating it they began to attack the sage, who opened his eyes and by his power, charred them all to death. Anshuman, Sagara's grandson through Keshini, found the bones and begged Kapila to revive them. The rishi said they could only be revived when the Ganga flowed over their bones. It was Anshuman's grandson Bhagiratha who by his penances and prayers to the god BRAHMA, succeeded in bringing Ganga down to earth. Finally she flowed to the required spot and revived Sagara's sons. The place was then known as Ganga Sagara and a temple of Kapila was built at the spot.

Gangamma A Hindu mother goddess worshipped in villages in parts of south India. Gangamma is a powerful deity, a form of DURGA, usually propitiated with animal sacrifices twice a year.

Gangaur A festival to honour the Hindu goddess GAURI, a form of PARVATI, held in March/ April in Rajasthan. It is both a harvest festival and a prayer for marital bliss. Unmarried girls worship Gauri to gain a good husband, while married women do so for the long life of their husbands and a happy married life. The festival begins on the first day of Chaitra, the day after Holi and continues for eighteen days. Images of Gauri and Isar (Shiva) are made and decorated and taken out in procession on the last three days of the festival. On the final day, the images are immersed in a well or tank.

Gangotri A sacred site located in Uttarakhand, at a height of 3048 m. It is worshipped as the source of the river GANGA, though the actual source is at Gaumukh, 18 km further up the Gangotri glacier. At Gangotri the Ganga is known as the BHAGIRATHI, named after King Bhagiratha of Hindu myths, whose prayers brought her down to earth. A temple is located at Gangotri; it is one of the Char Dham or four main Hindu shrines of the region. The present temple was constructed in the eighteenth century. Made of white stone, it has a gilded roof and a central spire. Nearby is a flat stone known as the Bhagiratha Shila, where Bhagiratha is said to have meditated.

Gangsar Gurdwara A GURDWARA or Sikh shrine with a sacred tank, located at JAITU in Punjab. According to the story associated with it, a pilgrim was once on his way to the river GANGA for a purificatory bath when he met Guru GOBIND SINGH. The guru told him he would acquire equal merit by bathing in the tank at Jaitu, because its water was as pure as the Ganga. The pilgrim bathed in the tank, which was then named 'Gangsar', or the 'tank with Ganga water'. Another Gangsar is located at KARTARPUR.

garbha-griha Literally, 'womb-house', it refers to the innermost or main shrine in a Hindu temple, where the image is kept.

Garcia, Gonzalo An Indian Christian who lived from 1557 to 97 and is the first Indian to have been canonized as a CHRISTIAN SAINT. Not much is known about his early life, but he was probably born in a local Christian family in Vasai district near MUMBAI.

He had a gift for languages and at the age of fifteen was taken by the JESUITS to Japan, where he became fluent in Japanese and acted as their interpreter. He worked in Macao and Manila, and in 1587 he became a Franciscan brother, returning to Japan in 1593 as a missionary. There was persecution against Christians in Japan, and in 1597 he and some other Japanese Christians were tied to crosses and executed. He was made a saint by Pope Pius IX in 1862.

garo demana A term for heaven in Zoroastrianism. According to the GATHAS, it is the house of song or truth, reached by the followers of truth. Later texts also have other terms for heaven, and ARDA VIRAF of the third century, describes seven heavens.

Garuda A divine bird associated with the Hindu god VISHNU. In the RIG VEDA, a celestial deity Garutman is mentioned, who has beautiful wings. In the *MAHABHARATA*, Garuda is said to be the same as Garutman and is the brother of ARUNA, who is the charioteer of the god SURYA. In the PURANAS, he is the son of the rishi KASHYAPA from his wife Vinata, with Aruna as his brother. Myths and stories narrate that Garuda glowed brilliantly when he was born and frightened the gods, who thought he was AGNI, the brilliant god of fire. They praised him as the highest being, a form of fire and the sun. Garuda is the chief of all the birds, and an enemy of NAGAS or serpents. The god Vishnu rides through the heavens mounted on him.

In early art, he is depicted as a large parrot-like bird, and he occurs on an architrave at SANCHI. On Gupta coins, he is shown as a plump bird, the capital on a column (Garudadhvaja). In later art, he is depicted with the head, wings and talons of an eagle, and the body of a man. He has a white face, red wings and a golden body. He usually has two arms and is also known as TARKSHYA. Some texts describe him with eight arms, the goddesses LAKSHMI and SARASVATI on either side of him. In general, there are two forms of Garuda, one as the capital of a column and the other as the VAHANA of Vishnu. Garuda often holds a snake as he flies through the air.

Garuda Purana A Sanskrit text, one of the eighteen major PURANAS of Hinduism. The introduction states that this Purana was revealed by the god VISHNU to GARUDA, who narrated it to the rishi KASHYAPA. It has some aspects of the five Puranic themes, but is more concerned with the worship of Vishnu, VAISHNAVA festivals and rites, and MAHATMYAS or accounts of sacred places. There are sections on SHAKTI worship and on the worship of the PANCHAYATANA or 'five gods', SHIVA, Vishnu, DURGA, SURYA and GANESHA. Like the *AGNI PURANA*, it is encyclopedic in character, with chapters on cosmography, astrology, astronomy, medicine, grammar and politics, as well as other subjects.

Gathas (1) In Zoroastrianism, a text which consists of verses composed mainly by ZARATHUSHTRA, the founder of the religion, who probably lived around

1500 BCE. Zarathushtra is said to have composed many more verses or songs, but most of them are lost, and only these fragments remain. It forms part of the YASNA, a text with seventy-two chapters or haiti, and includes seventeen hymns, divided into five *Gathas*, each with a different theme.

The *Gathas* are written in the AVESTA language, very similar to Rig Vedic Sanskrit. In fact, minor changes enable one to 'translate' or transpose much of the text into Sanskrit. Like the VEDAS, the verses were conveyed for hundreds of years through oral tradition. They were written down around 400 CE in a script specially composed for this purpose. By this time, the written language of Iran under the Sasanians was PAHLAVI, while the spoken language was known as Pazand. Because of the obscurity of the language, several *Gatha* scholars differ on their interpretation of the texts.

The five *Gathas* are:

(1) *Gatha Ahunavati*, the *Gatha* of Free Choice (*Yasna* 28–34). This includes the legend of GAUSH URVA, Zarathushtra's prayers for guidance to AHURA MAZDA, the creation of the twin mentalities, ANGRA MAINYU and SPENTA MAINYU, and the need for every individual to use his own discrimination and choose the right path. Finally, Zarathushtra dedicates his life and all his actions to Ahura Mazda.

(2) *Gatha Ushtavaiti*, the *Gatha* of Bliss and Enlightenment (*Yasna* 43–46). It begins by stating that those who bring light to others, gain light (enlightenment) themselves. It praises Ahura Mazda, who has directed Zarathushtra to instruct people in the path of truth (ASHA). Through a series of questions, Zarathushtra reveals how to use Ahura Mazda's powers to gain the strength to follow the right path. He comments on the twin spirits and the power of MANTHRA, the sacred word.

(3) *Gatha Spenta Mainyu*, the *Gatha* of the Holy Spirit (*Yasna* 47–50). This *Gatha* indicates how perfection (HAURVATAT) and immortality (AMERETAT) are attained by following the path of Spenta Mainyu, the good spirit, and of the best mind (*vahishta manangha*).

(4) *Gatha Vohu Khshathra*, the *Gatha* of Sovereignty or the Good Kingdom (*Yasna* 51). Here Zarathushtra comments on the wicked, who will be tormented by their own soul or conscience.

(5) *Gatha Vahishtoishti*, the *Gatha* of the Highest Wish or Fulfilment (*Yasna* 53). This short *Gatha* deals with the marriage of Zarathushtra's youngest daughter Pouruchista, probably to Jamaspa, though he is not mentioned in the text. It is not the work of Zarathushtra, but of someone close to him, written soon after his death. It asks the married couple to strive together to attain truth, and thus to lead a blessed existence. This text is still used in Zoroastrian marriage ceremonies today.

The *Gathas* contains the essence or basic principles of the Zoroastrian religion. Some of the daily prayers used today have passages from the *Gathas*, while others include Gathic concepts.

The text does not provide much historical information, though it mentions Kava VISHTASPA, the king who patronized Zarathushtra, and his ministers Frashaostra and Jamaspa Hvogva.

(2) *Gatha* is also a term used for certain texts or verses of other religions, including Islam, Hinduism and Buddhism.

Gaudapada A philosopher of ADVAITA, who lived between the sixth and eighth centuries and commented on the UPANISHADS. Though Advaitic ideas were known earlier, Gaudapada explained its principles in a systematic way.

He was the teacher of Govinda, who in turn was the guru of SHANKARA, who firmly established Advaita in India. Gaudapada's main work is the *Karika*, which has four sections. The first is the Agama, a commentary on the MANDUKYA UPANISHAD. The second, Vatathya, explains the phenomenal nature of the world. The third lays down the main principles of Advaita, whereas the fourth, Alatashanti, develops these principles further. This section gets its name from the analogy of a burning stick circled in the air, which creates the illusion of a circle of fire, alatachakra. The world with its various forms is said to be a similar illusion. Gaudapada's ideas were further elaborated by Shankara.

Gauri A name of the Hindu goddess PARVATI. Gauri means 'the fair one'. According to one story, SHIVA called Parvati by her name Kali (black). Parvati thought he was mocking her for having dark skin, so she meditated until she became Gauri, or fair, shedding her dark skin. This myth probably indicates the absorption of a dark tribal goddess into the Brahmanical pantheon, and her subsequent transformation into a form of Parvati.

Gaurishankara Temple A temple dedicated to Gaurishankara, the name of the Hindu deities SHIVA and PARVATI, located at Jagatsukh near Manali in Himachal Pradesh. This early temple has an image of four-armed DURGA killing Mahisha, the buffalo demon, with a trident that she holds in one of her hands. Though Durga holds the tail of the buffalo, her eyes are closed in serene contemplation.

This small square temple dates from the eighth or ninth century.

Gaush Urva In Zoroastrianism, a symbol of the suffering earth. Literally it means 'the soul of the cow', but the cow represents the whole earth. In the PURANAS too, the goddess of the earth, BHUDEVI, appears to VARAHA in the form of a cow, and pleads for help for the oppressed earth. In the BHAGAVATA PURANA she appears to INDRA, who sends KRISHNA to save the earth.

In the GATHAS, Gaush Urva appeals to AHURA MAZDA or God to send her a saviour because she was oppressed and surrounded by violence and aggression. In response, Ahura Mazda sent ZARATHUSHTRA to protect the earth.

In the later creation stories in PAHLAVI texts such as the *BUNDAHISHN* and *ZADSPRAM*, Gaush Urva is described in detail. When GAYODAD, the primeval bull, died because of the attack by the evil spirit, AHRIMAN, Gaush Urva arose as Gayodad's living soul. She went to Ahura Mazda, the stars, the moon and the sun for help. Ahura Mazda revealed to her the FRAVASHI, the spirit of Zarathushtra, who would soon come to help her. Gaush Urva, collecting the seed of Gayodad and GAYOMARD (man), repopulated the earth with the help of Mino Ram, spirit of peace. But once again it was attacked by Ahriman. Then finally Zarathushtra came down to earth, 'the man who would teach reverence and care for every living thing'.

Similar myths of the cow representing the earth attacked and oppressed in various ways, and then provided with a saviour, occur in other ancient cultures. One such story is in a Slavonic version of the *Book of Enoch*.

Gaya A city located in Bihar, 10 km north of BODH GAYA. According to tradition Gaya is one of the seven sacred cities of Hinduism. It has several temples, and is a major centre of pilgrimage. The existing temples were constructed in the eighteenth century or later, but there are numerous sculptures dating back to the ninth and tenth centuries and even earlier. Special rites are conducted here for the souls of ancestors. At Gaya, Hindu and Buddhist legends are intermixed. In ancient texts, Gaya is linked with the story of the king Gaya, and later the asura Gaya. The Vishnupada Temple was constructed here by Ahalyabai of Indore in the eighteenth century, on the site of a Buddhist temple. It is said to mark the spot where VISHNU placed his foot on the asura Gaya.

RAMA and SITA are said to have visited Gaya. There are numerous sacred sites and ghats along the Falgu river.

The Buddha is said to have preached the fire-Sermon (*Adittapariyaya Sutta*) here, to 1000 fire-worshipping ascetics, who immediately gained enlightenment

Gayatri A verse in the RIG VEDA and also a verse metre. The Gayatri verse or MANTRA is considered specially sacred, and is named after the metre, which has twenty-four syllables. It is a prayer to the sun as SAVITR, and reads 'Om bhur bhuva svaha, tat savitur varenyam, bhargo devasya dhimahi, dhiyo yo nah prachodayat'. (The first part is an invocation, the syllables being counted from 'tat'). This verse has been variously translated. One version is, 'We meditate on that excellent light of the divine sun; may he illumine our minds' (H.H. Wilson). Other verses too, can be composed in this metre, and are referred to with a qualifying term, such as Vishnu Gayatri, or Surya Gayatri.

Gayatri, goddess A Hindu goddess, a wife of BRAHMA. According to a story in the Puranas, Brahma and his consort SARASVATI went to perform a sacrifice at Pushkar. Sarasvati came late for the sacrifice, and

an impatient Brahma made Gayatri, a milkmaid, his consort. Despite Sarasvati's fury, Gayatri remained his wife. She is considered the mother of the VEDAS and the personification of the Gayatri Mantra.

Gayodad A white bull, a creation of Ohrmazd or AHURA MAZDA, described in later Zoroastrian texts. Gayodad suffered when AHRIMAN brought evil and disease to the earth. After he died his soul emerged as GAUSH URVA. He represents the life of the animal kingdom. The white bull NANDI, companion of the Hindu god SHIVA, also represents life and fertility, though other aspects of their myths are not similar.

Gayomard Primeval man, the creation of Ohrmazd or AHURA MAZDA, described in later Zoroastrian texts. When AHRIMAN attacked the world, Gayomard died, but with his last breath he prophesied that men would arise again from his seed.

Gelug (Dge-lugs-pa) One of the four main schools of TIBETAN BUDDHISM. The Gelug school was founded by TSONG KHAPA (1357–1419), who studied with masters of all traditions before founding this school. Tsong Khapa set up the Ganden monastery, the first of the major Gelug monasteries, in 1409. The Drepung monastery was founded in 1416 by one of his disciples and the Sera monastery was established in 1419. The first DALAI LAMA, Gyalwa Gendun Drup, founded the Tashi Lhunpo monastery at Shigatse in 1447, later the seat of the PANCHEN LAMA. Two Tantric colleges were also established. The Gelug tradition emphasizes ethics and monastic training, as well as knowledge and scholarship as a basis for meditation. Studies for a Gelug monk include the five major topics, the perfection of wisdom, the Middle Way, valid cognition, phenomenology and monastic discipline. These studies last fifteen or twenty years, after which one of the three levels of the GESHE (doctorate) degree is granted. Geshes can then join the Tantric college if they wish.

After 1959 the major Gelug colleges of Ganden, Drepung, Sera and Tashi Lhunpo were reestablished in Karnataka in India, while the Gyuto Tantric College has been set up at Bomdila in Arunachal Pradesh. The Gelugpa are commonly called the 'Yellow Hats' because of the type of hat they wear. They rejected the 'Red Hat' representing earlier Buddhist schools.

geshe An academic title for a Tibetan Buddhist monk of the GELUG or SAKYA sects, equivalent to a PhD Several courses of study, exams and debates have to be undertaken before this stage is reached, which can take up to thirty years.

Gesu Daraz, Mir One of the greatest SUFI saints of the CHISTI ORDER. Born in about 1321, his name was Syed Muhammad bin Yusuf al-Husaini, but he was popularly known as Khwaja Banda Nawaz or Mir Gesu Daraz. He was the leading disciple of NASIRUDDIN MAHMUD (Chirag) of DELHI. Though he was originally in Delhi at the time of Timur's invasion, he moved to Gujarat and later to Gulbarga in the Deccan. He wrote a number of works on Sufism, initially based on the WAHDAT AL-WUJUD doctrine, but later was convinced of WAHDAT AL-SHUHUD beliefs. His conversations are compiled in the *Jawami al-Kalim*, and short works on Sufism such as the *Miraj al-Ashiqin*. He died in 1422. His DARGAH at Gulbarga in Karnataka is a popular place of pilgrimage. Built in Indo-Saracenic style, it has paintings in Iranian and Turkish styles on the walls and dome.

getig A term for the physical world in Zoroastrianism. It is not considered separate from MENOG, the mental world, and both, forming one whole, are sacred. Thus neither the world nor the body are denied in Zoroastrianism, and asceticism and fasting are not advised. The physical world, including rocks, rivers, plants and animals, are to be cared for and protected. Food and sex are to be enjoyed, but without indulgence, as even these are sacred. Most Zoroastrians are meat eaters though some hold that the religion implies vegetarianism, an aspect that was later forgotten.

Ghalib, Mirza Asadullah Khan A great poet of Urdu and Persian. Ghalib was descended from a Persian-speaking Turkish tribe. His paternal grandfather Quqan Beg reached Lahore from Samarkand in 1750, and later settled in Agra, where Asadullah Khan was born in 1797. He lost his father in 1802 and his uncle a few years later, and came under the care of his maternal grandfather. He was married to Umrao Begum of Delhi in 1810 and by 1812 had settled in Delhi. Asadullah was writing poems by the age of eleven, first using the pen name Asad, and later Ghalib. Collections of his Urdu and Persian poems were ready in the 1830s and published in the 1840s. In 1854, he became the court poet of the last Mughal emperor, Bahadur Shah Zaffar II. His fortunes suffered after the 1857 revolt against the British, but from 1859 he received an allowance from the nawab of Rampur. Among his compilations are *Urdu Diwan*, a collection of his Urdu poems; *Mekhana-I-Arzoo, Panjabang, Dastambu,* an account of the 1857 revolt, in Persian; *Durafsh-e-Kaviyani*, earlier called *Qati-e-Burhan*, a criticism of a Persian dictionary; *Ud-e-Hindi* (Indian Harp) a collection of his Urdu letters; and *Urdu-e-Mualla*, another collection;. Ghalib's poems include ghazals (love songs) masnawis (mystical or moralistic verses), and qasidas (panegyrics), but through them all, his spirituality is revealed. For example:

The universe is nothing but
Thyself in peerless glory;
We exist, since Beauty takes
Delight in seeing Itself.

Though a Muslim, he saw the truth in all religions. He wrote:

God is One, That is our faith;
All rituals we abjure.

It is only when the symbols vanish
That belief is pure.

Ghalib died in 1869

ghat A Sanskrit term. Ghats are located at sacred sites near rivers and temples, and consist of stairs which lead down to the water. Devotees can use these to enter the water and perform religious rites, or to bathe. The term ghat also refers to a hill range or cliff.

Ghat Sahib Gurdwara A GURDWARA or Sikh shrine located at Nangal in District Rupnagar, Punjab. It is built at a spot visited by Guru GOBIND SINGH, who crossed the river Satluj at the ghat here.

Ghateshvara Temple A temple of the Hindu god SHIVA, dating to the ninth or tenth century, located at Baroli in Rajasthan. In the main shrine, natural LINGA-shaped stones are set in a square pedestal. One stone resembles an inverted *ghata* or pot, and this gives the temple its name. The shrine has a curvilinear tower and a columned MANDAPA adjoining it.

There are several beautiful sculptures, including images of Shiva, BRAHMA, VISHNU, CHAMUNDA, and guardian deities.

Ghazi Miyan's Dargah A DARGAH or shrine of a Muslim saint located at Bahraich in Uttar Pradesh. His name was Sayyid SALAR MASUD GHAZI, but he is popularly known as Ghazi Miyan. According to tradition, he was a nephew of the invader Mahmud of Ghazni, though his actual identity is unknown. He is said to have renounced the world, but was forced to fight and died in battle in 1033. His grave was guarded by his devotees and gradually became a shrine where miracles of all kinds were reported. Jasu Ahir, a Hindu blessed with a son while praying there, rebuilt the grave with cow's milk mixed with lime. Zahra Bibi, a woman blind from birth, regained her sight there, tended the grave till she died, and is buried nearby. The shrine was expanded by some of the DELHI sultans and other structures were built around it later. Saints and SUFIS paid tribute to Ghazi Miyan, and both Hindus and Muslims worship at the shrine, which continues to be popular.

The dargah, popular from the thirteenth century onwards, is now a large complex of three forts. Within the Sangi-Qila (stone fort) is Ghazi Miyan's tomb as well as that of his horse and dog. Around this is the Qila-i-Kalan, with the graves of his companions, and surrounding this, a huge outer complex entered through the Zanjiri Darwaza.

Pilgrims arrive at the dargah every day, but particularly on Islamic festivals, the URS of the saint in the Islamic month of Rajab, the BASANT fair in the month of Magha, and the Jyaishtha fair in the month of Jyaishtha.

All prayers are said to be answered here, but Ghazi Miyan's Dargah is specifically known as a place where lepers are cured. The water used in bathing the grave is said to have special powers to cure leprosy and other skin diseases.

The shrine has a large income and contributes to educational institutions in the district. It makes charitable gifts, and gives 6 per cent of its earnings to the UP Waqf Board. In terms of the numbers who come to visit it and its annual income, it is considered no less significant than the dargah of MUINUDDIN CHISTI at Ajmer.

Ghoshitarama An ancient Buddhist monastery in KAUSHAMBI, near Allahabad in present Uttar Pradesh. It was gifted to the BUDDHA by Ghoshita, treasurer of the king of the region. Remains of the monastery have been discovered in excavations.

Ghulam Ahmad, Mirza The founder of the AHMADIYA sect of Islam.

Born in 1836 at Qadian in District Gurdaspur of Punjab, his ancestors were from Khurasan.

Ghulam Ahmad was educated in Persian and Arabic and later joined govenment service at Sialkot in 1860. After his father's death he began to think about life, and to study various religions, including Islam, Hinduism and Christianity. He wrote the *Barhin-i Ahmadiya* (Proofs of the Ahmadiya), of which the first two parts were published in 1880, as well as a number of other works. In 1888, he received a divine revelation and founded the Ahmadiya sect the following year. A few years later, in 1891, he said that he was the MAHDI, as well as the Messiah predicted in Islam. He also claimed that he was like JESUS and KRISHNA. He wrote a book on Jesus in India, locating his grave in Kashmir. He provided a new interpretation of the QURAN and a theory of salvation.

Ghulam Ahmad was opposed by orthodox Muslims, Hindus and Christians. He died on 26 May 1908 at Lahore and was buried at Qadian. The Ahmadiya sect continues to exist in Pakistan and elsewhere, but remains controversial.

ginans Devotional verses and songs of the Nizari Ismaili sect of Islam. The term 'ginan' is derived from the Sanskrit 'jnana'. Ginans are composed in Urdu, Punjabi, Sindhi, Gujarati, and other languages.

Girija A name of the Hindu goddess PARVATI, referring to her origin in the mountains. Giri and Parvat both mean hill or mountain, and Parvati was the daughter of the mountain, her father being Himavat or HIMAVAN, a name of the Himalayas.

Girnar A sacred Jain site in Saurashtra, Gujarat. The Girnar Hill rises to a height of 900 m. More than halfway up, on a rocky outcrop at about 650 m, are sixteen Jain shrines of the ninth to thirteenth centuries. The largest of these is dedicated to ARISHTANEMINATHA, the twenty-second Jain TIRTHANKARA. At the top of the Gorakhnath Peak is a shrine of the goddess AMBIKA. Along the path leading to the peak are gateways, shrines and tanks. Girnar is described in the VIVIDHA

TIRTHA KALPA, a Jain text, and was also known as Ujjayanta or Revantaka. It was an ancient site and at the foot of the hill inscriptions of ASHOKA, the Mauryan emperor who ruled in the third century BCE, have been found.

Gita Govinda A Sanskrit text in verse, written in the twelfth century by JAYADEVA. It describes the divine love between the god KRISHNA and RADHA, his beloved. Radha, as she yearns for Krishna, represents every soul's yearning for god, and her union with him is the union of the soul with the divine. Composed in Bengal, the *Gita Govinda* has twelve chapters containing ashtapadis (songs) and shlokas (verses). The text can be seen at two levels, with erotic descriptions revealing the sacred. Beginning with a prelude, the poem then describes the ten well-known avataras of Vishnu, and identifies Krishna with Vishnu, and Radha with Shri. The rest of the poem deals with the pain of separation, longing, and reunion, of Radha and Krishna. Radha, as she yearns for Krishna, represents every soul's yearning for God, and her union with him is the union of the soul with the divine. In one verse, Krishna is described:

Sandal and garment of yellow and lotus garlands upon his body of blue,
In his dance the jewels of his ears in movement dangling over his smiling cheeks.
Hari here disports himself with charming women given to love!

In another verse, after uniting with him in love, Radha commands Krishna:

Make a pattern upon my breasts and a picture on my cheeks and fasten over my loins a girdle,
Bind my masses of hair with a beautiful garland and place many bracelets upon my hands and jewelled anklets upon my feet!
And so he who wore the yellow garments did as she told him. (Trans. George Kyt)

The text forms the basis for Radha-Krishna worship, and has inspired music, dance forms, and paintings.

Gitanjali A collection of spiritual verses written by Rabindranath TAGORE that won him the Nobel Prize for literature in 1913. Originally written in Bengali, the verses were translated into English by the author. The songs or verses are in the BHAKTI tradition, addressed directly to god. For Tagore, god is the Universal Self, the divine musician, singer and poet, the companion of the poor, the friend and lover, the mother and compassionate one. He longs to experience god, yet at times finds himself far away. Thus he says:

My heart longs to join in thy song, but vainly struggles for a voice. (Song III)

In another verse he writes of a moment of quietness:

I ask for a moment's indulgence to sit by thy side. The works that I have in hand I will finish afterwards.

Away from the sight of thy face my heart knows no rest nor respite, and my work becomes an endless toil in a shoreless sea of toil.

Today the summer has come at my window with its sighs and murmurs; and the bees are plying their minstrelsy at the court of the flowering grove.

Now it is time to sit quiet, face to face with thee, and to sing a dedication of life in this silent and overflowing leisure. (Song V)

Gnosticism　A form of religious thought considered an offshoot of Christianity, or one that has its roots in pre-Christian traditions. The term comes from *gnosis* or 'secret knowledge' in Greek, and Gnostics believe in attaining God or salvation through esoteric knowledge. A number of different Gnostic groups developed from around the second century CE. In general they affirmed that individual souls emerged from divine sparks and had to disentangle themselves from matter through knowledge of their true selves, and thus return to their source. Some schools put forward the idea of two separate entities of good and evil, matter being a creation of evil.

Gnostic philosophy was once known mainly from the writings of their opponents, but the finds of the scrolls at NAG HAMMADI have revealed the writings of Gnostics themselves. Medieval Gnostic schools include the Cathars and others. In the Christian Gnostic sects, JESUS is seen as the redeemer or teacher who provides true knowledge and who temporarily took on a material body, which had no true reality. Thus only the body was crucified, and not the essential spirit of Christ.

Gnostic ideas have been compared with ADVAITA, with its focus on self-knowledge and the concept of the world as MAYA or illusion, and also with SAMKHYA philosophy and the two principles of soul and matter, PURUSHA and PRAKRITI. A suggestion has been made that Gnosticism developed through Indian influence and was a result of Greek contacts with India. The ideas have also been compared with writings of the early Greek philosophers and with Zoroastrianism, particularly in its later dualistic form. Mani, a philosopher who founded a religion known as Manichaeism, based on Gnostic concepts, includes both Christian and Zoroastrian ideas. Parallels can also be seen in Buddhist theories, including that of the three bodies (TRIKAYA) of the BUDDHA, and in Jain concepts of the accumulation of KARMA on a pure soul or JIVA, as well as with other Indian philosophies emphasizing the purity of the soul as distinct from matter. A Gnostic group of the second century known as Naassenes, from the Hebrew *nahash* for serpent, believed snakes were symbolic of knowledge, similar to ideas in India and the concept of the KUNDALINI.

Some medieval Gnostic schools in Europe, particularly branches of the Cathars, incorporated the concept of spiritualizing matter instead of rejecting it, an idea later developed to its fullest extent by Sri AUROBINDO.

There are also Neo-Gnostic groups in the present age which have a variety of beliefs. The influence of Gnostic ideas is thus seen in a number of philosophies and sects.

Goa, Christians in　The state of Goa on the western coast of India has a Christian population of 26.7 per cent (2001), mainly Catholic, as well as a number of old churches. Christianity came to Goa with its conquest by the Portuguese in 1510. Before this, Goa had been under the sultan of Bijapur, Adil Shah. Though at first, freedom of religion was promised by the Portuguese, it was not followed for long. Initially Muslims in Goa were persecuted because the Portuguese saw them as a challenge to state power. Intermarriage with Indian women created the first Indian Christians in the region, and conversion of their extended families was encouraged. In 1517 a group of Franciscan friars came to Goa and by 1539, had established churches and converted a number of Hindus to Christianity. Members of other Catholic orders—Carmelites, Augustinians, Dominicans and JESUITS—also arrived in Goa, each group setting up churches and monasteries constructed in styles prevalent in Europe. Around 1540, the policy of conversion by persuasion was changed to one of conversion by force. The king of Portugal ordered that idols be destroyed and 'pagan worship' be stopped. A large number of forcible conversions took place and Goa became a Christian state. This policy was strangely known as the 'rigour of mercy'. Another Christian group, known as the 'Confraternity of the Holy Faith' worked to spread education and understanding of the religion, opening the famous college of St. Paul, the first Jesuit school in the world.

In 1560 an INQUISITION was established. It existed for more than 200 years before it was finally abolished.

Goa remained under the Portuguese till 1961, when it was taken over by India. Goan Christianity had also spread to MUMBAI and other parts of the western coast, and Christians in these areas were more Westernized than in other areas, using Western names and forms of dress. After 1961, several Goans took on Indian names, while some reverted to earlier religious practices.

Churches of Goa are still popular places of pilgrimage, notable among them being the BOM JESUS BASILICA, associated with ST. FRANCIS XAVIER.

Gobind Singh, Guru　The tenth and last Sikh guru. Born on 22 December 1666 at Patna (Bihar), Gobind Rai was the son of the ninth guru, TEGH BAHADUR, who at that time was touring Bengal and Assam. They returned to ANANDPUR, Punjab, in 1672, where Gobind began his education, studying Punjabi, Braj Bhasha (early Hindi), Sanskrit and Persian, and developing physical skills. On 11 November 1675, his father was killed by the Mughal emperor AURANGZEB and Gobind Rai was installed as guru in March 1676. He continued his education and from 1685 to 1688 stayed at Paonta on the banks of the Yamuna, before returning to Anandpur. To defend the Sikh position in Punjab, he fought battles against some of the Rajput hill rulers and the Mughal forces.

In 1698 he decided to enthuse the Sikhs and inspire them to further acts of bravery. To start with, he asked them not to acknowledge the MASANDS, or Sikh leaders, who by now had grown corrupt. He asked all Sikhs to come to him personally, calling them his 'Khalsa', a Persian term for crown lands, as opposed to feudal landholdings.

On BAISAKHI in 1699, which in that year occurred on 30 March, he created the Sikh KHALSA and laid down rules to give Sikhs a common identity and focus. The Khalsa added the word 'Singh' (lion) to their names, and the guru took the name Gobind Singh.

Battles with the Rajputs continued, and with the help of Mughal forces, Anandpur was besieged in May 1705. The siege lasted till December, when the Mughals promised the Sikhs safe conduct if they left the fort. However, as they came out they were attacked, and only five Sikhs survived, among them Guru Gobind.

Helped by some Muslim disciples, he made his way to Malwa in the Deccan. He composed an epistle to the emperor AURANGZEB, known as the ZAFAR NAMAH, on the need to observe moral principles even in battle.

After he had regrouped his forces, he returned to TALWANDI SABO in Punjab, in 1706. Here he spent nine months preparing a new recension of the Granth Sahib.

The emperor seemed touched by the *Zafar Namah* and asked to meet the guru, but Aurangzeb died in 1707, before a meeting could take place. His successor, Bahadur Shah I, was helped by the guru to win the war of succession. The guru accompanied Bahadur Shah to the Deccan, and while he was in Nanded in Maharashtra, was attacked and stabbed, probably by people sent by the nawab of Sirhind, who was jealous of his growing power. Though Gobind Singh fought off his attackers, he died a few days later from the wounds received, on 7 October 1708.

Before he died he stated that there would be no more gurus, and that only the Granth Sahib would be the guru, which was known as the GURU GRANTH SAHIB thereafter.

Gobind Singh is primarily remembered for his creation of the Khalsa and for building the Sikhs into a fighting force. Apart from the *Zafar Namah* he wrote the *Var Sri Bhagauti Ji Ki*, popularly known as *Chandi di Var*, a poem in Punjabi based on the battle between the gods and demons in the MARKANDEYA PURANA, and the autobiographical *Bachitra Natak*. The DASAM GRANTH, compiled by his disciple Bhai MANI SINGH, is a collection of his writings, thoughts and ideas.

Gobindpura Gurdwara A GURDWARA or Sikh shrine located at Ambala in Haryana. Guru GOBIND SINGH passed this way on his return journey from KURUKSHETRA, where he had gone at the time of a solar eclipse to preach the message of Guru NANAK.

godan The gift of a cow to BRAHMANAS on marriage, death, eclipses or other special occasions. It is said to bring merit and benefit to the giver.

Goindwal A sacred centre for Sikhs, located in the Punjab on the right bank of the river Beas, not far from Khadur Sahib. Guru Amar Das established, and helped in the construction of the gurdwara and baoli (step-well) here. *See* Chaubara Sahib Gurdwara.

Gokul A place located near MATHURA in Uttar Pradesh, which is a centre of pilgrimage of the Hindu god Krishna. KRISHNA grew up here and there are several sites in Gokul, associated with his childhood and youth. Gokul is also a centre of the VALLABHA sect, established in the fifteenth century.

Gokulnatha A leader of the Hindu VALLABHA sect. He lived in the sixteenth to seventeenth centuries and is known for two works on VAISHNAVISM, *Chaurasin Vaishnavan ki Varta* and *Do Sau Bavan Vaishnavan ki Varta*. He was the son of Vitthalanatha and grandson of Vallabha.

Golden Temple The popular name of the most sacred GURDWARA or shrine of the Sikhs, also known as Sri HAR MANDIR SAHIB (Golden Temple of the Lord), located at AMRITSAR in Punjab. Sikh authorities stated in 2005 that they did not approve of the popular name, and would prefer the term Har Mandir Sahib or Golden Gurdwara.

Goloka The name of a real and mythical place. It is the paradise of the Hindu god KRISHNA, said to be located on the mythical Mt MERU, where the divine cow SURABHI dwells. It is also another name for VRINDAVAN, a place in the region of MATHURA associated with Krishna.

Gommateshvara image, Shravana Belagola An image of BAHUBALI, the son of the first Jain TIRTHANKARA, also known as Gommata or Gommateshvara. Though there are several images of Bahubali, the one at SHRAVANA BELAGOLA in Karnataka, probably constructed around 983, is exceptional. Inscriptions on the statue and elsewhere state that it was erected by Chamunda Raya, a minister of the Western Ganga king Rachamalla or Rajamalla, who ruled the area from 974 to 984. Chamuda Raya was inspired by reading the *Adi Purana* of the Kannada poet PAMPA, and in a divine dream he received the message to erect this image. At 17.7 m tall, this free-standing stone sculpture carved out of a single rock on the Chandragiri hill can be seen from a distance of 10 km, and is reached by a climb of over 600 stairs. The nude image is a representation of the Kevalin or realized soul, conceived in DIGAMBARA style. The statue stands in the open and has withstood rain, heat and wind for over a thousand years. The standing saint gazes ahead with half-closed eyes, a peaceful expression on his face, while creepers grow around his feet. The figure has all the signs of a superior human being (*mahapurusha lakshana*) as described in texts, such as long arms, long-lobed ears and broad shoulders. On either side are *chauri*-bearers. The image is surrounded by a wall built in the twelfth century, enclosing small shrines with fifty-three images of TIRTHANKARAS and other deities, constructed at different dates. In front of the image is a pillared hall with intricately carved ceiling panels.

The mahabhisheka, or sacred bath of the image is a grand event which takes place once in twelve years. Hundreds of pots of curd, milk, honey, vermilion (kumkum) coconut water, turmeric paste, and even some gold and jewels are poured over the head of the deity at this time. This special festival attracts thousands of pilgrims.

gompa The term for a Tibetan Buddhist complex, including a monastery and shrines for worship. Large complexes have the tsomchen (great assembly hall), the dukhang (assembly hall), tratsang (colleges), lhakhang (temples/shrines), and clusters of lodgings. See TIBETAN BUDDHISM.

Good Friday A sacred day for Christians that commemorates the crucifixion of JESUS CHRIST. On this day Christians offer prayers, remembering that Jesus died to save the world. It is also a day of fasting and penance. Good Friday takes place some time in the month of April, and is followed by EASTER Sunday two days later.

Gopala Literally, 'cowherd'. A name of the Hindu god KRISHNA, who was a cowherd in his youth. In early Greek myths, Apollo was a goatherd, indicating some paralells between the two deities.

gopi A term for the female devotees of the Hindu god KRISHNA, particularly in the region of Vraja or MATHURA. Gopis were the female cowherds of the region who flocked around Krishna. RADHA, who was one of the gopis, was Krishna's favourite. The gopis represent BHAKTI, a selfless and pure love of god, beyond consideration of social norms, and beyond any thoughts of worldly gain, such as marriage, status or protection. The relationship of the gopis with Krishna is described in several texts, particularly the *HARIVAMSHA, BHAGAVATA PURANA* and *GITA GOVINDA*, and has been the subject of art, literature and music through the ages. Several VAISHNAVA groups emphasize that the devotee of Krishna should emulate the love of the gopis.

Gopi Krishna, Pandit A mystic and teacher. Born in 1903 in Srinagar, Kashmir, he moved to Lahore in 1914 with his family, and completed his school and college there. Later he returned to Kashmir and was employed in the public works department of the maharaja. He began meditating every day, and in 1937, he inadvertently aroused a powerful force in himself, which he recognized later as the KUNDALINI. He had several physical problems until the force finally reached the correct channel within the body. Some years later he resigned his job and began to write and express his experiences. He gave speeches, toured the West and wrote a number of books, including his autobiography.

Gopi Krishna believed that the kundalini was a force that every person could arouse which revolutionized the entire being. He said: 'The awakening of kundalini does not only mean the activation of a dormant force in the body, but also an altered activity of the entire nervous system and the opening of a normally silent centre in the brain.' He appealed for a scientific investigation of the phenomenon and wrote: 'Why science should ignore some of the most important issues of human existence, no one has dared to answer. And why religion should be satisfied with explanations for these riddles offered thousands of years ago . . . is equally unintelligible.'

He died at Srinagar in 1984.

gopuram A term for the gateway of south Indian temples. The temples could have one or more gateways, which are several storeys high, and are adorned with elaborate carvings.

Gorakhnatha/Gorakshanatha A yogi who lived in about 1120 at Gorakhpur in present Uttar Pradesh and is said to have been one of the founders of the NATHA or KANPHATA Yogis, a Hindu SHAIVITE sect. A disciple of the legendary MATSYENDRANATHA, he composed verses which were written down in a book called *Goraksha-Shataka*, which described the rituals and practices of the sect. These included YOGA asanas or physical postures, pranayama or breathing techniques, and explanations on how to energize the CHAKRAS or mystical energy centres and raise the KUNDALINI. These practices were said to give the disciples spiritual and other powers. Gorakhnatha himself is believed to have been a SIDDHA or perfected one. His description of different asanas has led him to be called the founder of HATHA YOGA, or the physical aspect of Yoga, though the basic system was also described earlier by PATANJALI.

Gosala Maskariputra The founder of the AJIVIKA sect. He lived in the sixth century BCE and was initially a disciple of MAHAVIRA.

Gospel An Old English term meaning 'good news', which in Christianity refers to the message of JESUS CHRIST. The four texts on his life that are considered most authentic are known as the Gospels of Matthew, Mark, Luke and John. They were written some time in the first century and form part of the NEW TESTAMENT.

Other texts known as Gospels are usually referred to as 'apocryphal Gospels', because though they are attributed to the APOSTLES and other contemporaries of Jesus, they are not acknowledged as canonical texts. Many of them were written from the second century onwards.

gotra A term used for a group or clan in Hinduism, technically an exogamous sept. It was first used to denote a clan in the ATHARVA VEDA. Initially, the BRAHMANA CASTE was divided into gotras and each gotra claimed descent from early RISHIS such as KASHYAPA and Bharadvaja. Later KSHATRIYAS and VAISHYAS also adopted gotras, usually from the brahmana priests who performed the rituals for their families. There were, in addition, non-brahmana or Laukika gotras. Marriage within the same gotra is not allowed.

Govardhan/Govardhana A town near MATHURA in Uttar Pradesh, where the Hindu god KRISHNA is said to have lived. It is also the name of a hill in the area. According to myth, Krishna raised the mountain Govardhan on his finger to shelter his fellow cowherds when INDRA sent a deluge of rain to challenge his power. Another story narrates how the god HANUMAN, transporting material to build a bridge across the ocean to LANKA, brought Govardhan from the Himalayas. Meanwhile RAMA sent him a message not to bring any more rocks and hills, and therefore Hanuman placed the mountain Govardhan near Mathura.

Govardhan is a sacred place and a centre of pilgrimage.

Govinda A name of the Hindu god KRISHNA.

Goyama Indabhuti (Sanskrit: Gautama Indrabhuti) The name of the chief disciple of MAHAVIRA, the twenty-fourth Jain TIRTHANKARA. Several Jain texts include dialogues between Goyama and Mahavira.

graha A term which indicates a planet. In Hinduism, the NAVAGRAHA are the nine planets traditionally known and depicted in art. Graha comes from the word grah, meaning to seize or overpower, and earlier, grahas were known as demons who possessed humans and caused illness.

grama devata A male or female deity who is the guardian of the village (grama). The deity is more often female and is prayed to for the protection of the village from disease and disaster. Sometimes animal sacrifices are conducted to appease her. A village may have its own unique deity, or there may be a common deity for many villages. GANGAMMA and MARIAMMA are some examples of female village deities, while DHARMA THAKUR is one of the male deities.

Granth Sahib A colloquial term used for the Adi Granth or GURU GRANTH SAHIB, the sacred book of the Sikhs.

granthi A term in Sikhism for a priest who reads the GURU GRANTH SAHIB or takes care of a GURDWARA.

Gridhrakuta An ancient Buddhist site located near RAJAGRIHA (modern Rajgir) in the Rajgir hills of Bihar. The BUDDHA used to meditate here. Several MAHAYANA texts give this place a mystical sanctity. For instance, the SADDHARMA PUNDARIKA states that the Buddha preached here surrounded by monks, nuns, BUDDHAS, BODHISATTVAS and various deities. As he began to speak, a ray of light from between his brows illuminated 18,000 Buddha lands, the regions where Buddhas live.

Griffiths, Bede A Christian monk who came to India and lived as an Indian SANNYASI. Bede Griffiths was earlier a monk of Prinknash Abbey and the Prior of Farnborough Abbey in England. He came to India in 1955 and remained here till his death in 1993. He became part of a group of Christians who live and dress in Indian style, like the much earlier Roberto de NOBILI. Initially Griffiths helped to establish the Syrian Christian Kurisumala Ashram in Kerala. In 1968 he went to Sachchidananda Ashram, another Christian ashram located at Shantivana in Tamil Nadu, where he lived in simple style, wearing the orange robes of a sannyasi. Here he created a centre where people of different religions could meet and hold discussions to understand the underlying unity and truth of all religions.

Bede Griffiths was a profound thinker who wrote a number of books, including *The Golden String*, *The Marriage of East and West*, *A New Vision of Reality*, *Universal Wisdom*, and *Return to the Centre*.

Grihadevi A village deity, also known as Jara. She was worshipped until medieval times, and was a rakshasi, a demonic being who could assume any form.

Grihya Sutras Sanskrit texts that form part of the KALPA SUTRAS and describe household or domestic ceremonies, that are to be performed by Hindus at every stage in life, beginning from the time a child is in the womb. These ceremonies are known as SAMSKARAS. The main Grihya Sutras are the *Ashvalayana*, *Baudhayana*, *Paraskara*, *Vaikhanasa* and *Varaha*. They were composed between about 400 BCE and CE 400.

Gudi Padva A New Year's day celebrated in March/April in Maharashtra. It marks the first day of the Hindu month of Chaitra, according to the Marathi calendar. On this day a pole or 'gudi' is erected, with an upturned decorated pot tied to the top. The gudi is worshipped after which the coconut within the pot is broken, symbolizing a good harvest and prosperity in the new year. New clothes are worn, and special food is prepared on this day.

Guga Pir A local deity worshipped by all castes and communities at a number of temples in Himachal, Punjab, Uttarakhand, Uttar Pradesh and Haryana. Guga Pir or Guga Devata is worshipped particularly to guard against snakes. There are several legends and stories associated with him, and his SAMADHI is revered at Nagar in Himachal and in Rajasthan. According to one story, Guga was born after his mother, who had no children, received a boon from Guru GORAKHNATHA. At the same time, a wonderful blue horse was born who became his constant companion. Guga and his horse could not be defeated. They had many powers and were immune to snakebite. Guga performed miracles and healed the blind, deaf and lame. Many were jealous of him and tried to kill him, even invoking the help of Vasuki Naga, the king of snakes, but Guga defeated them all. He vowed to exterminate all snakes, but Vasuki promised that no snakes would trouble him again.

Guga seems to have been a real person, deified after his death. According to some legends, he was a Rajput from the Bikaner region of Rajasthan and fought against Mahmud of Ghazni, the invader of the early eleventh century. Guga is also said to have killed his cousins who were against him, and as his mother was unhappy with this, he vowed to take samadhi , and to live beneath the earth. Gorakhnatha sent him to a Muslim PIR, Hajji Rattan, to learn the technique for this. He was given the name Zahir and taught Islamic prayers. Guga is thus one of the many syncretic deities or heroes, combining elements of Hinduism and Islam.

His small shrines are found in several villages, in which he is depicted as a figure on a horse. Special celebrations and fairs take place at his shrines in August.

Guha   A name of the Hindu god KARTTIKEYA. Guha is also the name of other people, including the king of the Nishadas in the *RAMAYANA*.

guhyakas   Minor Hindu deities who are attendants of the god KUBERA. They live on Mt KAILASHA and are said to be either half horse or half bird. All brave warriors who die in battle go to their abode.

Guhyasamaja Tantra   A Buddhist text belonging to the Anuttara-Yoga class of TANTRAS, attributed to ASANGA, but probably composed slightly later. It includes meditational and practical sections and is considered one of the oldest of the Buddhist Tantric texts. The text has eighteen chapters, and the first describes the main meditational mandala, with AKSHOBHYA at the centre, surrounded by other Buddhist deities. Other practices include a meditation on the Buddha VAIROCHANA, with four female deities Lochana, Mamaki, Pandara and TARA. Methods leading to enlightenment, along with Buddhist terms are explained. Bodhichitta, normally interpreted as the thought of enlightenment, is explained here as a combination of SHUNYATA (emptiness) and KARUNA or compassion. The text also deals with sexual union, which according to some interpreters, is only symbolic.

Gujjars, Van   A pastoral nomadic community, who though Muslims, are vegetarians and have several Hindu customs. Some of them now live a settled life, while others continue to be nomadic, building their temporary huts on the outskirts of forests. Gujjars live mainly in Jammu, parts of the Punjab, Haryana, Uttar Pradesh and Uttarakhand. Their origin is uncertain and similarities have been traced between them and the gypsies of Europe.

Van Gujjars are one of the many groups in India who follow a mix of Hindu and Muslim customs. There are also other Gujjar groups in north India, who are Hindus.

Gumanapantha   A minor sub-sect of the DIGAMBARA Jain sect. It was probably started in the eighteenth century by Pandit Gumani Rama or Gumani Rai, a son of Pandit Todarmal, who lived in Jaipur, Rajasthan. It was known as shuddha amnaya, that is, the pure and sacred tradition, and stressed purity, self-discipline and adherence to all the Jain precepts. Gumani was against the lighting of diyas or lamps in Jain temples, as he felt this violated the principles of AHIMSA or non-violence. This sect was once popular in Rajasthan but now has only a small following.

Gunabhadra   A Jain scholar of the ninth century who wrote the last part of the *ADI PURANA* and the whole of the *UTTARA PURANA*. Both these form part of the Jain *TRISHASHTILAKSHANA MAHAPURANA*. Gunabhadra, a pupil of JINASENA, was also the author of the *Atmanushasana*, a poem describing Jain ethics in 270 verses.

Gunadhara   A Jain scholar who wrote the *KASHAYAPRABHRITA*, a sacred text of the DIGAMBARA sect. He lived in the second century CE.

gunas   A Sanskrit term that is used in different ways, but means 'quality'. In Samkhya philosophy it refers to the basic qualities or characteristics according to which people can be classified. The three gunas are sattva or serenity and purity, rajas or energetic activity, and tamas or dullness. Most people have all these qualities, but one predominates in each individual. Ideally, a person should cultivate sattva. Certain foods are associated with these qualities. This theory of the gunas is also described in the BHAGAVAD GITA, and in other texts.

Gurdas, Bhai   A Sikh scholar, who helped the fifth guru, ARJAN DEV, in compiling the Granth Sahib. Bhai Gurdas was born around 1560 at Goindwal and was the son of Datar Chand, the younger brother of Guru AMAR DAS. He learnt the principles of Sikhism from Amar Das, and after his death was sent to AGRA by the next guru, RAM DAS, to spread the religion. Later he joined Guru Arjan Dev at AMRITSAR and helped the guru by transcribing the first version of the GURU GRANTH SAHIB. He also served the next guru, HARGOBIND, and while the guru was imprisoned, he and Baba BUDHA took care of the affairs of the Sikh community. He died in 1629 at Goindwal. Bhai Gurdas composed forty vars (poems) and 556 kabits (couplets), which while not part of the GRANTH SAHIB are considered sacred and recited by Sikhs.

gurdwara A Sikh temple or shrine. Each gurdwara, literally meaning 'the gateway of the guru' is linked with Sikh history and constructed at a place connected with the SIKH GURUS, other revered Sikhs, or a historic site. Though prayers can be offered anywhere at any time, gurdwaras bring the community together. As they are associated with Sikh history and often with legends of miraculous occurences, praying in a gurdwara has a special sanctity. In every gurdwara it is essential to have a room in which the GURU GRANTH SAHIB can be placed. The holy book is the main object of worship or reverence. Entrances are made on all four sides to indicate that people of all religions are welcome. The GRANTH SAHIB is on a pedestal under a canopy, cordoned off by a railing. The room is large enough to allow for congregational worship. Some such rooms have a deorhi, an entrance gateway, in the walls enclosing the gurdwara compound.

Architecturally, the ground-plan of a gurdwara is of one of four basic types: square, rectangular, octagonal or cruciform. Some are simple, single-storeyed structures, while others have two, three, five, or even nine storeys. Most of them are crowned with domes, which are often fluted or ribbed, while a few have a flat roof. In special gurdwaras, domes may be gold-plated or can be covered with bronze or copper gilt. Apart from the central dome, there are four or more smaller domes or cupolas. Parapets around the gurdwara are decorated and often have turrets and the entrance has floral, geometric and other designs. Building materials include marble, red stone, brick, brick-tile, lime mortar, and other materials available locally. Some gurdwaras also have galleries with works of art depicting scenes from Sikh history, and store artefacts connected with the gurus. A free community kitchen (LANGAR) is attached to gurdwaras. Many have libraries and schools, and run charitable dispensaries.

Gurdwara Reform Movement Another name for the AKALI MOVEMENT, which took place in 1920 to free the GURDWARAS or Sikh shrines from corrupt priests.

gurmukh A term in Sikhism for those who are pious and follow the path of the guru. The opposite is manmukh, those who follow their own path, enmeshed in delusion.

Gurmukhi A script in which the sacred texts of the Sikhs are written. It was said to have been first used by Guru ANGAD, the second Sikh guru, and was based on the Sharada script, a derivative of DEVANAGARI. The script is also used for the Punjabi language.

guru A Sanskrit term that literally means 'one who points the way'. Traditionally it is used as a respectful term for a spiritual teacher or preceptor. Though still used in this sense today, it also has a wider usage and can refer to a teacher of any kind.

Guru Ghantal Gompa A Buddhist monastery located on a hill above Tupchiling village in the LAHAUL region of Himachal Pradesh, at the confluence of the Chandra and Bhaga rivers. According to tradition, it was founded by the famous monk PADMASAMBHAVA in the eighth century. The temple is a wooden structure with pyramidal roofs and has wooden idols, including those of Padmasambhava, the BUDDHA, and various lamas. It is thought to have once been a Hindu temple, as there is also a black stone goddess image within, locally known as KALI. The Ghantal festival used to be held here in mid-June. Today the monastery is in disuse, most of its valuable items being kept in a gompa in the village.

Guru Granth Sahib The sacred text of the Sikhs. The Adi Granth or Guru Granth Sahib was compiled in 1603–34 by ARJAN DEV, the fifth Sikh guru. It was then known as the *Pothi Sahib* (Holy Book). Additions were made to it by the tenth guru, GOBIND SINGH. The text consists of the compositions and teachings of Guru NANAK, the founder of the Sikh religion, of the next four gurus and of the ninth guru, TEGH BAHADUR. (The sixth, seventh and eighth gurus did not write anything). Apart from this, it has the verses of some of the companions of the gurus and of sixteen other saints including KABIR, SURDAS, RAVIDAS, NAMADEVA and the Sufi saint Baba FARID. Altogether there are 5894 compositions by thirty-six holy people. The largest number of hymns are by Guru Arjan Dev (2218), followed by Guru NANAK (974).

Guru Gobind Singh gave the book the status it has today. He affirmed that there would be no successor to him. Instead, the sacred words contained in the Granth would be the guru. In GURDWARAS or Sikh shrines, the Guru Granth Sahib is the main object of worship and is kept on a throne under a canopy, wrapped in an embroidered cloth. Prayers and ceremonies are conducted every morning when it is opened and in the evening when it is closed. Devotees worship the book as the representative of god and the gurus, and pay obeisance to it.

The Granth opens with the Mul Mantra, the basic prayer composed by Guru Nanak, which states that God is truth. This forms the preamble to the JAPJI, the first prayer, also by Nanak. Other parts of the text include the Banis or songs of the gurus, followed by those of the saints, bhatts (bards), and other Sikhs. There are also verses in praise of the True Name and of thanks to the guru. The whole is arranged in thirty-one different RAGAS, in which it can be sung.

Several languages are used in the text. Those of the Sikh gurus are in Punjabi of the fifteenth and sixteenth centuries, while those of other saints are in old Hindi dialects, as well as in Marathi, Persian and Sanskrit. The tenth guru's hymns and writings are in a separate book, the *DASAM GRANTH*.

Guru Ka Bagh Gurdwara A GURDWARA or Sikh shrine located at Varanasi, at a spot where Guru

NANAK had discussions with a BRAHMANA named Pandit Chattar Das. Later, Guru TEGH BAHADUR also visited the place, and the brown Rajput-syle clothes he wore are preserved here.

Guruparb/Gurupurab (1) A Sikh festival that commemorates the birthday of Guru NANAK (1469– 1538), the founder of Sikhism. Though his birthday is celebrated in the month of Karttika (October– November), he is said to have been born in the month of Vaishakha (Baisakh) (March/April), and until 1815 his birthday was celebrated at this time. However, later celebrations began to be held in the month of Karttika, perhaps because he attained enlightenment at this time. The AKHAND PATH, a ceremonial reading of the GURU GRANTH SAHIB, begins two days before the festival. On the day of the festival processions are taken out and free food is served to all.

(2) The festival for the birthday celebrations of Guru GOBIND SINGH (1666–1708), the tenth Sikh guru, which takes place in the month of Pausha (December-January).

(3) Other Sikh festivals associated with the gurus, are also known as Guruparb.

Guruvayur Temple A temple of the Hindu god KRISHNA located at Guruvayur in Thrissur district of Kerala. Constructed in the sixteenth century, this temple is particularly sacred. The image in the inner shrine is of Narayana or VISHNU, dressed in yellow silk with a crown on his head, holding a disc, conch, mace and lotus in his four hands. On either side of the main deity are the goddesses SHRI and Dhara. According to the story connected with this image, it was one that Krishna himself worshipped at Dvaraka, and even earlier was worshipped by Vishnu in VAIKUNTHA. The image is thus considered very ancient. It was preserved by BRIHASPATI, guru of the DEVAS, and finally installed in the temple by VAYU, the wind god, and hence was known as Guruvayur. The temple has subsidiary shrines of GANESHA, SASTHA and BHAGAVATI.

Hundreds get married in this temple, as it is believed that it ensures a happy married life. Children are brought here for their first food-tasting ceremony. The temple has over forty elephants, as it is considered meritorious to present an elephant to the deity. Some of the elephants take part in processions and in a traditional elephant race.

There is a special annual utsavam or festival in February/March that lasts ten days.

Habba Khatoon A Kashmiri mystic and ascetic who lived in the sixteenth century. The Mughal emperor AKBAR captured her husband Yusuf Shah, a local ruler, and Habba Khatoon's grief at his absence led her to asceticism. She composed mystic verses and songs in Kashmiri that can be interpreted at two levels: as her yearning for her husband or as the higher yearning of every soul for God. Some of her verses can be compared to those of the BHAKTI saints, particularly worshippers of KRISHNA. For example:

He glanced at me through my window,
He who is lovely like my earrings;
He has made my heart restless;
I, hapless one, am filled with longing for him.

habs-i nafs A term in Islam used by SUFIS, indicating the method of meditating while controlling the breath. Habs-i nafs, similar to the yogic PRANAYAMA, was practised by a number of Sufi orders, including the CHISTI, KUBRAWIYA, SHATTARI and QADIRI.

Hadis/Hadith The Prophet MUHAMMAD's sayings and actions, and those of his companions. Second to the QURAN, these are the most important source of Islam. The Hadis or traditions consist of short stories or accounts of different incidents in the life of the Prophet, while the SUNNAH are the laws that are deduced from the Hadis. The Sunnah also refers to the whole collection of Hadis.

There are vast numbers of Hadis, and many of them were considered spurious, therefore scholars attempted to sort through them and put together those that were authentic. The contents of the Hadis of the SUNNI and SHIA sects are different. Muhammad bin Ismail al-Bukhari (810–70) compiled the most accepted version of Sunni Hadis, known as *Sahih* (Authentic). It has 2762 statements, the origins of which are given, and he is said to have chosen these from 6,00,000 traditions. Another authentic compilation is by Muslim ibn al-Hajjaj (d. 875). These two are considered the most reliable, though there are four other major Sunni Hadis, namely, those of Ibn Maja al-Qazvini (d. 886), Abu Dawud al-Sijistani (d. 888), Abu Isa al-Tirmizi (d. 892) and Abu Abdul Rahman al-Nasal (d. 915). The earliest biography of the Prophet is the collection of Hadis compiled by Muhammad ibn Ishaq of Medina (d. 768). Malik ibn Anas (d. 795) and Ahmad ibn Hanbal (d. 855), founders of two schools of law, were among others who compiled Hadis.

To be considered sound, the Hadis must include the name of each person who wrote it down, tracing it back to the Prophet. Each human link in the chain (*sanad* or *isnad*) has to be noted. Each compiler of Hadis had to decide on the merits and authenticity of the 'links'. Some Hadis may not be considered true but can be included when they convey a greater truth with a moral value.

Shia Hadis include stories of the Prophet and of Ali and the Imams. Among the compilations of Shia Hadis, that of Muhammad ibn Yaqub al-Kulayni (d. 940) is the earliest. Others include those of Ibn Babuya or Babawayhi (d. 991) and Muhammad al-Tusi (d. 1067).

hafiz A term in Islam for a person who can recite the whole QURAN. It comes from hafaza, Arabic for 'memorized'. Hafiz is also used as a name.

Haimavata A school of HINAYANA Buddhism which developed in the Himalayan region, and was a branch of the STHAVIRAVADA. This school denied any divine qualities of the BODHISATTVA.

Hairambas (Herambas) A TANTRIC sect that worships the Hindu god GANESHA, along with DEVI or SHAKTI as his consort. Heramba is one of the names of Ganesha.

Haj The term for pilgrimage to Mecca, which forms one of the FIVE PILLARS, or basic practices of Islam. The Haj is obligatory for all Muslims, at least once in a lifetime. The pilgrimage provides a reaffirmation of faith and belief, and of dedication of one's life to God. The person proceeding on the pilgrimage should have enough funds for it and enough for the family he leaves behind.

The Haj begins in the month of Zilhajja, the twelfth month of the ISLAMIC CALENDAR, on the eighth day of the month, and is completed on the twelfth day. Absolute purity and celibacy is to be maintained on the pilgrimage, and specific rituals are prescribed for each of the days. Before reaching Mecca, a particular type of clothing has to be worn, known as ihram which for men consists of two unstitched pieces of cloth wrapped around the waist and shoulders, and for women, a white headscarf, apart from full clothing. This symbolizes leaving behind the material world and focusing on spirituality. On the first day of the Haj, the pilgrims go around the nearby hills of Safa and Marwa seven times, and then proceed towards Mina, 6.5 km from Mecca. There they say their five daily prayers. On the second day they go to the plains of Arafat, 9 km away, recite special prayers and ask for God's mercy for their sins. In the evening they leave there and reach Muzdalfa, where they spend the night in the open, reciting prayers. On the third day they reach the three pillars near Mina, which represent IBLIS or Satan. Here Iblis tempted IBRAHIM not to offer his sacrifice. Ibrahim threw pebbles at Iblis, who then retreated. The pilgrims therefore throw pebbles at one of the pillars. As it is the day of BAKR-ID, they then offer the sacrifice, bathe and wear fresh clothes. Proceeding to Mecca, they circumambulate the holy KABA and later return to Mina. On the fourth and fifth days, they throw pebbles at the three pillars, symbolizing the defeat of evil. The pilgrims also have to stay in Medina, where the Prophet is buried, for eight days, either before or after the Haj, and offer their daily prayers.

In India large numbers go on the Haj pilgrimage every year, and discounted air-fares are offered to enable less affluent Muslims to fulfill the obligations of the religion.

Haji Ali Mosque A mosque along with a DARGAH, located at MUMBAI in Maharashtra. Haji Ali Shah Bukhari, a rich merchant who lived in the fifteenth century, gave up all his wealth after a pilgrimage to Mecca and was revered as a saint. His dargah is built at the edge of the sea and is approached by a causeway that is covered with water at high tide. The tomb is located in a marble courtyard, and a white mosque was added in the 1940s. Worshippers and pilgrims visit the popular mosque and dargah every day.

halal An Arabic term, literally, 'that which is untied or loose', or 'permissible'. In Islam, it refers to that which is lawful, as against that which is forbidden (haram). Halal includes lawful conduct and lawful food, such as meat from animals slaughtered in the prescribed manner.

Halebid A town in Karnataka which has temples of the twelfth and thirteenth centuries, built at the time of the Hoysala dynasty. The most important is the HOYSALESHVARA TEMPLE. Halebid was once known as Dvarasamudra and was the capital of the Hoysala dynasty.

Hali, Altaf Hussain An Urdu poet and writer. Born in 1837, he was educated in DELHI and later employed in Hisar. He also worked at the Government Book Depot in Lahore and taught at Chief's College, Lahore, and at the Anglo-Arabic School in Delhi. Influenced by GHALIB, he began to compose poetry, and wrote a number of works, including *Yadgar-i-Ghalib, Diwan-i-*

Hali, Watan, Munajat-i-Bewa and *Majalislal-i-Nisa*. His work *Musaddas* (The Ebb and Flow of Islam) had a wide impact and influenced Syed AHMAD KHAN.

He died in 1914.

Hallaj, Al A SUFI saint who lived in the ninth century and is still revered. Husain Ibn Mansur al-Hallaj was born in 857 in Tus or Bayza in Fars. In a state of ecstasy he realized the true Self within and stated, 'Ana al Haqq', or 'I am the Truth'. He travelled to various places, including northern and eastern India, and had a number of disciples. The ULAMA at the Abbasid court condemned him for heresy and though others defended him, he was tortured and executed in 922.

Hama ust A Persian term meaning 'All is He', i.e. all is God. It is a concept accepted by many of the SUFI saints.

Hamadani A branch of the KUBRAWIYA Sufi sect in Kashmir, founded by Mir Sayyid Ali Hamadani (d. 1385). Hamadani is said to have performed miracles, leading to the conversion of a priest of a KALI temple, and encouraged his disciples to convert Hindus. He gained support from Irani nobles, migrants to the area, who were struggling to gain administrative and political power. They attempted to achieve this by advocating conversion and thus removing BRAHMANAS from their traditional posts. Sultan Sikandar (1389–1413) of Kashmir, influenced by Hamadani's son Mir Muhammad, initially supported this. He demolished temples and introduced the JIZYA tax for the first time in Kashmir, but later changed his policy when be realized that it did not lead to political stability.

Another group of Kubrawiyas, known as Baihaqi Sayyids, were patronized by ZAINUL ABIDIN (1420–1506), one of the most enlightened rulers of Kashmir. This group worked to integrate Hindus and Muslims in Kashmir.

Hamiduddin Nagauri, Qazi A SUFI saint of the thirteenth century who belonged to the SUHRAWARDI order. His family had migrated to DELHI from Bukhara, and his father, Ataullah Mahmud, died in Delhi. Hamiduddin became the Qazi of Nagaur, but after a few years he left for Baghdad and became Shaikh Shihabuddin Suhrawardi's disciple. After visiting several places he settled in Delhi. Despite being a Suhrawardi, he was in favour of SAMA, the musical sessions of the CHISTI saints, and thus was opposed by the ULAMA. However, his knowledge of law and influence with Sultan Iltutmish enabled him to challenge the Ulama.

Hamiduddin composed a number of SUFI works, studied by both Chisti and Suhrawardi Sufis. Among them were *Lawaih* (Flashes of Light), now lost; *Ishqiyya*, in which he states that the Lover and the Beloved (God) are one; *Tawali-ul Shumus*, on the names of ALLAH; and *Risala Min Kalam*.

Hamiduddin, Shaikh, of Nagaur (Chisti) A SUFI saint of the CHISTI order, who lived in the thirteenth century and was a disciple of Shaikh MUINUDDIN CHISTI. He was a vegetarian and lived simply at Siwal, a village near Nagaur in present-day Rajasthan, cultivating a small plot of land hardly larger than what was required to pitch a tent, and subsisting on what he grew there. He refused a grant from the sultan because he did not want his spirituality diverted by the acquisition of material wealth. He was a learned scholar and the answers he gave to questions on religion are quoted in various texts, including the *Siyarul-Auliya* and *Akhbarul-Akhyar*. He died in 1274.

His son Shaikh Fariduddin Mahmud carried on his tradition and compiled a collection of his sayings. Later Sufis of his tradition are known for their simplicity. Among them, Khwaja Ziyauddin Nakshabi (d. 1350–51), a disciple of Shaikh Fariduddin Mahmud, was also renowned for his scholarship. He translated the *Suka Saptati*, a Sanskrit text written by Chintamani Bhatta, into Persian and called it the *Tuti Nama* (Stories of a Parrot).

hamkar A term in Zoroastrianism, meaning co-worker or helper. It implies that the righteous person is the helper and friend of AHURA MAZDA or God. Human beings are meant to work together with Ahura Mazda and his powers to bring about FRASHOKERETI, the renewal of existence. This implies consistently choosing the right path, and working for a better world. The word hamkar is not used in the GATHAS but the concept is clear even there.

Hamsa (1) A name of deities and a sacred bird, a wild goose or swan. It is also a mythical bird. In the RIG VEDA, it is said to be able to separate SOMA from water, and in later texts, milk from water, when the two are mixed together. This indicates its ability to separate the pure from the impure. The hamsa is the VAHANA or vehicle of the Vedic ASHVINS and of the Hindu deities BRAHMA, SARASVATI and VARUNA. It is identified with various deities, including VISHNU, SHIVA and SURYA. In the *MAHABHARATA*, KRISHNA is referred to as Hamsa.

(2) A PRAJAPATI and incarnation of the Hindu god VISHNU in the KRITA YUGA. He was also known as Yajna (sacrifice), and taught YOGA to Sanaka and other RISHIS.

(3) Hamsa is a term for yogis who meditate on 'Ham-Sah' (I am He, or I am That), signifying identification with the Supreme. Ham-Sah is mentally chanted with every inhalation and exhalation. The technique is described in the *Gheranda Samhita*, the *Vigyan Bhairava*, and by GORAKHNATHA. In more recent times, it was propagated by PARAMAHANSA YOGANANDA. The title Paramahansa is used by the highest grade of DASNAMI sannyasis.

(4) The white Hamsa symbolizes the purity of the soul or spirit. It is the ATMAN within the individual, and is like the flame of a lamp in a windless place. It is located in the ANAHATA CHAKRA and in the SAHASRARA CHAKRA.

(5) Among others known as Hamsa was a GANDHARVA born to the rishi KASHYAPA.

(6) According to the *BHAGAVATA PURANA*, in the old days there was only one VEDA, one God, and one CASTE known as Hamsa.

(7) In other ancient religions, too, the goose or swan is linked with the sacred. In ancient Egypt, the god Amon-Re is said to have flown over the waters in the form of a goose, and its honk was the first sound ever made.

Hanafi A school of ISLAMIC LAW, the largest of the four orthodox schools of SUNNI jurisprudence. It was founded by Abu Hanifa, who lived from 700 to 767. He was born in Kufa and died in prison in Baghdad. He was possibly imprisoned because he refused to serve as a Qazi (judge) or because he supported the Zaidi revolt that took place at that time.

Abu Hanifa laid the foundations for Islamic law by attempting to deal with various issues, problems and interpretations. Hanifa stated that a Muslim believer should not be condemned for wrong actions as long as he had not given up his faith. Thus faith and works were separated, though he did not go so far as to say that all Muslims are saved, regardless of what they do. He put forward this view in a letter to Usman al-Batti. In addition, the *Fiqh Akbar-i* (Greater Fiqh) with ten Articles, is attributed to him and provides guidelines for believers. It affirms predestination and disavows the SHIA and Kharija philosophies.

The Hanafi school of law is followed in India by most SUNNIS.

Hanbali A school of ISLAMIC LAW. It was founded by Ahmad ibn Hanbal, who lived from 780 to 855 and was a student of al-Shafi, founder of the SHAFI school of law. This school uses only the QURAN and SUNNAH for decisions of law. Hanbal himself compiled the *Musnad*, including 28,000 Traditions of the Prophet. The WAHHABIS of Saudi Arabia follow this school.

Hanuman A Hindu deity in the form of a monkey who is worshipped particularly on Tuesdays. Hanuman is described in various versions of the *RAMAYANA*, the *MAHABHARATA*, the PURANAS and other texts.

In the *Ramayana* of VALMIKI, Hanuman was a minister of Sugriva, the leader of the Vanaras, a monkey tribe in KISHKINDHA. When RAMA and LAKSHMANA reached Kishkindha in their search for SITA, who had been kidnapped by RAVANA, Sugriva sent Hanuman to meet them. After he met Rama, Hanuman became his devoted and loyal servant and disciple, and helped Rama to defeat Ravana and rescue Sita. He located Sita in LANKA, the city of Ravana where she was held in captivity, by a prodigious leap across the ocean. There he assured Sita that Rama would soon come to her rescue and managed to set fire to Lanka before escaping. He then helped Rama in his war against Ravana, with several extraordinary feats.

Hanuman could fly through the air, was extremely strong, could carry the heaviest loads, and vanquished several demons. He knew the art of healing and collected herbs from the Himalayas to heal the wounds of those who were injured in the battle against Ravana. In the Uttara Kanda, the last section of the *Ramayana*, there is a lengthy description of Hanuman. He was the son of VAYU, god of the wind, through ANJANA, the wife of Kesari, who lived on the mountain SUMERU. Unaware of his own strength, soon after he was born, he leapt, swifter than the wind, and tried to catch the glowing sun. He then tried to catch the shadow planet RAHU, but the god INDRA knocked him down with his VAJRA or thunderbolt. In response, Vayu was angry and withdrew himself from the world, so that all began to suffocate, for the wind is in the breath of every being. Then the god BRAHMA restored Hanuman to life and Vayu restored breath to the world. Following this, all the gods granted boons to Hanuman.

In other texts there are different myths about his origin. In one story, he was the son of SHIVA and PARVATI, who had once taken the form of monkeys. In another myth, Shiva sent his seed through the wind god Vayu to be implanted in the womb of Anjana, who was in the form of a monkey because of a curse. After Hanuman was born, Anjana returned to heaven.

The child monkey was intelligent and learnt the four VEDAS in no time. He was originally called Sundara, but because he was injured on his jaw (hanu) by Indra's vajra, he was known as Hanuman.

In the sixteenth century *RAMACHARITAMANASA* of TULASIDASA, the story of Hanuman is elaborated upon. The text has several devotional passages to Hanuman, which are recited even today. The forty verses of the *Hanuman Chalisa*, are particularly revered. In these verses he is said to have a golden body, curly hair, and to hold a vajra-like mace in one hand, and a dhvaja (flag or banner) in the other, with a holy thread made of a long reed on his shoulder.

The god Hanuman represents strength, loyalty and asceticism. He not only knows the Vedas, but is proficient in Sanskrit and other languages. He is celibate, but according to one account, a son known as Makaradhvaja was born through a drop of his sweat. His asceticism and celibacy made him immune to the affects of SHANI (Saturn), the planet believed to bring misfortune, and therefore he is worshipped when Shani is to be propitiated. He is immensely strong and is the patron deity of those engaged in feats of strength, particularly wrestlers. Worshipping him brings success in all ventures. He is also known as Bajrang (originally Vajrang). A popular deity, he is revered in all parts of India. He is depicted in human form, with a monkey-like face and a tail. In images, he has two or more hands and usually holds a club or mace in one hand and the mountain GOVARDHANA in the other, which, according to another myth, he had brought from the Himalayas and placed near MATHURA. Another form of Hanuman is as a bhakta or devotee, with his hands joined in prayer.

Images of Hanuman are found in Rama temples and in temples specially devoted to him. The prasad offered to him is usually besan ladoos (gram-flour sweets), while in the south offerings of butter are made. Worship also includes putting red paste or kumkum on the deity.

Among the most popular Hanuman temples today are: Hanuman Garhi Temple at AYODHYA, of about the sixteenth century; Sankat Mochana Temple at VARANASI, of the same date, where he is worshipped as the deity who solves problems and removes distress; Hanuman Dhara Temple at CHITRAKUTA; Sinhapaur Hanuman Temple at VRINDAVAN; Poonchari ka Launtha Temple at Govardhana; Luteriya Hanuman Mandir at GOKUL, where he is depicted as a child; and Hanuman Hatheelau Temple near Gokul. All the above temples are in Uttar Pradesh, the last four in the Mathura region. Some Hanuman temples elsewhere include the Hanuman Temple on Jakhoo hill, Shimla, and those at Sholingapuram and Suchindram in south India. Every Rama temple has a separate shrine for the god Hanuman. There are usually monkeys at Hanuman temples and shrines; they are also revered and fed.

Hanuman's other names include Anjaneya, son of Anjana; Mahabala, the strong one; Rameshta, the devotee of Rama; Vayuputra, or Vayunanadan, son of Vayu; Phalgunasakha, a friend of Phalguna (Arjuna); Pingaksha, with sallow-hued eyes; Ativikrama, supremely powerful; Udadhikramana, the leaper across the ocean; Sitashokavinashana, remover of Sita's grief; Lakshmanaprandhata, reviver of LAKSHMANA; Dashagrivasyadarpaha, attacker of the ten-faced one (Ravana); Rajatadyuti, the brilliant; Yogachara, with knowledge of YOGA; Maruti, son of Maruta, another name of Vayu; Siriya Tiruvedi, the one who carried Rama (in Tamil).

Scholars believe the Vanaras could have been a forest tribe with a monkey totem. Hanuman is also thought to have been a tribal deity, incorporated into the Brahmanical pantheon. The deity provides a bridge between VAISHNAVISM and SHAIVISM, as he is a son of Shiva, but a devotee of Rama, who is an incarnation of VISHNU.

Hanuman Nataka A Sanskrit play on the adventures of the monkey-god HANUMAN, compiled by Damodara Mishra in the eleventh century. Fragments of it are said to have existed earlier and even to have been seen by VALMIKI. They were collected and put together, the missing incidents being added by Damodara.

Har Krishan, Guru The eighth Sikh guru, Har Krishan was born on 7 July 1656 to Guru HAR RAI and his wife Krishan Kaur. Before his death in October 1661, Har Rai appointed the young child, then five years old, as the guru. His elder son, RAM RAI, who was friendly with the Mughal emperor. Aurangzeb, resented this and complained to the emperor. AURANGZEB asked that Har Krishan be brought to Delhi and sent Raja Jai Singh to escort him and assure him of his safety.

In 1664, Har Krishan, his mother and disciples came to DELHI and stayed in Jai Singh's palatial house. At this time small pox and cholera epidemics were raging in the city, and hundreds of people, including Sikhs, Hindus and Muslims, came to the young guru, hoping to be cured by his touch. The guru distributed medicines, food and clothes to the poor, and ordered all the money from the daily offerings to be used for the people. Miracles of healing were reported, but Har Krishan himself fell ill. He went to the banks of the YAMUNA, where he died on 30 March 1664, and was cremated there. Before dying, he murmured 'Baba Bakala' and this was taken as an indication that the next guru would be found in Bakala. Two GURDWARAS commemorate Har Krishan's life and work in Delhi, the BANGLA SAHIB GURDWARA, which was Jai Singh's residence, and BALA SAHIB GURDWARA, which marks the spot where he died.

Har Mandir Sahib, Sri   The most sacred GURDWARA of the Sikhs. Literally, the name means 'temple of God.' It is also popularly known as the Golden Temple, because of its gilded upper two storeys and dome. The Har Mandir is located at AMRITSAR. Guru AMAR DAS (1479–1574), the third guru, asked his successor, Guru RAM DAS, to set up a sacred *tirtha* or tank here. According to some sources, part of the land was granted by the Mughal emperor AKBAR. It was already a holy site, as Guru NANAK is said to have meditated here. Ram Das constructed the tank and the place was then known as Ramdaspur or Guru ka Chak. Guru ARJAN DEV (1563–1606) began the construction of the temple in the middle of the sacred tank. He asked the SUFI saint Hazrat Mian Mir of Lahore to lay the foundation stone of the Har Mandir, thus indicating the unity of all faiths.

The temple has four entrances to welcome all who wish to enter. The main gateway, Darshani deorhi, opens on to a marble causeway which leads to the temple across the water. The causeway has latticed balustrades and lamp posts with copper-gilded lanterns, while the walls of the temple are inlaid with semi-precious stones in floral patterns. There are frescoes depicting scenes from Sikh history and the ceilings are decorated with concave and convex glass. The doors are made of silver, replaced with golden doors on special occasions. The structure is covered with a gold-plated dome. At each corner are fluted cupolas, and several small domes decorate the parapet.

The GURU GRANTH SAHIB, first installed in the Har Mandir in 1604, is located on the ground floor, facing the entrance from the causeway.

Above the Darshani deorhi, is the Tosha-khana or treasure-trove, where the valuable gold doors are stored along with other precious items dating back to the time of Maharaja RANJIT SINGH.

The temple was damaged by the Afghan invader Ahmad Shah Abdali in 1762 but was later restored. Maharaja Ranjit Singh added to the temple, and

there is now a whole complex of buildings around it. Adjacent to it is the AKAL TAKHT, the supreme seat of Sikh religious authority.

More recently, in 1984, the Golden Temple was damaged in a battle between armed militants, who had made it their residence, and the Indian Army. It was rebuilt through voluntary labour (*kar seva*).

The Har Mandir is a place of pilgrimage not only for Sikhs, but for people of all religions.

Har Rai, Guru   The seventh Sikh guru. Born in 1630 at KIRATPUR in Punjab, he was the son of Baba Gurditta, the eldest son of Guru HARGOBIND. He became the guru in 1644 when Guru Hargobind died. He continued to consolidate the position of the Sikhs, but no major battles were fought while he was the guru. As long as the Mughal emperor Shah Jahan was alive, he had good relations with the Mughals and even cured Shah Jahan's eldest son, DARA SHIKOH, of an illness with some herbal medicine. During the struggle for succession when Shah Jahan was ill, Dara Shikoh fled from AURANGZEB and came to the guru for his blessings. However, Aurangzeb ascended the throne after killing all his brothers. Some time later, he asked the guru to come to his court, but the guru sent his eldest son RAM RAI, who impressed Aurangzeb favourably. Har Rai was not happy with Ram Rai's actions at the Mughal court and disowned him, appointing his infant son, HAR KRISHAN, as the guru.

Har Rai was known for his extreme sensitivity and care for plants and animals. He would not allow animals to be killed on a hunt, but kept those that were captured as pets.

Hara   A name of the Hindu god SHIVA. Hara was also the name of a DANAVA born to KASHYAPA, and, according to some PURANAS, of one of the eleven RUDRAS.

Harbhajan Singh, Yogi   A renowned Sikh spiritual leader, popularly known as Yogi Bhajan who founded the Sikh Dharma Movement in the West. Born in 1929 at village Kot Harkan in present Pakistan, he migrated to India at the time of Partition. He completed an MA in economics from Punjab University and joined the Customs Service, married and had three children. At the same time he studied Sikhism, received spiritual training and became proficient in HATHA YOGA and KUNDALINI techniques. In 1969 he began to teach in Los Angeles and also obtained a PhD in communications psychology from San Francisco. He set up the 3HO, the 'Happy, Healthy, Holy Organization', with the belief that every person had the right to be happy, healthy and holy, and that his organization could reveal how this could be achieved. He taught the principles of Sikhism, along with Kundalini Yoga, Hatha Yoga, MANTRA and meditation, and had thousands of followers, setting up 3HO centres worldwide. The SHIROMANI GURDWARA PRABANDHAK COMMITTEE gave him the title Siri Singh Sahib and entrusted him with disseminating knowledge about the Sikh religion in the West. From Los Angeles, Harbhajan moved to New Mexico and established Sikh Dharma in the Western Hemisphere, a non-profit organization. Members of the organization wear white clothes and turbans, and follow the principles of Sikhism, in addition to practising special meditation and other techniques. Yogi Bhajan wrote over thirty books on consciousness, spirituality and related topics.

Yogi Bhajan was not merely a guru, but a businessman and entrepreneur. His Sikh Dharma organization produces natural foods, health and beauty products. His food products alone had an annual revenue of over $60 million. He was the head of fourteen US corporations, including Akal Security, whose 12,000 employees provided security to military installations, airports and other sensitive sites in the US. He also conducted business seminars, helped entrepreneurs and fostered economic development of the area in which he lived. Yogi Bhajan died in New Mexico on 7 October 2004 after an illness. His followers include hundreds of thousands of Americans and Europeans.

He had interfaith dialogues with other world religious leaders and believed that: 'If you can't see God in all, you can't see God at all.'

Hardwar/Haridwar   A city in Uttarakhand that marks the point where the river GANGA enters the plains. It is one of the seven sacred cities of Hinduism, and there are numerous temples here, some dating back to the eighth century. Its early names were Gangadvara, or the gateway of the Ganga, Kapila, and Kankhal. Hardwar comes from Hara, a name of SHIVA, but because it is also sacred to VISHNU, it is sometimes called Haridwar (Hari = VISHNU).

Pilgrims come here from all over India to bathe in the Ganga, as the sacred waters are said to cleanse one of all sins. Hindus immerse the ashes of the dead in the river, and rites for ancestors are conducted here. Every evening at sunset, ARTI or worship with lights, chants and the ringing of the temple bells, is performed.

Numerous legends, stories and myths are narrated about Hardwar. The king DAKSHA performed a sacrifice here and did not invite his son-in-law, Shiva. The Daksha Mahadeva Temple at Kankhal nearby is said to mark the spot of Daksha's sacrifice. SATI, daughter of Daksha and wife of Shiva, killed herself because of the insult to her husband, giving rise to other myths. Parts of her body fell at different places, which are revered as SHAKTA PITHAS, charged with sacred feminine power.

Hardwar is also a centre of the KUMBH MELA, which takes place once in twelve years, with the *ardh* or half kumbh held every six years. According to the story related with this event, a drop of the sacred AMRITA, nectar of immortality, fell here after the ocean of milk was churned.

Hare Krishna Movement   The popular name of the INTERNATIONAL SOCIETY FOR KRISHNA CONSCIOUSNESS (ISKCON).

Hargobind, Guru   The sixth Sikh guru. Born in 1595 at village Wadali in Punjab, he was the only child of Guru ARJAN DEV. He became the guru on 25 May 1606, a few days before the martyrdom of his father. The ceremony for his initiation as guru was performed by Baba BUDHA, and instead of the traditional *seli*, or woollen cord worn around the head, the guru asked for a sword, and from this time onwards every guru wore two swords. This symbolized the Sikhs' transformation into a martial group and the concept that the guru had both spiritual and temporal power. Hargobind believed the Sikhs must fight against tyranny and gave instructions to the MASANDS and other Sikhs to make offerings of horses and weapons instead of money. Sikhs were trained in martial arts and soon an army of 1000 horses was raised. The spiritual side was not neglected, as the guru stated that one of his swords represented Shakti (strength) and the other Bhakti (devotion). The guru meditated every morning, and prayed along with his followers. Soon after his accession as guru, he laid the foundation of the AKAL TAKHT at AMRITSAR.

Hearing of the army of the Sikhs, the Mughal emperor Jahangir asked Hargobind to come to DELHI. He was charmed by the personality of the young guru and indebted to him when the guru saved him from a tiger on a hunt. However, later intrigues led to the guru being imprisoned in Gwalior fort, though he was released after a few months.

Guru Hargobind travelled to a number of places and preached the Sikh religion. After 1624, relations with the Mughals deteriorated and a major battle took place that year. Hargobind left Amritsar, settled at KARTARPUR near the river Beas, and built the city of HARGOBINDPUR. Later he moved to KIRATPUR, where he lived with a group of followers until his death in 1644.

The guru had several sons; Gurditta, b. 1613; Suraj Mal, b. 1617; Ani Rai, b. 1618; ATAL RAI, b. 1620; TEGH BAHADUR, b. 1622. He chose his grandson, HAR RAI, the son of Baba Gurditta, as his successor.

Hargobindpur   A town in district Gurdaspur, Punjab, constructed by the sixth Sikh guru, HARGOBIND. It was built with the help of the local people, in an open space near village Ruhela, on the right bank of the river Beas. The Mughals tried to prevent the construction of a fort here, and in 1630 a battle took place, in which the Mughal forces and some local rulers were defeated. A GURDWARA known as Damdama Sahib was built at this spot. A mosque was constructed in the village as well, indicating the open-mindedness of the guru. The house where the guru lived, known as Manji Sahib, is also preserved in this town. It is an important place of pilgrimage for Sikhs.

Hari   A name of the Hindu god VISHNU or of his incarnations. It is at times used as the name of other gods as well.

Haribhadra Suri   A Jain philosopher of the eighth century who belonged to the SHVETAMBARA sect and contributed to Shvetambara doctrines. He probably lived from 705 to 775. According to tradition he wrote 1444 works; eighty-eight texts with his name have been discovered, of which twenty-six are thought to have definitely been written by him. Haribhadra states in his own works that he was a pupil of Jinabhadra (or Jinabhatta) and Jinadatta of the Vidyadhara kula, and was born at CHITRAKUTA in a BRAHMANA family. According to stories in texts he was extremely learned and boasted of his erudition, stating he would become the disciple of any one who could say something that he did not understand. One day, a Jain nun, Yakini, recited a verse that fulfilled that criterion. For its explanation, she sent him to her teacher, Jinabhatta. Haribhadra then became a Jain monk and excelled in his knowledge of the Jain texts, and therefore was given the title Suri. He wrote in Sanskrit and Prakrit, in verse and in prose, and was the first to write commentaries on Shvetambara texts in Sanskrit. His commentaries include those on the AVASSAYA SUTTA and DASAVEYALIYA SUTTA.

Haribhadra is also famous for his dharmakatha or religious novel, the SAMARAICHCHA KAHA, written in Prakrit verse, in which, after a series of many lives, the main characters enter the Jain religious order.

Haridasa A name used by devotees of the Hindu god VISHNU and of his various forms, particularly KRISHNA. Several saints of different times adopted this name.

Haridasa, Swami A BHAKTI saint, poet and singer who lived in the fifteenth and sixteenth centuries and was a devotee of the Hindu god KRISHNA. According to some accounts, he was born in a village near VRINDAVAN, a place sacred to Krishna, in MATHURA district of present west Uttar Pradesh. He became a SANNYASI and lived in his ashram Nidhuvan, composing devotional songs on the love between Krishna and RADHA. He sang Vishnupadas, a form of the Dhrupad style of classical music, mainly about the life of Krishna. Approximately 128 of his compositions are available today. He was a brilliant singer. According to later sources, he was the guru of the renowned singer TANSEN, who lived at the court of the Mughal emperor AKBAR. Contemporary sources of Akbar's reign, however, do not mention Haridasa. According to the *Nijmat Sidhanta*, an eighteenth-century text, Swami Haridasa was associated with the NIMBARKA sect.

Haridasa started the Haridasa Sampradaya, for the worship of Krishna. Members sang devotional songs together, a type of congregational singing known as Samaj in the Mathura region. Swami Haridasa lived a simple, reclusive life with some close disciples who included Vitthal Dasa, Vipul Dasa, Viharin Dev and Krishna Dasa.

Haridasas A sect or group founded in the thirteenth century dedicated to the Hindu god HARI or VISHNU and his various forms. Some trace the origin of the sect to the ninth century, but the main founder was NARAHARI TIRTHA, a BHAKTI saint and a follower of MADHVA, who lived in the present region of Karnataka. Members of the group were against animal sacrifices, superstitions, caste and the worship of many gods. They also disapproved of astrology, the use of horoscopes and rituals. They tried to reform existing practices and preached to others in the local language, Kannada, and composed devotional songs. Among prominent Haridasas was the famous singer, PURANDARADASA. Other saints of this group included Vyasaraya, KANAKADASA, Vadiraja, Vijayadasa, Jagannathadasa, Vasudevadasa and Gopaladasa.

There was some opposition to the use of Kannada, and VAISHNAVAS in Karnataka came to be divided into the Vyasakuta and Dasakuta, the former being those who continued to use Sanskrit.

Haridasas still exist, and the songs of the earlier Haridasas remain popular.

Harihara A Hindu deity that combines the aspects of VISHNU and SHIVA, HARI being a name of VISHNU, and HARA of SHIVA. There were often conflicts between the two sects of VAISHNAVITES and SHAIVITES, and this deity represents an attempt to unite the two groups. This syncretic god seems to have been represented on a coin of the Kushana dynasty in the early centuries CE. In a later stone image from BADAMI, the god holds a battle-axe entwined with a snake in his right hand (representing Shiva), and a conch shell in his left (representing Vishnu). Attendants and consorts of the two gods are also placed to the right and left, and each half of the crown and head is differently carved. Several other images of the deity have been found in Bihar, Bengal and elsewhere. In some composite images, other deities and even BODHISATTVAS have been added, probably in an attempt to bring diverse groups together.

Harijan The name chosen by Mahatma GANDHI for the lower or 'untouchable' castes in Hinduism, today known as DALITS. Mahatma Gandhi worked to abolish untouchability and to get these castes accepted by Hindu society. He gave them this name, which literally means 'Children of God' to show that he held them in high regard. Today's dalits, however, consider it a patronizing term, and it is no longer used.

Hariti A Buddhist mother goddess. According to Buddhist texts, she was a ferocious goddess who used to devour children, but the BUDDHA transformed her and she became a protector of children. The *NISHPANNAYOGAVALI*, a VAJRAYANA text, describes her as yellow in colour. Hariti is also known as a YAKSHI, the consort of KUBERA or Panchika. She is depicted with Panchika or Jambhala in GANDHARA images, and with Kubera in MATHURA art of the first and second centuries CE. She appears on her own as well, along with one or more children. She was one of the most popular Buddhist deities in India.

Harivamsha A Sanskrit text which describes episodes from the life of the Hindu god KRISHNA. Consisting of 16,374, verses, it is an appendix to the *MAHABHARATA*, but is a later addition and is used as a separate text. It is similar to a PURANA, and has three parts or parvas. The first part, the *Harivamsha Parva*, contains creation myths as well as an account of the YADAVA dynasty, while the second, the *Vishnu Parva*, deals with the life of KRISHNA. The third part, the *Bhavishya Parva*, has prophecies of the future, as well as accounts of VISHNU and SHIVA.

Harivamsha Purana (1) A Jain text based on the *HARIVAMSHA*, the appendix to the *MAHABHARATA*. It was completed by Jinasena in 783. It tells the story of KRISHNA and BALARAMA in a Jain setting. Gautama (Goyama) the chief disciple of MAHAVIRA, is made the narrator of the Purana, and ARISHTANEMINATHA, the twenty-second TIRTHANKARA, is described as a cousin of Krishna. In this Purana, the KAURAVAS and Karna become Jains, and later the PANDAVAS too, become Jain ascetics. The descendants of the PANDAVAS and KAURAVAS, and of Krishna and Balarama, are described.

(2) Another Jain text of the same name, was composed by Salakirti and his pupil Jinadasa in the fifteenth century.

Harsha A king who patronized Buddhism. Harshavardhana of the Pushyabhuti dynasty ruled over much of northern India from 606 to 647. His ancestors were devotees of the Hindu god SHIVA, while his immediate ancestors were worshippers of Aditya or SURYA, and he himself is described as Parama-Maheshvara, a devotee of Shiva. In later life he was deeply influenced by Buddhism. He held a meeting at his capital of Kannauj to discuss MAHAYANA Buddhism, and thousands of monks as well as the kings of twenty countries gathered there. A huge golden image of the BUDDHA was placed in a tower and worshipped by the people, and the Chinese pilgrim XUANZANG explained Mahayana Buddhism to the audience. Harsha organized another meeting at PRAYAGA (Allahabad) that lasted for seventy-five days. On the first day a statue of the Buddha was set up and worshipped, on the second, of Adityadeva or Surya, and on the third of Ishvaradeva or Shiva. Large amounts of money were distributed in charity to Buddhist monks, BRAHMANAS, Jains, members of other sects, and wandering mendicants, after which alms were given to the poor, the orphans and the destitute, by which time Harsha's entire treasury was exhausted.

Haryashvas The name of 5000 mind-born sons of DAKSHA and ASIKNI described in Hindu texts.

Hashim Pir A SUFI saint who lived in Bijapur in the seventeenth century. According to legend, Muhammad Adil Shah III (1627–56), ruler of the kingdom of Bijapur, fell ill while supervising the construction of his tomb, later known as the Gol Gumbaz. He prayed to a Sufi saint, Sayyed Shah Hashiro Husaini of Bijapur, popularly known as Hashim Pir. The saint predicted that Muhammad Adil Shah would die in three days, but then offered his own life in place of the king's. Hashim Pir died and the king lived and completed the Gol Gumbaz.

Hastinapura An ancient city, identified with a village of the same name in District Meerut, Uttar Pradesh. In the *MAHABHARATA*, Hastinapura is the capital of the Kuru kingdom. The king DHRITARASHTRA ruled here, and the battle between the PANDAVA and KAURAVA cousins was over the territory of Kuru. After the Kauravas were defeated, YUDHISHTHIRA ruled here. According to the *Mahabharata*, a later king, Nichakshu, grandson of Janamejaya, moved his capital to KAUSHAMBI after Hastinapura was destroyed by a flood. Excavations reveal that Hastinapura was occupied from around 1500 BCE to CE 300, though not continuously. It was reoccupied between 1100 and CE 1500. There is evidence of desertion after a flood, tentatively dated to 800 BCE.

Hastinapura is also the birthplace of three Jain TIRTHANKARAS, and two Jain temples still exist here.

Hatha Yoga A system of YOGA or union with the divine, described in various texts. The essentials of Hatha Yoga form part of Patanjali's *YOGA SUTRA*, but more elaborate descriptions occur in later texts, including the *Hatha Yoga Pradipika* of Svatmarama, the *Goraksha Shataka* of GORAKHNATHA, and the *Gheranda Samhita*. Hatha Yoga is merely a different approach to Yoga and consists of first purifying the physical and subtle body through ASANAS or physical postures and PRANAYAMA or breathing techniques, before going on to higher techniques of concentration and meditation. Apart from ethical principles basic to all forms of Yoga, Hatha Yoga deals specifically with: (1) cleansing of the body (shodhana) by six processes; (2) attaining strength and firmness by asanas or bodily postures, as well as fortitude by specific positions (mudras); (3) steadying the mind by restraining the senses (pratyahara); (4) gaining lightness of the body by pranayama; (5) attaining realization (pratyaksha) through DHYANA or meditation; (6) achieving detachment (nirliptatva) in SAMADHI.

Hatim, Shah A SUFI poet of the eighteenth century. Shaikh Zahiruddin Hatim was born in DELHI in 1699 and was initially employed in the army but became a Sufi of the SUHRAWARDI sect and an ascetic. He was one of the most noted Urdu poets of his time. Hatim was a disciple of Shah Badal Ali, and after the latter's death, of Shah Taslim, both of Delhi. His poems do not reflect any particular school of SUFISM. It was a time of turmoil and conflict in Delhi, and in one of his verses Hatim wrote:

How can one be happy even for a moment in this age,
That is devoid of all that brings happiness.

In another verse he revealed the Sufi's detachment:

A darvesh does not seek favours from anyone;
Continued deep affliction is his sustenance.

Haurvatat A deity and a power of AHURA MAZDA, the name of God in Zoroastrianism. She is personified as an AMESHA SPENTA representing perfection. Her name can be compared to the Sanskrit sarva-tat (all is that). Haurvatat presides over the waters and her emblem is a lily. In later texts she is known as Khordad.

Hauz-i Shamsi A sacred tank constructed in DELHI in 1230, at the time of Sultan Iltutmish. According to the story associated with its construction, Delhi, even in those days, faced a shortage of water, and therefore the sultan wanted to construct a storage tank, but could not decide on a suitable location. The Prophet MUHAMMAD is then said to have appeared to the SUFI saint QUTBUDDIN BAKHTIYAR and to the sultan, and indicated in which area to build the tank. After the Hauz-i Shamsi was constructed, the area near it became a meeting place, a spiritual and cultural centre. In the monsoon, the water flowed from here into a garden. The tank, located in the Mehrauli area, still exists.

Hayagriva (1) An AVATARA or incarnation of the Hindu god VISHNU. Literally, the word means 'horse-necked'. There are different accounts of Hayagriva in various texts and legends. In the VEDAS, Hayagriva is a form of YAJNA (sacrifice), which in some texts is a term used for Vishnu. According to one story in the PURANAS, BRAHMA is said to have cursed Vishnu out of jealousy, because in a test he proved to be the greatest of the gods. As a result of the curse, Vishnu lost his head and attended a yajna of the DEVAS wearing a horse's head. After that he meditated, and with the blessings of SHIVA regained his original head.

(2) In another story, Vishnu took the form of Hayagriva to restore the Vedas, which had been stolen by two asuras, to Brahma. Alternatively, Hayagriva is the name of a DAITYA who stole the Vedas.

(3) Hayagriva was also the name of others, including a DANAVA who was the son of KASHYAPA, and of an ASURA killed by KRISHNA.

(4) In VAJRAYANA Buddhism, Hayagriva is the name of a deity, a form of the Buddha Vajrasattva.

Hayashiras/Hayashirsha A name of the Hindu god VISHNU, meaning horse-headed. According to the BHAGAVATA PURANA, Hayashirsha was the same as BHAGAVATA (a name of Vishnu). He was the colour of gold; the VEDAS and the sacrifice were his substance, while the god was his soul. The name probably relates to his incarnation as HAYAGRIVA.

Hazrat Bal Mosque A mosque in Srinagar, Kashmir. It is one of the most sacred places for Muslims as a hair of the Prophet MUHAMMAD is a holy relic in the mosque. The original mosque, which was destroyed by terrorists in the 1990s, was a white marble structure with a large dome and a minaret. The hair of the Prophet was brought to Srinagar in the seventeenth century by Nuruddin Ashwar, a Kashmiri trader, who obtained it from an Arab during his travels. It was originally housed in the Shah Hamadan mosque but that became too small to contain the crowds who came to pay reverence to it. The relic is displayed to the public on certain special days, including ID-I-MILAD. The mosque has been partially rebuilt.

Hazur Sahib Gurdwara A Sikh shrine or GURDWARA, known as Sachkand Sri Hazur Achbal Nagar Sahib, which houses one of the TAKHTS or centres of Sikh spiritual authority. It is located on the banks of the river Godavari at Nanded in Maharashtra and marks the spot where Guru GOBIND SINGH died in 1708. The two-storeyed building is in a style similar to the HAR MANDIR and was constructed at the time of Maharaja RANJIT SINGH, between 1832 and 1837. The inner room, known as the Angitha Sahib, has gold-plated walls, and the pinnacle on the polished dome is also gold-plated. In the gurdwara, the GURU GRANTH SAHIB is recited continuously, day and night. Some of the weapons of Guru Gobind Singh, including five golden swords, are preserved here. It was here that BANDA BAHADUR converted to Sikhism.

There are other gurdwaras in Nanded, including the Sangat Sahib Gurdwara, Shikhar Ghat Gurdwara, Nagina Ghat Gurdwara and Hira Ghat Gurdwara. They were all constructed to commemorate the visit of Guru Gobind Singh to these places.

Heart Sutra The popular name of a MAHAYANA Buddhist text, known in Sanskrit as the *PRAJNAPARAMITA-HRIDAYA-SUTRA*, one of the many PRAJNAPARAMITA or 'perfection of wisdom' texts.

Hemachandra Suri A renowned Jain scholar who wrote a number of texts. According to several accounts, Hemachandra was born in 1089 in Dhanduka, about 100 km south-west of Ahmadabad in present-day Gujarat, and was originally named Changadeva. His father was probably a SHAIVITE and his mother a Jain. A Jain acharya who came to Dhanduka was impressed with the boy, and with the consent of his parents, took the child with him. The boy was made a Jain monk in 1097 and given the name Somachandra. He soon became extremely learned and was therefore given the title Suri at the age of twenty-one, and later the name Hemachandra, for his face shone like gold (*hema*).

Hemachandra, who was a SHVETAMBARA, composed the *TRISHASHTISHALAKAPURUSHA CHARITRA*, the counterpart of the DIGAMBARA Purana of a similar name. He also composed the *Sidha-hema-shabdanushasana*, a grammar of Sanskrit and Prakrit; the *Kumarapala Charitra* on king Kumarapala of Gujarat, who was his patron; and four lexicons: the *Abhidhana Chintamani*, similar in style to the AMARAKOSHA; the *Anekarthasangraha*, a dictionary of homonyms; the *Nighantu*, on medicinal plants; and *Deshinamamala*, on commonly used words that are not derived from Sanskrit or Prakrit.

Hemis Gompa A Buddhist monastery in the region of LADAKH in Kashmir. It was probably constructed in the fifteenth century, during the reign of the legendary Sengge Namgyal, and is under the DRUGPA sect. It has a large dukhang or assembly hall, apart from the main temple. Among its treasures is one of the largest THANGKAS or scroll paintings in Ladakh, which is unfurled once every twelve years. A Buddhist festival takes place here every year in June to celebrate the birthday of PADMASAMBHAVA.

Hemkunt Sahib Gurdwara A Sikh shrine or GURDWARA located at Hemkunt in Uttara khand, at a height of 4636 m. An interesting story is connected with this gurdwara, narrated in the *Bachitra Natak*, the autobiographical account written by Guru GOBIND SINGH. In this the guru said that in his previous life he had meditated on the Hemkunt hill, also known as Sapta Shringa, a place where seven peaks are visible, and where once PANDU had meditated on the god YAMA. There God came to the guru-to-be and asked him to be born in the world to establish the path of truth.

The exact site was not known until Pandit Tara Singh, exploring the region in the 1930s, discovered the spot near a small, clear lake. A hut was built there in 1936 and a copy of the GURU GRANTH SAHIB was placed in it in 1937. Later a gurdwara was constructed in place of the hut. Near the Hemkunt Gurdwara, are natural forests of silver birch, fir and pine, and the water in the lake looks blue. The snow-covered Himalayas form the backdrop to this sacred site.

Heruka A Buddhist deity of VAJRAYANA Buddhism, described in the *NISHPANNAYOGAVALI* and other texts. He belongs to the Buddha family of AKSHOBHYA and is blue in colour. In some texts he is identical with the ADI BUDDHA.

Heruka is also a term for 'means of attainment' and in this sense there are eight Heruka *sadhanas* or methods of practice.

Hevajra Tantra A Buddhist text of the ANUTTARAYOGA class of TANTRAS. It begins with a dialogue between the Buddha Vajrasattva and the Bodhisattva Vajragarbha. The text, which includes philosophy, ritual and practice, was probably composed some time around CE 700. This Tantra is also important for its explanation of SANDHA-BHASHA, the secret or hidden language of Tantra.

Hidimba (Hidimbaa) A rakshasi who married BHIMA, one of the PANDAVA brothers of the MAHABHARATA, after Bhima had killed her brother Hidimba in battle. Their son was Ghatotkacha. A small temple of Hidimba known as the Dungri Temple exists above Manali in Himachal Pradesh. Here Hidimba is considered a form of the Hindu goddess DURGA, and is the first of the deities to be brought to Kulu for the annual DASHAHARA festival. Hidimba was the goddess of the former royal family of Kulu.

Hieun Tsang A Chinese pilgrim who visited India in the seventh century, during the reign of King HARSHA, and provided an account of Buddhism at this time. His name is also spelt XUANZANG.

hijrah An Arabic term referring to the departure of the Prophet MUHAMMAD from Mecca for Medina in 622. The Islamic calendar begins on this date.

Himalaya The mountain range across the north of India, also known in texts as HIMAVAN.

Himavan A name for the HIMALAYA in ancient texts. These mountains were considered sacred and were associated with the gods. According to Hindu mythology, Himavan or Himavat, the DEVA or god representing the mountain, was married to MENA or Menaka, and was the father of Uma or PARVATI and of GANGA. Several of the gods or devas live on Himavan as well as a number of RISHIS. Parvati and SHIVA live forever on the northern heights of the mountains, and GARUDA, the divine bird of VISHNU, as well as the DIKAPALAS, are among the other residents of these mountains. The sacred MANASAROVARA lake and the KAILASHA mountain were located north of Himavan.

Hinayana Buddhism One of the three main divisions of Buddhism. Hinayana Buddhism is the earliest form of Buddhism, based on the basic teachings of the BUDDHA. The term means 'Lesser Vehicle', while MAHAYANA means 'Greater Vehicle'. It is still used in academic works to describe early Buddhist sects, but is not used by Buddhists of this school, who consider it a pejorative term. The Hinayana school that exists today in Sri Lanka and other countries is the THERAVADA.

Hinayana accepts the basic principles of Buddhism: the FOUR NOBLE TRUTHS on suffering and its cause and the EIGHTFOLD PATH, which is the way to liberation. It also accepts the concepts of impermanence (anichcha, ANITYA), the non-existence of a permanent individual self, anatta (ANATMAN), the five aggregates (SKANDHAS) which create human existence, and the doctrine of patichcha samutpada (PRATITYA SAMUTPADA), or the law of dependent origination, in which one state of being arises out of the previous state.

After the death of the Buddha, differences of opinion began to appear, and a number of schools of Hinayana Buddhism developed. The two main schools were the STHAVIRAVADA and the MAHASANGHIKA, which had several offshoots themselves. By the first century BCE, there were about thirty different sects and schools. Some of these, such as the SARVASTIVADA, had their own ABHIDHARMA and VINAYA texts. The various schools differed in their understanding of the concept of the ARHAT and whether an arhat could regress; the nature of a BODHISATTVA; whether a Bodhisattva could be born in hell to lighten the sufferings of those there; the concept of an intermediate existence (antarabhava); and whether DEVAS were capable of practising BRAHMACHARYA, as well as other minor aspects. Most of these sects no longer exist.

The MAHAYANA form of Buddhism emerged by the first century CE. Though they also accepted the early Buddhist canon and its basic teachings, they developed their own texts and disagreed with the Hinayana view of the stages on the Buddhist path. They believed that enlightenment could not be sought only for oneself; a person following the Buddhist path must seek it for all living beings.

Hinayana texts include the PALI CANON, comprising the SUTTA PITAKA, ABHIDHAMMA PITAKA and VINAYA PITAKA. In addition, there are five different Vinaya Pitakas, of the Mahasanghika, MAHISHASAKAS, DHARMAGUPTAKAS, Sarvastivada and Mula Sarvastivada sects, mostly in Chinese translation, though some Sanskrit fragments are available. Of these, the Mula Sarvastivada Vinaya is the most extensive version, also available in Tibetan. The ABHIDHARMA PITAKA of the Sarvastivada, and the *Shariputra Abhidharma*, are preserved in Chinese translation; the second is probably of the Dharmaguptaka sect, with some Mahasanghika influence.

There are numerous commentaries on these texts, including the early works of BUDDHADATTA and BUDDHAGHOSHA. The Theravada that still survives today, developed additional texts.

Hindu calendar Several different calendars are used in Hinduism, both for astrological purposes and for calculating the dates of festivals. There is thus no single uniform calendar. The solar calendar is based on the *Surya Siddhanta*, a text from around CE 400. The rashi, which has its equivalent in the Western zodiac, is the basis of this calendar. The twelve rashis with their Western equivalents are: Mesha (Aries); Vrisha (Taurus); Mithuna (Gemini); Karkata (Cancer); Simha (Leo); Kanya (Virgo); Tula (Libra); Vrischika (Scorpio); Dhanus (Sagittarius); Makara (Capricorn); Kumbha (Aquarius); Mina (Pisces). However, these are not exactly the same as in the west. The solar year fluctuates slightly, by approximately six hours every year, which can affect the date on which the rashi begins. The twelve solar months correspond with the rashi divisions.

A lunar calendar is also used. The twelve lunar months are: Chaitra, Vaishakha, Jyaishtha, Ashadha, Shravana, Bhadrapada, Ashvina, Karttika, Margashirsha or Agrahayana, Pausha or Taisa, Magha, and Phalguna. The standardized lunar year begins in the third week of March, though there are other systems as well. Some lunar calendars are associated with the festival of HOLI, whereas several others begin in April. Another traditional calendar celebrates the day after DIVALI as the new year. Each lunar month consists of approximately 29½ solar days and is divided into thirty *tithis* or lunar days. The month has two halves of fifteen *tithis* each, related to the waxing and waning of the moon. The months have different names in various regions. There are also regional variations of the time that each month begins.

The year is divided into six seasons of two months each. These are Vasanta (spring), Grishma (summer), Varsha (monsoon), Sharad (autumn), Hemanta (winter) and Shishira (cool weather).

A seven-day week is used, adopted from the Greeks in the third century. The names of the days of the week in north India from Monday to Sunday are Somavara, Mangalavara, Budhavara, Brihaspativara, Shukravara, Shanivara and Ravivara. Each day is named after the sun, moon and planets, as in the West.

These calendars and their regional variants are used to calculate festival days, auspicious days for celebrating marriages and other events, as well as inauspicious times.

Hindu deities Hinduism has a number of deities, though all are considered aspects of the one God, or as emanations of BRAHMAN, the Absolute. The deities that are popular today have evolved over time. Terracotta female figurines have been found at settlements dating back to 4000 BCE or earlier. Some scholars believe that this suggests the prevalence of a mother goddess or fertility cult, though their actual significance is not clear. The INDUS CIVILIZATION, c. 2500 to 1800 BCE, has evidence of female figurines, a deity with a horned headdress seated in a Yogic position that has been variously identified, as well as possible evidence of the worship of certain animals and trees. The RIG VEDA, usually dated between 1500 BCE and 1000 BCE, describes a number of deities of which the most important are INDRA and AGNI. In the later VEDAS these deities change and evolve. By the first century BCE, new deities emerged, which included aspects of the earlier Vedic gods. These gradually crystallized into three main groups of deities which remain popular today: those connected with the god SHIVA; with the god VISHNU; and with SHAKTI or MAHADEVI, the great goddess. BRAHMA, though the creator deity, has a position inferior to these. SMARTAS worship a group of five or six deities, cutting across different sects, and certain groups worship SURYA. All these deities are described at length in the PURANAS and in several other texts. There are also references to Vedic deities in the Puranas, though here they have an inferior position. In addition, there are regional deities, as well as regional variations of the main deities, apart from local and village deities and various minor deities, such as YAKSHAS, YAKSHIS, NAGAS and spirits. Deities are connected with caste groups, and each caste or sub-caste worships its own particular deity.

Hindu life, four stages of Traditionally, there are four stages to be followed in Hindu life, also known as the ASHRAMA DHARMAS.

Hinduism Hinduism, also referred to as Sanatana Dharma, is the religion of over 80 per cent of the population of India, and has a variety of beliefs and practices, with a certain underlying unity. Broadly, it exists at two levels, the philosophical and that of popular belief.

Hindu philosophy is highly complex and continues to draw inspiration from the six classic systems of SAMKHYA, VAISHESHIKA, VEDANTA, MIMAMSA, NYAYA and YOGA. Of these the most widespread today is Vedanta, particularly the ADVAITA Vedanta of SHANKARA, though other forms are also well known. Aspects of Samkhya philosophy underlie various philosophical systems. Yoga is popular, though more so in its practical form than in its philosophy.

Hinduism at the popular level has different aspects. Most commonly, a variety of deities are worshipped and propitiated. Along with this is an acceptance of certain basic concepts. These include a realization that though different gods might be worshipped, there is one reality, which can manifest itself in an infinite number of ways. The whole of creation, including the gods, emanates from this One. Other basic beliefs include reincarnation or transmigration of souls (*punarjanama* or *avagamana*); the concept of KARMA, or of the results of one's actions; DHARMA, or right conduct and the way of life, and related to this the CASTE SYSTEM, which earlier provided everyone with a fixed role in life. ARTHA, or a 'rational pursuit of economic and political goals', as well as KAMA, a sexual life within prescribed limits, are considered part of the life of a householder, the second of the traditional four stages of life.

Finally, there is the ultimate goal of MOKSHA or liberation from the cycle of lives. Another aspect of popular Hinduism is reverence for a GURU or spiritual teacher, who may belong to the past or the present. The beliefs and practices of individuals are then based on those of the guru. Most gurus are those who have taken SANNYASA and many belong to one or the other of the various SADHU sects. As long as actual conversion is not demanded, the guru may even be non-Hindu in origin, such as NIRMALA DEVI or MEHR BABA, or may incorporate non-Hindu ideas. Hindus sometimes worship saints of other religions, including Muslim PIRS.

History: Hinduism has to be understood in the context of its history. It was not initially a well-defined religion, and the term itself was commonly used only from medieval times. Hindu, the Persianized form of Sindhu, the name of the river Indus, was used from about the eighth century to refer to the people who lived to the east of the river, i.e., in India. Later it was used to describe all those in India who did not consciously identify with any other religion.

Some of the aspects of Hinduism can be traced to Vedic or even pre-Vedic times. The history of the religion can be seen both through texts and through visual representations, in sculptures, coins, seals and temples.

Terracotta female images, dating to before 4000 BCE, are thought to be the first representations of a mother goddess or fertility deity, though some scholars question this. The INDUS CIVILIZATION, despite its undeciphered script, has representations on seals interpreted as male and female deities, considered by some scholars as proto-Hindu. The RIG VEDA, dated between 1500 and 1000 BCE, describes a number of deities, mainly personifications of nature, while the later VEDAS, dated between 1000 BCE and 600 BCE, describe sacrifices to gain power and control. The CASTE SYSTEM also began to develop at this time. The UPANISHADS which form the last part of Vedic literature, contain philosophical ideas, while the epics, particularly the *MAHABHARATA*, include stories and legends of the gods.

In the sixth century BCE, new philosophies emerged, two of which, Buddhism and Jainism, later grew into important religions. The six classic systems of philosophy, referred to above, also developed. By the second century BCE, images in stone began to be made, and deities were represented on coins. Deities included representations of Buddhist, Jain, and Brahmanical (Hindu) images. Coins from around the second century BCE show that local kings in north India used the names of deities mentioned in the Vedas, such as INDRA, SURYA, BRAHMA, PRAJAPATI, BRIHASPATI, in their own names, indicating that Vedic deities were still worshipped. Between the second century BCE and the third century CE, images depict YAKSHAS, YAKSHIS, NAGAS and various Brahmanical deities, apart from Jain and Buddhist deities. Some Greek and Zoroastrian deities were also depicted on coins of the Indo-Greeks and other dynasties, non-Indian in origin. From the first century CE, deities such as SHIVA, VISHNU, VARAHA, VAMANA, KARTTIKEYA, GANESHA, GARUDA, KRISHNA, BALARAMA, LAKSHMI, PARVATI and DURGA become more common. The PURANAS, which incorporate extensive myths about these deities, were written down slightly later, but their worship was already widespread, as indicated from sculptural and other finds at excavated sites. The transition had thus been made from the Vedic deities, who now had an inferior position, to the deities still worshipped today.

The major Puranas, written in Sanskrit by BRAHMANAS, redefined Hinduism, incorporating popular myths and legends, and bringing local cults into the mainstream. Puranic writers attempted to build links between the new deities and the Vedic gods, though some of the connections were tenuous. The new gods and their images were described, along with rules for erecting them and setting up temples. Simultaneously the DHARMA SHASTRAS were written, laying down rules of conduct. While these developments were taking place in north India, there were certain differences in the south and east. By this time north Indian deities were prominent in the south, though local gods remained popular. Northern myths were modified to suit southern traditions, and northern gods were given southern names. The *MANIMEKHALAI*, a Tamil text dated between the second and sixth centuries CE, describes the philosophies and sects present in the Tamil country at that time. These included Buddhism, Jainism, Mimamsa, Vaisheshika, Vedism, VAISHNAVISM, SHAIVISM, the AJIVIKAS and materialists. Slightly later, XUANZANG, the Chinese pilgrim who visited India in the seventh century, states that in Harsha's kingdom in northern India, apart from Buddhism, the three main Brahmanical deities worshipped were Aditya or Surya, Shiva and Vishnu. He also mentions the KAPALIKAS, Bhutas, Jutikas and followers of the Samkhya and Vaisheshika sects. Bana, writing around the same period, adds that the followers of KAPILA, KANADA and of the Upanishads (Vedanta) were present in the region.

By the seventh century, the two main sects of Vaishnavism and Shaivism in the south propagated BHAKTI, or loving devotion to god, through the ALVARA and NAYANAR saints. In the ninth century SHANKARA, later known as Adi Shankaracharya, established Hindu MATHAS or religious centres, and spread the message of Advaita, providing unifying institutions and a unifying philosophy that forms the basis of Hinduism today. RAMANUJA, MADHVA and others responded with different interpretations of Vedanta. Meanwhile the bhakti movement spread to Maharashtra, focusing on the worship of Vishnu, and from the fourteenth century prominent bhakti saints appeared in the north, many worshipping Krishna or Rama, while others worshipped the formless lord (nirguna bhakti). SUFI saints and the emergence of SIKHISM in the fifteenth century also influenced Hinduism.

A parallel development from around the eighth century was of TANTRISM, particularly in east India, and the corresponding importance given to SHAKTI, or female power.

Till the nineteenth century the term 'Hindu' was used mainly by those belonging to other religions. Hindus referred to themselves in terms of their caste or as adherents of Vaishnavism, Shaivism or other sects and deities. The attempt at self-identification was largely a response to Western stimuli. Reform movements such as the BRAHMO SAMAJ and ARYA SAMAJ emerged, while VIVEKANANDA, a follower of RAMAKRISHNA PARAMAHANSA and founder of the RAMAKRISHNA MISSION, gave speeches on Hinduism in the West. Leaders of the THEOSOPHICAL SOCIETY, particularly Annie BESANT, saw everything good in Eastern religions, and promoted Hinduism, Buddhism and Zoroastrianism. These movements provided Hindus with a consciousness of their own identity, and there was an attempt to emphasize the common aspects of different sects and deities. Sri AUROBINDO, another great philosopher, commented on Hindu texts and ideas, but in later years, clearly stated that his philosophy was beyond all sectarian beliefs.

The politics of the first half of the twentieth century and the partition of India in 1947, led to a heightened consciousness of being 'Hindu'. Mahatma GANDHI, leader of the freedom movement, emphasized his identity as a Hindu but put forward his own broad concept of what being a Hindu meant. Among other things, he believed that a Hindu must serve and help those of other religions. After Independence, Hindu organizations made an attempt to give all groups a Hindu identity and to include DALITS and tribals in the Hindu fold. The Rashtriya Swayamsevak Sangh (RSS), founded in 1925, and the Hindu Mahasabha (founded 1915), were among the early organizations promoting Hindu unity. The Vishwa Hindu Parishad (1964) and Bajrang Dal (1984) carried this process further. The earlier Arya Samaj also continued its attempts to provide a Hindu identity. Political parties with a Hindu ideology included the Bharatiya Jana Sangh (1951) and later the Bharatiya Janata Party (BJP, founded 1980), which used Rama as both a cultural hero and a divine figure, and a symbol of the new India.

Today, though there are new Vedantic movements and innumerable gurus, the average Hindu has a limited knowledge of the intricacies of Hindu philosophy. There is instead a revival of rituals and worship fuelled by popular media. The caste system still exists, though dharma or right conduct based on caste is beginning to change, leading to conflicts between the old and the new.

Despite the politically motivated rhetoric of some Hindu groups, most Hindus are in favour of a pluralistic and tolerant society, worshipping whichever deity appeals to them and following various gurus and sects. Hinduism remains a vast, complex and diverse religion that is not easy to define.

Key features: Some of the key features of the religion, apart from the underlying concepts of worship, dharma, karma, reincarnation and the caste system, are that the religion has no founder, no single canon and no supreme authority. It includes both high philosophy and simple worship of a deity.

Hindutva A popular term that is used in different ways. Though the term was used earlier, the concept was clearly explained by V.D. Savarkar in his book *Hindutva: Who is a Hindu?*, first published in 1923. To him Hindutva was the culture of Hindus, of those who lived in India or Hindustan and whose first allegiance was to the country of India. He connected Hindutva with Hindu customs and festivals, the ARYANS and their descendents, and the Sanskrit language. He believed that Muslims and Christians in India were originally Hindus, and thus could return to the fold.

In general Hindutva has been used as a synonym for the Hindu way of life, presupposing an underlying cultural unity in Hinduism despite divergent beliefs and sects.

Recently, attempts have been made to give the term a wider meaning, and to see it as a synonym for Indianness or Bharatiyata. A Supreme Court judgment of 1996, now usually quoted as a definition, states that Hindutva indicates 'a way of life of the Indian people'. The Bharatiya Janata Party, a political party that promotes Hinduism, states: 'Hindutva is not a religious or exclusivist concept. It is inclusive, integrative, and abhors any kind of discrimination against any section of the people of India on the basis of their faith.' However, since the term is derived from the word 'Hindu' and is related to the Hindu cultural ethos, its use continues to have Hindu, rather than Indian, connotations.

Hira Vijaya Suri   A prominent Jain of the sixteenth century who was invited by the Mughal emperor AKBAR to Fatehpur Sikri to hold discussions on Jainism. Hira Vijaya Suri, who reached the court of the emperor in 1582, was the head of the Tapa GACHCHHA. According to a Jain inscription at Palitana, dating from 1582–83, Akbar was persuaded to issue an edict forbidding the slaughter of animals for six months, abolishing certain taxes, releasing many captives, snared birds and animals, and presenting the sacred place SHATRUNJAYA to the Jains. A farman or edict of 1584 ordered officials not to allow the killing of animals for the twelve days of the PARYUSHAN festival wherever Jains were settled. Jain sources state that Hira Vijaya was given the title 'Jagad Guru' or 'world preceptor' by Akbar. He left Akbar's court in 1585, but other Jains of the Tapa Gachchha, including Shanti Chandra and later Bhanu Chandra, remained at Akbar's court. Vijayasen Suri, successor of Hira Vijaya Suri, was later invited to the court. Jains of the Kharatara Gachchha, particularly JINACHANDRA SURI, also influenced Akbar. Akbar was personally against killing animals, and therefore acceded to Jain requests concerning the slaughter of animals.

Hiranyagarbha   A Hindu deity first mentioned in the RIG VEDA, identified with PRAJAJPATI, and in later texts with BRAHMA. Hiranyagarbha means the golden womb, and is the cosmic womb from which all life originates. Hiranyagarbha is also identified with BRAHMAN, the ultimate reality.

Hiranyakashipu   A DAITYA, the son of DITI and KASHYAPA. He had received a boon from the god SHIVA, of sovereignty of the three worlds. He hated the Hindu god VISHNU, who had defeated and killed his brother, HIRANYAKSHA. However, Hiranyakashipu's son PRAHLADA was devoted to Vishnu. Finally Hiranyakashipu was killed by Vishnu in his form of NARASIMHA.

Hiranyaksha   A DAITYA, the son of DITI and KASHYAPA. He was the elder brother of HIRANYAKASHIPU, and attained great power. The residents of the three worlds feared him because he oppressed them all. He besieged heaven, and all the DEVAS ran away from him. He then dragged the earth under the ocean. Finally he was defeated and killed by VISHNU in the form of VARAHA.

Hitopadesha   A Sanskrit text consisting of ethical and moral stories, based on the earlier PANCHATANTRA. The *Hitopadesha* dates to between the twelfth and fourteenth centuries.

Hoi   A Hindu festival known as Hoi Ashtami, celebrated on the eighth day of the fortnight before DIVALI. On this day the goddess Hoi Mata is worshipped, particularly by women who desire children, or have received them through her blessing.

Hola Mohalla   A Sikh festival that commemorates the martial glory of the KHALSA, which was founded by Guru GOBIND SINGH. The festival is celebrated one day after HOLI, and at this time Sikhs dressed in martial clothes re-enact historic battles. Celebrations take place at several places associated with Sikh history, particularly at ANANDPUR SAHIB, where the KHALSA was first created.

Holi   A Hindu festival celebrated on the full moon day of the month of Phalguna (February–March). It is a spring and harvest festival especially popular in north India and is celebrated on two days, the first by lighting bonfires and the second by throwing coloured water and dry powdered colour on one another. According to some astrological calculations, the Hindu new year starts two days after the Holi fire is lit.

Several legends are associated with the festival, the most popular being that of Holika. Holika was the sister of HIRANYAKASHIPU, whose son PRAHLADA was devoted to VISHNU. She joined her brother in trying to kill Prahlada because of this devotion. She took Prahlada on her lap and entered a fire, believing she was beyond harm, but she was consumed by the fire, whereas Prahlada emerged unharmed. Thus, the night before Holi, fires are lit, symbolizing the burning of Holika and the triumph of good over evil.

Another legend links Holi with the defeat of KAMA, the god of love, by SHIVA, while according to one story it is a celebration of the marriage of Shiva and PARVATI.

The festival has a special significance in MATHURA, where Holi is celebrated for several days and is associated with the god KRISHNA. According to local tradition, Krishna used to throw spring flowers of different colours on the GOPIS, and thus the practice of throwing coloured water on one another began. In this area, 'Lath Mar' Holi is also celebrated, where women attempt to hit men with sticks, thus establishing their dominance for at least one day in the year. In Barmer in Rajasthan, groups throw stones at one another, and in Meera Ghat in Varanasi they attack one another with sticks. Wrestling and boxing matches also take place.

In rural areas Holi remains linked with the harvest. The harvested sheaves are roasted and offered to deities. In some regions, Holi dances are performed.

Special delicacies are made on Holi. Malpua, a sweet of bread and sugar syrup, gujiya, another sweet, and papri, made of corn flour, are popular in north India. In Maharashtra, puranpori, a kind of flat bread stuffed with sweet lentils, is common, and in Gujarat, flat millet bread. Traditionally bhang, an intoxicant, is also used, leading at times to wild behaviour. Holi is thus not only a spring festival, heralding spring with colour and song, but a time when conventions are broken in a spirit of freedom.

homa/haoma   A term in the AVESTA, the Zoroastrian texts, for a sacred juice used in rituals, known in Sanskrit as SOMA. The use of homa pre-dates ZARATHUSHTRA, who seems to have been against it. Vivanghvant, the father of YIMA, is said to have worshipped homa, and in later texts, four types of homa are described. They are: Homa Duraoshi, which keeps death afar; Homa Zairi, or golden homa; Homa Frashmi, the renewer; Homa Khvarenangha, or homa with kingly glory. Several scholars have identified homa or soma with the juice of the ephedra plant.

Home Church/House Church   A PROTESTANT Christian movement that has taken root in India and consists of spreading Christianity through small, local, unobtrusive 'home churches'. Any Christian can open their home for discussions and prayers among friends and family, thus forming a 'home church'. The movement has gained considerable popularity, particularly in Kerala, Gujarat, Uttar Pradesh, Madhya Pradesh and Rajasthan. The Home Church programme also exists in other countries. It is thought that early Christians in India had a similar method of worship.

Hormazd   A later term for AHURA MAZDA, the name of God in Zoroastrianism.

horses, sacred   Horses were associated with deities in India since early times.

The VEDAS have several references to horses, both associated with the gods and with rituals, probably because the Vedic people used the horse extensively. Horses usually draw the chariots of the gods and the horse seems to represent the sun's rays, fire and knowledge. Among the Vedic deities, the ASHVINS are closely associated with horses, while the KINNARAS have human heads with horse's bodies. Mythical or semi-mythical horses mentioned in the RIG VEDA include DADHIKRA, TARKSHYA and Paidva, a white horse. Etasha, meaning swift, is the name of a horse who draws the chariot of SURYA, the sun god. The horse is also symbolic of AGNI, the sacrificial fire. The rishi DADHYANCH's head was replaced by that of a horse, and in later texts HAYAGRIVA, an incarnation of VISHNU, had his head replaced by that of a horse. UCHCHHAISHRAVAS, the king of horses, appeared at the churning of the ocean for AMRITA.

The ASHVAMEDHA, or horse sacrifice, was conducted as a mark of kingly power. Horses were associated with warriors and revered, possibly for their role in battle. Guardian deities such as AYYANAR ride on horses and are usually depicted on a horse. In some areas, terracotta horses are offered annually at ancestor shrines.

Horses have a role in several other ancient and medieval cultures. In Europe, wooden horse heads were carved on house-gables for protection. Horses also occur in Greek, Roman and other myths.

hotr   One of the four main priests who officiate at Vedic sacrifices and ceremonies, described in the SHRAUTA SUTRAS and other texts.

Hoysaleshvara Temple   A temple of the Hindu god SHIVA constructed in the twelfth century, located at HALEBID in Karnataka. It was built at the time of the Hoysala rulers Vishnuvardhana and Narasimha, and is in the typical style of Hoysala temples. There are two identical structures, each with an inner shrine and a columned MANDAPA. The two mandapas are linked, forming a large space. The temple is raised on a high plinth, carved with rows of elephants, horses, lions, geese and makaras, as well as *MAHABHARATA* and *RAMAYANA* scenes. The sculptures on the outer walls include BRAHMA seated on a goose, a dancing SHIVA, and KRISHNA raising the mountain GOVARDHANA. In front of each mandapa is a NANDI image in a detached pavilion. Guardian deities flank the doorways.

Hujwiri   A SUFI saint. *See* Abul Hasan al-Hujwiri.

hukam-nama   A term for a Sikh edict, a command or request to the community or to a particular person. Hukam-namas were issued by the Sikh gurus, and those of the later gurus have been preserved. These provide information on spiritual questions, apart from being useful historical sources. Hukam-namas are still issued by Sikh religious authorities.

humata   A term in the AVESTA language of Zoroastrianism that means 'good thoughts'. The basic motto of the religion is: 'Humata, huvakta, huvarashta', or 'Good thoughts, good words, good deeds'. In the later Pahlavi, the words are 'Manashni, gavashni, kunashni'.

Hume, Allan Octavian   A Theosophist who was one of the founders of the Indian National Congress.

Born in 1829, Hume was an Englishman who joined the Indian Civil Service in 1849 and retired in 1882.

As a Theosophist, he claimed that he was in touch with a secret sect of mahatmas, or spiritual masters, and SANNYASIS, who told him that a revolt on a large scale was imminent in India unless the Indians were given an outlet to express their problems and demands. He said he had met Master KUTHUMI of the Theosophical hierarchy, and urged Lord Dufferin, the then viceroy, to meet him as well. Though Dufferin might not have met Kuthumi, he was persuaded by Hume to allow the founding of the Indian National Congress in 1885, to provide a forum of expression for educated Indians. Hume's role in founding the Congress is recognized, but his reasons for it and the alleged role of the secret masters have largely been forgotten.

Hume died in 1912.

Husain ibn Ali The grandson of the Prophet MUHAMMAD. Born in 626, he was the second son of Ali ibn Abi Talim and Fatima, the daughter of Muhammad. The SHIAS considered him and his elder brother Hasan as the successors of Ali in the leadership of the community. Ali's son Hasan was chosen as his successor but abdicated when opposed by Muawiya, the governor of Syria. Husain fought against Muawiya, and at a great battle at Karbala in Iraq, was defeated and killed. This took place on the tenth day (ASHURA) of the month of MUHARRAM in 680, since then observed as a day of mourning.

hvare kshaeta A term for the sun in the Zoroastrian *GATHAS*. The *Gathas* state that the light of the sun is precious in the eyes of the good mind (*Yasna* 50.10) and that the sun symbolizes truth and wisdom. The implication here is similar to statements made in the UPANISHADS. The later term for the sun, personified as a YAZATA, was Khorshed or Khursheed.

ibadat A term in Islam indicating God's commands regarding the basic duties of a Muslim. These include prayer, fasting, charity and HAJ or pilgrimage.

Ibadat Khana The name of a hall set up in 1575 by the Mughal emperor AKBAR (ruled 1556–1605) at Fatehpur Sikri for discussing aspects of religion. Initially only Muslims, particularly SUNNIS, were invited for these religious debates. Mulla Abdul Qadir Badauni, a Sunni who had joined Akbar's court in 1574, was among the first to be invited to the Ibadat Khana, along with ABUL FAZL. Both had been trained by Shaikh Mubarak, Abul Fazl's father. Early discussions included criticisms of the ULAMA of the court.

In 1577 Akbar had a mystical experience while on a hunting expedition, and on his return showed an interest in all religions. Representatives of Shias, Christians, Hindus, Jains and Zoroastrians all joined in debates and discussions at the Ibadat Khana. Akbar now believed that all religions contained divine truths, and thus founded his own method of worship, the DIN-I ILAHI or Tauhid-i Ilahi.

Iblis A term for a devil in Islam. Iblis was once an angel or a JINN, but refused to obey ALLAH when he was asked to bow down to Adam, though all the other angels did so. According to the QURAN, Allah then said, 'What prevented thee from prostrating when I commanded thee?' He replied, 'I am better than he; Thou didst create me from fire and him from clay.' (7.12–13). Then Allah cast him out of heaven. Iblis gained the power to lead unbelievers astray.

Some of the SUFI saints see Iblis in a different light, as one who loved God exceedingly and therefore would not bow down before Adam. For instance, Ainul Quzat, the Sufi saint martyred at Baghdad in 1098, wrote in the *Tamhidat*: 'That mad lover whom you call Iblis in this world—do you not know by what name he is called in the divine world? If you know his name, by calling him by that name you know yourself an unbeliever . . . This mad one loved God.' (Trans. A.J. Arberry)

Ibn al-Arabi Muhyiuddin A SUFI saint who put forward the doctrine of WAHDAT AL-WUJUD. Though he was not the first to describe the unity of God, he clarified this concept, and all future followers of this doctrine based their ideas on his works.

Born in 1165 at Murcia in the south-east of Spain, al-Arabi belonged to the Arab tribe of Tai. After a mystical vision, he became a Sufi and studied under several shaikhs and at the same time claimed that the truth was revealed to him by divine inspiration. He wrote a number of works and composed mystical poetry. Much of his philosophy is summarized in *Al-Futuhat al-Makkiya* (Meccan Discourses) and *Fusus al-Hikam* (Gems of Wisdom). To Ibn al-Arabi, the whole world is a manifestation of the divine. Thus all religions, irrespective of how they worship the Absolute, are identical. People who strive for true knowledge cannot reject other religions. Al-Arabi said that idol worship or polytheism is not wrong, as long as there is a recognition that it is a form or aspect of God, and that through it only the Absolute, or the One God, is being worshipped.

His ideas thus marked a turning point in Islamic philosophy. He died in 1240 at Damascus where he had settled, and his grave is still worshipped.

Ibn Sina An Islamic philosopher and physician who lived from 980 to 1037. He is also known as AVICENNA.

Ibrahim The Islamic name of Abraham of the BIBLE. According to the QURAN, he was one of the six prophets to whom ALLAH conveyed his special laws. Islamic tradition holds that he rebuilt the KABA and started the HAJ.

I-Ching/I-Tsing A Chinese Buddhist pilgrim who came to India in the seventh century and visited several Buddhist sites. He studied HINAYANA and MAHAYANA Buddhism at NALANDA. After spending twenty years in India he returned to China in 695, carrying with him more than 400 Mahayana texts. He is said to have translated fifty-six texts into Chinese.

Id A term in Islam which indicates a festival or festivity. It is said to be derived from the Arabic word *ood* or *oud*, meaning 'return' or 'coming again' because it returns every year.

Ida (1) A deity, also known as ILA.

(2) A passage of energy in the human body. The Ida Nadi is to the left of the SUSHUMNA, the central channel through which the KUNDALINI is said to rise.

Id-i-Milad A Muslim festival (also known as Bara Wafat or Milad-ul Nabi) that commemorates the birthday of the Prophet MUHAMMAD. It is the twelfth day of the month of Rabi-ul-awwal, when the Prophet was born. On this day prayers are offered and *Milad-Sharif*, or accounts of the Prophet's life, are recited. There are different versions of these in a mix of prose and verse, and the verse sections are usually sung in chorus. Sweets are distributed and the poor are fed.

Id-ul-Azha or Zuha A term for a Muslim festival, more commonly known in India as BAKR-ID, celebrated on the tenth day of the month of Zilhajja. Azha or Zuha comes from the word UZHAIYYA or sacrifice.

Id-ul-Fitr A special festival for Muslims that takes pace on the first day of the month of Shawwal, the tenth month in the ISLAMIC CALENDAR, when the fast of the month of RAMZAN ends. Fitr is a donation that is made on the breaking of the fast. On this day Muslims visit mosques to attend the Id prayers, wear new clothes, eat special food, and greet their neighbours and friends. Before the prayers, a donation of a certain amount of cereal is distributed to the poor. It is a day to recollect the spiritual benefits of abstinence during the fast, as well as a day of celebration and thanksgiving.

Traditionally, on the day of Id or one day before, sugar, milk, dry and fresh fruits, sweets and a gift of money are sent by brothers to their sisters, and by parents to their married daughters. Children receive 'Idi' or a small amount of money, which they can spend as they like.

iftar A term in Islam for the breaking of the fast every evening in the month of RAMZAN. Muslims fast from dawn and in the evening after sunset a siren or a gun shot indicates the time to end the fast for the day. The fast is broken with a few dates or other items, followed by the evening prayers and then the main meal.

ijma A term in Islamic law for consensus. Different interpretations of Islamic law are possible and therefore agreement is sought on various issues. Initially a consensus of the whole community was required, but later agreement among certain learned groups was sufficient. Ijma is one of the four main sources of SHARIA or Islamic law.

ijtihad A term in Islamic law that literally means 'exertion' but has been explained as 'the exertion of mental energy for a legal opinion to the extent that the faculties of the jurists become incapable of further effort'. It implies using reasoning by analogy (qiyas) and informed opinion (ra'y) on questions of law not dealt with in the QURAN and SUNNAH. Initially, any individual could attempt this, but later only the mujtahid (experts in law) could do so. Their consensus or IJMA on these issues became law. According to several modern scholars, by the tenth century the four orthodox schools of SUNNI law declared that

ijtihad was completed and should not be modified. Instead there was to be taqlid, or emulation, implying following what was already laid down, and therefore Sunni law was unchangeable from this time. Other scholars, including W.B. Hallaq and Muzaffar Alam, believe that in India ijtihad was not closed and that the four schools of Sunni jurisprudence continued to develop even in the Mughal period and later. In the early twentieth century, however, Muhammad IQBAL called for a reopening of ijtihad, indicating that at this time it was generally considered closed. Muzaffar Alam points out that it was colonial rule, not only in India but in other parts of the Islamic world, that led to rigid and stereotyped views of Islam.

Certain modern groups, including both moderates and fundamentalists, favour the reopening of ijtihad—the moderates in order to reinterpret laws in the light of changing times, and the fundamentalists to remove innovations that they consider incorrect.

As for SHIAS, mujtahids were allowed to continue ijtihad.

Ikshvaku A legendary king who ruled at AYODHYA in very ancient days. He was the son of MANU VAIVASVATA and the founder of the Suryavamshi or solar dynasties.

Ila/Ida (1) A goddess, mentioned in the RIG VEDA. The name means nourishment and Ila was the personification of the offering of milk and butter, which represents the nourishment provided by the cow. In the Rig Veda, she is called butter-footed and butter-handed, and AGNI is once said to be her son. In the *Shatapatha Brahmana*, she is the daughter of MANU or of MITRA-VARUNA. According to the *Taittiriya Samhita*, Manu sent her to see whether the sacrifice of the DEVAS and ASURAS had been conducted properly. She said their sacrifice was incorrect and described the correct way, as a result of which the devas attained prosperity. Through Ila, Manu gave birth to the human race.

(2) In later texts, Ila is a mythical person, both a woman and a man. She is described as the daughter of Manu Vaivasvata by his wife Shraddha. IKSHVAKU was her brother. According to the *BHAGAVATA PURANA*, Manu performed a sacrifice in order to get a son, but instead, Ila was born. He complained to the rishi VASISHTHA, who turned Ila into a boy named Sudyumna. By a curse of SHIVA he was again turned into a woman. The woman Ila met BUDHA (Mercury) and the two fell in love, married, and had a son named PURURAVA. However, Ila was not happy as a woman, and by the intervention of Vasishtha, Shiva agreed that she could be a man in alternate months. As Sudyumna, she was later taught by the rishi NARADA and attained salvation by worshipping the Hindu goddess DEVI.

(3) Ila was the daughter of the god VAYU, and married to DHRUVA. She had a son named Utkala.

Ilm-e-Khshnoom The 'Science of Spiritual Bliss', an esoteric Zoroastrian school founded by Behramshah

Navroz SHROFF (1857–1927). Behramshah claimed that he was taught the hidden truths of Zoroastrianism during his youth in a secret paradise that he visited, though he began to reveal these truths only in 1907–08. Later, Framroze Chiniwalla was authorized by Shroff to present the teachings. The Ilm-e-Khshnoom has an extensive literature that seeks to understand and explain the hidden meaning behind Zoroastrian stories and rituals. It has two main parts, the first presenting the principles and the second dealing with esoteric aspects. For instance, it states that the marriage of ZARATHUSHTRA represents only a mystical union with the divine, and his six children represent the AMESHA SPENTAS or powers of God. It divides the world into Hasti, the divine creation, and Nisti, the sphere of non-physical energies. Every word in the AVESTA is said to be a powerhouse of spiritual energy. The sect also believes in the observation of all ancient rituals. The three standard advanced textbooks of Khshnoom are known as Nikeez volumes and include interpretations of the prayers, YASHTS, *GATHAS* and other texts. The Khshnoom presents the mystical side of the religion and has a limited following among PARSIS in India.

imam   A title for Muslim religious leaders, used in different ways. Imam is a title for those who lead the prayers in mosques. In the QURAN, it refers to IBRAHIM and other religious leaders. Later it referred to the spiritual successors of the Prophet MUHAMMAD, and SUNNIS used it as synonymous with Caliph or Khalif. They acknowledge the first four Sunni Caliphs and the four founders of the orthodox schools of law as imams. Different SHIA sects recognize various imams. The ISNA ASHARI Shias follow twelve imams, of whom the twelfth is the hidden imam who will reappear as the MAHDI. The Zaidis believe that the fifth imam was Zaid ibn Ali (d. 740) and are his followers. The ISMAILIS take Ismail (d. 760) as the true seventh imam.

Imambara, Great   A huge vaulted structure located at Lucknow in Uttar Pradesh, constructed in 1784 by Nawab Asaf-ud Daula and dedicated to three early IMAMS: Ali, Hasan and HUSAIN. It is also known as the Bara Imambara or Asafi Imambara. The structure has a length of 50 m and a height of 15 m, the entrance being through a square gateway. To the west is the Asafi mosque, with two minarets, while an outer staircase leads to a series of labyrinths. The central hall is said to be the largest vaulted chamber in the world.

iman   An Islamic term for faith. There are SIX PRINCIPLES OF ISLAMIC FAITH, which are considered essential. These are belief in ALLAH, the angels, the prophets, the QURAN, the day of judgment and the Divine Decree.

Inayat Khan, Hazrat   A SUFI saint. Inayat Khan was born in Vadodara (Baroda) in 1882 in an atmosphere of spirituality and music. His father was Mashaik Rahmat Khan, while his mother, Begam Khadija, was from a landed family of Mysore. His grandfather, Maula Baksh, was the court musician of the maharaja of Baroda, and had founded a music institution known as Gayana Shala. From his father's side, Inayat was the descendent of a Muslim saint or PIR known as Jammashah.

Inayat studied music at the Gayana Shala and became a great singer. He also played the Sarasvati vina and performed and sang at the courts of various rulers in India. He became a disciple of the Sufi saint Syed Abu Hashim Madani of Hyderabad and was initiated into the CHISTI and QALANDAR orders by him.

In 1910, at the age of twenty-eight, he travelled abroad along with his brothers, who were also singers and musicians and performed Hindustani and Karnatak music at concerts all over Europe and America. Inayat also founded the Sufi Movement, preached on SUFISM and had a large number of followers. He returned to India in 1926 and died the following year in New Delhi. His speeches were later collected and published in twenty-four volumes. His brothers and other disciples continued the Sufi Movement that he had founded. The Hazrat Inayat Khan Memorial Trust was founded to spread his message and take care of his DARGAH.

Hazrat Inayat spoke on a variety of different topics, explaining the inner meaning of myths, symbols and concepts in all religions. His underlying theme is of love, unity and divine knowledge.

Indo-Aryan languages   A term for a group of languages spoken in India which have developed from Sanskrit, the language of the RIG VEDA. Regional and colloquial variants began to develop from early times and included PALI and various Prakrit languages, including Ardha Magadhi, Maharashtri and other variants. Languages of this group today include Hindi and its dialects including Hindustani, Rajasthani, Avadhi, Bagheli, Chhattisgarhi and Bihari, as well as Garhwali, Kumaoni and other hill dialects; Punjabi, Sindhi, Marathi, Konkani, Gujarati, Oriya, Bengali and Assamese. All these languages have local variants.

Kashmiri is also considered Indo-Aryan. Some believe it is derived from Dardic and not Sanskrit, but Dardic is also usually thought to be a branch of Indo-Aryan. Indo-Aryan is related to INDO-IRANIAN and INDO-EUROPEAN languages.

Indo-European languages   A term used for a group of languages which are today spread across Asia and Europe, and which are presumed to have originated from one language, termed Proto-Indo-European. The spread of the language has been related to the migration of people at an uncertain date in the distant past. Various dates have been suggested for the possible spread of Proto Indo-European in parts of Europe and the Middle East, including 6000 BCE, 4000 BCE, or even earlier. The diffusion into Iran and India is thought to have been later. The languages which are derived from Indo-European have been identified as: Germanic languages, including English, German, Dutch, Danish, Swedish, Norwegian, Icelandic; Romanic languages, including French, Spanish, Portuguese, Italian, Romanian and Greek; Balto-Slavic languages, including Russian, Polish, Ukranian, Czech, Slovak, Serbo-Croatian and Bulgarian; INDO-IRANIAN languages, including Persian and Sanskrit, and their derivatives. Armenian and Albanian are sometimes included in the latter group. Welsh, Irish and extinct Anatolian, Illyrian and Tocharian language groups are also part of the Indo-European family.

Several Indo-European groups have some common religious practices, such as the worship of sky and earth deities, deities associated with nature, and fire sacrifices. There are also similarities in myths. William JONES was one of the first to point out similarities in the languages, while G. Dumezil (1898–1986) was among those who revealed some of the common aspects of the various Indo-European groups and developed the TRIPARTITE IDEOLOGY.

Indo-Iranian language A term used for a language derived from INDO-EUROPEAN, from which both Iranian and INDO-ARYAN languages are thought to have developed. The close similarities between the languages of the *GATHAS* and of the RIG VEDA, as well as similarities between RIG VEDIC DEITIES and YAZATAS or Zoroastrian deities, have led scholars to presume that Iranians and Indo-Aryans were once a united people with a common homeland. The inverted use of some words, such as DAEVAS for demons in AVESTA (whereas DEVA is a god in the Rig Veda), and AHURA for god (whereas ASURA is a demon in later Hinduism), have led some scholars to believe there was an early conflict between the two groups, while others point out that there are more similarities than differences. Recent research on the Bactria–Margiana Archaeological Complex, extending from Margiana in southern Turkmenistan to Afghanistan and Baluchistan, suggests that this region may have been the early homeland.

Indra A Hindu deity. The most important deity in the RIG VEDA, Indra is described in this text as the god of thunder who conquers the demons of drought and darkness, bringing water and light. He is also the god of wars and battles, and is the dominant deity of the middle region, pervading the air. His weapon is the VAJRA or thunderbolt, which is golden and metallic. He is married to INDRANI, though sometimes other female consorts are mentioned. He is associated with the MARUTS and loves drinking SOMA. He is the slayer of the chief of dragons, VRITRA, who was obstructing the waters, and is also known as Purandara or 'breaker of forts'. He was the friend and defender of his worshippers. He had a female dog named SARAMA who helped him in one of his battles. In the *MAHABHARATA*, he is the father of ARJUNA, the third of the PANDAVA brothers.

In later texts, he became secondary to BRAHMA, VISHNU and SHIVA, and is one of the DIKAPALAS, the guardian of the eastern quarter. In the PURANAS, he is the eldest of the thirty-three sons of KASHYAPA and ADITI. There are several other stories about him, including one in which he lost a challenge to KRISHNA. He appears in a secondary position in Buddhist and Jain myths and sculptures.

Indra's mount is the white elephant AIRAVATA and his horse is UCHCHAISHRAVAS. His consort is also known as Shachi or Pulomaja. His city is AMARAVATI and his mansion is known as Vaijayanta. The trees in his heaven include Mandara, PARIJATA, Santana, Kalpavriksha and Harichandana. In images he is depicted holding a vajra and riding his elephant, or in scenes with other deities.

In the AVESTA, his name occurs twice as that of a demon, but also as the deity VERETHRAGHNA.

Indrani A Hindu deity, the wife of INDRA. She is mentioned in the RIG VEDA and the BRAHMANAS. In the PURANAS, she is the daughter of the DAITYA Puloma. She is worshipped as one of the MATRIKAS or mothers.

Indraprastha An ancient city that has been identified with a portion of modern DELHI. In the *MAHABHARATA*, it was the capital of the PANDAVAS. Settlements here have been dated from c. 1000 BCE to medieval times.

Indus Civilization, religion of An urban civilization that existed in the region of the river Indus and its tributaries, the river SARASVATI, and areas further south. It is also called the Indus Valley Civilization, Indus–Sarasvati Civilization and the Harappan Civilization, and can be dated between 2500 and 1800 BCE. The largest civilization of the contemporary ancient world, it covered an area of 12,99,600 sq. km, stretching from Baluchistan, Punjab and Sind in present-day Pakistan, and across Punjab, Haryana, Rajasthan, DELHI and Gujarat in India. The civilization had planned cities, brick-built houses and an elaborate drainage system. Among the major cities were Mohenjodaro and Harappa (now part of Pakistan), Kalibangan in Rajasthan, Dholavira and Lothal in Gujarat.

As its script has not been satisfactorily deciphered, most of the evidence for its religion comes from numerous stone or steatite seals. In addition, there are flat copper tablets, as well as figures depicted in bronze and stone, and a number of terracotta human and animal figurines. There are also certain unique architectural structures. On the basis of these, scholars have formed tentative and varying conclusions about the nature of the religion of the civilization. Some of the key features are given below.

(1) Horned deity: Some seals and copper tablets of the Indus Civilization depict a horned person, usually identified as a deity. The most famous of these depictions is a seal with a figure wearing a horned

headdress, seated in a yogic posture. On this seal he appears to be ithyphallic and possibly three-faced. It is not clear if the faces are human or animal. Under his seat are two goats or deer, and around him are a rhinoceros, a buffalo, a tiger and an elephant. Marshall, who first excavated Mohenjodaro, labelled this as a deity, a proto or early form of SHIVA. However, the identification of the deity with Shiva-Pashupati, the lord of animals, has been questioned, as Pashupati was the guardian of domestic animals and was not associated with wild animals. Others identified him with the Vedic AGNI or RUDRA. Shubhangana Atre, using in addition other seals with a similar deity, interpreted this as a form of the goddess Diana. Jains identify this deity with an early Jain TIRTHANKARA.

The deity shows a remarkable similarity to the early Celtic god Cernnunos, particularly to an image found on a cauldron at Gundestrup in Denmark, dated between the sixth and fourth centuries BCE (In New Age revivalism, Cernnunos is worshipped as the god of Wicca or witches, along with Diana as the goddess.)

In later times there were other horned deities in India, including tribal deities, NAIGAMESHA, a Jain deity, and several more. There are horned and forest deities in other parts of the ancient world as well.

(2) Mother goddess: Female figurines in terracotta, found at several sites, are thought to represent worship of a mother goddess, though this has been questioned. More questionable is the identification of 'ring stones' of various sizes with the YONI, or feminine emblem.

(3) Male images: Sculptures of men have been found at Mohenjodaro and lately at Dholavira in Gujarat, and a stone bust of an imposing bearded man is well known, though it is not clear if this was a deity or an important person. He has been thought by some to represent a priest-king. There are also phallic objects, sometimes identified as early LINGAS.

(3) Animals: There are numerous animal terracotta figurines, and animals are also depicted on seals. The terracotta figures include domestic animals and are generally thought to have been toys. On seals, the humped bull is the only domestic animal depicted, the rest being wild animals, including elephants, tigers, rhinoceros, buffalo, deer and antelope, a one-horned animal like a unicorn, as well as crocodiles and fish. In some seals, a bull or a unicorn is shown in front of an altar or incense brazier. There are also birds and hybrid half-human and animal figures.

(4) Trees: Trees are depicted, particularly pipal trees and leaves. Some seals have figures in trees, including a horned figure, who may be tree deities; tree worship could have taken place.

(5) Other: A tank-like structure at Mohenjodaro, commonly called the Great Bath, was possibly used for ritual bathing; fire pits found at Kalibangan are thought to suggest fire sacrifices.

Without the help of a written script, analyses of the religion of this civilization are many and varied. Some see in it proto-Hinduism; others identify the culture with that of the RIG VEDA, or with an indigenous Dravidian culture later displaced by the Vedic. Still others see elements of Shamanism, animism, or folk religions. No definite conclusions can be reached at present.

Inquisition The term for a Roman Catholic tribunal, to discover and punish heresy, that was set up in several parts of the world in medieval days. The Portuguese introduced the Inquisition in GOA in western India in 1560. King John III had earlier set it up in Portugal to prevent the REFORMATION and the ideas of Calvin and Luther from taking hold. In Goa the Inquisition aimed to eliminate 'superstitious' beliefs and idol worship. It was suspended in 1774 but revived in 1779, though not with the same fervour, and was finally abolished in 1812 on the recommendation of the British who had a garrison in Goa. Between 1561 and 1774, 16,172 cases were tried by the Goan Inquisition, of which 4046 were sentenced to various forms of punishment. About 119 'Acts of Faith' (trials by torture) were held, and 105 men and women were condemned to be burnt to death. Of these, fifty-seven actually were burnt.

The Inquisition building no longer exists. It was located in Old Goa, in what was previously the residence of the Portuguese viceroys. It has been described as a huge building with a large hall, as well as several other halls, rooms, and prison cells.

inshallah A phrase used in Islam, meaning 'if God wills'. It is often used even by non-Muslims.

International Society of Krishna Consciousness (ISKCON) A religious society set up in 1965 in New York by A.C. Bhaktivedanta Swami PRABHUPADA. The aim of the society, which has branches in many countries, including India, is to lead people towards the realization of Oneness or of unity with God. CHAITANYA MAHAPRABHU and the Hindu god KRISHNA form the inspiration for the movement. The texts of the movement include the early VEDAS, later Vedic literature, the MAHABHARATA, RAMAYANA and PURANAS, but above all the BHAGAVAD GITA. Bhaktivedanta Swami Prabhupada's extensive commentaries on some of these texts are also important for the philosophy of the sect. The sect uses the basic mantra 'Hare Rama Hare Krishna' and believes that the ultimate goal is union with Krishna. Swami Prabhupada states that realizing BRAHMAN is the first stage, though several philosophies take this as the ultimate goal. The second stage is the realization of Paramatma, the 'Supersoul', while the 'Supreme Personality of Godhead is the ultimate realization of the Absolute Truth'.

In another passage, he sums up his philosophy: 'In this present day, man is very eager to have one scripture, one God, one religion, and one occupation. So let there be one common scripture for the whole world—Bhagavad Gita. And let there be one God only

for the whole world—Sri Krishna, Krishna, Hare Hare/
Hare Rama, Hare Rama, Rama Rama, Hare Hare. And
let there be one work only—the service of the Supreme
personality of the Godhead.'

The organization soon spread throughout the world
and includes both lay followers and SANNYASIS. The
concepts of discipleship, the guru and an unbroken
parampara (spiritual lineage), form an important part
of ISKCON. Swami Prabhupada died in 1977 and after
his death a governing body was set up to look after
the affairs of the organization. ISKCON has a number
of branches in India and runs schools and hospitals
and disseminates information on Krishna and his
worship.

Iqbal, Muhammad   An Islamic philosopher and
a poet in Urdu and Persian. Born in 1877 in Sialkot,
now in Pakistan, he studied at Lahore and Cambridge,
and received a doctorate from Munich, Germany. He
also became a lawyer and was admitted to the bar in
London.

Iqbal was initially inspired by the SUFI thought of
IBN AL-ARABI and spoke of Hindu-Muslim unity. In
later years he was more influenced by the thought
of AHMAD SIRHINDI. After going to Europe, he began
to have a different perspective on Islam in India. In
1909 he said, 'I have myself been of the view that
religious differences should disappear from this
country . . . But now I think that the preservation of
their separate national entities is desirable for both the
Hindus and the Muslims.'

In his poem *Asrar-i-Khudi* (Secrets of the Self),
published in Persian in 1915 and later translated
into English, he put forward a concept of the
individual self or ego, a self with desire and purpose,
which must strive for development. He feels the self
should be 'massive in nature, like mountains', and
should become God's viceroy on earth. In his next
philosophical poem, translated as *The Mysteries of
Selflessness*, he said that the self-affirming individual
formed a part of the community and should act on its
behalf. He turned away from what he believed were
weaknesses, such as Christian meekness or Hindu
vegetarianism and non-violence. He also wrote and
spoke about reform in Islam. In a series of six lectures
entitled 'The Reconstruction of Religious Thought in
Islam' delivered in Chennai (Madras) in 1929, Iqbal
stated that he believed Islam should be reinterpreted
in the light of modern developments. He wanted
a reopening of IJTIHAD and a new look at scholastic
theology or *ilm-e-kalam*. He believed that the SHARIA
was not inviolable and should be reconstructed for
modern times. Only religious obligations or IBADAT
were beyond change. A reinterpretation of personal
law was definitely required.

His collections of poems include *Bang-i Dara* (Caravan
Bells), early poems in Urdu; *Bal-i Jibril* (Gabriel's Wing),
later Urdu poems; and his poems in Persian.

He is best remembered in India for his song, '*Sare
jahan se accha, Hindustan hamara*' (Of all places, India
is the best). Iqbal's philosophy can be summed up as
a call to action, a belief that individuals should not be
passive, but should act to create a better world.

He died in 1938.

Iravateshvara Temple   A temple of the Hindu
god SHIVA constructed in the eighth century, located
at KANCHIPURAM, Tamil Nadu. The small inner shrine
is square with a pyramidal roof. On the walls, Shiva
is depicted in different forms, in a yogic pose in the
north, as NATARAJA in the west and DAKSHINAMURTI in
the south.

Isa   A term for JESUS in India. Jesus is referred to by
this name in Islam and in some Indian languages.

Isha Upanishad   A Sanskrit text, a verse UPANISHAD
that can be dated between about 600 and 300 BCE.
This short Upanishad of eighteen verses, contains
the essence of Upanishadic philosophy. As one of its
verses states:

He moves, and he moves not. He is far and he is
near. He is within all and he is outside all.

Who sees all beings in his own Self, and his own Self
in all beings, loses all fear. (Trans. Juan Mascaro)

ishtadevata   A term in Hinduism for a personal
deity. It can refer to any deity the individual has
chosen as his/her own special deity. It can also be the
chosen deity of a family or group.

Ishvara   God, or lord, a name which can be applied
to any Hindu deity. Ishvara is considered a form of
BRAHMAN, the Absolute.

Islam   The religion of Muslims as revealed by the
prophet MUHAMMAD, who lived from 570 to 632.
Literally, Islam means 'submission' in Arabic, and
implies a total surrender to the will of ALLAH. Islam
accepts a series of Prophets beginning with Adam and
ending with Muhammad. All the Prophets transmit
the word of Allah, but at the time of Muhammad
people had forgotten God's words and gone astray,
therefore a new revelation was required. The word
of God as conveyed to Muhammad was compiled in
the QURAN, which contains 114 suras or chapters. The
Quran states, 'We believe in Allah and that which is
revealed unto us, and that which was revealed unto
Ibrahim (Abraham), and Ishmael, and Isaac, and
Yaqub (Jacob) and the tribes, and that which Musa
(Moses) and Isa (Jesus) received, and that which
the Prophets received from their Lord. We make no
distinction between any of them, and unto Him we
have surrendered'. The Quran defines the nature of
God and provides a new version of the earlier Biblical
Prophets and some of the stories in the Bible, and is
said to supersede all earlier texts. It includes beliefs,
religious duties (IBADAT) and right actions.

Another body of literature that grew around the Quran are the HADIS or traditions. They contain various accounts of Muhammad's life and actions, which are to be emulated. The truths of the Hadis are compiled in the SUNNAH.

The basics of Islam are contained in the SIX PRINCIPLES of the faith, which are belief in Allah, his angels, the holy books (of the Prophets), the Prophets, the last day or day of Judgement, and the decrees of God. In addition there are basic duties to be performed, namely, the FIVE PILLARS OF THE FAITH: the profession of faith, prayer, fasting in the month of RAMZAN, pilgrimage or HAJ, and charity. JIHAD, or striving in the way of God, is sometimes considered the sixth.

Differences in the interpretation of the religion, and on the successors of Muhammad, soon arose, and two main sects of SUNNIS and SHIAS emerged, each with their own schools of law and beliefs. Within them there were further divisions and subdivisions, while there were also several SUFI sects, with their own practices and ideas.

History Islamic sects and practices are linked with the history of Islam. The religion was born in Mecca, a city located to the north-west of the Arabian peninsula. The KABA, a cube-like shrine, was located here and was the centre of pilgrimage for tribals and city dwellers. About 450 km north of Mecca was Yasrib, later known as Medina. In this region there were Jewish clans, as well as various tribes, and Bedouins in the north-west. While the Jews followed their religious traditions, the tribes worshipped various deities. The Kaba had around it a number of idols propitiated by the tribes including that of the deity Hubal. After the new religion was revealed to MUHAMMAD, his wife Khadija and his cousin Ali were among his first followers. Muhammad began to preach this religion, with its emphasis on one God, Allah. He advocated social equality and justice and condemned idol worship. To differentiate his religion from those of the tribes, Muhammad advocated praying while facing the direction of Jerusalem. He accepted many of the Jewish laws, but the Jews could not accept Muhammad as the new Prophet. In Mecca, he and his followers faced persecution. In 622, Muhammad was persuaded to move to Yasrib (Medina). This immigration (HIJRAH) was later taken as the starting point of the Islamic era.

In 624, Jews were further alienated when Allah commanded Muhammad to pray facing the Kaba, instead of Jerusalem.

Muslims soon had to defend themselves against attacks from Bedouins, Meccans and Jews. After a series of successful battles, Muhammad re-entered Mecca in 630. He then destroyed the idols in the Kaba and established it as the centre of Islamic pilgrimage.

After Muhammad's death in 632, some of his followers elected Abu Bakr as Muhammad's successor.

He was known as the Caliph (meaning 'successor' in Arabic). Others felt Muhammad had stated that Ali, his cousin and son-in-law, was to be his successor, and did not accept Abu Bakr. They were known as SHIAS (partisans) of Ali. The first group later came to be known as SUNNIS.

Umar al Khattab succeeded Abu Bakr and was Caliph from 634–44. Syria, Palestine, Egypt, Iran and Iraq were conquered at this time. Umar was assassinated in 644 and Usman was elected Caliph. However, there was dissension among various groups and he was killed in 656. Ali was then persuaded to become the Caliph to save the community from disintegrating. Ali also had to face opposition and fight a number of battles, and was finally assassinated in 661. His son Hasan was chosen as his successor but was opposed by Muawiya, governor of Syria. Hasan abdicated and Muawiya ruled, founding the dynasty of Ummayads and making Damascus his capital. Muawiya nominated his son Yazid as his successor, but this was opposed by HUSAIN, brother of Hasan, and other prominent Muslims. A historic battle was fought at Karbala in Iraq, and Husain and his followers were killed. The tragic circumstances of Husain's death led to widespread unrest, and in 750 the Umayyads were overthrown. The Abbasids, who claimed descent from the Prophet's uncle Abbas, ruled from 750 to 1258. Both Ummayads and Abbasids were known as Caliphs but were in fact hereditary monarchs.

By this time the religion was well established and had spread to a number of other countries, including India.

Islam in India India has a population of 13,81,88,240 Muslims, comprising 13.4 per cent of the total population (2001 census). According to statistics, this is the third largest number of Muslims in any country in the world, the largest being in Indonesia. The influence of Islam in India was initially through Arab traders on the southern and western coasts. In 712, the Arabs invaded Sind and conquered the region, bringing Islam to the area. A further extension of Islam began in the eleventh century, with the invasion of India by Mahmud of Ghazni (Afghanistan), who retained control over the Punjab. Muhammad of Ghur followed in the twelfth century, and his successors established the rule of sultans at DELHI. The first sultan was a Turk, Qutbuddin Aibak (ruled 1206–10), who was followed by Iltutmish (1211–36), his daughter Razia, the noble Balban, and other weak rulers. Successive dynasties of sultans included the Khaljis, Tughlaqs, Sayyids and Lodis, who were all either Afghans or Turks. With the decline of centralized power, independent kingdoms were established. Those under Islamic rulers included kingdoms in Kashmir, Bengal, Gujarat, Malwa and Jaunpur. In the Deccan, the Bahmani kingdom emerged, later breaking up into the five kingdoms of

Bijapur, Ahmadnagar, Golkonda, Bidar and Berar.

The Lodis had already declined when Babar, a Chagatai Turk, invaded India and founded the Mughal empire in 1526. Babar was followed by Humayun, AKBAR, Jahangir, Shah Jahan and AURANGZEB. Humayun lost the throne for a while, during which time the Afghan Sur dynasty ruled.

The Mughals prospered till the time of Aurangzeb, after which the empire declined, but small independent or semi-independent states emerged, several under Muslim rulers. These included Avadh, Rohilkhand and Farrukhabad in the north, Bengal in the east, and Hyderabad in the Deccan. Further south, Haidar Ali established a kingdom in 1761, and was succeeded by his son Tipu Sultan.

By this time the British and other Europeans had made inroads into India and defeated a number of local rulers. The revolt of 1857 against the British was led by Bahadur Shah Zaffar, the last Mughal emperor, who was then sent into exile in Yangon (Rangoon). The British now ruled much of India, but Indian states, with some British control, continued to exist. Those under nawabs or other Muslim rulers included Bahawalpur, Tonk, Junagadh, Bhopal and Hyderabad.

Muslims lived in these states and in other provinces and states across India. Initially those in India consisted of Turks, Afghans and Iranians, as well as many indigenous converts. At the courts there were conflicts among the foreign and non-foreign nobles, and in some areas between Sunnis and Shias. Most Mughals were SUNNIS, while there were SHIAS in the Deccan.

With this political background, several levels and types of Islam existed in India. The ULAMA and orthodox theologians attempted to influence the kings but were usually overruled. Kings themselves largely believed in the principles of a just rule rather than conversion to Islam. Many married Hindu princesses and most celebrated Hindu festivals. With some exceptions, Hindus and other communities were protected by Islamic rulers and where conflicts did take place, there was often a political and territorial element involved. Muslim rulers who remained in power after the arrival of the British had peaceful states with less instances of communal riots than British India.

At a popular level, the SUFIS bridged the gap between Hindus and Muslims, and so did some of the BHAKTI saints. Sufi saints and PIRS were worshipped by Muslims, Hindus and other communities. In urban areas, Islamic principles were followed more strictly, while in rural areas converts continued with their original Hindu practices. Thus there were several sects with a mix of Hindu and Muslim beliefs.

Sikhism initially had both Hindu and Muslim adherents but gradually grew closer to Hinduism.

Within Islam in India there were indigenous developments. New sects emerged and a number of Islamic texts were composed. Urdu, a mix of Persian and Hindi, provided a bridge language and Islamic influence could be seen in the spheres of music, dress and customs.

Islam had a certain flexibility that adapted to local conditions and circumstances, but it became less flexible with the coming of the British, who put forward a rigid view of Islam that was gradually adopted by Muslims themselves. Islamic revivalism began in the nineteenth century with the establishment of MADRASAS, such as the DAR-UL ULOOM at Deoband, and a move towards purity and religious study. In the twentieth century, Syed AHMAD KHAN and Muhammad IQBAL were among those who advocated reform in the religion, but on the whole the orthodox prevailed.

After the Partition of India in 1947, the level of mutual interaction between Islam and other religions diminished, though in several areas syncretic cults and the celebration of each other's festivals continues. The shrines of Sufi saints remain popular centres of worship for people of all communities. Certain Hindu shrines, such as that of AYYAPPA in SABARIMALA, also incorporate shrines for Muslim saints. Islam in India today has several different facets, represented by different sects and political groups, but for the Sunni majority orthodoxy seems to prevail. There are Islamic political parties that are both extreme and moderate. In the personal sphere, ISLAMIC LAW has a significant influence on Muslims. Some of the issues of concern to Muslims in India today are:

- Deciding whether and to what extent, modernization and reform are required in their educational institutions, and in social norms;
- Examining the role of Islamic law and whether Muslims should accept a common civil code;
- Preventing misunderstanding by clarifying that the majority of Muslims are neither responsible for, nor associated with terrorist acts;
- Building bridges with other communities.

Sects: There are several Islamic sects in India. The two main groups are the SUNNI and SHIA. The majority of Muslims in India are SUNNIS. Various sub-sects or sub-communities include the AHL-E-HADIS, AHMADIYAS, BARELVIS, WAHHABIS, BOHRAS, KHOJAS, MEMONS and MOPLAHS. Many SUFI sects were once active in India, among which were the CHISTI, SUHRAWARDI, QADIRI, SHATTARI and NAQSHBANDI. Some Sufi sects still exist but are not so prominent, though Sufi music is popular. Intermarriage between sects may take place. Apart from these are a number of Muslims who do not follow traditional practices or identify with any sect.

Islamic calendar The Islamic calendar begins with the HIJRAH year, the year of the Prophet MUHAMMAD's flight from Mecca to Medina which took place in 622. All events in Islam are dated from that event, following a lunar calendar.

The lunar year has twelve months, beginning with the month of MUHARRAM, followed by Safar, Rabi-ul-awwal, Rabi-us-sani, or Rabi-ul-akhir, Jamadi-ul-awwal, Jamadi-us-sani or Jamadi-ul-akhir, Rajab, Shaban, RAMZAN (the holiest month), Shawwal, Zilqada and Zilhajja. The last two months are also known as Zul-qada and Zul-hijja, depending on the region and the pronunciation used. In addition, months are popularly known by the names of the main festivals that occur in them.

The Islamic day begins at sunset. In Arabic, Yaum indicates a day of twenty-four hours, and Nahar the day in contrast to the night. Friday is known as Yaum-ul-jumah (or jama), the day of assembly, when special prayers are held.

Islamic ceremonies In India, Muslims have a number of ceremonies or rituals, mainly related to birth, marriage and death, similar in concept to the Hindu SAMSKARAS. Recitations from the QURAN form an important part of most rituals. When a child is born, the AZAN or call to prayer is recited in its right ear, and Iqawat, a similar prayer, in its left ear. On the seventh day after birth, a ceremony known as aqiqa takes place, when the child is given a name and the hair on its head is removed. This can be observed later too. Circumcision of the male child is another essential ceremony which can take place soon after birth or at a later age. There are also traditional school-going ceremonies, but in modern times these are not necessarily observed.

Marriage or nikah is conducted in the presence of a Qazi and may include regional customs and rituals. Customs similar to those of Hindus, such as applying mehndi (henna) to the hands and feet of the girl before the marriage, the Baraat or marriage procession, and the Vidai or farewell to the girl are commonly observed. On the deathbed, the Islamic creed or KALIMA is recited, as well as Yasin, a sura of the Quran. Honey mixed with water or Ab-i-Zamzam, holy water from the well in Mecca, is dropped between the lips. After death the face is turned in the direction of the KABA. The body is buried after being bathed, accompanied by prayers. Several rituals follow death, including recitations from the Quran and gifts in charity.

Islamic festivals The Islamic year (see ISLAMIC CALENDAR) has several festivals and religious observances. The first month of MUHARRAM is a period of mourning for the Prophet's grandson HUSAIN and his followers, martyred at Karbala. In the third month of Rabi-ul-awwal, the Prophet's birthday is celebrated as ID-I-MILAD. In the sixth month of Jamadi-us-sani, is the feast of Ghausal Azam Sheikh Abdul Qadir Jilani, an eleventh-century SUFI saint of Baghdad. In the seventh month of Rajab, the birthday of Ali, son-in-law of the Prophet, the feast of the Imam, Jafar Sadiq, and the Urs of Shaikh MUINUDDIN CHISTI are important festivals. Another major festival is Shab-i-Miraj, commemorating Muhammad's visit to heaven. In the eighth month of Shaban, is SHAB-I-BARAT, when the souls of the departed come down to earth. RAMZAN, the ninth month, consists of an entire month of fasting and religious observances, ending in the festival of ID-UL-FITR. In the twelfth month of Zilhajja, all who can are supposed to go to Mecca for the HAJ pilgrimage. In the same month the festival of BAKR-ID takes place.

Apart from these festivals, the URS or death anniversaries of various saints are celebrated locally.

Islamic law Islamic law refers to the SHARIA, or the entire way of life for a Muslim, which includes FIQH or jurisprudence. Law is based on the QURAN and HADIS or SUNNAH, and there are four main schools of SUNNI law or Fiqh. Even in medieval days, Islamic law in India was never rigorously applied and was modified to suit local conditions. Except in Islamic countries, today Islamic law operates only in the personal sphere. Muslims in India have their own civil code and the All India Muslim Personal Law Board (AIMPLD), founded in 1972, decides on religious, social, educational, political and cultural issues. Certain groups feel they are inadequately represented in the AIMPLD and have formed new boards. In December 2004 the BARELVIS set up a separate All India Personal Law Board. In January 2005 the All India Shia Personal Law Board was formed, claiming that issues pertaining to SHIAS were being neglected. Shias, however, also remain part of the AIMPLD. An All India Muslim Women's Personal Law Board was formed in February 2005. These boards provide guidelines for personal law, but the laws are applied by the regular court system of civil courts, family courts, district courts, high courts and the Supreme Court. Some of the specific acts pertaining to Muslim law are the Muslim Personal Law (Shariat) Act 1937, Dissolution of Muslim Marriages Act, 1939, and Muslim Women (Protection of Rights on Divorce) Act, 1986. In India, mainly HANAFI fiqh is applied, along with some aspects of other schools, earlier legislation, precedent, custom, and the authority of certain texts, both classical and modern. Some Muslims feel new laws need to be enacted for modern times and proposals have been made for these, though no consensus has been reached.

Islamic saints Islam has a number of different types of saints, though they are not accepted by all Islamic sects or groups. Saints include secret or mystical saints, SUFI saints or others close to God, as well as legendary saints. PIR and wali are terms commonly used for Sufi saints, while qutb and ghaus denote saints of a high order. Faqir and shaikh are among the other terms used.

The concept of a hierarchy of secret saints was put forward by Islamic mystics. HUJWIRI summarized the prevailing beliefs about them. He wrote: 'God has made the saints the governors of the universe; they have become entirely devoted to his business, and have ceased to follow their sensual affections.

Through the blessing of their advent the rain falls from heaven, and through the purity of their lives, the plants spring up from the earth, and through their spiritual influence the Muslims gain victories over the unbelievers. Among them there are four thousand who are concealed . . . But of those who have power to loose and to bind and are the officers of the divine court, there are three hundred called akhyar, and forty called ABDAL, and seven called abrar, and four called autad, and three called nuqaba, and one called qutb or ghaus.' There is a similar concept of secret saints in Theosophy and other mystic cults.

Another view of Islamic saints was explained by IBN AL-ARABI. He said saints (walis) were perfect men who no longer identified with the ego, and thus reflected the Absolute. According to him, after MUHAMMAD there was a cycle of saints, of which he was the last.

Apart from these, there are innumerable Sufi saints as well as legendary saints, whose shrines or DARGAHS are worshipped.

Islamic thought

A number of questions arose on different aspects of Islam, giving rise to different schools of thought. Islamic ideas were also influenced by an interaction with other philosophies. Between the seventh and tenth centuries, the main schools of KALAM or scholastic theology developed.

Other philosophers emerged from the BAITUL HIKMAH, or House of Wisdom, set up by the Abbasid Caliph Al-Mamun (813–33), where Greek works were translated into Arabic. Greek philosophical concepts were introduced and equated with those of Islam. Among these philosophers were al-Kindi (c. 800–870), Ar-Razi (d. 932), Al-Farabi (875–950), Ibn Miskawayh (d. 1030) and AVICENNA or Ibn Sina (980–1037). Al Ghazali (1058–11) further commented on their work and attempted to reconcile theology with mysticism. Fakhruddin Razi (1149–1209) defended ASHARI theories.

In India there were further developments in philosophy and theology. Orthodox SUNNIS were against philosophers and believed they should be suppressed by the state. However, the work of philosophers was popular in India, particularly that of Avicenna. Intellectuals in India included Abul Fazl Gaziruni of Gujarat, who lived in the fifteenth century, Shaikh Mubarak, the father of ABUL FAZL Allami, who studied Avicenna's philosophy with Gaziruni, and several others. Philosophy became popular in DELHI and AGRA, particularly at AKBAR's court, leading to movements such as that of AHMAD SIRHINDI, which sought a return to orthodoxy. The Mughal emperors Jahangir and Shah Jahan continued to patronize philosophers. SHIAS had their own schools of thought, while various developments took place in SUFI ideology. In the eighteenth century, Shah WALIULLAH introduced new trends from which other Islamic movements emerged. Today different schools of thought exist in the AHL-E-HADIS, BARELVIS, Deobandis, and various Shia groups, as well as some Sufi sects.

Ismailis

A SHIA sect of Islam, which follows Ismail (d. 760), believing that he is the seventh and last IMAM. Ismail was the son of the sixth imam, Jafar al-Sadiq, and was initially chosen by his father to follow him. According to some accounts, however, he died before him, and according to others he was rejected because of his behaviour. Jafar al-Sadiq then appointed his other son Musa al-Kazim as imam, but one group of Shias did not accept him and believe Ismail is the true imam and will return as the MAHDI. They came to be known as Ismailis or Sabiya (Seveners).

Ismailis interpret the QURAN in two ways: exoteric (zahir) and esoteric (batin). The latter has several mystical aspects. The hidden meanings of the world are linked with the number seven; thus there are seven main Prophets: Adam, Noah, Abraham, Moses, Jesus, Muhammad and Ismail, while between each there are silent prophets. Certain secret doctrines are also taught to initiates through their DAIS or leaders. Ismailis themselves have a number of sects, the main sects in India being the BOHRAS and KHOJAS. The NIZARI ISMAILIS, of whom most Khojas form a part, differ from the others in that they accept the AGA KHANS, who trace their descent from Ismail, as spiritual leaders.

Isna Ashari Shias

A SHIA sect of Islam also known as the Imamis, Jafaris or 'Twelver Shias'. The Isna Ashari are numerically the largest of the Shia sects. Theologically, they believe that God is essentially good and that he has created human beings with free will in order that they might know Him. For their guidance God sent the Prophets and the divinely appointed IMAMS.

Isma Asharis believe in twelve imams, who are: Ali, son-in law of the Prophet (d. 661); Hasan, son of the Prophet (d. 669); HUSAIN, son of the Prophet (d. 680); Ali Zayn ul Abidin (d. 712); Muhammad ul-Baqir (d. 731); Jafar ul-Sadiq (d. 765); Musa ul Kazim (d. 799); Ali ul Razi or Riza (d. 818); Muhammad ul-Jawad (d. 835); Ali ul Hadi (d. 868); al Hasan ul Askari (d. 874); and Muhammad ul-Muntazar (d. 878).

According to the Isna Ashari, the twelfth imam, Muhammad ul-Muntazar did not die but remains concealed and continues to guide the world. He will appear ultimately as the MAHDI, restoring justice to the world. For sixty-two years (878–940) after his disappearance, four intermediaries acted as his representatives. After this period, the Shia ULAMA took over responsibility for guiding the community until his reappearance.

The sect was probably introduced in India in the fourteenth century.

Israel, Lost Tribes of

According to the Hebrew BIBLE and the history of Judaism, Jacob, grandson of Abraham, later known as Israel, had twelve sons, from whom the twelve tribes of Israel were descended. The names of Jacob's sons were Reuben, Simeon, Levi, Judah, Issachar, Zebulun, Dan, Gad, Napthali, Asher,

Joseph and Benjamin. The descendants of Levi did not form a tribe, as they were scattered in various places in service of the Lord. Joseph himself did not head a tribe, but tribes were formed by his two sons, Ephraim and Manasseh. In 922 BCE, after the death of Solomon, his assistant Jeroboam rejected the rule of Solomon's son Rehoboam and founded the kingdom of Israel with its capital at Samaria, supported by ten tribes (Zebulun, Issachar, Asher, Napthali, Dan, Manasseh, Ephraim, Reuben, Gad and some of Simeon). The tribes of Benjamin and Judah lived in the kingdom of Judah. When the Assyrians conquered Israel in 721 BCE, the tribes of Israel were scattered, and believed to be lost, though some had probably migrated into the southern kingdom of Judah. Modern historians feel that there were a number of nomadic tribes that combined together to form states, and that when

Israel was defeated, they were assimilated in other areas. They believe that the descent from Jacob, and the theory of lost tribes wandering to different areas is a myth. Nevertheless, it remains an important part of Jewish history and tradition.

The story of the lost tribes has significance in India, as the BNEI MENASHE claim to be the lost tribe of Manasseh and the BENE ISRAEL also claim to be a lost tribe. Others place the lost tribes in England, Europe or America, and believe that they will one day be rediscovered, and will return to Israel.

Itivuttaka A Buddhist text that forms part of the *KHUDDAKA NIKAYA* of the PALI CANON. It consists of 112 short pieces, which include prose and verse sayings ascribed to the BUDDHA. The Buddhist ideals of friendliness, charity, serenity, and the merits of following the Buddhist path are described.

J

Jabriya An Islamic school of theology, or KALAM, which said that human actions are ordained by God. Jabr means compulsion and this school stated that God being sovereign, all were compelled to obey him. Jahm ibn Dafwan (d. 746), one of the most important Jabriyas, claimed that even salvation was predetermined, in contrast to some of the other schools, that maintained that man was responsible for his own actions.

Jacobite Church A name by which the MALANKARA ORTHODOX SYRIAN CHURCH is known.

Jadi Rana A king of a region in Gujarat who according to PARSI tradition gave refuge to a group of Iranian Zoroastrians (later known as Parsis) fleeing from Islamic Iran. According to the *KISSAH-I-SANJAN*, Jadi Rana was 'liberal, sensible and wise'. The Dastur or head priest of the Zoroastrians presented him with a gift and, stating that they had heard of his benevolence, asked for permission to settle in his land. Jadi Rana then asked the high priest to first explain the religion. In addition, he said that they must give up their language and learn the local language; the women must wear clothes like the women of the region; all weapons must be laid aside; and marriages must be performed only in the evening. Dastur Neryosangha agreed to the conditions, and before explaining the religion he said, 'We shall be friends of the whole of India and we shall cut off the heads of your enemies'. They were then given a piece of land—a plot in the desert which they named SANJAN. The city of Sanjan still exists and is a sacred place for Parsis. On the basis of information in the *Kissah-i-Sanjan*, Jadi Rana seems to have ruled in the eighth century, and has been identified with Vanraj Chavda of Anhilwara (745–806), Vajjada Deva of the Shilahara dynasty or Vijayaditya (696–733) of the Chalukya dynasty. Others believe that the Parsis arrived in the tenth century and that Jadi Rana must therefore have been a tenth-century king.

Jagannatha A Hindu deity, literally 'the lord of the world'. Jagannatha was initially worshipped by the Savara tribe and later considered a form of KRISHNA. According to one story associated with the deity, after Krishna was killed by Jara, a hunter in a forest, his bones were collected and placed in a box by some people who recognized their sanctity. The king Indradyumna was then asked by VISHNU to make an image of Jagannatha and place the bones inside. VISHVAKARMA, the divine architect, began making the image for the king, but Indradyumna interrupted him before it was complete. Vishvakarma was annoyed by this and left the image unfinished, therefore it has no hands or feet. Then King Indradyumna prayed to the god BRAHMA, who promised to give a soul to the image and to make it famous. Thus Jagannatha was created. Another version is that the image itself was found floating in the water. Jagannatha is worshipped in Bengal and elsewhere, but the most important Jagannatha temple is at Puri, Orissa.

Jagannatha Temple, Puri A temple dedicated to the Hindu god JAGANNATHA, located at Puri, Orissa. It was constructed by Anantavarman Chodaganga, a king of the Eastern Ganga dynasty who ruled from 1076 to 1148, in place of another shrine which is said to have existed from CE 500. The main images in the temple are those of Jagannatha, a form of KRISHNA, as well as of Balarama, Krishna's elder brother, and SUBHADRA, his sister. There are different versions of the origin of the images. Nowadays the images are remade of special margosa wood every eleven or twelve years. They are carved in the primitive style of the original image, without legs and with short stumpy arms.

The temple has a series of festivals that take place throughout the year. The most important are the Dola Yatra, the Chandan Yatra, the Snana Yatra and the Rath Yatra. The Dola Yatra is held in the month of Phalguna (February–March), when the deities Dolo-Govinda (Krishna), BHU DEVI and SHRI DEVI are taken in a procession to Dolabedi outside the temple and special rituals are conducted. The Chandan Yatra is a forty-two-day festival, divided into two parts of twenty-one days each, beginning on the third day of Vaishakha (April–May). In the first part, the deities of the temple, along with SHIVA images from neighbouring temples, are anointed with a paste of sandalwood (chandan) and placed in decorated boats that are floated in the attached tank. The second part consists of rituals within the temple, not open to the public. The Snana

Yatra or Bathing Festival then takes place. Here Lord Jagannatha is given a ritual bath, after which he is said to get a cold and fever. No darshana or glimpse of the deity is allowed for fifteen days while he rests and recovers, and only offerings of fruit are received. The grandest festival of the Rath Yatra now takes place. The image of Jagannatha is placed in a huge decorated chariot and is taken out in a procession accompanied by smaller chariots with Subhadra and Balarama. Priests accompany the chariots, there are frenzied chants, bells are rung and cymbals and drums are struck as the procession moves through the streets with thousands watching.

Rath Yatras of the deity also take place in other cities.

Jaggayapeta Stupa A Buddhist STUPA located near AMARAVATI in Andhra Pradesh. It can be dated to the second century BCE and is one of the earliest surviving stupas, with a stylistic similarity to the SANCHI STUPA.

Jahanara Begam A daughter of the Mughal emperor Shah Jahan. Born in 1614, Jahanara was a year older than her brother DARA SHIKOH, and like him had a passionate interest in SUFISM. She was initially interested in the CHISTI order and wrote a biography of Shaikh MUINUDDIN CHISTI in Persian, in which she included descriptions of some of his disciples. This text is known as *Munish-ul-Arwah*, or 'Sympathizer of Souls'. Later she became a disciple of the saint Mulla Shah of the QADIRI ORDER and wrote *Sahibiyya*, an account of his life and teachings. Jahanara remained unmarried. She took care of her father when he was imprisoned by her brother AURANGZEB and after his death lived at Aurangzeb's court. She died in 1681.

jahannam A term for hell in Islam. Unbelievers and sinners are said to go to hell after death. According to some theologians, Muslims who sinned will spend only a limited time in hell, whereas others stated that they too could be condemned to hell forever. Commentators described seven hells, each for different groups or religions.

Jaimini The founder of the philosophical school of MIMAMSA who probably lived between the fourth and second centuries BCE. His *Mimamsa Sutra* forms the basis for this philosophy and has twelve chapters. The first discusses the sources of knowledge and the truth of the VEDAS. Other chapters describe various sacrifices and what can be gained from them, the theory of *apurva*, and some other philosophical concepts. *Apurva* is a concept related to action; it is the hidden force that brings, at some point in time, the result of the action performed. Jaimini also wrote *Samkarshanakanda* or *Devatakanda*, on methods of worship.

In myths Jaimini was a great RISHI and teacher, a disciple of VYASA. He is said to have received the knowledge of the *SAMA VEDA* from Vyasa.

Jain art and architecture Jain sacred sites, temples and sculptures exist all over India, but some have a special significance. In general, sacred sites include those associated with the lives of the TIRTHANKARAS, where major temples have been built. The *VIVIDHA TIRTHA KALPA*, a Jain text, provides descriptions of several sites, while others are known from temples that are still extant.

Among the earliest Jain temples are the cave temples at UDAIGIRI, KHANDAGIRI and elsewhere, dating to the first century BCE or earlier. They consist of simple caves carved in the hillside, some with pillared verandahs. Later, both rock-cut and structural temples were made, with increasingly complex decorative features. In the early centuries CE, Jain STUPAS were constructed at MATHURA. These have stone railings, decorative gateways, stone umbrellas and elaborate carved pillars. Several Jain temples are on hilltops or in secluded valleys. Jain temples of the sixth to tenth centuries CE have been found at AIHOLE, BADAMI and elsewhere in the Deccan. The Indra Sabha at ELLORA is among the later Jain cave temples. At KHAJURAHO there are a number of Jain temples, of which the shrine of PARSHVANATHA is the largest. Many more temples can be seen at SHRAVANA BELAGOLA in Karnataka, both in the town and on the Indragiri and Chandragiri hills. In Rajasthan, the DILWARA temples at Mt Abu are made of intricately carved white marble, while a different style of architecture is used at Ranakpur, with doorways on all four sides. Jain temple cities were constructed on the SHATRUNJAYA hills at Palitana and on the GIRNAR hill in Gujarat. PARASNATH hill in Bihar, where most of the Tirthankaras are said to have attained moksha or liberation, is another significant Jain site. Early Jain temples exist at several other sites in western and southern India, while modern temples can be found in almost every town or city that has a Jain population.

Jain sculptures generally consist of images of the Tirthankaras, either seated in a yogic pose or standing upright, and are made of stone or of metal. A Jain image found at Lohanipur (Bihar) is thought to be one of the earliest. A number of images and AYAGAPATTAS or inscribed slabs from the second century BCE to third century CE are found at sites in MATHURA, particularly at Kankali Tila, and at other sites in India as well. Jain images continued to be made and one of the most notable is the 17.7-m-high statue of BAHUBALI at Shravana Belagola. Jains are also known for paintings and were the first to produce illustrated manuscripts with detailed paintings. Some of their temples also have wall paintings.

Jain ascetics Jainism has both male and female monastic orders. There is some difference in the rules for DIGAMBARA and SHVETAMBARA monks, and between male and female ascetics. In general an ascetic follows the VRATAS or vows, which even a lay person takes, to a more extreme degree. AHIMSA or non-violence is the most important of these. All monks and nuns must observe the three guptis (care in thought, speech and action), the five samitis (vigilance over actions), and the six AVASHYAKAS (essential principles of conduct). Jain ascetics are strictly celibate.

Each ascetic is guided by a guru or teacher. Among Digambaras there are three categories of male ascetics: Anuvrata, Mahavrata, and Nirvana. Anuvrata ascetics leave home and live at the temple. Their hair is shaved, they dress in saffron clothes and carry an earthen vessel for alms. When walking, they sweep the ground in front of them with a broom made of peacock feathers, so as to not crush any insects underfoot. Mahavrata ascetics wear only loin cloths, have no vessel and eat rice once a day. The hair on their heads is pulled out from the roots. The Nirvana ascetic remains nude and has his hair pulled out by the roots. He eats rice in his palms if it is given to him voluntarily, without him asking for it. He many not move around after sunset. Female ascetics do not practise nudity, but generally live in monasteries.

Most Shvetambara ascetics wear white clothes. They cover their mouths with white cloth masks so as not to breathe in insects, and sweep the ground before them as they walk. Both monks and nuns have their hair pulled out by the roots. Some advanced Shvetambara monks also discard their clothes and use only their cupped hands as a bowl.

The highest and most advanced monks and nuns end their lives through the act of SALLEKHANA (death by starvation). This takes place in rare cases even today.

Jain Councils   Four Jain Councils were held in order to put together the original teachings of MAHAVIRA. The first was held at PATALIPUTRA in the fourth century BCE and the last at Vallabhi (modern Vala, near Bhavnagar in present-day Gujarat) some time between CE 453 and 466. At the latter the ANGAS and other JAIN TEXTS were written down. They are still used by the SHVETAMBARAS today.

Jain deities   Jainism does not believe in a supreme God who has to be propitiated, but nevertheless a number of Mahapurushas, or great beings, are worshipped. Chief among these are the twenty-four TIRTHANKARAS. Images of the Tirthankaras, standing or seated, are installed in Jain temples from the north to south of India. They are worshipped as ideals; by concentrating on them individuals are inspired to attain the qualities they represent: compassion, love and unity, and finally transcendence of all forms. Each Tirthankara also has attendant YAKSHAS and YAKSHIS, also known as Upasakas or SHASANA DEVATAS. Yakshas include KUBERA, while AMBIKA is among the prominent yakshis. The Tirthankaras form part of sixty-three significant figures described in texts. These include twelve Chakravartins or rulers of the world, nine Vasudevas, and nine Baladevas, together constituting the fifty-four MAHAPURUSHAS. Nine Prati-Vasudevas, who are negative forces, bring the total to sixty-three.

In addition, minor deities worshipped include nine Naradas, eleven RUDRAS and twenty-four Kamadevas, as well as four groups of deities: Bhavanavasis, or gods worshipped in the home, Vyantara Devatas or 'intermediate' deities, Jyotishkas (beings of light), and Vaimanikas or astral gods. VIDYADEVIS, or goddesses of learning, are also worshipped. Initially SARASVATI or Srutadevi was the head, but later a set of sixteen Vidyadevis emerged. DIKAPALAS and NAVAGRAHAS, known from Hinduism, are part of the Jain pantheon, as well as sixty-four Dikkumaris, or goddesses of the directions, similar to the sixty-four yoginis of Hinduism. However, these deities are not worshipped by all Jain sects. Temples of some sects have no images at all, while others revere only the Tirthankaras.

Jain festivals   Jains observe a number of Hindu festivals in addition to their own festivals. Among the latter are MAHAVIRA JAYANTI, the birthday of MAHAVIRA, observed in March–April; PARYUSHAN, observed in the month of Bhadrapada (August–September); Bhai Beej, a festival for brothers similar to BHAI DUJ. Other festivals include NAVAPADA OLI, nine days of fasting; Jnana Panchami, the celebration of knowledge; Ashadh Chaturdasi, the start of the monsoon and of the four-month period when Jain ascetics cease wandering and stay in one place; Karttika Purnima, when they begin their travels again; MAUNA EKADASHI, a day of silence; PAUSHA DASHAMI, the birthday of PARSHVANATHA; and Akshay Tritiya, when those who have been performing special austerities end them by sipping sugar-cane juice at the holy city of SHATRUNJAYA. There are also local festivals and other festivals related to the TIRTHANKARAS.

Jain texts   The sacred texts of the Jains are different for the two main sects of SHVETAMBARAS and DIGAMBARAS. Both sects use the term Siddhanta or Agama for their collection of texts.

Shvetambara texts: The Shvetambaras provide an account of the origin and compilation of their texts. The original teachings of MAHAVIRA were included in fourteen Puvvas (PURVAS, or old texts). This knowledge was preserved for six generations, but in the fourth century BCE, when many of the monks led by BHADRABAHU had moved to south India or elsewhere at the time of a famine, only STHULABHADRA in the north remembered the contents of the Puvvas. Therefore a council was convened at PATALIPUTRA to compile the knowledge available. Eleven ANGAS were compiled, which included the available knowledge, while additional information was incorporated in the twelfth Anga, the DITTHIVAYA. When the followers of Bhadrabahu returned, they refused to accept this canon and it gradually reached a state of disorder. Thus another council was held at Vallabhi in Gujarat in the fifth century CE, when the ANGAS were written down in their present form. By this time, the twelfth Anga was lost.

The Shvetambara canon dating back to this council includes a number of other texts, and lists of these vary in different Jain traditions. However, scholars believe that forty-five texts divided into six groups are the most important. These are the eleven ANGAS, twelve UVANGAS (Upangas), ten PAINNAS (Prakirnakas), six CHEYA-SUTTAS (Cheda Sutras), two individual texts (the *NANDI-SUTTA* and *ANUOGADARA*), and four MULA SUTTAS (Mula Sutras). The texts other than the Angas are also known as Anga-bahiya Agamas (texts outside the Angas) which are a total of thirty-four. The STHANAKAVASI sect of the Shvetambaras accepts only twenty-one of these.

Apart from these, there are several other non-canonical works written in Jain Maharashtri, a form of Prakrit, and in Sanskrit. Between the first and eighth centuries these include Pattavalis and Theravalis, or lists of teachers, NIJJUTTIS (Niryuktis) or commentaries, as well as longer commentaries known as Bhashyas and Churnis. Later, further commentaries were written by HARIBHADRA, Silanka, Abhayadeva, Malayagiri and others.

There are also a number of accounts, known as Charitras, of the sixty-three great personages and other Jain saints.

Digambara texts: The Digambaras recognize that there were fourteen Puvvas and twelve Angas, but do not accept the contents of the Angas and related texts as compiled by the Shvetambaras. Two Digambara texts are given canonical status. These are the KARMAPRABHRITA and the KASHAYA-PRABHRITA. Other Digambara texts include fourteen Anga-bahiya Agamas or Prakirnakas. The first four Anga-bahiyas, the *Samayika, Chaturvimshatistava, Vandana* and *Pratikramana*, are part of the second Mula Sutta of the Shvetambaras. Other Digambara Anga-bahiyas which occur in the Shvetambara canon are the *Dashavaikalika, Uttaradhyayana* and *Kalpa-Vyavahara*.

The Digambaras have additional texts, some of a later date, described as the 'four Vedas'. These texts were classified by scholars into: Prathamanuyoga or accounts of the past, which include the Jain PURANAS; Karunanuyoga or cosmological works, among which are the *Surya-Prajnapti, Chandra Prajnapti* and *Jayadhavala*; Dravyanuyoga or philosophical works, of which the writings of KUNDAKUNDA, the *Tattvarthadhigama Sutra* of UMASVAMI (Umasvati) and the *Aptamimamsa* of SAMANTABHADRA are important; Charananuyoga or ritual works, including the *Mulachara* and *Trivarnachara* written by Vattakera, and the *Ratnakaranda Shravakachara* written by Samantabhadra.

This remains a useful classification for the study of the texts, though Digambaras themselves do not use it. Out of these, the writings of Kundakunda and Umasvami are considered particularly sacred.

Other texts: Apart from these sacred texts, there are many others, including epics, stories, fables, plays and poems, usually illustrating religious themes. There are also Jain works on grammar, lexicography, mathematics, medicine, YOGA and other subjects. Jain scholars wrote in Sanskrit, Prakrit, and in regional languages such as Gujarati, Kannada, Tamil and Telugu.

Jainism The religion of the Jains, i.e., those who revere the Jinas or realized souls. Today there are 42,25,053 Jains in India (2001 census) comprising 0.41 per cent of the population. In early literature, Jains were known as Nirgranthas.

In historical times, Vardhamana MAHAVIRA, who according to tradition was born in 599 BCE, explained this religion, but he was not the first to reveal its principles, which are said to have always existed.

Philosophy and Ethics: Though Jainism has two main sects of SHVETAMBARAS and DIGAMBARAS, as well as several sub-sects, the basic philosophical concepts are common to all.

According to Jain theory, there is no creator god, but the universe exists by itself. The aim of every living being is to attain MOKSHA or liberation. This is possible by understanding the nature of the world and by following an ethical and ascetic path.

Jain ethics are different for the ascetic and the lay person. Even a lay person however, has to observe eight basic lifestyle disciplines, such as not eating after sunset, avoiding certain foods, and following twelve vows or VRATAS. Eleven PRATIMAS or stages in the life of a Jain householder are also laid down.

Similar to the EIGHTFOLD PATH of Buddhism, Jainism has three ideals of right belief (SAMYAK DARSHANA), right knowledge (SAMYAK JNANA), and right conduct (SAMYAK CHARITRA), known as the three jewels or RATNATRAYA. Right conduct includes truth, BRAHMACHARYA, AHIMSA and non-attachment to material possessions, similar to the five basic YAMAS or restraints of YOGA. These form part of the vratas or vows. The most important ethical aspect of Jainism is ahimsa or not harming any living being, including plants and insects. Ahimsa in Jainism has several aspects, including vegetarianism, and also a restriction on certain types of vegetarian food, such as root vegetables. Agriculture is forbidden as an occupation, since ploughing leads to the death of small creatures and insects.

Jain ascetics observe some of the same vows, at a higher level, as well as additional ones.

Jainism explains the nature of the world in detail. There are two main categories in the universe, JIVA (life or soul) and AJIVA (non-living substance). Various aspects of the universe are classified into ASTIKAYAS or basic realities, DRAVYAS or substances, TATTVAS or principles and PADARTHAS or categories. KARMA, which in Jainism is a material substance, prevents the jiva from attaining its natural blissful state. An ethical life, penance and austerities, are necessary to eliminate karma; this may take several lifetimes.

Jainism has a complex classification of JNANA or knowledge, and of the means of understanding reality. Scholars compare its logical approach to that of the SAMKHYA philosophy.

History Jain cosmology believes in a series of KALPAS or cycles of existence, in each of which there are twelve ARAS or periods of time. According to Jain tradition, Jainism is revealed anew in every kalpa through twenty-four TIRTHANKARAS.

In the current cycle, the first TIRTHANKARA was Adinatha or RISHABHA, and the twenty-fourth, MAHAVIRA. Some Jain scholars feel that the representations of the figure with a horned head-dress on seals of the INDUS VALLEY CIVILIZATION is either Rishabha or Suparshvanatha, the seventh Tirthankara. The twenty-second Tirthankara, ARISHTANEMINATHA, is said to have been a contemporary of KRISHNA, while the twenty-third, PARSHVANATHA, seems to have lived around the eighth or ninth century BCE.

According to Shvetambara tradition, Mahavira was married but left home at the age of thirty. He gained enlightenment after almost thirteen years and began to teach. He had eleven chief disciples known as GANADHARAS, of whom GOYAMA INDABHUTI was the foremost. According to some texts, by the time of Mahavira's death there was a community of 14,000 monks and 36,000 nuns, as well as lay disciples. In the third century BCE, or according to other sources the first century CE, his followers were divided into two groups, the Shvetambaras and the Digambaras, from which in turn sub-sects later emerged. At the time of Mahavira, Jainism remained mainly within the region of MAGADHA, or modern Bihar, and eastern Uttar Pradesh. Jain tradition holds that many contemporary kings, including BIMBISARA and AJATASHATRU of Magadha, the rulers of KAUSHAMBI, UJJAIN and Anga, and the heads of the Malla and Licchhavi republics, were among the patrons of Mahavira and the Jain monastic order. The Nandas who ruled in the fourth century BCE were also said to favour Jainism, while CHANDRAGUPTA MAURYA is believed to have become a Jain and ended his life at SHRAVANA BELAGOLA in south India. Though ASHOKA was a Buddhist, his grandson and possibly his successor King Samprati is said to have patronized Jainism. (It is not clear who succeeded Ashoka, Jain sources believe it was Samprati.)The inscriptions at KHANDAGIRI in Orissa from the second and first centuries BCE indicate that Jainism flourished there at the time of King Kharavela. MATHURA was another important Jain centre. Excavations there, particularly at the site of Kankali Tila, have revealed numerous Jain sculptures and inscriptions dated between the second century BCE and the third century CE. After the end

of the Mauryan dynasty, Jainism and Buddhism lost importance in Magadha but continued at Mathura and Ujjain, and was also prevalent in western India, other places in the Deccan, and south India. The fourth JAIN COUNCIL was held in the fifth century at Vallabhi (in Gujarat) in western India, when the Shvetambara Jain canon was put into writing. In this region, Jainism was at its height in the twelfth century at the time of the Chalukya or Solanki king, Siddharaja, and his successor, Kumarapala. In the Deccan, Jainism flourished under the Chalukyas of Vatapi (BADAMI) (c. 550–740), the Western Chalukyas and the Rashtrakuta dynasty (750–1000), particularly under King Amoghavarsha of the ninth century. The renowned Digambara Jain teachers JINASENA and Gunasena lived at this time. In Andhra, the Eastern Chalukyas (c. 625–1100) patronized the Jains. In the Karnataka region, some of the Kadamba rulers (c. 345–560) patronized Jainism, as well as kings and ministers of the Western Ganga dynasty (c. 400–1100). Some kings, such as Nitimarga (853–870), Nitimarga II (907–935), Marasinha III (960–974) possibly became Jains, and Marasinha is said to have died by the vow of SALLEKHANA. It was under this dynasty that the great image of BAHUBALI at SHRAVANA BELAGOLA was built. Under the Hoysala dynasty, Jain temples were built, as some Hoysala ministers were Jains. In the Tamil region, MADURAI, KAVERIPATTINAM and other places were centres of Jainism. Jains, or Nirgranthas, are mentioned in the Tamil texts *MANIMEKHALAI* and *SHILAPADDIGARAM* of the sixth century or earlier. The *Pattinapalai*, another Tamil text, refers to Jain and Buddhist temples in one part of the city of Puhar, with BRAHMANA temples on another side. XUANZANG, the Chinese pilgrim of the seventh century, visited KANCHI and saw Nirgranthas there. There are several Jain inscriptions of the eighth and ninth centuries, mainly in the Madurai–Tirunelvelli area, after which there seems to have been a decline. Two important Jain centres in Tamil Nadu today are at Tirumalaipuram and Tiruparuttikunram, the latter a suburb of Kanchi.

On the whole Jains had good relations with the sultans of northern India and with the Mughal emperors, particularly AKBAR, though also with Jahangir, Shah Jahan and even AURANGZEB, who issued a decree giving Jains rights over the sacred site of SHATRUNJAYA. Jainism flourished under the Malwa sultans and the Vijayanagara kingdom, and later in the various small states of Rajasthan.

The wealth of Jain merchants and bankers helped to ensure the status and prestige of the community as the Mughals and other Muslim rulers often depended on them for loans. Even the British took loans from Jain bankers.

Jain sects: The two main sects of Jainism are the SHVETAMBARAS and DIGAMBARAS, with various sub-sects of these developing later on. A third sect that existed from about the fourth to the fifteenth centuries was the YAPANIYA. The Kurchakas are also mentioned in inscriptions, though little is known about them. Later sects include the KANJIPANTHA and KAVIPANTHA. There is also evidence of Jain TANTRISM in the medieval period, and the Jain VIDYADEVIS have some similarities with Buddhist and Hindu Tantric deities.

Differences between the Shvetambaras and Digambaras include:

(1) The acceptance of different texts.
(2) More rigid rules for ascetics among Digambaras.
(3) Different views on a Kevala or Tirthankara: according to Digambaras these no longer need food, while Shvetambaras believe they do; also according to Digambaras a woman cannot achieve this state, according to Shvetambaras she can.
(4) Different views on MAHAVIRA: the Digambaras hold that he was not married, the Shvetambaras that he was married and had a child.
(5) Different types of images: those of the Shvetambaras are decorated, those of the Digambaras are plain.

Jainism and other religions: Jainism has several similarities with Buddhism. In a historical context, it flourished at the same time as Buddhism and in the same areas; like Buddhism, it was against caste, animal sacrifices, and rituals. There were also similar views on God, and even similar names. Thus while Gautama Siddhartha, later the BUDDHA, had a wife named Yashodhara, Mahavira's wife was Yashodha. Goyama (Gautama) was the name of MAHAVIRA's chief disciple; Siddhartha was the name of Mahavira's father. In fact some Western scholars initially believed that they were actually one religion, though later they realized the two were distinct and different. Gradually Jainism became closer to Hinduism and absorbed many Hindu customs, as well as the concept of caste and forms of worship. Rites known as Kriyas, similar to the SAMSKARAS, are observed by traditional Jains, beginning with ceremonies from before birth up to death. These are described in the Jain *ADI PURANA* and in later texts.

Scholars believe that Jainism absorbed certain aspects of Islam, particularly the sects that emerged in the medieval period, the STHANAKAVASI sub-sect of the SHVETAMBARAS and the TERAPANTHI of the DIGAMBARAS, both of which rejected idol worship.

Jains today   Jains today live in all parts of the country, though they are more prominent in Gujarat, Rajasthan and Karnataka.

Jaitu   A town in Punjab that is a sacred site for Sikhs. It is associated with Guru GOBIND SINGH and with the AKALI MOVEMENT. The GANGSAR GURDWARA and the Tibbi Sahib Gurdwara are located here. In 1923–24, Jaitu, then a small village, was part of Nabha state. Maharaja Ripudaman Singh had been forced to abdicate by the British, as he was sympathetic to the Sikhs and the Indian National Congress. To protest against this, Akali Sikhs gathered at the Gangsar Gurdwara in 1924 and started a non-stop recitation of the GURU GRANTH SAHIB. The AKALI DAL was declared an illegal organization and the recitation was stopped by the government. As more and more Sikhs joined in a peaceful protest they were fired upon and several Akalis were arrested. Ceremonies are held at Jaitu in memory of this day.

jajmani   A traditional system of relationships among various groups in a village. In this system each CASTE, community or group had a specific occupation, and services were exchanged or paid for in kind. This led to social and economic stability, but each person had little or no choice, and had to function according to fixed hereditary roles. With modernization, the system has been modified.

Jakhs   A term that specifically refers to a group of seventy-two people who came to the region of Bhuj in Gujarat at the time of King Punara or Punarvo, a local ruler of about the tenth century. They landed here because of a shipwreck and the general belief is that they were a group of Iranian Zoroastrians, while some believe they were Greek. The Jakhs, seventy-one men and one woman, were healers who rode around on horseback, helping the local people. They were said to be fair foreigners, helpers of the poor and messengers of God. However, Punara did not like their influence and hunted them down, finally killing them all. To commemorate their martyrdom, seventy-two idols were made and erected on a hillock near Puraneshwar. A big fair is held every year at Kakkad Bhit in Munjal in their honour, on the second Monday of Bhadrapada (August–September). There are other local temples and fairs honouring them.

Jakh is also a colloquial term used for YAKSHAS or guardian spirits. A similar name for god and spirit, 'Jok', was used by the ancient Nilotic people who lived in parts of Africa.

Jalakateshvara Temple   A temple of the Hindu god SHIVA located at Vellore in Tamil Nadu, constructed in the sixteenth century. The temple is within a fort and was built by Chinna Bomma, a governor under the Vijayanagara dynasty. The main temple has two shrines that open into a common MANDAPA or hall. To the west is a shrine with a Shiva LINGA and to the north a shrine with NATARAJA. There are guardian images in the doorways and a NANDI image in front of the east wall of the mandapa. On the outer walls are images of SHAIVA saints and of GANESHA. To the north-west is a small DEVI shrine. The temple is enclosed with walls and entered through a GOPURAM or gateway on the south. Around this is a much larger enclosure with another towering gopuram on the south. Within this is another mandapa, famous for its magnificent sculptures. The outer piers are in the form of rearing lion-like beasts and horses with riders. The ceiling is intricately carved; the central panel depicts a fruit surrounded by parrots.

The whole temple has been renovated and a new pyramidal tower has been built. It remains a popular and important Shiva temple today.

Jalaluddin Bukhari, Syed A SUFI saint of the SUHRAWARDI order popularly known as Makhdum-i Jahaniyan (Lord of the World's People). Born in 1308, he lived mainly at Uch in the north-west, but made frequent trips to DELHI and is also said to have travelled to several places in different parts of the world, where he met other leading Sufis. Sultan Muhammad bin Tughlaq made him the head of a KHANQAH in Siwistan in Sind, but he had a closer relationship with Sultan Firuz Shah Tughlaq, and all his recommendations were accepted by the sultan. His sayings were compiled by his disciples in a book known as *Khulasatul-Alfaz Jamiul-Ulum*. Jalaluddin objected to Hindu practices in Islam, exploding crackers at festivals and referring to ALLAH by Hindu names such as Thakur (Lord) or Kartar (Creator). He believed Sufis should maintain relationships with rulers and officials so that they could intercede on behalf of the poor. He died in 1384 and was buried at Uch.

Jalaluddin Rumi A renowned SUFI saint. Born in 1207 in Balkh in present Afghanistan, he later lived with his father in Turkey in the city of Rum (today known as Konya). At the age of fifteen he had a mystical experience. Later he studied in Baghdad and travelled to different parts of the world. His most famous work is his *Masnawi*, which consists of 26,660 couplets in six volumes. This text has stories interspersed with Sufi and mystical concepts. Parts of it are similar to the verses of the BHAKTI saints, and his 'Song of the Reed Flute' in the *Masnawi* is reminiscent of songs to KRISHNA. In one of these verses, he says:

Listen to the pain of the reed flute, complaining of the pain of separation;

and in another verse:

The reed is comrade to him who has lost his Friend,
Its strains rend the veil from our hearts . . . ;
It tells of the mystic path of blood,
It recounts the love of Majnun for Layla.

He founded the Mawlawi (Mevlevi) Sufi order, known for their whirling dances through which ecstasy can be achieved. Rumi influenced Sufi saints in all parts of the world, including India, and his *Masnawi* is probably the best-known Sufi text today.

jalarupa A fish or MAKARA associated with the Hindu god KAMA.

Jama Masjid A large number of mosques all over India are known as Jama Masjid, Jami Masjid or Jumma Masjid. The term has sometimes been translated as 'Friday Mosque' but the word jama and its alternate spellings merely means 'congregation'. The Arabic term for Friday is also Jama, as Friday is the day for special prayers held in congregation. Several of these mosques are historically or architecturally significant.

Jama Masjid, Delhi A mosque located in DELHI, constructed between 1650 and 1656 by the Mughal Emperor Shah Jahan. It is the largest mosque in India, built of red sandstone with inlays of white and black marble. The mosque is constructed on a high platform and has a huge courtyard of 100 m each side, accessed by three gateways. Within are a basin and fountain, with the prayer hall to the west. The facade has eleven bays, with three white marble domes, and two minarets, each with a height of 39 m. The mosque was designed by Ustad Khaliq; 5000 or more artisans and workmen were involved in its construction. A small pavilion in the north-east corner of the courtyard contains relics of the Prophet.

This popular and beautiful mosque is still in use.

Jamaat-Khana Mosque A mosque located in DELHI near the tomb of the SUFI saint Hazrat NIZAMUDDIN AULIYA. It was constructed by Khizr Khan, son of Sultan Alauddin Khalji, who ruled from 1296 to 1316. The mosque is made of red sandstone and consists of a rectangular prayer hall with three chambers entered through archways. The central chamber, about 11.5 m each side, is said to have been built as a tomb for Nizamuddin, but he declined to be buried there.

Jamadagni A BRAHMANA described in ancient texts, who was descended from the rishi BHRIGU. He was the son of Richika and Satyavati. He married RENUKA, daughter of King Renu or Prasenajit, and had five sons, the youngest and most famous of whom was PARASHURAMA an incarnation of the Hindu god VISHNU. Jamadagni was killed by the sons of King KARTAVIRYA, in response to which Parashurama annihilated all the KSHATRIYAS.

Jamali The pen-name of the SUFI saint Shaikh Hamid bin Fazlullah of the SUHRAWARDI order, an eminent poet who was admired by Sultan Sikandar Lodi and by the Mughal emperor Babar. During his lifetime he travelled to a number of places, including Mecca, Medina, Syria, Palestine, Iraq and Iran. He accompanied Babar's son Humayun on an expedition to Gujarat and died there in 1536.

Jamali composed a number of poems, including the masnawi *Mihr wa Mah*, a love story with a mystic theme. His *Siyarul Arifin*, written between 1530 and 1536, contains an account of the CHISTI and Suhrawardi Sufi saints of his day.

Jamali-Kamali Mosque A mosque located in DELHI near the twin tombs of Jamali and Kamali, from which it gets its name. It was constructed between 1528 and 1535 by Jamali, the name used by the saintly poet Shaikh Fazlullah, who was also known as Jalal Khan. No one knows who Kamali was. The mosque, located in a courtyard in the Mehrauli area, has a rectangular prayer-hall entered through five decorated arches. There are Quranic inscriptions on the western wall and an ornamented parapet on the second floor. Two octagonal towers are at the rear.

Jambavan/Jambavat The king of the bears in Hindu mythology. According to Valmiki's RAMAYANA, he lived in the kingdom of SUGRIVA, chief of the VANARAS. He had great energy and brought with him ten crore bears to help RAMA in his search for SITA.

In another story, he took possession of a wonderful gem called Syamantaka, which KRISHNA wanted. Finally Jambavan surrendered it to him and also gave Krishna his daughter Jambavati in marriage.

Scholars suggest that Jambavan was actually a leader of a tribe with a bear totem. Jambavan is also referred to as a vanara and as kapi (monkey) and in the *Ramayana* of Valmiki it is unclear whether he was a bear or a monkey. In most later texts, however, he is referred to as a bear.

Jami Masjid, Ahmadabad A large mosque located in Ahmadabad, Gujarat, constructed by one of the sultans of Gujarat, Ahmad Shah I, who ruled from 1411 to 1441. It was completed in 1424. This huge mosque measures 63 m by 30 m within an even larger courtyard of 87 m by 72 m. Inside there are fifteen bays divided by 300 pillars, and five mihrabs. The mosque is considered one of the most beautiful and imposing in the world.

Jami Masjid, Bijapur A mosque constructed in the sixteenth and seventeenth centuries, located in Bijapur, Karnataka. It was begun by the Bijapur sultan Ali Adil Shah (1558–80). Additions were made by Muhammad Adil Shah (1627–56), but the mosque was completed only in 1686.

The largest mosque of Bijapur, it is within a courtyard of about 137 m by 68.5 m. The mosque is about 47 m each side, with seven arches on every side, leading into corridors and a prayer-hall on the west. It has a façade of nine bays crowned with a huge dome. The gilded MIHRAB is inscribed with Persian verses.

Jami Masjid, Champaner A mosque located in Champaner, Gujarat, constructed in 1523 by the sultan of Gujarat, Mahmud Begarha.

Architecturally, it is considered one of the most significant mosques in Gujarat. It is enclosed in a courtyard, with the prayer hall to the west. Its façade has five pointed arches and two minarets, and oriel windows in between. The open court in front has arched cloisters on three sides, and the entrance is through three porches. The exterior is richly ornamented, with traceried openings, and on the upper balconies are stone seats for meditation.

Jami Masjid, Fatehpur Sikri A mosque located in Fatehpur Sikri, the city constructed by the Mughal emperor AKBAR near Agra, in Uttar Pradesh. The mosque was completed in 1572 and dedicated to the SUFI saint Shaikh SALIM CHISTI. Also known as the Dargah Mosque, it is usually entered from the east, through the Badshahi Darwaza or gateway, which led to Akbar's palace. The main entrance, however is via a large central arch said to be based on that of Mecca Masjid.

Within the mosque, there are seven bays while above is a huge dome painted on the interior. On the west, the prayer-hall measures 88 m by 20 m. The famous Buland Darwaza, the victory gateway built by Akbar, is at the rear of the complex. The white marble tomb of Shaikh Salim Chisti, who died before the mosque was completed, is in the court of the mosque.

Jami Masjid, Gulbarga Fort A mosque located in Gulbarga fort in Karnataka. It was constructed in 1367, during the reign of Muhammad Shah (1358–75), and resembles the Great Mosque at Cordoba. An inscription at the entrance states that it was built by one Rafi, son of Shams, son of Mansur of Qazvin.

This large mosque conforms to the usual orthodox mosque plan but has no open courtyard and is entered through a narrow gateway on the north. There are wide cloisters with arches on three sides and a prayer-hall on the west. It is covered by a dome on a square base, and in addition has four corner domes and seventy-five smaller ones.

Jami Masjid, Jaunpur A mosque built by Hussain Shah (1458–79), the last ruler of the Sharqi dynasty of Jaunpur (Uttar Pradesh). It is similar to the Atala Mosque but much larger, the largest mosque in the area, and the last great mosque built at Jaunpur.

It is constructed on a raised platform approached by flights of steep stairs. The courtyard measures 66 m by 64.5 m and the prayer-hall is a square chamber covered by a large dome. The side aisles have vaulted roofs, while the three entrance gateways have halls surmounted by domes.

Jami Masjid, Mandu A mosque located at Mandu, Madhya Pradesh. It was begun by Hoshang Shah (1406–35), one of the Mandu sultans, and completed by Mahmud Shah I in 1454.

It is a monumental structure, similar to the Great Mosque at Damascus, covering a large area measuring 97.4 m each side. On the east is a huge domed porch. The building is raised on a platform, with arched chambers on the sides. It has an open court of 50 m each side, enclosed by pillared halls and arched openings, with the prayer hall on the west. There are seventeen niches on the qibla wall, the central one with inscriptions from the QURAN.

The main entrance is approached by a wide staircase and was once decorated with glazed tiles, while to the north are two more entrances, one for women. The roof consists of three large domes on the prayer hall and 158 small domes.

Jami Masjid, Mangrol A mosque located at Mangrol in the Saurashtra region of Gujarat. It was constructed in 1384 by Izzud-Din, an official of Firuz Shah Tughlaq, the sultan of DELHI. The stone mosque has a pillared corridor in two storeys around three sides of an open court. The prayer-hall has rows of pillars and ten almost conical domes on the roof. In the north-west corner is a stone step-well.

Jami Masjid, Srinagar A mosque located in Srinagar, Kashmir. It was first erected in 1393–94 by Sikandar, sultan of Kashmir, and expanded by his son, Zain-ul-Abidin, in 1402. Between the fifteenth and seventeenth centuries, it was rebuilt thrice after being burnt down. This typically Kashmiri-style mosque is constructed of wood. It has a court of about 73 m each side surrounded by pillared aisles. There are over 370 pillars, and each of these is 7.5 m to 15 m high and is made out of a single trunk of deodar wood. Four arched openings on each side are covered by pyramidal roofs, and there are three pagoda-shaped minarets.

Jamshed A legendary king of ancient Iran particularly revered by Zoroastrians. He was known as YIMA in the AVESTA and Jamshed in PAHLAVI texts.

Janaka (1) A mythical king who was the son of Nimi, and grandson of IKSHVAKU. Cursed by VASISHTHA, Nimi lost his body and became videha (without body). As he had no sons, the RISHIS churned (mathana) his body, and obtained a child, who was therefore known as Mithi Janaka (born of churning). His city was then known as MITHILA, and the country as Videha. According to some accounts, all succeeding kings were known as Janaka, though they had other names as well.

(2) A descendant of the first Janaka and father of SITA, described in the *RAMAYANA*. He was also known as Shiradhvaja.

(3) Apart from a description in the *Ramayana*, there are several stories about Janaka in the MAHABHARATA and PURANAS, though some of these may refer to other Janakas.

According to accounts in texts, the rishi YAJNAVALKYA was his priest and advisor. Janaka was against the role of the BRAHMANAS and performed sacrifices himself. Because of his pure life, he became a Brahmana and rishi, though he was born a KSHATRIYA. Janaka is said to have met the sage Ashtavakra and had a diaologue with him, later known as the ASHTAVAKRA GITA. Janaka also had several conversations with other rishis or sages. Among the rishis he conversed with were Ashmaka, Mandavya and Parashara.

Janaka was compassionate and pious. A story in the *PADMA PURANA* states that he visited one of the numerous hells and by his piety saved those who were there.

All the Janakas had great renown as scholars, teachers, and philosophers.

Janam Sakhis Hagiographic accounts of the life of Guru NANAK, the founder of the Sikh religion, written after the death of the guru. Bhai GURDAS (1560–1629) is said to have written the first Janam Sakhi in his *var*, or poetic composition. The *Bhai Bala Janam Sakhi* is the most popular and is attributed to BALA, one of the two closest companions of Guru Nanak. This text however, seems to be of a much later date, and some scholars even doubt the existence of Bala. The *Puratan*

Janam Sakhi is possibly the earliest, written about eighty years after Nanak's death.

The *Meherban Janam Sakhi* is attributed to Sodhi Meherban (1581–1640), son of Prithi Chand, the elder brother of Guru ARJAN DEV. Prithi Chand was against Arjan becoming the guru, therefore though this Janam Sakhi is learned and well-written, its traditions have been questioned. The *Bhai Mani Singh Janam Sakhi* was written by MANI SINGH, who lived at the time of Guru GOBIND SINGH. Asked to write an authentic Janam Sakhi, to remove interpolations in the other accounts, he based his account on Bhai Gurdas's var as well as popular accounts prevalent at the time he lived.

The Janam Sakhis do not agree on details. Some provide an account of two udasis or missions, others of four. According to the *Meherban* and *Mani Singh Janam Sakhis*, Nanak travelled not only all over India but to several other countries, including Palestine, Turkey and Syria. Despite these problems the Janam Sakhis are important sources for the life of Guru Nanak and for Sikh history.

Janamashtmi A Hindu festival celebrating the birthday of the god KRISHNA, which occurs on the eighth day of the dark half of the month of Bhadrapada (August–September). Images of KRISHNA, particularly as a baby, are made and set up in homes and temples. Scenes from his life are also enacted at this time. This festival is celebrated all over India, but particularly in the region of MATHURA, the area of his birth and early life.

Janamejaya A king described in the MAHABHARATA and other texts. He was the son of Parikshit and great-grandson of ARJUNA, one of the PANDAVAS. His father was killed by the bite of a snake, and Janamejaya held a great snake sacrifice (SARPA SATRA) at which thousands of snakes were killed before the sacrifice was stopped. The *Mahabharata* was recited to him by the rishi VAISHAMPAYANA.

jannah/jannat An Arabic term used in Islam for heaven. In Persian, the term is bihisht, while Firdaus, another Persian term commonly used for paradise, refers to one particular heaven. Jannah literally means 'garden', and heaven is described as a garden with flowing streams and fruit-bearing trees. The QURAN mentions eight heavens, and some take these as different names of one paradise, while others believe there are eight graded heavens or stages. In some texts seven heavens are described. Those who reach the higher heavens will recline on carpets lined with rich brocade and see chaste maidens, untouched by man or JINN. The Prophet MUHAMMAD, in his MIRAJ or night journey to heaven, went through seven levels that are described in detail.

Jap Sahib A sacred prayer in Sikhism, composed by Guru GOBIND SINGH. It consists of 199 short verses, and forms part of the *Dasam Granth*, a collection of the Guru's writings. Many of the verses of the Jap Sahib, describe the nature of God, who has no form, shape, dwelling place, colour or caste. It also indicates the supreme and universal nature of God, the creator of all. Thus one of its verses states:

You are the source of all light,
The object of all praise;
You are the Supreme Lord,
The moon of the universe. (v.119).

The Jap Sahib is one of the daily prayers for Sikhs, and is recited after the JAPJI of Guru NANAK.

japa A term for the repetition of a holy name, word, phrase or MANTRA. Japa can be silent, the word being repeated mentally, or spoken aloud. Malas or rosaries are often used to count the number of repetitions. Traditionally repetitions are uttered 108 or 1008 times, or more.

Japji A sacred prayer in Sikhism, that forms part of the GURU GRANTH SAHIB. It was composed by Guru NANAK and contains the essence of the faith. The Japji, recited every morning by devout Sikhs, has thirty-eight pauris (hymns) and two shlokas (verses), and begins with the Mul Mantra, which states that there is One God, whose name is Truth, who is beyond time, and is self-existent. Contemplating and listening to the name of God brings peace and divine knowledge, revealing hidden mysteries.

Jara In Hindu myths, the name of a hunter who was responsible for the death of the god KRISHNA. Like Achilles, Krishna's only vulnerable spot was his heel. Jara, hunting in the forest, saw what he thought was a deer and shot an arrow. It struck Krishna and resulted in his death, or at least the end of his earthly existence.

jashan A Zoroastrian ceremony or sacrificial ritual. It is performed on special occasions or festivals in front of the sacred fire, when blessings are sought for the created world. The fire in the afarghan or receptacle is fed with sandal and incense, while two or more priests chant the prayers and perform the ritual. Water, symbolizing life, milk, symbolizing the animal kingdom, and fruits and flowers, representing the vegetable kingdom, are among the items placed on a tray and offered to AHURA MAZDA. Nearby there are additional trays of flowers, fruit and special food. After the ceremony the blessed food is distributed to the congregation. Amal, or cosmic energy, is believed to permeate these food items through the priests, and those who eat the food thus partake of this divine energy.

Jatakas A collection of Buddhist texts that form part of the *KHUDDAKA NIKAYA* of the PALI CANON. The Jatakas, stories of the former births of the BUDDHA, number around 500. In each, the Buddha appears as a BODHISATTVA, i.e., one who would be a Buddha in future. This collection, in a mixture of prose and verse, includes fables, folktales, short anecdotes, long narrative stories of adventure and romance, moral and ethical stories, legends and myths. Many of these were probably stories that already existed and are known from other sources, but here they are given a Buddhist flavour. Stories with animal characters are common. In one of them, the Bodhisattva, then a male gazelle offers himself to the king as food, to save a pregnant gazelle from being killed. Touched by his noble generosity, the king henceforth protects the gazelles and gives up hunting. There are many stories of kings who renounced the world and became hermits. In the *Jataka of Prince Kanha*, the prince gives away everything to live as a hermit. Sakka offers him a boon, and the boon he asks for is: 'Let none on my account be harmed, whether in mind or body, at any time or place.' In one of the most famous Jatakas, the *Vessantara Jataka*, Prince Vessantara gives up everything, including his wife and children, because he has vowed never to refuse anything that is asked of him. Stories in which the characters include giants and divine beings, such as YAKSHAS, GANDHARVAS and KINNARAS, all form part of the Jatakas.

Jataka stories are depicted in reliefs at BHARHUT, SANCHI, AMARAVATI and elsewhere, and occur in the cave paintings at AJANTA. There are also other Jataka collections, which include some of the stories from the Pali Jatakas, as well as some which are not found here. Jataka tales are still popular in India.

Jatayu A divine bird in Hindu mythology, the king of the vultures. In the RAMAYANA he tried to prevent RAVANA from carrying away SITA but was wounded and killed. RAMA and LAKSHMANA performed his last rites, and he ascended to heaven in a chariot of fire. In the PURANAS, he helped the king DASHARATHA and saved him from being consumed by SHANI (Saturn).

jati Another word for CASTE. VARNA is an earlier term, first used in the RIG VEDA, and some scholars feel that jatis developed later from the broader category of varna. Others trace the origin of jatis to early social groups such as clans. Today there are innumerable jatis, including castes and sub-castes.

Jawahir-i Khamsa A mystical SUFI text written by Shaikh MUHAMMAD GHAUS of the SHATTARI order, who lived in the sixteenth century. The *Jawahir* is considered his most significant text and was written in 1522–23, and revised and enlarged in 1549–50. The text has five sections known as Jawahir (gems), which are: forms and methods of worship for devotees; forms and methods for ascetic practices; conditions for the invocation of the great names of ALLAH; discipline of the Shattars; devotional practices for advanced mystics.

Invocation, known as DAWA or dawat-i asma, was a complicated practice for which certain preconditions had to be followed rigorously. Truthfulness, humility, avoidance of certain food items, celibacy, fasting, living in seclusion, and wearing unsewn garments were among the many conditions for this practice. Failure to observe these placed the practitioner in jeopardy.

Jayadeva The composer of the *GITA GOVINDA*, a verse text on the divine love between RADHA and KRISHNA. According to some accounts he was the court poet of Raja Lakshmana Sena (1178–1205) of Bengal, while according to others he came from Mithila or Orissa.

Jehovah's Witnesses A Christian denomination that has a following in India. The sect was founded by Charles Taze Russel (1852–1916) of Alleghany, Pennsylvania, USA. It uses the Hebrew name of God, Yahweh, or Jehovah in English. The sect believes that Christians departed from the true faith after the death of the last Apostle. Russel, a Presbyterian who started a study circle, was thought to have gained a true understanding of the scriptures, and the Watch Tower Society was founded by him and his associates in 1881. After Russel's death, changes took place in the Watch Tower and Bible Tract Society, as it was then known, and some of Russel's associates left. In 1931, when Joseph Franklin Rutherford (d. 1942) was the president, those who remained gave themselves a new name, Jehovah's Witnesses. The sect interprets the BIBLE literally and rejects the concepts of the Trinity, immortality of the soul, and eternal punishment in hell. Instead they believe that the earth will one day (after Armageddon, the final battle) become a paradise, and the wicked will be eliminated. A somewhat similar concept, the FRASHOKERETI, or the renewal of existence, exists in Zoroastrianism.

Jehovah's Witnesses believe that while Jehovah is the supreme God, JESUS is a form of the Angel Michael, who is also a God. Adherents practise political neutrality, do not join military service, and refuse to sing the National Anthem or salute the National Flag. They do not use any images or icons, not even the cross, and do not allow blood transfusions. They also believe that theirs is the only true faith.

Jesuits The Society of Jesus, a Catholic monastic order popularly known as Jesuits, was founded in Paris by Ignatius Loyola, a Spaniard, in the 1530s. It was introduced in India by Francis Xavier, also a Spaniard, who was later made a saint. Xavier arrived in GOA in May 1542 and converted people to Christianity there and on the coast of the Tamil region in south India. He left India in 1548. There were several other Jesuits in India, mainly in Goa, some of whom were invited to the court of the Mughal emperor AKBAR in the sixteenth century to explain the principles of Christianity to the emperor. The Jesuits became extremely powerful in the Christian world, and Catholic rulers in Europe resented their influence. They were also accused of accumulating undue wealth. As a result, Portugal banned the Jesuits in 1759, France in 1764 and Spain in 1767. In 1773, pressure from Catholic rulers led to Pope Clement XIV suppressing Jesuits in all countries. However, the suppression was never completely effective and the order was restored in 1814. In India today there are a number of Jesuits teaching in educational institutions, while the most famous Jesuit, ST. FRANCIS XAVIER, is still revered.

Jesus Christ The founder of the religion that came to be known as Christianity. According to traditional accounts, found mainly in the Gospels of the NEW TESTAMENT, Jesus was a Jew born in Bethlehem in Judea, when Herod was king. By the grace of God, he was born to MARY, a virgin, who was married to Joseph. Herod, informed by wise men that a great king was born, feared a threat to his kingdom and ordered the killing of all children under the age of two in Bethlehem and surrounding areas. Jesus was taken by his parents to Egypt to escape the massacre, and later they dwelt in the city of Nazareth, in Galilee. John the Baptist, a preacher who baptized people with water, predicted that one much greater than he would come, and Jesus fulfilled this prophecy. When Jesus grew up, he gathered twelve disciples who would be his main companions and began to teach the people about love, forgiveness and compassion. The essence of his teachings is in a speech he delivered known as the SERMON ON THE MOUNT. Jesus also healed the sick, opened the eyes of the blind and enabled the paralyzed to walk. He was said to be the son of God, and he taught with the authority of divine knowledge. The Jews feared a threat to their authority; Jesus was questioned by them, and at their request he was executed by the Roman authorities, just outside Jerusalem. The method of execution was crucifixion. After three days Jesus was resurrected, that is, he rose from the dead, and was seen by his disciples. Jesus suffered and gave up his life so that others may be saved.

According to estimates, he was born around 4 BCE, and was crucified around 30 CE.

Over the years there has been considerable controversy about the life and nature of the historical Jesus, including on the virgin birth, and whether or not he was married. Ancient documents known as the Dead Sea Scrolls throw new light on the times in which he lived, but these texts have not yet been fully studied. Whatever the historical truth may be, it does not detract from or alter the essential truth of his teachings.

Jesus in India According to Indian tradition, Jesus came to India between the ages of twelve and thirty. As a young man he visited Kashmir, Punjab, Tibet, Varanasi and other places, preached to the people in India, and also studied with Indian yogis and gurus. There is no historical evidence for this, but it remains a strong tradition, and books have been written on it by Indians and Westerners. Of course, among Western esoteric groups there are also traditions, unsupported by any evidence, that at this time Jesus was initiated and transformed in the pyramids of Egypt.

In other accounts, Jesus came to India again after his crucifixion. According to this theory, he did not die on the cross but was taken down and revived. He then returned to India and ended his days in Kashmir.

Claims have been made on the location of his tomb there, and one researcher claims to have found both his tomb and that of his mother MARY. His tomb has been identified with that of one Yus Asaf, located in Khaniyra in the northern part of Srinagar, though there are other identifications as well. Some even locate the tomb of Moses in Kashmir. Jesus's name had many variations in different languages, and one of them, ISA, which occurs in Islamic texts, is similar to Isha or Ishvara, a term commonly used for God in India.

Apart from local oral traditions, books have been written on these themes since the late nineteenth century. One of the earliest is a French book written in 1894 by Nicolas Notovitch, a Russian journalist, later translated as *The Unknown Life of Jesus*. Notovitch claimed knowledge of a Buddhist account of Jesus' life in India, narrated to him when he was recovering from an injury at the HEMIS GOMPA. Mirza GHULAM AHMAD, founder of the AHMADIYA sect, wrote an account of Jesus in India after the crucifixion, published in Urdu in 1899. Since then there have been many more such books.

Several spiritual leaders in India have pointed out similarities between Jesus and KRISHNA, stating that both 'Christ' and 'Krishna' are derived from the same root word. In addition, the story of Jesus's life has at least one similarity with that of Krishna. At Krishna's birth, King Kamsa of MATHURA ordered all children below the age of one to be killed, as it had been prophesied that Krishna would kill him.

At a popular level, Jesus is often worshipped along with other deities, even by non-Christians.

Jesus in Islam Jesus, known in Islam as ISA, is recognized as a Prophet, a messenger of God, but is not considered the same as God. He was born of MARY, without a father, but is not the son of God, because ALLAH is One and therefore cannot have a son. According to Islam, Jesus was not crucified; only a likeness of him was executed. Several Muslims in India subscribe to the theory that Jesus lived in India for some time and died in Kashmir.

Jetavana A Buddhist monastery located in SHRAVASTI, in present-day Uttar Pradesh. It was donated to the SANGHA by Anathapindika, a wealthy banker who lived at the time of the BUDDHA and was his disciple. The site is said to have been selected by SHARIPUTRA, a close disciple of the Buddha. The Buddha lived here during the monsoon season in the last twenty-five years of his life.

Jewish calendar and festivals The traditional Jewish year has twelve lunar months, each having twenty-nine or thirty days. There are approximately 354 days in a year. An extra lunar month is added every few years to bring it in line with the solar calendar. The new year is celebrated in September/October, with the festival of ROSH HASHANAH; YOM KIPPUR occurs eight days later followed by SUKKOTH, or the Feast of Tabernacles.

It concludes with Simchat Torah (the rejoicing of the Torah). CHANUKAH, the festival of lights, takes place next, usually in December. Ten weeks later is Purim, while at the beginning of spring the PASSOVER is celebrated to commemorate the Exodus from Egypt.

Jews in India Jews, who follow the religion of JUDAISM, lived in India since ancient times, but after the creation of Israel in 1948 most of them gradually migrated there. At the same time, however new Jewish groups are emerging. According to the 1991 census, there were 5271 Jews in India.

It is not known when Jews first settled in India, though based on legendary and traditional accounts, there may have been Jews on the Kerala coast as far back as 1000 BCE. The Bene Israel and tribal groups claiming a Jewish ancestry also believe they were here since ancient times. The main groups of Jews in India were the KERALA JEWS, the BENE ISRAEL, the MARRANO JEWS from Spain and Portugal, the PERSIAN-SPEAKING JEWS, the BAGHDADI JEWS, and the ASHKENAZIM. Among other groups claiming Jewish ancestry are the BNEI MENASHE and the ANDHRA JEWS.

Clear evidence of Jewish settlements on the western coast exists only from the eleventh century. Jews reached their height in population and wealth at the time of British rule in India.

Jewish SYNAGOGUES were constructed from the twelfth century onwards. Today many of them are abandoned, while others have difficulty in putting together a minyan or quorum for the service. There are also insufficient members for various traditional ceremonies. Other groups, however, such as the Bnei Menashe, are growing. Some Israeli Jews in search of spiritual peace, are also setting in India.

jihad A term in Islam that means 'striving' or 'effort in the way of God'. Jihad has both an outer and an inner meaning. The outer meaning is to wage war against unbelievers, to strive to get people to accept the way of Islam. As Judaism and Christianity originally enjoyed some acceptance in Islam, this striving or effort was against those who did not follow a sacred book or believe in one God. Later it implied warfare against those who did not accept Islam, but in India this policy was not followed. Iltutmish (ruled 1211–36), one of the early sultans of DELHI, was asked why he did not convert Hindus by the sword. He replied that for the present Hindus were just too many, when numbered against his officers and soldiers.

On the whole Islamic rulers in India attempted to understand indigenous religious ideas and concepts, and to protect people of all religions, though at times conversion by force did take place.

The internal meaning of jihad is to wage war against the evils within oneself, and thus to strive in the way of God. This interpretation is favoured by most adherents of Islam today, with the exception of a few extremist groups.

Jina A term that literally means 'conqueror', used for a liberated being who has conquered himself. The term is specifically used in Jainism for the TIRTHANKARAS, but also in other religions for those who are enlightened. Thus Jina is a term also used as an epithet of the BUDDHA.

Jinachandra Suri A Jain scholar of the Kharatara GACHCHHA, who lived in the sixteenth century and influenced the Mughal emperor AKBAR. Jinachandra was invited for discussions by Akbar and reached his court in Lahore in 1592, along with other Jain monks. He was given the title Yuga Pradhan (Lord of the Age) by Akbar. Some of his disciples accompanied Akbar to Kashmir, and on their request Akbar passed orders protecting all living beings there, including fish, for eight days. Jinachandra's noted disciples at the court included SAMAYASUNDARA, Gunavinaya and Jinasimha Suri.

Jinadasagani A Jain scholar of the seventh century who wrote a Churni or commentary on the *AVASSAYA SUTTA (Avashyaka Sutra)*. This commentary also contains a long description of MAHAVIRA's travels during the years after he became an ascetic and before he achieved enlightenment. The account is probably based on earlier sources.

Jinasena A Jain scholar who wrote a large part of the Jain *ADI PURANA* in the ninth century, in the time of the Rashtrakuta king Amoghavarsha (815–77). Jinasena was a pupil of the Jain scholar Virasena and was honoured by Amoghavarsha.

jinn A term for a spirit in Islam. According to the QURAN, jinns were created before human beings, from the fire of a scorching wind. They have some free will.

Jinnah, M.A. A Muslim leader who spear-headed the movement for the creation of Pakistan. Born in Karachi (now in Pakistan) on 25 December 1876, he initially joined the Indian National Congress but later became a leader of the Muslim League, a party primarily for Muslims. After 1937 he opposed the Congress and worked for a separate state for Muslims, though in his personal life he had secular beliefs. In 1947, his dream came partially true with the creation of two separate countries of India and Pakistan. Jinnah became the governor general of Pakistan, but died at Karachi soon after, on 11 September 1948. This division into two countries led to riots in which about one million people were killed and ten million displaced, and worsened the relations between Hindus and Muslims. Jinnah believed that Muslims would be at a disadvantage in the new India, but despite the creation of a separate state, there are more Muslims in India than in Pakistan.

jiva (1) A Sanskrit term which implies a living being.

(2) It also signifyies the individual soul. In SAMKHYA philosophy, the jiva is the Self, distinct from the senses and the body. According to SHANKARA, the jiva is in essence identical with the absolute ATMAN or BRAHMAN. For RAMANUJA, the individual soul is a form of the Supreme, yet is unique, endowed with intelligence and self-consciousness. It remains unchanged through a series of lives, retaining its identity, and is distinct from the body, the breath or the intelligence. According to MADHVA, the number of jivas is infinite, and they are different from Brahman. NIMBARKA believed that the jiva is both different from, and united with Brahman. These are broadly the main views in Hindu philosophy, with other philosophers varying in the details.

jiva, in Jainism In Jain thought, everything in the universe is classified into two categories, jiva and AJIVA, which broadly mean life and non-life.

Jiva signifies the soul. The nature of the jiva is chetana, or chitsvarupa, that is, it has the qualities of perception and knowledge. It performs actions and reaps the fruit of its actions. There are an infinite number of jivas, which exist for eternity. The jiva joins together with PUDGALA, or matter, to form a body and after death enters another body. Each jiva goes through a series of births and deaths, from rock to plant to animal, evolving all the time. Freeing itself from ajiva and from the cycle of birth and death through its own efforts, it achieves MOKSHA (liberation), and is known as a SIDDHA, or perfected being.

The jiva exists in plants, animals and people, as well as in natural substances, such as wind or water. When linked to a body or to some form of matter, jivas can be classified into different groups. Ekendriya jivas are those with one sense organ, that of touch, and comprise the whole vegetable kingdom. Microscopic ekendriya jivas also exist in earth, air, water and light. Worms, termites and similar creatures represent jivas with two sense organs (touch and taste), while ants, beetles and moths are included in the third group, which also have the sense of smell. Bees, locusts and scorpions are among those in the fourth category, while panchendriya jivas have five senses, including the mind. This latter category includes higher animals, of which humans are the highest. Jivas are also classified according to their states of existence, i.e. divine beings, human beings, dwellers in hell, and others, including animals and plants. All these constitute SAMSARA, and moksha represents the escape from this cycle of samsara. The liberated or Siddha Jiva is akin to a god. This perfected being has infinite knowledge, vision and bliss, but does not intervene in life on earth. Thus a Kevala, TIRTHANKARA or Siddha Jiva serves as an inspiration to others to pursue the same goal, and worshipping them is a mark of reverence, and of dedication to achieve the same end.

Jivandhara A character in the Jain *UTTARA PURANA* that forms part of the ninth century *Trishashtilakshana Mahapurana*.

Jivandhara's story is popular in Jain texts and is retold several times, both in Sanskrit and in Tamil. He was the son of Queen Vijaya, wife of King Satyandhara of Rajapura. The king was killed before the child was born, but protected by a YAKSHI, the queen gave birth in a cremation ground. The child was given to the merchant Gandhotkata and his wife Nanda to rear, while the queen lived in a hermitage. Nanda's son, as well as other children of the king and his followers, all grew up together. Of these seven children, Jivandhara was the wisest and most remarkable. As a young man he married eight beautiful women and performed several remarkable feats. He tamed a wild elephant and rescued a dog who turned into a yaksha and became his protector. With a magic ring given to him by the yaksha he could take on any form he liked. After many adventures he reclaimed his father's kingdom, but after meeting MAHAVIRA he abdicated in favour of his son and became a Jain monk. His eight wives and his mother became Jain nuns.

In Tamil, this story is known as the *Shivakachintamani* or *Civakachintamani*.

jizya A tax levied on non-Muslims by Muslim rulers. In India, it was first imposed in Sind, conquered by the Arabs in 712. After 1200 the DELHI sultans extended the tax to parts of north India. The tax was payable according to the wealth of the assessees. Originally members of the BRAHMANA caste were exempted from payment, but from the reign of Sultan Firuz Shah Tughlaq (1351–88), brahmanas were included. The Mughal emperor AKBAR abolished the jizya in 1564, but it was reimposed by his great-grandson AURANGZEB in 1679.

It was abolished again by the Mughal emperor Farrukhsiyar in 1713 and reintroduced by him in 1717. In theory, it continued to be levied by succeeding Mughal emperors, but in practice it was discontinued from the time of the emperor Muhammad Shah (1719–48).

In other parts of India, the jizya tax was levied by Muslim rulers from time to time. In Kashmir, it was abolished by the enlightened ruler Zain-ul-Abidin (1420–70). In the Deccan, Ibrahim Qutb Shah (1550–80) of Golkonda did not impose the tax. The payment of the tax guaranteed protection by the state.

jnana A Sanskrit term that means knowledge. Jnana Marga is the path of knowledge leading to the realization of god. Jnana Yoga is a similar term, a means of achieving union with the divine through knowledge. To use knowledge to attain divine unity it is necessary to understand the nature and structure of knowledge. Thus all the ancient schools of philosophy, the SAMKHYA, NYAYA, VAISHESHIKA, VEDANTA, YOGA and MIMAMSA, analyse knowledge extensively. These analyses differ in details, but in general they distinguish between valid and invalid knowledge, and attempt to classify the means of valid knowledge, or pramanas. Three means of valid knowledge, accepted by most of these schools are perception, inference, and scriptural testimony.

In Jainism, jnana or knowledge is an intrinsic part of JIVA, the soul. In its pure state the soul has perfect knowledge, but this is limited by the accumulation of KARMA. Jnana is basically of five kinds: mati, shruta, avadhi, manah-paryaya and kevala.

Mati jnana is the usual inferential knowledge, based on sense perceptions. Shruta jnana is what is revealed by the scriptures. Avadhi jnana is knowledge beyond the senses, or clairvoyance. Manah-paryaya jnana is the knowledge of other's thoughts, obtained through yoga and TAPAS (austerity). Kevala jnana is perfect or infinite knowledge.

In Jainism, objects are real and not illusory as in Advaita. However, the perceptions of the same object can vary. The concepts of ANEKANTAVADA, or relativity, NAYA, or the different ways of looking at a thing, and SYADVADA, or the 'probable' but not definite nature of what seems real, form an important part of Jain theories of knowledge.

In Buddhism, Jnana or knowledge is analysed in a number of different ways by the various Buddhist schools. In MAHAYANA Buddhism, it is one of the ten perfections (PARAMITAS).

Jnaneshvara A BHAKTI saint who was probably born around 1275 at Alandi in present Maharashtra. His grandparents were followers of GORAKHNATHA. His father Vitthala, named after the god VITTHALA at PANDHARPUR, had taken SANNYASA, but returned to his married life on the advice of a saint. The BRAHMANAS of Alandi criticized this, and after the birth of four children, Vitthala ended his life at PRAYAGA on their advice. Soon after, his wife Rukmini followed him. Jnaneshvara's elder brother Nivrittinatha then became his guru after being initiated by a saint. At a young age, Jnaneshvara attained perfect knowledge. When he was fifteen, he explained the BHAGAVAD GITA in Marathi, and his commentary was written down and known as *Jnaneshvari*. He then wrote a philosophical work, *Amritanubhava*. His other works are *Changdeva Pasashti*, in which he gave advice to Changdeva, a well-known yogi, *Haripatha, Naman*, and several ABHANGAS. When he was just twenty-two he is said to have voluntarily entered SAMADHI at Alandi.

His best-known work is the *Jnaneshvari*, which is alternatively called *Bhavartha-Dipika*. It focuses on BHAKTI Yoga, and is notable as it is the first great text written in Marathi. *Amritanubhava* also deals with the path of Bhakti and describes the beauty of natural devotion. *Haripatha* has twenty-eight abhangas, which are recited every day by devotees of Vitthala, while *Naman* explains the importance of prayer.

Jnaneshvara explains that the ATMAN is self-luminous and self-conscious. The Self, and the knower of the Self, are like a god and goddess who are inseparable and united. In this he differs from the SAMKHYA theory of PURUSHA and PRAKRITI, which have different qualities. Jnaneshvara also challenged SHANKARA's views and said that the world was real, and a reflection of God.

He taught that ethical behaviour and bhakti lead to a realization of the divine Self.

Jnaneshvara was the first in a line of bhakti saints in Maharashtra. He was also known as Jnanoba Mauli, or the mother of devotees.

Jogeshwari Cave Temple A temple of the Hindu god SHIVA located at Jogeshwari in Maharashtra. This rock-cut temple dates back to the time of the Chalukya dynasty in the sixth century. Two flights of stairs lead up to the temple, which is entered through a square MANDAPA with rock-cut pillars. In the centre of this hall is the main shrine. Very few of the original sculptures still exist, among them being a NATARAJA figure and a scene of SHIVA and PARVATI playing dice.

Jones, Sir William An Englishman who founded the Asiatic Society of Bengal, and whose study of languages later led to the theory of a common INDO-EUROPEAN LANGUAGE.

Born in 1746 in England, he was educated at Oxford and studied various languages including Arabic, Persian, Hebrew, Chinese, French and other European languages. He also studied law.

In 1783 he became the judge of the Supreme Court at Kolkata (Calcutta). His interest in oriental languages and texts led him to establish the Asiatic Society of Bengal in 1784 to encourage the preserv-ation and study of India's rich heritage. He learnt Sanskrit and translated some Sanskrit texts into English, including the *Abhijnanashakuntalam* of KALIDASA, the *MANU SMRITI*, the *HITOPADESHA* and the *GITA GOVINDA*. His other works include a translation of an account of the life of Nadir Shah of Persia who invaded India in 1739, from Persian into French; a *Grammar of the Persian Language*; the *Muhammadan Law of Succession*; and the *Muhammadan Law of Inheritance*.

His most important contribution was his comparative study of Sanskrit, Greek and other languages, which other scholars used to formulate the theory of a common parent language, Proto Indo-European.

Judaism Judaism, the religion of the Jews, originated and developed outside India, but there was at one time a sizable Jewish population in the country. Today the number of Jews has diminished, though there are new Jewish groups emerging and developing. (see JEWS in INDIA).

History: Judaism can be traced back to ancient times, and is linked with its history, partly revealed in the Hebrew BIBLE, and supported to some extent by archaeology. The early Hebrews were nomadic, and according to tradition, Abraham migrated from Mesopotamia to Canaan (later called Palestine). His grandson, Jacob, was renamed Israel ('striver with God') and had twelve sons, ancestors of the twelve tribes of Israel. Joseph, one of Jacob's sons, was sold into slavery in Egypt. He prospered there and was joined by his brothers and father, but later their descendants were enslaved. Around the thirteenth century BCE, MOSES delivered them from slavery, and led an exodus to Canaan. They crossed the Red Sea and went to Mount Sinai, where the Ten Commandments were revealed to Moses. The TORAH, or the first five books of the Bible, is also attributed to Moses.

Around the eleventh century the dynasty of David was founded and King Solomon built the first Jewish temple in c. 950 BCE. After his death two kingdoms emerged: Israel in the north, with ten of the twelve tribes, and Judah in the south with two tribes. The northern kingdom was destroyed by the Assyrians in 721 BCE, but the southern kingdom lasted till the defeat of Jerusalem by the Babylonians and the destruction of the temple in 587–86 BCE, when most Jews were deported to Babylon. Cyrus, the ruler of Persia, defeated Babylon in 539 BCE and allowed the Jews to return to Jerusalem and rebuild the temple. By this time, the ten tribes of the northern kingdom had been lost and scattered. (see ISRAEL, LOST TRIBES OF). The Jewish community that returned were the people of Judah. They remained under the Persians and later the Greeks, but were able to practice their religion in peace, though one of the Greeks, Antiochus Epiphanes (ruled 174–64 BCE) attempted to prevent them. He was defeated by a rebellion led by Judas Maccabees and his family, known as the Hasmoneans, and the Jewish Temple was rededicated in 164 BCE. This event is celebrated in the festival of CHANUKAH. The Hasmonean priests ruled the area until the Romans occupied Palestine in 63 BCE. The temple continued to flourish and was even enlarged, but was finally destroyed by the Romans in 70 CE.

After the destruction of the temple most Jews had to leave Palestine and were scattered throughout the world. In the twentieth century, a movement to create a homeland for the Jews was started. At this time Palestine was an Arab state under a British mandate. After the Second World War and the Holocaust that took place under Hitler, there was increasing pressure to create a separate state for Jews. In 1948, before leaving the area, the British partitioned Palestine, creating the separate state of Israel in part of it. The ensuing conflict between Israelis and Palestinians continues till today.

Religion Like other religions, Judaism has several phases of development. Though Jews trace their religion back to Biblical days, many of the beliefs and practices of Judaism developed after the destruction of the second temple in 70 CE. It was at this time that Christianity separated from Judaism. The synagogue became the meeting place of the community and the leaders or Rabbis were lay teachers and not priests. This phase is known as Rabbinical Judaism, as it is based on texts compiled by the Rabbis, including the MISHNAH, the TALMUD commentaries, and the MIDRASH. Other sources of Judaism, include the later writings of several theologians.

Jews believe in one God, Yahweh, and in a covenant that he made with his people. The Jews were chosen by God to follow His commandments and to be a model for the human race. Jewish laws, known as MITZVAH, are contained in the Torah and permeate every aspect of life.

Describing the Jewish religion, Arthur Herzberg writes, 'The emphasis of Jewish faith . . . is on human action . . . Every man plays his role, for good or ill, in the redemptive history of mankind, for man is God's partner in the work of creation.' Though God is omnipotent, man has free will and is responsible for his own actions and the well-being of society. The essential goal of the religion is to be like God, to walk in his footsteps.

Man cannot know or understand God's plans, or the reasons for suffering, but finally a MESSIAH will come and God will create a second world, where people will be rewarded for their deeds, though God does not leave his people entirely without reward and punishment in this world.

In the nineteenth century there were attempts to reform Judaism and the main Jewish groups outside Israel today are divided into followers of Orthodox, Reformed and Conservative Judaism. Orthodox, refers to a number of Jewish groups that accept traditional beliefs and practices. Reformed Judaism has dropped a number of traditions, while Conservative Judaism retains the essentials of traditional Judaism, with some modernization. In addition, Reconstructionist Judaism attempts to review the basic principles of the religion, in the context of modern developments and social change. There are several sub-groups within these broad categories. In Israel, however, there are basically two divisions, between those who observe the Jewish laws strictly, and those who do not. Apart from these groups, there are mystical aspects of Judaism, including the MERKABAH and KABBALAH.

Both Christianity and Islam recognize the Prophets of Judaism, and the Hebrew Bible, with some variations, is also a basic Christian text.

There are also some similarities with Zoroastrianism, especially in the emphasis on human responsibility and the ultimate creation of a new world.

Junnar A town located in Maharashtra. On the hills around it are more than 150 Buddhist rock-cut CHAITYAS and VIHARAS, dated between the second century BCE and the second century CE. The caves are classified into various groups. Cave 3 of the Tulja Lena group, 2 km west of Junnar, has a circular chaitya hall with twelve octagonal pillars around a plain hemispherical STUPA. Cave 40 of the Bhuta Lena group on the Manmodi hill has a large chaitya hall, its arched doorway carved with reliefs of LAKSHMI, elephants and other images. Cave 7 of the Ganesha Lena group on the Lenyadri hill has a vihara with nineteen cells.

Jvalamukhi Temple A temple located in the Kangra Valley in Himachal Pradesh, built around natural flames emanating from gases in the ground and worshipped as the Hindu goddess Jvalamukhi, a form of SATI, consort of SHIVA. The flames are considered to be sacred fire coming from the mouth of the goddess (jvala = fire, mukhi = mouth). The temple attracts numerous pilgrims, particularly during April/ May, when a special festival is held.

Jyeshtha A Hindu mother goddess who was once popular in south India, but is hardly worshipped there now. The *Bodhayana Grihya Sutra* has a whole chapter on the worship of this goddess. She is said to have 'lions attached to her chariot and tigers following her'. Her other names are given as Kapila-Patni, Kumbhi, Jyaya, Hastimukha, Vighnaparshada and Niririti. In the VISHNUDHARMOTTARA and other texts she is described as two-armed and long-nosed, with long and pendulous breasts. She holds a lotus in her right hand and is surrounded by her children. She has a crow-banner and holds a broom, while her son has the face of a bull. In one text she is described as riding a donkey. In Tamil texts her names are Mugadi, Tauvai, Kaladi and Mudevi, meaning crow-bannered and ass-rider. Myths indicate that she was once a local deity, absorbed later into the VAISHNAVITE pantheon. She is also known as ALAKSHMI and was originally malefic. It is said that she should be propitiated by women.

jyotisha The science of ASTROLOGY and astronomy, which forms one of the VEDANGAS or Vedic sciences.

Ka A Sanskrit word that means 'who?', and came to represent a deity, particularly PRAJAPATI. A hymn in the RIG VEDA (10.121) asks which god (Ka) should be adored. It begins:

In the beginning rose HIRANYAGARBHA, born only lord of all created beings. He fixed and holdeth up this earth and heaven. What god shall we adore with our creation?
Giver of vital breath, of power and vigour, he whose commandments all the gods acknowledge: the lord of death, whose shade is life immortal. What god shall we adore with our oblation? (Trans. R.T.H. Griffith)

Each verse ends with this question; the end of the hymn provides the answer: 'Prajapati! Thou only comprehend all these created things, and none beside thee.' In the later VEDIC SAMHITAS and BRAHMANAS, Ka is used both as a name of Prajapati and a name of the Supreme Deity.

Kaba The main shrine of all Muslims, located at Mecca. It is a cubical structure enclosing a black stone and is said to have been made by Ibrahim (Abraham), at the spot where he had been prepared to sacrifice his son at the command of God. Ibrahim's construction supersedes an earlier structure made by Adam. The Kaba building is about 12 m by 10 m and 15 m high. Within it, on the east, is the black stone, at a height of 1.5 m. According to tradition, the black stone, which is an object of veneration and looks like a meteorite, was placed there by Adam and later by the angel Gabriel. The Kaba was destroyed in warfare and rebuilt several times. In 930 a SHIA group, the Qarmatians, invaded the area and took away the stone. It was restored in 951, but had broken into seven pieces; it is now held together by silver rings. The whole building is covered in black cloth with gold embroidery, or partly with white at the time of Haj, and is changed every year. Muslims all over the world pray facing the direction of the Kaba. A large mosque, known as the Grand Mosque, surrounds it, and can accommodate two million pilgrims.

The Kaba has a long history and initially had a number of idols around it, that were worshipped by local tribes. At one time, to differentiate his religion from those of the tribes, MUHAMMAD advocated praying while facing the direction of Jerusalem. In 630 he destroyed the idols in the Kaba and established it as the centre of Islamic pilgrimage.

Kabbalah A Jewish mystical tradition that originated in the middle ages. Its main text is the *Zohar*, compiled in Spain in the thirteenth century. There are several commentaries and elaborations on this text; Isaac Luria (1534–72) is considered one of the most important Kabbalah mystics who developed its ideas further. The Kabbalah reinterprets Jewish texts and beliefs in an esoteric, symbolic way. It describes ten Sefirot, or emanations of God, which represent the inner reality of the world. The Sefirot are depicted in a symbolic tree and are connected by twenty-two pathways. The mystical rituals of the Kabbalah, aim to reveal the SHEKHINAH, the divine presence within.

Kabir A BHAKTI saint probably of the fifteenth century. His verses, written in simple colloquial Hindi of his times, are non-sectarian and have universal appeal. There are different stories regarding his early life, but a popular version is that he was a Hindu child adopted by Muslim parents. His dates of birth and death are also uncertain, though it is likely he was born around 1398 in KASHI or Varanasi. He was of the Julaha caste, a caste of weavers who can be either Muslim or Hindu, therefore, this too, does not provide any clear information on his religion. This ambiguity about his origin is reflected in his popularity in both communities.

Kabir is said to have been a disciple of the VAISHNAVA saint RAMANANDA, and to have been inspired by SUFI saints and NATHA YOGIS. He was not learned and had not studied sacred texts but was divinely inspired, and spoke about the One Reality, beyond form. He was against distinctions between different religions and castes, worship in temples and mosques, idol worship, rituals and ceremonies, and advocated truth, love and compassion. His songs were written down by his followers, who are known as Kabir Panthis. *Bijak*, a compilation of his verses, is considered a sacred text today. His verses were also included in the GURU GRANTH SAHIB, the sacred scripture of the Sikhs, and the *Kabir Granthavali* based on the *Panchvani*, a text of the followers of DADU, the Dadu Panthis of Rajasthan.

There are also several compositions assigned to him that were probably written by others. His compositions were basically of two kinds: dohas, or two-line couplets, and padas or songs. In addition, he composed Ramainis, verses with esoteric meanings.

Though Kabir spoke of RAMA or HARI, he used these as names of the Absolute and not of personalized incarnations. In one of his dohas, he says:

Him whom I went out to seek,
I found just where I was;
He has now become myself,
Whom before I called Another! (Trans. C. Vaudeville)

In another song he talks of the Lord of Kabir, which lies in the heart:

The Jogi cries, 'Gorakh, Gorakh!',
The Hindu repeats the name of Rama,
The Muslim says, 'There is One God',
But the Lord of Kabir
Is in all.

Kadam/Kadampa A school of TIBETAN BUDDHISM, also spelt Bka-gdams-pa, founded by DROMSTON (1008–64), the disciple of ATISHA. Dromston built a STUPA and monastery housing the relics of Atisha. The main text of the school was the *Bodhipatha Pradipa* of Atisha, and a strict monastic discipline was followed. SHAKYAMUNI BUDDHA, the Bodhisattva AVALOKITESHVARA, his consort TARA, and the protective deity Achala were revered. The school emphasized the practices of both Sutras (traditional texts) and TANTRAS in a graded path (LAM-RIM), and had a series of instructions on developing the bodhichitta or 'thought of enlightenment'. The Kadam school died out by the fourteenth century, but some of its teachings were preserved in the GELUG and KAGYU schools.

Kadimi/Kadmi A Zoroastrian sect that means 'ancient' and which arose among the PARSIS in India in the eighteenth century, after a dispute regarding the calendar. As a lunar calendar is followed, it was earlier the practice to add an extra month to the calendar every 120 years. Parsis in India claimed this practice was followed from the twelfth century. As contacts with Zoroastrians in Iran revived, they realized the Iranian calendar was one month behind. In 1745 a group of Parsis therefore corrected their calendar according to this, and called themselves Kadimi, the followers of the ancient practice. Most Parsis opposed this and were known as SHAHENSHAHIS, followers of the 'royal' traditional calendar. Conflicts between the two groups took place, and inter-marriage between members of the two sects was rare.

Though the two sects still exist, there are no longer any conflicts. Festival dates fall on different days for each, with a third set of festivals following the Fasli calendar (*See* Zoroastrian Calendar).

Kadru In Hindu mythology, one of the wives of the rishi KASHYAPA, and a daughter of DAKSHA. She is the mother of a thousand serpents, among whom are Shesha and Vasuki.

Kagyu One of the four main schools of TIBETAN BUDDHISM, also spelt Bka-brgyud-pa, which traces its origin to two Indian Buddhists, TILOPA and NAROPA. Marpa (1012–97), a Tibetan Buddhist, travelled to India to study from them. After returning to Tibet, he laid the foundations of this school, advocating the practice of the Mahamudra or 'great seal', and the 'Six Yogas of Naropa'. His disciple was MILARASPA (Milarepa), whose student Gampopa (1079–1153) organized the teachings into a lineage known as Dakpo Kagyu, or the mother lineage of the Kagyu school. In the twelfth century, four major schools arose from this, founded by disciples of Gampopa. These were the Tsalpa Kagyu, Barom Kagyu, Phagmo Drupa or Phagtru Kagyu and Kamtsang or Karma Kagyu. Eight sub-schools of the Phagtru Kagyu developed, of which three are still active today. They are the DRIGUNG KAGYU (Brigung), the TAGLUNG KAGYU and the DRUGPA KAGYU (Brugpa). These three, as well as the KARMA KAGYU, were re-established in India after 1959. Another major Kagyu school is the Shangpa Kagyu, established by Khyungpo Nyaljor (978–1079). Monks in all sub-sects of the Kagyu tradition study the Perfection of Wisdom (PRAJNAPARAMITA), and MADHYAMIKA philosophy, as well as theories of valid cognition, discipline and phenomenology, with some variations of interpretation in each school. They also focus on interpreting the Mahamudra through the SUTRAS and TANTRAS, and on the practice of the Six Yogas.

Kagyur A term for a collection of the Tibetan Buddhist canon, also spelt Bkagyur or Kanjur. In TIBETAN BUDDHISM the texts are divided into two groups, known as Kagyur and TANGYUR. The Kagyur includes thirteen volumes of Vinaya texts, twenty-one volumes of PRAJNAPARAMITA texts, six volumes of Avatamshaka texts, six volumes of Ratnakuta texts, thirty volumes of Sutras, which include 270 texts, and twenty-two volumes of TANTRAS incorporating more than 300 texts.

Kailasha mountain A mountain located in Tibet, that is considered sacred by Hindus, Buddhists and Jains. To its south lies MANASAROVARA, a sacred lake. Kailasha is also called Gana Parvata and Rajatadri (silver mountain). The gods SHIVA and PARVATI are said to reside here and it is sometimes identified with Mt MERU of Hindu myths. In Buddhist texts, it is said that the BUDDHA, along with 500 BODHISATTVAS, still lives here. Legendary accounts state that four footprints of the Buddha can be seen on the four sides of the mountain. According to Jain texts, the mountain is known as Ashtapada, and the first Jain TIRTHANKARA, Adinatha or RISHABHA, attained liberation here.

Pilgrimages to the mountain have taken place since ancient times, and even today pilgrims from India visit the mountain every year.

Kailasha Temple A temple of the Hindu god SHIVA located at ELLORA in Maharashtra, constructed in the eighth century at the time of the Rashtrakuta dynasty. This remarkable monument is the largest and finest of the rock-cut temples in India, made like a structural temple, raised on a solid base. Steps lead up to the temple, which opens on the west into a large columned MANDAPA or hall, with three porches. The ante-chamber on the east leads to the inner shrine, and around it there are five small shrines on an open terrace. The pyramidal tower reaches a height of 32.6 m above the level of the court, while the roof is formed by an octagonal dome. Elaborate sculptures decorate all the walls, including scenes from the MAHABHARATA and RAMAYANA, along with depictions of Shiva and other deities. Some murals can still be seen on the porch ceilings. In front of the temple is a NANDI pavilion and on either side of it are monolithic columns, 17 m tall, as well as two elephants. On the outside is a screen wall with a gateway. The temple is built in Dravidian style.

Kailashnatha Temple A temple of the Hindu god SHIVA located in KANCHIPURAM in Tamil Nadu, constructed in the eighth century, at the time of the Pallava ruler Rajasimha. The main shrine has a multi-faceted Shiva LINGA and a SOMASKANDA panel on the rear wall. This is surrounded by a narrow passageway. The whole temple is raised on a basement, which is carved with GANAS or Shiva's attendants, and with foliage. Images of Shiva decorate the outer walls. On the north is an image of BHAIRAVA, and on the south, Shiva emerging from a linga, with VISHNU and BRAHMA on two sides. The shrine has a pyramidal roof and is constructed mainly from sandstone.

kala A Sanskrit term for time. The concept of Kala has been extensively analyzed in philosophy. In the NYAYA and VAISHESHIKA, systems, kala is one of the DRAVYAS or substances. According to the Vaisheshika, it is an eternal substance, the cause for change in non-eternal substances. In Jainism, too, kala is one of the six dravyas or substances of the world. It pervades the whole universe and continues from the past into the present. Kala is eternal time, without beginning or end, and from it proceeds relative time, known as samaya. Samaya can be seen through change and motion, through creation and destruction. In SAMKHYA philosophy, space and time can be both eternal and limited, and eternal time is part of PRAKRITI. According to SHANKARA, time has reality only in the world of experience. In the PURANAS and other texts, there are varying views of time, as either eternal or limited. Time has also been subdivided into minuscule units, or expanded into vast cosmic ages, such as YUGAS and KALPAS. Kala is also time which destroys all things.

Kala, deity A name of YAMA, the god of death in Hinduism. The gods BRAHMA and SHIVA are sometimes also referred to as Kala.

Kalachakra 'The wheel of time', a mystical and occult system in Tantric Buddhism (See TANTRA, BUDDHIST). According to tradition, the mysteries of the Kalachakra were taught by SHAKYAMUNI BUDDHA, to King Suchindra, who was an emanation of the Bodhisattva Vajrapani and came from the hidden land of SHAMBHALA. He then returned there, and the teachings were transmitted through the Kalkis (leaders) of Shambhala and later reintroduced into India and then into Tibet. The teachings are described in the *Kalachakra Tantra*, a text of about the tenth or eleventh century, thought to have been composed in Central Asia, and later written in Sanskrit. It is classified as an ANUTTARAYOGA TANTRA, or one of the highest Tantras. There are also commentaries and explanations on the text.

Three Kalachakras or wheels are described: the outer, the inner, and the 'other' that unites the first two.

The system of the Kalachakra is taught through a series of initiations, before which certain codes of conduct and other practices must be observed. This is considered the highest of all occult initiations and can only be performed by a DALAI LAMA. The present Dalai Lama regularly conducts the Kalachakra initiation ceremony, in which the Kalachakra, symbolizing the BUDDHA and other deities, is visualized. A Kalachakra temple has been constructed at Siliguri.

Kaladi A town in Kerala, the birthplace of Sri SHANKARA, who is also known as Adi Shankaracharya, the ninth-century philosopher of ADVAITA. Located on the river Alwaye, the town has a number of temples, among which are one with an image of Shankara and another of the goddess SHARADA. There is a KRISHNA temple nearby.

Shankara Jayanti, the birthday of Shankara, is an important festival celebrated here on the fifth day after the new moon in April/May.

Kaladungar Temple A Hindu temple on the Kaladungar hill in the Rann of Kachchh in Gujarat. According to tradition, the rishi DATTATREYA lived for twelve years on this hill before attaining SAMADHI. While he lived here, he used to distribute the temple prasada (food offerings) both to his devotees and to the jackals who live in this barren region. At a time of famine, when he had no prasada to distribute, he offered the starving jackals his own hand. According to one version of the story, the jackals refused it, upon which Dattatreya said that the noble jackal was henceforth his symbol, and his devotees must offer them prasada for the fulfilment of their wishes. Thus even today, prasada consisting of sweet rice is offered to the local jackals twice a day.

Kalahastishvara Temple A temple of the Hindu god SHIVA, in the town of Kalahasti in Andhra Pradesh.

It is located at the foot of the Kailasgiri hill, called the 'southern KAILASHA'. First constructed in the eighth century at the time of the Pallava dynasty, major additions were made by the Cholas, and later, by the Vijayanagara rulers. In 1912 the temple was partly reconstructed and assumed its present form. Kalahastishvara is famous as the main shrine contains the Vayu LINGA, representing the element of air. The linga is shaped like the trunk of an elephant and when viewed from the top, looks like a snake. The base appears like a spider. According to legend, an elephant, a snake and a spider were the first worshippers of the linga, but accidently killed each other. Because of their devotion to him, Shiva granted them all MOKSHA or liberation. Apart from the main shrine, there are other shrines as well. An underground shrine is dedicated to the god GANESHA, here known as Patala Vinayaka.

The temple has images of Shiva, other deities, and of SHAIVITE saints, including Kannappa, a NAYANAR devotee who gave his eyes to the lord, but whose eyesight was later restored. He is said to have attained salvation by worshipping the linga here. There is a large MANDAPA built in Vijayanagara times, and the whole complex is enclosed by high walls, entered by a GOPURAM or gateway on the south. The pyramidal tower has a height of 36.5 m. The nearby hills have a number of small temples and shrines.

The temple is historically important as it has several early inscriptions. It is still a major centre of pilgrimage, where Shaivite festivals take place. Among them, Maha SHIVARATRI is the most important, celebrated here for ten days. In another festival on the third day of Sankranti in January, the deity is taken in a procession round the Kalahasti hills.

Kalakacharya A Jain monk who probably lived in the first century BCE. According to the *Kalakacharya Kathanaka,* a Prakrit text, he organized local rulers to overthrow King Gardhabilla of Ujjain, who had captured his sister, a Jain nun. The date of this text is not known, but it is thought to have been based on older traditions and to have a historical basis.

kalam An Arabic term literally meaning 'word' or 'speech'. It is also a technical term used for scholastic theology in Islam. Several theological and philosophical discussions and different theological schools existed from the earliest days. Points of divergence were free will, predestination, reason and rationality, wrong actions, and the fate of the sinner.

One controversy revolved around judgment and sin. The Kharija who were initially followers of Ali were among the first divergent groups. However, Ali submitted to arbitration in his dispute with Muawiya, and the Kharija broke away from him, asserting that judgment belonged only to God. An extreme branch, the Azraqiya, stated that Ali was an unbeliever (kafir) who should be destroyed. The Murjiya stated that a believer, even if he sinned, should not be condemned because judgment must be left to God.

Another problem concerned free will. The Qadariya stated that each person could decide between good and evil actions. A modification of this view was held by the MUTAZILA, who were rationalists. The JABRIYA (jabr = compulsion) said that a person had no free will; everything was ordained by God. The ASHARIYA placed revelation over reason, while the MATURIDI felt that predestination and free will could exist together. The ASHARIYA school formed the basis of orthodox doctrines.

Kalamukha (1) A Hindu SHAIVITE sect with TANTRIC practices. They wore a black mark on their foreheads, and hence were called Kalamukha, or 'black face'. They were once prominent in Karnataka, but later the LINGAYATS or Virashaivas became more popular there. (2) In ancient texts Kalamukhas were those born from human males and RAKSHASA females.

Kalan Mosque A mosque located in DELHI within the area of Turkman Gate. It was constructed in 1387 by Khan-i Jahan, the title of Junan Shah, the prime minister of Sultan Firuz Tughlaq. This fortress-like mosque has rounded bastions at the corners and a projecting entrance, reached by a flight of stairs. The mosque is on the upper storey and is built in orthodox style, with a prayer hall on the west.

Kali A Hindu goddess, a ferocious form of DURGA or PARVATI.

Myths of Kali are contained in the PURANAS, and she is mentioned in texts from around the sixth century. In the *DEVI MAHATMYA,* a part of the *MARKANDEYA PURANA,* she appears from Durga's forehead, when she is attacked by the asuras Chanda and Munda, and is a form of Durga's anger. She also helps Durga to defeat the asura Raktabija. In the *LINGA PURANA,* she appears from Parvati, who has been asked by SHIVA to destroy a demon. She is also also one of the MAHAVIDYAS, created by SATI at the time of DAKSHA'S sacrifice. In other texts, she is worshipped by tribals, or away from settled villages. The Thags, a now-extinct band of robbers, used to worship a form of Kali before killing their victims.

Kali is described in most texts as black or dark, with dishevelled long hair. Her skirt is made of severed arms, and severed heads adorn her neck. Sometimes she is adorned with skulls and has blood-smeared lips. She dwells in cremation grounds and battlefields, and holds a severed head in her hand. She is worshipped on her own but is also associated with Shiva. She is his consort, particularly in his form as Mahakala, eternal time, for Kali also represents time that devours all things. According to the TANTRAS, Kali is even the destroyer of time. In one story she was challenged by Shiva to a dance and was defeated by him, yet in most images she is shown in a superior position, standing on a prone Shiva. Thus she is SHAKTI, the active aspect of the passive PURUSHA or male principle, represented by Shiva. Occasionally, Kali is represented as a beautiful woman with a gentle smile.

According to some theories, Kali was a tribal deity who was absorbed into the Brahmanical pantheon. Psychological theories suggest that she represents the 'bad mother', who nevertheless has to be propitiated. Kali is also the dark side or the 'shadow' of each individual, and by worshipping her, this darkness can be eliminated.

Kali worship became widespread from early medieval days, and she remains a popular deity all over India, particularly in Bengal. Kali is often, though not always, propitiated with animal sacrifices. In TANTRISM, worship of Kali enables a transformation of negative energies and a defeat of demonic forces. According to the *Mahanirvana Tantra*, she is black and unclothed as she represents the primordial substance, and by worshipping her, all names and forms disappear. In south India, KORRAVAI has similarities with Kali, and so do certain other forms of Durga, such as CHANDI and CHAMUNDA. Among the many worshippers of Kali, RAMAKRISHNA PARAMAHANSA is the best known in relatively recent times.

Major Kali temples include the KALIGHAT TEMPLE, Kolkata; THE DAKSHINESHVARA TEMPLE, West Bengal; the Kalika Devi Temple, Kalka, Himachal; and the Kalka Temple, DELHI. There are other Kali temples all over India.

Kali Yuga In Hindu mythology, the fourth and last YUGA or period of time, when one MAHAYUGA comes to an end. The Kali Yuga follows the DVAPARA YUGA and is the yuga that exists today. It marks a general decline, and during this age, there is only one-quarter of the righteousness that existed in the first yuga. Its main scriptures are the TANTRAS, and people focus on the body instead of the mind. It is a time of anger, hatred, discord and strife. Humans live for various periods of time, and some reach one hundred years. The Kali Yuga is said to have begun in 3102 BCE and will last for 1200 divine years, equal to 4,32,000 human years. It is symbolized by the colour black. After this yuga a new cycle of the mahayuga will begin, starting again with the KRITA or Satya Yuga.

Kalidasa A poet and dramatist who wrote in Sanskrit and belonged to the fourth or fifth century. His plays include: *Malavikagnimitram; Vikramorvashi*, the story of PURURAVAS and URVASHI; and *Abhijnanashakuntalam*, the story of Dushyanta and Shakuntala, considered the best of his plays. Both the latter texts are based on mythical stories. His long poems are *Kumara Sambhava*, on the god Kumara or KARTTIKEYA; *Raghuvamsha*, the story of RAMA; *Ritu Samhara*, on the seasons; and *Meghaduta* (Cloud Messenger), the story of a YAKSHA banished for a year from the divine city of KUBERA, chief of the Yakshas. Several other works of his are no longer extant. Kalidasa is considered the greatest Sanskrit poet of all time.

Kalighat Temple A temple dedicated to the Hindu goddess KALI, located near the river Hughli at Kolkata.

The temple was constructed in 1809 by the Sabarna Roy Chaudhurys, a BRAHMANA family of the region. Legends suggest the existence of an earlier temple in the same area. The region was known for Kali worship from medieval days, and according to some accounts, the Kali image worshipped here, had been worshipped for centuries before the temple was built. The place is also recognized as a SHAKTA PITHA, a sacred site of SHAKTI, or feminine energy. One story states that long ago, a brahmana named Atma Ram found a piece of stone shaped like a human toe in the BHAGIRATHI (Ganga) river. In a dream he was told this was the toe of SATI and began worshipping it nearby; the site was considered sacred from that day. The image in the inner shrine of the temple is of Kali in her ferocious aspect. Animal sacrifices take place here every day.

Kalika Purana A Sanskrit text, a minor PURANA or UPAPURANA, dealing with the worship of the Hindu goddess PARVATI in different forms, as DURGA, SATI and KALI. It describes the marriage of SHIVA, the sacrifice of DAKSHA, the death of Sati and the emergence of SHAKTA PITHAS where parts of her body fell. The animal and human sacrifices to be offered to KALI are described, as well as sacred places associated with the goddess in Kamarupa (Assam), where Durga is worshipped in the form of KAMAKSHI. The text has TANTRIC aspects.

Kalima/Kalma The Islamic creed recited by all Muslims. The Kalima is 'La-ilaha illallah Muhammadur rasulallah', meaning 'ALLAH is the only god, and MUHAMMAD is his Prophet'. Reciting the Kalima is the first of the FIVE PILLARS OF ISLAM.

Kalki An incarnation of the Hindu god VISHNU, which will appear at the end of the KALI YUGA. Kalki will come as a man riding on a white horse, holding a flaming sword. His appearance will lead to the rejuvenation of the world, the beginning of a new yuga, the KRITA or Satya Yuga, which will be a glorious golden age. This is a late myth and paralells have been drawn with the concept of the MESSIAH in Judaism, the descriptions in the book of Revelation in the BIBLE, Zoroastrian concepts of the FRASHOKERETI, and the Bodhisattva MAITREYA in Buddhism.

Kalki Purana A Sanskrit text, a minor PURANA or UPAPURANA that describes the Hindu god VISHNU's incarnation as KALKI.

kalpa A Sanskrit term with many meanings, including a period of time, and a ritual or prescribed manner of action.

kalpa (time) A period of cosmic time. According to Hindu cosmology, a kalpa is one day of the god BRAHMA's life, comprising fourteen MANVANTARAS. Each manvantara has 71 mahayugas, hence there are 994 mahayugas in a kalpa. Sometimes, however, a kalpa is said to comprise 1000 MAHAYUGAS, amounting to 4320 million years of human beings. One month of Brahma has thirty kalpas, twelve months equal one year, and one hundred such years form the lifetime of Brahma. We are now said to be in the fifty-first year of Brahma's life. At the end of each kalpa, the universe is destroyed and recreated.

Jainism also has a concept of kalpas or cycles of time. These cycles are endless, and in each there is a period of evolution and growth or UTSARPINI, followed by a period of decline or AVASARPINI. Each of these periods is subdivided into six parts known as ARAS. Currently, the world is in the fifth sub-period of AVASARPINI, which began on the death of MAHAVIRA. All the twenty-four TIRTHANKARAS lived in the fourth sub-period.

The kalpa is also a concept in Buddhism.

Kalpa Sutra A Jain text of the SHVETAMBARA canon. It is ascribed to BHADRABAHU, but some parts are distinctly later. Section I of this Sutra contains the *Jinacharitra*, with biographies of the TIRTHANKARAS, particularly MAHAVIRA. Section II consists of the *Theravali* and has a list of schools (GANAS), with their heads or leaders (GANADHARA) and their branches (shakha). Section III, probably the oldest, has the Samachari or rules for ascetics during the rainy season (Pajjusan, or Paryushan in Sanskrit). The text is still read out on the PARYUSHAN festival celebrated by Jains. For the lay Shvetambara, the *Kalpa Sutra* is the most important sacred text.

Kalpa Sutras A term for Sanskrit texts of Hinduism which deal with kalpa or ritual. The texts have three categories: the SHRAUTA SUTRAS, which provide instructions for the agnihotra and other sacrifices; the GRIHYA SUTRAS, which describe domestic sacrifices; and the DHARMA SUTRAS, which explain laws and customs.

kalpa-vriksha/kalpa-druma According to Hindu mythology, a divine tree located in DEVALOKA, the heaven of the gods, which can fulfill all desires. There are actually five kalpa-vrikshas, known as Mandana, Parijata, Santana, Kalpa-Vriksha and Harichandana, all of which grant various wishes.

According to Jain mythology, in the first three ARAS of the descending era (AVASARPINI), kalpa-vrikshas provided all that was needed, but towards the end of the third ara, the yield from them diminished. Eight types of these trees are described in some texts, each of which provided different items. Thus from the Madyanga tree delicious and nutritious drinks could be obtained; from the Bhojananga, wonderful food; from the Jyotiranga, light more radiant than the sun and moon; while from Dipanga came indoor light. Other trees provided houses, musical instruments, plates and dishes, fine clothes, garlands and perfumes.

Kalyanaka A term in Jainism for an auspicious event in the life of a TIRTHANKARA. The Kalyanakas are: (1) Chyavana Kalyanaka, when the Tirthankara's soul departs from its previous existence and is conceived in the mother's womb; (2) Janma Kalyanaka, when a Tirthankara is born; (3) Diksha Kalyanaka, when the Tirthankara renounces the world and becomes a monk or nun (according to DIGAMBARAS, nuns cannot become Tirthankaras); (4) Kevaljnana Kalyanaka, when the Tirthankara attains kevaljnana or absolute knowledge after destroying the four ghati karmas; he then delivers his first sermon and reinstates the Jain religion; (5) Nirvana Kalyanaka, when the Tirthankara's soul is liberated from the world, the four aghati karmas are destroyed (see KARMA), and NIRVANA or salvation is attained. Before the final birth as a Tirthankara, the soul has gone through several incarnations, until it reaches the last and final birth. According to Digambaras, only men can become Tirthankaras, and a very pious woman would be reborn as a man in the final birth. According to SHVETAMBARAS, both men and women can be Tirthankaras.

Kama (1) The Hindu god of love, similar to Cupid. There are numerous myths and legends associated with Kama. A verse in the ATHARVA VEDA states that Kama is a supreme deity, unequalled by gods, PITRIS (ancestors) or men. Kama is sometimes identified with AGNI, the god of fire. In the *Taittiriya Brahmana*, he is said to be the son of DHARMA DEVA by his wife SHRADDHA. According to the HARIVAMSHA, he is the son of the goddess LAKSHMI. There are more accounts of him in the PURANAS. He is said to be born from the heart of BRAHMA, or to be self-existent, and therefore Aja, 'unborn'. His wife is RATI (passion) or Reva, and he is the lord of the APSARAS. He is depicted as a handsome young man with a parrot as his vehicle. Apsaras surround him, and one of them holds his banner with his emblem, the Jalarupa, a fish or MAKARA on a red background. Kama's arrows, made of flowers, strike the hearts of people and cause them to fall in love. His bow is made of flowers or of sugarcane, his bow-string consists of a line of bees, and each arrow is tipped with a flower.

In a well-known story, he tried to get the god SHIVA to fall in love with PARVATI, but was burnt to death by a flash of Shiva's third eye, though later he was revived. According to one account he was reborn as PRADYUMNA, son of KRISHNA.

Kama is also known as Mada or Madana; Rama or Ramana; Smara, remembrance; Abhirupa, the beautiful; Kamana, desirous; Shringarayoni, the source of love; Kusumayudha, armed with flowers; Pushpasara, whose arrows are flowers; Vama, the handsome; as well as by many other names.

(2) Kama means love or desire, and is one of the three components of life, the others being DHARMA and ARTHA, following one's duty and gaining wealth, respectively.

Finally, all aspects of life are abandoned for moksha or liberation.

Kama Shastras A term used for texts that deal with human love in its various aspects. The earliest extant text is the *Kama Sutra*, written by Vatsyayana in the third century. Several commentaries were written on it. Some later texts include the eleventh-century *Samaya-Matrika* (Life of a Courtesan), written by Kshemendra, the *Nagar Sarvasa* of Padmasri (c.1350), *Ratiratna-Pradipika* of Devaraja (c.1400), and the *Ananga-Ranga* of Kalyanamalla (d.1530). Though all these works are on erotic love, there are an implicit underlying assumption that love is a route to god. TANTRIC texts see a symbolic or real sexual union, under certain strict conditions, as a pathway to god. BHAKTI and SUFI saints inculcated love of the divine in their hearts, but often used the imagery of human love in their poems and songs.

Kamadhenu   A divine cow said to fulfill all wishes. The *MAHABHARATA, RAMAYANA* and PURANAS have various stories about Kamadhenu. Though several Kamadhenus are mentioned, all seem aspects of one divine cow.

When the ocean was churned for AMRITA, Kamadhenu emerged from it. Another story relating to Kamadhenu is about her life at the ashram of the rishi VASISHTHA. King VISHVAMITRA was attracted by her powers and tried to capture her, after Vasishtha refused to sell her to him. But Kamadhenu assumed a different form, and warriors emerged from her. Vishvamitra was so impressed by this that he gave up his life as a king and became a RISHI himself.

Kamadhenu is also known as Surabhi and Nandini, though some feel these are different cows. All cows are said to be descended from Surabhi. According to the *MAHABHARATA*, Surabhi went to Mt KAILASHA and worshipped the god BRAHMA for 10,000 years. Then Brahma said to her, 'Surabhi, I have made you a goddess. You are above the three worlds, and your world, Goloka, will be famous.'

Kamakhya Temple   A temple of the Hindu goddess Kamakshi or Kamakhya (a form of DURGA) located on a hill near Guwahati in Assam. The site is a SHAKTA PITHA, i.e., one of the places where SATI's dismembered body is said to have fallen. An ancient temple existed at this spot; it was reconstructed in the sixteenth century by Malladeva or Naranarayana, one of the kings of the Koch kingdom of the region, and by his brother Sukladeva or Chilarai. The inner shrine has a YONI or female emblem, and there are three MANDAPAS. Sculptures on the walls, include those of GANESHA and CHAMUNDA, as well as scenes of devotees, dancing figures, and animals. High curved towers rise above the shrine and mandapas.

The temple remains popular today, and animal sacrifices take place here. Among the temple festivals, the most important are DURGA PUJA, the Ambubachi festival, and the Debaddhani festival. At Ambubachi or Ameti, held in June/July, the temple is closed for three days, as the earth, represented by Kamakhya, is said to become impure because of menstruation. On the fourth day lakhs of devotees worship at the temple. The Debaddhani festival is connected with the worship of the goddess MANASA. Dances and songs take place at this time.

Though people of all affiliations worship at the temple, it is of particular importance for TANTRISM.

Kamakshi Amman Temple   A temple of the Hindu goddess Kamakshi (a form of DURGA) located at KANCHIPURAM in Tamil Nadu. It was constructed mostly between the sixteenth and seventeenth centuries. The main shrine is of the goddess Kamakshi, with other small shrines around it. To the north of the temple is a large columned MANDAPA or hall. The whole complex is enclosed and can be entered through four GOPURAMS or gateways. A small SHIVA temple of the Chola period is nearby.

Kamakshi/Kamakhya   A Hindu goddess, a form of DURGA or DEVI.

Kamala   Another name of the goddess LAKSHMI, and also one of the ten MAHAVIDYAS or TANTRIC goddesses. She is described as beautiful and with a golden complexion.

Kamalashila   A Buddhist philosopher of the MAHAYANA school who lived between c. 740 and 790. He was a disciple of SHANTIRAKSHITA and continued the latter's work in Tibet. He wrote three books on meditation and the BODHISATTVA path, each known as *BHAVANAKRAMA,* which are recognized as being among the best of Buddhist thought. He also wrote commentaries on the work of Shantirakshita and DHARMAKIRTI.

Kamban/Kampan   A Tamil poet who wrote the RAMAYANA in Tamil. Some scholars place him in the ninth century, while others believe he lived at the court of the Chola kings in the twelfth century. His Ramayana is based on VALMIKI's work, with some differences. It raises RAMA to the level of a divinity, but simultaneously explores the psychology of the characters. A dialogue between Rama and VALI suggests that without SITA, Rama has lost his soul, his conscience, and thus cannot act in a fair and balanced way. RAVANA is depicted as a man with a helpless passion. He says of Sita, 'I dread to give up thoughts of you . . . Every name is Yours, every face is You . . . Who can see I die a daily death?' Known as *Iramavataram* or the *Kamban Ramayana* and written in Sanskritized Tamil, it is a popular sacred text.

Kamsa ka Mela   A Hindu festival held at MATHURA and AGRA in October/November every year. It celebrates the ancient story of the victory of the god KRISHNA over King Kamsa. This event is re-enacted by actors dressed as Krishna and BALARAMA who shoot arrows at an effigy of Kamsa, which then goes up in flames.

Kanada, Uluka   The founder of the VAISHESHIKA school of philosophy, who probably lived between the third century BCE and the early centuries CE. He wrote the *Vaisheshika Sutra.*

Kanakadasa   A BHAKTI saint of the sixteenth century, who belonged to the HARIDASA sect in the Karnataka region and was a contemporary of PURANDARADASA. Kanakadasa, a shepherd by birth, was a disciple of Vyasaraya, who may also have been Purandaradasa's teacher. Kanakadasa sang philosophical songs of devotion in Kannada, seeing HARI or god everywhere. In one of his songs, still popular today, he says:

This body is yours, so is the life within it;
Yours too are the sorrows and joys of our daily life.
Whatever sweet word or Veda or story that we hear,
The power to hear them is yours.
The eye that gazes on the beauty of form,
That vision too is yours.

When a dog entered his house and stole some bread, Kanakadasa, who saw all beings as forms of the Lord, ran after it with ghi and jaggery, calling 'Lord, have this on your bread too'.

Kanaka is associated with the KRISHNA temple in UDUPI. Despite his devotion, he was not allowed within the temple because of his low caste. He is said to have stood outside its western wall and sung to the deity that he was unable to see. And one day the wall cracked, a chunk fell out of it, and the deity turned his face to the west, so that Kanaka could see him. Even today, the image remains in that position, and is viewed through a grilled window on the western wall.

Kanchipuram A city in Tamil Nadu, one of the seven sacred Hindu cities. Located along the Palar river, it has Hindu temples dating back to the eighth century, as well as Buddhist and Jain monuments. Most of the SHIVA temples are located in a suburb to the north of the city, while VAISHNAVA temples are at another end of the town. Across the river to the south is a group of Jain temples. Among the Shiva temples is the KAILASHNATHA TEMPLE of the eighth century. The Vaikuntha Perumal is a VISHNU temple of the same period. Chola temples include the KAMAKSHI, EKAMBARESHVARA and Varadaraja, though these were reconstructed under the Vijayanagara rulers and the Nayakas.

Stories about Kanchi are narrated in ancient texts, and it was a centre of pilgrimage from the earliest days. At different periods, Jains, Buddhists and Vedic scholars lived here. RAMANUJA (1017–1137) was one of the noted scholars who studied here.

Kanchi is the seat af a SHANKARACHARYA who claims to belong to the direct lineage of Adi Shankaracharya. According to this tradition, SHANKARA himself settled here and attained SAMADHI at Kanchi. Before this he established a MATHA, of which he became the first Shankaracharya. In 1743 this matha, the Kanchi Kamakoti Peetham, shifted to KUMBAKONAM, at a time when there was warfare in the region, though Kanchi remained the nominal centre. In the nineteenth century, the temple of the matha was reconsecrated at Kanchi. However, the SRINGERI Shankaracharyas put forward a different tradition and do not count Kanchi among the original Mathas established by Adi Shankaracharya.

At the Kanchi Matha, the deity Chandramoulishvara, a form of Shiva, is particularly worshipped.

Kandariya Mahadeva Temple A temple of the Hindu god SHIVA, located at KHAJURAHO in Madhya Pradesh, constructed in the eleventh century. This is the largest and most intricately carved of the many temples here, constructed on a platform with a height of 8.4 m. Two MANDAPAS open into the GARBA-GRIHA, or inner shrine, which houses a LINGA. Towers rise above the mandapas, the highest reaching 30 m from the base. There are Shiva images on the walls of the garba-griha and on the mandapa walls. Sculptures also include DIKAPALAS, other deities and goddesses. Panels on the outer walls depict couples in sexual postures.

Kandh Sahib Gurdwara A GURDWARA or Sikh shrine located at Batala in Gurdaspur district, Punjab. Within it is a wall enshrined in glass, on which Guru NANAK is said to have once leaned while listening to discussions on his forthcoming marriage to Bibi Sulakhni. He was warned that the crumbling wall was about to fall, but stated that by the will of God it would not fall for hundreds of years. This gurdwara is a celebration of the fact that his words came true, and also commemorates his marriage. Every year a procession takes place on his marriage anniversary.

Kanheri A place where over a hundred Buddhist rock-cut CHAITYAS and VIHARAS are located, along the Western Ghats in Maharashtra. The site was occupied from around the first century BCE to the eleventh century CE. Some of the caves have BUDDHA and BODHISATTVA images, as well as attendant figures and other deities. Cave 41 has an unusual image of AVALOKITESHVARA with four arms and eleven heads.

Kanishka A king of the Kushana dynasty who ruled much of northern India and Afghanistan from c. CE 78 to 103, with his capitals at Purushapura (modern Peshawar in Pakistan) and MATHURA. The fourth BUDDHIST COUNCIL was held during his reign, in around CE 100. According to XUANZANG, the seventh century Chinese pilgrim, it was held at Kundalavana in Kashmir, whereas other accounts state that it was held in GANDHARA or Jalandhara. Five hundred monks of the SARVASTIVADA school debated at this council. According to Buddhist tradition, ASHVAGHOSHA, the Buddhist scholar, converted Kanishka to Buddhism, who then became a great patron of the religion and a builder of STUPAS. Kanishka's coins, however, depict a variety of deities, including Greek, Zoroastrian, Hindu and Buddhist gods. Two schools of art flourished at this time, in Gandhara and MATHURA, in which Buddhist images were made.

Kanjipantha A sub-sect of the DIGAMBARA Jain sect, started by Kanji Swami (1889–1980), originally a Shvetambara-STHANAKAVASI. He was an extremely learned monk who studied all the SHVETAMBARA texts, but felt that something was lacking in these. It was only when he read the works of the Jain scholar Kundakunda, held in high regard by the Digambaras, that he believed he had discovered the true source of knowledge. In 1934 he left the Sthanakavasi sect, proclaimed that he was now a Digambara, and began to teach and comment on the texts of KUNDAKUNDA, particularly the *Samayasara*. He also appreciated the writings of the Jain scholars Todarmal and Rajachandra (founder of the KAVIPANTH) and did not bother about rituals, but emphasized the importance of understanding the Truth and the nature of the soul.

He has a number of followers particularly in Sonagarh in Gujarat and Jaipur in Rajasthan.

Kanjur A collection of Buddhist manuscripts. *See* Kagyur.

Kannagi/Kannaki A Hindu goddess worshipped in Tamil Nadu. Kannagi is a heroine in the *SHILAPPADIGARAM*, a Tamil epic dated between the second and sixth centuries. She was married to Kovalan, who was also involved with the dancer Madhavi. However, she remained chaste and faithful to him, and when he was unjustly executed by the king of MADURAI, she burnt down the city in her anger and grief. Her elevation to the status of a goddess is based on her chastity and devotion to her husband, which bestowed divine strength on her. She is considered a form of DURGA.

Kanniyakumari A Hindu goddess who is worshipped alone, without a male consort. A town at the southermost tip of India is named after her, and a temple is dedicated to her there. She is a 'virgin goddess' but is also considered a form of PARVATI or of DURGA. Several stories are narrated about her. According to one, she was named Pushpakashi. She loved the god SHIVA and wished to marry him, and like Parvati, meditated on Mt KAILASHA for hundreds of years. She was then granted her wish, entered heaven and became Shiva's companion. But soon Shiva asked her to go down to earth again, to the southernmost point, to vanquish the Asura Bana, and then to wait for him. She did so, as she had great powers, yet Shiva has not appeared to her again, and she still awaits him.

According to another story, Kanniyakumari and KALI were created by Shiva to defeat the two demons, Bana and Muka. Kanniyakumari was sent down to the southern tip of India and successfully defeated Bana. She was so beautiful that the god Suchindra Perumal, at a nearby temple, fell in love with her and wanted to marry her. But the other gods were against this, as the goddess', powers would diminish if she married. At their request, the rishi NARADA put obstacles in the way, so that Kanniyakumari gave up and cursed the food items that had been brought to feed the marriage guests, which turned into sea-shells and sand. These are worshipped at eleven holy ghats or tirthas around her temple. Another

story states that PARASHURAMA established her image here for the protection of the land.

The processional deity in the temple is known as Tyagasundari, while the deity ready for marriage is Syamasundari.

The stories connected with Kanniyakumari indicate the power assigned to virginity. Most Hindu goddesses are powerful on their own, but passive when with their consorts.

Swami VIVEKANANDA used to meditate on a hill near the Kanniyakumari temple, now known as Vivekananda hill. A Vivekananda Memorial is constructed on a rock in the sea.

Kanphata Yogis A SHAIVITE sect founded by MATSYENDRANATHA and GORAKHNATHA in the twelfth century. It was an esoteric TANTRIC sect, and its adherents wore huge earrings which split their ears, giving the sect its name (kanphata = torn or split ear). Their practices include HATHA YOGA.

They were also known as Nathpanthis, or NATHA YOGIS.

Kanvariyas A term for those who participate in a ritual that consists of carrying water from a sacred river to offer to a Hindu temple. Often the water is carried from the GANGA and offered in a temple of the god SHIVA. Traditionally, the water is in two covered pots, tied to a pole, and carried on the shoulders. Devotees walk from a point on a sacred river to a temple of their choice. They should not enter any vehicle or place the pots on the ground at any time. The journey may take several days or even weeks; participants walk all day, resting at night. The ritual is undertaken for the fulfilment of a vow, or merely as an offering to the deity. In the old days it was an individual ritual, but now it has grown in popularity, with lakhs of devotees participating in it during the month of Shravana (July–August), while some undertake it before SHIVARATRI in January–February. At this time special facilities are arranged for the pilgrims, free food and water is offered along the way, wooden stands are set up to place their pots on while they rest, and temporary shelters are made for them to rest at night. For a few crucial days, even the national highways are closed to traffic to allow the Kanwariyas to walk freely. On the last day processions are taken out, in which people dressed like Shiva's GANAS or attendants, dance and sing devotional songs.

Kapal Mochan A site sacred to Hindus and Sikhs, located near Jagadhri in Haryana on the river Ghagghar, which is identified with the ancient SARASVATI river. Kapal Mochan is mentioned as a tirtha in the MAHABHARATA and PURANAS. The god SHIVA is said to have dropped a skull (kapala) at this place, leading to its sanctity. A GURDWARA was built here after a visit by Guru GOBIND SINGH in 1579.

Kapaleshvara Temple A temple of the Hindu god SHIVA located at Chennai in Tamil Nadu, constructed in the seventeenth century, with additions made later. An earlier temple was destroyed by the Portuguese. The main shrine has a large Shiva LINGA. Nearby is another shrine with the image of Subrahmanya or KARTTIKEYA, and a smaller DEVI or goddess shrine.

The goddess here is known as Kalpakavalli. There are several legends associated with the temple. According to one story, the god Brahma once met Shiva and Parvati in Kailasha, but did not pay respect to them, and Shiva in anger, cut off one Brahma's heads. To pacify Shiva, Brahma came to this spot and set up a lingam and worshipped it. As Brahma had lost one of his heads (kapala) the linga was known as Kapaleshvara, and the place Kapali-nagara.

Kapaleshvara is still an important shrine, visited by thousands of pilgrims.

Kapaleshvara Tirtha   A tirtha or sacred spot, located 2 km north of TIRUPATI in Andhra Pradesh, where a natural waterfall descends from the hills. A small pond has been constructed to hold the water of the fall, and a shrine has been built into a rocky ledge. At the entrance a LINGA, sheltered by a NAGA, is worshipped as SHIVA in the form of Kapaleshvara, or lord of the KAPALIKA. Within the shrine is an image of VISHNU with his consorts, SHRI DEVI and BHU DEVI.

Kapalika   A SHAIVITE sect with TANTRIC practices also referred to as Kapala or Mahavrata. The name is derived from kapala, a human skull. Kapaleshvara, lord of the Kapalikas, is a name of the Hindu god SHIVA, while in the MAHABHARATA, Kapalin is also a name of one of the MARUTS. According to a story in the PURANAS, Shiva quarrelled with the god BRAHMA and cut off one of his heads. Thus he committed the sin of brahmahatya, the killing of Brahma, who was a BRAHMANA. To expiate this sin Shiva vowed to wander as an ascetic for twelve years, using only the skull of Brahma as his begging bowl. This is known as Mahavrata, the great vow. Finally Shiva ended his penance at KASHI (Varanasi) at Kapala-mochana Tirtha. Kapalika ascetics use a skull as their begging bowl and sometimes also carry a Khatvanga, a skull mounted on a stick. They are smeared with ashes, wear bone or skull ornaments, and have their hair in matted locks.

The sect seems to have existed from around the fifth century. They are mentioned in negative terms by various writers, such as Mahendravarman of the seventh century and Krishnamishra of the eleventh century. Their philosophy included achieving divine union through the PANCHA-MAKARAS, the five elements used in TANTRISM.

However, the kapala, in addition, has a symbolic meaning, and in the secret language (SANDHA-BHASHA) of TANTRA it can represent the universe, the supreme deity, or the great void (SHUNYA).

Skulls were also used by Buddhist Tantrics.

Kapila   An ancient RISHI, the traditional founder of the philosophical system of SAMKHYA. A historical Kapila probably did exist, around the seventh or sixth century BCE, but the text attributed to him, the *Samkhyapravachana Sutra,* has been assigned a date as late as the fourteenth century CE. The *Tattvasamasa* is another late text that he is said to have written. These probably had earlier versions, while other texts written by him may not have survived.

There are several myths and stories about Kapila in ancient texts. He is considered the son of the Hindu god BRAHMA, an incarnation of VISHNU, or an incarnation of AGNI. He meditated in a cave at GANGA SAGARA, and a temple of Kapila Muni is located there.

Karaga   A Hindu festival celebrated during the month of April in Karnataka in honour of DRAUPADI, wife of the PANDAVAS. At this festival, Vira Kumaras, young men armed with swords, march in a moonlight procession.

karah prasad   The prasad or sacramental food distributed at Sikh GURDWARAS. It is so-called because it is prepared in an iron vessel or karahi.

Karam   A tribal festival celebrated in August/ September, mainly in Jharkhand. A karam tree is planted at a special spot in the village. At the time of the festival, tribals dance and sing around the tree, drinking rice beer. This ceremony is to ensure prosperity for the village.

Karchi Puja   A Hindu festival celebrated in July at Agartala in Tripura, in honour of the goddess DEVI or SHAKTI. The main celebrations last for seven days and take place at the temple of Chaturdashi Devata, which contains fourteen images of Shakti.

Kardang Gompa   The largest Buddhist monastery in Lahaul in Himachal Pradesh. Kardang village was once the capital of Lahaul, and the monastery is located above the village on the left bank of the river Bhaga. It was founded about 900 years ago, but lay in ruins until it was reopened by a monk named Lama Norbu in 1912. There are both monks and nuns here, and lamas are allowed to marry and visit their families in the summer to work in the fields. It has a fine library with all the volumes of the KAGYUR and TANGYUR collections, as well as a number of THANGKAS, musical instruments and old weapons. The walls have murals, and there are several statues, including YAB-YUM images. Lama Norbu died in 1952, and his relics are contained in a silver CHAITYA. The monastery belongs to the DRUGPA KAGYU sect.

Karle   The site of several rock-cut Buddhist CHAITYAS and VIHARAS dating from about 100 BCE to the fifth century CE, located along the Western Ghats in Pune District of Maharashtra. Cave 8, from the first century CE, has the largest and best preserved chaitya hall of the early monuments in this area. At the entrance is a monolithic pillar with a capital of four lions. Other columns within have capitals with elephants, on which embracing couples are seated. The STUPA has a hemispherical dome and is capped by a wooden umbrella.

karma A Sanskrit word from the root 'kri', meaning 'to do', karma literally means 'that which is done' or 'action', but is also a philosophical doctrine. In simple terms, it is the law of cause and effect, the principle that 'as you sow, so shall you reap'. Every action has a result, and good or bad fortune is said to be the result of one's own actions. The concept of karma is linked with that of reincarnation, in that the effect of actions can last through several lifetimes. Karma can be changed or modified through right action, and a state beyond the effects of karma is achieved through union with the divine. There are many subtle interpretations and modifications of this concept, but its basic philosophy is accepted not only in Hinduism, but also in Buddhism, Jainism and Sikhism, and permeates Indian life.

In Hindu texts certain types of karma are mentioned. Among these are:

Prarabda karma, which determines into which body the soul will be born, and how long it will live. It is the cumulative result of all past actions.

Sanchita karma, translated as 'seed karma', which constitutes the characteristics and aptitudes of a person, dependent on those in his past life. They can be modified with right practices and thoughts.

Agami karma or the karma that is being created for the future by one's present actions.

Karma also simply means action, and the best form of action is nishkama karma, something done without desire or thought of a reward.

The concepts of karma and of rebirth are accepted in Buddhism. Many Buddhist schools reject in theory the idea of a permanent Self or entity that is reborn, yet all schools of Buddhism accept stories of the past births of the BUDDHA, and the idea that through good actions in several lives the stage of Buddhahood can be reached. Both negative and positive actions have results; negative actions are those motivated by lust (raga), hatred (dvesha) or delusion (moha), while positive actions include the opposite of these, as well as actions for the welfare of all beings. Without a permanent Self, how karma is transmitted from one life to another is not clear. Yet both concepts are recognized.

Jainism has a unique concept of karmic matter and the karmic body. Karma is part of PUDGALA or matter, and creates the subtle body or karmana sharira, which attaches itself to the JIVA or soul. The physical body dies, but the karma body accompanies the jiva through its lives. Karma molecules are attracted to the jiva according to its actions, and this inflow is known as ASRAVA. It then becomes bound or fixed to the body (bandha), but can be eliminated when the jiva realizes it is distinct from the material world. Even after this realization, it is not easy for the jiva to free itself. The first step is samvara or stopping the inflow (asrava)

of karmic matter. The next is tapas, consisting of meditation or concentration on one's true nature. The process by which the karmic body then disintegrates is known as NIRJARA. Finally, MOKSHA is reached.

To help in extinguishing karma, Jains believe a thorough understanding of it is necessary, and describe eight types of karma. Four of these are destructive or ghati karmas: mohaniya karma, which is delusory; jnana-avaraniya karma, which obscures knowledge; darshan-avarniya karma, which interferes with sense perception; antaraya karma, which obstructs the energy of the jiva. Another four are non-destructive or aghati karmas. These are: vedaniya karma, which produces feelings; nama Karma, which determines the nature of a person's rebirth; ayu karma, which determines the lifespan; gotra karma, which determines the status.

Karma is a concept also accepted in Sikhism. It determines one's birth, but salvation is attained not only through actions, but through grace.

Though the same term may not be used, karma as the law of cause and effect is accepted in other religions, including Christianity, Judaism and Zoroastrianism. In Zoroastrianism, the *GATHAS* (*Yasna* 43.5), states: 'You maintain that words and deeds bear fruit, evil comes to the evil, a good reward to the good.'

Later thinkers provided new interpretations of karma, notable among them being Sri AUROBINDO, who had a somewhat different interpretation of the concept. He saw karma as something that takes place to help the individual soul on its path, rather than as a mechanism of cause and effect or reward and punishment.

Karma Kagyu A school of TIBETAN BUDDHISM, a sub-sect of the main Kagyu school. It was founded by Dusum Khyenpa (1110–93), who became the first Karmapa, or head of the school. The sixteenth Karmapa, Ranjung Rigpe Dorje (1924–81) was appointed the head of the whole Kagyu tradition while in exile. The present head is the seventeenth Gyalwa Karmapa Ogyen Drodul Trinley Dorje, who is living in exile in DHARAMSALA in Himachal Pradesh after escaping from China in 2000. After some initial hesitation, the DALAI LAMA recognized him as the Karmapa. The school has re-established its headquarters at the Rumtek monastery in Sikkim, but because there are rival claimants to the position, the seventeenth Karmapa has not taken over officially at Rumtek.

Karma Mimamsa Another name of Purva MIMAMSA, an ancient school of philosophy.

Karma Yoga The path of union with the divine through KARMA or action. Patanjali's *YOGA SUTRA* describes Kriya Yoga, another term for Karma Yoga, as action dedicated to the divine. The BHAGAVAD GITA explains that any action performed should be offered to the Supreme, without looking for its fruits or rewards. It also speaks of different types of actions and of work or action that is silence. Swami VIVEKANANDA is among those who explained the path of Karma Yoga in detail.

Karmaprabhrita A Jain text sacred to the DIGAMBARAS. It is said to be based on the lost DITTHIVAYA text, the twelfth ANGA which no longer exists. The text deals with KARMA and is also called the *Shat Khandagama Sutra*. According to tradition, Dharasena, who lived in the first or second century at GIRNAR in Gujarat, sent a message to the Jain monks in south India stating that true knowledge of the Jain Canon was disappearing. Two scholars, Pushpadanta and Bhutavali, were sent to him and compiled this text based on his teachings. It was completed on the fifth day of the bright fortnight of Jyaishtha, and this day is celebrated every year as Shruta Panchami, the day when the teachings were received.

Karna The name of the first of KUNTI's sons in the *MAHABHARATA*. He was thus the brother of the PANDAVAS. Karna was born through the sun god SURYA, but was not acknowledged by Kunti who was then unmarried, and was brought up by a charioteer. As he grew up, he learnt the art of warfare from DRONA and PARASHURAMA and became a great warrior. As he was apparently of low birth, he was humiliated by ARJUNA, though he was befriended by DURYODHANA. He remained Duryodhana's loyal friend and was killed in the great war by Arjuna. Finally Kunti revealed that Karna was in fact Arjuna's brother.

Kartarpur The name of two towns sacred to Sikhs. (1) A town founded by Guru NANAK on the right bank of the river Ravi, opposite DERA BABA NANAK. A large community of the guru's followers settled here. (2) A town in Jalandhar district of Punjab, founded by the fifth Sikh guru ARJAN DEV. The guru came here in 1598; planting his sandalwood walking-stick in the ground, he stated that it would be the support of the faith in this place. Nearby a well was dug, named Gangsar, as the water from the GANGA was miraculously said to flow here. One of Arjan Dev's disciples is said to have lost his lota (vessel) in the Ganga at HARDWAR, but found it here. The town prospered and grew with the blessings of the guru. Around the stick (tham) the Tham Sahib Gurdwara was built with funds granted in 1833 by Maharaja RANJIT SINGH. Guru HARGOBIND visited this place after a battle fought nearby, and Guru TEGH BAHADUR was married here.

Kartavirya A mythical king of the Haihayas, described in the PURANAS and other texts. He worshipped the rishi DATTATREYA and obtained a boon of a thousand arms and a golden chariot that could travel anywhere according to his will. He ruled the earth for 85,000 years, and there was peace, prosperity and justice. He visited the ashram of JAMADAGNI and stole a sacred cow, after which PARASHURAMA cut off his arms and killed him. According to one version,

as his rule was oppressive, the Hindu god VISHNU was incarnated as Parashurama for the specific purpose of killing him.

Karttika Festival A Hindu festival that involves the worship of the god SHIVA in the form of the five elements—earth, water, fire, air and ether. It is celebrated at Shiva temples, mainly in south India, in November/December.

Karttikeya A Hindu god, also commonly known as Skanda and Kumara. In the south he has several names, including Subrahmanya and MURUGAN. His other names include Mahasena, Shakha, Vishakha, Guha, Brahmanya and Naigameya.

According to myths, he was born in order to destroy the asura TARAKA. Taraka was troubling the gods, but they were unable to defeat him, because he had received his powers through a boon from the god BRAHMA. It was predicted that only a son of SHIVA could destroy him. However, Shiva, after the death of his wife SATI, was in retreat, meditating, not wishing to marry again. Sati had been reborn as Uma (PARVATI) and she too sat in meditation till Shiva noticed her and married her.

After the marriage, Shiva and Parvati engaged in love-play on Mt KAILASHA and Shiva dropped his seed, which was accepted by the god AGNI. Unable to hold it, Agni gave it to the river GANGA, who transferred it to the six Krittikas, the wives of sages. They threw their foetuses back in the Ganga, who threw it into a forest of reeds, and there Karttikeya was born, named after the Krittikas, and with six faces as he had six mothers. Then Uma and Shiva took back their child.

He grew into a handsome young man, and riding on a peacock, he led the gods and defeated Taraka. He became the commander-in-chief of the divine forces.

Karttikeya's younger brother was GANESHA. To decide who would marry first, their parents asked them to travel around the world. Whoever returned first would be married first. Strong Karttikeya set off on his peacock, while Ganesha slowly walked around his parents, saying that to him they were the world. Ganesha was married first, and Karttikeya felt unhappy. Therefore, it is said, he went to the south and never returned to north India again.

Today Karttikeya is worshipped primarily in the south, particularly in his form as Murugan, but at one time he was popular in north India as well. He is depicted on coins of the Yaudheyas, who ruled between the second century BCE and the third century CE in the area of Haryana and Garhwal. The *MAHABHARATA* and *MAHAMAYURI* record that he was the god of Rohitaka (Rohtak, Haryana). He is also depicted on the coins of the Kushana ruler Huvishka (second century CE) and the Gupta ruler Kumaragupta (CE 412–55), and in inscriptions of Skandagupta (CE 455–67), there are references to temples dedicated to Karttikeya. In Bengal, several images of him have been found dated between the eighth and eleventh centuries. In south India he was the tutelary deity of the Kadamba dynasty. As Subrahmanya he is depicted at AIHOLE and ELLORA.

Myth and iconography indicate that Skanda-Karttikeya is a composite god, originally with YAKSHA affinities. In some texts he is even identified with SANAT KUMARA, the mind-born son of Brahma. He is also identified with MANGALA, or Mars.

In the BRIHAT SAMHITA he is described as riding a peacock and holding a shakti (spear). In the VISHNUDHARMOTTARA he is said to be six-faced and four-armed, riding a peacock, and dressed in red. In his two right hands he holds a cock (kukkuta) and a bell (ghanta), in his left hands a victory flag (vaijayanti pataka) and a spear. His consort is Devasena, while in the south, his two consorts are Devayanai and Valli or Mahavalli. In the north he is often considered unmarried.

Karttikeya is worshipped mainly in Shiva temples, though there are independent Murugan temples in the south. One of the places sacred to Karttikeya is the SRISAILAM hill, where he is said to have gone immediately after leaving home; there is a shrine dedicated to him here. He is worshipped in Shiva shrines in Bhubaneswar (Orissa), and along with DURGA in Bengal. There are a number of subsidiary shrines dedicated to him, prominent among them being those in the KAPALESHVARA TEMPLE in Chennai, and in the NATARAJA TEMPLE at CHIDAMBARAM.

karuna A Sanskrit term meaning compassion, which is important in Buddhism. Along with prajna or wisdom, it is one of the two main attributes of a BODHISATTVA.

Karva Chauth A day-long fast observed by Hindu women for the welfare of their husbands. The fast is popular in the north and normally takes place in October on the fourth day of the fortnight before DIVALI. On this day women wake early and eat and drink water before sunrise. They then neither eat nor drink anything until the rise of the moon. In the evening women wear jewellery and fine clothes and wait for their husbands to take them out to see the moon. The couple then eats together, celebrating marriage and togetherness.

Kashayaprabhrita A Jain text sacred to the DIGAMBARAS. It was compiled by Gunadhara in the second century CE, based on the lost DITTHIVAYA text. It deals with desires or passions and their pitfalls. Later commentaries by Virasena in the eighth century and JINASENA in the ninth century are also respected texts.

Kashful-Mahjub A SUFI text written by ABUL HASAN AL-HUJWIRI. The Kashful Mahjub is the first-known manual on SUFISM in Persian. In this text, Hujwiri, who lived in Lahore in the eleventh century, explained and commented on a number of Sufi sects and practices prevalent at the time.

Kashi The ancient name of VARANASI, a sacred city. It is particularly sacred to the Hindu god SHIVA. According to the PURANAS and other texts, all the sacred places or tirthas associated with Shiva are also represented here.

The Kashi Khanda, a section in the SKANDA PURANA, describes early Shiva temples located in and around Kashi.

Kashi Vishvanatha Temple A temple of the Hindu god SHIVA located at VARANASI in Uttar Pradesh. Originally an ancient shrine, the temple was reconstructed in 1585 but demolished during the reign of the Mughal emperor AURANGZEB, when a mosque was built at the spot. In 1777 the temple was rebuilt adjacent to the mosque. The LINGA in the inner shrine is said to be the original one, which was thrown into the nearby well when the temple was destroyed. The walls are intricately carved, and above the temple are a series of spires. There are other small shrines in the courtyard, with lingas and images of deities. Behind is the Jnana Vapi well whose waters are said to provide JNANA or wisdom. The adjacent mosque is named after it.

Kashyapa An ancient RISHI or sage, one of the seven great rishis, said to be the grandson of the Hindu god BRAHMA and the progenitor of human beings. He was the father of Vivasvat and grandfather of MANU. Some of the Vedic hymns are attributed to him, and in Vedic texts he is also a mythical being associated with the sun. In the MAHABHARATA and PURANAS, he is a rishi who married thirteen daughters of DAKSHA, through whom all beings in the world were descended. Among his wives were ADITI, mother of the ADITYAS and of Vivasvat. VAMANA, an incarnation of VISHNU, was also born to her. Other wives included Danu, mother of the DANAVAS; DITI, mother of the DAITYAS; and KADRU, mother of the NAGAS or serpents. Khasa was the mother of YAKSHAS and RAKSHASAS. Others were mothers of demons, birds and various beings. Thus through Kashyapa all living beings were born. He is also called PRAJAPATI.

Kashyapa/Kassapa A close disciple of the BUDDHA, also known as Maha-kashyapa, who presided over the first BUDDHIST COUNCIL at RAJAGRIHA.

Kashyapiya A HINAYANA Buddhist sect, a branch of the STHAVIRAVADA, alternatively known as Suvarshakas. They held a position between the SARVASTIVADA and other Sthaviravada sects, regarding the nature of existence. The Sarvastivada believes that past, present and future all exist, while the Sthaviravada that only the present exists. The Kashyapiya said that when the fruits of the past have been realized, those aspects of the past ceased to exist, while the rest of the past continued to exist.

Katarmal Surya Temple A temple of the Hindu god SURYA located at Katarmal near Almora in Uttarakhand, constructed in the twelfth century. In the main shrine is an image of Surya, about 1 m high, made of brownish stone. The temple is in a dilapidated state.

Katha Upanishad A verse UPANISHAD that can be dated between 600 and 300 BCE. This is one of the most popular Upanishads, that tells the story of Nachiketa, a pious boy. Seeing his father offering old and barren cows to BRAHMANAS, he questioned him, saying, 'To whom then will you give me?' He asked again and again, till his angry father said, 'I will give you to death'. The boy dutifully went to the house of YAMA, god of death, who happened to be away. He waited for him for three days, and when he returned, Yama granted him three boons, in apology for his absence. For the first boon, Nachiketa asked that his father, Gautama, be pacified. For the second, Nachiketa asked for the knowledge of the fire (AGNI) that leads to heaven and immortality, and Yama taught him the fire sacrifice, which was then named after him. For the third boon, Nachiketa said, 'There is that doubt when a man is dead—some say he is, some say he is not—this I should like to know.' Then Yama taught him the truth about life and death, and about the ATMAN, knowing which all is known, and neither grief nor fear remain.

SHANKARA, the ninth-century philosopher of ADVAITA, is among those who have commented on this Upanishad.

Kathavatthu A HINAYANA Buddhist text that forms part of the ABHIDHAMMA PITAKA of the PALI CANON. This text is ascribed to Tissa Moggaliputta, who presided over the third BUDDHIST COUNCIL held in the third century BCE. Some scholars accept this, while others reject it; a third group believes the core could have been compiled by Tissa, with later additions. The text has twenty-three sections. Each section has eight to twelve questions, consisting of views held by opposing sects. Typical questions are: 'Does everything exist?' 'Do the pupils of the Buddha share in his superhuman powers?' 'Can animals be reborn among the gods?' After a dialogue, the correct answer according to Buddhist principles is given. The text is important for an understanding of the views of different sects.

Katyayana A Sanskrit scholar and grammarian. He wrote a commentary on the Sanskrit grammar of PANINI, as well as the *Katyayana Shrauta Sutra* and the *Yajurveda Pratishakya*. A DHARMA SHASTRA is also attributed to him. Katyayana has been variously dated between the fourth and first century BCE, and was also known as Varuruchi.

Kaula A term for a TANTRIC sect. Kaula refers to the family (kula) of initiates. It is specifically used for the Shaivite Tantric school that focuses on raising the KUNDALINI. It uses the PANCHA-MAKARA, and attempts to transcend desire (kama) through meditation on it.

Kaumudi A Hindu deity, the wife of Chandra or SOMA, the moon, who represents moonlight. She is also known as Jyotsna.

Kaurava The descendants of King Kuru of ancient texts. The name Kaurava particularly applies to the hundred sons of DHRITARASHTRA in the MAHABHARATA, of whom DURYODHANA was the eldest. Technically it also applies to the PANDAVAS, their cousins, as both groups were descended from Kuru.

Kaushambi An ancient city with Buddhist and other remains, located near the river YAMUNA, not far from ALLAHABAD in Uttar Pradesh. This historic site is mentioned in several ancient texts, including the BRAHMANAS, the MAHABHARATA, the RAMAYANA, Buddhist Pali texts, Jain texts, and the PURANAS. It was occupied from about the seventh century BCE to the sixth century CE. According to the Puranas, Nichakshu, a descendant of Parikshit, the grandson of ARJUNA, moved his capital here from HASTINAPURA. Archaeological excavations have unearthed a wealth of material, including structures, coins, sculptures and terracotta images. It was also the site of an ASHOKAN PILLAR, later shifted to Allahabad.

At the time of the BUDDHA, Kaushambi was a prosperous town, the capital of the state of Vatsa. Among the important structural remains are those of the Buddhist Ghoshitarama vihara or monastery, well known from Pali texts. It was constructed in the sixth century BCE for the BUDDHA and his disciples by Ghoshita, treasurer of the king of Vatsa. There is a STUPA and CHAITYA hall here, enlarged in the third century BCE at the time of the Mauryan emperor ASHOKA, and a later shrine of the Buddhist mother goddess, HARITI. Buddha and BODHISATTVA images dated from the first century CE onwards, both in stone and terracotta, as well as relief panels are among other artefacts found here.

There are also Brahmanical and Jain sculptures and hundreds of terracotta images of various deities. In addition, the excavator G.R. Sharma, felt there was evidence to indicate a site of the Purushamedha or human sacrifice described in Vedic texts.

Kaushambi was an important city up to about the sixth century CE. Today, a small settlement of the same name exists at the ancient site.

Kaustubha A jewel obtained at the time of the churning of the ocean for AMRITA or divine nectar. The jewel adorns the Hindu god VISHNU or his incarnation, KRISHNA.

Kava-Ushan A legendary sage and king described in the AVESTA. A halo of light surrounded him, and thus he was known as Ashvarechao (of full radiance). Through his prayers and saintliness he gained great powers. He could fly through the air with the help of a divine bird. In the VEDAS a RISHI with a similar name, Kavya-Ushanas, is associated with the god INDRA, another indication of similarities between the texts of the RIG VEDA and the Avesta of Zoroastrianism.

Kavipantha A Jain sect or spiritual movement that emerged in the nineteenth century and sought to find the true principles of Jainism. It was started by Rajachandra, a Jain saint, who believed that too many sects and divisions had led to the downfall of Jainism. He said he did not belong to any sect, but to the true Self or soul. He wrote about 800 letters, which collected together form the sacred text of the sect. In a short poem written to his friend Sobhagbhai in 1896, he explained his six basic principles: the soul exists; the soul is eternal; the soul is the agent of action; the soul is the experiencer of action; the state of deliverance exists; the means of gaining it also exists. According to Rajachandra experiencing the true Self or the soul was the same as attaining MOKSHA or liberation, and his letters explain how to attain this state beyond attachment, hatred or fear. He was against rituals, but later accepted that image-worship could be used as an aid to spiritual growth. Rajachandra had a close relationship with Mahatma GANDHI and is said to have influenced his thinking.

Kaviyur Rock Temple   A temple of the Hindu god SHIVA, located in a cave carved into the rock at Kaviyur, District Alleppey, Kerala. It can be dated to the eighth or ninth century.

kayotsarga   A term in Jainism for a standing posture in which penance is practised. Several TIRTHANKARAS and Jain ascetics are depicted in this posture.

Kedarnatha Temple   A temple of the Hindu god SHIVA located at Kedarnath in Uttarakhand, at a height of 3581 m. Kedarnatha is one of the names of Shiva. A natural Shiva LINGA is located here, and is one of the twelve jyotir lingas.

There are a number of myths and legends regarding the temple. It was said to have been constructed in ancient times by NARA and NARAYANA, two RISHIS who were incarnations of VISHNU and worshipped Shiva here. Other stories relate the temple to the PANDAVAS, who often came here to pray to Shiva. After the great war, they searched for Shiva to obtain his blessings, to free them from the guilt of killing their relatives, but the god remained elusive. He changed into a bull or buffalo, and at Kedarnath dived under the ground, leaving his hump behind. Other parts of him appeared nearby, his arms at Tungnath, his navel at Madhmaheshvara, his face at Rudranath, his head and hair at Kalpeshvara. These places also have shrines, and together with Kedarnath are known as the Panch-Kedar (five Kedars). Another story narrates that when the Pandavas set out for heaven, they reached this peak and were blessed by Shiva. ARJUNA first thought Shiva was a local hunter, but then he realized who he was and constructed this shrine in his honour.

SHANKARA, the ninth-century philosopher, is said to have attained SAMADHI here.

Kedarnath is a major centre of pilgrimage; along with BADRINATH, GANGOTRI and YAMUNOTRI, it is one of the Char Dham, or four main temples in the western Himalayan region.

Ker Puja   A Hindu festival held in Tripura seven days after KARCHI PUJA. At Agartala, the main centre of the festival, seven BRAHMANA priests chant MANTRAS, while a huge pole is raised in the air by ropes and then lowered to the ground. This is believed to bring prosperity to the area.

Kerala Jews   A group of Jews that lived in the Kerala region, and traced their origin to ancient days. There are several different versions on the origin of these Jews. According to one tradition, Jews settled on the south-west coast in present-day Kerala soon after the destruction of the second temple in 70 CE. Other versions are that they arrived as traders at the time of King Solomon, or that they were one of the lost tribes of Israel. The Jews first lived in Kodungallur (Cranganore) in several different groups. The early group came to be called Meyuhassim or Privileged, and alternatively Malabari Jews or Black Jews. Another group consisted of merchants who arrived later from various countries and were known as Paradesi or 'foreign' Jews, also known as White Jews. A third group were the slaves of Jewish merchants who were converted to Judaism and later released from slavery, and were known as Meshuhararim or 'released'. The Paradesi Jews looked down on the others, but all three groups lived together on land granted by the local king. This grant was recorded on copper plates, said to date to the fourth century CE, though some scholars believe the plates are considerably later. In the fourteenth century two brothers quarrelled for chieftainship of the Jewish province, leading to the intervention of other local rulers, and many of the community moved to Kochi (Cochin). The remaining Jews lived peacefully in Kodungallur until the sixteenth century, when they were attacked by Moorish Arab traders who had the support of the local ruler of Kozhikode (Calicut), mainly because the Jewish merchants were prominent in the pepper trade. All the Jews then moved to Kochi, where they were given a piece of land by the local king. Around the same time the Portuguese arrived on the western coast and more Jews reached Kochi because of persecution. However, the Portuguese were eventually displaced by the Dutch in 1660, followed by the British in 1795, and under both these, the Jewish settlement prospered. Though there was some British control, Travancore and Cochin were under Indian rulers and the Jews continued to flourish there. In 1947, there were seven functioning synagogues in the state of Cochin and one in Travancore, and a community of around 2500 Jews in the two states. With almost all the Jews emigrating to Israel, only the Paradesi SYNAGOGUE at Kochi is now able to function, while the North Parur synagogue is taken care of by one family. Today there are less than thirty Jews in Kochi, and perhaps another thirty elsewhere in Kerala.

Kerala, Christians in   Kerala is closely associated with the history of Christianity in India. ST. THOMAS, an Apostle of Christ, is said to have reached the Kerala coast in 52 CE. He was followed by CANAI THOMA and the Syrian Christians in the fourth century, as well as other Christian groups in the ninth and thirteenth centuries, the Portuguese in the sixteenth century, and later other European communities. About 19 per cent of the population of Kerala remains Christian (2001 census), belonging to the ORTHODOX CHURCHES, ROMAN CATHOLIC CHURCHES, and Protestant Churches; the latter are mainly under the CHURCH OF SOUTH INDIA.

Keshava Deva Temple A temple of the Hindu god VISHNU located at MATHURA in Uttar Pradesh. It was erected by Raja Bir Singh Bundela at the time of the Mughal emperor Jahangir. Under AURANGZEB's orders, the temple was destroyed in 1670, and a mosque was constructed in its place. The temple was rebuilt later.

Keshava Temple A temple of the Hindu god VISHNU located at Somnathpur in Karnataka, constructed in 1268 by Somnath, a general of the Hoysala ruler Narasimha III. The temple has three shrines dedicated to Vishnu, surrounded by a passageway within a rectangular enclosure. A pillared MANDAPA extends eastwards. The structure is a typical Hoysala temple, with a star-shaped ground plan, a high plinth, and carved panels on the basements, representing elephants, horses with riders, mythological scenes, geese and MAKARAS. Above on the walls are carvings of Vishnu, his incarnations and consorts, as well as of other deities. Among notable sculptures are a dancing Vishnu and GANESHA, Vishnu and LAKSHMI riding on GARUDA, and INDRA and his consort Shachi on their elephant.

The temple is made of green-grey chloritic schist. An inscribed stone slab on the eastern gateway records its dedication by Somnath.

kesh-dhari A term in Sikhism for a Sikh who follows the rule of wearing long or uncut hair. This is one of the five principles of the KHALSA.

Ketu One of the NAVAGRAHA or nine planets. Ketu is a 'shadow' planet, represented in astronomy by the descending node of the moon. It is the other end of RAHU, which is the ascending node. According to myth, Rahu is fixed in the sky with the head of a dragon, while Ketu is the dragon's tail. Comets and meteors are said to arise from it. Like Rahu, Ketu is said to be a DANAVA, or a DAITYA, the son of Viprachitti and Simhaka. His chariot moves across the sky, drawn by eight dusky red or dark coloured horses.

Kevali/Kevala-jnani A term used for a TIRTHANKARA or realized soul in Jainism, meaning one who is omniscient. A Kevala-jnani knows the past, present and future, and is perfect in every way. Apart from the Tirthankaras, certain Jain acharyas or leaders also attained this level. Lists of these, given in Jain texts, differ for the SHVETAMBARAS and DIGAMBARAS.

Key Monastery A Buddhist complex in Spiti in Himachal Pradesh, probably constructed in the eleventh century, but partly destroyed during the Dogra invasion of 1834. The complex has five GOMPAS, each with a BUDDHA statue, on either side of which are small wooden niches where Tibetan scriptures are stored. On the walls are beautiful THANGKAS or scroll paintings. Other images include those of TARA and the Bodhisattva AVALOKITESHVARA. The monastic complex belongs to the GELUG sect of TIBETAN BUDDHISM.

Khadur Sahib A village near Goindwal in Punjab where there are several GURDWARAS associated with the lives of the second and third Sikh gurus, ANGAD and AMAR DAS. Guru Angad lived here for some time and Amar Das served him before he himself became the guru. The Mal Akhara Gurdwara is located where Guru Angad finalized the GURMUKHI script. The Darbar Sahib or Angitha Sahib Gurdwara marks the sport where guru Angad was cremated. Amar Das used to go to the river Beas every day, a distance of 10 km, and bring back water in a vessel for Guru Angad. Two gurdwaras are connected with this daily journey. The Killa Sahib Gurdwara marks the spot where Amar Das briefly rested the vessel along the way. The Khaddi Sahib Gurdwara is where Amar Das fell into a hollow, a weaver's pit, (khaddi) while carrying the vessel, yet managed not to spill a drop of water. Another important shrine is the Thara Sahib Gurdwara, where Amar Das was anointed as guru by Baba BUDHA.

Khajuraho A town located in Madhya Pradesh, famous for its temples, many of them with erotic sculptures. The temples were constructed mainly between the tenth and twelfth centuries under the rulers of the Chandella dynasty. There are both Hindu and Jain temples here, and about twenty-five temples are still extant, constructed in a distinctive style. Most of them are erected on high platforms and are entered through an open porch, followed by a MANDAPA or hall, a larger mandapa with lateral transepts, and a vestibule leading to the inner shrine. Above is a SHIKHARA or tower, and some of the temples have a number of subsidiary shikharas, clustered together. The temples are decorative and inricately carved with sculptures of all kinds, deities, semi-divine figures or minor deities, sura-sundaris or beautiful young women representing APSARAS or divine nymphs, dancers, musicians, couples in erotic postures, and various animals. Among the Hindu temples, the earliest is the Chausath Yogini Temple of the late ninth century, while the most imposing is the KANDARIYA MAHADEVA TEMPLE, dedicated to SHIVA. Among other Hindu temples are the Lakshmana, Vishvanatha, Jagdambi, Chitragupta and VAMANA temples. Jain temples, include those of Adinatha or RISHABHA, Shantinatha and PARSHVANATHA, the latter being the best of the Jain group. Some of the temples have both Hindu and Jain deities.

Khalsa A term referring to a Sikh community of highly committed Sikhs or to a member of this community. The Khalsa was created by Guru GOBIND SINGH on BAISAKHI Day in 1699 (celebrated in that year on 30 March) at ANANDPUR SAHIB. The guru asked for Sikhs to offer their lives in sacrifice; when the first Sikh came forward, he pretended to cut off his head behind a curtain and returned with a sword dripping in blood. Even so four more Sikhs came forward, and these five are known as the PANJ PYARE, or 'Five Beloved Ones'. They provided an example for all Sikhs to emulate, through their dedication to the guru, the religion and the community. Such Sikhs were known as Khalsa and rituals were established for their initiation. This included sipping water that had been placed in an iron bowl, with batasas or sugar crystals added to it, and stirred with a double-edged dagger or sword, while prayers were recited. This water, known as AMRIT or divine nectar, was sprinkled on initiates as they recited 'Waheguruji ka khalsa, Waheguruji ka fateh' (the Khalsa belongs to God, may He be victorious). This initiation ceremony was termed KHANDE DI PAHUL.

In addition, initiates were given certain marks of identity that would set them apart from others. Each male member of the Khalsa had the suffix 'Singh', meaning 'lion' and indicative of bravery, attached to his name. They had to wear five items beginning with 'k', i.e., kesh, or long hair; kanga, a small comb; kachha, under-shorts; kara, a steel bracelet; kirpan, a sword. Certain dietary and other principles were laid down. These included not cutting or removing hair, not using tobacco or other intoxicants, not eating the meat of an animal slaughtered slowly, not committing adultery, even in their thoughts. They were to chant certain prayers every day, believe in One God, and not worship idols. They should defend their faith, help the poor, and protect the weak. They should forget about caste and religious differences as they now all belonged to one community.

The first five Khalsa then initiated the guru, who now also took the name 'Singh'. Thousands more were initiated in the next few days.

Through the creation of the Khalsa, the Sikhs were unified. Simultaneously Guru GOBIND SINGH ended the institution of MASANDS. The Sikhs became a well-defined community with a distinct identity, though some Sikhs remained outside the Khalsa.

Khalsa is taken to mean 'the pure', but was the term used in those days for 'crown lands', or lands belonging to the king, and thus indicates that members of the Khalsa were people out of the ordinary, who belonged to the guru and to God.

Khan, Syed Ahmad *See* Ahmad Khan.

Khandagiri A hill located in Orissa, noted for its ancient Jain caves and later Jain temples. The early caves, cut into the sides of the hill, can be dated to the second and first centuries BCE and were meant as simple residences for Jain monks. Some of these were converted into temples between the eleventh and fifteenth centuries, with the addition of carvings of the TIRTHANKARAS and other deities. There are about fifteen caves altogether. On top of the hill is a temple constructed in the nineteenth century and dedicated to RISHABHA, with a white marble image added in the twentieth century. The nearby hill of UDAYAGIRI has similar caves.

Khande di Pahul A term in Sikhism for the KHALSA initiation ceremony. Literally it means 'initiation with the two-edged sword'. This ceremony still takes place, usually on BAISAKHI, though it is not compulsory for Sikhs.

Khandoba A Hindu deity who is worshipped in Maharashtra and Karnataka, and is generally considered a form of SHIVA. He is also known as Mallari, Malharai, Mailar, Mhalsakant, Ravalnath, and Yelkoti Mahadeva. Medieval texts such as the *Jayadri Mahatmya*, *Martand Vijaya* and *Malhari Mahatmya* provide legends about the origin of Khandoba. According to these texts, after the DAITYAS MADHU and Kaitabha were killed by VISHNU, two more appeared from their remains, named Mani and Malla. They obtained boons from SHIVA for the conquest of all the LOKAS, DEVAS, ASURAS and people. Shiva asked for a boon in return and stated that they would finally be destroyed by him. After Mani and Malla had conquered all the worlds, the great battle between them and the DEVAS led by Shiva as Martand Bhairava took place, and they were finally defeated and killed. Martand, also known as Khandoba, then began to be worshipped. As they begged pardon from Shiva, Mani and Malla are worshipped with Khandoba.

Khandoba is a warrior deity, often depicted on a horse or represented as a LINGA. A dog is associated with the deity. The four-armed god normally holds a khanda (sword), trishula, damaru (drum) and bowl. His consort is Mhalsa, who holds a lotus. Another consort of his is Banai or Palai. As a warrior or king, he has a minister known as Hegadi, who is also worshipped.

Khandoba is sometimes identified with SKANDA because of his warrior nature. In addition, there are certain Vaishnava elements in his worship; like the goddess LAKSHMI, Mhalsa holds a lotus, and some Khandoba temples have tortoise platforms outside, possibly indicating some relationship with KURMA. There are also similarities with the deity DHARMA THAKUR of Bengal. Khandoba was worshipped by the Marathas and is still a popular deity who is said to grant all wishes.

The most important shrine of this deity is the KHANDOBA TEMPLE at Jejuri in Maharashtra. Another popular shrine is at Pal in Satara district of Maharashtra. There are several other Khandoba temples in Maharashtra, and in Karnataka, where the name Mailar is more popular.

Khandoba Temple A temple of the Hindu god KHANDOBA located at Jejuri in Maharashtra.

The temple was probably built in the fourteenth century, with later additions. There are two shrines here, one known as Gad-Kot and the other as Karhe-pathar, the latter said to be the older of the two. Gad-Kot stands on a hill, enclosed by strong fort-like walls. All along the route to the temple are offerings made by pilgrims, as well as memorial stones of warriors killed in battle. The temple faces the east, and in the porch is a khanda or sword, the emblem of Khandoba. The porch opens into a MANDAPA or hall, in which there are two stone horses, one with Khandoba mounted on it. In the inner shrine are two LINGAS, one representing Khandoba, the other his consort, Mhalsa. There are other Khandoba-Mhalsa images within the shrine or GARBHA-GRIHA. In these images, donated to the temple at different times, Khandoba holds a sword, trishula (trident), damaru (drum) and bowl, while Mhalsa holds a lotus flower or bud. Outside the temple is a brass-plated stone tortoise, almost 9 m in diameter, used as a platform for singing kirtans and BHAJANS. Nearby is a giant image of Mani, as well as shrines of other deities. The Karhe-Pathar temple is similar.

khanqah   A SUFI residence or monastery headed by a SUFI saint, a SHAIKH or PIR. The khanqah generally had a large hall and other rooms, enclosed within a courtyard. There was an entrance gate through which visitors could enter freely at certain times. The hall or jamaat khana, was used both for prayers and as a dormitory, and often guests and residents slept on the floor. Some khanqahs had separate rooms for guests, and beds were provided as a mark of special favour. An administrator, who was appointed to supervise daily life at the khanqah, often had considerable power. The pir had a separate cell for meditation. Mosques and madrasas were often attached to khanqahs. Khanqahs normally supplied food and shelter to all who came there.

khatib   A religious preacher in Islam. The khatib is the IMAM who preaches to the congregation in the mosque.

Khilafat Movement   A movement started in India in 1920, that formed part of the freedom struggle. It was essentially a religious movement aiming to preserve the power of the Caliph or Khalifa, considered the leader of all Muslims, who was also the sultan of Turkey. Turkey had suffered losses in the First World War (1914–18), and Muslims wanted reassurance that the power of the Khalifa would not be reduced. As the threat was from Britain, Mahatma GANDHI thought it would be useful to combine a movement for the Khalif with the freedom struggle. This would lead to harmony between Hindus and Muslims, who would be joined against their common enemy, the British. Thus, with Gandhi's initiative, the Indian National Congress and the Khilafat movement, led by the brothers Shaukat Ali and Muhammad Ali started the Non-Cooperation Movement together in 1920.

While the Non-Cooperation Movement was part of a series of struggles against the British, the Khilafat movement ended when Turkey became a secular state and the office of the Khalifa was abolished in 1924.

Khirki Masjid   A mosque named after its location in Khirki village in New Delhi. It was constructed by Junan Shah, also known as Khan-i Jahan, the prime minister of Sultan Firuz Shah Tughlaq (1351–88).

The mosque is a double-storeyed building covering an area of 87 m each side, made from rubble stone and plaster. There are entrance gateways on three sides, covered by domes, with tapering minarets on each side. The main entrance is to the east and opens into a cruciform courtyard with twenty-five squares, each subdivided into nine smaller squares. Small domes cover most of the squares, with a few being left open for light. Altogether there are eighty-five domes.

The lower storey of the mosque consists of a basement with vaulted cells and bastions at the corners, while the upper storey has perforated windows.

Khizr, Khwaja   A legendary Islamic saint. He is said to have attained immortality, and therefore makes an appearance in every age. He is believed to have been the guide of Moses, and according to some traditions, a companion of Alexander the Great. He is a spiritual guide of SUFIS and saves people in desperate situations. Merchants and travellers appeal to him in times of distress. In some Arabic sources he is connected with the sea, and in others with vegetation. In India he is worshipped as a river god, or as a deity of wells and streams. Khwaja Khizr is sometimes identified with another legendary saint, Pir Badr, or worshipped along with him as one of the PANCH PIRS. Both the deities were said to occasionally travel on a fish.

Khojas   A Muslim community that includes both SUNNIS and SHIAS. The majority belong to the NIZARI ISMAILIS, a Shia sect who follow the AGA KHAN and believe in Ismail, one of the sons of Imam Jafar Sadiq, the sixth apostolic IMAM. The Khojas were a Hindu group who lived in Sind and according to traditional accounts, were converted to Islam in the fourteenth century by Pir Sadr-ud-din, a Persian saint. The new faith then spread to Gujarat, where the Lohana community was among those who accepted it.

Most Khojas speak Sindhi, the Kutchi dialect, or Gujarati.

Khordad   An AMESHA SPENTA in Zoroastrianism, the later form of HAURVATAT.

Khordeh Avesta   The 'little Avesta', a book of daily prayers for Zoroastrians. The prayers include passages from the GATHAS, as well as later prayers.

Khorshed   A YAZATA or minor deity in Zoroastrianism, a personified form of the sun.

khratu   A term in the GATHAS of Zoroastrianism that signifies mental energy and wisdom, and the will or purpose of AHURA MAZDA in creation. Such khratu is known as hu-khratu or good khratu. But there is also dush khratu or the evil intellect, which belongs to those who plan evil acts.

Khshathra A deity and a power of AHURA MAZDA, the name of God in Zoroastrianism. It is personified as an AMESHA SPENTA representing strength, power and sovereignty. Khshathra is the divine strength and power that exists in each person. Also known as Khshathra Vairya, he presides over metals, representing strength, and his symbolic flower is the royal basil. Later, he came to be known as Shahrevar. In the YASHTS, he is described as the compassionate protector of the poor.

Khuddaka Nikaya A collection of fifteen Buddhist texts that form part of the Sutta Pitaka of the PALI CANON. The texts are: *KHUDDAKA-PATHA, DHAMMAPADA, UDANA, ITIVUTTAKA, SUTTANIPATA, VIMANAVATTHU, PETAVATTHU, THERAGATHA, THERIGATHA, JATAKA, NIDDESA, PATISAMBHIDA-MAGGA, APADANA, BUDDHAVAMSHA,* and *CHARIYA PITAKA.* This miscellaneous group of texts was composed between the fifth century BCE and the second century CE.

Khuddaka-Patha A Buddhist text that forms part of the *KHUDDAKA NIKAYA* of the PALI CANON. Literally the title means 'short recitals', and the *Khuddaka-Patha* has nine short suttas (sutras), probably used as meditation exercises and prayers. Important principles of Buddhism are conveyed through these suttas. The first sutta is to proclaim faith in Buddhism. The second is a list of ten rules for monks. The fifth indicates what the BUDDHA considers the best mangalas or auspicious ceremonies. Among them are 'honouring mother and father, cherishing of child and wife, and a peaceful occupation'. The eighth sutta describes the best treasure, which is that of good works; the ninth, the *Metta Sutta,* describes friendliness to all living beings as the true Buddhism. This text is still studied today, particularly in Sri Lanka.

khutba A term used in Islam for the discourse preached by the KHATIB or IMAM at the Friday prayer in mosques. It usually has a formalized content.

kimpurushas A class of semi-divine or minor Hindu deities. In later texts the term was synonymous with KINNARAS.

kinnaras Minor Hindu deities who have horse's bodies and human heads, or sometimes the reverse. They are musicians associated with the GANDHARVAS and sing praises to the gods. They live in KUBERA's heaven on Mt KAILASHA. It is said that they are the sons of KASHYAPA, or that they emerged along with other YAKSHAS from the toe of the god BRAHMA. They are also mentioned in Buddhist texts. It is thought that the word 'kinnara' may be related to the Greek *kentauros* or centaur.

Kiratpur Sahib A town in district Rupnagar, Punjab, sacred to Sikhs. Guru HARGOBIND, the sixth guru, lived here and founded the town. The seventh and eighth gurus, HAR RAI and HAR KRISHAN, were born here. The tenth guru, GOBIND SINGH, also lived here for some time. The head of the martyred guru, TEGH BAHADUR was received here by Guru Gobind Singh before being taken to ANANDPUR SAHIB for cremation. The Babangarh Sahib Gurdwara marks this spot.

Kishkindha The city and region of the Vanaras described in the RAMAYANA. In Valmiki's *Ramayana,* the city is said to be located in an extensive cave. It was full of precious stones and other precious items, flowering groves, mansions, palaces and temples, and scented highways. Traditionally, Kishkindha has been located in Karnataka.

Kissah-i-Sanjan The 'Story of Sanjan', a short text written in 1600, that provides an account of the migration of Zoroastrians to India, and their first few hundred years in this country. The text has 864 lines in verse and was written in Persian by Bahman Kaikobad Hormuzdyar Sanjana. Later it was translated into Gujarati and then into English. Bahman, son of Kaikobad, who was a SANJAN priest at NAVSARI, wrote that he heard this story from Dastur Hoshang.

Beginning with an invocation and praise of God, the poem sums up the history of the religion until the departure to India from the city of Ormuz. Men, women and children travelled by ships and arrived at Diu, where they stayed nineteen years, and then went to Gujarat, where they were given a tract of land by the Hindu raja JADI RANA, which they named Sanjan. There they reinstalled their sacred fire. Around 300 years passed, during which some Zoroastrians moved to different cities in Gujarat, including Bharuch and Navsari. For 700 years after their arrival they lived happily, but then disaster struck the families at Sanjan. A Muslim sultan took over Champaner and sent a force to Sanjan under Alif Khan. According to tradition, the sultan was Mahmud Begdo (i.e., Mahmud Begarha, ruled 1459–1511). The raja asked for help and 1400 Zoroastrians armed themselves and joined him in battle. As the battle went on, the Hindu soldiers fled, but the Zoroastrians continued to fight, led by Ardashir, and drove back the attackers. However, Alif Khan rearmed and advanced again. This time the raja, Ardashir and many other Zoroastrians were killed. Those who survived fled to the Bahrot mountains. After twelve years there they went to Bansda. Then Changa bin Asa or Changa Shah of Navsari, a pious Zoroastrian dastur (priest), thought of bringing the sacred fire, which had been preserved first in Bahrot and then in Bansda, to Navsari. This was done, and the Sanjan community settled in Navsari.

The *Kissah* ends there and does not describe the later conflicts between the Sanjan and Navsari priests.

While some consider it a fairly authentic history, others see it as a 'historical novel' or even an invented tale to glorify the Sanjan priests who were in conflict with their Navsari counterparts. Most PARSIS in India, however, accept this account and base their history on this text.

Knanaya Christians A term for a group of SYRIAN CHRISTIANS who trace their origin to Knai Thomman or CANAI THOMA, a rich merchant who came to Kodungallur (Kerala) in the fourth century with 400 Syrian Christians. These included members of seventy-two families and seven clans, as well as priests, deacons and a bishop of the East Syrian Church. As the Christians claimed to be descended from the two Jewish tribes of Judah and retained many of their Jewish customs, they were known as Jewish Christians. They were also called Southists (Thekkumbhagar) as they lived on the southern side of Kodungallur, while the ST. THOMAS Christians lived to the north. Another explanation is that they were known as Southists because they came from the southern state of Judah. In 1882 a separate Knanaya Committee was set up, and in 1910, a Knanaya diocese. There are now sixty-three Knanaya parishes in India, as well as some in North America. Though most Knanaya Syrian Christians are Jacobites (see JACOBITE CHURCH), there are also some Catholics, and a separate diocese for Knanaya Catholics was set up in 1911. The two Knanaya groups intermarry and retain some Jewish customs.

Konarak Sun Temple A temple of the Hindu god SURYA, god of the sun, located at Konarak in Orissa. It was constructed in the late thirteenth century by King Narasimha Deo Langoraja of the Eastern Ganga dynasty. This grand temple was built in the form of a chariot with twelve large pairs of wheels drawn by seven horses, thus representing Surya's chariot as described in ancient texts. Each wheel, about 3 m high, is richly ornamented and is carved on the sides of a raised platform. The main temple is on the platform, and a staircase leads up to it, while the horses are on the sides of the staircase. The temple is in Orissa style, with a sanctuary or GARBHA-GRIHA, here known as a deul. This opens into the jagmohan or pillared porch, and is surmounted by a curvilinear tower. The deul once had a large image of Surya that no longer exists. There are two other images of Surya in green chloritic schist, in which he is standing in a chariot and riding a horse. Aruna, his charioteer, as well as donors, attendants and VIDYADHARAS, are also carved.

The sides of the platform have friezes, including images of elephants in the forest, processions of elephants, horses and camels, hunting scenes and caravans. There are sculpted panels with YAKSHIS and MITHUNA couples, NAGAS and Nagis, ascetics, warriors and princes. East of the temple is a pillared hall.

Images from the temple preserved in the adjacent museum include those of Surya, AGNI, VARAHA, Trivikrama and BHAIRAVA.

The temple is weathered and damaged but has partly been restored. Though no longer in use, it is still a magnificent sight and is considered one of the most beautiful medieval temples. Surya worship takes place on the sea-side near the temple.

Kooka/Kuka A Sikh sect, also known as NAMDHARI.

Korravai A Hindu goddess worshipped in south India, where she is considered the mother of MURUGAN, a form of KARTTIKEYA. She is a fierce goddess associated with the battlefield. Korravai was later identified with PARVATI.

kosha A Sanskrit term meaning a sheath or body. In YOGA texts, each person is said to have 'pancha kosha', or five bodies. The material body, that is visible to us, is known as the annamaya kosha. It is surrounded by the pranamaya kosha, or vital body. Around this is the manomaya kosha, the body of memory and the conscious mind. This is followed by the vijnanamaya kosha, of knowledge or super-consciousness. The highest is the anandamaya kosha, the cosmic body whose nature is bliss.

Koshala An ancient kingdom located in eastern Uttar Pradesh, described in texts of the sixth century BCE and earlier. According to the RAMAYANA, King DASHARATHA ruled here, with his capital at AYODHYA. Later RAMA ruled the kingdom, and after his death it was divided between his twin sons, LAVA and KUSHA.

Kratu One of the PRAJAPATIS, also referred to as a great RISHI or sage, and a mind-born son of the Hindu god BRAHMA. According to the VISHNU PURANA, 60,000 Valakhilyas were born from his wife Samnati. These were tiny RISHIS, each the size of a thumb.

Krishna A popular Hindu deity, an incarnation of VISHNU.

Krishna is first mentioned in the RIG VEDA, though in this text he may not be the same as the later deity. In the *Chhandogya Upanishad*, Krishna, son of DEVAKI, is a great scholar. Krishna was also the name of an ASURA.

There are several myths and stories relating to Krishna as an incarnation of VISHNU. Krishna is described in the MAHABHARATA and in the BHAGAVAD GITA, he is a divine being, a form of the Supreme. His life is described in more detail in the HARIVAMSHA, an appendix to the *Mahabharata*, and in the PURANAS, particularly the BHAGAVATA PURANA. Krishna is also described in later BHAKTI literature, such as the GITA GOVINDA and the poems of CHANDIDAS, CHAITANYA MAHAPRABHU, and others. A summary of his life story, as celebrated in art, music, dance and literature, is given below:

Birth: Krishna was descended from YADU, one of the sons of the mythical YAYATI, and thus was a YADAVA. Myths about his birth narrate that the earth was full of wickedness, and that he was born in order to save it. Specifically, he would rid the earth of Kamsa, usurper of the throne of MATHURA. DEVAKI, cousin of Kamsa, was married to VASUDEVA. Soon after the marriage, a celestial voice announced that her eighth son would kill Kamsa. According to one version of the story, Kamsa immediately put Devaki and Vasudeva in prison and killed their first six children as soon as they were born. The seventh embryo was whisked away by divine intervention and born to Rohini, another wife of Vasudeva who lived in GOKUL. This child was BALARAMA, Krishna's elder brother. At the same time that Krishna was born, YASHODA, wife of NANDA, a cowherd in Gokul, gave birth to a girl, who was actually the goddess YOGAMAYA. She was substituted for the baby Krishna, who was given secretly to Yashoda and Nanda. Kamsa went to kill Yogamaya, but she flew into the air and before disappearing said that Kamsa's killer had already been born. Kamsa then ordered all children below the age of one to be killed, but Krishna escaped.

Childhood: Krishna grew up in Gokul and VRINDAVAN, as the much-loved child of Yashoda and Nanda. He was both lovable and naughty, and at the same time endowed with tremendous strength. He played a number of pranks stealing butter, playing, and also vanquished several ferocious demons. The little child was loved by all around, particularly the GOPIS (cowgirls) from whom he would often demand milk and butter.

Youth: Krishna the youth was beautiful. He played his flute and enchanted the world. Cows, birds, the gopis and all who were near him were entranced by his beauty. With the gopis he became more demanding, breaking their vessels to take milk and hiding their clothes when they bathed in the river. Finally he became their lover, and they adored him; all wanted to spend their nights with him. (RADHA, the gopi most dear to him, is described only in late texts.)

Manhood: When Krishna grew up, he went to MATHURA and achieved his life's aim of killing Kamsa and installing the rightful king Ugrasena on the throne. But Kamsa's wives were the daughters of Jarasandha, king of MAGADHA. Jarasandha vowed to defeat Krishna and attacked Mathura seventeen times. Krishna and Balarama defended the city, but the repeated attacks caused great hardship to the inhabitants. Krishna and the Yadavas then decided to settle in DVARAKA on the western coast.

Family: Krishna married RUKMINI and later had several other wives. Among them were Jambavati, daughter of JAMBAVAN, and Satyabhama, daughter of Satrajit. Krishna also married the 16,000 wives of NARAKASURA, a demonic king of Pragjyotishpur, after killing the king. He did so in order to give protection to these women. His sons included PRADYUMNA from RUKMINI, Shamba from Jambavati, ten sons from Satyabhama, and thousands of others. Charumati was his daughter from Rukmini.

Mahabharata War: While he was at Dvaraka, the PANDAVAS and KAURAVAS became involved in their grand conflict. They came to Krishna for help, and he became ARJUNA's charioteer, but at the same time deputed his army to help the KAURAVAS. On the battlefield, as the war was about to start, the famous dialogue between Arjuna and Krishna, which forms the Bhagavad Gita, took place.

Dvaraka: Returning to Dvaraka, Krishna continued to rule over the Yadavas. After some time the Yadavas began to quarrel and fight with one another. They destroyed themselves, Balarama departed from his life in meditation, and Krishna was accidentally shot with an arrow by a hunter. Dvaraka was submerged under the sea.

Analysis: Krishna's life is seen as an amalgamation of different deities and heroic figures, yet it forms a unified whole. There have been different analyses of his story from a religious point of view, to investigate the spiritual symbolism of each of his attributes and actions. His flute, for instance, represents the body; the seven notes notched on it reflect the inner CHAKRAS. In the *Masnawi* of the SUFI saint JALALUDDIN RUMI there is a similar symbolism of the flute, which sings of the pain of separation from the divine. The devotion of the gopis to him is a perfect example of BHAKTI, devotion to god. As one surrenders to god, the bliss of divine union is awakened, and their union with him is nothing but the inner union with god. In the Bhagavad Gita, Krishna is the supreme deity, the synthesisizer of philosophy. However, as an incarnation, Krishna is not infallible, and can also be human and vulnerable.

Krishna is a friendly god, not a stern, inaccesible deity. He helps whomever he can, and though he kills Kamsa and several demons, he never condemns his friends and devotees. He is worshipped as a child, a lover, a friend, and a supreme deity.

Krishna in literature and art Krishna's myth has been endlessly elaborated on in literature. Jayadeva in his *Gita Govinda*, a romantic and erotic poem, describes the relationship between Krishna and RADHA. There are several works of Krishna Bhakti, including those of Chandidas, Chaitanya Mahaprabhu, the GOSWAMIS, VALLABHACHARYA, VIDYAPATI, MIRA and SURDAS.

Krishna and his story are depicted in painting, sculpture and other art forms, from the miniature paintings of the medieval period to folk and regional forms of art, and in calendar and popular art. One of the particular forms of depicting Krishna at Mathura is through paper cuts. In modern times, Krishna is often depicted as blue in colour, dressed in yellow clothes, playing on a flute, with one or more cows near him. Sometimes he is with Radha under flowering trees, or shown raising the GOVARDHANA mountain.

In sculpture, there are images of Krishna in temples all over the country. They depict scenes from his life or show Krishna as an incarnation of Vishnu. Some of the main Krishna temples are located in areas associated with his life: Mathura, Vrindavan, Gokul and Dvaraka. The Gita Temple at KURUKSHETRA is said to mark the spot where Krishna taught the Bhagavad Gita. Among other famous temples are the NATHDWARA TEMPLE in Rajasthan; the Gopeshwar

Temple at Datia, Madhya Pradesh; the Radheshyam Temple at Bilaspur, Himachal; the Gopal Mandir at Ujjain; the Kunj Behari Temple at Jodhpur, Rajasthan; the shrines at BISHNUPUR, West Bengal; the Krishna temples at GURUVAYUR, Mavelikara, Ambalapuzha, and KALADI in Kerala; and the Krishna Temple at UDUPI in Karnataka.

Songs of Bhakti or love and devotion to Krishna are numerous, and the separation and union of Krishna and Radha are depicted in both classical and folk dance forms.

Names: Krishna is known by a number of different names. The following are the names from the AMARAKOSHA: Vishnu, Narayana, Vaikuntha, Vishtarashravas, Damodara, Hrishikesha, Keshava, Madhava, Svabhu, Daityari, Pundarikaksha, Govinda, Garudadhvaja, Pitambara, Achyuta, Sharngi, Vishvaksena, Janardana, Upendra, Indravaraja, Chakrapani, Chaturbhuja, Padmanabha, Madhuripu, Vasudeva, Trivikrama, Devaki-nandana, Shauri, Shripati, Purushottama, Vanamali, Balidhvamsi, Kamsarati, Adhokshaja, Vishvambhara, Kaitabhajit, Vidhu, Shrivatsalan-chana. There are several more names in other texts, as well as local and regional names. Some of his other names are Gopala, Gopendra, Venugopala, Madhusudana, Vrajanatha and Vrishnishreshtha. Krishna is also worshipped in particular forms, such as VITTHALA and JAGANNATHA.

Similarities with other cultures: Of all Hindu deities, Krishna has been most compared with religious figures and heroes of other cultures. Some compare him with Christ, pointing out that the name Christ has the same root as Krishna. PARAMAHANSA YOGANANDA believes the two represent aspects of the same consciousness. There are also similar stories of the killing of children at the time of the birth of JESUS and Krishna. Krishna's heroic episodes, such as the killing of various demons, have close parallels with hero myths in other parts of the world. The worship of Herakles (Hercules) at MATHURA is mentioned by Megasthenes, the Greek ambassador of the fourth century BCE, and it is presumed Krishna is meant, as his exploits are similar to those of Herakles. Krishna's only vulnerable body parts were the soles of his feet, and like Achilles, he was killed by an arrow in his heel.

Sects: There are some sects specifically devoted to the worship of Krishna, both in historical times and in the present. These include the mystical PANCHARATRA, the followers of Chaitanya and Vallabhacharya, the more recent ISKCON, and other bhakti sects.

Krishna Dvaipayana A name of the ancient rishi, VYASA.

Krishna Lila An enactment of scenes from the life of the Hindu god KRISHNA. The scenes usually enacted are those from his early life and childhood, his youth, and his killing of King Kamsa.

Krishnamurti, J. A renowned twentieth-century philosopher. Jiddu Krishnamurti was born on 11 May 1895, at Madanapalle, a small town in present Andhra Pradesh. His mother died when he was young; after retiring from government service, his father volunteered to work for the THEOSOPHICAL SOCIETY and moved to its headquarters at Adyar, Chennai (Madras). At this time the Theosophists were searching for a 'vehicle', that is, a pure being into which the Messiah would incarnate. Krishnamurti, around fourteen years old and considered somewhat vague and dull, was identified by Charles W. Leadbeater, a leading Theosophist, as the coming Messiah, the World Teacher. Krishnamurti was then trained by Leadbeater and Annie BESANT to fulfill this role.

In 1911, the Order of the Star in the East was founded, with Krishnamurti at the head. Krishnamurti led the order for some time and had certain spiritual experiences, but gradually grew disenchanted with Theosophy. The turning point came after the death of his brother Nitya in 1929, after which Krishnamurti lost faith in the mystical Theosophical hierarchy. On 2 August 1929, the opening day of the annual Star Camp at Ommen, Holland, Krishnamurti dissolved the Order before 3000 members. On that day he said, 'I maintain that Truth is a pathless land, and you cannot approach it by any path whatsoever, by any religion, by any sect.'

Krishnamurti continued to develop his own philosophy over the years, gave talks all over the world, and developed a large following. Krishnamurti Foundations were set up in England, the USA and India to disseminate his teachings, and schools were opened to try to bring about a new type of human being. Krishnamurti spoke about the 'religious mind' that comes into being in silence, and of 'freedom from the known' when conditioned thought has ended.

In 1980 he summed up his own teaching beginning with the following words: 'The core of Krishnamurti's teaching is contained in the statement he made in 1929 when he said: "Truth is a pathless land." Man cannot come to it through any organization, through any creed, through any dogma, priest or ritual, not through any philosophic knowledge or psychological technique. He has to find it through the mirror of relationship, through the understanding of the contents of his own mind, through observation and not through intellectual analysis or introspective dissection.'

He ended by saying, 'Total negation is the essence of the positive. When there is negation of all those things that thought has brought about psychologically, only then is there love, which is compassion and intelligence.' Krishnamurti died on 17 February 1986, but his Foundations and schools still exist. The collected works of his talks and writings amount to hundreds of volumes. Krishnamurti's philosophy is non-sectarian and appeals mainly to the educated elite.

Krishnamurti, U.G. A twentieth-century philosopher whose thought is similar to that of J. KRISHNAMURTI, though more radical. Uppaluri Gopala Krishnamurti, popularly known as 'UG', was born on 9 July 1918 in the town of Masulipatnam in present Andhra Pradesh. His early years were spent in the nearby town of Gudivade. UG's mother died when he was only seven days old, and he came under the care of his grandfather, T.G. Krishnamurti, who was a Theosophist, though he at the same time retained his orthodox BRAHMANA culture. Between the ages of fourteen and twenty-one, UG tried several spiritual techniques and engaged in self-enquiry, rejecting traditional beliefs. He joined the THEOSOPHICAL SOCIETY, and in 1941, he worked for some time in C.W. Leadbeater's library at Adyar, but was disappointed that Leadbeater did not recognize his potential. He began to lecture for the Theosophical Society, and his talks were well received. Like J. Krishnamurti, he left the Society after a few years. Despite the similarities, he seemed in constant rivalry with J. Krishnamurti, whom he met frequently in the early part of his career. UG married in 1943 and had three children, though his marriage later broke up. In 1967 he had a transformatory experience, in which he felt he died, and was reborn a different person.

UG did not give formal lectures or write books, but had a number of disciples, some of whom recorded their conversations and dialogues. He said that each person should be their own teacher, and that no guru is required. His biographer, Mahesh Bhatt, says of him: 'UG shuns religious persons, ridicules social reformers, condemns saints, speaks with disgust about sadhakas (spiritual aspirants), detests the chanting of the Vedas or the recitation of the Upanishads and is full of rage when one speaks of Shankara or the Buddha.'

Though he did not acknowledge it, such rejection is similar to the Buddhist concept of negation, and to the thoughts of several other philosophers. Through the rejection of all tradition, the mind drops its conditioning and reaches a state of freedom.

UG died in March 2007.

Krista Purana A text on the life of JESUS written in the sixteenth century in the style of the PURANAS. It was composed in Konkani, the local language of Goa and parts of the western coast, by an English Jesuit, Father Thomas Stephens, who came to India in 1579. The text contained 10,962 verses and was popular among the local Christians of GOA. It was first printed in 1616. Stephens also compiled a Konkani grammar.

Krita Yuga The first of the four yugas or periods of time, which together comprise one MAHAYUGA. It is also known as the Satya Yuga, or 'age of truth'. The Krita Yuga was the golden age of truth and righteousness. Negative emotions, such as envy, malice, hatred and deceit, did not exist. All people were equal and worshipped the same deity, and there was only one Veda, known as the *Brahma Veda*. Humans lived for 4000 years, were the size of giants, and had vastly superior mental powers. Children were born through the power of the mind and not through sex. The yuga lasts for 4800 divine years, equal to 17,28,000 human years, and is symbolized by the colour white. It is succeeded by the TRETA YUGA. After the KALI YUGA, the present corrupted age, the Krita Yuga will appear again.

Kriya Yoga A type of YOGA described in Patanjali's *YOGA SUTRA* and other texts. According to Patanjali, tapas (austerities), svadhyaya (self-study and inquiry) and ishvara pranidhana (surrender to god) form Kriya Yoga, or the union with god through action (kriya). Within this broad sphere, the term is also used for various breathing and other techniques that foster divine union. PARAMAHANSA YOGANANDA taught a special set of exercises and PRANAYAMA, known as Kriya Yoga. Kriya is a synonym for KARMA, and the path of KARMA YOGA, or selfless action, is best described in the BHAGAVAD GITA.

Kriyayogasara A Sanskrit text that forms part of the *PADMA PURANA*, but is also considered a separate UPAPURANA, or minor PURANA. It deals with the worship of VISHNU, the celebration of festivals dedicated to him, and pilgrimages to sacred places on the river GANGA.

Krodha (Krodhaa) A daughter of the rishi DAKSHA in Hindu myths. She was one of the wives of KASHYAPA and the mother of the Bhutas or spirits. Her name means 'anger'.

kshatriya The second of the four main Hindu castes, who were initially warriors and kings. Kshatriyas were generally inferior to BRAHMANAS in Vedic tradition, but had a close relationship. There were instances of kshatriyas practising austerities and becoming RISHIS, normally the preserve of brahmanas. In Buddhism and Jainism, kshatriyas seem to have been considered superior. A Jain myth records that though MAHAVIRA was conceived in the womb of a brahmana, he was transferred to that of a kshatriya. Later myths tell the story of PARASHURAMA's annihilation of the kshatriyas, possibly indicating a conflict for status and power between kshatriyas and brahmanas. Through YAJNAS (sacrifices) brahmanas conferred kshatriya status on outsiders or non-kshatriyas, as revealed through the AGNI KULA and other myths. Today there are a number of divergent kshatriya castes.

Kshetrapala A group of guardian deities in Hinduism, who are said to protect temples and the area around them. They are worshipped particularly in south India. According to some texts, there are forty-nine Kshetrapalas. Kshetrapalas are also worshipped by Jains.

Kshitigarbha A BODHISATTVA who assists those who suffer in hell, as well as those in other realms. He is known as Jizo in Japan and Ti-tsang in Chinese. He is usually depicted holding a staff in one hand and a jewel in the other. He looks after children who have died untimely deaths, and helps in their rebirth.

Kubera A Hindu deity, the guardian of the northern quarter, associated with wealth and treasure. Kubera also appears in Jain and Buddhist sculptures. In some text, he is known as Vaishravana. He is the son of Vishravas, though he is sometimes called the son of Pulastya. His city Alaka is located in the Himalayas; it is described in early texts and in the *Meghaduta* of KALIDASA. His garden, Chaitraratha, is on Mt MANDARA, where the KINNARAS are his attendants. According to other sources, he lived on Mt KAILASHA, in a palace built by the divine architect Vishvakarma, or on the GANDHAMADANA mountain. He was the half-brother of RAVANA. At one time the city of LANKA belonged to him, but he was displaced by Ravana.

Kubera performed austerities and received a boon from the god BRAHMA, by which he became the guardian of the north and the lord of all treasures, gold, silver and gems. He was given the PUSHPAKA vimana, in which he could travel through the air.

Originally a YAKSHA, a semi-divine spirit or guardian deity, Kubera is the lord of all the yakshas. His consort is known as Bhadra, Charvi or Kauveri, the daughter of the DANAVA Mura. His sons are Manigriva or Varnakavi, and Nalakubera or Mayuraja; his daughter is Minakshi. He is also known as Yaksharaja, Mayuraja, Rakshasendra (lord of rakshasas), Ratnagarbha (belly of jewels), Vaishravana, Ishasakhi (friend of SHIVA), and by many other names.

Incorporated into Brahmanism, Kubera is depicted along with Shri or LAKSHMI, goddess of fortune. In Buddhism, his consort is the mother goddess HARITI, and in northern Buddhism he is known as Panchika. Kubera is similar to the Buddhist deity Jambhala, whose consort is Vasudhara. In Jainism, he is the yaksha associated with the TIRTHANKARA Mallinatha.

In texts he is described as two- or four-armed, holding a club and mace, accompanied by a shankha (conch) and padma (lotus), with his VAHANA or mount being a man or sometimes a lamb. However, in most sculptures Kubera is depicted as a pot-bellied figure or a dwarf, holding a money-bag and drinking wine. He sometimes holds a mongoose or a bunch of grapes. Sculptures of Kubera in his various forms occur from around the second century BCE.

Kubrawiya A SUFI sect that was a branch of the SUHRAWARDI. The Indian Kubrawiya branches were known as the FIRDAUSI and HAMADANI. The founder of the sect, Najmuddin Kubra, whose full name was Abul Jannab Ahmad bin Umar al-Khiwaqi, was born in Khwarizm in 1145–46. He travelled to various places to study HADIS, and after a mystical experience in Alexandria, became a Sufi. He then became a disciple of several Suhrawardi saints and later founded his own KHANQAH in Khwarizm. He wrote a number of books on SUFISM, including *Al-Usul-al-Ashra* in Arabic, which contains the ten basic guidelines for Sufis; the *Sifatul-Adab* in Persian, on rules for Sufi initiates; and *Minhajus-Salikin* in Arabic, an advanced manual for Sufis.

He died in 1221 when the Mongols invaded the city, after making a token attempt to stop their advance by throwing stones at them.

Kukadaru, Dastur A saintly Zoroastrian priest who lived in the nineteenth century and was given the title 'Dastur', or high priest, after his death. Jamshed Sohrab Kukadaru, was born at Surat, Gujarat, in 1831 and died in 1900. He was known to have been able to predict the future, heal the sick, and perform various miracles. He was a vegetarian and an ascetic who ate only once a day. He knew AVESTA and PAHLAVI, and translated parts of the DINKARD. He is revered by PARSIS and particularly by the ILM-E-KSHNOOM sect.

kuladevata A family deity (kula = family). Several Hindu communities, castes and clans worship a kuladevata, a deity specific to that clan or group, in addition to the other major deities.

Kulika A NAGA or serpent king in Hindu mythology. He is described as dusky brown, with a half-moon on his head.

Kumara A name of the Hindu god KARTTIKEYA.

Kumarajiva A Buddhist philosopher who lived from 344 to 413. He was the son of an Indian father, Kumara or Kumarayana, and a princess of the kingdom of Kucha in Central Asia, whose name was Jiva. He lived in Kucha and in Kashmir, and became a Buddhist monk when he was twenty years old. In Kucha he was renowned as a teacher of Buddhism. In 401 he was captured and taken to China, as the emperor Yao Hsin wanted him to teach Buddhism in China. He stayed in Changan for the rest of his life, translating Buddhist texts into Chinese, helped by Chinese scholars. Among the ninety-eight texts he translated were the *PRAJNAPARAMITA* and the *SADDHARMA PUNDARIKA*. He was also the teacher of FA-HSIEN.

Kumaran Asan A scholar and poet who wrote mainly in Malayalam on religious and social themes. Born in 1873, he joined Sri NARAYANA GURU, the social and religious reformer, in Kerala. He learnt YOGA and VEDANTA from him, and later studied Sanskrit, set up a Sanskrit school, and came to be known as Asan, or teacher. After the setting up of the Sri Narayana Dharma-paripalana Yogam, he worked as its secretary for sixteen years and edited its journal. He was a prolific poet, his poems combining Hindu and Buddhist ideas. Among his longer poems are *Chinta Vishtayaya Sita* (Sita in Meditation), *Duravastha* (Evil Plight), and *Karuna* (Compassion). There are several other collections of his poetry, and he also translated Edwin Arnold's *Light of Asia* into Malayalam. He died in 1924.

Kumaras The mind-born sons of BRAHMA, who are eternally young, pure and innocent. They are SANAT

KUMARA, Sananda, Sanaka and Sanatana. According to some accounts, they remain five years old, while according to others they are fifteen or sixteen years old.

Kumarila Bhatta A teacher of the Purva MIMAMSA school of philosophy who lived in the eighth or ninth century, though some assign him an earlier date. He believed in the authority of the VEDAS and wrote commentaries on Mimamsa philosophy. His disciple MANDANA MISRA was defeated by SHANKARA in a philosophical argument.

Kumbakonam A city located in the Kaveri delta in Tamil Nadu, known for its temples. It was the capital of the Chola dynasty in the seventh century. Among the many temples here is that of Lord Sarangapani (VISHNU) and his consort Kamala (LAKSHMI). This temple, with a towering GOPURAM, was erected by the Nayakas in the seventeenth century. The KUMBHESHVARA TEMPLE, dedicated to SHIVA, is one of the most sacred Shiva temples. There is a temple of Vinayaka (GANESHA), as well as sacred tanks, including the Lakshmi Tirtham and MAHAMAHAM tank.

Kumbh Mela A Hindu festival held in rotation at four sacred places: PRAYAGA (ALLAHABAD), HARDWAR, NASHIK, and UJJAIN. At each place the festival takes place once in twelve years, while an Ardha Kumbh, or half-Kumbh, is held every six years, and a Maha Kumbh every third year. Thus there is a Kumbh Mela at one of the four places every three years. According to the legends associated with the festival, when AMRITA or divine nectar was received from the ocean of milk, the ASURAS and DEVAS struggled for its possession. In the course of the struggle, twelve drops fell on the earth, four of them at the above places, and the Kumbh Mela commemorates this event. Another tradition states that SHANKARA established this mela, to serve as a meeting place for sadhus, yogis, and ascetics. It is also originally said to have been a fertility festival, in which pots of grain were dipped in the river to ensure a good harvest. Each Kumbh Mela, spread over several weeks, is visited by lakhs of people, and it is considered particularly auspicious to bathe in the sacred river at these places.

Kumbheshvara Temple A temple of the Hindu god SHIVA located at KUMBAKONAM in Tamil Nadu, constructed in the seventeenth century at the time of the Nayaka dynasty. According to the legend associated with this temple, the kumbha or vessel containing AMRITA or divine nectar was washed here by currents at the time of the great deluge. Shiva came here disguised as a hunter and shot an arrow at it, which broke the pot and the nectar spread all round. Out of the pieces of the pot Shiva made a LINGA, which he himself entered, and which is said to be the one enshrined in the temple. The linga is known as Adi Kumbheshvarar, the first lord to enter the kumbha. The goddess here is known as Mangala Nayaki. The temple covers a large area in the centre of the town, its GOPURAM rising to a height of 58 m. Within the temple there are several carvings and sculptures. Notable among these is one of Subrahmanya (KARTTIKEYA) with six heads but only six accompanying hands. In the Navaratri Mandapam is a single block of stone carved with the twenty-seven NAKSHATRAS and twelve rashis (astrological signs). There are several shrines around the temple, including those dedicated to VINAYAKA, Subrahmanya and LAKSHMI. In addition are five shrines sacred to Shiva, located around Kumbakonam, where drops of nectar are said to have fallen. They are Tiruvidaimarudur, Tirunageswaram, Tirudharasuram, Tiruvoragam and Tirupadalavanam, which are visited by pilgrims before going to the Kumbheshvara Temple.

Kumuda A NAGA or serpent king. He had a sister, Kumudvati, who married KUSHA, one of the twin sons of RAMA.

Kundakunda A Jain scholar and ACHARYA particularly revered by the DIGAMBARA sect. Kundakunda probably lived in the first century CE; according to his own writings, he was a disciple of BHADRABAHU II. (According to DIGAMBARA lists he was the fourth ACHARYA after Bhadrabahu II, but one interpretation is that all four may have been Bhadrabahu's disciples.) He was known by other names, including Vakagriva, Elacharya, Gridhrapincha and Padmanandi. According to one tradition, he was born in village Kondakunda or Konkakunda near Guntakal in present Andhra Pradesh, close to the Karnataka border. He is also associated with KANCHI in Tamil Nadu, where he is said to have lived. He composed some of the main philosophical texts of the Digambaras, writing in Prakrit.

His works are held in very high regard by Digambaras. Among his main texts are *Pravachanasara*, on ethics, *Samayasara*, on fine entities, *Niyamasara*, on rules for monks, and six *Prabhritas* on various religious topics. The *Samayasara* is considered the most important of his works.

kundalini A hidden source of energy within the human body, which when activated leads to super-human powers. The kundalini is described in Tantric and other texts, as a coiled serpent located at the base of the spine. Spiritual, breathing and physical techniques are prescribed to arouse the sleeping kundalini and lead it through the CHAKRAS or energy centres to the crown of the head. The *Shat Chakra Nirupana*, a Sanskrit text, describes kundalini, on the Svayambhu (self-created) LINGA of the god SHIVA, in the MULADHARA CHAKRA. It states: 'Over it shines the sleeping kundalini, fine as the fibre of the lotus stalk. She is the world-bewilderer (jagan-mohini, the creator of maya), gently covering the mouth of Brahma-dvara (the head of the linga) by her own. Like the spiral of the conch-shell, her shining snake-like form goes three-and-a-half times around Shiva, and her lustre is as that of a strong flash of young lightning. Her sweet murmur is like the indistinct hum of swarms of love-mad bees. She produces melodious poetry and all other compositions in prose or verse, in Sanskrit, Prakrit, and other languages. It is she who maintains all the beings of the world by means of inspiration and expiration, and shines in the cavity of the Mula Chakra like a chain of brilliant lights.'

Kunti The mother of KARNA and the PANDAVAS who is described in the MAHABHARATA. She was the daughter of King Shurasena and the sister of VASUDEVA, the father of KRISHNA. She was named Pritha, but was adopted by Shurasena's cousin King Kuntibhoja and was renamed Kunti. She received a secret MANTRA from the rishi DURVASAS, by which she could invoke any god she liked. Before her marriage she invoked SURYA, and Karna was born. After her marriage to PANDU, who could not have children of his own, she used her mantra to give birth to the three elder Pandavas, YUDHISHTHIRA, BHIMA and ARJUNA, who were born from various gods. She also conveyed the mantra to Pandu's second wife, MADRI, who had two children using this mantra. After Pandu's death Madri joined him on the funeral pyre, while Kunti stayed alive to take care of the five boys. When GANDHARI and DHRITARASHTRA went to live in the forest at the end of the great war, Kunti went with them, though the Pandavas tried to dissuade her. She died along with Gandhari and Dhritarashtra in a forest fire.

kurahit A term in Sikhism for an infringement of the RAHIT or code of conduct of the KHALSA. The four kurahit are: cutting the hair; eating meat of an animal killed according to Islamic ritual (halal or kuttha); extra-marital sex; and smoking.

Kural A sacred text in Tamil verse, also known as the Tirukural (tiru = sacred, kural = short rhyming verse) said to be written by TIRUVALLUVAR. It has been variously dated between the first century BCE and the fourth or fifth century CE. Its 1330 verses are arranged in three sections; the first deals with worldly life, the second with wealth, politics and related themes, and the third with love. Though there are not many references to god or a life devoted to spirituality, all the verses describe the ideal actions of a life founded in spirituality and ethics. Several commentaries have been written on this text.

Kurma A deity, an incarnation or avatara of the Hindu god VISHNU, in which Vishnu took the form of a tortoise. Kurma is first mentioned in the *Shatapatha Brahmana* as a form of BRAHMA, but in later texts he is associated with Vishnu. Vishnu became Kurma at the time of the churning of the ocean to extract AMRITA, or divine nectar. The divine tortoise formed the stable base for the churning rod, which was the mountain MANDARA.

As Kurma, Vishnu is usually depicted as half-man and half-tortoise, the lower half being that of a tortoise, but sometimes simply as a tortoise. When he is half-man, his four arms have the usual attributes of Vishnu. Kurma is depicted in Vishnu temples, and has a special place in the Shrikurmam Temple in Andhra Pradesh, where there is an image of a tortoise in the inner shrine, along with an image of Vishnu. The tortoise's back faces the entrance, and this is said to be because a Bhil king worshipped him from outside the back wall, and Kurma turned around to face him.

Kurma may have once been a tribal deity or a totem, and DHARMA THAKUR, a local deity in Bengal, is also sometimes worshipped as a tortoise. The tortoise has been linked with Buddhism, as its shape resembles a STUPA.

Kurma Purana A Sanskrit text, one of the eighteen major PURANAS of Hinduism. It once had four parts, but only one of these, the *Brahmi Samhita*, is available now. The Purana deals with the five Puranic themes. The story of VISHNU as KURMA is narrated, along with other Vishnu legends. Though the text relates to Kurma, it is considered a SHAIVITE text, because in it SHIVA is said to be the highest deity. The worship of SHAKTI is described, and DEVI as the Shakti of Shiva is praised with 1008 names. There are MAHATMYAS describing the sacred sites of KASHI and PRAYAGA. The *Ishvara Gita*, which prescribes techniques of meditation to reach Shiva, and the *Vyasa Gita*, where VYASA teaches the path to the highest knowledge, form a part of this Purana. In addition, the text narrates a story of SITA's rescue from RAVANA by the god AGNI.

Kuru The name of a king and of a kingdom in ancient India. According to mythical stories, King Kuru was descended from Puru, son of YAYATI, while the KAURAVAS and PANDAVAS of the MAHABHARATA were descended from him. The kingdom of Kuru forms the setting for the *Mahabharata*. Both HASTINAPURA and INDRAPRASTHA were cities in this kingdom, and KURUKSHETRA, where the great war took place, was also located here. The Kuru kingdom is also described in Buddhist and other sources.

Kurukshetra A city in Haryana, considered sacred, as it is said to be the place where the great MAHABHARATA war was fought and where KRISHNA preached the BHAGAVAD GITA. According to legends in Hindu texts, the place was sacred from ancient times, as King KURU practised austerities here, while later myths state that Kuru sacrificed himself here. The river SARASVATI flowed through Kurukshetra, and the PURANAS describe numerous sacred tirthas here. According to the MATSYA PURANA, a visit to Kurukshetra on the day of the eclipse, when RAHU attacks the sun, brings spiritual bliss to the devout.

A huge tank, the Brahmasagar or Brahmasarovar, has been constructed here, and pilgrims bathe in it on auspicious occasions. The Gita Temple, a modern temple with a life-size marble statue of Krishna, is said to mark the spot where Krishna preached the Bhagavad Gita. There are several other temples and bathing ghats, as well as the sacred tomb of Sheikh Chilli Jalal (d. 1582), mosques and GURDWARAS.

Kurukshetra remains an important place of pilgrimage, particularly at the time of a solar eclipse.

Kusha A son of RAMA and SITA. His twin brother was LAVA. After the death of Rama, Lava ruled north Koshala, and Kusha ruled the southern part of the kingdom. Kusha built the city of Kushasthali, also called Kushavati, in the Vindhyan hills, and made it his capital. He married Kumudvati, a NAGA princess, sister of KUMUDA.

kusha grass A type of grass that is considered sacred and is used in Vedic SACRIFICES. It is sometimes identified with darbha grass. Kusha grass is probably either *Desmostachya bipinnata* or *Poa cynosuroides*.

Kushinagara An ancient site in northern Uttar Pradesh where the BUDDHA is said to have attained NIRVANA. It is located in a suburb of the present town of Kasia. In the sixth century BCE, Kushinagara was the capital of the Malla state. The Buddha came here at the time of his death, and reclining between two sal trees, continued to teach until he passed into Nirvana. He was cremated on the seventh day and a memorial mound, an early form of a STUPA, was erected over his remains. A huge stupa located at Kasia is thought to mark this spot.

Excavations have revealed eight monasteries here, though most seem to have been of the Kushana period (first to third centuries) or later. The Mahaparinirvana Vihara, probably from the time of ASHOKA, the Mauryan emperor, was one of the earliest. A large image of Buddha reclining has also been found, dating to the Gupta period. Kushinagara continued to be occupied till the eleventh century. It is one of the most sacred sites for Buddhists, visited by pilgrims from all over the world.

kusti A term for the sacred thread worn by Zoroastrians. According to tradition, it was introduced in ancient days by YIMA (Jamshed), and when the Prophet Zarathushtra left home at the age of twenty, it was given to him by his father to protect him. The kusti is first worn by both boys and girls, after the NAVJOTE or ceremony for initiation into the religion. It is made of seventy-two strands of fine wool, representing the seventy-two chapters of the YASNA, and is woven only by members of priestly families. It is worn over the SUDREH or sacred shirt, and wrapped three times a round the waist. The tying of the kusti is a ritual to be performed by each individual at least twice a day, along with the recitation of prayers.

Kuthumi, Master A guru revered by Theosophists. According to Madame BLAVATSKY and other Theosophists, two gurus in the astral world were in charge of India. These were the Masters Kuthumi and MORYA, under the supervision of the Rishi AGASTYA. Kuthumi had the body of a Kashmiri BRAHMANA and was the teacher of J. KRISHNAMURTI who wrote *At the Feet of the Master* under his guidance. Later Krishnamurti rejected the concept of the Masters.

Kutsa An ancient rishi, the author of some hymns in the RIG VEDA.

Ladakh A region in the state of Jammu and Kashmir that has a number of Buddhist sects, as well as GOMPAS or monasteries, mainly associated with TIBETAN BUDDHISM.

Among the sects in Ladakh are the NYINGMA, based on the teachings of PADMASAMBHAVA (Thak-Thok Monastery); the SAKYA, with its oracle monks at MATHO; the DRUGPA KAGYU and DRIGUNG KAGYU at Phiyang and Lamayuru; and the GELUG headed by the DALAI LAMA.

Gompas include the Tekse Gompa, HEMIS GOMPA, Lamayuru Gompa, Shankar Gompa, Shay Gompa, and Tsemo Gompa, as well as others at BASGO, Spituk, Rezong, Deskit, Samur and elsewhere. Ladakh also has a number of SHIA Muslims who live in harmony with the Buddhists.

Lahaul and Spiti A district in Himachal Pradesh that has a number of Buddhist monasteries and was once under the control and influence of Tibet. The GURU GHANTAL monastery here dates back to the eighth century, while several others were founded in the eleventh and twelfth centuries, though they were reconstructed later. Buddhism is still the predominant religion in the area.

Lailat al-Qadr A term in Islam that means 'the night of power'. According to Islamic tradition, it was on this night in the month of RAMZAN of 610 that the Angel Gabriel first spoke to the Prophet MUHAMMAD, and the QURAN descended from the lowest heaven. This event is celebrated during the last few days of Ramzan and special prayers are said. The fate of a person for the rest of the year, is decided on this night. In India this night is known as SHAB-E-QADR.

Lakkundi A town in Karnataka, with ancient Hindu and Jain temples of the eleventh and twelfth centuries. Seventeen temples, constructed at the time of the Western Chalukya dynasty, still exist. These are richly decorated, and have pyramidal roofs. Many of them have open porches with multi-faceted pillars. Among Hindu temples, the Kashi Vishveshvara is notable; it has two shrines linked by an open porch, a pyramidal roof, and intricate carvings. The Jain Basti is the largest Jain temple here, with two MANDAPAS or halls opening into the shrine, and a five-storeyed pyramidal tower, capped by a square roof.

Lakshana Devi Temple A temple of the Hindu goddess DURGA, located at Brahmaur in the Chamba Valley of Himachal Pradesh. This wooden temple dates to the ninth century, but was largely reconstructed later. The inner shrine has a metal image of Durga holding MAHISHASURA, the buffalo demon, by the tail. At the doorway are male and female couples, or MITHUNA, the goddesses GANGA and YAMUNA, and the NAVAGRAHA. Other images include a three-headed VISHNU on GARUDA. The temple forms part of a group known as the Chaurasi temples.

Lakshmana The half-brother of RAMA, considered a partial incarnation of the Hindu god VISHNU, who is described in the RAMAYANA. According to the ADHYATMA RAMAYANA, he was an incarnation of Adi Shesha, or ANANTA. Lakshmana was the son of King DASHARATHA by his wife Sumitra, and the twin of SHATRUGHNA. He was married to Urmila, sister of SITA, and had two sons, Angada and Chandraketu. He accompanied Rama and Sita into exile, and helped Rama in the battle to recover Sita from RAVANA. He was always a friend and helper of Sita. When his time on earth came to an end, he went to the banks of the river Sarayu and was conveyed to heaven by the gods. He is known for his loyalty and devotion to Rama and Sita, and is considered an ideal brother. Lakshmana is depicted along with Rama and Sita in Rama temples and in art.

Lakshmana Siddha A sacred site located near Dehra Dun in Uttarakhand. According to tradition, the site has a dual significance. It is said to have been established by Lakshmana, a disciple of DATTATREYA, as a sacred centre of power. In addition, Lakshmana, brother of RAMA, is believed to have performed penances here. A small temple is located at the site.

Lakshmi A popular Hindu deity, the goddess of fortune. She is the wife of VISHNU and is worshipped both with him, and separately. Lakshmi is known as Shri, which indicates riches, prosperity and fortune, and this term frequently occurs in the VEDAS. In the *Shatapatha Brahmana*, Shri is referred to as a goddess, born because of the austerities of PRAJAPATI. In the *Shri-Sukta*, a hymn in praise of Shri, which possibly dates from the sixth century BCE, Shri is described as radiant and glorious, shining like the moon, invoked for fame and prosperity. She is seated on a lotus, a symbol of spiritual growth and purity. In the PURANAS, she is primarily the consort of Vishnu, but is sometimes associated with the god DHARMA, or with INDRA, and at times KUBERA. Lakshmi is mentioned in some versions of the story of the churning of the ocean for AMRITA. As she emerged from the ocean, she was chosen by Vishnu and became his loyal wife, remaining his partner in all his incarnations. Thus she is SITA when he is RAMA, and RUKMINI when he is KRISHNA. As BUDDHA is an avatara of Vishnu, she is also YASHODHARA, his wife.

Lakshmi is normally depicted as a beautiful woman with two or four arms. She usually holds two or four of the following objects: a lotus, a wood apple, a conch shell, a vessel of amrita or divine nectar, a citron fruit, a shield or a club (kaumodaki). As GAJA LAKSHMI she is seated on a lotus with an elephant on each side sprinkling water on her. She is shown with Vishnu in Lakshmi-Narayana images, where she is often seated on his thigh, one arm around his neck. In some images the two are merged into one figure. Other sculptures show Lakshmi and BHUDEVI standing on either side of Vishnu.

Lakshmi represents the social order and settled married life. She is described in texts as well-dressed and decked with ornaments. In SHRIVAISHNAVISM, she is not only Vishnu's consort, but the mediator for devotees, and embodies compassion. In relation to prosperity, Lakshmi is known to be as fickle as wealth, and if she can be persuaded to stay in one place, riches and fortune follow. In a myth associated with the CHARMINAR in Hyderabad, Lakshmi is said to have come there and fallen in love with a guard. The guard left, asking her to wait for him, and never returned, so that Laksmi continues to wait and brings prosperity to the city.

Laksmi is associated with several festivals. She is worshipped at DIVALI, along with GANESHA, for wealth and prosperity, and is also connected with the harvest. In Orissa, she is associated with crops and fertilty, and worshipped at the Kaumudi Purnima festival. In some areas, she is one of the goddesses worshipped at DURGA PUJA.

Though Lakshmi's VAHANA or vehicle is usually Vishnu's bird, GARUDA, she also rides on an owl, generally an inauspicious bird in Hindu mythology. Her opposite is ALAKSHMI, an inauspicious goddess.

Lakshmi is usually secondary to Vishnu, but in some texts and images she is the supreme deity. In the *Lakshmi Tantra*, she is both creator and destroyer. As MAHALAKSHMI, she is similar to MAHADEVI, the supreme goddess.

Lakshmi is depicted from the second century BCE onwards, a form of her being found in early Buddhist shrines. In later temples, Gaja Lakshmi was worshipped in a separate niche, or carved above the doorway. She remains widely worshipped in several temples, both modern and ancient.

Lakshmi-Narayana Temple   A temple of the Hindu deities LAKSHMI and VISHNU, located in New Delhi. It was constructed in 1938, and as it was financed by the industrialist Raja Baldev Birla, it is popularly known as the Birla Temple. From the beginning the temple had no caste restrictions, and the first PUJA was therefore attended by Mahatma GANDHI. It is a grand Orissa-style structure in white marble and red sandstone with tall shikharas or towers, capped with domes. The inner shrine has images of Lakshmi and Vishnu. Outside, there are gardens and fountains.

The temple is extremely popular, and elaborate celebrations take place at the time of JANAMASHTMI and other festivals.

There are several similar temples in other cities.

Lakulisha   The founder of the Shaivite PASHUPATA sect who lived in the second century and was said to be an incarnation of the Hindu god SHIVA. An inscription mentions that he lived in Kayarohana, which has been identified with Karvan in Kathiawar in Gujarat. His four main disciples were Kushika, Mitra, Garga and Kaurushya, who are said to have founded four sub-sects of the Pashupatas.

Lal Darwaza Mosque   A mosque located in Jaunpur, Uttar Pradesh, constructed in the time of the Sharqi dynasty in c. 1450, by Bibi Raji, the queen of Sultan Mahmud Shah (1436–58),for her own private use. This mosque is one of the smallest in Jaunpur, though with a design similar to the huge ATALA MOSQUE.

It has a rectangular prayer hall, opening into a courtyard on the east, with three gateways. The main entrance gateway is made of red sandstone, hence the mosque is known as Lal Darwaza (red gateway). The mosque has ornamental and decorated arches. Special prayers are still held here on Fridays, which are believed to bring peace of mind.

Laleshvari (Lal Ded)   A BHAKTI poet from Kashmir, also known as Lalla Arifa or Lal Ded, who is still held in high esteem in Kashmir.

Laleshwari was probably born between 1300 and 1335 at Pandrethan or Sempor near Srinagar, and married at the age of twelve into a Pandit (BRAHMANA) family of Padmapura, a few kilometres away. In childhood she was influenced by the family priest, and after marriage, ill-treated by her in-laws, she maintained an inner detachment from the world. She left home and lived in forests and mountain caves, composing verses to God, and finally achieving union with God. Her collected verses, in Kashmiri, are known as *Lala Vak*, vak being a Kashmiri verse form. They were transmitted orally, and later written down. Her verses indicate that she worshipped god in all forms, but particularly in the form of the Hindu god SHIVA. She was against animal sacrifices and rituals, and believed that all religions were essentially the same. In one verse she writes:

Whatever work I did, that was worship
Whatever I did, that became a mantra
This recognition entered every fibre of my being
As the essence of the knowledge of Parama Shiva.

Laleshwari is revered by both Hindus and Muslims, and according to tradition inspired the famous NURUDDIN RISHI and other wandering saints. Her verses still constitute many of the proverbs and sayings of Kashmir.

Lalita A Hindu mother goddess identified with the supreme goddess, MAHADEVI. The *Lalita-Sahasranama* contains a thousand names of the goddess. Lalita is also a form of the goddess SHARADA or SARASVATI. As one of the MAHAVIDYAS, she is represented by the goddess SHODASHI.

Lalitavistara A biography of the BUDDHA written in Sanskrit in about the second century CE. It is considered relatively accurate and records his life up to the time of his first sermon in the Deer Park at SARNATH. Its twenty-seven chapters also contain accounts of some of his past lives.

lama A term in TIBETAN BUDDHISM for an advanced monk, scholar or teacher. It can be used as a generic term for a monk. There are different types of lamas; some may be founders of various Buddhist orders, or great teachers. Without a lama one cannot receive Buddhist teachings, and thus lamas may be revered more than BUDDHAS or deities. The DALAI LAMA is one of the most respected.
Various types of lamas include a Rinpoche, or high-ranking lama, a Tulku, or incarnate lama, and a Khenpo, who is the abbot or head of a monastery.

lam-rim A term in TIBETAN BUDDHISM for 'stages of the path', the successive steps on the spiritual path. The graded path of lam-rim was explained in the KADAM school, and later formed part of other Tibetan Buddhist schools. TSONG KHAPA's *Lam Rim Chen Mo*, or *The Graduated Path to Enlightenment*, is a major fourteenth century text, describing this path.

langar In Sikhism, a term for the community kitchen attached to every GURDWARA, from which free food is served to all. It also refers to the free meal served from such a kitchen, or from elsewhere on special occasions. The system of the langar, in which all communities and castes ate together without distinction, was based on an earlier tradition that existed in the Sufi KHANQAHS.

Lanka A city, the capital of RAVANA, described in the *RAMAYANA*. It is usually located in present Sri Lanka, though archaeologists and historians have suggested other locations as well. Alternatively, it could have been a mythical city. Lanka is described as a grand city with seven moats and seven high walls of stone and metal. It was built by the divine architect VISHVAKARMA for the god KUBERA but was appropriated by Ravana. According to the *BHAGAVATA PURANA*, Lanka was originally on Mt MERU but was broken off by the god VAYU and hurled into the ocean.

Lankavatara Sutra A MAHAYANA Buddhist text of the YOGACHARA school, probably composed around 400 CE. It discusses various Yogachara concepts through a dialogue between the BUDDHA and the Bodhisattva Mahamati. The text has ten chapters, nine in prose and one in verse. It explains SHUNYATA or emptiness, the theory of 'eight types of consciousness' or vijnanas, and the TATHAGATA-GARBHA theory, i.e., that the essence of the BUDDHA is present in all living beings.

Latin Catholic Church A CATHOLIC CHURCH that has 119 dioceses and 16 Archdioceses in India. It has existed in India since the thirteenth century, when missionaries including MONTECORVINO, a Franciscan, Jordan Catalani, a Dominican, and John Marigloni, another Franciscan, came to south India. Pope John XXII established the diocese of Quilon with the Cathedral Church and nominated Cataloni the first Latin bishop of Quilon (present-day Kollam in Kerala). Its jurisdiction comprised all the Latin Churches in India and Southeast Asia. However, there were few Catholics in India until the coming of the Portuguese in the sixteenth century. The Portuguese received their authority from the PADROADO, an agreement between the Pope and the king of Portugal that gave the Portuguese authority to convert the local people. Francis XAVIER, who arrived in 1542, particularly helped in spreading Catholicism. Portuguese Catholics in the Kerala area attempted to bring the SYRIAN CHRISTIANS under Catholicism and initially had some success. In the sixteenth century, JESUITS from Goa were invited to the court of the Mughal emperor AKBAR, and though they did not manage to convert him, they spread Catholicism in the north, establishing Catholic settlements at AGRA, DELHI, Lahore, Jaipur, Nawar and Patna. There were some Catholic missions in the north-east as well, though at this time they did not have much effect. In 1662, Pope Gregory XV attempted to counteract the influence of the Portuguese and founded the Congregation of PROPAGANDA. Three Apostolic Vicariates and a Prefecture were created in India in the seventeenth century. The Vicariate of Malabar included both Syrian and Latin Catholics. In 1886, Pope Leo XIII constituted the Catholic Hierarchy of India. There were seventeen ecclesiastical units under the Propaganda and two under the Padroado (Goa and Mylapur). Two Apostolic Vicariates for the Syrian Christians were established in 1887 at Thrissur and Kottayam. The Propaganda tried to promote local priests, but this was opposed by the Padroado, and the first Indian head of a Latin-rite diocese was appointed in 1923. In 1944 the Indian missionary bishops formed the Catholic Bishops' Conference in India, and in 1948 Pope Pius XII established the Internunciate in India, which was raised to a Nunciate in 1967. An Archbishop is appointed as Apostolic

Nuncio (ambassador of the Vatican) to India. The Conference of Catholic Bishops of India, formed in 1988, now represents the Latin Church.

The Latin Church exists all over India and follows the Latin rite. GOA, parts of KERALA and MUMBAI have a number of Latin Catholic churches. Churches dedicated to MARY, mother of Jesus, are among the most popular.

Lava A son of RAMA and SITA, the twin of KUSHA. After the death of Rama, he ruled north Koshala, with his capital at Shravasti. According to tradition, the *RAMAYANA* was narrated to Lava and Kusha by VALMIKI, and they popularized it by travelling to various places and reciting it.

Lavan A four-stanza hymn composed by the Sikh guru, RAM DAS. It forms part of the Anand Karaj or Sikh marriage ceremony. Each stanza is read as the couple circumambulate the GURU GRANTH SAHIB. The hymn invokes God's blessing for the marriage but also has a deeper meaning, signifying the unity of the soul with God. The fourth stanza states: 'In the fourth round the mind receives divine knowledge and is inwardly united with god. Through the grace of the guru this blissful state is reached. The sweetness of the beloved pervades us, body and soul. The lord God is united with his holy bride.'

Lent A period of forty days of fasting and penance in Christianity. The forty days of Lent begin with Ash Wednesday and end on the eve of EASTER. Lent commemorates Christ's sojourn in the wilderness, when he fasted and prayed.

leshya A concept in Jainism. Leshya, signified by a colour, indicates the condition of the soul, which is affected by various types of KARMA. The six main leshyas, with a number of shades or tints in between, are black, blue, grey, red, yellow (or pink) and white. Black, blue and grey are negative states. A cruel and wicked person develops a black leshya; one who expresses greed, anger and other negative qualities has a blue leshya; a dishonest person has a grey leshya. Red, yellow and white are positive leshyas. A humble, honest, restrained person develops the red leshya; one who in addition devotes himself to studies and duties, the yellow leshya; and one who is totally controlled, free from passion, calm and with senses subdued, has the white leshya. These leshyas lead the soul to different forms and courses in life.

lhakhang A term for a Buddhist temple in TIBETAN BUDDHISM.

linga A term for the emblem of the Hindu god SHIVA. The linga is the depiction of Shiva in a column or pillar form. It represents the phallus, but at the same time, is a representation of the cosmos, and a symbol of fertility, life and regeneration. Myths connected with the linga narrate that Shiva appeared in this form as a column of fire, the top and bottom of which could not be seen.

Some trace the first depiction of the linga to the INDUS CIVILIZATION. The emblem was also depicted on coins and seals from the second century BCE onwards, while an early linga in stone, found at Gudimallam near Renigunta in Andhra Pradesh, is thought to belong to the second or first century BCE. Textual references seem to indicate that the cosmic significance of the linga was introduced at a later date to make its worship more acceptable.

SHAIVA AGAMAS describe different types of lingas. The *Kamika Agama* mentions six types: svayambhuva, or self-created; daivaka, or made by the gods; arshaka, made by the RISHIS; ganapatya, made by the GANAS; manusha, made by people; and bana lingas or natural objects that look like lingas. These are all sthiralingas, or fixed lingas.

Manusha lingas, and how they should be made, are extensively described. Each has three parts: Brahmabhaga, a square lowest section; Vishnubhaga, an octagonal middle section; and Rudrabhaga or Pujabhaga, the top section, which is generally cylindrical, and is the portion that is worshipped. The two lower sections are usually inserted into the ground or in a pedestal. There are several different categories of manusha lingas, based on the type of carving on the upper section. Particularly sacred out of these are the ashtottarashata, with 108 lines, and the sahasra linga with 1000 lines. One to five faces of Shiva, representing his different aspects, may be carved on the linga.

From a fairly early period, the linga was the main object of worship in several SHAIVITE shrines and temples, with depictions of the god used as accessories on the walls. Lingas enshrined in temples follow the standards laid down in texts, but can also be classified according to the elements they represent. Most sacred are the twelve jyotir lingas, or lingas of light, enshrined at SOMANATHA, in Gujarat; KEDARNATHA in Uttaranchal; KASHI VISHVANATHA in Varanasi, Uttar Pradesh; Mahakaleshvara at Ujjain, Madhya Pradesh; OMKARESHVARA, in Madhya Pradesh; Mallikarjuna at SRISAILAM, Andhra Pradesh; Vaidyantha or Baijnath at Deogarh in Jharkhand; Ghushmeshvara, in Maharashtra; Bhima-shankara, in Maharashtra; Tryambak-eshvara, also in Maharashtra; Nageshvara, in Gujarat; and RAMESHVARAM in Tamil Nadu. There are also lingas of other elements, vayu or air, prithvi or earth, jala or water, akasha or space as well as lingas representing yajna or sacrifice, Soma or the moon, and Surya or the sun. Important among these are the Vayu linga at the KALAHASTISHVARA TEMPLE in Andhra Pradesh; the Tejas or fire linga in TIRUVANNAMALAI; the Akasha linga at CHIDAMBARAM; the Jala linga at Jambukeshvara at Tiruvanaikaval, Tamil Nadu; and the Prithvi linga at the Ekambareshvara Temple in KANCHIPURAM. An ice linga is worshipped at AMARNATH.

Lingas can be made by individuals in their homes, and there are rules laid down for making and consecrating them. Temples enshrining lingas are found in all parts of the country and range from the huge and vast to small, mud structures.

The linga is worshipped by all Shaivites, but it is the special emblem of the LINGAYATS or Virashaivas, a Shaivite sect.

Linga Purana A Sanskrit text, one of the eighteen major PURANAS of Hinduism. The *Linga Purana* has two parts, Purvardha and Uttarardha, It begins with an account of the holy places visited by the rishi Narada, who finally rearches Naimisharanya. Suta Lomaharshana reaches there and reaches there and rectites this Purana at the request of the rishis. The text focuses on the consecration and worship of the LINGA, and of Shiva along with his five forms of Ishana, Aghora, Vamadeva, Tatpurusha and Jata. It describes SHIVA as the creator of the universe. Twenty-eight incarnations of Shiva are described.

Lingaraja Temple A temple dedicated to the Hindu god SHIVA, located in Bhubaneswar, Orissa. The temple is said to have been first constructed in the seventh century, but the present structure dates back to the eleventh century, with some later additions. It is a typical Orissa-style temple, with the inner shrine, known as the deul , the hall or jagmohan, the dance hall or nat mandir, and the bhog mandir or hall where offerings are made. The linga in the shrine rises about 20 cm above the ground, and is over 2 m (8 ft) in diameter. The whole complex is in an enclosure, entered from the east. The outer walls have two levels, divided by mouldings with sculptured niches. The tower over the shrine, reaches a height of 38.5 m. There are other small shrines in the enclosure, as well as a temple of the goddess PARVATI, dating to the thirteenth century.

According to legends, Parvati came here in disguise, as the area had been praised by Shiva. Here two asuras wished to marry her, but she defeated them. Shiva then appeared and constructed a lake, now known as the Bindusagar, for her to quench her thirst. He took the form of Lingaraja, and began to live near the lake. Later, the temple was constructed around his linga form.

The temple is still in use, and there are twenty-two daily ceremonies in worship of the deity.

Lingayats A SHAIVITE sect, also known as Virashaivas. The sect was founded in the twelfth century by BASAVANNA in the region of Karnataka, and may have developed as a reaction against BRAHMANA dominance and discrimination. Lingayats rejected the sanctity of the VEDAS and the authority of Brahmanas, and were against caste, sacrifices and pilgrimages. Certain Vedantic principles were accepted but were reinterpreted with Shaivite terminology. Thus SHIVA was recognized as the eternal principle, self-existent and beyond all attributes. Shiva's divine symbol was the LINGA, and no other image worship was allowed. The *Shunyasampadane,* written on Allama Prabhu, a saint of the sect, throws more light on their practices.

In some texts six progressive stages of worship are described. Briefly, the first stage consists of simple BHAKTI; the second of nishthe, or discipline, enduring temptations and ordeals; in the third, avadhana bhakti, the devotee recognizes that the lord is everywhere and 'receives' or acknowledges Shiva's presence in the world. The fourth stage is anubhava bhakti, in which the devotee sees Shiva within herself and others and is filled with compassion. The fifth stage is one of ananda or bliss, when the devotee is united with Shiva as a lover. However, at this stage separation from the divine, can still take place. In the sixth stage there is samarasa, when the devotee and Shiva are one, and all worship is ended. Later writers subdivided these stages into several more, though different aspects of each can be present at the same time. Apart from Basavanna and Allama Prabhu, other notable saints included Ekantada Ramayya, Kasimayya, Siddharama, Machideva, Bomayya and MAHADEVIYAKKA, a woman. These saints composed songs or vachanas of love and devotion to Shiva, many of which are preserved. A religious centre (the Anubhava Mandapa) was set up, where the saints of the new sect met and exchanged ideas.

Lingayats are still a practising sect, but caste distinctions gradually reappeared, and the sect itself became a caste, located mainly in Karnataka. Jangamas, or hereditary priests became a part of the sect.

Lingayats have five main MATHAS or religious centres at Kedarnath, SRISAILAM, Balehalli, UJJAIN and VARANASI. All members are attached to one of these centres and initiated by a guru. Each carries a small linga and wears a white dot on the forehead. The dead are buried instead of being cremated. Certain daily rites, such as worship of the linga, and some samskaras, such as initiation of male children, are practised. Their philosophy is described as Visheshadvaita.

The literature of the sect is in Sanskrit, Kannada and Telugu. Some Shaiva Agamas contain aspects of the philosophy, but the most important literature is in Kannada.

Lohri A harvest festival celebrated on 13 January in north India, particularly in Punjab, Haryana, Delhi and Himachal. Similar festivals, such as MAKARA SANKRANTI and PONGAL, are celebrated elsewhere on 14 January, when the sun enters the constellation Makara (Capricorn) according to the Hindu calendar. Lohri marks the beginning of spring and has its own local rituals. The first Lohri after a couple is married is considered a special occasion for them, as well as the first Lohri after a son is born.

On the evening of Lohri, bonfires are lit and people dance and sing around them. Sweets made of sesame or til, along with puffed rice and popcorn, are thrown in the fire, and handfuls of this mixture are distributed to the poor. Small coins are also thrown, and wishes are made for wealth and prosperity in the future. In some areas songs are sung about Dulha Bhatti, a legendary person similar to Robin Hood, who, long ago, robbed the rich and distributed their wealth to the poor.

loka   A term used in Hindu, Buddhist and Jain mythology, signifying a type of world, or a division of the universe into different worlds. In Hinduism there are various classifications of the different worlds. Triloka, or three worlds, are commonly mentioned and consist of heaven, earth and hell. In some PURANAS, fourteen worlds are mentioned as part of the BRAHMANDA or cosmic egg. There are seven in the upper world and seven in the nether world. The seven upper worlds are: Bhuloka, the earth; Bhuvarloka, between the earth and the sun, where munis, SIDDHAS and perfected ones live; Svarloka, the heaven of INDRA; Maharloka, where saints such as BHRIGU live; Janarloka, where BRAHMA's mind-born sons, Sanaka, Sananda, Sanatana and SANAT KUMARA are; Tapoloka, the home of Vairaja; Satyaloka, the heaven of Brahma, where one is freed from rebirth. The seven lower worlds are: ATALA, ruled by Bala or Mahamaya; VITALA, ruled by Hatakeshvara, a form of SHIVA; SUTALA, under MAHABALI; TALATALA, under Maya; MAHATALA, the residence of Nagas; RASATALA, where some of the enemies of the DEVAS live; PATALA, in which Vasuki is the ruler and the chief NAGAS or serpent gods dwell. The seven lower realms are together referred to as Patala. These are not the same as NARAKAS or hells. When the rishi NARADA visited these worlds, he said they were wonderful, and better than Indra's heaven. There are different lists of these lokas in various PURANAS. In some texts there are eight lokas: Brahmaloka, where the higher deities live; Pitriloka, where the PITRIS, RISHIS and PRAJAPATIS dwell; Somaloka, with the moon and other planets; Indraloka, where the lesser deities dwell; Gandharvaloka, which has GANDHARVAS and similar beings; Rakshasaloka, the world of the Rakshasas; Yakshaloka, of the YAKSHAS; Pishachaloka, of the PISHACHAS.

In Buddhism the different worlds include dhatus and lokas. The PALI CANON describes three realms: the Kamadhatu or realm of desire, where six classes of gods, humans and animals live, apart from anti-gods, hell-beings and hungry ghosts; the Rupadhatu, or realm of forms, where there are gods who have practised various types of DHYANA or meditation; the Arupyadhatu, or formless realm, for those who have achieved the state beyond form. Each realm has several heavens, and up to twenty-six heavens are described. Apart from these there are a number of hells, for which the term naraka is usually used. Eight hot hells and eight cold hells are often described.

The *ABHIDHARMAKOSHA* of Vasubandhu describes two sets of heavens above the earth, and six cold and six hot hells below.

MAHAYANA and VAJRAYANA texts describe a number of heavens ruled over by Celestial BUDDHAS.

Jain texts state that there are several lokas within the universe. Madhyaloka, the middle world, has various continents, of which Jambudvipa, which includes India, is the most important. Below is Adhaloka, which has seven levels, while above is Urdhvaloka, with two types of heaven, one for ordinary (but good) souls, and the second for those close to emancipation. At the apex is Siddhashila, the place of the SIDDHAS or liberated souls. There are also numerous hells.

Lokacharya, Pillai   A Vaishnavite philosopher who belonged to the TENGALAI school of VAISHNAVISM. According to some accounts he flourished in the second half of the thirteen century, and was born in 1205 while according to others he was born in 1130 in south India. He was influenced by the BHAKTI songs of the ALVAR saints and believed that though bhakti, and a total surrender to God, salvation could be attained through the grace of god. The collection of hymns of the Alvar saints, the *NALAYIRA DIVYA PRABANDHAM* is the main sacred text of this school. Lokacharya's works are mainly written in Sanskritized Tamil, put together as the *Ashtadasha-rahasya*. Of the individual texts, *the Tattva-traya, Tattva-shekhara, Arthapanchaka* and *Shrivachanabhushana* are among the most important.

Lokapalas   Guardian deities in Hinduism, also known as DIKAPALAS, guardians of the directions. In a different context, Lokapalas are sometimes referred to as a group of five deities, including Vedic and later deities. These five are GANESHA, DURGA, VAYU, DYAUS and the ASHVINS.

Lokayata   A Sanskrit term indicating materialistic schools of philosophy. It is specially used for the CHARVAKA school.

Lonka Shaha   A Jain of the fifteenth century who founded the Lonka GACHCHHA from which other SHVETAMBARA sects developed. Lonka lived in Ahmadabad in the Gujarat region, though according to some sources he was originally from Kathiawar. At first an official in the government, he gave up his job when he felt pain at the sight of birds being caught in a trap. Instead, he began to make a living by copying Jain manuscripts, and as he studied Jain texts further, he started teaching the truths of the Jain religion. He soon gained a large following, and though he remained a layperson he was popularly known as Muni Dayadharma, while the sect he founded was known as the Daya Gachchha. Several of his disciples became *munis* (monks). Lonka was succeeded by Rupa Rishi, followed by Jiva Rishi. A sub-group of the Lonka Gachchha, the Bijamata, was founded in 1513 by a person named Bija, while the main group came to be known as STHANAKAVASI.

Lonka was against the worship of images in temples, a common practice in Jainism.

Losar The Tibetan new year, usually celebrated in February. At this time lamps are lit in Buddhist temples, offerings are made and prayers chanted. Dances and other festivities take place. The festival is celebrated in Tibetan Buddhist temples in India (See Tibetan Buddhism).

lotus A flower that is considered sacred. Spiritual texts state that a person should be like a lotus that grows with its roots in mud, yet rises above, pure and untainted. In Sanskrit texts, the lotus has a number of names, including kamala and padma.

Several Hindu deities are associated with the lotus, particularly the goddess LAKSHMI. A lotus grows out of VISHNU's navel, hence he is known as Padmanabha (with a lotus navel). BUDDHAS and BODHISATTVAS are often depicted seated on a lotus. The lotus represents fertility, growth and purity.

Lotus Sutra A popular English name for the *SADDHARMA PUNDARIKA*, a MAHAYANA Buddhist text.

Lumbini The birthplace of the BUDDHA in Nepal, known today as Rummindei. According to the story of the Buddha's birth, his mother Mahamaya was on her way from Kapilavastu to her parents' home. While resting in the Lumbini gardens she gave birth to Siddhartha, later to become the BUDDHA. The Mauryan empereor ASHOKA set up a pillar here in the third century BCE. An inscription on the pillar, which is still standing, records that this was where the Buddha was born.

lungta A term in TIBETAN BUDDHISM for a 'wind horse', an image often depicted on tar-chok or prayer flags. The horse is a symbol of good luck, with the emblem of the three jewels of Buddhism on its back. The galloping horses cross the sky, spreading Buddhist teachings and taking prayers to heaven as the flags blow in the wind. The lungta image is sometimes printed on parchment or thin paper, and scattered on mountain tops or in sacred places.

Lutheran Church A Protestant Church based on the teachings of Martin Luther (1483–1546), who started the REFORMATION in Germany. Luther was against a number of Catholic practices of the times, among them the system of buying indulgences, or making cash payments for sins committed. He stated that the Catholic Church was not the only channel of communication with God, and that salvation was attained by grace, and not by works. Lutheranism spread through Europe and later North America, and a number of Lutheran Churches emerged. As they had no substantial philosophical differences, many joined together in unions. The Lutheran World Federation was set up in 1947.

Lutheranism also spread to India, where there is a united forum of these churches known as the United Evangelical Lutheran Church in India, with twelve member churches from all parts of the country. In Lutheran Churches, the basic unit is the congregation, administered by an elected council headed by a pastor or a layman elected by the council.

Ma (Maa) A word that means 'mother', but is often used for any Hindu goddess, particularly MAHADEVI, PARVATI, DURGA, or one of their forms.

Machhiwara A town in Ludhiana district of Punjab associated with the tenth Sikh guru, GOBIND SINGH. After the battle of CHAMKAUR, the guru escaped through thick forests and came to Machhiwara. He rested briefly in a garden and then spent one night at the house of Masand Gulab Rai. Three GURDWARAS commemorate Gobind Singh's stay at Machhiwara. The Machhiwara Gurdwara, also known as the Chubara Sahib Gurdwara, is located at Gulab Rai's house, while the Charan Kanwal gurdwara is built in the garden. This gurdwara is named after the Guru's feet, which are compared with a divine lotus. Another gurdwara is the Uchch da pir Gurdwara. The guru briefly stayed in a room here, and disguised as the pir of Uchch, was helped to escape from Machhiwara by his Pathan disciples Ghani Khan and Nabi Khan.

Madana A name of the Hindu god of love, KAMA. Madana is also a name of the god KRISHNA.

Madar, Shah A saint whose followers are the MADARIS or Madariyas. ABDUR RAHMAN CHISTI, wrote a biography of Madar, known as *Mirat-i Madari*, though according to some scholars, this account is based on legends and is not authentic.

Chisti states that Shah Madar, also known as Shaikh Badruddin, was born in 1315 at Aleppo in a Jewish family, but later went to Mecca and Medina and converted to Islam. Finally he reached India, and after visiting Ajmer, Jaunpur and other places, he settled at Makhanpur near Kanpur in present Uttar Pradesh. He lived here for several years, and according to legendary accounts, did not eat for twelve years. As he remained pure and unpolluted, he did not need to bathe or change his clothes. He had great spiritual powers and attracted a number of disciples. His DARGAH at Makhanpur is visited by both Hindu and Muslim devotees.

Madaris (1) A SUFI sect, the followers of Shah MADAR. Madaris are of different kinds; the ascetics wander naked with matted hair, use intoxicants and rub ash on their bodies. Influenced by certain NATHA YOGI practices, they are said to have great power. Their slogan is 'Dam, Madar' which can be translated in different ways, as 'Madar is life'; 'Madar is spirit'; or 'Control the breath'. By their ascetic practices, Madaris are able to perform various feats, such as walking on burning coal. (2) Another group of Madaris, including both Hindus and Muslims, are acrobats, jugglers, and those who train monkeys and bears for entertainment. Shah Madar is their patron saint.

Madhava Kandali An Assamese poet who lived in the fourteenth century and translated the RAMAYANA into Assamese. Not much is known about Madhava. He states that the translation was done at the request of the Varaha king Srimahamanikya, who was possibly a ruler of the Kachari dynasty. The Adi and Uttara Kandas, i.e., the first and last books of the *Ramayana*, are missing in Kandali's work. The rest is in Assamese verse and keeps close to the original, with some modifications. His translation formed the basis for later Ramayanas in Assamese, including the *Giti Ramayana* of Durgavara (sixteenth century), the *Ramayana* of Ananta Kandalai (sixteenth century), and the prose *Ramayana* of Raghunatha Mahanta (late eighteenth century). In all these the first and last books are missing. SHANKARADEVA rewrote the Uttara Kanda in Assamese verse.

Madhavacharya The probable original name of VIDYARANYA, who lived in the Vijayanagara kingdom in the fourteenth century.

Madhavi A goddess of the earth mentioned in the Uttara Kanda of the RAMAYANA of VALMIKI. SITA had originated from the earth, and at the end of her life, Madhavi arose from the earth to take Sita back. Throughout her life Sita had faced much sorrow. After being rescued from LANKA and undergoing a fire ordeal to prove her innocence, she lived for a while with RAMA, but was then banished to the ashrama of Valmiki. When Rama met their twin sons, LAVA and KUSHA, he wanted Sita once again to prove her purity before the people. Sita who came to the gathering wearing a brown garment, said, 'As I have not contemplated anyone but Rama, so may the goddess Madhavi provide space to me.' A divine throne arose from the earth, borne on the head of NAGAS, adorned with gems. The earth goddess was seated on it and welcomed Sita, making her sit with her, and descended once again into the earth. Rama was then filled with grief, but he was assured they would be united in heaven.

As Sita was born from the earth, her return to it is symbolic, in keeping with her earlier role as an agrarian deity.

Madhavi is also a name of the goddess LAKSHMI.

Madhu-Kaitabha The name of two DAITYAS or ASURAS who emerged out of the ear-wax of the Hindu god VISHNU. They are described in the MAHABHARATA and PURANAS. According to the DEVI BHAGAVATA PURANA, they worshipped DEVI and received a boon that they would not die except when they wished. They grew extremely powerful and stole the VEDAS from the god BRAHMA. Finally Vishnu managed to kill them by tricking them into granting him a boon.

Madhva The founder of the DVAITA system of philosophy, who lived in the thirteenth century. Madhva was also known as Ananda Tirtha or Purna Prajna.

Born in 1199 near Udupi in present Karnataka in a BRAHMANA family, he had exceptional abilities; by the age of five he is said to have had a complete knowledge of the VEDAS and all branches of Vedic knowledge. He studied ADVAITA, but gradually developed his own theories. He toured the sacred sites of north India and spent some time meditating in the Himalayas. In VARANASI, he is reputed to have walked on water and to have performed other miracles similar to JESUS. Returning to the south, he founded a Krishna Temple at UDUPI, and wrote a commentary on the BRAHMA SUTRA. His Dvaita philosophy was developed in several works, collectively known as the *Sarva-Mula Grantha,* and including at least thirty-seven texts. He believed in the reality of the world, rejecting the theory of MAYA or illusion, and in a permanent individual self, unlike the ADVAITA theory of only One Reality. He stopped sacrifices in temples and was against the DEVADASI practice. Some of his ideas are thought to have been influenced by Nestorian Christians who lived in south India in those days.

Madhva died in 1278. According to one legend he was the incarnation of the wind god VAYU and disappeared into the air while meditating.Though these dates of his birth and death are generally accepted, some place him in the eleventh century, and others, between 1238 and 1317.

There are still several followers of Dvaita in Karnataka and elsewhere.

Madhyamika/Madhyamaka A school of MAHAYANA Buddhism that literally means 'the middle way'. Founded by NAGARJUNA in about CE 150, its main text is his *Madhyamika Karika.* The school rejects both affirmations and negations of all metaphysical systems, and sees Shunyata as the middle way between being and non-being. SHUNYATA (void) is the only reality, SAMSARA and NIRVANA being the same and unreal. Cosmic change is unreal, and the consciousness

that perceives it has no reality either. Yet the world has a qualified practical reality, and Shunyata is the essence that pervades the world, which according to some texts, is identified with the ADI BUDDHA, and the source of bliss. Nagarjuna's disciple ARYADEVA also made notable contributions to this school. By about 500-50, two branches of Madhyamika developed, the PRASANGIKA and SVATANTRIKA. Later, Madhyamika absorbed other philosophies, including that of YOGACHARA.

madrasa/madarsa/madrassa (1) An Islamic educational institution. The focus is on Islamic subjects such as jurisprudence, theology and philosophy, though some other subjects are also taught. There are a number of madrasas in India, some dating back to medieval times, and each is usually attached to a mosque. The earliest madrasas in north India were established in the thirteenth century and by the fourteenth century, Delhi alone had one thousand. In the eighteenth century, the Dars-i-Nizamiya of Mulla NIZAMUDDIN, based on the Quran and HADIS, became the standard syllabus, later used in the DAR-UL-ULOOM, Deoband, and the NADWAT-UL-ULAMA. Madrasas still exist all over India, though there are suggestions that they should be modernized and their curriculum revised.

(2) The term is also used for Zoroastrian institutes for training priests, but is usually spelt 'madressa'.

Madrasa, of Mahmud Gawan A MADRASA or Islamic college located at Bidar in Karnataka, founded in the fifteenth century. It was constructed in 1472 by Khwaja Mahmud Gawan, the minister of Muhammad Shah III (1463-82), ruler of the Bahmani kingdom.

The madrasa had a grand reputation that attracted theologians, philosophers and scientists, who discussed and debated various issues. Its library had over 3000 manuscripts.

The three-storeyed madrasa, probably designed by architects from Iran, was a rectangular structure occupying an area of 68 by 60 m. The main entrance was on the east. Large reading halls were attached to it, with semi-octagonal chambers. The facade was once covered in glazed tiles, with a band of Quranic inscription inlaid with gold. Two tall minarets rose to a height of about 30 m.

Though the structure is still standing, it is a shadow of its former self. It was taken over by Aurangzeb before he become the Mughal emperor, in 1656 when he was governor of the Deccan, and used as military barracks. Gunpower stored in some of the rooms exploded and damaged the building. Part of it was also damaged in 1696 by lightning.

Madri The second wife of PANDU, the mother of the twins NAKULA and SAHADEVA, described in the *MAHABHARATA.* When Pandu died, Madri ascended the funeral pyre of her husband, an instance of SATI in the *Mahabharata.*

Madurai A city in Tamil Nadu famous for its temples, the most important being the seventeenth century MINAKSHI TEMPLE. Located on the Vaigai river, Madurai has ancient origins, and was the capital of the Pandya dynasty. From the fourteenth century, it was included in the Vijayanagara empire. The Nayakas (local governors) took over after the downfall of Vijayanagara in the sixteenth century.

There are several legends about the sanctity of the city. The Pandyas were worshippers of the Hindu god SHIVA, and a drop of nectar is said to have fallen here from Shiva's hair, hence the name 'Madurai' or 'the sweetest'. The movement of a great NAGA or serpent marked the boundaries of the city, and the Minakshi Temple was built where its tail and head met.

Madurai was a great centre of Tamil literature. Three literary sangams (meetings) were held here in early days, producing a body of work that is popularly referred to as SANGAM LITERATURE. The city is described in other texts as well, including the SHILAPPADIGARAM, an early Tamil epic.

Magadha A state in ancient India described in early texts, that covered part of present Bihar, extending to the east and south. In the MAHABHARATA, Magadha is said to have been ruled by King Jarasandha, who became an enemy of KRISHNA, and was finally killed by the Pandava BHIMA. However, Magadha is particularly important in the history of Buddhism and Jainism. At the time of the Buddha, King BIMBISARA was the ruler and became a follower and patron of the BUDDHA. He was succeeded by AJATASHATRU, a patron of both Jainism and Buddhism. ASHOKA Maurya (269–232 BCE), the king most responsible for spreading Buddhism, had his capital at PATALIPUTRA in Magadha. Apart from Pataliputra (modern Patna), RAJAGRIHA, VAISHALI, Uruvela (BODH GAYA), and other major sites associated with Buddhism are located here. MAHAVIRA, the Jain TIRTHANKARA, was born near Vaishali, and CHANDRAGUPTA MAURYA, grandfather of Ashoka, was a patron of Jainism. One of the most sacred Jain sites, the PARASNATH HILL, is located in the region of ancient Magadha.

The term Maga or Magha, still used for some of the local people, particularly Magha Brahmanas, is thought by some to be derived from Magi, a class of early Zoroastrian priests. This has led to the theory that Zoroastrians once settled here, and were absorbed into Hinduism. This is both because of the similarity with the word MAGI and because of some of the practices of these brahmanas.

Later, the great monasteries of Buddhism, NALANDA and VIKRAMSHILA, were located in Bihar, which itself is derived from the word for a Buddhist monastery, 'vihara'.

Magha Mela A Hindu festival held once a year at ALLAHABAD, the ancient PRAYAGA, in the month of Magha (January/February). At this time pilgrims come from all over for a dip in the sangam, the confluence of the rivers GANGA and YAMUNA.

magi The high priests of the Medes, who were later absorbed into Zoroastrianism. When the Median empire of western Iran was overthrown by the Achaemenian king Cyrus in 550 BCE, the magi began to influence Zoroastrianism, gradually gaining acceptance as Zoroastrian priests. They are thought to have introduced new elements into Zoroastrianism, including reverence for the elements of nature, which were to be kept pure and undefiled. This led to the exposure of dead bodies, rather than burial or cremation. They also had a role at the time of the Sasanian dynasty, when the office of the Magupatan Magupat, chief of the magi, existed. The magi are described in Greek and Roman accounts, and in the Christian tradition, the wise men who visited the baby JESUS, were magi. They lost their importance after the decline of the Sasanians in the seventh century.

Mahabali A DAITYA king who had many good qualities but was sent by the Hindu god VISHNU into PATALA or the nether world.

Mahabali, also known as Bali, was the son of Virochana and the grandson of PRAHLADA who was known for his devotion to Vishnu. Several stories are narrated about Bali in the PURANAS and other texts. He succeeded his father to the throne and was the king of the ASURAS when the ocean was churned for AMRITA. He was killed in the battle against the DEVAS, but was brought to life again through the use of sacred herbs. Bali then drove the devas out of heaven and ruled in their place. Everyone was happy under his rule, except the devas and the BRAHMANAS who lost their privileges. The devas appealed to Vishnu, who said that though Bali was devoted to him, he would solve their problems after being born as VAMANA. After some time, ADITI, mother of the devas, gave birth to Vishnu as Vamana.

While Mahabali was offering a sacrifice on the river NARMADA, Vamana appeared to him in the form of a young hermit and requested as much land as he could cover in three steps. Bali agreed, against the advice of his teacher and priest SHUKRACHARYA. Vamana began taking the three steps, and as he did so, he grew enormously in size. The first step covered the whole earth, the second, the whole of heaven. Mahabali then offered his own body for the third step, because a promise given can never be broken. Placing his foot on his head, VAMANA pushed Bali into Patala, the nether world, where he has reigned ever since.

This story may represent the conflict between the people of south India and the Brahmanic traditions of the north, which gradually overlaid early south Indian culture.

In Kerala, Mahabali is still considered an ideal king. He is said to have ruled there and to have made the land prosperous and peaceful. Vamana allows him to come out of the earth for one day every year, and that traditional day is celebrated in Kerala as the festival of ONAM. Mahabali is also revered in several other places across India.

Mahabalipuram   A city in Tamil Nadu, also known as MAMALAPURAM.

Mahabharata   An early Indian epic, written in Sanskrit and consisting of 1,00,000 verses. It is still popular today, and contains the BHAGAVAD GITA, one of the most sacred Hindu texts. The *Mahabharata*, with eighteen parvas or sections, has a main story and a number of subsidiary stories. It includes legends, myths and advice on living an ethical life, as well as philosophical and spiritual practices. In fact, it is said, there is nothing the *Mahabharata* does not contain.

The story: The central story is about two sets of cousins, the KAURAVAS and PANDAVAS, descendants of KURU. DHRITARASHTRA, PANDU and VIDURA, were three sons of the rishi VYASA, from different mothers. According to the story associated with their birth, Shantanu, a king of the Chandravamsha or lunar dynasty, had two wives, Ganga and Satyavati, Devavrata was the son of Shantanu through Ganga, but he renounced his succession to the throne, and was them known as Bhishma. Vyasa was born to Satyavati through a rishi, without her losing her virginity, while she had two more sons from Shantanu, known as Chitrangada and Vichitravirya. Chitrangada died young; Vichitravirya married two daughters of the king of KASHI, Ambika and Ambalika, but also died without any children. Satyavati therefore asked Vyasa to continue the line by begetting children through the two wives of Vichitravirya. Terrified at the sight of Vyasa, Ambika shut her eyes, and thus Dhritarashtra was born blind. Ambalika turned pale at the sight of the rishi, and so Pandu was born pale. Vidura was born through a servant maid who found Vyasa quite congenial, and thus Vidura was intelligent and wise.

They all lived at HASTINAPURA, the capital of the Kuru country. Dhritarashtra was married to GANDHARI and had one hundred sons, known as the Kauravas, the eldest of whom was DURYODHANA. As Dhritarashtra was blind, Pandu became the king of Hastinapura. Pandu had two wives, KUNTI and MADRI, but as it was dangerous for him to have children, his five sons, the Pandavas were born through the help of the gods. Pandu died young and Dhritarashtra took over the throne, taking care of the Pandavas as if they were his own sons. However, there was intense rivalry between the Pandavas and Kauravas, which reached a height when Dhritarashtra, in a fit of generosity, chose YUDHISHTHIRA, the eldest Pandava, as his successor. Games of dice between Yudhishthira and Duryodhana led to Yudhishthira losing his kingdom and all he possessed, and going into exile with his brothers and wife. Many years of conflicts between the two groups culminated in a great war, in which practically all the kings of Bharata (India) took part, on one side or the other. The god KRISHNA, in his human form, played a part in the war, and the BHAGAVAD GITA is a dialogue

between him and the third Pandava brother, ARJUNA, on the battlefield, as the war was about to start. The Kauravas were defeated in the war, and all of them were killed. The Pandavas too suffered losses, and all the children of DRAUPADI, their joint wife, were killed. Yudhishthira, at first filled with grief at the destruction caused by the war, was persuaded to take over the Kuru kingdom, which he ruled for many years, ensuring peace and prosperity.

Dhritarashtra could not get over the loss of his sons. He and Gandhari lived in Yudhishthira's capital for fifteen years and were consulted on affairs of state and treated with great respect by all the Pandavas except BHIMA. Bhima could not forget that the dice game that began all their troubles was assented to by Dhritarashtra. Finally Dhritarshtra and Gandhari, accompanied by Kunti and some of their ministers, went to live in an ashrama in the forest. Two years later they died in a forest fire. After some time Yudhishthira abdicated his throne, and all the Pandavas left for INDRA's heaven on Mt MERU which they ultimately reached.

The eighteen parvas of the *Mahabharata* are: (1) Adi Parva: the beginning, a description of Dhritarashtra, Pandu and their families; (2) Sabha Parva: life at the court; Yudhishthira is defeated in a game of dice, and is forced to go into exile for thirteen years, the last of which had to be spent incognito. The five Pandavas and their joint wife, Draupadi, set out for their exile in the forest; (3) Vana Parva: the life of the Pandavas in the Kamakhya forest; (4) Virata Parva: the thirteenth year of exile is spent in the kingdom of King Virata, with all of them in disguise; (5) Udyoga Parva: both sides prepare for war; (6) Bhishma Parva: Duryodhana refuses to accept their return or even to divide the kingdom, or to give the Pandavas the five villages for which they asked. The war begins at the battlefield of KURUKSHETRA. The BHAGAVAD GITA is composed. BHISHMA commands the armies of Duryodhana, and on the tenth day he falls to an arrow; (7) Drona Parva: DRONA takes charge of the Kaurava army. He is killed after some days; (8) Karna Parva: KARNA takes command of the Kaurava army. He is killed; (9) Shalya Parva: Shalya takes charge of the Kaurava army; (10) Sauptika Parva: most of the warriors of the Pandava army are killed while they sleep; (11) Stri Parva: all the women lament on the battlefield; (12) Shanti Parva: Yudhishthira becomes the king. Bhishma, still alive, lying on a bed of arrows, tells him the duties of kingship; (13) Anushasana Parva: Bhishma discourses on various topics; (14) Ashvamedhika Parva: Yudhishthira conducts the ASHAVAMEDHA sacrifice; (15) Ashramavasika Parva: Dhritarashtra, Gandhari and Kunti retire to live in an ashrama in the forest. After two years they die in a forest fire; (16) Mausala Parva: Krishna was of the YADAVA clan. He and his clan lived at DVARAKA. The

Yadavas begin to quarrel. KRISHNA and his brother BALARAMA die. Dvaraka is submerged in the sea; (17) Mahaprasthanika Parva: Yudhishthira hands over the kingdom to his successor. The Pandavas and Draupadi set out for Mt Meru; (18) Svargarohana Parva: The Pandavas and all their relatives are in heaven.

The HARIVAMSHA is appended to the *Mahabharata*, but is of a later date.

Date: The date of the *Mahabharata* is not easy to define. In general, scholars believe it was composed around the fourth century BCE, with additions being made up to 400 CE. There are several versions of the *Mahabharata*, with different recensions, from all parts of the country. A critical edition has been compiled identifying the earlier portions of the text. Though it is an epic and not history, the war and some of the other events are thought to have actually taken place, though not in the manner described. The traditional date of the war is 3102 BCE, while based on geography and archaeological excavations of the cities described, a date of 1000–900 BCE seems more likely.

Geography: The *Mahabharata* refers to people and kings from all parts of India, but most of the events of the main story take place in present Haryana, western Uttar Pradesh, Delhi and Rajasthan, and other parts of north-west India. Places in these areas and in Uttarakhand are still associated with the Pandavas.

Archaeology: Several of the places of the core area mentioned in the *Mahabharata*, such as Hastinapura, have the same or similar names today. Excavation and exploration at these sites link the period of the *Mahabharata* with that of the Painted Grey Ware Culture, datable to between 1200 and 600 BCE. Some scholars believe that such linkages are not merely tenuous but incorrect, as a mythical epic cannot be placed in a historical context. However, most of the early history of India available through contemporary literary sources is interspersed with myths and legends.

Links with other epics: Some scholars find parallels between the great war of the *Mahabharata* and the Trojan War, as each was the central point for traditional accounts of history.

Other versions: The story also appears in Jain and Buddhist texts, and is retold with variations in tribal and other cultures.

It was translated into Persian and into all the regional languages of India, with the addition of local themes.

Mahabharata, in Jainism Several versions of the MAHABHARATA occur in Jain literature. Among the earliest is the HARIVAMSHA PURANA of Jinasena, composed in 783 CE, which tells the story of the *Mahabharata* in a Jain setting. Many other Harivamsha Puranas were written, among them one by Sakalakirti and Jinadasa, composed in the fifteenth century.

Devaprabha Suri wrote the *Pandava Charita* around 1200; it has eighteen sargas or sections, following the eighteen parvas of the *Mahabharata*. Shubhachandra composed the *Pandava Purana* in 1551. *Mahabharata* stories are also included in other texts and are even found in the ANGAS.

Mahabodhi Society of India A society set up in 1891 to promote and revive Buddhism in India. It was founded by ANAGARIKA DHARMAPALA (1864–1933), the name adopted by Don David Hewaviratne from Sri Lanka, earlier a Christian. The society has a library of books on Buddhism and publishes Pali and Sanskrit Buddhist texts, as well as translations. It brings out two monthly magazines on Buddhism: *Mahabodhi* in English, and *Dharma Duta* in Hindi.

Mahabodhi Temple A Buddhist temple at BODH GAYA, erected near the spot where the BUDDHA gained enlightenment. First constructed around the fourth century, it has been rebuilt and expanded several times. The Chinese pilgrim XUANZANG visited the temple in the seventh century and left a description of it. He said that it was located east of the BODHI TREE, and was the equivalent of about 50 m high, made of bricks and coated with lime, with tiers of niches in which there were golden images. The main image of the Buddha here was said to have been made by the Bodhisattva MAITREYA, disguised as a BRAHMANA.

The temple was again reconstructed in the ninth century and several times after the twelfth century. The most extensive rebuilding was towards the end of the nineteenth century. Some aspects of the original structure have survived from the seventh century.

The temple is built on a broad terrace, the sides of which have niches with plaster sculptures. The walls of the main shrine have sculptured panels between pilasters. At the entrance is a sixth-century Buddha image. Above the shrine, a pyramidal tower rises to a height of 55 m. Subsidiary shrines on the four corners of the terrace replicate the structure of the main temple.

Behind the temple is the Bodhi Tree (not the original), and beneath it a carved stone seat marking the spot where the Buddha sat. The seat possibly dates back to the third century BCE. Around it are posts dating to the Shunga period (second century BCE), which were probably once connected by a railing enclosing the sacred site. There are also later posts of the Gupta period. Two shrines from the eighth century located within the temple compound are of the goddesses ANNAPURNA and TARA. In addition there are several STUPAS of the Pala period.

Other temples have been recently constructed at Bodh Gaya, including a Tibetan Buddhist temple and a Japanese Buddhist temple.

Mahadeva A name of the Hindu god SHIVA, and of one of the RUDRAS.

Mahadeva Temple A temple of the Hindu god SHIVA located at Ettumanur, Kerala. It was constructed in the sixteenth century, with additions being made later.

The square inner shrine contains a LINGA and is enclosed in a circular pillared mandapa. Both have conical timber roofs with metal tiles, and a brass pot finial. Around the MANDAPA is a circular passage with a carved wooden screen depicting scenes from the *RAMAYANA* and the life of KRISHNA. The mandapa has a wooden ceiling with twenty-five panels adorned with various deities. The porch at the western entrance has seventeenth-century paintings, including one of Shiva as NATARAJA. The temple is in typical Kerala style.

Mahadevi A Hindu goddess who combines aspects of other goddesses, and is considered a supreme deity. The concept of Mahadevi emerged around the sixth century, and has the characteristics of the Absolute, superior to all other deities. Texts deal with this concept in two different ways; firstly, to take a goddess such as DURGA or LAKSHMI, and assign to her the attributes of a supreme deity, with all other gods and goddesses being inferior; and secondly to describe a universal goddess, known as DEVI, Mahadevi or BHAGAVATI. In the *Lalita-Sahasranama*, the various names of Mahadevi include Jagatikanda (root of the world), Vishvadhika (one who transcends the universe), Nirupama (without equal) and Parameshvari (supreme ruler). She is Mahabuddhi (supreme knowledge), Prajnatmika (the soul of wisdom), and Gurumurti (the form of the guru). Several other names and epithets are given in various texts. In the *DEVI BHAGAVATA PURANA*, Mahadevi is said to be the ruler of all beings and the creator of BRAHMA, VISHNU and SHIVA. Mahadevi represents SHAKTI, or divine power, and is identified with PRAKRITI, nature or the feminine creative principle, and MAYA or illusion. Mahadevi's most common form is Durga. According to the *Devi Bhagavata Purana*, Mahadevi is NIRGUNA, or beyond all qualities and forms, but can assume any form she pleases. In the *Saundarya Lahiri*, a text assigned to SHANKARA, Devi is described as an extremely beautiful lady, though Mahadevi can also have ferocious forms. Mahadevi thus represents the supreme feminine principle, which can take on a particular form, either benevolent or terrifying.

Mahadeviyakka A female SHAIVITE saint who lived in the twelfth century in south India. She joined the Virashaiva or LINGAYAT sect and was accepted into it by Allama Prabhu, a senior member of the sect. According to some accounts, she was married against her will to Kaushika, a chieftain of the land, while according to others, she had rejected marriage, despite persuasion. She lived as a wandering ascetic, discarding her clothes and composing songs (vachanas) of devotion to the Hindu god SHIVA as MALLIKARJUNA, a form worshipped in her birthplace (village Udutadi). In her songs, she referred to Shiva as her husband and her lord. In one of her songs, she said:

I love the Beautiful One
With no bond nor fear
No clan, no land
No landmarks
For his beauty.
So my lord, white as jasmine, is my
husband.
Take these husbands who die,
Decay, and feed them
To your kitchen fires! (Trans. A. K. Ramanujan)

Mahakala A name of the Hindu god SHIVA, as lord of time. Mahakala is also the name of a jyotir LINGA worshipped as Mahakaleshvara at UJJAIN.

Mahakuta A place near BADAMI in Karnataka where there are several early temples of the Hindu god SHIVA, constructed between the sixth and eighth centuries, at the time of the Chalukya dynasty. Temples include the Mahakuteshvara and the Mallikarjuna, the Sangameshvara and the Naganatha or Adakeshvara. There is also a tank, fed by a natural spring, with a small shrine housing a four-faced LINGA in the middle. In the late sixth century, Mahakuta became a great Shaiva centre. A pillar inscription here dated between 592–605, records the dedication of ten villages, by Queen Durlabhadevi to the deity Mahakuteshvara Natha, a form of Shiva. Another slightly later inscription records a grant of jewels and a silver umbrella to the deity. High walls and a gateway have been built around it in recent times. Beyond is another gateway with the deities CHAMUNDA and BHAIRAVA, carved in the form of skeletons. There are more temples nearby, including a NAGA temple 2 km away.

Mahalakshmi A form of the Hindu goddess LAKSHMI in which she represents the supreme goddess, also known as MAHADEVI. Mahalakshmi is usually depicted holding a citrus, mace, shield and skull, with a snake, a LINGA and a YONI on her head. All the three GUNAS or qualities are manifest in her. According to the PURANAS, at the time of the dissolution of the universe, the goddess Mahakali emanated from her, in whom tamas guna, or the quality of darkness, predominates. Mahasarasvati, representing sattva guna, the quality of purity and light, also emanates from her. These deities are described in the *DEVI MAHATMAYA*.

The primary centre for the worship of Mahalakshmi is at Kolhapur in Maharashtra, where there are shrines of Mahalakshmi, Mahakali and Mahasarasvati, along with a number of other deities. There is also a large Mahalakshmi Temple in MUMBAI, as well as smaller temples elsewhere.

Mahamaha/Mahamakha A Hindu festival celebrated at KUMBAKONAM in Tamil Nadu once every twelve years. A sacred tank is located here, near the river Kaveri. It is surrounded by shrines, and it is believed that at the time of the festival, the water of all the sacred rivers unite in this tank. The festival, also known as the Kumbhareshvara, takes place when the sun is in Aquarius (Kumbha), Jupiter is in Leo (Simha) and the moon is in conjunction with the constellation of Magha. Pilgrims from all over come to bathe in the tank on this auspicious occasion. The tank was constructed in the seventeenth century.

Mahamaya (1) A revered person in Buddhism, Maya or Mahamaya was the mother of Gautama Siddhartha, who later became the BUDDHA. The wife of King Shuddhodana of the Shakya clan, she had mystical dreams indicating that she would give birth to a divine being. Proceeding from Kapilavastu to her parents' house, she gave birth to Siddhartha in LUMBINI gardens. Though she died seven days after his birth, there are several legends concerning her in Buddhist texts. Among them are that the Buddha once visited heaven to preach the DHARMA to her, and stayed there three months. At the time of his passing she came down from heaven and wept.

(2) A goddess, a from of DURGA.

Mahamayuri (1) A Buddhist text. It consists of a list of deities followed by magical spells (dharanis) to bring about rain, conquer enemies, remove sickness, etc. It was translated into Chinese by the fourth century.

(2) The name of one of the PANCHARAKSHA, or five protective spells.

(3) Mahamayuri is the name of a Buddhist deity, a goddess of wisdom.

mahant A title of the head of a Hindu temple.

Mahanubhava A religious sect founded by Chakradhara in 1263. It has a voluminous literature in Marathi and is devoted to the worship of five deities including the god KRISHNA and DATTATREYA.

Mahaparinibbana Sutta A discourse in the DIGHA NIKAYA, a HINAYANA Buddhist text of the PALI CANON, that deals with the last days of the BUDDHA's life, his final sermon, and his relics. Additions were probably made to it at different times, but its core is quite ancient. The text contains the famous words of the Buddha to ANANDA, when asked what would happen after he was gone, and who would lead them. The Buddha replied, 'Be your own Light; Be your own refuge; Hold to the Dharma as your Light, Hold to the Dharma as your refuge.' This Sutta is different from the later Sanskrit text, the MAHAPARINIRVANA SUTRA.

Mahaparinirvana Sutra A Buddhist MAHAYANA text in Sanskrit, probably composed between the second and fourth centuries CE. It describes the last sermon of the BUDDHA and explains various Mahayana concepts. According to this text, the essence of Buddhahood, which is in every person, is eternal, blissful and pure, an interpretation similar to the Upanishadic concept of BRAHMAN. It also states that NIRVANA is a permanent

and joyous state. This lengthy text thus has concepts different from other Buddhist texts, and claims that these represent the secret teachings of the BUDDHA.

Mahaprajapati The aunt and foster-mother of Gautama Siddhartha, the BUDDHA. She married his father Shuddhodana after the death of his mother MAHAMAYA. The Buddha was known as Gautama because Mahaprajapati was called Gautami. After ANANDA, one of the chief disciples of the Buddha, persuaded him to allow women into the SANGHA or monastic community, she became the first *bhikhuni*, or nun.

mahapralaya In Hindu mythology, a term for the dissolution of the universe, which takes place at the end of a KALPA. All the worlds, as well as BRAHMA, the creator, come to an end. *See* pralaya.

mahapurushas A term in Jainism for great beings that exist in the world. There are sixty-three mahapurushas or 'Great Men' listed and described in a number of texts. These include twenty-four TIRTHANKARAS, twelve Chakravartins or rulers of the world, nine Vasudevas and nine Baladevas, together constituting fifty-four mahapurushas. Nine Prati-Vasudevas were added, later bringing the total to sixty-three. The first Chakravartin of the current descending cycle was BHARATA, and the twelfth, Brahmadatta. The Vasudevas represent incarnations of KRISHNA, and the Baladevas incarnations of BALARAMA. The Prati-Vasudevas are powerful but wicked beings who are defeated and killed by the Vasudevas. One of each of the Vasudevas, Baladevas and Prati-Vasudevas live at any one time. Thus RAMA (Vasudeva), LAKSHMANA (Baladeva) and RAVANA (Prati-Vasudeva) lived between the time of the Tirthankaras Munisuvrata and Naminatha, while KRISHNA, BALARAMA and Jarasandha (Prati-Vasudeva) were contemporaries of the Tirthankara ARISHTANEMINATHA.

Mahasanghika A Buddhist HINAYANA sect. About one hundred years after the death of the BUDDHA, the community of monks split into the STHAVIRAVADA, or 'elders', and the Mahasanghikas, or 'members of the great community'. According to some accounts this split took place at the time of the second BUDDHIST COUNCIL at VAISHALI, while according to other sources it happened soon after this. The Mahasanghikas differed on the principles to be followed by monks and on the nature of the ARHAT. According to them, even those Arhats who had attained NIRVANA in this lifetime, could be subject to defilements, and still had vestiges of ignorance. The Mahasanghikas are known to have existed in north-west and west-central India near the river Krishna, and are mentioned in inscriptions at AMARAVATI, NAGARJUNAKONDA, MATHURA and elsewhere. After the basic division, other sects emerged, differing on minor points. Among the sects that evolved from the Mahasanghika were the Ekavyavaharika, Lokottaravada, Gokulika, Bahushrutiya, Prajnaptivada,

Chaitika, Purvashaila, Aparashaila/Uttarashaila, Rajagirika and Siddharthika. The Chaitikas were in north-west and central India, especially the latter. The Bahushrutiyas, Purvashailas, Rajagirikas and Siddharthikas were all located in the lower Krishna valley, where they constructed STUPAS and other monuments. In the seventh century, a prominent sect was the Lokottaravada, who had settled in Bamian in present Afghanistan. There is little information on the differences in philosophy of the sub-sects. The Prajnaptivada asserted that things did not really exist but arose through linguistic convention, that is through naming them, while the Lokottaravada believed the BUDDHAS are superior and extraordinary beings. The MAHAVASTU is a Lokottaravada text.

Later splits and developments among the Mahasanghika led to the MAHAYANA form of Buddhism.

Mahashveta A Hindu deity, a goddess of the earth. The name means 'brilliant white', and is also applied to DURGA, SARASVATI, and a consort of SURYA.

mahasiddha A term for a great SIDDHA, one who has attained perfection through a mastery of all SIDDHIS (powers). Traditionally, eighty-four great siddhas are revered by certain Hindu and Buddhist sects and described in texts on YOGA and TANTRA. Lists vary in different texts and include both men and women. In Tibetan Buddhist sources, the mahasiddhas listed lived mainly before the eleventh century.

Mahatala In Hindu mythology, the fifth of the seven divisions or LOKAS of the nether world or PATALA. The Kadraveyas or children of KADRU live here. They are long, lean and bad-tempered NAGAS who fear GARUDA, the divine bird and vehicle of the Hindu god VISHNU. Among them are Kuhaka, TAKSHAKA, Sushena and Kaliya.

mahatma A term for a great soul. It has been applied to several spiritual leaders, but is most commonly used as a title for M.K. GANDHI, who led India's freedom movement, basing it on the principles of non-violence and peaceful resistance.

mahatmya A Sanskrit term for an account of a sacred place, region, river, or shrine. The PURANAS include mahatmyas of specific areas, and there are in addition, more recent mahatmyas. Mahatmyas generally recount myths and legends, and describe the sacred TIRTHAS in the area. Mahatmyas may also describe saintly people, deities or sacred obejects.

Mahavagga (1) A Buddhist text of the Pali VINAYA PITAKA. It is the first of the two Khandakas (sections) that form the second part of the *Vinaya*, dealing with various regulations for the SANGHA. Its ten sections include rules for admission, for the Uposatha and Pavarana celebrations, for life in the rainy season, as well as rules for footwear, clothing, medicines and for settling disputes. The second Khandaka, the *Chulavagga*, contains other rules for the various aspects of the monastic life.

(2) A section of the Buddhist DIGHA NIKAYA (Book II) is known as *Mahavagga* because of its length, and contains suttas that mostly begin with *maha*.

(3) The third section of the SUTTANIPATA is also known as the *Mahavagga*.

Mahavamsha A Buddhist text that deals with Buddhism in Sri Lanka and provides an account of the history of the island up to the fourth century CE. It is attributed to King Mahanama of the fifth century, but also contains later details. It describes the creation of the Mahavihara there, the planting of a shoot of the BODHI TREE, and various historical conquests. It is important for the history of Buddhism.

Mahavastu A Buddhist text in hybrid Sanskrit that probably originated in the second century BCE, though it was enlarged later, and has references to incidents in the fifth century CE. The *Mahavastu* states that it was a book of the VINAYA PITAKA, according to the text of the Lokottaravada sect of the MAHASANGHIKA. It is actually the oldest surviving biography of the BUDDHA, and has three sections. The first section describes the life of Gautama Buddha in his previous incarnations as a BODHISATTVA, and the earlier BUDDHAS who lived in those times. The second section describes the Tushita heaven. Reborn there, the Bodhisattva planned his birth on earth in the womb of MAHAMAYA. The third section is similar to the MAHAVAGGA of the *Vinaya Pitaka* and describes the first disciples of Gautama Buddha, and the rise of the SANGHA. Inserted into the account of the Buddha's life, are JATAKAS, Avadanas and Sutras, some of which are unknown from other sources. Though it is a HINAYANA text, the *Mahavastu* has some MAHAYANA concepts, and thus marks a transitional phase between the two major schools.

Mahavibhasha A Buddhist text, the short name by which the *Abhidharma Mahavibhasha* is usually known. It is a commentary on the *Jnana-prasthana*, which forms part of the ABHIDHARMA PITAKA of the SARVASTIVADA school. It was composed at the time of the Fourth BUDDHIST COUNCIL held in c. 100 CE, during the reign of King KANISHKA.

Mahavidyas A term for ten Hindu goddesses who are forms of SATI or PARVATI. The ten forms usually mentioned are: KALI, TARA, CHINNAMASTA, BHUVANESHVARI, BAGALA, BHAIRAVI, DHUMAVATI, KAMALA, MATANGI and SHODASHI. According to the related myth, Sati, the wife of SHIVA assumed these forms in order to get Shiva to allow her to go to the sacrifice of her father DAKSHA. Shiva had refused to let her go, as he was not invited. Overwhelmed by the ten forms, some of which are fearsome, Shiva gave her permission. Another story in the *Shiva Purana* associates these deities with the goddess DURGA, who created them to defeat the demon Durgama. Mahavidya means 'great wisdom' and each of these goddesses represents an approach to the attainment of divine wisdom. In some texts, such as the *Guhyati-guha Tantra*, the Mahavidyas are related to the ten AVATARAS of VISHNU, who are said to have emerged from these deities. Thus, for instance, KRISHNA came from Kali, and NARASIMHA from Chinnamasta. Both these myths indicate the supremacy of the goddesses over the male deities.

Special methods of worship are prescribed for each, including the use of MANTRAS and YANTRAS. The goddesses form a part of Tantric worship focused on SHAKTI or feminine energy, and are propitiated mainly to gain power over others, as well as for the destruction of enemies, and for the conquest of one's own Self.

The Mahavidyas have their counterparts in Buddhism, while the VIDYADEVIS are similar goddesses in Jainism.

Mahavira The twenty-fourth Jain TIRTHANKARA who revitalized and organized Jainism. He was the successor of PARSHVANATHA, the twenty-third Tirthankara. According to tradition, Vardhamana, later known as Mahavira, was born in 599 BCE, though according to modern scholars, a more likely date would be 540 BCE. His father, Siddhartha, was a KSHATRIYA and prince of the Jnatr clan. His mother is known in various texts by different names, including Trishala, Videhadinna or Priyakarini. According to a legend contained in the KALPA SUTRA and other texts, his real mother was Devananda, a BRAHMANA lady. Vardhamana was conceived in her womb, but the embryo was transferred to Trishala by Harinegamesi or NAIGAMESHA, a minor deity, on the orders of Shakra (Indra).

Vardhamana was born at Kundagrama, a suburb of VAISHALI in present Bihar. He was the second son and was brought up in luxury. He married Yashoda, had a daughter named Anojja or Priyadarshana, and lived the life of a householder until the age of thirty, when his parents died. According to Jain tradition, his parents were followers of the ascetic order of Parshvanatha, and died through self-starvation, as prescribed by the order. Vardhamana then left home to search for enlightenment. According to some traditions, he too joined the Nirgranthas, the sect founded by Parshvanatha. He practised extreme asceticism and endured great hardship for over twelve years. Initially he wore a single garment, but then he discarded it. A passage in the AYARAMGA SUTTA describes his life: 'He wandered naked and homeless. People struck him and mocked him, unconcerned he continued in his meditations . . . In winter he meditated in the shade, in the heat of summer he seated himself in the scorching sun. Often, he drank no water for months. Sometimes he took only every sixth, eighth, tenth or twelfth meal, and pursued his meditations without craving.' In the thirteenth year he attained enlightenment. Now he was known as Mahavira (great hero), Kevali (omniscient, alone), Nirgrantha (free from bonds), and Jina (conqueror).

For the next thirty years he taught the truth he had discovered, wandering to different places. His followers were known as Nirgranthas, the term Jain being used later.

Mahavira systemitized and elaborated on earlier Nirgrantha beliefs and practices, and laid down the main principles of Jainism as it is practised today, along with guidelines for Jain monks and nuns. Liberation was possible only through extreme asceticism and total non-violence.

He died in 527 BCE, at the age of seventy-two, according to the traditional date, at Pava, identified with Pavapuri in Bihar.

This story is based on the SHVETAMBARA scriptures. DIGAMBARA texts differ in certain details. They reject the story of Vardhamana being conceived in the womb of Devananda, and believe that he never married.

Descriptions of Mahavira's life appear in the Jain Canon, and there are several biographies of him in various Jain texts. Among the notable biographies are those in the ADI PURANA; the Trishashtishalakapurusha Charita; the Mahavira Chariyam in Prakrit, written in 1082 by Gunachandra Ganin; and another text of the same name composed in 1085 by Devendra Ganin or Nemichandra.

Mahavira Jayanti A Jain festival that celebrates the birth of MAHAVIRA, the twenty-fourth TIRTHANKARA. The festival takes place on the thirteenth day of the fortnight of Chaitra (March–April). At this time Jain shrines are visited and ceremonies are held in temples. Jain scriptures are recited, and processions are taken out with the image of Mahavira carried in a ratha or chariot. A special celebration takes place at Kundagrama, his birthplace in Bihar, now known as Kshatriya Kunda. On this day Jains rededicate themselves to follow the teachings of Mahavira.

Mahayana Buddhism A term for a form of Buddhism that probably began to develop from the first century BCE. Mahayana literally means 'the great vehicle' (to enlightenment) and is a term used by later adherents to distinguish themselves from the earlier form of Buddhism, which they named HINAYANA.

Mahayana accepts the Hinayana tradition but differs from it primarily in its development of the concept of the BODHISATTVA and in the worship of multiple BUDDHAS. In Hinayana Buddhism, the Bodhisattva is the historic BUDDHA, or later any Buddha, in his prior lives. In Mahayana Buddhism, every follower of the path is a Bodhisattva, a potential Buddha. But while Buddhahood is an attainable goal, the Bodhisattva does not seek to attain it immediately; enlightenment is voluntarily postponed, until every last being is free of suffering and has attained salvation. The Bodhisattva thus dedicates his life to helping others, to suffering for the sake of others.

A number of Buddhas and Bodhisattvas are worshipped. The Mahayana Buddhas and celestial Bodhisattvas have superhuman and divine qualities and can help all beings. Other deities are also part of the Mahayana pantheon, though the concept of deities and the role they play was further developed in VAJRAYANA Buddhism.

Mahayana developed additional concepts, including that of the TRIKAYA, or three 'bodies' of a Buddha, of which the DHARMAKAYA is the eternal aspect.

Three main Mahayana schools emerged, though there are only subtle differences between the three. The two most important are the MADHYAMIKA and YOGACHARA. NAGARJUNA was the founder of the Madhyamika school, whereas MAITREYANATHA and ASANGA elaborated the principles of the Yogachara school. Some of the differences were so minor that at NALANDA these two virtually coalesced. Another Mahayana school explained the TATHAGATA-GARBHA theory, stating that Buddhahood, or the Tathagata, is innate in everyone.

In India the Mahayana declined in the seventh and eighth centuries and the Vajrayana gained prominence, though several aspects of Mahayana were incorporated into this. By this time Mahayana Buddhism had spread to other countries, and still exists today in different forms in Nepal, Tibet, India, Mongolia, Japan, Vietnam and Korea, while there is some revival of its practices in China.

Mahayana texts   Despite some common characteristics, there are several different types of MAHAYANA Buddhist texts.

(1) The earliest Mahayana texts are various PRAJNAPARAMITA SUTRAS, or the 'perfection of wisdom' texts. These put forward the Mahayana concept that to attain wisdom, one must realize that nothing exists and that the only reality is SHUNYATA (emptiness). Nagarjuna systemized Prajna-paramita thought, which was further developed in the MADHYAMIKA school.

(2) The *AVATAMSAKA SUTRA*, also known as the *Buddhavatamsaka Sutra*, is an important Mahayana text on the BODHISATTVA path, and explains how enlightenment is to be achieved. Its main sections were probably composed by 150 CE.

(3) Texts relating to the Buddha AMITABHA, his compassion and his ability to help living beings, form another group. Amitabha created Sukhavati, commonly translated as 'Pure Land', where those who worshipped him would be reborn. The *Sukhavativyuha Sutra* and other texts are important among Pure Land schools of Buddhism in Japan and East Asia.

(4) One of the most important Mahayana sutras is the *SADDHARMA PUNDARIKA SUTRA*, commonly known as the *Lotus Sutra*.

(5) Other texts: There are a number of other Mahayana texts. Several describe various Buddhas and Bodhisattvas while the *MAHAPARINIRVANA SUTRA* is said to reveal secret teachings of the BUDDHA. The *Maha-ratnakuta Sutra* is a collection of texts, some of which are early, while the *Mahasamnipata Sutra* includes seventeen Mahayana texts. Some groups of Mahayana sutras deal with the path of meditation and the doctrine of the transmigration of living beings. Another group describes protective spells or dharanis.

Many more texts were composed within each of the schools as they developed.

Mahayana Samgraha   A MAHAYANA Buddhist text of the YOGACHARA school, composed by ASANGA. Originally written in Sanskrit, only Tibetan and Chinese versions are available today. It explains various Yogachara concepts.

mahayuga   A period of cosmic time. A mahayuga or 'grand yuga' consists of four yugas in succession, KRITA or Satya, TRETA, DVAPARA, and KALI. Each successive YUGA is shorter and reflects a decline in morals and in the way of life. The four yugas consist of 4800, 3600, 2400 and 1200 years of the gods, and each such year extends for 360 human years. Together they comprise 12,000 years of the gods, which are equal to 43,20,000 human years. At the end of one mahayuga, the cycle of yugas begins again. The mahayuga is part of a larger cycle of time, the MANVANTARA. Each manvantara contains approximately seventy-one mahayugas. The manvantara, in turn, is part of the KALPA.

Mahdawi Movement   An Islamic movement started in the fifteenth century, based on the concept of the MAHDI, a term for a Messiah. Several people at various times claimed to be the Mahdi, but in India the most important was Sayyid Muhammad, born in 1443 at Jaunpur (in present Uttar Pradesh) during the reign of Sultan Muhammad of the Sharqi dynasty. Sayyid Muhammad traced his descent to Musa al-Kazim, the seventh IMAM of the ISNA ASHARI Shias. Muhammad was said to have been a child prodigy who completed his Islamic education by the age of twelve. After a visit to Mecca in 1495–96, he stated that he was the Mahdi. He went to Gujarat and acquired several followers there, but was condemned by the ULAMA. Initially he aimed to bring about a spiritual regeneration at a time of moral decay, and to achieve harmony between different Islamic sects. He set up *dairahs* (centres for spiritual practice), for this purpose Gradually his ideas became more extreme, and he even recommended the imposition of the JIZYA or poll tax on Muslims with divergent beliefs. Mahdawis in *dairahs* strictly followed the laws of the SHARIA and were not allowed to mix with or marry non-Mahdawis. Facing opposition in India, Muhammad moved to Afghanistan, where he died in 1505, but the movement continued after his death. He was succeeded by his son, Sayyid Mahmud (d. 1512), followed by the latter's brother-in-law Khwandamir (d. 1524). By this time *dairahs* had been set up in Sind, Gujarat, Rajasthan and the Deccan, and the movement posed a threat to political authority. Shaikh Abdullah Niyazi and Shaikh ALAI were important leaders during the reign of Islam Shah Sur, and Shaikh Alai was executed in 1550. The Mughal emperor AKBAR was initially keen on suppressing the Mahdawis, but did not take concrete steps towards this. AURANGZEB tried to crush the movement, and the centre moved further south, but Mahdawis continued to exist.

There are still some Mahdawi groups in India, particularly in Hyderabad and further south.

mahdi A term in Islam which signifies a spiritual redeemer or messiah. Literally it means 'the guided one', or 'one who guides' or is fit to direct others. It is believed that the mahdi is a future messiah, who will make an appearance when Muslims are oppressed and divided, and will unite them and bring peace to the world.

Sunnis and Shias have different views on the mahdi. Sunnis are divided on the issue, and some Sunni scholars and groups totally reject the mahdi concept.

The term mahdi is not in the QURAN, but is mentioned in some Sunni Hadis. These Hadis provide various details on the MAHDI. Putting them together it would seem that the mahdi will be a descendent of the Prophet Muhammad through his daughter Fatima; he will have the same name as Hazrat Muhammad; he will rule for seven years, and spread peace and justice in the world; he will lead a prayer at Mecca, and Jesus would also be present there. According to some Hadis, the mahdi would be helped by the abdals, the hidden mystics.

There are several more statements on the mahdi, which are disputed by Islamic scholars, or not considered authentic.

ISNA ASHARI Shias have a different concept, and believe that the twelfth IMAM did not die, and remains hidden. He will return as the mahdi and rule personally, providing a true interpretation of Islam and spreading the religion.

Over time, several people in various parts of the world have claimed to be the mahdi including some within India. During the reign of Sultan Firuz Shah Tughlaq (1351–88) a man named Rukn called himself the mahdi, but was killed along with his followers by the sultan. The most important claimant however, was Sayyid Muhammad of Jaunpur, of the fifteenth century who started the MAHDAWI MOVEMENT. Mirza Ghulam Ahmad, founder of the Ahmadiya movement in the nineteenth century, was another claimant.

The mahdi concept is similar to that of Kalki in Hinduism, the saoshyant in Zoroastrianism, the Bodhisattva Maitreya in Buddhism, and the messiah in Christianity and Judaism.

Mahesh Yogi, Maharishi A guru who revealed the method of TRANSCENDENTAL MEDITATION to the world. There are some conflicting accounts of his early life. His date of birth is not exactly known, but he is thought to have been born in 1911, or according to his own disciples, 1917 or 1918. He studied at Allahabad University, and around 1939 found his guru Swami Brahmananda Sarasvati in the HIMALAYAS. Swami Brahmananda was the Shankaracharya of the Jyotir Matha in Badrinath from 1941 till his death in 1953, and Mahesh became his secretary and studied with him during this time, learning and exploring meditation techniques. He was named Bal Brahmachari Mahesh. After the Swami's death, Mahesh continued to live in the Hinalayan regions, for another two years. He formulated the simple theory of transcendental meditation (TM) which, in its first stage, consists of the mental repetition of a short MANTRA. He then visited south India, and was instructed by Swami Brahmananda in a dream to spread the technique and message of TM. In 1957 he founded the Spiritual Regeneration Movement in Chennai (Madras). In 1958 he went to Myanmar and some other East Asian countries, and in 1959 he began to tour the world to spread his message. His form of meditation reached a height of popularity in the sixties and seventies. He still has several adherents, though with the emergence of other systems, TM has declined in popularity. The Maharishi's books include a commentary on the Bhagavad Gita; *The Science of Being*, and *Meditations*, while several others have written on the theory and practice of TM. The Maharishi also started universities and educational institutions in India and abroad, and a political party in England. He claimed that if even 1 per cent of the population practices TM, a transformation would take place in the world. The Maharishi moved to the Netherlands in 1990. In January 2008, he announced that his work in the world was over, and transferred administrative control of all his organizations to his disciples. He died on 5 February 2008.

While TM is a practical technique, a sadhana, Mahrishi also gave talks on various philosophical topics. In these, he largely followed the theories of ADVAITA. He stated that life was bliss, but it was the non-apprehension of true reality that led to sorrow. TM was one method of discovering the true blissful Self within, but was not the only method. Maharishi said that any mode of experience could be used as a path to realization. Yet this path was 'pathless', meaning that it was not at some far distance, but could be realized immediately. He said: 'Meditation is a process of leading the mind towards the realization of the Self, a process by which the pathless path can become reality for the individual.' Meditation was neither contemplation nor concentration, but a subtle means to reach the divine inner self.

Maheshvara A name of the Hindu god SHIVA.

Maheshvara Sutra A Sanskrit text that deals with the means of attaining realization through four sciences, which in this text are attributed to the Hindu god SHIVA. They are YOGA, VEDANTA, language and music, which are all said to emerge from the sound of Shiva's damaru or drum. It is an esoteric text.

Mahishasaka A HINAYANA Buddhist sect, an offshoot of the STHAVIRAVADA. Mahishasakas differed on certain points: they stated that a gift to the SANGHA or monastic community produced a 'great fruit', and was better than worshipping or making offerings to a

STUPA. However, Dharmaguptikas and others said that in worshipping a stupa one was paying reverence to the BUDDHA, who was far superior to any monk in the Sangha. Mahishasakas believed in the simultaneous penetration into truth, and in the non-existence of the past and future. That is, they believed that only the present is real. Regarding ARHATS, they felt they were perfected beings, incapable of regression. Another point of divergence was their views about the gods; they denied that a holy life (BRAHMACHARYA) was possible for the DEVAS.

Some scholars believe there were two different Mahishasaka schools, the first, which had much in common with the Sthaviravada, originating at the time of the First BUDDHIST COUNCIL at RAJAGRIHA. and another later group which branched off from the SARVASTIVADA.

Mahishasura   The buffalo ASURA or demon vanquished by by the Hindu goddess DURGA. In a story in the *MAHABHARATA*, it is Skanda (KARTTIKEYA) who kills this demon.

According to accounts in the PURANAS, Mahisha was the son of the Danava Rambha and a female buffalo, Mahishi, and was born as the result of a boon granted by the god AGNI. Agni had promised that the child could not be defeated either by the DEVAS or the asuras. According to another account, BRAHMA had granted him a boon by which he could not be killed except by a woman. Mahisha became extremely powerful. He defeated the devas and they all ran away from him, so that the asuras gained control of devaloka, the world of the gods. Finally the Devas created Durga, a beautiful and poweful woman, to kill him. In some accounts, at the very first sight of Durga, Mahisha fell in love and wanted to marry her. Durga stated that she would marry him only if he could defeat her in battle, but he was unable to do so and was killed by her.

Sculptures of Durga killing Mahisha (known as Mahishasuramardini) appear from the first century CE onwards. In a few, Mahisha is depicted as a man with horns, while in most he is a buffalo, often with a human head.

This mythological theme once again reveals the conflict between the devas and asuras. In this case it could indicate attempts to incorporate a tribal deity into the Brahmanical pantheon. Before Agni awarded him a boon, Rambha worshipped the YAKSHA Malavata and lived among the yakshas after marrying Mahishi, indicating the connection of Mahishasura with yakshas or non-Brahmanical deities.

Mahmud Faruqi Jaunpuri, Mulla   One of the greatest Muslim philosophers of India. His *Shams al-Bazigha*, a text that deals with physics and metaphysics, is still used in MADRASAS in India. He died in 1652.

Mahuli   A town located near Satara in Maharashtra, at the confluence of the Krishna and Yenna rivers, noted for its Hindu temples of the eighteenth and nineteenth centuries. The temples are built in Maratha style. The largest is the Vishveshvara Mahadeva Temple, constructed in 1735. Among others are the Radhashankara Temple, the Bilveshvara Temple, the Rameshvara Temple and the Sangameshvara Mahadeva Temple. Near the temples are some tombs and memorials, including one of a favourite and brave dog of Raja Shahu (1761–72).

Ram Shastri Prabhune, the spiritual and political preceptor of the fourth peshwa Madhavaro (1761–72) was born at Mahakuta adding to the sanctity of the place.

Mai Than Gurdwara   A GURDWARA or Sikh shrine located at AGRA in Uttar Pradesh. Agra was visited by Guru NANAK and Guru RAM DAS, but this gurdwara is associated particularly with the ninth guru, TEGH BAHADUR. On his visit here, Mai Jassi, a devout disciple, invited him to stay at her house, and as he agreed, the house was later sanctified and revered as a gurdwara.

Mainaka   A mountain mentioned in the PURANAS and other texts; it seems to refer to both a mythical and a real mountain. Most Puranas suggest that it was in the lower Himalayas, while some state it was to the north of KAILASHA. Mainaka is personified as the son of HIMAVAN and Menaka, the brother of Uma or PARVATI.

According to the *RAMAYANA*, Mainaka was located in the ocean, and provided a resting point to HANUMAN, when he leapt to LANKA. Once, it is said, all mountains had wings, but INDRA began cutting them off. The god VAYU saved his friend Mainaka from having his wings cut, by placing him in the ocean. In return, Mainaka helped Hanuman, the son of Vayu.

Maitreya   (1) A BODHISATTVA, said to be the future BUDDHA, who lives in the Tushita heaven. He is the saviour to come, and the next Buddha to be born on earth. When he comes to earth, he will bring peace, prosperity and salvation, and will teach the path that will save all sentient beings. Maitreya is described in a number of MAHAYANA sutras and is an important deity in Mahayana Buddhism. His concept is similar to that of KALKI in Hinduism, of the MAHDI in Islam, as well as of Messiahs of other religions. Maitreya also forms a part of the Theosophical divine hierarchy; according to this he is said to reside in the mystical land of SHAMBHALA.

(2) Maitreya was also an ancient RISHI, the son of Kusharava and a disciple of Parashara.

Maitreyanatha   A teacher of ASANGA and the founder of the YOGACHARA school of MAHAYANA Buddhism. According to some accounts, Maitreyanatha was a name used by Asanga to compile the teachings revealed to him in a vision by the Bodhisattva MAITREYA, while according to others the two were different, and Maitreyanatha lived between c. 270 and 350 CE. The works composed by Maitreyanatha are the *Yogacharabhumi*, the basic Yogachara text; the *Mahayanasutralankara*, explaining the stages of the BODHISATTVA path; the *Madhyantavibhaga*, a discussion of Yogachara concepts; the *Abhisamayalankara*, which summarizes the *Ashtasahasrika*; the *Dharamadharmata-vibhanga* on how 'unreal imagination' produces existence; and the *Vajrachchhedikavyakha*, a commentary on the VAJRACHCHHEDIKA SUTRA. The first two texts are sometimes attributed to Asanga, and part of the third to VASUBANDHU. The TATHAGATA-GARBHA theory, the theory of vijnaptimatrata, or the concept that what appears real is only a representation in one's consciousness, and the TRIKAYA theory, are among the concepts discussed in his works.

Majjhima Nikaya   A HINAYANA Buddhist text of the PALI CANON, literally 'medium-length suttas or discourses'. The *Majjhima Nikaya* forms part of the *SUTTA PITAKA* and has 152 suttas that cover all kinds of topics, including Buddhist ideas as well as myths and legends. There are stories that reveal the benefits of following the Buddhist path and passages on the purity and equality of all castes. While some suttas explain the FOUR NOBLE TRUTHS, KARMA and NIRVANA, others critically comment on the different and strange sects existing at the time, for instance the dog ascetic or ox ascetic, who lived the way a dog or ox would.

As in the *DIGHA NIKAYA*, the BUDDHA is at times described as an extraordinary human being, showing the way to truth, at other times as a divine power with the ability to perform miracles.

Majnu ka Tila   A GURDWARA or Sikh shrine located on the banks of the river YAMUNA in DELHI. A Muslim boatman once lived here and used to take people across the river free of charge. He constantly spoke of his love and yearning for God, and thus came to be known as 'Majnu', the name of the legendary lover, always pining for his love. Guru NANAK came here and blessed the boatman, who attained the divine vision for which he yearned, and became a disciple of Nanak. His dwelling was called Majnu ka Tila, and many came to visit it. Guru HARGOBIND and Guru RAM RAI were among those who briefly stayed here. In 1783, General BAGHEL SINGH lived here and erected a small shrine at the place. Later Maharaja RANJIT SINGH built a small marble gurdwara at this spot. This still stands, along with a new and larger gurdwara constructed in 1950.

makara   (1) A mythical sea-creature, often depicted in sculptures and in temples. It is the emblem of the Hindu god KAMA and of the goddess GANGA, and the vehicle of the god VARUNA. It is usually depicted with the head and forelegs of an antelope or a goat, and the body and tail of a fish or crocodile. It is also called kantaka, asitadamshtra (with black teeth), and jalarupa (water form). The term makara has sometimes been translated as a shark, dolphin or crocodile. A somewhat similar symbol occurs in twelfth-century churches in Spain and France.

(2) Makara is the name of the sign of Capricorn.

Makara Sankranti   A Hindu festival that takes place on 14 January and marks a change of season, or the

end of winter. According to the Hindu calendar, the sun enters Makara (Capricorn) on this day. The festival is important in Maharashtra and is also celebrated in Karnataka, Bihar and other states. In Maharashtra it is specially auspicious and lasts for seven days. Women share kumkum (red powder), bangles, combs and metal pots with their friends and distribute til (sesame) sweets. On the seventh day, milk is boiled in earthen pots and offered to the rising sun. A female deity is worshipped riding on an animal, the animal for the year being decided by astrological calculations. This indicates the prospects for the coming year. PONGAL, celebrated in Andhra Pradesh and Tamil Nadu, and LOHRI in Punjab, are similar festivals.

Makara Vilakku   A Hindu festival that takes place at the temple of the god AYYAPPA at SABARIMALA, beginning with the sighting of the Makara Jyoti on 14 January. The same night the deity Malikappurathuamma, from a nearby temple, is brought in a procession to the steps of the Ayyapa temple, then returning to her own abode. A seven-day festival follows, during which offerings are made to forest deities.

makaras   Five items that are used in TANTRIC rites. *See* Pancha-makaras.

Makhdum-i Jahaniyan   The popular name of JALALUDDIN BUKHARI, a SUFI saint of the SUHRAWARDI order who lived in the fourteenth century.

Makka (Mecca) Masjid, Hyderabad   A mosque located in Hyderabad, Andhra Pradesh, constructed in orthodox style. It was begun in 1617 by Sultan Muhammad Qutb Shah (1612–26) and added to by his sucessors, Abdullah (1626–72) and Abul Hassan (1672–87), and finally completed in 1693–94 under the direction of the Mughal emperor AURANGZEB. The mosque measures about 68.5 m by 55m. It has fifteen arches, five on each of three sides, while the fourth wall has the mihrab. The five arched facade was carved from a single piece of granite, flanked by two granite columns. In front is a courtyard, in which there is a room believed to contain a sacred relic, a hair of the Prophet Muhammad. More than 8000 people are said to have worked for seventy-seven years to build this grand mosque, that is now a heritage structure.

mala   A term for a rosary of sacred beads used while chanting MANTRAS, or worn around the neck. A mala also denotes any garland or necklace.

Malabar Independent Syrian Church   A Church of the ORTHODOX tradition of SYRIAN CHRISTIANS, with its headquarters at Thozhiyur, Kerala, founded by Kattumangattu Mar Koorilose in 1772. He was consecrated Metropolitan of the Malankara Church at Mattancherry by Mar Gregorius of Jerusalem, but was opposed by other church leaders. He therefore went to Malabar, where he settled at Anjoor in Thrissur district and founded a separate Church. The Church has a strength of about 21,000, with followers primarily in Kerala.

malaika The term for angels in Islam. According to the QURAN, they are messengers of God, with two, three or four pairs of wings. A HADIS states that the angels consist of light, except for IBLIS, who alone is made of fire, and who was banished from paradise because he disobeyed God. The angels of Islam correspond to some extent with those mentioned in the various books of the BIBLE, and the term karubiyam (cherubim) is also used. Jibril (Gabriel) was the messenger who appeared to the Prophet MUHAMMAD. Mikail (Michael) provides knowledge and food. Israfil is the angel who will sound the trumpet on the day of judgement, while Izrael or Azrail is the angel of death. Munkir and Nakir interrogate the dead in their tombs. Harut and Marut were two angels sent to earth by God, but they became sinful themselves and taught people magic, without warning them not to use it for evil.

Apart from these, each believer has two recording angels known as Kiramul-Katibin, who record his good and bad deeds. Iblis, the Islamic Satan, has similarities with Lucifer. Different accounts of angels in Islamic texts mention a number of other angels, including guardian angels, eight angels who support the throne of god, and nineteen angels in charge of hell.

Malankara Orthodox Church A Church of the ORTHODOX tradition. The church emerged because of the crisis faced by SYRIAN CHRISTIANS in Kerala with the coming of the Portuguese and later the British. Seeking freedom from Portuguese domination after the revolt of COONEN KURISU, the Church appealed to the Syrian Patriarch for help, who sent Mar Gregorius of Jerusalem to India, and confirmed Mar Thoma I as Bishop of the Church. The Church began to grow and develop, but soon after the British took over Malabar in 1795, ANGLICAN influence threatened its traditional culture. Finally the church split into three, one section joining the Anglicans, one forming the separate MAR THOMA CHURCH, and the third remaining as the Malankara Orthodox Church (Jacobite). However, conflicts within the church continued, resulting in another split in 1911, followed by a period of peace after 1958, and the appointment of the Catholicos of the East in 1964, with administrative jurisdiction limited to India. After yet another split in 1975, one section has its headquarters at Devalokam, Kottayam, Kerala and another at Muvattupuzha.

Malik Mughis' Mosque A mosque located in Mandu, Madhya Pradesh. It was built in 1432 by Malik Mughis, the prime minister of Hoshang Shah, sultan of Mandu.

The mosque is constructed on a raised platform, enclosed in a courtyard and surrounded by colonnades. A projecting porch on the east forms the main entrance, and there is an arched corridor in front with a domed turret on each side. The open prayer hall has numerous pillars with pointed arches supporting the roof. In the western wall are niches with MIHRABS, decorated with blue tiles and floral designs.

Malika Jahan's Mosque A mosque constructed in 1587, located at Bijapur in Karnataka. It was built by Ibrahim II of the Adil Shahi dynasty, who ruled from 1580 to 1627, for Princess Jahan Begam, after whom it is named. It is a small mosque, consisting of a rectangular hall, constructed on a high plinth. Its façade has three arches with tall minarets and a parapet of perforated stone screens. The prayer hall is covered by a large dome. The mosque has intricate and delicate carvings, and despite its small size is considered the gem among medieval Bijapur monuments. As it is decorated with hanging chains, it is also known as the Zanjiri (chain) Mosque.

Mallikarjuna A name of the Hindu god SHIVA and of one of his jyotir LINCAS, located at SRISAILAM.

Mallinatha The nineteenth Jain TIRTHANKARA, who according to SHVETAMBARA texts was a woman, the only female among the twenty-four Tirthankaras. However, DIGAMBARAS reject this, stating that Malli was a man, as according to them, only men can attain enlightenment. According to stories in Shvetambara texts, Malli was a great beauty, the daughter of the king of MITHILA (north Bihar). Six princes from different states were in love with her, but the king refused their offers of marriage. At this, they combined and planned to attack Mithila. Malli thought of a solution and asked her father to agree to each of their offers. She had a special house built, in which she placed a replica of herself, and filled its head with remains of food, which gradually rotted. While the princes contemplated the beauty of the replica, believing it to be her, she opened its head and a terrible stench emanated from it. The princes naturally retreated in disgust. Malli then preached to them on the transient nature of the body, saying that though she may appear beautiful, within her too was dirt, blood and pus. Then she narrated her former lives and stated that she was about to become a nun. The six princes too renounced the world.

Mamalapuram A city in Tamil Nadu, also known as Mahabalipuram, famous for its rock-cut temples and reliefs, as well as for other temples. The early temples date back to the seventh and eighth centuries, when it was a port of the Pallava dynasty. These include eight rock-cut shrines, known as rathas, of which the five PANDAVA RATHAS are the most important. A rock relief, known as ARJUNA'S PENANCE, is carved in intricate detail. Among structural temples, the SHORE TEMPLE dates back to the eighth century. On a nearby granite hill there are rock-cut cave temples. Other temples are located to the north and west. According to tradition, the asura Mahabali once ruled here and the place was named Mahabalipuram after him. As Mahabali oppressed the people, he was defeated by Vishnu as Vamana. Later, the place was renamed Mamalapuram, after the Pallava king Narasimha Varman I, who was known as Mamalla (the great wrestler). Mamalapuram is also associated with Bana, son of Mahabali.

Manasa A Hindu goddess associated with snakes. She is usually depicted as a woman with seven snake hoods above her head, and she often holds a snake as well. Manasa brings prosperity, protects worshippers from snakes, protects children, and is worshipped to obtain a child. She is a popular deity in Bengal, where Manasa Mangalas, texts dating to the sixteenth or seventeenth centuries, narrate stories and legends about her, and describe methods of worship. She was probably initially a folk deity. In mythology, she is the sister of the Naga king Shesha or ANANTA and the wife of the rishi Jaratkaru. She is worshipped in other parts of India as well, particularly in Himachal. Though a snake deity, she is in a different category from other Naginis, or snake goddesses. She has similarities with the goddesses Janguli of Buddhism and Padmavati of Jainism.

Manasarovara A sacred lake north of Mt KAILASHA. Like the mountain, the lake is revered by Hindus, Buddhists and Jains, and there are several myths relating to it. The god BRAHMA created it through his mind (manasa). In Buddhist texts, it is known as Anotatta or Anavatapta, the lake which is calm and without heat. It is mentioned in Jain texts as Padmabrida. The explorer Sven Hedin (1865–1952) described the lake: 'The oval lake lies like an enormous turquoise embedded between two of the finest and most famous mountain giants of the world, the Kailasha in the north and Gurla Mandhatta in the south, and between huge ranges above which the mountains uplift their crowns of bright white eternal snow.'

Manatunga A Jain poet who probably lived in the ninth century or later, though according to Jain lists of teachers, he could have lived as early as the third century. His work, the *Bhaktamara Stotra,* is revered by both SHVETAMBARAS and DIGAMBARAS, and its verses are used as protective MANTRAS or spells. According to legend, he had himself locked in a house, bound by forty-two fetters, but by composing this *Stotra,* freed himself, thus proving its power. The poem praises RISHABHA, the first TIRTHANKARA, as the highest deity:

Thou art Buddha, because the gods praise the awakening of thy mind.
Thou art Shankara, because thou workest out the salvation of the three worlds;
Creator art thou, because through thy doctrine thou hast created a path to salvation;
Thou, O Lord are Purushottama, the highest of all beings.

Manatunga also composed the *Bhayahara Stotra,* a poem in praise of PARSHVANATHA, the twenty-third Tirthankara.

mandala A circle or diagram that represents some aspect of mystic power—a deity, a hierarchy of deities, a cosmic principle, or the whole cosmos. Mandalas are used for worship, for protection, and to arouse one's own power. They usually form part of TANTRIC worship, but are used in other systems as well.

Mandana Mishra A disciple of KUMARILA BHATTA and an exponent of the Purva MIMAMSA philosophy. He wrote the *Vidhiviveka* and *Mimamsanukramani* on Mimamsa. According to tradition, he was defeated by Sri SHANKARA in a philosophical argument and became his follower. He was then known as Sri Sureshvara Acharya and was installed by Shankara as head of the SRINGERI Matha. As sureshvara, he wrote commentaries on Shankara's works, including the *Manasola Varttika,* on the *Dakshinamurti Stotra.* His *Naishkarmya Siddhi* summarizes the teachings of Shankara. In addition he wrote the *Balakrida,* a commentary on the *Yajnavalkya Smriti,* and elucidated Shankara's commentaries on the *Taittiriya* and BRIHADARANYAKA UPANISHADS.

mandapa A term for an assembly hall in a Hindu temple. A temple may have one or more mandapas, which are connected or adjacent to the inner shrine.

Mandara A mythical mountain used by the gods, for the churning of the ocean to obtain AMRITA. Mandara has been identified with real hills, including one located about 45 km south of Bhagalpur in Bihar. This isolated hill, about 220 m high, has a groove around its middle, said to be the mark left by the serpent VASUKI, who was used as a rope in the churning of the ocean. On the hill are remains of Buddhist, Jain and Hindu shrines, among them a temple of VISHNU known as Madhusudana, an image of NARASIMHA carved in a cave, and a huge image of VAMANA and of the daityas MADHU-KAITABHA. At the foot of the hill is a sacred tank known as Papaharini.

In the MAHABHARATA and some PURANAS, Mandara is located in the Himalayas, with Badarika ashrama on it, or to its south.

Mandi Gurdwara A GURDWARA or Sikh shrine located at Mandi in Himachal Pradesh. Here Guru GOBIND SINGH held discourses while seated on a large flat stone near the river. A gurdwara marks the spot.

Mandukya Upanishad An UPANISHAD commented upon by GAUDAPADA and SHANKARA, that can be dated to between the sixth and third centuries BCE. It gets its name from the rishi Manduka and is attached to the ATHARVA VEDA. This short Upanishad elaborates on the nature of BRAHMAN or the Absolute, and the sacred word OM, which represents Brahman. Gaudapada's *Karika* or commentary explains ADVAITA in the context of this Upanishad, while Shankara further elucidates the basic Advaitic principles.

Mangala One of the NAVAGRAHA or nine planets in Hindu mythology. Mangala represents the planet Mars, and according to some myths, was born from the god SHIVA through a drop of his blood or sweat. Other accounts state that Mangala was the son of BHU DEVI and VISHNU. The deity is also identified with the god KARTTIKEYA, but is depicted differently. Mangala's vehicle is a ram and he is red in colour, with four arms. He is worshipped in temples, usually along with the other Navagraha. He is considered the protector of landed property and of wives.

Mangala also means 'auspicious'.

Mangala-Kavya Literally, 'auspicious poems', Mangala Kavyas consist of verses praising and narrating the myths and legends of deities in Bengal. MANASA, DHARMA THAKUR and SHITALA are among the deities who have Mangala Kavyas. These are both written and oral texts, which are sung in praise of the deities, and modified by the singer. They date back to medieval days.

Mangu Math Gurdwara A GURDWARA or Sikh shrine located at Puri, Orissa. Guru NANAK is said to have come to the JAGANNATHA TEMPLE here and watched the evening ARTI in the temple. Inspired by this, he sang a song of devotion nearby, indicating that the best arti is that performed by nature. His song, named 'Arti', is recorded in the GURU GRANTH SAHIB. The first few lines state: 'The sky is the silver plate/The sun and moon the lamps/The stars are jewels/the wind conveys the incense of all the flowers on earth.' The gurdwara was built to mark the place where he sang.

Mani Singh, Bhai A Sikh scholar who was closely associated with Guru GOBIND SINGH. Born in 1670 in village Sunam in Punjab, he was the younger brother of Bhai Dyala, who was martyred in 1675 along with Guru TEGH BAHADUR. Mata Gujri, the mother of Guru Gobind Singh, took care of Mani Singh, and the two boys grew up together. Mani Singh spread the message of Sikhism and wrote down the final version of the GURU GRANTH SAHIB on the guru's instructions. This task was completed in 1705 and remains the version that is used today. In 1721 Mani Singh became the head granthi of the HAR MANDIR (Golden Temple) at Amritsar, and wrote a number of works on Sikhism. He also compiled the *DASAM GRANTH* based on the teachings of Guru Gobind Singh. He was arrested and executed by the Mughal authorities at Lahore in 1737.

mani stones A term in TIBETAN BUDDHISM designating a pile of stones painted with Buddhist images or carved with the Buddhist MANTRA, 'Om Mani Padme Hum'. They can range from small stones to massive rocks. Once found all over Tibet, they can still be seen near some Buddhist monasteries in India. Carving piles of stones with images is said to have been a pre-Buddhist custom in Tibet, later absorbed into Buddhism.

Manibhadra A YAKSHA chief mentioned in several texts and known through inscriptions and images. According to the MAHABHARATA, the yaksha Manibhadra stayed at the court of KUBERA and was worshipped particularly by merchants and travellers. ARJUNA too once worshipped this yaksha. Manibhadra is also mentioned in Buddhist and Jain sources. In the Buddhist *Samyutta Nikaya*, the yaksha Manibhadra is said to live in Manimala Chaitya in MAGADHA (Bihar). The later MAHAMAYURI states that Purnabhadra and Manibhadra, two yaksha brothers, were worshipped in Brahmavati. In the Jain *Surya Prajnapti*, an early text, it is said that a Manibhadra Chaitya was located to the north-east of the city of Mithila (north Bihar). One of the earliest images of this deity was found at Pawaya in Madhya Pradesh and can be dated to the first century BCE. An inscription states that the image was erected by Manibhadra worshippers. Several other Manibhadra images dating to the early centuries CE have been found at MATHURA and elsewhere.

manikhor A term in TIBETAN BUDDHISM for a prayer wheel. The 'wheel' is a hollow cylinder that contains within it Buddhist scriptures, and is turned by the faithful. Small wheels are held in the hands, while huge ones kept in temples require more than one person to turn them.

Manikkavachakar A BHAKTI saint of the ninth century who was associated with the NAYANARS and worshipped the Hindu god SHIVA. Born near MADURAI in the Tamil region, he was a minister of the Pandyan king, but became absorbed in his devotion to Shiva. As he abandoned his duties, the king put him in prison, and after he was released he became a wandering ascetic, singing of his love for Shiva. His verses are collected in the *TIRUMURAI* and include the *Tiruvachakam*, with 654 verses in 51 hymns, and the *Tirukkovaiyar*, with 400 verses. In one verse, he wrote:

You are my lord
Melting my bones
You entered my heart
And made it your shrine.

Manikyanandin A Jain philosopher of the eleventh century known for the *Parikshamukha Sutra*, a work on logic, based on the earlier *Nyayavinishchaya* of AKALANKA. In DIGAMBARA sources Manikyanandin is said to have lived in the sixth century, while in other sources he is a teacher of the eleventh century. There were probably two Manikyanandins.

Manimekhala A goddess of the ocean described in the Tamil epic, the *MANIMEKHALAI*.

Manimekhalai A Tamil epic, the sequel to the *SHILAPADDIGARAM*, which has been dated by various scholars between the second and sixth centuries CE. This philosophical epic, said to have been written by the merchant Shattan, tells the story of Manimekhalai, the beautiful daughter of Kovalan and the dancer Madhavi. After Kovalan's unjust death, Madhavi, once a courtesan, became a Buddhist nun. Despite her beauty, Manimekhalai shunned the pleasures of the world and sought truth, finally gaining ultimate knowledge. The story is set in the second century CE in the Tamil region, when the Cholas ruled the area. The text consists of thirty verse chapters.

The epic begins in the city of Puhar, where the festival of INDRA is taking place. Both Madhavi and Manimekhalai do not participate in the festival, as they have become disciples of the great Buddhist teacher, Aravana Adigal, who has explained to them the FOUR NOBLE TRUTHS and the basic rules of conduct (shila). Along with a friend, Manimekhalai visits a garden where the BUDDHA's footprints are enshrined, and Udayakumara, prince of the Chola dynasty, sees her and falls in love. Manimekhalai is attracted to him as well, but the goddess MANIMEKHALA appears, takes her away, and explains her true destiny to her. She also gives Manimekhalai a magic bowl that can provide unlimited quantities of food.

Wherever she goes, Manimekhalai feeds the poor with her magic bowl. She pursues her studies, and dressed like a man, she goes to different places, learns about various philosophies and enters into erudite discussions with philosophers. Convinced of the truth of Buddhism and guided by Aravana Adigal, she gains supreme wisdom.

The text describes the society, religion and philosophy of the times. It mentions a number of deities, particularly SHIVA and MURUGAN, as well as sects and philosophies including the Jains, AJIVIKAS, LOKAYATS or materialists, the SAMKHYA, VAISHESHIKA and others, against the backdrop of Buddhism. It is an important text for the history of religion, apart from being an interesting account of an intelligent young woman who chooses her own path in life.

Maninaga   A deity sometimes identified with MANIBHADRA, but who is actually a different deity, as he is not a YAKSHA but a NAGA. Maninaga is mentioned in texts and inscriptions.

Manipura Chakra   One of the seven main CHAKRAS or hidden energy centres within the body. The Manipura Chakra, in the solar plexus region above the navel, is described in TANTRIC and other texts. It is a shining lotus of ten petals, the colour of heavy-laden rain clouds. On the petals are the Sanskrit letters da (cerebral) to pha, of the colour of the blue lotus, with the nada and bindu above. Within is the region of fire, triangular in shape, shining like the rising sun. Outside the triangle are three svastikas.

By meditating on this, one acquires the power to destroy and create, as well as the wealth of knowledge.

manji   A preaching office of the early Sikh panth or community, and also a territorial division for spiritual purposes. Guru AMAR DAS established twenty-two manjis, each consisting of a group of Sikhs under a spiritual leader. This system helped him to keep in touch with Sikhs, as the Sikh population had increased considerably. Sangats or congregations in each manji were addressed by the sangatia or preacher, also known as the manji, and offerings from the sangat were used for the LANGAR, or community kitchen serving free meals.

Manjushri   A BODHISATTVA who embodies supreme wisdom. Manjushri is described in a number of MAHAYANA Buddhist sutras, including the AVATAMSAKA SUTRA and the *Surangamasamadhi Sutra*. According to these, long ago, even before the Buddha SHAKYAMUNI was born, he had sufficient merit to become a BUDDHA, but he chose to remain a Bodhisattva, tirelessly being reborn and helping others on the path.

In images, Manjushri is depicted holding a sword to destroy ignorance, and a book to reveal divine knowledge.

Manjushri Mula Kalpa, Arya   A Buddhist text that is considered one of the earliest TANTRIC texts, though it describes itself as a MAHAYANA sutra. In this text the Bodhisattva MANJUSHRI, the Buddha SHAKYAMUNI and the goddess Vijaya describe how to use MANTRAS and other rites for protection, for the destruction of enemies, and to attain all things. It falls in the class of Kriya Tantras.

Manmatha   A name of the Hindu god KAMA.

manthras   A term used in Zoroastrianism, similar to the Sanskrit MANTRA. Manthras are sacred words of power. In the GATHAS, the Prophet ZARATHUSHTRA says that he is a Manthran, or one who teaches manthra. He states that manthra, meaning 'the word of God', should be followed (*Yasna* 45.3) and that his manthra is the greatest of all truths (*Yasna* 28.5). Later, Manthra Spenta, the holy manthra, was personified and known as Marespand. Some texts mention specific manthras, such as Fashusho Manthra, the manthra for animals.

mantra   A sacred sound, word, or verse. The word in Sanskrit means 'instrument of thought', and mantras are used in all religions in different ways, either to invoke deities or powers, or in meditation. They may be used alone, or along with an image, MANDALA or YANTRA. Mantras are given to a disciple by a guru at the time of initiation, though some mantras can be used without initiation or transmission by a guru. Mantras are generally shorter than prayers, and their power is revealed through repetition and concentration. In Hinduism, OM is considered one of the most powerful mantras, as it is the original word and the origin of all. The GAYATRI MANTRA, mantras for SHIVA, VISHNU, RAMA, KRISHNA, GANESHA and other deities, are commonly used. Mantras are frequently used in Buddhism. They include protective spells known as dharanis, described in MAHAYANA Buddhist texts, as well as other mantras. Mantras form a major part of VAJRAYANA Buddhism. In TIBETAN BUDDHISM, 'Om Mane Padme Hum', is a popular mantra. There are also Jain mantras invoking the TIRTHANKARAS.

The repetition of any deity's name is considered a mantra, while specific mantras are used to invoke particular deities or powers. There are mantras which are said to be able to kill or give life, to guard and protect, cure disease, or grant any desire. Among different types of mantras, bija or seed mantras are sounds or syllables that represent a deity or concept. NIRGUNA (without attributes) mantras are those such as Om, invoking the universal Absolute, while SAGUNA (with attributes) mantras invoke a particular deity. Mantras are also prescribed in TRANSCENDENTAL MEDITATION and other newer systems. Apart from conferring powers or qualities, physiological changes such as relaxation, freedom from stress and reduced blood pressure, can be experienced while using mantras.

Mantra Yoga Mantras or sacred words can be used for different purposes, but in Mantra Yoga, the aim is union with the divine. The basic ethical principles are followed, as in other forms of YOGA, and then a mantra is prescribed, which may be used along with other visual aids, such as images or symbols. Swami Paramahansa Muktananda, a renowned yogi, said that as a MANTRA is repeated, it first purifies the outer body and then the subtle body. Correctly practised, the mantra finally permeates the whole being, leading to total transformation.

Mantrayana A term for the VAJRAYANA school of Buddhism, which uses MANTRAS of various kinds. Mantrayana is also sometimes distinguished from Vajrayana, as being that part of the latter that uses only mantras, and not any other rites.

Manu A term referring to the first man, or to an archetypal man. It is also the name or title of fourteen mystical rulers of the earth. According to Hindu myths and cosmological stories in the PURANAS and other texts, BRAHMA, creator of the world, has a beginning and an end. One lifetime of his is known as a mahakalpa, at the end of which there is a MAHAPRALAYA, or great deluge. One day of his is known as a KALPA. A kalpa consists of fourteen MANVANTARAS, each presided over by a Manu.

The names of the fourteen Manus in each kalpa are usually given as: Svayambhuva; Svarochisha; Uttama (Auttami); Tamasa; Raivata; Chakshusha; Vaivasvata; Savarni or Savarna; Dakshasavarni or Dakshasavarna; Brahmasavarni or Brahma-savarna; Dharmasavarni or Dharmasavarna; Rudrasavarni or Savarna; Rauchyadevasavarni; Indrasavarni or Bhautya or Bhaumi.

The seventh, MANU VAIVASVATA, rules the world today.

Manu Smriti A Sanskrit text, also known as the *Manava Dharma Shastra*. It consists of laws, customs and ethics of the Hindus. Its core was probably composed in the first few centuries CE, though it is attributed to the mythical Manu Svayambhuva, the spiritual son of the god BRAHMA. There are several similar texts, but the *Manu Smriti* gained popularity as it was chosen by Warren Hastings, governor-general of India from 1774 to 1784, to act as a guide for officials of the East India Company in their interactions with Hindus.

Additions and changes were made to it over the years; in its present form, it has between 2685 to 2694 verses divided into twelve sections. Laws, customs and duties of kings, BRAHMANAS, other castes and women

are recorded. However, the status of the higher castes is not merely based on birth. For instance, an ignorant brahmana is said to be as useless as an elephant made of wood. Customs and laws relating to inheritance, birth, marriage, death and the four traditional stages of Hindu life are described. Strict rules for each of the four stages are prescribed. For instance, a Brahmachari, that is, one in the student stage, should never criticize his teacher, should always speak respectfully to him, should rise earlier and go to bed later than him, should be seated at a lower level, etc. Though he should respect the teacher's wife, if she is young and he has reached the age of twenty, he should not greet her by touching her feet. After he has completed his studies, he should return home and marry a wife of equal caste.

These and other minute details of behaviour are laid down, with similar details being provided for the householder and for the next two stages of life. Penances and punishments are also prescribed for violating the laws. Towards the end of the book there is a description of the mind, the JIVA or individual soul, and the means of union with the ATMAN.

Though many laws have been altered in modern times, the *Manu Smriti* is still referred to for customary Hindu practices. It has been criticized, however, for the secondary position it gives to women and SHUDRAS.

Manu Vaivasvata According to Hindu mythology, the name of the seventh MANU who presides over the current MANVANTARA or epoch. Manu Vaivasvata was the son of Vivasvat, another name of SURYA or the sun, and all living beings are descended from him. A great flood took place during his time, and he was saved from it by the god VISHNU, in the form of MATSYA (a fish). According to the *VISHNU PURANA*, in the manvantara over which he presides the gods or DEVAS are the ADITYAS, RUDRAS and VASUS, the name of INDRA is Purandara, and the seven rishis are VASISHTHA, KASHYAPA, ATRI, JAMADAGNI, Gautama, VISHVAMITRA and BHARADVAJA.

manvantara A period of cosmic time. According to Hindu mythology, there are approximately seventy-one MAHAYUGAS in a manvantara and fourteen manvantaras in one KALPA, which is one day in the life of BRAHMA, the creator. At the end of each manvantara, constituting 30,67,20,000 years, the world is destroyed and re-created. A manvantara is presided over by a MANU, and each manvantara is assigned a different Manu. Different sets of deities and RISHIS are born in successive manvantaras, including seven rishis (saptarishis) known as PRAJAPATIS.

Manyu A deity who personifies anger, mentioned in the RIG VEDA. He glows like fire and bestows wealth. United with Tapas, or ascetic fervour, he grants victory to his worshippers and slays their foes.

Mappila/Moplah A community of Muslims of Kerala, who speak Malayalam and are concentrated in the districts of Kudungallur, Kozhikode and Palakkad. The word Mapilla or Moplah has been interpreted in different ways. It may be derived from 'mapillai', an abbreviated form of 'maha pillai' meaning great respected person, or from mopilla which means husband in colloquial Malayalam, and son-in-law in Tamil. Early Muslim immigrants (Arabs and others) on the Kerala coast, who married into local families were possibly referred to as Mapillai. Mapillas are generally SUNNIS. They have incorporated local customs in their way of life.

Mar Thoma Church An independent church that combines elements of Eastern Syrian Christianity and Anglicanism.

Named after Mar Thoma or ST. THOMAS, it was formed in 1889 as a result of ANGLICAN influence on a section of SYRIAN CHRISTIANS of India. It belongs to the family the Lesser Eastern ORTHODOX Churches and retains the essential character of the Orthodox Church in its liturgy, mode of worship, ceremonies and rituals, but also has Protestant aspects.

The first Anglican mission (CMS) started to work in Kerala in 1816. A group of Jacobites of the Syrian Church, influenced by the Anglicans and led by Palakkunnath Abraham Malpan of Maramon (1796–1845), a professor at Kottayam Seminary, and Kaithayil Geevarghese Malapan of Puthuppally, attempted to bring about some reforms in the Syrian Church. In 1836, this group was excommunicated. Malpan then sent his nephew, Deacon Mathew, to the Jacobite Patriarch at Mardin, Syria, who consecrated him bishop. The new bishop, Mathew Mar Athanasius, reached Malabar in 1843 and carried on with the reforms. Conflicts in the Syrian Church intensified and reached a head after Patriarch Pathros III visited Malabar in 1876, and convened a Synod that condemned the reformists. After a period of confusion and litigation, the Mar Thoma Church was established, initially with only three churches attached to it. The church then developed independently.

In 1927 new liturgical books in accordance with the reformed theology were published. In 1952 another split took place, with a breakaway group forming the St. Thomas Evangelical Church of India. However, the Mar Thoma Church continued to grow, and today it has over 9,00,000 members, 1062 parishes, 11 dioceses and 680 priests in different parts of the world, including India, West Asia, Africa, North America and Western Europe.

The Church has a democratic system of administration with the Metropolitan as the head, assisted by an Episcopal Synod, Executive Council and Prathinidhi Mandalam. Its headquarters is at Thiruvalla, in Kerala.

Mara The one who destroys. In Buddhism Mara is considered the tempter of the BUDDHA, just as Satan tempted JESUS. While Siddhartha, the Buddha-to-be, sat in meditation under the BODHI TREE, Mara tried to prevent and distract him. Mara is said to have offered Siddhartha the rulership of the world, and when he refused, Mara sent an army of demons to threaten him, and then his own daughters to attract him. (The details of Mara's attempts vary in different texts.)

Mara actually represents the inner struggle between good and evil. In one passage in the PALI CANON Siddhartha tells Mara, 'Lust is your first weapon; the second is dislike for a higher life; the third is thirst and hunger; the fourth is desire; the fifth is laziness and sloth; the sixth is fear; the seventh is doubt; the eighth is hypocrisy; the ninth is seeking praise, honour and false glory; the tenth is exalting oneself and despising others.' He adds that bliss can be attained only by conquering these shortcomings. Siddhartha was able to conquer them, thus defeating Mara and achieving Buddhahood, as he had attained all the PARAMITAS (virtues or perfections).

Mardana, Bhai The companion and close disciple of Guru NANAK, the founder of Sikhism. Mardana was born in 1459 at Nanakana Sahib. His parents, Bhai Badre and Mai Lakho were Muslims and were part of a community of musicians and dancers. Mardana accompanied the guru on all his journeys and sang and played the rabab, a stringed instrument, composing some of the music for the guru's hymns. Three of Mardana's own compostions are included in the GURU GRANTH SAHIB. After accompanying the guru for forty-seven years, Bhai Mardana died in 1520. According to some sources, the guru was returning from Mecca and Medina, and Mardana died near the river Khurram in Afghanistan, while according to other sources, it happened at KARTARPUR near the river Ravi when they were back home. Guru Nanak performed his last rites himself, and then asked Mardana's son, Shahzada, to accompany him instead. There are many stories about Mardana in the JANAM SAKHIS.

Mariamma A Hindu mother goddess worshipped in villages in south India. There are several local myths associated with Mariamma. According to one story, she was once a village girl, born in a BRAHMANA family. A lower caste youth, pretending to be a brahmana, married her. When she discovered his real identity, she killed herself, and after her death she was worshipped as a goddess. Another myth is similar to that of ELAMMA-Renuka, but here she has a brahmana head and an 'untouchable' body. Both these myths are related to the inclusion of DALITS in Hindu rituals, and the conflicts arising out of this.

Marichi (1) An ancient RISHI, a mind-born son of the god BRAHMA, and one of the PRAJAPATIS. His wives included Kala, Urna and Sambhuti, and the most famous of his children was the rishi KASHYAPA, born from his wife Kala.

(2) Marichi is mentioned as the chief of the MARUTS.

Marichi, goddess A Buddhist mother goddess described in TANTRIC texts. She is said to be a consort of the Buddha VAIROCHANA, and is invoked in the morning, in connection with the rising sun. She has some similarities with the god SURYA who is also known as Marichimali, meaning, 'one with a number of rays'. Marichi is depicted with several arms, and rides across the sky in a chariot drawn by seven pigs, whereas Surya's chariot is drawn by seven horses.

Markandeya   A RISHI or sage who gained eternal youth and according to tradition, composed the MARKANDEYA PURANA. In Hindu myths, he was the son of Mrikandu, born after the latter had performed tapas (austerities) to please the god SHIVA. Finally, Shiva appeared to him and asked whether he would prefer a long-lived, dull son, or a wise and virtuous one who would live only till the age of sixteen. Mrikandu chose a wise son, and Markandeya was born. From childhood he knew all the VEDAS and SHASTRAS, and when he was almost sixteen, he learnt of his impending death and began worshipping Shiva. When YAMA, god of death, came to take him away, his attendants having failed to do so because of the boy's radiance, Markandeya clung to the idol of Shiva, and Yama's noose caught it as well. Angry at this, Shiva killed Yama, but later revived him, and also made Markandeya an eternal youth of sixteen. Thus, the story says, Shiva received the name Mrityunjaya, conqueror of death. Markandeya lived in the Himalayas in his ashrama known as Pushpabhadra for over ten crore years, survived the MAHAPRALAYA or great deluge, and is said to be still alive. According to some texts, his wife was DHUMRORNA or Dhumra (usually the wife of Yama), otherwise known as Murdhanya, and his son was Vedashiras. He was also known as Bhargava, Bhrigukulashardula, Brahmarishi, Viprarishi and Dirghayu.

Markandeya Purana   A Sanskrit text, one of the eighteen major PURANAS of Hinduism, named after the rishi MARKANDEYA, who is said to have composed it. It begins with Jaimini, a disciple of VYASA, praising the *MAHABHARATA* and asking Markandeya four questions that are not answered in that text. The questions are referred to four wise birds who provide the answers. This is followed by a dialogue between a father and son on the life of a BRAHAMANA. Stories and legends are narrated, including that of King Vipaschit, who visited hell and refused to leave until all the sufferers there were released. Feasts, sacrifices and ceremonies related to various deities are also described in this Purana. Its ancient origin is clear, as there are hymns to the gods INDRA, AGNI, SURYA and BRAHMA, who were more important in Vedic times, with less emphasis on VISHNU and SHIVA. One section, the *DEVI MAHATMYA*, focuses on the worship of the goddess DURGA.

Markandeyeshvara Temple   A temple of the Hindu god SHIVA located at Bhubaneswar, Orissa. It was built originally in the eighth century, but has been partially reconstructed. It has a square shrine with a tower, and a rectangular MANDAPA or jagmohan. There is a a dancing Shiva in a medallion on the front of the tower, and NAVAGRAHAS above the doorway. On the door jambs are images of BRAHMA, AGNI and VARUNA.

Marpa   A Tibetan Buddhist who lived from 1012 to 1097 and studied at NALANDA under the Buddhist scholar NAROPA. His most famous disciple was MILAREPA. He forms part of the lineage of the KAGYU school of TIBETAN BUDDHISM.

Marrano Jews   A small group of Jews that once lived in India. 'Marrano' was a term for Jews from the Iberian peninsula who were forced to convert to Christianity in the fourteenth and fifteenth centuries. Despite their outer conversion, they maintained their Jewish practices in secret. They were expelled from Spain in 1492 and from Portugal in 1499. Marrano Jews from Spain and Portugal reached GOA in the sixteenth century and later settled in Kochi, Kerala, as they faced persecution from the Portuguese. There are scattered references to these Jews in India, and no trace of them remains today.

Martand Surya Temple   A temple of the Hindu god SURYA located at Martand in Kashmir. It was constructed in the eighth century during the reign of Lalitaditya, a king of the Karkota dynasty. The inner shrine opens into an ardha-mandapa, with images of GANGA and VISHNU in niches. Apart from the main shrine, there are also two minor shrines. The temple is built on a high basement, at one end of a rectangular court that has a collonnade of fluted pillars. The gabled roofs are charactersistic of the architecture of this region. The place was probably named after the temple, as Martanda is a name of Surya.

Martanda   A Hindu deity, a name of SURYA, the sun god. In the RIG VEDA, Martanda was one of the eight ADITYAS.

Maruts   A group of Hindu deities prominent in the RIG VEDA. According to this text, they were the sons of RUDRA, associated with thunder, lightning and rain. They formed a gana or group, and their number was said to be three times seven, or three times sixty. They were closely connected with the goddess Rodasi and were probably married to her. They wore spears on their shoulders, anklets on their feet, golden ornaments on their breasts and golden helmets on their heads. They rode across the sky in golden chariots, drawn by horses with golden feet, as swift as thought. They were invoked not only for rain, but also to bring healing remedies from seas, mountains and rivers. They were called singers and were associated with the god INDRA. They were self-luminous, shining and brilliant, of the same age, and born at the same place. The Maruts are also mentioned in the *RAMAYANA*, PURANAS and other texts. According to a Puranic story, they consisted of forty-nine gods, the sons of KASHYAPA and DITI. Diti, mother of the daityas HIRANYAKSHA and HIRANYAKASHIPU, was unhappy when her sons were killed by VISHNU. Bala another of her sons,was killed by Indra,and therefore Diti asked Kashyapa for a child strong enough to kill Indra. A child was conceived in her womb after various austerities, but Indra entered her womb and cut it into forty-nine pieces, which were later born as the Maruts and became the servants of Indra. They were called Maruts because when the child cried, Indra said 'ma-ruda', do not cry. There are also other variants of this story, which seems to be an attempt to explain their name and their connection with Rudra.

MARICHI is said to be the head of the Maruts, and their world, known as Maruta, is one of the heavens.

Mary   Mary, mother of JESUS, also known as the Virgin Mary, is prominent in India, particularly among CATHOLICS, and there are several churches dedicated to her. Among the more important, is the Church of Our Lady of Health in Velankanni, Tamil Nadu, known as the Lourdes of south India. Pilgrims of all religions come here with their prayers for healing, and mircaulous cures are said to have taken place. St. Mary's Basilica at Mount Mary, Bandra (MUMBAI) is another popular church, with all communities participating in the Feast of the Virgin, held in September. The Church of Our Lady, Mother of Divine Grace at Mokameh (Patna Diocese) also attracts thousands, particularly at the main feast held in November.

Mary in India   According to Indian tradition, not only did JESUS come to Kashmir after surviving his crucifixion, but so did his mother MARY, and her grave is said to be located here too. Another local tradition in Tamil Nadu states that the goddess KANNIYAKUMARI, is actually the Virgin Mary.

Mary in Islam   Mary, mother of JESUS, is highly respected in Islam, and is known as Mariam. Islam believes that a son was born to her through the spirit of God, but Muslims do not call her 'Mother of God', because God or ALLAH is only one and cannot be divided.

masand   A term in Sikhism for a spiritual or administrative deputy. The term masand comes from the Persian word 'musannad', meaning exalted or most high. From the time of Guru RAM DAS, this term was used for Sikh deputies who collected funds for the community and organized worship. Masands thus replaced the earlier MANJIS. Masands were not paid a salary, but retained a portion of the community's contributions to support themselves. Gradually, masands began to appoint deputies; the office became hereditary, and a number of them became corrupt. Because of this they were disbanded by Guru GOBIND SINGH in 1699, after the creation of the KHALSA.

masjid   The Arabic term for a MOSQUE, literally a 'place of prostration', implying prostating oneself before God, or surrendering to God.

Masjid-i Ala   A mosque located near the palace of Tipu Sultan, ruler of Mysore, in his capital town of Srirangapatnam. It was constructed by Tipu Sultan in 1786–87.

The mosque, built on a raised platform, has a large closed prayer-hall with a flat roof supported on arches, and an open pillared verandah in front. The mihrab in the hall has an inscription with the ninety-nine names of Allah. Scriptures in fine calligraphy decorate the walls and ceilings. At the front entrance are two tall octagonal minarets, with three sections separated by balconies. Above are turnip-shaped domes and balconied terraces providing a panoramic view of the town. These huge and unusual minarets make this otherwise simple mosque unique.

mass   A Christian form of worship, important for CATHOLICS. The mass celebrates the Lord's Supper, the Last Supper that JESUS shared with his disciples before he was betrayed. Catholics are supposed to attend Mass on Saturday evenings or on Sundays, and on other holy days.

The mass has two main parts. In the first part, the liturgy of the Word, a petitition is made for forgiveness of sins, after which there are hymns, prayers, Bible readings, a sermon, and a declaration of faith. The second part is the liturgy of the EUCHARIST, where bread and wine are offered to God in remembrance of Jesus, who offered these to his disciples at the Last Supper. These are then symbolically changed into the body and blood of Christ, as was indicated by Jesus. The worshippers experience Christ through Holy Communion by consuming a wafer of the consecrated bread and a few drops of wine.

There are also different types of mass, including a shorter mass, a 'dry' mass, a high or more elaborate mass, and a requiem mass for a dead person.

Apart from Catholics, the mass is celebrated by some PROTESTANT groups, particularly ANGLICANS.

Mata Sundri Gurdwara   A GURDWARA or Sikh shrine located in New Delhi near Ajmeri Gate. Mata Sundri and Mata Sahib Kaur, the wives of Guru GOBIND SINGH, stayed for many years at a haveli (house) here while the guru was in the Deccan. They were authorized to issue HUKAM NAMAS or orders in the name of the guru. After the guru died, Mata Sundri was looked up to by the Sikhs as their leader. She sent instructions to the Khalsa Panth and made Bhai MANI SINGH the head priest of the HAR MANDIR. Mata Sundri died in 1747, and later a gurdwara was constructed at the site of the haveli. Some weapons belonging to the guru are preserved here.

Matangi   (1) A Hindu goddess, one of the ten MAHAVIDYAS. She is related to the divine word and to the goddess SARASVATI, and is described as dark green, seated on a throne of grass, sweet of speech, representing wisdom and music. In some TANTRIC sources she is depicted differently and is described as an outcast, black, passionate, and reeling about in intoxication, thus representing knowledge beyond the ordinary.

(2) A daughter of DAKSHA and wife of the rishi KASHYAPA, from whom all elephants were born. The word Matangi means 'female elephant'.

(3) Matangi is also a term used in some villages in south India for a woman who enacts the role of the local village goddess.

Matarishvan A deity mentioned in the RIG VEDA, sometimes equated with AGNI. He seems to have been a personification of Agni, though a later commentary associates him with the god VAYU.

matha (math, muth) The term for a Hindu monastery or religious centre. Sri SHANKARA, also known as Adi Shankaracharya, the philosopher of the ninth century, is said to have first established mathas. Later, a number of mathas belonging to all schools of thought were established in various parts of India, and became centres of religious study and learning.

Matho Monastery A Buddhist monastery in Ladakh belonging to the SAKYA sect, constructed in the early sixteenth century. It is still a popular monastery and is known for its Oracles Festival, which takes place between February and March. Two Buddhist monks known as the Oracles, spend several months in fasts and purificatory rites, after which they are said to be possessed by a deity. At the Matho Festival, they are blindfolded and cross a narrow parapet 30 m high on top of the monastery. They then answer questions put to them by the people gathered at the festival, and are said to be able to predict all aspects of the future. Matho also has a museum with THANGKAS or scroll paintings dating back to the sixteenth century.

Mathura A city in Uttar Pradesh particularly associated with the life of the Hindu god KRISHNA, but also known for its vast stock of sculptures relating to Hinduism, Buddhism and Jainism. According to the *Ramayana* and Puranas, the city was founded by SHATRUGHNA, brother of RAMA. Archaeology indicates it was occupied from at least 1000 BCE, and several ancient sites have been excavated here. In the sixth century BCE it was the capital of the Shurasena kingdom, while later it was a centre of the Indo-Greeks, Mauryas, Shakas and Kushanas, followed by the Guptas and other dynasties. Innumerable Hindu, Buddhist and Jain images, as well as YAKSHA and NAGA images dating from the second or first century BCE onwards, have been found at various sites within and around the city area.

A distinctive school of art developed at Mathura between the second century BCE and the third century CE, known as the Mathura School of Art. Most of its images were made of red sandstone, and the deities were well-rounded, while later images had a more delicate style. Inscribed images provide information on deities and their donors. Buddhist sects of the MAHASANGHIKAS, SARVASTIVADA, SAMMATIYA and VATSIPUTRIYA are mentioned, while Jain images list names of shakhas, kulas and ganas (various sects or groups).

In the early eleventh century there were reported to be more than 1000 wealthy temples in the region. This affluence attracted the invader Mahmud of Ghazni (Afghanistan), who looted a number of temples. Mathura later came under the sultans, the Mughals and the Jats, before being taken over by the British.

Despite its early importance as a Buddhist and Jain centre, it is today most important for its temples and holy sites associated with Krishna. It is also a centre for followers of CHAITANYA MAHAPRABHU and VALLABHACHARYA, as well as of ISKCON. Among the notable temples today are the KESHAVA DEVA TEMPLE, said to mark the spot where Krishna was born, the Rangeshvara Mahadeva Temple, where according to legend, King Kamsa worshipped the god SHIVA, and the Dvarkadhish temple, constructed in 1814 and managed by the followers of Vallabhacharya.

Myths and legends regarding the ancient city, occur in various texts. RAVANA is said to have performed austerities in Mathura to gain mystic powers, and MAHABALI performed a sacrifice here to gain control of the universe. Around the city of Mathura are GOKUL, VRINDAVAN and other sacred places connected with Krishna and RADHA.

Apart from Krishna temples and those of other Hindu deities and sects, there are also Jain temples, mosques and churches. Historic mosques include the Jami Masjid constructed in 1660–61, and the Katra Masjid, built by AURANGZEB on the earlier site of the Keshav Deva Temple. The Roman Catholic Church of the Sacred Heart was built in 1860, its architecture incorporating local elements. Mathura Museum, founded in 1874, stocks thousands of sculptures and other artefacts of the city and its neighbourhood.

Matri Mandir A non-sectarian temple, located at AUROVILLE in Pondicherry (Puducherry). Matri Mandir, literally meaning 'Temple of the Mother' and signifying the Universal Mother, was established by the MOTHER, who was closely associated with Sri AUROBINDO. It is constructed as a large golden sphere which appears to rise out of the earth, indicating a new consciousness, and was seen by the Mother as the 'symbol of the Divine's answer to man's aspiration for perfection' and as 'the central cohesive force' for the growth of Auroville. The inner chamber in the upper hemisphere of the structure is white, with white marble walls and white carpeting. In the centre is a pure crystal-glass globe, which suffuses a ray of electronically guided sunlight falling on it, through an opening at the apex of the sphere. According to the Mother this is a place of silence, 'a place for trying to find one's consciousness'.

Matrikas A term for a group of Hindu mother goddesses. Matrikas are mentioned in the *MAHABHARATA* and other texts, but are extensively described in the PURANAS. There are numerous such goddesses, but used collectively the term specifically refers to certain female deities worshipped as a group. The number of Matrikas is usually seven or eight, though later texts list sixteen. A myth in the DEVI MAHATMYA states that they were created by the male gods to help the goddess DEVI or MAHADEVI defeat the demons against whom she was battling; a similar story about their origin appears in the DEVI BHAGAVATA PURANA. In one passage in the *Devi Mahatmya* they are referred to as forms or aspects of Devi, and according to the VAMANA PURANA they were created from Devi. In the MATSYA PURANA they were said to be created by the god SHIVA to defeat the ASURA Andhaka.

Matrikas are also mothers associated with children. Myths narrate that some of these fierce goddesses initially attacked children but later became their protectors. One story associates them with the god KARTTIKEYA, who was looked after by the six Krittikas or mothers.

In sculptures they are often depicted in a panel of three or more goddesses, but they can be depicted separately. The goddesses have children on their laps or standing nearby. Early sculptures show a variety of women with various animal or bird heads, holding or surrounded by children. Only later were they formalized according to Puranic myths.

Matrikas commonly listed in the PURANAS and depicted in later images are Aindri or Indrani, Brahmi or Brahmani, Maheshvari, Kaumari, Narasimhi, Varahi, Vaishnavi, while other Matrikas mentioned include Kauberi, Vainayaki, Varuni, and Yami. As the wives or Shaktis of male gods with similar names (INDRA, BRAHMA, etc.), they are usually depicted in human form, mounted on the VAHANA or vehicle of their male counterpart, while Narasimhi and Varahi have the faces of a lion and a boar, respectively.

In some panels, they are depicted with Virabhadra (SHIVA) and GANESHA standing behind them. Animal-headed or other mother goddesses with children are worshipped even in Buddhism and Jainism.

In Chalukya inscriptions they are referrred to as sapta-matrikas (seven mothers), the descendants of HARITI, who is a Buddhist mother goddess.

Matrikas thus have two aspects: as powerful deities who defeat demons, and as protectors of children. Groups of Matrikas are depicted in temples all over India.

Matsya   One of the ten main incarnations of the Hindu god VISHNU. In this form Vishnu's lower body is that of a fish (matsya), while his torso and face are human. According to the myth associated with this form, Vishnu became a small fish at the time of a great flood. He then came to MANU, the progenitor of the human race, and asked him to get into a boat, which he would tow to safety. As Matsya pulled the boat along, he grew larger and larger, finally assuming an enormous size. Matsya took the boat to safety and instructed Manu to tie it to a peak of the Himalayas. This done, he swam away. In one version of the story, Matsya has a horn onto which the rope towing the boat can be tied. In the BHAGAVATA PURANA, Matsya fights against the demon HAYAGRIVA, who has stolen the VEDAS from the god BRAHMA, while he slept.

The story of Manu and the flood has parallels with that of Noah and the ark in the Judeo-Christian tradition. There are also similar flood stories from ancient Sumeria and Babylonia, the Greek writer Hesiod, the Maya of Central America and the Yoruba of Africa.

Matsya is generally considered the first incarnation of Vishnu, and is said to represent the first stage of evolution, as life emerged in the ocean. However, Puranic lists differ, and it is only in later texts that Matsya is placed first.

The deity Matsya is normally depicted with four arms, two holding a conch and discus or wheel, the emblems of Vishnu, with the other two holding a lotus and a mace, or in the protection- and boon-granting mudras or gestures.

Matsya Purana   A Sanskrit text, one of the eighteen major PURANAS of Hinduism. It is one of the older PURANAS, and begins with the story of a great flood that devastated the world, in which the god VISHNU took the form of a fish, MATSYA, and pulled MANU and his ship to safety. While Manu is being drawn through the waters, a dialogue takes place between him and Matsya, which forms the core of the Purana. This Purana has the five usual Puranic themes, along with geographical, chronological and astronomical sections. The genealogical details, particularly on the Andhra dynasty, are considered fairly authentic. There are other topics covered, including the duties of a king, omens and portents, ceremonies when building a house, rules for making images of deities and for constructing temples. Festivals of both VAISHNAVAS and SHAIVAS, as well as 108 names of DEVI as Gauri, are given. It also has MAHATMYAS or descriptions of PRAYAGA and KASHI, as well as of those along the river NARMADA. The Purana has between 13,000 and 15,000 verses in available recensions.

Matsyendranatha   The traditional tenth-century founder of the Hindu NATHA YOGI sect, also known as the KANPHATA sect. Matsyendranatha is said to have obtained his knowledge directly from the god SHIVA, by taking the form of a fish (matsya) and listening to Shiva instructing PARVATI on the means of attaining the divine. He was one of the eighty-four MAHASIDDHAS or perfected ones, and one of the nine Nathas or masters worshipped by the Natha Yogis. Not much is known of Matsyendranatha's life, but there are several legends and stories about him. According to these, he went to Nepal, where he is still worshipped, and spread his teachings there. He also went to Sri

Lanka; though he was an ascetic, he had two sons through a woman there. These two sons, known as Parosenatha and Nimnatha, became leaders of Jainism. Matsyendranatha searched for a successor, and found one in GORAKHNATHA.

Matsyendranath and Gorakhnatha are both considered founders of the Natha or Kanphata Yogis, and of HATHA YOGA. Their teachings are a mix of Hatha Yoga, TANTRIC practices, and meditation, that lead to the attainment of perfection, the mastery of all SIDDHIS or powers, and total control of the body and mind.

Mattan Gurdwara A GURDWARA or Sikh shrine located at Mattan in Kashmir, associated with the life of Guru NANAK. Here the guru met Pandit Brahmdas, a BRAHMANA scholar who spent his time studying various religious texts. The guru recited couplets on the futility of too much study. He said that one may study thousands of books, and read throughout one's life up to one's last breath, but, 'There is one Truth, His Name only, All else is vanity of the egoistic mind'. Brahmdas recognized the truth of what Nanak said and became his disciple.

A gurdwara was built here to commemorate the guru's visit.

Maturidi A school of Islamic thought founded by Abu Mansur al-Maturidi, a theologian from Samarkand (d. 944). According to this school, predestination and free will exist together. In legal matters the HANAFI school was followed.

Maudgalya Purana A late PURANA dealing with the worship of the Hindu god GANESHA, also known as the *Mudgal Purana*. It was compiled by Shri Ganesh Yogindra, who died in 1805. According to legendary accounts Yogindra lived for over 200 years and was a worshipper of the god Ganesha at the MORESHVARA TEMPLE in Morgaon. He studied ancient texts and came to believe that there existed a Purana written by Mudgal rishi, revealing the secrets of the worship of Ganesha. Unable to locate it, he continued to worship Ganesha, and was then given portions of the Purana by a BRAHMANA who was said to be the god Ganesha himself.

These legendary accounts increase the sanctity of the Purana compiled by Yogindra, who also wrote the *Ganesha Vijaya*, describing the various aspects of the god. A MATHA was set up by his followers; it continues the tradition of study and worship of Ganesha.

Maudgalyayana One of the first disciples of the BUDDHA, known in Pali as Moggallana. He gained enlightenment soon after joining the Buddha and was known for his miraculous powers.

Mauna Ekadashi A Jain festival also known as Mauna Agiyaras, which consists of a day of silence. It takes place on the eleventh day (Ekadashi) of the month of Margashirsha (November–December). On this day Jains fast and observe total silence (Mauna).

They worship the gods, TIRTHANKARAS and saints and meditate on five holy beings, a monk, religious leader, teacher, ARHAT and SIDDHA.

Maya According to Hindu mythology, a DAITYA who ruled in TALATALA, one of the LOKAS, and fashioned the ASURAS, just as VISHVAKARMA, the divine architect, fashioned the DEVAS. Maya was a great architect, and in the *MAHABHARATA*, he is said to have constructed the city of INDRAPRASTHA, while according to the PURANAS he also built Tripura, the triple city. He was the son of Viprachitti and the father of Mandodari, the wife of RAVANA. Vajrakama and Chhaya were his other daughters. He lived in the Devagiti mountains.

maya (maayaa) A Sanskrit term that indicates the illusory nature of the world. Originally the word meant art or wisdom, secrecy, extraordinary power or sorcery. Maya as a philosophical concept forms an important part of ADVAITA. The philosophers GAUDAPADA and SHANKARA, spoke about the One Reality as the only truth, the world and all creation being illusion or maya. The word is most commonly used in that sense today. Other philosophical systems do not see the world as totally unreal, and interpret maya as God's creative power, through which the world came into being. According to RAMANUJA, the world is real but is called maya because it attracts people and draws them away from God. Maya has also been identified with PRAKRITI, the material nature of the universe, the seed from which creation emerges. Among more recent philosophers Sri AUROBINDO stated that though there is One Reality, there are also individual souls. The world is not maya or an illusion, but real, and needs to be perfected through the spiritual and material evolution of every living being.

Mayon A Hindu deity popular in Tamil Nadu, also known as Mal, Tirumal, Perumal, Mayavan, and other local names. The name literally means 'one of a black complexion', the Tamil version of KRISHNA. Though initially a folk deity, Mayon is usually worshipped as VISHNU or Krishna, and was popular with the ALVAR saints and later VAISHNAVITES. He is worshipped as a folk deity as well.

Mazdayasnan/Mazdayasni A term for Zoroastrians. Many Zoroastrians call themselves Mazdayasni or Mazdayasnan, that is, worshippers of Mazda (God).

Mazhar Jan-i Janan, Mirza A SUFI saint and poet of the NAQSHBANDI order who lived in the eighteenth century (d. 1784). He was a follower of the WAHDAT AL-SHUHUD doctrine, but tried to reconcile differences among various groups. He considered the VEDAS divinely inspired and wrote favourably about Hindu beliefs, pointing out similarities between Hinduism and Islam. He compared idol worship to the Sufi adoration of PIRS or saints, for he said it was not the idol itself that was worshipped, but the essence of the saint or deity that it represented. He wrote that Hindus 'believe in the Vedas and the oneness of God . . . Their religious leaders are masters of their own religion and rational sciences, methods of self-discipline and sublimation of the human soul.'

He also wrote verses in Persian and Urdu describing his experience of the divine, including the one below:

In the dazzling morning sun in all its glory
I saw God's presence in all its splendour.

Meghalaya, traditional religion The dominant population in Meghalaya are the Khasi, Jaintia and Garo or Achik tribes. The majority are Christians converted by missionaries in the nineteenth and twentieth centuries, but earlier they followed their own deities, and still have some parallel beliefs. Khasis believed in the creator U Blei Nongthaw, with subordinate water, mountain and nature spirits. Both Khasis and Jaintias are known as the Hymniewtrep people and claim to be descended from Ki Hymniewtrep or Hynniew Trep. Traditional festivals are still celebrated by these groups to appease ancestral spirits, and in connection with sowing and harvesting. Ka Pomblang Nongkrem, popularly known as the Nongkrem dance, is one of the most important Khasi festivals; it is a thanksgiving for the harvest, as well as a prayer for peace and prosperity. Behdiengkhlam, the most significant festival of the Jaintias, is celebrated annually at Jowai in the Jaintia hills, in July. Wangala is the prominent festival of the Garos, to honour and offer sacrifices to their principle deity Saljong (sun god).

Meharji Rana, Dastur A Zoroastrian DASTUR or priest from NAVSARI (Gujarat) who lived in the sixteenth century, visited the court of the Mughal emperor AKBAR and was granted land by the emperor. Meharji Rana, son of Rana Jesung, was born at Navsari in 1514. According to tradition, he initially met AKBAR when the latter besieged Surat in 1573. Impressed by the Dastur, Akbar invited him to his court, where Meharji Rana explained the Zoroastrian religion to him. Akbar incorporated some elements of Zoroastrianism in his DIN-I ILAHI and kept a sacred fire burning at his court. He granted 200 bighas of land in Gujarat to Meherji Rana as a *Madad-i-Maash* grant. In 1579 Meherji Rana was recognized by the community as the first high priest of Navsari, which then became a hereditary post. The celebrated singer TANSEN composed a song, still preserved today, on Meherji Rana, describing the priest's long beard and radiant face. A few years after Meherji Rana's death in 1591, Akbar granted another tract of land to Meherji's son Kaikobad.

Mehr Baba A spiritual teacher, who has a large number of followers worldwide. Mehr Baba was originally a Zoroastrian. Born at Pune (Poona) on 25 February 1894, he was named Mehrwan Sheriar Irani. At the age of nineteen, he was awakened to his innate spirituality by the touch of a Muslim woman known as Hazrat Babajan, who was a realized soul. He became her disciple and also met other spiritual teachers, including SAI BABA of Shirdi, Hazrat Tajuddin Baba of Nagpur, Narayan Maharaj of Kedgaon, and Upasini Maharaj of Sakori. He lived for seven years with Upasini Maharaj, and gradually developed his own philosophy through the guidance of his teachers and his own intense meditation, and experienced Self-realization, a state that he said was one of continuous and infinite knowledge, power and bliss. He began to attract followers, who, impressed by his compassionate nature, gave him the name 'Meher Baba', or 'Compassionate Father'. He believed that love, compassion and the awareness of the divine were the essential aspects of spirituality.

In 1922 he set up the Manzil-e-Meem or House of the Master, in Mumbai, where his disciples began to gather. In 1923, he set up Mehrabad near Ahmadnagar, which would become the permanent centre of his teachings. From 1925 he stopped speaking, and lived in silence for the rest of his life as he believed that the highest knowledge could best be conveyed in silence. He stated that he observed silence because people through the ages had remained deaf to God's teaching and precepts.

When necessary, he communicated through writing, and later through an Alphabet board, and after some time only through gestures.

In the 1930s he began a series of visits to Europe and USA, and gained numerous followers. In India he focused on a special group known as 'masts', those who were God intoxicated, and who appeared deranged to ordinary mortals. In 1949–52 he organized 'The New Life' where he and his select disciples moved through towns and villages in India in disguise, spreading his messaage in different ways. In 1954, he called himself an avatara, an incarnation of the divine.

After two road accidents in 1952 and 1956, he suffered from ill-health and passed away in 1969.

Mehr Baba developed his own philosophy, which incorporates aspects of Advaita, Sufism as well as esoteric Zoroastrianism.

According to his philosophy, the individual soul experienced various stages, first being incorporated in stone or metal, then proceeding through plant to animal form, culminating in the human state. In this final stage, love, service and meditation enabled the soul to be united with God, and realize its true nature.

People belonging to different religions from all over the world became his followers, and even after his death on 31 January 1969, his disciples continue to increase. Meher Baba temples have been erected in a number of places, and annual celebrations of his birthday take place. His followers have a sense of oneness and community.

His ideas are recorded in his *Discourses* in five volumes; *God Speaks*, which he said was one of the most important books of this age; *The Theme of Creation and Its Purposes;* and *The Everything and the Nothing*

Meiteis, traditional religion Meiteis form the dominant population of the plains of Manipur. They worship Hindu deities, particularly KRISHNA, as well as indigenous deities and spirits. In earlier times, however, they followed the Sannamahi religion, and recently there have been attempts to revive their traditional beliefs.

According to these beliefs, when there was nothing in the universe, it was known as Ting-Ka-Kok or total emptiness. Yaibirel Sidaba, also known as Atiya Kuru Sidaba, representing the eternal, asked his elder son Sannamahi to create life, and Sannamahi, who was the sun god, did so. Then his father sent his younger son, Pakhangba, to protect and sustain life on earth. Gradually kings took on the name Pakhangba, as protectors of the earth. Pakhangba was also symbolized by a dragon and associated with a dragon god. Two types of worship became common: the Sannamahi Laishon, which involved prayers, chanting and singing, and the Pakhangba Laining or meditation, performed only by scholars, kings and nobles. The worship of VISHNU started in the region in the fifteenth century, and the kings converted to VAISHNAVISM in the eighteenth century, by which time most of the Meiteis began to follow Hinduism. The Chaitanya sect became popular here.

From the eighteenth century onwards, indigenous deities developed Hindu counterparts. Thus Pakhangba became SHIVA, the dragon god became ANANTA, and Panthoibi, god of prosperity and war, was equated with DURGA. Thangjiang, the supreme god of the Moirang kingdom, was equated with Vishnu, and Nongpok Ningthou, of the eastern hills of Imphal, became VARUNA, while Atiya Kuru Sidaba began to be called Atiya Guru Sidaba.

Yaosang, a great festival of the Meitis, became popular in the eighteenth century, and traditional festivals are still celebrated.

Memons A community of Muslims, settled mainly in western and southern India. There are different accounts of their origin, based on oral traditions. According to one account, they originally lived in Sind and were Hindus of the Lohana community, who were merchants and traders. Around 1422 a SUFI saint, Pir Yusufuddin, or Yusuf Alauddin Qadiri, is reported to have reached Thatta in Sindh and converted around 700 Lohana families to Islam. He asked them to settle on the banks of the river Varaya. Regarding their name, one theory states they were not socially accepted by Hindus, and therefore initially took refuge with Baluch chieftains. Thus they came to be called Mamoon, which in Arabic means 'Safe at Peace'. Another theory is that they were descended from Arab soldiers who came to Sind with Muhammad bin Qasim in 712. They were known as Maymenah, the right-wing of the army, which later became 'Memon'. Alternatively it is said the term Memon comes from Moman, meaning the preacher of iman or truth.

While some remained in Sind, unrest in the region led groups of Memons to migrate to Kachchh and Kathiawar in Gujarat. One story is that they were first invited to settle in Bhuj by a sixteenth century king, and later moved to other parts of Gujarat, the port towns of west and south India and particularly to MUMBAI (Bombay) where they were involved in trade and commerce and became extremely prosperous. Memons are SUNNIS, but in India are culturally more similar to BOHRAS and KHOJAS, who are SHIAS. Their dialect, Memoni, is a mixture of Kachchi and Sindhi and does not have a script.

As a wealthy community they have set up charitable trusts, which fund hospitals and educational institutions. There are still a number of Memons in India, though after Partition in 1947, many moved to Pakistan. Initially, Memons preferred to marry within their own community, but now marriage to other Muslims is common. The All India Memon Jamat Federation takes care of their interests in India, while there are other regional and local Jamats. Memons also live in all parts of the world.

Mena, Menaka (1) In Hindu myths, the wife of HIMAVAN and mother of Uma (PARVATI), GANGA and a son named MAINAKA. In the RIG VEDA, she was a daughter of Vrishanashva.

(2) An APSARA who attracted the rishi VISHVAMITRA. From her, Shakuntala was born.

Menander An Indo-Greek king who ruled parts of north and north-west India in the second century BCE. He is known for the conversations he is said to have had with the Buddhist philosopher NAGASENA, which are compiled in the *MILINDA PANHA*, a Pali text.

Mennonite A PROTESTANT Church, an offshoot of the Anabaptist Christian movement of the sixteenth century, which preached adult baptism and organized independent congregations.

The Church is named after Menno Simons (1496-1561), a Dutch Catholic priest who left the Catholic Church and led a reform movement that gained a number of followers.

Because of persecution, many Mennonites fled to Russia in 1860; others moved to America between 1860–1929. In 1889 Rev. Freser J. Abraham and his wife who came from Russia, became the first Mennonite missionaries in India. They were followed in 1899 by Hubert, the first American Mennonite to reach India. More American missionaries followed later.

There are six Mennonite groups in India today. The Mennonite Brethren Church of Andhra Pradesh has the largest following. The five smaller Mennonite Churches are: Mennonite Church of India; Dhamtari

Brethren in Christ Church; Britain United Missionary Church; Bharatiya General Conference, Raipur, M.P.; Bihar Mennonite Mandali.

Apart from India, Mennonites exist all over the world, with congregations in Angola, Austria, Brazil, Canada, China, Colombia, Germany, Japan, Mexico, Panama, Paraguay, Peru, Russia, the United States, Uruguay and Zaire.

menog A term in Zoroastrianism for the mental world, which forms a whole along with GETIG, the physical world. To perfect the mental world people are advised to think for themselves, to use their conscience to make the right choices, and to be guided through insight by AHURA MAZDA. In one passage 'silent meditation' is mentioned as the best.

Meos A tribal group in north India who were originally Hindus, but converted to Islam. They follow a mix of Hindu and Muslim practices, and at the Nikah, or Islamic wedding ceremony, they circumambulate fire, like the Hindus. They celebrate both ID and DIVALI and follow most local customs. Before Independence they lived in the states of Alwar and Bharatpur, along with the Minas, some of whom are also Muslims. Both groups initially retained their Hindu names, or added Khan to their original names. Apart from the traditional worship of ALLAH, they worshipped several saints and deities, including the PANCH PIR, and the goddess CHAMUNDA, also called Khera Deo, to whom sacrifices were offered. The SUFI saint Muinuddin Chisti, MADAR Shah and SALAR MASUD GHAZI are also venerated by them. Meos have their own versions of the *Ramayana* and *Mahabharata* and revere Rama and Krishna.

Merkabah An esoteric and mystical tradition in Judaism, in which a vision of the divine throne or chariot (merkabah) is attained. The vision of the throne is first described in the BIBLE, in the Book of Ezekiel; it is supported by four beings, each with four faces, of a man, a lion, an ox and an eagle, and with four wings. The throne had the appearance of 'a sapphire stone', and is also described in other texts. Merkabah mysticism invloves attaining a vision of the throne under the guidance of a teacher. Merkabah meditation leads one through seven stages, each guarded by an angel and a password.

Though a traditional Jewish system, it has been popularized as a form of New Age meditation in India. The seven stages can be compared to the seven CHAKRAS, or the seven levels of NAFS in SUFISM.

Meru, Mount A mythical mountain, also known as Sumeru, described in the PURANAS and other texts. This golden mountain marks the centre of Jambudvipa, the island or continent that contains Bharatavarsha or India. It extends upwards to the heavens and downwards to the depths of the earth. The mountain is composed entirely of gold and gems. BRAHMA, the creator, lives on its peak, and other celestial beings often gather on it. Around the mountain are the various dvipas or lands. Flowing from heaven, the river GANGA reaches the mountain, and then continues to the surrounding world in four streams. The guardians of the four quarters live on the four sides of the mountain.

The name seems to refer to both a mythical and a real mountain. As for its location, the MATSYA PURANA says Uttara Kuru is to the north, and Bharatavarsha (India) to the south. The PADMA PURANA says the Ganga starts from this mountain and flows into Bharatavarsha.

The Kedarnath mountain in Garhwal is known as Sumeru, and some identify Mt Meru with this mountain. Scholars have also identified it with Mt KAILASHA, the Rudra Himalaya in Garhwal, the Hindu Kush mountains, and the highland of Tartary, to the north of the Himalayas.

Merutunga A Jain scholar of the thirteenth to fourteenth centuries. He composed a number of texts, including the *Mahapurusha Charitra* on five TIRTHANKARAS: RISHABHA, Shantinatha, ARISHTANEMINATHA, PARSHVANATHA and MAHAVIRA; the *Theravali*, a list of Jain teachers; and the *Prabandhachintamani*, which has semi-historical stories and legends.

messiah, in Judaism The Hebrew BIBLE contains several references to the messiah (in Hebrew, mashiach), and according to Judaism, the messiah is yet to come. The Jews will then be gathered in the Holy Land, there will be divine judgement, and the dead will be resurrected.

Methodist Church A Christian denomination with a number of followers in India.

The Methodist Church was founded by John Wesley, an ANGLICAN priest (1703–91), who believed in frequent attendance at Holy Communion, serious study of the Bible and social work, including regular visits to prisons. Wesley led a group called the Holy Club and the members were known as Methodists, as they followed a regular way of life. Later, John Wesley was joined by the Anglican clergyman George Whitefield, and the Methodists formed a society within the Church of England. Though Wesley did not want to leave the Church, a break took place in 1795. After this, Methodists developed rapidly from a society to a Church, within which several different branches emerged. A movement to reunite the Methodist groups began at the end of the nineteenth century, and in 1907 the United Methodist Church was formed. In 1932 the Wesleyan Methodist Church, the Primitive Methodists and the United Methodist Church came together to form the Methodist Church. The Methodist Episcopal Church came to India in 1856 with William Butler, a missionary from America who began his missionary work in Bareilly (Uttar Pradesh). In 1870 the famous evangelist William Taylor, was invited to India to hold special revival meetings, which led to the growth of Methodists in India. In 1870 the arrival of two women missionaries—Isabella Thoburn, an educationist, and Clara Swain, a doctor—further contributed to its growth. In 1930 the Central Conference of Southern Asia elected Jaswant Rao Chitamber the first Indian Bishop, marking the beginning of a new era. Some groups of Methodists joined the CHURCH OF NORTH INDIA, while in 1980 the autonomous Methodist Church in India was affiliated with the United Methodist Church of the United States.

The supreme legislative body of the Church is the General Conference, which meets once in four years and takes all major decisions, including the appointment of Bishops. Ministerial laymen and deaconess delegates are members of the General Conference. The Church is divided into the six episcopal areas of Bangalore, Bareilly, MUMBAI, DELHI, Hyderabad and Lucknow, and members number over six lakh.

Meykanta Shastras Texts connected with the Hindu god SHIVA, written in Tamil in the thirteenth and fourteenth centuries. They were composed by SHAIVITE theologians, of whom the most important was Meykanta Tevar. His main work, the *Shivananapotam* (*Instructions on the Knowledge of Shiva*) contains twelve verses summarizing essential concepts, along with a commentary. These Shastras form part of the texts of the SHAIVA SIDDHANTA.

midrash A Jewish term for biblical exegesis, contained in the TALMUD, the Targum or Aramaic translations of the Hebrew BIBLE, and in other midrash collections. The midrash attempts to reconcile contradictory texts and to explain the Bible within its social context.

mihrab A niche in the wall of a mosque that marks the QIBLA, or direction of the KABA.

This arched concave recess indicates the direction of Mecca towards which Muslims must turn when they offer prayers. In India, the direction is to the west. The mihrab is usually ornamented with inscribed verses from the QURAN.

Milad ul-Nabi An Islamic festival that celebrates the birth anniversary of the Prophet MUHAMMAD. It takes place on the twelfth (barah) day of the month of Rabi-ul-awwal, and thus is also known as Barah Wafat, and because it is a festive occasion, as ID-I-MILAD.

Milarepa/Milaraspa A Buddhist who lived from 1040 to 1123 and was a disciple of MARPA. His student Gampopa founded the KAGYU school of TIBETAN BUDDHISM. Milarepa is known for his extreme asceticism and the powers he gained through this. He was able to fly through the air, transcend the world, and meet the BUDDHAS in different realms. He lived for long years in solitude and composed a number of verses and songs reflecting his teaching.

Milinda Panha A Buddhist text written in Pali and attributed to NAGASENA. It was probably composed between the second century BCE and the first century CE. It consists of a series of philosophical questions posed by Milinda (the Pali form of MENANDER, an Indo-Greek king) and answered by Nagasena. The book begins with an account of the past lives of Menander and Nagasena, and the reasons for their meeting again in this life. Menander, a deep thinker, could find no one to answer his questions, until he met the monk Nagasena. Impressed by this calm and serene monk who went from door to door begging for food, Menander began a conversation with him. Nagasena answered Menander's questions in a series of dialogues that explain Buddhist concepts. The *Milinda Panha* is a great work of prose, and a profound Buddhist text. While the core of the book is early, analysis shows that there are also later additions.

Mimamsa One of the six classical systems of philosophy in ancient India. JAIMINI, who lived between the fourth and second centuries BCE, is said to have founded this school, and his work, the *Mimamsa Sutra,* explains its philosophy. This early form of Mimamsa, known as Purva Mimamsa or Karma Mimamsa (analysis of action) focused on the VEDAS as the ultimate source of divine knowlegde, and on the correct performance of rituals and sacrifices. The interpretation of the Vedas was only possible through the understanding of each shabda or word. Other commentators elaborated on Jaimini's text. Shabara, who has been variously dated from the first century BCE to the sixth century CE, was the chief commentator, with all later Mimamsa writings being based on his work. He said that not only right knowledge, but DHARMA and right conduct were essential. KUMARILA of the eighth century, MANDANA MISHRA, his disciple, and Prabhakara were among other commentators. Prabhakara's followers belonged to two schools of thought, while a third school is associated with the name of Murari, though its details are not known. In the seventeenth century, Apadeva and Khandadeva also wrote texts on Mimamsa.

Purva Mimamsa examines the nature of DHARMA and tries to show that every part of the Vedic texts can be related to dharma. It believes in a plurality of selves, and the early writers do not concern themselves with MOKSHA or ultimate liberation; they accept a number of deities, the worship of which leads to heaven. Later commentators began to deal with higher philosophical concepts, and their philosophy became almost identical with VEDANTA and was known as Uttara Mimamsa, or later Mimamsa. Badarayana's *BRAHMA SUTRA* is also known as Uttara Mimamsa. According to some commentators, Jaimini's Purva Mimamsa and Badarayana's Uttara Mimamsa formed one whole, the former emphasizing dharma, ethics and ritual, and the latter, philosophical aspects.

Purva Mimamsa, with its emphasis on dharma, is an important source of Hindu law.

mimbar A term for a raised platform in a mosque from which the KHATIB or preacher delivers his KHUTBA or Friday sermon.

Minakshi A Hindu goddess, the wife of Sundareshvara, a name of SHIVA. She is worshipped mainly at MADURAI in Tamil Nadu, and elsewhere in south India. Though worshipped as Shiva's wife and a form of PARVATI, legends connected with her are entirely different. According to one legend, she was born to the king of Pandalam in the Tamil region, as a girl with three breasts. Upset, the king went to his priest, who instructed him to raise her as a boy. Thus she dressed and acted like a boy, and, after ascending the throne on her father's death, she went on a campaign to bring the whole world under her rule. Leading her army, she won battles everywhere, until she reached Mt KAILASHA, the abode of Shiva. There she fell in love, her third breast disappeared and she became Shiva's wife. Her brother ALAGAR (VISHNU) was late for the marriage, and it took place without him. This drama of the marriage, with Minakshi's brother arriving late, is re-enacted every year.

According to another legend, Minakshi said she would only marry someone who could defeat her in battle. After vanquishing several suitors, she was defeated by Shiva in the form of Sundareshvara, and then lived with him happily ever after. This story is similar to DURGA myths, though Durga remained undefeated.

Minakshi means 'fish-eyed' and the fish was once the emblem of the Pandyan dynasty.

Minakshi Temple A temple of the Hindu deities MINAKSHI and Sundareshvara (PARVATI and SHIVA), located at MADURAI in Tamil Nadu. It was initially built by the Pandya dynasty, and reconstructed in the seventeenth century, during the time of the Nayaka dynasty. This elaborate temple complex actually has two temples, one dedicated to Shiva as Sundareshvara, the other to Minakshi. The inner shrine of the Shiva temple has an image of Sundareshvara. A MANDAPA and ardha-mandapa are attached, and above the shrine is a small SHIKHARA or tower. The Minakshi temple is similar, on a smaller scale. The temple walls have sculptures of deities, and along the passages are murals of Shiva, who is said to have performed sixty-four acts (lilas) in Madurai. The ceilings are painted with large medallions. Apart from these, there is a huge hall known as the Hall of a Thousand Pillars, and a tank called the Pool of Lilies, as well as other mandapas and shrines. Steps descend into the tank, which is surrounded by a pillared porch. The whole complex is enclosed by high walls, with twelve elaborately carved GOPURAMS or gateways, four of which are over 45 m high. The gopuram on the south reaches a height of 65 m.

There are innumerable carvings on the walls and in the various mandapas and shrines in the complex; according to one estimate they amount to 33 million. Sculptures include depictions of the story of Minakshi, various forms of Shiva and scenes from his life, the NAYANARS and other Shaiva saints, deities including KALI, GANESHA, the DVARAPALAS, and the Utsava Vigrahams or processional deities.

Precious jewels and ornaments donated over the years are used to decorate the deities at various festivals.

At the Teppam festival in January, images of the deities are floated in a huge tank nearby. The marriage festival is held here in April/May, when Sundareshvara and Minakshi are decorated with jewels and pearl crowns, and taken out in procession. The god ALAGAR (VISHNU) then comes to give his sister Minakshi in marriage to Sundareshvara. He is late again, as he was when the marriage first took place, because he was dallying elsewhere with a princess. Thousands of devotees and pilgrims watch the ceremonies.

minaret A tower of a mosque, from which the MUAZZIN sounds the call to prayer. The minaret has different architectural forms and can be of varying height. It sometimes stands adjacent to a mosque.

Minjar festival A Hindu festival related to agriculture and fertility, celebrated in Chamba in Himachal Pradesh. The festival takes place in the month of Shravana (July–August), and lasts for a week. Minjar is a word for the silky upper section of maize, and at this festival people tie these plants on their clothes, sing, dance and worship the rain god VARUNA. This is said to ensure good rains and a plentiful crop in the coming year.

Mir Dard A SUFI poet who wrote in Urdu and lived from 1719 to 1785. His lineage included two Sufi saints, and he was descended on his father's side from Bahauddin Naqshband of the NAQSHBANDI order, and on his mother's side from Abdul Qadir Jilani, founder of the QADIRI order. His father, Muhammad Nasir, had a vision of Imam Hasan, grandson of the Prophet MUHAMMAD, which guided him on a mystical path and led him to found the Tariqa-i-Muhammadiya, a branch of the Naqshbandis. Dard became his father's disciple and propagated his teachings.

Dard's family lived in DELHI, and after the devastation of the city in 1739 by the invader Nadir Shah, they were provided a house by AURANGZEB's daughter. Dard was not only a poet, but also wrote on philosophical and mystical themes. Despite the repeated devastation of Delhi, Dard continued to live there, bearing all hardship like a true Sufi.

Though they were Naqshbandis, he and his father had a liberal attitude to SAMA or Sufi music, and were against orthodoxy. In one of his verses, Dard wrote:

Dard you may omit the pilgrimage
To Kaba and the temple
Only try to win
The hearts of the downtrodden.

Another verse reflects his mystical view of the world:

O Dard, clear the mirror of your heart of
impurities;
The universe will then manifest itself in all its
beauty.

Mir Taqi Mir   A SUFI poet who lived from 1722 to
1810. Mir, the son of a darvesh, was born in Akbarabad,
lived in DELHI for many years and left after the invasion
of Ahmad Shah Abdali around 1757, moving first
to the Jat kingdom nearby, and ending his life in
Lucknow. His autobiography, *Zikr-i-Mir*, provides an
account of his life and sufferings. He began writing in
Urdu around 1740. He was not attached to any Sufi
order, but his poems reflect his mystical quest:

I wandered around in search of God
Not knowing that realization of the Self
Means a union with Him.

Not concerned with orthodoxy, he claimed:

I the intoxicated one, am not concerned
with Sharia,
I forced the Shaikh to silence in the
mosque.

Mira Bai   A BHAKTI saint who was a devotee of
the Hindu god KRISHNA. Not much is known about
her life, and there are conflicting versions and
traditions about her birth, marriage and death. She
was probably born in 1498, in a Rathod family of
Marwar in Rajasthan, and married Bhojraj, the rana
or ruler of Udaipur or Mewar. Her mother died when
she was young, and from childhood she was devoted
to Krishna. An unhappy marriage ended when her
husband died, and despite the persecution of her
brothers-in-law, she became a wandering ascetic,
singing songs of devotion to Krishna. She went to
MATHURA and VRINDAVAN, places sacred to Krishna, and
lived there for some years. Here she is believed to have
met Jiva Goswami of the Chaitanya tradition, but did
not become a follower of CHAITANYA, or of VALLABHA,
whose disciples were also in Mathura. She then
moved to DVARAKA, where she is said to have merged
with Krishna in about 1546. According to other
accounts she left Dvaraka at this time and continued
her wanderings, meeting the musician TANSEN, the
Mughal emperor AKBAR, TULASIDASA, and other noted
saints, before dying a natural death at the age of over
seventy. Her verses, composed in Rajasthani, Braj-
bhasha (Hindi) and Gujarati, the languages of the
three regions in which she lived, provide some hints
on her life, but on the whole are pure Bhakti. Some
of her verses are included in the GURU-GRANTH SAHIB,
and her songs are still popular in north India. In one
of them, she sings:

Come to my house, O Krishna,
Thy coming will bring peace.
Great will be my joy if I meet Thee
And all my desires will be fulfilled.

You and I are one,
Like the sun and its heat.
Mira's heart cares for nothing else,
It only wants the beautiful Shyam. (Trans. A.J.
Alston)

Mira Behn   An Englishwoman who became a
disciple of Mahatma GANDHI and lived at his ashram
in Sabarmati. Her original name was Madeline Slade,
and she was born in 1892 in England, the daughter of
Admiral Sir Edmond Slade. She grew up in luxury and
loved music particularly Beethoven, but was inspired
by Romain Roland, to come to India and meet
Mahtama Gandhi. She reached India in 1925, and
after meeting Mahatma Gandhi, her life changed. She
became his disciple, took the vow of BRAHMACHARYA,
and wore the orange robes of a SANNYASI, giving up
all worldly possessions. Gandhi gave her the name
Mira Behn. She worked in the villages, and joined in
political activities and in India's struggle for freedom.
She was imprisoned for some time during the Civil
Disobedience Movement (1930–34) and again
detained during the Quit India Movement (1942–44).
After this she moved to Rishikesh in Uttar Pradesh
and started an ashram to help the villagers, as well as
a home for old cows and bulls, called Pashulok. She
left India in 1959, and lived in a village near Vienna
where she devoted the rest of her life to the study of
Beethoven. She died in 1982.

Her writings include: *Gleanings Gathered at Bapu's Feet*;
New and Old Gleanings; and her autobiography, *The
Spirit's Pilgrimage*.

miraj   A term in Islam for the mystical night journey
of the Prophet MUHAMMAD to heaven, which took
place in the Islamic month of Rajab. Miraj literally
means 'climbing the ladder', but in this context it
indicates climbing to heaven. The QURAN mentions it
briefly in Sura xvii.1, which states: 'Praise be to Him,
who carried his servant by night from the Masjidul-
Haram (Mecca) to the Masjidul-Aqsa (the Temple of
Jerusalem).' Several HADIS comment on this journey
and it is described in a number of texts. Basing itself
on al Baghawi's Hadis, the *MISHKATUL MASABIH*, describes
the journey in detail, as narrated by Muhammad.
Muhammad is reputed to have said that when he was
sleeping, he was visited by the Angel Jibrail (Gabriel),
who removed his heart and washed it in zamzam
water, and filled his heart with faith and science. He
then brought him an animal with wings to ride on,
named BURAQ, and took him through seven heavens.
In the first heaven he saw Adam; in the second, John
and Jesus; in the third, Joseph; in the fourth, Enoch;
in the fifth, Aaron; in the sixth, Moses, and in the
seventh, Abraham. There he saw the tree called Sidratul
Muntaha, with fruit like water-pots and leaves like
elephant ears; four rivers, of which two were hidden;
the Baitul Mamur (inhabited house, said to be directly
above Mecca Masjid); and vessels of honey, milk and

wine. There he also received the divine orders for the daily prayers, which at first were fifty times a day, but then were reduced by God to five. Other texts vary regarding the details of this journey.

Miratul Makhluqat   A text written by the SUFI saint ABDUR RAHIM CHISTI (d. 1683). Literally 'Mirror of the Creatures', it is a translation and commentary into Persian of a Hindu text, consisting of a conversation between Mahadeva (SHIVA), PARVATI and VASISHTHA. In this work Abdur Rahim explains Hindu legends, though he is also at times critical of Hindu beliefs. He describes the various YUGAS, and says that Hindu deities were divine messengers who existed before the Prophet MUHAMMAD, and that the eternal truth, which was earlier manifested in Mahadeva and KRISHNA, attained its final form in Muhammad.

miri-piri   A term in Sikhism indicating that both temporal and spiritual power rests with the guru. It is said to have originated with the sixth guru, HARGOBIND, who wore two swords at the time of his initiation as guru, one representing his authority as the guru, and the other, the spiritual power of his ancestors.

Mishkatul Masabih   A text on HADIS, compiled by Shaikh Waliuddin Muhammad (d. 1342). Its name means 'Niche for Lamps' and it is based on an earlier work of Hadis known as the *Masabih ul-Sunnah* (Lamps of the Tradition), compiled by Imam Husain al-Baghawi (d. c. 1132), a Hadis scholar of the Shafi school. Waliuddin added a chapter to each section and revised the book, with the aim of providing an authoritative compendium of Hadis. It became a popular text used in SUNNI seminaries in India. Several commentaries were written on it, most notable among them being that of Shaikh ABDUL HAQQ Muhaddis Dihlawi, who wrote commentaries both in Persian and Arabic, in the time of the Mughal emperor AKBAR (ruled 1556–1605).

Mishnah   A Jewish text compiled at the end of the second century CE by Rabbi Judah the Prince and his companions. It has six sections: agrarian laws and blessings; Chagim or festivals; laws regarding women; civil laws; holy things; laws regarding ritual purity. The TALMUD consists of commentaries on much of the *Mishnah*.

misls   A term in Sikhism for divisions of the Sikh army in the mid-eighteenth century. There were initially twelve misls: Bhangi, Ahluwalia, Ramgarhia, Suker-chakia, Kanheya, Nakkai, Phoolkia, Singhpuria, Nishania, Krora Singhia, Dulewalia and Shahid. Each misl was in charge of a particular area and at first had a democratic character. By the time of RANJIT SINGH, who belonged to the Sukerchakia misl, most of the misls were weak. Ranjit Singh eliminated the misls and established a unified Sikh kingdom, which he ruled from 1800 to 1839.

Mitakshara   A text dealing with Hindu law. It is a commentary by Vijnaneshvara on the *Yajnavalkya Smriti*, a DHARMA SHASTRA. It deals with customary Hindu laws and is used for laws of inheritance. Vijnaneshvara lived at the court of the Chalukya emperor Vikramaditya VI (c. 1075–1127).

Mithila   An ancient city, the capital of Videha, a region of north Bihar. It was the capital of King JANAKA, father of SITA, in the *Ramayana*. The area is still known as Mithila, and the story of RAMA and Sita is an integral part of life there, celebrated in traditional folk art and in songs.

Mithra   A YAZATA or minor Zoroastrian deity, similar to the Vedic MITRA. Mithra was a solar deity, who probably predated the *GATHAS*, though he is not mentioned in them. KHURSHED, the sun, is closely associated with Mithra, and in later texts, he is also one of those, along with Rashnu, who judges departed souls. After Alexander conquered Persia in the fourth century BCE, Mithra began to be worshipped in the Hellenic world, and later in the Roman empire. From the second century CE onwards, there are numerous dedicatory inscriptions to Mithra. In the third and fourth centuries CE, it became an important cult, a rival to Christianity. Two Roman emperors, Commodus and Julian, were followers of the cult. In 307, Diocletian built a temple to Mithra, 'Protector of the Empire,' on the Danube river. By now there were a number of myths associated with the deity. He was born of the earth, near a sacred stream, and under a sacred tree. In his hands he held a flaming torch and a knife. He killed the cosmic bull, whose blood fertilizes vegetation. Bull sacrifices took place, and Mithra killing the bull is depicted in Hellenic art. Mithra as the god of light was associated with Helios, the Greek sun god, and with Sol Invictus, the Roman deity. He is also associated with Anahita, a fertilizing deity.

mithuna   A term for a male and female couple, frequently depicted in temples. Mithuna images symbolize the divine union of male and female, and may be erotic. The YAB-YUM images of TIBETAN, BUDDHISM, though depicted somewhat differently, have a similar symbolism.

Mitra   A deity mentioned in the VEDAS, associated with the god VARUNA. In the RIG VEDA, he is said to 'bring men together uttering his voice', while other hymns state that he supports heaven and earth and sustains all gods. In the later BRAHMANAS, he is considered a god of the daytime. In some texts, Mitra is one of the ADITYAS.

He is similar to the Zoroastrian MITHRA, a god of light and of the sun, the guardian of friendship and faithfulness.

Mittani Inscription   An inscription with names of Rig Vedic deities found at Bogazkoi (present Bogazkale in Turkey), dating to the fourteenth century BCE. The Mittani state was established in this area in about

1500 BCE by the Hurrians, but they were defeated by the Hittites around 1380 BCE. An inscription recording an agreement between the two groups, includes as Mittani deities, names similar to INDRA, AGNI, MITRA, VARUNA and the ASHVINS. Some scholars feel that Rig Vedic Aryans ruled the Mittani kingdom, while others believe similar deities worshipped in different areas had a common origin.

mitzvah A term in Judaism for 'commandment'. According to tradition, there are 613 commandments in the Pentateuch, the first five books of the Hebrew BIBLE, which the Jews are required to obey. These include the Ten Commandments or Decalogue. The Ten Commandments are ethical precepts, while the rest relate to Jewish law, diet, ritual, festivals and ceremonies.

Not all mitzvah are followed today, and Reform Judaism has modified many of them.

Mizos, traditional religion Mizos, residents mainly of Mizoram, consist of a number of tribes who speak similar Mizo languages. Among them are the Kukis, Lushais, Pawis, Paithes, Raltes, Pang, Himars, Maras, Lakhars and others. Most Mizos are Christians, though there are other groups in the state, such as the Chakmas, who are Buddhists and speak the Chakma language. Despite the predominance of Christians, some aspects of Mizo traditional beliefs still co-exit with Christianity.

Mizos believed in a supreme god known as Pathian, as well as in nature spirits known as Huai. Illness or disease was believed to be the result of a Huai's evil influence, who then had to be propitiated with the offering of a pig, chicken or other animal. The priest or Puithiam had an important role, and made the offering amidst traditional chants.

Each family had a personal deity, a sort of guardian angel, a spirit who was always there to protect them. This was known as a Sakhua, and sacrifices and offerings had to be made to appease the spirit.

After death people went to Mitthikua, the dead men's village, on the other side of which was Pialral, the abode of bliss.

There was a strong code of ethics, of which the central theme was Tlawmngaihna, which meant that all should be kind, helpful and hospitable. Community work was practised, known as Hnatlang. There is a move to revive these practices today, while traditional festivals are still celebrated, mostly in connection with agriculture.

Chapchar Kut, a spring festival, takes place in March after clearing the land for cultivation (traditionally Mizos practised slash-and-burn cultivation, though now this is changing); Mimkut, the maize festival in August/September, occurs after the harvest of maize; Pawkut, another harvest festival, is in December/January.

Modhera Surya Temple A temple of the Hindu god SURYA, located at Modhera in Gujarat. It was constructed in the eleventh century, at the time of King Bhimadeva of the Solanki dynasty. The main temple has an inner shrine, a closed MANDAPA and a porch. There is also a large detached hall, known as the sabha mandapa, with central pillars arranged in an octagon. Nearby is a tank with miniature shrines. The tower of the temple, here known as the jangha, has numerous sculptures, including several of Surya. This intricately carved temple is one of the most beautiful in the state.

Mohini The Hindu god VISHNU in female form. When the ocean was churned for AMRITA, Vishnu took this form to distract the ASURAS, who had stolen it, so that the DEVAS could retrieve it. In another story, VISHNU took the form of Mohini to test the chastity of a group of RISHIS living in the Darukavana (Daruka forest).

He took this form on other occasions, and the god AYYAPPA is the son of Vishnu in the form of Mohini, with SHIVA as the father. AYYANAR in Tamil Nadu is a similar deity.

Various gods, such as Indra, also assume female forms at times. Such instances are described in the myths of other countries as well. For instance, the Scandinavian god Thor became a beautiful woman and thus cheated the giants of their fee, after the building of Valhalla.

moksha A Sanskrit term, implying liberation or release from the cycle of birth and death. It has different connotations in the various philosophical schools of Hinduism. In ADVAITA Vedanta, moksha implies union with the One Reality, BRAHMAN, where the individuality disappears. In VAISHNAVISM and SHAIVISM, it indicates a close association with the deity of one's choice, while individual consciousness is retained. The term moksha is also used in Buddhism and Jainism, and is similar to the concept of NIRVANA in Buddhism. Ancient materialistic schools denied the concept of moksha, while the twentieth-century philosopher Sri AUROBINDO believed that the goal of life was not moksha, but evolution to a higher state.

Monserrate, Father Antonio A Jesuit priest who visited the court of the Mughal emperor AKBAR. Akbar, who wished to understand all religions, asked the Portuguese to send some Christian priests to his court. Three priests arrived at his court in 1580: Father AQUAVIVA, Father Monserrate and Father Henriques. Monserrate lived there for several years, joined in discussions at the court, and taught Portuguese to Prince Murad, Akbar's second son. He wrote a book in Latin, called *Commentarius*, about his mission and his work; it includes a description of Akbar's court and the life and customs of the people.

Montecorvino, Giovanni da One of the earliest ROMAN CATHOLIC missionaries in India. Born in Sicily in 1247, he joined the Franciscan order and was sent to attempt to unify the Greek and Roman churches in Asia. From Armenia and Persia, he moved into south

India and wrote an account of the Coromandel Coast in 1292–93. He recorded the existence of NESTORIAN Christians in India and set up a Roman Catholic mission. He soon moved on to China and was made Archbishop of Peking (Beijing) and Patriarch of the Orient. He died in Beijing in 1328.

Moplahs *See* Mappila.

Moral Rearmament A Christian movement that was promoted in India in the 1960s and early 70s. It was founded in the 1920s by Frank N.D. Buchman (1878–1961), a Lutheran from the USA, and gradually spread to other parts of the world. Its aim was to bring about a moral regeneration by asking people to cultivate moral principles and values, and to pledge themselves to the 'Four Absolutes' of honesty, purity, unselfishness and love.

Moreshvara Temple A temple of the Hindu god GANESHA located at Morgaon in Maharashtra. It is the most important of the Ashtavinayaka temples, i.e., the eight temples specially dedicated to the worship of Ganesha in this state. According to a legend, in one incarnation in the TRETA YUGA, Ganesha broke an egg laid by Vinita, mother of GARUDA. A peacock (mor or mayura) emerged and attacked him, but then became his disciple or vehicle. In this place, therefore, Ganesha took the name Moreshvara or Mayureshvara, lord of the peacock, though usually it is his brother KARTTIKEYA who is associated with a peacock.

According to tradition, the Moreshvara or Mayureshvara Temple was constructed by Moreshvara Gole, a local official, probably in the eighteenth century. It is built on a platform about 4.5 m high. Outside is a shrine with a large image of a mouse, Ganesha's vehicle, and also a large NANDI. Within the temple, in the garbha-griha or inner shrine, is a large four-armed Ganesha image with Siddhi and Buddhi, his two wives, on either side. The image is somewhat roughly made, known as a svayambhu, or self-created image. In front are sculptures of a mouse and a peacock. There are two MANDAPAS or halls, within which are images of Ganesha in different forms, as well as additional shrines, including one of a guardian deity, Nagnabhairava. Other shrines include those of Moraya Gosavi, a devotee of the fifteenth century, and Shri Ganesh Yogindra, who compiled the *MAUDGALYA PURANA*. This is one of the most popular Ganesha temples, visited by pilgrims throughout the year.

Morya, Master A guru revered by Theosophists. He was one of the two gurus of the astral world said to be in charge of India, the other being Master KUTHUMI. Morya had the body of a Rajput prince and was the guide of Madame BLAVATSKY.

mosques, architecture Mosques in India are said to date back to the seventh century, but the earliest extant mosques are from the end of the twelfth century. Mosques follow the general plan of these structures elsewhere in the world, but also have indigenous features.

In general, a mosque consists of an open courtyard enclosed by colonnades on three sides, and a prayer hall on the fourth. The hall may be open, supported by pillars, or enclosed, and often has a domed roof. One or more MINARETS usually form part of the structure. Within the mosque is the MIHRAB, or prayer niche, indicating the QIBLA, or direction facing which prayers are to be offered. There is also a MIMBAR, a pulpit or platform where the KHATIB or preacher gives his sermon. In the courtyard is a well or fountain, providing water for ablutions.

The earliest mosques, such as the QUWWATUL ISLAM MOSQUE at DELHI and the ARHAI-DIN-KA JHONPRA MOSQUE at Ajmer, both from the last decade of the twelfth century, have indigenous aspects, particularly in the dome and corbelled arches, and even in the structure of the walls, pillar capitals and ceilings. By the thirteenth century, mosques were being built in Islamic style, such as the Jamaat-Khana Mosque in Delhi, though this has only a prayer hall without a courtyard. Under the Tughlaq dynasty (1320–1413), the Delhi mosques looked almost like fortresses, with arches at the entrance, thick walls, sloping minaret-like buttresses, and multi-domed roofs. Inside they were decorated with paintings and coloured tiles. Mosques of the later Lodi and Sur dynasties, such as the Bara Gumbad, MOTH KI MASJID and QALA-I-KUHNA MOSQUE are more refined, with better building material and rich decoration.

Other types of mosques include:

Mughal mosques The emperors of the Mughal dynasty were great builders of all kinds of structures. The true dome, little known in India earlier, was commonly used, but there were indigenous features as well, particularly the narrow pillars, corbel brackets and ornamental features. Mosques were located in symmetrical gardens with fountains, flowers and trees. In AKBAR's time, architecture at Fatehpur Sikri, included Hindu, Iranian and Turkish influences. The Jami Masjid here is a notable mosque, while in some structures there were gods of other religions. Thus the Panch Mahal, a five-storeyed palace, had paintings of RAMA and HANUMAN, whereas MARY and JESUS were depicted elsewhere. Akbar also allowed the use of plants, flowers and animals in decoration, a practice frowned upon in traditional Islam.

Shah Jahan (ruled 1627–58), the greatest builder, constructed most of his monuments in white marble, among these being the TAJ MAHAL and the MOTI MASJID (1654) at Agra. The mosque at this time was refined and delicate, the arches with a multi-foil or cusped shape, pillars with many-sided tapering shafts and foliated bases, and bulbous domes. Some mosques had lavish pietra dura work or inlay of semi-precious stones, in black or white marble. During the time of AURANGZEB, architectural monuments declined, but his Moti Masjid built in DELHI fort in 1659, and the Badshahi Mosque at Lahore (1673–74) are notable.

Regional mosques   There were also regional mosque building styles. In Bengal, the earliest extant mosque, the ADINA MASJID at Pandua (1369), is in standard imperial style, but later mosques were in both orthodox and regional styles. Most were built of brick; some had decorated terracotta panels on the walls. The Jaunpur style, developed under the Sharqi rulers (c. 1394–1484), had an orthodox plan with large dimensions, and no surface decoration. Gujarat mosques are built mainly of stone and are both of orthodox and single-prayer-hall type, but have indigenous features, with pillars and lintels, arches and domes. The prayer hall often has a clerestory in the centre, with perforated stone screens all round. The minarets are tall and graceful, with delicately carved stone surfaces.

Malwa mosques are similar to those of the Tughlaqs, and include MALIK MUGHIS' MOSQUE and the Jami Masjid at Mandu.

Mosques in the Bahmani kingdom in the Deccan had Persian features. After the kingdom broke up, each of the resulting five kingdoms constructed mosques with different features. Mosques in the Bijapur kingdom had almost spherical domes, with a band of petals encircling the drum, tall and slender minarets and projecting cornices on intricately carved brackets. Golkonda mosques had rich surface decoration in cut plaster, as well as small turrets and cupolas used for decorative effect.

In Kashmir, mosques were constructed of wood and had pyramidal roofs in tiers, crowned by a spire. In Kerala too, some mosques were built of wood.

Modern mosques   Mosques today are constructed in different styles, both small and large, but the more popular and prominent mosques are those dating back to medieval times.

Moth ki Masjid   A mosque located in Moth village in New DELHI. It was constructed by Miyan Bhuiya, the prime minister of Sultan Sikandar Lodi (ruled 1488–1517). According to the story connected with the origin of the mosque, it was built from the money gained by the sale of moth (lentils). Sultan Sikandar is said to have given a single grain of moth to the minister, who sowed it. Soon it multiplied, so that he had a whole field, and its sale generated enough for the mosque.

The structure is built with red sandstone, white marble and coloured tiles. To the east is an ornamental gate. The mosque is to the west of a raised platform, enclosed by a low wall, with arched cells in front. The front angles have octagonal kiosks once inlaid with blue tiles. The prayer-hall is rectangular, about 38 m by 8 m with five arched openings, while the roof has three domes. The MIHRAB has inscriptions from the QURAN. Despite its relatively early date, the mosque has many features of the later mosques of Mughal days.

mother goddess   A type of deity commonly worshipped in India. 'Mother goddess' is a broad term used for most female deities, representing fertility and feminine energy or SHAKTI. She can also literally be a 'mother' figure, surrounded by children. Some scholars trace the worship of such deities back to the INDUS CIVILIZATION or even earlier. Mother goddesses are common in Hinduism and in Buddhism. They may be referred to by their individual names or known by generic terms such as Ma, Mata, Amma, or Devi. In Hinduism, a specific group of such goddesses are known as MATRIKAS.

Mother, The   The name by which Mirra Richard, the companion of Sri AUROBINDO, was known. Mirra Alfassa was born in Paris in 1878, and was the second child of an Egyptian mother and a Turkish father who settled in France. She had spiritual experiences even as a child, and in her twenties, she studied occultism and worked with different spiritual groups. She heard of Sri Aurobindo in 1912, and in 1914, visited him in Puducherry (Pondicherry) along with her second husband, Paul Richard. She recognized Aurobindo as the guru she had seen in her dreams. She returned in April 1920 to join him in Puducherry and lived there for the rest of her life. She took charge of his followers, and from 1926 organized his ashram, continuing his work after his death in 1950. In 1952 she set up the Sri Aurobindo International Centre of Education to provide a different kind of education to young people. In 1968 she founded the international township of AUROVILLE.

She continued Sri Aurobindo's work for the manifestation of a higher consciousness, termed the 'Supermind' or 'the Supramental', which would result not only in a new species, greater than the human beings of today, but in a modification of all creation. She wrote commentaries on Sri Aurobindo's teachings, and her collected works run into over thirty volumes. Speaking of the new consciousness, the Mother said, in words similar to J. KRISHNAMURTI, 'The failure of religions is . . . because they were divided. They wanted people to be religious to the exclusion of other religions, and every branch of knowledge has been a failure because it has been exclusive. What the new consciousness wants (it is on this that it insists) is: no more divisions.'

From 1958 she became deeply involved in 'Yoga of the body', an experiment in the transformation of the physical cells in the body. An account of her experiences in the course of this work is given in *The Mother's Agenda*, a thirteen-volume work. She died at Puducherry on 17 November 1973.

Moti Bagh Gurdwara   A GURDWARA or Sikh shrine located at Moti Bagh, New Delhi, associated with Guru GOBIND SINGH. He came here in 1707 to help Prince Muazzam, later the Mughal emperor Bahadur Shah I, in his struggle for the throne. From here the guru shot two arrows to the Red Fort. The first announced his arrival, the message on the second said, 'It is not magic, but skill in archery'. A gurdwara was built around the platform from where he shot the arrows. Later, a new marble gurdwara was constructed here, though the old one is still preserved.

Moti Masjid, Agra   A mosque constructed in the seventeenth century by the Mughal emperor Shah Jahan. The 'Pearl Mosque' at AGRA, in Uttar Pradesh, is one of the most beautiful specimens of Mughal architecture. It took seven years to build and was completed in 1665. The mosque, located in Agra Fort, is made of white marble, erected on a red sandstone platform. The open courtyard is about 48 m each side enclosed by low arched cloisters. On the west is the prayer hall, which has seven arched openings and three domes. Inside there are rows of arches emerging from massive piers, intersecting to form the ceiling vaults, and four octagonal kiosks at each corner of the hall. The main entrance is on the east, approached through two flights of stairs.

There are other mosques known as Moti Masjid, including those at DELHI and Bhopal.

Mount Malayattoor, Church of   A Christian shrine located in the hill ranges of Kerala, dedicated to ST. THOMAS, an Apostle of Christ. According to tradition, St. Thomas came to the region in 52 CE and meditated at this spot, in the midst of thick forests. After his death, a cross and perennial spring were found here, and a shrine was built. It has been reconstructed several times after being damaged by wild elephants, and remains an important centre of pilgrimage. MASS is conducted here on Sundays by a priest of a parish located nearby, and an annual festival takes place on the first Sunday after EASTER, visited by thousands of pilgrims. Several people come here to seek the blessings of the saint, particularly the newly-wed among the Syrian Catholics.

mountains, sacred   Mountains are considered sacred, particularly in Hinduism, Buddhism, Jainism and tribal religions. Other religions too, have stories regarding the sanctity of specific mountains. As mountains and hills rise above the land, they symbolize the yearning of the soul for the divine. Practically all hills, hillocks and mountains are considered sacred, with one or more shrines built upon them, but some have a special sanctity.

Mountains considered specially sacred in Hinduism are MERU or Sumeru and Mt KAILASHA, also sacred to Buddhists and Jains. KEDARNATH, BADRINATH, NANDA DEVI, Chitrakut, Mahendragiri, MANDARA and GOVARDHAN are among the many others. Mountains sacred to Jains include the PARASNATH hill in Bihar, SHATRUNJAYA in Gujarat and Mt ABU in Rajasthan, as well as the Indragiri and Chandragiri hills at SHRAVANABELAGOLA in Karnataka.

There are myths and legends about mountains, which are often personified. Thus HIMAVAN, personifying the Himalayas, was married to Mena, and was the father of Parvati.

A myth in the Puranas recounts that in the KRITA YUGA, all mountains had wings, and flew over the earth as swift as VAYU, the wind. The DEVAS and RISHIS were afraid of them, because at any minute they could land on their heads and squash them. They complained to the god INDRA, who began cutting off the wings of the mountains. Only the mountain MAINAKA escaped.

Mrigavati   A story reflecting SUFI ideals, written in 1503 in Hindi by Shaikh Qutb Ali Qutban, a SUHRAWARDI saint. The story is based on a local folktale about the love between Mrigavati and the prince Raj Kunwar. On his death Mrigavati and the prince's other wife, Rukmini, both commit SATI. The introduction states that Mrigavati represents eternal beauty, a symbol of the divine, and explains the story in a Sufi context, while using Hindu terms.

muazzin/muezzin   A term in Islam for the person who calls the faithful to prayer by reciting the AZAN. In Islam prayer is obligatory five times in every twenty-four hours. At these times, the muazzin calls from the MINARET of large mosques, or the door of small mosques, or any high point near a mosque. The call begins with the Arabic words, 'Allahu Akbar', or 'God is great'.

Mubarak Ghazi   A local Islamic deity once popular among woodcutters and fishermen in the Sunderbans region of Bengal. Mobrah or Mubarak Ghazi was said to have been a FAQIR who rode a tiger in the forest, and whom all the animals obeyed. The local ruler therefore said that every village should have a shrine dedicated to him. Woodcutters never ventured into the forest without praying to Ghazi, and faqirs would accompany them to mark out a circle where they could work, safeguarding that area with magical chants. It was a syncretic cult, as Jagbandhu (lord of the world, VISHNU), Mahadeva (SHIVA), MANASA Devi and other deities were worshipped alongside Ghazi.

The cult must have emerged because of the nature of the tigers in the region, which are known to be particularly ferocious. A similar deity was Baghai Devata, who was worshipped right across the Himalayan foothills.

Mudabadri   A town in Karnataka, a sacred centre for Jains. A Jain temple, the Parshvanatha Basadi, was established here in the early eighth century, but Mudabadri became a major centre of Jainism a little later, from the thirteenth to the seventeenth centuries. At this time a number of temples were constructed, of which the most notable is the thousand-pillared temple, known as the Tribhuvana-Tilaka-Chudamani, built by a group of Jain merchants in 1430. These temples also stored important Jain manuscripts. A large BAHUBALI image is erected here.

mudra   (1) A symbolic gesture or position of the fingers or hands that conveys a meaning. Images of deities depict different types of mudras, such as abhaya-mudra, to dispel fear, or varada-mudra to indicate granting of boons. Mudras are used in meditation, to bring about a particular state of mind. In classical dance forms, mudras convey an idea or indicate an animal, such as a deer in the forest or some other object.

(2) In yoga, particularly HATHA YOGA, mudras are certain specific postures or techniques, used along with ASANAS and PRANAYAMA for self-transformation. Mudras include bandhas or locks, which are methods of controlling PRANA, the breath. Using mudras leads to fortitude, steadiness and better health, and helps in arousing the KUNDALINI.

mufti A term in Islam for a specialist in Islamic law who gives a legal opinion or FATWA on a question raised.

Muhammad The founder of the religion of Islam. Muhammad was born in Mecca in 570, in the Arab Quraishi tribe, and was the son of Abdullah of the Hashimite clan. His father died before he was born, and his mother died when he was six years old. Two years later, his grandfather, who was taking care of him, died. He was brought up by his paternal uncle, Abu Talib, and later worked for Khadija, a wealthy widow, managing her caravans and trade. After some time, in 595, he married Khadija, who was fifteen years older than him, and settled in Mecca. He was spiritually inclined, and when in retreat at Mt Hira (near Mecca), the angel Jibril (Gabriel) appeared to him and began to reveal the word of God, later written down as the QURAN. The first revelation took place in 610, in the month of RAMZAN. The angel conveyed to him that there was only one God, ALLAH, and that Muhammad was his messenger or Prophet. His first converts were Khadija, his cousin and son-in-law Ali, and Abu Bakr, who later became the Caliph. As Muhammad's influence grew, the Quraish in Mecca, who were in positions of power, turned against him, as his message threatened their way of life and worship. Both Abu Talib, who had been his protector, and Khadija died in 1619, after which Muhammad faced more problems. He was then invited by the people of Yasrib (later Medina) to head the community there. Muhammad went to Yasrib along with some followers, and the date of his departure (HIJRAH) from Mecca in 622, marks the beginning of the Islamic era. Muhammad now began to gain more followers, married women of different groups to gain their allegiance, and gave his three daughters in marriage to three of his closest disciples. A conflict now started between the people of Mecca and Muhammad and his followers, as Mecca and Medina had emerged as rival centres of power. After a series of successful battles, Muhammad re-entered Mecca in 630, destroyed the idols in the KABA, and established it as the centre of Islamic pilgrimage. He then sent letters to neighbouring rulers, promising them safety if they became his followers. By the time of his death in 632 most of Arabia was unified under Islam, through a combination of military expeditions and marriage alliances.

During his lifetime, Muhammad made significant social and administrative reforms, putting an end to tribal warfare and revenge killings, and granting women certain rights that improved their condition in those days.

He continued to receive divine revelations, which were compiled in the Quran. Each action of his was believed to be worthy of emulation, and was remembered by his followers, later forming the HADIS and the basis for the SUNNAH. Thus Muhammad laid the basis for a new reformist religion that came to be known as Islam.

Muhammad Abid, Haji Syed A SUFI saint of the Chisti SABIRI order, who was also attached to the DAR-UL-ULOOM, Deoband, and was for some years its manager. Born in 1834, he studied the QURAN and Persian, before proceeding for higher studies to DELHI. There, however, he was drawn to the Sufi path, and became the disciple of various Sufi saints, including Mianji Karim Baksh Rampuri and Hazrat Haji Imdadullah Mahajir-e Makki, acquiring the Khilafat (succession) from both of them. He lived in the Chhata Mosque for sixty years, never missing the daily prayers, and was renowned for the amulets he gave to those in need, which were said to have great healing power.

Muhammad Abid was manager of the Dar-ul-Uloom in 1866–67, 1869–71, and 1890–92. After this, he continued with his spiritual pursuits, until his death in 1912.

Muhammad Ghaus, Shaikh A sixteenth-century SUFI saint who belonged to the SHATTARI order. Muhammad Ghaus was the younger brother of Shaikh Phul, a noted saint whose disciple was the Mughal emperor Humayun. Shaikh Phul had been killed by Humayun's brother Hindal. Both Ghaus and his brother, were disciples of Shaikh Zuhur Hajjid Hamid, who specialized in mysticism.

After meditating for many years in the Chunar caves in Mirzapur (southern Uttar Pradesh), Muhammad Ghaus settled in Gwalior. He temporarily moved to Gujarat at the time of Afghan rule under Sher Shah (1540–45), but returned to Gwalior later. There he owned a large tract of land, as well as cattle and other livestock. In his KHANQAH, he taught the mystical techniques described in his book, the *JAWAHIR-I KHAMSA*. His other works include the *Bahrul-hayat*, the *Kalid-i Makhazin*, the *Zamair*, the *Basair*, the *Kamzul Wahdat*, and the *Risala-i Mirajiyya*. In the *Risala* he claimed he could ascend to heaven and converse with God, and therefore was condemned by the ULAMA and the orthodox. He died in 1563, and an imposing tomb was built over his grave in Gwalior. Muhammad Ghaus was one of the most influential Shattaris.

Muhammad Ishaq, Shah A noted HADIS scholar of the nineteenth century, the grandson of Shah Abdul Aziz and great-grandson of Shah WALIULLAH. He took over the Madrasa Rahima from Shah Abdul Aziz and taught there until he migrated in 1841 to Mecca, where he died a few years later. He translated the MISHKATUL MASABIH into Urdu. With the addition of a commentary added by his pupil Maulana Qutbuddin Khan, this text is known as the *Mazahir-e Haq*. His other works include the *Miat Masail* and *Rasail-e Arbin*.

Muhammad Qasim Nanautavi, Maulana An Islamic scholar, who was one of the main founders of the DAR-UL-ULOOM Deoband. Born at Nanauta near Saharanpur in 1832, he was educated at Deoband, Saharanpur and DELHI, and also studied HADIS with Hazrat Shah Abdul Ghani Mujaddidi, the successor of MUHAMMAD ISHAQ at Abdul Aziz's MADRASA. Thus he was well-trained in Hadis and in the teachings of Shah WALIULLAH, and was soon considered as learned as Muhammad Ishaq.

Muhammad Qasim worked in an Islamic press in Delhi and later in Meerut, collating and editing Islamic texts, and simultaneously taught Hadis. In 1857 he took part in the revolt against British rule.

Seeing the decline of Islam in India and the challenges it faced at this time from Christian missionaries, he helped to establish a number of MADRASAS, the most prominent being the Dar-ul-Uloom. In the Dar-ul-Uloom he developed the teaching of Hadis from original sources instead of translations, and favoured the HANAFI school of law. He joined in public debates with Christian and Arya Samaj preachers, putting forward the Islamic point of view. He is considered one of the greatest Islamic scholars, who strictly followed the SHARIA and SUNNAH. He died in 1880 at the age of forty-nine.

Muharram The first month of the Islamic calendar, which is considered specially sacred. In this month certain special events are said to have taken place, including the acceptance of the vows of Adam by ALLAH, the freeing of Moses and his followers from the persecution of the Pharaoh of Egypt, and the disembarcation of Noah from his ark.

This month also commemorates the martyrdom of Hasan and HUSAIN, the grandsons of the Prophet MUHAMMAD. It is a month of mourning and fasting, particularly for SHIAS. *Majlises* (congregations) meet and *marsias* (elegies) are recited, about Husain's life, the events of the battlefield of Karbala, and his death. The historic battle of Karbala took place between Yazid, son of Muawiya of the Umayyid dynasty, and Husain, ending in the tragic death of Husain and his followers. They were encircled on the plains of Karbala from the first day of Muharram, and denied even water in the last few days.

Shias also mourn Hasan, who was poisoned earlier. Shia women break their bangles and remove their ornaments, as they do when a death occurs. Both Sunnis and Shias observe the tenth day, ASHURA as a day of mourning, as this was the day on which Husain was killed. Mourners take out processions with TAZIYAS (models of Husain's tomb), *alams* (the standards of his army), as well as models of his horse, Duldul. While walking, they cry out, 'Ya Hasan! Ya Husain!' Identifying with Husain's suffering, they beat themselves with whips and cut themselves with swords. Later, the taziyas are buried in Muslim graveyards.

In earlier times it was common for Hindus to join in these processions.

Muhibullah, Shaikh An Islamic thinker who lived in the seventeenth century (d. 1648) and wrote on similarities between Hinduism and Islam. His *Risala-i Taswiyya* (Treatise on Equality), was condemned by the orthodox during his lifetime, and later by AURANGZEB. Shaikh Muhibullah emphasized the similarities between SUFI and yogic practices, and believed there was much to be learnt from yogis.

muhpatti A white cloth worn across the mouth by SHVETAMBARA Jain ascetics to prevent them from breathing in insects or minuscule forms of life, or to prevent pollution while performing rituals. All Shvetambara ascetics wear them while performing rituals, while the Sthanakavasi and Terapanthi ascetics wear them constantly.

Zoroastrian priests wear a similar cloth while performing rituals. Both Jains and Zoroastrians were once prominent in Gujarat, and thus may have influenced each other.

Muinuddin Chisti, Hazrat A SUFI saint who founded the CHISTI order in India. Born in 1142 in Sijistan, he traced his descent from the Prophet MUHAMMAD. Always religiously inclined, he left home at the age of fifteen and went to Bukhara, where he studied Islam with learned ULAMA. It is likely that he came to India in 1191 and after staying in Multan, Lahore and Samana, reached Delhi in 1206. Later he went to Ajmer, where he married and settled down. According to other accounts, he reached Ajmer in 1191, when Prithviraj Chauhan was ruling there, and was not welcomed, but by performing a number of miracles, gained the confidence of the people. Among his miracles were the changing of a revered idol into a human being, who then recited the KALIMA or Islamic creed. He is also said to have caused the defeat and capture of Prithviraj by the invader Muhammad Ghori in retaliation for Prithviraj's animosity toward him. (Prithviraj was defeated in 1192, though he continued to rule at Ajmer for some time after this). These are probably later legends, created both to add sanctity to the saint, and to provide legitimacy to Islamic rule.

Some of Muinuddin's sayings have survived and show that he was a simple, pious man, with an awareness of mystical truths.

Khwaja Muinuddin died in 1236, and by this time had acquired a large following. His main disciples included Sheikh QUTBUDDIN BAKHTIYAR KAKI (d. 1235) and Sheikh HAMIDUDDIN (d. 1267). The Mughal emperor frequently visited Muinuddin's tomb, and had a mosque built nearby.

Muinuddin's DARGAH at Ajmer is perhaps the most popular SUFI shrine in India, visited by Hindu and Muslim pilgrims even today. Thousands come here, particularly at the time of his URS or death anniversary, which takes place in the first six days of the Islamic month of Rajab. Prayers and requests made to him are said to be miraculously granted.

mujadid A term in Islam for one who reforms or renews the faith. Among those known as Mujadid in India were AHMAD SIRHINDI (1564–1624) and Mirza GHULAM AHMAD, founder of the AHMADIYA sect. There were several others who used this title.

mujahid A term in Islam for one who struggles against unbelievers on behalf of the religion. It comes from an Arabic word meaning to 'exert oneself vigorously against, to fight against'.

mujtahid A term in Islam for one who is well versed in canon law. Among SUNNIS it refers to the founders of the four orthodox schools of law (FIQH). Among SHIAS, the mujtahid, through IJTIHAD or effort, can formulate new rules based on the QURAN and SUNNAH.

Muktad A ritual in Zoroastrianism, practised by PARSIS, in which prayers are offered for the Fravashis of ancestors or others who have died, and for the FRAVASHIS of all righteous souls. Ten days of prayers take place before the Zoroastrian new year, beginning on Roz Ashtad, the twenty-sixth day of the last month of Spendarmad, until the day of the *Vahishtoishti Gatha*. On the last day the Fravashis are said to descend to earth and bless those who offer prayers. In Zoroastrian temples, silver vases containing flowers are marked with the name of the person prayed for. Some offer the prayers in their own homes. The concept is similar to the SHRADDHA ceremonies in Hinduism and the term Muktad is said to be derived from the Sanskrit 'mukti-atma' or liberation.

The Muktad ceremonies take place at different times, depending on the calendar used (see ZOROASTRIAN CALENDAR).

Muktananda, Swami A guru or teacher of SIDDHA YOGA who popularized this system in the West. Born in 1908, he became a disciple of Swami NITYANANADA, after meeting him in 1947. In 1970 he went to the USA to convey his teachings and founded a large organization there. Branches soon spread to other countries. After his death in 1982, he was succeeded by Swami Chidvilasananda.

Mukteshvara Temple A temple dedicated to the Hindu god SHIVA, located in Bhubaneswar in Orissa, constructed in c. 975 at the time of the Eastern Ganga dynasty. The inner shrine houses a LINGA, and above the doorway are an image of LAKSHMI and a NAVAGRAHA panel. The temple is small, only 13.5 by 7.5 m, with a tower of 10.5 m, but is intricately carved. The attached MANDAPA has a pyramidal roof.

The whole is surrounded by an enclosure with other small shrines. The gateway on the west is decorated with reliefs of plants, reclining women, and human heads in medallions. The walls have women or YAKSHIS standing under trees, and NAGAS or snakes wound around pillars. On the ceiling are gods and goddesses, warriors and VIDYADHARAS.

Muktsar A town in Punjab, sacred to Sikhs. It gets its name from the Muktas or 'liberated' Sikhs, martyrs who died fighting against Wazir Khan, the nawab of Sirhind. The battle took place in 1705, and the Sikh forces were led by Guru GOBIND SINGH. The Shahid Ganj Gurdwara was built here in honour of the martyrs, and thousands of pilgrims come here every year. Other GURDWARAS in the town include the Tibbi Sahib Gurudwara, located at the Tibbi or mound from where the Guru shot arrows at the Mughal forces; the Tambu Sahib Gurdwara, in memory of a ruse of the Sikh soldiers, who made bushes look like tambus or tents; and the Darbar Sahib Gurdwara, first constructed in 1743 and rebuilt in the 1980s.

Mula Suttas (Mula Sutras) A group of Jain texts of the SHVETAMBARA canon. They are: *Uttarajjhayana (Uttaradhyayana); Avassaya (Avashyaka); Dasaveyaliya (Dashavaikalika); and Pimdanijjutti (Pinda-Niryukti)*. The last sometimes appears in the list of CHEYA SUTTAS, while some give the third and fourth Mula Suttas as *Ohanijjuti (Ogha-Niryukti)* and *Pakkhi (Pakshika Sutra)*, respectively.

Muladhara Chakra One of the seven main CHAKRAS or hidden energy centres within the body. The Muladhara Chakra, at the base of the spine, is described in texts as a lotus of four crimson-red (shona) petals with the Sanskrit letters va, sha (palatal), sha (cerebral), and sa, in colours of gold. In the centre is a yellow square or cube, signifying the earth. Eight spears or arrows point outwards from it. Within it is a lightning-like triangle, and within that is the Svayambhu (self-created) LINGA, dark in colour, with the KUNDALINI coiled three-and-a-half times around it. Meditating on this one becomes lord of speech, an adept in all types of learning. One is free of all diseases, and the inner self or ATMAN is filled with joy.

mulla A title in Islam, for a spiritual teacher or preacher. It is also used for instructors in MADRASAS.

Mulla Feroze A renowned PARSI scholar who lived from 1758 to 1830. The son of Kaus bin Rustam Jalal of a DASTUR (priestly) family of Bharuch, Gujarat, he was initially named Peshotan. At a young age he accompanied his father to Iran, where Kaus had been sent with a list of questions to be answered by the learned Dasturs of Iran. The father and son spent twelve years in Iran, and during this time Peshotan studied various languages, including AVESTA and PAHLAVI, as well as Zoroastrian and other scriptures. At one time, studying in an Islamic MADRASA in Ifsahan when he was about twelve years old, he surpassed all the other students and thus was named 'Feroze' or 'victorious'. Later, the Caliph of Baghdad, impressed by their erudition and learning, conferred on both father and son the honorary title of MULLA, normally given to learned Muslim ULAMA.

On returning to India, Mulla Kaus started a Kadimi ATASH BEHRAM in Mumbai (consecrated in 1783), and became its first Dastur. Mulla Feroze brought back to India a number of rare books and manuscripts, and continued to acquire more, soon founding a vast library. He became a trader and businessman, but also continued with his scholarly studies, taught Persian, and even wrote a Persian epic in verse about the British in India, known as the *George Namah*. His other scholarly works include the *Pand Nameh-e Mulla Feroze* and the *Din-e-Khered-e-Mauzume*, which provide answers to the questions his father had taken to Iran; a brief autobiography, *Kuliyat-e-Farsi*; and several other books. Mulla Feroze also succeeded his father as Dastur.

The Mulla Feroze Madressa for teaching Avesta was established in his memory in 1854. In 1916, his valuable library was relocated to the K.R. Cama Oriental Institute, which is named after another noted Parsi scholar.

Mumbai   A major city, the capital of the state of Maharashtra, and India's financial capital. This vibrant and fast-paced city is also known for its Hindu and Jain temples, mosques, churches, synagogues and Zoroastrian fire temples. Buddhism was once prominent in the region, and though it had declined and almost disappeared, it was revived by neo-Buddhists in the late 1950s.

Mumbai, then known as Bombay, developed as a city only from the seventeenth century, when it came under the British, but the area was occupied from ancient days. The early Buddhist rock-cut caves at KANHERI are about 42 km away, while there are Hindu cave temples at ELEPHANTA Island nearby, dating from the sixth century CE.

The city is named after a local goddess, Mumba Devi, initially worshipped by Koli fishermen, but now popular with other groups as well. An earlier temple of the goddess was destroyed in 1737 and a new one was later constructed. Among hundreds of other temples, those of the Hindu goddess MAHALAKSHMI, the SIDDHI VINAYAKA (Ganesha) Temple and the Valkeshvara Temple are significant. The latter was constructed at a spot where RAMA is said to have worshipped a LINGA that he made from sand (valkeshvara = sand god). The Surya Narayana temple, built of white stone and constructed in 1899, the Babulnath Temple, where SHIVA is worshipped as Babulnath, and the ISKCON Hare Krishna Temple are among other popular shrines.

There are several Jain temples, of which the marble temple constructed in 1904 on Malabar hill is one of the best.

Among notable Islamic shrines are the Jumma Masjid, HAJI ALI Dargah, and the shrine of Makhdum Fakir Ali Paru, who died in 1413.

There are a number of churches, including the AFGHAN Church, also known as St. John's Church, and several churches of Mother Mary, the Mount Mary Church at Bandra being one of the most popular. The St. Thomas Cathedral was opened to the public in 1718.

Once the centre of BENE ISRAEL, BAGHDADI and other Jews, there are old synagogues in the city. It is also home to the majority of Parsi Zoroastrians, and among Zoroastrian temples there are four ATASH BEHRAMS and forty-six others, more than in any other city.

In addition, Mumbai has been a focal point of the DALIT movement associated with B.R. AMBEDKAR, and lakhs of dalits pay homage to Ambedkar on his birth anniversary, and on the anniversary of his conversion to Buddhism.

Mundas, religion of   A tribal group found mainly in south Bihar and central India, Mundas worship a number of deities, of whom Sing Bonga is the supreme being. Among others, the guardian deities of the village, known as Hatubongako, play an important part in daily life, and are worshipped for prosperity and a good harvest. The Orabongako are household deities and spirits of ancestors. After the death of a person, a ritual takes place to enshrine their spirit in the house in which they once lived. These ancestors are then considered powerful protectors.

There are also nature spirits, including spirits of trees, streams and mountains. The Pahan or village priest plays an important part in religious rituals.

muni   A term for a sage or RISHI, a holy or learned person.

Muntazar, Muhammad al   The twelfth Shia Imam, who according to the ISNA ASHARI Shias, will finally reappear as the MAHDI. He disappeared in 878, and remains hidden since then.

murid   A term in Islam for a disciple of a SUFI master. The master is known as a SHAIKH, MURSHID or PIR.

murshid   One of the terms in Islam for a SUFI master or spiritual teacher.

murti   A Sanskrit word for an image or form of the divine.

Murti Pujaka   A SHVETAMBARA sect of Jainism. They are so-called because they worship idols (*murtis*) of the TIRTHANKARAS and their attendants, adorn them with rich clothes and jewels, and make offerings to them of flowers, fruit, saffron, and incense. Ascetics of this sect stay in temples or in special residences termed upasrayas.

Murti Pujakas are alternatively referred to as Pujera (worshippers), Deravasi or Chaityavasi (dwellers in temples or special residences), or Mandir-margi (those who go to temples).

Murti Pujakas are now spread all over India, though their initial area of concentration was Gujarat .They consist of the main group among Shvetambaras.

Murugan A Hindu deity, one of the names of Skanda or KARTTIKEYA in south India, also known as Subrahmanyam, Swami Mahasena, or Shanmukham. In his earlier form, he was a local god of the Tamil region, associated with the mountains, with war and with fertility. He is described in SANGAM LITERATURE as a god of Kurinji or hilly regions, and is depicted holding a *vel* or spear, sometimes in a frenzied dance, or with his mother KORRAVAI on the battlefield. As he was associated with war, he was later identified with Skanda.

There are a number of shrines and temples dedicated to Murugan in the south, particularly in Tamil Nadu, of which six are considered the most sacred. These are: (1) The Murugan Temple at Palani near MADURAI, where Murugan is said to have meditated after being defeated by his brother in the competition of going around the world. The image here is of an unknown age and is said to have healing properties; (2) A shrine at Tiruchendur marks the spot where Murugan defeated the asura Surapadman. Here the demon turned into a peacock and became Murugan's vehicle; (3) A temple on the Tiruttani hill at the spot where Murugan meditated after his battle with other demons; (4) Tiruparankunram, a hill near MADURAI where Murugan's marriage took place; (5) Swamimalai Temple near Kumbakonam, where Murugan instructed his father SHIVA on the meaning of the word OM; (6) There is some dispute about the sixth shrine, but it is often described as that above the ALAGAR temple on the Paramthirsolai hill near Madurai or at Tirukkazhakunram.

While in the north Karttikeya is usually considered unmarried, in the south he has two wives, Devasena or Devayanai and Valli. Devayanai is said to be the daughter of INDRA and Indrani. According to some accounts, both were daughters of VISHNU, but Devayanai was so named because she was brought up by Indra's elephant (yanai = elephant). Murugan is also associated with kadamba trees. In his later form he is depicted with a peacock mount, like Karttikeya.

Karttikeya is said to have left the north because he was upset with his parents' preference for GANESHA. Thus he settled in south India, and is especially popular there.

Mutazila The rationalist school of SUNNI Islam, influenced by Greek philosophy. It was based on the views of Wali ibn Ata, who lived in Basra in the eighth century.

The Mutazila stated that God has given people free will, therefore they are rewarded for good deeds and punished for evil ones. God is not the creator of evil. Knowledge, power and speech may be divine attributes, but are not different from God's essence. God has no eternal attributes, and references to his face, hands and eyes in the QURAN, are to be taken as metaphors, not literally. There is no uncreated word of God, but the word of God is that power of language that God has bestowed in order to communicate with man. The Quran as the word of God, is what God wants man to know.

Later, some of the ideas were modified, and Al-Mutawwakil (847–61) abandoned the concept of the createdness of the Quran, as orthodox schools of thought generally accept that the Quran is uncreated.

Naba Barsha A Hindu festival that takes place on 14 April in West Bengal, marking the beginning of the new year. Houses are decorated, and people sing and dance and take out processions. Many perform PUJA (worship) and take a dip in a tank or river.

nabi A term in Islam for a Prophet to whom God has given a message, through an angel, a vision or dream, or directly to the heart. A similar term is rasul, or messenger, but a rasul receives a Holy Book, not merely a message.

nada A Sanskrit word meaning 'sound' or 'tone'. The *Sangita Bhashya*, a text on music, says: 'Nada (intelligible sound) is the treasure of happiness for the happy, the distraction of those who suffer, the winner of the hearts of hearers, the first messenger of the god of love . . . The fifth approach to the eternal wisdom, the VEDA.' Sound can also be of divine origin. Thus Anahata Nada is the unstruck or divine sound and can be heard within oneself, particularly in the ANAHATA CHAKRA, the hidden energy centre representing the heart.

nadis A Sanskrit term for hidden channels of energy within the body, said to be like light waves or sound waves. Texts on YOGA normally mention 72,000 nadis, while the *Yoganushasanam* states that there are 3,50,000. Of these, three are considered most important, the Ida, Pingala and Sushumna. The Sushumna is the central channel that runs from the base of the spine (the MULADHARA CHAKRA) along the spinal cord, through the other main CHAKRAS, up to the crown of the head. According to some TANTRIC texts, it then curves downwards, like the handle of a walking stick, to the nostrils. Within it is the vital essence, known as vajra-nadi, and within that the Chitrini, brilliant and subtle. Inside this is the Brahma nadi, representing pure intelligence, shining like the minds of sages, revealing pure knowledge. On either side are Ida, to the left, cool and white, representing the moon, and Pingala, to the right, red and hot, representing the sun and fire. Texts give different descriptions of these nadis, and according to some, they cross each other like the caduceus and end in the nostrils. Along these central nadis rises the KUNDALINI, the serpent power or sacred energy. The other nadis pervade the subtle body, bringing consciousness and energy to every cell. The nadis are energized and purified in various ways, by yogic and Tantric techniques, particularly PRANAYAMA, or specific breathing techniques.

According to the *Hatha Yoga Pradipika*, a fifteenth-century text, when the nadis are purified, a person becomes happy, peaceful, optimistic and enthusiastic. The body is slim and radiant, and the mystic fire is aroused.

Nadwat-ul-Musannifin An institution for Islamic study located at DELHI, established in 1938. Its scholars belong mainly to the DEOBAND school. It publishes a number of works on Islam, as well as an Urdu monthly, *Burhan*.

Nadwat-ul-Ulama, Lucknow An institution for Islamic research and study. The Nadwat-ul-Ulama Association was first established at Kanpur in 1893. It moved to Lucknow in present Uttar Pradesh in 1898, where a Dar-ul-Uloom was founded. Its main aims were to bring harmony among Muslims of different groups, to create an atmosphere of unity and cooperation, and to modernize the syllabi of the Arabic MADRASAS. Maulana Shibli Numani was the first academic supervisor of the Dar-ul-Uloom, succeeded by Maulana Syed Sulaiman Nadwi, followed by the well-known scholar Maulana Abul Hasan Ali NADWI. Its syllabus focuses on the QURAN and SUNNAH, but modern sciences and languages are also studied. It has produced outstanding scholars and remains an important institution with over a thousand students. It also has a large library and a research and publications department.

Nadwi, Abul Hasan Ali An Islamic philosopher, historian and scholar. Born in 1914 at Takia Kalan in Rai Bareili, in present Uttar Pradesh, he was educated by his mother and brother, his father having died when he was young. In 1926 he joined the NADWAT-UL-ULAMA at Lucknow and specialized in HADIS, later joining Lucknow University. He also studied for a few months at Deoband, and with the SUFI saint Shaikh Abdul Qadir Raipur. In 1934 he became a teacher in the Nadwat-ul-Ulama, and in 1954, director of education. He had joined the Jamat-i-Islami in 1941 but resigned because he did not agree with its principles. Nadwi was proficient in English and Arabic, and became a noted scholar who travelled to many parts of the world, giving learned lectures in Arabic and English, on Islam. His speeches were listened to by the Muslim elite in Islamic countries, and by other scholars in the West, and collected in books. Collections of his speeches include the *Islamic Concept of Prophethood*, *Western Civilization*, and *Islam and Muslims*. Possibly his most widely read book, is *What the World Lost Through Muslims' Deterioration*, while his *Saviours of the Islamic Spirit*, originally in Arabic, is popular among Muslims. Nadwi commented on the lack of education among Muslims and their ignorance of true Islam. He received a number of awards and honorary degrees and was a member of a number of Islamic organizations, highly respected by ULAMA and other scholars, both in India and abroad. He died in 1999.

nafs A term in Islam usually interpreted as the soul, which is immortal and non-material. Alternatively, nafs has been translated as 'human conscience', and also means 'animal life', substance, or desire. Certain SUFIS interpret nafs as the lower soul that has to be purified, while Qalb, the heart, is the higher soul in which the divine light can be seen. Other Sufis see seven stages of nafs, the lowest belonging to ordinary human beings, and the highest, Nafs al-Kamila, to the perfected Sufi. This concept indicates that while the essence of the soul may be eternal, its qualities can be modified.

Nag Hammadi documents Ancient documents found in 1945 at Nag Hammadi in Egypt, that relate to eastern or Coptic Christianity, and reflect Gnostic ideas. (See GNOSTICISM). They have usually been dated to between the second and fourth centuries, though they are attributed to earlier authors, and some scholars believe they incorporate earlier traditions. Among the documents is the *Gospel of Thomas*, which contains sayings of JESUS and provides information on ST. THOMAS, who according to Indian tradition came to India and died here. In addition there are the *Gospel of Philip*, the *Gospel of Truth*, the *Secret Book of James* and other texts. Scholars such as Edward Conze, an authority on Buddhism, have suggested Indian influence, both Hindu and Buddhist, in the ideas of these texts, which differ from mainstream Christianity. Though more research is yet to be done on this, some passages do seem to indicate either Indian influence or an expression of universal ideas and concepts which underlie different religions. For instance, a text called *Thunder, Perfect Mind*, contains verses reminiscent of the BHAGAVAD GITA:

I am the silence that is incomprehensible,
I am the utterance of my name.

The *Trimorphic Protennoia* contains a passage similar to a description of BRAHMAN, the Absolute. The text begins: '[I] am [Protennoia the] Thought that [dwells] in [the Light] . . . [she who exists] before the All . . . I move in every creature . . . I am the Invisible One within the All.' (Quotes from Elaine Pagels, *The Gnostic Gospels*).

naga deities A number of naga and nagi deities, male and female snake gods, are described in texts and represented in images. They form part of the Hindu pantheon, but some are also worshipped in Buddhism and Jainism. Such deities represent power, wisdom and fertility.

The worship of snakes probably dates back to pre-Vedic times. In the RIG VEDA, AHI BUDHNYA is mentioned, meaning 'the serpent of the deep'. In the *ATHARVA VEDA* there are references to snake deities, among them being Tirashchiraji, Pridaku, Svajo, Kalmasagrivo and Svitro, who were the guardians of the south, west, north, east and upper regions. TAKSHAKA, prominent in later texts, is also mentioned. In the *MAHABHARATA* and PURANAS, several snake deities are described, including Takshaka, Karkotaka, Padma, Mahapadma and Kulika. The *Mayasamgraha*, a Sanskrit text, states that nagas or naga deities have two tongues, two arms and seven hoods embedded with jewels. They hold an akshasutra (bead rosary) and have curling tails. Their wives and children have one to three heads. In the much later *Shilpa Ratna*, a text of the seventeenth century, nagas are said to be human in form above the navel, and snake-like below.

According to some of the PURANAS, the nagas are the children of KASHYAPA and KADRU. They live in PATALA, also known as Nagaloka, a beautiful world, with its capital at Bhogavati.

Several Hindu deities are associated with snakes or with snake divinities. The god VISHNU rests in the waters on ANANTA or Shesha Naga in the intervals between creation. BALARAMA is depicted holding a plough and a snake, both representing fertility, and is said to be a form of Ananta Naga. On the other hand, GARUDA, the vehicle of VISHNU, is an enemy of snakes. KRISHNA, in one of his heroic episodes, struggled with and defeated the serpent Kaliya, probably representing the subordination of a snake cult. SHIVA is associated with snakes and is depicted with a snake around his neck. Nagas and nagis are often shown worshipping deities such as Vishnu.

In Jainism, the Tirthankara PARSHVANATHA is associated with snakes and is surmounted by a canopy of seven hoods. In Buddhism, nagas are depicted on the pedestals of some BUDDHA images. There are MAHAYANA texts dealing with the prevention of snake bite, and with the benefits of friendliness towards snakes.

Independent snake deities existed from early days, and are depicted in sculptures and mentioned in inscriptions. Among such deities are Dadhikarna, and MANINAGA, while among female snake deities MANASA is the most prominent and is still worshipped today. There are several other local deities associated with snakes or the prevention of snake bite, such as GUGA in northern India.

Snakes are associated with wisdom and with the KUNDALINI, the hidden energy in the human body, said to be like a coiled serpent at the base of the spine.

Texts also mention snake SACRIFICES that took place in ancient times. (*See* Sarpa Satra).

Snakes are still worshipped all over India. NAGAPANCHAMI, a special festival for snakes, is popular in north India. It probably originated in an earlier ritual, known as Sarbapali, described in the GRIHYA SUTRAS, and performed during the rainy season to honour and ward off snakes.

Two snakes intertwined in the shape of caduceus are often carved on stones and placed outside temples or under trees. Cobras particularly are considered sacred, and killing them is said to bring ill fortune.

Snakes are prominent in other ancient civilizations. In ancient Mesopotamia, for instance, there was a serpent god that was half-man, half-serpent.

A Naga dynasty existed in early northern India, though their name was possibly derived from the Scythian word for leader or chief.

Naga people, religion of The Naga people, who are now mainly Christians, consist of tribes and sub-tribes who probably originally migrated from southern China to the hills of Myanmar and north-east India. Today they live mainly in the state of Nagaland, extending into neighbouring states and into Myanmar. Among the main tribes settled in different parts of Nagaland are the Angami, Ao, Chakhesang, Chang, Khiamungan, Konyak, Kuki, Lotha, Phom, Pochury, Rengma, Sangtam, Sema, Yimchunger and Zeliang. Other tribes include the Kabui (Rongmei and Puimei) and the Kacha (Liangmai and Zeme).

There are different interpretations of the term Naga in this context. According to one theory, Naga is derived from the Burmese word naka, meaning people with perforated ears, as they used to pierce their ears with large wooden plugs. Another theory is that it is related to a Tibetan word, that means mountain people. The term 'Naga was initially used for these tribes by people of the plains, and later adopted by the tribes themselves.

Nagas retain many of their traditional customs, as well as their traditional form of dress, which is unique to each tribe. Each tribe has its own language and legends, and once had its own traditional deities. In general, there was a supreme, benevolent god, and a number of lesser deities and spirits. The Angamis had a supreme deity known as Ukepenuopfu, whose abode was in the sky. There were special gods for hunting and fishing, as well as a god of death and a god to be propitiated in case of nightmares. Stones and animals were believed to possess spirits. Head-hunting, killing members of enemy tribes in war, and bringing back their heads as trophies, was a common practice among all Naga tribes. These practices died out with the introduction of Christianity but their legends and traditional festivals are still popular. Several tribes trace their origin to mythical ancestors. For instance, Gairemong is the legendary ancestor of the Rongmei Nagas. He was born from a union between a human

mother and the Master of the World, who came to her in the form of a charming python. Later, the father bequeathed the land, plants, animals and birds to his son, who ruled the land ensuring peace and prosperity.

Some of the tribal festivals still celebrated (with the name of the tribe in parentheses) are: Sekrenyi (Angami), Ngada (Rengma), Nga-Ngai (Zeliang), Mimkut (Kuki), Tsukhenyi (Chakhesang), Nazu (Pochury), Moatsu (Ao), Aoling (Konyak), Monyu (Phom), Miu (Khiamngan), Nkanyulum (Chang), Metemneo (Yimchunger), Amongmong (Sangtam), Tokhuemong (Lotha), Tuluni (Sema).

See also North-east, Christianity in.

Naga sadhus A sect of SADHUS or holy men, said to have been founded by the ninth-century philosopher SHANKARA, though their actual origin is unclear. Divided into akharas, loosely translated as 'regiments', they were once a martial group and fought against the British during the revolt of 1857. They practise extreme asceticism, many of them always remaining naked even in the coldest weather. Naga sadhus usually carry sticks, spears, swords or tridents, remnants of their martial origin, that now have a symbolic significance, representing conquest of the Self. They remain celibate, often smear their bodies with ash, and are known to consume bhang or ganja (cannabis).

There are ten main Hindu akharas, seven Shaivite and three Vaishnavite, as well as additional akharas. Of the Shaivites, the Mahanirvani akhara, Niranjana akhara and Juna akhara are the best known, the sadhus of the last always remaining naked, clothed only in ash. Other Shaiva akharas are the Anand, Atal, Avahana and Agni. Vaishnavite akharas were founded somewhat later, according to tradition by Shri Balanandji Maharaj. These consist of the Nirmohi akhara, Nirvani akhara and Digambar akhara, all of which have split into sub-sects. These ten akharas are together known as the Dasnami, but are different from the DASNAMI sadhus attached to the MATHAS, and in the hierarchy of sadhus are second to them.

Apart from these there are the akharas of Sikh origin, including the Udasin akhara, and the Nirmala Panchayati akhara.

The akharas are under a supreme head known as the Acharya Mahamandaleshvara, while individual akharas are under a Mahamandaleshvara. Each akhara is based at one place, but the sadhus may travel wherever they like. Naga sadhus are prominent at the KUMBH MELAS, where bathing areas are reserved for them at specific times.

Nagapanchami A Hindu festival in which snakes or NAGAS are worshipped. Panchami means 'fifth', and this festival takes place on the fifth day of the bright half of the month of Shravana (July/August). It is associated with ANANTA, the serpent on whom VISHNU rests in the intervals between dissolution and creation. It is also a festival to appease and honour all snakes.

At the festival, stone and other images of snakes are worshipped, and images of snakes are made from cloth, or drawn on various surfaces. Rice, flour and bowls of milk are placed near snake holes, and snakes that emerge to accept the food, are said to bring good fortune. No snakes are killed on this day, and fields are not ploughed in case snakes are accidently injured. Naga Panchami is celebrated particularly in north and east India, and has different local forms. In MATHURA the defeat of the Naga Kaliya by the god KRISHNA is celebrated.

In Bengal the Ashtanagas (eight nagas), which include Vasuki, TAKSHAKA, Shesha and Ananta, are worshipped, as well as the goddess MANASA.

The celebration of this festival is said to provide protection from snakes in the coming year.

Nagara   A style of temple architecture. *See* Temples.

Nagari   A north Indian script, also known as DEVANAGARI, which is considered a script of the DEVAS or gods.

Nagarjuna   A MAHAYANA Buddhist philosopher who probably lived between 150 and 250 CE. He was born in the region of present Andhra Pradesh and was originally a BRAHMANA, but later became a Buddhist. He wrote the *Madhyamika Karika*, which formed the basic text of the MADHYAMIKA school of Mahayana Buddhism. Nagarjuna propounded the basic doctrine of SHUNYATA or emptiness, and tried to show how conclusions reached on the basis of different schools of thought are actually unreal. Among other works attributed to him are the *Yuktashashtika* or Sixty Arguments, the *Shunyata-Saptati*, or Seventy Verses on Shunyata, the *Pratitya-Samutpadahridaya* on 'dependent origination', the *Dvadasha-dvara Shastra*, the *Vigrahavyavartani*, and many more, which may not actually be his. Nagarjuna is a revered figure in Buddhism and is considered the patriarch of several Japanese Buddhist schools.

Nagarjunakonda   An early Buddhist settlement located in present Andhra Pradesh. A large STUPA, 18 m high and 32 m in diameter, constructed in the second century BCE but rebuilt in the third century CE, is located here. During the third to fourth centuries CE, it was the capital of the Ikshvaku dynasty, covering an area of approximately 23 sq km, near the Krishna river. A number of Buddhist monuments and shrines were constructed at this time, for various Buddhist sects. Among these were votive stupas, with a brick-and-rubble filling, overlaid by plaster or lime stucco, often placed within CHAITYA halls. Viharas or monasteries had cells arranged around a courtyard. Several Buddhist sculptures have been found here, and there are Hindu shrines as well.

The Nagarjuna Sagar Dam has submerged the original site, but most of the monuments have been carefully relocated on a nearby hill top.

Nagasena   A Buddhist philosopher who lived in the second century BCE and had a series of dialogues on Buddhism with King MENANDER, which form the *MILINDA PANHA*. According to the *Milinda Panha*, Nagasena was famed far and wide for his wisdom, and no one could rival him. He settled in an ashram in Sakala, King Menander's capital in north-west India, where he met the king, who was searching for answers on philosophical questions.

Nageshvara Temple   A temple of the Hindu god SHIVA, located at KUMBAKONAM in Tamil Nadu. It was constructed during the reign of the Chola ruler Parantaka I (907–40), and though small in size, is among the finest Chola temples. According to legend, when Adishesha or ANANTA Naga was groaning under the weight of the world, he came here, performed penances and worshipped Shiva as Nageshvara or lord of the snakes. Shiva and PARVATI appeared to him, blessed him and gave him strength. A temple was built at this spot, consisting of a shrine attached to a columned MANDAPA, both raised on a basement.

The inner shrine has a LINGA, as well as various images on the walls. To the north is Shiva as DAKSHINAMURTI, to the west ARDHANARISHVARA, and to the south, BRAHMA. In between there are life-size sculptures, probably of donors or worshippers. On the mandapa walls are other images, including those of DURGA and of Shaivite saints, which are beautifully carved. The basement has panels of lotus petals and epic scenes.

Above the shrine is a pyramidal tower with a hemispherical roof that has been renovated recently. The whole is enclosed in a courtyard, in which there is also a NATARAJA shrine. The basement of this is remarkable, with richly decorated rearing horses and large wheels, the spokes of which are made up of tiny figures. A well in the complex is known as Naga Tirtham.

nagi/nagini   Female snake deities, the counterparts of NAGA DEITIES. Nagis often accompany nagas and are depicted in temples.

Nagore Dargah   The DARGAH of a popular SUFI saint, Meeran Sahib Abdul Qadir Shahul Hamid Badshah (d. c. 1560), located at Nagore in Nagapattinam district of Tamil Nadu. The dargah covers an area of about five acres, enclosed with walls and with four impressive entrances. In front of the western gate is a tower 40 m high known as Periya Minar, constructed by Pratap Singh, king of Thanjavur, in about 1760. Within the enclosure, the dargah has a golden dome covering three tombs, of the saint, his son, and his daughter-in-law. A large mosque that attracts a big gathering on Fridays is located nearby. The Vanjur shrine 2 km away, marks the spot where the saint meditated in a cave, whereas another shrine connected with the saint is located at Silladi. Meeran Sahib was said to be a disciple of a SHATTARI saint of Gwalior, but later settled in the south. A fourteen-day festival known as Kandhuri Urs is held every year, and attracts thousands of pilgrims of all religions. Prayers here are said to be answered through the miraculous power of the saint.

Naigamesha A Jain deity, also known as Negamesha, Nemesa, Naigameshin, and other variants. Naigamesha is mentioned in the KALPA SUTRA and other Jain texts, and depicted in sculptures in the first few centuries CE. Sculptural representations show him as an antelope or goat-headed deity associated with children. In the *Kalpa Sutra*, Negamesi or Harinegamesi, on the instructions of INDRA, transferred the embryo of MAHAVIRA from the womb of Devananda, a BRAHMANA, to that of Trishala, a KSHATRIYA lady, through whom he was born. In the *Neminathacharitra*, a SHVETAMBARA text on the life of the Tirthankara ARISHTANEMINATHA, the god KRISHNA is said to have worshipped Naigamesha to obtain a son for Satyabhama, his second wife. In other texts, Satyabhama worshipped the deity.

Naigamesha is depicted in narrative panels showing him transferring the embryo, or independently, jewelled and seated on a throne, accompanied by one or more children on his lap or shoulders, and sometimes by a goat-headed female or female attendants. Several images of the first to third centuries CE have been found at MATHURA and other sites.

The BRAHMANAS, GRIHYA SUTRAS and some medical texts mention a deity with a similar name who had a ram's head. Naigamesha is also one of the names of the god Skanda or KARTTIKEYA, and thus was probably both a Jain and a Brahmanical deity.

The name of the deity has been variously interpreted. Harinegamesi is said to be Negamesi, general of Hari or Indra, or to come from harina (deer), while mesha means ram. The deity was worshipped to obtain children, but after around the third century, his images are rare.

naivedya A term for offerings or oblation in Hindu temples.

Najmuddin Kubra The founder of a SUFI sect known as the KUBRAWIYA, who lived in the twelfth century. The Kubrawiya was a branch of the SUHRAWARDI, and its Indian branches were known as the FIRDAUSI and HAMADANI.

Nakhoda Mosque A mosque located in Kolkata in West Bengal; it is the largest in the region, with space to accommodate ten thousand people. Its two minarets reach a height of 50 m, and a huge dome covers the mosque.

nakshatra A word that literally means 'star', but in the Hindu calendric system refers to a lunar mansion, in which the moon is placed during a twenty-four-hour day. The nakshatra divisions are named after the most prominent constellations in the lunar segment. There are twenty-seven nakshatra divisions, each covering 13.20' on the ecliptic, and 2¼ nakshatras

equal one rashi. The nakshatras are: (1) Ashvini; (2) Bharani; (3) Krittika; (4) Rohini; (5) Mrigashira; (6) Ardra; (7) Punarvasu; (8) Pushya; (9) Aslesha; (10) Magha; (11) Purva Phalguni; (12) Uttara Phalguni; (13) Hasta; (14) Chitra; (15) Svati; (16) Vishakha; (17) Anuradha; (18) Jyeshtha; (19) Mula; (20) Purvashadha; (21) Uttarashadha; (22) Shravana; (23) Dhanishtha; (24) Sata-bhisha; (25) Purva Bhadrapada; (26) Uttara Bhadrapada; (27) Revati.

They are used in astrological calculations for fixing the dates of festivals. Other parts of the ancient world also used twenty-seven or twenty-eight similar divisions. A twenty-eighth nakshatra was added in India, but twenty-seven are used currently. In early days, the day was named after the nakshatra, but later the TITHI or lunar day, based on the lunar phase of the moon, came into use.

Nakula One of the five PANDAVA brothers, described in the MAHABHARATA. Nakula was the son of MADRI, born along with his twin brother SAHADEVA, by Madri invoking the ASHVINS, who were twin deities. Nakula was very handsome and an expert horseman and sword-fighter. He took part in the great war, and when YUDHISHTHIRA became king, he was appointed chief of the army.

Naladiyar A Tamil text that forms part of the collection of the PADINENKILKANKKU, or eighteen minor works. The *Naladiyar,* an anthology of 400 verses, has wise sayings and can be compared to the Buddhist DHAMMAPADA. For instance:

Better to have hatred than the friendship of fools;
Better to have death than chronic illness.

Nalanda Monastery An extensive Buddhist monastery, that existed between the fifth and twelfth centuries, and possibly later, located near the ancient city of RAJAGRIHA (modern Rajgir) in Bihar. XUANZANG, the Chinese pilgrim, visited it in the seventh century and provided a description of it. He said it was founded by Shakraditya and expanded by succeeding kings, including Buddha Gupta, Tathagata Gupta and Baladitya. Shakraditya has been identified with Kumara Gupta I (414–55), a ruler of the Gupta dynasty. Xuanzang also wrote that there were thousands of monks here, all of great ability and learning, and several foreign students. In and around Nalanda were a hundred sacred monuments, including STUPAS and large temples, as well as beautiful BUDDHA images. There was a copper Buddha about 29 m high in a six-storeyed building. Shilabhadra was the head of the monastery, which specialized in MAHAYANA Buddhist studies.

Buddhist texts state that other topics were taught as well, including various systems of philosophy, logic, grammar, medicine and even the VEDAS. The monastery was flourishing in the ninth century when Viradeva, originally a BRAHMANA from Jalalabad, became its head. At this time the king of Java, who belonged to the Sailendra dynasty, built a monastery here for Javanese students with the permission of the Indian king. A number of students from Tibet and China studied here, and the scholars at Nalanda had a profound influence on TIBETAN BUDDHISM.

Between the eighth and twelfth centuries, Buddhist art flourished at Nalanda and in neighbouring areas. Bronze images of Buddhist deities and fine paintings on palm leaf manuscripts were made. These influenced art in Nepal and Tibet, and even in China and Japan.

According to some accounts, the monastery was destroyed by a general of Muhammad Ghori in the twelfth century, but this is contradicted by the account of a Tibetan Buddhist monk, Dharmasvamin. He visited it in the thirteenth century and said that there were more than eighty viharas in and around Nalanda, where Buddhist teachers and their disciples lived.

The remains of Nalanda can still be seen today.

Nalayira Divya Prabandham   A collection of the works of the ALVAR saints, who composed songs of love and devotion to the Hindu god VISHNU. The name means 'The Divine Four Thousand', and the *Prabandham* has four thousand verses, most of them composed to be sung or set to music. They are verses of BHAKTI or devotion and love of Vishnu as a personal god. The verses include praises of the deities of 108 Divya Desams, or Vaishnava temples in south India. The text is divided into four parts: the Mudaliyiram, Periya Tirumozhi, Tiruvaymozhi and Iyarpa. Several commentaries have been written on the *Prabandham*, and some commentators provided a theological framework for the text, naming the parts according to themes. The first two parts are thus also known as Tirumantra, or the divine mantra, and explain the mantra *Om Namah Narayanaya*, in praise of Vishnu. The third part is classified as Charamashloka, or the verse of death, and is concerned with ways of seeking refuge in the universal soul, while the fourth, known as Dvayamantra, focuses on the ultimate goal and its realization.

Nam simaran   Remembrance of the True Name, a term for meditation in Sikhism. In Sikhism, God is recognized as NIRGUNA or without attributes, and at its highest Nam simaran is a meditation on the formless God, leading finally to divine bliss. According to Guru NANAK, meditation on Nam, the True Name, is worship.

Another form is Nam japa or repeating the name of God, and is based on the transforming power of the word. Different names are used for God in Sikhism, including Satnam, Hari, Ram, Mohan, Allah, Khuda, Rabb, but usually the term Satnam (True Name) or Wahe Guru (victory to the guru) is used as a mantra. Reciting Sikh prayers is another form of Nam simaran.

Namadeva   A BHAKTI saint of the Maratha region. There are some conflicting views of his life.

Namadeva was the son of a tailor named Damasheti. According to some accounts, his parents moved to Pandharpur when he was still a child, while according to others, they had moved there even before his birth. He was probably born in 1270, either in the village of Narasi-Vamani in Satara district of Maharashtra, or in Pandharpur. He married young, and had four sons and a daughter. Namadeva initially followed his father's profession, but after facing losses in business, he is said to have become a thief and a murderer. He was transformed, according to some accounts, by a meeting with the saint JNANESHVARA, and according to others because he was touched by the grief of the wife of one of his victims.

Other versions of his life deny this story, and state that he was a devotee of the god Vitthala from childhood.

He received a divine vision and then spent his time singing ABHANGAS or verses in praise of the god VITTHALA or Vithoba, a form of VISHNU. He lived mostly at PANDHARPUR, the centre of the Vithoba temple, but also travelled with Jnaneshvara. His verses, in simple Marathi and Hindi, are still popular, and reflect his pure love for god. He died in 1350.

namaz   A term for prayer in Islam, referred to as salat in Arabic. Namaz is one of the basic duties of Islam, compulsory for every Muslim adult who is in good health. The five prayers that must be offered daily are known as Fajr, Zuhar, Asr, Maghrib and Isha. Fajr is offered before dawn, Zuhar (actually considered the first) in the afternoon, the third between Zuhar and sunset, the fourth after sunset but before night, and the fifth any time during the night, but preferably before midnight.

An AZAN or call to prayer is made from mosques for each of the five daily prayers to indicate the correct times. Men go to the mosque to pray whenever possible, while women pray at home. Wuzu or ablutions are made before prayers.

On Fridays (juma) a special juma (congregation) prayer is offered in place of the Zuhar, which is preceded by the khutba or sermon. There are also special prayers on ID and other festivals. Prayers are offered facing the QIBLA (direction of Mecca).

Nambi Andar Nambi   A BHAKTI saint and worshipper of the Hindu god SHIVA, who lived in the tenth and eleventh centuries at the time of the Chola ruler Rajaraja. He put together a collection of the hymns of the NAYANARS or Shaivite saints, to which additions were made later. This collection is known as the *TIRUMURAI* and includes his own verses on the saints SAMBANDAR and APPAR, as well as those in praise of Vinayaka (GANESHA) and of CHIDAMBARAM. Nambi also composed the *Tiruttondar-Tiruvantadi*, an account of their lives, based on Sundaramurti's *Tiruttondattogai*.

Nambudiri, Cherusseri   A sixteenth-century writer in Malayalam who composed a long poem,

Krishna Gatha, based on stories of the life of the Hindu god KRISHNA in the tenth Skandha of the *BHAGAVATA PURANA*. His work is recognized as a religious and poetic masterpiece.

Namdhari A Sikh sect also known as Kukas. It was founded in the 1840s by Bhagat Jawahar Mal and his disciple Baba Balak Singh, who lived at Hazro in the North-West Frontier Province. Their aim was to revive and purify Sikhism, which by then had accumulated several non-Sikh practices and Hindu customs, and had lost its simplicity. Their centre was the Jagiasi Abhiasi Ashram at Hazro, and as the movement gained followers, Baba Balak Singh (d. 1862) came to be known as the eleventh guru. His successor Ram Singh (1815–85) moved the centre to Bhaini in Ludhiana, Punjab, and laid down several rules for his disciples, including not eating meat or drinking alcohol, not coveting another's wife or property, not practising female infanticide or allowing marriages to take place before the age of sixteen, and not joining government service or patronizing government facilities. In addition Namdharis were to rise at dawn and meditate and pray, and to distinguish themselves from other Sikhs, were to wear their turbans straight across the forehead, instead of the two ends meeting at an angle.

Namdharis came to be known as Kukas, for when they assembled for Chandi ki Path, a reading of certain scriptures, they reached a state of ecstacy, emitting cries (*kuks*).

Ram Singh divided the Punjab into Kuka districts, each in charge of a disciple known as a Subah. As Namdhari influence spread, some became fanatical and organized protests against cow slaughter that often led to violence. In 1872 they came in conflict with the British, after which Ram Singh and some others were exiled and the Namdharis suppressed. Though reduced in strength, Namdharis continued to exist and had a series of gurus. Their guru still resides at Bhaini, while the headquarters of the sect is at Sri Jiwan Nagar, Hisar, Haryana. They follow the principles laid down by Ram Singh and revere him as an incarnation of Guru GOBIND SINGH (d. 1708).

Namdharis view their historical past not merely as a purificatory movement, but as a nationalist struggle against the British.

Namgyal Institute of Tibetology An institute for the study of Buddhism, located at Gangtok in Sikkim. Opened in 1958, the institute has a collection of BUDDHA and BODHISATTVA images, fine THANGKAS, and a large library of books on Buddhism, including Tibetan, PALI, Sanskrit and Burmese texts, as well as translations and scholarly works in English. There are a number of Tibetan manuscripts, and writings from the KANGYUR and TANGYUR collections. The institute has initiated research on various aspects of Buddhism, the history of Tibet, and the structure and phonetics of the Tibetan language. It also edits and publishes ancient texts.

Nammalvar One of the ALVAR saints, who composed songs of love and devotion to the Hindu god VISHNU. He was born in Tirunagari, the son of a local chief named Kariyar and his wife Udayamankayar, and was initially named Maran, and later Shathakopa and Nammalvar. Always spiritually inclined, he is said to have renounced the world at the age of thirty-five, devoting himself to the worship of Vishnu.

Legendary accounts present a different picture. According to these, the child did not speak or move at birth, and considering him divine, the parents left him at the Vishnu temple nearby in a golden cradle, under a tamarind tree. He stayed there without speaking or moving for sixteen years until the Alvar saint Mathura or Madhura Kavi saw him and recognized his greatness, after which Nammalvar began to sing songs of praise to Vishnu. Madhura Kavi then became his disciple. According to this account, he continued to compose and sing songs of devotion under the tamarind tree, until he left the world at the age of thirty-five. His compositions, include *Tiruvaymozhi*, that forms part of the NALYIRA DIVYA PRABANDHAM. They are not only devotional hymns, but are deeply philosophical, later commented on by exponents of VISHISHTADVAITA.

Nanak, Guru The founder of Sikhism. Nanak was born in 1469 at Talwandi (now known as Nankana Sahib) in Punjab, in present Pakistan, to Mehta Kalu Chand and his wife Tripta.

Nanak's life is known mainly through the JANAM SAKHIS, which were composed later. According to these, even as a child, Nanak was reflective and spiritually inclined, and though he studied with a Hindu pandit and learnt Persian with a Muslim Maulvi, he was not interested in studies, or later in business. His father despaired of him, but his sister Nanaki and the village landlord Rai Bular believed he was a saint. Nanaki was married to Jairam of Sultanpur, and later Nanak went there and worked as a store-keeper. Meanwhile he was married to Sulakhni, daughter of Mula, and had two sons, SRI CHAND in 1494 and Lakshmidas in 1496. Soon after this, Nanak had a mystical experience when he went into the Bein river to bathe, and disappeared. All had given him up for dead, but he reappeared after three days, and the first words he is reported to have said are: 'There is no Hindu and no Mussalman.' The essence of the teachings he was soon to reveal, were received by him in a divine vision. He left Sultanpur and began travelling in order to spread his divine message.

According to some Janam Sakhis, he made four Udasis or divine missions over a period of twenty-three years, accompanied by MARDANA, his Muslim disciple. Some accounts state that BALA, his Hindu disciple, also went with him. GURDWARAS or shrines are located at most of the places he visited, and stories and legends are associated with each of these places.

In his first Udasi he travelled to various places in Punjab and then moved towards DELHI. On the way he met the SUFI saint, ABU ALI SHAH QALANDAR in Panipat, and in Delhi he stayed with a Muslim faqir named Majnu. The MAJNU KA TILA GURDWARA marks his visit here. He then went to HARDWAR, KEDARNATH, BADRINATH, JOSHIMATH, AYODHYA, VARANASI and PRAYAGA. Along the way he came across people of different sects, commented on superstitious practices, and indicated the true path to those he met. He also went to GAYA, Bengal, Assam and Orissa before returning to Sultanpur in 1509. After this he visited a few towns in Punjab, before beginning his second Udasi around 1510. He crossed through Rajasthan, the Deccan and south India, and reached Sri Lanka. On the return journey he passed through Gujarat and Multan. His third Udasi probably began in the summer of 1517. Some time before this, around 1516, he founded a settlement of Sikhs at KARTARPUR. In the third Udasi, he is said to have visited some Himalayan regions, reached Mt KAILASHA and MANASAROVARA, and according to some accounts, crossed into Nepal and Sikkim. He then went to Tibet and returned through Ladakh. On his fourth Udasi, Nanak went to Baluchistan, and from the port of Miani sailed for Mecca. Here he had discussions with QAZIS and MULLAS, before proceeding to Medina. According to some accounts he even visited Palestine, Turkey and Syria, though most accounts state that he went to Baghdad and then returned via Iran and Afghanistan. He settled down in Kartarpur along with MARDANA, and a growing community of his followers. Here he met Lehna, whom he chose as his successor, naming him ANGAD. After this he made a few short trips, including one to Achal, where he conversed with YOGIS and SIDDHAS. The ACHAL SAHIB GURDWARA marks this spot. Guru Nanak died at Kartarpur in 1539. According to legend, his Muslim and Hindu disciples quarrelled about how to dispose of the body. The body was covered with a sheet, and when the sheet was lifted, only flowers remained.

The historical Nanak This account of his life is based on the Janam Sakhis, which are hagiographical, written some years after his death, and contain legends and stories of miracles that are doubted by historians. Some scholars do not believe that he visited all the places described in his Udasis, while others point out that there is evidence for most of these visits.

Nanak's teachings are conveyed through his verses in the GURU GRANTH SAHIB, and through accounts provided in the Janam Sakhis and other texts. The most important of his verses in the Granth Sahib is the JAPJI, containing the Mul Mantra. Others include the Asa di Var and SIDDHA GOSHT. Nanak spoke of one universal God, eternal and beyond form. He emphasized that all people were equal and that rituals were unnecessary, most important being good actions. Superstitions, magical practices, TANTRISM and too much book learning led nowhere.

The religion of Sikhism is founded on his basic teachings, which were added to by the later gurus.

Nanak Jhira Gurdwara A GURDWARA or Sikh shrine located at Bidar in Karnataka. According to the JANAM SAKHIS, Guru NANAK came here on his second udasi or missionary tour of south India. He stayed on the outskirts of Bidar town, where there were several Muslim faqirs who listened to his teachings with interest and reverence. People from the surrounding areas gathered to hear him. There was a shortage of drinking water in the area, and Nanak, with his compassionate heart, wished to help them. He moved some rubble on the side of a hill, and a spring of sweet water was miraculously revealed. The place was then known as Nanak Jhira (jhira = stream). The water is collected in a white marble tank and is said to have healing properties. The Nanak Jhira Gurdwara was built nearby. A LANGAR or free kitchen serves the pilgrims who visit the place, and Sikh festivals, particularly the birthday of Guru Nanak are celebrated here.

Bidar is also remembered for one of the PANJ PIARE, Bhai Sahib Singh, who was originally from here.

Nanak Matta Gurdwara A GURDWARA or Sikh shrine located in Udham Singh Nagar District of Uttarakhand. Guru NANAK came here on his way to Mt KAILASHA. At that time Gorakhpanthis, followers of the Yogi GORAKHNATHA, lived here, and the place was known as Gorakh Matta. Guru Nanak had a discussion with them about the true religion, and they became his followers. The name of the place was changed to Nanak Matta, and a shrine in memory of the guru's visit was maintained here. Some Gorakhpanthis resented this and wanted the place restored to them. In the seventeenth century, they tried to destroy the shrine and burnt the pipal tree near it. However, Guru HARGOBIND went there and the Gorakhpanthis, impressed with his discourses, allowed the shrine to exist. Later, a gurdwara was built there.

Nanak Panth A term for the followers of Guru NANAK, the founder of Sikhism. In early years the term included all Sikhs, but later it came to signify those who were not members of the KHALSA.

Nanak Piao Gurdwara A GURDWARA or Sikh shrine located in DELHI, at the place where Guru NANAK is said to have stayed in around 1505. Many people came to see him and brought him food and offerings, which he distributed to the poor. At this time Sultan Sikandar Shah Lodi was ruling Delhi. A story is told, related to the guru's stay here. Elephants were tethered near where the guru was staying, and when one of them died, the mahout began to lament. Guru NANAK asked him to pray instead, and the elephant revived. The sultan then came to him and demanded that he kill it and revive it in front of him, but the guru refused, and the angry sultan imprisoned him. SUFI saints convinced the sultan that Nanak was a holy man, and simultaneously a great earthquake took place in Delhi, which many people connected with the imprisonment of the guru. Nanak was released, and later a gurdwara was built here. A well from which Nanak used to serve water to the poor, exists here.

Nand Lal 'Goya', Bhai A Sikh poet who was a disciple of Guru GOBIND SINGH. Born in 1633 in Ghazni (Afghanistan), he wrote poems in Persian and Arabic. He married a Sikh girl, came in contact with Guru Gobind Singh and became his disciple, living with him from 1697. He wrote a number of works on Guru Gobind Singh and his code of conduct, and his writings are considered sacred. Several RAHIT-NAMAS are attributed to him, including the *Tanakhah-nama*, the *Prashan-uttar*, and a prose Rahit-Nama. In the first two verse namas, questions asked by Nand Lal are answered by the guru. For instance, Nand Lal asks what deeds a Sikh should perform, and the guru replies that only those deeds, which reflect the divine name, charity and purity. Nand Lal died at Multan in 1715.

Nanda A cowherd who raised the god KRISHNA. According to one account in the *BHAGAVATA PURANA*, in a previous birth he was one of the eight VASUS, who because of a mistake he made, was reborn as a cowherd. After praying to BRAHMA, he was told he would be liberated when he was born as Nanda and took care of Krishna. According to the *SHIVA PURANA*, he was earlier born in a cowherd family but gained great merit by worshipping SHIVA, and thus became the foster-father of Krishna. Along with his wife YASHODA, he cared for KRISHNA until he reached adulthood.

Nanda Devi A Hindu deity, a mountain goddess, after whom Nanda Devi mountain in the Himalayas is named. There are a number of Nanda Devi temples in the western Himalayas, at Nauti, Chandpur, Kurur, Srinagar (Garhwal), Nandaprayaga, Gopeshwar, Almora, Baijnath, Ranikhet and other places.

The origin of the deity is not clear, and she is not mentioned in the PURANAS. According to some accounts, she is a form of PARVATI, while according to others, she is YOGA MAYA, the daughter of the cowherd NANDA. Folk songs, however, describe her as a local princess. A popular Nanda Devi festival takes place once a year in the month of Bhadon or Bhadrapada (August-September), when Nanda Devi goes to visit her mother's home, escorted in a procession known as the Nanda Jat. Once in twelve years, an even more elaborate festival, the Nanda Raj Jat, is held, said to have been started in the fifteenth and sixteenth centuries by the rulers of Garhwal and Kumaon. In this festival the deity is accompanied by a four-horned ram who, when the goddess returns home, is said to proceed on its own to Mt Trishula. This festival still takes place, and the four-horned mountain ram, a rare creature, really does inexplicably walk off on its own in the direction of the mountain, leaving behind the goddess and accompanying villagers. The goddess Naina Devi at Nainital, and Naina in Himachal, are thought to be variants of Nanda Devi.

Nandana The grove of the Hindu god INDRA, where the PARIJATA tree grows, located in Devaloka, the world of the gods. Good people go there after death, particularly those who have controlled their senses and have not killed any living beings.

Nandi (1) A white bull, associated with the Hindu god SHIVA. Nandi is the chief of all Shiva's GANAS and the guardian of four-legged animals. He is alternatively known as Nandin or Nandikeshvara. Other names are Shalankayana, Nandideha, and Tandava-tilaka. He was earlier sometimes depicted in human form, or as a form of Shiva known as Rishabha (bull).

Nandi images are found in or outside most Shiva temples. The largest such image is near the VIRABHADRA TEMPLE at Lepakshi, Andhra Pradesh, that is over 6 m high and 9 m long. Another large Nandi image is near the Mahanandi Shiva temple in Andhra Pradesh, while in a radius of about 6 km around Mahanandi are nine Nandi temples, known collectively as the Nava Nandi. In some temples, Shiva is depicted as seated on Nandi.

There are several stories regarding how Nandi came into being. According to the *Vayu Purana*, he was the son of Kashyapa and Surabhi. In a story in the *Linga Purana*, Nandi was the son of the rishi Shilada.

(2) A name of the god Shiva and of Vishnu.

Nandi Sutta A Jain text of the SHVETAMBARA canon. Sometimes listed with the PAINNAS, it is usually not connected with any group of texts. According to tradition, this Sutta was written by Devarddhi, who presided over the Jain Council at Vallabhi, when the texts were written down.

It is an encyclopedic work that begins with a verse in praise of MAHAVIRA. It then describes the twenty-four TIRTHANKARAS, the eleven GANADHARAS or heads of schools, followed by a Theravali or list of teachers, the last of whom was Dusagni, the teacher of Devarddhi. It also surveys the whole Jain canon and summarizes everything that a monk needs to know.

Apart from this, it discusses different fields of knowledge, including texts and concepts of other religions, mathematics, drama, poetry and grammar.

Nandini A divine cow in Hindu mythology, sometimes considered the same as Surabhi and KAMADHENU, or thought to be the mother or offspring of Surabhi.

Nannaya A poet who lived from 1023 to 1063 and translated part of the *MAHABHARATA* into Telugu. He was the priest and court poet of King Rajaraja Narendra of the Eastern Chalukya dynasty, who ruled the country of Vengi, with present Rajahmundry in Andhra Pradesh as its capital. Nannaya was asked by the king to translate the *Mahabharata* and he translated the Adi Parva, Sabha Parva, and part of the Aranya Parva, but could not complete the whole work. Though meant to be a translation, Nannaya introduced certain changes, which made it rather a retelling of the original story.

The translation was later continued by TIKKANA and Yerrapragada.

Naoroji, Dadabhai A prominent PARSI in the freedom movement, and the first Indian MP in Great Britain who lived from 1825 to 1917. He was also involved in the reform of Parsi society and customs. He was a founding member of the the Rahnumae Mazdayasnan Sabha, an organization for Parsi reform, and in 1851 started the *Rast Goftar*, a Gujarati newspaper putting forward liberal views. He believed that the purity and simplicity of the GATHAS should be revived, and initiated a 'Back to the *Gathas*' movement.

Naqshbandi Order A SUFI order that originated from the Khwaja order founded in Central Asia, its main principles being established by Khwaja Abdul Khaliq (d. 1220), who lived near Bukhara. It came to be known as Naqshbandi, named after Khwaja Muhammad Bahauddin Naqshband (1317–89), one of the members of the order. The order became popular in India with the arrival of Babar, who became the first Mughal emperor in 1526, and was a follower of one of the Naqshbandi saints. It gained prominence when Khwaja Baqi Billah (1563–1603), a Naqshbandi saint from Kabul, came to DELHI in 1599, and popularized the order in the four years before his death. Naqshbandis were orthodox and were initially against SAMA and the liberal policies of the Mughal emperor AKBAR. Baqi Billah's disciple Shaikh AHMAD SIRHINDI (1564–1624) was one of the most important Naqshbandis who was critical of Akbar's liberalism. He condemned Sama, and put forward WAHDAT AL-SHUHUD concepts. His ideas were opposed by SHIAS and other Sufis, and though the Mughal emperor AURANGZEB supported the order and was even initiated into it in 1665, opposition to it remained strong, leading to its decline. Two Naqshbandis, Mirza Mazhar and his son MIR DARD, revived the order in the eighteenth century, with a broader and less rigid philosophy.

The sons of Baqi Billah, Khwaja Khurd and Khwaja Kalan, were opposed to Sirhindi and had a different school of thought, following WAHDAT AL-WUJUD beliefs. Shah WALIULLAH, the famous philosopher of the eighteenth century, was influenced by them.

Narada An ancient RISHI or sage, the author of some hymns in the RIG VEDA, described in the *MAHABHARATA*, PURANAS and other texts. Narada lived in svarga or heaven, but made frequent trips to earth. According to the *Mahabharata*, he visited the PANDAVAS a number of times and advised them on right action and conduct, and also tried to persuade DHRITARASHTRA to get DURYODHANA to make peace, but failed.

Narada narrated the *BRIHHANNARADIYA PURANA*, and the *NARADIYA PURANA*, to suta.

In the Puranas, Narada is a complex character. He was one of the seven rishis created by BRAHMA, but had a number of odd births, partly because of his mischievous nature. In one life he was born as a GANDHARVA, in another as a worm. After he had persuaded the sons of DAKSHA to wander over the earth, he was reborn as his son. He was once changed into a monkey, and on another occasion into a woman. But Narada continued to wander between heaven and earth, predicting the future and giving advice, both good and bad.

Other stories about him state that Narada played the vina, which became the musical instrument of the world. He supported the DEVAS in their struggle against the ASURAS over AMRITA or divine nectar, and protected the pot of Amrita. He inspired VALMIKI to compose the *RAMAYANA*, and according to the *CHHANDOGYA UPANISHAD*, he gained divine wisdom from SANAT KUMARA. The *Narada Dharma Shastra* is attributed to him. He was known by various other names, including Devarishi, Parameshthi and Surarishi.

Naradiya Purana A Sanskrit text, a minor PURANA or Upapurana, describing the worship of the god VISHNU. It includes the *RUKMANGADACHARITA*, the story of a king named Rukmangada, who was devoted to Vishnu. Another text of the same name forms a major Purana, but is usually known as the *BRIHANNARADIYA PURANA*, to distinguish it from the *Naradiya Purana*.

Narahari Tirtha A BHAKTI saint who probably lived from 1241 to 1333 , and is said to have been a disciple of MADHVA. According to various accounts, Narahari Tirtha was a regent of the Gajapati kings of Kalinga (Orissa) for twelve years, but later settled on the banks of the Tungabhadra river in the south. He was an ascetic, composing songs of love and devotion. In one of the first songs he composed, he said, 'Call on god to whom all creation submits, and give up the enemies within the Self'. He asked people to live a true life, without deceiving themselves. He is also considered the founder of the HARIDASA sect, devotees of the Hindu god VISHNU or Hari, based in the region of Karnataka. Among the Haridasas were KANAKADASA and PURANDARADASA, whose compositions are still sung today.

naraka A name for hell in Hindu mythology. It is the most commonly used name for hell even today, though ancient texts mention several others. According to the *MANU SMRITI*, there are twenty-one hells, while other texts give varying figures. The *VISHNU PURANA* describes twenty-eight hells to which people are assigned by YAMA on the basis of their misdeeds. There are hells for those who have cheated or robbed others, and for those who kill and harm others. The hell of Lalabhaksham, for lustful people, consists of a sea of semen; Vatarodham is for those who have harmed creatures of the forest.

Narakasura An ASURA king who ruled over Pragjyotisha (Assam). He was the son of the daitya HIRANYAKSHA and PRITHVI, goddess of the earth. He obtained a divine weapon from the Hindu god VISHNU, and could not be killed as long as he kept this with him. He married 16,000 princesses who, according to one story, were his daughters in a previous birth. Narakasura treated his wives badly and caused terror and devastation in the world. Finally he was killed by the god KRISHNA, who married all his wives to provide them with protection and status.

Nara-Narayana Two ancient RISHIS. The Sanskrit word Nara literally means 'man', while NARAYANA later became a name of the Hindu god VISHNU. There are several stories about these rishis in the MAHABHARATA and PURANAS. According to a legend in the DEVI BHAGAVATA PURANA, BRAHMA created DHARMA from his breast, and Dharma married ten of the daughters of DAKSHA. Among their sons were HARI, KRISHNA, Nara and Narayana. The first two became YOGIS, and Nara and Narayana became rishis. According to some accounts, they were the sons of Dharma and Ahimsa, and are said to be forms of KRISHNA and ARJUNA.

Various texts state that they lived in the Himalayas in Badarikashrama for a thousand years. Though they were rishis, they were good warriors. They once defeated SHIVA in battle, and the axe that they threw at Shiva was the one he gave to PARASHURAMA. They also defeated PRAHLADA and according to the VAMANA PURANA, Prahlada then realized that Narayana was actually the same as Vishnu.

Narasimha A Hindu deity, one of the ten main AVATARAS or incarnations of the god VISHNU. In this, Vishnu took the form of a half-man, half-lion (nara = man, simha = lion) in order to defeat the daitya HIRANYAKASHIPU. The latter, who was the father of PRAHLADA, and brother of HIRANYAKSHA, had practised great austerities and obtained a boon from the god BRAHMA. By this boon, he could not be killed by man, god, demon or animal; he could not die in the day or in the night, neither inside his home nor outside, neither in the earth nor in the sky. Having obtained apparent immortality, he began to rule the world as a tyrant. He was angry with Vishnu, who had already killed his brother; his anger increased because of Prahlada's devotion to Vishnu. Finally Vishnu assumed the shape of Narasimha, which was not a man, animal or demon, and killed him at dusk, when it was neither day nor night, in the courtyard of his house, which was neither within nor really outside, and just a little above the ground, which was neither on earth nor in the sky.

Narasimha is always depicted with the face of a lion and the body of a man, but there are several variations, with different expressions and moods. A number of images show him in combat with Hiranyakashipu, or emerging out of the pillar in which he was concealed. In some texts, nine forms are described, but his images in different temples reveal even more. Among his forms are: Prahladavarada Narasimha, in which Narasimha is shown blessing Prahlada; Yogananda Narasimha, or a peaceful and tranquil Narasimha teaching YOGA to Prahlada; Guha Narasimha, where Narasimha conceals himself; Kroda or Ugra Narasimha, the angry form; Vira Narasimha, a warrior form; Malola or Lakshmi Narasimha, where he is with his consort LAKSHMI; Jvala Narasimha, where he emits flames of anger; Sarvatomukha Narasimha, with a number of faces; Bhishana Narasimha, a ferocious form; Bhadra Narasimha, another fierce form; Mrityormrityu Narasimha, or Narasimha as the defeater of death.

Narasimha images and temples are found all over India and became popular from around the fourth century. Early images can be seen at ELLORA, MATHURA, Garhwa (near Allahabad) and elsewhere, but later he was most popular in south India.

In Andhra Pradesh, Narasimha temples are found at AHOBALAM, Dharmapuri, Mangalagiri, Simhachalam, Khammam and other places. In Karnataka there are a number of temples dedicated to the deity, but the most outstanding is the free-standing image carved out of a rock at Vijayanagara, today known as Hampi. Made in the sixteenth century, this reaches a height of almost 7 m. A well-known Narasimha temple in Tamil Nadu is located at Namakkal, while other famous temples are at Joshimath in Uttarakhand, Charthana in Maharashtra, and Nrusinghanath in Orissa. Narsimhapur, a town in Madhya Pradesh, is named after a Narasimha temple located here, constructed in 1800.

As one of Vishnu's AVATARAS, Narasimha represents a stage in evolution from the animal to the human.

Narasimha Mehta A Vaishnava BHAKTI saint and poet, also known as Narsi Mehta, who belonged to Gujarat, and probably lived from 1414 to 1480(alternative dates 1408–75). Born in Talaja village near Junagadh in an orthodox Nagar brahmana family, he married Manekbai and had a daughter and son. He was originally a worshipper of the Hindu god SHIVA, but Shiva himself is said to have revealed to him a vision of KRISHNA. After this he worshipped Krishna, chanting his name continuously and envisaging himself as one of the GOPIS. He saw Krishna as the one beyond form, eternal and unknowable. Through bhakti or love, Krishna could be seen without eyes, through an internal vision. Narasimha Mehta, through his vision of god, transcended caste, and composed devotional poems in Gujarati, singing of the joy of union with god. Men and women of all castes gathered around him, but the traditional BRAHMANAS rejected him.

Narasimha's compositions include autobiographical poems, verses to Krishna, and to the god beyond form. One of his bhajans *Vaishnava Jana*, was a favourite of Mahatma GANDHI, and the first few lines can be translated as: 'Who venerates each one in the world, who speaks ill of none, whose senses and mind are disciplined, blessed is the mother who gave birth to him. Him we call a Vaishnava.'

Narayan Guru A guru and leader of the Ezhava community of Kerala, who was born in 1854 or 1856 at Chempazhanti near Thiruvananthapuram, in Kerala. He was extremely learned and knew Sanskrit, Tamil and Telugu, apart from Malayalam. He spoke against the caste system and worked to raise the social and economic status of the Ezhavas, who were a backward caste, setting up the Sri Narayana Dharma Paripalana Yogam for this purpose. He had a large following before his death in 1928, and continues to be revered by the Ezhavas and others.

Narayana A name of the Hindu god VISHNU. Narayana was probably an independent deity whose concept was later merged with that of Vishnu. In early texts, Narayana was a name given to both BRAHMA and PRAJAPATI. The *MAHABHARATA* states that Prajapati first rested in the waters, known as Naras as they were the sons of Nara, and therefore Prajapati was called Narayana. The same principle is expressed in the *RIG VEDA*, which states that the waters contained the embryo of the gods. Narayana, resting on the waters, was later represented by Vishnu in his Sheshashayana form, resting on Shesha or ANANTA.

NARA-NARAYANA, two ancient RISHIS, were said to be brothers of HARI and KRISHNA, both names or forms of Vishnu.

As the concept of the god Vishnu developed, Narayana began to be used as an alternative name for him.

Narmada river A river in central India, that has a number of sacred sites along its banks. Rising at AMARKANTAK in Madhya Pradesh, it flows between the Vindhyan and Satpura Ranges, and after covering a distance of 1300 km, enters the Arabian Sea. According to the *PADMA PURANA*, it is the purest of rivers in the three worlds, and DEVAS, ASURAS, GANDHARVAS and RISHIS who bathe in it attain eternal bliss. The same text states that there are 60 crore and 60 thousand sacred ghats along the river.

Naropa A Buddhist scholar who lived from c. 956 to 1040, and was the teacher of MARPA. Naropa was originally at NALANDA, but left to study with TILOPA (989–1069), who was known as a MAHASIDDHA. Tilopa's esoteric teachings were transmitted through Naropa to Marpa, and are known as the 'Six Dharmas', or 'Six Yogas' of Naropa. These, termed Naro Chodrug in Tibetan, form an essential part of the KAGYU school of TIBETAN BUDDHISM. They include techniques for producing inner heat; experiencing the body as illusory; entering the dream state; perceiving the clear light; experiencing the state between birth and death; and transferring one's consciousness.

Nasatyas A name of the ASHVINS, deities described in the RIG VEDA.

Nashik A city in Maharashtra, located on the river Godavari. It is one of the sacred cities of Hinduism, and has several shrines and temples. The northern part of Nashik is known as Panchavati, identified with the Panchavati of the *Ramayana*, where Rama lived while in exile. Two Rama temples, Kala Rama and Gora Rama, are located here. The Sita Gumpha cava, is said to be the place from which Ravana abducted Sita. Rama Kund is a sacred site on the Godavari where Rama is said to have bathed. Nashik is also one of the places where the KUMBH MELA is held every twelve years. Among other temples here are the Sundara Narayana Temple of the god Vishnu and the Modakeshvara Ganesha Temple. Rock-cut Buddhist caves locally known as Pandu Lena, dating back to the first century BCE, are located in hills to the west of the city. Tryambakeshvara, 22 km away, has one of the twelve jyotir lingas of the god SHIVA.

Nasiruddin Mahmud, Shaikh A SUFI saint of the CHISTI order, a disciple of NIZAMUDDIN AULIYA. Nizamuddin appointed a number of Khalifas or deputies, but his chief successor in DELHI was Shaikh Nasiruddin Mahmud, who came to be known as Chiragh-i Dilli, or the lamp of Delhi.

Nasiruddin was born in 1276–77 in the region of Avadh, and by the age of twenty-five, had renounced the world and become a Sufi, fasting, praying and living in isolation. He was forty-three years old before he decided to come to Delhi, where he was welcomed by Shaikh Nizamuddin. He became a prominent Sufi of Delhi, and a supporter of Sultan Firuz Tughlaq. Once attacked by a QALANDAR, Nasiruddin received eleven knife wounds, but forgave his attacker and would not allow him to be prosecuted. He died in 1356, and a tomb was built on his grave by Sultan Firuz, with further enclosures and a mosque erected by the Mughal emperor Muhammad Shah (1719–48).

His teachings, which were compiled in the *Khairul Majalis* by Shaikh Hamid Qalandar, represent the height of Chisti philosophy. He said that a Sufi should fast, pray and practise ZIKR, inwardly withdrawn from the world, even when in company. Control of the breath was an important part of Sufi practice, and the perfect Sufi was a master of the breath. His tomb, known as CHIRAGH-I DILLI'S DARGAH, remains a place of pilgrimage.

Nasks A division of Zoroastrian literature. According to tradition, twenty-one Nasks were collected at the time of the Sasanian dynasty of Iran (226-651 CE). These included books in three groups: seven on religion, seven on statecraft and seven on medicine. With the coming of the Arabs most of these texts did not survive, though summaries exist in Pahlavi. The *DINKARD* describes the contents of the Nasks and explains how the Nasks were composed, each related to the twenty-one words of the AHUNA VAIRYA prayer. Two Persian RIVAYATS also describe the Nasks. The only surviving Nask is the *VENDIDAD*, while fragments of some others exist.

nastika A term indicating non-orthodox schools of Indian philosophy, i.e., those which do not base themselves on Vedic literature. Buddhism, Jainism, the philosophy of the AJIVIKAS and of other materialist schools, are thus in this category. Some scholars include only materialistic schools which do not believe in an afterlife, and thus exclude Buddhism and Jainism.

Nataraja A form of the Hindu god SHIVA. In this form, Shiva is the god of dance and the lord of the universe. Images of Nataraja are many and varied, as Shiva performs various dances described in the NATYA SHASTRA. These include the nadanta or tandava, lalita, lalatatilaka, katisama, talasamphotita and others. In the most common form, Shiva is depicted in the tandava pose, the dance of destruction. In this pose, he stands with his right leg on a dwarfish figure, crushing him under his feet. This figure represents Asmarapurusha or Muyalaka, the embodiment of illusion or MAYA. Shiva's left leg is raised and bent at the knee. He has four hands; the front right hand is in Abhaya Mudra, the gesture to dispel fear, while the back right hand holds a kettledrum, known as a damaru. The front left hand points downwards towards the raised foot, while the other holds fire. The whole is encircled in flames. The *Chidambaram Mumanikovai*, desccribes the inner meaning of this form, in a verse in praise of the deity: 'O my Lord, thy hand holding the sacred drum has made and ordered the heavens and earth and innumerable souls. Thy lifted hand protects both the conscious and unconscious order of thy creation. All these are transformed by thy hand bearing fire. Thy sacred foot planted on the ground, gives an abode to the tired soul struggling in the toils of causality. It is thy lifted foot that grants eternal bliss to those that approach thee. These five actions are indeed thy handiwork'. The sound of the drum thus is shabda, the 'word' from which creation arises. The dance represents all movement in the universe, and the conquest of illusion. On his head Shiva wears a symbol of the moon and of the river GANGA contained in his matted hair. The moon represents the light of the ATMAN, and the Ganga the flow of wisdom. Thus the main aspects of Shiva are contained in this image. Some images have six, eight, ten, sixteen or more arms, and are in different dance postures. Under the Chola dynasty of south India, bronze and stone images of Nataraja were made, and a number of temples or shrines were dedicated to the deity, the most important being the NATARAJA TEMPLE at Chidambaram. Gangaikondacholapuram, a city of the Cholas, has temples with exquisite Nataraja images. The Nataraja form was popular in Bengal between the eighth and twelfth centuries, and several SHIVA temples in Bengal have images of Nataraja, with a separate shrine or hall dedicated to the deity.

Nataraja Temple A temple of the Hindu god NATARAJA, a form of SHIVA, located at Chidambaram in Tamil Nadu. It was constructed mainly in the twelfth and thirteenth centuries, during the time of the Chola dynasty, with later additions.

However, the origin of the temple dates back to the sixth century.

This huge temple complex has several shrines within an area of twenty-two hectares. There are four enclosure walls, the outermost constructed in the seventeenth century, at the time of the Nayaka dynasty. The main shrine, known as the Chit Sabha, has an image of Nataraja in the dance form known as Ananda Tandavam. According to traditional accounts, Shiva performed his famous dance in a forest exactly at this spot, at the request of the gods and RISHIS. Nearby is an image of the goddess Shivakami or Shivakama Sundari, a form of PARVATI.

Five stone steps lead to the Chit Sabha, representing the five syllables of the Shiva mantra, *namah shivaya*. On the silver-plated doorposts are representations of Vyaghrapada (a RISHI who was granted a boon of having a tiger's feet, so that he could climb trees to collect flowers for the deity) and PATANJALI, who worshipped Shiva here. There are several other halls and shrines, among them the Kanaka Sabha or golden hall; the Nritta Sabha or dance hall, in the form of a chariot; the Deva Sabha with images of various deities; and the Raja Sabha or thousand-pillared hall used for festivals. Other shrines include the Shivakami Amman shrine and a temple of Subrahmanya or MURUGAN. There are four towering GOPURAMS as well as numerous sculptures of Shiva, other deities and Shaivite saints. The 108 dance forms described in the NATYA SHASTRA are depicted in the temple.

Chidambaram is said to be the centre of the universe, representing the ATMAN or soul within the heart. The area was earlier known as Tillai or Ponnambalam, which remain some of the alternate names of the temple.

Festivals take place all through the year and there is a constant flow of pilgrims to the temple. The most important festival is the ten-day festival in the month of Marghazi (December to January), concluding on the day of the full moon.

Natha yogis A Hindu SHAIVITE sect, said to have been founded in the tenth century by MATSYENDRANATHA and GORAKHNATHA who formulated various practices that would lead to the transformation of the mind and body. The aim of the yogi was to enable people to become Nathas or masters, to rise above bondage, sorrow and limitation, and attain complete control over oneself, even to the extent of conquering death. Hatha Yoga and Tantric practices were combined, based on earlier systems. The adherents were also known as Kanphata Yogis because of the earrings they wore, which split their ears (kanphata = torn ear). There were nine traditional Nathas or leaders. Nathas worship SHIVA in the form of BHAIRAVA, as well as HANUMAN and DATTATREYA.

Nathas seem to have been prominent around the fifteenth and sixteenth centuries, and are mentioned in Sikh literature. Guru NANAK is said to have had discussions with yogis of this sect, and to have convinced them of his philosophy, as described in the SIDDHA GHOSHT section of the GURU GRANTH SAHIB. Natha yogi sects still exist.

Nathamuni A BHAKTI saint and devotee of the god VISHNU, also known as Ranganatha Muni, who lived between 824 and 924. He was the son of Ishvara Muni, and the first of the VAISHNAVA acharyas, the successors of the ALVAR saints. He put together the hymns of the Alvar saints in the NALAYIRA DIVYA PRABANDHAM and popularized them in Vaishnava temples of south India. His Yogarahasya and Nyayatattva form the beginnings of the VISHISHTADVAITA philosophy, which was fully formulated and developed by RAMANUJA. Nathamuni was the first acharya of the SRIRANGAM temple. His grandson was the scholar and philosopher YAMUNACHARYA.

Nathdwara Shrinathji Temple A temple of Shrinathji, a form of the Hindu god KRISHNA, located at Nathdwara, 50 km north-east of Udaipur in Rajasthan, on the Banas river. The image here is said to be Svayambhu, or self-created, and represents Krishna raising the mountain GOVARDHANA, to protect his fellow cowherds from the deluge sent by the god INDRA. The image was intitially enshrined near Govardhana in the MATHURA region, but was brought to the state of Mewar in the seventeenth century to protect it from possible destruction by AURANGZEB. According to legend, as the chariot carrying the image rolled along, it stuck at this point, and therefore this was considered the right place to install the image. Shrinathji was worshipped by VALLABHACHARYA, and his followers still take care of the temple, which attracts a number of pilgrims.

National Council of Churches of India An association of Churches of India, that began as the National Missionary Council, founded in 1914. Various Christian agencies and Churches were associated with it over time. In 1923 it became the National Christian Council of India, Burma and Ceylon, and after 1947, the National Christian Council of India. It was renamed the National Council of Churches of India in 1979. Its headquarters are at Nagpur. Most of the PROTESTANT and ORTHODOX CHURCHES are members of this body. ROMAN CATHOLIC Churches are not part of the Council, but coordinate with it.

Natya Shastra A Sanskrit text of the first or second century, that describes various forms of dance, drama and music, in great detail. The text is said to have been written by Bharata, and emphasizes the divine nature of all art forms. Classical dance forms, as well as temple dances, were originally described in this text.

Nau Ruz A term for the BAHAI new year celebrated on 21 March, which marks the end of a nineteen-day period of fasting. Celebrations include prayers and festivities, which are adapted to local customs. The Bahai scriptures state that the equinox marks the rejuvenation of life, and symbolizes a new spiritual birth. Thus the sun at the equinox can be compared to the spiritual suns, the great spiritual leaders and prophets who appear from time to time to rejuvenate and purify life on earth. The same term is used for the Iranian and Kashmiri new year. See NAVROZE.

Navagraha A group of nine planets, which are considered deities in Hinduism. They are SURYA, the sun; SOMA, the moon; MANGALA or Mars; BUDHA or Mercury; BRIHASPATI or Jupiter; SHUKRA or Venus; SHANI or Saturn; and the two shadow planets, RAHU and KETU. Surya has a number of separate temples, while the others are often depicted in groups or in separate shrines within temples. Among the notable Navagraha temples are the NAVAGRAHA TEMPLE, GUWAHATI, the Navagraha Temple at Ujjain, and the series of NAVAGRAHA TEMPLES in Tamil Nadu.

In temples the Navagraha are depicted as sculptures, on panels in relief, by their symbols, or in the form of LINGAS.

Navagrahas are important in astrology and are believed to have ill or good effects depending on their placement in a person's astrological chart or horoscope. Separate rituals, prayers and MANTRAS are recommended for propitiating each of the planets.

Navagraha Temple, Guwahati A Hindu temple located on Chitrachal hill, near Guwahati in Assam, constructed in 1752 during the reign of Rajesvar Singh. In this temple, the NAVAGRAHA, or nine planets, are symbolized by LINGAS, each covered by a different coloured cloth, representing the colours associated with the planets. The original garba-griha or inner shrine still exists, while the tower or shikhara has been rebuilt after its destruction in an earthquake.

Navagraha Temples, Tamil Nadu The NAVAGRAHA, or nine planets, are very sacred in Tamil Nadu, and worshipping them is said to bring great benefits. Separate shrines dedicated to individual grahas are located in a number of temples. They include the shrine of MANGALA or Mars at Vaitheeswaran Koil, BUDHA or Mercury at Thiruvenkadu, KETU at Keezhaperampallam, SHANI or Saturn at Thirunallaru, Jupiter at Alangdi, SOMA or the Moon at Thingalur, RAHU at Thiruganeswaram, SURYA at Surianar Koil, and SHUKRA or Venus at Kanchanur. All these are located within a radius of 60 km, and the whole circuit can be completed within three days.

Navapada Oli A Jain ritual and festival. Ayambil Oli, also known as Navapada, takes place twice a year for a period of nine days, in the months of Chaitra (March–April) and Ashvina (September–October). Ayambil refers to a penance of semi-fasting, consisting of one meal a day of simple food, without spices, milk, sugar, salt, oil, butter, fruits or vegetables. At the same time meditation on the Navapada or nine pious entities is practised, and worship to them is offered. The Navapada are arihants, siddhas, acharyas, upadhyayas and sadhus (together constituting the Pancha Parameshthi or five holy beings), as well as jnana (knowledge), darshana, charitra (character), and tapa (austerities). Oli is connected with the story of SHRIPALA and Mayana, who lived in ancient times. Shripala was cured of leprosy after practising Oli nine times, and its practice is believed to be helpful in curing and preventing diseases. The story of Shripala and Mayana is enacted during this festival.

Navaratra A festival of nine nights during which DURGA PUJA, or the worship of the Hindu goddess DURGA, takes place. The festival occurs before DASHAHARA in October/November. Another Navaratra or period of Durga worship for nine days takes place in spring. According to some PURANAS, only ghi (clarified butter) should be eaten at the start of the puja on a new moon day. An open temple with sixteen pillars should be constructed, and a platform made in the middle on which a throne should be placed, covered in white silk. The image of DEVI or Durga is to be placed here and worshipped. Nine young virgin girls should be worshipped on these days.

Worship during the Navaratras remains popular, with several regional variations.

Navjote The term for the thread ceremony of Zoroastrians. Literally it means 'new birth'. The ceremony originates in the concept that each person should understand the religion, and choose it for themselves, after which they can be initiated into the religion. However, it is now a ritual, usually performed for children between the ages of seven and fifteen. The child is given a ritual bath, after which the main ceremony takes place, when the priest or priests, along with the child, recite prayers in front of the sacred fire. During this recital, the sacred vest, SUDREH, and sacred thread, KUSTI, are put on the initiate for the first time, as a formal induction into the religion. In Zoroastrianism both boys and girls undergo the Navjote ceremony. After this initiation the prayers are to be recited at least twice a day.

Navroze A term for the Zoroastrian new year. The same term is used in Kashmir, Iran and elsewhere, and is often spelt Naoroz or NAU RUZ. Because of variations in the Zoroastrian calendar in India, there are three different new years, of the Fasli, KADIMI, and SHAHENSHAHI sects. The Fasli new year, also known as Jamshedi Navroze, and according to tradition started by the legendary king, JAMSHED, is based on a solar calendar and is observed every year on 21 March. This day is celebrated in Iran and a number of other countries, indicating the continuation of Zoroastrian traditions even after its decline.

The Kadimi and Shahenshahi are based on a lunar calendar and take place on varying dates in July and August respectively. Most PARSIS celebrate Jamshedi Navroze as well as one other new year. On Navroze prayers are said and JASHANS are held, and friends and family celebrate with feasts.

Traditionally, Navroze was celebrated for fourteen days, beginning on the eve of the new year. On Navroze morning, a white cloth was spread on a table, and seven items beginning with 's' were placed there: sib (apple), sabzi (vegetable), sir (garlic), sambol (hyacinth), serteah (vinegar), samukh and sumnool (herbs). They represented fertility and prosperity for the coming year. A live fish was placed in a bowl of water, and a lamp lit for each member of the family. All stood around the table to greet each other. Wheat was grown in small pots, and on the thirteenth day after Navroze, the pots were floated in a nearby river or other water source. Thus both water and plants, the givers of life, were revered. Similar ceremonies still take place in Iran, though Parsis in India today usually limit the celebrations to one day.

Navsari A town in Gujarat sacred to PARSIS. The sacred fire was moved here from SANJAN in the twelfth century, and a Dar-e Mehr or AGIARY was constructed, while an ATASH BEHRAM was consecrated in 1765. There is also an institute for training priests.

naya A concept in Jainism, that forms part of the Jain theory of knowledge. Naya deals with different ways of perception. Most commonly, there are seven types of naya, though others are mentioned in various texts. The seven types are: (1) Naigama-naya, in which something is looked on as a whole; for instance, going to gather wood and lighting a fire are parts of what constitutes cooking. According to another view, Naigama-naya consists of looking at general and specific characteristics together; (2) Samgraha-naya looks at the common features of something, thus placing it in a class; (3) Vyavahara-naya is the usual way of perception, based on empirical knowledge; (4) Rijusutra-naya sees things in the moment, without taking into consideration continuity and identity; (5) Shabda-naya bases itself on the name of the item, and the images which come to mind through its name; (6) Samabhirudha-naya is connected with Shabda-naya, and analyzes things through the root meaning of the word; (7) Evambhuta-naya is a refined version of Samabhirudha-naya, looking at only one relevant aspect of the root meaning.

Naigama has the widest application, and Evambhuta the narrowest. Nayas are also divided into the dravyatirthaka, or substance, and the paryatirthaka or modification of the substance. Nishchaya-naya is an integration of all nayas. Some aspects of this categorization of methods of perception also exist in other philosophies, including the NYAYA, VAISHESHIKA, SAMKHYA, ADVAITA and Buddhist systems, but the Jain system is more complete. The naya approach leads to SYADVADA or satbhangi, the seven different approaches to a thing or its attributes. It is also related to the Jain concept of ANEKANTAVADA or relativity.

Nayadhammakahao (Jnatadharmah-katha) A Jain text, the sixth of the twelve ANGAS. It is divided into two sections, called *Naya* and *Dhammakaha*, the first with nineteen chapters or suyakkhandas, and the second with ten vaggas. The first has stories or parables, many of which are fairy tales or adventures to which a moral has been added, conveying Jain teachings. The stories include that of MALLI, the female TIRTHANKARA, and of Dovai (DRAUPADI), the wife of the PANDAVAS. The second section consists mainly of legends of Jain saints.

Nayanars/Nayanmars A term for SHAIVITE saints who probably lived between the seventh and tenth centuries, though some scholars assign them an earlier date. They followed the path of BHAKTI and devotion to the Hindu god SHIVA, and some of them composed verses and songs in praise of the god. They were called leaders (Nayanars) because of their knowledge and devotion, though they thought of themselves as servants of the deity. Traditionally, sixty-three Nayanars are recognized. Their songs were collected in the TIRUMURAI, in eleven books. Among these, the *Tevaram* includes seven books, and contains verses by three of the main saints, APPAR, SAMBANDAR and Sundarar or SUNDARAMURTI, while the *Tiruvasagam* contains verses by the later saint, MANIKKAVACHAKAR. Among other saints, Karaikkal Ammaiyar was a woman. Kannappar, a hunter, was known for his extreme devotion; he removed one of his eyes and offered it to the lord when he saw that the eye of the Shiva idol was bleeding. Sirutonttar even cooked and served his son to the deity, who later restored the boy to life; others worshipped Shiva in simple ways. The saints were of different ages, castes and professions, but united in their extreme love of, and devotion to the deity. Some of them were ascetics, while others were householders.

Various accounts of the saints have been written, including Sundaramurti's *Tiruttondattogai*, NAMBI ANDAR NAMBI's *Tiruvantadi* and Sekkilar's *Tiruttonda-puranam*, also known as the PERIYA PURANAM, and considered the twelfth book of the *Tirumurai*. Images of the saints, with brief accounts of their deeds, are found in Shiva temples in the Tamil region.

The songs of the Nayanars are still sung in temples in Tamil Nadu, and images of the saints are taken out in procession on special occasions.

The Nayanar texts form the base for the SHAIVA SIDDHANTA philosophy.

Nazir Akbarabadi An Urdu poet who lived from 1735 to 1830. Born in DELHI, his real name was Wali Muhammad. He later moved to AGRA and became a school teacher and tutor, and thus used Hindi and Braj Bhasha (a Hindi dialect of the region) in his poems. His father was a SUNNI, but his mother was a SHIA, and Nazir probably became a Shia too. He was not sectarian in his approach, and some of his poems are on Hindu deities, including one in praise of the god KRISHNA.

Nazranis A term for the early Christians of KERALA, so-called because they were followers of the Nazarene (Jesus). Later they were absorbed in the SYRIAN CHRISTIANS.

Nechung Monastery A Tibetan Buddhist monastery at DHARAMSALA. Here the Tibetan state oracle resides, and predicts the events of the coming year.

Nemichandra A Jain scholar of the DIGAMBARA sect, who lived in the tenth century and was a friend of Chamunda Raya, a minister of the Ganga dynasty, responsible for the construction of the GOMMATESHVARA image at SHRAVANA BELAGOLA. He wrote a number of books, of which three are considered important, *Trilokasara*, a work on Jain cosmography, and *Labdhisara* and *Gommatasara* on Jain philosophy.

Neminatha A name by which the twenty-third Jain Tirthankara, ARISHTANEMINATHA, is popularly known.

Neo-Buddhists A term referring to new Buddhist converts. Neo-Buddhists exist all over the world, but in India the term specifically refers to converts to Buddhism, which began with B.R. AMBEDKAR's conversion in 1956 along with 2,00,000 people from backward castes. Over the years conversions to Buddhism have continued, leading to a revival of the religion and a considerable rise in numbers. At the conversion ceremony, Neo-Buddhists declare their faith in Buddhism and agree to abide by the twenty-two vows laid down by Ambedkar. The Bharatiya Baudha Mahasabha is an organization of Neo-Buddhists.

Neryosang, Dastur (1) According to oral tradition, the name of the Zoroastrian DASTUR or priest who led the first group of Zoroastrians to SANJAN and conversed with the king, JADI RANA. He is said to have set up the first ATASH BEHRAM and invoked lightning for the atash (sacred fire) through the power of his prayers.

(2) Another dastur of the same name is said to have translated the Avestan texts into Sanskrit in 1200.

Nestorian A term for a Christian doctrine named after Nestorius, Patriarch of Constantinople (428–31) who held that there were two separate substances or persons in JESUS, the human and the divine, and only the human was crucified. This view was condemned by the orthodox. Nestorian ideas existed among Christians in India and were predominant in Asia up to about the thirteenth century. The Nestorian Patriarch was in Mesopotamia and was recognized by some Muslim rulers. With the Mongol expansion under Chengiz Khan (1206–25), Nestorian centres in Mesopotamia were destroyed and Nestorianism declined in India as well.

Netti-Pakarana   A Buddhist text written in Pali, that probably belongs to the first century BCE, though it contains earlier material. It is also known as the *Netti-Gandha,* or *'The Book of Guidance'* and is attributed to Mahakachchana, a disciple of the BUDDHA. The text is the first to provide a connected account of the teachings of the Buddha. The *Petakopadesa* is also attributed to Mahakachchana and is a continuation of the *Netti.*

New Apostolic Church   A PROTESTANT Christian church that began in Europe in the nineteenth century, and was introduced in India in the 1970s. It now has twenty-seven centres. The 'Chief Apostle' is the name of the head of the church, below whom there are Apostles, bishops, district elders and others. Its headquarters is at Bangalore, Karnataka.

New Testament   A sacred text of Christians, based on the teachings of JESUS. It forms the second part of the Christian BIBLE.

Nidana-Katha   A Buddhist text that is an introduction to the fifth-century JATAKA commentary, the *Jatakatthavanana.* It provides a biographical background of the BUDDHA in the THERAVADA tradition. *Nidana-Katha* means 'Story of Beginnings' and consists of three sections: *Durenidana,* referring to the remote past, when the Buddha Shakyamuni was a person named Sumedha and was guided by the Buddha Dipankara and finally reborn in the Tushita heaven; *Avidurenidana,* the life of the Buddha after his descent from the Tushita heaven, up to his attaining Buddhahood; *Santikenidana,* the beginnings of the present from the Buddha's enlightenment to the construction of the Jetavana monastery by ANATHA-PINDAKA.

The text thus presents an account of the life of the Buddha in a connected sequence, and includes passages from the *BUDDHAVAMSHA* and *CHARIYA PITAKA.*

Niddesa   A Buddhist text that forms part of the *KHUDDAKA NIKAYA* of the PALI CANON. It consists of a commentary on some sections of the *SUTTA NIPATA* in two parts, the *Maha-Niddesa* and *Chulla-Niddesa.* The *Niddesa* includes explanations for technical terms, words and phrases, and synonyms. It is much earlier than other Pali commentaries.

Nihang   A Sikh warrior group said to have been founded by Guru GOBIND SINGH. They wear dark blue clothes and a peaked turban, sometimes affixed with a steel disc, and carry steel weapons. This group of special soldiers was important in the time of RANJIT SINGH under the leadership of Phula Singh.

Nihangs still exist and observe all the principles of the KHALSA, though they are no longer warriors.

Nijjuttis (Niryuktis)   A category of Jain texts consisting of commentaries on the canonical texts of the SHVETAMBARAS. Some of the early Nijjuttis form part of the canon, and the *Ogha Nijjutti* was said to be based on one of the lost PURVAS. They are written in Jain Maharashtri and later in Prakrit.

nikaya   A Pali and Sanskrit term, commonly used in BUDDHISM, where it can mean a collection or group of texts, or a school or sect.

Nilakantha   A name of the Hindu god SHIVA, literally meaning 'blue-throat'. According to the myth connected with the churning of the ocean for AMRITA or divine nectar, at this time poison also emerged from the ocean and was swallowed by Shiva and kept in the region of his neck, so that it would not injure anyone. This turned his neck blue.

Nilamata Purana   A Sanskrit text, a minor PURANA or Upapurana. It describes the wise sayings of a NAGA king who lived at a place called Nila in Kashmir. It is important for the study of Kashmir, as it narrates its early history, festivals and ceremonies.

Nimbarka   A philosopher and mystic who probably lived in the twelfth century.

Nimbarka was born in a Telugu BRAHMANA family at Nimbapuri in present Karnataka, but spent most of his life in VRINDAVANA near MATHURA. He advocated the worship of RADHA and KRISHNA, as he believed BRAHMAN or the Absolute was also a personal god who transcended all limits. He felt that Radha was the eternal consort of Krishna, and lived with him in GOLOKA, or the highest heaven. He stated that god, the soul and the world were identical yet distinct.

His philosophy is called DVAITADVAITA and is considered one of the schools of VEDANTA.

nirakara/nirankara   A term used to describe god or BRAHMAN. It means 'without form'.

nirang   A term in Zoroastrianism used in different ways, for something that is sacred.

(1) Gomez, the urine of a special white bull, is known as nirang after its consecration and purification, and is used in rituals.

(2) Nirang are also sacred formulae or chants. They can be inscribed on amulets, or recited to ward off disease and evil.

niranjana   A term used to describe god or BRAHMAN. It means stainless, untainted, or pure.

Nirankari   A Sikh sect which began as a purificatory movement within Sikhism. It was started by Baba Dyal (1783–1855), who though a Sikh, was not one of the KHALSA. Baba Dyal was against the Hindu customs that had crept into Sikhism, and particularly against idol worship, including the existing practice of worshipping the gurus through idols or pictures. He believed this went against the basic tenet of Sikhism, that God was beyond form, or Nirankar. He settled at Rawalpindi (present Pakistan) and built a temple there, but because of opposition from other Sikhs, he later moved to the outskirts of the town. Maharaja RANJIT SINGH is said to have appreciated his teachings. Baba Dyal's son, Bhai Dhara or Darbara Singh (d. 1870), succeeded him and collected his father's teachings in a book known as *Hukam Nama*. He set up over forty centres to spread these teachings, and was responsible for eliminating several Hindu customs. Sikh birth, marriage and death ceremonies, as practised today, are based on his reforms. Bhai Dhara was succeeded by his brother Rattan Chand (d. 1908), followed by the latter's son Gurdit Singh (d. 1947). A succession of gurus followed, and Nirankaris still have a large following. They do not accept militant Sikhism and greet each other with the words 'Dhun Nirankar'. Orthodox Sikhs oppose them because of their different views, and because they follow other gurus in addition to the traditional ten. Their headquarters is now at Chandigarh. The SANT NIRANKARI, despite their similar name, is a different sect.

nirguna A term that means 'beyond attributes' and applies to the Absolute, the deity that transcends all qualities. In Hinduism, BRAHMAN is said to be nirguna; the concept of god in Sikhism is similar. Nirguna, or that which is beyond form or specific qualities, can also take on attributes and become SAGUNA.

nirjara A term in Jainism, for the process through which KARMA is removed. It includes fasting, meditation and various auterities and penances. Two types of nirjara are recognized, akam and sakam, passive and active. Akam is the shedding of karma by passive suffering, for instance, fasting when there is no food to eat, while sakam is taking active steps to end karma, such as fasting even when food is available.

Nirmala A Sikh sect that, according to tradition, came into existence at the time of Guru GOBIND SINGH. It is said to have developed through the views of five Sikhs who were sent by the guru to VARANASI to study Hindu theology. Some scholars, however, feel that the sect originated later. Nirmalas follow the GURU GRANTH SAHIB but have their own ideology and GURDWARAS, and their tenets include celibacy. They were particularly important in the nineteenth century, and Baba Nand Singh was one of their noted gurus

Nirmala Devi The founder of the system of SAHAJA YOGA.

Nirmala Devi was born on 21 March 1923 in Chhindwara, in present Madhya Pradesh, to Prasad and Cornelia Salve, a Christian couple. Her father was a renowned scholar, who is said to have known fourteen languages. Always spiritually inclined, Nirmala married C.P. Srivastava, a civil servant, shortly before Independence in 1947, and had two daughters.

Though she was aware of her own spirituality, it was only in 1970 that through a divine vision, she discovered a simple method by which she could enable people to reach self-realization. Thus she started teaching and propagating Sahaja Yoga (spontaneous union with the divine), which soon became a worldwide movement.

Nirmala Devi has also set up hospitals to help in curing serious diseases including cancer, through Sahaja Yoga, as well as other charitable institutions.

Nirmala Jhara temples A complex of four Hindu temples located at Khallikote in Orissa. Here a stream of pure water from a natural spring flows through stone channels into a pond, around which the temples are located. The Patitpavan Temple is dedicated to Patitpavan, a form of the god VISHNU worshipped in Orissa. The flowing water from the spring is said to be the sacred river GANGA, flowing from the foot of Vishnu. The Vimala Temple has a beautiful image of a four-handed DURGA holding a conch and chakra. The Radha–Krishna Temple depicts RADHA and KRISHNA, as well as the Dashavataras and scenes from Krishna's life. The Shiva Temple is the smallest of the four. There are other images near the pond, notable being those of Vishnu, a meditating ascetic, and a huge crocodile. Sculptures carved in black granite decorate the walls of the temples.

nirmanakaya The first of the TRIKAYA or the concept of the three bodies of the BUDDHA, in MAHAYANA Buddhism.

Nirriti (1) A Hindu deity first mentioned in the RIG VEDA, in association with YAMA, god of death. He later became one of the DIKAPALAS, the guardian of the south-west. He is also described as one of the eleven RUDRAS and is said to be the son of Sthanu and grandson of BRAHMA. According to the *AGNI PURANA,* he is depicted holding a sword in his hand and is seated on an ass.

(2) Nirriti is also a goddess who signifies destruction.

Nirukta A Sanskrit text that explains and comments on the words used in the VEDAS. Nirukta, in the sense of etymology or glossary, is one of the VEDANGAS. There must have been several Niruktas, but the one that is still extant is that of Yaska, who probably lived before PANINI. The *Nirukta* based itself on the Nighantus or lists which have three parts: the Naighantuka, which consists of words with synonyms; Naigama, words found only in the Vedas; Daivata, names of deities, and words connected with them and with sacrifices. There are several other lists of words, followed by a commentary, in which Yaska explains the words with illustrative passages of how they were used.

nirvana A term normally used in Buddhism, indicating the blissful state of liberation from rebirth and the cycle of lives, achieved by transcending desires and passions. Literally it means 'blowing out'. It is also used in Hindu texts, though the more common term there is MOKSHA. In Hinduism it signifies union with, or realization of, the divine.

Nisargadatta Maharaja A realized soul who lived a simple life in MUMBAI (Bombay) and preached his philosophy to all who came to see him. He is considered a modern exponent of ADVAITA.

Born in Mumbai in 1897, he was named Maruti and was the son of Shivaram Pant, who had come from the village of Kandalgaon in Maharashtra and worked for some time as a domestic servant. Shivaram returned to his village to cultivate his land, and was helped by Maruti and his other children. Maruti did not have a formal education but took an interest in spirituality and imbibed religious ideas from a BRAHMANA friend of his father. His father died when he was eighteen and Maruti again went to Mumbai and opened a shop selling children's clothes, tobacco and bidis. He married and had four children. At the age of thirty-four he met Siddharameshwar Maharaj, a NATHA YOGI, who instructed him and gave him a MANTRA. After his guru's death in 1936, Nisargadatta, as he was now known, left his home and became an ascetic, but was convinced by another Natha yogi that renunciation in the midst of life was a better option. Nisargadatta returned to Mumbai and continued to run his shop until his death from cancer in 1981, meeting people in search of spiritual answers, in his simple home. The discussions that took place reflect his self-realization. He spoke only in Marathi, but his followers included a number of foreigners, and other disciples helped to translate his words.

Nisargadatta said that his guru told him he was the Supreme Reality, and as he thought about this, he realized its truth and understood the True Self, free of all desires and beyond the body and mind. He recommended the same practice to his followers. He said 'Just keep in mind the feeling "I am", merge in it till your mind and feeling become one.' The first collection of his talks translated into English, *I Am That*, gave him international fame. Other collections include *The Nectar of Immortality*, *The Ultimate Medicine*, and *The Quintessence of My Teaching*.

Nishpannayogavali A VAJRAYANA Buddhist text in Sanskrit. It describes more than 500 Buddhist deities and assigns them to various BUDDHA families.

Nityananda, Swami or Bhagwan A renowned guru, Swami Nityananada was born some time before 1900. He was abandoned in a forest as a baby, but was found and cared for by a local woman, Uniamma, and after her death by her employer, Ishwar Iyer, who lived in Kozhikode (Calicut). The child was named Ram and was always spiritually inclined. He lived for some time at Udupi and Mangalore in Karnataka, and was recognized as a realized soul, and took the name Swami Nityananada. He then set up his own ashram at Ganeshpuri in Maharashtra in the 1930s.

Swami Nityananda was known to be a simple man who did not teach any particular philosophy, but guided all towards the realization of the True Self. His presence was said to bring peace to all who were near him, and miracles of healing were reported. He died on 7 August 1961, and his conversations and teachings, compiled from the notes of his disciples, are collected in the *Chidakash Gita*. The best-known of his disciples was Swami Muktananda Paramahamsa, who popularized the system of SIDDHA YOGA, a simple method of self-realization, in India and abroad. Swami Muktananda was succeeded after his death in 1982, by Swami Chidvilasananda.

Nivedita, Sister An Irish woman named Margaret Noble who became a disciple of Swami VIVEKANANDA and took the name Sister Nivedita.

Born in Ireland in 1867, she was an educationist who followed the then-new ideas of Froebel and Pestallozzi. After meeting Swami Vivekananda in London in 1890, she came to India, joined the RAMAKRISHNA MISSION as a nun, and dedicated her life to the service of India. She started a girls' school in Kolkata (Calcutta), wrote against British policies in India, and was associated with Sri AUROBINDO. She left the Mission after Vivekananda died, but continued to work selflessly for India. She died in 1911 at the age of forty-six. She wrote about Vivekananda in *The Master as I saw Him*, while among her other writings are *The Cradle Tales of Hinduism*.

niyama Five positive principles that form part of the practice of YOGA. They are shaucha (purity), santosha (contentment), tapasya (ascetic practices), svadhyaya (self-study), and Ishvara pranidhana (surrender to God). The *Hatha Yoga Pradipika* and some later texts list ten niyamas.

Nizamuddin Auliya, Shaikh A SUFI saint of the CHISTI order, who was a disciple of Baba FARID. Nizamuddin was born in 1238 in Budaun in present Uttar Pradesh, and was saintly even as a child. At the age of sixteen, he came to DELHI along with his mother in order to complete his education, and studied both HADIS and FIQH. He lived in poverty, and though he qualified for a post as QAZI, he decided to follow the Sufi path. He visited Baba Farid at Ajodhan, who prescribed various ascetic practices for him. On his third visit to the KHANQAH of Baba Farid in 1265, Nizamuddin was appointed his khalifah (deputy), and the Baba blessed him and said, 'You will be a tree under whose shadow people find rest.'

Shaikh Nizamuddin settled in Delhi and became one of the most renowned Sufis. Around 1286 he moved to Ghiyaspur on the outskirts of the city. He lived simply and ate only before dawn and in the evening. Countless people came to him with their problems, and he helped them all. His LANGAR, or free kitchen, was open to both Hindus and Muslims. Nizamuddin laid down six conditions for a SUFI to reach the goal of realizing God. These were: retiring to a lonely cell, and remaining there; always existing in a state of performing wuzu (ablutions); perpetual fasting; maintaining silence except for the practice of ZIKR; continuosly reciting zikr while remembering one's PIR in one's heart; expelling all thoughts except those of God.

Among his noted disciples were AMIR KHUSRAU and Ziauddin Barani. Nizamuddin appointed a number of Khalifahs, but his chief successor in Delhi was Shaikh NASIRUDDIN MAHMUD, who came to be known as Chiragh-i Dilli, or the lamp of Delhi.

Nizammuddin died in 1325, and his DARGAH in Delhi is still a popular place of pilgrimage.

Nizamuddin, Mulla A theologian of the eighteenth century (d. 1784), who formulated a MADRASA curriculum known as Dars-i-Nizamiya. This, based on the QURAN and HADIS, became the standard syllabus for madrasas, including the DAR-UL-ULOOM, DEOBAND.

Nizari Ismailis An Islamic SHIA sect, a branch of the ISMAILIS. They were followers of Nizar, one of the sons of the Fatimid Kaliph Mustansir (d. 1094). Imam Nizar escaped from prison after being deposed by supporters of his brother Imam Mustali. Most KHOJAS form a part of the Nizari Ismaili sect.

Nobili, Roberto de A Christian missionary in India, who was one of the first to Indianize Christian rituals, in order to attract more people to Christianity. Born in 1576, he came to south India and studied the customs of the area, as well as Sanskrit and Tamil. He felt the best way to convert Indians to Christianity was to make himself less alien to them, and therefore began to dress like an Indian SANNYASI, with a saffron robe, sacred thread, and sandal paste on his forehead. He referred to himself as a 'Roman brahmana' and managed to convert a number of high-caste Hindus. He also laid the foundations for a community of Christian sannyasis who lived and worked like him. He was opposed by his own colleagues, but was revered and respected by Indians. He died at Mylapore, Chennai, in 1656.

North-east, Christianity in Christianity predominates in three states of the north-east—Nagaland, Meghalaya and Mizoram. These areas, occupied by tribal groups, had their own beliefs, and had not been particularly influenced by religions in other parts of India. Some Christians settled here in the seventeenth and eighteenth centuries but did not have much impact. The first Christian missionary in the region was Krishna Chandra Pal (1764–1822), an Indian from the Serampore mission, while more PROTESTANT missionaries arrived in the 1820s and 30s. The Baptist Missionary Society, dominated by American Baptists, had considerable success in spreading Christianity in Nagaland, while the Welsh Presbyterian Mission worked with the Mizos and Khasis. Later, ROMAN CATHOLIC missions also preached in the area.

Despite large-scale conversion to Christianity, most of these groups retain many of their traditional customs, festivals and modes of dress. (*See* also MEGHALAYA, TRADITIONAL RELIGION; MIZO, TRADITIONAL RELIGION; NAGAS, RELIGION OF.)

Nuruddin Mubarak Ghaznawi, Syed An Islamic scholar who lived in DELHI in the thirteenth century, and was against the philosophical school of Islam, represented by AVICENNA and others. He stated that kings could not attain salvation, unless the philosophers were banished from the kingdom.

Nuruddin Rishi A SUFI saint of Kashmir, popularly known as Nund Rishi, who started a Sufi order of RISHIS.

Born in 1377–78, Nuruddin did not have a formal education. He became a mystic, living in a cave at Kaimuh near Srinagar, eating only wild leaves. Some accounts state that he was initiated into the HAMADANI Sufi order, a branch of the KUBRAWIYA, or that he was an UWAISI. Nuruddin composed verses on the mystical union with God, reached through the heart of love. Some of his verses are similar to those of LALESHVARI, the SHAIVITE saint of Kashmir. He was a vegetarian, as he believed cruelty to animals should be avoided. He advocated simplicity, asceticism and celibacy, and had both Hindu and Muslim disciples, though some of the former converted to Islam. His disciples carried on the order after his death in 1439, but about a century later they began to live in KHANQAHS, acquiring wealth and property.

The Rishi order is considered a reflection of the syncretic nature of Islam in Kashmir. Nuruddin's verses in Kashmiri have been collected in two volumes, the *Rishinama* and *Nurnama*. His tomb, known as CHARAR-E-SHARIF, is located at Charar, 32 km from Srinagar.

Nur-ul-Muhammadiya A Persian term in Islam for the divine light of the Prophet MUHAMMAD, known in Arabic as the Haqiqa-ul-Muhammadiya. The realization of this light is a concept in several SUFI orders. According to a HADIS, the Prophet said, 'The first thing created was the light of your Prophet, which was created by the light of God.' ISNA ASHARI Shias believe that Nur, or this divine light, was inherent in the twelve Imams.

nyaesh A term for certain Zoroastrian prayers, usually to individual YAZATAS (divine beings). For instance, the Khorshed Nyaesh praises the light of the sun. The Atash Nyaesh praising fire is one of the most popular nyaeshes.

nyasa An ancient technique that involves activating power in one's own or another's body through touch, accompanied by MANTRA and meditation or concentration. Nyasa is used by the PANCHARATRAS, SHAIVITES, and various Tantric sects.

There are several different types of nyasa. One type involves assigning parts of the body to various deities and activating them by touching the body. Anga nyasa consists of touching different parts of the body with the hands or fingers, while reciting a MANTRA to stabilize the body, before starting meditation. In Kara nyasa the hands and fingers are touched by those of the other hand. Nyasa is also done to activate the CHAKRAS or energy centres. There are texts dealing with nyasa, but the actual process has to be learnt from a guru.

Nyaya   One of the six classical schools of philosophy. Nyaya literally means 'that by which the mind reaches a conclusion', and is based on logic and analysis.

According to tradition, it was founded by Akshapada Gautama, who probably lived between the third century BCE and first century CE, though some hold that Akshapada and Gautama were two different people, who both contributed to Nyaya philosophy. The basic text is Gautama's *Nyaya Sutra.* It deals with sixteen topics and analyses religious concepts and means of knowledge. Its five main subjects are: pramana, the means to right knowledge; prameya, the object; vada, dialogue or discussion; avayava, parts of the syllogism; and anyamata-pariksha, a comparison with different systems. Nyaya also distinguishes between nine DRAVYAS or substances that comprise the world.

The *Nyaya Bhashya* of Vatsyayana, probably of the fourth century, is an important commentary on the *Nyaya Sutra*. The Nyaya philosophy continued to develop over the years, and among other notable works are Uddyotakara's *Nyayavarttika* of the sixth century, Vachaka's *Nyayavarttika-tatparyatika* of the ninth century, and Udayana's *Nyaya-tatparyatika-parishuddhi* of the tenth century. Gangesha's *Tattvachintamani* (eleventh century) is the standard text of the modern school. Nyaya developed further at Navadvipa, a centre of learning in Bengal, in the sixteenth century and later. Both Nyaya and Vaisheshika put forward the theory that the natural world is composed of atoms, which are eternal, unalterable, and have an independent existence. In its explanation of creation and matter, Nyaya seems to be a forerunner of modern physics. Regarding the soul, Nyaya states that there are eternal souls attached to a body from time to time, but each soul is individual and independent. Neither knowledge nor intellect forms the soul. The individual is neither the soul nor the body, but the result of their union.

Later Nyaya became similar to VAISHESHIKA and also became theistic, with SHIVA as the chief deity and the cause or origin of the universe. The rigorous analytical methods of Nyaya contributed to other philosophical systems, and its categories are still used in philosophical debate and discussion.

Nyingma   A school of TIBETAN BUDDHISM, which literally means 'the Ancient Ones'. Though the school is known only from the eleventh century, it traces its origin to PADMASAMBHAVA of the eighth century. At a time of persecution in Tibet, sacred texts and teachings of Padmasambhava were concealed, and these secret texts were known as gterma (treasures). The texts were revealed later, and form the basis for this school. Gterma can also refer to wisdom attained through insight and intuition. The school divides Buddhist teachings into nine vehicles or categories, the first six of which are common to other schools of Tibetan Buddhism. The three additional categories are classifed as the innermost Tantras, known as Mahayoga, Annuyoga and Atiyoga. In Mahayoga, the ordinary level of perception and attachment is transcended; through Annuyoga, primordial awareness is aroused; finally, in Atiyoga, also known as Dzogcheng, the practitioner transcends ordinary time, activity and experience. These special teachings are said to have been conveyed by the Buddha SAMANTABHADRA. Among the hundreds of teachers who revealed the gterma or sacred treasures, five are specially revered. These are: Nyangral Nyima Ozer (1124–92): Guru Chowang (1212–70); Dorje Lingpa (1346–1405); Padma Lingpa (b. 1405); and Jamyang Khyentse (1820–1892). Nyingma texts, preserved in their monasteries, consist of thousands of TANTRAS that are not included in the KANGYUR and TANGYUR COLLECTIONS.

Among the new Nyingma monasteries established in India after 1959 are: Thekchok Shedrub Dargye Ling, in Bylakuppe, Karnataka; Ngedon Gatsal Ling in Clementown, Dehra Dun; Palyul Chkher Ling, and E-Vam Gyurmed Ling in Bir, Himachal; Nechung Drayang Ling at Dharamsala, Himachal; Thubten E-Vam Dorje Drag at Shimla, Himachal.

The Nyingma tradition is headed by a Rinpoche.

Ohrmazd A later name of AHURA MAZDA, or God in Zoroastrianism. In Pahlavi texts he was known as Ohrmazd or Hormazd.

Olcott, Henry Steele One of the founders of the THEOSOPHICAL SOCIETY. Born in New Jersey in 1832, he was interested in the occult and along with Madame BLAVATSKY and W. Judge, set up the Theosophical Society in New York in 1875. He came to India with Madame Blavatsky and helped to found the Theosophical Society of India at Adyar in Chennai. He settled in Sri Lanka, became a Buddhist and worked to promote Buddhism there. He was the inspiration for the founding of the MAHABODHI SOCIETY in India. He died in 1907.

Old Testament A text sacred to Christians that forms the first part of the Christian BIBLE. The same text, with some variations, forms the whole Hebrew BIBLE.

Om A sacred word, also spelt Aum, used at the beginning of all Hindu prayers and ceremonies, said to be the greatest of MANTRAS, and to possess mystic power. It is a compound of three syllables, 'a', 'u' and 'm', which traditionally represent the first three VEDAS. The *MANDUKYA UPANISHAD* is among the texts that provides a description of Om. It states that all that is past, present and future, is Om. Om represents the nature of BRAHMAN, the Absolute, and is the symbol of the Supreme, the beginning, middle and end of all things. It is also the ATMAN, and its three letters reflect the waking, dreaming and sleeping states of consciousness. Those who know the Om that is beyond its individual parts reach TURIYA, the fourth state of consciousness. A person with such knowledge is a great sage. Om is the god (ISHVARA) seated in the heart; meditating on this, the Self transcends sorrow. The *KATHA UPANISHAD* states that Om is BRAHMAN, the highest, and one who has a true knowledge of this word obtains all desires (II.16). Later texts state that its three letters, a, u, and m, symbolize the three divine aspects of creation, preservation and destruction, or the three Hindu deities, BRAHMA, VISHNU and SHIVA.

Omkareshvara A small island located at the confluence of the NARMADA and Kaveri rivers in Madhya Pradesh. It is said to be shaped like the symbol OM and is a sacred site for Hindus. There are several temples here, dating back to medieval days. The SHIVA temple of Omkareshvara Mahadeva, which has one of the twelve jyotir LINGAS, is specially venerated. It was reconsructed by the Maratha peshwa Baji Rao II in the eighteenth century. Two major festivals take place here every year, that of Karttika in November and SHIVARATRI in February/March, attracting pilgrims from all over India.

Onam A festival celebrated in Kerala in August-September, marking the traditional day when MAHABALI, who according to legend ruled the area in ancient times, visits from the underworld. It is also a harvest festival. The Malayalam era (Kolla Varsham) new year begins with the month of Chingam. Year-long farming activities usually ended on 1 June before the advent of the monsoon. Paddy is sown before this and becomes ripe for harvest in the month of Chingam for the Onam festival. Other agricultural produce was also harvested at his time. The surplus produce was used to buy new clothes and special food was prepared from the newly harvested crops. Now there is a change in farming practices and an increase in non-farming activities, but onam is still celebrated with great joy and splendour. On this day special clothes are worn, houses are decorated with flowers, and elaborate meals are prepared. Games are organized, including the famous snake-boat race (Vallumkali) held at Aranmulai, Kottayam and other places, in which each of the long boats is rowed by a hundred people. The day ends with dances, feasts and other festivities.

Opus Dei A conservative CATHOLIC Christian religious order, founded by Josemaria Escriva de Balaguer. In India, it has centres in DELHI and MUMBAI.

Oraons, religion of Oraons, a tribal group found mainly in Jharkhand and Orissa, believe in a number of deities and spirits of whom the most important is Dharmesh, the sun god, creator and destroyer of the world. Dharmesh is not worshipped in any temple, but Oraons have a sacred grove where other deities, belonging to ten different levels or grades, are worshipped. Offerings and sacrifices are made by the village priest, known as the Pahan, sometimes assisted by the Pujar. Oraons also worship Hindu deities, including a form of SHAKTI named Devi Mai, but give them somewhat different characteristics. Some Oraons have become Christians, though they retain their tribal identity.

Oriyur A town in Ramanathapuram district, Tamil Nadu, sacred to Christians. The Portuguese Jesuit St. John de Britto was martyred here in 1693. A shrine with a Portuguese-style façade is located here, with a statue of Arul Anandar, as St. John was popularly known, where he is depicted offering his head to the executioner.

According to legend, the sand turned red when he was beheaded. This red sand can still be seen and is said to have healing powers. Thousands of pilgrims visit the site every year.

Orthodox Church A group of Churches that broke away from the Western ROMAN CATHOLIC Church in the fifth century and later. Before the 400s there was only one Christian Church, but within it there were different nationalities and some divergent beliefs. At the Christian Council of Ephesus (431 CE), the Church condemned the teaching of the Patriarch Nestorius, who had said there were two natures in Christ (see NESTORIAN), leading to the separation of the East Syrian Church. Following this, at the Council of Chalcedon (451), the nature of Christ was redefined, as 'truly God and truly man . . . in two natures . . . without separation', thus leading to a rejection of Monophysite teachings, which said only one nature existed after the incarnation. The Armenian Church, the Coptic Church of Egypt, the Ethiopian Church and the Syrian Jacobite Church then broke away from the main group. After a series of disputes between the Patriarch of Constantinople and the Pope, a further schism took place in 1054 between Churches that followed the Byzantine rite and those that followed the Latin rite. Later some Orthodox Churches reunited with the Catholics, and they are now known as Eastern Catholics or Orthodox Catholics.

The Orthodox Church includes the four ancient Patriarchates of Alexandria, Antioch, Constantinople and Jerusalem, as well as Orthodox Churches in eastern Europe, Russia, Africa, Australia and Asia.

In general, these churches believe that God is one and cannot be known, but that he is present in all creation through his energy. The human being was created in the image of God, but because of the sin of Adam, he became less than perfect, and death came into the world. Jesus, through his death and resurrection, provided for new life through his holy Spirit. Orthodox rituals include the seven Mysteries, similar to the SACRAMENTS.

In India the Orthodox Churches follow the traditions of ST. THOMAS and of Christians who came from Syria in ancient times and are known as SYRIAN CHRISTIANS. They include two Catholic Churches, while the others are linked with the Churches of West Asia. The main Orthodox Churches are the SYRO-MALABAR CHURCH (CATHOLIC); the SYRO- MALANKARA CHURCH (CATHOLIC); the MALANKARA ORTHODOX CHURCH, also called the Jacobite Church, or Orthodox Church; the Malankara Orthodox Christian Church; the ASSYRIAN CHURCH OF THE EAST, also known as the Chaldean Syrian Church of the East; and the MALABAR INDEPENDENT CHURCH. There are other Orthodox Churches that are offshoots of these.

Orthodox Churches in India are also referred to as Eastern Orthodox, Lesser Eastern Orthodox, or Oriental Orthodox.

Oshadhipati A Hindu deity, another name of the moon, literally meaning 'lord of herbs'.

Osho A philosopher and religious leader also known as Rajneesh, who has a considerable following both in India and abroad.

Born in 1931 at the village of Kuchwada in present Madhya Pradesh, his original name was Chandra Mohan Jain. He was rebellious in school, though intellectually and artistically gifted. After leaving school, he dabbled in politics, worked in a newspaper and studied for some time at a college. Simultaneously, he was developing his own philosophical ideas, meditating, practising austerities and seeking self-discovery. He claimed to have become enlightened on 21 March 1953, and to be a reincarnated saint who had lived 700 years ago. He then studied philosophy, obtaining BA and MA degrees, and going on to teach at Raipur Sanskrit College. In 1960 he was appointed professor at the University of Jabalpur. He began giving public talks on various issues and also organized meditation camps. He resigned from the university in 1966. In 1970 he moved to MUMBAI and soon started attracting disciples, using the title Bhagwan Shri Rajneesh. In the seventies he started an ashram at Pune, where both Indian and Western disciples lived. Though it was in some ways a typical ASHRAM, with duties assigned to everyone and several rules, in other ways it was unique. One disciple wrote, 'The ashram is crazy, it's chaotic . . . It's a funhouse and a madhouse. A bawdyhouse and a temple. There's music and dancing and laughter. There's silence and reverence and stillness.' Dynamic Meditation was held every morning, several different techniques and methods were made available, and sex was one of the paths to enlightenment, as in traditional TANTRISM. Orthodox neighbours objected to the activities at the ashram, and in 1981 Rajneesh moved to Oregon, USA, founding a commune called Rajneeshpuram. The ashram was extremely prosperous, but new controversies arose and local people complained against it. Rajneesh returned to Pune in 1985, and at his ashram there he continued to introduce new and esoteric techniques. He claimed that his Mystic Rose Meditation was the greatest breakthrough in 2500 years. In 1989 he took the name Osho, by which he is still known. He had suffered from ill-health even before going to the US, and after his return his health steadily declined. He died on 19 January 1990.

During his life he wrote over a hundred books interpreting ancient texts and explaining his own philosophy. He was charismatic and learned, and believed in inner exploration and in freeing and opening the mind, but in contradiction to this, he demanded surrender and obedience. His ideas are in some ways similar to those of J. KRISHNAMURTI, and Osho is still one of the most popular gurus of modern times, as well as one of the most innovative. Many of his meditation techniques, such as Dynamic Meditation or Enlightenment Intensive, are used today, without acknowledgement, by a variety of different teachers and spiritual groups.

Our Lady of Dolours, Church of   A church located in Thrissur, Kerala, one of the largest in India, built in Indo-Gothic style and dedicated to the Virgin MARY. The interior has eleven altars in a row, and is richly decorated with large statues, murals and painted ceilings, while above it has a domed roof and belfry towers. It is a popular place of pilgrimage, and a tourist attraction.

Our Lady of Graces, Church of   A ROMAN CATHOLIC church located in Sardhana, in Meerut district of Uttar Pradesh, built by Begam SAMRU in 1822. The church is linked with the history of the Begam, a Muslim who later became a Catholic.

The church was earlier known as St. Mary's Church, dedicated to the Virgin MARY, and once functioned as a cathedral. It is built in a combination of styles, designed by an officer in the Begam's army, Antonio Reghelini of Padua. A marble monument dedicated to the Begam was added in 1848.

The church was renamed Church of Our Lady of Graces, after a new image of the Madonna was installed there in 1957, blessed by Pope Pius XII. In 1961, the church was raised to the status of a minor Basilica. The image of Our Lady is credited with miraculous powers, and the church is a centre of pilgrimage not only for Christians, but for those of other religions as well. A special feast is held on the first Sunday of November every year.

Begam Samru also left a legacy of several lakh rupees to be used by Christian churches and missions, both for their upkeep and for providing for the poor.

Padartha A term in ancient philosophical systems, literally meaning a category. All early philosophical systems attempted to classify the material and non-material world into a variable number of padarthas or categories. ADVAITA recognizes two padarthas, ATMAN and ANATMAN, the soul and that which is not-soul, while VISHISHTADVAITA has the above two as well as God. SAMKHYA sees PURUSHA and PRAKRITI as padarthas, and MIMAMSA describes five padarthas. NYAYA and later VAISHESHIKA have seven padarthas. The term is also used in Buddhism and Jainism.

The terms tattva and prameya are sometimes used in the same way as padartha. Depending on the context in which it is used, there can be varying classifications of padarthas, even within the same philosophy.

Padinenkilkanakku A collection of eighteen minor works in Tamil which have been variously dated. While some place them between the fifth and eighth centuries CE, others feel they are much earlier. Out of these, the two most famous are the *TIRUKURAL* and a Jain text, the *NALADIYAR*, which contain wise or moral sayings on life and religion. Among others that have ethical or moral statements are the *Nanmanikkadigai* by Vilambi Naganar, a VAISHNAVA poet, and the *Palamoli*, another Jain work with proverbs illustrated by stories. The *Trikadukam, Eladi* and *Shiru-panchamulam* are three similar works that provide advice on curing the diseases of the mind and body. The first is by a Vaishnava, while the other two are by Jains. The *Asarakkovai* is a SHAIVITE work.

These texts provide an idea of the diverse religious traditions of the times.

Padma A Sanskrit term for a lotus. It is the name of various goddesses, including LAKSHMI and MANASA, as well as of other people. In Jain texts, Padma is a name of RAMA.

Padma Purana (1) A Sanskrit text, one of the eighteen major PURANAS of Hinduism. It has six books or sections, the sixth being a late addition. Book I, the *Shrishtikhanda*, states that Lomaharshana, the suta, sent his son Ugrashravas to recite this Purana to the RISHIS in the Naimisha forest. The Purana had earlier been recited to Ugra by Pulastya, son of BRAHMA. It is named Padma after the lotus (padma), in which Brahma appeared at the time of creation, and the highest god is said to be Brahma. Nevertheless, the Purana glorifies the god VISHNU. The rest of Book I has creation myths, followed by explanations of PITRI (ancestor) worship, as well as descriptions of dynasties, myths of the conflicts between the gods and the demons, and an account of sacred places.

Book II, the *Bhumikhanda*, has stories and legends, beginning with that of Somasharma, who was later reborn as PRAHLADA. Book III, *Svargakhanda*, describes the world of the gods, as well as of the BHUTAS, PISHACHAS, GANDHARVAS, VIDYADHARAS, APSARAS and others. Book IV, the *Patalakhanda*, describes the subterranean regions in which NAGAS or snake gods live. Stories of RAMA and of KRISHNA are also narrated. Book V, the *Uttarakhanda*, deals mainly with the myths and rituals of VAISHNAVISM. In one chapter here, RADHA is identified with LAKSHMI. The sixth book, the *Kriyayogasara*, is also considered an UPAPURANA, and prescribes methods of Vishnu worship. In its final form the *Padma Purana* is a late work, but has an earlier core.

(2) A Jain *Padma Purana* provides a version of the RAMAYANA.

Padmanabha Temple A temple of the Hindu god VISHNU, located in Thiruvananthapuram, Kerala. Originally of the seventeenth century, the shrine was reconstructed in the eighteenth century, in the time of Martanda Varma, ruler of Travancore. The inner shrine has an image of a reclining Vishnu, around which is a passageway and a columned MANDAPA or hall. Other shrines are dedicated to KRISHNA, NARASIMHA and GARUDA. The temple has a double-tiered gabled roof and is notable for its murals on the outer walls. The GOPURAM on the east has a soaring tower.

Padmapani A Buddhist deity, another name of the Bodhisattva AVALOKITESHVARA.

Padmasambhava A Buddhist monk of the eighth century, originally from Kashmir, who laid the foundations of Buddhism in Tibet. He also founded monasteries in Ladakh and in Lahaul and Spiti. Not much is known of the life of Padmasambhava, but he succeeded in spreading Buddhism in Tibet, whereas earlier scholars such as SHANTIRAKSHITA failed because of their philosophical and scholastic approach. At this time the Bon religion was widespread in Tibet, and its deities and priests were thought to have great power.

Padmasambhava defeated them using mystical and magical techniques, and at the same time revealed Buddhist teachings. The NYINGMA school of TIBETAN BUDDHISM is based on his teachings.

Padmavati A story in verse written in Hindavi or early Hindi in the sixteenth century by Malik Muhammad Jayasi, which expresses SUFI ideals.

The story is based on a tale from Rajasthan and describes the life of the queen Padmavati. It begins with an invocation to ALLAH and the Prophet MUHAMMAD, mentions the emperor who was ruling at the time, Sher Shah Sur (ruled 1540–45), and pays reverence to the author's PIRS.

The main story is divided into two parts, beginning with Padmavati's early life in Simhala Dvipa (Sri Lanka), and her love for her parrot who was stolen from her and somehow reached the court of Ratna Sena, king of Chittor (Rajasthan). There the parrot kept describing the beauty of Padmavati, and leaving his wife Nagmati, the king took the parrot and set off to find Padmavati. On the way he was helped by NATHA YOGIS and the eighty-four SIDDHAS. Finally he brought Padmavati back to Chittor, but the DELHI sultan Alauddin Khalji (ruled 1296–1316) heard of her beauty and captured her husband. Though Ratna Sena was rescued, he later died in battle against another Rajput chief, and Padmavati and Nagmati, his two queens, joined him on the funeral pyre.

Through this story Jayasi brings in Sufi sayings and concepts, and makes innumerable comparisons between the Sufi path and that of the yogis and siddhas, pointing out several similarities. He believed GORAKHNATHA was a counterpart of the MAHDI.

Jayasi, also known as Muhaqqiq-i-Hind (Researcher of Indian Truth), was born in 1494-95, and was originally a Sufi of the CHISTI order, but later became a MAHDAWI. He wrote a number of other works in early Hindi, of which the *Padmavati* is the best known.

Padroado A Portuguese term meaning 'patronage', referring specifically to the right granted by the Pope to kings and nobles of Europe to promote religious activity in areas under their rule. In 1418 Pope Martin V granted the Portuguese these rights in their overseas territories, and it was later used by the Portuguese to promote Christianity in India. The Padroado prevailed in India till 1953, when an agreement was signed between the Holy See in Rome and Portugal, bringing it to an end.

Pahlavi The written language of the Sasanian dynasty (225 to 651) of ancient Iran, in which several ZOROASTRIAN TEXTS were composed. At this time the ancient AVESTA texts were copied, re-edited and translated, and new texts based on ancient traditions were written. The final versions of many of these date to the ninth century.

Paila An ancient RISHI who was a disciple of VYASA, and was one of the five disciples who narrated the *MAHABHARATA* to others. He visited BHISHMA while he was lying on his bed of arrows, and attended the RAJASUYA sacrifice of YUDHISHTHIRA.

Painnas (Prakirnakas) A series of Jain texts that form part of the SHVETAMBARA canon. The ten Painnas, known in Sanskrit as Prakirnakas, are: *Chausarana* (Skt: *Chatuhsharana*) by Virabhadra; *Aurap-achchakkhana (Aturapratyakhyana); Bhattaparinna (Bhakta-Parijna); Samthara (Samstara); Tamdulaveyaliya (Tandul-avaitalika); Chamdavijhaya; Devimdathaa (Devenrastava); Ganivijja (Gani Vidya); Mahapachchakkhana (Maha-Pratyakhyana);* and *Viratthaa (Virastava)*. These miscellaneous texts deal with various aspects of the Jain religion. The *Chausarana* discusses the six essentials (AVASHYAKAS) and four refuges (chausarana or chatuhsharanam) of Jainism. The *Devimdathaa* provides a classification of the kings of gods. Some of the texts describe methods of SALLEKHANA or voluntary death of a sage. Astrology, time, anatomy and physiology are among the other subjects discussed in the texts.

Other texts are sometimes added to the list of Painnas, which then exceed twenty.

Pali Canon A collection of Buddhist texts written in PALI. These are the basic Buddhist texts, particularly important for HINAYANA Buddhism, but also used by other schools. The three groups of texts, also called the Tipitaka or three baskets, are the SUTTA PITAKA, VINAYA PITAKA and ABHIDHAMMA PITAKA. The *Sutta Pitaka* includes five NIKAYAS, of which the first four contain discourses of the BUDDHA, while the fifth is a collection of miscellaneous texts. The VINAYA PITAKA has rules for the monks and nuns of the SANGHA, and the *Abhidhamma Pitaka* explains various philosophical concepts. These texts have been variously dated, but the *Vinaya Pitaka* and the first four Nikayas of the *Sutta Pitaka* were probably composed by the third century BCE, and contain material not far removed from the time of the BUDDHA. According to a tradition in Sri Lanka, all the texts were written down by the first century BCE.

Pali language An early Indian language in which HINAYANA Buddhist texts were written. It was closely related to Sanskrit and is considered a literary form of PRAKRIT, but probably had a mixed origin. The language spread along with the PALI CANON to Myanmar, Thailand, Laos, Cambodia and Vietnam, but died out in India.

Palitana A town in Gujarat sacred to Jains, where the SHATRUNJAYA hill is located. Palitana was granted to SHANTIDAS, a rich Jain banker, for the use of Jain pilgrims, by Murad Baksh, son of the Mughal emperor Shah Jahan, in 1656. Later the grant was confirmed by the emperor AURANGZEB.

Pampa A Kannada poet of the tenth century. Born in 902 or 903, he was the court poet of Arikesari, a feudatory of the Rashtrakuta dynasty, who ruled at

Lembalapataka, now called Vemulavada in present Karnataka. He probably grew up in or around Banavasi and had BRAHMANA ancestors, though his father Bhimapayya had become a Jain. Pampa is known for two major works, the *ADI PURANA* and the *Vikramarjuna Vijaya* or *Pampa Bharata*. While the *Adi Purana* is a Jain text, the *Vikramarjuna* is a retelling of the MAHABHARATA story, much abridged and with some variations. Pampa makes ARJUNA the hero of the story, and also identifies Arikesari with Arjuna. Pampa inspired other retellings of the *Mahabharata* in south India.

panch pir A group of five Islamic saints of India, revered by both Hindus and Muslims. The panch pir were worshipped collectively and often not individually identified. Shrines of the five saints were once prominent in northern and eastern India. Sometimes the names of these saints are listed, and usually include Ghazi Miyan or Salar Masud, Zinda Ghazi, Shaikh Farid, Khwaja Khizr and Pir Badr. These PIRS were historical people around whom legends were later woven. SALAR MASUD was a saintly warrior who died in battle; Shaikh Farid refers to Baba FARID, the SUFI saint; Pir Badr-i-Alam, or Shaikh Badruddin, the patron saint of sailors, was prominent in East Bengal and Bihar, and like Khwaja KHIZR, whom he was closely associated with, was said to travel on a floating rock or a fish. He died in 1440, and his grave is in Bihar. WARIS SHAH, the eighteenth-century SUFI poet, provided a different list, identifiying the Panch Pir as Khwaja Khizr, Baba Farid, Lal Shahbaz Qalandar, Shaikh BAHAUDDIN ZAKARIYYA and MAKHDUM-I JAHANIYAN.

pancha shila A term in Buddhism for five moral principles that all Buddhists are meant to observe. They are similar to the YAMAS in YOGA.

pancha-makara A term in TANTRISM. It refers to the five (pancha) makaras or five items beginning with the 'Ma' sound or letter. These are maithuna or sex, mamsa or meat, matsya or fish, madya or liquour, and mudra, parched grain or kidney beans. These five makaras are used in Tantric rites and by using or doing that which is often prohibited, Tantrics seek to liberate the mind, eliminate desire, and transcend the material world.

pancharaksha A term in MAHAYANA Buddhism for five protective spells or dharanis. They are the Maha-Pratisara, for protection against sin, disease and various evils; the Maha-Sahasrapramardini, against evil spirits; the Maha-Mayuri, against snake bite, and also against disease; the Maha-Shitavati, against wild animals, insects and the negatively aligned planets; and the Maha. Mantranusari, against diseases. These protective spells were once commonly used.

Pancharatra A Hindu VAISHNAVA sect that believes in the theory of *vyuhas* or cosmic emanations. According to this theory, Vasudeva-KRISHNA, who is the same as VISHNU, is the source of the universe. Sankarshana or BALARAMA emanates from him and represents PRAKRITI or nature. From Krishna and Sankarshana emerges PRADYUMNA, who in other sources is the son of Krishna. Pradyumna represents Manas or the mind. Aniruddha, who is Krishna's grandson, comes from Pradyumna, and is identified with Ahamkara, the ego or the conscious self. In the Pancharatra system, each of these deities is worshipped individually, though they emanate from one.

The followers or the pancharatra practice ancha-kala or five observances every day. These are : abhigaman, that is approaching the god, referring to morning prayer and ablutions; upadana, collecting the materials for worship; ijya, sacrifice, i.e., worship; svadhyaya, study; yoga, meditation. The word Pancharatra is first used in the *Taittiriya Samhita*, where a man named Babara Pravinhi is said to have used the Pancharatra sacrifice to gain rhetorical power. In the *Shatapatha Brahamana*, a Pancharatra sacrifice conducted by Narayana, is mentioned. Through this sacrifice Narayana describes the vyuhas to Narada. A vast Pancharatra literature emerged from around the fifth century, and the sect was prominent between the fifth and ninth centuries, though it continued in succeeding centuries.

Some of the texts that describe the sect's practices are the *Ahirbudhnya Samhita* and the *Ishvara Samhita*, as well as various *Pancharatra Sutras*.

Panchashikha An ancient RISHI. According to the PURANAS, he was also known as Kapila, as his mother's name was Kapilaa. He lived at the court of JANAKA and was revered as his guru.

Panchatantra A Sanskrit text containing fables and stories, probably written in the fifth century, but with an earlier origin. It was compiled by Vishnusharman to provide guidance to the sons of kings. The text consists of a series of connected stories. Vishnusharman, a BRAHMANA, was asked by a king to teach his sons, and he did this through fables with animal characters. The stories reveal the common human failings of greed, envy, malice, vanity and treachery, and warn against being too trusting. They provide guidelines on living life wisely. By the tenth century or earlier, the book had been translated into Persian, Arabic, Syrian, Greek and Turkish, and was known in European countries. *Aesop's Fables, La Fontaine's Fables* and other similar collections derived many of their stories from the *Panchatantra*. A later version in India is the *Hitopadesha*.

panchayatana A Sanskrit term used in different ways, that normally refers to five shrines, or to five aspects or elements. Among the ways in which the term is used are : (1)Panchayatana puja: the worship of five Hindu deities, VISHNU, SHIVA, DURGA, GANESHA and SURYA. Such worship transcends sectarian divisions, and is common among the SMARTAS.

(2)According to the *PADMA PURANA*, the term Panchayatana refers to an image of the god SHIVA in

KASHI (Varanasi), which has five ayatanas or aspects: shanti (peace), atitashanti (that which is beyond peace), paraparavidya (transcendent knowledge), pratishtha (fame) and nivritti (recession).

Panchen Lama A term for a line of lamas within the GELUG sect of TIBETAN BUDDHISM. In the seventeenth century, the fifth DALAI LAMA gave this title to his tutor, who was the head of the Tashi Lhunpo monastery in Tibet. He is considered the fourth Panchen Lama, as three earlier lamas obtained the title retrospectively. Panchen means 'great scholar', and the lamas are believed to be incarnations of the Buddha AMITABHA. From the seventeenth century onwards, the Panchen and Dalai Lamas initiated one another in turn, the older serving as a tutor for the younger. When a Panchen Lama died, his incarnation was searched for in the same way as for a Dalai Lama. So far (2005), there have been eleven Panchen Lamas. The tenth, born in China in 1938, was not confirmed till the age of eleven. He died in 1989, and a conflict arose over the eleventh Panchen Lama. In 1995, the Dalai Lama recognized Gedhun Choekyi Nyima, a six-year-old boy, as the Panchen Lama, while the Chinese government chose Gyaltzen Norbu. The latter is the official Panchen Lama, with the religious name of Bainqen Erdini Qoigyijabu.

Some Tibetan Buddhists revere them more highly than the Dalai Lama, because Panchen Lamas are purely spiritual and not involved in government, though they have taken part in political activities. Foreigners called them 'Tashi Lamas', from the name of the monastery.

Panchika A name by which the yaksha KUBERA was known in the early centuries CE in the GANDHARA region. Kubera or Panchika had a son named Panchalika who was granted a boon by the Hindu god SHIVA.

Panchika is a Buddhist deity, and in Gandhara art he is depicted both alone and with his consort HARITI.

Pandava rathas Five monolithic rock-cut shrines located at MAMALLAPURAM, dating to the seventh or eighth century. These shrines were later named 'Pandava rathas' because there are five of them together, but they have really nothing to do with the PANDAVAS. The Draupadi ratha is a small, hut-shaped shrine with a standing lion in front and an image of the goddess DURGA on the back wall. To the south is the Arjuna ratha, a two-storeyed shrine with images of SHIVA, NANDI, VISHNU, GARUDA and INDRA on the outer walls. The Bhima ratha, shaped like a chariot, has pillars with lion bases. The Dharmaraja ratha has three storeys, with several images on the inner walls, including those of Shiva, BRAHMA and KARTTIKEYA. The Sahadeva ratha is located in front of the others, with a carved elephant behind it.

Pandavas Five brothers, the descendants of PANDU, whose lives are described in the MAHABHARATA. They were YUDHISHTHIRA, BHIMA, ARJUNA, NAKULA and SAHADEVA.

They were not actually born from PANDU, who could not have children, but through his first and second wives, KUNTI and MADRI, invoking the gods. Sacred sites associated with the Pandavas are mainly in northern India, though they are depicted in temples both in the north and in the south.

Pandharpur A town in Maharashtra on the river Bhima. It is a centre of pilgrimage, known particularly for its temple of the Hindu god VITTHALA or Vithoba, a form of VISHNU or KRISHNA.

In early texts and inscriptions, Pandharpur is known by various names, including Pandhari, Pandurangpur, Pandarangapalli, Pandarange, Phaganipur and Pundarik Kshetra. The god Vitthala is also known as Pandurang, and Pundarik or Pundalik, who was responsible for the deity staying here. Pandharpur has a number of other temples apart from that of Vitthala, as well as TIRTHAS or holy sites along the Bhima, locally known as the Chandrabhaga. A short distance from the Vitthala Temple is the SAMADHI of Pundalik, while behind the temple is another of Rakhumai (local name of RUKMINI), with shrines nearby of Satyabhama and Rahi (RADHA). The Vishnupada Temple in the middle of the Bhima, which is usually submerged during the monsoon, enshrines footprints said to be of the god Krishna and his cow, as well as images of Krishna and Vishnu. There are numerous other temples and shrines, including those of SHIVA, DEVI, GANESHA and HANUMAN.

In a poem praising Pandharpur, the Maratha saint NAMADEVA says:

Pandhari was created first, only then Vaikuntha-nagari (heaven of Vishnu).
Pandharpur existed even when there was nothing else, neither life nor non-life.
The Chandrabhaga was there even when the Ganga and Godavari were yet to be born;
Blessed is the auspicious Pandhari that stands on the banks of the Chandrabhaga.
Pandharpur remains undisturbed, even if the rest of the world is destroyed;
Its foundation is the Sudarshana-chakra (of Vishnu).
Oh Shri Hari, I have seen this Pandhari with my own eyes, says Nama.

Pandharpur is the centre of the VARKARI sect, who are followers of the god Vitthala, and of the Maratha saints.

pandit A term for a holy or learned man.

Pandu The brother of DHRITARASHTRA and the father of the PANDAVAS, described in the *MAHABHARATA*. His name means 'pale'. Pandu married KUNTI, also known as Pritha, and later married MADRI, daughter of the king of Madra. Wandering in the forest, he saw a pair of mating deer and killed one of them. But the deer were actually the rishi Kindama with his wife, and as he died the rishi cursed Pandu, stating that he would fall dead if he ever mated with his wives.

Pandu went to the Himalayas to do penance, and along with his wives he visited a number of holy places. When Kunti revealed to him that she knew a divine MANTRA by which she could invoke the gods to have children, he was happy. YUDHISHTHIRA, BHIMA and ARJUNA were born to Kunti, who then conveyed the mantra to Madri, to whom NAKULA and SAHADEVA were born.

One fine spring day, despite Madri's protests, Pandu, carried away by the scent of flowers and the gentle breeze, tried to make love to Madri, and died. Both wives wanted to end their lives with him, but Kunti was asked to live to take care of the children, while Madri joined him on the funeral pyre. Later, they all lived happily together again in Indraloka, the heaven of the gods.

Panhavagaranaim (Prashna-Vyakara-nani) A Jain text, the tenth of the twelve ANGAS. It describes the five mahavratas or great vows and the five virtues that a Jain monk should possess. The information in the *THANAMGA*, another of the Angas, indicates that its contents were once different.

Panini A Sanskrit grammarian of ancient days. He wrote the *Ashtadhyayi*, that is said to be most perfect grammar of any part of the ancient world. The grammar has short aphorisms that have been commented on and explained by PATANJALI and others. Not much is known of his life, but Panini is thought to have lived some time between the seventh and fourth centuries BCE. He was possibly born in the village of Shalatura in the north-west region of GANDHARA, but lived mainly in PATALIPUTRA. According to legend he was inspired to write the grammar by the Hindu god SHIVA and by the sound of his damaru or drum, which reveals the true word.

panj pyare A term in Sikhism, literally 'five beloved ones', for the first five Sikhs to be initiated into the KHALSA by Guru GOBIND SINGH. They were Daya Ram, Dharam Das, Mukham Chand, Himmat Rai and Sahib Chand, who were then given the title Singh and were closely associated with the guru. Bhai Daya Singh (1669–1708) helped Guru GOBIND SINGH to escape from the battle fought at CHAMKAUR in 1704. He delivered the guru's letter, titled *ZAFAR NAMAH*, to the Mughal emperor AURANGZEB, and was with the guru at Nanded, where he died in 1708. Bhai Dharam Singh (1666–1708) was also with the guru at Chamkaur, and it is not clear if he died there or later at Nanded. Bhai Mukham Singh (b.1663), Bhai Sahib Singh (b. 1662) and Bhai Himmat Singh (b. 1661) were all killed in the battle of Chamkaur in 1704.

Panjokra Sahib Gurdwara A GURDWARA or Sikh shrine located at Ambala in Haryana, constructed in memory of the eighth guru, HAR KRISHAN. The guru stayed here for a few days and blessed hundreds of people who came to meet him. He then made a sand platform or ridge and said that whoever stood there and prayed with purity would have his desires granted. Later a gurdwara was built over this spot.

panth A path or way; a community observing a particular system of religious belief. The term particularly refers to the Sikh community.

Paonta Sahib Gurdwara A GURDWARA or Sikh shrine located at Paonta on the banks of the Yamuna in Himachal Pradesh, in the foothills of the Himalayas. Here the tenth guru, GOBIND SINGH, spent some happy and peaceful days wandering in the nearby forests, composing poems, reading and writing. The guru also invited a number of poets who recited their poems to him.

A large gurdwara has been built to commemorate his stay here, and thousands of pilgrims come here particularly during the HOLA MOHALLA festival. A Kavi Darbar, or meeting of poets is an annual affair.

Papanatha Temple A temple of the Hindu deity SHIVA, located at Pattadakal in Karnataka. It is a typical Chalukyan temple of the sixth or seventh century. The inner shrine has a coiled NAGA on the ceiling and is connected to a MANDAPA and porch, while a tower rises above it. The mandapa has images of DURGA and GANESHA, while the outer walls have scenes from the RAMAYANA and MAHABHARATA.

Paramahansa Yogananda A spiritual leader who set up organizations in India and the West. Born in 1893 in a Bengali family in Gorakhpur in present Uttar Pradesh, his original name was Mukunda Lal Ghosh. His parents were disciples of Lahiri Mahasaya (Shyama Charan Lahiri, 1828–95) and Mukunda had spiritual aspirations from childhood. In 1910 he met his guru, Swami Sri Yukteswar Giri (originally Priya Nath Karar, 1855–1936), was initiated into his religious order and given the name Swami Paramahansa Yogananda. After completing a BA degree from Calcutta University at the insistence of his guru, Yogananda began to spread his teachings, with a particular emphasis on KRIYA YOGA. He set up the Yogoda Satsanga Society of India at Ranchi, Jharkhand, and an international organization, the Self-Realization Fellowship, at Los Angeles, USA. Both these continue to have a large following and to spread and teach Kriya Yoga. Yogananda died on 7 March 1952.

paramita A Sanskrit term used in Buddhism, meaning 'perfections'. These perfections are essential on the Buddhist path, particularly in MAHAYANA Buddhism. Six paramitas or perfections are described in early PRAJNAPARAMITA literature. They are dana (giving), shila (morality), kshanti (patience), virya (vigour), dhyana (meditation) and prajna (wisdom). Four more were added later: upaya (skill in action), pranidhana (vow of surrender or renunciation), bala (strength or power), and jnana (knowledge). The ten paramitas are essential for all those who aspire to become BUDDHAS, and for those on the BODHISATTVA path. They were an integral part of Gautama Siddhartha, which is why he could defeat MARA and attain enlightenment.

Parashurama A Hindu deity, one of the ten main incarnations of the god VISHNU. Vishnu took the form of Parashurama in order to defeat all the KSHATRIYAS, the caste to which kings and warriors belonged. According to the BRAHMANDA PURANA, the earth, in the form of a cow, appealed to Vishnu to save her from the atrocities of kshatriya kings, and therefore he was born as Parashurama. (There is a similar story regarding Vishnu's incarnation as VARAHA). According to another story, it was actually the curse of a RISHI that led to Parashurama's birth and the destruction of the kshatriyas. Once the god AGNI went to a king, KARTAVIRYA, and asked for food. The king gave him food, but Agni (fire) began to consume everything around him, including the hermitage of a sage, who then cursed him, and along with him all kshatriyas.

Parashurama was born as a BRAHMANA to the rishi JAMADAGNI, and thus was also known as Jamadagnya. One of his ancestors was the rishi BHRIGU, and therefore he was known as Bhrigupati or Bhargava. When he was born his name was RAMA, but after pleasing the god SHIVA he received from him a divine weapon, a parashu or axe. He was never without his axe, and so he was called Parashurama.

There are several stories about Parashurama. As a young man, his father Jamadagni asked his sons to cut off their mother RENUKA's head, because she had for a moment harboured a desire for someone else. Parashurama's four brothers refused to do so, but he complied with his father's wishes. Pleased, his father granted him a boon, and he asked for her to be restored to life.

Parashurama was a renowned archer and taught archery to a few select pupils, among them being DRONA and KARNA. In his long life he had many exploits, but the most important was his destruction of the Kshatriyas, which of course was pre-ordained. The immediate provocation was when Jamadagni's ashram was raided by King Kartavirya. Later, Parashurama killed this king, who had a thousand arms. Kartavirya's sons then killed Jamadagni, and Parashurama vowed to exterminate all kshatriyas. He fought and killed most of them, but some always remained alive, and when they became strong again, Parasharuma began another attack. Thus, he rid the earth of kshatriyas twenty-one times. He stored their blood in five lakes known as Samantapanchaka in KURUKSHETRA, and performed a YAJNA (sacrifice), praying that the lakes become holy and he be freed of the sin of killing.

According to one story, the rishi KASHYAPA then asked him to go and live somewhere else, and Parashurama settled on the western coast, reclaiming a strip of land from the sea. This area is known even today as Parashurama Kshetra.

Parashurama lived at the same time as another incarnation of Vishnu, the god RAMA, and they met when Rama won SITA's hand in marriage by stringing Shiva's bow. Parashurama objected to this, but later blessed Rama. According to the MAHABHARATA and the BHAGAVATA PURANA, Parashurama also met KRISHNA and blessed him.

Scholars believe there is a historical basis for some of these legends, which may record the memory of a major conflict. Some try to equate the name Parashurama with Pars or Persia, and with early Zoroastrians, or other settlers from Iran on the western coast.

Parashurameshvara A name of the Hindu god SHIVA, who received this name when he was worshipped by PARASHURAMA. There are a number of temples dedicated to Shiva as Parshurameshvara, among the early temples being those at Bhubaneswar (Orissa) of the seventh century and at Gudimallam in Andhra Pradesh. The latter temple was originally constructed in the ninth century, with later additions. The inner shrine is apsidal-ended, and has an ancient LINGA said to date back to the second or first century BCE. This 1.5-m-high linga, with a figure of Shiva carved on the shaft, is one of the earliest representations of the linga in art. The shrine and attached ardha-mandapa are from the ninth century, while the adjoining MANDAPA and passageway are from the Chola period, around the twelfth century. The gateway and outer mandapa are in Vijayanagara style.

Parasnath A hill in Jharkhand sacred to Jains, known in texts as Samet Shikhara. The twenty-third TIRTHANKARA, PARSHVANATHA, is said to have attained MOKSHA or liberation here, when he was a hundred years old. Eighteen other Tirthankaras also attained moksha here. The hill has a number of Jain temples, including one of Parshvanatha at the summit, and is one of the most sacred Jain sites.

pardah Literally, a term that means a curtain or veil. It refers to the custom of veiling women, or keeping them in seclusion, which was once common in Islam and in some Hindu castes. In India some Muslim women still wear a burqah, while the custom of covering the head with the sari and veiling the face with one end of it, is prevalent among Hindus in rural areas.

Parida, Sidheswar An Oriya poet who worshipped the goddess Sarala Devi and took the name SARALA DASA.

parijata A divine tree in Hindu mythology. It was one of the five trees that emerged out of the ocean when it was churned for AMRITA, and it was kept in the heaven of the god INDRA but was later taken by the god KRISHNA to his city of DVARAKA. After Krishna departed from the world, the tree returned to Indra's heaven. This tree had a wonderful fragrance, and the scent of its blossoms perfumed the world. It has been identified with a real tree, the Indian coral.

Parjanya A deity described in the RIG VEDA. He is the god of rain clouds and sheds rain. He brings thunder and lightning, and is rich in clouds and water. His chariot is watery, and he nourishes vegetation. More important rain gods in the VEDAS are the MARUTS and INDRA.

Parshvanatha The twenty-third Jain TIRTHANKARA, who probably lived in the ninth or eighth century BCE. According to Jain tradition he preceded MAHAVIRA (b. 599 BCE) by 250 years and was the son of King Ashvasena and Queen Vama of KASHI (Varanasi). SHVETAMBARA texts state that he married Prabhavati, daughter of King Prasenajit, but left home to become an ascetic at the age of thirty. After practising austerities for eighty-three days, he reached Omniscience on the eighty-fourth day, and then wandered for seventy years, preaching his doctrines. Finally he attained MOKSHA or liberation at Samet Shikhara (PARASNATH hill in Jharkhand). He founded the Nirgrantha ('free from bonds') sect. He explained some of the Jain beliefs and laid down the four basic vows of not killing, not lying, not stealing, and not owning more than necessary. At the time of Mahavira, his followers were headed by one Keshi Kumara. Mahavira, according to some accounts, at first joined the sect, but then left it, having developed his ideas further. Keshi Kumara and others then became disciples of Mahavira.

Parshvanatha's symbol is a serpent, and he is usually depicted with a serpent hood above his head.

Parshvanatha Temple, Khajuraho A Jain temple dedicated to PARSHVANATHA, the twenty-third TIRTHANKARA. It was constructed in 954 by Pahila, during the reign of King Dhanga of the Chandella dynasty. The temple has a rectangular ground plan, with axial projections on the shorter sides. It is richly carved, and the main hall has sculptured bands and latticed windows. The present image of Parshvanatha, made of black marble, was installed in 1860. The temple also has some Hindu images, including a head of SHIVA on the outer walls.

Parsis A term for Indian Zoroastrians. According to traditional history, supported by the *KISSAH-I-SANJAN*, a document of 1600, the Parsis are descendants of a group of Zoroastrians who came to the western coast of India in the eighth century, fleeing persecution in Iran. This is the traditionally accepted date, though scholars have pointed out that there is little evidence of religious persecution at this time, and therefore a tenth-century date is more likely. An account written in 1826 provides a date of 716 (Samvat 772), though some read this as Samvat 972, thus again providing support to both theories.

Most Parsis accept the story of this migration, though some feel the traditional history is wrong and Parsis had settled here from ancient days. While there is evidence of Zoroastrians having been in India from ancient times, they seem to have been absorbed into the local culture and were not distinguished as a separate group; the Parsis as a distinctive group are probably later migrants.

Some time after reaching SANJAN, the Parsis settled in different parts of Gujarat, and an account of their life there, the establishment of a fire temple, and their early problems are narrated in the *Kissah-i-Sanjan*. At this time they were mainly farmers, toddy-planters, weavers and carpenters. They began to speak Gujarati and adopted some local customs. With the coming of the British they became more prosperous, as lack of caste and food restrictions enabled them to mix more easily with Westerners. Many moved to MUMBAI (Bombay) and became merchants, traders and professionals. By the nineteenth century they had adopted liberal Western ideas, and also attempted to reform Parsi society, which had incorporated several Hindu customs. Later, prominent Parsis joined in the freedom struggle against the British.

The number of Parsis in India reached a height in 1941, when the census recorded a figure of 1,14,890. This, of course, was for undivided India. In 1951 there were 1,11,791, after which there has been a decline. According to the 2001 census, there are now 69, 601.

Who is a Parsi?: Parsi are governed by the Parsi Marriage and Divorce Act of 1936. Yet the question of who or what is a Parsi is still being debated.

This question had been raised in the nineteenth and twentieth centuries in response to some prominent Parsis marrying non-Parsis, and the subsequent conversion of the non-Parsi spouse to Zoroastrianism. In general, Parsis today agree with the definition provided by the Daver-Beaman judgement, 1908. According to this, Parsis are: (1) the descendants of the original emigrants into India from Persia, who profess the Zoroastrian religion; (2) descendants of Zoroastrians in Persia who were not among the original emigrants, but who are of the same stock, and have since that date, from time to time, come to India and settled here, either permanently and temporarily, and who profess the Zoroastrian religion. (3) the children of a Parsi father by an alien mother, if such children are admitted into the faith of the father and profess the Zoroastrian religion.

In 2003 the Parsi high priests, with one exception, stated that in their view the children of a Parsi father and non-Parsi mother are not Parsis, and that such a marriage has no religious sanctity. Their views have not been accepted by most. As for children of a Parsi mother, only a few north Indian Anjumans accept them as Parsis and allow their NAVJOTE or thread ceremony to be performed.

Some issues: There are several issues that concern this small community. The decline in numbers is the most important issue and is related to the question of conversion, and whether conversion of any kind should be allowed. In other countries, conversion does take place, but in India it is hotly debated. Other issues include the means of disposal of the dead and whether an acceptable alternative can be found to the DAKHMA system, which is not operating well due to the paucity of vultures; the necessity or not of rituals; joining in or cooperating with a world body of Zoroastrians; whether adoption should be allowed. Even questions on religion bring forth different responses, with some stating that Zoroastrianism is a monotheistic religion, and others that it is dualistic. There are also some who believe the GATHAS is the only authentic text, while others include all the later texts. Which calendar to follow (*see* Zoroastrian calendar) is another matter of debate.

Despite these internal controversies, Parsis are recognized as having enriched India in various ways, and apart for a few early local conflicts, have lived peacefully in India.

Parthasarthy Temple   A temple of the Hindu god KRISHNA, located in Chennai in Tamil Nadu. It is not known when the temple was first constructed, but it was revered by the ALVAR saints and renovated at the time of the Pallava dynasty, with further additions made later.

The image of Parthasarthy, or Krishna as the charioteer of ARJUNA, (Partha = Arjuna, sarthy = charioteer), discoursing on the BHAGAVAD GITA, is made of black granite, and according to legend, was brought here by the rishi Atreya. The presiding deity of the temple is Krishna, known here as Sri Venkatakrishna Swami or Gitacharya. Krishna's wife RUKMINI and younger brother Satyaki are to his right and left, his elder brother BALARAMA is to the right of Rukmini, while images of his son PRADYUMNA and grandson Aniruddha are also in the inner shrine or GARBHA-GRIHA.

There are additional shrines of RANGANATHA (VISHNU), Sri Tellia Singha-Perumal (NARASIMHA), Sri Chakravarti Tirumagan (RAMA), HANUMAN, ANDAL, and some other deities and saints.

A tank in front of the temple, known as Karveni, is said to provide prosperity and happiness to all who bathe there.

The philosopher RAMANUJA was particularly fond of this temple, and according to legend, he was an incarnation of Parthasarthy.

Parvati   A Hindu deity, the wife of the god SHIVA. Parvat means 'mountain', and she was named Parvati because she was the daughter of the Himalaya mountain, personified as HIMAVAN, and of his wife Mena. There are several myths and legends in ancient texts regarding Parvati, but many of these developed only after the fifth century.

Parvati is not mentioned in the VEDAS, though there are references to AMBIKA, one of her later names. In some Vedic passages SHIVA'S wife is referred to as Rudrani. The KENA UPANISHAD mentions a goddess named Uma Haimavati, which is possibly a reference to Parvati. The MAHABHARATA and RAMAYANA tell the story of Parvati and her previous incarnation as SATI, and this is further elaborated on in the PURANAS.

The central story regarding this goddess states that in her previous birth she was Sati, daughter of DAKSHA, who killed herself when her father insulted her husband Shiva. After a period of grief, Shiva retreated into ascetic meditation; meanwhile, an ASURA known as TARAKA was threatening the world. Taraka, it was said, could not be killed except by an offspring of Shiva, but how was Shiva to be persuaded to start a family? Sati was reborn again as Parvati, to unite with her beloved once again, and to enable a child to be born who would kill Taraka.

Shiva was deep in meditation and initially was not attracted by the beautiful Parvati. KAMA, the god of love, attempted to awaken his desire but Kama was burnt to ashes by a flash of Shiva's third eye. Parvati then decided that the only way to attract Shiva was to become an ascetic herself. She meditated and practised TAPAS or austerities for thousands of years on Mt KAILASHA. Finally Shiva noticed her and fell in love, and they married and lived together on the mountain, making love and playing dice, and produced two children, KARTTIKEYA and GANESHA.

Parvati's role is usually as the wife and counterpart of Shiva, providing a domestic aspect to his asceticism and wildness, but she is also worshipped in different ways. She is part of him, and thus Shiva is worshipped as ARDHANARISHVARA, half-man and-half woman. She is his feminine aspect, his SHAKTI or power. In some Tantric texts she transcends Shiva and is worshipped as the supreme deity. In the SHAIVA SIDDHANTA system, she is Shiva's grace (arul). In a number of texts, she is Shiva's disciple, asking Shiva questions and learning divine truths from him. Some devotees of Shiva identify with Parvati, just as devotees of KRISHNA identify with RADHA. By the medieval period, all these aspects of Parvati had developed, reflected in her various names. Parvati also has different forms and can manifest herself as MAHADEVI, the MAHAVIDYAS, and other deities. In her fierce form she is DURGA or KALI.

Parvati is also worshipped in her essential feminity, as the YONI. Once the RISHIS caused Shiva's LINGA to fall to earth, and by its power it burnt everything before it. It could only be held in Parvati's yoni, thus the linga and yoni are worshipped together. Parvati tames Shiva and brings his sexuality within acceptable limits, and also reduces his asceticism.

The AMARAKOSHA, a Sanskrit text, has the following synonyms for Parvati: UMA, Katyayani, GAURI, KALI, Haimavati, Ishvari, Shivaa, Bhavani, Rudrani, Sarvani, Sarvamangala, Aparna, DURGA, Mridani, Chandika, AMBIKA, Arya, Dakshayani, Girija, Menakatmaja, Chamunda, Karnamoti, Charchchika, Bhairavi. She is also called ANNAPURNA (giver of food) or Mata (mother). In the south she has other names, including MINAKSHI.

Paryushan A Jain festival held in Bhadrapada (August–September), which begins on the twelfth day of the fortnight of the waning moon. The festival lasts for eight or ten days and Jains at this time fast or eat a restricted diet. Shvetambaras celebrate it for eight days, while Digambaras celebrate it for ten days, beginning on the last day of the Shvetambara festival. Digambaras refer to it as Dash-Lakshana Parva. During these days, Jain texts are read out and explained, particularly the KALPA SUTRA for SHVETAMBARAS. Jains recollect and rededicate themselves to the basic virtues of Jainism, including truthfulness, non-violence, self-restraint and simplicity. There is a special emphasis on forgiveness, and the last day is one of atonement, dropping all feelings of enmity, forgiving others and mentally asking others for forgiveness. A prayer recited at this time says:

I forgive all living beings;
May all living beings forgive me.
All in this world are my friends,
I have no enemies.

An effort is also made to actively prevent the slaughter of animals, and free those in captivity.

Pashupata A Hindu SHAIVITE sect, probably founded in the second century by LAKULISHA, who is said to have been an incarnation of the god SHIVA. The *Pashupata Sutra* and the *Ganakarika* describe the principles of this sect. Three aspects of creation were Pashu, the individual soul, Pati, god or the lord, and Pasha, which indicates bondage or the world. These three were separate and distinct. The path to enlightenment had five stages, the first two being external, and the next three involving meditative and other internal practices. Despite all one's efforts, enlightenment finally could be achieved only by the grace of God. The sect existed until the end of the fifteenth century.

Pashupati A name of the Hindu god SHIVA. Pashupats has two aspects. In the Pashupata sect, he is the supreme deity. As a form of Shiva, he is the protector of animals, particularly of domestic herds. He is also the patron of reproduction in all forms of life. In south India he is represented in this form as a four-armed man, holding an axe and a small deer.

Passover A Jewish festival known in Hebrew as Pesach. It commemorates the Exodus from Egypt and the liberation of the Jews from slavery, which took place around the thirteenth century BCE, when Moses led them to Canaan. It is known as the Passover because God passed over their houses when he unleashed a plague that killed the first-born of the Egyptians after the Pharaoh had refused to release the Jews. He asked them to mark their houses by sprinkling the blood of a lamb on their doorposts. The lamb should then be roasted and eaten. God Himself is said to have redeemed the people from bondage, and they left Egypt so quickly, that their dough for baking bread had no time to rise, and they ate unleavened bread (matzoth). Therefore, at this time Jews eat matzoth for seven days, as well as bitter herbs (maror), as the Egyptians embittered the lives of their forefathers, and a roasted lamb drained of blood. The Passover is also a harvest festival.

The festival takes place in the Jewish month of Nisan (March–April), and the main Passover festival is between the 14th and 15th of Nisan. The Passover begins with a service in the synagogue, followed by the Seder (literally, order), a ritual meal, and readings or a retelling of the Exodus story. On this night four questions are asked about the symbolism of the meal by the youngest child present, and four cups of wine, symbolizing four aspects of divine redemption, are drunk. A special cup filled with wine, the Kos-shel Eliyahu, the cup of the Prophet Elijah, is kept because, according to tradition, the Prophet visits every Seder.

Patala The seventh LOKA of the netherworld in Hindu mythology. The Nagalokadhipatis, or lords of the NAGAS, live here. Among them are VASUKI, Shankha, Dhananjaya, and others. Their hoods vary in number from five to one hundred, and the shining jewels on them keep Patala brightly illuminated. Patala is described in texts as a beautiful place. After visiting it, the rishi NARADA stated that it was better than the heavens of the gods. Patala is also used as a generic term for all the seven lower Lokas or worlds, which are: Atala, Vitala, Sutala, Talatala, Mahatala, Rasatala and Patala. Below Patala is Adishesha or ANANTA, the serpent on which the god VISHNU rests. These worlds are 10,000 yojanas below the earth.

Pataliputra The ancient name of Patna, today the capital of Bihar. Earlier a village, it was an important centre from about the sixth century BCE, and the capital of the kingdom of MAGADHA. By the third century BCE became it was a prosperous city, the capital of the Mauryan empire. It was associated with Buddhism, and the Third BUDDHIST COUNCIL was held here in the time of ASHOKA Maurya. Archaeological excavations indicate that the site was occupied from around the sixth century BCE to the third century CE, and some parts of it until the sixth century CE. It was then deserted and reoccupied in the medieval period.

Patanjali A philosopher who wrote the YOGA SUTRA, the basic Sanskrit text describing the system of YOGA. Another Patanjali composed the *Mahabhashya*, a commentary on PANINI's grammar known as the *Ashtadhyayi*. According to tradition, both texts were written by the same person, but scholars believe they were composed by two different Patanjalis, for while the *Mahabhashya* can be dated to the second century BCE, the *Yoga Sutra* in its present form, is somewhat later.

pathashala A traditional school. Literally it means 'house of recitation', and in the past students had to memorize long passages from Sanskrit texts and recite them. The system is still followed in religious schools attached to temples or MATHAS.

Patimokha A term in Buddhism for a list of actions forbidden to Buddhist monks. The *Patimokha* (Sanskrit: Pratimoksha) forms part of the *VINAYA PITAKA* and is also used as a separate text. A good monk is said to be 'restrained by the restraints of the *Patimokha*.' The *Patimokha* list was recited twice a month in the SANGHA (the community of monks and nuns), at which time they had to confess their transgressions. This was known as the Uposatha ceremony, and probably started at the time of the BUDDHA.

Patisambhida-Magga A HINAYANA Buddhist text that forms part of the *KHUDDAKA NIKAYA*, the fifth NIKAYA of the *SUTTA PITAKA* of the PALI CANON. Literally 'the path of analysis', it has three sections, each divided into ten treatises on various aspects of Buddhist principles and ideals. Among its topics are the seventy-three kinds of knowledge, the FOUR NOBLE TRUTHS, and the merit of friendliness towards all creatures.

Pattadakal A place in Karnataka that has several temples from the time of the Chalukya dynasty of the sixth to eighth centuries. Among these are the Sanameshvara, Virupaksha, Mallikarjuna and PAPANATHA temples, as well as a later Jain temple.

Patthana-Pakarana A HINAYANA Buddhist text that forms part of the *ABHIDHAMMA PITAKA* of the PALI CANON. It has two parts, the *Tika Patthana* and the *Duka Patthana*, and analyzes twenty-four kinds of relationships. Except for NIRVANA, which is absolute and therefore unrelated, everything else has a relationship of some kind that can be classified into the twenty-four types mentioned here. Thus there are relationships between cause and effect, subject and object, ruler and ruled, etc. This book is important for understanding Buddhist ideas and for philosophical concepts.

Pattupattu Literally, 'The Ten Idylls', a series of Tamil texts that form part of SANGAM LITERATURE. They date from about the third to sixth centuries CE, and are slightly later than the eight texts of the ETTUTOGAI. Similar in style to the former, they consist of ten longer poems and provide information on the Tamil country and early kings. One of the poems, the *Tirumuruka-narrupatai*, describes the god MURUGAN and his shrines.

Paumchariyam A Jain version of the *RAMAYANA*, composed by Vimalasuri. It is said to have been written 530 years after the death of MAHAVIRA and is composed in a Prakrit dialect, Jain Maharashtri. Despite the date given in it, scholars date it between the first and third centuries CE. Pauma, or Padma in Sanskrit, is another name of RAMA. The epic depicts a world full of Jains and begins with the time when King Seniya (BIMBISARA) was ruling at MAGADHA. The king doubts some of the fantastic stories contained in the *Ramayana*, and asks

GOYAMA, disciple of Mahavira, to tell him the truth. Goyama then narrates this story, which was revealed to him by Mahavira.

The story begins with the history of RISHABHA, the first TIRTHANKARA. An account of the second Tirthankara is followed by a description of Kishkindhapura (KISHKINDHA), the capital city of the monkeys. These monkeys are really VIDYADHARAS (here meaning a community of people), but are called vanaras (monkeys) because they have monkeys depicted on their gates and banners. The RAKSHASAS, among whom RAVANA is born, are also vidyadharas. There was a great vidyadhara hero named Rakshasa, after whom they were named. The vidyadharas were not demonic; they followed the principles of AHIMSA or non-violence, and did not even kill animals. Ravana was a devotee of the Jinas who propagated the Jain faith and restored Jain shrines. He was a great ascetic with magic powers, and accounts of his heroic deeds are given. The god INDRA, when defeated by Ravana, became a Jain monk. HANUMAN also became a Jain, helped Ravana in his exploits, and received a thousand wives in return.

After all this, King DASHARATHA is mentioned, and the main *Ramayana* story begins, which in its essentials follows Valmiki's *Ramayana*, though the details are different. SITA is born in a natural way, the daughter of JANAKA and his wife Videha. Padma (Rama) helps Janaka in his fight against his enemies and hence is betrothed to Sita. The later episodes are largely the same: Sita is abducted by Ravana, Hanuman helps Padma in rescuing her, after her return she is banished and her twin sons are born. In between are several secondary stories. Finally Padma (Rama) enters NIRVANA. Ravana is sympathetically portrayed, his only weakness being his desire for Sita.

There are also other Jain *RAMAYANAS* (*See Ramayana*, in Jainism).

Pausha Dashami A Jain festival that celebrates the birthday of the twenty-third TIRTHANKARA, PARSHVANATHA. The festival starts on the twelfth day of the month of Pausha and involves pilgrimages, fasting, and the recitation of scriptures.

Pavaka The name of a son of the Hindu god AGNI. Agni and his wife Svaha had three sons, Pavaka, Pavamana and Shuchi. These three had forty-five sons, and they were all also known as Agni. Thus there were forty-nine Agnis.

Pentecostal Church of God, Indian The Indian Pentecostal Church of God was founded in 1924 by Pastor K.E. Abraham at Mulakuzha, Chengannur. Later it spread to several parts of India and shifted its base to Kumbanad, Kerala. It now has 3500 churches and over five lakh members.

Pentecostal Churches A group of Protestant Churches. The Pentecostal movement in Christianity began in Los Angeles (USA) in 1906, and spread to other countries. The movement takes its inspiration from the descent of the Holy Spirit on the APOSTLES on the day of the Pentecost, when they began to speak in many tongues. It is based on approaching God through simplicity and invoking the divine spirit of God, which can lead to spontaneous speech and spiritual healing.

Pentecostal Churches in India include the Indian PENTECOSTAL CHURCH OF GOD, Assemblies of God; the CHURCH OF GOD (FULL GOSPEL); the Church of God, founded 1914; The New India Church of God, an indigenous church established in 1976; the New India Bible Church, founded in 1973; the Sharon Fellowship Church, founded in 1953; Church of God in South India, founded 1910; and the World Missionary Evangelism of India, originally founded in 1940 and established in India in 1969.

Periya Puranam The popular name of the *Tiruttondapuranam*, a Tamil SHAIVITE work, composed by Sekkilar in the twelfth century. It provides an account of the lives of the sixty-three NAYANAR saints. It is considered a literary and religious masterpiece.

Persian-speaking Jews A number of Persian-speaking Jews from Afghanistan, Khorasan and Iran came to India from the eleventh century onwards and were associated with the DELHI sultans and the Mughals. Some Jews came along with Mahmud of Ghazni and Muhammad Ghori in the eleventh and twelfth centuries. These Jews were both traders and courtiers, and scattered references to them occur in texts. The Mughal emperor AKBAR had discussions with Jews, and during his time a SYNAGOGUE was constructed at Agra. DARA SHIKOH, son of the Mughal emperor Shah Jahan, had a Jewish tutor. Both Dara and his tutor were executed by the emperor AURANGZEB. Other Jews were traders in various parts of the Mughal empire, and there were Jewish settlements in northern India, including in Kashmir.

Perumal A term usually used for the god VISHNU in Tamil. It is also applied to other deities, as well as to kings in south India.

Petavatthu A Buddhist text that forms part of the *KHUDDAKA NIKAYA*, the fifth NIKAYA of the *SUTTA PITAKA*, of the PALI CANON. It deals with the negative results of wrong actions. A peta (Sanskrit: preta) is the spirit of a dead person, roaming the world as a ghost. This text is mainly in the form of dialogues, where NARADA or another sage asks a peta the reasons for its misfortunes, and the peta recounts its wrong deeds.

Phalakaksha The name of a YAKSHA or divine being, who was a member of the court of KUBERA.

Phul Walon ki Sair A festival representing harmony between communities, also known as SAIR-E-GUL FAROSHAN.

Pillai Lokacharya *See* Lokacharya.

pinda A term for offerings made to the PITRIS or ancestors, usually consisting of balls of rice or flour.

Pingala An attendant of the Hindu god SURYA.

Pingala Nadi A hidden passage of energy in the human body. The Pingala Nadi is said to exist to the right of the KUNDALINI, while to the left is the Ida Nadi. Pingala represents heat, fire or the sun, while IDA is cool, representing the moon.

Pippalada An ancient RISHI who founded a school of the *ATHARVA VEDA*, which was named after him. In the *PRASHNA UPANISHAD* he guides other rishis on the path to enlightenment. According to a story in the *PADMA PURANA*, he sat in meditation without moving for 3000 years, though an ant-hill grew around him and cobras circled him. Then BRAHMA gave him a boon, the SIDDHI or power of obtaining all he desired, and he became extremely proud, until Brahma again appeared to him in the form of a swan and told him that there was a person named Sukarma who possessed more knowledge than he. Pippalada met Sukarma and acknowledged his greatness, which was due to the merit he had gained by taking care of his parents.

pir A term in Islam for a SUFI master or spiritual teacher. Other terms used are Shaikh or Murshid.

pishachas A class of lower spirits in Hindu mythology. They are associated with RAKSHASAS, and sometimes with YAKSHAS and ASURAS. In early texts, they are said to have been created by BRAHMA, or to have emerged from the PRAJAPATIS. In different passages of the *MAHABHARATA*, they are said to worship KUBERA, SHIVA, or Brahma; another passage in the *Mahabharata* states that their food is flesh and their drink is blood. A number of pishachas were also incarnated as kings. In the PURANAS, they are described as descended from the rishi KASHYAPA through one of his wives, either Krodhavasha or Pishacha, or Kapisha. While earlier their nature was ambivalent, in later texts they are bloodthirsty and aggressive beings.

Pitamaha A name of the Hindu god BRAHMA, in the sense of father of all. Literally it means paternal grandfather.

Pitra Paksh A Hindu festival to pray for the souls of ancestors or PITRIS, held during the dark fortnight of the month of Ashvina (September/October). These fifteen days are also known as SHRADDHA. At this time, ceremonies are performed in which the eldest son and other male relatives have an important role. Food, including PINDA (rice balls), and khir is fed to BRAHMANAS, in the belief that this reaches the departed soul. In some areas, food is also offered to a cow, a dog and a crow. The ceremonies are performed for both males and females. Offerings to ancestors were common among ancient Egyptians, Sumerians and Jews, as well as in China and Japan. In Zoroastrianism, the MUKTAD is a similar ritual.

pitris (1) A term in Hinduism usually used for ancestors or manes. Pitris are human ancestors who have died and for whom ceremonies have been performed with proper rites. YAMA, the god of the dead, is the lord of the pitris and performing sacrifices for the pitris, brings blessings. The period of SHRADDHA or PITRA PAKSH is when ancestors are formally revered.

(2) There are also other types of pitris, including the ten PRAJAPATIS. According to one story, pitris include the sons of the gods. When the gods offended BRAHMA, he cursed them, and they became fools, but then he allowed them to be re-instructed by their sons, who were therefore called Pitris.

(3) Other pitris are minor deities, or sages who reached a high level and transcended ordinary life. In the RIG VEDA, there are two classes of pitris, while according to the PURANAS there are seven classes of pitris, three without form, though they can assume any form they like, and four with form. According to one text, those without form are the Vairajas, the Agnishvattas and the Barhishads, while those with form are the Sukalas, Angirasas, Susvadhas and Somapas. Variant names are also given for all these.

Ponda Mosque A mosque located in Ponda, Goa, also known as the Safa Shahouri Masjid. It was constructed in 1560 by Ibrahim Adil Shah, sultan of Bijapur. It was once the largest of the twenty-seven mosques in Ponda Taluk, and the only one that still survives. Next to it was a masonry tank and an extensive garden decorated with fountains, which was destroyed at the time of the Portuguese. The mosque gradually crumbled and decayed, but it has been partially restored. The renovated mosque is still in use and attracts crowds, particularly on the ID festivals. It is the oldest standing mosque in Goa.

Pongal A Hindu festival celebrated in Andhra Pradesh and Tamil Nadu in January. The main festival is on 14 January, but ceremonies extend over three days. Pongal, a dish of sweetened rice and dal, is made at this harvest festival, to celebrate the bounty of the harvest. On the first day, a feast is prepared for family and relatives; on the second day, SURYA is worshipped. The third day is known as Mattu Pongal, and is dedicated to cattle, in thanksgiving for the work they have done during the year. Cattle are bathed, their hooves are oiled, and their horns polished and painted. Garlands of flowers are placed around their necks and they are given special food and a day of rest. In some areas, they are made to run races after the rest day. In parts of Tamil Nadu, the game of jallikattu is played, in which bundles of money are tied to the horns of bulls, who are forced to run while young men chase them and attempt to retrieve the bundles.

SANKRANTI, a similar festival, is celebrated on 14 January in other states, while LOHRI is celebrated on 13 January in Punjab and some other parts of north India.

Ponna A Jain poet who lived in the tenth century and wrote in Kannada. His main work is the *Shanti Purana*, an account of the sixteenth TIRTHANKARA,

Shantinatha. He also wrote the *Jinaksharamala*, a poem praising Jains, and the *Bhuvanai-Karamabhyudaya*, which no longer exists, but is known through quotes in other texts.

Pooram A Hindu festival named after the Pooram constellation. It takes place in April/May and lasts for thirty-six hours. The grandest Pooram festival is celebrated at Thrissur in Kerala, in honour of the deities of two temples, Paramakkavu Devi (Bhagavati) and Thiruvambadi Devi. Elephants are adorned and decorated with gold and jewels, mantras are chanted, and processions are taken out from the two temples, accompanied by musicians playing *panchavadyam* (five instruments). The two processions meet in an open space near the VADAKKUNATHAN TEMPLE, where the ceremony of unfurling silk parasols takes place. Three hundred brightly-coloured parasols are unfurled by the two groups in quick succession. At night there are fireworks, and the following morning the festival ends after another musical recital. Thousands of pilgrims come from all over to join in the festival, in which all castes and communities participate.

Potana A poet who lived from 1400 to 1475. He wrote the *Bhagavatam*, a translation of the BHAGAVATA PURANA, with some modifications and elaborations. Potana lived in the Andhra country and is said to have been an agriculturalist who refused the patronage of kings. He was a SHAIVITE who later became a follower of the ADVAITA philosophy. In the *Bhagavatam*, a work of BHAKTI, he uses Sanskritized Telugu, and shows equal devotion to RAMA, VISHNU and SHIVA. Another work by him is *Virabhadra Vijayam*, which is based on the story of DAKSHA's sacrifice, as narrated in the *VAYU PURANA*. His *Bhagavatam* is popular even today.

Prabhas Patan A town in Gujarat that has several temples, among which the SOMANATHA TEMPLE of the Hindu god SHIVA is particularly famous. Prabhas Patan has been a sacred place and centre of pilgrimage since ancient times and is the site of one of the jyotir LINGAS of SHIVA. There are other old and new shrines, sacred wells, and tanks. The town is mentioned in the MAHABHARATA and the PURANAS. Those who bathe in the holy pond here are taken up to heaven in divine vehicles (vimanas), where with their songs they awaken the celestial maidens. The YADAVAS fought against one another and destroyed themselves here, and KRISHNA and BALARAMA merged in the supreme here. YUDHISHTHIRA, the eldest of the PANDAVAS, practised austerities in this place. As the god AGNI is said to reside here, those who bathe here enjoy the benefit of the Agnishtoma (fire) sacrifice.

Prabhupada, Swami A devotee of the god KRISHNA and the founder of the INTERNATIONAL SOCIETY FOR KRISHNA CONSCIOUSNESS (ISKCON). Born in Kolkata (Calcutta) in 1896, he was initially known as Abhay Charan De. After his initiation, he came to be called Abhay Charanaravinda Bhaktivedanta, and later

Swami Prabhupada. He had a degree in chemistry, ran a pharmacy business, was married and had one son. He became a devotee of the god Krishna, and left his business and family in 1954, devoting himself to the worship of the deity. In 1959 he was initiated into a SANNYASI sect and became a Swami. He set up ISKCON at New York in 1965 with the aim of spreading the message of the BHAGAVAD GITA and the worship of Krishna. He wrote over fifty books, including commentaries on the BHAGAVAD GITA, *Srimad Bhagavatam* (29 volumes), and *Sri Chaitanya Charitamrita* (17 volumes). His organization soon spread throughout the world, and though he died in 1977, the movement he started has continued to grow and expand.

Pradyumna   A son of the Hindu god KRISHNA by his wife RUKMINI. According to one legend in the *BHAGAVATA PURANA*, he was the incarnation of the god KAMA, who had been burnt to ashes by the god SHIVA. When Kama was killed, his wife RATI was filled with grief, but was informed by the goddess MAHADEVI that Kama would be reborn, and that she, Rati, would again be his wife. Meanwhile Rukmini was longing for a child, and Krishna, after being blessed by the rishis NARA-NARAYANA, went to Mt KAILASHA and asked Shiva for a child. Thus Pradyumna was born, and when he was six or seven days old, he was stolen by the ASURA Shambara, who had been told that the child would grow up to kill him. Shambara threw him into the ocean, where he was swallowed by a fish. The fish was caught and by a coincidence sold to Shambara. The child was found inside the fish and reared by Shambara's wife Mayadevi or Mayavati, who was actually an incarnation of Rati. The rishi NARADA told her the truth about the child's birth, and when he grew up, she fell in love with him and told him how he had come to her house. Pradyumna then killed Shambara in battle and married Mayavati. Both then flew through the air to see his parents. Later, Pradyumna also married Kakudmati, and had a son, Aniruddha. In addition, he married Prabhavati, daughter of the asura Vajranabha. Along with other YADAVAS, he died during the conflicts that took place at DVARAKA. According to another story, he was the son of Kama and Rati, while according to the *MAHABHARATA*, he was a partial incarnation (AMSHA-AVATARA) of SANAT KUMARA, the son of BRAHMA, and after his death he merged with Sanat Kumara. He is one of the deities worshipped in the PANCHARATRA system.

Prahlada   A DAITYA who was a great devotee of the Hindu god VISHNU. His story is narrated in the PURANAS and other texts. His father was the daitya HIRANYAKASHIPU and his mother was Kayadhu. Vishnu had killed the brother of Hiranyakashipu and there was a deep enmity between them. While Hiranyakashipu was fighting against the devas, Kayadhu, who was pregnant, was captured by INDRA, but she was rescued by the rishi NARADA. Narada kept Kayadhu with him

for some time and his spiritual discourses were heard by Prahlada, while still in the womb, and he was born with a devotion to Vishnu. As he grew up, this devotion angered his father. Unable to persuade Prahlada to give it up, Hiranyakashipu called on various powers to torment and torture the boy. He was thrown from mountains, trampled by elephants and placed in a pit of fire, but he remained constant in his devotion and emerged unharmed. After Prahlada survived being left in the ocean with mountains pressing down above him, Hiranyakashipu was for some time reconciled to his son's devotion to Vishnu, but later began his persecution again, and was finally killed by Vishnu in the form of NARASIMHA.

Prahlada then became the king of the daityas and danavas in PATALA, but soon had further adventures. According to the *VAMANA PURANA*, he went to Naimisharanya, the forest of Naimisha, one of the most sacred sites, where he met the rishis NARA-NARAYANA. Thinking they were fake SANNYASIS, he began a battle with them, but they remained undefeated. Learning of their true nature from Vishnu, he went to Badarikashrama in the Himalayas and began to propitiate them, leaving his cousin Andhaka on the throne. Even after returning to Patala, he remained an advisor to Andhaka and did not take over the throne again.

In battles between the DEVAS and ASURAS, Prahlada tried to make peace, but finally was forced into combat with the devas.

Prahlada is also connected with the festival of HOLI. His grandson was the emperor MAHABALI.

Prajapati   A deity in the VEDAS. In the RIG VEDA, he is described in a hymn in the tenth or latest book, where he is praised as the creator of heaven and earth, of the waters and of all that lives, of the one god above all other gods. In some later Vedic texts, he is recognized as the chief god, or father of the gods, the creator of the DEVAS and ASURAS, and the first sacrificer. He is also known as 'KA' or 'who', as the verse praising him in the Rig Veda uses this pronoun to ask who the greatest god is. Later BRAHMA took the place of Prajapati, and in the SUTRAS he is identified with him.

Prajapatis   In Hindu mytholgy, RISHIS or sages descended from the god BRAHMA, from whom all people are descended. Different texts state that there were seven, ten or twenty-one Prajapatis. The names of the ten Prajapatis that are usually listed are: MARICHI, ANGIRAS, ATRI, PULASTYA, Pulaha, Kratu, VASISHTHA, DAKSHA or Prachetas, BHRIGU and NARADA.

Prajnaparamita, goddess   A Buddhist goddess representing wisdom. She is the mother of all BUDDHAS, who awakens the mind; she is also present in the wisdom texts, the PRAJNAPARAMITA SUTRAS.

Prajnaparamita Sutras   A category of Buddhist MAHAYANA texts. Literally, the term means 'perfection of wisdom'. These form the earliest MAHAYANA texts, which explain that to attain the Buddhist goal, one must realize the PARAMITAS or perfections, and particularly the perfection of wisdom (prajna). True prajna shows that nothing exists and that the only reality is SHUNYATA (emptiness). All else is MAYA, or illusion. All things exist because of causal factors, through the law of dependent arising (PRATITYA-SAMUTPADA), but have no permanent Self or nature of their own (svabhava). The goal is not NIRVANA, but an understanding of shunyata, and of the real nature of things as dharmata or tathata (suchness), i.e., things as they are. Perfect wisdom thus frees one of all concepts and attachments.

These texts also describe ten stages through which enlightenment can be reached. Prajnaparamita ideas existed from the first century BCE, but the earliest text, the *Ashtasahasrika-Prajnaparamita Sutra* (The Perfection of Wisdom in Eight Thousand Verses) was composed in the first century CE. The *Panchavimshatisahasrika Prajnaparamita Sutra (The Perfection of Wisdom in Twenty-Five Thousand Verses)* was composed by the early third century. The *Mahaprajnaparamita Sutra*, an even larger text, was translated into Chinese in the seventh century by the Chinese pilgrim XUANZANG. Sections of it were compressed into separate books, such as the *PRAJNAPARAMITA-HRIDAYA SUTRA*. The philosopher NAGARJUNA systematized Prajnaparamita thought, which was further developed in the MADHYAMIKA school.

Prajnaparamita-Hridaya Sutra

A MAHAYANA Buddhist text in Sanskrit, popularly known as the *Heart Sutra*. It is one of the many PRAJNAPARAMITA texts, and consists of a summary of the key Prajnaparamita concepts. This short text consists of a dialogue between Shariputra and the Bodhisattva Avalokiteshvara, said to have taken place on the Gridhrakuta hill in RAJAGRIHA. AVALOKITESHVARA explains how to attain 'perfection of wisdom' by viewing even the five SKANDHAS or aggregates as empty of inherent existence. He states, 'Form is emptiness, emptiness is form'. Further he says: 'In emptiness (SHUNYATA) there are no sufferings, sources, cessations and paths; no exalted wisdom, no attainment, and also no non-attainment.' Relying on this profound wisdom, minds are without obstruction and without fear. Commentaries explain that 'form is emptiness', i.e., all things are empty, is a notion based on the concept of 'dependent arising' (PRATITYA SAMUTPADA), which indicates that things have no inherent existence of their own. Avalokiteshvara's discourse ends with a MANTRA of perfection of wisdom: '*Tadyate gate gate paragate parasamgate bodhi svaha*', which has been translated as 'Proceed, proceed, proceed beyond, thoroughly proceed beyond, be founded in enlightenment', (trans. by DALAI LAMA). This *Sutra* has been extensively analysed and commented upon, as it contains the essence of MADHYAMIKA philosophy. It is recited and meditated upon daily by monks who follow the Mahayana path.

Prakrit A term for a number of local dialects and languages that developed from Sanskrit. Among them were Sauraseni, Magadhi, Jain Maharashtri, Paishachi and Apabhramsa. The present regional languages of India originated from the various Prakrit languages.

Prakriti A term for nature or matter. Prakriti and PURUSHA, the twin principles of creation, are extensively described in SAMKHYA philosophy. Prakriti represents feminine energy, and is the active principle of creation, as opposed to Purusha, the passive principle. The PURANAS provide various explanations of the term. Pra, it is said, means 'principal', and kriti, 'creation', thus it is the principal cause of creation. Alternatively pra = sattva, kr = rajas, and ta = tamas, thus all the three GUNAS or qualities are reflected in the word. In another interpretation, pra = before, and kriti = creation, therefore Prakriti is that which existed before creation.

According to the *DEVI BHAGAVATA PURANA*, the supreme spirit consists of Purusha and Prakriti, which separated to bring about creation. Prakriti then took the form of the goddesses DURGA, LAKSHMI, SARASVATI, SAVITRI and RADHA. To RAMANUJA, Prakriti is one of the non-conscious substances of the world, the others being Kala or time, and Shuddhatattva or pure matter. To SHANKARA Prakriti belongs to the world of experience, and thus is essentially unreal. Other philosophies have subtly different interpretations of the term.

pralaya A Sanskrit term that refers to the dissolution or ending of objects. Most commonly, pralaya refers to the end of the world after a KALPA or a cycle of YUGAS, also known as Brahma-pralaya, but there are other types of pralaya as well. Nitya-pralaya is the destruction of living and non-living things that happens on a daily basis. Prakrita-pralaya is the great deluge or flood caused by nature (PRAKRITI) that ends creation. Atyantika-pralaya is the dissolution of the individual through union with the divine.

pramana A philosophical term that has been translated as the 'means of attaining reliable knowledge'. Among the various types of pramanas, are pratyaksha or perception, anumana or inference, upamana or inference through analogy or comparison, and shabda or the word, indicating the words of an authoritative text. According to VEDANTA, other means of knowledge are arthapati, which can be translated as intuition or presumption, and anupalabdhi, or non-perception.

prana The life-force or breath. It denotes the vital force of every living being, or the spirit of life. In the *ATHARVA VEDA* there is a hymn to prana, who is personified. In yogic texts, the pranic body, known as the Pranamaya KOSHA, is said to surround the material or visible body. Ten forms of prana are described: prana, apana, vyana, samana, udana, naga, kurma, krikara, devadatta and dhananjaya. Of these, prana is the vital function through which air is drawn into the body;

apana is the force controlling ejection or elimination; vyana is concerned with the distribution of the force; samana with assimilation; udana is related to the voice and sound. The other five are subsidiary pranas, that control belching, eyelid movement, hunger and thirst, yawning and hiccups.

Pranami Panth   A syncretic sect that has both Hindu and Muslim practices. Its foundation was laid by Shri Devchandra in the seventeenth century, while his disciple Mahamati Prannath (1618–94) of Jamnagar, Gujarat, further explained its concepts and spread its teachings. The sect is based on the worship of the Hindu god KRISHNA, as revealed in the BHAGAVATA PURANA, but also contains ideas and concepts from Islam. Mahamati Prannath, whose original name was Mehraj Thakur, composed the *Qulzam Swarup*, the basic text of the sect, which runs into fourteen volumes and has 18,758 verses. It explains the unity of religions and the universality of religious teachings, conveyed through quotes from the VEDAS, other Hindu texts, and the QURAN. It believes in the worship of the Uttam Purush, the supreme lord identified with Krishna, to attain divine bliss. The text with its quotes uses five languages: Hindi, Gujarati, Kachhi, Sindhi and Arabic, as well as some Persian words. The sect promotes basic ethical principles, the avoidance of meat, fish and alcohol, and honour and respect for all religions. Prannath aimed to establish a universal religion, which he named Nijanand Dharma. He had both Hindu and Muslim disciples, and his most prominent disciple was Maharaja Chhatrasal of the Bundela dynasty at Panna in present Madhya Pradesh. Panna remains the main centre of the faith while Pranami temples also exist in DELHI, Chandigarh, Gujarat, other states of India, Nepal, and Western countries. All Pranami temples contain the *Qulzam Swarup*. The sect has a series of gurus who continue to promote its ideals.

pranayama   A term often translated as 'breath-control', (prana = breath, yama = control), though according to the AMARAKOSHA, it means 'breath-lengthening' (prana = breath, ayama = length, or expansion). Pranayama are breathing techniques that form part of the practice of YOGA, particularly HATHA YOGA. Pranayama implies gaining control over the natural process of breathing. By understanding different types of PRANA and controlling the breath in prescribed ways, health is maintained, diseases are cured, energy and vitality are increased, and at higher levels, various SIDDHIS or powers are achieved. In Kundalini Yoga, prana awakens the KUNDALINI and causes it to rise. Breathing techniques are also prescribed in SUFI systems.

Prarthana Samaj   A religious society that worked for social reform in Hinduism. It was founded in MUMBAI (Bombay) in 1867, by a group of people led by Atmaram Pandurang, with the inspiration of Keshab Chandra Sen of the BRAHMO SAMAJ. The members of the Prarthana Samaj, literally the 'Society of Prayer', worshipped the Maratha BHAKTI saints. Like these saints, they were against caste distinctions. They started educational institutions and worked to improve the position of women and to remove untouchability. The Deccan Education Society was among the notable institutions they founded.

prasada   A Sanskrit word that literally means 'grace'. It refers to consecrated food, offered to the deities in temples and then distributed among worshippers.

Prasangika   A branch of the MADHYAMIKA school of MAHAYANA Buddhism. BUDDHAPALITA (c. 470–540) and later CHANDRAKIRTI (c. 600–650) put forward the views of this school, stating that a Madhyamika exponent should point out the errors in another's argument, but not present positive views. BHAVAVIVEKA (490–570) opposed this and advocated a positive rather than a negative approach, thus founding the SVATANTRIKA school.

Prashna Upanishad   An UPANISHAD that can be dated to before the third century BCE, and has a commentary by SHANKARA. It consists of questions (prashna) asked of the rishi PIPPALADA about the methods to reach the supreme BRAHMAN. In response to the first question, Pippalada describes two paths, that of those who undertake pious works but have a family life, and the greater path of those who follow the inner spirit with steadfastness and purity. Through the first path, the pale regions of the moon are reached, and through the second, the radiant regions of the sun. Pippalada then answers other questions, describing how the individual spirit merges into the Supreme Spirit, where name and form disappear.

pratimas   A term in Jainism for the stages in the life of a householder. Eleven stages are described in texts. In the first stage, the individual should understand and believe in Jainism, and follow its basic principles. Gradually, the person follows the principles more strictly, and takes a number of vows. By the eleventh stage he abandons all property and worldly activity, and begs for his food, refusing anything specially prepared for him.

Pratishakhyas   Sanskrit texts that describe how the verses in the VEDAS are to be pronounced. They were composed later than the Vedas. Those available today include the *Rig Veda Pratishakhya*, ascribed to Shaunaka; the *Taittiriya Pratishakhya* of the Black YAJUR VEDA; the *Vajaseniya Pratishakya* of the White Yajur Veda, said to be written by KATYAYANA; and the *Shaunakiya Chaturadhyayika* of the ATHARVA VEDA, attributed to Shaunaka.

pratitya-samutpada   A doctrine of Buddhism, the principle of 'dependent arising'. According to this, what we see as the Self is something conditioned, and everything conditioned arises from certain circumstances or causes. Understanding the cause from which something arises, in other words, the origin of all things, brings freedom from sorrow.

Pratyabhijna A philosophical concept in SHAIVISM, implying a recognition of the world as a manifestation of SHIVA. ABHINAVAGUPTA, Somananda and Utpaladeva were among those who propagated this philosophy.

Prayaga A sacred city for Hindus, the ancient name of the city of ALLAHABAD in Uttar Pradesh. Prayaga marks the confluence of the GANGA and its main tributary, the YAMUNA. According to legend, a third river, the SARASVATI, which cannot be seen, joins the two rivers here. Thus Prayaga is also known as Triveni, the meeting place of three rivers. The site of the confluence, known as the sangam, is especially sacred. The city has several temples. Metaphysically, the three rivers represent the KUNDALINI and the two main NADIS, IDA and PINGALA, which lead to enlightenment when united with the SUSHUMNA.

According to ancient texts, ending one's life at Prayaga by jumping into the river was a sacred act, bringing merit in the next world or life. The Kalachuri king Gangeyadeva, along with a hundred wives, as well as many others, are said to have done this. Alternatively it was also meritorious to enter a fire of cow dung cakes here.

These religious sacrifices are described by the seventh-century Chinese traveller XUANZANG, as well as in the PURANAS, and in several inscriptions.

prema A word that means love. In some Hindu BHAKTI sects, prema refers to the pure love felt by an individual for the divine.

Presbyterian Church A Protestant Church that arose out of the Reformed Church of the 1500s. Presbyterian Churches are administered by ministers and presbyters or elders, and have Synods or associations in which both priests and lay people participate.

The Presbyterian Church of India developed out of the Presbyterian Church of Wales. The Rev. Thomas Jones and his wife, of the Welsh Calvinist Methodist or Presbyterian Church of Wales, came to India as missionaries in 1914 and settled in the Khasi–Jaintia area of present Meghalaya. Their missionary work soon spread to the Cachar hills of Assam, Mizoram and Manipur, and in 1926 the Synod of the Presbyterian Church in Assam was formed. In 1935 the Synod was renamed the Assembly, and in 1992 it came to be known as the Presbyterian Church of India. The Presbyterian Assembly, under which there are six Synods, is the supreme body, with authority over all the churches under it. The Church is prominent in the north-east, in the states of Assam, Meghalaya, Manipur, Tripura and Arunachal Pradesh, but it also has churches in other parts of the country. According to 1998 statistics, it has 8,23,456 members and 2568 local churches.

preta (1) In Hindu mythology, a term for a ghost or evil spirit, which is said to be able to enter dead bodies and animate them. Graveyards are among its favourite haunts.

(2) It is also said to be the temporary state of a dead person, for whom ancestral rites have not yet been performed.

Prithvi A Hindu deity, the goddess of the earth. She is first described in the RIG VEDA, and later in the *ATHARVA VEDA*. She is paired with DYAUS (heaven), and Dyaus-Prithvi is thus the deity of heaven and earth. She is the kindly earth mother who bears the weight of the mountains, supports the trees of the forest, and scatters the rain. In later texts, Prithvi is an alternative name for BHUDEVI.

Propaganda, Congregation of A Roman Catholic missionary organization founded in 1662 by Pope Gregory XV to spread Christianity abroad. The Portuguese, through the PADROADO, had the authority to convert people in their overseas territories, but were themselves in decline, and the Propaganda was created when Portugal was under the Spanish crown. More Catholic missionaries gradually arrived in India, and initially the two missionary organizations co-operated, but later tensions arose. The Pope began to appoint 'Vicars Apostolic', church officials similar to, but with not quite the same power as Bishops, even in areas that were under the Padroado. Conflicts took place between the two groups, particularly in MUMBAI (Bombay), but also in other areas. In 1886, Pope Leo XIII constituted the Catholic Hierarchy of India, with seventeen ecclesiastical units under the Propaganda, and two under the Padroado, thus to some extent resolving the conflicts.

Protestantism A form of Christianity with hundreds of different denominations or sects, that developed after the REFORMATION, which took place in the sixteenth century. The term is derived from the Latin word 'protestans', or 'one who protests', and was first used in Germany in 1529, when in a Diet (assembly) German leaders protested against the Roman Catholic attempts to stop the spread of Lutheranism. Gradually the word came to be used for all Western Christian groups who separated from the Roman Catholic Church. While Protestants have some common beliefs with Roman Catholics, certain beliefs differ. Like Catholics they believe in One God, and most accept the concept of the TRINITY. However, they oppose the Roman Catholic doctrine of salvation, which gives importance to both God's grace and good works, and stress the importance of faith instead of good deeds. They emphasize the BIBLE rather than the traditions of the Church that developed over time, do not adhere to all the SACRAMENTS, have less elaborate forms of worship, and less dependence on priests, with a greater involvement of lay people. While some

Protestant denominations are very liberal, others can be puritanical.

Broadly, Protestant denominations have been divided into five main groups: (1) the conservative reform movements that broke away in the 1500s, including the LUTHERAN, the Reformed or PRESBYTERIAN, and the ANGLICAN; (2) the radical reform movements of the 1500s and 1600s, including Anabaptists, Quakers, Separatists and Shakers; (3) the Free Church movement of the 1500s and 1600s, which developed into the CONGREGATIONAL and BAPTIST Churches; (4) the METHODIST movement of the 1700s, which was related to evangelical movements, and the Holiness Movement, from which PENTECOSTAL Churches developed; (5) the unity movement of the 1800s and 1900s, which is still continuing, where groups of churches made attempts to resolve differences and join together in various types of unions.

Protestants in India Protestantism is widespread in India. The first Protestant church in India, ST. MARY'S CHURCH in Chennai, was built in 1680, though Protestant missions were established only in the eighteenth century. In 1706 Frederick IV, king of Denmark, sent two Lutherans from Halle in Germany, Bartholomew Ziegenbalg and Henry Plutschau to set up a Protestant mission in Tranquebar in present Tamil Nadu. They were supported by British associations, including the Society for the Propagation of Christian Knowledge and the Society for the Propagation of Gospel. The British East India Company, which had begun taking over territory in India, had initially banned missionaries. William CAREY, an Englishman who came to India in 1793, started the Baptist Mission in 1799 at Serampore, which was under the Danes. He was assisted by Joshua Marshman and William Ward. Another missionary movement was started by Alexander DUFF in Kolkata (Calcutta) soon after the removal of the Missionary Clause of the East India Company in 1814. Missions of a wide variety of Protestant denominations followed, mainly from Europe and America, and today almost all Protestant denominations are represented in India. Protestants exist all over India, but are more prevalent in the north and east.

Among the Protestant Churches in India are the two groups of the CHURCH OF NORTH INDIA and the CHURCH OF SOUTH INDIA, the BAPTIST CHURCH, the EVANGELICAL CHURCHES, the LUTHERAN CHURCH, the METHODIST CHURCH, the MENNONITE CHURCH, the NEW APOSTOLIC CHURCH, the PRESBYTERIAN CHURCH, the SEVENTH DAY ADVENTIST CHURCH and the PENTECOSTAL CHURCHES.

pudgala (1) A concept in some schools of HINAYANA Buddhism. According to this, in each individual there is a permanent entity called pudgala, which transmigrates from life to life. The VATSIPUTRIYA and their subdivisions followed this concept, which was strongly opposed by other schools that did not believe in any permanent entity.

(2) In Jainism, one of the six DRAVYAS or substances of the world. Pudgala is matter, the physical substance of the world. It includes everything that can be experienced through the senses and the mind. According to the DASAVELIYA SUTTA, 'sound, union, fineness, grossness, shape, division, darkness, and image, with lustre and heat, are modifications of the substance known as pudgala.' Undifferentiated pudgala consists of atoms or paramanus, and these combine in various ways to form skandhas, which are aggregates or compounds. The whole world is a maha-skandha. Atoms are infinite and eternal. They are formless, but can be perceived by the enlightened. AKASHA or space, DHARMA or movement, and ADHARMA or the principle of rest, enable them to combine.

(3) Pudgala also has other meanings, and is a name of SHIVA.

Puggalapanati A Buddhist HINAYANA text that forms part of the ABHIDHAMMA PITAKA of the PALI CANON. Literally a 'description of human individuals', it has some passages similar to the texts of the SUTTA PITAKA. Most of it describes in detail the nature of different types of people, such as an angry person, a crafty person or a good person. For instance, 'What sort of person is angry? What then is anger? That which is anger, being angry, and the state of being angry, hatred, hating, hatefulness, malice, the act of being malicious, maliciousness, hostility, enmity, rudeness, abruptness, resentment of heart—this is called anger. He who has not got rid of this anger is said to be an angry person.' (Trans. B.C. Law)

puja The act of worship in Hinduism, which may take place in a temple or at home. Prayers, along with offerings such as fruit, flowers or incense, are made to the image of a deity, or to a symbol of the divine. Puja may be done either according to prescribed rituals, or in a spontaneous way.

Pulastya A mind-born son of the Hindu god BRAHMA, one of the PRAJAPATIS or great RISHIS. Some of the PURANAS were revealed to him by Brahma. He was the father of Vishravas, who in turn was the father of KUBERA and RAVANA.

Puranas Sanskrit texts sacred to Hindus that include myths, legends, methods of worship, geographical and historical details and a lot more. They probably originated before the first century CE, but in the form available today they date from the second to fourth centuries and later. According to tradition, they have five main topics: sarga or creation; pratisarga, or re-creation, after the periodic destruction of the worlds; (alternatively, 'secondary cretaion') vamsha or genealogy, here referring to the genealogies of gods and RISHIS; manvantarani, an account of the MANVANTARAS or great periods of time, each headed by a MANU, the ancestor of all humans; vamshanucharita, the history of dynasties, whose mythical origins are traced back to the sun or the moon (SURYAVAMSHA and CHANDRAVAMSHA dynasties, respectively).

The Puranas vary in nature. Some of them contain aspects of the five topics listed above, while others do not. Many are associated with a particular deity or sect.

Eighteen Puranas are listed as Mahapuranas or great Puranas, and they are the most important. These are: (1) BRAHMA PURANA; (2) PADMA PURANA; (3) VISHNU PURANA; (4) VAYU or SHIVA PURANA; (5) BHAGAVATA PURANA; (6) BRIHANNARADIYA or NARADIYA PURANA; (7) MARKANDEYA PURANA; (8) AGNI PURANA; (9) BHAVISHYA PURANA; (10) BRAHMAVAIVARTA PURANA; (11) LINGA PURANA; (12) VARAHA PURANA; (13) SKANDA PURANA; (14) VAMANA PURANA; (15) KURMA PURANA; (16) MATSYA PURANA; (17) GARUDA PURANA; (18) BRAHMANDA PURANA.

Apart from these, there are said to be eighteen Upapuranas or minor Puranas, as well as several other works called Puranas. Lists of Upapuranas vary, but most commonly consist of the following: (1) Sanatkumara Purana; (2) Narasimha Purana; (3) NARADIYA PURANA; (4) SHIVA PURANA; (5) Durvasas Purana; (6) Kapila Purana; (7) Manava Purana; (8) Ushanas Purana; (9) Varuna Purana; (10) KALIKA PURANA; (11) Samba Purana; (12) SAURA PURANA; (13) Aditya Purana; (14) Maheshvara Purana; (15) Devi Bhagavata Purana; (16) Vasishtha Purana; (17) VISHNUDHARMOTTARA PURANA; (18) NILAMATA PURANA. Out of these the Shiva Purana and Devi-Bhagavata Purana, are often considered Mahapuranas or major Puranas.Some other Puranas listed as Upapuranas are the Kalki Purana, Chandi Purana, Ganesha Purana, and Brihaddharma Purana. Various later accounts and temple records also use the name Purana, but are different from the traditional Puranas.

Puranas, Jain A number of texts composed by Jains are known as Puranas. Among these Puranas are the Padma Purana (a version of the RAMAYANA), the Jain HARIVAMSHA PURANA, and the TRISHASHTI-LAKSHANA MAHAPURANA.

Purandaradasa A sixteenth-century singer who composed devotional songs in Kannada, to the Hindu god VITTHALA, a form of VISHNU.

Born in 1484 in Purandargarh near the city of Vijayanagara in present Karnataka, Purandara was married to a saintly woman, Sarasvati Bai, when he was sixteen years old. Initially Purandara lived a life of luxury, but influenced by the piety of his wife, he became a disciple of Vyasaraya, a guru of the HARIDASA sect, and a devotee of Vitthala. Purandara believed in the grace of god, a god who would understand all frailties and never condemn a devotee, no matter what his or her faults. In one song he compares himself to an insect who has fallen into the fire. It is only god who can save him. He asks god why he sent him to the earth, why he could not love and care for him in heaven. In a similar song he says, 'Having assumed the title of protector of devotees, should you not be on hand for them?'

In later songs he seems more at peace, sure of the protection of the Lord, and sings, 'When I am dwelling in thought of you, what can the wicked do to me?'

He asked people to do their best in the world, to provide food and charity to the poor, help others and give up attachments. He was against the caste system and believed true caste was based on character, not on birth. Sacrifice did not imply the slaughter of animals, but the slaying of one's own bad qualities.

Purandaradasa is the best known of the Haridasas. His songs of BHAKTI and devotion, composed in classical RAGAS, are still sung today.

Puri A town in Orissa, with more than a hundred early temples, including the celebrated JAGANNATHA TEMPLE. Puri is also the site of one of the four mathas founded by SHANKARA.

purohita A BRAHMANA priest. In ancient times the purohita was often the royal priest, an official who influenced the policies of the king.

Puru A king of the CHANDRAVAMSHA or lunar dynasty mentioned in the MAHABHARATA and other texts. He and YADU were among the sons of YAYATI, and were the founders of two main branches of the Chandravamsha: the Pauravas, who were descendants of Puru, and the Yadus or YADAVAS. Both the KAURAVAS and PANDAVAS were Pauravas.

Pururavas/Pururava A person mentioned in Hindu texts and known in myths and stories for his association with the APSARA Urvashi. According to the VEDAS, he was connected with the sun and dawn, while the MAHABHARATA states that he was the son of BUDHA (Mercury) by ILA, daughter of MANU. There are other versions of his parentage as well. The story of Pururavas and Urvashi is first described in the RIG VEDA and elaborated on in several later texts. The fifth-century playwright KALIDASA made it the subject of his play Vikramorvashi. The story recounts how Pururavas fell in love with Urvashi, who had descended from heaven. She agreed to stay with him but laid down certain conditions, one of which was that he never see her undressed, or she would have to depart. By a trick of the GANDHARVAS, Pururavas did see her, and Urvashi vanished. Finally, however, the Gandharvas granted his wish to live with her. The story is said to be based on a myth, with Pururavas representing the sun and Urvashi the morning mist, or Urvashi as the dawn and Pururavas as twilight. It has some parallels with the Greek myth of Psyche.

Purusha A Sanskrit term meaning 'man', soul, or Self. It represents the eternal male principle, the passive or fixed aspect of creation. Purusha is the eternal Truth that sets creation in motion. It is beyond form and shape, the subtle essence of creation.

Its counterpart is PRAKRITI, nature or matter, the active principle. Purusha and Prakriti are extensively described in SAMKHYA philosophy. In the *RIG VEDA*, Purusha represents primeval man, from whom creation emerged.

Purva Mimamsa Another name of MIMAMSA, one of the six ancient systems of philosophy.

Purvas/Puvvas A term for the original Jain texts containing the teachings of MAHAVIRA, which were lost long ago. Purva means 'previous' or 'former', and there were fourteen such texts. The twelve ANGAS, of which one is lost, sacred to the SHVETAMBARA sect, were compiled based on what was remembered of the Purvas. The DIGAMBARA sect, however, believe the Angas are not authentic.

According to the Shvetambara tradition, the Purvas were known up to the time of STHULABHADRA, the fourteenth Jain leader after Mahavira.

Pushan A deity in the RIG VEDA, who later declined in importance. Pushan is described as the lord of all things, and the guardian of all. He has braided hair and a beard, and carries a golden spear, along with an awl or a goad. His chariot is drawn by goats and he eats gruel. He was married to Surya (Suryaa), daughter of the sun god, SURYA. He is described as 'glowing' and is the guardian of roads, leading the dead to the distant abode of the fathers. He makes hidden things easy to find and protects cattle. He is one of the ADITYAS.

Pushkar A sacred place in Rajasthan that has several shrines, including a temple of the Hindu god BRAHMA, and a holy lake. Here Brahma is said to have performed a sacrifice after killing a demon. Pushkaranya, the forest of Pushkar, is described in the PURANAS and other ancient texts. According to the texts, the full benefits of visiting other places of pilgrimage is obtained only by bathing in the lake here. In modern times Pushkar is also known for its annual camel and cattle fair.

Pushpaka A vimana or aerial chariot described in the RAMAYANA. It was very large and could contain a whole palace or even a city. It was a gift from the Hindu god BRAHMA to KUBERA, but was appropriated by Kubera's half-brother RAVANA. After RAMA killed Ravana, he used the chariot to carry SITA, LAKSHMANA and all his allies back to AYODHYA, and then returned it to Kubera. VALMIKI's *Ramayana* has the following description of the Pushpaka: 'The aerial car was furnished with pillars made of gold; its portals were of cat's-eye gems; it was hung with nets of pearls and planted with fruit-bearing trees; it was swift as the mind, could go anywhere one wanted, and assume any form; its stairways were of gems and gold; it was a celestial vehicle and not subject to wear and tear.' It had been constructed by the divine architect VISHVAKARMA.

Pushtimarga A Hindu sect based on the teachings of VALLABHACHARYA. The sect worships the god KRISHNA with love and devotion. It believes that since Krishna created the world, worldly pleasures should be enjoyed and not avoided.

Puttaparthi A place in Andhra Pradesh where the ashram of Sri Sathya SAI BABA is located. Prasanthi Nilayam, the abode of peace at Puttaparthi, has developed as a vast complex consisting of prayer halls, temples, and secular institutions. Here all religions are respected, reflecting the philosophy of Sai Baba.

Qadiri A SUFI order founded by Abdul Qadir al-Jilani (d. 1166), who was also known as Ghaus-ul Azam. The Qadiriyas revered their founder as an embodiment of the divine, as he was a direct descendant of the Prophet MUHAMMAD, through the Prophet's daughter Fatima. The order follows the WAHDAT AL-WUJUD doctrine, as IBN AL-ARABI, its greatest exponent, had once joined them.

The Qadiri order was introduced in India by Mir Nurullah bin Shah, a grandson of Shah Nuruddin Nimatullah, a noted Sufi who had settled in Iran. Nurullah came to the Deccan soon after 1424 at the request of Sultan Ahmad Shah I of the Bahmani kingdom, who even built a town called Nimatabad near Bidar in his honour, and gave him his daughter in marriage. The Qadiriyas were thus very influential in the Deccan. In the north, a Qadiri KHANQAH was established at Uch near Multan in the second half of the fifteenth century, by Shaikh Muhammad al-Husaini al-Jilani. Among other noted Qadiriyas in northern India were Shaikh Dawud (d. 1574–75), who was known for his miraculous powers and spread Qadiri influence in the north, Shaikh Abul Maali (1553–1615), who was a renowned poet, and Shaikh Mahdo (d. 1646–47), who was a BRAHMANA converted to Islam. Shaikh ABDUL HAQQ MUHADDIS and his disciples formed a line of Qadiriyas who tried to find a middle path between the SHARIA and Sufi ideals. Miyan Mir (1535–1635) and his disciples were mystics and ascetics. Among them Mulla Shah (1564–1628/29) was the PIR of DARA SHIKOH and JAHANARA, the son and daughter of the Mughal emperor Shah Jahan. Qadiriyas also spread to Gujarat, Malwa, Bengal and Avadh, and remained important until the eighteenth century.

A prominent Sufi of the seventeenth and eighteenth centuries was Saiyid Shah Abdul Razzaq Bansawi, who lived at Bansa near Lucknow and was said to be a friend of Hindus as well as Muslims, both SHIAS and SUNNIS. Though he remained a devout Muslim, he had visions of KRISHNA, RAMA and LAKSHMANA, and believed that the same truth could be perceived in different ways, and that others' beliefs must be respected. Thus there were several different trends in the order.

Qala-i-Kuhna Mosque A mosque located in DELHI, constructed in 1541 by the Afghan emperor Sher Shah. Its prayer hall measures 51 m by 15 m and has five arched entrances. The tall central arch is recessed within another archway, set in a rectangular frame, and decorated with an inlay of coloured stones.

There are octagonal double-storeyed turrets at the rear, with arches and galleries at each level. The mosque represents a transitional style between Lodi and Mughal monuments.

Qalandars A term for wandering SUFI saints who rejected the organization and discipline of most Sufi orders, as well as Islamic laws. Their origin is unclear, but they are known from the eleventh and twelfth centuries, when they existed in Syria, eastern Iran and Transoxiana.

An eleventh-century Sufi, Baba Tahir, wrote a verse describing them. Written in the first person, it says:

I am the mystic gypsy called Qalandar;
I have neither fire, home nor monastery.
By day I wander about the world;
At night, I sleep with a brick under my head.

The Qalandars belonged to different groups. Some shaved their heads and discarded their clothes, while others wore blankets. They were known for the use of intoxicants and for their wild behaviour, and in India they borrowed some of the customs of the NATHA YOGIS and NAGA SADHUS. Early Qalandars were against the KHANQAH form of life of other orders, and against the veneration given to a SHAIKH or PIR. In their wanderings they often visited khanqahs, creating problems for the residents. Qalandars were both feared and revered, as though they had rejected all norms, many were known to have miraculous powers. By the thirteenth century, some Qalandars began to live settled lives, though others continued to wander and despise established pirs. Among the Qalandar groups were the Haidaris, who originated in Iran. Shaikh Abu Bakr Tusi Haidari lived in DELHI on the banks of the Yamuna in the thirteenth century. He was visited by the Delhi sultan and various Sufis, and was said to have great powers.

Some Qalandars joined the CHISTI and SUHRAWARDI orders, and thus Qalandar-Chisti and Qalandar-Suhrawardi orders developed. Among the noted Qalandar-Chistis was ABU (BU) ALI SHAH of Panipat.

Qalandars remained prominent in India, at least till the sixteenth century.

qazi A term in Islam for an Islamic judge or author of law books. Qazis were judicial officials in the time of the sultans and Mughals, and in other Islamic states in India. Qazis still have a role today.

qibla A term for the direction of the KABA at Mecca. Wherever they are, Muslims turn towards this direction while praying. In India, the direction is west.

Quran The sacred text of Islam, composed in Arabic. It is believed to be a divine revelation that supersedes previous revelations in the Hebrew and Christian BIBLES. The words of God in the Quran were revealed to the Prophet MUHAMMAD over a period of twenty-three years while Muhammad was in Mecca and Medina. In the first revelation, the Angel Jibril (Gabriel) came to Muhammad in 610 in the month of RAMZAN, and subsequent revelations followed. According to some sources, however, the first revelations were through dreams.

Muhammad himself is said to have arranged the text into suras or chapters, and chosen their titles. The whole was memorized by his companions while he was still alive, and thus has the authenticity of teachings as revealed to him. According to a HADIS, Abu Bakr, the Caliph from 632–34, arranged and wrote down the Quran, though a final version is said to have been compiled at the time of the third Caliph, Usman (ruled 644–56). The Quran has 114 suras and 6236 verses, according to the Kufah method of numbering, generally followed in India, though there are also different methods of counting the verses, leading to different results. The term Quran comes from the Arabic qara, similar to the Hebrew kara, meaning to read or recite. One commentator has listed fifty-five alternate titles of the Quran, among them being *Al-Kitab* (*The Book*); *Al-Quran* (*The Reading*); *Al-Mubin* (*The Enlightener*); *Al-Mubarak* (*The Blessed*) and *Al-Hikmah* (*The Wisdom*). The first chapter of the Quran has the FATIHA, a prayer recited at every new beginning. The Fatiha begins with an invocation to God, and asks for guidance on the right path, which is blessed by God.

The Quran provides a guide to an ethical life, where God is remembered, and deals with a number of different aspects of life, both religious and social. It states that there is one God, ALLAH, who formulated the laws of the universe, and Muhammad is his Prophet. As God is One, no idols should be worshipped, nor should people or other created beings be deified. There are angels who are helpers or messengers of God, as well as a judgement day, heaven and hell. There are passages dealing with the basic duties of a Muslim—prayer, fasting, charity and pilgrimage—as well as the main principles a Muslim should follow. It also deals with civil and criminal laws relating to marriage, inheritance, adultery, theft and murder.

A number of its traditions can be traced to Talmudic Judaism, prevalent in Arabia at the time of Muhammad; stories of the Biblical Prophets Abraham, Moses and others are also narrated in the Quran. It has references to JESUS, MARY and Christian beliefs, though the concepts associated with them are reinterpreted. Some trace these interpretations to Gnostic sources, or to Eastern or Syrian Christianity.

The Quran, along with the SUNNAH, forms the basis for Islam. There are numerous commentaries and different interpretations of the text, and though it is normally studied in its original Arabic, it has been translated into a number of languages.

A Hadis of al-Bukhari states: 'The best person amongst you is he who has learnt the Quran and teaches it.'

Qutb Minar A tall tower located in DELHI, built in the thirteenth century and later. It probably served as a MINARET for the QUWWATUL ISLAM MOSQUE constructed nearby, but it may have also been a tower of victory. The tapering tower, begun by Sultan Qutbuddin Aibak (ruled 1206–10) was completed by Sultan Iltutmish (1211–36). It reaches a height of 73.7 m with a diameter of approximately 14 m at the base and somewhat less than 3 m at the top, and has five storeys. It was struck by lightning twice, and was repaired by Sultan Firuz Shah Tughlaq in 1368 and later by Sultan Sikandar Lodi in 1503. Further repairs were carried out by the British in the nineteenth century. A winding staircase with 379 steps leads to the top. The Minar is built in Saracenic style; the first three stories are made of red sandstone and are fluted, the next two are made of marble with belts of sandstone and are plain. There are four projecting balconies, the fourth at a height of 66 m. The whole is beautifully carved and embellished, and is considered one of the grandest towers in the world.

Qutbuddin Bakhtiyar Kaki, Khwaja A SUFI saint of the CHISTI order, the chief disciple of Shaikh MUINUDDIN CHISTI. Born in Ush in the province of Jaxartes, he met Muinuddin Chisti when he was in Baghdad and became his disciple. Later he came through Multan to DELHI, arriving there soon after 1221, and was welcomed by Sultan Iltutmish (ruled 1211–36). When Muinuddin visited DELHI, Qutbuddin went with him to Ajmer, but returned to Delhi because of the people's affection for him. Iltutmish was said to be devoted to him and often came to him for advice. According to tradition, the spot for the HAUZ-I SHAMSI water tank was chosen after consulting him. The ULAMA, however, were opposed to him, and did not appreciate the Chisti practice of SAMA (music).

Qutbuddin lived in simplicity and poverty, and advised his disciples to assist the needy. He is said to have never had enough money for his own family's needs, but one day after sitting in deep meditation, bread began to miraculously appear in his house, and thus he was known as Kaki, or 'man of bread.' He died in 1235 in a state of ecstasy aroused by Sama. Among his chief disciples was Shaikh Fariduddin, popularly known as Baba FARID, whose successor was NIZAMUDDIN AULIYA.

Qutbuddin's DARGAH is located in the Mehrauli area of Delhi, and is a place of pilgrimage. In the festival of SAIR-E-GUL FAROSHAN or Phul Walon ki Sair, a procession starts from his tomb and proceeds to the YOGA MAYA TEMPLE.

Quwwatul Islam Mosque A mosque located in DELHI, which is the earliest mosque of the Delhi sultans. It was constructed by Qutbuddin Aibak before he became the sultan, between 1191 and 1196, on the orders of Muhammad Ghori. Later it was extended by Iltutmish, who ruled from DELHI between 1211 and 1236, with further additions made by Alauddin Khalji (1296–1316). The mosque, built in orthodox plan, has a large court, 43 m by 33 m, enclosed by pillars. Some materials from earlier Hindu structures were used in the mosque, including carved pillars. To the west is the prayer hall. In front is an arched screen, carved with passages from religious texts and floral patterns. Nearby is the QUTB MINAR.

R

Rachol Seminary A Catholic seminary located in Rachol fortress in village Raia, GOA. It was initially established at Margao in 1574, with funds provided by the king of Portugal, Dom Sebastiao, but was destroyed by the rulers of Bijapur. It was shifted to Rachol, back to Margao, and finally relocated at the current site where it was constructed in 1606. It functioned as a college under the Jesuits, who conducted classes in theology, Portuguese, and other subjects. In 1762, after the Jesuits were expelled from Portuguese territory, it was turned into a Diocesan seminary for the education of the clergy.

The seminary building has solid granite pillars and houses a treasury of Renaissance art including a large picture of Sebastiao, who was killed in a battle in 1578. According to local legend, the ghost of Dom Sebastio, mounted on a white horse, rides through the seminary at night, and hence a lighted lamp is always placed in the gateway.

A church dedicated to St. Ignatius of Loyola, and a chapel are attached to the seminary.

Radha A Hindu deity who symbolizes love and longing for God. She is the divine lover and consort of the god KRISHNA, though she is not married to him. In early texts describing the life of Krishna, Radha is not specifically mentioned, though Krishna's affairs with the GOPIS are described. Radha is referred to in texts of the ninth and tenth centuries, and the love between Radha and Krishna is fully described in the twelfth-century *GITA GOVINDA* and narrated in several later texts. As a young man, Krishna lived in the Vraja region, the area around MATHURA. There he danced and played with the gopis, as the wives and daughters of the cowherds of the region were called. Radha was his favourite among them, and they often met in the forests and glades of VRINDAVAN, amidst spring flowers and natural beauty. Radha was already married, thus her desire for Krishna and their long separations, form a unique part of this relationship. Radha's longing is said to reflect the yearning of the individual soul for union with god. Radha is worshipped along with Krishna by several VAISHNAVA sects, among them being the followers of VALLABHACHARYA, CHANDIDAS and CHAITANYA MAHAPRABHU. In the fifteenth century VIDYAPATI composed beautiful poems on Radha and Krishna. Their love has been depicted in art, music and literature. However, some temples and worshippers of Krishna, particularly in south India, prefer to worship Krishna along with his legitimate wives, particularly RUKMINI.

Radhasoami/Radhaswami sect A religious sect founded by Swami Shiv Dayal Singh in 1861, which today has many offshoots and branches. Originally its headquarters were in a locality near AGRA in present Uttar Pradesh, which came to be known as Swami Bagh. The sect focuses on Surat Shabd Yoga, union with the divine through inner sound, and prescribes meditative practices to lead the individual to higher stages of consciousness and finally to Anami Lok, the nameless world or state. In this sect, the supreme being is known as Radha-soami, and chanting this name brings one close to the divine. Three requirements of the Radhasoami way are: (1) the necessity for a living guide, the Satguru or true guru; (2) the Satshabda or true word, the inner sound revealed to the disciple by the guru; (3) the Satsang or right association or religious order. Related to these is Satanuraga, or true love and obedience to the guru. Followers are to practise Surat Shabd Yoga meditation for two to three hours every day, obey the living guru, and lead a moral life. This includes not consuming meat, fish, eggs, alcohol or drugs, and not having sex outside marriage. All people, regardless of caste or religion, are welcome to join.

Swami Shiv Dayal was recognized as the first Satguru. After his death in 1878, there was confusion about who should succeed him, and soon six different groups were formed. Among these were two in Agra and one at Beas in the Punjab. Today there are about thirty offshoots of the sect, though the two main centres are at Beas and Agra. Among the many notable leaders over the years was Kirpal Singh, who had a large following abroad and started Manav Kendra, with somewhat different principles.

The sect and its branches have thousands of followers of all communities in India and other parts of the world.

raga A musical form that has five, six or seven notes. Each raga has certain fixed notes and some variable themes. Ragas are said to exist naturally, and are not created, but only discovered. Thus they represent the hidden sounds of creation and are linked with mysticism and religion. Both Hindustani and Karnatak (Carnatic) music have a number of ragas. Ragas have also been personified and are represented in art along with their consorts, known as Raginis.

Raghava A name of the Hindu god RAMA, who was a descendant of RAGHU and is therefore known as Raghava.

Raghu A famous king of the Ikshvaku dynasty. He was the grandfather of DASHARATHA and great-grandfather of the Hindu god RAMA. Rama thus belonged to the family of Raghu, or the Raghuvamsha.

Ragniya Temple A temple dedicated to the Hindu goddess Ragniya, located 22 km from Srinagar in Kashmir. The shrine of this local goddess is surrounded by natural springs. The Khir Bhavani festival is held here in the month of Jyaishtha (May–June), when milk, khir (rice cooked with milk and sugar) and flowers are offered to the deity.

Rahim A noted BHAKTI poet. Abdul Rahim Khan-i Khanan, popularly known as Rahim, was a noble at the court of the Mughal emperor AKBAR in the sixteenth century. He took part in several military campaigns, but was also a scholar and poet who knew Persian, Arabic, Turkish, Sanskrit and Hindi.

A number of poems in Hindi, including short couplets or *dohas* are attributed to him, though scholars doubt whether these were all his. There are legends about Rahim's devotion to Srinathji, a form of the Hindu god KRISHNA, and his poems include those on love, on Bhakti or devotion to Krishna, along with wise moral sayings. TULASIDASA is said to have been inspired by Rahim's form of composition when he wrote the *RAMACHARITAMANASA*.

rahit A code of discipline observed by KHALSA Sikhs. Sources for the rahit include both scriptures and tradition.

Rahit-namas A term for written sources of the RAHIT, or the code of discipline for Sikhs who follow the KHALSA. Kahn Singh of Nabha (1861–1938), a Sikh scholar, listed twenty-eight Rahit-namas, including the GURU GRANTH SAHIB and the JANAM SAKHIS. There are also texts specifically dealing with rahit as laid down by Guru GOBIND SINGH when he founded the Khalsa. Among these are Rahit-namas attributed to his associates NAND LAL, Daya Singh (one of the PANJ PYARES) and others. These texts, however, cannot be dated precisely nor can their authorship be confirmed. In 1915, the SINGH SABHA put together a Rahit-nama based on earlier texts, named *Gurmat Prakash Bhag Sanskar*, but it did not gain widespread acceptance. The SHIROMANI GURDWARA PRABANDHAK COMMITTEE published a new Rahit-nama in 1950, entitled the *Sikh Rahit Maryada*, laying down the code of discipline for Sikhs. A Sikh who follows the Khalsa is one who

believes in the ten gurus and the GURU GRANTH SAHIB, while different Sikh sects have their own rules. The Namdharis, for instance, have their own *Namdhari Rahit-nama*.

Rahu One of the NAVAGRAHA, or nine planets in Hindu mythology. Rahu does not correspond to a real planet, but is called a shadow planet. In astrology, Rahu represents the ascending node. Rahu is also said to be the king of meteors, the cause of eclipses, and even the word used for an eclipse. He is a DAITYA or a DANAVA the son of Viprachitti and Simhika. According to myths in texts, at the time of the churning of the ocean for AMRITA, Rahu came in disguise and stole some of the divine drink. The sun and moon saw him and told the god VISHNU, who cut off his head and two of his arms, but as he had drunk amrita, he was immortal. His body was placed in the spheres, the upper part with a dragon's head and the lower (KETU) with a dragon's tail. Rahu takes revenge on the sun and moon by swallowing them now and then, causing an eclipse. His chariot moves across the sky, drawn by eight black horses. Rahu is depicted in Navagraha panels in temples. In astrological charts or horoscopes, Rahu is usually not considered an auspicious planet.

Rahula The son of Siddhartha Gautama, the BUDDHA. Rahula was born shortly before Siddhartha left his home in search of truth. His name literally means 'rope' or 'fetter', one more tie binding Siddhartha to the world. Despite this, Siddhartha left and achieved enlightenment after six years. Later, persuaded by Shariputra, a close disciple of the Buddha, Rahula joined the SANGHA at a young age, without the knowledge of his mother YASHODHARA. Upset by this she requested that no child should be allowed to become a monk without the permission of his parents. The Buddha agreed that this would be followed in future.

Raidas A Hindu saint, who was also known as RAVIDASA.

Raikot Gurdwara A GURDWARA or Sikh shrine located in Ludhiana, Punjab, associated with the life of Guru GOBIND SINGH. It marks the spot where the guru stayed with his Pathan disciple Rai Kalla, and where he heard the sad news of the death of his sons, Zorawar Singh and Fateh Singh. In response to the news, the guru said that his sons had been a gift of God and had now returned to God.

Rajagriha The ancient name of the town of Rajgir in Bihar. It is associated with Buddhism and Jainism, and has several sacred sites within the town, and nearby in the Rajgir hills. In the sixth century BCE, it was the capital of the kingdom of MAGADHA, and the first BUDDHIST COUNCIL is said to have been held here. The BUDDHA spent many years here, living in a shelter on Gridhrakuta peak. When King AJATASHATRU ruled Magadha there were at least two Buddhist monasteries here. There are also Jain caves and temples in the hills. The Maniyar Matha, dating back to the time of the Gupta dynasty (fourth to sixth century), has a shrine of a Naga deity, MANI NAGA, while rock-cut shrines nearby dated to the third or fourth century are associated with Jainism and Buddhism.

rajarishi A term for a RISHI or sage who was originally a king or raja, or who was of the KSHATRIYA caste. Though sages of all kinds are described in the UPANISHADS, traditionally, Kshatriyas could not be rishis. Rishis in the olden days are supposed to have had great powers. Some exceptional Kshatriyas practised intensive austerities until their purity and ascetism enabled them to become rishis. VISHVAMITRA was one such rajarishi, described in ancient texts.

rajasuya One of the four main consecration rituals for kings in Vedic days. The Rajasuya sacrifice (YAJNA) is described in detail in the *Shatapatha Brahmana*. The rituals began with presents to the chief queen and court officials, followed by the abhisheka or sprinkling with consecrated water. This was a mixture of seventeen different types of water, including water from the river SARASVATI, from a pond, a well, a whirlpool, sea-water and dew. After invoking the gods and sprinkling the water, the king walked towards the different directions, indicating that his rule extended everywhere. Next he trod on a tiger-skin to gain the strength of a tiger. After this the hotr or priest recited the story of SHUNAHSHEPA, following which a mock battle or cattle raid was enacted. The king was then enthroned and played a game of dice, which he was made to win. These rituals blessed the king and were symbolic of his rule over the four quarters, and the strength and luck he required for his successful rule. Other consecration rituals or SACRIFICES included the vajapeya, punar abhisheka, and aindra abhisheka.

Rajgir The modern name of RAJAGRIHA, a town in Bihar associated with Buddhism.

Rajneesh A philosopher and religious guru, now known as OSHO.

Raka (1) A Hindu goddess first mentioned in the RIG VEDA. She is associated with fertility, and in the PURANAS she is one of the daughters of the rishi ANGIRAS by his wife Smriti. According to the VISHNU PURANA, she is the presiding deity on the day of the full moon.

(2) The name of a rakshasi, the wife of Vishrava and mother of Shurpanakha, the half-sister of RAVANA.

Rakabganj Gurdwara A GURDWARA or Sikh shrine located in DELHI. It was first constructed in 1783, to commemorate the martyrdom of the ninth guru, TEGH BAHADUR, who was executed by order of the Mughal emperor AURANGZEB in 1675. The execution took place on 11 November in Chandni Chowk, and a great dust storm is said to have arisen at this time. The resulting poor visibility enabled his son and one of his disciples, to remove the headless body and

cremate it, by placing it in their own house in Raisina and setting fire to the whole building. The ashes were then collected in an urn and buried there. Sardar BHAGEL SINGH had a small shrine built over them when he invaded Delhi in 1783, dismantling a mosque in the area. After Bhagel Singh explained the sacred nature of the site, the Mughal emperor Shah Alam II (1759–1806) himself granted the land to the Sikhs for the construction of the gurdwara, and the Sikh army withdrew from Delhi.

The Rakabganj Gurdwara, later reconstructed in white marble, remains an important Sikh shrine and a place of pilgrimage.

Raksha Bandhan A Hindu festival that celebrates the bonds between brothers and sisters. It occurs on the full-moon day of Shravana (July/August). On this day, girls and women tie a rakhi, a decorated strand of thread, on the wrists of their brothers. They worship the family deity and pray for the protection of their brothers. In return, the brothers give them gifts and promise to protect them in all situations. Rakhis can be tied even on those who are not related, who are then considered brothers. According to the legend associated with it, a rakhi was first tied by the consort of the god INDRA on his wrist, to give him protection and strength in his fight against the demons.

Raksha Bandhan means 'bond of protection'. Another brother-sister festival is BHAI DUJ.

rakshasas A term generally used for demons, but which also refers to other beings. Broadly, three types of rakshasas are mentioned in texts:
(1) Semi-divine beings, similar to YAKSHAS, and on the whole, benevolent.
(2) Giants or enemies of the gods.
(3) Demonic beings.

This last class harasses people, particularly those who are pious, disturbs sacred rites, eats human beings, and enters the bodies of the dead, apparently giving them life. They can take on any shape and form, and have magical powers. In the Hindu tradition, RAVANA belonged to this category. One view is that rakshasas represented indigenous groups, different from the so-called Aryans, and their representation as demons reflects the conflict between the two groups.

According to the RAMAYANA, rakshasas were created by the god BRAHMA to protect the waters (raksha = protection). The VISHNU PURANA has a similar story, and also states that they were the descendants of KASHYAPA and Khasa, one of the daughters of DAKSHA, through their son Rakshas.

Ram Das, Guru The fourth Sikh guru. Ram Das was born at Lahore in 1534 to Hari Das and Anup Devi, and was known as Jetha, meaning the 'first-born'. He always associated with religious people and ascetics; one day he went to meet Guru AMAR DAS at Goindwal and became his disciple. Jetha was chosen by Amar Das to explain the Sikh religion to the Mughal emperor AKBAR, who then waived the land revenue of the Punjab for one year. Jetha married Guru Amar Das's younger daughter, known as Bibi Bhani, and they had three sons, Prithi Chand, Mahadev and ARJAN DEV. Amar Das chose him as his successor and renamed him Ram Das.

After becoming guru, Ram Das continued building Ramdaspur, the city now known as AMRITSAR, and constructed two sacred tanks there. He composed a number of hymns, among them being the LAVAN, verses still used in the Sikh marriage ceremony. He used MASANDS to collect funds and spread the Sikh faith.

Ram Rai, Guru   The eldest son of the seventh Sikh guru, HAR RAI. Though by this time the line of succession had become hereditary, Ram Rai did not succeed his father as guru, as Har Rai was displeased by his interaction with the Mughal emperor AURANGZEB. Aurangzeb had asked Har Rai to come to his court, but the guru sent Ram Rai instead. Ram Rai is said to have agreed to delete a verse of the GURU GRANTH SAHIB that was unfavourable to Muslims, and to have performed a miracle of walking across a sheet spread over an open well, to prove the powers of his faith. Aurangzeb was impressed by him, but Har Rai was upset by his behaviour in the court and disowned him, appointing his infant son, HAR KRISHAN, as the guru.

Ram Rai was then given a grant of land by Aurangzeb in the area of Dehra Dun, in present Uttarakhand, and attracted many followers. However, while he was seated in meditation, in deep SAMADHI, he was cremated by some of his enemies who claimed he had died.

Ram Rai still has followers, and the Ram Rai Gurdwara in Dehra Dun is a popular place of pilgrimage.

Rama   A Hindu deity, one of the ten main incarnations of the god VISHNU. The story of Rama is briefly told in the *MAHABHARATA* and at great length in the *RAMAYANA* of VALMIKI, followed by innumerable other versions of the *Ramayana*. According to Valmiki's *Ramayana*, Rama was the eldest of the four sons of King DASHARATHA of AYODHYA, the other three being BHARATA, LAKSHMANA and SHATRUGHNA. Dasharatha had three wives: Kaushalya, the mother of Rama; Kaikeyi, the mother of Bharata; and Sumitra, mother of Lakshmana and Shatrughna. All four boys grew up together, but from the beginning Rama and Lakshmana were specially close. While they were still young, the rishi VISHVAMITRA asked Dasharatha to allow Rama to go with him to help him eliminate the RAKSHASAS, who were growing more powerful. Reluctantly, Dasharatha agreed and Rama and Lakshmana went to Vishvamitra's ashram and helped him to kill the rakshasi Tataka. Vishvamitra later took all four brothers to Mithila, to the court of King JANAKA, where, by breaking the god SHIVA's bow, Rama won the hand of Janaka's daughter, SITA. Rama's three brothers were married to Sita's sister Urmila and her two cousins.

As preparations were made at Ayodhya for Rama's coronation as successor to Dasharatha, Kaikeyi, inspired by her female servant Manthara, tried to win the throne for Bharata instead. She reminded Dasharatha that he had promised her a boon and asked him to redeem the promise. When Dasharatha agreed, she asked that he banish Rama to the forest for fourteen years. Despite his grief, Dasharatha was unable to go back on his word, and Rama, accompanied by Lakshmana and Sita, left for the Dandaka forest. Crossing the YAMUNA river, they reached Chitrakuta, where they lived for a while in the rishi VASISHTHA's ashram. Meanwhile Dasharatha died in despair at the loss of Rama, and Bharata refused to ascend the throne, instead placing Rama's sandals on it and acting as regent. For ten years Rama wandered through forests, staying at different ashrams, and then reached Panchavati on the banks of the river GODAVARI. This region was infested with RAKSHASAS. Shurpanakha, a rakshasi, was attracted to Rama, but when he rejected her, she threatened Sita, upon which Lakshmana cut off her ears and nose. Her brother Khara, along with Duhsana came to avenge her, but were killed themselves. Shurpanakha then appealed to her half-brother RAVANA, who came from LANKA in his aerial car and charmed by Sita, managed to abduct her and take her to Lanka. In despair and grief, Rama and Lakshmana went in search of her and were helped by Sugriva and his group of monkeys, and particularly by his minister, HANUMAN. After a prolonged struggle and fierce battles, Sita was rescued. Rama asked her to undergo an ordeal by fire to prove her purity, and Sita did so, emerging unscathed. Rama then ruled at Ayodhya, with Sita by his side. The seventh part of the *Ramayana*, the Uttara Kanda, believed to be a later addition, continues the story. When aspersions were cast on Sita, Rama banished her, and Lakshmana left her at Valmiki's ashram. There she had twin sons, LAVA and KUSHA. They grew up and met Rama, who recognized them as his sons. He then asked Sita to publicly prove her purity once again, so that she could return to him, but Sita instead appealed to the earth goddess to take her back into the earth. The goddess MADHAVI appeared, and Sita, seated on a throne, descended into the earth. Rama was disconsolate, but was assured that they would be reunited in heaven.

In much of the text, Rama is represented as an ideal king rather than a deity, but in the first and seventh kandas, he is clearly depicted as an incarnation of Vishnu. Innumerable later texts describe the story of his life, with many variations. The most popular of these in north india is the sixteenth-century *RAMACHARITAMANASA*.

Rama temples: Rama temples exist all over India, but among the more prominent are: the Raghunatha Temple, Jammu, constructed in 1835 at a traditionally sacred site, where Rama is seen with his brothers, along with Sita and Hanuman; several Rama temples in Ayodhya, the traditional capital of Rama in Faizabad district in Uttar Pradesh, among which is the Kanak Bhavan, where the non-stop recitation of the *Ramacharitamanasa* takes place; Ram Raja Temple, Orchha, Madhya Pradesh, where Rama is worshipped in his form as a king; Raghunathji Temple, Devaprayag, Uttarakhand: here Rama is said to have done penance for killing Ravana, who was a BRAHMANA; several shrines in Nashik, which is believed to represent the ancient Panchavati; shrines at Rameshvaram in Tamil Nadu. Among historic Rama temples are those at Kumbakonam in Tamil Nadu, constructed in the sixteenth and seventeenth centuries during the time of the Vijayanagara and Nayaka rulers, and the RAMACHANDRA TEMPLE at Vijayanagara.

Rama devotees: Among the innumerable devotees of Rama known in history, some of those who stand out are BHADRACHALAM RAMDAS, RAMADAS of the seventeenth century, and RAMANANDA.

Rama and history Historians question Rama's existence as a historical king, and also the story of his journey to Lanka. According to tradition Rama ruled at Ayodhya in the distant past, millennia ago, but excavations at Ayodhya indicate that occupation does not go back beyond the seventh century BCE. Others believe there was another Ayodhya, which existed long ago in the region of Afghanistan, and that Rama ruled there. Afghanistan was once part of the Indo-Iranian homeland and in Zoroastrianism, Rama is the deity of the twenty-first day of the calendar, his name signifying 'abounding peace'. This gives credence to the theory that Rama ruled in Afghanistan. All these theories are perhaps irrelevant, as each deity represents a real or essential truth, even if not a historical truth.

Rama today: The story of Rama is a part of the popular imagination, particularly in Uttar Pradesh and Bihar. Rama temples are found across the length and breadth of India; places mentioned in the *Ramayana* have their own traditional location and are pointed out even today. Of course, Rama is not the only popular deity. KRISHNA, SHIVA and DEVI temples are also found all over the country.

Rama, however, differs from these in being monogamous, righteous and ethical. Though today he is a deity who appeals to all castes, there was earlier opposition to him, particularly in south India. In one passage in the *Ramayana*, he cut off a shudra's head for practising austerities. Rama has also been criticized for his treatment of Sita. However, all these aspects of the *Ramayana* cannot be judged through modern concepts of right and wrong. Times were different and for those days Rama was an exemplary king. 'Rama Rajya' is a commonly used term even today, signifying an ideal system of government.

Rama and other kings: Other cultures too have stories of semi-mythical exemplary kings. For instance, a perfect king in Western mythology was King Arthur, and there are some similarities in the development of the mythology around him and Rama, though Arthur legends originate later. Arthur, too, captured the popular imagination, and variations of stories on his life are numerous. Arthur, too, was forced to condemn his wife, though he did not wish to do so. Ayodhya and Camelot, Arthur's city, are similarly described, as perfect cities, perfectly ruled.

Rama in other countries: The story of Rama is popular in a number of other countries, and is described in local *Ramayanas*.

Rama Gita A Sanskrit text, a section of the ADHYATMA RAMAYANA, which is used as a separate text in the worship of the Hindu god RAMA.

Rama Lila A term for the enactment of scenes from the life of the Hindu god RAMA. Literally it means 'Rama's sport or play'. While such enactments can take place at any time, they are an essential feature of the nine days before the DASAHRA festival in September/October. At this time episodes from Rama's childhood, marriage, stay in the forest, rescue of SITA and other events of his life, are portrayed in cities, towns, villages and localities, particularly in north India. Some are grand productions with elaborate costumes, sets and effects, while others are simple affairs. All evoke BHAKTI, or devotion to Rama, HANUMAN, and Sita. On the tenth day of Dasahra, effigies of RAVANA are burnt, symbolizing the triumph of good over evil.

Rama Setu Another name for ADAM'S BRIDGE, the stretch of shoals connecting India and Sri Lanka, said to have been crossed by RAMA in order to rescue SITA from captivity.

Rama Tirtha, Swami A guru who spread VEDANTA in the West. He was born in 1873 in village Murariwala in Punjab. A brilliant student, he studied mathematics, and after completing his degree he became professor of mathematics at Forman Christian College. At this time he began to read the BHAGAVAD GITA. He was also inspired by the teachings of the SHANKARACHARYA of DVARAKA and of Swami VIVEKANANADA. In 1901 he took sannyasa, and then went to Japan and the USA to spread Vedantic teachings. Returning to India, he died in 1906 at the young age of thirty-three. His speeches and writings have been collected in seven volumes, entitled, *In the Woods of God Realization*.

Ramachandra Temple A temple of the Hindu god RAMA, also known as the Hazara Rama Temple, located at the medieval city of Vijayanagara in Karnataka. It was constructed in the fifteenth century as the royal temple of the Vijayanagara dynasty. The inner shrine is attached to the ante-chamber and MANDAPA. The brick tower rising above, as well as the mandapa walls, have scenes from the *RAMAYANA*. Among the episodes depicted are the battle between Rama and RAVANA, HANUMAN accepting a ring from Rama, and then taking it to SITA. The temple is enclosed in a rectangular compound. The inner walls have more *Ramayana* scenes, while the outer walls have friezes of elephants, horses, soldiers and dancing girls. Another small temple is located to the north-west, with two shrines and carved panels with scenes from the life of Rama and of KRISHNA.

Ramacharitamanasa A text in Hindi verse on the life of the Hindu god RAMA, composed between 1574 and 1577. The text was written by TULASIDASA and is a work of BHAKTI or devotion. Using VALMIKI's *RAMAYANA* as the base, Tulasidasa recreates the epic, making Rama the representation of VISHNU on earth. He says, 'For the sake of his worshippers, Rama, the Blessed Lord, assumed the form of a king, and played his most holy part as an ordinary man.' The text begins with invocations to deities, gurus, saints and holy people, and to all living beings, since everything is permeated by Rama and SITA. It speaks of the glory of the name of Rama, tells the story of his life, and intersperses it with philosophical and devotional verses. Tulasidasa says, 'The story of Rama is like the moonbeams, and the saints are the partridges that drink from them.' The verses are still popular all over north India, and are sung and chanted not only in Rama temples, but by ordinary villagers.

Ramadasa A Maratha saint of the seventeenth century who was the guru of the Maratha ruler, Shivaji. Born in 1608 at Jamb on the river Godavari in a BRAHMANA family, he was named Narayan. At the time of his marriage, as the priest was chanting prayers, one word of the Sanskrit chants stood out and seemed to him like a divine command. It was 'svadhan' or 'be constant', and Narayan felt God was telling him to be constant and serve him. He became a devotee of the Hindu god RAMA and began wandering through the region as a SANNYASI, establishing MATHAS, erecting temples, and preaching love and devotion to Rama. His book, *Dasbodh*, teaches ethics, morality and love of all. He wrote a number of other books, as well as songs and poems. He was revered throughout the Maratha kingdom and still has a number of followers. He died in 1681.

Ramakrishna Mission A religious organization founded by Swami VIVEKANANDA to spread the teachings of Sri RAMAKRISHNA PARAMAHANSA. On 1 May 1897 Vivekananda founded the Ramakrishna Mission Association. In 1899 he started a MATHA, a religious centre and monastery at BELUR near Kolkata (Calcutta). The matha has spiritual leaders as well as monks and nuns. It is controlled by a number of trustees, initially set up by a Deed of Trust in 1901. In 1909 the Society of the Ramakrishna Mission was set up for charitable and educational works. The Mission runs hospitals, health centres, orphanages, schools and colleges, and members work to spread health and education among the poorer sections of society. They also provide relief at times of natural disasters and epidemics. The Society has branches all over India and abroad, and has set up temples where all castes and religions are welcome. The Ramakrishna Mission is based on the thoughts of Ramakrishna, who, though he was devoted to the Hindu goddess KALI all his life, recognized her as one form of the Supreme, encompassing all religions and forms. The Ramakrishna Matha and Mission are two separate but related organizations.

Ramakrishna Paramahansa A saint and religious leader of the nineteenth century. Born in 1836 in a BRAHMANA family at village Kamarpukar in present West Bengal, his original name was Gadadhar Chatterji, but he was later known as Ramakrishna. His father died when he was seven years old, and he was looked after by his mother and his brother, Ramkumar. From a young age Gadadhar went into spiritual trances, enacted stories from the life of KRISHNA, and associated with wandering mendicants. He soon abandoned all concepts of caste and saw everyone as the same.

After his brother became a priest of the DAKSHINESHVARA TEMPLE, he assisted him with his duties and took over as priest on his brother's death, when he was twenty years old. He was devoted to the worship of KALI, the temple deity, seeing her as a living, breathing being, and not an image. He began to have visions of Kali, and said he could even feel her breath on his hands. His ecstatic and emotional behaviour affected his health, and in 1859 he was persuaded to return to his village for a while. Attempts were made to get him married, but Ramakrishna had a vision of his divine consort, then a child of five named Sarada Devi. At the age of fourteen, she began to stay with him, initially for short periods, and later, permanently. They lived as spiritual partners without a physical relationship.

Returning to Dakshineshvara, he met a brahmana Bhairavi (female tantric) in 1861–62, who taught him the intricacies of TANTRA. Later, through a VAISHNAVA monk, Jatadhari, he had visions of Rama Lala, the child form of RAMA. The secrets of ADVAITA Vedanta, meditation on the formless, were revealed to him by a Vedantist, Tota Puri. Thus he attained a state of supreme illumination and identity with BRAHMAN.

Seeking to understand other religions, he contemplated SUFISM and Islam, and in 1866 through a Muslim PIR, he had a vision and realization of the formless God of Islam. In 1874, after listening to the readings of the BIBLE, he understood Christianity, and had a vision of JESUS.

Ramakrishna attracted many disciples, the most important of whom was Narendranath Dutta, known as Swami VIVEKANANDA, who established the RAMAKRISHNA MISSION. Worn out by his ecstacies and his constant fervour in helping others, Ramakrishna died of throat cancer in 1886. His wife Sarada Devi, revered in her own right, passed away in 1920.

Ramakrishna had understood the truth behind all religions and said: 'I have practised all religions—

Hinduism, Islam, Christianity, and I have also followed the paths of the different Hindu sects. I have found that it is the same God towards whom all are directing their steps, though along different paths.' He did not advocate any particular rituals but believed in communicating the divine truth and serving and helping others.

Ramana Maharshi, Sri A spiritual guru of the twentieth century. Born in 1879 in a village near MADURAI in present Tamil Nadu, in a Shaivite BRAHMANA family, his original name was Venkataraman Ayyar. After losing his father when he was twelve, he and his family moved to Madurai. At the age of sixteen, when alone in his uncle's house, he was transformed through an intense spiritual experience that occurred spontaneously. A few weeks after this he left his family and went to Tiruvannamalai, at the foot of the sacred hill, Arunachala or Arucachalam. Traditionally, Arunachala was associated with the Hindu god SHIVA, and Ramana felt that the hill represented god. Initially he lived in the ancient Shiva temple there, and then in various shrines and caves on the hillsides. A radiance emanated from him and he soon attracted followers, one of whom renamed him Bhagavan Sri Ramana Maharshi. An ASHRAM was set up at Tiruvannamalai at the base of Arunachala, and his inner light and simplicity brought followers from all over the world.

He lived in a communal hall and was available to all visitors. According to David Godman, who was associated with him for several years, 'When visitors came to see him—it made no difference whether they were VIPs, peasants or animals—they would all be treated with equal respect and consideration. His egalitarian concern even extended to the local trees; he discouraged his followers from plucking leaves or flowers off them and he tried to ensure that whenever fruit was taken from the ashram trees it was always done in such a way that the tree only suffered a minimum amount of pain.'

Usually he communicated in silence, with a powerful silent presence, but at times he answered the questions of those who insisted on answers. He spoke in Tamil, Telugu and Malayalam, and his replies to questions were noted down and also translated into English.

His words reveal the Advaitic nature of his thought, that ultimately only the Self is real, beyond birth and death. He had not studied ADVAITA but realized the truth by constantly enquiring into the nature of the individual, particularly using the question, 'Who am I?' At the request of his disciples, he also translated a number of Sanskrit texts, mainly into Tamil.

Ramana died in 1950. His ashram at Tiruvannamalai is still popular, and brings out a journal, *Mountain Path*. His answers to questions and translations of texts have been compiled into several volumes of his *Collected Works*.

Ramananda A fifteenth-century saint and devotee of the Hindu god RAMA. According to some accounts he was born in 1299, and according to others in 1390 probably at Allahabad in present Uttar Pradesh. He became a disciple of Raghavananda, in the lineage of RAMANUJA, the VAISHNAVA philosopher who founded the system of VISHISHTADVAITA, but later preferred to devote himself to the worship of Rama. After wandering through north India and visiting sacred places, he went to the south and settled there. Alternatively, he is believed to have settled in Kashi. He advocated BHAKTI or devotion to Rama as a representative of the One Supreme God. His sect was open to people of all castes and religions, as he believed god loved all people equally. Among his disciples were a woman, Padmavati, KABIR, a Muslim, and RAVIDAS, of a low caste. The Ramananda Sampradaya is still popular today. Followers worship Rama with love and devotion and wear on their bodies the sacred marks of the god VISHNU, of whom Rama is one of the main incarnations. The Rasikas, a branch of the Ramanandis, visualize the ancient city of AYODHYA, and Rama as he lived in those days, just as worshippers of KRISHNA visualize him and the scenes of his life.

Ramananda Tirtha, Swami A twentieth-century guru who was also a nationalist. Born in 1903 at Chirmalli in the then state of Hyderabad, but now in Karnataka, in a Maharashtrian family, his original name was Venkatesh Bhavan Rao Khedikar.

In 1921 he joined the Non-Cooperation Movement, part of the freedom struggle against British rule, and later became involved in trade union activities. In 1929 he was imprisoned after organizing a textile-workers' strike.

In 1931 he joined the Swami RAMA TIRTHA sect and received the name of Swami Ramananda Tirtha. Even after this, however, he continued his political activities, working to spread Congress ideas and policies in Hyderabad. He remained involved in politics till 1962. His other activities included founding educational institutions and establishing Marathwada University at Aurangabad. He also worked for lower castes, presided over the Adamjati Sevak Sangh, and helped Vinoba Bhave in the Bhudan Movement. He thus combined social and political activities with his spiritual and religious beliefs. He died in 1973.

Ramanathaswamy Temple A temple of the Hindu god SHIVA in his form as Ramanatha, located on the island of Rameshvaram at the southern tip of India. The temple, said to have first been constructed in the twelfth century, was reconstructed between the seventeenth and nineteenth centuries. According to tradition, it was built by the god RAMA. After slaying RAVANA in LANKA, Rama came here to worship Shiva in order to expiate the sin of killing a BRAHMANA. SITA made one LINGA from sand, while HANUMAN brought another from KAILASHA. The first is enshrined in the main sanctuary, as the linga of Sri Ramanatha.

The second, known as Vishvalinga, or the linga of Vishvanatha, is also worshipped in the temple. Apart from these two shrines there are others dedicated to Vishalakshi, consort of Vishvanatha, PARVATI, consort of Ramanatha, and VISHNU, known here as Setumadhava. There are also twenty-two sacred wells or tirthas here. The huge temple extends over 264 m from east to west, and 200 m from north to south. The main GOPURAM reaches a height of 54 m. Three corridors surround the shrine, and along the third there are over 1200 granite columns. Sculptures within the temple include a large NANDI, 6.7 m long and 5 m high, as well as portraits of the Nayaka rulers, under whom the major part of this temple was built. It remains a popular pilgrimage site.

Ramanavami   A Hindu festival that celebrates the birth of the god RAMA, the king of AYODHYA. The festival takes place on the ninth day of the bright fortnight of the month of Chaitra (March–April). The nine preceding days are known as the NAVARATRAS, and fasts and rituals are practised on these days, particularly on the first and eighth days. On the ninth day, or Navami, processions depicting aspects of Rama's life are taken out, and special worship is offered to Rama in temples, and to SITA, LAKSHMANA and HANUMAN. It is an important festival in north India, particularly at Ayodhya.

Ramanuja   The founder of the philosophical system of VISHISHTADAVAITA, a school of Vedantic thought. Ramanuja advocated the worship of VISHNU, and Vishishtadvaita can be translated as qualified monism. According to tradition, he was born in 1027 in Sriperumbudur in present Tamil Nadu. Spiritually inclined from childhood, he went to KANCHI, where he studied ADVAITA with the philosopher Yadavaprakasha, but gradually diverged from classical Advaita and came to his own conclusions. After travelling all over India, including to Kashmir, and visiting innumerable sacred sites, he settled at Srirangam in Tamil Nadu, then under the Chola dynasty. The Cholas were known for their devotion to the god SHIVA, and facing hostility there, Ramanuja moved to Hoysala territory. The king of the Hoysalas, Bittiga, was a Jain. Ramanuja successfully converted him to VAISHNAVISM. Bittiga took the name Vishnuvardhana and constructed grand Vishnu temples at Belur and Halebid. Ramanuja converted others to Vaishnavism, and restored several Vishnu temples. Later he returned to Srirangam and lived there until his death in 1137.

Ramanuja stated that the individual soul emerges from BRAHMAN or god, and is therefore eternal and the same in essence. Yet even when recognizing the truth of its eternal nature, it retains its self-consciousness and separateness, while enjoying a close communion with god. He based his philosophy on the UPANISHADS, BHAGAVAD GITA and *BRAHMA SUTRA*, and was also influenced by the *VISHNU* and *BHAGAVATA PURANA* and the devotional hymns of the ALVARS. He believed that god, in his form as Vishnu, his AVATARAS and his consort LAKSHMI, should be worshipped with love and devotion. All castes could become his followers, known as Ramanujas or Sampradaji, but had to follow certain rules and principles. For instance, food had to be prepared and eaten in privacy.

According to tradition, he founded seven hundred MATHAS, of which one still functions at Melkota in Karnataka. He also initiated seventy-four gurus, whose descendants would inherit the mantle from them. His philosophy is described in his writings, which include *Vedantasara*, written together with his disciple Kuruttalvara, *Vedarthasamgraha*, *Vedantadipa*, and *Shribhashya*, a commentary on the *Brahma Sutra*, as well as *Gitabhashya*, a commentary on the BHAGAVAD GITA.

Ramappa Temple   A temple of the Hindu god SHIVA located at Palampet in District Warangal of Andhra Pradesh. It was constructed in 1213 by Rudra Samani, a general of King Ganapatideva of the Kakatiya dynasty. It stands on a star-shaped platform, 1.8 m high. The inner shrine has a LINGA, nearly 3 m high. There are several other subsidiary shrines, as well as a MANDAPA, all enclosed in a compound wall. The temple has both Dravidian and Nagara shikharas or towers, and is known for its intricate and profuse carving. There are scenes from the *RAMAYANA* and *MAHABHARATA*, processions of dancers, elephants and warriors, and stories from the PURANAS. Outside is a NANDI image, 2.7 m high. Nearby are two other Shiva temples in dilapidated condition. A large tank dates back to the same period, created by making an earthen dam connected to a semi-circular hill range. The temple is named after the sculptor, Ramappa. Pilgrims visit the temple particularly on Maha Shivaratri, celebrated here for three days.

Ramayana   A Sanskrit epic that tells the story of RAMA. There are several versions of the *Ramayana*, but the earliest is that of VALMIKI.

Valmiki's *Ramayana* has 24,000 shlokas or verses, divided into seven kandas or sections. The kandas are: (1) Bala Kanda, the childhood of Rama and his brothers; (2) Ayodhya Kanda, life in AYODHYA and the banishment of Rama; (3) Aranya Kanda, the life of Rama, SITA and LAKSHMANA in the forest, and the abduction of Sita by RAVANA; (4) Kishkindha Kanda, Rama at KISHKINDHA, the capital of Sugriva, the monkey king; (5) Sundara Kanda, the crossing of the ocean by Rama and his allies to reach LANKA; (6) Yuddha Kanda, the fight against Ravana, his defeat and death, the rescue of Sita, the return to Ayodhya and coronation of Rama; (7) Uttara Kanda, Rama as king of Ayodhya, Sita's banishment, the birth of their sons, their reunion, and Sita's departure into the earth; Rama goes to heaven. The last and the first are often considered to have been added later.

Date: The date of the text is controversial. Some date it as far back as 3000 BCE, while others place it in the first century CE. The core of the story is narrated in the MAHABHARATA, the other great north Indian epic, which has led some to believe it was earlier than the *Mahabharata*. Other scholars point out that there are numerous interpolations in both texts, and therefore its mention in the *Mahabharata* is no evidence of an early date. The type of society described in the *Ramayana* also represents a later stage than that of the *Mahabharata*. C. Rajagopalachari was probably right when he said, 'It would appear that the story of Rama had been in existence long before Valmiki wrote his epic and gave form to a story that had been handed down from generation to generation.'

Location: The controversial date is linked with controversies about the location of places in the text. Traditionally Ayodhya is identified with the place of the same name in Faizabad district of Uttar Pradesh, and Ravana's Lanka with Sri Lanka. All other places are located along the way. Archaeology, however, does not date Ayodhya earlier than the seventh century BCE. H.D. Sankalia, a renowned archaeologist, believed that all the places could be located between Uttar Pradesh and Madhya Pradesh, while others have identified the sites in Afghanistan.

As religion: In the religious context, only the traditional locations are important, with myths, legends and sacred sites having grown up around them over centuries. The Ramayana has been retold innumerable times, and in its later versions it remains a popular religious text today.

Other versions: By the time of TULASIDASA's *RAMACHARITAMANASA*, devotion to Rama as a god had reached a height.

Some other major narratives of Rama in the Hindu tradition are the *ADHYATMA RAMAYANA*, KAMBAN *Ramayana*, and sections in the PURANAS. The story of Rama has been narrated with variations in every regional language of India and has been translated into several other languages. In Jainism, the *PAUMCHARIYAM* tells the story of Rama somewhat differently. In Buddhism, there is a version in the *Dasharatha Jataka* as well as in other texts. The *Ramayana* also reached other countries, and Thailand, Indonesia, Malaysia, Laos and Cambodia are among those that have their own versions of the story.

The *Ramayana* has been compared to the great heroic epics, the Iliad and the Odyssey.

Ramayana in Jainism The *RAMAYANA* had an important place in Jain literature and was retold several times. The earliest Jain version of the *Ramayana*, is the *Paumchariya* or *PAUMCHARIYAM* of Vimala-suri, written between the first and third centuries. Among others are the *Padma Purana* of Ravishena of the seventh century, which, though written in Sanskrit, is similar to the *Paumchariyam*. The *Paumachariu* of Svayambhu was composed in the eighth century. The *UTTARA PURANA*

also contains within it the story of Rama, in Parvan 68, while Parvan 7 of the *Trishashti-shalakapurusha Charitra* of Hemachandra is popularly known as the Jain *Ramayana*. Another notable version is the *Rama-Charita*, written in Sanskrit prose by Devavijayaganin in 1596. Several other Jain texts include the *Ramayana* story, indicating its widespread popularity.

Rameshvara Temple, Nashik A temple of the Hindu god SHIVA located at NASHIK in Maharashtra, constructed in the eighteenth century. It has one of the twelve great jyotir LINGAS, which according to tradition was installed at this site by RAMA. The temple is within an enclosure. Next to the linga shrine is a MANDAPA with carvings on the walls. Near the temple is a tank where Rama is said to have performed funerary rites for his father.

Rameshvaram An island considered sacred by Hindus, located at the southern tip of India in the Gulf of Mannar. Rameshvaram is connected to the mainland by a 1 km bridge. RAMA is said to have worshipped the god SHIVA here after recovering SITA from LANKA, and the island has a number of sacred shrines. The main temple here is the RAMANATHASWAMY TEMPLE, with one of the jyotir LINGAS of SHIVA. Originally constructed at the time of the Cholas, the present temple is mainly of the seventeenth to nineteenth centuries. One hundred metres away is the Agni Tirtham, where Rama worshipped Shiva to remove the sin of killing RAVANA, who was a BRAHMANA. Further north is the Gandhamadana hill, where a footprint of Rama is enshrined in a small temple. To the south-east of the island is the spot where Rama is said to have bathed, known as Dhanushkodi after Rama's bow. It was destroyed in a cyclone in 1964, but the Kothandaraswamy Temple marking the spot where Vibhishana, brother of Ravana, declared his allegiance to Rama, is still standing. Rameshvaram is an important centre of pilgrimage for both SHAIVITES and VAISHNAVITES. Twenty-four kilometres away at Erwadi is the tomb of a SUFI saint and a centre of Muslim pilgrimage.

Ramsar Gurdwara A GURDWARA or Sikh shrine located at AMRITSAR, near the Ramsar pool to the north-east of the HAR MANDIR or Golden Temple. It marks the spot where the fifth guru, ARJAN DEV, lived along with Bhai Gurdas when he was compiling the Granth Sahib. The sacred book was then installed in the Har Mandir Sahib in 1604. The tenth guru, GOBIND SINGH, made some additions to the Granth, and stated that henceforth this book would be the guru.

The gurdwara was later expanded, and now has five storeys. It retains its importance regarding the sacred text, as all authorized versions of the Guru Granth Sahib are printed and distributed from here.

Ramtek A town in Maharashtra that has several temples of the Hindu god VISHNU. On a hill to the east is a Maratha fort, where some shrines are located, while others are at the foot of the hill, near a lake. Most of the temples date from the eighteenth century, the time of the Marathas, while some are as early as the fifth century. Others are more recent. The ancient temples consist of small GARBHA-GRIHAS or sanctuaries, and open MANDAPAS that were later enclosed. They are made mainly of red sandstone. Images include those of NARASIMHA and VARAHA. Three recent shrines are dedicated to RAMA and LAKSHMANA. Ramtek was earlier known as Ramagiri and is described in the writings of Kalidasa.

Ramzan   A month of fasting and self-purification in Islam. Ramzan is the ninth month of the Islamic calendar, considered the holiest of all the months. Muslims fast from dawn to sunset for the thirty days of the month, in remembrance of the time the Prophet MUHAMMAD spent in the desert.

Food can be consumed before sunrise, after which not even a sip of water is taken until the evening, when the fast is broken. The main meal is eaten after offering prayers. On certain nights during the month of Ramzan, special prayers are offered. The twenty-sixth night commemorates the martyrdom of Ali, the son-in-law of the Prophet. Between the twenty-first and twenty-seventh nights is SHAB-E-QADR, a time considered particularly holy, when prayers have great efficacy. The twenty-ninth day is the last Friday of the lunar month. After the sighting of the new moon, ID-UL-FITR is celebrated, and the holy month of Ramzan comes to an end.

Ranakpur   A town in Rajasthan, with a number of Jain temples built in Solanki style. The temples are richly decorated with beautiful sculptures and intricately carved ceilings and pillars. The most notable is the Chaumukha Temple constructed in 1438.

Randhir Singh, Bhai   A Sikh teacher who gathered a group of followers around him, and can be considered to have started a sub-sect of the KHALSA Sikhs. Born in 1878 in Narangwal village near Ludhiana, Punjab, Randhir Singh was a Jat who fought against the British and spent long periods in jail. He strictly observed Khalsa discipline, was a vegetarian, and would only eat food cooked in an iron vessel and prepared by an orthodox Sikh. The story of his life in prison is told in his *Jehl Chitthian* (literally, 'Letters from Prison'). Randhir Singh's followers have their own Rahit Maryada or rules, and emphasize Kirtan or the singing of religious songs. NAM SIMARAN for them consists of recitation of the term 'Waheguru'; the Khalsa initiation is also done in a special way. Meat is forbidden, and Keshki, a small under-turban, is to be worn by both men and women. Randhir Singh died in 1961, but his followers still exist. The Akhand Kirtani Jatha, founded by Amarjit Kaur, hold all-night singing sessions of Kirtans (hymns) and are inspired by him.

Ranganatha   A name of the god VISHNU in south India.

Ranganatha Temple   A temple of the Hindu god VISHNU, known here as Ranganatha, located at Srirangam in Tamil Nadu. The goddess here is known as Ranganyaki. It was constructed mainly between the thirteenth and seventeenth centuries. This huge temple complex covers an area of sixty-three hectares and has seven concentric rectangular enclosures. There are GOPURAMS along the four sides, decreasing in size towards the inner enclosures. Roads lead through the gateways towards the centre. The southern outer gateway, enlarged in 1987, now reaches a height of 72 m, probably the largest in south India. Each enclosure has a number of structures. In the fourth enclosure is the interesting Rangavilasa Mandapa, with carvings all over the walls, as well as a Venugopala (KRISHNA) temple of the sixteenth century. The same enclosure also has a museum, with stone and bronze sculptures, and ivory plaques.

Legends and stories regarding the temple are collected in the *Sriranga Mahatmya*.

rangjung   A term in TIBETAN BUDDHISM for sacred objects that occur naturally. Rangjung means 'self-arising' and can consist of rocks on which a Buddhist image occurs miraculously, or other similar phenomena.

Rani Sabri's Mosque   A mosque in Ahmadabad, Gujarat, one of the most notable monuments in the city. This small mosque, measuring just 14.6 m by 6.1 m, was, according to an inscription on the central MIHRAB, constructed in 1514 by Rani Sabri, during the reign of Sultan Muzaffar II of Gujarat. She is said to have been the mother of Abu Bakr Khan, who was the son of Sultan Mahmud Begarha, and who, according to other sources, was poisoned. The mosque is only two bays deep, with a row of double pillars in front and ornate decoration on the stone tracery windows. The prayer hall has an open façade, with slender minarets in four sections, three above roof level. Because of the delicate and jewel-like carvings and the fine detail of the traceries, it has been referred to as a 'gem' of a mosque. According to J. Fergusson, who wrote on the architecture of Ahmadabad, it is 'one of the most exquisite buildings in the world'. The tomb of the queen is located in front of the mosque.

Ranjit Singh   A Sikh leader who organized the Sikhs into a kingdom in the Punjab. Born in 1780, in 1792 he succeeded his father, Maha Singh, as the head of a group of Sikh MISLS with a small territory, and by 1798 had occupied Lahore. He was recognized by Zaman Shah, the Afghan ruler, as governor of Lahore, but soon became independent and expanded his territory, using a series of alliances and conquests to consolidate his hold on the Punjab. By the time of his death in 1839, the Sikh state was at the height of its power. Its decline, particularly after 1850, gave rise to a number of new Sikh movements, including attempts to purify and revive Sikhism.

Ranjit Singh is revered as a hero by Sikhs.

Ranna A Jain poet of the tenth century who wrote in Kannada. Born in 949, he lived at the court of the Chalukya king Taila II, and of his successor. Ranna wrote the *Ajita Purana* in verse on the life of the second TIRTHANKARA Ajitanatha, and the *Sahasabhimavijaya* or *Gadayuddha*, which tells part of the story of the MAHABHARATA, focusing on the fight between BHIMA and DURYODHANA during the great war. In addition he describes the wars of a local king, whom he compares with Bhima. His other works, including the *Parashurama Charita* on PARASHURAMA, have not survived, though a lexicon, *Ranna Kanda*, is sometimes attributed to him. PAMPA, PONNA and Ranna are considered the three 'gems' of Kannada poetry.

Ras Khan A poet and devotee of the Hindu god KRISHNA in his form as Srinathji. Not much is known about Ras Khan, who is said to have been a Muslim from a village near Hardoi, in present Uttar Pradesh, and to have been born sometime between 1528 and 1558. He later moved to DELHI and then to the MATHURA region, where he became a devotee of Srinathji, at that time enshrined in a temple at GOVARDHANA. The *Vaishnavon-ki-varta*, a VAISHNAVA text, provides some legends about him, whereas his own work, *Prem-Vatika*, has fifty-three dohas or couplets, describing the life of Krishna and the GOPIS, and the love which is the essence of BHAKTI.

Ras Khan is thought to have died some time in the first quarter of the seventeenth century.

Rasatala The sixth of the seven divisions or LOKAS of the nether world or PATALA, in Hindu mythology. Here the Nivatakavacha-Kalakeyas live, who were enemies of the DEVAS.

Rati A Hindu deity, the wife of KAMA, the god of love. She is sometimes worshipped along with him. Among her other names are Reva, Kamapriya and Priti.

Ratnakuta Sutra A MAHAYANA Buddhist text that is a collection of forty-nine sutras.

Ratnasambhava A celestial BUDDHA, also known as a DHYANI BUDDHA. Literally, the name means 'jewel-born'. Ratnasambhava is associated with the southern direction. His colour is yellow, and his right hand is in varada mudra, the boon-granting gesture. His BODHISATTVA is Ratnapani, and his SHAKTI or consort is Mamaki. Among the deities that emanate from him are Jambhala, Ucchushma-Jambhala, Mahapratisara, Vasudhara, Gandhavajra, Gandahasti, Gaganaganja, Jambuki, Jnanaketu, Khagarbha, Khandaroha, Lasya, Lama, Prajnantka, Patalavasini, Pushpa, Pratibhanakuta, and the twelve Paramitas. All deities that are yellow, placed in the south or in the south-west are also associated with him.

ratnatraya The three ideals (literally, 'jewels') of Jainism, also known as the triratna, which consist of right belief (samyak darshana), right knowledge (samyak jnana) and right conduct (samyak charitra). All three, practised together, are essential on the path to enlightenment.

Ratri A deity mentioned in the RIG VEDA, the daughter of heaven and the goddess of the star-lit night. Only one hymn is addressed to her. Ratri fills the valleys and heights, driving away the darkness with her light.

Raushaniya movement A religious and political Islamic movement in the north-west of India, founded by Miyan Bayazid Ansari (d. 1580). Bayazid described a path leading to internal illumination, and stated that religious rites had to be understood through their symbolism. His followers led ascetic lives, but as the movement spread among the north-west tribes, there were conflicts with the Mughals. After Bayazid's death his son Jalal led the movement. He was captured by the Mughals but escaped and harassed travellers in the north-west. In 1600 Jalal was killed, and the movement died down, though some followers remained.

Ravana The king of the RAKSHASAS, known chiefly for his abduction of SITA, described in the RAMAYANA. Ravana was the grandson of the RISHI Pulastya and the son of Vishrava by his wife Kaikasi or Nikasha, who was the daughter of the rakshasa Sumali. Thus from his father's side, Ravana was a BRAHMANA. He was well-versed in Sanskrit and the VEDAS. He had many wives, but his chief consort was Mandodari. His sons were Meghanada, also known as Indrajit, Ravani, Aksha, Trishiras, Devantaka, Narantaka and Atikaya. Ravana propitiated the god BRAHMA and gained from him various boons—he could not be killed either by the gods or by demons. According to some accounts, he had ten heads and could assume any form he liked. He ruled from the magnificent city of LANKA, which he had appropriated from his half-brother, KUBERA. Charmed by the beauty of Sita, Ravana assumed a disguise and abducted her in his PUSHPAKA Vimana (aerial chariot) when she was alone in the forest. He took her to Lanka and tried to persuade her to love him, but Sita remained true to RAMA. Finally, after a great battle, Rama killed Ravana, who was then cremated with Brahmanical rites. In south India and in Sri Lanka, Ravana is seen in a more favourable light than in north India, where he is thought to be demonic.

Ravi A name of the Hindu sun god SURYA, as well as a name of the sun.

Ravi Shankar, Sri Sri A spiritual guru who runs the ART OF LIVING Foundation and has followers all over the world. Born in 1956 in Papanasam, Tamil Nadu, he studied Vedic literature with spiritual teachers, and also obtained a degree in physics. Later he received an honorary doctorate from Kuvempu University, Karnataka. He studied with Maharishi MAHESH YOGI in Rishikesh. In 1982, in silent meditation, he is said to have discovered the Sudarshan Kriya, a particular breathing technique. He then began to teach special breathing techniques, which form part of his Art of Living course, including a series of techniques said to prevent disease and to lead to rejuvenation and vitality. In 1982 he set up the Art of Living Foundation, one of the largest voluntary organizations, providing education to the underprivileged and to women, rehabilitation in prisons, and help and relief in a number of other spheres, in 140 countries worldwide. He aims at creating a physically, mentally and spritually healthy person through meditation, health, educational and other programmes. In 1992 he set up the Prison SMART Foundation (Stress Management and Rehabilitative Training). In 1997 he founded the International Association for Human Values, which has development projects in over 25,000 villages helping people to become self-reliant. His 5H programme focuses on Health, Hygiene, Homes, Harmony and Human Values. His organization has also undertaken relief projects in Bosnia, Afghanistan, Iraq and other countries, apart from India. Sri Ravi Shankar has travelled all over the world and has been presented with a number of awards.

His main ASHRAM is on the outskirts of Bangalore, known as Ved Vignan Mahavidya Peeth Bangalore International Centre.

Ravidas A Hindu saint of the fourteenth and fifteenth centuries who was also known as Raidas. He was born in 1376 or 1377, at the village of Mandoor Garh near Varanasi, in a chamar family. He was named Ravidas because he was born on Ravivar, a Sunday. The chamar caste of leather workers were considered untouchables, but when Ravidas began to worship VISHNU in the form of SHALAGRAMA, Ramananda, a VAISHNAVITE saint, accepted him as his disciple. The BRAHMANAS and pandits were against this because of his caste, but gradually he attained a reputation as a saint and gained a large following. He was against caste and ritual, and composed devotional poems and songs, some of which are included in the GURU GRANTH SAHIB and are popular even today. His disciples are known as Raidasis or Ravidasis. Ravidasis are usually householders, but constantly remember and invoke the name of god, and also try to help others and perform acts of charity. They include both Hindus and Sikhs, and now have declared that they are a separate religion.

Red Hats The colloquial name of some Tibetan Buddhist sects related to the KARMAPA sect. The name is derived from the red hats that the monks wear.

Reformation A movement in CHRISTIANITY that led to the division of Christians all over the world into Roman Catholics and Protestants. In the 1500s there were many problems in the Catholic Church, despite earlier attempts at reform. The Roman Curia who assisted the Pope were corrupt, the bishops and even the monastic orders amassed wealth, and the local priests were largely ignorant, though there were still some who were widely respected and learned.

In 1517, Martin Luther put forward his 'Ninety-Five Theses' at Wittenberg in Germany, in which he criticized various aspects of the Church's functioning. Luther pointed out the prevailing corruption, and attacked the church system of selling 'indulgences', i.e., allowing individuals to pay for the remission of sins. He also focused on theological doctrine, particularly the importance given to good works rather than to salvation through faith and the grace of God. John Calvin, a French lawyer who left France for Switzerland, was another important reformer. His *Institutes of the Christian Religion*, first published in 1536, provided a systematic exposition of the concepts of the reformers. The movement snowballed, leading to large groups and entire countries breaking away from the Roman Catholic Church and setting up their own 'Protestant' Churches. By the middle of the sixteenth century, northern and eastern Europe were dominated by Protestantism. In England, Henry VIII declared himself head of the Church of England in 1534, after he was refused a divorce by the Pope, and England soon turned Protestant, though there were later attempts to revive Catholicism.

The Counter-Reformation eliminated many of the abuses in the Catholic Church, but Christianity remained divided. (*See* Roman Catholicism, Protestantism).

Reiki A Buddhist technique for healing, revitalizing and transmitting positive energy. This system was rediscovered and simplified for the common person by a Japanese Buddhist named Mikao Usui (1862–1926) in the late nineteenth century, and is based on the Shingon Buddhist school of Japan. It was introduced in India by 1989, and today there are thousands of teachers and practitioners in urban India. It consists of a simple technique of transmitting energy through the hands, similar to NYASA techniques described in indigenous Tantric texts.

Renuka The wife of the rishi JAMADAGNI, and the mother of PARASHURAMA, an incarnation of the Hindu god, VISHNU. At the request of his father Jamadagni, Parashurama cut off her head, as she was once unchaste in thought, and desired a GANDHARVA. In most accounts in texts, Parashurama then received a boon from his father, and restored her to life. Renuka is worshipped in some temples as a goddess, while ELAMMA-Renuka is a composite deity revered in south India.

Revanta A Hindu deity, who was one of the sons of SURYA, the sun god. According to the *MARKANDEYA PURANA*, Revanta guards people in forests and lonely places, saves them from enemies and robbers, and provides his worshippers with comfort, intelligence, happiness, health, wealth and fame. The *VISHNUDHARMOTTARA*

PURANA states that he is to be depicted riding a horse. Images of Revanta have been found mainly in Bengal and Gujarat.

Revati The wife of the Hindu god BALARAMA. She was the daughter of King Raivata, and extremely beautiful. Raivata believed no one was worthy of her and went to consult the god BRAHMA in heaven about her husband. He spent a long time there, and Brahma finally directed him to Balarama, at DVARAKA. Many ages had passed, though Raivata did not realize this. Revati was still beautiful and very tall, but other humans had grown short. Balarama first shortened her with his ploughshare, and then she became his wife.

Rewalsar Lake A lake that has seven floating islands, located in Himachal Pradesh. Near it are sacred Buddhist, Hindu, and Sikh sites. In Tibetan, the lake is known as Tso-Pema or Lotus lake, and is associated with PADMASAMBHAVA, who is said to have meditated here. According to legend, a local king feared his powers and ordered that he be burnt alive. A huge pyre was constructed around him and lit, but by the powers of Padmasambhava, the burning pyre turned into a lake. A NYINGMA monastery is located here. In Hindu myths, the rishi Lomasha is said to have worshipped Shiva here. There are temples dedicated to Lomasha, SHIVA and KRISHNA near the lake. A gurdwara is also located here, constructed in memory of a visit by Guru GOBIND SINGH.

Ribhu A name of various Hindu gods, including INDRA, AGNI and the ADITYAS. Ribhu was also the name of one of the four Kumaras, or mind-born sons of the god BRAHMA.

Ribhus A group of semi-divine beings of the Vedic pantheon, associated with the god INDRA. There are three Ribhus, whose names are Ribhu or Ribhukshan, Vaja and Vibhuvan. They are sons of Sudhanvan and are helpers of Indra. According to some passages, they were originally men, but because of their skilful deeds, became immortal. The Ribhus are also mentioned in later texts.

Riddhi The name of a Hindu goddess, the wife of KUBERA, who is the god of wealth. It is also a name of PARVATI and of a wife of GANESHA. Literally, the word means 'prosperity'.

Ridvan A BAHAI festival. The word literally means 'paradise'. BAHAULLAH, the founder of the Bahai religion, faced persecution and many tribulations, but for a brief period in his life he lived in perfect peace. He and his companions once spent twelve days in a garden near Baghdad, on the banks of the Tigris river, from 21 April to 2 May 1863. This was later known as the Garden of Ridvan. It was here that he announced his divine mission, and wrote: 'This is the paradise, the rustling of whose leaves proclaims: O ye that inhabit the heavens and the earth! There hath appeared what hath never previously appeared. He, who, from everlasting, had concealed His face from the sight of creation, is now come.' To commemorate this event the Ridvan festival is held every year between 21 April and 2 May. During this time prayers are offered, festivities and celebrations are held, and the Bahais join with others to proclaim the fellowship of the world. The first, ninth and twelfth days are considered particularly sacred.

Rig Veda The first of the four VEDIC SAMHITAS, which has a total of 1028 hymns, divided into ten mandalas or sections. Most of the verses in the SAMA and YAJUR VEDAS are derived from it. Each hymn has the name of a RISHI, such as VASISHTHA, VISHVAMITRA, BHARADVAJA, and others to whom it was divinely revealed. It is not known when the Rig Veda was first written down, and the hymns were transmitted orally for generations.

The text provides an account of the religion, society and economy of those times, in the region of the Sapta Sindhava, or seven rivers, namely, the Indus and its tributaries, along with the SARASVATI and Drishadvati, all located to the west of the YAMUNA. Some hymns, which are considered slightly later than the others, mainly in the tenth mandala, express a vague concept of one supreme being, but most of them are addressed to individual deities, often personifications of nature or of an attribute or ideal. YASKA, a later commentator on the Rig Veda, classified the main deities into three categories: terrestrial, celestial and atmospheric. Among the terrestrial deities are the rivers Sindhu, Vipasa, Shutudri and SARASVATI; PRITHVI, the earth, AGNI, fire, BRIHASPATI and SOMA. Celestial deities include DYAUS, VARUNA, MITRA, SURYA, SAVITRI, PUSHAN, VISHNU, VIVASVAT, the ADITYAS, USHA, and the ASHVINS; atmospheric deities are INDRA, TRITA APTYA, APAM NAPAT, MATARISHVAN, AHI BUDHNYA, Aja Ekapad, RUDRA, the MARUTS, VAYU-VATA, PARJANYA and AGNI. Agni is a deity who belongs to several categories. Other gods include DHATR, VIDHATR VISHVAKARMAN, TVASHTR and PRAJAPATI. Though female deities are not very important, a number of them are mentioned apart from Sarasvati, Prithvi and Usha. RATRI and ARANYANI have separate hymns dedicated to them. Groups of deities or semi-divine beings include RUDRAS, VASUS, ANGIRASAS, RIBHUS, APSARAS, and GANDHARVAS. There are also ASURAS, RAKSHASAS and PISHACHAS. While the latter two are usually demonic, in the Rig Veda ASURA is normally used interchangeably with DEVA, indicating a divine being. Wise and powerful rishis are referred to, as well as divine and mythical animals. These deities are elaborated on in later Vedic texts.

A famous hymn that is considered a late part of the text seeks to understand creation:

Then even nothingness was not, nor existence
There was no air then, nor the heavens beyond it.
What covered it? Where was it? In whose keeping?
[. . .]

He, who surveys it all from the highest
heaven
He knows, or maybe even he doesn't know.

The People: The Rig Vedic people refer to themselves as arya, meaning 'noble'. In English they are commonly called ARYANS, thought to be connected with INDO-IRANIANS and INDO-EUROPEAN groups of people.

Date: The text is usually dated to between 1500 BCE and 1000 BCE, though some scholars believe it is much earlier.

Location: Most of the places mentioned in the text have been analysed and identified with sites to the west of the YAMUNA, extending into Punjab, present Pakistan and Afghanistan. A few scholars believe all places mentioned should be located in Afghanistan, but have not carried out a detailed identification of sites there.

Indus Civilization and the Rig Veda: No archaeological culture has been satisfactorily identified with that of the Rig Veda. As the location of the INDUS CIVILIZATION is partly coterminous with the places mentioned in the Rig Veda, some scholars feel it represents that culture, or a pre-Indus Culture.

Rinchen Zangpo A Tibetan Buddhist associated with the revival of Buddhism in the eleventh century. According to tradition he set up 108 Buddhist monasteries in present Himachal Pradesh and Ladakh, and translated Buddhist texts into Tibetan.

Rishabha The first Jain TIRTHANKARA, also known as Adinatha or the first Lord. According to legend, he lived millions of years ago, towards the end of the third ARA of the descending cycle. According to SHVETAMBARA Jain texts, he was born at AYODHYA, earlier known as Vinita, in present Uttar Pradesh, a place also sacred as the birthplace of the Hindu god RAMA. At this time, according to Jain cosmology, all people were born as twins, one male and one female, and on reaching adulthood, the twins became husband and wife, lived a happy life together, and died at the same time. But, as it was the end of the Ara, certain discrepancies took place, and Rishabha married his twin Sumangala as well as another girl, Sunanda, whose twin had died. Sumangala gave birth to BHARATA, Brahmi, and ninety-eight other sons, while BAHUBALI and Sundari were born from Sunanda. Rishabha, ruling at Ayodhya, became the first king of the age, and introduced the alphabet, writing, all arts and crafts, laws and methods of administration. He brought education and civilization to the world, laid down funeral ceremonies, and taught seventy-two accomplishments to men, and sixty-four to women.

After a long time he left the kingdom and became an ascetic, and practising asceticism for one thousand years, he attained enlightenment and became a Jina, or one who has conquered the Self. He taught spiritual truths, morality and ethics before attaining MOKSHA (liberation) on Mt KAILASHA and departing from the world.

Rishabha's symbol is a bull (rishabha), reflecting his name.

rishi A Sanskrit term for a sage. The word is derived from the Sanskrit rish (to see), and the rishi is the wise sage who can see the truth. Rishis are first mentioned in the RIG VEDA, where the various hymns were revealed to them. According to early texts, seven rishis, or saptarishis, also known as PRAJAPATIS, preside over each MANVANTARA or age of the universe. According to the *Shatapatha Brahmana,* they were Gotama, BHARADVAJA, VISHVAMITRA, JAMADAGNI, VASISHTHA, KASHYAPA and ATRI, while according to the MAHABHARATA, those of the first manvantara were Marichi, Atri, Angiras, Pulaha, Kratu, PULASTYA and Vasishtha. Rishis of later manvantaras are listed in the HARIVAMSHA and in the Puranas. The PURANAS describe several other great rishis, including BHRIGU, DAKSHA, Kanva, NARADA, VALMIKI, VYASA and Vibhandaka. The constellation of the Great Bear, which has seven stars, is known as Sapta Rishi, or seven rishis. The seven rishis are thought to symbolize the seven chakras or seven senses. Later, nine or ten main rishis were listed. The nine rishis of the present manvantara, according to the VISHNU PURANA, are Vasishtha, Kashyapa, Atri, Jamadagni, Gautama, Vishvamitra, Bhrigu, Daksha and Bharadvaja. There were thousands of other rishis; the main classes of rishis were Brahmarishis, Devarishis and RAJARISHIS. Others were Maharishis, Paramarishis, Shrutarishis and Kandarishis.

Rishyashringa A rishi described in ancient texts. He was the son of the rishi Vibhandaka, and grandson of KASHYAPA, while his mother was a deer or antelope. According to the story regarding his birth, Vibhandaka once saw the beautiful apsara Urvashi, and his semen fell in the water and was swallowed by a deer, who then gave birth to Rishyashringa. Thus he had a horn on his forehead, from which he got his name (rishya = male antelope). He grew up in the forest and met no one but his father, until he became a young man.

At this time the kingdom of Anga, ruled by King Lomapada, was suffering from drought. The BRAHMANAS there informed the king, that if a rishi who had never seen a woman came to the kingdom, rain would fall. After much searching by the king's men, Rishyashringa was discovered. Beautiful young girls were sent to bring the rishi, who was astounded when he saw a woman for the first time. They did not have much trouble in persuading him to accompany them, and in the kingdom of Anga, Rishyashringa was married to Shanta, the daughter of King DASHARATHA, who had been adopted by Lomapada. Rishyashringa performed a yajna or sacrifice, that brought rain to the parched kingdom. He also performed a sacrifice through which king Dasharatha's sons, including RAMA, were born.

Rivayats Zoroastrian texts in Persian, which are collections of letters exchanged between Zoroastrian priests in India and Iran. These letters were written between 1478 and 1766, and consist of answers to questions posed by the Indian priests. There are twenty-six Rivayats, of which the best-known is that of Darab Hormazyar.

rivers, sacred India has innumerable rivers, all of which are considered sacred in some way. Traditionally, the seven most sacred are the Indus, GANGA, YAMUNA, SARASVATI, NARMADA, GODAVARI, and Kaveri. The Indus was known in early texts as the Sindhu. Rising in the Himalayas and flowing into the Arabian Sea, with a length of 2880 km, it is one of the longest rivers of the world. Its main tributaries are the Jhelum, Chenab, Ravi, Beas and Satluj. The GANGA also begins as a Himalayan river and flows into the Bay of Bengal, with a length of 2525 km. Apart from the YAMUNA, its main tributaries are the Ramganga, Gomati, Ghaghara, Gandak and Kosi, which start in the Himalayas or their foothills, while the Betwa, Ken, Sone and others join it from the south. The Chambal flows into the Yamuna from the south. The SARASVATI is sometimes considered a mythical river. Today it is identified with the Ghaggar, a semi-dry river in Haryana, whose dry river bed extends into Pakistan, where it is known as the Hakra. Its ancient remains have alternatively been traced in Gujarat. The Godavari, Narmada and Kaveri are rivers of the peninsula, with respective lengths of 1465, 1312, and 800 km.

Rodasi A goddess mentioned in the RIG VEDA, associated with the MARUTS. As she is always mentioned with them, she is thought to have been their wife.

Roman Catholicism A form of Christianity that traces its origin to the earliest days of the development of the religion. The spiritual leader of the Roman Catholic Church is the Pope, known as the Bishop of Rome, who governs the Church from Vatican City, a small independent state within Rome. Catholic beliefs are based on the BIBLE and on church traditions and doctrines, which include declarations of church councils and popes, and short statements or creeds, that summarize Catholic beliefs. Around the beginning of the second century CE, the NEW TESTAMENT was accepted as representing the authentic teachings of JESUS Christ.

Catholics believe in the TRINITY—that there is One God within whom there are three persons. Humanity was created by God and for God, but the original sin of Adam's disobedience affected God's plan for humanity. The son of God, Jesus, the second person in the Trinity, therefore came to earth to save them from sin. However, salvation has to be brought to each person, therefore Jesus's Apostles and missionaries are there to teach the word of God.

Catholics worship only one God, but revere other holy people, such as MARY, mother of Jesus, and various saints. The seven SACRAMENTS, ceremonial signs of God through which his grace is received, form an essential part of Catholicism. Of these, the Eucharist is the most important.

History: The first Christians who were the followers of Jesus, were Jews, but the early Church gradually drew away from Judaism, though it accepted the BIBLE, known in Christianity as the OLD TESTAMENT. Paul (d. 65 to 67) spread Christianity to the gentiles, the non-Jews, and by about 140 CE the centre of Christianity moved from Jerusalem to Antioch in Syria, Alexandria in Egypt, and Rome. Initially Christians faced persecution from the Romans, and also had to deal with divergent doctrines, such as GNOSTICISM, which they termed heresies. After the Roman emperor Constantine the Great accepted Christianity in the fourth century, the religion spread further. Conflicts with different doctrines of the Eastern Church began in the fifth century, leading finally to the separation of what came to be called the ORTHODOX CHURCH. Meanwhile, the monastic system began to develop, with various Christian monastic orders. Scholars analysed Christian doctrines and a huge body of Christian literature arose.

There are numerous other historical developments in Church history, but the most important was the REFORMATION, in the early 1500s, which led to the growth of PROTESTANTISM, and a long-lasting division of the Church. Protestants do not accept the authority of the Pope.

Roman Catholics reformed their own Church through a Counter-Reformation and the Council of Trent (1545–63) brought in changes that resolved doctrinal issues and other problems. However, religious wars followed, and through a long history of conflicts, Catholic revival and decline took place.

The Popes had acquired territory around Rome from the fourth century onwards, but their sovereignty over these states was often threatened and dependent on prevailing political conditions. With the unification of Italy in the nineteenth century, the existing papal states became part of Italy, though the Vatican continued to be occupied by the Pope. The Lateran Treaty of 1929 recognized the Vatican within Rome as an independent city-state.

Church Organization: The Pope, at the head of the Church, is assisted by the Roman Curia, a term for the papal bureaucracy. The Cardinals, a special class of clergy including bishops, priests and deacons, are the chief officials of the Curia. Cardinals are appointed by the Pope, but also form the electoral body for the new Pope.

The basic unit of Church organization is the diocese. The Pope appoints bishops, who are considered the successors of the APOSTLES, and have the responsibility to teach and guide members of the Church. A Bishop, leads a diocese, which serves the Catholics in a particular geographical area, and is assisted by other bishops. A diocese is divided into parishes, headed by a pastor or priest. A number of dioceses are grouped into an Archdiocese under an Archbishop.

Monastic orders have their own leaders.

Catholicism in India: In India, the Portuguese were chiefly responsible for the spread of Catholicism (*see* Goa). Later other Catholics entered India as missionaries and even today are respected for their educational institutions.

There are two types of Catholic Churches in India, the Roman or LATIN CATHOLICS, and the Eastern Catholics, who are associated with the ORTHODOX CHURCH.

Rosh Hashanah A Jewish festival that marks the beginning of the new year according to the Jewish calendar, on the first day of Tishri (September to October), the first month. On this day prayers are offered at synagogues and the *shofar* or ram's horn is blown one hundred times. Rosh Hashanah begins a period of repentance, ending ten days later with YOM KIPPUR, but is also a day of celebration. Special food is eaten, including sweetened apple, beetroot, fish, dates, white pumpkin and the head of a goat or lamb. This symbolic food represents good fortune in the coming year. In the intervening days before Yom Kippur, God is said to judge the world, based on acts committed in the preceding year. However, there is also faith that God forgives those who are repentant. The prescribed prayers praise God, and state that God sets the measure of every person's life, 'decreeing its destiny'. But God accepts repentance because He desires 'not the death of the sinner but that he turn from his way and live'.

Roy, Ram Mohan The founder of the BRAHMO SAMAJ who attempted to bring about social and religious reform in India. Born in 1772 at Radhanagar in District Hughli of present West Bengal, he came from a rich and orthodox family of Bengali zamindars. After his early education, he studied Sanskrit literature and Hindu philosophy at Varanasi, as well as the QURAN, Persian and Arabic at Patna in Bihar. He also learnt Pali, Latin, Greek, Hebrew and French.

In 1814 he started the Atmiya Sabha, a society for the study of religious truth. In 1828 he founded the Brahma Sabha (Society of God), later known as the Brahmo Samaj. Ram Mohan was influenced by the VEDAS and UPANISHADS and by his study of Islam and Christianity. He was opposed to idol worship, caste and rituals, and believed that VEDANTA was the best system of Indian thought. In 1820 he published the *Precepts of Jesus*, in which he praised the ethical values of the NEW TESTAMENT, which he felt should be incorporated in Hinduism.

He tried to reform Hindu society, and campaigned against SATI, polygamy and child marriage. He advocated equal property rights for women and a better status for widows. He promoted modern education and published journals in Bengali, Persian, Hindi and English. Among these were the *Mirat-ul-Akhbar*, the *Samvad Kaumudi* and the *Bengali Herald*.

In addition, he focused on political issues and on the reform of the administration, and raised other social and economic questions. In 1830 he was bestowed the title 'Raja' by Akbar II, the Mughal emperor, and tried to help him obtain a pension from the British by pleading his case in England. He died in Bristol in 1833.

Rudra A Vedic deity, usually regarded as a storm god, and an early form of the Hindu god SHIVA. Rudra is described as dazzling, shining like the sun, copper-coloured or red, blue-necked and blue-tufted. He dwells in mountains and is clothed in skin. He is young, fierce, strong, unassailable and wise, and though beneficent, his wrath is to be feared. He has a fierce and formidable nature, but is also a healer.

Rudras A group of gods, the sons of the god RUDRA. They were gods of the air and are said to number either eleven or thirty-three. Various texts give different lists of the Rudras. According to the MAHABHARATA they are Mrigavyadha, NIRRITI, Ahirbudhnya, Pinaki, Sarpa, Ajaikapat, Dahana, Ishvara, Kapali, Bharga and Sthanu. They were born to Sthanudeva, the son of BRAHMA. In the VISHNU PURANA, the eleven Rudras are listed as Hara, Bahurupa, Tryambaka, Aparajita, Vrishakapi, Shambhu, Kapardi, Raivata, Mrigavyadha, Sharva and Kapali. At least one hundred names of Rudras are mentioned in the PURANAS. Several of these are also the names of the god SHIVA.

Rukmangadacharita A Sanskrit text that glorifies devotion to the Hindu god VISHNU. It is a part of the NARADIYA PURANA, a minor PURANA, but is also used as a separate text. In it, a king named Rukmangada promises his daughter Mohini that he will grant any wish of hers. She asks him to either break his fast on *ekadashi*, the eleventh day of a fourteen-day fast sacred to Vishnu, or to kill his own son. Rukmangada decides to kill his son rather than break his vow to Vishnu.

Rukmini One of the chief wives of the Hindu god KRISHNA. She is worshipped as a deity along with Krishna in some temples, particularly in south India. According to the story in the MAHABHARATA, she was the daughter of the king of Vidarbha. Though her brother Rukmi wanted her to marry the king Shishupala, she loved Krishna, who, on her request, abducted her while she was on her way to a temple. PRADYUMNA was their son. When the PANDAVAS went into exile, Rukmini looked after DRAUPADI's children, and when Krishna died she burnt herself on his funeral pyre along with his other wives. In the PURANAS she is considered an incarnation of the goddess LAKSHMI.

Sabarimala The name of the summit of the Neelimala hill in Kerala, known for its temple of the Hindu god AYYAPPA, the Sannidhanam, and for the great Ayappa pilgrimage that takes place every year.

Preparations for the pilgrimage begin forty-one days in advance and include austerities such as wearing black, blue, or saffron clothes, sleeping on the floor and remaining celibate. The pilgrimage is open to men and to women after the age of menopause, or to young girls below the age of ten. For the *abhisheka* (anointing of the god), the pilgrim carries clarified butter on his head, filled in coconut shells, placed in *irumudi*, a particular kind of cloth bag with two compartments. The pilgrimage concludes around the end of December. After a few days' break, the temple reopens to prepare for the Makara Vilakku festival. Thousands of pilgrims reach the temple in a steady stream, chanting *Swamiye Sharanam Ayyappan*, the chant reaching a crescendo. On the evening of 14 January, known as MAKARA SANKRANTI, the grand spectacle of a natural light, the Makara Jyoti, appears to the north-east of the temple on the opposite hill. This light is believed to come from an ARTI performed by DEVAS and RISHIS who live at a place called Kantamala on this hill. After this the festival of Makara Vilakku continues until the closure of the temple on 20 January. The Ayyappa shrine here is open only from mid-November to January, and for the first five days of every Malayalam month.

The present shrine was reconstructed in 1950, after a fire destroyed the old temple. After a 3 km trek up the hill, the shrine is approached by the Patinettampadi, the holy eighteen stairs. The temple has an inner shrine with a gold-plated roof, topped by four gold finials, two MANDAPAS and the *belikalpura*, which contains the altar. The deity, about half-a-metre tall, is made of an amalgam of five metals.

At the foot of the eighteen stairs are shrines of Karuppaswamy or Karuppan, a local deity, and Kaduthaswamy, said to have been a warrior devoted to Ayyappa. Near the stairs is also the shrine of Vavarswami, a Muslim who was Ayyappa's close companion. Here a Muslim priest conducts the PUJA, and the deity is represented by a stone slab. A green silken cloth and an old sword hang across the wall, and the special offering here is green pepper. Some pilgrims come to this shrine along with a goat, which they believe helps them to reach the temple safely. The goats are later auctioned by the temple.

There are several other shrines near the temple, including that of GANESHA, known here as Kannimula Ganapati. The temple of Mallikappurathamma, which contains the shrines of DEVI and Kaduthaswamy is nearby. On the way is the holy tank, the Bhasma Kulam, where the ascetic Sabari entered a fire to end her life, and after whom the peak is named. To the left of the Mallika temple are shrines of the snake deities, Nagaraja and Nagayakshi.

Sabarimala is open to all castes, religions and nationalities.

Sabbath/Shabbat In Judaism, the Sabbath, or weekly day of rest, is observed very strictly. The Pentateuch, comprising the first five books of the BIBLE, states that on this day there must be a total abstention from work. God laboured for six days to create the world and then rested, therefore man must do the same, and it is only by refraining from work that the spiritual state necessary on the Sabbath can be created. A passage in the Bible says: 'Remember the Sabbath day, to keep it holy. Six days you shall labour, and do all your work; but the seventh day is a Sabbath to the Lord your God; in it you shall not do any work, or your son, or your daughter, your manservant or your maidservant, or your cattle, or the sojourner who is within your gates.' (Ex 20.8–11).

In Judaism the Sabbath is observed on a Saturday, but it begins on Friday evening because the religious day (as in Islam) starts in the evening. Special prayers are prescribed before the Friday night meal, after which the kitchen fire is not lit until Saturday evening. At the end of the Sabbath the Havdalah is recited, a prayer over wine, spices and fire; wine symbolizing the joy of the Sabbath, spices to raise the spirits of people who are saddened by its end, and fire to indicate that the working week begins.

Sabiri A SUFI order that was a branch of the CHISTI order. Its founder, Shaikh Alauddin Sabir, is said to have been a disciple of Baba FARID. He settled at Kaliyar in present Uttar Pradesh, his DARGAH being known as Kaliyar Sharif. His immediate successor was Shaikh

Shamsuddin Turk of Panipat, who was succeeded by Shaikh Jalaluddin Mahmud of Panipat. Among the notable later saints of the order was Shaikh Ahmad Abdul Haqq of Rudauli (d. 1433). His teachings have been explained in the *Anwar al-Uyan*, written by Shaikh ABDUL QUDDUS GANGOHI (d. 1537), another Sufi of the order. Shah Muhibullah of Allahabad (d. 1648), Shah Abul Maali (d. 1700), and Shah Abdul Hadi of Amroha (d. 1776) were among other leading saints. This order combined adherence to the SHARIA with metaphysics, and experiences of divine ecstasy.

sachkhand   A term in Sikhism describing the state of bliss and final union with God. The Sikh prayer, the JAPJI, provides an account of stages on the path. The first stage is dharamkhand, where a person acts according to DHARMA or right conduct. The second stage is jnanakhand, where by seeking JNANA or knowledge, insight and understanding grows. The third stage is saramkhand, which has been interpreted in different ways, but is generally taken to mean 'effort'. The fourth stage is karamkhand, which indicates the stage of action or of finally overcoming KARMA, either through one's own actions or through God's grace. Finally sachkhand, the true state, is reached.

sacraments   Holy ceremonies that take place in Christianity, particularly in ROMAN CATHOLICISM. The seven sacraments of Roman Catholics are BAPTISM, confirmation, the EUCHARIST, penance, holy orders, marriage, and extreme unction or anointing of the sick. Baptism signifies initiation into the faith, while confirmation indicates spiritual adulthood. The eucharist, forming part of the MASS is a special method of worship. Penance is also called confession; Catholics confess their sins to a priest, who forgives them in the name of God. Holy orders is the sacrament by which individuals choose to serve the church and become its ministers. The marriage sacrament helps couples to fulfill the obligations of marriage. Extreme unction or anointing of the sick is for those who are very ill or on the verge of death, when the priest anoints the dying person with oil and prays that they may be freed from sin, strengthened in soul, and restored to health. The sacraments of baptism, confirmation and holy orders take place only once in a lifetime. Marriage normally takes place only once, unless the partner dies, divorce not being permitted for Catholics. Confession of sins and holy communion, which form part of the eucharist, are essential at least once a year.

PROTESTANTS do not follow all the sacraments, and various Protestant denominations disagree on what to follow. Baptism is common to most Protestants.

The ORTHODOX CHURCH follows the seven mysteries, which correspond to the seven sacraments. They are: baptism, chrismation, confession, eucharist, marriage, euchelaion and ordination. Chrismation corresponds to confirmation, and euchelaion to extreme unction.

sacred places   Every village and city in India is associated with sacred shrines, but in each religion there are some particularly sacred places. Seven cities are considered the most sacred centres of pilgrimage for Hindus. They are: AYODHYA, MATHURA, GAYA, KASHI, KANCHIPURAM, UJJAIN and DVARAKA. In addition there are several sacred places in the Himalayan region, sacred sites along rivers all over India, and the great sacred centres of the south, which include KUMBAKONAM, KANCHIPURAM and MADURAI. In Islam the DARGAHS of SUFI saints are centres of pilgrimage, particularly those of Shaikh MUINUDDIN CHISTI at Ajmer and Shaikh SALIM CHISTI at Fatehpur Sikri, though there are several others. In Christianity, particular churches associated with miraculous cures or prayers answered are visited by all communities, among these being the shrine of Our Lady of Health at Velankanni, OUR LADY OF GRACE at Sardhana, and Catholic churches in Goa. Buddhism reveres sites associated with the life of the BUDDHA, particularly BODH GAYA, while Jain sacred sites include the PARASNATH hill, the SHATRUNJAYA hill, and SHRAVANA BELAGOLA in south India, among others. For PARSIS there are sites mainly in Gujarat, associated with their arrival in India, and the earliest Zoroastrian temples erected in the country.

sacred thread   A thread signifying belonging to the religion, worn by certain Hindu castes, as well as by Zoroastrians. In Hinduism, the thread, known as the yajnopavita, is conferred traditionally at the UPANAYANA ceremony, the time when a young male of any of the three upper castes begins his studies with his guru. In modern times it may be conferred later. In Zoroastrianism the sacred thread is known as the KUSTI; it is conferred on both males and females at the NAVJOTE ceremony, the time of formal initiation into the religion.

sacrifices   Sacrifices, known in Sanskrit as YAJNA, take many different forms. At a sacrifice, a ritual fire is lit, and offerings may be made of fruit, flowers, grain, milk, water, or sometimes of animals. Among the sacrifices conducted in ancient times in India, there were several to increase or assert the power of a king, such as the ASHVAMEDHA or horse sacrifice, the RAJASUYA, vajapeya, punar abhisheka and aindra mahabhisheka. The darsha-purnamasa, or new and full moon sacrifices, pinda-pitra-yajna, or sacrifices to the ancestors, chaturmasya, or four monthly seasonal sacrifices, and Soma sacrifices are described in ancient texts. Other sacrifices included fire sacrifices of the agnihotra, agnishtoma, and daily household sacrifices. Sacrifices of animals were common in ancient times and are still practised in some Hindu temples. Large-scale sacrifices involving hundreds of animals are described in the RAMAYANA and other texts; the SARPA SATRA or snake sacrifice also involved killing living beings. The purushamedha, or human sacrifice, is mentioned though some feel this was only symbolic. Buddhism and Jainism rejected animal sacrifices and so did VAISHNAVISM and several later Hindu sects. Sacrificial rituals are believed to bring about a connection with the divine. Today there is an attempt in some cases to substitute a real animal with a terracotta figurine or a pumpkin, though daily animal sacrifices still take place in certain KALI temples. Biannual sacrifices at DEVI temples in rural areas later turn into feasts in which the whole village participates. The sacrifice of animals also takes place in other religions, including Islam.

Other types of sacrifices, such as offering lights, incense, flowers, etc., along with ritual prayers occur in all religions.

Sadashiva A name of the Hindu god SHIVA, meaning the 'eternal one'.

Saddharma Pundarika A MAHAYANA Buddhist text composed in Sanskrit, in about the second century CE, possibly in the region of GANDHARA or Kapisha. Literally, the name means 'The Lotus of the True Law', and it is popularly known as the *Lotus Sutra*. The *Sutra* has been described as a narrative drama, with a series of dialogues between BUDDHAS, BODHISATTVAS and ordinary people. The text states that all living beings who believe in the BUDDHA and follow his DHARMA will attain Buddhahood.

The first half of the *Sutra* deals with three traditional paths, that of the Shravaka (HINAYANA path), of the Pratyeka Buddha (solitary Buddha, one who achieves Buddhahood on his own), and the path of the BODHISATTVA. All these are different aspects of the one path and goal. The second half of the text represents the fully developed theory of the Buddha in Mahayana Buddhism. According to this the Buddha is eternal, and has always existed. He is the essence of Buddhahood, free from all concepts of being or non-being. As he is eternal and unchanging, he never attained NIRVANA, for there was nothing to be attained. His life in the world is only a cosmic drama, a device through which the Truth is to be understood. This concept was later accepted by VAJRAYANA Buddhists.

The theory of the eternal essence of Buddhahood is also similar to that of the ATMAN or BRAHMAN in some of the UPANISHADS, clearly explained by SHANKARA in his theory of ADVAITA.

The *Saddharma Pundarika* was first translated into Chinese by the third century. It is one of the most influential Mahayana texts and the main text for several schools of Buddhism, including the Tendai and Nichiren schools of Japan. A branch of the Nichiren school, the SOKKA GAKAI, is active in India.

sadhana A Sanskrit term that usually refers to a daily purificatory practice. It can involve the worship of, or devotion to, a deity, religious rites of some kind, contemplation, meditation, or any other practice. It can also refer to non-religious disciplines. The term has several meanings, including 'the act of mastering, accomplishment, fulfilment, achievement and perfection'.

sadhu A saint or a holy person. There are several formal sadhu sects, such as the DASNAMIS and the NAGA SADHUS, though sadhus need not belong to any sect. Sadhu is often used as a synonym for SANNYASI. Literally, the word in Sanskrit means 'good' or 'virtuous', and it is also used in this sense in ancient texts.

Sadhyas A class of semi-divine beings. In the RIG VEDA they are called the 'gods of old', and in the *Taittiriya Samhita* they are said to have existed before creation. According to the PURANAS, they are the sons of DHARMA and Sadhya, who was a daughter of DAKSHA. They were associated with the ASHVAMEDHA or horse sacrifice, and with the Pushyasnana, the sacred bath before the annual consecration ceremony of a king. Twelve Sadhyas are named in the *AGNI PURANA*: Manas (mind), Manta (thought), Prana (life-force or breath), Nara (man), Apana (a type of breath), Viryavan (brave), Vibhu (powerful), Haya (horse), Naya (prudent), Hamsa (swan), Narayana (refuge of man), Prabhu (lord). In some Puranas, seventeen Sadhyas are listed.

Safa Shahouri Masjid The oldest mosque located in Goa, also known as the PONDA MOSQUE.

Sagar Island An island in the GANGA delta on the river Hughli, which is a centre of pilgrimage. *See* Ganga Sagara.

Saguna Brahman BRAHMAN, a term for the Absolute in Hinduism, can be known in two ways— without form and with form. Saguna Brahman is the representation of Brahman through different forms or deities. Literally it means 'with attributes', and thus each deity has various qualities or attributes, but still reflects Brahman.

Sahadeva The youngest of the five PANDAVAS, the twin of NAKULA, described in the *MAHABHARATA*. Sahadeva and Nakula were born when their mother MADRI invoked the twin deities of the ASHVINS. Sahadeva studied astronomy with DRONA and was an expert at managing cattle. His son from Draupadi was Shrutasena or Shrutakarman. In addition, he married Vijaya and had a son named Suhotra.

Sahaja Yoga A system of union with the divine, founded by Mata NIRMALA DEVI. Sahaja Yoga implies a spontaneous union, or Self-realization, through the raising of the KUNDALINI. Nirmala Devi is said to have devised a method by which the kundalini could be raised instantly, for a number of people at one time. 'Self-realization is the first encounter with reality', she says. Sahaja Yoga is transmitted through a simple initiation process, performed by Nirmala Devi or her senior disciples. After the first initiation, practitioners of Sahaja Yoga meditate every day to enable the divine power to flow through them.

There are Sahaja Yoga temples and hundreds of thousands of Sahaja Yoga followers all over the world. According to Nirmala Devi, 'Sahaja Yoga establishes the proof of Truth and enables you to experience it.'

Sahaj-dhari A term in Sikhism for a Sikh who does not belong to the KHALSA.

Sahajiya A Tantric system of worship in Hinduism, similar to the SAHAJIYANA of Buddhism. The name comes from sahaja, which means 'easy' or 'natural'. Sahajiyas believe that the innate and natural functions of the body, such as sex, should not be suppressed, but should be experienced, and their power used for divine transformation. For VAISHNAVA Sahajiyas, KRISHNA and RADHA are the role models, while for SHAIVITES or SHAKTAS the examples are SHIVA and SHAKTI. Several BAULS were also part of the Sahajiya movement. The BHAKTI saint CHANDIDAS is said to have been a Sahajiya, on the basis of some poems attributed to him, though probably these belong to a later date.

Sahajiyana, Buddhist A branch of Buddhist TANTRA that is said to have originated with Lui-pa, a yogi from Kashmir (c. 750–800). The earliest texts are from Bengal, the *Dohakosha* being written in Apabhramsa, a form of Prakrit, and the *Charyagita* in early Bengali. The basic doctrine is that Sahaja is the same as the Bodhichitta, the innate thought of enlightenment, which can be realized by combining *prajna* (wisdom), with *upaya* (skillful means). The same concept exists in VAJRAYANA, but the Sahajiyas also used the outer interpretation of *prajna* and *upaya*, as the feminine and male principles, the union of the two being achieved through sex. Sahajiyanas were against the settled Buddhist establishment, the SANGHA, with its rules and norms, and were homeless wanderers travelling from place to place, often accompanied by their female consorts. They rejected all accepted norms of conduct or fixed rules, unlike the Vajrayana, who formalized Tantric thought into academic disciplines. Sahajiyas can be compared in some ways with the later QALANDARS of Islam.

Sahasrara Chakra One of the seven main CHAKRAS or hidden energy centres within the body. The Sahasrara Chakra is at the crown of the head and is described as a lotus of a thousand petals, with its head downwards, lustrous and whiter than the full moon. Its clustered filaments are of the colour of the rising sun, and within it is the full moon, shining like lightning, spreading its rays, moist and cool like nectar. Inside this is a shining triangle, and within that shunya, the void, which represents the sun that destroys ignorance and delusion. People call it by different names, but it is the highest abode, and the one who knows this place with a controlled mind, possesses the power to do anything, has divine knowledge and is not affected by actions. The Supreme, as subtle as the ten-millionth part of the end of a hair, resides here, and through her flows a stream of love and a knowledge of the Truth. The KUNDALINI should be led to this chakra, and all things should be absorbed in her.

Sahibzadas A respectful term that refers to the four sons of Guru GOBIND SINGH, who all died in the cause of Sikhism, and who are remembered every day in the ARDAS prayer. Baba Ajit Singh (b. 1687) and Baba Jujhar Singh (b. 1689), the guru's elder sons, were both killed fighting in the battle of CHAMKAUR in 1704. At the time of the battle, the two younger sons, Baba Zorawar Singh (b. 1696) and Baba Fateh Singh (b. 1698) were captured by Nawab Wazir Khan, the governor of Sirhind, and given the choice of death or conversion to Islam. The two small children refused to convert and were bricked up in a wall.

Sai Baba, of Shirdi A saint of the nineteenth and early twentieth centuries, who settled at Shirdi in Maharashtra. There are different versions of his early life, with some claiming he was born a Muslim, and others a Hindu. According to one version, he was born to Hindu BRAHMANA parents in the state of Hyderabad, but after they died he was adopted and brought up by a Muslim faqir or saint. Later he also had a Hindu guru. At some time, it is not clear when, he came to Shirdi, and was addressed by someone as 'Sai', meaning holy or good, and soon came to be known as Sai Baba. He loved singing KABIR's songs, and wandered around Shirdi before settling down in an old mosque. He referred to god as ALLAH, but was familiar with Hindu deities and methods of worship.

He lived simply and answered philosophical questions on Advaitic lines (*see* Advaita), helped people with their material problems and was said to have miraculous powers. He soon attracted crowds of devotees and followers who claimed that he cured diseases and fulfilled wishes and desires. He was not in favour of doing this, but his love and compassion did not allow him to turn anyone away. He never changed his simple life, shared the food given to him with others, and cultivated a small garden himself, where he meditated and prayed in private. After his death in 1918, the mosque where he had stayed and his SAMADHI continued to attract thousands of pilgrims. His comments and discussions were noted down and translated into English from the original Marathi by Narasimhaswami as *Sri Sai Baba's Charters and Sayings*, available in several books and pamphlets. *Sri Sai Satcharita*, a hagiographic biography in Marathi verse by G.R. Dabholkar, provides an account of his life.

Sai Baba asked people to meditate on the question 'Who am I?', as many other Vedantic teachers have done. He said he was the formless Absolute, who came into the world because of the action of KARMA. 'The world is my abode. BRAHMAN [the Absolute] is my father and MAYA [illusion] my mother. By their interlocking I got this body.'

He also referred to Brahman as Suddha Chaitanya, the origin and essence of all life that permeates the universe.

Sai Baba, Sathya A saint of the twentieth century. Born on 23 November 1926 at Puttaparthi in present Andhra Pradesh, his original name was Sathyanarayana

Raju. He began to reveal exceptional powers by the age of eight, and by the age of fifteen he renounced the world. When he was twenty-one years old, he founded an ASHRAM, Prasantha Nilayam, at Puttaparthi and attracted a number of disciples. He is known for his apparent ability to produce objects out of the air, gifting them to his devotees, and also for the Vibhuti, or sacred ash, that seems to fall out of photographs of him. His disciples consider him an incarnation of SAI BABA OF SHIRDI.

Sathya Sai Baba has founded schools, colleges and institutes of higher education, hospitals, and a number of other philanthropic institutions. He is revered by millions in India and abroad. His teachings are based on universal truth and Oneness. He encourages people to recognize the Atman within, and realize Prema or divine love, leading to selfless service for all.

Sair-e-Gul Faroshan (Phul Walon ki Sair) A festival that takes place in the Mehrauli area of New Delhi in the month of Bhadrapada (August to September). It symbolizes harmony between Hindus and Muslims who jointly participate in the festival, which is said to have been started by one of the later Mughal emperors, Muhammad Shah 'Rangila' (1719–48), also known for his patronage of music and musicians. Large hand-fans of palm leaves, made specially for this occasion, are strung with flowers and decorated with tinsel and carried in a procession by Hindus and Muslims together, first to the DARGAH of the SUFI saint QUTBUDDIN BAKHTIYAR KAKI and then to the YOGA MAYA TEMPLE. The fans are presented to the temple and kept there till the following year. After this, people gather to listen to qawwalis and Sufi music, representing the spirit of oneness. The celebration of the festival had declined but was restarted in 1961 by the prime minister, Jawaharlal Nehru, and continues to be celebrated every year.

Saiyyid/Sayyed Also spelt Syed or Saiyad, Saiyyid was initially a respectful term, but later was used by Muslims who claim descent from the Prophet MUHAMMAD through his daughter Fatima. In India Saiyyid families maintain genealogies to prove their descent. Saiyyids can be either SUNNIS or SHIAS.

Sakya Lama The head of the SAKYA order of TIBETAN BUDDHISM.

The current head (in 2005) is the forty-first Sakya Lama, who came to India in 1959 at the age of fourteen. Sakya Lamas are allowed to marry, and the title is inherited either by his son or his nephew.

Sakya order A school of TIBETAN BUDDHISM that has several monasteries in India. The Sakya order traces its origin to the Indian yogi Virupa, who is one of the eighty-four MAHASIDDHAS. Drogmi (Brogmi) Shakya Yeshe (992–1074) travelled to India and received the teachings of this yogi as well as of other Indian masters. One of his teachers was Shantipa at the VIKRAMSHILA university. His disciple Khon Konchok

Gyalpo founded a monastery in 1073 in central Tibet, named Sakya, from which the school took its name. In the thirteenth century, the Sakyas gained political control in Tibet. Later, several subsects of the Sakya order emerged.

Sakya teachings combine esoteric and exoteric disciplines, and its concepts are known as 'lambras', or 'the path and its fruit'. It believes that there is no difference between SAMSARA and NIRVANA, as both are products of the mind. Right meditation and other practices are prescribed. Their texts include eighteen major works on monastic discipline, the PRAJNAPARAMITA or perfection of wisdom texts, logic, as well as the HEVAJRA, *Chakrasambhara* and other TANTRAS.

After the migration of Tibetans to India in 1959, a number of Sakya monasteries have been established in India. These include Tsechen Tenpai Gatsal and Ngor-e-vam Chodhen in Dehradun, Uttarakhand; Ngor-e-vam Shadrup Dargye Ling in Bir, Himachal Pradesh; and Tsechen Dhongag Choeling in Mundgod, Karnataka. The SAKYA LAMA, the head of the order in India, resides in Dehradun.

Salar Masud Ghazi, Sayyid A Muslim saint whose shrine or DARGAH is worshipped at Bahraich in Uttar Pradesh, and who is popularly known as Ghazi Miyan. According to traditional accounts of his life, compiled in the seventeenth century by ABDUR RAHIM CHISTI in his *Mirat-i Masudi*, Ghazi Miyan was born in 1015, the nephew of Sultan Mahmud of Ghazni, who invaded India in the early eleventh century. Scholars, however, feel this is an invented story, and that Ghazi Miyan was an unknown warrior. Legends state that he accompanied Mahmud on his expedition to Somanatha, but was against the plunder that took place there, and decided to follow a spiritual path. He became the disciple of a PIR, wandered through the plains of north India, and finally reached Bahraich. Meanwhile his mother, father, and revered teacher all died, and Ghazi Miyan decided to spend his days in worship and prayer in the forests of Bahraich. He was revered as a spiritual leader, and as his fame grew he was challenged by a local raja who feared a threat to his throne. Though he assured the raja that he had no worldly ambitions, the raja was not convinced, and Ghazi Miyan was forced to fight a series of battles and was finally killed in 1033, at the young age of nineteen. A shrine soon grew around his tomb, and stories of miracles were reported. An annual pilgrimage to GHAZI MIYAN'S DARGAH began, in which all communities participated. It still takes place every year in May–June.

Some kings were against this pilgrimage and both Sultan Sikandar Lodi (ruled 1489–1517) and the Mughal emperor AURANGZEB tried to stop the pilgrimage to his tomb, while the emperor AKBAR blessed it. Apart from his main shrine at Bahraich, there are several others in Uttar Pradesh and Bihar, among them being shrines at Meerut, Sambhal in Moradabad, Satrikh, Maner in Bihar, and elsewhere.

The saint seems to have been well known by the thirteenth century and the time of Sultan Iltutmish (ruled 1211–36). His dargah is mentioned by AMIR KHUSRAU and was visited by Sultan Muhammad bin Tughlaq (ruled 1325–51).

Whatever his actual ancestry, he seems to have been a military adventurer from Central Asia or Afghanistan, known for his bravery and piety.

Salim Chisti, Shaikh A SUFI saint who belonged to the CHISTI order and lived in the fifteenth and sixteenth centuries. Sheikh Salim was a descendant of the Sufi saint Faridud-din Ganj-i-Shakar (c. 1175–1265), popularly known as Baba FARID, of Pak Patan, now in Pakistan. Born in DELHI in 1479–80, Salim and his family moved to Sikri near AGRA, when he was still a child. In 1524–25 he went on a pilgrimage to Mecca and visited several other Arab countries, returning to Sikri in 1537–38. He married and had several children from his many wives. In 1563, when he was over eighty years old, he began the construction of a KHANQAH (residence for Sufi disciples) and mosque on the Sikri ridge.

In 1556 the Mughal emperor AKBAR succeeded his father Humayun and began to rule from Agra. Akbar had no children, and it was after the blessing of Sheikh Salim, whom he met in 1568, that three children were born to him. The first was named Salim after the Shaikh, and later became the emperor Jahangir.

Akbar built a whole city, Fatehpur Sikri, near the residence of the saint. After Salim Chisti's death in 1572, a beautiful tomb was erected over his cell. The deserted city, with the DARGAH of the saint within it, can still be seen. People from all religions come here to make offerings and seek blessings at the tomb of Sheikh Salim.

sallekhana A term for the rite of religious suicide in Jainism. This rite consists of death through starvation and is the ideal end for the advanced Jain monk or nun. All food contains life, and water too contains minute forms of living beings, therefore refraining from these frees one from the KARMA, which is generated by taking life. Sallekhana in ancient days could be performed standing, or lying on a bed of thorny grass, but today it can be undertaken on a simple bed. Usually, the person first refrains from food, purifying the mind with prayers and meditation, and then ceases to take even water. Sallekhana still takes place, and is considered extremely meritorious.

Salvation Army A Christian movement that has a presence in India. It was started by William Booth (1829–1912) in 1865 in London, and was originally known as the Christian Mission. Booth's wife Catherine and eldest son William Bramwell Booth are considered co-founders of the movement. It was renamed the Salvation Army in 1878. Booth was initially a priest in the METHODIST New Connection Church. The Salvation Army symbolizes 'spiritual warfare', and uses uniforms, ranks, badges, flags and bands like a real army, and is an evangelical movement with a focus on social work. The flag, of blue, red and yellow, represents the TRINITY, while bands and music help to attract people. The leaders, who are ministers of religion, are known as commissioned officers, and the highest leader is a general, elected by the High Council. Women have an equal status. High moral standards are advocated, including abstinence from alcohol and tobacco. The headquarters is at London, and the movement exists in over ninety countries.

The organization was introduced in India in 1882 in Mumbai (Bombay) by Frederick George De Latour Tucker, previously in the Indian Civil Service, who took the name Fakir Singh and adopted an Indian lifestyle. The organization spread to Travancore by 1889, and then expanded further. It provided relief in natural calamities, opened educational institutions and started cottage industries to provide employment. In India, its main office is at DELHI.

sama A term used in SUFISM, literally 'listening'. It implies a focus on songs and music, which lead to divine ecstasy. Sama was popular particularly with the CHISTIS, and was frowned upon by some SUFI orders as being non-Islamic.

Sama Veda One of the four VEDIC SAMHITAS. It consists of hymns to be chanted at sacrifices, and has 1810 verses or 1549 without repetitions, most of which can be found in the RIG VEDA, with some variations. Priests who chant the *Sama Veda* are known as udgatris.

samadhi (1) A Sanskrit term indicating union with the divine. Samadhi is a state of deep meditation, in which Oneness or non-duality is experienced. It is described as the eighth and final stage in the system of Raja YOGA. The term is used in Buddhism and other philosophies as well.

(2) A samadhi is also a place where a saint or yogi is buried or enshrined after death. In several SANNYASI sects a person who has attained a high stage of communion with the divine is entombed after death seated in a yogic posture. Other saintly people are also enshrined in this way and not cremated, as is otherwise the custom in Hinduism. Pilgrims then visit the samadhi and gain the blessings of the saint. The DARGAH of a saint in Islam has a similar function.

Some saints are believed to have never died, remaining in samadhi in a cave or somewhere beneath the ground, meditating for thousands of years, for the good of the world.

Samantabhadra, Buddhist A celestial BODHISATTVA associated with the Buddha VAIROCHANA. He is usually depicted as blue in colour and is often seated on a six-tusked white elephant.

Samantabhadra, Jain A Jain scholar and philosopher who, according to the DIGAMBARA sect, lived in the second century CE. A twelfth-century inscription at SHRAVANA BELAGOLA states that he was a disciple of Balakapichha, a pupil of UMASVAMI. Some scholars, however, place him in the eighth century. Samantabhadra wrote a number of books, including a commentary on Umasvami's *Tattvarthadhigama Sutra*, known as the *Devagama Sutra* or *Aptamimansa*. Only the introduction of this text exists today. The text explained the SYADVADA philosophy and was commented on by non-Jain philosophers such as KUMARILA (eighth–ninth centuries) and Vachaspatimishra.

Samaraichcha Kaha A Jain *dharma katha*, or religious novel, written by HARIBHADRA SURI in the eighth century, in PRAKRIT prose (Jain Maharashtri), interspersed with verse. It contains a number of stories that trace the successive lives of people through adventures and romance, until they finally understand the true meaning of life and become Jain monks and nuns. There are numerous other such novels in Jain literature.

Samavayamga A Jain text, the fourth of the twelve ANGAS. Much of it is arranged in numerical groups, like the *THANAMGA*, though instead of using groups from one to ten, there are number groups that exceed one hundred and even reach one million. Thus it deals with two Rasis, two types of hellish creatures, three types of Vedas, and other subjects grouped together. Its later date is indicated by the eighteen types of Brahmi script mentioned under the number eighteen. The text lists the contents of the fourteen PURVAS and provides an account of the ANGAS.

Samayasundara A Jain scholar of the Kharatara GACHCHHA who lived in the sixteenth century, and was conferred the title of Upadhyaya by the Mughal emperor AKBAR. Samayasundara accompanied JINACHANDRA SURI to Akbar's court, and on one occasion he read out to the emperor a work composed by him, known as *Ashtalakshi*. He explained how a sentence of three Sanskrit words, '*Rajno dadate soukhyam*' (the king alone can bestow pleasure), could be interpreted in 8,00,000 ways. Grammatically, the sentence had 10,22,407 meanings.

This indicates the great learning of Jain scholars, which extended beyond Jainism to several other fields.

Sambandar (Campantar) A BHAKTI saint of the seventh century who was one of the NAYANARS and worshipped the Hindu god, SHIVA. Born in a BRAHMANA family in the village of Sirkazi near CHIDAMBARAM in the Tamil region, he was a devotee of Shiva and PARVATI from childhood. He composed hymns and songs to Shiva, which are included in the *Tevaram*, a sacred SHAIVITE text which forms part of the TIRUMURAI.

sambhogakaya A term for one of the three bodies (TRIKAYA) of the BUDDHA, a concept that developed in MAHAYANA Buddhism.

Samet Shikhara A sacred Jain site, another name of the PARASNATH HILL in Jharkhand, where most of the TIRTHANKARAS are said to have attained MOKSHA or liberation.

samhita A term in Sanskrit that means 'putting together' and refers to a collection or compilation. A number of early texts are known as Samhitas. Among them are the first section of the VEDAS, which have hymns or verses. The four VEDIC SAMHITAS are: the *Rig Veda Samhita*, the *Sama Veda Samhita*, the *Yajur Veda Samhita* and the *Atharva Veda Samhita*. They are generally referred to as the RIG VEDA, SAMA VEDA, YAJUR VEDA and ATHARVA VEDA. The Brahmanas and other Vedic texts are attached to the Vedic Samhitas.

Samkhya One of the six classical systems of ancient Indian philosophy, said to have been founded by the sage KAPILA. In early texts, the term Samkhya is used in the sense of philosophical reflection, and this system reaches its understanding by reflecting on the nature of the world. It sees the world as a result of two principles, PURUSHA and PRAKRITI. The latter is the active principle, the potentiality of all nature, through which the material and psychic world comes into being. It is not exactly the same as matter, and it has three components through which it arises: sattva, rajas and tamas. Sattva is potential consciousness and indicates perfection, goodness and happiness. Rajas is the source of all activity, producing enjoyment as well as restlessness and pain. Tamas resists activity, leading to indifference and slothfulness. The three are never separate, but one or the other predominates. Sattva is the essence of that which is to be realized, tamas the obstacle preventing its realization, and rajas the force that overcomes the obstacle. Prakriti evolves for the sake of Purusha. It develops into buddhi, higher intelligence, thought, and the objects of thought, as well as the ego. Purusha can be translated as soul and is similar to the concept of BRAHMAN. In each living being there is a Purusha, yet essentially all Purushas are the same. According to S. Radhakrishnan, it is 'not the mind, life or body, but the informing and sustaining soul, silent, peaceful, eternal'. It illuminates all the activities that take place, but does not participate in them. Purusha is eternally free, but to realize its nature one requires virtue, including unselfish activity, and vairagya or detachment, as well as higher knowledge. With right discrimination (viveka), freedom from bondage is achieved. Prakriti provides the experiences that enable Purusha to free itself.

The Samkhya system is against sacrifices and caste, but believes in the path of liberation through knowledge and understanding. Elements of the Samkhya philosophy are found in the UPANISHADS and the *MAHABHARATA*, and are also explained in the BHAGAVAD GITA.

The legendary Kapila is said to have existed some time between the seventh and sixth centuries BCE, but the texts attributed to him, the *Samkhyapravachana Sutra* and the *Tattvasamasa*, seem to have been written much later. In fact the former is dated by some scholars to the fourteenth century CE, though there was probably an earlier version. The earliest available text seems to be the *Samkhya Karika* of the third century CE, written by Ishvarakrishna. Among other major works explaining Samkhya philosophy are Vachaspati's *Samkhyatattvakaumudi* of the ninth century, and Vijnanabhikshu's *Samkhya-pravachanabhashya* of the sixteenth century.

Sammatiya A school of HINAYANA Buddhism that emerged out of the VATSIPUTRIYA. Like the Vatsiputriya, it believed in the PUDGALA concept, the essence of a person, not identifiable with its components. However, it implied that the Pudgala, though real, is undefinable. Regarding ARHATS, it believed an Arhat can fall from the perfect state. Sammatiyas also emphasized acts of charity or generosity, which provide merit to the giver.

XUANZANG, the Chinese pilgrim of the seventh century, records their existence in numerous monasteries from north-west to western India, and they are also said to have existed in eastern India, up to the time of the Pala dynasty in the eleventh century.

Samru, Begam A Muslim woman who became a Catholic and founded a Catholic church. Farzana, a young Muslim girl of fifteen, later known as Begam Samru, married Walter Reinhardt, a mercenary from Luxemburg who became the commander of the army of Najaf Khan, a local Afghan ruler. Reinhardt was known as 'Le Sombre' because of his dark and pensive appearance. This name turned into 'Samru' in Hindustani, and thus Farzana became Begam Samru. Reinhardt was given the *pargana* of Sardhana neer Meerut in present Uttar Pradesh, by Najaf Khan, and after his death in 1778 it came to Begam Samru, who ruled over it. In 1781 she became a Roman Catholic and was renamed Joanna. In 1793 she married Le Vessault, the French commander of her artillery, but he died a tragic death. Begam Samru successfully took care of her territory until her death in 1836, despite the political intrigues and conspiracies in the area. She built St. Mary's Church, dedicated to the Virgin Mary, which once functioned as a cathedral, and is now known as the Church of OUR LADY OF GRACES.

samsara A Sanskrit term for the concept of reincarnation or transmigration of the soul in Hinduism. According to this concept, the soul occupies a series of bodies, from plant to animal to human life, though it always remains the same, untouched, eternal and pure. When the individual realizes the truth of the eternal soul and ceases to identify with the ego, MOKSHA, freedom from the process of rebirth, is achieved. In Jainism, the term refers to the cycle of transmigration, leading to the entanglement of the JIVA or soul, in matter.

samskara A Sanskrit term that has a number of meanings, but is broadly used in two ways: it indicates ceremonies and rituals practised in Hinduism, as well as the tendencies and qualities that accumulate around a person in succeeding lives, and influence his fate. The two meanings are connected, as the correct practice of rituals generates new qualities. In orthodox Hinduism, samskaras in the form of rituals are to be practised from before birth to after death, mainly by the three higher castes. Texts prescribe different numbers of samskaras, ranging from ten to forty-eight or more. Later authorities recommended sixteen essential ceremonies. Many of these, relating to birth, marriage and death, are still in use.

samudramanthana The term for the churning of the ocean of milk, a myth in Hinduism related to the obtaining of AMRITA or divine nectar by the DEVAS. The story occurs in the MAHABHARATA and PURANAS, with some variations.

samyak charitra One of the TRIRATNA, the three jewels or ideals of Jainism. Samyak charitra means right conduct and is based on the other two jewels, SAMYAK DARSHANA (right belief) and SAMYAK JNANA (right knowledge). When these two are understood, conduct is perfected, by following all Jain ethical principles, particularly that of AHIMSA or non-violence.

samyak darshana One of the TRIRATNA, the three jewels or ideals of Jainism. Samyak darshana is translated as right belief or faith, or sometimes right perception. Samyak darshana is of two kinds, belief with attachment and belief without attachment, through the purity of the soul. Right belief can be attained through intuition or by acquiring knowledge from external sources.

samyak jnana One of the TRIRATNA, the three jewels or ideals of Jainism. Samyak jnana, or right knowledge, is of five kinds: (1) knowledge derived through the senses or the mind; (2) knowledge through the study of scriptures; (3) direct knowledge of matter; (4) direct knowledge of others thoughts; (5) perfect knowledge.

Samyutta Nikaya A Buddhist text of the PALI CANON, literally 'the grouped discourses or suttas'. The *Samyutta Nikaya* is part of the SUTTA PITAKA, and has five sections or vaggas, subdivided into fifty-six groups (samyuttas) of suttas. Among the *samyuttas* is the *Devata Samyutta*, with diverse sayings attributed to Devatas or deities. The *Bhikkuni Samyutta* has ten stories of bhikkunis or nuns, who resisted the temptations of MARA. The *Naga Samyutta* has fifty suttas on NAGAS (snake deities) and on snakes. There is some beautiful poetry in this *Nikaya*, as well as discourses in the form of riddles.

Sanat Kumara (1) A mind-born son of the Hindu god BRAHMA, that is, a son born through the power of his mind. His other mind-born sons are usually mentioned as Sanaka, Sananda and Sanatana, while some texts list a total of seven. According to Puranic myths, these sons refused to marry because they were created from the pure element of Sattva. They remained innocent and celibate eternally, and some PURANAS state that they never grew beyond the age of five. They had mastered all the VEDAS and travelled together to VAIKUNTHA, the heaven of VISHNU.

In the hierarchy of deities acknowledged by the THEOSOPHICAL SOCIETY, Sanat Kumara is at the apex, and was eternally sixteen years old. In his young days J. KRISHNAMURTI, is said to have visited him in his astral body. He recounted: 'He is a boy not much older than I am, but the handsomest I have ever seen, all shining and glorious, and when He smiles it is like sunlight. He is strong like the sea, so that nothing could stand against him for a moment, and yet he is nothing but love, so that I could not be in the least afraid of Him.' Sanat Kumara is also mentioned in TANTRAS.

(2) In one passage of the MAHABHARATA Sanat Kumara is equated with KARTTIKEYA. He is mentioned in the CHHANDOGYA UPANISHAD, where he instructs the rishi NARADA in Brahmavidya. Here he is described as the same as Skanda, another name for Karttikeya.

(3) In Jainism, Sanat Kumara is the fourth of the twelve Chakravartins or world rulers, a contemporary of the fifteenth TIRTHANKARA, Dharmanatha. According to stories in Jain texts, Sanat Kumara ruled for 3,00,000 years before he renounced the world, and after practising asceticism, reached the Sanat Kumara heaven.

(4) Sanat Kumara is a name sometimes applied to other great ascetics.

sanatana   A term that means 'eternal'. Hinduism is often described as Sanatana Dharma, the eternal religion.

Sanchi Stupa   A Buddhist STUPA located at Sanchi in Madhya Pradesh, which dates back to the third century BCE. Additions were made to it in the second and first centuries BCE. The stupa has a diameter of 36 m and a height of 16.5 m, and is a hemispherical dome with a flattened top. Decorated plaster once covered it. There are two processional paths and four carved gateways, which support architraves with sculpted panels depicting scenes from the JATAKAS and from the BUDDHA's life. While the Buddha is indicated only by symbols (such as an empty throne, an open umbrella, or footprints), animals, birds and people are realistically carved.

Sanchi was an important centre of Buddhism, with several monasteries dating from the third century BCE to the twelfth century CE. Among them is the Devi Vihara, where Devi, a queen of the Mauryan emperor ASHOKA, lived.

sandha-bhasha   A term for the secret language of TANTRA. Several Tantric texts are written in symbolic language that can be understood only by initiates.

Sangam Literature   A term for a group of Tamil texts, probably composed between the last few centuries BCE and the early centuries CE. According to traditional accounts, three great literary gatherings (sangams or cankams in Tamil) were held at MADURAI in ancient times. Gods and sages participated in the first, but their compositions are lost. At the second and third, there were saints and sages, as well as poets and writers. The *Tolkappiyam*, a Tamil grammar, is attributed to the second sangam. At the third Sangam, the ETTUTOGAI was composed as well as several other texts. The eight texts of the Ettutogai, have over 2000 poems written by 200 poets. The PATTUPATTU, or ten idylls, are in a similar style. There are differing views on the dates of these texts, but much of the Ettutogai and parts of the Pattupattu are believed to date between the third century BCE and the third century CE. These texts throw some light on the early history of the Tamil country, including aspects of caste and religion.

Other texts included by some scholars in Sangam literature, though they are somewhat later, are the PADINENKILKANAKKU, or eighteen didactical texts. These texts also provide information on the early history of south India.

sangha, Buddhist   The Buddhist monastic order, first established at the time of the BUDDHA. On joining the Sangha, the initiate took certain vows and gave up his worldly life. The texts of the VINAYA PITAKA provided the rules and precepts of the monastic order, and the basic vows included celibacy and refraining from all intoxicants. Initially, only monks were admitted into the order, but ANANDA, the Buddha's closest disciple, advocated the admittance of women. The Buddha was against this, but finally agreed. The first woman to be admitted was his foster mother and aunt, MAHAPRAJAPATI. Both monks and nuns of the sangha, wore yellow robes and had their heads shaved. Elaborate rules for every aspect of their lives were worked out and recorded in the *Vinaya*, but differences arose and several schisms took place in the sangha. Some sects formulated their own *Vinaya Pitakas*, while others continued to use the texts of the PALI CANON.

sangha, Jain   In Jainism, the Sangha is a term for a community or group of Jains. Sometimes, the term is also used for a sect. Sanghas are headed by acharyas and within each sangha there are smaller groups, such as GANAS, kulas and shakhas, while GACHCHAS form another subdivision. Jain inscriptions from the first and third centuries CE at MATHURA, have numerous references to ganas, kulas and shakhas, though sanghas are not mentioned. The term seems to have been used later and to have been more popular in south India. According to texts and inscriptions of the fourteenth to sixteenth centuries, Arhadvali, a Jain acharya who was the second acharya after BHADRABAHU II, divided the Mula Sangha or original sangha into four sanghas: Sinha, Nandi, Sena and Deva. Gunaratna, a

SHVET-AMBARA scholar of the fifteenth century, states that the DIGAMBARAS were divided into four sanghas, but provides a different list: Kastha, Mula, Mathura and Gopya or YAPANIYA. In Karnataka after the ninth century, various sanghas and the ganas that belonged to them, are mentioned. The Sena Gana and Balatkata were said to be part of the Mula Sangha; the Mathura, Ladabagada, Bagada and Nanditata Gana of the Kastha Sangha. These ganas are mentioned before the twelfth century, but were not then connected with sanghas. From the lists provided, the terms sangha and gana seem to have been used interchangeably. A sangha could also represent a sect or a smaller community.

Sanjan   A town in Gujarat sacred to PARSIS, where they are said to have settled after their migration from Iran in the eighth or tenth century. The story of their arrival and of the later problems they faced is narrated in the *Kissah-I-Sanjan*. The traditionally accepted date for arrival is 716, and for first consecrating the sacred fire here, 721 CE. An arrival date of around 785 is considered more likely, while some place it as late as the tenth century.

Sankisa/Sankasya   A village in District Farrukhabad in Uttar Pradesh which is an ancient site, sacred to Buddhists. Excavations have revealed that the early settlement here, dates from about 1000 BCE to the eighth century CE. Buddhist texts state that from here the BUDDHA ascended to the heaven of the thirty-three gods, where he met his mother, MAHAMAYA, who had died when he was just seven days old, and preached to her the message of DHAMMA. After three months in heaven, when he decided to return, the god INDRA created triple stairways for his descent. The middle one was of gold, the left of crystal, and the right of silver. While the Buddha descended on the gold stairs, BRAHMA, holding a white whisk over him, accompanied him on the right stairway, and Indra on the left. Then all the DEVAS or gods showered flowers on them. Buddhist legends recount that these stairs existed for several centuries. Later, kings set up stairs at the same site, of brick and stone inlaid with precious substances, and several STUPAS and monasteries were erected here. When the Chinese pilgrim XUANZANG, visited Sankisa in the seventh century, he recorded that there were four Buddhist monasteries with 1000 monks, all of the SAMMATIYA school. There were also Hindu SHAIVITE temples.

The site has remains of stupas and a monastery, as well as an ASHOKAN PILLAR.

sannyasi   A person who has renounced the world and become a wandering ascetic. There are broadly two categories of sannyasis. (1) In the four-fold system or the four ASHRAMAS of traditional Hindu life, that of the sannyasi represented the fourth stage. At this time the person left his life in the forest and became a homeless wanderer. This stage thus helped to free a person of all attachments, focus on god, and prepare for death and the next life. Thus, according to this interpretation, every male person of the higher castes, became a sannyasi towards the end of his life. This is no longer followed.

(2) A person in search of spiritual truth could leave home and become a sannyasi, renouncing a worldly life, at any point of time. This was usually motivated by a genuine spiritual search, but in a social system where one's role in life was determined by one's birth, it was also the only legitimate means of opting out of society. The same role was played by the Buddhist SANGHA where many of the women who joined wrote of their relief at escaping oppressive lives. In the ninth century the philosopher SHANKARA founded the DASNAMIS, ten orders of sannyasis, giving them a formal structure, but sannyasis also existed outside this structure. The Dasnami and other sannyasi orders still exist. Sannyasis at times became involved in political movements, particularly in the freedom movement against the British.

The terms sannyasi and SADHU are often used interchangeably.

Sanskrit   One of the main languages of ancient India, considered a divine language. According to most scholars it was derived from a common language known as INDO-EUROPEAN, while some believe it is of Indian origin. Proto-Dravidian words of the languages of south India also occur in Vedic Sanskrit.

The earliest extant Sanskrit text is the RIG VEDA, usually dated to between 1500 and 1000 BCE. Later Vedic texts, the north Indian epics of the *MAHABHARATA* and *RAMAYANA*, the DHARMA SHASTRAS, DHARMA SUTRAS and PURANAS, are among the vast body of sacred Hindu literature composed in Sanskrit. MAHAYANA Buddhist texts, as well as some Jain texts, were also written in Sanskrit, though earlier Buddhist and Jain texts used PALI or some form of PRAKRIT, respectively. Texts continued to be composed in Sanskrit, though as regional languages arose, much devotional literature was composed in them. In medieval days Sanskrit texts were translated into Persian and Arabic, while from the eighteenth century, they became known in European languages. Sanskrit is still an important language for the study of religion and ancient texts, and is used in ceremonies and sacrificial rituals.

sant   A term for a holy man or saintly person.

Santhal religion   Santhals, a large tribal group, live mainly in Bihar, Jharkhand, West Bengal and Orissa, and speak Santhali, a MUNDA language. Some have converted to Christianity, while others are influenced by Hinduism, though at the same time they worship their own deities. According to one of their myths, the first people originated from the eggs of a wild goose. The whole world was full of water, and Pilchu Haram and Pilchu Budhi, born from the eggs, had no place to stand. Then Thakur (god), with the help of a crocodile, fish, tortoise, crab, and other aquatic creatures, brought earth up from the bottom of the ocean, and created a place for them. Pilchu Haram and Pilchu Budhi married, and had seven boys and seven girls, who in turn married each other, and had children. The descendants of each of the seven couples then became seven clans, who did not marry within the clan. Today there are twelve clans, as well as sub-groups.

The chief deity is Sing Bonga, the sun god, also referred to as Thakur, who is both creator and destroyer. Marang Bonga is second in importance, while there are a number of other Bongas (deities or spirits) who are worshipped. The main festivals include Sohrai in November December; Baha, in February–March, heralding the flowering of the sal tree and the beginning of spring; and Bandhana Puja, in April–May, when all the gods are worshipped together. SHIVA and DURGA are among the Hindu deities that are often incorporated in their pantheon.

The naik or village priest has a central role in the ceremonial worship of the deities.

Sant-Nirankari   A Sikh sect that traces its origin to Baba Buta Singh (1873–1943). Along with his disciple Avtar Singh, he founded the Sant Nirankari Mission in 1929–30. After Partition, Avtar Singh moved the headquarters of the Mission from Rawalpindi to Delhi. The Sant Nirankari Mandal was founded in 1948, and branches were soon established in other cities. In 1962–63 Avtar Singh made Baba Gurbachan Singh the guru, preferring to remain an ordinary devotee. Orthodox Sikhs opposed the sect, and conflicts led to the assassination of Gurbachan Singh in April 1980. He was succeeded by his son Hardev Singh (b. 1954), who is still the guru. New branches were established by Hardev Singh, and the Mission spread to other countries. Baba Buta Singh was originally a NIRANKARI, though the Sant Nirankari is not accepted by the Nirankaris or by other Sikh groups. The sect reveres the GURU GRANTH SAHIB and the ten Sikh gurus, and uses Sikh symbols, but apart from this has certain differences from other Sikh sects. It has additional texts, including the *Avtar Bani*, a collection of verses by Avtar Singh, and reveres its own leaders as much as the early gurus.

The Sant Nirankari welcomes people from all communities and religions, and its followers include a number of non-Sikhs.

Santoshi Ma   A Hindu goddess whose worship became popular in the 1960s and '70s. Santoshi Ma, the goddess of fulfilment or contentment, was virtually unknown before the 1960s. At that time some pamphlets describing the goddess were circulated, and her worship began to spread in parts of western and northern India. According to the myths which were generated, she was the mind-born daughter of the god GANESHA.

It was, however, a Hindi film, *Jai Santoshi Ma*, released in 1975, that really made her popular. Elaborating on the myths in the pamphlet and introducing a parallel story of a suffering Bahu (daughter-in-law) who achieved happiness by worshipping the deity, the film was a great success, and led to the widespread worship of Santoshi Ma. Such worship could be done at home, without the intervention of a priest, and involved offering gur (unrefined sugar) and channa (chickpea) to the deity, and observing a partial fast on Fridays, for the fulfilment of a wish. Temples dedicated to Santoshi Ma were erected in many parts of the country. Though Santoshi Ma is a relatively new deity, she is not considered new, as she is another manifestation of divine feminine power, or SHAKTI. The film introduced myths that led to her acceptance by other female deities, such as LAKSHMI and PARVATI, and she soon became a recognized part of the Hindu pantheon. A new film on Santoshi Ma was made in 2006, but did not gain the same popularity as the first one.

saoshyants   A term used in Zoroastrianism, indicating a guide or saviour. In the GATHAS, the term applies to all who attempt to establish good in the world, who struggle to uphold truth and justice and perform right actions. In later Zoroastrianism, the term came to mean a future saviour who will guide the people towards the truth. In PAHLAVI texts it is stated that saoshyants will appear at the end of the cycle of creation, and bring about the FRASHOKERETI or renewal of existence. The idea of a future saviour in Judaism, Christianity and Islam was probably derived from Zoroastrianism. The concept of MAITREYA in Buddhism and of KALKI in Hinduism, are also thought to have Zoroastrian origins.

Sarala Dasa   A poet of the fourteenth or fifteenth century who rewrote the MAHABHARATA in colloquial Oriya, using a local background. Its characters are ordinary people in familiar settings. He also wrote the *Vilanka Ramayana*, a version of the RAMAYANA, and the *Chandi Purana*, which were popular in the Orissa region. His real name was Sidheswar Parida, but he took the name Sarala Dasa, as he worshipped the deity Sarala Devi, a local goddess.

Sarama   A name used in ancient texts.

(1) In the RIG VEDA, she is the dog of the god INDRA. In later texts, she is the mother of the SARAMEYA, the two dogs who accompany the god YAMA.

(2) In the BHAGAVATA PURANA, Sarama is one of the daughters of DAKSHA, from whom all wild animals are descended.

(3) Another Sarama is mentioned in the RAMAYANA. She was the wife of Vibhishana, the brother of RAVANA, and was kind to SITA when she was captured by RAVANA.

Saramati   A Buddhist philosopher who lived between 350 and 450, and founded a school of MAHAYANA Buddhism based on the TATHAGATHA-GARBHA concept. Saramati systematized this theory and wrote a commentary on the *Ratna-gotravibhaga*, a text attributed in Tibetan Buddhism to MAITREYANATHA, but thought by some scholars to have been composed by Saramati.

Sarameya Two watchdogs of the Hindu god YAMA, the god of the dead. They had four eyes each, and their names were Shabala and Shyama. Their mother was SARAMA, the dog of INDRA. In several ancient religious myths, dogs are associated with the underworld and the dead. In Zoroastrianism, YIMA, the counterpart of YAMA, had four dogs. In Zoroastrian traditions, when a person died, a four-eyed dog was brought to view the dead body, while in the *Arda Viraf Namah*, a Zoroastrian text, Zerioug Goash is a dog that guards the CHINVAT BRIDGE. In Greek myths, the dog Kerberos (Cerberus) guards the underworld; he has three heads, a dragon's tail and snakes on his back. In Egyptian myths, Anubis, with a jackal's head, was called the 'opener of the way' to the land of the dead.

Sarasvati A Hindu deity, goddess of music and learning. In the RIG VEDA she is the goddess of the river SARASVATI, but in the BRAHMANAS she is also associated with Vach or speech and with healing. Later she became the goddess of wisdom and music. She is the wife of BRAHMA, and sometimes his daughter.

According to the *MATSYA PURANA*, Brahma created her from his own effulgence, and her other names are Shatarupa, SAVITRI, GAYATRI and Brahmi or Brahmani. According to the *SKANDA PURANA*, Gayatri, Savitri and Sarasvati, are three different deities. The *DEVI BHAGAVATA PURANA* states that she is one of the five Shaktis of Krishna. In some myths she is associated with VISHNU and is his second wife, representing spiritual values, while LAKSHMI represents power in the material world. Sarasvati has a number of names indicating her various aspects. Thus she is Smritishakti, the power of memory; Jnanashakti, the power of knowledge; Kalpanashakti, the power of imagination; Pratibha, intelligence; Vedagarbha, the source of the Vedas, as well as other similar names. Sarasvati is also known as Lalita and SHARADA. In sculpture and art she is depicted as a graceful young woman, holding a vina (a traditional stringed instrument), a mala or string of beads, a water pot, and a book. Her VAHANA is a white swan. Though the wife of Brahma, she is usually worshipped independently, and is a popular goddess even today. All musical performances begin with an invocation to her, and she is worshipped by writers, poets and students.

Sarasvati, river A sacred river, first mentioned in the RIG VEDA as a mighty river flowing into the sea. According to later Vedic literature, the Sarasvati disappeared in the sands of the desert. This river is usually identified with the Ghaggar, a semi-dry river that begins in the Shivalik hills to the west of the YAMUNA. Its dry river bed crosses Rajasthan and flows onward as the Hakra. The Sarasvati has alternatively been identified with a dry river flowing through Gujarat. Other identifications include a river in Afghanistan.

It is also possible that the same name was used for different rivers, and the historical importance of the original Sarasvati led to the name being used in a generic sense for a number of sacred rivers. The *MARKANDEYA PURANA* states that all sacred rivers are the Sarasvati, all sea-going rivers are the GANGA (1V.11.30). The *MAHABHARATA* states that the Sapta Sarasvati (seven Sarasvatis) covered the universe, and wherever she was summoned she made her appearance. Thus she appeared under different names at PUSHKARA, Naimisha, GAYA, northern Koshala, KURUKSHETRA and Himavat, usually at the time of a sacrifice. At DAKSHA's sacrifice at Gangadvara, she appeared by the name Surenu.

The seven Sarasvatis and the seven Gangas are frequently referred to; the Sarasvati is also mentioned as one of the seven Gangas. The Sapta Sindhava, referring to the seven rivers of the area west of the YAMUNA, is another common term.

According to later texts, the Sarasvati joined the GANGA and YAMUNA at PRAYAGA. As there is no such river here, this has been taken to have a symbolic meaning, with the Sarasvati representing the SUSHUMNA and the GANGA and YAMUNA the two NADIS on either side of it.

Sarhul A festival celebrated by the MUNDA tribe in the Jharkhand region, when all the Munda deities are propitiated. It takes place in March/April and continues for several days. The Pahan, or village priest, leads the worship while devotees offer sal flowers.

Sarkar, Prabhat Ranjan The founder of the ANANDA MARGA, a spiritual organization. He was also known as Shri Shri Anandamurti. Born in 1921 in Bihar, he became a railway official, but at the same time experimented with various spiritual practices. He developed a modern form of TANTRA Yoga, and established the Ananda Marga in 1955. In addition he had a number of different ideas and concepts. His philsophy of Neo-Humanism, aimed at inculcating a love of all, including animals, plants and inanimate objects. He started a global plant exchange programme to save and propagate plant species, and founded some animal sanctuaries. Another of his ideas was the Progressive Utilization Theory (PROUT) for collective welfare, which aimed at the maximum utilization and distribution of resources, physical, mental and spiritual. Despite these valuable programmes, he and his followers were said to be engaged in sectarian violence, though they claimed they were being persecuted because of their growing influence. Sarkar was arrested in 1971 and imprisoned, and released only in 1978.

After his release, he developed new ideas, including that of Microvita, the theory of emanations of pure consciousness, which are the building blocks of life. He died in 1990, but the Ananda Marga continued to grow in strength.

Sarnath An ancient site near VARANASI in Uttar Pradesh, sacred to Buddhists, but also associated with Hinduism and Jainism.

Here the BUDDHA preached his first sermon in a Deer Park (Mrigadava). According to Buddhist texts, the Buddha once lived here in a previous life, as king of a herd of deer. He was then named Sarangnatha, from which the name Sarnath is derived. A previous Buddha, named Kashyapa, once lived here as well. The place also used to be called Isipatana, or in some texts, Rishipatana. The first SANGHA or community of Buddhist monks was founded here by the Buddha. ASHOKA, the Mauryan emperor, erected a STUPA here, known as the Dharmarajika Stupa, and near it a pillar with a capital of four lions back to back, which today forms India's National Emblem. On the pillar is an inscription regarding a schism in the sangha, stating that dissenting monks and nuns would be excommunicated.

Several other stupas, shrines and VIHARAS or monasteries were constructed here at different times, and flourished up to the twelfth century. FA-HSIEN, the Chinese pilgrim of the fifth century, recorded that there were four stupas and two viharas here. XUANZANG, who came here in the seventh century, said there was a vihara here with eight divisions and 1500 Buddhist brethren, all belonging to the SAMMATIYA school. There was also a Buddhist temple and a life-size image of the Buddha. Later, Sarnath was protected by the Pala kings (750–1050). Kumara-devi, a queen of the Gahadavala dynasty, gave a donation to the site in the first half of the twelfth century.

Subsequently, Sarnath was neglected and destroyed. In the nineteenth century, sixty cartloads of carved stone were taken from the site and used to build an embankment. Many of the rich Buddhist artefacts at Sarnath have been lost, including a green marble relic casket, though a number of images and remains are preserved at the site and in the site museum. Among the remains is the Dhamekh Stupa, probably constructed in the fourth or fifth century, and the Chaukhandi Stupa, of uncertain date. There is a brick temple, erected on the spot where the Buddha preached, dated to around the same time as the Dhamekh Stupa. A colossal BODHISATTVA image belongs to the time of KANISHKA (first century CE), and there are numerous Buddha and Bodhisattva images of the Gupta period (fourth to sixth centuries), which, with their fine carving and depiction of inner serenity, represent the height of Buddhist art.

This is one of the four holiest places for Buddhists, who come here from all over the world. The Deer Park has been recreated and there are modern Buddhist structures here, including the Mulgandha-kuti Vihara of the MAHABODHI SOCIETY.

According to Jain tradition, this was the birthplace of the eleventh TIRTHANKARA, known as Shreyansa, and the place was called Simhapuri.

As nearby Varanasi is important for SHAIVISM, there is some SHAIVITE influence here, and miniature LINGAS are among the artefacts found. According to Hindu tradition, Sarangnatha is the name of a form of the god SHIVA, installed in a temple here.

sarpa satra Ancient texts record snake sacrifices (sarpa satra), where snakes were killed in large numbers, not to propitiate the gods, but as a form of revenge. One example is the sacrifice of King Janamejaya, described in the MAHABHARATA, undertaken because his father Parikshit was killed by the bite of a snake. Priests recited MANTRAS that compelled snakes to come from all over and throw themselves into the sacrificial fire. TAKSHAKA, king of the snakes, took refuge with the god INDRA, but finally was compelled to reach the sacrifice. Meanwhile the serpent VASUKI asked his sister Jaratkaru to find a way to save them, and she sent her son Astika, a young RISHI to whom Janamejaya owed a favour. Astika asked the king to stop the sacrifice, and he had to agree because he had promised to grant any wish of his. Takshaka was thus saved. Astika then blessed the snakes that had been killed, so that they might all attain salvation. The story also appears in the BHAGAVATA PURANA. Snake sacrifices have been recorded in other ancient cultures.

Sarvastivada A Buddhist sect of the HINAYANA tradition. The Sarvastivada probably developed from the STHAVIRAVADA around the middle of the third century BCE. According to a Chinese tradition, their philosophy was formalized in Kashmir and MATHURA at the time of KANISHKA, the Kushana ruler of the first century CE, when the fourth BUDDHIST COUNCIL was held. The Sarvastivada were prominent all over the north-west, Kashmir and the upper Ganga plains until the seventh century. Their ideas are summarized in the MAHAVIBHASHA. They believed that everything exists (*sarvam asti*) and always will exist, while the Sthaviravada hold that the past and future are non-existent. The Sarvastivada state that the past, present and future coexist, or else it would not be possible to think of them in the present. Nor would it be possible for KARMA to ripen over time. Even so, there is no individual soul or underlying being. One of their other differences with the STHAVIRAVADA was a belief that ARHATS could regress from the perfect state. VASUBANDHU was initially one of the greatest authorities of this school, and wrote the *ABHIDHARMAKOSHA*.

The Saravastivada had a Sanskrit canon of their own. No complete canon is now available in Sanskrit, but fragments and quotes are found in other texts. The main texts were translated into Chinese by the Chinese pilgrim I-CHING between 700 and 712, but there were earlier Chinese translations as well. The Sarvastivada *Vinaya*, in addition to rules for monks, contains legends relating to the spread of Buddhism in Kashmir and north-west India. The NIKAYAS were known as Agamas; for example, *Dirghagama* corresponds to the *Digha Nikaya*. These have some differences from the Pali texts. The Sanskrit ABHIDHARMA PITAKA of the Sarvastivada is entirely different from the Pali ABHIDHAMMA PITAKA.

Among the branches of the Sarvastivada were the VAIBHASHIKA, named after the *Mahavibhasha*. The SAUTRANTIKA contradicted Vaibhashika theories by appealing to the authority of the early sutras. The Sarvastivada no longer survives, but its sub-school, the Mula Sarvastivada, has an importance in TIBETAN BUDDHISM, which follows their Vinaya or code of monastic discipline.

Sastha A Hindu deity mentioned in the PURANAS. He is considered the northern counterpart of the god AYYAPPA in the south as well as of AYYANAR. Dharma Thakur, a village deity of Bengal was also absorbed into the concept of Sastha.

Satbis Deori A Jain temple located in Chittorgarh, a fort in Rajasthan. This fifteenth-century temple gets its name from the twenty-seven (satbis) small shrines that surround it. There are several Jain images in niches and some finely carved decorations. A tower rises above the sanctuary. Another Jain temple nearby is the Shringara Chauri temple, constructed in 1456 and dedicated to PARSHVANATHA.

sati An ancient practice in which a Hindu woman joined her husband on the funeral pyre when he died. It was mainly practised by the higher castes, and was supposed to be a voluntary act of devotion to the husband. The act of sati is named after the god SHIVA's wife, who killed herself because of an insult to her husband.

Vedic texts do not mention sati. There is one instance in the *RAMAYANA* in which Vedavati's mother is immolated. In the *MAHABHARATA*, PANDU, the father of the Pandavas, had two wives, and when he died his second wife, MADRI, immolated herself along with him, though the RISHIS present tried to dissuade her. In the same text, Sairandhri is forcibly burnt with her husband Kichaka. However, these are exceptional instances, as none of the numerous other widows created by the great war in the *Mahabharata* commit sati. The first definite literary evidence of the custom of sati is provided by Greek historians of the time of Alexander (fourth century BCE) who witnessed some examples of it in north-west India. The *Vishnu Dharmasutra*, which can be dated to the first century CE or later, mentions the custom but does not regard it as a duty. Several of the PURANAS, including the *VISHNU PURANA, PADMA PURANA, BHAGAVATA PURANA* and *BRAHMA PURANA*, cite instances of sati, which suggests that it was slowly emerging between CE 400 and 600.

Later texts looked on it as a meritorious act, though certain groups always opposed it. The first inscriptional evidence of it appears in the sixth century. By around 1000, it became an accepted practice among higher castes, particularly Rajput KSHATRIYAS. Through this act, both husband and wife were said to gain religious merit and attain salvation. Many women, including young widows, voluntarily committed sati, partly because it was glorified and praised, and partly because the life of a widow was often made miserable by social restrictions. In other cases, women were forced to burn themselves against their will. AKBAR, the Mughal emperor of the sixteenth century, was one of the kings who banned and tried to prevent forcible sati.

Though sati was more common in the north, it also took place in southern India. According to detailed accounts of travellers in the Vijayanagara kingdom, which existed between the fourteenth and sixteenth centuries in the region of Karnataka, women voluntarily burnt themselves on the funeral pyres of their husbands. When the king died, all 500 of his wives were burnt along with him. In some sects where burial took place, the women were buried alive with their dead husbands.

Reform movements of the nineteenth century attempted to stop sati. Ram Mohan ROY of Bengal, founder of the BRAHMO SAMAJ, tried to prevent the burning of widows, though he was socially ostracized for this. Lord Bentinck, the British governor-general, supported his efforts, and a law was passed in 1829, applicable to all British Indian territories, making sati an act of homicide. Other reformers too, tried to improve the condition of women and prevent sati. Sati continued to take place in the latter half of the nineteenth century in territories under maharajas, particularly in Rajasthan, but gradually was controlled. The Commission of Sati (Prevention) Act of 1987 made all types of sati illegal, even if it was claimed to be voluntary. Stray incidences of sati still take place, and though illegal, temples are set up at the site, and the women venerated as deities. There are several older sati temples as well.

Practices similar to sati were known in other cultures. Herodotus, the Greek historian, reported that the Scythians had a custom of slaying the wives and attendants of deceased chieftains and others of high rank. In Viking myths, when the god Balder was killed, his wife Nanna joined him on his funeral pyre. There are other accounts of wives accompanying their husbands in death, from ancient communities in North America, Africa, Oceania, China, Japan and Korea.

Sati, goddess A Hindu deity, a form of the goddess PARVATI. According to myths, the god SHIVA was married to Sati, daughter of DAKSHA. Daksha did not care for his son-in-law and organized a sacrifice to which he invited all the gods, except Shiva. Several legends recount this sacrifice. In one, Shiva took the ferocious form of Virabhadra to destroy the sacrifice. In another, Sati insisted on going to the sacrifice, and when Shiva did not want her to go, took on the ten ferocious forms of the MAHAVIDYAS. A third story states that upset with the insult to her husband, Sati killed herself. Shiva, in tremendous grief, roamed the world carrying her dead body until VISHNU dismembered it and it fell to the earth. Wherever the pieces of her body fell, a SHAKTA-PITHA, a sacred site of great power, was created. Some texts list 108 sites, some name only four main sites, while others have varying numbers of such sites.

sattva One of the three GUNAS or qualities described in SAMKHYA philosophy. Sattva is the quality of purity, calmness and peace.

satyagraha A form of protest that was developed by Mahatma GANDHI, and included using truth and non-violence, even in political protests.

Satyapir A legendary sage, who is supposed to have lived in the fifteenth century, and who incorporated both Hindu and Muslim traditions. His worship was popular in Bengal and Orissa, and there are numerous mythical stories of his exploits in folk literature. Satyapir is said to have been an incarnation of Satya Narayana, a form of the Hindu god VISHNU, and of a Sufi PIR. He wore the Brahmanical sacred thread, and a scarf representing Islam. He could perform all sorts of miracles, and worshipping him brought prosperity and protection from harm.

Sauda, Mirza An Urdu poet who lived from 1713 to 1781. He was born in DELHI, the son of a prosperous merchant from Kabul. After the invasion of the Afghan, Ahmad Shah Abdali in 1757, he moved to Farrukhabad and later to Lucknow.

Though he was not attached to any SUFI order, his poems, as in the example below, reflect his mysticism and Sufi ideals:

We turned to the Kaba and the temple
In search of God,
Not realizing
He is in our hearts.

Saura Purana A Sanskrit text, an Upapurana or minor PURANA, which claims to be a supplement of the *BRAHMA PURANA*. The *Saura Purana* (Saura = sun) explains the LINGA cult, glorifies the Hindu god SHIVA, and links the worship of Shiva with that of the sun god, SURYA. It includes myths and legends, as well as three chapters criticizing the ideas of the philosopher MADHVA. It is an important text for the study of SHAIVISM, and in its final form can be dated to the thirteenth century.

Sautrantika A school of HINYANA Buddhism that developed from the SARVASTIVADA around the middle of the second century BCE, so-called because it focussed on the Sutras rather than on other texts. It rejected the Sarvastivada ABHIDHARMA PITAKA and used mainly their *Sutra Pitaka*. They denied that everything exists (sarvam asti) and stated that the subtlest SKANDHAS (aggregates) transmigrate from life to life, but they did not adopt the PUDGALA concept of an underlying permanent entity. They said that at the attainment of NIRVANA, the Skandhas cease to exist. Some identify the Sautrantika with the Darshtantika, so-called because they illustrated their discussions with comparisons (drishtanta), and who are criticized in SARVASTIVADA texts. Vasubandhu's *ABHIDHARMAKOSHA* summarizes some of their ideas.

Savitr, god A deity mentioned in the RIG VEDA, a sun god. Golden in colour, he is said to illumine the air, heaven, and earth. He is associated with PRAJAPATI, PUSHAN, MITRA and BHAGA, and sometimes seems identical with SURYA, but in other passages is distinctly different. He stimulates or arouses all that lives, protects worshippers and bestows immortality. Some scholars believe that in the Rig Veda, Savitr reflects the divine power of the sun in a personified form, while Surya represents the sun in a more concrete way. The sacred GAYATRI MANTRA is recited to this deity.

Savitri and Satyavan An ancient tale first narrated in the *MAHABHARATA*. According to this, King Ashvapati and his wife Malati prayed to the goddess SAVITRI for a child. After eighteen years their prayer was granted, and they named their beautiful daughter Savitri. When she grew up, Savitri chose to marry Satyavan, son of king Dyumatsena. Dyumatsena, however, was blind and had lost his kingdom, and Satyavan lived in the forest along with his parents. The rishi NARADA told Ashvapati that Satyavan had every good quality, but would die within a year. Nevertheless Savitri insisted on marrying him. After the year was over, the god of death, YAMA, came to take his soul away, but Savitri followed Yama, and finally she obtained, through her persistence, several boons, through which Satyavan was restored to life. In addition, Dyumatsena's sight and his kingdom were restored.

The story has been retold many times, and Savitri represents the ideal of a wife's love for her husband. In modern times Sri AUROBINDO recreated the story in his poetic epic, *Savitri*, which has 24,000 lines.

Savitri, goddess (1) A Hindu goddess, daughter of the sun, who was married to the god BRAHMA. Brahma was married to SARASVATI, Savitri and GAYATRI. According to some PURANAS, these were all names of the same goddess, but according to others they were different.

(2) Savitri is a name of the Gayatri mantra, dedicated to the god SAVITR.

Sayana A commentator on the RIG VEDA. He lived in the fourteenth century, and was a minister of several kings of the Vijayanagara empire. Sayana wrote commentaries on Vedic literature, as well as texts on grammar.

Sé Cathedral A large cathedral located in the city of Old Goa, constructed in the seventeenth century. A Latin inscription records that Dom Sebastiao (ruled Portugal 1557–78) ordered it to be built for the use of the Dominicans. The construction began in 1562 and took almost one hundred years. The body of the cathedral was ready by 1619, while the altars were completed only in 1652.

The cathedral is constructed on a laterite platform and measures 76 m by 55 m, with a 35 m high façade. Though it is rectangular in shape, the interior layout is cruciform in plan. It has a grand vaulted ceiling and is divided into a nave and two aisles by two rows of Corinthian pillars. Apart from the main altar, dedicated to St. Catherine of Alexandria, the church has six additional altars in the transept and eight chapels along the aisles. The additional altars are dedicated to St. Anna, Our Lady of Dolours, St. Peter, Our Lady of Sorrows, Our Lady of Three Necessities and Our Lady of Hope, while the chapels are dedicated to Our Lady of Virtues, St. Sebastian, the Blessed Sacrament, Our Lady of Life, St. Anthony, St. Bernard, the Cross of Miracles and the Holy Ghost. The Cross of Miracles was earlier located in a separate church and is so-called because it is said to have grown miraculously in size, till it reached its present height of 6.4 m.

The exterior of the cathedral is a mix of Doric and Tuscan styles, and the whole is influenced by the Renaissance architecture of Europe. It once had two bell towers, but only one remains today.

Sen, Keshab Chandra   The founder of a new branch of the BRAHMO SAMAJ and of the Nava Vidhan, a new religious sect.

Born in 1838 at Coolootola near Kolkata (Calcutta), after studying at Hindu College (1854–56), he went on to study philosophy and then worked in the Bengal Bank and later in the Calcutta Mint.

Right from his college days he was interested in religion and spirituality, and was continuously seeking new ways to express his ideas. In 1857 he set up the Goodwill Fraternity, an organization for students based on Unitarian theological ideals. The same year he met Debendranath TAGORE and joined the Brahmo Samaj, soon becoming its leading member. He introduced the concept of volunteer missionaries and inspired them to work to remove caste distinctions, child marriage and polygamy, and to improve the position of women. He advocated women's education and widow remarriage. He also founded a journal, *Indian Mirror*, to spread these ideas. These programmes brought him into conflict with Debendranath, who was still the head of the Samaj, and who believed social change should be a gradual process. In 1866 Sen founded a new Samaj, named Bharatbarsiya Brahmo Samaj (Brahmo Samaj of India). Tagore's branch came to be known as the Adi Brahmo Samaj. A new text, the *Shloka Samagraha*, was formulated for Sen's Samaj, putting together ideas from Hindu, Buddhist, Christian, Jewish, Islamic and Confucian texts, and a place of worship was built, combining the symbols and architectural features of a temple, a mosque and a church. Sen's Brahmo Samaj was open to all.

After visiting England in 1870, Sen, inspired by reformist activities there, returned to India and founded the Indian Reform Association. Under this association he set up educational institutions, including those for girls and for promoting adult literacy, as well as for vocational training. He also set up the Temperance Society and opened medical centres in Kolkata and its suburbs. He began publishing *Sulabh Samachar*, a weekly newspaper that highlighted the problems of the poor and underprivileged, and had a large circulation until 1877. The passing of the Brahmo Marriage Act in 1872, a liberal act allowing inter-caste and widow marriage, and prohibiting child marriage, was mainly the result of his reformist zeal.

From 1872, however, Sen underwent a change. Gradually he became more inclined towards a mystical and inward spirituality; he began to give spiritual initiations and to act on the basis of divine messages. He was associated with RAMAKRISHNA PARAMAHANSA for several years, which may have influenced him. Going back on his earlier beliefs, he married his minor daughter to the maharaja of Koch Bihar. In 1881 he renamed his organization Nava Vidhan (New Dispensation) and created a composite symbol for it, consisting of a cross, crescent and trident. Twelve disciples were appointed to spread its message, for he wanted it to become a universal religion. By this time, a group that found his new policies regressive had broken away from him, and founded the Sadharan Brahmo Samaj in 1878.

Sen's new religion did not find much favour, and he became disturbed and depressed, and though he was still revered, his influence declined. He died in 1884.

Septuagint   A term for the Greek version of the Hebrew BIBLE. The translation from the Hebrew was begun at Alexandria in the third century BCE. This is the standard version of the Bible for Greek-speaking Christians, and it includes other books that are not part of the Hebrew BIBLE, but are in the Christian text.

Sermon on the Mount   A term for the teachings of JESUS Christ as contained in the NEW TESTAMENT in the Gospel of Mathew, Chapters 5–7. These chapters are based on a sermon given by Jesus, probably on a mountain near Capernaum. The sermon begins with the Beatitudes, also found elswhere in the Gospel, that describe the qualities that are considered blessed. Each of the nine Beatitudes starts with the term 'Blessed' and the first Beatitude states 'Blessed are the poor in spirit, for theirs is the kingdom of heaven'. Other concepts considered central to Christianity are contained in the sermon, including the Lord's prayer and various ethical precepts. The sermon puts forward the ideal of love, even for one's enemies, instead of the old law of revenge, and recommends forgiveness of all. It was a favourite text of Mahatma GANDHI.

Setu Bandha   Another name for the line of shoals connecting India and Sri Lanka, also known as Rama's Bridge or ADAM'S BRIDGE.

Seventh Day Adventist Church   A Christian church that arose out of the Millenarian Movement of the 1840s, which believed that JESUS Christ will come again and rule over the world for a period of 1000 years. The term 'Adventist' thus refers to the advent or second coming. Seventh Day Adventists, who celebrate the Sabbath on Saturday, believe in salvation through faith in Christ, and focus on the message provided in Revelation, the NEW TESTAMENT text. Founded in 1860 and officially recognized in 1863, it was introduced in India in 1890. The world headquarters is at Silver Spring, Maryland, USA, and in India the main centre is at Pune, Maharashtra.

Shab-e-Barat An Islamic festival held in the middle of Shaban, the eighth month of the Islamic calendar. It celebrates the visit of the Prophet MUHAMMAD to Jannat ul-Baqt, one of the heavens. It is a day of worship and sanctity because, according to some accounts, on this day the wicked are purified and sins and merits are judged. Happiness and suffering are then allotted for the coming year, and decisions are made on who should die or be born. The whole day therefore is devoted to fasting and prayer, and some pray through the night as well. Ancestors are remembered at this time and FATIHA prayers offered at their graves. In India local customs were introduced: fireworks are set off and lamps placed on the newly whitewashed graves.

On this day halwa (sweet) is lovingly prepared and served, for it is said MUHAMMAD lost a tooth on this day, and so ate halwa.

This is considered a minor festival as it is not mentioned in the QURAN, but in the HADIS. In Judaism the festival of ROSH HASHANAH, ending in YOM KIPPUR, is similarly the time when God is said to judge the world.

Shab-e-Qadr An Islamic festival, the term commonly used in India for the LAILAT AL-QADR, or night of power. The festival takes place in the last ten days of the month of RAMZAN. The date is not fixed, and it can be on any odd-numbered day, that is, the 21st, 23rd, 25th, 27th or 29th, but normally takes place on the 23rd or 27th of Ramzan.

Shabuoth A Jewish festival, also known as the Feast of Pentecost, observed fifty days after PASSOVER on the sixth day of Sivam (May–June). It lasts for two days and is connected with the harvest festival of early times, when people offered the first fruits of their harvest to God. Shabuoth is also the day when God revealed the Ten Commandments to Moses on Mt Sinai, and thus marks the spiritual birth of Israel.

shadavashyakam A term for the six AVASHYAKAS or essentials in Jainism.

Shah Namah A text written by Firdausi, completed in CE 1010. It traces the legendary history of Iran from ancient times up to the coming of Islam. Legends include those of mythical Zoroastrian kings, such as Jamshed (Yima), Lohrasp and others, as well as of later kings known to history. The text states that kings are the representatives of God on earth, and describes a God who is omnipotent and omniscient, the creator of Zoroastrians, Jews, Christians and Muslims. Stories from the text form part of Zoroastrian legends, but the *Shah Namah* is also important in Islam, its theory of kingship being accepted by Islamic kings. Written in verse, it consists of 60,000 couplets.

Shahenshahi A Zoroastian sect that emerged in India in the eighteenth century in opposition to the KADIMI. The division into two sects was created by a dispute over the calendar. In 1745 a group of PARSIS adjusted their calendar according to the calendar prevailing in Iran, pushing the lunar calendar one month back. They came to be known as Kadimis, followers of the 'ancient' tradition, while those who opposed the move were known as Shahenshahis, followers of the 'royal' traditional calendar. Initially there were conflicts between the two groups, but now they live in harmony, though they observe different festival dates. The majority of PARSIS are Shahenshahis and most Zoroastrian temples follow the Shahenshahi calendar.

Shah-i-Hamadan Mosque A mosque located in Kashmir on the river Jhelum, not far from Srinagar, originally constructed in 1395. This wooden mosque was twice destroyed by fire and rebuilt in 1479 and 1732. Constructed on a masonry plinth, the mosque is a cube-like structure with a pagoda-style roof. Shah Hamadan is identified with Mir Sayyid Ali Hamadani (d.1385), who founded the HAMADANI sect. According to legends associated with the mosque, he flew through the air from Hamadan to Kashmir, to the place where the mosque stands.

shaikh/sheikh In Islam, a learned and holy man, a title given to many Islamic saints in India. It specifically refers to a leader of a SUFI order.

Shaiva Agamas Sanskrit texts that deal with the worship of the Hindu god SHIVA. There are twenty-eight Shaiva Agamas, said to have been composed by Shiva after the creation of the world, though they probably date to the seventh century CE and later. Each Agama has a number of Upagamas, or minor Agamas. The SHAIVITE sects who follow these texts include the SHAIVA SIDDHANTA, the Virashaiva or LINGAYAT, and the Kashmir Shaivas.

Shaiva Siddhanta A SHAIVITE school of thought that developed between the seventh and fourteenth centuries. Literally it means 'the doctrine of the followers of SHIVA'. It bases its philosophy on the VEDAS, the UPANISHADS and the SHAIVA AGAMAS, which are all Sanskrit texts, as well as the Tamil texts of the NAYANAR saints, the TIRUMURAI, and the MEYKANTA SHASTRAS, apart from other Shaivite works. It sees the supreme reality as Shiva, who is both the formless Absolute and the personal god and saviour representing love. Shiva operates through his SHAKTI, which, though a part of him, forms the link between pure consciousness and matter. Through Shakti, knowledge, action and desire come into being, creating the world and the individual souls. Shiva is Pati, the lord, and all the souls are pashu (literally, cattle). They are in bondage pasha, to the world, or material existence. Acting in the world, the souls, which are eternal, and have knowledge and the ability to act, become bound by false ideas and wrong actions. Destroying these bonds by right action and devotion to Shiva, the soul is freed from impurities and united with Shiva, though it retains its separate identity. Divine knowledge is obtained through Shiva, either directly through intuition, or through a guru. The four stages on this path are said to be charya, or external acts of worship, kriya or action, yoga or union, and jnana or knowledge, though these can exist simultaneously as well. Daily rituals are an essential part of this school. Certain principles of this school, i.e., of the three forms of Pati, pashu and pasha, are the same in the PASHUPATA form of SHAIVISM.

Shaivism   One of the three main sects of Hinduism, the others being VAISHNAVISM and SHAKTISM. Shaivism centres around the worship of the god SHIVA in his various forms, of the LINGA, his emblem, and of other deities associated with him, particularly PARVATI, GANESHA and KARTTIKEYA. Certain SHAKTA sects are also considered a part of Shaivism. There are innumerable Shaivite texts, as well as Shaivite sub-sects and cults.

Rudra, an early form of Shiva, is mentioned in the RIG VEDA, whereas Shiva is first referred to in the *Shvetashvatara Upanishad*. Shiva is described in the MAHABHARATA and the PURANAS. Several Upapuranas or minor Puranas also deal with the worship of Shiva, particularly the *Shiva Purana*. The *Shiva Gita* and the *Nanmarai* are other early texts dealing with the worship of Shiva. The BHAKTI movement brought in new trends, and the NAYANARS of the seventh to tenth centuries wrote devotional hymns to SHIVA in Tamil. Their collected verses are included in the TIRUMURAI, of which the Tevaram forms a part.

The *SHAIVA AGAMAS* and the *MEYKANTA SHASTRAS* are among other Shaivite texts, while additional texts are associated with various Shaivite sects. Among early sects is the PASHUPATA, said to be founded by LAKULISHA. Later sects include the Virashaiva or LINGAYAT of Basavanna, and various branches of Kashmir Shaivism. Another important school of Shaivism in south India is the SHAIVA SIDDHANTA. The KALAMUKHA, KANPHATA or NATHA YOGIS, Aghori and KAPALIKA, are also associated with Shiva, and are considered Tantric sects. Other Tantric or SHAKTA sects are those that worship Shiva along with Parvati as SHAKTI or female energy.

Within Shaivism, Parvati is also worshipped separately in her many different forms, as DURGA, KALI and other goddesses, and so are GANESHA and KARTTIKEYA. Shaivite temples, many of them with inscriptions, are found all over India. In south India, the Chola dynasty in particular, were patrons of Shaivism. SHANKARA was said to be a Shiva devotee and founded the DASNAMIS, Shaivite SANNYASI orders.

In Kashmir several branches of Shaivism were prevalent from around the eighth century, including Trika Shastra or the monistic school propagated by VASUGUPTA, Kallata, SOMANANDA, UTPALADEVA, ABHINAVAGUPTA, Kshemaraja and others, and often termed 'Kashmir Shaivism'. In this school, Shiva is the sole reality, but his energy or Shakti is worshipped in three forms, as Para, a benign goddess, and Parapara and Apara, two fierce goddesses who are forms of Kali. The PANCHA-MAKARA were used in the lower stages, but higher stages involved only meditative practices. The Trika was later absorbed into Kaula Tantrism. Krama Shaivism, another branch, included mystical cults of the goddess Kali and also used the Pancha-makara. There was another dualistic school, which worshipped Shiva as Svacchandabhairava, along with his consort Aghoreshvari. All these schools had Tantric aspects, but at the same time developed significant philosophical concepts.

Among Shaivite festivals, Shivaratri is the most important.

Shaivite/Shaiva   A follower of the Hindu god SHIVA or of any of the sects of SHAIVISM.

Shakambhari   A Hindu deity, a name of DURGA in her form as goddess of vegetation.

shakha   Literally, 'a branch', which in Hinduism refers to a branch or school of the VEDA. Each shakha had a different version and interpretation of the texts. According to Shaunaka's *Charana Vyuha*, an early text, there were five Rig Vedic schools: the Shakala, Bashkala, Ashvalayana, Shankhayana and Mandukayana. The term shakha is also used in different ways, and can refer to a branch of any sect or group.

shakinis   Female spirits who were attendants of the Hindu deities SHIVA and DURGA.

Shakta   A Hindu sect based on the concept of SHAKTI or divine feminine energy. Shaktas, those who primarily worship Shakti, see the feminine principle represented by DEVI or MAHADEVI as inherent in every aspect of the universe. The Shakta sect not only worships the outer form of the deity, who can transform herself into all forms, but the inner aspect as well. Thus the KUNDALINI is identified with Shakti, and the advanced Shakta attempts to raise it from the MULADHARA to the SAHASRARA CHAKRA. The SAMKHYA theory of PURUSHA and PRAKRITI is incorporated in Shakta philosophy, where SHIVA represents Purusha, and Shakti represents Prakriti. The sect has ascetic, philosophic, and Tantric practices, and was initially prominent in Bengal and Assam, though the worship of Shakti is widespread all over India. Other ancient civilizations, including Mesopotamia, Anatolia, Syria and Egypt also had the concept of a female generative principle. The principle exists even in later sects such as the Jewish KABBALAH and the medieval Christian Cathars.

Shakta Pithas   Sacred sites in Hinduism that are repositories of divine feminine energy. According to myths, Shakta Pithas occur where parts of the body of the goddess SATI fell when it was cut into pieces after her death. One hundred and eight such sites are mentioned in texts, along with the different forms of DEVI or Sati. Among the places and forms mentioned are VARANASI, where she is known as Vishalakshi, and PRAYAGA (Allahabad), where she is known as Kumuda. At HASTINAPURA she is called Jayanti, and at Kanyakubja (Kannauj), Gauri. She is KALI at Kalanjara, Ratipriya at Gangadvara (HARDWAR) and SITA at Chitrakuta. One of the most important centres is at Guwahati, where she is known as KAMAKHYA. Temples exist at several of these sites, and at other places as well, where local traditions state that a portion of Sati's body fell. Such sites are said to be very powerful, storing the energy or SHAKTI of Devi. They are also known as Pitha Sthanas or Devi Sthanas.

Shakti   The principle of female energy. The worship of the female principle has been traced back to the INDUS CIVILIZATION and even earlier, where 'mother goddess' figurines, and ring stones, thought by some to represent the YONI, have been found. Without textual corroboration, however, it is not possible to say whether these items were worshipped, or in what way. In the *Devi Sukta* hymn of the RIG VEDA, (X.125) the concept of feminine energy inherent in creation is explained. The goddess or DEVI is supreme and all-pervading. In this hymn the goddess says: 'I am the kingdom, the giver of wealth, the knower of all. I am the first of all rituals . . . I dwell in all things.' Two *Durgastotras* in the MAHABHARATA and the *Aryastava* in the HARIVAMSHA further expand the concept, while the DEVI-MAHATMYA section of the MARKANDEYA PURANA is the most important text describing different forms of Shakti. In the SAMKHYA philosophy, PRAKRITI is the equivalent of Shakti. Other PURANAS too contain passages on Shakti. Shaktis are named as consorts of some of the gods and depicted in images as the MATRIKAS. These represent aspects of one supreme feminine deity. Two texts, the *Saundarya Lahiri* attributed to the philosopher SHANKARA, and the *Lalita-sahasranama*, are expositions on the powers and aspects of Shakti. Shakti is most commonly associated with SHIVA, but also forms a part of other sects and religions. In VAISHNAVISM, eight Shaktis are named as channels for the energies of the gods. They are: Shri, Bhu, Sarasvati, Priti, Pushti, Tushti, Kirti and Shanti. The feminine principle is an integral part of VAJRAYANA Buddhism and is seen in Jainism in the VIDYADEVIS and SHASANA DEVIS. Reverence and worship of Shakti forms a part of all Tantric cults.

Shaktism   A term for sects that worship SHAKTI or female power, also known as SHAKTA sects.

Shakyamuni   A name by which the historic BUDDHA is commonly known. It means 'a sage (*muni*) of the Shakya clan'. Shuddhodana, the father of Gautama Siddhartha, later known as the BUDDHA, belonged to the Shakya clan.

Shalagrama   A type of ammonite or fossil that represents the Hindu god VISHNU. These fossils of an extinct species of molluscs, are found mainly along the river Gandak. They are said to be pervaded by the divine energy of Vishnu and are of different colours, marked with spirals. They are considered auspicious, and keeping them in the house and worshipping them brings good fortune.

Shambhala   A mythical Buddhist kingdom where the Bodhisattva MAITREYA and other BUDDHAS are said to reside. In TIBETAN BUDDHISM, it is said to be located to the north of Tibet, where the practitioners of the KALACHAKRA live. Shambhala is mentioned in Hindu texts, including the VISHNU PURANA and the BHAGAVATA PURANA, where it is said to be a village where KALKI, the future incarnation of the god VISHNU, will be born. Madame BLAVATSKY of the THEOSOPHICAL SOCIETY also described Shambhala, and it is a popular concept in New Age sects.

Shambuka   A SHUDRA described in the RAMAYANA of VALMIKI. After a BRAHMANA boy died in RAMA's kingdom, Rama, rising up in his PUSHPAKA vimana or aerial vehicle, searched the land for evidence of unrighteousness that could have caused the boy's death. He found Shambuka, a shudra, practising ascetic penances and chopped off his head with a sword. The gods praised Rama, as it was not right for a shudra to try and reach heaven, and the brahmana boy was restored to life.

This episode was used by the DRAVIDIAN MOVEMENT to condemn the *Ramayana* as an upper-caste text. Conversely, however, Valmiki, the traditional author, is worshipped by some lower-caste groups. Those who justify this incident state that modern concepts cannot be applied to the past, where the king had to maintain order according to prevailing customs and laws.

Shani   One of the NAVAGRAHA or nine planets, representing the planet Saturn. In Hindu mythology, Shani is the son of SURYA and Chhaya, or of BALARAMA and Revati. He is known as Ara, Kona and Kroda, and is depicted as a black man wearing black clothes, with a vulture as his VAHANA or vehicle. Sometimes he is associated with a crow. In astrology, Shani's influence is generally malefic, though it can alternatively lead to spiritual and mystical heights. In north India, Shani is propitiated on Saturdays.

Shankara, deity   A name of the Hindu god, SHIVA.

Shankara, Sri (Adi Shankaracharya)   One of the greatest philosophers of India, an exponent of the ADVAITA school of VEDANTA. There is some controversy about the date of his birth, but most scholars believe he was born in 788 and died in 820 CE. Though there are many myths, stories and conflicting accounts of his life, the broad outlines are given below.

He was born at village Kaladi in present Kerala. His parents, Shivaguru and Aryamba, were Nambudiri BRAHMANAS and devotees of the Hindu god SHIVA. His father died when he was a young boy, and he was then brought up by his mother. He displayed extraordinary intelligence, soon mastered all the ancient texts and philosophies, and somehow persuaded his mother to allow him to take sannyasa. He then went in search of a guru, and found him in Govinda Bhagavatapada. Govinda had been the disciple of GAUDAPADA and taught Shankara the Advaita philosophy that he had learnt from his own guru. Govinda then advised him to go to KASHI, and there Shankara composed commentaries on the *BRAHMA SUTRA*, *BHAGAVAD GITA* and UPANISHADS. After this he travelled through the country to restore true religion based on the Vedas and Upanishads. He defeated many philosophers in debate and converted them to his point of view. Notable among these was MANDANA MISHRA, the disciple of KUMARILA BHATTA. Mandana then became Shankara's disciple. To ensure that his principles and ideas were not forgotten, Shankara set up four MATHAS, or centres of religious authority and learning: the Jyotir Matha at BADRINATH in the north, the Sharada Matha at SRINGERI in the south, the Kalika Matha at DVARAKA in the west, and the Govardhana Matha at PURI in the east. According to some accounts, he set up a fifth Matha at KANCHIPURAM. He established the DASNAMI, or ten orders of SANNYASIS attached to these Mathas.

After completing this immense task, Shankara died at the young age of thirty-two, at KEDARNATH in the Himalayas.

Shankara's works include commentaries on ancient texts, including on the *Brahma Sutra*, ten or eleven Upanishads and the Bhagavad Gita; the *Upadeshasahasri*, and the *Vivekachudamani* are important philosophical texts. Other works attributed to him are the *Dakshinamurti Stotra*, *Harimide Stotra*, *Saundarya Lahiri*, *Dashashloki*, *Atma Bodha* (Knowledge of the Soul) as well as several others, though some scholars doubt whether all these works were his.

Shankara's philosophy has permeated Indian consciousness. The idea of the One Reality, BRAHMAN, of its identity with the ATMAN or individual soul, and of the world as MAYA or illusion, as well as the concept of KARMA, were known before Shankara, but it was he who explained each with indefatigable logic and established them in the Indian mind. Even today, every person in India is familiar with these concepts, though they may be understood at different levels and interpreted in various ways.

Though Shankara believed in the One Reality, he upheld certain traditional practices. He did so in order to remove Tantric practices that had crept into Hinduism, as well as to combat the threat posed by Buddhism. Some of his ideas are considered similar to those in Buddhism, and by reinterpreting these in a Hindu context, the importance of Buddhism was diminished. He maintained the traditional structure of caste and advocated LINGA worship.

His ideas were challenged by several later philosophers, chief among them being RAMANUJA and MADHVA.

shankaracharyas   A title by which the religious heads of the MATHAS established by the philosopher SHANKARA are known. The first four shankaracharyas of the four traditional mathas were chosen from among his disciples and were Padmapadacharya, Totakacharya, Hastamalakacharya and Sureshvara Acharya, earlier known as Mandana Mishra. The head of the Kanchipuram MATHA also uses the title shankaracharya. Later, other mathas began using this title, including Jain mathas.

Shankaradeva   A BHAKTI saint of the fifteenth and sixteenth centuries who worshipped the Hindu god VISHNU in his various forms.

Born in 1449 at village Bardowa in the present district of Naogong in Assam, his father was the shiromani or overlord of a number of local chieftains known as Bhuyans. The boy was born after prayers to the god SHIVA in a local temple, and hence was named Shankara. He lost his parents when still a child and was looked after by his grandmother and educated at the gurukula of a learned pandit, Mahendra Kandali. When he grew up his relatives insisted he take over as shiromani, and got him married, though his inclinations were for a religious life. After the death of his wife, he handed over his duties to his uncles and set off on a religious pilgrimage in 1481. He visited sacred places, including GAYA, PRAYAGA, MATHURA and PURI, and here became a devotee of Lord JAGANNATHA. He began to compose lyrical verses (bargitas) to Jagannatha and to Vishnu in his various forms. Returning to his hometown in 1493, he was persuaded to remarry but spent all his time in a temple, composing verses of devotion and reading and discoursing on sacred texts.

At this time in Assam there were several warring groups. As the Bhuyans faced problems from the Kacharis and the Koch kingdom, Shankara and his followers moved to the island of Majuli in Ahom territory, but after facing problems there too, they went to the Koch kingdom. Here he had initial difficulties, but finally the king, Naranarayana, befriended him. Shankaradeva then lived mainly at Barpeta, and is said to have died in 1568, when he was around 120 years old.

His life has to be seen in the context of the troubled and warlike conditions in Assam, and of the prevailing religion, which was based on SHAKTA and Tantric rites and involved massive animal sacrifices. Shankara was against all this, and his form of VAISHNAVISM gradually became the religion of at least a part of Assam. His philosophical base was Vedantic, but he believed in BHAKTI, prayers and worship. He was against caste and his followers included lower castes and tribals. Helped by his main disciple Madhavadeva, he composed songs and verses, and wrote books and plays. Among his songs were bargitas, compositions with different ragas or melodies, ghoshas, or couplets, and bhatimas or eulogistic songs. His plays *Rukmini-harana, Parijata-harana* and others on Vaishnavite themes, are still enacted in Assam. In his books *Bhakti-pradipa* and *Niminava-siddha-samvada* he explains the principles of bhakti. He also wrote other books, including *Harishchandra Upakhyana, Amrita Manthana*, and *Balichalana,* in which he retold stories from the PURANAS in simple verse.

Shankaradeva set up satras, Vaishnava religious centres or monasteries, for organizing and spreading Vaishnavism in Assam.

He is still revered as a great saint and reformer of Assam.

shankha The Sanskrit term for a conch. The shankha is considered sacred and is an emblem of the Hindu god VISHNU. It is sometimes personified as a Shankha Purusha, a male figure. Conches are blown at the time of prayers and on any auspicious occasion.

Shanti Durga Temple An eighteenth-century temple dedicated to the Hindu goddess DURGA, in the form of Shanti Durga. It is located a little outside the town of Ponda in Maharashtra. The main shrine has an image of the goddess, and an octagonal domed tower rises above. There is a secondary shrine and a rectangular MANDAPA with a gabled roof. The temple has glass chandeliers, wooden ceilings and silver screens with embossed doorways.

Shanti Suri A Jain philosopher of the eleventh century (d. 1040) who wrote a commentary named *Shishyahita* on the UTTARAJJHAYANA SUTTA. It formed the basis for later commentaries on this text.

Shantidas Jawahari A seventeenth-century Jain jeweller and banker from Ahmadabad, who was influential at the Mughal court. Shantidas constructed poshalas, or places where Jains stayed while fulfilling vows, and built a large Jain temple at Ahmadabad. In 1629 the Mughal emperor Shah Jahan granted the land where the poshalas were constructed, to the Jains. In 1654, AURANGZEB, then governor of the Deccan, built a MIHRAB in the temple, thus converting it into a mosque. When Shantidas appealed to Shah Jahan, the temple was restored. In 1656, Murad Baksh, another of Shah Jahan's sons who became governor of Gujarat, granted PALITANA to Shantidas for the use of Jain pilgrims, and Shah Jahan confirmed the grant. Murad took a large loan from Shantidas, which he later ordered to be repaid from the Gujarat revenues. Before it could be repaid, however, Aurangzeb imprisoned Murad. Later, Aurangzeb ordered the repayment and asked for Shantidas's help in conciliating merchants and others in Ahmadabad. In 1660 Aurangzeb in another farman or decree, acknowledged the help given by Shantidas to the army in the form of provisions. He also confirmed the Palitana grant.

Shantideva A Buddhist scholar and poet of the MAHAYANA school, who lived between the seventh and eighth centuries. His *Bodhicharyavatara* is essential reading on the path of the BODHISATTVA. Among his other works is the *Shiksha-samuchchaya*, a summary of Mahayana practice and thought, and *Sutra-samuchchaya*, an anthology of sutras from Mahayana texts. A verse by Shantideva epitomizing the compassion of the BODHISATTVA is often meditated upon by Buddhists. It states:

As long as the sky exists
And there are sentient beings in the world,
May I remain to help them
To relieve them of their pain.

Shantirakshita A Buddhist philosopher of the MAHAYANA school who lived from 680 to 740. He combined the ideas of the YOGACHARA-SVATANTRIKA and MADHYAMIKA schools and took Buddhism to Tibet, but did not have much success in spreading it there, as his concepts were too rational and analytical. His work was carried on by KAMALASHILA, but it was PADMASAMBHAVA who combined mystical techniques with rational concepts and succeeded in establishing Buddhism in Tibet. Shantirakshita wrote several texts, including the *Tattvasamgraha* and the *Madhyamakalankara.*

Sharada A name of the Hindu goddess SARASVATI. Sharada is also the name of the universal mother, the supreme deity representing the absolute.

Sharada Temple A temple dedicated to the goddess SHARADA, in her form as the supreme deity, located at SRINGERI in Karnataka. The present temple dates to 1916, but is a reconstruction of an earlier temple. The first structure is said to go back to the time of Sri SHANKARA in the ninth century, and consisted of a YANTRA, a sacred diagram, drawn by Shankara on a rock in the middle of the Tunga river. A sandalwood image was installed on this, and it was covered with a thatched roof. VIDYARANYA, the guru of the founders of the Vijayanagara empire, installed a golden image and added a tiled roof. The modern construction was started in 1907.

Sharada is the main deity of the Sringeri Matha. She represents the Absolute and has no consort. In her hands the goddess holds a jar of AMRITA, the divine nectar of immortality; a book, representing supreme knowledge; and a mala or rosary, symbolizing the aksharas, the divine syllables from which forms are created. The fourth hand is in chin mudra, a gesture indicating the identity of the individual soul with BRAHMAN. Sharada is another form of the goddess Lalita Raja Rajeshvari and is worshipped through the recitation of the *Lalita Sahasranama*. She is also called Sharada Parameshvari. Sharada transcends the three deities Brahma, Vishnu and Shiva, along with their Shaktis, and encompasses all these.

The temple has a GARBHA-GRIHA housing the deity, and a small ante-chamber in front, enclosed in granite. Around this is a passageway, and in front a large MANDAPA or pillared hall.

Sharaf-ud-din Yahya Munyari, Shaikh A SUFI saint of the FIRDAUSI ORDER who was popular in Bihar. He is also known as Shaikh Maneri because he lived in Maner in Bihar. Shaikh Munyari was saintly and liberal in his approach. He admired IBN AL-ARABI, but did not totally accept the WAHDAT AL-WUJUD doctrine, as he said the union of man and God was not possible. He was influenced by the Sufi saints, Attar, Rumi, and Iraqi.

Munyari initially studied with an orthodox scholar, Maulana Sharaf-ud-din Tauma, at Sonargaon. He came to DELHI in search of a PIR and became the disciple of Shaikh Najibuddin Firdausi. He meditated in a cave in the Rajgir hills, visiting Maner on Fridays for prayers, and became known as a spiritual ascetic. A small KHANQAH was built for him in Maner by his disciples, and later a large one by order of the Delhi sultan, Muhammad bin Tughlaq, but Sharaf-ud-din remained an ascetic by temperament. He had a good relationship with the Delhi sultan, and later with the sultan of Bengal. His disciples included both learned and ordinary people. He wrote the *Maktubat-i-Sadi*, a collection of one hundred epistles, while the first collection of his discourses is known as the *Madan al-Maani*. His disciple, Shaikh Zain Badr Arabi, compiled the *Khwan-i-Pur Nimat* on his teachings, and the *Malfuzat*, a collection of Munyari's utterances.

Shaikh Munyari died in 1381 and is still renowned in Bihar.

sharia/shariat A term for law in Islam, which includes codes of conduct for every aspect of life. Islamic law is based on the QURAN and the SUNNAH, along with IJMA (consensus of the learned) and qiyas or reasoning by analogy. IJTIHAD, 'the exertion of mental energy by jurists', was also used. The four main schools of SUNNI law (FIQH) were formed by the eighth century and consist of the HANAFI, the Shafi, the Maliki and Hanbali. The Hanafi code is most commonly used by Sunnis in India, while some follow the Shafi code.

The SHIAS of the ISNA ASHARI sect depend on the Quran, the Sunnah, and the traditions of the IMAMS, as well as ijma of Shia jurists, and aql (reason). Qualified scholars, the MUJTAHID, can make decisions after ijtihad. The *Al-kutub al-arbaa* (four books) are the main books for Shia law.

In India ISLAMIC LAW operates only in the personal sphere.

Shariputra A disciple of the BUDDHA. He was originally a BRAHMANA, but after listening to the discourse of a Buddhist monk he joined the SANGHA. He was close to the Buddha and quickly gained enlightenment.

shasana devata A term for a male guardian deity of a TIRTHANKARA. Each TIRTHANKARA has its own shasana devata and SHASANA DEVI.

shasana devi A term for a female deity who is a guardian deity of a TIRTHANKARA. Each TIRTHANKARA has its own SHASANA DEVATA and shasana devi, also known as a YAKSHA and Yakshini.

The shasana devis, though termed yakshis, are actually goddesses in Jainism. The shasana devis of the twenty-four Tirthankaras in sequence are: (1) Chakreshvari; (2) Rohini; (3) Prajnapti, (4) Vajrashrinkala; (5) Purushadatta; (6) Manovega, (7) Kali, (8) Jvalamalini or Jvalini; (9) Mahakali; (10) Manvi; (11) Gauri; (12) Gandhari; (13) Vairoti; (14) Anantamati; (15) Manasi; (16) Mahamanasi; (17) Jaya or Vijaya; (18) Tara; (19) Aparajita; (20) Bahurupini; (21) Chamunda; (22) Amra or AMBIKA; (23) Padmavati; (24) Siddhayika.

They are similar to the Jain VIDYADEVIS and have their counterparts among Hindu and Buddhist deities.

Shastra The name of a certain category of Sanskrit texts. Shastra, a Sanskrit word, originally meant an order, command or rule. It can also refer to teaching or good advice or council. Shastras include religious or sacred texts, scientific manuals and books of rules or precepts. For instance, DHARMA SHASTRAS are texts on right conduct, sanctified by customary religious law; SHULVA SHASTRAS provide information on measurement for sacrificial altars.

Shat Khandagama Sutra A Jain text sacred to the DIGAMBARA sect, also known as the *KARMAPRABHRITA*.

Shatrughna The son of the king DASHARATHA and half-brother of RAMA, described in the *RAMAYANA*. His mother was queen Sumitra, and he was the twin of LAKSHMANA. He was married to Shrutakirti, who was related to SITA. In later versions of the *Ramayana*, Shatrughna was said to be a partial incarnation (AMSHA-AVATARA) of the god VISHNU, to the extent of one-eighth.

Shatrunjaya A Jain temple city on Shatrunjaya hill, near PALITANA town in Gujarat. The hill reaches a height of 600 m and has a number of Jain temples. The *Shatrunjaya Mahatmya*, a work of about the eleventh century written by Dhaneshvara, describes the shrines and legends associated with the sacred city. It is also described in the *VIVIDHA TIRTHA KALPA*, a later text.

According to the traditional accounts in these and other texts, RISHABHA, the first Jain TIRTHANKARA, visited this hill, and the temple of Marudeva located here was first made by Rishabha's son BAHUBALI. Pundarika, a disciple of Rishabha, attained enlightenment here. Other Tirthankaras and Jain saints also visited the place, and according to the *Vividha Tirtha Kalpa* the five PANDAVAS, along with KUNTI, attained perfection here.

The existing temples were constructed in the sixteenth century and later.

Temples and smaller shrines are located on two ridges and in the valley between them, mostly clustered together in fortified enclosures known as *tuks*. They were founded mainly by wealthy merchants, and in general have plain exteriors, double-storey porches, elaborate gateways, corner bastions, and high towers. The sacred hill is visited by pilgrims every day.

Shattari   A SUFI order that came to India in the fifteenth century. The order was founded in the eighth century and was known as the Ishqiya in Iran and Central Asia, and the Bistamiya in Turkey. Shah Abdullah, who came to India from Central Asia in the fifteenth century, named it the Shattari, meaning 'fast runner', as he claimed it was the quickest way to reach perfection. He travelled across north India and Bengal, finally settling in Mandu, where Sultan Ghiyasuddin Shah (1469–1500) became his disciple. He died there in 1485. He wrote a text known as the *Lataif-i-Ghabiyya*, in which he explained the basic Shattari teachings. Among his most notable disciples was Shaikh MUHAMAMAD GHAUS, author of the *JAWAHIR-I KHAMSA* and other texts, and his elder brother Shaikh Phul. Other prominent Shattaris were Shaikh WAJIHUDDIN AHMAD (d. 1589–90) of Gujarat, Shaikh Isa, and Shaikh Burhanuddin of the seventeenth century, both of Burhanpur. Shattaris preached a mystical approach to God, accompanied by the control of breath, diet restrictions, and invoking the names of ALLAH under specific conditions. The order remained popular in Bengal, Gujarat and the Deccan until the seventeenth century, and even spread to Mecca, Medina, Syria, Malaysia and Indonesia.

shekhinah   A Hebrew word meaning 'dwelling' or 'presence'. In Judaism the term indicates God's presence in the world. The term can be translated as the 'divine light' or 'glory' of God.

Shesha/Sheshanaga   The king of the NAGAS or serpents, described in Hindu mythology. He ruled in PATALA, one of the LOKAS or worlds, and had a thousand heads. He is also called ANANTA. The god VISHNU sleeps on Shesha or Ananta in the intervals between creation and in this pose is known as Sheshayana. BALARAMA is said to be an incarnation of Shesha.

Sheshayana   A form of the Hindu god VISHNU when he sleeps on the serpent ANANTA or SHESHA.

Sheth Hathisingh Temple   An ornate Jain temple located in Ahmadabad, Gujarat, constructed in 1848 by a Jain merchant. The temple is in a rectangular court, entered through an elaborate gateway, and has three shrines, each with an image of the fifteenth TIRTHANKARA, Dharmanatha. Attached to the shrines are several MANDAPAS, and along the outer walls are other small shrines. Three spires rise above the shrines, while the mandapas have domed roofs. The temple has intricate carving and decoration.

Shia   One of the two main sects of Islam, the other being the SUNNI. Shias differ from Sunnis primarily in their views on the rightful successors of the Prophet MUHAMMAD. They revere Muhammad's relatives, including Fatima, his daughter; Ali, his son-in-law and cousin; and his grandsons, Hasan and HUSAIN. They also consider the IMAMS who followed as infallible. They do not acknowledge the Prophet's successors, Abu Bakr, Omar and Osman, and believe that Ali should have been made Caliph after the Prophet. The Imam has a spiritual function exceeding that of the Sunni Caliphs and is the interpreter of the law. Shias reject the Sunni belief that the Divine Being will be seen by the pious on the day of judgement.

In India, Shias first settled in Sind in the late tenth century and ISMAILI Shias remained prominent in part of lower Sind until the fourteenth century. Most north Indian Islamic rulers favoured SUNNIS. In northern India in the time of Sultan Razia (1237–40), a Shia, Nur Turk, tried to start a revolt, but did not succeed. In Sind and Gujarat the BOHRAS and KHOJAS were converted to the Ismaili Shia sect in the thirteenth or fourteenth centuries. ISNA ASHARI Shias seem to have been introduced in India in the fourteenth century, and according to some accounts they were patronized by Sultan Muhammad bin Tughlaq, but suppressed by Firuz Tughlaq.

After Timur's invasion (1398), Shias migrated from Iran to the Deccan. Sultan Yusuf Adil Shah of Bijapur (1490–1510) made the Isna Ashari faith the state religion. More Shia scholars came from Iran to the Deccan, and Shias were favoured by the Qutb Shahi rulers of Golkonda. In Kashmir, Shias came in conflict with Sunnis.

On the whole, Shias did not face problems from the Mughal emperors, not even AURANGZEB, who was a staunch SUNNI, but at times were persecuted because of opposition from the ULAMA. After the downfall of the Mughal empire in the eighteenth century, Shias and Sunnis became more hostile to each other.

There are over five crore Shia Muslims in India. In January 2005, Shia representatives formed the Shia Muslim Personal Law Board, breaking away from the all-India body, as they felt it was not tackling their problems. Separate Shia Waqf boards (charitable trusts) already exist in Uttar Pradesh and Bihar, and they want similar Waqfs established in other states.

Shia sects include the Isna Ashari or Imami, Zaidi, and Ismaili, among whom are the Bohras and Khojas.

shikhara   A term for the tower rising above a temple. It is particularly used for TEMPLES of the north Indian or Nagara style. Literally, the term means the peak of a mountain.

shiksha   The science of phonetics, one of the VEDANGAS or additional branches of the VEDA. It deals with the correct pronunciation and recitation of the Vedas.

shila   A term that means 'principle', but in Buddhism refers specifically to moral precepts. The pancha-shila or five precepts, similar to the five YAMAS of Hinduism, are to be followed by all Buddhists, while there are five additional precepts for monks and nuns. These additional precepts are: not eating solid food after noon; avoiding music, dance and drama; avoiding perfumes and other adornments; not using high beds; not touching gold or silver. In MAHAYANA Buddhism there are other shila for the BODHISATTVA path, including the PARAMITAS or perfections.

Shilappadigaram A Tamil epic, sometimes considered part of SANGAM LITERATURE, though usually assigned to a later date. The name *Shilappadigaram* can be translated as 'The Jewelled Anklet'. The author is said to be Ilangovadigal, the grandson of Karikala, a king of the Chola dynasty who ruled in the first or second centuries CE. References in the text indicate it could be somewhat later and some scholars assign it to the sixth century.

This verse epic narrates the story of Kovalan and KANNAGI, a married couple. Kovalan fell in love with the dancer Madhavi and spent all his money on her. Kannagi, however, remained faithful to Kovalan, and penniless, the couple reached the city of MADURAI. Kannagi then took off one of her anklets and gave it to Kovalan to sell, but in the market he was accused of being a thief because the queen had lost a similar anklet. The falsely accused Kovalan was put to death, and Kannagi, when she heard of it, stormed through the city in grief. Finally she was taken to the king, and when she showed him her remaining anklet he realized he had wrongly condemned an innocent man. 'I am no king,' he said, and in shock he fell down dead. Kannagi then tore off one of her breasts and threw it in the city, which went up in flames. Thus she destroyed the king and his city, and finally retreated to a hill where she died a few days later, rejoining her husband in heaven. Kannagi is worshipped as a goddess in the Tamil region, a symbol of a wife's chastity, devotion and loyalty to her husband. The *MANIMEKHALAI* is a sequel to this epic.

Shiromani Gurdwara Prabandhak Committee (SGPC) An organization founded in 1920 to look after the affairs of Sikh GURDWARAS. The SGPC is an elected body that exercises direct control over most of the historic Sikh gurdwaras, gives rulings on religious issues, runs some educational insitutions, trains Sikh preachers and publishes material on Sikhism. Sikhs contesting SGPC elections are normally backed by political parties.

Shitala A Hindu mother goddess worshipped in rural Bengal for protection from disease, particularly smallpox. Shitala is usually depicted dressed in red, seated on a lotus or a donkey. She was more popular in the days when smallpox was widespread.

Shiva One of the two most important gods in Hinduism, the other being VISHNU. Three gods, BRAHMA, Vishnu and Shiva, represent creation, preservation and destruction respectively, but Brahma is less important than the other two. Shiva is not only part of the trinity, but also a supreme deity, the ultimate source and goal. The Pashupata, Shaiva Siddhanta and some other sects view Shiva as equal to, or even greater than, BRAHMAN.

As part of the trinity, Shiva is a complex deity with several different aspects. According to A.L. Basham, Shiva's character, unlike that of Vishnu, is 'ambivalent', as he can be a moral and paternal god, or a god of outsiders, of those outside the Brahmanical maintream, worshipped in various ways. Several Tantric cults are also associated with Shiva.

Though some associate Shiva with the INDUS CIVILIZATION, this is only a conjecture, that has been challenged by other scholars. Historically, Shiva is not mentioned in the VEDAS, but an earlier form of the deity is thought to be the Vedic RUDRA. In the *YAJUR VEDA*, Rudra's other names are given as Kapardin, Sharva, Bhava, Shambhu, Shankara and Shiva, thus leading to his later identification with Shiva.

In the *Shvetashvatara Upanishad*, probably dating from the sixth century BCE, Rudra is described as Eka-deva, the One God, and is also known as Hara, Isha, Mahapurusha, Ishana, Bhagavat, Shiva and Maheshvara. The worship of Shiva is extensively described in the *MAHABHARATA*. Megasthenes, the Greek ambassador to the court of Chandragupta Maurya in the fourth century BCE, mentions the worship of Dionysius, thought to be his term for Shiva. A large Shiva LINGA found at Gudimallam in the Deccan is dated to the second or first century BCE, suggesting that there was linga worship at this time. PATANJALI, of about the same period, mentions Shiva Bhagavatas. These seem to be similar to the PASHUPATAS of the *Mahabharata* and later texts. Several PURANAS describe Shiva, his worship and the legends associated with him, while the SHAIVA AGAMAS and hymns of the NAYANARS are among other Shaivite texts.

Inscriptions, coins and Shiva sculptures are numerous from the first century CE, and increase at the time of the Gupta dynasty (300–550), though the Gupta kings were inclined towards VAISHNAVISM. Shaivism flourished in the Deccan and western India at this time, and from the seventh century onwards became popular in south India.

There are numerous myths and legends about Shiva in the Puranas and other texts. According to one story of his origin, Shiva, blue and white in colour, was born from Brahma and was known as Rudra, while according to another, he was born from Vishnu.

Shiva is depicted with anything up to five faces and always has three eyes. These represent his knowledge of the past, present and future. The third eye is in the centre of his forehead; a crescent moon above it indicates time measured through the phases of the moon. Around his neck is a garland of skulls, symbolizing destruction, or sometimes a snake, symbolizing fertility or the recurrent cycle of years. His hair is matted and gathered into a topknot or coil. Above it is the personification of the river GANGA, which he is said to have received into his hair. Thus he is also known as Gangadhara, the bearer of the Ganga. His throat is blue from the poison he swallowed at the time of the churning of the ocean for AMRITA. His consort is PARVATI or Uma, who has many forms, and was earlier born as SATI. The myth of the sacrifice of DAKSHA, father of Sati, and Shiva's exclusion from it is connected with the worship of SHAKTA PITHAS.

Shiva's other wife is Ganga, and his two sons are KARTTIKEYA and GANESHA. According to some myths, HANUMAN is also his son.

Shiva is most commonly worshipped in the form of a linga, which is both a phallic symbol and a representation of cosmic order and regeneration. There are several different types of lingas. His VAHANA or vehicle is NANDI, a white bull, and his favourite weapon is a TRISHULA or trident.

In general, Shiva exists outside established society. As a wandering ascetic, he has to be lured by PARVATI into a domestic setting with a family. Even so, they never live in a settled home, but in caves, mountains and forests. In the Himalayas are several places where Shiva is said to have lived, and which he visits even now, though his main abode is on Mt KAILASHA. Thus Shiva is a god of the mountains, untrammelled and free. He often sits in meditation, and his TAPAS or austerities are so intense that in one myth his veins are said to have ashes instead of blood.

Shiva's principal function is that of destruction and he fought a number of battles, defeating various demons. One flash of his third eye could reduce a person or god to ashes. But though he is the god of destruction, he is also the god of regeneration, known for his sexual vigour.

Shiva has different forms and names, each related to one of his various aspects or exploits. Among these are: NATARAJA, the god of dance; DAKSHINAMURTI, literally 'the south-facing', who is the univeral teacher; BHAIRAVA, the ferocious one; PASHUPATI, lord of animals, or lord of souls; Lingaraja, the personification of the eternal reproductive power of nature; Yogiraja, the god of ascetics who sits in meditation on Mt Kailasha, his hair matted and his body smeared with ash, his eternal meditation upholding the world; Augadh, the carefree reveller, worshipped particularly by Tantrics; Mahakala, the god of time, also known as Mahamrityunjaya or the conqueror of death; Shankara or Shambhu, the giver of happinesss, health and wealth; Mahesha or Mahadeva, the Supreme Lord; SADASHIVA, the eternal; BHUTESHVARA, lord of bhutas, which are goblins or ghosts and various other beings; Tripuraghati, Tripurantaka or Tripuranashana, as he destroyed the three cities (Tripura) of the demons; Jatandhara, as he has matted hair; Andhakaghati, the killer of the Asura Andhaka.

He has many more names, including Umapati or Girjapati, the consort of UMA or Girija, Kashinatha, lord of Kashi, Kedarnatha, Somanatha, lord of the moon, Ramanatha, lord of Rama, TYAGARAJA, etc.

Shiva can be worshipped along with PARVATI or alone. A special form with Parvati is ARDHANARISHVARA, where the two are conjoined. Shiva is also depicted in family scenes, along with his wife and sons.

Shiva temples are located all over India. VARANASI, the ancient KASHI, is a city particularly important for Shiva worship. Among the most important Shiva temples are the sites of the twelve jyotir lingas, at SOMANATH, KEDARNATH, KASHI VISHVANTHA, Mahakaleshvara at UJJAIN, OMKARESHVARA, MALLIKARJUNA, Vaidyantha or Baijnath dham, Ghushmeshvara, Bhimashankara, Tryambakeshvara, Nageshvara, and RAMESHVARAM.

Historically, the Cholas of south India were the dynasty most closely associated with Shiva. The Cholas built grand Shiva temples, including the BRIHADESHVARA TEMPLE and those at Darasuram and CHIDAMBARAM. Among modern-day Shiva temples is a huge monument at Chhattarpur on the outskirts of DELHI. Other significant temples include the Jogeshwari Cave Temple at ELEPHANTA. There are innumerable small Shiva temples, some of which consist only of a mud hut with a linga. See SHAIVISM.

Shiva Purana A Sanskrit text, a PURANA, which deals with the worship of the Hindu god SHIVA. Traditionally, the Purana consisted of twelve samhitas or books, but today has six or seven samhitas in different versions.

Shiva Sutra A text written in the eighth century by VASUGUPTA. It describes the basic principles of Kashmir SHAIVISM. It has short aphorisms on the non-dual nature of reality. Several commentaries were later written on this text.

Shivadvaita A monistic school of philosophy, based on the worship of SHIVA as the one deity, who, along with SHAKTI, is identical with BRAHMAN. This system was developed by SHRIKANTHACHARYA in the twelfth century.

Shivaratri A Hindu festival celebrated to honour and worship the god SHIVA. The festival takes place in February or March. On this night, Shiva is said to manifest himself as a jyotir LINGA, or pillar of light. Devotees fast during the day and chant a series of MANTRAS through the night. They gather at Shiva temples, that are decorated with flowers and lights, and make offerings to the LINGA. The following day there are feasts, songs and celebrations.

shloka A term for a Sanskrit verse. Shlokas are of different kinds and can include chants to deities, proverbs, short statements, or any kind of verse that is part of a longer composition. In a specific sense, shloka refers to a particular metre of verse.

Shodashi A Hindu goddess, who is one of the ten MAHAVIDYAS or great Tantric goddesses. In some texts she is called Tripura Sundari or Rajarajshvari. As Shodashi, she is a girl of sixteen and is depicted with a red complexion, or as a beautiful woman with the crescent moon in her hair.

Shoghi Effendi A leader of the Bahai religion, the grandson of ABDUL BAHA. Born in 1897, Effendi studied at Balliol College, Oxford. Before his death Abdul Baha appointed him his successor and the 'Guardian of the cause of God'.

Shoghi Effendi officially took over the leaderhip of the Bahai community in 1921, but because he was still in his early twenties he felt he needed time to prepare for the responsibility. Meanwhile his great aunt, Bahiyyih Khanum, the sister of Abdul Baha, helped him, and continued to support him until her death in 1932. Shoghi Effendi continued as Guardian until his own death in 1957. As he had no heirs and was unable to find a suitable successor, his writings became a source of authority for the future.

Shore Temple A temple of the Hindu god SHIVA located at MAMALLAPURAM in Tamil Nadu. It was constructed between CE 700 and 800 by Rajasimha of the Pallava dynasty and is named the Shore Temple, because of its location on the coast. It has a solid masonry structure that has withstood the storms and waves for centuries. The temple has three shrines: the shrine in the centre has an image of VISHNU sleeping on the serpent ANANTA; on the east is a shrine with a multifaceted LINGA carved from basalt stone. There is a SOMASKANDA panel on the rear wall. The third shrine, on the west, has SHIVA images. The two Shiva shrines have pyramidal towers with octagonal domes and the whole was once enclosed by a massive wall.

Conservation work has been carried out to preserve this ancient structure.

Shraddha A Hindu goddess. Shraddha means faith, which was personified as a deity in the RIG VEDA. In the BRAHMANAS, she is said to be a daughter of the sun god SURYA, or of PRAJAPATI.

shraddha (shraadha) A term in Hinduism for rites performed for ancestors. Daily, monthly and annual ceremonies can be performed, the last being known as PITRA PAKSH. During these ceremonies pinda or balls of rice are offered to ancestors, or PITRIS. The ancestors are of two types, distant and mythical, and immediate. The second category includes the father, grandfather and great-grandfather on both sides of the family. Shraddha is also performed for women. These rites are said to enable the ancestors to live in Pitri Loka, along with other Pitris.

Shrauta Sutras Sanskrit texts that deal with Vedic sacrifices and further explain the sacrifices described in the BRAHMANAS. Shrauta Sutras are attached to each of the VEDIC SAMHITAS. The RIG VEDA thus has the *Ashvalayana, Shankhayana* and *Shaunaka*; for the *SAMA VEDA* there are the *Mashaka, Latyayana* and *Drahyayana*. The *TAITTIRIYA SAMHITA* or *Black Yajur Veda* has the largest number—the *Apastamba, Baudhayana, Satyasadha-hiranya-keshin, Manava, Bharadvaja, Vadhuna, Vaikhanasa, Laugakshi, Maitra, Katha* and *Varaha*. The *VAJASANEYI SAMHITA* or *White Yajur Veda*

has the *Katyayana*; the ATHARVA VEDA has the *Kushika*. Another Shrauta Sutra attached to the *Atharva Veda* is the *Vaitana*, which is anonymous. The Shrauta Sutras form part of the texts known as KALPA SUTRAS.

Shravana Belagola A sacred Jain town in District Hasan, Karnataka, where there are a number of Jain temples, as well as the largest statue of BAHUBALI or GOMMATESHVARA.

The temples at Shravana Belagola are located within the town and on two granite hills that rise above it. Indragiri hill rises 143 m above the plain south of the village, and shrines line the 650 steps that lead to the summit, where the 17.7 m high monolithic image of Bahubali is located. Chandragiri hill to the north also has a number of temples. The images in these DIGAMBARA temples are mainly carved in black stone. Of particular interest among the many scattered temples here is the small 'ant temple', where offerings are made to ants, with the request that they do not enter the homes of the people making the offerings.

A Digambara Matha is located in Shravana Belagola, headed by a BHATTARAKA, where students study Jain scriptures as well as secular subjects. The matha has a collection of miniature Jain images created out of gold, silver and precious and semi-precious stones.

The religious monuments at Shravana Belagola were constructed from the ninth century onwards at the time of the Western Ganga dynasty. A number of temples were constructed in the twelfth century by Gangaraja, an officer of the Hoysala dyansty, while others were added by the later Vijayanagara and Wodeyar dynasties. Several inscriptions here provide historical information as well as information on Jainism.

Shravana Belagola remains a popular centre of pilgrimage for Jains.

Shravasti A town located in Shravasti district in Uttar Pradesh, sacred to Buddhists. Texts record that the Buddha often spent the rainy season here in the Jetavana vihara. Later legends recount miracles performed by the Buddha here. According to these, while seated on a thousand petalled lotus, he displayed a million manifestations of himself. To commemorate the Buddha's association with this place, two pillars and a stupa were constructed here in the third century BCE by the Mauryan emperor Ashoka. These were still standing in the seventh century when the Chinese pilgrim Xuanzang visited the site.

According to Jain sources, the third Tirthankara, Sambhavanatha, was born here, and his birthday is celebrated here every year at the time of the full moon in the month of Karttika (October–November). Shravasti reached its height by the first century CE, and exacavations reveal it was a prosperous town covering a large area.

Shridevi or Shri A Hindu goddess, a name of LAKSHMI. Literally, it means 'auspicious' or 'prosperous'. The name first occurs in the RIG VEDA, while the

Shatapatha Brahmana states that Shri emerged from PRAJAPATI.

Shrikanthacharya A philosopher who lived in the twelfth century, and was the founder of the philosophical system of SHIVADVAITA.

Shripala A saintly person revered by Jains, whose story is connected with the ritual of NAVAPADA OLI, which takes place twice a year.

According to the story in Jain texts, Shripala was the son of a king, but after his father died, his uncle coveted the throne and wanted to kill the child. His mother therefore fled with Shripala, then only five years old, and in desperation left him with a group of lepers. Shripala grew up to become their leader, and was known as Umar Rana, but unfortunately contracted leprosy.

Mayana Sundari, the daughter of another king, was married to Shripala by her father in a fit of anger, because she affirmed that everything was due to KARMA, and that her father though a king, had no say in her destiny. 'Suffer your karma, then,' said the king, marrying her to the leader of the wandering leper group. Mayana took care of Umar Rana and lived with him as a devoted wife. Accumulating good karma, the couple then met a Jain acharya, Muni Chandra, who advised them to practise Ayambil Oli, which can cure all diseases. After practising Oli nine times, Umar Rana was cured. Later, his throne too was restored to him, and the two lived happily ever after.

Shrivaishnavism A form of Vaishnavism in which the goddess SHRI or LAKSHMI is considered an inseparable part of the god VISHNU. Shrivaishnavism is based on the poems and teachings of the ALVARS, compiled by NATHAMUNI in the tenth century in the *NALAYIRA DIVYA PRABANDHAM*. Nathamuni's grandson, YAMUNACHARYA, translated some of these into Sanskrit in his text *Stotraratna*. His disciples were among the teachers of RAMANUJA. Ramanuja modified the teachings and made Shrivaishnavism a part of the Vedantic tradition. Thus Shrivashnavism has been called the socio-religious manifestation of Ramanuja's Vishishtadvaita. After his death the sect split into two groups, known respectively as the VADAGALAI (northern) and TENGALAI or Tenkalai (southern). The northern school, led by VEDANTA DESIKA, preferred the use of Sanskrit and believed that to achieve liberation or MOKSHA, human effort was necessary. The southern school, led by LOKACHARYA Pillai, used Tamil texts and affirmed that god's grace was sufficient to attain moksha. The centre of the sect is the Vishnu temple at SRIRANGAM.

shrivatsa A sacred mark or sign that indicates divinity or greatness. It is depicted as a whorl on the chest of VISHNU or KRISHNA, but has other forms, including a triangle or a cruciform flower. The shrivatsa appears on several deities including Buddhist and Jain images. It is associated with the goddess SHRI, indicating good fortune or auspiciousness.

Shroff, Behramshah Navroz The founder of the Zoroastrian ILM-E-KSHNOOM sect. Behramshah was born in a priestly family at MUMBAI (Bombay) in 1857, and did not have much formal education. He became a preacher of esoteric Zoroastrian wisdom around the age of fifty, on the basis of an incident that took place in his youth. According to his story, he left home at the age of eighteen and finally reached Peshawar. There he met a group of radiant-looking men who wore the SUDREH and KUSTI, emblems of Zoroastrianism, and took him with them to the Daemavand mountain in the Alburz range, where they lived in a community of about 2000, including men, women and children, in a secluded place named Firdaus (paradise). Some of these people were those who had eternal life and had been the MAGI at the birth of Christ. Behramshah stayed with them for three years, during which time they taught him the hidden meaning embedded in Zoroastrian rituals, stories and legends. The Ilm-e-Kshnoom has a group of followers in India, though many PARSIS remain sceptical about its claims. Its teachings are similar to the Theosophical ideas that spread in the early twentieth century. Behramshah died at Surat in 1927.

Shruti literature One of the two categories of sacred literature in Hinduism, the other being SMRITI. Shruti is that which is heard or divinely revealed, while Smriti is remembered or composed through divine inspiration. Shruti literature, which is the most sacred, comprises the VEDIC SAMHITAS, the BRAHMANAS and also usually the ARANYAKAS and UPANISHADS.

Shuddhadvaita A system of philosophy founded by VALLABHACHARYA in the sixteenth century. Shuddhadvaita is explained as pure non-dualism. According to this world, the individual soul, KALA or time, and PRAKRITI or MAYA, are eternal and part of BRAHMAN. Thus the world is not an unreal illusion as stated by SHANKARA, but is as real as Brahman, and the individual thus has the same essence as Brahman. This essence can be realized through BHAKTI or devotion to the Hindu god KRISHNA, who is identified with Brahman. The whole universe is Krishna, therefore everything is an object of devotion. Since the world is Krishna, every aspect of it is also to be enjoyed.

shudra The lowest of the four traditional castes in Hinduism. Acording to a late verse in the RIG VEDA, they emerged from the feet of PURUSHA, the primeval man. In Vedic times, the four castes were relatively equal. The *Mimamsa Sutra* of JAIMINI states that shudras could perform Vedic sacrifices, study the scriptures and wear the sacred thread. Later, however, they were barred from all this. Over the centuries, numerous sub-castes emerged and shudras who were peasants attained a higher status, while other groups who were considered untouchables were not allowed to mingle with higher castes, and were denied all rights.

Several saints and religious leaders, including some of the Maratha BHAKTI saints, the ALVARS and the

NAYANARS, denied the importance of caste, while reform movements of the nineteenth century, such as the BRAHMO SAMAJ and ARYA SAMAJ, worked to remove untouchability. Mahatma GANDHI tried to improve the status of the lowest castes and renamed them HARIJANS, or children of God. B.R. AMBEDKAR, a leader from the Mahar caste, felt that no real change could take place within Hinduism and led them in a mass conversion to Buddhism.

The lowest castes were listed in a schedule in 1935, which was incorporated into the Constitution in 1949–50, and therefore are known as Scheduled Castes. Since the 1970s they have called themselves DALITS, and are still engaged in a struggle for equality.

Other shudras are included in a category known as Other Backward Classes (OBCs). Dalits are sometimes considered outside the shudra category and are referred to as a fifth caste, or outside the caste system. Both OBCs and dalits today have a significant role in politics.

Shukra One of the NAVAGRAHA or nine planets in Hindu mytholgy, and a name of the planet Venus. Shukra literally means 'the bright one' and comes from the Sanskrit root shuch, to shine. It also means semen, sperm or seed.

Shukracharya The name of the preceptor of the ASURAS, who is sometimes identified with the planet SHUKRA, or is considered its regent. He is also known as Kavya Ushanas, who is mentioned in the RIG VEDA in association with INDRA, and is similar to KAVA-USHAN of Zoroastrian texts. In some Puranas, Shukra is said to be the strongest of the seven sons born to Bhrigu and Puloma. He restored to life those asuras who were killed in battles with the DEVAS, and was the guru of PRAHLADA as well as of MAHABALI. Other stories in the Puranas narrate how he fell in love with an APSARA and thus lost his merit, and was reborn many times before he regained his original form. Shukra lived with other asuras on Mt MERU.

Shulva Sutras/Shulba Sutras Sanskrit texts that form part of the KALPA SUTRAS. They consist of methods of measuring and constructing the Vedic sacrificial altars, and are among the oldest texts dealing with the principles of geometry in India. The *Baudhayana* and *Apastamba Shulva Sutras* are the most important.

Shunahshepa A RISHI to whom some hymns of the RIG VEDA are attributed. His story is narrated in later texts, including the later VEDAS, the *MAHABHARATA* and the PURANAS, with some variations. According to the *Aitareya Brahmana*, Shunashepa was offered as a sacrifice in place of Rohita, the son of Raja Harishchandra, but as he recited verses in praise of deities, he was saved. He then became part of the family of the rishi VISHVAMITRA.

shunyata A Sanskrit term meaning emptiness or void, used particularly in the MADHYAMIKA school of MAHAYANA Buddhism. It is related to the doctrine of dependent arising (PRATITYA SAMUTPADA) and implies that there is no permanent reality.

Shvetambara One of the two main Jain sects, the other being the DIGAMBARA. Shvetambara literally means 'those who wear white clothes'. In the fourth century BCE, one group of Jains migrated to south India and later came to be known as Digambaras, while Shvetambaras, led by STHULABHADRA, were those who lived in the north. They abandoned the practice of nudity and wore white clothes, unlike the Digambaras. Though their basic doctrines were the same, certain other differences arose over the centuries (see JAINISM for the differences between the two sects). The Shvetambara canon consists of the twelve ANGAS and associated texts.

The Shvetambara sect has a number of sub-sects. The main body of Shvetambaras is known as the MURTIPUJAKAS (worshippers of idols), and alternatively as Deravasi (temple residents), Chaityavasi, and Mandira-margi. Other sects are the STHANAKAVASI and TERAPANTHI. In addition there are groups known as GACHCHHAS.

siddha One who has attained perfection. A siddha refers to a person who, through various practices, has gained powers and attained mastery over life and death. Siddhas are thus those who have perfected all the SIDDHIS, or supernormal powers, through ascetic and other practices.

There are any number of siddhas or perfected beings in the Indian tradition. The term is also specifically used for two groups, the MAHASIDDHAS and the TAMIL SIDDHAS.

Siddhas are also a class of semi-divine beings in Hindu mythology. They are pure, holy and have great powers, and live in the sky, between the earth and the sun.

In Jainism, siddhas are higher than ARIHANTS, having destroyed all KARMAS. They live in Siddhashila, at the top of the universe.

Siddha Gosht A section in the GURU GRANTH SAHIB, that records Guru NANAK's dialogue with SIDDHAS and NATHA YOGIS, which took place during the course of his travels. Such discussions are said to have taken place at Mt KAILASHA, at ACHAL SAHIB, at the spot marked by the NANAK MATTA GURDWARA, and perhaps at other places as well. The *Siddha Gosht* has seventy-three verses of six lines each, dealing with the basic concepts of Sikhism. In this text Nanak speaks about detachment and about the freedom of the spiritual man who has no desires, and is united with the true name.

Siddha Yoga A system of Yoga founded by Swami MUKTANANDA, a disciple of Swami NITYANANDA. Siddha Yoga is a simple method of self-realization, which includes meditation and other practices. After his death in 1982, Muktananda was succeeded by Swami Chidvilasananda, also called Gurumayi. The headquarters of the organization in India is at Ganeshpuri in Maharashtra, and in the West, in the Catskill mountains near South Fallsburg, New York.

siddhi A supernormal power attained through YOGA, TANTRA or other practices. Eight siddhis have to be perfected before one can be called a SIDDHA. They are: anima, the ability to become as small as an atom; mahima, the ability to bicome huge; laghima, the ability to become as light as a feather; garima, the ability to become heavy; prapti, the ability to attain anything one wants; prakamya, the power to succeed in any endeavour; vashitva, gaining control over all objects and situations in the material world; ishitva, to possess or control anyone or anything according to one's will. In his *Yoga Sutra*, PATANJALI described other powers that could be gained by focusing on someone or something, including the power to know the past, present and future. Some YOGIS believe such powers are a distraction on the path to SAMADHI, others that they are as essential as the normal functions of the senses and body that one takes for granted, such as walking, seeing or hearing.

Siddi Sayyid Mosque, Gujarat The popular name of a mosque located at Ahmadabad, Gujarat, constructed in 1572–73 by Shaikh Said Sultani, a noble at the court of the Gujarat sultan. Though a small mosque, it has exquisite carving, both in its ten semi-circular tracery windows and in its perforated stone screens. In the two western windows, the entire window space is carved with trees, foliage and floral designs. The interior of the mosque measures 21 m by 11 m, with eight pillars that create fifteen sections, each with inner domes in varying styles.

The mosque was in a state of decline but has been restored.

Sikh A term for a follower of the Sikh religion, which comes from the Sanskrit word shishya, or disciple. Originally the followers of Guru NANAK were known as Shishyas, which later became Sikhs. According to the *Rahit Maryada*, a guide to Sikhism, 'A Sikh is any man or woman who believes in one God, in the ten gurus, the teachings of the GURU GRANTH SAHIB and the gurus, who has faith in the AMRIT of the tenth guru and who professes no other religion.' However, this definition does not include all Sikhs, as there are different groups and sects which do not conform to these principles. Amrit refers to the KHALSA ceremony, and Amritdhari Sikhs are those who follow the Khalsa, while the SAHAJDHARI are those who do not. There are also sects, including the NAMDHARIS and the NIRANKARIS, who are Sikhs but who follow their own gurus. Sikhs share some Hindu customs, but are distinct in their reverence for the Guru Granth Sahib, and for their GURDWARAS. The majority of Sikhs follow the five Ks of the Khalsa.

Sikh gurus Sikhism was founded by Guru NANAK, who was followed by nine other gurus. The tenth guru, GOBIND SINGH, stated that he was the last guru, and henceforth the Granth Sahib, the collection of sacred verses, would be known as the GURU GRANTH SAHIB and would take the place of the guru. These ten gurus are recognized and accepted by all Sikhs. They are: Guru NANAK (b. 1469, d. 1539), who founded the religion; Guru ANGAD (guru from 1539–52); Guru AMAR DAS (1552–74); Guru RAM DAS (1574–81); Guru ARJAN DEV (1581–1606); Guru HARGOBIND (1606–44); Guru HAR RAI (1644–61); Guru HAR KRISHAN (1661–64); Guru TEGH BAHADUR (1664–75); Guru GOBIND SINGH (1675–1708). Some Sikh sects such as the NAMDHARIS also follow and accept other gurus.

Sikhism The religion followed by Sikhs, founded by Guru NANAK (1469–1539). After a mystical vision around 1496, Nanak emerged from the the Bein river, where he had gone to bathe, and stated: 'There is no Hindu and no Mussalman.' He realized the inherent truth and oneness of all religions, and began to teach what had been revealed to him. The essence of his teaching is in the JAPJI, the prayer with which the GURU GRANTH SAHIB begins.

The Mul Mantra, the opening verse of the Japji, states that there is One god, whose name is Truth and who is eternal and self existent. God has no form or substance and cannot be known. The rest of the Japji provides other details on the nature of God and his creation, and the means of salvation. God, the creator, created the world, and the world is not an illusion, but is real. Each soul can attain salvation by striving to eliminate lust, anger, greed, attachment and pride; the soul moves through various stages until it attains SACHKHAND, the state of truth, bliss and union with God. God's grace, through meditation on the divine name, helps in attaining this state. As the world is real, good works are to be performed in it, and isolation and renunciation are not recommended. Charity and sharing are also advised. Rituals, MANTRAS and pilgrimages are said to be useless without inner purification, and all people are considered equal. Thus castes, sects and different religions have no meaning.

At KARTARPUR, Guru Nanak started the institution of LANGAR, community meals in which all ate together and worked together in preparing the food. Each succeeding guru contributed something to the practical aspects of the religion. The fifth guru, ARJAN DEV, compiled the sacred teachings in what was later known as the Guru Granth Sahib, while Guru GOBIND SINGH, the tenth guru, gave the religion its final form, introduced the KHALSA and the symbols of Sikhism, and ended the line of gurus. Gobind Singh introduced certain new concepts in his compositions, including the symbolism of the sword. Thus in the *Jap Sahib*, a prayer composed by him and forming part of a Sikh's daily prayers, he says, 'Salutations to God who wields the sword; salutations to God who hurls arrows.' This symbolism is repeated in other writings as well. Despite this, and despite the prevailing conflicts with the Mughals, Sikhism retained its universal approach. Another verse in the *Jap Sahib* states: 'God has no country, dress, form, limit or hue; God is omnipresent, his universal love is everywhere.' (Trans by Gopal Singh). Guru Gobind Singh also emphasized God as the timeless one, both creator and destroyer.

Sikhs have a series of daily prayers, the daily prayer routine being known as nitnem. NAM SIMARAN, meditation on the True Name, is very important. The name of God used can be just Nam, signifying the 'true name', or the name of any form of God.

Sikhs believe in the doctrine of KARMA and the transmigration of souls, and are against idol worship. Drugs and alcohol are frowned upon. Their temples are known as gurdwaras, and the Guru Granth Sahib is enshrined in them on a throne. There are over 200 historic gurdwaras connected with the lives of one or the other of the gurus, as well as several others, constructed in all areas where Sikhs live. All castes and communities are welcome in gurdwaras.

Sikhism is generally seen as a religion that drew from both Hinduism and Islam, and initially formed a bridge between the two, but gradually became closer to Hinduism. Some scholars, however, believe Sikhism is almost exclusively derived from the Hindu sant tradition, the tradition of the BHAKTI saints, and uses mainly Hindu terminology. Despite the use of such terminology, the first view seems more correct, as several Sikh concepts are similar to those in Islam. Among these are concepts such as the One God, eternal and without form; no idol worship; the practice of NAM SIMARAN, which can be compared to the Sufi ZIKR; even the LANGAR, so much a Sikh institution today, was earlier customary in Sufi KHANQAHS.

Sikh history   The Sikh religion is closely linked with history. The three gurus after Guru Nanak followed, and expanded on, his principles. After the fifth guru, ARJAN DEV, was executed by the Mughal emperor Jahangir in 1606, the nature of the Sikh community began to change, and Sikhs began to organize themselves as a military force. This process intensified after the martyrdom of Guru TEGH BAHADUR in 1675. Guru GOBIND SINGH, the tenth guru, founded the KHALSA and promoted the concept of the sant-sipahi, or saint-soldier. Following Gobind Singh's death in 1708, BANDA BAHADUR was the main Sikh leader, but it was RANJIT SINGH who later was able to establish a strong Sikh state. Not long after his death in 1839, between 1845 and 1849, the British took over the Sikh territories. The subsequent decline of Sikh ideals, coupled with memories of an independent state, led to new Sikh movements, such as the SINGH SABHA and later the AKALI MOVEMENT, as well as the rise of purificatory sects such as the NAMDHARIS and the NIRANKARIS. New problems arose after Independence and Partition in 1947, when thousands of Sikhs left west Punjab in Pakistan and settled mainly in east Punjab in India. The demand for a separate Punjabi-speaking state within India was spearheaded first by the AKALIS led by Master Tara Singh and then by Sant Fateh Singh. In 1966 two states of Punjab

and Haryana were created out of the existing state of Punjab, with the new Punjab being primarily Punjabi-speaking. A separatist movement arose in the early 1980s with a demand for an independent state to be named Khalistan, leading to a conflict between government troops and armed Sikhs in the HAR MANDIR at AMRITSAR in 1984. Conflicts continued until the suppression of the militants in the 1990s.

Sikhs are now more assertive about their identity as a distinct group, unrelated to Hinduism. Earlier there were close relations between Sikhs and Hindus, and a number of Hindu families routinely made one of their sons a Sikh.

Sikh festivals   Among Sikh festivals are several that revolve around the gurus and their lives, and include a celebration of their birthdays and a commemoration of their death anniversaries. These are broadly known as GURUPARB or Gurparb. Other Sikh festivals include the HOLA MOHALLA festival, BAISAKHI day, when the KHALSA was formed, and DIVALI, which in Sikhism commemorates the founding of the HAR MANDIR or Golden Temple at AMRITSAR.

silsila   A term used in Islam for a SUFI order, for instance, 'Qadiri silsila'. Literally, it means 'chain' or 'series', and here refers to a lineage chain, the transmission of a particular tradition through a series of people. Usually, a lineage is traced back to the Prophet MUHAMMAD, through Ali or Abu Bakr. Each silsila had its own rules and systems for leading disciples along the Sufi path. The head of a silsila, known as SHAIKH, murshid or PIR, appoints his chief disciple as his Khalifah or successor.

simha   The Sanskrit word for lion. In Indian mythology, the lion is associated with sovereignty and power. Simhasana, means the royal seat, and was a term indicating the king's throne, and also the seat of certain deities. VISHNU, in his form as NARASIMHA, is half-man and half-lion. The lion is the VAHANA or vehicle of the goddess DURGA, reflecting her strength and power. In Jainism, it is the emblem of MAHAVIRA. The lion figures in several other cultures as well. It was associated with the Babylonian Ishtar and the great goddess of Phyrgia. Sekmet, an Egyptian goddess, had the head of a lion.

Sindhu   The Sanskrit name of the river Indus. The term 'Hindu' is the Persian form of Sindhu, and was used from around the eighth century to refer to the people who lived to the east of the river, i.e., in India.

Singh Sabha Movement   A Sikh reform movement that began in the latter half of the nineteenth century. At this time a number of Sikhs were following Hindu practices and customs, while others were influenced by Christian missionaries. The mahants or priests of the Sikh temples were mainly UDASIS, a sect within the Sikhs who had never accepted the symbols of the KHALSA. In 1873 Thakur Singh Sandhanwala founded the Sri Guru Singh Sabha, the aim being both to purify the Sikh religion and to educate Sikhs regarding their scriptures and true religion. Books on Sikh history were written in the Gurmukhi script, and commentaries on Sikh scriptures were composed. In 1879 Gurmukh Singh founded a Singh Sabha at Lahore, and a joint board was formed for coordinating the activities of the two branches. The two groups worked in harmony till 1886, when differences arose, leading to a separate association being set up at Lahore. Sikhs from both groups succeeded in spreading the message of Sikhism, taught Sikhs about the Khalsa, and attempted to remove non-Sikh practices such as child marriage, female infanticide, and the prevalence of caste. A number of Sikh writers contributed to the growth of Sikh literature, including Bhai VIR SINGH, who wrote novels and poems. He also founded the Khalsa Tract Society, which published pamphlets on Sikhism, as well as a journal, the *Khalsa Samachar*. Kahan Singh of Nabha compiled an encyclopaedia of the Sikh religion.

In 1902 the two associations joined together under the name Chief Khalsa Diwan, and in 1908 an educational committee was formed. By this time Sikh schools and colleges had been founded, and the true aspects of the religion had been explained to both Sikhs and Hindus.

Within the Singh Sabha there were still two groups with differing views, one known as the Sanatan Sikhs, which saw Sikhism as a religion closely related to Hinduism, or even a part of it, and the Tat Khalsa, or 'Pure' Khalsa, who denied any relationship.

The Singh Sabha was gradually replaced by the AKALI MOVEMENT, which formally began in 1920, but the Sabha's contribution to Sikhism was immense. It redefined the religion and customs of the Sikhs, laying the foundation for the form of Sikhism that is practised today.

Sinivali   A Hindu goddess who personifies the new moon. Three other lunar phases are represented by the goddesses Kuhu, Anumati and Raka. They are all related to childbirth and fertility, and in Vedic days, to cattle.

Sis Ganj Gurdwara   A GURDWARA or Sikh shrine located in DELHI, first constructed in 1783 by Sardar BHAGEL SINGH, and reconstructed in 1930. The gurdwara marks the site where the ninth guru, TEGH BAHADUR, was executed by the Mughal emperor AURANGZEB on 11 November 1675. The trunk of the tree under which he was beheaded is preserved in this gurdwara. Another Sis Ganj Gurdwara is located at ANANDPUR SAHIB.

Sita   A Hindu goddess, the wife of the god RAMA. The story of Rama and Sita is first narrated in the *RAMAYANA* of VALMIKI, a Sanskrit text probably compiled between the fourth century BCE and the first century CE, though the core may be earlier. In this, Sita is the ideal wife of an ideal king, and in certain late passages, is considered a goddess. By the time of the

RAMACHARITAMANASA, written in the sixteenth century, she attains divine status as the incarnation of LAKSHMI. In the PURANAS, too, Sita is described as an incarnation of Lakshmi.

However, Sita as a fertility deity and goddess of the earth, existed even before Valmiki's *Ramayana*, and is mentioned in the RIG VEDA. In the *Kaushiki Sutra* she is the wife of Parjanya, and in the *Paraskara Sutra*, the wife of INDRA.

In the *Ramayana*, Sita is the daughter of JANAKA, the king of Mithila. However, she was not born in any ordinary way. Janaka, in Valmiki's *Ramayana*, narrates how when he was ploughing a plot for a sacrifice, a female baby was discovered in the furrow and was named Sita (Sita = furrow). She married Rama, the eldest son of King DASHARATHA of Koshala. She followed Rama into exile in the forest, and even when she was kidnapped by RAVANA, she remained true to Rama. When she was rescued, Rama accepted her only after she had undergone an ordeal by fire to prove her purity. However, when his subjects continued to gossip about her, Rama had her abandoned in a forest, even though she was pregnant. The rishi Valmiki took her into his ashram, and twin sons, LAVA and KUSHA, were born to her. After some years, Rama asked her to return, but first to undergo another ordeal to prove her innocence. Sita asked the earth goddess MADHAVI to take her if she was pure, and the earth opened, a throne rose up, and Sita descended. Rama had an image made of her in gold, which he always kept near him, and the two were later reunited in heaven.

This story is said to symbolize the union of kingly virility with the fertility of the earth, leading to prosperity and abundance, but in the popular imagination, Sita reflects the perfect wife. She blames herself for any disasters that take place, always reveres Rama, and never wavers in her devotion to him. She is held as an example to all women, particularly in rural areas. In temples, she is worshipped along with Rama, or with HANUMAN, but never on her own.

Sita's life is full of sorrow, and later texts provide stories to account for this. The *PADMA PURANA* states that Sita once met a pair of parrots who were narrating the story of Rama. She insisted on keeping the female parrot, who was pregnant, near her, thus separating her from her mate. Sita too was therefore deprived of Rama when she was pregnant.

Sittanavasal Cave Temple   A rock-cut Jain temple located at Sittanavasal in Tiruchirapalli District of Tamil Nadu. It was probably constructed at the time of the Pallava dynasty and renovated in the eighth century by a king of the Pandya dynasty. In the inner shrine are images of TIRTHANKARAS, and on the outer wall is a sculpture of PARSHVANATHA. The walls, ceiling and pillars were once decorated with paintings, traces of which remain. One pillar has a painting of a king with his queen, while on the ceiling is a lake with lotuses, and swimming geese and fish.

Sivananda, Swami   A renowned religious leader and guru. Born on 8 September 1887, he studied VEDANTA, but in his desire to help people he qualified as a medical doctor and practised for some time in Malaysia. Later, he renounced the world, became a SANNYASI, and settled at Rishikesh in 1924. In 1932 he started the Shivananda Ashram, in 1936 the DIVINE LIFE SOCIETY, and in 1948 the Yoga-Vedanta Forest Academy, to train teachers and spread the knowledge of YOGA and VEDANTA. He wrote over 300 books and had disciples of all religions, nationalities and castes. He died on 14 July 1963, but his ashram and the Divine Life Society continue to grow and flourish.

six principles of Islamic faith   A follower of Islam is one who adheres to six basic principles of the faith. They are: belief in ALLAH, in the angels or MALAIKA, in the Books (of the Prophets), meaning the QURAN, in the Prophets (Rasul), in the day of judgment and in the Decrees of God.

Skanda   A Hindu deity, another name of KARTTIKEYA.

Skanda Purana   A Sanskrit text, one of the eighteen major PURANAS of Hinduism. This Purana is very voluminous and has seven khandas or parts. It is said to have once been even larger, with six SAMHITAS (books) divided into fifty khandas. The six samhitas were the *Sanat Kumara Samhita, Suta Samhita, Brahmi Samhita, Vaishnavi Samhita, Shankari Samhita* and the *Saura Samhita*. The seven khandas existing today are the following: *Maheshvara, Vishnu, Brahma, Kashi, Avantya, Nagara* and *Prabhasa*.

This is a SHAIVITE Purana, said to have been narrated by SKANDA. It contains legends relating to SHIVA and describes methods of worshipping Shiva, as well as ceremonies and festivals. The *Kashi Khanda* focuses on Shiva temples in KASHI (VARANASI), and there are several other MAHATMYAS or accounts of sacred places. The *Gangasahasranam* lists one thousand names of the sacred river GANGA.

The *Skanda Purana* has 84,000 verses.

Skanda Shashthi   A festival of the Hindu god SKANDA, also known as KARTTIKEYA. The festival takes place in SHIVA and Skanda temples, particularly in Tamil Nadu, and celebrates Skanda's victory over the three ASURAS, Simhamukha, Supradman and TARAKA. This victory is said to have taken place on the sixth day (shashthi) of the bright half of the month of Karttika (October/November), which is the Tamil month of Aippasa. At this time, devotees worship Skanda for six days. Two major temples for Skanda worship are at Tiruparankundram and Tiruchendur.

skandha   A term commonly used in Buddhist texts, meaning a group or bundle, but usually translated as 'aggregate'. It applies to five aspects that create a person or a personality. Early Buddhism has no concept of a soul or ATMAN, which transmigrates through time. Instead individuals consist of five skandhas, which dissolve at the time of death. They are rupa or form, vedana or feeling, samjna or perception, samskaras or mental constituents or attitudes, and vijnana or consciousness. This concept was elaborated and modified in different ways in the various Buddhist sects, while some schools later put forward the concept of a permanent underlying entity. In Jainism, skandhas are combinations of atoms which form the basis of matter. *See* ajiva.

Smarta   A Hindu sect that follows SMRITI literature, particularly the *RAMAYANA, MAHABHARATA*, DHARMA SHASTRAS and PURANAS. They believe that all gods are aspects of the One, and therefore worship five deities known as PANCHAYATANA; VISHNU, SHIVA, DURGA, GANESHA and SURYA. One of the five is chosen as the ishta devata, or personal deity, and the other four are arranged around it when PUJA is performed. Worship combines Vedic mantras with methods prescribed in the Shastras. The sect traces its origin to SHANKARA and mostly follows Advaita philosophy.

Smriti literature   A term for texts of Hinduism that are remembered or inspired, rather than SHRUTI, which are directly revealed. In its broad interpretation, it includes the VEDANGAS, SUTRAS, *RAMAYANA, MAHABHARATA*, PURANAS and DHARMA SHASTRAS. According to the *MANU SMRITI*, it refers only to the DHARMA SHASTRAS. Some texts fall in two categories, for instance the BHAGAVAD GITA, which is technically Smriti literature, but considered SHRUTI by BHAGAVATAS.

snakes, sacred   *See* nagas.

Soka Gakkai   A Buddhist sect based on the teachings of Nichiren Daishonen, a Japanese Buddhist who lived from 1222 to 1282 and advocated the study of the *SADDHARMA PUNDARIKA* or *Lotus Sutra*, known in Japanese as *Myoho Renge Kyo*. A school of Buddhism known as Nichiren-shu grew around his teachings. A modern version of this, the Nichiren Shoshu Soka Gakkai, is popular in urban India today.

Its practices include chanting the mantra *Nam Myoho Renge Kyo*, which means 'Reverence to the *Lotus Sutra*', meditating on the Gohonzon or scroll on which these words are written, and studying the *Saddharma Pundarika* in its Japanese version.

Soma   A Hindu deity, god of the moon, who is also known as Chandra, and is one of the NAVAGRAHA or nine planets. He originated in the RIG VEDA, where he represented a divine drink made from the Soma plant.

In the Rig Veda, Soma is one of the most important deities. All the 114 hymns of the ninth book are dedicated to him, both as a deity and in his form as a plant. The method of extracting juice from the plant is described in detail, as well as the nature of the juice, which is said to be the equivalent of AMRITA, the drink of immortality. The drink had an exhilarating and invigorating effect, along with medicinal properties, and this led it to be considered divine. It is the same as the AVESTAN Haoma or Homa, from the Haoma plant.

Soma is also the lord of the plants or of the woods (Vanaspati). He is the king of the rivers and of the earth, and the father of the gods.

The soma plant has been variously identified, the most common identification being with ephedra.

In post-Vedic literature, Soma is the name of the moon. Some scholars believe Soma is connected with the moon even in the Rig Veda, while others believe the identification is made only in later texts. Like the Soma plant, the moon is drunk by the gods, thus explaining its waning. In the PURANAS, Soma, as Lord of the moon and of Monday (Somavara), is the son of ATRI and grandson of BRAHMA. He kidnapped TARA, wife of BRIHASPATI, and through Tara his son BUDHA (Mercury) was born. As a Navagraha, Soma is depicted as a white deity, holding a mace in one hand, seated in a three-wheeled chariot, drawn by three horses.

Somananda   A philosopher of the Kashmir school of SHAIVISM who lived from c. 875 to 925. He founded the PRATYABHIJNA system, further elaborated by UTPALADEVA and ABHINAVAGUPTA.

Somanatha   A name of the Hindu god SHIVA, particularly of his LINGA installed at the SOMANATHA TEMPLE in Gujarat. Literally it means 'Lord of the Moon'.

Somanatha Temple   A temple of the Hindu god SHIVA located at PRABHASA PATAN near the port of Veraval, in the region of Saurashtra in Gujarat. The main shrine has a LINGA, considered the first of the twelve jyotir lingas, or lingas of light. Somanatha at Prabhasa is mentioned in the MAHABHARATA, SKANDA PURANA and other texts.

According to myths, twenty-seven daughters of DAKSHA were married to SOMA, the moon, but his favourite was Rohini. As he neglected the others, Daksha cursed him to wane into nothing. Soma then came here and worshipped Shiva in the form of his Sparsha Linga, and Shiva blessed him so that he could regain his light again after waning. Thus the moon waxes and wanes.

As Soma worshipped Shiva here, the linga was known as Somanatha. A temple was constructed probably in the tenth century, though it had earlier origins. This was destroyed by Mahmud of Ghazni in 1026 and immediately rebuilt by King Bhima of Gujarat and by Bhoja of Malwa. It was destroyed and rebuilt again several times. After its destruction by AURANGZEB in 1703, the temple was rebuilt nearby by Ahilyabai, a Maratha queen, in 1783. In 1951 a new temple was constructed at the original site.

The temple is a major centre of pilgrimage. To the east is a place where three rivers meet, known as the Triveni Tirtha, said to mark the site where the god KRISHNA's funerary rites were performed.

Somaskanda   A term for an image of the Hindu god SHIVA, where he is depicted along with his wife Uma (PARVATI) and SKANDA. The name comes from the Sanskrit 'Sa-Uma-Skanda', i.e., 'with Uma and Skanda'.

Sonabhandara shrines   Jain rock-cut caves located near Rajgir, ancient RAJAGRIHA, in Bihar. According to a Sanskrit inscription found in one of them, they were constructed by Muni Vaira. A SHVETAMBARA leader of this name attained MOKSHA in 57 CE, and the inscription possibly refers to him, though some scholars feel the two caves are not earlier than the third or fourth century CE. Alexander Cunningham, the great archaeologist, believed the caves were very early, and identified the western cave with the place where the first BUDDHIST COUNCIL was held, 100 years after the death of the BUDDHA.

Soundararajaswamy Temple   A temple of the Hindu god VISHNU located at Nagapattinam in Tamil Nadu. According to the legend associated with this temple, a local prince here had a daughter who was born with three breasts. He was upset, but was told that when she met her future husband her third breast would disappear. One day she came across Nagaraja, the king of the NAGAS, and knew he was to be her husband when her third breast dropped off. As Nagaraja was worshipping Vishnu, she joined him and they worshipped the deity together. Finally Vishnu appeared in a beautiful form, enshrined in the temple here. Because of his beauty, he is known as Soundararaja. Vishnu's consort here is Sundaravalli Tayar. The place was named Nagapattinam, after Nagaraja, and is one of the sacred sites for VAISHNAVITES. TYAGARAJA, a form of SHIVA, is also installed in the temple.

A similar story about a girl with three breasts is narrated about the goddess MINAKSHI.

Spendarmad   An AMESHA SPENTA in Zoroastrianism, the later term for Spenta ARMAITI, Spenta meaning holy, pure, or blessed.

Spenta Mainyu   A term in Zoroastrianism for the good spirit that permeates the universe and exists in every individual. According to the GATHAS, it was the twin of ANGRA MAINYU, the evil spirit, who was opposed to it in every way. The implication in the text is that both were created by AHURA MAZDA or God. Later, Spenta Mainyu was considered identical with Ahura Mazda, Angra Mainyu or AHRIMAN having an independent and separate existence. This led to the concept of ZURVAN or time, as the progenitor of both good and evil, and of Zoroastrianism being a dualistic religion.

Sraosha   A YAZATA or divine being in Zoroastrianism, personifying the conscience or inner voice, that listens to the word of AHURA MAZDA or God. Sraosha is first mentioned in the GATHAS, where he is said to bring rewards and blessings for those who follow the true path, and is accompanied by ASHI VANGHUI. In later texts, he is also the guardian of souls and protects them for three days after death. On the fourth day, along with Rashnu and Meher, divine beings who act as judges, he leads the souls to the CHINVAT BRIDGE. Sraosha's weapons are MANTHRAS or holy chants, and his emblem is the cock, which crows at dawn and thus dispels darkness.

There is some similar imagery in the mystical KABBALAH of Judaism. According to a Kabbalah text, a spark of the fire of God strikes the Angel Gabriel, whose cry awakens the cocks, and as they crow spirits and demons become powerless. Here, too, like Sraosha, the Angel Gabriel is associated with judgement.

Sri Chand The elder son of Guru NANAK. Born in 1494, Sri Chand or Siri Chand was spiritually inclined from childhood, and as he grew up, led an ascetic and simple life. Guru Nanak did not choose him as his successor, because the Guru advocated remembering God while living a householder's life and was thus not in favour of asceticism. Sri Chand had his own group of followers, known as UDASIS.

Srinagar Gurdwara A GURDWARA or Sikh shrine located at Srinagar, Kashmir, said to have been first constructed by the sixth guru, HARGOBIND, when he visited Kashmir in 1620. At this time the MASAND here was one Seva Das; his old mother made a gown for the guru with her own hands, which he wore after blessing her. The guru remained here for three months, during which Mai Bhagbari, the old mother, fell ill and died. The guru waited for her last rites to be performed. Before leaving he asked Masand Seva Das to continue to preach the true faith.

Sringeri A town in Karnataka that has ancient temples and a MATHA of a SHANKARACHARYA.

Sringeri is located on a plateau of the Western Ghats, near the river Tunga. SHANKARA, the philosopher of the eighth-ninth centuries, when searching for a place to build a matha, was struck by the sanctity of this place. According to tradition, here on the banks of the river, he saw a strange sight—it was hot and sunny, and in this treeless spot a cobra was spreading its hood to shelter a female frog about to give birth. A place where natural enemies became friends must be sacred, he thought, and constructed a temple and later a matha here.

Another legend links Sringeri with the ancient sage RISHYASHRINGA, after whom a neighbouring hill is named, and who is said to have merged into a LINGA, still worshipped at a nearby village.

The temples here include the SHARADA TEMPLE of the goddess Sri SHARADA, the VIDYA SHANKARA TEMPLE, an ancient temple dedicated to Mahavishnu or Janardana, the temple of Shankara or Sri Adi Shankaracharya, as well as several smaller temples that are the SAMADHIS of the various shankaracharyas of Sringeri, over which lingas have been installed.

The matha serves as a gurukula, where students study the ancient texts. Thousands of pilgrims visit Sringeri, and food is served to all who come here, free of cost.

Srirangam A town on the outskirts of Tiruchirapalli in Tamil Nadu, which has several temples. The largest is the Ranganatha Temple, a temple of the Hindu god VISHNU, constructed mainly between the thirteenth and seventeenth centuries, with some modern additions. The inner shrine has an image of Vishnu. The whole complex is enclosed in seven concentric walls with twenty-one GOPURAMS, the tallest being a modern structure, 73 m high. The image is taken out in a procession once a year in January. Another temple here is the Shri Jambukeshvara temple, dedicated to SHIVA. In the GARBHA-GRIHA is a LINGA immersed in water that flows from a spring. This temple has five concentric walls and seven gopurams.

Srisailam A place located in the Nallamalai hills of Andhra Pradesh, known for its Mallikarjuna Temple, which contains one of the jyotir LINGAS of the Hindu god SHIVA. In addition there is a DEVI temple here, a SHAKTA PITHA where the goddess is known as Bhrarambha, as well as a number of other shrines, including a NANDI shrine and other linga shrines. The temples, on top of Srisailam hill, are enclosed in a courtyard and were constructed in the fourteenth century and later. The site, however, has an ancient sanctity and is mentioned in the PURANAS. The main temple has a small shrine with a linga and a pillared porch; a large MANDAPA was added in the fifteenth century.

The CHENCHU tribe has a role in the rituals of the temple and refer to Mallikarjuna as Chenchu Malliah. This temple is unique because all castes are allowed to perform the abhisheka or worship of the linga. Srisailam is also a centre of the LINGAYATS or Virashaivas, and is thought to have once been a Buddhist site.

St. Cajetan, Church of A church located in the city of Old Goa, opposite the Sé Cathedral, constructed in the seventeenth century. It is built of lime-plastered granite blocks. The façade has Corinthian columns, while towers on each side serve as the belfry. The building is rectangular, the inner plan in the shape of a Greek cross. The main altar is dedicated to Our Lady of Divine Providence, and there are six other altars, three on each side, dedicated to the Holy Family, Our Lady of Piety, St. Clare, St. John, St. Cajetan, and St. Agnes. The altars are in baroque style, decorated with angels, gilded and intricately carved, while the church as a whole is in Corinthian style, modelled on the original design of St. Peter's in Rome.

The church was constructed by Italian friars of the Order of Theatines. Originally they were sent by Pope Urban III to Golkonda in the Deccan to spread Christianity there. As they were not allowed to preach there, they came to Goa in 1640, and later were granted some land for this church.

St. Francis Xavier A sixteenth-century Jesuit who spent a long time in India and was later canonized as a saint. Francisco de Xavier y Jassu was born on 7 April 1506 in Castle Xavier, in the kingdom of Navarre in Spain. He studied in Paris, obtained a degree in arts in 1530, and took up a teaching post. After a meeting with Inigo (Ignatius) de Loyola who later founded the Society of Jesus, Xavier dedicated his life to work for the salvation of souls. He and Inigo met Pope Paul III and Francis was ordained as a priest in 1537. The king of Portugal, John III, requested the Pope to send some priests to India, and though Francis was initially not one of the chosen ones, he reached Goa in May 1542. In the same year he went to the Malabar coast and Mylapore in south India, preaching to the local people, and converted several Paravas and Mukkuvars, who were fishermen. He frequently returned to Goa, which remained his base. Here he converted and baptized a number of people, and was associated with the College of St. Paul. For a while he went to Malacca to convert people there. Returning to Goa in 1548, he left soon after for Japan, but found the people there unresponsive to Christianity. On his way to Goa again, he stopped at Sancian, an island near China, where he died after an illness on 3 December 1552, at the age of forty-six. His body was first buried at Sancian, later taken to Malacca, and finally brought to Goa on 16 March 1554. The fresh condition of the body was considered miraculous, and he was declared a saint. After his canonization, his body was placed in a silver casket and kept in the BOM JESUS BASILICA. Several parts of his body were, over the years, taken by different groups as sacred relics. The body is exposed to public view about once every ten years, at which time miracles are said to take place.

St. James Church An ANGLICAN church located in DELHI, initially constructed in 1836 by Colonel James Skinner. Skinner, the son of a Scotsman and an Indian woman, was a soldier in the forces of the Maratha Scindias, and was seriously injured in a battle. He vowed that if he survived, he would build a church. He recovered, and before the beginning of the Anglo-Maratha war in 1803, left the Marathas and joined the English East India Company. He raised his own cavalry regiment, known as Skinner's Horse, as he was not accepted in the army because of his mixed parentage. He managed to accumulate money for the church, and finally it was constructed in the style of a church in Venice. Skinner lived mainly in Hansi, along with several wives, but often visited DELHI. He died in 1841 and is also remembered for his memoirs, which he wrote in Persian.

During the revolt of 1857, the church was damaged, but later rebuilt. Its ground plan is that of a Greek cross, around an octagonal central enclosure, with projecting porches. The central portion is surmounted by a large dome, topped by a copper ball and cross.

St. John de Britto A Portuguese Christian Jesuit martyred at ORIYUR in 1693. The parish of Sakthikulangara in Kerala is dedicated to this saint.

St. John's Church A church in Kolkata, constructed in 1787 in the style of St. Martin-in-the-Fields,

London. A tall steeple was intended, but it had to be shortened because the foundation could not bear the weight. Originally opening to the east, the entrance was shifted to the west, with the addition of a porch in 1797. Verandahs were added on the north and south in 1811, as well as Corinthian capitals on the columns. The interior has a number of monuments from British times, along with an interesting painting of the Last Supper by Johann Zoffany (1733–1810), in which well-known residents of Kolkata are depicted as the APOSTLES.

St. Mary of the Angels, Cathedral of A ROMAN CATHOLIC cathedral located in Chennai. The date 1642 is inscribed on the door, though the cathedral was probably completed in 1775. It is known for its oil paintings of Mary Magdalene and of the crucifixion.

St. Mary's Church, Chennai A church located in Chennai, constructed in 1680. It was the first church constructed by the English in India, and was built by Streynsham Master, the governor of Madras. Made of solid masonry, the church measures 24 m by 17 m, with three aisles covered by semi-circular roofs. A tower was added in 1701, and a steeple in 1710. Other extensions were made later, though the original design is maintained. The Altarpiece is a painting of the Last Supper made by a pupil of Raphael. It was captured in 1761 from the French, and then installed here. Governor Elihu Yale, who later endowed Yale University, was married in this church and donated a silver alms dish in 1687. Robert Clive was also married in this church in 1753. There are several old monuments and tombs from British times, both in the church and in the nearby graveyard. It is the earliest surviving church in the Eastern world associated with ANGLICANS.

St. Paul's Cathedral An ANGLICAN cathedral located in Kolkata, constructed in 1847. This was the first Anglican cathedral to be erected in India, and was patronized by the governor-general and later the viceroy of British India, who were based in Kolkata (Calcutta) till 1911. The cathedral, in Indo-Gothic style, is 75 m long and 25 m wide. The western window of stained glass is a memorial to Lord Mayo, viceroy in 1869–72, and is considered one of the finest in the world. The original steeple was destroyed in an earthquake, but has been restored.

St. Thomas An APOSTLE of JESUS Christ who came to India to spread Christ's teachings. This is not mentioned in the NEW TESTAMENT, and some doubt its historical veracity, but his arrival in India is accepted as a fact by all Christians in the country.

An account of St. Thomas is provided in an apocryphal text, the *Acts of St. Thomas*. According to this text dated between the second and third centuries CE, Thomas first went to the court of Gondophernes, an Indo-Parthian ruler in the north-west. A stronger tradition states that he reached Kodungallur (Cranganore, ancient Muziris, near Kochi) on the Kerala coast in 52 CE. Here he is said to have founded seven churches and converted a number of people to Christianity. He went to other parts of south India and was martyred at Mylapore (Chennai) around 72 CE. Two Christian writers, Jerome in the fourth century and Gregory of Tours in the sixth century, mention that Thomas came to India. All SYRIAN CHRISTIANS revere St. Thomas. There are several monuments and churches dedicated to him, among them ST. THOMAS'S MOUNT in Chennai and MOUNT MALAYATTOOR in Kerala.

St. Thomas Christians   A term for Christians in India who trace their origin to ST. THOMAS. They are also known as SYRIAN CHRISTIANS, and are now divided into many groups.

St. Thomas's Mount   A hill located in Chennai, with a monument on it dedicated to ST. THOMAS. At a height of 91 m, the monument can be reached by 132 steps. Below is St. Thomas's Church, built in 1547 by the Portuguese, with later additions. The Apostle ST. THOMAS is said to have been attacked at the spot where the altar is built. Behind the altar is a cross, known as 'the bleeding cross' which is supposed to have bled when he was killed. It has an inscription dated to c. 800, written in PAHLAVI, indicating its NESTORIAN connections. It reads: 'Ever pure is in favour with Him who bore the cross'. There is also a picture of the Virgin MARY, which, according to tradition, was painted by St. Luke and brought here by St. Thomas. About 3 km away is Little Mount, a rocky outcrop also associated with St. Thomas. A church was constructed here in 1612 by Antonio Gonsalves from Goa. Beneath the altar is a cave where St. Thomas is said to have lived, and behind the church is a spring, believed to have miraculous healing powers. A short distance away, a stone cross marks the spot where he preached.

Sthanakavasi   A SHVETAMBARA Jain sect that developed from the Lonka GACHCHHA, founded by LONKA SHAHA in the fifteenth century. According to some accounts, Sthanakavasi was the name given to the main group of Lonka's followers, some time after the Bijamata broke away in 1513. According to other accounts, it was started in 1652 by Lava or Vira of the Lonka gachchha, because ascetics of the sect were not adhering to strict rules. The origin of the name is unclear, but it may be derived from the monks being resident at one place (sthanaka) or by worship being conducted in community halls or sthanakas, instead of temples. The Sthanakavasis are also called Battisis (battis = thirty-two), as they follow only thirty-two out of forty-five of the Shvetambara texts, and reject thirteen. Another name for them is Dhundiya, meaning 'seekers', or Sadhu-margi, followers of sadhus or ascetics. In the eighteenth century another group, the TERAPANTHA, emerged from the Sthanakavasi. Sthanakavasis who did not join the Terapanthis were known as Vaistola.

Sthanakavasis are against the worship of images and believe in a purified form of Jainism. They do not believe in pilgrimages and do not follow the usual religious festivals. Ascetics always cover their mouths with strips of white cloth.

Sthaviravada   One of the two main early schools of HINAYANA Buddhism, the other being the MAHASANGHIKA. The Sthaviravada claimed that they closely followed the BUDDHA's teachings and those of his first disciples, and retained their purity. They denied that ARHATS could have any imperfections as claimed by the Mahasanghikas. Sthaviravada, Sanskrit for the Pali Theravada, meant 'those who speak as the elders, or who 'teach the doctrine of the elders'.

Over the years, several sects emerged from them. Among these were the SARVASTIVADA, prominent in northern India, and the THERAVADA, which formed the rest of the Sthaviravada. According to some sources, the Vibhajyavada, 'those who teach discrimination', were identical with the Theravada, while according to others they were closely associated. The Theravada and Vibhajyavada were settled in Sri Lanka and southern India. The MAHISHASAKA were a branch of the Vibhajyavada, and so were the DHARMAGUPTAKA. Both were located in north-west India, though the Mahishasaka were also known from the region of the Deccan, near the river Krishna. Branches of the Theravada include the Mahavihara, Abhayagirivasa and Jetavaniya. Other Sthaviravada schools were the KASHYAPIYA, HAIMAVATA, VATSIPUTRIYA, Dharmottariya and Bhadrayaniya. The SAMMATIYA emerged out of the Vatsiputriya and was an important sect in the seventh century; in addition there were the Sannagarika, Avantaka, Kurukulla, SAUTRANTIKA, and Mulasarvastivada.

The Sthaviravada texts at times praise the Buddha as a deity, but on the whole describe him as a simple human being. They follow the accounts of his life and philosophy in the PALI CANON. The three concepts of ANATMAN, ANITYA and Dukha are emphasized: the first states that there is no permanent soul or entity, the second that all things are evanescent and transitory, and the third that sorrow or Dukha is a part of all experiences.

KARMA is threefold, physical, verbal and mental, and arises as avidya or ignorance, which leads to desire or craving, known as trishna.

Of all these sects, the Theravada are prominent today.

Sthulabhadra   A leader of SHVETAMBARA Jains who lived in the fourth to third centuries BCE. At this time one group of Jains went to south India and came to be known as the DIGAMBARA, while Sthulabhadra took charge of the Jains of the north, later known as Shvetambaras. He organized a Jain council at PATALIPUTRA in Bihar to reconstruct the Jain texts, parts of which were already lost. The twelve ANGAS were compiled at this time, though they were put together in their final form only in the fifth century. These texts form the main part of the Shvetambara canon.

stupa A Buddhist monument that contains the relics of the BUDDHA, a Buddhist teacher or saint, or any other sacred object. Stupas are erected at sacred Buddhist sites. Initially stupas were also constructed by Jains, though later they focused on building temples.

Subhadra The name of the sister of the Hindu god KRISHNA, described in the *MAHABHARATA* and other texts. She was the wife of ARJUNA and mother of Abhimanyu. Subhadra is worshipped in the JAGANNATHA TEMPLE at Puri, as well as at some other temples, along with Krishna.

Subrahmanya A name of the god KARTTIKEYA or SKANDA in south India. He is called MURUGAN in Tamil. Subrahmanya was probably an earlier folk deity who was later absorbed into the cult of Skanda-Karttikeya. He was also known as Mahasena, Kumara and Guha. Swami Mahasena was worshipped by the Kadamba dynasty, and was said to live in a kadamba tree.

Suchindram Temple A Hindu temple located at Suchindram in Tamil Nadu. The temple is associated with the story of the rishi DATTATREYA, considered an incarnation of VISHNU. Three deities—BRAHMA, Vishnu and SHIVA—are worshipped here in the form of LINGAS, though Vishnu is the main deity in the inner shrine. According to the story connected with this site, they had appeared here to Anasuya, wife of the rishi ATRI, in the form of brahmanas, making the preposterous demand that they be fed by Anasuya after she had removed her clothes. Unable to refuse a BRAHMANA, Anasuya by her power converted them into three babies and then fed them. When they returned to their normal forms, they granted her a boon. She requested that all of them be born to her, and thus Dattatreya was born who incorporated the qualities of all three gods. (In another account the three deities were incarnated separately, as three children of Atri and Anasuya.) Suchindram is also associated with the purification (suchi) of the god INDRA, after his misbehaviour with Ahalya, wife of the rishi Gautama.

The temple is entered through a huge GOPURAM, while the main temple is guarded by DVARAPALAS and YALIS. This opens into the Champakaram Mandapam, with thirty-two carved pillars depicting the story of Anasuya, and of parts of the *RAMAYANA*.

There are at least thirty shrines of various deities and unique images at this temple, including a giant HANUMAN shrine, a shrine of Uma or PARVATI, known here as Dharmasamvardhini, one who promotes DHARMA, a NAVAGRAHA Mandapam, as well as images of Vinayaka or GANESHA, and of KRISHNA.

The processional deity is Suchindra Perumal, and there are three main festivals: Marghazi Utsava (December–January), Chaitra Utsava (April–May) and Avani Utsava (September–October).

Sudarshana Chakra A weapon of the Hindu god VISHNU, shaped like a discus. It was sometimes personified as an AYUDHA PURUSHA, represented as a male figure.

sudreh A sacred vest, usually made of white muslin, worn by Zoroastrians. It is first worn after the NAVJOTE ceremony, and the KUSTI or sacred thread is tied over it. The sudreh has a V-shaped neck, with a 'pocket' at the base, one inch square. This is known as the kisseh-i-kerfeh, or pocket of good deeds. It is there to remind the individual of the good deeds to be done every day. It also indicates that all the good deeds of a person only amount to one inch when compared with those of God.

Sufis A term for followers of the esoteric branch of Islam. According to one theory, the word is derived from the Arabic suf, or wool, as these ascetics at one time wore woollen garments. Other theories are that it comes from suphia, wisdom, or safam, meaning purity. Sufis trace their origin to an 'inner circle' of disciples of the Prophet MUHAMMAD, to whom he taught secret and hidden truths that were not revealed to all. Living with total dedication and devotion to God, they realize God within their hearts, experiencing mystic visions and uniting with the divine.

In the eighteenth century Shah WALIULLAH, summarized the Sufi movement, dividing it into four epochs. In the first, dating from the time of the Prophet Muhammad to the ninth century, Sufis devoted themselves to prayer, fasting and ZIKR (remembering God's name). In the second stage through continuous meditation and contemplation they attained intuitive insights. They reached the height of ecstasy through SAMA or devotional music, and lived in poverty to avoid material desires. In the third stage, in the eleventh and early twelfth centuries, they focused on living in a state of tawajjuh, or union with the divine. In the fourth stage, they discovered the way that Wajibul-Wujud (Necessary Being) could descend into the world. These stages overlapped, and also existed simultaneously. By the thirteenth century Sufis were divided into fourteen orders or SILSILAS.

In the second epoch, Sufis were divided into different sects. Many of them came to India at this time and settled in the Punjab after Mahmud Ghazni's conquest of the region. More arrived after the sultans had seized political power.

Most Sufis lived in KHANQAHS headed by a PIR or shaikh, and practised various disciplines according to the nature of their order. The pir chose his khalifahs or successors from the best of his disciples. When a pir died, a DARGAH or shrine was erected around his tomb and revered by his disciples and others. Though today there are not many notable Sufi saints, the dargahs of the early Sufis are still worshipped.

Orthodox SUNNIS do not accept the worship of tombs and the decoration of graves, while the BARELVIS support this practice. Despite the official view, the shrines of saints are visited by people of all communities and religions, particularly at the time of the annual URS.

Sufis in India were of several different kinds. Some lived in poverty, others acquired wealth and property. Some sects strictly followed the SHARIA, others did so in varying degrees. Some of the saints were involved in the political intrigues of the times, while others lived in isolation as ascetics. Several were influenced by yogic practices, and particularly by NATHA YOGIS.

The main Sufi orders in India included the CHISTI, SUHRAWARDI, FIRDAUSI, SHATTARI, QADIRI and NAQSHBANDI, as well as the more loosely organized groups of the Gurzmars, Jalalis, QALANDARS, MADARIS and Haidaris.

Sufism   A term for the ideas and practices of SUFIS.

Sugriva   A vanara or monkey king described in the RAMAYANA. He had been deposed by his brother Vali, but was restored to the throne by RAMA. Sugriva ruled at KISHKINDHA, and his advisor, HANUMAN, as well as his subjects, the vanaras, helped Rama to recover SITA from LANKA.

suhl-i kuhl   A term in Islam that means 'universal peace'. It was a popular concept among the SUFI saints.

Suhrawardi   An order of SUFI saints founded by Shaikh Shihabuddin Umar Suhrawardi of Baghdad (d. 1234). The order was introduced in India by his disciple Jalaluddin Jabrizi, who lived in Bengal and converted a number of Hindus. However, Shaikh Bahauddin Zakariyya (d. 1262) organized the SILSILA in India.

Among his disciples was Shaikh Fakhruddin Ibrahim Iraqi, a poet who composed an important Sufi work, *Lamat* (Flashes) on the WAHDAT AL-WUJUD doctrine. Bahauddin was succeeded by his son, Shaikh Sadruddin Arif. A disciple of Arif, Amir Husain, wrote *Zadul-Musafin* and other works that elaborated on the Wahdat al-Wujud doctrine. However, Suhrawardis did not follow the CHISTI practice of bowing before the SHAIKH, and unlike the Chisti saints most Suhrawardis led a comfortable life, believing there was no harm in wealth if one remained unattached.

Bahauddin set up a KHANQAH at Multan and attracted disciples from Sind and elsewhere. It reached its height under his grandson Shaikh Ruknuddin Abul Fath (d. 1335), while there was another branch at Uch. A renowned saint of the Uch branch was Syed JALALUDDIN BUKHARI, popularly known as Makhdum-i Jahaniyan (d. 1384). He had a close association with Sultan Firuz Shah Tughlaq. A grandson of Jalaluddin, Qutb-i-Alam (d. 1553), settled near Ahmadabad. His son, Syed Muhammad, known as Shah Mahjhan or Shah-i-Alam (lord of the universe) was very famous.

Other disciples of Shaikh Shihabuddin settled in India, among them Sayyid Nuruddin Mubarak Ghaznawi (d. 1234–35). Not much is known of his early life, but he was famous in DELHI and had good relations with Sultan Iltutmish. Another was Qazi HAMIDUDDIN NAGAURI, who composed a number of important Sufi works, and Shaikh Samauddin of Delhi. His disciple, a poet, was known as JAMALI. His two sons Shaikh Abdul Hayy (d. 1551–52) and Shaikh Gadai (d. 1569) were also prominent in the order.

After this the Suhrawardi declined, partly because of lack of court patronage. Suhrawardis had always been associated with kings and even accepted some political posts, because they believed this helped them to perform their functions effectively.

Later the sect merged with the QADIRI order.

Sukkoth   A Jewish festival also called the Feast of Tabernacles or the Feast of Booths, which was earlier an agrarian festival marking the end of the harvest. The festival begins five days after YOM KIPPUR and takes place from the fifteenth to the twenty-third day of the Jewish month of Tishri (September-October).

During the harvest festival, people lived in tents in the fields in order to complete the work before the rains began. This was adapted to Jewish beliefs, and the Sukkoth festival recalls the time when the Jews wandered in the desert for forty years after they escaped from Egypt, living in temporary shelters. A passage in the BIBLE says: 'From the fifteenth day of the seventh month, when you shall have gathered in all the fruits of the land, you shall celebrate the feast of the Lord seven days; on the first day and the eighth day there shall be a solemn rest . . . You shall dwell in booths seven days . . . that your posterity may know that I made the children of Israel dwell in booths, when I brought them out of the land of Egypt' (Lev. 23.39–43). On this festival therefore the Jews make huts of plants and leaves (Sukkah), and offer four species of plants: ethrog (citron) and lulav (branches of palm, myrtle and willow bound together). According to a thirteenth-century text, the *Sefer Hahinukh*, these plants symbolize the body; the ethrog is like the heart, the temple of the intellect that is offered to God; the lulav together represent the spinal cord, meaning that the entire body is offered to God. Myrtle is like the eyes, which should not be led astray; the willow represents the lips, indicating control of speech. On the seventh day, known as Hoshana Rabba (great hosanna), seven circuits of the synagogue are made, holding the four plants. The eighth day is known as Shemini Atzeret (day of the solemn assembly) and is also called Simhat Torah (rejoicing of the law). Throughout the year the Five Books of Moses are read consecutively, and on this day the reading is completed and begins anew. The Scrolls of the Law, which are kept in the ark in the synagogue, are taken in procession, and everyone is called at the reading desk to say a blessing over some part of the TORAH. The eighth day is thus one of celebration and thanksgiving.

Sultan Bahu   A SUFI poet who wrote in Persian and Punjabi. Born in 1629–30 in the village of Sherkot in

Punjab, his real name was Sultan Muhammad, but he was called Bahu because he ended his verses with this phrase (hu = a term for God). He later became a disciple of Abdur Rahman Qadiri in DELHI. He wrote about twenty treatises in Persian, as well as Persian poetry, but is best known for his verses in Punjabi. He died in 1691.

Sultanpur Lodhi   A town sacred to Sikhs located near Kapurthala in Punjab. Guru NANAK, the founder of Sikhism, lived here, and several shrines associated with him are located here. The Ber Sahib Gurdwara is near the Bein stream where Guru Nanak used to meditate and where he attained divine illumination. He planted a ber tree near the river, and it was here that he first began his teaching. A shrine was erected at the spot and a large marble-and-mosaic GURDWARA was constructed in 1942. The Hatt Sahib Gurdwara marks the site where Guru Nanak worked for some years in the storehouse of Nawab Daulat Khan Lodi. Eleven stone weights, said to have been used by the guru in weighing the supplies, are preserved here. Nearby is a sacred tank.

The guru's two-storeyed house is still standing and is now a place of pilgrimage. His children, SRI CHAND and Lakshmi Chand, were born here. Another Sikh shrine in the town, known as Kothi Sahib, consists of a single room where Guru Nanak was confined for a short period of time by Daulat Khan Lodi, governor of the region. Daulat Khan had received false reports about the guru, but soon released him and apologized to him.

The Sikh Janam Sakhis describe Guru Nanak's daily life here. He used to rise before dawn, bathe in the Bein river, and meditate for some time, before attending to his work in the store.

Sumeru   Another name of the mythical mountain MERU.

Sumitra   One of the three wives of King DASHARATHA, in the *RAMAYANA*. She was the mother of LAKSHMANA and SHATRUGHNA.

Sumtsek Temple   A Buddhist shrine located at ALCHI in Ladakh. Constructed in the late eleventh century, the temple has three floors. The ground floor has BUDDHA images in niches, as well as large standing images, more than 4 m high, of three BODHISATTVAS: MANJUSHRI, AVALOKITESHVARA and MAITREYA. Fine, detailed painting covers the images. Small medallions on their robes are intricately painted with scenes from the BUDDHA's life, depictions of the DHYANI BUDDHAS and of eighty-four traditional MAHA-SIDDHAS, and other scenes. Smaller images of Buddhas, devotees and celestial figures are carved near them. There are seated Bodhisattva images, and a large image of Mahakala on a corpse at the entrance. The walls of the next two levels are covered in MANDALAS, painted with Bodhisattvas, goddesses and other figures. The ceilings are painted as well. Blues, reds and bright colours predominate in all the paintings.

Sundar Singh, Sadhu   A Sikh who became a Christian preacher. Born in 1889 in the Punjab at a time of missionary influence, Sundar Singh was originally against Christianity and even burnt a BIBLE at his Christian school. As a teenager he became confused about the meaning and purpose of life, and in 1905 he contemplated suicide. That night he received a vision of JESUS Christ, who asked him to follow him. Transformed by this experience, Sundar Singh left home and wandered through mountain villages dressed as a SANNYASI, preaching the message of Jesus. There are legendary accounts of him, and he is said to have gone to Tibet and returned and to have visited other countries, including Myanmar, Singapore, Japan, China, North America, Europe and Australia. In 1929 he set out again for Tibet, but never returned.

Sundar Singh was known as a charismatic speaker who used local stories as parables, and thus made Christ acceptable and understandable to ordinary villagers.

Sundaramurti/Sundarar (Cuntarar) A BHAKTI saint of the eighth century, who was one of the NAYANARS and worshipped the Hindu god SHIVA. Born in the Tamil region, he was earlier known as Nambi Arurar, and later as Sundarar or Sundaramurti. His life is described in several texts, including the *PERIYA PURANAM*. He composed verses of love and devotion to SHIVA, which are incorporated in the *Tevaram*. He also wrote the *Tiruttondattokai*, an account of the NAYANAR saints.

Sunnah   The Prophet MUHAMMAD's sayings and actions, and those of his companions. Second to the QURAN, they are the most important source of Islam. The HADIS or traditions consist of short stories or accounts of different incidents in the life of the Prophet, while the Sunnah are the laws that are deduced from the Hadis. Sunnah also refers to the whole collection of Hadis.

Sunni   One of the two main sects of Islam, the other being the SHIA. The two sects arose soon after the death of the Prophet MUHAMMAD in 632. Some of his followers elected Abu Bakr as his successor, who was known as the Caliph (or Khalif, meaning 'successor' in Arabic). Others felt Muhammad had selected Ali, his cousin and son-in-law, as his successor, and therefore did not accept Abu Bakr. They were known as Shias (partisans) of Ali. The first group later came to be known as Sunnis, the 'people of custom and community' (ahl-us-sunnah wul-jamaa), and are known to be more orthodox. Sunnis form 80 per cent of the Muslim population in the world.

Sunnis accept the first four Caliphs as the rightful successors of the Prophet Muhammad, while Shias accept only Ali. Sunnis also accept the Umayyad and Abbasid Caliphs, and differ from Shias in the concept of the IMAM. Sunnis accept the six 'authentic' books of the HADIS, and follow any of the four schools of Muslim law—Hanafi, Shafi, Maliki and Hanbali.

Sunnis believe that the suras or chapters of the QURAN were ordained by God and put together by Muhammad, while Shias believe there is a logical and chronological order of suras.

The majority of Muslims in India are Sunnis, and most of the north Indian Islamic kings in medieval times were Sunnis.

Suparna A name of the divine bird GARUDA. According to a story in the *MAHABHARATA*, Garuda snatched the divine nectar or AMRITA from paradise. As he flew away with it, the god INDRA hurled his thunderbolt at him, and one of his feathers fell on earth. It was so beautiful that people became happy when they saw it, and therefore Garuda was named Suparna, i.e., the one with beautiful wings.

Surabhi A divine cow who emerged at the time of the churning of the ocean for AMRITA. All cows are descended from her. She is often considered the same as KAMADHENU, the wish-fulfilling cow.

Surdas/Surdasa A BHAKTI singer and poet, a devotee of the Hindu god KRISHNA. Details of his life are not clear, but he was probably born in 1478 at the village of Siri near DELHI, and died in 1563. According to all accounts, he was blind from birth and constantly searched for truth. He wandered from place to place and settled at Gau Ghat on the banks of the river YAMUNA, between MATHURA and AGRA. Surdas composed and sang songs of love and devotion to Krishna in Braj Bhasha, a Hindi dialect. He sang mainly of Krishna's childhood and youth. His verses are collected in the *Sur Saravali, Sahitya Lahiri*, and *Sur Sagara*. Some of them are included in the GURU GRANTH SAHIB.

Surya The sun, as well as a Hindu deity, the sun god. He is first mentioned in the RIG VEDA, and in some cases in that text Surya refers only to the sun, not to its personification as a deity. In the Rig Veda it is said that Surya shines for the whole world, prolongs life and drives away sickness, disease and evil dreams. He is born of the gods, and the seven horses who draw his chariot represent the rays of the sun. He is a bird traversing space, or a brilliant white steed. Sometimes his chariot is drawn by a single horse called Etasha. In Vedic times SAVITR, PUSHAN, BHAGA, MITRA, VIVASVAT and ARYAMAN were sometimes used as synonyms, though they were also individual deities. The ADITYAS too, represented solar deities.

Surya continued to be worshipped after the Vedic period. The symbol of the sun appears on coins, and some early kings incorporated the word Surya in their names. In the first few centuries CE, Surya was depicted as a man, dressed in a tunic and boots, or in a long coat with trousers, suggesting Greek, Iranian or Scythian influence, but from the fourth century onwards he is depicted in Indian attire.

Early Surya temples still exist at KATARMAL, KONARAK, MARTAND, MODHERA and other places. Surya worship is incorporated in daily rituals and in several festivals and ceremonies. CHHATH puja, popular in Bihar and eastern Uttar Pradesh, is one of the major festivals focusing on sun-worship. Surya worshippers are known as Sauras, and the *Saura Purana*, a minor or Upapurana, is dedicated to this deity.

There are several myths and stories regarding Surya in the PURANAS. Surya, also known as Vivasvan, was the son of KASHYAPA by his wife ADITI. He married Samjna, daughter of VISHVAKARMA, and had three children, MANU, YAMA and YAMI, and three other children by Chhaya, the maid of Samjna, who tricked him into believing she was his wife. However, according to the *KURMA PURANA*, he had four wives: Samjna, Chhaya, Rajni and Prabha.

Though Surya is worshipped independently, he is also one of the NAVAGRAHA or nine planets, and is important in Indian astrology. He is known as Ravi, the lord of Ravivara (Sunday). According to the *AMARAKOSHA*, Surya was also known as Dvatashatma, Arka, Mihira, Aruna and Mitra, as well as by a number of other names.

Sun gods and goddesses exist in ancient myths of all cultures. The Hittite word for sun was 'surias'.

Surya (Suryaa) The daughter of the sun god SURYA, mentioned in the RIG VEDA. She was married to the ASHVINS, though in later myths the Ashvins were sons of SURYA.

Suryavamsha Ancient Indian dynasties that trace their descent from SURYA or the sun. According to the *DEVI BHAGAVATA PURANA*, Marichi, one of the mind-born sons of the god BRAHMA, was the father of KASHYAPA, who, in turn, fathered VIVASVAN, the sun. Vivasvan had ten sons, IKSHVAKU, Nabhaga, Dhrishta, Sharyati, Narishyanta, Pramshu, Nriga, Dishta, Karusha and Prishadra. Various dynasties were descended from all these. According to other accounts, Vaivasvata Manu was the son of Vivasvan, and Ikshvaku was born from him, all solar dynasties being descended from Ikshvaku. Several later kings traced their ancestry to the sun to give themselves an exalted status, while others traced it to the CHANDRAVAMSHA, or moon family.

Sushruta A fourth-century author of a text on Ayurveda, the Indian system of medicine. Medicine was considerd a gift of the gods, and Sushruta was said to have studied with DHANVANTARI, the legendary founder of the medical system. He was also said to be the son of the rishi VISHVAMITRA. His *Sushruta Samhita*, along with the earlier *Charaka Samhita*, is one of the two main texts that laid the foundation of Ayurveda.

Sushumna A NADI or hidden current of energy described in yogic and Tantric texts. It is located along the spine. When aroused, the KUNDALINI, rises along the Sushumna. On either side of it are the IDA and PINGALA nadis.

suta A bard or court poet. The PURANAS were usually narrated to a suta, who then retold them. Lomaharshana

Suta is frequently mentioned in the Puranas. Sutas also had a prominent part in Sanskrit plays.

Sutala The third of the seven divisions or LOKAS of the nether world or PATALA, in Hindu mythology. MAHABALI rules there, meditating constantly on the god VISHNU. Recognizing that he was wrong in sending Mahabali away from the earth, Vishnu acts as the doorkeeper here. According to the *VISHNU PURANA*, Patala has wonderful regions, occupied by DAITYAS, DANAVAS and YAKSHAS.

sutra A Sanskrit term meaning a thread or string, or a short composition or series of compositions, held together as if on a thread. It usually refers to a short verse, expressing a complex idea. Hindu texts have a number of sutras on all topics, but sutras also refer to groups of texts, such as the KALPA SUTRAS or GRIHYA SUTRAS. In early Buddhism the term used is the Pali SUTTA, referring to a text with a discourse or sermon, while later the Sanskrit word sutra was used. Jainism also has sutra texts.

sutta The PALI form of the Sanskrit word SUTRA.

Sutta Pitaka A term for a series of Buddhist texts, divided into five Nikayas or groups. They are the most important texts of the PALI CANON, and consist of the *DIGHA NIKAYA, MAJJHIMA NIKAYA, SAMYUTTA NIKAYA, ANGUTTARA NIKAYA* and *KHUDDAKA NIKAYA*. The last includes fifteen miscellaneous texts.

Suttanipata A HINAYANA Buddhist text that forms part of the *KHUDDAKA NIKAYA* of the PALI CANON. It consists of poetical SUTTAS in five sections. The language and subject matter indicate that this is one of the earliest Pali texts. The first four sections have fifty-four shorter poems, while Section V has one long poem. Among the significant suttas, the *Brahmana-Dhammika-Sutta* (II.7) says that RISHIS of the olden days were 'true BRAHMANAS', but later animal sacrifices, wealth and luxury led to their corruption and decline in purity. The *Dhaniya Sutta* (I.2) describes the serene joy of the BUDDHA, who is homeless, without possessions, and free of all bonds. The *Amagandha Sutta* (II.2) criticizes the brahmana who considers dietary restrictions the highest moral law. Worse than eating meat, it says, are 'Torturing living creatures, murder, killing, tyranny, theft, lies, fraud', etc. The text includes narrative passages on the Buddha's life.

Suyagadamga A Jain text, the second of the twelve ANGAS. It describes the doctrines of other sects and warns monks to keep away from them, following only the Jain path. For instance, criticizing BRAHMANA rituals, it says that if perfection were to be attained by ablutions of water, then fishes, tortoises and snakes would also attain them, and if by the daily lighting of fire, then blacksmiths and artisans would be the holiest. It warns monks against women, who can ensnare them and lead them away from the path. It describes various hells and torments for those who stray from the path.

This text is historically important, as it describes other religious sects and practices prevailing at the time.

Svadhishthana Chakra One of the seven main CHAKRAS or hidden energy centres within the body. The Svadhishthana Chakra, a little above the MULADHARA CHAKRA at the base of the spine, is at the root of the genitals. According to Tantric texts, it consists of a lotus of six petals, vermilion in colour. On the petals are the Sanskrit letters ba, bha, ma, ya, ra and la, of the colour of lightning. Within the lotus is a white, eight-petalled lotus, with a half-moon in the middle, a shining, watery region of VARUNA. One who meditates on this lotus is freed of all inner enemies, such as lust and anger. He is a lord among yogis and shines like the sun, removing the darkness of ignorance.

svaha (1) A Sanskrit term used at the end of Hindu MANTRAS, as well as in Buddhist rituals. According to the *Shatapatha Brahmana*, it has magical powers.

(2) Svaha is personified as a goddess and is the daughter of DAKSHA and the consort of AGNI. Agni and Svaha had three sons, Pavaka, Pavamana and Shuchi. Svaha is sometimes identified with UMA or PARVATI.

svarga A common term for heaven. In Hindu mythology, it also refers to the specific heaven of the god INDRA, located on Mt MERU.

svastika An auspicious symbol, particularly in Hinduism. It is in the form of a cross, with the ends of its four arms bent at right angles. In the twentieth century, it was adopted by Hitler and used as his symbol for the Aryan race and thus had negative connotations. However, it remains an important symbol in India.

Svatantrika A branch of the MADHYAMIKA school of Buddhism that developed in the sixth century. Its main exponent was BHAVAVIVEKA (490–570), who differed with NAGARJUNA, the founder of the Madhyamika school, on the methodology of argument.

svayambhu A term that means 'self-existing', that which has not been created but exists by itself. In the UPANISHADS it signifies BRAHMAN. In the PURANAS, SVAYAMBHUVA is the creator, born from svayambhu. Among the forms of SHIVA's LINGA is the svayambhu, or self-existent. In Buddhism, the Adi Buddha, or the first BUDDHA, is also called self-existent. In ancient Egypt, the god Ptah was 'self-begotten'.

Svayambhuva The name of the first MANU.

swami/svami A term for a guru or religious leader. It applies particularly to heads of the DASNAMI sannyasi orders, but it can be adopted by the head of any religious group. Swami is also used as an honorific title for deities and holy men.

Swaminarayan Sampradaya The sect started by the guru SWAMINARAYAN in the nineteenth century. The sect is divided into northern and southern sections, and is led by householders, i.e., married men.

All disciples have to follow five basic principles: no alcohol or intoxicating drugs; no meat of any kind; no stealing; no debauchery or adultery; and purity of food and drink, which leads to purity of body and mind. Swaminarayan advocated good moral conduct, and the reading of SHASTRAS and sacred books. His followers were asked to end the practice of female infanticide and SATI.

Though the sect is open to all castes and religions, disciples are divided into three categories based on caste. Women and men are always segregated in places of worship, as Swaminarayan felt that even SANNYASIS would lose their spiritual focus if they associated with women. The wives of the ACHARYAS or heads of the sect, give initiations to women.

Apart from opening temples, the sect organizes social work, runs hospitals and schools, and works for village and rural development. Swaminarayan temples are located in all parts of the world, and there are thousands of followers in all countries.

Among the main temples are the AKSHARDHAM at Gandhinagar, Gujarat; several others in Gujarat; the Akshardham in DELHI; and a Swaminarayan temple in England.

Swaminarayan, Sri The founder of a religious sect and a guru of the nineteenth century, earlier known as Shri Sahajananda Swami. Born in a BRAHMANA family in 1781 at village Chhapiya, north of AYODHYA in present Uttar Pradesh, as a child he was known as Krishna, Harikrishna or Ghanshyam. His family moved to Ayodhya, and Ghanshyam's early years were spent there. He studied with his father and had a prodigious intellect, mastering all the VEDAS and other sacred texts at a young age. Both his parents died by the time he was eleven years old, and Ghanshyam left home and travelled first to Nepal and then to temples and sacred sites throughout India. At the age of eighteen, when he was in Gujarat, he was initiated by Sri Ramananda Swami and given the name Shri Sahajananda Swami. In 1802 he was installed as the guru at Jetpur in Junagadh.

He advocated the chanting of the name Swaminarayan, the true name of god, and soon came to be known as Swaminarayan himself. He travelled from village to village, setting up temples and initiating disciples, and established the SWAMINARAYAN SAMPRADAYA. His writings include a selection and annotation of texts that he is said to have completed by the age of ten, as well as the *Shiksha Patri*, or ethical precepts and guidelines of the Sampradaya, and the *Desh Vibhag no Lekhe*, the constitution of the sect. Swaminarayan's philosophy is thought to be similar to VISHISHTADVAITA, with some minor differences. He believed in non-duality and the worship of the one god in the form of Swaminarayan. God alone was One, without a second. Souls were eternal, but were not the same as the One. Swaminarayan provided food and shelter to the needy, preached respect to all life and stopped animal sacrifices. He died in 1830.

He is revered by his followers and considered an incarnation of VISHNU.

swan A bird considered particularly sacred in Sanskrit texts, in which it is known as HAMSA. Swans are said to dwell in lake MANASAROVARA. They are the VAHANA or vehicle of the Hindu deities SARASVATI and BRAHMA. Hamsa is also a MANTRA used for meditation, and yogis who practise it are known as hamsas.

syadvada A concept in Jainism related to the theory of knowledge and to the NAYA concept. It examines different ways of viewing something and concludes that all knowledge is 'probable' and not definite. Seven statements can be made about a thing or its attributes. Each statement it is preceded by syad, which means 'probably' or 'may be'. The statements are: (1) syad asti: probably, it is; (2) syad nasti: probably, it is not; (3) syad asti nasti: probably, it is and it is not; (4) syad avaktavya: probably, it cannot be described; (5) syad asti avaktavya: probably, it is, but it cannot be described; (6) syad nasti avaktavya: probably it is not, but it cannot be described; (7) probably it is, and it is not, and it cannot be described. Taking the example of a jug, the first statement sees the jug existing at a particular time and place. But from a different time and place, the jug does not exist. The third statement thus shows that the jug both exists and does not exist, thus leading to the fourth statement, where its existence cannot be described, and then to variations of this statement.

The syadvada concept was criticized by the philosophers SHANKARA and RAMANUJA, who said that contradictory characteristics could not coexist. However, syadvada attempts to point out that things are complex and not always as they seem. Only the real can reconcile differences and see the truth. Syadvada is related to the concept of ANEKANTAVADA or relativity.

Syamantaka A celebrated jewel in Hindu mythology. The sun god, SURYA, presented it to Satrajit, his friend, who praised Surya after seeing him in his true form. The Syamantaka was the source of all good fortune if the wearer was good, but brought disaster to a bad person. Satrajit gave it to his brother Prasena, who was killed by a lion. The lion was killed by JAMBAVAN, king of the bears, who carried off the gem, which was later retrieved by the god KRISHNA, who returned it to Satrajit. After more adventures and deaths, the gem ended up with Akrura, an uncle of Krishna. Because of the brilliance of the gem, Akrura looked like the sun, wearing a garland of light.

synagogue A term for a Jewish place of worship. Synagogues are thought to have first been used when the Jews were in captivity in Babylonia in the sixth century BCE. When the Jews returned to Jerusalem they rebuilt their temple, and the synagogues had a minor role until the destruction of the temple in CE 70, after which the synagogue was again the main centre of study and worship.

A traditional synagogue has a bimah or platform in the centre, from which the TORAH is read, and an ark, i.e., a cupboard on the wall that faces Jerusalem, used to store the scrolls of the Torah. The *ner tamid*, a small lamp representing eternal light, is kept burning in a synagogue.

There are a number of synagogues in India, though not all are regularly used. At the time of Independence in 1947, Kerala had seven active synagogues. Today only the Paradesi Synagogue at Kochi, constructed in 1568, is well maintained. In north Parur, a synagogue constructed in 1164 and rebuilt in 1616 is still in use, while other synagogues in Kerala are either empty or converted to other uses.

In MUMBAI, synagogues include the Shaar-ha-Rahamim or Gate of Mercy Synagogue (constructed 1796) in Mandvi; the Shaare Rason (1840); Tifereth Israel (1886); Magen Hasidim Synagogue (1904); the Magen David Synagogue (1863); the Keneseth Eliyahoo Synagogue (1883); the Kurla Bene-Israel Prayer Hall (1946); Rodef Shalom (1925), the only synagogue of Reform Judaism; and the Etz Haeem Prayer Hall (1888). The Indian Council of Jewry is also located in Mumbai. The Beth-El Synagogue (1849) is at Panvel, Maharashtra, while the Shaar Hashamaim (Gate of Heaven) Synagogue (1879) is in Thane, Maharashtra. In Pune, the Succath Shelomo Synagogue of the BENE ISRAEL community was built in 1921 and is still active; the Ohel David Synagogue (1863), with a tower rising to a height of 28 m, was constructed by David Sassoon, a BAGHDADI JEW. In Gujarat the Magen Abraham Synagogue, built in art-deco style in 1934, is located at Ahmadabad, and still functions.

In Kolkata are the Neveh Shalom (1831), the Beth El Synagogue (1856), and the Maghen David Synagogue (1884), while there were once two other small synagogues. New Delhi has the Judah Hyam Hall Synagogue, where prayers are held on festivals and holy days. There are also small synagogues formed by the new Jewish groups in India.

In many of the synagogues no longer in use, there are ancient Torah scrolls, intricately carved arks, and other valuable material that needs to be preserved.

Syrian Christians A group of Christians who trace their origin to ST. THOMAS, Apostle of Christ, and to CANAI THOMA or Thomas of Canan, a merchant who came to India along with some Syrian Christian bishops and others in the fourth century. Both groups settled in Kerala. The earlier St. Thomas Christians, known as Nazranis, gradually merged with the new group, and all came to be known as Syrian Christians. Some of the new immigrants, however, kept apart, and even today there are two groups: the 'southerners', who claim they came from Syria and did not mix with the locals, and thus have racial 'purity'; and the 'northerners', who trace their descent from the original St. Thomas Christians. Another group

of Syrian Christians came from Syria in the ninth or tenth centuries and settled in Kollam (Kerala). These groups of Christians seem to have been fairly united until the coming of the Portuguese. They maintained contacts with West Asia, and their bishops came from Mesopotamia and Persia. They adopted the customs, mode of worship and even the Syriac language of the Syrian Church. When the Portuguese came to India in the sixteenth century, they established control over the Syrian Christians and prevented their contacts with West Asia. In 1653, the Syrians organized a protest against this, an event known as the revolt of COONEN KURISU. They were partially successful in their attempt, but not all Syrian Christians wanted to sever ties with the Portuguese. Thus a number of Syrian Christian groups arose, including Syrian Catholics and ORTHODOX CHRISTIANS, and even within these there are further divisions.

Syro-Malabar Church A CATHOLIC Church that follows some Eastern rites and is headed by a Major Archbishop based in Ernakulam–Angamali. It was raised to the status of a Major Archiepiscopal *sui juris* (autonomous) Church in 1993. The Church traces its origin back to the ST. THOMAS CHRISTIANS and the later group of SYRIAN CHRISTIANS, which then came under Portuguese influence. After the revolt of COONEN KURISU in 1653, one group retained its Catholic ties and came to be known as the Syro-Malabar Church. European bishops from the Latin Church were appointed, and the Church was under their rule till 1896, when three Apostolic Vicariates were set up, which were made dioceses in 1923. In the same year the Syro-Malabar hierarchy was established. Some KNANAYA CHRISTIANS joined the Church, but have separate dioceses.

A Major Archiepiscopal Church is relatively autonomous under the Holy See. The only other Catholic Major Archepiscopal Church is the Ukranian Church of the Byzantine tradition.

In the Syro-Malabar Church there are fifteen dioceses under the Archbishop, and eleven directly under the Pope. However, all form part of the Synod of Bishops of the Church, which is the second-largest Catholic Church under the Oriental Churches. Some groups in the Church want a reformed liturgy based on Indian traditions, while others want a revival of the pure Chaldean rites.

Syro-Malankara Church A CATHOLIC Church with some Eastern rites, presided over by the Metropolitan Archbishop of Thiruvananthapuram, Kerala. The Church traces its origins to ST. THOMAS and the later SYRIAN CHRISTIANS. After the revolt of COONEN KURISU in 1653, one section of the Syrian Christians adopted the Jacobite or West Syrian liturgical tradition. Another group wanted to revive their ancient traditions, and therefore in 1926 the Metropolitan Mar Ivanios entered negotiations with the Pope. In 1932 Pope Pius XI erected the Syro-Malankara Catholic Hierarchy, which consisted of the Metropolitan Eparchy (Diocese) of Trivandrum and the Eparchy of Tiruvalla. Gradually parishes of the Church were established in various parts of India and the USA. According to the new Code of Canons of the Eastern Churches, the Syro-Malankara Church has the status of a Metropolitan autonomous Church. The Metropolitan or head of the Church, is appointed by the Pope. Thus the Church retains both its Catholic connections and its autonomy.

The Church today has four Eparchies and six bishops, with about 5,00,000 members.

Tabo Monastery   A Buddhist complex located near the Spiti river in Lahaul and Spiti, Himachal Pradesh. An inscription records that it was founded in 996 by RINCHEN ZANGPO, a Tibetan scholar who came to India to study Buddhism at the time of the Guge dynasty of western Tibet. Tabo has several temples, twenty-three CHORTENS, monks' chambers and an extension with nuns' chambers. The main Lakhang or shrine has an image of the Buddha VAIROCHANA, below which are two images of Rinchen Zangpo, as well as other BUDDHAS and BODHISATTVAS. The complex has stucco images and colourful murals, on account of which it has been called the 'Ajanta of the Himalayas'. Painted frescos tell the story of Prince Novsang, a Bodhisattva, and of the Buddha SHAKYAMUNI. Nearby is a contemporary monastic structure.

Taglung Kagyu   A school of TIBETAN BUDDHISM, a sub-sect of the KAGYU lineage. It was founded by Taglung Thangpa Tashe Pel (1142–1210). The current head (2005) is Shabdrung Rinpoche who now lives in Sikkim.

Tagore, Debendranath   A leader of the BRAHMO SAMAJ, as well as of other socio-religious organizations. Born in 1817, he was the son of Dwarkanath TAGORE of Jorosanko, Kolkata (Calcutta) in present West Bengal. Growing up in luxurious surroundings, with a relatively liberal atmosphere, he was sensitive to social ills and yearned to do something for society. In 1839 he founded the Tattvabodhini Sabha to spread the knowledge of the true religion of the VEDAS. In 1843 he modified his ideas on the Vedas and became the leader of the Brahmo Samaj, merging his Sabha into this. In 1866 modern reformers broke away from the Samaj and started their own group. The group led by Debendranath was then known as the Adi Brahmo Samaj.

Debendranath was involved in a number of other activities. He acquired land and founded an ASHRAM, later devoloped by Rabindranath TAGORE into Santiniketan. In 1846 he founded the Hindu Hitarthi Vidyalaya to counteract the effects of Christian missionaries and promote Hindu and nationalist education. He was also part of the British Indian Association, one of the first groups to put forward the views of Indians to the British. He wrote a number of books on philosophy and religion, among them being *Brahmo Dharma,* on the ideas of the Brahmo Samaj. He was respected for his simple way of life and involvement with spirituality, and was affectionately called 'Maharishi'. He died in 1905.

Tagore, Dwarkanath   A leader of the BRAHMO SAMAJ. Born in 1784, he grew up in his ancestral home at Jorosanko, Kolkata (Calcutta). He was fluent in English, Arabic and Persian, and became an official in the British East India Company. He also ran a number of flourishing business concerns.

He supported Ram Mohan ROY in his reformist ideas and joined the Brahmo Samaj, leading the organization up to 1843, when the leadership was taken over by his son, Debendranath TAGORE. Dwarkanath died in England in 1846. His extravagant way of life led him into debt, though he was popular with all who knew him, appreciated for his generosity, his learning, and his liberal and progressive outlook.

Tagore, Rabindranath   A multi-faceted person, a mystic and visionary, who won the Nobel Prize for Literature in 1913. He was the first Indian to win a Nobel Prize in any field. Rabindranath was also a writer, poet, artist, musician and educationist.

Born on 6 May 1861 at Jorosanko, Kolkata, he was the fourteenth child of Debendranath TAGORE. He was educated partly at home and partly in school, and from an early age demonstrated that he was gifted, talented and mystical. He began composing poems from the age of thirteen, and from around the age of sixteen he had mystical visions. He read the texts of various religions and was inspired by the UPANISHADS, the BHAKTI poets, Buddhist texts and the songs of the BAULS. He was also inspired by Western liberalism and was against orthodoxy and superstition.

During his lifetime he composed more than 2000 songs, hundreds of long poems, as well as plays, essays, short stories and novels. Many of his poems and songs had mystical themes, and his collection *GITANJALI* earned him the Nobel Prize.

Taittiriya Samhita   A term for one version of the *YAJUR VEDA,* also known as the *Krishna* or *Black Yajur Veda.* The *Taittiriya Brahmana, Taittiriya Aranyaka* and *Upanishad* are attached to it. There is also a *Taittiriya Pratishakhya.*

Taj Mahal The most notable monument of the Mughal dynasty (1526–1857) in India, which is said to represent 'the ultimate expression of earthly love'. Though the Taj Mahal is a tomb, it also has mosques attached to it. The huge structure, constructed entirely in pure white marble, was built on the banks of the YAMUNA at AGRA in present Uttar Pradesh by the Mughal Emperor Shah Jahan (1628–66) in memory of his favourite queen, Arjumand Banu Begam, known as Mumtaz Mahal (d. 1629). The graves of both Shah Jahan and Mumtaz Mahal are within the structure.

The Taj took over twenty years to complete and is thought to be the most perfect building in the world. The main entrance is from the west, though there are two more gates on the east and south. Outside the western gate is the Fatehpuri Mosque, which is still in use, as well as other structures and tombs. The gateway is inscribed with passages from the QURAN, and the main building is approached through a symmetrically laid out garden with fountains.

Built on a square platform measuring 95 m by 95 m, the main tomb is square. Each side measures 56.6 m, and has a large central arch around which are Quranic inscriptions, with smaller double arches on either side. The central dome is 56.9 m high, topped with a finial of 17.1 m. On the walls are inscribed verses from the Quran in ornate script, inlaid in black marble on the white marble walls. Each corner of the structure has a small dome and at each end of the platform is a tall tapering minaret, 41.6 m high. The screens around the tomb are finely carved, and there is also pietra dura work, where white marble plates are inlaid with precious and semi-precious stones, creating beautiful intricate floral designs. On either side of the Taj are two mosques in red sandstone, in a style similar to that of the entrance gateway.

The Taj is visited by thousands of tourists every day.

Taj-ul Masjid An imposing mosque located in Bhopal, Madhya Pradesh. It was begun in 1878, by the ruler of the state, Jehan Begum but remained unfinished and was completed only in 1971. The huge mosque dominates the city and has a vast prayer hall, three large white-painted domes, and two minarets, each with eighteen storeys.

Takht A centre of Sikh spiritual authority. Apart from the AKAL TAKHT at AMRITSAR, the supreme seat of spiritual authority, there are four other Takhts:
(1) Takht Sri Harmandir Sahib, at Patna in Bihar. It marks the birthplace of Guru GOBIND SINGH.
(2) Takht Sri Keshgarh Saheb at ANANDPUR, Punjab. It marks the place where Guru Gobind Singh created the Khalsa.
(3) Takht Sri Damdama Sahib at TALWANDI SABO, Punjab.
(4) Takht Sachkhand Huzur Sahib at Nanded, Maharashtra. This marks the place where Guru Gobind Singh died.

Takshaka A NAGA deity, the king of snakes in Hindu mythology. According to the ATHARVA VEDA, he was descended from Vishala, while in the VISHNU PURANA he is the son of Kadru. In the MAHABHARATA he was said to live in the Khandava forest, and when it was burnt by ARJUNA, Takshaka was saved by INDRA, though his wife was killed. During the SARPA SATRA or snake sacrifice of King Janamejaya, he took refuge with the god Indra. Takshaka lives in PATALA. The deity is still worshipped in some areas in the rainy season, to ward off snake bite.

Tala Kaveri A sacred spot where the river Kaveri originates, located at a height of 1350 m on the Brahmagiri peak in Karnataka. The river rises here from a spring, around which there are three shrines. It is a popular place of pilgrimage, particularly at Tulasankranti. The river soon goes underground again, reappearing a kilometre later.

Talatala The fourth of the seven divisions or LOKAS of the nether world or PATALA, according to Hindu mythology. MAYA, a great asura, who was blessed by SHIVA, rules here.

Talmud A text in Judaism, a commentary on the MISHNAH. There are two versions of the *Talmud*, the Palestinian or Jerusalem *Talmud*, compiled at the end of the fourth century, and the Babylonian *Talmud* from the end of the fifth century, which is considered more authoritative. Both were composed in Aramaic. The *Talmud* contains both halakhah, information on legal and ritualistic matters, and aggadah, or theology and ethics explained through stories and parables. Traditional Jews follow the halakhah of the Babylonian *Talmud*. Both these *Talmuds* have several commentaries.

Talwandi Sabo A town sacred to Sikhs, in Bathinda district of Punjab, where the TAKHT Sri Damdama Sahib, a centre of Sikh spiritual authority, is located. Talwandi is also associated with Guru GOBIND SINGH, who in 1706, lived for some time in a spot close to Talwandi village and composed verses that were then compiled by Bhai MANI SINGH. Here the final version of the Granth Sahib was written down by Mani Singh. According to some accounts the guru stayed here for nine months, while according to others he was here for about three years. The Sri Damdama Sahib Gurdwara was built at this spot. Two GURDWARAS associated with the ninth guru, TEGH BAHADUR, who visited this place, are known as Wada Darbar Sahib and Gurusar.

tamas One of the three main GUNAS or qualities, said to exist in all human beings. Tamas is inertia, negativity or darkness, obstacles that have to be overcome in order to proceed in any activity. The gunas are mentioned in several texts, but they are best described in SAMKHYA philosophy.

Tamil New Year's Day A new year's day celebrated according to the Tamil calendar, in March/April in Tamil Nadu. Festivities take place in homes and in temples. Tiruvadamarudar (near KUMBAKONAM), Tiruchirapalli and KANCHIPURAM, are among the areas where large-scale celebrations take place.

Tamil siddhas In the Tamil tradition, eighteen saints are recognized as SIDDHAS (Tamil: Cittar), or perfected ones. The names of the siddhas vary in different texts, and there were many more than eighteen, the traditional mystical and symbolic number. Among the siddhas were TIRUMULAR, also a NAYANAR, but considered the founder of the Tamil siddha tradition, as well as Akkapey-cittar, Sivavakkiyar, Pattinattar, and Pampatti-cittar. Tirumular lived in the sixth or seventh century and Sivavakkiyar in the eighth century, while the others were later. Pampatti-cittar has been placed between the fifteenth and eighteenth centuries.

The siddhas were usually wandering ascetics, and were against BRAHMANAS, rituals, caste, formal worship and social norms. They emphasized meditation on the god within the Self, as well as various YOGA and TANTRIC practices, to reach their goal. They composed songs in colloquial Tamil about liberation, immortality, and the divine soul within the heart, and each siddha reflected his own experiences in his songs. Tirumular's verses are varied, and are collected in the *Tirumantiram*. The songs of Akkapey-cittar are reminiscent of the thoughts of the Buddhist philosopher NAGARJUNA. In one composition Akkapey said:

I do not exist,
The Lord too, is non-existent;
The Self is non-existent
The Teacher does not exist . . .
All actions
Are really the Void.
That which does not exist
Will appear in Nothingness.

Pattinattar, though he sang in several different moods, prayed to the Lord of MADURAI and experienced the divine truth, also realized the void, in which nothing remained. Sivavakkiyar's *Patal*, or *Song*, has 527 stanzas, in which he describes the Light, and the Ultimate or Absolute, which is beyond all forms.

Other siddhas include Kudambai-cittar, Kaduveli-cittar, and Azhuhini-cittar. Though most of the siddhas were from the Hindu tradition, Gunankudi Masthan was originally a Muslim. As siddhas, they transcended formal religion, though they used some of its terminolgy in their compositions.

Tanakh A term for the Jewish BIBLE. The Hebrew BIBLE is divided into three parts: TORAH, Nevi'im and Ketuvim. Tanach or Tenakh is an acronym based on the first letters of these parts. According to Jewish tradition, the Tanakh consists of twenty-four books. The Torah has five books, Nevi'im contains eight books, and Ketuvim has eleven.

tandava A term for the Hindu god SHIVA'S cosmic dance, which he dances in his form as NATARAJA.

Tangyur/Tanjur A collection of Buddhist texts, forming the second part of the canon of TIBETAN BUDDHISM. These texts were composed by various individuals and consist of a volume of Stotras which has sixty-four texts, commentaries on the TANTRAS in eighty-six volumes, incorporating 3055 texts, and commentaries on the Sutras in 137 volumes, incorporating 567 texts.

Tansen One of the most famous musicians and singers of India, who lived in the sixteenth century. Though India has had renowned musicians of all kinds, Tansen was one who was able to realize the legendary powers of music. Born in 1506, Tansen, originally known as Ramatanu, became the court musician of the Mughal emperor, AKBAR. His music was so perfect that he was said to have been able to light a lamp or bring rain by singing the appropriate RAGA. He died in 1580 and was buried at Gwalior, near the tomb of his spiritual guru, the great saint known as Muhammad Ghaus.

Tantras A class of texts of both Hinduism and Buddhism. Tantras focus on the manifestation of divine energy within the body, through various practices. See TANTRISM.

Tantric That pertaining to TANTRA or TANTRISM.

Tantrism, Buddhist Tantric Buddhism developed in India by the seventh or eighth centuries, though there are also earlier texts relating to Tantric practices. Despite different techniques being used, the aim of Tantric Buddhism remains the same as for MAHAYANA Buddhism, i.e., to gain the power to help all sentient beings. Tantric Buddhism has been divided into the three broad groups of VAJRAYANA, SAHAJIYANA and KALACHAKRA, though this is a somewhat artificial division. Tantra and Vajrayana are sometimes used as synonyms, while early forms of Vajrayana are also referred to as MANTRAYANA.

From the monasteries of VIKRAMSHILA, NALANDA and Odantapura in India, this form of Buddhism spread to Tibet and was preserved there. Since 1959, with the escape of the DALAI LAMA to India, some of its practices have been revived here, particularly in Tibetan enclaves and institutes.

The revealed TANTRAS translated into Tibetan were collected in two groups, translated works known as KAGYUR (Bka-gyur), and commentaries, or TANGYUR (Bstan-gyur). Four types of literature were identified within this division: Kriya Tantras, Charya Tantras, Yoga Tantras and ANUTTARAYOGA TANTRAS, representing different methods of Tantra. These groups have two types of approaches. The first two provide methods which all practioners can use to attain Buddhahood, while the second two are based on a classification into Buddhist families headed by a BUDDHA (see DHYANI BUDDHAS). People are assigned to these families on the basis of the predominant vice that remains in them on the purificatory path, and thus different practices can be provided for different types of people. Practitioners usually use a mix of outer rituals and inner practices. In addition there are works known as *Sadhanas*, to invoke a particular deity, as well as texts on MANDALAS or cosmic diagrams, and on MAHASIDDHAS, or adepts who had attained various powers. The NYINGMA school divides Anuttarayoga Tantras into three additional categories: Mahayoga, Anuyoga and Atiyoga (dzogchen).

Tantric Buddhist texts include the *GUHYASAMAJA TANTRA; Arya MANJUSHRI MULA KALPA*, the oldest available Buddhist Tantra; *NISHPANNAYOGAVALI; Ratna-gotra-vibhaga-mahahanottara-Tantra*, on the worship of the Dhyani Buddhas; the *Kalachakra Tantra* and several others.

Tantrism, Hindu A form of religion or spiritualism which originated in ancient days but gained popularity by the eighth century. The word may come from the Sanskrit root tan, 'to spread' or tanu, 'body' or tadantara, 'inner'.

As a method of religious practice, its exact origin is not known, but certain concepts and practices can be traced back to the *ATHARVA VEDA*.

Tantrism aims to gain control over all the forces of nature and to obtain the power to accomplish any task. At its highest level it seeks union with the divine, while at its lowest, its powers can be used to harm others.

There are numerous Tantric texts describing various practices, as well as a number of Tantric sects, many of which still exist. Extant Hindu Tantric literature includes a vast number of texts dating from the seventh to the seventeenth centuries, much of which is still untranslated. TANTRAS contain both high philosophy and practical methodology. The texts are composed in Sanskrit and in regional languages. The main topics in Tantras are: theories regarding the creation and destruction of the world; methods of worship of various deities; attainment of all objects as well as all SIDDHIS; methods of uniting with the Supreme.

Some important Hindu Tantric texts are the *Aghori Tantra; Bagala Tantra; Gayatritantra*, on how the GAYATRI MANTRA can be used for protection; *Kalavilasa-Tantra*, on the goddess KALI; *Kularnava-Tantra*, of the KAULA sect; *Maheshvara-Tantram*, a SHAIVITE text; *Matrikabheda-Tantra*, on the meditational use of syllables of the alphabet; *Pranatoshini-Tantram*, 'the Tantra that satisfies the vital force'; *Prapanch-sara-Tantram*, 'Tantra of the essence of the phenomenal universe', attributed to SHANKARA; *Saundarya-lahari*, also attributed to Shankara; *Tantraraja-Tantra*, which describes the Shri-yantra.

Sects can be divided broadly into two categories: those that use MANTRAS or sacred chants, meditation on YANTRAS or cosmic diagrams, and other meditative and breathing practices; and those that negate and overturn all normal practices. The former are known as the right-hand sects, and the latter as the left-hand sects, though there is some overlap between the two. The real objective of Tantra is to sublimate desire by first acceding to it. In the 'left' (vamachara) path, physical union is prescribed under strict conditions. The Tantric method includes sadhana or practice, shuddhi or purification, uddhara or elevation, and chaitanya, the reaffirmation of identity in consciousness.

All Tantric sects seek to raise the KUNDALINI, the hidden energy centre at the base of the spine, to the SAHASRARA CHAKRA at the top of the head, arousing other CHAKRAS along the way.

Left-hand sects particularly use the PANCHA-MAKARA or panchatattvas, commonly known as the five Ms. They are madya or wine, matsya or fish, mamsa, meat or flesh, mudra or parched grain, and maithuna or sexual union.

There are seven Tantric paths included in orthodox Hindu Tantric texts, among them the Shakta, Shaiva, Vaishnava, Saura and Ganapatya forms. The KAPALIKAS and KALAMUKHAS were among the SHAIVITE Tantric sects, while NATHA YOGIS have some Tantric practices. Among VAISHNAVA sects the PANCHARATRA and SAHAJIYA follow Tantric practices. Traditionally, Hindu Tantra is attributed to the god SHIVA, and several texts consist of a dialogue between Shiva and PARVATI.

tapas/tapah A term for heat, which generates power. Tapas is the heat generated by ascetic practices. Special powers can be attained through it, as well as spiritual development.

taqiya A term in Islam that refers to the practice of dissimulation or concealment of belief. SHIAS are allowed to practise this if their lives are in danger. This was at one time practised by MAHDAWIS in Gujarat, who pretended to be orthodox Muslims to escape persecution.

Tara A goddess who has Hindu and Buddhist forms.

(1) In Hinduism, she is one of the ten MAHAVIDYAS or Tantric goddesses, and is similar to KALI. She is said to be dark. She is draped in a tiger skin, wears a necklace of severed heads, and has her foot on a corpse.

(2) Tara was also the wife of the rishi BRIHASPATI, and was abducted by SOMA. She was restored to her husband after a war. BUDHA, Mercury, was her son through Soma.

(3) In the *RAMAYANA*, another Tara is the wife of the vanara king, VALI.

(4) In Buddhism, Tara has many forms. According to legend, she was born from the tears of the Bodhisattva AVALOKITESHVARA. There are twenty-one different forms of Tara, including Green and White Taras. Tara is depicted in her various forms in Buddhist temples, particularly those of TIBETAN BUDDHISM.

Taraka A DAITYA, who had gained great powers by practising austerities and worshipping the Hindu god SHIVA. Soon, however, he became arrogant and oppressive, and a threat to the gods. Only a son of

SHIVA could kill him, thus KARTTIKEYA, the son of Shiva and PARVATI, was born in order to destroy him, and succeeded in doing so.

Taraknatha Temple   A temple of the Hindu god SHIVA, located at Tarakeshvara in Bengal. It is the most important Shiva shrine in the region and was constructed in the eighteenth century, with additions made later. The inner shrine houses a LINGA, while the adjoining MANDAPA is a late construction. The walls of the temple have terracotta plaques depicting various deities, while the roof is curved and double-tiered.

Worshippers of Shiva from all over the country visit this temple throughout the year. Thousands arrive for the two main festivals of SHIVARATRI in February/March and Gajan in April. On these occasions pots of water are carried from the river GANGA 35 km away and poured on the image. The water is not allowed to touch the ground; the water pots are attached to poles balanced on the shoulders. Similar rituals take place in other parts of India in the month of Shravana.

Tarana Svami   The founder of a Jain DIGAMBARA sub-sect, the TARANAPANTHA. He was also known as Tarana-Tarana-Svami and lived from 1448 to 1515. He is said to have been influenced by Islamic ideas and by the teachings of LONKA SHAHA, the founder of the STHANAKAVASI sub-sect of the SHVETAMBARAS. He wrote fourteen books expounding his ideas. He died at Malharagarh in present Madhya Pradesh.

Taranapantha   A sub-sect of the DIGAMBARA Jain sect, founded in the fifteenth century and named after its founder, TARANA SVAMI. It is also known as Samayapantha, because the adherents of this sect worship samaya, or sacred books, instead of images of deities. Taranapanthas follow the texts sacred to Digambaras, as well as the fourteen texts by Tarana Svami. They reject idol worship, caste and religious differences, and outer religious practices, believing in an inner spirituality. There are not many Taranapanthas, but some live in Madhya Pradesh and Maharashtra. Malharagarh in Madhya Pradesh, where Tarana Svami died, is their main centre of pilgrimage.

Taranatha   A Tibetan Buddhist (b. 1575) who wrote a number of texts on Buddhism in Tibetan, including the *History of the Kalachakra*, and the *History of Buddhism in India*. These are still considered important texts on Buddhism.

tar-chok   A term in TIBETAN BUDDHISM for coloured prayer flags that are tied to the roofs of Tibetan houses, monasteries and sacred places. Passages from Buddhist texts are printed on them, and thus they are said to spread the teachings while they flutter in the wind. The LUNG-TA, or wind horse, is another common motif on these flags.

tariqa   The path, a term used in Islam for the SUFI way. Tariqa has several stages, including repentance,

conversion or a resolve to adhere to the new path, renunciation and trust in God. The PIR or shaikh prescribes the path for each disciple.

Tarkshya   (1) The name of a divine horse in the RIG VEDA, described in terms similar to DADHIKRA. He is swift as a bird, and in later texts, is identified with GARUDA, the vehicle of the Hindu god VISHNU.

(2) An ancient RISHI described in the MAHABHARATA and other texts.

Tarn Taran Sahib Gurdwara   A GURDWARA or Sikh shrine, also known as Darbar Sahib, located at Tarn Taran in Punjab, 22 km south-east of AMRITSAR, first constructed by the fifth guru, ARJAN DEV, in memory of Guru RAM DAS. At this time the gurdwara was a small hut, with a tank dug adjacent to it. However, the lining of the tank that was begun at the time of Guru Arjan Dev, could not be completed till 1778. The present gurdwara was largely constructed in the time of Maharaja Ranjit Singh. Built in Mughal style, the three-storeyed gurdwara is richly ornamented, its dome covered in copper gilt. The entrance has a double-storeyed arch, with projecting balconies on the facade. The large tank nearby measures 300 sq. m, larger than that of the Harmandir Sahib. Its waters are said to have healing properties, and are believed to cure leprosy. Every month, on Amavas day, a fair is held here, when hundreds of pilgrims visit the holy shrine.

Tasawwuf   A term used in Islam for SUFISM.

Tathagata   A term used to refer to the BUDDHA; literally, one who realizes the true nature of things, their 'suchness' (TATHATA).

Tathagata-garbha   A school of MAHAYANA Buddhism expounded by SARAMATI (350–450). It refers to the presence of the TATHAGATA, the BUDDHA essence, in all beings. It states that Buddhahood, or the Tathagata, is innate in everyone, and shows how it can be realized. This concept is subtly different from that of SHUNYATA, with its focus on emptiness devoid of qualities, and also different from the consciousness theories of the YOGACHARA school. Instead it focuses on positive attributes and the realization of the Absolute (dharmadhatu) in the world. Saramati wrote a commentary on the *Ratnagotravibhaga*, a text attributed to MAITREYANATHA, where he explained how this innate essence becomes manifest in the world. Thus the BODHISATTVA, according to him, is not one who abstains from liberation in order to help others, but rather a manifestation of the Absolute in the world.

tathata   A MAHAYANA Buddhist term translated as 'suchness'.

Tattva Samasa   A Sanskrit text dealing with the SAMKHYA philosophy, which is ascribed to KAPILA.

Tattvarthadhigama Sutra   A Jain text written in Sanskrit by UMASVAMI, translated as *A Manual for Understanding the True Nature of Things*. This manual is recognized as an authority by both SHVETAMBARAS and DIGAMBARAS, and includes the logic, psychology, cosmography, ontology and ethics of Jainism. The commentary on this text, also attributed to Umasvami, is not accepted as authentic by the Digambaras, though another commentary by the scholar Siddhasena Divakara is accepted by both sects.

tattvas A term for an element or elementary property, or for the principles of PRAKRITI or matter. The term also refers to categories of various phenomena. Tattvas are classified in the early schools of philosophy as well as in Buddhism and Jainism.

tattvas, in Jainism A term for the basic principles or constituents recognized by Jainism. The seven tattvas include JIVA and AJIVA, life and non-life, as well as ASRAVA, bandha, samvara, NIRJARA and MOKSHA. Asrava is the inflow of KARMA; bandha, the bondage of the soul through asrava; samvara, stopping the inflow; nirjara, gradually removing karma, leading finally to moksha or liberation.

Tawang Monastery A Buddhist monastery located in Arunachal Pradesh. Tawang monastery, also known as Galden Namgyal Lhatse, stands on a hill 3096 m high. It was founded in 1860–61, by Merak Lama Lodre Gyamsto, and has the capacity to house 700 monks.

The Dukhang is the main temple building, containing a large image of the Buddha. A silver casket holds special thangkas of the goddess Palden Lhamo, the main deity of the temple. On the walls are murals of Buddhist deities and saints.

The monastery is entered from the north, along the ridge. Apart from the temple and the residential quarters, Tawang has a large library and a centre for Buddhist cultural studies.

The monastery is closely connected with the fifth Dalai Lama, Ngawang Lobsang Gyatso, and was constructed on his request. The goddess thangkas are said to be painted with blood drawn from his nose, giving it a living quality, while the boundary wall was protected by yarn given by the Dalai Lama to Merek Lama.

This is one of the most important monasteries in India, and belongs to the GELUG sect of TIBETAN BUDDHISM.

taziya A term in Islam for the model of the tomb of HUSAIN, grandson of the Prophet MUHAMMAD. Taziyas made of wood and paper are decorated and carried in MUHARRAM processions, and then taken to the local graveyard, or immersed in water. Taziya also refers to enactments of the life and death of Husain, that take place during Muharram.

Teej A Hindu festival celebrated at the beginning of the monsoon, in June/July, mainly in Rajasthan and Madhya Pradesh. Dressed in bright colours, groups of people sing, dance and take out processions, which include decorated elephants, horses or camels.

The festival also re-enacts the daughter's departure for her husband's house. An image of the goddess DEVI (PARVATI) is kept in the house for two days and worshipped, after which a ceremony takes place, similar to that when the real daughter leaves home.

Tegh Bahadur, Guru The ninth Sikh guru, from 1664 to 1675. The youngest son of Guru HARGOBIND and his wife Bibi Nanaki, Tegh Bahdur was born at AMRITSAR in 1621. He was trained in the religious tradition and in martial arts, but after a battle at KARTARPUR in 1634, he felt nothing could be gained through bloodshed and became a renunciate, later settling in village Bakala, where he lived a reclusive life in constant meditation. Guru Hargobind therefore chose his grandson, HAR RAI, the son of Baba Gurditta, as his successor, and Har Rai was succeeded by HAR KRISHAN, who, however, died when he was still a child. On his deathbed, Har Krishan is said to have muttered 'Baba Bakala', indicating that the next guru would be found in village Bakala. A number of people from Bakala claimed to be the guru, and the succesor of Har Krishan, but through the efforts of Makhan Khan Lubana, a trader of Bakala, the true guru was discovered. Tegh Bahadur now became an active leader of the Sikhs, though he faced opposition from rival claimants. He travelled across Punjab but was refused entry into the HAR MANDIR at Amritsar, which was controlled by a descendant of Prithi Chand, an elder brother of ARJAN DEV. He therefore built a new township of Chak Nanaki, later known as ANANDPUR SAHIB. Accompanied by his wife and mother, Tegh Bahadur is said to have visted DELHI, AGRA, KURUKSHETRA, PRAYAGA, VARANASI, GAYA, PATNA and other places, spreading the message of Sikhism. Leaving his wife at Patna he moved further east, crossing Bengal and Assam, where he was able to negotiate a peace settlement between the Ahom ruler and the Mughal forces. By this time, his son Gobind Rai, later the tenth guru GOBIND SINGH, had been born at Patna. Guru Tegh Bahadur and his family returned to Anandpur Sahib in 1672–73. Meanwhile the Mughal emperor AURANGZEB was ruling at Delhi. He was known to be intolerant of other religions, and some of his local governors were even more oppressive. According to Sikh tradition, certain Hindu pandits of Kashmir approached the guru asking for his help, and the guru proceeded to Delhi to meet the emperor. There Guru Tegh Bahadur is reported to have told the emperor, 'Hinduism may not be my religion . . . but I would fight for the right of Hindus to live with honour and practise their faith according to their own rites.' When asked to convert to Islam, he said, 'For me there is only one religion, the religion of God, and whoever belongs to it, whether a Hindu or a Muslim, him I own and he owns me. I neither convert others by force, nor submit to force to change my faith.' The guru and the three disciples who had accompanied him, Bhai Mati Das, Bhai Dyala and Bhai Sati Das, were tortured and killed, the guru himself being executed on 11 November 1675. A huge storm took place, darkening the city of Delhi and enabling some of his disciples to remove his head and body. His head was cremated at Anandpur Sahib. The BABA BAKALA GURDWARA, RAKABGANJ GURDWARA and SIS GANJ GURDWARA, are among the shrines associated with the guru.

tejas A term for fiery energy or spiritual power. It sometimes refers to semen.

temples, Hindu Temples are sacred shrines, where the divine spirit, embodied as a deity or a great saint, is said to dwell. They vary from a tiny shrine beneath a tree to immense and elaborate structures, but in one form or the other, they are found all over India.

Small shrines are set up at places considered sacred and can have many forms: a mud hut with a stone or figure representing a deity; an image placed beneath a tree; or just a natural stone that has acquired sanctity over the years. Larger temples, however, are often constructed according to fixed principles, laid down in texts.

The main parts of a constructed temple are:
(1) The GARBHA-GRIHA, literally 'womb house', also called the cella or sanctum. This is the innermost shrine, housing the main deity. It is usually a small, square structure, dark inside, with its doorway facing east.
(2) The tower, also known as the SHIKHARA or vimana, which rises above the roof of the garbha-griha, and can reach great heights.
(3) The antarala, or vestibule. The door of the cella opens into this, which connects the cella with a pillared hall or MANDAPA.
(4) The mandapa or hall where devotees gather, which can be of varying sizes.
(5) The ardha-mandapa, literally 'half-mandapa', which is the outer porch through which devotees enter.
(6) The maha-mandapa, a transept on each side of the central hall. Only the larger temples have this.
(7) There may be additional towers over the mandapas.
(8) Outside the temple there may be other subsidiary shrines.
(9) The whole complex is often enclosed by high walls, entered through a gateway.

Not all temples have these components. Small temples may have only a garbha-griha, or a garbha-griha along with an ardha-mandapa. Large temples may have additional features, including extra towers. The style and structure of a temple varies considerably over time, and in different regions. Some different temple styles are given below.

Cave and rock-cut temples: Natural caves were used to make Brahmanical and Jain temples, as well as Buddhist CHAITYAS and VIHARAS. Often the walls and roofs were carved, and additions made with wood.

Among the earliest such Brahmanical temples are the temples at Udaigiri in Madhya Pradesh; AIHOLE, BADAMI, ELLORA, ELEPHANTA and Jogeshvari in Karnataka and Maharashtra; Vijayawada, Bhairavakonda and other sites in Andhra Pradesh; Pallavaram and MAMALLAPURAM in Tamil Nadu. In addition there are rock-cut temples such as the PANDAVA RATHAS at MAMALLAPURAM, and the KAILASHNATHA TEMPLE at Ellora. There are also some rock-cut temples in Himachal and elsewhere.

Early structural temples: In early days, temples were probably made from simple posts and thatch, or from a combination of brick and wood. One of the earliest surviving temples is at Bairat, near Jaipur in Rajasthan, dated to about 250 BCE. Next are some small north Indian temples built between CE 300 and 500, most of them flat-roofed, except for the Deogarh temple, which has a small tower. In the sixth and seventh centuries there were experimental styles; some had flat roofs, others spires or curvilinear towers.

Later temples: In succeeding centuries, regional styles developed. Three main styles recognized in the Shilpa Shastras, texts on architecture, were the Nagara, Vesara and Dravida.

Nagara style: The Nagara style developed a curvilinear tower and had a cruciform ground-plan. This type, with some variations, is found from the north to the Deccan, and from the west to the east. The Orissa temple is closest to the classic Nagara style. Uttar Pradesh, central India, Gujarat (Solanki temples), Rajasthan, Himachal Pradesh, Uttarakhand and Bengal all had variants of this style, built between the eighth and thirteenth centuries.

Orissa temples: In Orissa temples, found at Bhubaneswar, Puri, Konarak and elsewhere, the inner shrine is a cubical structure known as the deul. Above it is a tall, beehive-shaped tower. The shrine opens into the hall or antarala, also known as the jagmohan, which is usually square, with a pyramidal roof. One or two more halls are often added, such as the nat mandir or dance hall, and the bhog mandir.

Malava temples: Malava temples were an offshoot of the Nagara style, and reached its height under the Paramara dynasty in the western Deccan, between the tenth and twelfth centuries. In this style, because of the diversity of the exterior walls, the inner shrine and the MANDAPA often appear to be diagonally connected.

Dravida style: Typical of the Dravida style in the Tamil region are pyramidal roofs and huge, elaborately carved GOPURAMS.

Vesara style: The Vesara style, found in the Deccan, is an intermediate style, with Dravida and Nagara elements.

Kerala and Kashmir: Kerala and Kashmir had somewhat different styles. Typical Kerala temples are built mainly of laterite stone bricks and have roofs covered with tiles. Some are multi-roofed, whereas others are circular structures with pointed, upturned cone roofs. In Kashmir, wood was often used.

There were several other local styles, which were variants of these. In modern times temples have been constructed in eclectic styles, while some retain traditional forms.

Tengalai school One of the two schools of Shrivaishnavism or southern VAISHNAVISM, which emerged in the twelfth or thirteenth century, the other being the VADAGALAI. The writings of the ALVARS are their main sacred texts. Tengalais admitted all castes and preached in the local language, Tamil. One of its major proponents was Pillai LOKACHARYA. The Tengalai school believes in the doctrine of prapatti or complete resignation and surrender to god, and states that nothing else is required because a person is saved by the grace of god.

Teppam A Hindu festival celebrated in Tamil Nadu, in which deities placed on decorated floats (teppam) are floated in the temple tanks, while priests chant shlokas. The festival takes place in January/February at a number of temples. In Chennai the main temples involved in the celebrations are the KAPALESHVARA TEMPLE and the PARTHASARTHY TEMPLE. Perhaps the grandest Teppam is at the Minakshi Temple in Madurai.

Terapantha (Digambara) A sub-sect of the DIGAMBARA Jain sect, different from the SHVETAMBARA Terapantha. In north India several Digambara Jains were opposed to the control of the BHATTARAKAS, and in 1627, founded a separate sect, denying their authority. The sect rejected certain practices, such as worshipping deities other than the TIRTHANKARAS and making offerings of sachitta items, i.e., items with life, such as fruits and flowers. Their offerings consisted of sacred rice, cloves, sandal, almonds, dry coconut, dates and similar items. Devotees stand while worshipping and do not usually perform ARTI or distribute prasad. Digambara Terapanthas live mainly in Uttar Pradesh, Rajasthan and Madhya Pradesh.

Terapantha (Shvetambara) A sub-sect of the SHVETAMBARA Jain sect that emerged from the STHANAKAVASI. It was founded in 1760 by Bhikhan or Bhikkana, who was a Sthanakavasi ascetic, in the Marwar area of Rajasthan. There are different versions of the origin of the name, the popular version being that it is derived from the sect following thirteen (tera) main principles of Jainism, the five VRATAS or vows, the five samitis or rules of conduct, and three guptis, of control of thought, speech and action. Another explanation is that as tera also means 'yours', it refers to 'your path', that is, the path of MAHAVIRA. Terapanthas are a closely knit group under the guidance of an acharya. The first acharya was Bhikkana, and the ninth, Tulasi, was born in 1914. Acharya Tulasi started the Anuvrata Andolan, a movement to spread the basic vratas to the masses.

After his death in 1997, Acharya Mahapragya became the tenth acharya.

All ascetics and members of the sect follow the orders of the acharya. Once a year they observe a festival known as Maryada Mahotsava, held on the seventh day of the bright half of the month of Magha, when all members of the sect, both ascetics and lay disciples, meet to discuss various issues and problems. Terapanthas believe in simplicity, do not worship idols, and have strict rules for ascetics. The sect has limited numbers and is concentrated in Rajasthan.

Teresa, Mother A ROMAN CATHOLIC originally from the Loretto Order of Nuns, who founded a new order, the Missionaries of Charity, to work for the poor and destitute. Born in 1910 as Agnes Gongxha Bojaxhiu in Shkup, Albania, Ottoman empire (now Skopje, Macedonia), in 1928 she joined the Institute of the Blessed Virgin Mary in Ireland, but soon after came to India as part of the Bengal mission of Loretto nuns. After her novitiate in Darjiling, she taught at a school in Bengal. In 1946 she became convinced through a spiritual experience that her mission was to help the poor. Obtaining permission from Pope Pius XII, she founded her new order in 1948, which was given official sanction in 1950, and began working in the slums of Calcutta. In 1965 the order was made a pontifical congregation, responsible only to the Pope.

Her order grew and expanded; schools for poor children, orphanages, shelters for the terminally ill, abandoned people, lepers and the mentally ill were opened in several parts of India. The order has also spread to other countries of the world. The nuns of the order wear white saris with blue borders, and are often helped by volunteers.

During her lifetime, Mother Teresa received a number of awards, including the first Pope John XXIII Peace Prize (1971), the Nobel Peace Prize (1979) and the Bharat Ratna (1980), India's highest civilian award.

She died in September 1997 and was beatified in 2003.

thags/thugs A sect of robbers who worshipped the goddess Bhavani, a form of KALI, before robbing and killing their victims. Muslims also became thags, but had their own groups and rituals. Thags were eliminated by the British in the nineteenth century. Some doubt the descriptions of thags and their rituals provided by British officials.

Thanamga (Sthananga) A Jain text, the third of the twelve ANGAS. It deals with religious topics grouped according to numbers from one to ten, as in the Buddhist ANGUTTARA NIKAYA. Thus, under four there are four kinds of teachers, four kinds of mendicants, and four kinds of men. The text also has a list of the contents of the DITTHIVAYA, the lost twelfth ANGA.

thangkas A term for Buddhist scroll paintings depicting Buddhist deities. The paintings can be of different sizes and with various themes, and are found in every Tibetan Buddhist temple, monastery or family shrine. The painting is usually made on cotton canvas and framed in silk brocade. Some scrolls have fine embroidery instead of painting. Thangkas were first made in Tibet around the tenth century. The concept of scroll painting was probably borrowed from China, while the painting style may have been derived from Nepal or Kashmir. The paintings include BUDDHAS, BUDDHIST DEITIES, MANDALAS and other Buddhist themes. Apprentice painters learn the art from experienced lamas to ensure that every detail is correct. Each painting is consecrated before being installed. The paintings are used by lamas for meditation, while lay Buddhists install them for protection against spirits. Several old and new monasteries have beautiful thangkas, and the art is kept alive in India by Tibetan refugees.

Thanjavur A city in Tamil Nadu that has a number of temples and is a major centre of pilgrimage. The temples date back to the Chola period; the most important is the BRIHADESHVARA TEMPLE constructed in the early eleventh century.

Theosophical Society of India A society dedicated to exploring the hidden truths that are the source of all religions. The Theosophical Society was first founded in New York in 1875 by H.P. BLAVATSKY, Col. H.S. OLCOTT and W. Judge.

Blavatsky and Olcott visited India and Sri Lanka in 1878, and in 1882–83 they set up the Theosophical Society of India at Adyar in Chennai (Madras). Blavatsky's writings, particularly *The Secret Doctrine* and the *Voice of the Silence,* laid the basis for Theosophical thought.

Annie BESANT joined the Society in 1889, and came to India in 1893. She wrote extensively on Indian religions, particularly Hinduism and Buddhism, stating that these religions put forward greater truths than those of the West. In a time of rising nationalism and anti-British feelings, this helped to give Indians a sense of pride. Besant also joined the freedom movement and was elected president of the Indian National Congress in 1917. Another prominent Theosophist in India, C.W. Leadbeater, was responsible for choosing J. KRISHNAMURTI as the new messiah. Allan Octavian HUME, a British civil servant and Theosophist, assisted in starting the Indian National Congress in 1885. Rukmini Arundale, married to George Arundale, was among other Theosophists who made major contributions to Indian life and society.

Several prominent Indians joined the society in the early decades of the twentieth century. They followed the Society's principles of dropping caste and religious differences, a major achievement particularly in south India, where Brahmanical traditions were very strong.

Around 1930 the society went through a crisis, soon after J. Krishnamurti rejected its principles. Many left the society to follow Krishnamurti, though they retained their Theosophical ideals.

The society continues to exist today. At its sprawling wooded grounds in Adyar there are a number of activities and programmes attended by visitors from India and abroad. A large and well-stocked library provides facilities for research on the society and on all religions. There are also branches in VARANASI, DELHI, MUMBAI and other cities, where meetings are held, but its greatest impact on India was in the first few decades of the twentieth century.

The aims of the society have been summarized in three principles: (1) to form a nucleus of the universal brotherhood of humanity, without distinction of race, creed, sex, caste, or colour; (2) to encourage the study of comparative religion, philosophy and science; (3) to investigate unexplained laws of nature and the powers latent in man.

The society has a separate esoteric section. In the early days, Madame Blavatsky and her associates formulated an occult hierarchy based on Tibetan Buddhist and Tantric texts, as well as on Puranic myths. According to this hierarchy, SANAT KUMARA, an eternal youth, was at the head of the universe. Below him was the BUDDHA. At the third level were the three heads of the Logos: the Bodhisattva MAITREYA, representing compassion, the Mahachohan, representing buddhi or the higher intellect, and the MANU, representing skilful action. At the fourth level were the Mahatmas or Masters. There were several of these and Master Koot Hoomi or KUTHUMI and Master MORYA were in charge of India. Below this level were the Adepts, but to reach this stage an individual had to be guided by a Master through a series of initiations and to be committed to selfless action. These ideas still have an impact on a number of Western spiritual societies.

Theragatha A HINAYANA Buddhist text that forms part of the KHUDDAKA NIKAYA of the PALI CANON. The *Theragatha*, literally 'songs of the elders', contains verses composed by monks. It has 107 poems, with 1279 stanzas. The beautiful poems describe the experiences of the monks, the peace attained through giving up a worldly life, as well as Buddhist principles and concepts. As the monks live in VIHARAS (monasteries) away from the towns and cities, they are close to nature, and describe the changing seasons. One example is given below:

When the drum of the clouds thunders in
heaven,
and all the ways of the birds are thick with rain,
the monk sits in the hills in ecstasy
and finds no greater joy than this. (Trans. A.L.
Basham)

The *THERIGATHA* is a similar text, consisting of songs by women.

Theravada A Buddhist sect of the HINAYANA school, that is still popular in Sri Lanka, Myanmar, Thailand, Cambodia and Laos. They were an offshoot of the STHAVIRAVADA sect, the sect of the elders. One group of the Sthaviravada was known as Vibhajyavada and settled in south India and Sri Lanka by the third century BCE, where they took the name Theravada, the Pali word for Sthaviravada. According to other sources, the Theravada and Vibhajyavada were similar and closely related, but not identical. Three branches developed in Sri Lanka, named after their monastic centres, the Mahaviharika, Abhayagirika and Jetavaniya. Later Theravada Buddhism spread to Myanmar and other countries.

The Theravada follow the PALI CANON, like other HINAYANA schools, but certain beliefs distinguish them from other schools. Among their main differences are the denial of the concept of an intermediate existence linking death and rebirth, and of the notion that an ARHAT could regress or that a BODHISATTVA could be born in hell. They also said it was possible for the DEVAS or gods to practise BRAHMACHARYA (celibacy), a concept denied by other schools.

Therigatha A HINAYANA Buddhist text that forms part of the *KHUDDAKA NIKAYA* of the PALI CANON. The *Therigatha*, literally 'songs of the women elders', are verses composed by Buddhist nuns, and consist of seventy-three poems with 522 stanzas. These verses depict the joy of the monastic life, but also narrate their own life stories and how they came to choose this path. A few, such as the courtesan Ambapalli, joined the order after being influenced by the BUDDHA and his path, while others found peace and a new understanding after great grief and loss. Some long poems are narrative stories in verse.

Thirupurantakeshvarar Kshetram A temple of the Hindu god SHIVA in his form as Thirupurantakeshvara, located in Andhra Pradesh on a hill along the Guntur-Kurnool road. In this form Shiva destroyed the three cities (Tripura) of the ASURAS. His consort here is PARVATI in the form of Thirupurasundari. Over 260 inscriptions have been found in the temple. BUDDHA images and the remains of a STUPA are nearby.

Thomas of Canan A Christian from Syria who came to India around 345 CE, and is also known as CANAI THOMA.

Thomas, St. *See* St. Thomas.

Thousand-Pillared Temple A temple of the Hindu god SHIVA located on the hills of Hanamkonda near Warangal in Andhra Pradesh. It was constructed in 1163 by Prataparudradeva, a king of the Kakatiya dynasty, and derives its name from the number of columns in its MANDAPAS. Though primarily a Shiva temple, there are actually three shrines dedicated to three deities, Shiva, VISHNU and SURYA. They open into a columned mandapa, its platform extending southwards, where there is a large NANDI carved in granite, 2.7 m high. Beyond this is another mandapa with a number of columns. The columns or pillars in the mandapas are remarkable, carved in black stone with multi-faceted shafts. The ceiling has elaborate decorations around a central NATARAJA image. The temple is constructed mostly in green-grey basalt.

Thraetona A sage in the AVESTA texts. He cured diseases with the help of MANTRAS and was a great physician and healer and had the epithet Athwya. He slew a three-headed demon, Azhi-Dahaka. His Vedic counterpart is TRITA APTYA, while Traitana, who slew a three-headed monster, is also mentioned in the VEDAS. In the SHAH NAMAH he is known as Faridun, the heroic king who defeated Zohak, a tyrant.

Thyagaraja/Tyagaraja A great musician of south India, also considered a saint. Born in 1767 at Tiruvarur in present Tamil Nadu, a town known for its temple of SHIVA in his form as TYAGARAJA, Thyagaraja is said to have married twice and had one daughter. He then took a vow of poverty and began wandering through the streets, singing songs of BHAKTI or devotion to god, accepting a few handfuls of rice in return. His favourite deity was the Hindu god RAMA, and many of his compositions are in praise of him. He also sang about the joy of reciting the divine name, and about music itself, which could lead one to MOKSHA or liberation. Most of his songs are in Telugu, as his ancestors came from the Andhra region. He contributed greatly to Karnatak music by popularizing the kriti, a particular type of composition, and leaving behind over 700 songs in 200 different ragas, which are still sung today. He died in 1847.

Tibetan Buddhism An important form of Buddhism in India today, that incorporates MAHAYANA, TANTRIC and VAJRAYANA Buddhism. Several Indian Buddhists went to Tibet to spread Buddhism there, and Tibetan Buddhists came to India to study.

Buddhism is said to have been introduced in Tibet in the second century CE, though it was King Songtsen Gampo (608–50) who firmly established it there. The next prominent Buddhist king was Trisong Detsen (755–97). He invited famous teachers from India to Tibet, including SHANTIRAKSHITA and PADMASAMBHAVA. A later king, Lang Darma (836–42) attempted to extinguish Buddhism, and for more than a hundred years, Buddhism almost disappeared in Tibet. However, some monks preserved the practices and gradually, it began to revive. From western Tibet, Lha Lama Yeshe O dispatched Tibetans to Kashmir, where Buddhism still flourished. The best known of these was RINCHEN ZANGPO (958–1055). Tibetan Buddhists studied in Kashmir and founded a number of monasteries in India before returning to Tibet.

From the time of the founding of the first monastery in Tibet to the eleventh century, there were no separate orders in Tibet. In the eleventh century, ATISHA, an

Indian Buddhist, came to Tibet, helped in the revival of Buddhism and began the translation of Tibetan texts into Sanskrit. His disciple, DROMSTON (Bromston) set up the first distinctive monastic order with the founding of the Rwa-sgren monastery in 1056. This was known as the KADAMPA (Bka-gdams-pa) or Kadam order. In 1073 another monastery was founded in the principality of Sakya (Saskya) by Kon-chog-ryal-po, a disciple of DROGMI. This laid the foundation for the SAKYA order. Another major school of Tibetan Buddhism, the KAGYU order, soon arose. The NYINGMA (Rnin-ma-pa) emerged in the twelfth century, but traced its origin to Padmasambhava. These groups also competed for political power.

In the fourteenth century, TSONG KHAPA started the GELUG school (Dge-lugs-Pa), which became the most important order, of which the DALAI LAMA is the head.

All these orders and their offshoots exist in India today. Most of the orders have a basic similarity. All Tibetan orders accepted the VINAYA or monastic rules of the Mulasarvastivada school, a sub-school of the SARVASTIVADA. They base their teachings on late Mahayana, Tantric and Vajrayana texts, and also incorporate some aspects of the earlier Bon tradition. Differences that exist among the Tibetan schools emerged in a historical and political context.

Buddhism continued to flourish in Tibet until the Chinese occupation of the 1950s. In 1959, the Dalai Lama, followed by thousands of Tibetan Buddhists, came to India to escape persecution. Here they set up a government in exile, founded new monasteries, and continued the practice of their religion.

Over 1,20,000 Tibetan Buddhists are still in India, though there is some revival of the religion in Chinese Tibet.

Tikka A Hindu festival, another name for BHAI DUJ, celebrated in Punjab and Haryana.

Tikkana A poet who lived from 1220 to 1300 (or 1208–1288), and rewrote the *RAMAYANA* and *MAHABHARATA* in Telugu. He was a minister of the king Manumasiddhi in the Nellore region of present Andhra Pradesh. His *Ramayana* in verse is known as the *Nirvachanottara Ramayana*. However, his work on the *Mahabharata* is better known. Completing the work begun by NANNAYA, he began his translation from the *Virata Parva*, recreating several passages and introducing his own thoughts and ideas. Telugu by this time was highly Sanskritized, but Tikkana limited his use of Sanskrit, using mainly colloquial Telugu. His work remains popular today.

Tilopa A Buddhist MAHASIDDHA who lived from 989 to 1069. He was an expert in the Tantric tradition and esoteric teachings. His teachings, along with those of his chief disciple, NAROPA, resulted in the founding of the KAGYU school of TIBETAN BUDDHISM. The six teachings of Naropa are well known in this school.

Tipitaka (Tripitaka) A name for the Buddhist PALI CANON, which literally means 'three baskets', referring to three groups of texts, namely, the VINAYA PITAKA, SUTTA PITAKA and ABHIDHAMMA PITAKA.

tirtha A term used for a sacred site or place of pilgrimage (usually Hindu). Tirthas are often along rivers but can be elsewhere as well.

Tirthankara A Jain religious leader, a saviour who has attained enlightenment. Literally it means 'ford-maker' or 'ford-finder', one who builds a ford or bridge, i.e., points out the way to cross beyond the cycle of birth and death. Twenty-four Tirthankaras appear in every age or YUGA. Those of the present age are: Adinatha or RISHABHA, Ajitanatha, Sambhavanatha, Abhinandanatha, Sumatinatha, Padmaprabha, Suparshvanatha, Chandraprabha, Pushpadanta or Suvidhnatha, Shitalanatha, Shreyamsanatha, Vasupujya, Vimalnatha, Anantanatha, Dharmanatha, Shantinatha, Kunthunatha, Aranatha, MALLINATHA, Munisuvrata, Naminatha, ARISHTANEMINATHA, PARSHAVANATHA, and MAHAVIRA. The first Tirthankara existed millions of years before the twenty-fourth.

Tirthankaras have perfect knowledge of the past, present and future. Each Tirthankara reorganizes the Jain religion to suit the changing times and reinstates the four-fold order, consisting of sadhus (monks), sadhvis (nuns), shravakas (male householders) and shravikas (female householders).

When a Tirthankara is to be born, his mother has fourteen (or according to some texts, sixteen) auspicious dreams.

Five auspicious events, known as kalyanaka are celebrated in every Tirthankara's life. These are: (1) Chyavana Kalyanaka, when the Tirthankara's soul enters the mother's womb; (2) Janma Kalyanaka, his birth; (3) Diksha Kalyanaka, when the Tirthankara renounces the world and becomes a monk or nun (according to DIGAMBARAS nuns cannot become Tirthankaras); (4) Kevaljnana Kalyanaka, when the Tirthankara attains kevaljnana or absolute knowledge, after destroying the four ghati KARMAS; he then delivers his first sermon and reinstates the Jain religion; (5) Nirvana Kalyanaka, when the Tirthankara's soul is liberated from the world, the four aghati karmas are destroyed, and NIRVANA is attained.

The Tirthankaras who have passed beyond life and death are not capable of helping living beings today, though their philosophies are there for guidance. Images of Tirthankaras are worshipped in temples, as a form of reverence to them and to remind one of the path. The lives of each of the Tirthankaras is described in later Jain texts, including the *TRISHASHTISHALAKAPURUSHA-CHARITRA*, the *TRISHASHTILAKSHANA MAHA-PURANA*, and several individual Charitras and PURANAS. Some details of the parents, place of birth and death, and emblems of the Tirthankaras are given in the corresponding table.

Name	Mother	Father	Place of Birth	Place of Nirvana	Emblem
1. Rishabha (Adinatha)	Maru-Devi	Nabhi-raja	Ayodhya	Mt Kailasha	Bull
2. Ajitanatha	Vijaya Devi	Jita Satru	Ayodhya	Mt Parasnath	Elephant
3. Sambhavanatha	Sena	Jitari	Shravasti	Samet Shikhara	Horse
4. Abhinandanatha	Siddhartha	Samvara	Ayodhya	Samet Shikhara	Monkey
5. Sumatinatha	Sumangala	Megh-Prabha	Kanchanpur	Samet Shikhara	Chakravaha or red goose (curlew)
6. Padmaprabha	Susima	Dharana (Sidhara) Kaushambi		Samet Shikhara	Red Lotus
7. Suparshvanatha	Prithvi	Supratishtha	Varanasi	Samet Shikhara	Svastika
8. Chandraprabha	Lakshmana	Mahasena	Chandrapuri	Samet Shikhara	Crescent moon
9. Pushapadanta or Suvidhnatha	Rama (Supriya)	Sugriva	Kakendrapur	Samet Shikhara	Crocodile or makara or dolphin
10. Shitalanatha	Sunanda	Dridharatha	Bhadalpur	Samet Shikhara	Wishing tree or flower
11. Shreyamsanatha	Vishnudri (Vishna) Vishnu		Sinhpur	Samet Shikhara	Garuda or rhinoceros
12. Vasupujya	Vijaya (Jaya)	Vasupujya	Champapuri	Samet Shikhara	Buffalo
13. Vimalnatha	Suramya (Syama)	Kritvarman	Kampilapur	Samet Shikhara	Boar
14. Anantanatha	Sarvavasa	Simhasena	Ayodhya	Samet Shikhara	Porcupine or bear
15. Dharmanatha	Suvrata	Bhanu	Ratnapuri	Samet Shikhara	Thunderbolt
16. Shantinatha	Achira	Vishvasena	Hastinapura	Samet Shikhara	Antelope or deer
17. Kunthunatha	Sri Devi	Surya (Sura)	Hastinapura	Samet Shikhara	Ram
18. Aranatha	Mitra (Devi)	Sudarshana	Hastinapura	Samet Shikhara	Fish
19. Mallinatha	Rakshita	Kumbha	Mithilapuri	Samet Shikhara	Pinnacle or water pot
20. Munisuvrata	Padmavati	Sumitra	Rajagriha	Samet Shikhara	Tortoise
21. Namimatha	Vapra (Vipra)	Vijaya	Mithilapuri	Samet Shikhara	Blue lotus
22. Arishtaneminatha or Neminatha	Sivadevi	or Mathura Samudravijaya	Sauripura or Dvaraka	Shatrunjaya	Conch shell
23. Parshvanatha	Vama	Ashvasena	Varanasi	Samet Shikhara	Snake
24. Mahavira	Priyakarni (Trishala)	Siddhartha	Kundapura	Pavapur	Lion

Tiruchirapalli A city in Tamil Nadu which has a number of historic temples, and is a centre of pilgrimage. Temples include cave temples of the Pallava kings, as well as structural temples of the Chola and Nayaka dynasties. On one side, a huge rock, 82 m high, is notable for its stone elephants and pillars with carved capitals. Just 3 km to the north is the famous SRIRANGAM temple.

Tirukkalukunram A place in Tamil Nadu famous for its SHIVA temple, located on top of a hill. The temple, at a height of 152 m, is reached by steps. Two white kites are said to have been coming here for centuries. They would fly to the temple each morning around 11 am, were fed by the priests, and then departed. Tradition says that they embodied the souls of two ancient saints who rested at the temple on their way from RAMESHVARAM to VARANASI. However, according to recent reports, they are no longer seen.

Tirukural A Tamil text also known as *KURAL*, written by TIRUVALLUVAR.

Tirumalai A sacred hill, a place of Hindu pilgrimage in Andhra Pradesh. Located 10 km from Tirupati. Tirumalai, also known as Upper Tirupati, is the site of the famous temple of Lord VENKATESHVARA, the richest and perhaps the most popular temple in India.

Tirumalai is part of a group of seven hills known as Venkatachalam or Sheshachalam. The hills are said to represent the seven hoods of ANANTA or Adishesha, the lord of the serpents.

Tirumangai A VAISHNAVA Alvar saint whose verses, including the *Periya Tirumozhi*, form an important part of the NALAYIRA DIVYA PRABANDHAM. In these verses he glorified more than eighty-four sacred VAISHNAVA sites.

Tirumular A SHAIVITE saint who probably lived in the sixth or seventh century, and is known for his collection of three thousand verses, the *Tirumantiram*. This text forms part of the *TIRUMURAI*, which includes verses by the Hindu SHAIVITE saints of south India.

Not much is known about his life. Some date him much earlier as far back as the second century BCE. According to tradition, he came from the region of the KAILASHA mountain in the far north and settled in south India. Originally a siddha, he entered the body of a shepherd named Mulan or Mular, and was later known as Tirumular (tiru = sacred). He was an expert in YOGA and TANTRA, and is considered the founder of the SHAIVA SIDDHANTA school of thought, as well as one of the NAYANARS or Shaivite BHAKTI saints, and one of the eighteen TAMIL SIDDHAS. His work explains the principles of Shaiva Siddhanta and focuses on the similarities between the SHAIVA AGAMAS and the VEDAS. He uses the term Vedanta Siddhanta to signify their essential unity.

Tirumurai A collection of verses composed in Tamil by SHAIVITE saints and compiled by NAMBI ANDAR NAMBI in around CE 1000. The whole comprises eleven books, while a twelfth book, the *PERIYA PURANAM*, is often included. The first seven books are known as the *Tevaram* or *Devaram* and contain the hymns of Sambandar, Appar and Sundarar.

Tirupati A sacred city located to the south of Andhra Pradesh. Nearby is the hill of TIRUMALAI, with the renowned temple of Lord VENKATESHVARA. Other temples in Tirupati include that of Sri Kodanda Ramaswami. Three kilometres away at Tiruchanur is the temple of the goddess Alamelumanga, the consort of Lord Venkateshvara.

Tiruvalluvar A Tamil poet who lived between the second century BCE and the fourth or fifth centuries CE and composed the *TIRUKURAL*. Not much is known about his life. He lived in Mylapur (Chennai). According to some accounts he had a BRAHMANA father and a SHUDRA mother, while according to others he was born in a shudra family of cultivators or weavers. In Mylapur he lived near a Christian community, and some see traces of Christian influence in his work.

Tiruvannamalai A city in Tamil Nadu known for its SHIVA temple. A huge festival takes place here in November/December, when thousands of pilgrims arrive. A bonfire is lit on top of the hill and is visible for days, thought to represent Shiva's fire LINGA. There are other temples and shrines in the town, including those dedicated to DURGA and SUBRAHMANYA, as well as tanks with sacred TIRTHAS associated with three of the LOKAPALAS or guardian deities. The ASHRAM of RAMANA MAHARSHI is nearby, on the outskirts of the city.

Tiruvaymoli/Tiruvaymozhi A Tamil text composed by the ALVAR saint NAMMALVAR in the eighth or ninth century. It consists of poems of devotion to, and longing for, the Hindu god VISHNU.

Tiruvembavai-Tiruppavai festival A Hindu festival that unifies SHAIVITE and VAISHNAVITE sects, and was once very popular in south India. At this time the *Tiruvembavai* hymn of the Shaivite saint Manikavachakar and the *Tiruppavai* hymn of ANDAL, the ALVAR saint, are recited together.

Tishtriya A yazata or minor deity in Zoroastrianism representing a star. A hymn to the deity in the Yashts records that every year Tishtriya, in the form of a white-adorned horse, defeats Apaosha, a demon of drought, near the sea Vourukasha.

tithi A lunar day, a unit of time in the Hindu calendric system. Thirty tithis form one lunar month, the equivalent of about twenty-nine-and-a-half solar days. The tithis can begin at any time of the twenty-four-hour day.

Toda religion Todas, a tribal group that live in the Nilgiri mountains near Udhagamandalam in Tamil Nadu, venerate the buffalo, and their religious practices revolve around the sacred buffalo and dairy. Every aspect of the life and care of the buffaloes has a ritual element, and there are special rules concerning their milking, taking out to the pasture, naming, introducing new items in the dairy, or even rebuilding the dairy. Even their deities are connected with the buffalo. In general, Toda deities are known as Towtit, or gods of the mountains, and the most important of these is the goddess To-kisy, who is said to have divided the sacred buffaloes and dairies among the various clans and sub-clans. Great importance is given to the Tow-nor or sacred places (the dairies) that are sometimes anthropomorphized as deities. These special dairies are located apart from the settlements, while there are other buffaloes and dairies that are not in the same category. The sacred dairies often resemble the dwelling-huts of the tribe, but have carvings of buffaloes, the sun and moon, and sometimes of the PANDAVAS. The concept of the sacred buffalo originates in its economic importance, for the once pastoral tribe. The priest-dairyman offers prayers for the welfare of the whole tribe.

Torah A term in Judaism for the divine teaching or revelation that is often translated as 'law'. In a narrow sense the Torah refers to the first five books of the Hebrew BIBLE, but in a broader sense it includes the rest of the Bible, the oral teachings, and sometimes the whole body of Jewish law and custom.

Totapantha A minor sub-sect of the DIGAMBARA Jain sect. It came into existence to try to bring about a reconciliation between the BISAPANTHA (twenty-sect) and the TERAPANTHA (thirteen-sect), hence it was known as the Sadesolah (sixteen-and-a-half) sect, or Totapantha. It did not succeed in bringing the two sects together. Members of the sect follow a mix of BISAPANTHA and TERAPANTHA ideas. There are few members, mostly in Madhya Pradesh.

Transcendental Meditation A form of meditation propagated by Maharishi MAHESH YOGI. It was extremely popular in the 1970s and 80s and is still practised in several parts of the world. According to the Maharishi, this meditation was taught to him by his guru Brahmananda Sarasvati, who later came to him in a vision and urged him to reveal it to the world.

Transcendental Meditation has several levels. In the first stage, a simple two-syllable MANTRA is given to the disciple after a small initiation ceremony, by teachers trained by the Maharishi. This is repeated twice a day, morning and evening for twenty minutes each. Great benefits of freedom from stress, calmness, and positivity have been reported from this practice. Higher stages of meditation are revealed by the teacher and can lead to the development of various SIDDHIS (powers). Several practitioners reported that they achieved some kind of levitation.

The Maharishi believed the widespread practice of this meditation would change the world in a positive way, creating peace and harmony.

trapa The term for the lowest-ranking monk in a Tibetan Buddhist monastery. Trapas can study and advance to a higher level.

Treta Yuga The second of the four YUGAS or periods of time, in Hindu mythology, which together comprise a MAHAYUGA. The Treta Yuga follows the KRITA YUGA, and in it the righteousness that existed in the first yuga is reduced by one-fourth. Its primary virtue is knowledge. Four VEDAS have now appeared, sacrifices and rituals have started, and people have begun to seek rewards for their work. Humans live for 3000 years and still have superior powers. Children are born through a simple touch between two people, and not through sex. The yuga lasts for 3600 divine years, which are equal to 12,96,000 human years, and is symbolized by the colour red. It is succeeded by the DVAPARA YUGA.

tribal religions India has a tribal population of around 8 per cent. Tribal groups are found all over India, though particularly in the north-east and in central India. The largest broad tribal groups in India are classified as Bhils, Gonds, Oraons, Mundas and Santhals. Among others are: Apatani, Badaga, Baiga, Bhot, Bhotia, Chakma, Chenchu, Gaddi, Garo, Gujjar, Jarawa, Khasi, Kol, Lepcha, Lushai, Muria, Naga, Shompen, Todas and Warlis. Many of the tribes have been influenced by Hinduism, while others have converted to Christianity. However, even these retain some of their original practices and festivals. In general, tribal groups revere a creator deity, or a pair of deities, apart from a number of other spirits and ancestral deities. The names of their deities, and the festivals associated with them, are unique to each tribe.

Trika Shastra A name of a branch of non-dual SHAIVISM that was popular in Kashmir.

trikaya The three bodies of a BUDDHA, an idea that developed in MAHAYANA and VAJRAYANA Buddhism. Earlier a concept of two bodies, the rupakaya and the dharmakaya, the material body and the eternal body, had evolved. This concept was expanded into that of the trikaya, or three bodies. According to this, the Nirmanakaya, literally the magical body, the body that is only an apparition, is the physical body in which the BUDDHA (Shakyamuni) appeared on earth, or the body of all historical BUDDHAS. The sambhogakaya is the enjoyment or bliss body, the Buddha that appears in paradises and is the form that is worshipped. The dharmakaya is the eternal Buddha, the origin and source, the TATHAGATA.

The trikaya also has an esoteric symbolism and in Tantric Buddhism corresponds to certain stages on the Tantric path. Thus the nirmanakaya corresponds to a stage where bliss can be sought through a union of two people; the dharmakaya reflects the internal union of the male and female principles; the sambhogakaya, the internal state of bliss. A fourth body or stage is also mentioned, the mahasukhakaya, which is beyond all these.

Trimurti The triple form of the three main gods of Hinduism, BRAHMA, VISHNU and SHIVA, who represent creation, preservation and destruction, respectively. These are three aspects of the One supreme reality. In iconography, the Trimurti form is depicted with one body and three heads or as a composite image. The deities are also depicted separately and have their own temples and forms of worship.

Trinity A ROMAN CATHOLIC concept that God is One, yet consists of three persons: the Father, the Son and the Holy Spirit. The concept is also accepted by most Protestant denominations.

tripartite ideology A theory put forward by George Dumezil (1898–1986) regarding the society and religion of the INDO-EUROPEANS. According to this theory, there was a hierarchical three-fold (tripartite) structure in society, of priests, representing spirituality and sovereignty, warriors, and productive workers, common to all members of the Indo-European group. This was reflected in religion and myth, and similar aspects could be traced in the myths and deities of the ancient cultures of this group.

Tripura (1) A wonderful triple city of gold, silver and iron, constructed by the great asura architect MAYA. It was destroyed by SHIVA. (2) Tripura today is the name of a state in India.

Tripura Bhairavi A Hindu goddess who is the SHAKTI of SHIVA. She emerged from his LINGA, which was divided into three parts.

Tripura Sundari A Hindu goddess identified with DURGA or with SHODASHI. She was the fairest being in heaven, earth and air.

Tripureshvari Temple A Hindu temple in the town of Udaipur in Tripura. It was constructed in the fifteenth century and is a SHAKTA PITHA, one of the places where a part of SATI's body is said to have fallen. A major festival takes place here at the time of DIVALI.

triratna, of Buddhism Literally, 'the three jewels', the triratna form the basics of the Buddhist religion. They are related to: (1) the BUDDHA: worshipping or recognizing the Buddha as the Enlightened One; (2) the DHARMA: understanding his dharma and teachings; (3) the SANGHA: being a part of the sangha or monastic community. These are also the three refuges (trisharana), which should be relied on and are expressed even today in the Buddhist formula: 'Buddham sharanam gachchhami; Dharmam sharanam gachchhami; Sangham sharanam gachchhami'; meaning, 'I take refuge in the Buddha, the dharma and the sangha.'

triratna, of Jainism The three jewels of Jainism, which consist of SAMYAK DARSHANA, SAMYAK JNANA and SAMYAK CHARITRA, or right belief, right knowledge and right conduct. Right conduct depends on both right belief and right knowledge. These are also known as the ratnatreya.

Trishashtilakshana Mahapurana A Jain text that describes the lives of the sixty-three great men of Jainism from a DIGAMBARA perspective. It is divided into two parts, the *ADI PURANA* and *the UTTARA PURANA*. The text was composed in the ninth century by JINASENA and GUNABHADRA.

Trishashtishalakapurusha Charitra A Jain text written by Hemachandra Suri between 1160 and 1172, which contains an account of the sixty-three great men of Jainism. The text is divided into ten sections or parvans, beginning with the life of the first TIRTHANKARA, RISHABHA. The tenth parvan, also used as an independent text, is the *Mahavira Charitra*, describing the life of MAHAVIRA. The appendix, known as the *Parishishta Parvan* or *Sthaviravali Charitra*, describes the lives of the disciples of Mahavira and of the Dashapurvin, those who once had the knowledge of the ancient texts known as the PURVAS. The whole text is interspersed with semi-historical and mythical stories. These accounts are taken from earlier sources, but the text forms the base for all later accounts of the Tirthankaras in SHVETAMBARA sources.

trishula The term for a trident, the emblem and weapon of the Hindu god SHIVA.

triskandhaka A Buddhist MAHAYANA ritual that has three steps: (1) confessing one's sins; (2) rejoicing at the merit of others; (3) requesting all BUDDHAS to remain in the world to help all suffering beings. This ritual was to be performed three times in the day and three times at night. It is an extension of the earlier PATIMOKKHA ritual and was to be performed in monasteries interspersed with regular periods of meditation.

Trita Aptya A Vedic deity usually associated with INDRA and connected with SOMA. He slew a three-headed, six-eyed dragon. His name signifies 'the third'. His counterpart in the AVESTA is Thrita, the third man to prepare haoma (Soma), or THRAETONA, who slew a serpent. He has been considered a god of lightning, or of wind and water, or of the moon. Others believe he was a healer who was later deified.

Triveni A name of PRAYAGA, modern Allahabad. Literally, it means 'three streams'. The name comes from the fact that the GANGA and YAMUNA unite at Prayaga, and according to tradition, a third river, the SARASVATI, unites with them underground, though there is actually no third stream here. The myth of the three rivers is said to symbolize the three passages of energy in the human body, the PINGALA, IDA and SUSHUMNA.

Tryambakeshvara A name of SHIVA and of one of his jyotir LINGAS.

Tsong Khapa The founder of the GELUG school of TIBETAN BUDDHISM, who lived from 1357 to 1419. He was initially a monk of the Kadam school, but began the Gelug school, which has some differences from the former, emphasizing monastic discipline as well as the study of texts. He wrote a number of works, including the *Lam-rim chen-mo*, describing the stages on the Buddhist path.

Tsuglagkhang Temple A Buddhist temple located at DHARAMSALA in Himachal Pradesh, constructed after the arrival of Tibetans in India. It has a hall where the DALAI LAMA delivers discourses, in which there are images of SHAKYAMUNI, AVALOKITESHVARA and PADMASAMBHAVA. Another temple nearby has a mural of a KALACHAKRA mandala, as well as sand mandalas that are regularly created and destroyed.

Tukaram A Maratha saint of the seventeenth century who was a devotee of the god VISHNU in his form as VITTHALA or Vithoba. Born in 1607 in Dehu near Pune in present Maharashtra, he was the son of Bolhoba, a farmer who owned some land. Though they were quite well off, they were considered SHUDRAS by the orthodox BRAHMANAS. Tukaram's parents died when he was young. When he grew up he married Rakhma, and though he was very fond of her, he took a second wife as she was always ill. They had six children.

A great famine took place in 1629 and Tukaram watched helplessly as his wife Rakhma died of starvation and illness. After this he withdrew from his family and work, and began to worship Vitthala at a dilapidated shrine in his village, which he restored. He sang songs composed by earlier saints, and after a vision of the saint NAMADEVA and of the god Vitthala he began to compose ABHANGAS himself. Over 4000 abhangas by Tukaram are known, and some scholars believe there are many more. His devotion to the god and his BHAKTI compositions attracted many followers.

In 1649, Tukaram disappeared. While his disciples believed he had been taken to God in a chariot, scholars speculate that he was murdered by the brahmanas who did not like the rise and popularity of a low-caste person, or that he left for some unknown destination, to end his life in solitude.

His abhangas deal with his early life, his search for God, his despair, and finally his realization of the divine.

tulasi (1) A sacred plant, basil (*Ocimum sanctum*). Tulasi can grow to a height of one metre, and leaves of the plant are used as offerings to deities. (2) According to Hindu mythology, Tulasi was the name of a woman loved by the god VISHNU. In some versions of the story she was the same as the goddess LAKSHMI, but in others she was a different woman, of whom Lakshmi was jealous. Lakshmi therefore turned Tulasi into a plant, while Vishnu became the SHALAGRAMA stone to keep her company.

Tulasidasa A devotee of the Hindu god RAMA, who composed the Shri RAMACHARITAMANASA in Hindi in the sixteenth century. The text is still sung with love and devotion by worshippers of Rama in all parts of the country.

Not much is known about Tulasidasa's life. He was born in the sixteenth century, according to some accounts at Rajapur in Banda district in southern Uttar Pradesh, and according to others, at Soron or Sukarkhet in Gonda district in northern Uttar Pradesh. His parents died when he was young, and he was brought up by a holy man, Naraharidasa. He married Ratnavali and was extremely fond of his wife. Once, when she had gone to her parents' house, he crossed a flooded river to visit her, but she told him it would be better if he devoted himself to the god Rama instead. He went to AYODHYA and KASHI (Varanasi) and began to worship Rama, resulting in several compositions on the god. The *Ramacharitamanasa* was completed in 1575.

He also wrote the story of Rama in other books, including *Gitavali* (1571), *Kavitavali* (1612) and *Barvairamayana* (1612). In addition, his *Vinaya Patrika* or *Petition to Rama* contains a number of hymns to the deity. Tulasidasa died in 1623.

tulku A term in TIBETAN BUDDHISM for an incarnate lama who is highly revered.

Turaga A divine horse in Hindu mythology. According to the MATSYA PURANA, Turaga was a white horse that emerged at the churning of the ocean. It was taken by the god SURYA. Another such horse was UCCHAISHRAVAS.

turiya A state of consciousness. According to the philosophy of YOGA, waking, sleeping and dreaming are the three states of consciousness normally known. The fourth state, turiya, exists beyond all these, and is the state of an advanced yogi. The *AVADHUTA GITA*, as well as some other texts, describes a state beyond these four, known as turiyatita.

Tushitas A class or GANA of divine beings. Their number is given as thirty-six or sometimes twelve. In the seventh manvantara they were reborn as the ADITYAS.

Tvashtr A Vedic deity whose nature is somewhat obscure. He has been considered a solar deity, a god of the year, or an abstract god. Most commonly, he is considered the divine artisan.

Tvashtr is described as holding an axe. He gave all beings their form, fashioned the bolt of INDRA, sharpened the axe of Brahmanaspati, and formed a new cup that held the food of the ASURA (here meaning a divine being). His daughter was Saranyu, wife of VIVASVAT, from whom YAMA and YAMI were born. In the *ATHARVA VEDA* he is described as an old man, carrying a bowl of SOMA. The *Shatapatha Brahmana* states that he produced and nourished a great variety of creatures, whereas in the PURANAS he is identified with VISHVAKARMA, and sometimes with PRAJAPATI.

tyaga A Sanskrit word for renunciation.

Tyagaraja (1) A term for a form of the Hindu god SHIVA in south India. The term came to be used from the sixteenth or seventeenth century and in this form, Shiva is said to grant all prayers. One of the largest Tyagaraja temples is located at Tiruvarur in Tamil Nadu, where Shiva is depicted as SOMASKANDA, that is, along with his wife UMA and son SKANDA, as well as in the form of a LINGA.

Originating during the time of the Chola ruler Rajajraja I in the eleventh century, this temple complex was constructed mainly in the fourteenth century, with additions being made up to the seventeenth century, as well as recent renovations. The main shrine, with an emerald linga placed in a silver casket, is surmounted by a pyramidal tower with a square roof. Adjacent is another shrine with a Somaskanda image and a tower with a hemispherical roof. There are also some goddess shrines attached to large columned MANDAPAS. The mandapas have painted ceilings, some depicting the story of King Muchukunda, who is said to have brought the Tyagaraja image down from heaven. The whole complex is enclosed in an area of about 20 acres, and can be entered through several GOPURAMS.

There are seven sacred Tyagaraja shrines in Tamil Nadu, known as the Sapta Vitanka. Tyagaraja at Tiruvarur was earlier referred to as Aruran or Vidhivitankar. Other notable Tyagaraja shrines are at Nagapattinam, Tiruvanmayur and Tiruvotriyur.

(2) A great singer. *See* Thyagaraja.

Uchchhaishravas (1) A divine horse in Hindu mythology, which emerged from the ocean when it was churned for AMRITA. It is the white horse of the god INDRA, and the king of all horses.

(2) Uchchhaishravas was also the name of an ancient king.

Udaigiri Cave Temples Rock-cut cave temples located at Udaigiri near SANCHI in Madhya Pradesh. There are around twenty temples, made in the fifth century and later. Most are Hindu temples, though one of them is possibly Jain and has an inscription mentioning the Tirthankara PARSHVANATHA.

Many of the caves consist of rectangular niches cut into the rock, with sculptures placed there. Images of VISHNU resting on the serpent Shesha and of VARAHA are among the notable sculptures. There is also a larger temple with a rock-cut inner shrine and a porch with structural pillars, as well as a circular monolithic temple surmounted by a large flat stone, locally called the Tawa (griddle) Temple.

Udana A Buddhist text that forms part of the *KHUDDAKA NIKAYA* of the PALI CANON. The *Udana* has eight vaggas or sections, each of which has ten suttas or sutras. Each sutta narrates a story ending with a moral contained in a short verse, which is ascribed to the BUDDHA. A typical verse is given below:

The wheel is broken, since he has become desireless;
The river is dried up and flows no more,
No longer does the broken wheel roll on
The end of sorrow is attained. (VII.2)

Udasi (1) A Sikh sect founded by SRI CHAND, the son of Guru NANAK. The term comes from the Sanskrit word *udas*, meaning 'to renounce'. Udasis live a life of asceticism and celibacy. Baba Gurditta, the eldest son of Guru HARGOBIND later became a leader of the sect, which was popular in north and east Punjab. Udasis do not accept the symbols of the KHALSA, remain clean shaven, and have similarities with Hindu ascetics. They were once prominent as mahants of the Sikh GURDWARAS, but after the AKALI MOVEMENT they became separated from mainstream Sikhs. The sect still exists, and their main temple is located at AMRITSAR.
(2) A term used for Guru Nanak's preaching missions.

Udayagiri The site of early Jain rock-cut temples. *See* Khandagiri.

udgatr A Vedic priest who chanted the prayers from the *SAMA VEDA* during a sacrifice or YAJNA.

Udupi A town in Karnataka, renowned for its temples. Though primarily a centre of VAISHNAVISM, it also has SHAIVITE and other temples. It is famous as the birthplace of MADHVA, the thirteenth-century saint and philosopher. Udupi is best known for its KRISHNA Temple, with eight MATHAS founded by the disciples of MADHVA.

The whole town is considerd divinely protected, and around it are a number of temples, including those of DURGA as Mahishasuramardini, of Indrani Devi, Vishnumurti and Mahakali. Two major SHIVA temples are of the deity as Ananteshvara and Chandramoulishvara respectively.

The former has an interesting story, linking SHAIVISM and VAISHNAVISM. According to texts, the city formed part of Parashurama Kshetra, the area said to be claimed by PARASHURAMA from the sea. Legends state that a king named Ramabhoja worshipped Parashurama here in the form of a LINGA, which then manifested itself on a silver seat (rajata pitha), and was installed in the Shiva temple. Thus in Sanskrit texts, the city is known as Rajata Pitha.

There are many more Hindu temples in the city, both old and new, as well as a Jain temple.

Udvada A town in Gujarat sacred to PARSIS, where the Iran Shah, the sacred fire brought from Iran, is enshrined in an ATASH BEHRAM. This Atash Behram is considered the most sacred of the Zoroastrian temples because it contains the fire that was consecrated when the PARSIS first arrived in India at SANJAN, and was later moved to Udvada.

Ugadi A new year's day celebrated in Karnataka and Andhra Pradesh in March/April. On this day celebrations, prayers and feasts take place.

Ujjain One of the seven most sacred cities of the Hindus, located on the Shipra river in Madhya Pradesh. The city has a number of temples. A KUMBH MELA is held here once in twelve years, and according to myths, the god SHIVA killed the demon Tripura here. Archaeological excavations indicate that the earliest settlements here date back to around 700 BCE, after which the area was occupied continuously.

ulama The plural of ALIM, the term for a Muslim religious scholar. Under Muslim dynasties in India, the ulama or religious officials interpreted Islamic law and attempted to control and direct the rulers. Though they had some political influence, most kings acted independently of them.

uluka The Sanskrit term for an owl. Though often considered an inauspicious bird, the owl is sometimes associated with the goddess LAKSHMI. In Greek mythology the bird is sacred to the goddess Athena.

Uluka Kanada The traditional founder of VAISHESHIKA, one of the six orthodox systems of Indian philosophy, who was also known as KANADA, Kanabhuj or Kanabhaksha. His real name is thought to have been Kashyapa.

Uma A name of the Hindu goddess PARVATI. Literally, it means 'light'.

Umasvami/Umasvati A Jain scholar and ACHARYA, revered by both DIGAMBARAS and SHVETAMBARAS. According to the Digambaras, his name was Umasvami, and he lived from 135 to 219 CE. He was also known as Ghridhrapincha or Ghridhra-piccha, which was one of the names of KUNDAKUNDA as well. According to the SHVETAMBARAS, his name was Umasvati, and he was the disciple of Ghosanandi Kshamashramna. He wrote the *TATTVARTHADHIGAMA SUTRA*, a scholarly text explaining various aspects of Jainism; it is popular among both sects even today. This text was composed in PATALIPUTRA, though he is said to have lived in south India. According to tradition, Umasvami wrote 500 books, of which very few are known today. The Digambaras believe that the *Pujaprakarna Prasamarati* and the *Jambudvipasamasa* are among his works.

Universal Syrian Orthodox Church (Jacobite) An Orthodox Church headed by the Patriarch of Antioch. The Church was the first to be established outside Jerusalem, and thus has a very ancient origin. It uses the Syro-Aramaic liturgy and has twenty-nine dioceses, of which ten are in India. The president of the Episcopal Synod in India is based in Kothamangalam, while the Metropolitan is in Damascus, Syria.

Upali A close disciple of the BUDDHA. He was a specialist in matters of monastic discipline, and at the first BUDDHIST COUNCIL held at RAJAGRIHA soon after the Buddha's death, he recited the whole *VINAYA PITAKA*.

upanayana A Sanskrit term for the initiation ceremony, when upper-caste Hindu boys are invested with the SACRED THREAD. This is considered a new birth, and they are then known as dvija or twice born.

The ceremony takes place for BRAHMANA, KSHATRIYA and VAISHYA boys, but is conducted differently for each caste.

The upanayana ceremony is linked with the beginning of the boy's education. Literally, it is a Sanskrit term meaning 'leading to' or 'bringing near' and originally signified the guru taking on the education of a boy and leading him on a spiritual path. The child then entered the first stage of Hindu life, BRAHMACHARYA, and studied the VEDAS and other sacred texts with his guru. The texts state that the ceremony should be conducted for a brahmana boy in his seventh or eighth year, a kshatriya in his eleventh year, and a vaishya in his twelfth year, but it can take place at a later age. Though the ceremony still takes place, today it is largely a formal ritual.

The thread ceremony also takes place in some groups of Jains.

Upanishads Sanskrit texts that form part of Vedic literature. The word upanishad is said to mean 'sitting near the feet of a master', from upa = near, and nishad = sitting down. Another interpretation takes shad as 'destruction' and upanishad as 'that which destroys ignorance'. The original meaning, however, was 'secret doctrine'.

These texts form the latter part of the BRAHMANAS and are attached to the VEDIC SAMHITAS. They are called Vedanta, 'the end of the VEDAS', both because they form the last part of the Vedas, and because in them, the Vedas reach the ultimate or highest philosophy. The earliest Upanishads, in their present form, date back to the sixth or seventh century BCE, while altogether fourteen have been dated to before the third century BCE. The earliest are said to be the *Aitareya, Kaushitaki, Taittiriya, Brihadaranyaka, Chhandogya* and *Kena*, while slightly later are the *Kathaka, Shvetashvatara, Mahanarayana, Isha, Mundaka, Prashna, Maitrayaniya* and *Mandukya*.

At least 280 Upanishads are known today, of which 108 are recognized in classic texts. These 108 are uneven in quality and character.

Of the 108 recognized Upanishads, the number attached to the various Vedic Samhitas is given in the *Muktika Upanishad*, a late text, as: RIG VEDA: 10; *White YAJUR VEDA*: 19; *Black Yajur Veda*: 32; SAMA VEDA: 16; ATHARVA VEDA: 31. Other sources differ on this classification.

SHANKARA, the leading philosopher of the ninth century, commented on eleven major Upanishads: *Isha, Kena, Katha, Prashna, Mundaka, Mandukya, Taittiriya, Aitareya, Chhandogya, Brihadaranyaka*, and *Shvetash-vatara*. He is also said to have commented on the *Atharvashikha, Atharvashiras* and *Nrisimhatapaniya* Upanishads. A number of other Upanishads also contain the highest philosophical ideas while some deal with various rituals, deities, or aspects of yoga.

Most of the early Upanishads have gone beyond all external forms of worship and seek the supreme goal through an exploration of ideas, leading to ultimate knowledge. Yet they have different aspects and have been interpreted to support ADVAITA or monism, DVAITA or dualism, and VISHISHTADVAITA or qualified monism. There are also Upanishads which are sectarian and focus on deities as a means of realizing the Truth.

BRAHMAN, the One Reality, ATMAN, the soul, which is often identified with Brahman, KARMA, reincarnation, and the nature of the universe, are some of the concepts discussed in the Upanishads.

Sri AUROBINDO called the Upanishads 'the supreme work of the Indian mind'. Upanishadic ideas form the basis for several later streams of thought in India, and are similar to some SUFI concepts, as well as to certain ideas in the works of Plato, Pythagoras, the Gnostics and other profound philosophies.

Upapurana A minor or secondary PURANA. There are eighteen main Upapuranas, as well as several more. (*See* Puranas).

Upavedas A term for Vedas, or branches of knowledge, that are not connected with the VEDIC SAMHITAS or revealed Vedic texts. Four classes of Upavedas are: Ayurveda, the science of medicine; Gandharvaveda, concerning music and dancing; Dhanurveda, the art of archery or military science; Sthapatyaveda, the science of architecture.

urs A term in Islam for the death anniversary of a SUFI saint. Literally, the word means 'wedding' or 'union', for through physical death the saint is thought to be reunited with the divine. Urs are celebrated at the DARGAHS or tombs of saints and involve prayers, offerings of flowers and embroidered cloth, and the singing of qawwalis or special Sufi songs.

Not merely Muslims, but Hindus and members of other religions travel long distances to participate in the urs of certain saints, particularly of Shaikh MUINUDDIN CHISTI at Ajmer. Urs of other saints too, are celebrated by people of all religions.

Uruvela A town in the region of MAGADHA, connected with the life of the BUDDHA. At the village of Senanigama nearby, the Buddha practised severe austerities for six years. Realizing that this would not help him, he again began to eat simple food. He then sat under a pipal tree and meditated until he gained enlightenment at Uruvela, the place now known as BODH GAYA.

Urvashi An APSARA or divine nymph who fell in love with PURURAVAS. The story has been retold many times in Indian literature.

Usha A deity in the RIG VEDA, the goddess of the dawn. About forty hymns are dedicated to her in the Rig Veda and she is mentioned in several more.

In the Vedic hymns, Usha is said to be shining and resplendent, ancient yet born again and again, the one who drives away the darkness and awakens all life. Her chariot radiates brilliance and is drawn by ruddy steeds, or by bulls or cows. In one passage, she is said to arrive in a hundred chariots, reflecting the way the dawn illuminates the sky, with hundreds of rays. She is closely associated with SAVITR and SURYA, and is the sister of BHAGA, an ADITYA.

Ushanas In Hindu mythology the name of the planet Venus, or of its regent. It is also called SHUKRA.

Utpaladeva A philosopher of the Kashmir school of SHAIVISM who lived from c. 900 to 950. He developed the doctrine of PRATYABHIJNA or 'recognition', in which the individual recognizes the world as a manifestation of the Hindu god SHIVA. His works include the *Ishvara-pratyabhijna-karika*, as well as a number of verses in praise of SHIVA.

Uttara Mimamsa A school of philosophy that developed out of PURVA MIMAMSA and is considered similar or identical to VEDANTA. Purva Mimamsa and Uttara Mimamsa are said to form one whole and to present an integrated philosophy.

Uttara Purana A Jain text that forms the second part of the *TRISHASHTILAKSHANA MAHAPURANA*. While the first part, the *ADI PURANA*, deals with the life of RISHABHA and the first Chakravartin, the second part contains an account of the lives of all the other sixty-three great persons of Jainism. The *Uttara Purana* was composed by GUNABHADRA in the ninth century, and contains a number of additional stories and legends. Among the most popular is the story of JIVANDHARA, retold several times in Sanskrit and Tamil.

Uttara Rama Charita A Sanskrit play about the second half of the life of RAMA, written by BHAVABHUTI, who lived in the eighth century. The first half is described in the *Mahavira Charita*. The plays are based on the story in the *RAMAYANA*.

Uttarajjhayana Sutta (Uttaradhyayana) A Jain text of the SHVETAMBARA canon, one of the four MULA SUTTAS. This text has thirty-six sections and contains the teachings of MAHAVIRA, along with various aspects of Jain religion and philosophy. Several parables, stories and legends are narrated, as well as rules, regulations and principles of the religion.

Uvangas (Sanskrit: Upangas) A series of twelve Jain texts that are secondary to the ANGAS. The texts are written in Ardha-Magadhi and are listed below with the Sanskrit title in brackets: *Uvavaiya (Aupapatika)*, *Rayapasenajja (Rajaprashniya)*, *Jivabhigama*, *Pannavana (Prajnapana)*, *Surapannati* or *Suriyapannati (Surya-Prajnapti)*, *Jambudivapannati (Jambudvipa-Prajnapti)*, *Chamdapannati (Chandra- prajnapti)*, *Nirayavali*, *Kappavadamsiao (Kalpavatamsika)*, *Pupphiao (Pushpikah)*, *Pupphachuliao (Pushpachulikah)*, *Vanhidasao (Vrishnidashah)*.

The Uvangas deal with various aspects of Jainism, and with astronomy, cosmology and geography. They contain stories of Jain saints, explanations of doctrines, prayers, and descriptions of heavens and hells.

Uvasagadasao (Upasakadasah) A Jain text, the seventh of the ten ANGAS. It consists of stories of Jain saints, particularly of ten pious Jain merchants who, though they were householders, practised certain forms of asceticism and self-denial. They attained miraculous powers, died by the vow of SALLEKHANA, and were reborn in heaven. Among the stories is one with some historical interest, about a potter who was first a disciple of Gosala Makkhaliputta (GOSALA MASKARIPUTRA, the founder of the AJIVIKA sect), but later became a follower of MAHAVIRA.

uwaisi   A term in Islam that refers to initiation in a SUFI order through spiritual means, by SHAIKHS who have passed into the next world. Those who claim to receive initiation in this way, in a dream or vision, are known as uwaisis.

Vach A Hindu goddess, later identified with SARASVATI. In the RIG VEDA, Vach is the personification of speech, through whom divine knowledge is communicated. In the *Taittiriya Brahmana*, she is the wife of INDRA and the mother of the VEDAS, while in the *Shatapatha Brahmana* and *Kathaka Upanishad*, she is associated with PRAJAPATI. In the *MAHABHARATA* and most of the PURANAS, Vach is identified with Sarasvati. However, according to the *PADMA PURANA*, Vach was one of the daughters of DAKSHA and a wife of KASHYAPA. Through her, the GANDHARVAS and APSARAS were born.

Vachaspati Mishra A scholar who lived in the ninth century in the Mithila region of present north Bihar. He wrote commentaries on each of the six classical systems of philosophy. His *Tattvakaumudi* is a work on SAMKHYA, while his text *Bhamati* elaborates on SHANKARA's commentary of the *BRAHMA SUTRA*. His works on NYAYA include the *Nyayakanika* and *Nyaya-varttikatatparyatika*.

Vadagalai/Vadakalai One of the two schools of Shrivaishnavism or southern VAISHNAVISM, which emerged around the thirteenth century, the other being the TENGALAI. The main proponent of this school was VEDANTA DESIKA. Unlike the Tengalai, this group promoted the use of Sanskrit and used both the Tamil and the Sanskrit Vaishnava texts. They believed that BHAKTI and surrender were not sufficient to reach god, but that a combination of KARMA, JNANA, bhakti and prapatti (surrender) were required. They established a MATHA at AHOBALAM where Jiyars, a class of priests, provide leadership to the followers of the school.

Vadakkunathan Temple A Hindu temple located at Thrissur in Kerala, constructed in the twelfth century, with later additions. This interesting temple has three shrines within a rectangular court, dedicated to Vadakkunathan (SHIVA), Shankaranarayana and RAMA, respectively. According to legend, PARASHURAMA meditated here on the god Shiva, but when he opened his eyes, he saw an image of Rama. He installed this and continued his meditation, when a Shiva LINGA appeared to him. After further meditation, Shankaranarayana, the combined form of Shiva and VISHNU, was revealed. The Rama shrine has a square sanctuary surrounded by a square passageway attached to a pillared MANDAPA. The other two shrines have square sanctuaries surrounded by circular passageways, attached to open mandapas. Behind the Shiva shrine is a PARVATI shrine.

Vadakkunathan is worshipped by pouring *ghi* (clarified butter) over the linga. Over the years, this has grown into a high and solid mound, which somehow does not melt.

There is a small GANESHA shrine to the south of the Vadakkunathan and beyond this seven MATRIKA altars. In addition there are shrines to Vettakkorumakan, a Kerala guardian deity, Dharma Sastha (AYYAPPA) and Gopalakrishna, as well as a roofless shrine with a shankha (conch) and chakra, commemorating SHANKARA or Adi Shankaracharya. The shrines have conical roofs made from timber and covered with metal sheets, capped by a pot finial. There are carved timber screen walls and murals on the shrine walls, most of which date to the eighteenth century. Vishnu on ANANTA, NATARAJA, and scenes from the *MAHABHARATA* are among the paintings. The whole complex covers nine acres, surrounded by a high wall, with GOPURAMS on each of the four sides. The main entrance is from the west, near which is a large theatre hall (Koottambalam). The temple is still popular, and SHIVARATRI is the most important festival. The POORAM festival also takes place here, though it is not associated with the temple deities.

vahana Literally, 'vehicle', it usually indicates an animal or bird associated with a Hindu deity. The vahana either accompanies the deity or serves as a mount. Some of the vahanas of deities are: HAMSA, a swan or goose, associated with the god BRAHMA; GARUDA, the divine bird, with VISHNU; NANDI, a white bull, with SHIVA; AIRAVATA, a white elephant, with INDRA; a mouse, with GANESHA; a peacock, with KARTTIKEYA; a parrot, with KAMA; a tiger or lion, with DURGA; a fish or MAKARA, with VARUNA; a buffalo, with YAMA; a ram, with AGNI; an antelope, with VAYU; a vulture, with SHANI. Gods of other ancient cultures had similar animal associations.

Vaibhashika A school of HINAYANA Buddhism, the orthodox branch of the SARVASTIVADA. It was based on the *Abhidharma-mahavibhasha-shastra* (known as the *MAHAVIBHASHA*), which was a commentary on the *Jnana-prasthana*. A number of texts were composed on the Vaibhashika viewpoint, which was opposed by the SAUTRANTIKAS.

Vaidyanatha A name of the Hindu god SHIVA, as lord of the physicians, and of one of his jyotir LINGAS, located at Deogarh in Jharkhand.

Vaijayanti A necklace worn by the Hindu god VISHNU. It has five precious gems: pearl, ruby, emerald, sapphire and diamond, said to represent the five elements.

Vaikuntha The heaven of the Hindu god VISHNU. It is said to be on Mt MERU and is built of gold and precious stones. It is also a name of VISHNU and was earlier associated with the god INDRA. Those who dwell in Vaikuntha enjoy bliss and freedom from KARMA.

Vaikuntha Ekadashi A Hindu festival that celebrates the opening of the gate to the god VISHNU's heaven, VAIKUNTHA. It takes place in November/ December and is popular in Andhra Pradesh and Tamil Nadu. At the temple in SRIRANGAM, celebrations last for twenty days. According to popular legend, Mohini, a divine beauty and a form of Vishnu, urged King Rukmangada to break his fast to Vishnu. The king prayed to Vishnu, who took him to Vaikuntha to save him from temptation. The gates of Vaikuntha are said to open every year on this day, to those who worship at Vishnu temples.

Vaikuntha Perumal Temple A temple of the Hindu god VISHNU located at Kanchipuram in Tamil Nadu. It was constructed by King Nandivarman II (CE 731–96) of the Pallava dynasty.

This unique temple is three-tiered, with three Vishnu shrines, one above the other. Attached to these is a pillared MANDAPA, while a passageway surrounds the temple. An entrance hall was added at the time of the Vijayanagara dynasty (fourteenth to sixteenth centuries). The plastered outer walls have jutting eaves and parapets, and there is a pyramidal tower surmounted by an octagonal roof. The temple has several sculptures of Vishnu in his various incarnations.

Vairochana A celestial BUDDHA, also known as a DHYANI BUDDHA. His name literally means 'shining out'. Vairochana is located in the centre of the universe and is sometimes identified with the ADI BUDDHA, or first Buddha. His colour is white and in the cosmic MANDALA he is located in the centre, with the four other celestial BUDDHAS around him. His right hand is usually held in dharmachakra mudra (the teaching pose). His symbol is a pair of discs, and his VAHANA or vehicle is a pair of dragons. His BODHISATTVA is SAMANTABHADRA and his SHAKTI or consort is Vajradhatvishvari. A number of deities emanate from him. These include the Bodhisattvas KSHITIGARBHA and MAITREYA, as well as MARICHI, Ushnisha-vijaya, Sitapatra-Aparajita, Mahasahasrapramardini, Vajravarahi, Kamini, Lalaratri, and Rupavajra. All deities that are white in colour are assigned to this family.

Vaishali An ancient city associated with Buddhism and Jainism. It is identified with village Basarh in Muzaffarpur district, Bihar, and excavations indicate its occupation from the sixth century BCE. The second BUDDHIST COUNCIL took place here, and here the BUDDHA spoke to his disciple ANANDA about the length of his life. FA-HSIEN, the Chinese pilgrim, visited in the fifth century CE and recorded the existence of several Buddhist shrines and monasteries. The twenty-fourth Jain Tirthankara MAHAVIRA was born near Vaishali.

Vaishampayana A rishi or sage who was a student of the rishi VYASA. According to tradition, the MAHABHARATA was narrated to him by Vyasa, and he in turn narrated it to King Janamajeya. The HARIVAMSHA was also narrated by him.

Vaisheshika One of the six classical systems of Hindu philosophy. The traditional founder was the rishi KANADA, also known as ULUKA KANADA, who probably lived between 250 BCE and 100 CE. His real name is said to have been Kashyapa, and he composed the *Vaisheshika Sutra*, which forms the basis for this philosophy. Several writers later elaborated and commented on the *Sutra*, the most prominent being Prashastapada of the fourth century. Later writers include Shridhara, Udayana and Shivaditya. The term Vaisheshika comes from Vishesha, or 'particularity'. It has similarities with the NYAYA system of philosophy, and by the medieval period the two schools had almost merged.

Vaisheshika deals with physics, metaphysics, logic and methods of knowledge, and its central feature is considered its theory on the atomic structure of the universe. It recognizes four valid methods of knowledge, perception, inference, remembrance and intuition (arshajnana). These are subdivided into various categories. Vaisheshika uses intensive methods of analysis to understand the components of the world. Central to these methods is the theory of PADARTHAS, or categories, literally, the meaning of a word, an object which can be thought of and named. Objects can be analyzed according to substance (dravya), quality (guna), activity (karma), generality (samanya), particularity (vishesha) and inherence (samavya), to which a seventh aspect of non-existence (abhava) was added later. Substances can also be eternal, and include souls, which according to this philosophy are several, are bound by their own deeds, and can attain liberation. The supreme soul is distinct from these individual souls.

Other DRAVYAS or substances include earth, air, water, light, space and time. Earth, air, water and light are concrete and are made up of atoms (paramanus) which combine to form objects but are never destroyed, even when the world ends. Atoms have both a primary and a secondary nature, and thus have different qualities. True knowledge, that is, recognizing the atomic nature of the world, is essential for liberation.

Vaisheshika also speaks of DHARMA, ethics and the right way of life. Kanada's *Sutras* do not directly refer to god, though Prashastapada sees Ishvara (god) as the cause of the universe. Later writers accepted a divine principle because of existing contradictions in the philosophy. Summimg up this philosophical system, S. Radhakrishnan says, 'The many-sided context of human life is ignored by the Vaisheshika, and its physical philosophy and moral and religious values are not worked into a unified interpretation. An atomistic pluralism is not the final answer to the intellectual demand for a rational interpretation of the universe.'

Vaishnavism One of the three main sects of Hinduism, the other two being SHAIVISM and SHAKTISM. Vaishnavism focuses on the worship of the god VISHNU, which can be traced back to the RIG VEDA, and of his incarnations, which developed over time. Vaishnavism includes not only devotion and worship, but also a complex philosophy.

An early Vaishnava sect was the BHAGAVATA, focusing on the worship of Vasudeva Krishna. A later development was the PANCHARATRA, with its theory of emanations or vyuhas. Between the seventh and tenth centuries the ALVAR saints worshipped Vishnu with BHAKTI or love and devotion. The Alvars were followed by the Vaishnava acharyas, including NATHAMUNI and YAMUNACHARYA. RAMANUJA in the eleventh century took over from them and established the most influential Vaishnava philosophy, known as VISHISHTADVAITA; MADHVA founded the school of DVAITA in the thirteenth century. Two branches of southern Vaishnavism around this time were the TENGALAI and VADAGALAI, while the HARIDASA sect focussed on Bhakti. Meanwhile in Bengal, JAYADEVA wrote the famous *GITA GOVINDA* in the twelfth century, on the love between RADHA and KRISHNA, which contributed to the growth of Radha-Krishna cults.

Another major sect was established by VALLABHACHARYA (1481–1533). In central India, including Maharashtra and Karnataka, the cult of VITTHALA, a form of Vishnu, was important. He was worshipped by JNANESHVARA, NAMADEVA, TUKARAM and others, while in north India RAMANANDA, RAVIDAS, MIRABAI, and SUR DAS were among the noted Vaishnava saints. Among others there were NIMBARKA, Nabhadas (c. 1525), Biharilal (1603–63), Ramdas (1608-81) and Jagjivan Das (1632–1720). CHANDIDAS, CHAITANYA MAHAPRABHU and SHANKARA DEVA were Vaishnava saints in eastern India. In modern times, ISKCON carries on the tradition of Krishna worship. Nimbarka, Vidyapati, Umapati, Chandidas and Chaitanya Mahaprabhu are among those who focus on Radha-Krishna worship influenced by SHAKTISM.

The VEDAS, UPANISHADS, the *BRAHMA SUTRA*, *HARIVAMSHA* and PURANAS, are all utilized in the development of Vaishnava philosophy, while the BHAGAVAD GITA, *Pancharatra Agamas*, the Bhakti compositions of all the saints and writers, and the complex works of the philosophers form part of Vaishnava literature. The PURANAS describe the myths, stories and attributes of Vishnu in his various incarnations. Among the Puranas, the *VISHNU PURANA* and the *BHAGAVATA PURANA* are primarily concerned with the worship of Vishnu. Simultaneously the iconography, symbolism and forms of worship for the various incarnations of Vishnu developed and Vaishnava temples were constructed in all parts of India, the earliest extant temples dating to the fifth century. Thus Vaishnavism includes a number of different sects, methods of worship, incarnations, myths, legends and philosophy. Vishnu therefore is said to exist in five different forms of the Absolute: as images (archa), incarnations (vibhava), emanations (vyuha), in subtle (sukshma) form, and as the inner ruler (antaryamin).

Vaishnava sects include the Pancharatras, SAHAJIYAS, VARKARIS or worshippers of Vitthala, SHRIVAISHNAVAS, and followers of the various Vaishnava saints and philosophers, including Chaitaniya Mahaprabhu, Vallabhacharya, Ramanuja, Madhva, and Ramananda.

Vaishnavite/Vaishnava A term for a follower or adherent of Vaishnavism.

Vaishno Devi A temple dedicated to the Hindu goddess Vaishno Devi, located at Udhampur in Jammu and Kashmir. The cave shrine, at a height of 1640 m, has representations of the goddess in her three aspects of creation, preservation and destruction. This popular shrine is visited by thousands of pilgrims.

vaishya A term for the third broad caste division within Hinduism. Vaishyas were originally merchants and traders, but branched into a number of different professions. Though they also have the UPANAYANA or sacred thread ceremony and are among the dvija or twice born, they were considered inferior to BRAHMANAS and KSHATRIYAS. Ancient texts referred to them as avaricious, but they were also recognized as playing a useful and essential role in society. Vaishyas include business communities such as Agarwal, Maheshwari, Oswal, Jaiswal, Poswal and Mahajan; Banias, originally grain dealers, who have a number of sub-castes and are known by different names in different regions; Marwaris; and several others.

Vaivasvata The name of the seventh MANU, who, according to Hindu mythology, rules the world at present.

Vajasaneyi Samhita The name of a version of the YAJUR VEDA, also known as the *White Yajur Veda*.

vajra A weapon, a thunderbolt used by the Hindu god INDRA. The term is also used in Buddhism, where it has a complex and symbolic meaning.

Vajrachchhedika-prajnaparamita-sutra A MAHAYANA Buddhist text, popularly known as the *Diamond Sutra*. The text has thirty-two chapters, with themes similar to other PRAJNAPARAMITA or perfection-of-wisdom texts. The terms used are complex, and the correct understanding of the text requires an advanced teacher.

Vajranabha   A weapon, the name of a chakra or discus used by the Hindu god KRISHNA. It was given to him by the god AGNI, so that he could defeat INDRA and burn the Khandava forest.

Vajrayana Buddhism   A school of Buddhism that developed in India in the seventh century, though its basic elements can be traced back to the fourth century. It forms part of the system of TANTRA. Vajrayana and Buddhist Tantra are often used as synonyms, though Vajrayana is sometimes considered Tantra formalized into academic disciplines. A form of Vajrayana focusing on the use of MANTRAS is called MANTRAYANA. The term Vajrayana comes from vajra which means diamond or thunderbolt, and indicates strength, hardness and brilliance, representing the underlying BUDDHA nature.

Vajrayana developed out of MAHAYANA philosophy and includes some aspects of it. Initially, Vajrayana Buddhists abandoned the SANGHA and wandered around as ascetic SIDDHAS, but later they followed established patterns and lived along with Mahayana monks. They, too, took the vows of the BODHISATTVA, but used different rituals. Vajrayana arrived in China in the eighth century and then spread to Japan. The school became popular in Tibet, where Tantric literature was translated and classified.

Vajrayana uses mantras and yantras or MANDALAS, ritual techniques and meditation, as well as the visualization and internalization of a deity to bring about a spontaneous awakening of enlightenment or Buddhahood.

Sexual symbolism is a part of both Vajrayana and other forms of Tantra. For instance, the thought of awakening is symbolized by semen, wisdom or prajna is a female deity who can also be a real woman, while skilful means or upaya is her male consort. The union of upaya and prajna can be expressed in real terms as by SAHAJIYAS, but in Vajrayana traditional vows and rules are normally maintained.

Vali (Vaali)   The ruler of KISHKINDHA described in the RAMAYANA. He was of the vanara or monkey tribe and was said to be the son of the Hindu god INDRA. He was defeated and killed by RAMA, who placed his brother Sugriva on the throne. This act of Rama's has been dealt with in different ways in later versions of the Ramayana.

Vallabhacharya   A VAISHNAVA philosopher, whose system of philosophy is known as SHUDDHADVAITA.

Born in 1481 in a Telugu BRAHMANA family, he is said to have had a complete knowledge of the VEDAS, the six classical systems of philosophy and the eighteen major PURANAS by the age of seven. He went to VARANASI to study, and then to VRINDAVAN and MATHURA. At Mathura he had a divine vision in which he saw the god KRISHNA,

and this led him to develop his philosophy. He accepted the authority of the UPANISHADS, the BHAGAVAD GITA, *BRAHMA SUTRA* and *BHAGAVATA PURANA*, as well as the works of Vishnusvamin, a philosopher of the thirteenth century. His writings include *Anubhasya*, *Siddhanta-rahasya* and *Bhagavata-tika-subodhini*. His philosophy of Shuddhadvaita is considered pure non-dualism. Vallabha sees God as the whole and the individual as the part, but both have the same essence and hence are essentially the same. Yet the highest goal for the individual is not union with God, or liberation, but the service of Krishna.

Vallabha travelled to different parts of the country and became known as ACHARYA or teacher. He started a sect known as Pushtimarga, which flourished in western and central India. This sect is still important today. He also established the worship of Krishna as Shrinathji, the main temple being located today at NATHDWARA in Rajasthan.

His son VITTHALANATHA was his successor, and had seven sons, the descendants of whom are the leaders of the sect, known as Goswamis.

Valmiki   A RISHI or sage, and the traditional author of the earliest known RAMAYANA. Not much is known of Valmiki's life, though according to the text, he was a contemporary of RAMA. In the Uttara Kanda, the last part of the *Ramayana*, he states that he was the tenth son of Pracheta. Pracheta is another name for VARUNA, who according to the *Shatapatha Brahmana* and some of the PURANAS, had two sons, BHRIGU and Valmiki. According to one myth, Varuna's semen fell on an ant hill (valmika) and Valmiki was born from this. The *MAHABHARATA* mentions a Valmiki born in the Bhargava gotra or family.

According to popular legend, Valmiki was once a hunter who became a robber. This is first clearly stated in the *SKANDA PURANA*, dated around 800, and therefore considered too late to be an authentic story. This story was elaborated in different texts, and a long version appears in the *ADHYATMA RAMAYANA* (fourteenth century), in which Valmiki states that he was born a BRAHMANA but was brought up by Kirata (forest-dweller) parents. He used to hunt in the forests, and made an attempt to rob seven rishis or sages, who prevented him from doing so and gave him a mantra, 'Mara'. As he kept repeating this, the word became 'Rama'. An ant hill grew around him, and after ages the rishis returned, dug him out of there, and called him Valmiki because he came from an antheap (valmika). This story seems a mix of different legends. It was unlikely that Valmiki was ever a hunter, as his *Ramayana* recounts that he began composing verse in a moment of deep compassion, when a hunter killed a male heron, and he saw the grief of its desolate mate.

In the sixteenth century, TULASIDASA said that Valmiki was of a very low caste but attained a high status as he worshipped SHIVA. This story accounts for the worship of Valmiki in north India by DALITS even today.

When SITA was banished from AYODHYA, she stayed at his ASHRAM, which was located at CHITRAKUTA. When LAKSHMANA left her there, he described Valmiki as a friend of his father DASHARATHA and a learned brahmana. Rama and Sita's twin sons, LAVA and KUSHA, were educated by Valmiki, who taught them the *Ramayana*. The dates of both Valmiki and his *Ramayana* remain uncertain, but its composition, including later sections, was probably complete by the first century.

Vamana A Hindu deity, one of the ten main incarnations of the god VISHNU, in which Vishnu took the form of a dwarf. He assumed this form in order to defeat MAHABALI. Mahabali, the great-grandson of HIRANYAKASHIPU, was a good king but was against the DEVAS and BRAHMANAS. Vishnu therefore was born from ADITI as Vamana.

While Mahabali was offering a sacrifice on the river NARMADA, Vamana appeared as a young hermit, and asked for some land, an area he could cover in three steps. Bali agreed, and Vamana began taking the three steps, but as he did so, he grew enormously in size. The first step covered the whole earth, the second, the entire heaven. Mahabali then offered his own body for the third step, because a promise given can never be broken. Placing his foot on his head, Vamana pushed Bali into PATALA, the nether world, where he has reigned ever since.

Mahabali was allowed to rule only in the underworld, but was given permission to appear on earth once a year. In the epoch when VISHNU appeared as Vamana, LAKSHMI was said to have appeared as a lotus.

Vamana is depicted either as a dwarf or as a giant, with his foot on Mahabali's head. Images of him occur in Vishnu temples, while separate temples dedicated to him are located mainly in south India.

Vamana Purana A Sanskrit text, one of the eighteen major PURANAS of Hinduism. It begins with the story of VAMANA, the dwarf incarnation of VISHNU, while other incarnations are described in succeeding chapters. There is an account of LINGA worship and legends of SHIVA, including the story of the marriage of Shiva and PARVATI, as well as the birth of GANESHA and KARTTIKEYA. The five Puranic themes are barely mentioned, and it seems to be a fairly late text. It has some similarities with the *VARAHA PURANA*.

Van Yatra A Hindu festival associated with the god KRISHNA, celebrated in August/September at MATHURA and neighbouring sites associated with Krishna. According to legend, when INDRA sent down a deluge in this month, Krishna raised the mountain GOVARDHANA to protect himself and his fellow cowherds. To commemorate this, followers of Krishna make a pilgrimage to all the places connected with his life and re-enact the scenes that took place.

vanaprastha The third stage of traditional Hindu life, following the life of a householder. In this stage, a man should live in the forest, preparing for the life of a SANNYASI.

vanara The Sanskrit term for a monkey, a term used in the RAMAYANA for VALI and Sugriva, the ruler of KISHKINDHA, and for their subjects, including HANUMAN. Some scholars feel the term refers to a tribe with a monkey totem.

Vande Mataram The National Song of India. It was composed in Sanskrit by Bankim Chandra Chatterjee around 1875 and published in his book, *Anand Math*, in 1882. Literally, the first line means 'Mother, I bow to thee' and refers to India as a divine mother. During the national movement and later, BHARAT MATA temples, where India is worshipped as a goddess, were erected.

var A term for a poetic composition in Punjab, a heroic ballad. Sikh literature has a number of vars; three vars by Guru NANAK are included in the GURU GRANTH SAHIB. The *Asa di var*, with some additions by the gurus ANGAD and RAM DAS, is considered the most profound. In it Nanak speaks about the nature of God and about a life dedicated to truth and service, and states that the guidance of a true guru is needed on the path. He also praises women and describes their importance in the world.

Varaha A Hindu deity, one of the ten main incarnations of the god VISHNU. In this, Vishnu took the form of a boar (varaha), and descended to the depths of the ocean to rescue the earth. There are different versions of this story in the PURANAS. According to one version, the daitya HIRANYAKSHA practised austerities for many years and obtained a boon from the god BRAHMA, that he would become lord of the world, and no animal or person would be able to harm him. Hiranyaksha gradually began to inflict all kinds of torments on the earth and its inhabitants, and the earth sank down into the ocean. Assuming the form of a cow, the earth (Prithvi or BHUDEVI) appealed to Vishnu to save it. When Hiranyaksha had listed the animals that could not harm him, he missed out on the boar, or varaha. Therefore Vishnu assumed the form of a boar, with great white tusks, and descended into the ocean. After a battle of 1000 years, he defeated Hiranyaksha and raised the earth up again on his tusks.

Some parallels can be seen in a Zoroastrian story, where GAUSH URVA, the cow representing the suffering earth, appeals to AHURA MAZDA for help.

Varaha is depicted in two ways: either fully in animal form or as a four-armed human with a boar's head. His consort is Varahi. Varaha images occur in Vishnu temples as well as in some independent shrines. The story is also related to creation myths and to the evolution of life from water.

Varaha Purana A Sanskrit text, one of the eighteen major PURANAS, of Hinduism. It is said to have been narrated to the goddess PRITHVI by VISHNU in the form of VARAHA. It has some creation myths and genealogies, but is primarily concerned with the worship of Vishnu. There are stories of SHIVA and of GANESHA, and of the MATRIKAS or mother goddesses. SHRADDHA ceremonies for ancestors are described. The *Ganesha Stotra*, which forms part of it, is used for the worship of the god Ganesha, and the *Mathura Mahatmya*, on the sacred places of MATHURA, is important for the worship of KRISHNA.

Varahamihira The author of works on astronomy, astrology and religion, who lived in the sixth century. His *BRIHAT SAMHITA* has chapters on iconography, the materials to be used in making images, and the methods for their installation, as well as sections on omens, natural and celestial events, astronomy and mathematics. He wrote two works on astrology, the *Hora Shastra* and *Laghu Jataka*, as well as the *Pancha Siddhanta*, a summary of five older astronomical texts.

Varanasi A city in Uttar Pradesh known in ancient days as KASHI. It is one of the most sacred cities in Hinduism.

There are innumerable temples here, the most famous being the KASHI VISHVANATHA, a SHIVA temple. Though Varanasi is associated primarily with the god Shiva, there are legends and temples of other deities as well. VISHNU is said to have created the Kashi LINGA at this place. BRAHMA performed the Dasashvamedha sacrifice at Dasashvamedha Ghat. Varanasi was once important for Buddhism, and nearby SARNATH is where the BUDDHA preached his first sermon. Under the Pala dynasty of the ninth to eleventh centuries, Buddhism revived.

The river GANGA flows through Varanasi, which is known for its ghats, or stone stairs, constructed on the banks of the river. From here pilgrims descend to the river to bathe and perform various rituals. Some of the ghats are used exclusively for burning the dead. There are altogether about seventy-four ghats, including the Dashashvamedha and Manikarnika ghats.

Several mosques were built later and co-exist with the Hindu temples in this holy city.

Vardhamana Temple A temple of the Hindu god VISHNU located at KANCHIPURAM in Tamil Nadu. It was constructed in the twelfth century at the time of the Chola dynasty, though several additions were made later in the sixteenth century, during the time of the Vijayanagara dynasty.

Within the temple is a sacrificial altar on a high platform. According to legend, Vishnu came to reside in this place after the god Brahma prayed to him. The temple is in a rectangular walled enclosure with GOPURAMS on the east and west. A smaller gopuram on the inner walls on the west leads to the main temple. There is a large pillared MANDAPA of the Vijayanagara period, with ninety-six columns intricately carved with scenes from the life of Vishnu in his various incarnations. Two sacred tanks are located near the temple, one to the north and the other to the east.

Varkaris A name for the worshippers of the Hindu god VITTHALA, a form of VISHNU or KRISHNA. Varkaris also revere Pundalik, JNANESHVARA and other early devotees of Vitthala. Varkaris converge at PANDHARPUR at the Ashadha and Karttika fairs. One month before the Ashadha festival, devotees set off for Pandharpur on foot, accompanying the palkis or palanquins of the saints, which contain their images or padukas (sandals). The palki of Jnaneshvara comes from Alandi, of TUKARAM from Dehu, of Nivrittinatha (brother of Jnaneshvara) from Tryambakeshvara, and of EKNATHA from Paithan. Altogether there are sixty palkis from all over Maharashtra, accompanied by Dindis or BHAJAN-singing groups, who reach Pandharpur on the tenth day of the latter half of the month of Ashadha (June-July), one day before Ekadashi, the eleventh day, when the festival takes place. In everyday life Varkaris do not wear special clothes and are householders, but are bound to participate in the twice-yearly festivals. At this time they carry tals or small cymbals in their hands, wear TULASI malas (garlands) and hold saffron flags on short sticks. Varkaris follow ethical precepts and are strict vegetarians. They are initiated by a guru or spiritual leader, after which they wear the special tulasi mala. They observe fasts on Ekadashi and often form mandalis or groups wherever they live, singing bhajans or ABHANGAS in praise of Vitthala, composed by the Maratha saints and others. Later spiritual leaders of the Varkaris include Shri Gadge Maharaj and Manmadkar, a woman. Recently attempts have been made to start a mass movement to propagate Varkari philosophy and methods of worship. Varkaris include women and people of all castes.

varna A term indicating CASTE in Hindu texts. Literally, varna means 'colour'. In the *ATHARVA VEDA* varna or colour is associated with caste. White is said to be the colour of the BRAHMANA, red of the KSHATRIYA, yellow of the VAISHYA and black of the SHUDRA. Later, and even today, varna is used for caste without any association of colour. However, from the original four castes, there are several thousand today. As caste was associated with occupation and with types of people, the concept of caste represented as a colour, has some similarity with the Jain concept of LESHYAS. JATI is another term used for caste.

Varuna A Hindu god, lord of the waters and guardian of the western quarter. He was a major deity in the RIG VEDA, where he is usually mentioned along with MITRA. Both Mitra and Varuna were connected with water and worshipped as lords of rain. They lived in a golden abode in heaven. They were guardians of the moral order, known as rita. Varuna's chariot shone like the sun, and was drawn by well-yoked steeds. He was omniscient, and he knew the flight of the birds, the path of ships, the course of the wind, and all the secrets of the world. A highly ethical god, he punished any infringement of his law or ordinances. He was known as an ASURA, a word which in early days meant a divine being. His nature and character have led some scholars to see him as similar to AHURA MAZDA, the name of God in Zoroastrianism (asura = ahura in Persian). Semitic concepts have also been suggested for his origin. In post-Vedic times, he lost his importance but retained his connection with water. He became a DIKAPALA, the guardian of the western quarter.

The MAHABHARATA states that he was the son of KASHYAPA and ADITI, and was one of the twelve ADITYAS. According to the VISHNU-DHARMOTTARA PURANA, he is the god of the waters and rides a chariot drawn by seven swans. He is to be depicted with four hands that hold a lotus, noose, conch shell and jewel box. His consort is Gauri, who sits on his lap, and to his right and left are the river goddesses, GANGA and YAMUNA. In most sculptures, however, Varuna has two arms and sits or stands on a MAKARA, a mythical sea-creature. Other texts state he had several wives, chief of whom were Gauri and Varunani, and a number of children. Myths also connect him with the rishi VALMIKI. His semen fell on a valmika (white ant-hill), from which Valmiki was born.

Vasanta Panchami A Hindu festival celebrating spring. *See* Basant Panchami.

Vasishtha An ancient RISHI or sage. Many hymns of the RIG VEDA are ascribed to him. He is said to be one of the seven great rishis, and one of the ten PRAJAPATIS. In one of the hymns of the Rig Veda, he and the rishi AGASTYA are described as the offspring of MITRA and VARUNA. The rivalry between him and the rishi VISHVAMITRA is often described. Vasishtha owned Kamadhenu or NANDINI, a wish-fulfilling cow, who provided him with all he needed. The story of how Vishvamitra, then a king, attempted to take away his cow, and having failed, practised austerities and became a rishi himself, is described in the RAMAYANA and other texts. There are several stories about Vasishtha in the PURANAS. In the VISHNU PURANA, he is married to Urja, one of the daughters of DAKSHA, while according to the BHAGAVATA PURANA, he was married to Arundhati. He is described as the family priest of King Harishchandra, and of the King IKSHVAKU and all his descendants for sixty-one generations. Vasishtha probably represented one of a line of rishis or priests.

vastushastra The traditional science of architecture, the Indian counterpart of the Chinese feng shui. There are several ancient texts on vastu shastra.

Vastupurusha According to the AGNI PURANA, Vastupurusha was the name of an enormous ghost. Feared by all other ghosts, he was buried in the ground, where he still remains. He is the deity of all that is built on earth, and offerings are made to him after a house is built.

Vasubandhu A Buddhist scholar who lived in the fourth century, and is thought to have been the younger brother of ASANGA. He first belonged to the SARVASTIVADA school of HINAYANA Buddhism and wrote the *ABHIDHARMAKOSHA*, which some scholars believe presents SAUTRANTIKA views. Later he joined the YOGACHARA school of MAHAYANA Buddhism founded by his brother Asanga, and wrote two texts on the theory of consciousness, *Vimshatika* and *Trimshika*.

Vasudeva (Vaasudeva) A name of the Hindu god KRISHNA derived from the name of his father, Vasudeva.

Vasugupta A SHAIVITE philosopher, the founder of a school of Kashmir SHAIVISM. He lived in the eighth century and wrote the *SHIVA SUTRA*, which his followers believe is the result of a divine revelation.

Vasuki A king of the NAGAS or serpents in Hindu mythology, who lives in PATALA. He was one of the sons of KASHYAPA from his wife KADRU. There are several stories regarding him in various texts. When the ocean was churned for AMRITA, Vasuki, whose length was tremendous, was used as the rope. For the protection of serpents, he gave his sister Jaratkaru as wife to the rishi Jaratkaru. (Both the rishi and his wife had the same name.) Their son Astika saved the snakes at the time of Janamejaya's SARPA SATRA or snake sacrifice. In the MAHABHARATA, Vasuki is said to be one of the seven nagas who uphold the earth. He stayed in the palace of the god VARUNA and worshipped him.

Vasumitra A Buddhist scholar of the orthodox SARVASTIVADA school, which was also known as the VAIBHASHIKA. He was present at the BUDDHIST COUNCIL held at GANDHARA in c. 100 CE, and his views were important in the preparation of the *MAHAVIBHASHA*.

Vasus A group of semi-divine beings associated with AGNI. The number of Vasus given in different texts varies from eight to 333. According to one account, the eight Vasus are connected with the goddess GANGA. In the KRITA YUGA, it is said, the wife of the eighth Vasu desired KAMADHENU, the sacred and magical cow of the rishi VASISHTHA. On her insistence, the Vasus stole the cow, but were cursed by the rishi to be reborn on earth and lose their divine status. As they begged for forgiveness, he modified the curse, saying that the first seven could return to heaven as soon as they were born, but the eighth would live a long and celibate life. As the Vasus could not be born to an ordinary mortal, Ganga took the form of a woman and appeared on earth. She married King Shantanu, and all the eight Vasus were born to her. She threw the first seven into the river Ganga as soon as they were born, while the eighth grew up, and was known as BHISHMA.

Vata A name of the Hindu god VAYU. Vata literally means wind or air.

Vatsiputriya A school of HINAYANA Buddhism that developed from the STHAVIRAVADA around the beginning of the third century BCE. Its divergence from other schools was regarding the concept of the PUDGALA. It stated that the pudgala was a permanent entity, a 'person' not the same as the five SKANDHAS, nor different from them. Without the pudgala there could be no transmigration. Though not identified with the ATMAN, their concept of the pudgala was somewhat similar and not accepted by other early Buddhist schools. Several branches of the Vatsiputriya, including the SAMMATIYA, flourished in India.

Vayu A Hindu deity, god of the wind, first mentioned in the RIG VEDA, where he is also known as Vata. Here Vayu seems to be the personified form of Vata, the wind. In the VEDAS, his chariot is said to have a golden seat; it touches the sky and is drawn by reddish horses. As Vata, he is the breath of the gods, goes where he likes, and cannot be seen. Vayu bestows fame and wealth to his worshippers, disperses their enemies, and protects the weak. In the MAHABHARATA, Vayu is the father of BHIMA, the second PANDAVA brother. In the RAMAYANA he is known as the father of HANUMAN. In the PURANAS, he is one of the DIKAPALAS, the guardian of the north-west. The VISHNUDHARMOTTARA states that he is two-armed, and holds in his hands the ends of the scarf he wears. His clothing is inflated by the wind, and his hair is disshevelled. Some other texts state that he has a banner in his right hand and a staff or elephant goad in his left. He also has a simhasana (lion seat, indicating royalty). In later texts, he has four hands and a stag as his VAHANA or vehicle. According to the *Rupamandana*, his vahana is an antelope. Of his four hands, one is in varadamudra (boon-giving pose), while the others hold a banner, a flag and a waterpot. His colour is green. In early medieval temples, he is usually shown riding a stag and holding a flag, positioned in the north-west corner of the structure.

Vayu Purana A Sanskrit text, one of the eighteen major PURANAS of Hinduism. It is sometimes known as the *Shiva Purana*, as it is dedicated to the worship of SHIVA. It deals with the five Puranic themes, including creation myths and genealogies, but is mainly a glorification of Shiva. Shiva's heavenly city of Shivapuri is described, which can be reached by one who loses himself in contemplation of Shiva.

The original Purana is quite early, the present version probably of the fifth century. It has 14,000 verses and is narrated by VAYU, the wind god.

Vaz, Joseph An Indian who was a ROMAN CATHOLIC missionary. Joseph Vaz was born in Benaulim in Goa in 1651 and worked to promote Catholicism in the region of Karnataka (Mysore) and Sri Lanka. He lived like a Buddhist for over twenty-three years in Sri Lanka, secretly propagating Catholicism, and died there in 1711. He was beatified in 1995.

Veda A term for a group of Sanskrit texts, which are the most sacred texts of Hindus. Veda comes from the Sanskrit root vid, to know, and the word Veda implies divine knowledge. They are said to be 'SHRUTI' or texts divinely revealed to the ancient RISHIS and sages. They have two broad divisions, the SAMHITAS and

BRAHMANAS. The four Vedic Samhitas are the RIG VEDA, *SAMA VEDA, YAJUR VEDA* and *ATHARVA VEDA*. These contain the MANTRAS and prayers to be chanted and used in YAJNAS or sacrifices. The BRAHMANAS are texts attached to each of the Samhitas, and describe sacrificial rituals, while the ARANYAKAS and UPANISHADS are philosophical texts, which are appendages to the Brahmanas, and sometimes considered a part of them. While the Rig Veda can be dated between 1500 and 1000 BCE, the three later Vedas are dated between approximately 1000 and 600 BCE. Some of the attached texts also belong to this date, while others are later.

The VEDANGAS can also be included in the broad category of Vedic texts.

Vedangas A group of texts dealing with six subjects that are considered essential for an understanding of the VEDAS. The subjects are: shiksha, phonetics or pronunciation; vyakarana, grammar; chhandas, metre; nirukta, etymology or glossary; jyotisha, astronomy and astrology, essential to fix the right time for ceremonies and sacrifices; kalpa, or rules for sacrifices. The texts consist mainly of sutras, or short aphorisms.

Vedanta One of the six main schools of ancient Indian philosophy. The term Vedanta is most commonly used for ADVAITA, but includes all those schools of philosophy that use the UPANISHADS, the last part of the Vedas, as their ultimate authority. (Vedanta = Veda + anta (end or last)).

BADARAYANA (fifth to third century BCE) summarized the main teachings of the Upanishads in the *BRAHMA SUTRA*, also known as the *Vedanta Sutra*, a text reinterpreted by later scholars in varying ways. The most notable school of Vedanta is Advaita, which originated earlier, but developed between the seventh and ninth centuries. VAISHNAVA Vedanta schools include VISISHTADVAITA, DVAITA, DVAITADVAITA, and SHUDDHADVAITA. A Shaiva school of Vedanta is Shivadvaita.

Vedanta Desika The founder of the VADAGALAI sect of SHRIVAISHNAVISM, who lived in the thirteenth century. He was also known as Venkatanatha, and is considered one of the greatest successors of RAMANUJA. Born in KANCHIPURAM, he spent most of his life in SRIRANGAM, and wrote works on a number of subjects. His philosophical texts include *Pramatabhanga* and *Rahasyatrayasara*, written in Tamil. *Pancharatraraksha* and *Sachcharitraraksha* describe the PANCHARATRA school of Vaishnavism. His other works are the *Tattvatika*, a commentary on the *Shribhashya;* the *Tatparyachandrika*, a commentary on Ramanuja's commentary of the BHAGAVAD GITA; *Sheshvara Mimamsa* on MIMAMSA philosophy; *Nyayasiddhanjana* on NYAYA; *Tattvamuktakalapa*; and *Shatadushani*, in which he criticizes the philosophy of ADVAITA.

Vedanta Sutra A Sanskrit text that summarizes the main principles in the UPANISHADS and is used as a base by all schools of VEDANTA. It was written by BADARAYANA, and is also known as the *BRAHMA SUTRA*.

Vedartha Prakasha A Sanskrit text that provides a commentary on the RIG VEDA. It was written by SAYANA. Another text of the same name forms the commentary of MADHVA on the *TAITTIRIYA SAMHITA*.

Veda-Vyasa A name of the rishi VYASA, who is said to have arranged the VEDAS.

Vedic Samhitas A term for the first part of the VEDAS. The four Vedic Samhitas are the RIG VEDA, *SAMA VEDA, YAJUR VEDA* and *ATHARVA VEDA.*

Vendidad (1) A Zoroastrian text that forms part of the AVESTA, also known as the *Videvdat*. The *Vendidad* begins with an account of the sixteen lands created by AHURA MAZDA, and goes on to the story of YIMA, the first man, who sheltered people, plants and animals in a vara or enclosure, when ice and snow covered the world. The text has rituals, ceremonies and prayers, and describes methods for the disposal of the dead. Part of the text consists of various punishments for misdeeds and rewards for good acts. Some scholars believe the excessive punishments described must often have been converted into monetary payments. A number of things were considered wrong, including tilling land in which a corpse had been buried for less than a year, drinking water immediately after giving birth, or covering a dead man's feet with cloth. The high regard given to dogs is also revealed in the text. For instance, serving bad food to a shepherd's dog deserves a punishment of 200 stripes, while killing a man leads to only ninety.

In Hindu texts, killing a cow or a BRAHMANA deserved the highest punishment. Other parts of the ancient world, such as Greece, also had extreme punishments. Nevertheless, the *Vendidad* indicates the long distance the religion had travelled from the prayers and ideals of the *GATHAS.*

(2) Vendidad is also the name of a purificatory ritual in which the entire text is recited.

Venkateshvara A Hindu deity, a form of the god VISHNU in south India.

Venkateshvara Temple A temple of the Hindu god Venkateshvara, a form of VISHNU. It is located at Tirumala, near the city of Tirupati in Andhra Pradesh. This extremely popular and sacred temple dates back to the tenth century, though several additions were made by the later Vijayanagara kings, as well as in modern times. Within the main shrine is a standing image of Venkateshvara, also known as Srinivasa, and popularly called Balaji. The ornaments and crown of the image are made of pure gold, inlaid with precious stones. Above the sanctuary is a tower, a later construction with a gold-covered dome. The adjoining MANDAPA with carved pillars has gold sheets over the overhanging eves.

The temple has been expanded and renovated to accommodate the large number of pilgrims that visit every day. It is enclosed in walls, entered through a towered GOPURAM on the east, probably first constructed in the Vijayanagara period, but later rebuilt. Sheets of embossed silver cover the lintels. Inside the gateway is a columned porch with life-size images of the Vijayanagara rulers. Those of Krishnadeva Raya and his two queens are in copper, while Achyuta Raya and his queens are carved in stone. Left of the gateway are two mandapas with small shrines within. Rearing horses and images of VAISHNAVITE deities, including NARASIMHA and KRISHNA, are depicted. In the centre of the enclosure is a flag column and an altar covered with sheets of gold.

Verethraghna A YAZATA or divine being in Zoroastrianism, considered the Zoroastrian counterpart of the Hindu god INDRA, one of whose titles is Vritrahan, the slayer of VRITRA. Verethraghna had a number of incarnations, one of which was a bull. He also takes the form of Varaghna, the swiftest of birds. He was later known as BEHRAM.

vetala A ghost or spirit in Hindu mythology. Vetalas are said to haunt cremation grounds and enter dead bodies, bringing them to life.

Vettekkaran A Hindu deity, a hunter god, worshipped in Kerala. He is considered a form of SHIVA, as the Kirata hunter. His son, Vettakorumakkan, is a different form of the same deity.

Vibhajyavada A school of HINAYANA Buddhism which formed the rest of the STHAVIRAVADA when the SARVASTIVADA broke away. They took this name, meaning 'those who teach discrimination' to distinguish themselves from the Sarvastivada. They had a number of branches, including the MAHISHASAKA, the KASHYAPIYA and the DHARMAGUPTAKA. Some of the Vibhajyavadas settled in Sri Lanka and were called THERAVADA, the PALI for Sthaviravada. Branches of the Theravada include the Mahavihara, Abhayagirivasa and Jetavaniya.

Vibhanga A Buddhist HINAYANA text that forms part of the *ABHIDHAMMA PITAKA* of the PALI CANON, and has three sections. The first describes basic Buddhist principles, the second, the knowledge derived by sense impressions, which gradually leads to higher knowledge, while the third section describes the obstacles preventing the attainment of knowledge.

Vibhishana A RAKSHASA, the younger brother of RAVANA, described in the *RAMAYANA*. He allied with RAMA and became the king of LANKA after the death of Ravana.

Viceroy's Church A popular name for the ANGLICAN Cathedral Church of Redemption, located at New Delhi. It was consecrated in 1931, but completed in 1935. Originally designed as a grand church for the new British capital, financial problems toned down the project, though it is still an imposing structure. The church, located near Rashtrapati Bhavan, which was originally the viceroy's house, was designed by H.A.N. Medd. It is built of buff-coloured Dholpur stone, with a red sandstone roof, and has a silver cross donated by the British king. A picture at its east end was donated by the then-viceroy, Lord Edward Irwin and his wife, in thanksgiving for their escape in an attempt to blow up their train in 1929.

Vidhatr A Sanskrit word, meaning the creator. It is a name of various Hindu deities, including BRAHMA, VISHNU, and VISHVAKARMA.

Vidisha A city in Madhya Pradesh, which in ancient days, was an important religious centre. Buddhist VIHARAS and shrines, as well as VAISHNAVITE and other monuments, are located here.

Vidura A son of the rishi VYASA, and the half-brother of PANDU and DHRITARASHTRA in the *MAHABHARATA*. He sided with the PANDAVAS in the great war.

Vidya Shankara Temple A temple located at SRINGERI in Karnataka. It was built over the SAMADHI of the tenth SHANKARACHARYA of the Sringeri Matha, Vidya Tirtha, by his two close disciples, the brothers Bharati Tirtha and VIDYARANYA. The main shrine of the temple has an image representing Vidya Tirtha, and a LINGA. According to the story associated with this temple, Sri Vidya Tirtha entered a chamber for samadhi. Before doing this, he showed his disciples an image. He asked them to keep the chamber sealed for twelve years, during which time he would be in Lambika Yoga (a form of meditation). At the end of this, they should open the chamber and would find him in the form of the image. Unfortunately, a curious person opened the chamber after three years. Vidya Tirtha had disappeared, but his transformation was not complete—only a part of a linga had appeared. The original image and a linga were thus installed here, and a temple built over them. In front of the inner shrine is a remarkable MANDAPA or hall. Twelve pillars within it, each representing a sign of the zodiac, are arranged in a circle and covered with a dome. Three small low gateways provide openings on the east, north and south. The whole is so scientifically designed that the rays of the rising sun hit only that pillar which represents the rashi or zodiac sign through which the sun is passing at that time. Each month when the rashi changes, the sun's rays move on to the next pillar.

According to legend, Vidya Tirtha still sits in the inner chamber, in Lambika Yoga.

Vidyadevis A class of deities in Jainism, consisting of sixteen goddesses of knowledge. Initially SARASVATI was the chief deity, but later new goddesses emerged. The names of the sixteen are: Rohini, Prajnapti, Vajrashrinkhala, Vajrankusha, Apratichakra, Purushadatta, Kali, Mahakali, Gauri, Gandhari, Sarvastra-Mahajvala, Manavi, Vairotya, Achchhupta, Manasi, and Mahamanasi. These are depicted in some Jain temples, including the DILWARA temples at Mt Abu. These sixteen are not depicted with attributes of

Sarasvati, but are thought to be Tantric deities, similar to Buddhist and Hindu Tantric goddesses. The Jain SHASANA DEVIS are in some cases identical.

Vidyadharas (1) A class of semi-divine beings in Hindu mythology who lived between the earth and the sky. They were attendants of INDRA, but also had kings of their own. Their female counterparts were Vidyadharis. They are depicted on early Buddhist and Jain monuments, as well as in Hindu temples.

(2) Jain texts indicate that Vidyadharas were also a group of people.

Vidyapati A poet who wrote in praise of Hindu deities, as well as on other themes, but is most famous for his poems of the love between RADHA and KRISHNA. Vidyapati was born in about 1360, in village Bisaphi of Darbhanga district in Bihar. The area is known as Mithila and the Maithili language here is a Hindi dialect, in which Vidyapati mainly composed his works. He also wrote in Avahatta (an earlier form of Maithili) and in Sanskrit. Vidyapati was patronized by kings of the Oinibara dynasty who ruled in this area and became their court poet. Some of his poems are written in praise of the kings Maharaja Kirti Singh (ruled 1402–05) and Maharaja Shiva Singh (ruled 1407–1416). In 1416 the latter mysteriously disappeared, and Vidyapati lived with Queen Lakhima till 1429. Most of his works were composed in this period. Apart from the verses in praise of kings, he wrote the *Danavakyavali*, a guide to the types of *dana* or religious gifts to be made; the *Bhuparikrama*, on various places of pilgrimage; the *Gayapattalaka* on rites to be performed at GAYA; the *Gangakyavali*, regarding rites relating to the river GANGA; the *Shaivasarasvasara*, consisting of songs of devotion to the god SHIVA; and the *Durgabhaktitarangini*, a work of devotion to DURGA. There were also other secular texts, as well as his love poems, with erotic imagery. These were appreciated and popularized by CHAITANYA MAHAPRABHU and influenced the later VAISHNAVA poets of Bengal, Assam, Orissa and Nepal. In these poems Vidyapati describes Radha as a young girl, her growth to maturity, and her beauty, as well as the beauty and charm of Krishna. The images of human love in his poems reflect love for the divine.

Vidyaranya A philosopher of the fourteenth century. The identity of Vidyaranya is not clear. His original name is thought to have been Madhava, and he is often identified with Madhavacharya of the fourteenth century. However, according to the records of the Sringeri Matha, he was born in about 1296 in Ekasila Nagara, present Warangal in Andhra Pradesh, and took the name Vidyaranya after he became a SANNYASI in 1377. He was the elder brother of Sri Bharati Krishna Tirtha, whom he succeeded as the twelfth ACHARYA of the SRINGERI Matha, from 1380 to 1386. Vidyaranya was involved in the foundation of the Vijayanagara kingdom in 1336. He wrote a number of texts, including *Jivanmukti Viveka* and *Panchadashi* on ADVAITA VEDANTA. These provide clear guidelines for sannyasis and spiritual aspirants, and have quotes from earlier Vedantic texts. He also wrote *Dhatu-vritti* on Sanskrit grammar, *Jaiminiya Nyayamala* on MIMAMSA, and *Parasara-smritivyakhya*, a commentary on the *Parasara-smriti*. Other texts attributed to him are *Smriti Sangraha, Vyavahara Madhava, Sri Vidyartha Dipika, Vivarana-prameya Sangraha, Drig Drishya Viveka, Aparokshanubhuti Tika*, as well as commentaries on the UPANISHADS. According to some sources, not all the texts were solely written by him, and Bharati Tirtha contributed to the *Panchadashi*. In spreading the truths of Advaita, Vidyaranya had a reputation that came close to that of SHANKARA. Vidyaranya died in 1386 at Sringeri.

vihara The term for a Buddhist monastery. Viharas were made from the time the Buddhist SANGHA was founded. Early viharas often consisted of rock-cut caves, with a rock platform for a bed and a niche in the cave wall for a lamp or book. Structural viharas usually had individual cells around a central courtyard. Most viharas had an assembly hall and a temple or shrine for worship, which usually consisted of a STUPA at one end of a hall, known as the CHAITYA, or hall of worship.

Vijnanavada A term by which the YOGACHARA school of MAHAYANA Buddhism is also known. Vijnana means 'consciousness', and thus Vijnanavada refers to 'theories of consciousness'.

Vikramashila A Buddhist monastery and university located in Bihar, which flourished between the eighth and twelfth centuries. It was founded at the time of Dharma Pala (780–815), a king of the Pala dynasty. The monastery was also a centre of learning that specialized in VAJRAYANA Buddhism. Monks and scholars from different countries, including Tibet, studied here.

Vimanavatthu A Buddhist text that forms part of the KHUDDAKA NIKAYA of the PALI CANON. It seems to be a relatively late text and deals with the merit of good actions through a series of dialogues attributed to Mogallana (MAUDGALYANA), a close disciple of the BUDDHA, and various divine beings.

Vinata The mother of the divine bird GARUDA in Hindu mythology. She was one of the daughters of DAKSHA and a wife of the rishi KASHYAPA. According to another version, she was a wife of Garuda.

Vinaya Pitaka A group of Buddhist texts that deal with rules for the conduct of monks. The term usually refers to the texts that form part of the PALI CANON of HINAYANA Buddhism, though there are also other Vinaya Pitakas.

The Pali or Hinayana *Vinaya* has the following texts: *Suttavibhanga*, consisting of the *Mahavibhanga* and the *Bhikkuni-vibhanga*; the *Khandakas*, which include the *Mahavagga* and the *Chulavagga*; the *Parivara* or *Parivarapatha*.

The PATIMOKKHA, a list of actions that are forbidden to monks, as well as atonements if a monk happens to perform any of the forbidden actions, forms the base of the *Vinaya* and the *Suttavibhanga* is a commentary on these. The *Mahavibhanga* provides a commentary on rules for the monks, and the *Bhikkunivibhanga* on rules for bhikkunis, or nuns. The *Khandakas* deal with the way monks and nuns should lead their daily lives, and go into great detail. Both the *Mahavagga* and the *Chulavagga* have ten sections each, the tenth section of the *Chulavagga*, being specifically for nuns. The *Parivara*, probably a later work, has nineteen short texts.

Along with the rules for monks and nuns, the *Vinaya* texts contain stories of the BUDDHA's life and some of his teachings.

Among the other *Vinayas*, that of the Mulasarvastivada, a branch of the SARVASTIVADA, is a voluminous compendium of biographical traditions of the Buddha, dated between the fourth and fifth centuries CE. This formed a source for later MAHAYANA schools, and is also used as the *Vinaya* by all schools of TIBETAN BUDDHISM.

Mahayana Buddhism formulated its own monastic rules, which did not replace earlier *Vinayas* but added to them. Texts which recorded these rules include the *Bodhisattva-pratimoksha* and other texts on the path of the BODHISATTVA.

Vinayaka A name of the Hindu god GANESHA, popularly used in Maharashtra and south India.

Vindhyavasini A name of the Hindu goddess DURGA. In this form she is a forest goddess, a dweller of the Vindhyas.

Vipassana (Vipashyana) A Buddhist method of meditation, which consists of focusing on the breath and watching the mind, its desires and emotions. Being a witness and not reacting to events or to what one thinks or feels, leads to calmness, an ending of negative emotions, and the rise of love, friendliness and compassion. This ancient technique was reintroduced in India by a businessman, S.N. Goenka, who studied the technique in Myanmar. Ten-day courses are conducted to teach the basic technique.

Viprachitti A chief of the DANAVAS in Hindu mythology. He was the son of KASHYAPA and DANU.

Vir Singh, Bhai A Sikh who was part of the SINGH SABHA movement of Sikhism, and was also a noted Punjabi poet and novelist. Born in 1872, Vir Singh grew up in a spiritual atmosphere and from 1892 became involved in the Singh Sabha. He founded the Khalsa Tract Society, which disseminated pamphlets on Sikhism, as well as a journal, the *Khalsa Samachar*. He wrote novels with themes of Sikh heroism and chivalry, which were extremely popular. These include *Sundri, Raja Lakhdata Singh, Baba Naudh Singh, Vijay Singh*, and *Satwant Kaur*. An epic poem, *Rana Surat Singh* (1905), was written in blank verse, which was unique in those days. He wrote a number of other poems in short quatrains, of which his last collection, *Mere Saian Jio,* interprets Sikh themes in a modern idiom. He also composed biographies of Guru GOBIND SINGH, known as *Kalghidar Chamatkar*, and of Guru NANAK, the *Guru Nanak Chamatkar*.

He was awarded a doctorate by Punjab University and received several awards, including the Padma Shri.

Bhai Vir Singh died in 1957.

Virabhadra Temple A temple of the Hindu god SHIVA located at Lepakshi in Andhra Pradesh, built in Vijayanagara style in the sixteenth century. The temple complex is surrounded by two sets of enclosure walls. The outer enclosure contains a number of inscriptions of the Vijayanagara period. The main temple is in the inner enclosure entered through two GOPURAMS. Virabhadra, a form of Shiva, is in a shrine facing north, while there are two other shrines with images of Shiva and VISHNU. Nearby is a huge Nagalingam carved out of a granite block, consisting of a LINGA surmounted by a seven-headed cobra, as well as an enormous NANDI carved out of a single block. There are also some half-completed shrines and MANDAPAS.

According to the legend associated with this temple, it was built by Virupanna, treasurer of King Krishnadeva Raya of the Vijayanagara dynasty. Virupanna used the money from the king's treasury, and when he discovered this, the king ordered him to be blinded. Virupanna then blinded himself and died soon after, thus the grand temple was never completed.

The temple has a number of sculptures and is particularly known for its murals, which cover parts of the walls and ceilings, depicting stories from the epics and PURANAS.

Virashaiva Another term for the LINGAYAT sect started by BASAVANNA.

Virji Vohra A rich and prominent Jain merchant and banker of the seventeenth century. He gave loans to several important people, including the Mughal emperor Shah Jahan's son, Prince Murad. He represented the Surat merchants and was invited to Shah Jahan's court to explain their grievances against the governor. He also gave huge loans to the English. It was partly because of merchants and bankers like him and SHANTIDAS that the Mughals gave concessions and grants to the Jains.

Vishishtadvaita A system of philosophy founded by RAMANUJA in the eleventh century. Vishishtadvaita is defined as 'qualified monism'. According to this philosophy, BRAHMAN, the Absolute, pervades all creation, including matter and the individual soul. The soul is created by god from his own essence. It shares the divine nature and is eternal, but always remains distinct from god, with a consciousness of itself. If it

were to lose this, it would not exist. Through worship and BHAKTI, the soul attains eternal communion with god. The material world is also a part of god, but is not an illusion. Out of love and compassion for his creation, God incarnated in different forms to show them the path to salvation. According to Ramanuja, RAMA was the highest of these incarnations.

According to the philosopher S. Radhakrishnan, SHANKARA and Ramanuja were both great exponents of VEDANTA, examined the same texts, and based their ideas on the same assumptions, yet reached different conclusions. He says, 'Ramanuja trusts firmly in the religious instinct, and sets forth a deeply religious view which reveals god to man through creation.'

In its social and religious manifestation, Vishishtadvaita is known as Shrivaishnavism.

Vishnu A Hindu deity, one of the two most important gods in Hinduism, the other being SHIVA. BRAHMA, Vishnu and Shiva are the lords of creation, of whom Vishnu is the preserver. Vishnu is first mentioned in the RIG VEDA, where he joins the god INDRA in his battles. In other Vedic texts, he is mentioned as a god who takes three steps, traversing heaven and earth, which later becomes the story of his incarnation as VAMANA. His incarnations, however, are not directly mentioned in the VEDAS. In the MAHABHARATA, MATSYA, later one of his incarnations, is identified with PRAJAPATI.

The name Vishnu is said to come from the word vish, to pervade, as Vishnu pervades the world. According to Puranic myths, after the great deluge when creation ends, and before the next cycle of creation begins, there is deep silence, and Vishnu sleeps on a banyan leaf on the surface of the water, in his form as Bala Mukunda. Slowly he awakes, a lotus stalk grows from his navel, and on it appears Brahma, who gains from Vishnu the power to create. Other myths state that between cycles of creation Vishnu sleeps on the serpent ANANTA. The developed form of Vishnu incorporates earlier deities, including NARAYANA, later one of his names.

Vishnu lives in a heaven known as VAIKUNTHA and is married to LAKSHMI, also known as SHRI DEVI. Another consort is BHUDEVI. Through his mind Vishnu once created a son named Viraja, but more important is his son Sastha, actually born through Shiva when Vishnu took the form of a woman, Mohini. Sastha is popular in south India as AYYAPPA. Vishnu's VAHANA or vehicle is the bird GARUDA.

Vishnu is born in the world in different forms, which are known as his incarnations or AVATARAS. The ten main incarnations of Vishnu listed in the *AGNI PURANA, VARAHA PURANA* and other texts are: MATSYA, KURMA, VARAHA, NARASIMHA, VAMANA, PARASHURAMA, RAMA, KRISHNA, BUDDHA and KALKI. Some of these are only partial incarnations, that is, they do not embody the complete essence of Vishnu, but only a part of it. Some texts provide lists of twenty-two and even thirty-nine incarnations, while others state that there are thousands of incarnations. The twenty-two incarnations given in the *BHAGAVATA PURANA* are: (1) SANAT KUMARA, the eternal youth; (2) Varaha; (3) the rishi NARADA; (4) the two saints, NARA and Narayana; (5) the rishi KAPILA; (6) DATTATREYA; (7) Yajna, personification of sacrifice; (8) Rishabha, a king; (9) Prithu, the first ruler; (10) Matsya; (11) Kurma; (12) DHANVANTARI, the divine physician; (13) Mohini, the divine enchantress; (14) Narasimha; (15) Vamana; (16) Parashurama; (17) the great rishi VYASA; (18) Rama; (19) BALARAMA; (20) Krishna; (21) Buddha; (22) Kalki. Each of his incarnations has its own myths and legends.

His main consort, Lakshmi, takes different forms in his various incarnations.

Vishnu is normally depicted as a youth, dark blue in clour. In his four hands he holds a SHANKHA or conch; the SUDARSHANA CHAKRA or Vajranabha, a discus; a gada or club known as Kaumodaki; and a padma or lotus. He wears the jewel Kaustubha on his breast, as well as a particular mark, known as the SHRIVATSA. He is often depicted with his consort Lakshmi, seated on a lotus. He is also shown sleeping or resting on the serpent Shesha or Ananta, or riding on Garuda.

Vishnu is known by many other names. Some of them are connected with his incarnations, while others are less specific. Among these are: Pitambara, he who wears yellow silk; Janardana, who destroys birth and death; Chakrapani, he who carries the chakra in his hand; Padmanabha, the one who has a lotus in his navel; Shripati, the husband of Shri; Vishvambara, he who rules over the world (vishva); Mukunda, the one who gives salvation; Jalshayi, he who lies in water. One thousand names of Vishnu are listed in the *Mahabharata* and the *PADMA PURANA*.

Vishnu Purana

A Sanskrit text, one of the eighteen major PURANAS of Hinduism. It is one of the main texts for the worship of the god VISHNU, and is probably one of the earliest Puranas. It includes the five traditional themes of a Purana and has six sections. It begins with a dialogue between Parashara, the grandson of the rishi VASISHTHA, and his student Maitreya, on the origin of the universe. Parashara then narrates what Vasishtha had told him. This includes an account of the creation of the world, of gods, demons, heroes, ancestors and ancient kings. Next, the seven continents and oceans of the world are described, where Jambudvipa is located and where on the golden mountain, MERU, the gods dwell. Here too, is Bharatvarsha (India), once ruled by the king BHARATA. Other themes include cosmic time, measured by MANVANTARAS and YUGAS, methods of achieving MOKSHA or liberation from the bonds of the world, Vishnu rituals and legends, and stories of the life of KRISHNA. The dynastic details in the fourth section have some historical value. There are few references to temples or sacred sites.

Vishnudharmottara Purana

A Sanskrit text of Hinduism, a minor PURANA or Upapurana, which is sometimes considered a part of the *GARUDA PURANA*. It deals with the worship of VISHNU and has the usual five Puranic themes, apart from several other topics. These include politics, medicine, the science of war, astronomy, astrology, grammar, poetry, music and dance, and rules for the making of images and the construction of temples. This Purana was probably composed between the seventh and tenth centuries.

Vishrava/Vishravas

A son of Pulastya, a PRAJAPATI, in Hindu mythology. According to one text, Pulastya reproduced half of himself to create Vishrava. According to the *Ramayana*, Vishrava was the father of the god KUBERA or Vaishravana by his wife Ilabida or Ilabila, and of the RAKSHASA family consisting of RAVANA, Kumbhakarna, VIBHISHANA, and Shurpanakha, by his wife Kaikasi, also known as Nikasha.

Vishtaspa, Kava

A king of Bactria and Iran. He patronized ZARATHUSHTRA, the Zoroastrian prophet, and promoted his teachings. His father, Lohraspa, was the king when Zarathushtra was born. The ministers of Vishtaspa, the brothers Frashaostra and Jamaspa, are specifically mentioned in the *GATHAS*. Zarathushtra's daughter Pouruchista was married to Jamaspa.

Vishu

A New Year's Day celebrated in Kerala in March/April. At this time people wear new clothes, prepare special food and greet each other. A particular custom consists of giving gifts of money to dependants and children.

Vishuddha Chakra

One of the seven main CHAKRAS or hidden energy centres within the body. According to Tantric texts, the Vishuddha Chakra, located in the centre of the throat, consists of a lotus of sixteen shining petals of a smoky purple. Within them, in shining crimson, are the sixteen Sanskrit vowels. In the lotus is the region of ether, circular and white. One who meditates on this becomes a knower of BRAHMAN, gains a knowledge of the Shastras without reading them, is constant, steady, gentle, modest, courageous, forgiving and self-controlled, freed from all vices.

Vishvadevas

A class of semi-divine beings. In the VEDAS they are said to be preservers of men and bestowers of rewards. Ten or more are listed in various texts: Vasu, Satya, Kratu, Daksha, Kala, Kama, Dhriti, Kuru, Pururava and Madrava. Others are Rochaka or Lochana, and Dhuri or Dhvani.

Vishvakarma/Vishvakarman

The divine architect in Hindu mythology. In the RIG VEDA he is considered an all-seeing god, four-faced and four-armed, the creator of heaven and earth. In the BRAHMANAS he is identified with PRAJAPATI. In post-Vedic times, he is considered both the architect of the universe and the artificer of the gods. He also made their weapons and chariots. In the *MAHABHARATA* he is said to be the lord of all arts and handicrafts, carpenter of the gods, fashioner of all ornaments, the most eminent of all artisans, who made the chariots of the deities. In the RAMAYANA, he is said to have built the city of LANKA. In the PURANAS, he is the son of one of the VASUS. His daughter Samjna was married to SURYA, the sun, but was unable to bear his brilliance. Therefore Vishvakarma cut off one-eighth of its brightness, and from this he made the weapons of the gods, including the discus of VISHNU and the trident of SHIVA. He also made the image of JAGANNATHA at Puri.

Vishvamitra An ancient RISHI. According to the RIG VEDA, he was the son of Kushika. But according to later texts, he was the son of Gadhi, king of Kannauj, and a descendant of PURU, and was himself a king. His intense rivalry with the rishi VASISHTHA is described in several texts. When Vishvamitra undertook severe austerities to become a rishi, the gods were afraid of his power and sent the APSARA Menaka to seduce him. She succeeded, and a daughter, Shakuntala, was born. Vishvamitra then realized his error and sent Menaka away. In the Rig Veda, the hymns of the third mandala are attributed to him. In the RAMAYANA, he asked for the help of RAMA and LAKSHMANA, when they were still young, to subdue the RAKSHASAS of the forest.

Vishvarupa A name of the Hindu god VISHNU, as well as of other deities.

Vishveshvara A name of the Hindu god SHIVA and of his LINGA at VARANASI. Literally it means 'lord of the world'.

Vismapana A heavenly city of the GANDHARVAS, described in Hindu mythology. It can magically appear and diasappear.

Vitala The second of the seven divisions or LOKAS of the nether world or PATALA, in Hindu mythology. Here Hatakeshvara, who is the same as SHIVA, rules. He is accompanied by Bhavanidevi, surrounded by his Pramathaganas, and worshipped by DEVAS. The divine essence flows here as the river Hataki.

Vitthala A name of the Hindu god VISHNU or KRISHNA, also known as Vithoba. The origin of the name of the deity is uncertain. According to some scholars, the name Vitthala was probably derived from Bittideva, a Hoysala king also known as Vishnuvardhana (1117–37), who erected the VITTHALA TEMPLE at PANDHARPUR. Other traces the origin of the name to 'vitha', a term for a brick.

Though Vitthala is worshipped mainly in Maharashtra, Namadeva calls him a 'Kanada' and possibly he originated in the Karnataka region, through the Hoysalas. Vitthala is mentioned in inscriptions from the thirteenth century onwards, and in Kannada literature of the sixteenth century and later.

There are a number of stories regarding the setting up of the image at Pandharpur, which is the chief centre of the deity. According to a story in the *Pandurang Mahatmya* of the PADMA PURANA, once Shachi, INDRA's wife, approached Vishnu, saying she was in love with him. Fearing Indra's anger, Vishnu could not approach her, but assured her that he would take the form of KRISHNA, and she of RADHA, so that they could be together. According to this version, Krishna met Radha not only in his youth, but even after he married RUKMINI. Rukmini, seeing them together, ran away. She sat in meditation in a forest near Pandharpur, and when Krishna came to find her, would not respond, therefore he too stood in meditation nearby. Thus they remained for twenty-eight YUGAS, until another incident took place.

A young man named Pundalik, who had once neglected his parents, was now devoted to them, and Krishna was so impressed that he went to his house to reward him. But Pundalik first had to tend to his parents, and therefore he threw a brick for Krishna to stand on and wait. Finally he went to Krishna and worshipped him, and Krishna offered him a boon. Pundalik only asked that Krishna always remain there, and thus Krishna, named Vitthala, stands on a brick in the temple.

Worshippers of Vitthala, known as VARKARIS, revere Pundalik as the first great devotee of Vitthala. Several Maratha saints, including JNANESHVARA, NAMADEVA, EKNATHA and TUKARAM, composed ABHANGAS or verses in praise of the god in Marathi. Bhanudasa, Janabai, Chokha Mela, Gorahkumbhar and Savata-mali are among other well-known devotees of medieval times. Thousands of Varkaris still exist today.

Vitthala Temple, Pandharpur The most important temple of the god VITTHALA, located at PANDHARPUR in Maharashtra. Constructed in the twelfth century, and later expanded and renovated, the temple attracts thousands of pilgrims every year.

The temple was set up by Bittideva, a Hoysala king, also known as Vishnu-vardhana (1117–37).

The deity was frequently removed from the temple and returned, first by Krishnadeva Raya of Vijayanagara (1510–26) and later by others, but never diminished in sanctity. Royal grants were made to the temple from the time of the Maratha Rajaram, grandson of Shivaji.

The Vitthala temple stands on a platform, surrounded by high walls with eight gateways. The whole covers an area of 108 m by 53 m. The main entrance is through the eastern gate, known as the Namadeva Gate, in front of which are images of NAMADEVA and his family or disciples. Nearby is the SAMADHI of Chokha Mela, another devotee of Vitthala. The Namadeva gate leads to a passage opening into a large quadrangle used for gatherings at festivals, which in turn leads into a MANDAPA or hall, with three elaborately carved doorways. The central doorway leads into the Solahkhamba or hall with sixteen pillars, which has a number of cells with various deities. From this hall one can enter the Chaukhamba, a hall with four pillars, attached to an ante-chamber, opening into the GARBHA-GRIHA or inner shrine. A niche in the northern wall of the Chaukhamba contains the shejghar or bed-chamber of the deity, which has a silver couch.

In the garbha-griha, the deity on a stone pedestal, is a little more than one metre high, made of black stone. It has two arms, holding a conch and lotus, and stands on a square block or brick. The headdress is said by the priests to represent a Shiva LINGA.

A verse of TUKARAM describes the deity:

The beautiful form stands on a brick; arms rest on the hips.
Around his neck is the tulasi mala; his garment is the pitambara (yellow silk dhoti);
In his ears shine makara-kundalas, the Kaustubhamala adorns his neck.

The Badavas are the hereditary priests of the temple. The routine worship of the god takes place five times a day, and there are two special festivals in the months of Ashadha and Karttika, when thousands of VARKARIS and other pilgrims visit the temple.

Vitthalanatha The son of VALLABHACHARYA, who lived between 1518 and 1588. Vitthalanatha, also known as Gosainji, propagated his father's teachings, was a devotee of the god KRISHNA, and established a centre in GOKUL near MATHURA. He and his group of disciples composed poems and songs on Krishna. The traditions of Vallabhacharya were carried on through Vitthalanatha's seven sons, whose descendants are the leaders of the sect, known as Goswamis.

Vivagasuyam (Vipaka-Shrutam) A Jain text, the eleventh of the twelve ANGAS, which has stories related to KARMA, retribution and rebirth, and is mainly a dialogue between MAHAVIRA and GOYAMA INDABHUTI, his disciple. Goyama asks Mahavira to explain the reasons for the suffering he sees around him, and in each case Mahavira gives an account of the former lives of the person, and what has led to their suffering. There are ten stories on this, and another ten on the results of good deeds. The text also describes some of the cities of northern India and local deities or YAKSHAS.

Vivasvat/Vivasvan A deity in the *RIG VEDA*, the father of the ASHVINS, of the god YAMA, and of MANU. Vivasvat or Vivasvan is a god of light or of the rising sun. He is similar to the Iranian Vivanghvant, father of YIMA, and probably originated in the Indo-Iranian period. Some scholars feel he cannot be considered a deity, but only the ancestor of human beings. In the BHAGAVAD GITA, KRISHNA says, 'I revealed this Yoga to Vivasvat.' Vivasvat is usually identified with SURYA.

Vivekananda, Swami A spiritual leader and the founder of the RAMAKRISHNA MISSION.

Born in Kolkata in 1863, his original name was Narendranath Dutta. After completing a BA degree, he explored various aspects of Indian and Western philosophy, and began some spiritual practices, though he remained a sceptic. His first meeting with RAMAKRISHNA PARAMAHANSA in 1882 changed his life. He became Ramakrishna's closest disciple and surrendered to him completely, and before Ramakrishna's death, underwent a spiritual experience and was transformed. Shri Ramakrishna chose him to continue his work. Vivekananda set up the Ramakrishna Order of SANNYASIS and organized Ramakrishna's disciples. In 1893 he attended the World Parliament of Religions in Chicago and spoke on Hinduism and VEDANTA, making a profound impression on the Western delegates. In 1895 he set up a centre for Vedantic learning at New York and gave lectures in London and other parts of Europe before returning to India in 1897. He then set up the Ramakrishna Mission, and in 1898, the BELUR MATHA.

He wrote texts on BHAKTI YOGA, RAJA YOGA and other forms of YOGA, including a commentary on Patanjali's *Yoga Sutra*. He said, 'Religion is realization; not talk, nor doctrine, nor theories, however beautiful they may be. It is being and becoming, not hearing or acknowledging; it is the whole soul becoming changed into what it believes.' He believed in the essential unity of all religions, and said that the only hope for India lay in 'a junction of the two great systems, Hinduism and Islam'.

Vivekananda stressed not only the ideals of Vedanta, freedom from CASTE prejudices and superstition, but also the need for service to the people of India. He wrote, 'The only god in whom I believe, the sum total of all souls, is above all, my god the wicked, my god the afflicted, my god the poor of all races.' Thus the Ramakrishna Mission has set up schools, hospitals, orphanages and other welfare institutions, and Sannyasis of the Mission work to improve the condition of the common people.

Vividha Tirtha Kalpa A Jain text that describes Jain TIRTHAS or sacred sites, and was composed between 1326 and 1331 by Jinaprabha Suri. The text, written in a mix of Sanskrit and Jain Maharashtri, has authentic as well as legendary accounts of these places. Among the places described are HASTINAPURA, MATHURA, AYODHYA, VARANASI, PATALIPUTRA and SHATRUNJAYA. The names of those who founded the sites and the kings associated with them are provided, along with accounts of TIRTHANKARAS and other Jain saints who were associated with these places.

Vohu Mana A power of AHURA MAZDA, the name of God in Zoroastrianism. It is personified as an AMESHA SPENTA and the name means the 'Good Mind'. Each person should use his own Vohu Mana to choose the right path and perform good actions. In the *GATHAS*, ZARATHUSHTRA realizes the wonder of Ahura Mazda through the power of the Good Mind. In later texts Vohu Mana is the guardian of the animal kingdom, and is often represented by a white cow. His symbolic flower is myrtle and his opposite is Ako Mana, or the evil mind. In later times Vohu Mana came to be known as Behman or Bahman. A YASHT or hymn of praise is dedicated to him.

Vraja A name of the region of MATHURA, where the god KRISHNA lived in his youth.

vratas, Jain Jainism has five basic vows or vratas, which are the same as the five YAMAS of YOGA. Thus the vratas are AHIMSA or non-violence, satya or truthfulness, asteya or not stealing, aparigraha or non-acquisition, and BRAHMACHARYA or chaste living. These are followed by both ascetics and lay persons, but in different ways. For ascetics the vows are termed mahavratas or 'great vows' and are followed strictly, while lay persons follow the anuvratas or 'lesser vows' while living normal family lives.

vratya A Sanskrit term that literally means 'one who has taken a vow'. It refers to a group of ascetics who were different from the Vedic ARYANS.

Vrindavan/Vrindavana A sacred place in the region of MATHURA, connected with the youth of the god KRISHNA. Vrindavan today is a town in MATHURA district with several Krishna temples and sacred sites.

Vritra An ASURA or danava in the RIG VEDA. Vritra caused drought and darkness. He was defeated by the god INDRA, who released the waters. Scholars have different interpretations of Vritra. He is said to represent the clouds, which, struck by Indra's vajra or thunderbolt, released the rain. Alternatively, the term is thought to refer to human enemies, and possibly to the people of the INDUS CIVILIZATION. Indra was known as Vritrahan, defeater of Vritra, a name equated with the Zoroastrian Verethraghna, whereas Vritra's counterpart in Zoroastrian myths is Azi Dohak.

Vyasa A RISHI of ancient days. According to tradition, Vyasa arranged the VEDAS, compiled the *MAHABHARATA*, and was the author of the PURANAS. His life is described in the *Mahabharata* and other texts.

He was the son of the rishi Parashara and Satyavati. He was dark in colour, and so was known as Krishna, and being born on an island (dvipa) he was also known as Dvaipayana. Satyavati later married King Shantanu and had two sons, one of whom died in battle, and the other, Vichitravirya, died leaving two childless widows. Though he was a rishi, it was his duty to see that they had children, therefore through Vyasa, DHRITARASHTRA and PANDU were born. Before approaching the wives, Vyasa wanted time to make himself presentable, but at Satyavati's insistence he went to the women unkempt and in his rishi's garb. Ambika, one of Vichitravirya's wives, was so terrified at the sight of the rishi that she shut her eyes, and therefore Dhritarashtra was born blind, whereas the other wife, Ambalika, turned pale out of fright, which led to PANDU being born pale. Only the maid servant was unperturbed and through her the wise Vidura was born.

Vyasa was also called Veda Vyasa because he divided the VEDAS, which originally were one, into four smaller texts. Four pupils, Paila, Sumantu, Jaimini and Vaishampayana, memorized and narrated one Veda each, while Lomaharshana Suta memorized and transmitted the Puranas.

Vyasa is also listed as an incarnation of VISHNU.

Vyasa seems to be a title of many of the authors and compilers of ancient texts. Several Vyasas are mentioned in the Puranas, as incarnations of Vishnu or of SHIVA. They were born in successive ages to arrange and propagate the Vedas.

vyuha A Sanskrit word meaning 'a manifestation'. It is used particularly by the Vaishnava PANCHARATRA sect.

Wahdat al-Shuhud An Islamic concept conceived by Alaud-Daula Simnani (d. 1336), an Iranian SUFI who rejected the WAHDAT AL-WUJUD concept. Whereas IBN AL-ARABI identified all existence with God, Simnani said that it was an attribute of God. The highest stage was not union with the divine but ubudiyya or servantship of God. This was later known as Wahdat al-Shuhud or Wahdatus-Shuhud, or Unity of Appearance.

Wahdat al-Wujud An Islamic concept that dates back to the twelfth century and was formulated by the SUFI saint IBN AL-ARABI, who used existing Sufi ideas to present a coherent doctrine. It has been translated as the Unity of Being, a belief in the nature of primordial unity, in which only God exists, similar to the ADVAITA of VEDANTA. The doctrine has been interpreted by Western scholars, alternatively as monism or as Islamic pantheism.

In Islam the relationship between God and creation has been interpreted in different ways. Ibn al-Arabi states that the One and the Many are two aspects of the One. Absolute reality is both passive and active, male and female. He said, 'The one and same reality variously determines and delimits itself, and appears immediately in the forms of different things.' He introduced the concept of the Perfect Man, who reflected God and the Absolute, and embodied all the attributes of the universe. As in Advaita, he stated that mystical union was the realization of an already existing state. Inherent in this concept was that the same divinity existed in all religions.

This idea is also expressed by nirguna BHAKTI saints such as KABIR. The WAHDAT AL-SHUHUD doctrine was opposed to this concept.

Wahhabi A Muslim puritan revival movement founded in Najd, Central Arabia, in the eighteenth century by Muhammad ibn Abd al-Wahhab (1703–92). Wahhab's ideas were conveyed in the *Kitab-al-Tauhid* (Book of Unity). He believed the only sources of Islamic law were the original doctrines of the Prophet MUHAMMAD as revealed in the QURAN and early HADIS, and rejected the four schools of SUNNI law. He was against SUFIS, saints and intermediaries between God and the people. From 1744 Wahhabi ideas dominated the Saudi dynasty, which later founded Saudi Arabia.

Wahhabi ideas were introduced in India in the early nineteenth century, but the person closely linked with Wahhabi thought was Sayyed AHMAD BARELVI. Recent scholars however, believe his somewhat similar ideas were developed independently. After returning from Mecca in 1822, Sayyed Ahmad resolved to reclaim north India and bring it under true Islam. Some of the Muslims in India looked up to him as the MAHDI, and he gained thousands of followers. In 1826 he started a war against the Sikhs of the north-west, hoping to unite Muslims from Central Asia under his banner. However, his attempts failed and Sayyed Ahmad was killed in 1831. His followers settled across the border but were suppressed by the British in 1863, though a small group continued to exist even after this. The AHL-E-HADIS are considered a Wahhabi group, as they are successors of the Tariqa-i-Muhammadiya, founded by Sayyed Ahmad Barelvi. Wahhabis call themselves Muwahhid or Unitarians.

Wajihuddin Ahmad, Shaikh A SUFI saint of the SHATTARI order who lived in the sixteenth century in Gujarat. Born in 1496–97, he was initially a noted Islamic scholar, in religious, literary and philosophical subjects, who kept apart from the world, teaching his disciples in his own house. At the age of thirty-eight he became the disciple of MUHAMMAD GHAUS and popularized the Shattari order in Gujarat and central India. He died in 1589 at Ahmadabad.

Waliullah, Shah An Islamic reformer who lived in the eighteenth century. Born in 1703, in the last years of the reign of the Mughal emperor AURANGZEB, his father was a teacher in a MADRASA. Waliullah knew the whole QURAN by the age of seven, and after his father's death in 1717, became a teacher himself. Later he went to Mecca and studied further. Returning to DELHI in 1731, he gave speeches and sermons, and wrote books on different aspects of Islam. Among his books are *Hujjat, Al-Badrul Bazigah, Al-Khairul Kathir, Tafhimat* and others. He combined both SUFI and KALAM traditions in his writings, differentiating between esoteric and exoteric Islam, and believed Islam should be reinterpreted in the light of reason. He translated the Quran into Persian and encouraged the study of the HADIS.

His sons, Shah Abdul Aziz, Shah Rafiuddin and Shah Abdul Qadir, carried on his work.

Shah Waliullah died in 1762, but his ideas had a profound influence on Islam in India.

Waris Shah A SUFI saint of the CHISTI order who lived in the eighteenth century. He is known for his Punjabi verse retelling of the story of Hir and Ranjha, an earlier folk tale on doomed love. The work was completed in 1766, and in it Waris Shah also philosophized on love, and described yogic practices as well as the PANCH PIRS. Born in village Jandyala Sher Khan near Gujranwala in Punjab, Waris Shah fell in love with a village girl of Pak Patan, but because he was a Saiyyid, a superior class, he was driven out of his village. He settled in another village and wrote this story, which to some extent reflected his own feelings.

Xavier, St. Francis *See* St. Francis Xavier.

Xuanzang A Chinese Buddhist pilgrim who visited India in the seventh century, travelled to Buddhist sites, and carried a number of Buddhist scriptures back to China. His record of his travels is important for the history of Buddhism in India, and also provides information on other aspects of life in India.

Xuanzang was born in 602 in a learned Chinese family at Chenlu in China. He studied Confucianism but later converted to Buddhism. He discovered many discrepancies in Buddhist texts and decided to travel to India to discover more about Buddhism. Leaving Suchuan (Szechwan) secretly in 629, as he could not get a travel permit, Xuanzang crossed high mountains to reach India, travelling on foot with some helpers and supplies carried on mules. Moving through Tashkent, Samarkand and Bactria (Afghanistan), he crossed the Hindu Kush mountains and reached India after one year. He stayed in India for over thirteen years, travelling from Taxila (now in Pakistan) in the north-west across northern India up to Assam in the east, and down to KANCHIPURAM in the south. He was welcomed by King HARSHA in the north and spoke at a MAHAYANA Buddhist meeting organized by Harsha. Wherever he went, Xuanzang noted the state of Buddhist VIHARAS and temples, described the monasteries and the Buddhist sects to which they belonged, and commented on the existence of other temples and on the nature and characteristics of the people.

He began his return journey in 643–44 and reached Changan, the capital of the Tang dynasty of western China, in 645. He brought with him 657 sacred Buddhist texts, which he began translating into Chinese.

He was most interested in the YOGACHARA school of Buddhism, and he and his disciple Kuei-chi (632–82) founded the Fa-hsiang, also known as the Wei-shih or Consciousness school of Buddhism in China. Though it declined in China, it was transmitted to Japan, where it became known as the Hosso school.

Xuanzang died in 664, by which time he was a much-venerated person in China. His name is also spelt Hieun Tsang, or Yuan Chwang, in addition to other variations.

Yab-Yum A guardian deity, a type of YIDAM in Tibetan Buddhism, depicted as a twin mother-and-father deity, representing the union of male and female, and of wisdom and compassion. The Yab-Yum can be in benign or ferocious form. Usually the twin deity is shown in the form of a male seated in padmasana, with a female on his lap.

Yadava A descendant of YADU in Hindu mythology. The god KRISHNA was a Yadava, and the story of the Yadavas is given in the MAHABHARATA. At first the Yadavas and Krishna lived in the region of MATHURA and were pastoral cowherds. Later, Krishna established a kingdom at DVARAKA in western india, and the Yadavas came to live there. Gradually they began to drink, quarrel and fight with one another, and finally destroyed themselves. Krishna too died, and Dvaraka was submerged in the ocean.

A dynasty of south India was also known as Yadava, and had their capital at Devagiri.

Yadavaprakasha A VAISHNAVA philosopher who lived in the eleventh century and was for some time the guru of RAMANUJA. Yadavaprakasha put forward the theory of Brahmaparinamavada, or the 'transformation of BRAHMAN' or the Absolute. According to him, Brahman is transformed into ISHVARA or God, chit or spirit and achit or matter. These, however are only different states, not different substances, thus even while Brahman is transformed, its intrinsic purity is retained. This doctrine is termed BHEDABHEDAVADA, or the doctrine of simultaneous difference and non-difference. His ideas are slightly different from those of BHASKARA, another exponent of this theory, who held that Brahman is to some extent modified, though identity is maintained. Ramanuja, however, said that Ishvara is the ultimate, and no distinction can be made between Brahman and Ishvara.

Yadu A son of YAYATI, who was a king of the CHANDRAVAMSHA dynasty, tracing its descent from the moon. His descendants were known as YADAVAS. The Hindu god KRISHNA was a Yadava.

yajna A Sanskrit term that means sacrifice. A yajna is usually performed according to the methods described in Vedic texts. Yajnas can be undertaken for any purpose, including conferring blessings, purifying a house or place, curing illness, or bringing rain. They are conducted at various rituals performed in temples or sacred places, or at the samskaras or rituals of daily life, including those connected with birth, marriage and death.

Yajnavalkya An ancient RISHI, who is said to have composed the *Vajasaneyi Samhita* or *White Yajur Veda*, as well as the *Shatapatha Brahmana*, the *Brihadaranyaka*, and the *Yajnavalkya Smriti*. It is unlikely that he was the author of all these texts, as they are of different dates. According to the MAHABHARATA, he attended the RAJASUYA sacrifice of YUDHISHTHIRA, while according to the RAMAYANA, he was attached to the court of King JANAKA. He was against the prevailing religious practices of the time, and defeated many BRAHMANAS in argument. He advocated meditation and asceticism. His two wives were Maitreyi and Katyayani, and the former, at her request, was instructed by him in the philosophy of BRAHMAN.

yajnopavita A term for the sacred thread in Hinduism. The thread is conferred on the three upper castes at the UPANAYANA ceremony.

Yajur Veda One of the four VEDIC SAMHITAS. The *Yajur Veda* consists of hymns arranged for the performance of sacrifices (YAJNAS), and is for the use of priests. Many of the hymns are taken from the RIG VEDA, with some variations, and there are also some prose passages. There are a number of different schools or shakhas for this VEDA, and two main versions are the *White Yajur Veda* and the *Black Yajur Veda*. The first consists of the *Vajasaneyi Samhita* that is said to have been revealed to YAJNAVALKYA by the sun. The *Black Yajur Veda* has four closely related recensions, known as the *Kathaka Samhita*, the *Kapishthala-Katha Samhita*, the *Maitrayani Samhita* and the *Taittiriya Samhita*. The *Yajur Veda* priests were known as adhvaryus.

yakshas and yakshis A class of semi-divine beings described in Hindu, Buddhist and Jain texts, and represented in iconography. According to the art historian A.K. Coomaraswamy, yaksha literally meant 'a wondrous spirit'. In general, yakshas and yakshis include a number of folk and guardian spirits, some of whom were incorporated into the

Hindu and Buddhist pantheon as deities. KUBERA, alternatively known as Vaishravana or Panchika, is the king of the Yakshas and also a DIKAPALA. Other yakshas and yakshis include Ajakalaka, Chulakoka, Gangita, MANIBHADRA, Purnabhadra, Suchiloma, Sudasana, Supavasa, Vriudhaka Dharana, Vajrapani, Mudgalpani, Sudarshana, Dhanya, Ganditinduya, and Layava. Several images of Manibhadra occur up to the second century CE, with identifying inscriptions. An important yakshi is HARITI, consort of Kubera, and also a Buddhist mother goddess. The *Mayasamgraha*, a Sanskrit text, states that yakshas are depicted as pot-bellied, two-armed and fierce, holding nidhi (treasure) in their hands. The earliest extant sculptures have been identified as yakshas, while the MAHABHARATA refers to two famous yakshi shrines at Munjavata and RAJAGRIHA. Yakshas are often depicted with animal faces, accompanied by dwarfs, or dwarfish themselves, and associated with children. Yakshis are also associated with children, as well as with trees. A common form of yakshi depicted in ancient sculptures is the Shalabhanjika yakshi, a woman shown touching a tree which sprouts leaves and flowers through her touch. Yakshas and yakshis are depicted in Buddhist sculptures at SANCHI, Amravati and elsewhere, and are described in Buddhist texts. They are also carved on the railings of Buddhist STUPAS.

In Jainism they are the guardian deities of the TIRTHANKARAS and are known as SHASANA DEVATAS and SHASANA DEVIS. The Tirthankaras do not answer prayers, as they have attained MOKSHA and are beyond the world. However, their guardian deities are more accessible and respond to the prayers of devotees.

Yakshas can be depicted in a number of ways, including as free-standing images or deities, as tree spirits, as attendants or GANAS of the god SHIVA, or as decorative devices in art, supporters of architectural structures, or holders of bowls.

yali A mythical animal depicted in temples, which has the features of a lion combined with an elephant or other animal.

Yama A Hindu deity, the god of the dead. According to the VEDAS, the spirits of those who died went to his abode. He was the son of VIVASVAT or Vivasvan, and had a twin sister named YAMI or YAMUNA. In some passages they are the progenitors of the human race, from whom all people are born. Another hymn states that Yama was the first man to die, and the first to find his way to the other world, so that others could later follow his path. In the MAHABHARATA, he was the son of SURYA by Samjna and the brother of Vaivasvata, the seventh and present MANU. As he is identified with Dharma Deva, he is sometimes considered the father of YUDHISHTHIRA.

By this time Yama became known as the judge of the dead. His chief assistant, Chitragupta, records the deeds of each person in a huge register called Agrasandhani. Yama judges the dead and assigns them to different regions. According to its deeds, the soul is sent to the world of the PITRIS, or is reborn, or is sent to one of twenty-eight hells or NARAKAS.

In later texts, Yama is the guardian or DIKAPALA of the southern quarter, and is therefore named Dakshinapati. Among his wives are DHUMRORNA, Hemamala, Sushila, and Vijaya. He lives in Pitriloka, in his city of Yamapuri, where he has a huge palace called Kalichi. Apart from Chitragupta, his two main attendants are Chanda or Mahachanda, and Kalapurusha. He has two four-eyed dogs known as SARAMEYAS, descended from INDRA's dog SARAMA. His messengers, known as Yamadutas, help him to bring the souls of the dead.

There are innumerable stories about Yama in ancient texts. Among the most significant is that in the KATHA UPANISHAD, where Yama explains the secret of life and death to Nachiketa. Another important story is of SAVITRI, who brings her husband Satyavan back to life after a dialogue with Yama.

In iconography Yama is depicted riding on a buffalo. He holds a mace and a noose, which he tightens around his victims. Though often shown as a two-armed deity, the VISHNUDHARMOTTARA gives a detailed description of Yama with four arms. Seated on a buffalo, his consort Dhumrorna sits on his left lap. His right hands hold a staff and a sword, while his left hands have a trident with flames and a mala or rosary. To his right stands Chitragupta, his chief attendant, in northern dress (udichyavesha), and Kala or time, holding a noose, stands to his left. Some texts state that he is green in colour, and dressed in red clothes. His dogs are sometimes shown with him.

Yama has several names, including Mrityu (death), Kala (time), Pashi (one who carries a noose), and Dharmaraja (lord of DHARMA).

In Zoroastrianism, his counterpart is YIMA.

Yamaka A HINAYANA Buddhist text that forms part of the ABHIDHAMMA PITAKA of the PALI CANON. Like the KATHAVATTHU, it has questions and answers on Buddhist doctrine, but here each question is approached in two different ways.

Yami The twin sister of the god YAMA in Hindu mythology. She was also known as YAMUNA and was a personification of the river of the same name.

Yamuna, goddess A Hindu goddess, the personification of the river YAMUNA. According to myth, she is the daughter of VIVASVAN, the sun, and the sister of the god YAMA and of MANU VAIVASVATA. She is also known as YAMI. Her other names are Suryatanaya, Suryaja and Ravinandini. Yamuna is depicted in temples from the Gupta period onwards, usually along with GANGA at entrances or on door jambs. She holds a water pot and stands on a kurma or tortoise. In medieval miniature paintings she is shown as a beautiful young woman, standing on the banks of the river. In myths she is associated with the festival of BHAI DUJ and with the god KRISHNA.

Yamuna, river   A sacred river, the main tributary of the river GANGA, that is also personified as a goddess. Flowing from the Yamunotri peak in the Garhwal Himalayas, the river has a course of almost 1400 km before it joins the Ganga at Allahabad. Sacred places along the Yamuna include Yamunotri, MATHURA, Bateshvar and PRAYAGA (Allahabad). The Yamuna is closely associated with the god KRISHNA's early life and is revered by devotees of Krishna. The *PADMA PURANA* states that the Kalindi (another name of the Yamuna) is like the SUSHUMNA, the secret channel in the body, carrying the highest form of nectar.

Yamunacharya   A VAISHNAVA acharya, a grandson of NATHAMUNI, who lived in the eleventh century. Yamunacharya, also known as Alavandar attempted to correlate the Vaishnava samhitas and works of the ALVARS with the VEDAS. He wrote a number of books, among which are: *Siddhitrayam, Gitarthasamgraha, Agamapramanya, Mahapurushanirnaya, Chatushloki* and *Stotraratna*. He was the forerunner of RAMANUJA who founded the VISHISHTADVAITA school of philosophy.

yantra   A term used for a mystical diagram, also known as a MANDALA. Yantras, symbolizing the cosmos or a divinity, are used in TANTRISM. A yantra can also be an astronomical or other instrument.

Yapaniya   A Jain sect that existed in Karnataka between the fifth and fourteenth centuries. The first available reference to them is in a Kadamba inscription of the fifth century. According to Devasena, a Jain scholar of the tenth century, the Yapaniya Sangha was started in the third century and was associated with the SHVETAMBARA sect. The Shvetambara author Gunaratna, of the fifteenth century, stated that Yapaniyas or Gopyas were one of the four DIGAMBARA Sanghas. Yapaniyas had a mixture of Shvetambara and Digambara beliefs and practices. They accepted the Shvetambara texts and agreed with the principle that women can achieve salvation, but worshipped nude images like the Digambaras. Their ascetics followed the rules of the Digambaras. Yapaniyas are believed to have been later absorbed in the Digambara sect.

Yashoda   (1) The foster mother of the Hindu god KRISHNA and the wife of the cowherd NANDA. Yashoda brought up Krishna with great love and care. She was also the mother of YOGA MAYA, who was substituted for Krishna at his birth.

(2) Yashoda was the name of the wife of the Jain Tirthankara MAHAVIRA.

Yashodhara   The wife of Siddhartha Gautama, who later became the BUDDHA. Siddhartha and Yashodhara had one son, RAHULA, but soon after he was born Siddhartha left the house at night and did not return home for many years, while he was searching for the Truth. After attaining enlightenment he returned to meet his family, and all came out to meet him except Yashodhara, whom he then went and met in her apartments. When Rahula joined the SANGHA at a young age, without the knowledge of his mother, she was upset and asked that no child should be allowed to become a monk without the permission of his parents. The Buddha agreed that this would be done in future.

Yasht   A term for sacrificial songs and verses in praise of divine beings in Zoroastrianism. Yashts form part of the AVESTA texts.

Yaska   The author of the *NIRUKTA*, a Sanskrit text, which is the oldest known etymology or glossary of the VEDIC SAMHITAS. Yaska probably lived before PANINI but was not the first to compose a Nirukta.

Yasna   (1) A Zoroastrian text with seventy-two chapters. The five GATHAS are contained in it, forming *Yasna* 28–34, 43–51, and 53. The *Yasna Haptanhaiti*, the *Yasna* of seven chapters, is placed between the first and second *Gathas*, and is of about the same date. It may have been composed soon after the Prophet ZARATHUSHTRA's death, and according to some scholars, even before. Between the fourth and fifth *Gatha* is *Yasna* 52, which describes the physical, mental and spiritual attributes of an individual.

The rest of the text includes prayers and invocations to AHURA MAZDA, the AMESHA SPENTAS, and various minor deities. It also has descriptions of methods of worship.

(2) The Yasna is a sacred ritual in Zoroastrianism, during which the whole *Yasna* text is recited.

yatus/yatudhanas   A class of spirits in Hindu mythology which take on various forms. Generally considered evil spirits, they were initially distinct from the RAKSHASAS, but later were associated with them. The *VAYU PURANA* lists twelve yatudhanas, who were born from KASHYAPA, through his wife Surasi.

Yayati   The name of an ancient king in Hindu mythology who belonged to the CHANDRAVAMSHA or lunar dynasty. From his two wives Devayani and Sarmishtha he had five sons, YADU, PURU, Druhyu, Turvasu and Anu. The two great lineages of the YADAVAS and KAURAVAS were descended from the first two. Yayati was cursed by SHUKRA, Devayani's father, with premature old age and decrepitude, because of his amorous nature. Of all his sons, Puru agreed to take on the curse and restore his father's youth. Later Puru's youth was also restored. Yayati and his five sons were all RAJARISHIS.

yazata   A term for heavenly beings in Zoroastrianism, similar to deities in Hinduism. Some scholars believe the concept of yazatas was absorbed by Judaism, Christianity and Islam as angels. Yazatas have been classified broadly into three categories: personified divine powers; the deities of the ancient Iranians, later incorporated into Zoroastrianism; and the personifications of the powers of nature. The last two categories often overlap. In the GATHAS, apart from the six powers or AMESHA SPENTAS, only ASHI VANGHUI, SRAOSHA and ATAR are mentioned, all of whom were later considered yazatas. Yazatas of pre-Zoroastrian Iran, incorporated into Zoroastrianism at a later date, include Mithra, Verethraghna (later Behram), and Anahita (later Anahid), a female yazata. Months and days are named after them, and YASHTS are dedicated to them. Vayu, Nairyosangha, the messenger of AHURA MAZDA, and a SAOSHYANT or saviour, Armaiti, Baga, Airyaman and Haoma are among the other yazatas.

Apart from comparsisons with Vedic deities, Zoroastrian yazatas have been related to Buddhist deities and to the gods and goddesses of ancient Greece and Rome.

Yellow Hats A term for a school of Tibetan Buddhism. 'Yellow Hats' is a popular name for the GELUG school, the predominant Buddhist school in Tibet after the fifteenth century. The term is derived from the yellow hats that the monks wear. The line of DALAI LAMAS comes from this school.

yidam A guardian deity in TIBETAN BUDDHISM. Palden Lhamo is the yidam for the whole of Tibet, and is outwardly a ferocious-looking deity with a bull's face, though he is a form of the Bodhisattva MANJUSHRI. In addition, Buddhist lay persons, monks and temples, each have their own yidam. The consort of a yidam is a dakini.

Yima A mythical Zoroastrian hero, the son of Vivanghvant and the third ruler of the world. Yima is mentioned in the GATHAS, but there he is criticized by ZARATHUSHTRA for permitting the bull sacrifice. Yima had a sister Yimak, whom he married. In later Zoroastrian texts he is known as JAMSHED and is a heroic ruler and leader. Informed by AHURA MAZDA (God) that the world is about to be destroyed by snow and ice, he is asked to build a vara, a cave or shelter, and to go there along with a group of chosen people, the seeds of the trees, fruits, and flowers, and a pair each of the best and most useful animals. These are used later to repopulate the world.

Jamshed is described in the BUNDAHISHN, SHAH NAMAH and other texts, and lived, according to the texts, for between seven hundred and a thousand years. According to the *Shah Namah*, he was the third king of the Pishdadian dynasty. However, after a long reign he was murdered by the tyrant Zohak (the later form of Azhi Dahak).

The myths of Yima have similarities with those of YAMA and MANU in Hindu texts, in which Yama, Yami or YAMUNA, and Manu are the children of VIVASVAT or Vivasvan, considered the same as the Zoroastrian Vivanghvant. The vara in which Jamshed saved the plants and animals, can be compared with the role of Manu during the great flood.

Yoga One of the six classical systems of philosophy,

first fully explained by PATANJALI in his *YOGA SUTRA*. Yoga literally means union, implying the union of the individual self with the divine. This is attained when the individual self, the ATMA or Jivatma, realizes its true being by stilling the mind and body. Patanjali's Yoga was later called Raja Yoga to distinguish it from other forms of Yoga. This form is also known as Ashtanga Yoga, or the yoga with eight limbs or eight parts, sometimes translated as eight steps. The eight parts are: (1) Yama, or the five ethical restraints of AHIMSA (non-violence), satya (truth), asteya (non-stealing), BRAHMACHARYA (always being aware of god, often translated literally as celibacy), aparigraha (non-greed); (2) NIYAMA, or five positive observances, which are shaucha (purity), santosha (contentment), tapasya (ascetic practices), svadhyaya (self-study), Ishvara pranidhana (surrender to God); (3) ASANA, or various postures to stabilize and improve the body; (4) PRANAYAMA, or breathing practices; (5) Pratihara, or withdrawal of the senses from the outer world; (6) Dharana, or concentration; (7) DHYANA, or meditation; (8) SAMADHI or union. These are explained in the *Yoga Sutra* and in numerous commentaries, and form the basis for all later systems of Yoga. Later texts on Yoga include the *Gheranda Samhita*, the *Goraksha Samhita* of GORAKHNATHA, and the *Hatha Yoga Pradipika*, among others. These texts do not exactly follow Patanjali, and some list ten yamas and niyamas. Other texts explain various forms of Yoga in detail, such as HATHA YOGA, MANTRA YOGA, BHAKTI YOGA, JNANA YOGA, Kundali Yoga, Likhita Yoga, Laya Yoga, Siddha Yoga, Integral Yoga, Tantra Yoga, as well as several modern hybrid forms, such as Power Yoga. All traditional forms of Yoga are not mutually exclusive, each employing some of the techniques used by other forms, though the emphasis is different. The pre-requisites of each form are basic ethics, morality (DHARMA) and discipline or regular practice (SADHANA).

Yoga Maya A Hindu goddess. Yoga Maya is considered the sister of KRISHNA, though she was actually the daughter of YASHODA and the cowherd NANDA. She was substituted for Krishna at his birth. When King Kamsa came to kill Yoga Maya, she flew up in the air and disappeared, returning to heaven. Yoga Maya is worshipped as a goddess of austerity and purity. Among temples dedicated to the goddess, the Yoga Maya temple in DELHI, located not far from the QUTB MINAR, is connected with the SAIR-E GUL FAROSHAN festival symbolizing Hindu-Muslim unity. According to tradition the shrine was first constructed by YUDHISHTHIRA of the MAHABHARATA, but the existing temple was built in 1827 by Syed Mal, a noble at the time of the Mughal emperor Akbar II. The small temple, along with other buildings, is in a large walled enclosure and has a pyramidal roof topped with a pinnacle, reaching a height of about 13 m. Two stone tigers in a cage are the guardians of this shrine. A sacred stone is located in a square room, placed over a small marble well less than half- a- metre high, and covered with a cloth. Above it are suspended the pankhas or fans presented to the shrine at the Sair-e gul Faroshan festival. This annual festival is the main event at the temple, but a mela is also held every Tuesday. White flowers and sweets are offered to the deity, and her devotees do not consume meat or alcohol.

Yoga Sutra A text on YOGA written by Patanjali. It consists of short sutras or verses on the method of yoga or union with the divine. The terse sutras have been commented on and explained by several scholars.

In the second verse of the text, Patanjali describes yoga as 'Chitta vritti nirodhah', that has been interpreted as 'a state of mind that is still and without thought'. This state enables the experience of divine intelligence, and the ultimate union with the divine. The rest of the text describes the methods of attaining this union. Patanjali's system, with eight limbs or stages, is normally called Raja Yoga. The text forms the base for all later yoga texts and developments in yoga.

Yoga Vasishtha A Sanskrit text, said to have been composed by VALMIKI. It records the philosophical teachings given to RAMA by the rishi VASISHTHA. The text discusses the nature of the mind and how to control it. The mind has great potential, and by gaining control over it, its inherent powers can be developed. It guides the individual to think for himself, rather than to depend on the authority of the Shastras, a guru, or divine grace. To one who has gained control over the mind, everything in life can be achieved, including health, wealth, power and position. Both liberation and bondage are only states of mind.

Yogachara A school of MAHAYANA Buddhism. It expresses the importance of cultivating the self, particularly through meditation. According to this school, there is nothing but the mind, or what is perceived by the mind. Meditating and analyzing the mind, reveals the source of consciousness. The school basically consists of theories of consciousness (vijnana) and therefore is called Vijnanavada. Its main exponents were MAITREYANATHA, ASANGA (310–90) and VASUBANDHU (320–400).

Yogacharabhumi, the basic text of the school, is attributed to Maitreyanatha, or sometimes to Asanga. The school explains the ideas of consciousness derived from the practice of meditation. In deep meditation, ecstacy is experienced, indicating that the world is nothing but mind (chittamatrata), or else something that is perceived by the mind (vijnaptimatrata). When meditating, one becomes aware of different levels of the mind, and deep within is the alaya vijnana, the storehouse of consciousness, containing the seeds of past actions, and therefore of KARMA. Vasubandhu focuses in his writings on the nature of the mind, while Asanga deals more with the storehouse of consciousness.

There were subtle differences in the various branches of the Yogachara school, particularly at NALANDA and Vallabhi. The Vallabhi school, led by Sthiramati (500–60), held that the storehouse of consciousness is pure and has no forms, while the Nalanda school, systemized by DHARMAPALA (530–61) and based on the work of DIGNAGA, stated that consciousness does contain forms. The Yogachara school spread to China in the seventh century, through the Chinese pilgrim XUANZANG.

Yogananda, Paramahansa *See* Paramahansa Yogananda.

yogi A term for an ascetic, or one who is adept at YOGA.

Yogi Bhajan *See* Harbhajan Singh, Yogi.

yogini (1) the feminine form of YOGI, an ascetic or adept in YOGA.

(2) A class of semi-divine beings, attendants of DURGA. They are said to number eight, twelve, sixty-four or sixty-five. There are several temples dedicated to the chausath yoginis, or sixty-four yoginis.

Among the Chausath Yogini temples are two located in Orissa, one at Hirapur near Bhubaneswar, and another at Ranipur–Jharial in Bolangir district. They are circular and roofless, and have an image of Bhairava in the centre, surrounded by the sixty-four yoginis in individual niches. At Hirapur each yogini is distinctive, even with different hairstyles.

yoni The female organ, a symbol of SHAKTI or divine power. It is worshipped alone, or along with the LINGA.

Yudhishthira The eldest of the five PANDAVAS, described in the *MAHABHARATA*. He was the son of DHARMA DEVA, usually considered the same as the god YAMA, and was also known as Dharmaputra. Yudhishthira was made the heir apparent by DHRITARASHTRA at HASTINAPURA, capital of the Kuru kingdom, but this was resented by DURYODHANA, the eldest son of Dhritarashtra, and the kingdom was divided into two, with Yudhishthira ruling from INDRAPRASTHA. Indraprastha and the surrounding area prospered under his rule, and Yudhishthira conducted the RAJASUYA sacrifice to consolidate his power. The jealous Duryodhana then managed to win the kingdom from him through a game of dice, and Yudhishthira, along with his brothers and their wife DRAUPADI, were forced to go into exile for thirteen years. Many adventures took place during these years, after which Yudhishthira claimed his kingdom, but as Duryodhana did not accept the claim, a great war took place, leaving countless dead on both sides. Duryodhana and all his brothers were killed, and Yudhishthira was crowned king. After many years, he appointed Parikshit, grandson of ARJUNA as his successor and then proceeded towards heaven, along with his brothers and their wife, accompanied by a dog who turned out to be DHARMA DEVA. After more adventures, he and all his relatives finally entered Divyaloka, a heavenly world.

Yudhisthira and his brothers are worshipped in certain temples. Yudhishthira is considered the epitome of justice and wisdom, and is also known by other names, including Ajamidha, Kurushreshtha, Mridangketu, Panduputra, and Pandava-shreshtha.

yuga　A period of time in the the Hindu system of cosmic time. Four yugas, the KRITA, TRETA, DVAPARA and KALI, comprise one MAHAYUGA.

The concept of four ages is also described by the Greek writer Hesiod. The *BUNDAHISHN*, a Zoroastrian text, describes four ages of the world, each of 3000 years, in the last of which the SAOSHYANT will appear.

Zadspram A Zoroastrian text of the ninth century written in Pahlavi. It deals with various Zoroastrian themes on the basis of earlier AVESTA and Zand (commentary) texts. It includes legends of creation, the assault of AHRIMAN on the world, the life of ZARATHUSHTRA, his conversations with OHRMAZD and his powers, and other similar subjects. Some aspects of it are based on ZURVAN sources.

Zafar Namah Gurdwara A GURDWARA or Sikh shrine located in Kangar village of Bathinda district in Punjab. It is said to mark the spot where the tenth guru, GOBIND SINGH, composed his letter, the ZAFAR NAMAH, to the Mughal emperor AURANGZEB. One of Gobind Singh's disciples then delivered it to Aurangzeb, who was in the Deccan. Some scholars believe the letter was actually written at Dina.

Zafar Namah A letter in Persian verse written by the tenth Sikh guru, GOBIND SINGH, to the Mughal emperor AURANGZEB. In this document the guru accuses the emperor of making promises and pledges that he did not keep. In the siege of Anandpur, for example, the Sikhs had been promised safe conduct if they left the fort, but the promise was not kept. The guru goes on to say, 'When there is no other course open to man, it is but righteous to unsheath the sword.' He says that such a person, who cannot keep his word, obviously does not believe in ALLAH, nor in his Prophet. He adds, 'If the Prophet MUHAMMAD were here, I would present to him this vile deed of your treachery.' The letter continues in this vein, and towards the end the guru says, 'You have an empire, wealth and pomp, a generous disposition and warlike qualities, but are far from religion.' On receiving this letter Aurangzeb asked the guru to come and meet him, but before they could meet, the emperor died. According to Sikh sources, Aurangzeb was deeply moved by this letter, particularly because he was condemned by a holy man. Sikh tradition believes this led to his despairing last letters to his sons, where he says, 'I have lost hope in myself . . . I have gravely sinned and know not what torment awaits me.'

Zain-ul Abidin An enlightened Muslim ruler of Kashmir of the fifteenth century. Zain-ul Abidin ruled from 1420 to 1470, rebuilt some temples that had earlier been destroyed and restored the BRAHMANAS to their high posts in the government. He also promoted the study of Hindu literature and philosophy, and had the MAHABHARATA and the *Rajatarangini*, the account of the kings of Kashmir, translated into Persian, while Persian works were translated into Sanskrit.

zakat One of the essential duties of Islam, zakat is translated as 'charity' or 'poor due'. The QURAN has several passages on the importance of zakat. One passage states: 'Lo! Those who believe and do good deeds and establish prayer and pay the zakat, their reward is with their Lord.' (2:227).

Zakat is said to lead to the purification of the soul, as it checks the greed for wealth. It also helps the poor and provides basic necessities to those who do not have them. Thus the *MISHKAT* says: 'One who eats to his full appetite while his neighbour starves is not a true Muslim.' Another objective of zakat is to help Islam, and it can be used to support or protect the religion.

Zanjiri Mosque A historic mosque located in Bijapur, Karnataka, constructed in 1587 by Sultan Ibrahim Adil Shah II, also known as MALIKA JAHAN'S MOSQUE, popularly called the Zanjiri Mosque because of its hanging chain ornaments.

Zarathushtra A prophet of ancient Iran, known as ZOROASTER in Greek, who was the founder of the Zoroastrian religion. The dates of Zarathushtra's life remain controversial, but most scholars now accept that he lived sometime between 2000 BCE and 1000 BCE. While Zoroastrian tradition placed him even earlier than this, Western scholars once assigned him to around 600 BCE, based on a late Sasanian account stating that he lived 258 years before Alexander. There were also accounts of Zarathushtra at the court of King Vishtaspa, taken to be the father of the Achaemenian King Darius (522–486 BCE). However, the close linguistic similarity with the RIG VEDA makes a date later than 1000 BCE improbable. In addition, the genealogy of the Vishtaspa mentioned in association with Zarathushtra is different from that of the later Achaemenian king.

Zarathushtra was the first to preach a monotheistic religion, with one God, and to introduce the concept of good and evil, and the importance of living an ethical life.

Fragments of his own writings survive in the GATHAS, but do not tell us much about his life. In the *Gathas*, AHURA MAZDA (God) says that Zarathushtra was the only man who 'listened to our decrees'. He is sent to the earth to guide the people on the right path (*Yasna* 28). He refers to himself as a zaotar (Sanskrit: hotr), a priest (*Yasna* 33.6). He is a Master of Righteousness and an erishi (Sanskrit: rishi) endowed with visionary insight (*Yasna* 31.5, 10). He is also called a Manthran (teacher of MANTHRAS), Ratu (guide) and Saoshyant (saviour), and in later texts an Athravan (priest).

Legendary accounts of his life, with some variations, are provided in later Pahlavi texts. According to these, Zarathushtra, meaning 'he of the golden light', was born in Arak in Azerbaijan to the north of present Iran, in the Spitama family, to Pourushaspa, son of Paitiraspa, and Dughdova, daughter of Frahim-rava. The baby laughed when he was born and the vibrations in his brain were so powerful that none could touch his head. People feared his potential power, and a wicked magician, Dorasarun, made several attempts to kill him, but the child always miraculously escaped. (There are some parallels here with the KRISHNA legend.) Always sensitive and thoughtful, at the age of fifteen he turned away from worldly life and pondered the mysteries of life, death and suffering. A few years later he went to Mt Ushidaran, where he lived in a cave, eating roots and berries, and drinking the milk of a she-goat who came there voluntarily to feed him. There, around the age of thirty, he received enlightenment and conversed with AHURA MAZDA in a vision. He returned to the world and began to convey his vision.

The religion of Iran at this time seems to have been similar to that of the Rig Veda. There were multiple deities, sacrifices, and the cult of Haoma (Vedic SOMA). Preaching against these, he did not find many followers, and at first only his cousin Maidhyomaongha believed what he said and followed him. Zarathushtra then left his home and reached Bactria, where Kava Vishtaspa was the king. His courtiers plotted against Zarathushtra and got him imprisoned, but the king released him after his horse, Aspa Siha, became ill and was cured by Zarathushtra. Vishtaspa then became a follower of the new religion. By this time Zarathushtra was about forty-two years old. He married Havovi and had six children, three sons named Isatvastar, Urvatatnar and Khurshid-chichar, and three daughters, Freni, Thriti, and Pouruchista.

He then travelled on horseback from place to place to spread his teachings. According to tradition, he even visited Tibet and China. He returned to Balkh, capital of Bactria (Afghanistan) and settled there. At the age of seventy-seven, while he was praying in a temple, he was stabbed by Tur-bara-tur, the leader of a hostile Turanian tribe. As Zarathushtra died, his attacker is said to have fallen dead. In esoteric interpretations Tur-bara-tur is seen not as an individual but as the embodiment of evil, which was shattered in Zarathushtra's last moments on earth.

Zatra A Christian festival held at Kansaulim in Goa on 6 January every year. It celebrates the visit of the MAGI to the baby JESUS at Bethlehem, but is more like a carnival than a religious festival. Three men dressed in wigs and bright clothes enter a church with an image of the baby Jesus, and pay their respects to him. After this, the festival starts with dancing, music and various games.

zikr A term in Islam for recollection or remembrance. Zikr, performed primarily by SUFIS, is a continuous focus on God, either in solitude or in a community, and can be performed mentally or in a low voice (zikr khafi), or loudly (zikr jali). It involves repetition of the names of God or of parts of the QURAN, and a rosary or tashih can be used for counting. The breath is controlled during zikr, and there are also body movements or sometimes rhythmic dancing. Zikr often includes the phrase 'La-illaha-illa-allah', meaning, 'There is no God but Allah', half of it repeated while exhaling and the other half while inhaling. There is an account of a saint who used to exhale after the afternoon prayers and inhale only at the next set of prayers, thus holding his breath for three hours, while others inhaled only once or twice through the whole night. Zikr may be followed by meditation (muraqabah) on some verse of the Quran.

These practices are similar to various YOGA techniques.

Zoroaster A Greek term for ZARATHUSHTRA, from which the term Zoroastrian is derived. In Greece, ZARATHUSHTRA or Zoroaster was considered extremely wise and a spiritual adept. A number of later texts were written in the name of Zoroaster though they have nothing to do with Zarathushtra.

Zoroastrian calendar Three different calendars are followed by PARSI Zoroastrians in India. The Fasli calendar, also used in Iran, begins on 21 March every year, a date that is celebrated as NAVROZE or New Year. The KADIMI and SHAHENSHAHI calendars do not have fixed dates, but the new year starts some time in July and August respectively, when another Navroze is celebrated.

In all the calendars, there are twelve lunar months in the following order: (1) Farvardin; (2) Ardibehesht; (3) Khordad; (4) Tir; (5) Amardad; (6) Shahrevar; (7) Meher; (8) Ava/Avan; (9) Adar/Atar; (10) Dae; (11) Behman; (12) Spendarmad/Asfandarmad. Each month has thirty days, and each day is dedicated to and named after a power of God or of nature, personified as a YAZATA or deity. The days, which follow the same order in every month, are: (1) Ohrmazd/Hormazd; (2) Behman/Bahman; (3) Ardibehesht; (4) Shahrevar; (5) Spendarmad; (6) Khordad; (7) Amardad; (8) Daepe-Adar; (9) Adar/Atar (fire); (10) Ava (water); (11) Khursheed/Khorshed (sun); (12) Mohor (moon); (13)

Tir (star); (14) Gosh (animals); (15) Dae-pe-Meher; (16) Meher (light/mercy); (17) Sraosha (wisdom); (18) Rashnu; (19) Farvardin (Fravashi); (20) Behram (victory); (21) Ram/ Mino Ram (peace); (22) Govad (wind); (23) Dae-pe-Din; (24) Din (religion); (25) Ashishvangh (Ashi Vanghui); (26) Astad; (27) Asman (sky); (28) Zamyad (earth); (29) Marespand (Manthra); (30) Aneran (Anagra Raocha).

At the end of the year five days are added, named after the GATHAS, to bring the total to 365 days. To give an example of the different calendars, 21 March 2004 would be Farvardin month, Hormazd day (Fasli); Ava month, Shahrevar day (Shahenshahi); Adar month, Shahrevar day (Kadimi).

The use of three calendars in India causes some confusion in festival dates. At one time there were major conflicts between the Kadimi and Shahenshahi, but now most Parsis happily celebrate at least two new years. The celebration of the other festivals depends on the nature of the AGIARY or Zoroastrian temple; most temples follow the Shahenshahi calendar for festivals. Kadimis are prominent in Surat, and Fasli temples are few.

Zoroastrian festivals and ceremonies

Zoroastrian festivals include NAVROZE, the new year; Khordad Sal, the birthday of the Prophet ZARATHUSHTRA, celebrated five days after the new year; Pateti, the last day of the year, actually a day of repentance; six GAHAMBARS, or seasonal festivals; and celebrations on special days of the month, particularly when the deity of the month and the day coincide.

Sacred ceremonies include the ijashne or YASNA, the VENDIDAD, the navar and martab for initiation of priests, as well as various rituals from the time of birth to death, of which the most important are the NAVJOTE, and the marriage and death ceremonies. JASHANS are held in celebration on festival days or other auspicious occasions.

Zoroastrian temples Zoroastrian temples in India are of three grades, the ATASH BEHRAM, ATASH ADARAN, and AGIARY. The grade of the temple depends on the nature of the sacred fire within, an ATASH BEHRAM requiring purificatory ceremonies that can go on for more than a year. The fire is always kept burning in a temple, and there is great emphasis on purity and on its preservation from 'pollution'. In Iran non-Zoroastrians can enter fire temples, and in ancient days some of the temples were open fire altars, but in India entry is forbidden to non-Zoroastrians.

The temple is normally a simple structure consisting of a rectangular hall. At one end is a section where the sacred fire (ATAR or atash) is kept burning in an afarghan, a metal container shaped like an inverted bell. The BOI ceremony takes place five times a day, in which the priest prays and feeds the fire with sandalwood and incense.

The hall contains pictures of revered Zoroastrians.

Ceremonies such as JASHANS, or special prayers, take place in the hall.

Zoroastrian texts Sacred texts of the Zoroastrian religion include the AVESTA texts in two categories, older and younger, and the Pahlavi texts. AVESTA texts are the YASNA, including the GATHAS, the *Visperad*, VENDIDAD, the YASHTS, and NYAESHES; prayers taken from these as well as others are included in the *Khordeh Avesta*, the book of prayers. Among Pahlavi texts are the ARDA VIRAF NAMAH, the BUNDAHISHN, the DINKARD, the *Menog-i-khrad*, the *Shkandgumanig Vizar*, the DADESTAN-I-DENIG, the ZADSPRAM, *Shayast-al-Shayast*, and the later Persian RIVAYATS. The PARSIS of India have added collections of prayers, translations, commentaries, and the works of the ILM-E-KSHNOOM.

Zoroastrianism Zoroastrianism is an ancient religion with a complex history, preserved in India by the PARSIS. The religion was founded by ZARATHUSHTRA around 1500 BCE, and his own words are recorded in the GATHAS or songs, of which only fragments are available today. The religion developed and changed over time, and these changes are reflected in the various ZOROASTRIAN TEXTS composed in older and younger Avestan, in Pahlavi and Persian. The later texts provide a number of myths, legends, descriptions of creation, and semi-historical accounts. Thus, depending on the texts used, the religion can be interpreted differently.

Fundamental principles: The *Gathas*, the Songs of Zarathushtra, state that there is one God, AHURA MAZDA, who represents truth and cosmic order, and guides the world through his powers, the AMESHA SPENTAS. Ahura Mazda created twin spirits, SPENTA MAINYU and ANGRA MAINYU, the good and the bad, and gave each person the freedom to choose between them.

A person has to choose rightly, and thus help God in creating a perfect world. A human being is considered God's hamkar or helper, and the body and mind are to be dedicated to God. Thus life is perfected over time, leading to the FRASHOKERETI, the renewal of existence. The basic ethics of the religion are summed up in the term Humata, huvakta, huvarashta, or good thoughts, good words and good deeds. After death one crosses the CHINVAT BRIDGE to reach the other world and attains the rewards of one's actions. According to the *Gathas* (*Yasna* 30.11), 'There will be a long period of suffering for the wicked, and salvation for the just, but thereafter eternal bliss shall prevail everywhere.'

Additional principles: Later texts contain myths of creation (BUNDAHISHN) and several concepts not contained in the *Gathas*. A clear division between good and evil led to the idea of everything in the world being divided into these two categories, including the animal world. Thus, instead of preserving life as enjoined by Zarathushtra, it was considered meritorious to kill so-called 'noxious creatures', such as snakes and insects.

The concept of purity also became important, similar to the Brahmanical concept, though interpreted differently. There was a belief that death, as well as all disorder, comes from the evil spirit.

The purity of fire was to be maintained, therefore dead bodies should not be burnt, because they pollute fire. In India, the orthodox believe a glance of a non-Zoroastrian pollutes the sacred fire, an idea that can be compared to the Hindu practice of not allowing non-Hindus into certain temples.

Reform movements attempted to go 'Back to the Gathas', and to ignore the later texts, similar to the 'Back to the Vedas' movement in Hinduism.

Monotheism or dualism?: Some scholars using later texts interpret Zoroastrianism as dualistic, with God, known as HORMAZD or Ohrmazd, and the evil spirit AHRIMAN being constantly at war. This interpretation is often followed by new converts to the religion.

History: The history of Zoroastrianism has been put together through later texts, legends, myths, as well as excavations, coin finds and inscriptions. Linguistic analysis plays a role in dating the religion.

According to Avestan texts there were seven regions of the world, of which Airyana Vaeja (the land of the Airyas) was the centre. Airya is the same as the Sanskrit 'arya', and later Airyana was abbreviated to Iran.

Legendary history talks of the Pishdadian dynasty of pre-historic days. Among the kings of this dynasty was YIMA (JAMSHED), a great king whose pride led to his downfall. Azhi Dahak (later known as Zohak) then conquered Iran and oppressed the people. He was defeated in a struggle led by Kava, a blacksmith and THRAETONA, the true heir. After a time of warfare, the Kayanian dynasty is said to have followed. Kava Vishtaspa, patron of Zarathushtra, belonged to this dynasty. Soon after this the Medes rose in northern Iran.

At the time of Zarathushtra, many deities seem to have been worshipped. Out of these Zarathushtra gave supreme importance to AHURA MAZDA, and put forward the concept of one God for the first time. The *Gathas* mention King Vishtaspa and his two ministers, but not much is known of those early years. Vishtaspa ruled over Bactria.

History is clearer after the sixth century BCE. Between 558 BCE and 330 BCE, the Achaemenid dynasty emerged in Iran. Darius (522–486 BCE), a Persian monarch of the Achaemenid dynasty, the son of another Vishtaspa, expanded his empire. It extended across west Asia to Egypt, present Afghanistan, and north-west India. North of Afghanistan the Persian empire included parts of Russia. There are records that at this time, Ahura Mazda was worshipped, along with other Vedic-Iranian deities. The MAGI, a priestly class of the Medes, were powerful under the Achaemenians. In 330 BCE, Iran was conquered by Alexander, and the great library at Persepolis containing Zoroastrian texts is said to have been destroyed. The Parthian Arsacids (160 BCE–CE 225) revived Zoroastrianism. The compilation of the AVESTA was begun and completed under the Sasanians (CE 225 to 651). The last Sasanian ruler, Yazdagird III, was defeated by the Arabs, after which a group of Zoroastrians fled to the mountains of Kohistan. Some time later, according to the KISSAH-I-SANJAN, they reached India, where they came to be known as PARSIS.

Organizations: There are a number of Zoroastrian organizations in the world today. In India there are the Parsi Punchayets (Panchayats) and the Federation of Parsi Punchayets. Outside India, organizations include the World Zoroastrian Organization (WZO), based in London, and the Federation of Zoroastrians of North America (FEZANA). A proposal for a world body including all Zoroastrians was opposed by some in India who instead formed the World Alliance of Parsi and Irani Zarathoshtis (WAPIZ), believing that all others are not true Zoroastrians.

Zoroastrians A term for the followers of the religion of the Prophet ZARATHUSHTRA, known in Greek as ZOROASTER. Zoroastrians themselves more often use the term Zarathushtris, Zarathoshtis, or Mazda-yasnis. Zoroastrians originated in Iran, but for centuries the religion has been best preserved in India. Today there is a revival of interest in Zoroastrianism, with new converts in a number of countries.

In Russia and the former Soviet states, particularly Tajikistan and Uzbekistan, there are a number of groups claiming Zoroastrian ancestry, and keen on following the religion. Excavations indicate forms of the religion existing in the past in Sogdiana and elsewhere. A group of Kurds, originally from Iraq, and now in Germany, also claim to be Zoroastrians. There is also a revival of Zoroastrians in Iran. In Europe and America, individuals are converting to the religion, inspired by its ideals.

Orthodox Parsi Zoroastrians believe most of these (except in Iran) are not true Zoroastrians. Some individual Parsis, however, have tried to provide them support, texts, and acceptance.

There are 69,601 Zoroastrians in India (according to the 2001 census); between 30,000 and 90,000 in Iran, where some who call themselves Zoroastrians are officially counted as Muslims, 10,000–15,000 in the USA; approximately 6000 in Canada; 5000 in the UK, mostly in England, 2600 in Australia, 2200 in the Persian Gulf; about 2000 in Pakistan, 1000 in Europe and Central Asia, and 900 in New Zealand.

Zurvan A concept in Zoroastrianism. As the religion came to be seen as dualistic, with two separate powers of good and evil, the concept of Zurvan, meaning time, came into being. Zurvan was seen as a kind of godhead from which the two powers emerged. This is thought to have been the dominant tradition in Sasanian times, but was not an important concept in India. Lately, the idea of Zurvan has been revived.

Select Bibliography

Books

Ahmad, Aziz, *An Intellectual History of Islam in India* (Edinburgh: Edinburgh University Press, 1969).

Ahmad, Aziz, *Islamic Modernism in India and Pakistan 1857-1946* (London: Oxford University Press, 1967).

Ahmad, Aziz, *Studies in Islamic Culture in the Indian Environment* (Oxford: Clarendon, 1964).

Ahmad, Mohiuddin, *Saiyid Ahmad Shahid: His Life and Mission* (Lucknow: Academy of Islamic Reasearch and Publ., 1975).

Alam, Muzaffar, et.al.,eds., *The Making of Indo-Persian Culture: Indian and French Studies* (Delhi: Manohar, 2000).

Alam, Muzaffar, *The Languages of Political Islam in India c.1200-1800* (Delhi: Permanent Black, 2004).

Alston, A.J. trans., *The Devotional Songs of Mirabai* (Delhi: Motilal Banarsdass, 1980).

Arberry, A.J. ed., *The Cambridge History of Iran*, 7 vols., (Cambridge: Cambridge University Press, 1968-91).

Arberry, A.J., *An Introduction to the History of Sufism* (Oxford: Oxford University Press, 1962).

Arberry, A.J., *Muslim Saints and Mystics* (London: Routledge and Kegan Paul, 1966).

Archaeological Remains, Monuments and Museums Pt I and *II* (New Delhi: Archaeological Survey of India, 1964).

Asad, Majida, trans. M.R. Sharma, *Indian Muslim Festivals and Customs* (New Delhi: Publications Division, 1988).

Atiya, A.S., ed., *The Coptic Encyclopaedia*, 8 vols (New York: Maxwell Macmillan International, 1991).

Atre, Shubhangana, *The Archetypal Mother: A Systemic Approach to Harappan Religion* (Pune: Ravish Publishers, 1987).

Aurobindo, Sri, *Songs of Vidyapati* (2nd ed., Pondicherry, Aurobindo Ashram, 1974).

Aurobindo, Sri, *The Integral Yoga: Selected Letters of Sri Aurobindo* (Pondicherry: Sri Aurobindo Ashram, 1996).

Aurobindo, Sri, *The Message of the Gita: with Text, Translation and Notes* (1938; reprint, Pondicherry: Sri Aurobindo Ashram, 1977).

Aurobindo, Sri, *The Synthesis of Yoga* (1914-21; reprint, Pondicherry: Sri Aurobindo Ashram, 1998).

Aurobindo, Sri, *The Upanishads: Texts, Translations and Commentaries* (2nd edn., Pondicherry: Sri Aurobindo Ashram, 1981).

Aurobindo, Sri,*The Life Divine* (5th imp.,Pondicherry: Sri Aurobindo Ashram, 1993).

Ayyar, C.V. Nayanar, *Origin and Early History of Saivism in South India* (1936; reprint, 1974).

Baird, Robert D., ed., *Religion in Modern India* (4th edn., New Delhi: Manohar, 2001).

Banerjea, J.N., *The Development of Hindu Iconography* (3rd edn, New Delhi: Munshiram Manoharlal, 1974).

Bapat, P.V., ed., *2500 Years of Buddhism* (New Delhi: Publications Division, 1956).

Barrett, David B., et al., *World Christian Encyclopedia: A Comparative Study of Churches and Religions in the Modern World*, AD 1900 –2000 (2nd edn., New York: Oxford University Press, 2001).

Barton, J., *Reading the Old Testament: Method in Biblical Study* (London: Darton, Longman and Todd, 1984).

Barua, D.K., *An Analytical Study of Four Nikayas* (New Delhi: Munshiram Manoharlal, 2003).

Barua, R.K., and H.V. Sreenivasa Murthy, *Temples and Legends of Assam* (Bombay: Bharatiya Vidya Bhavan, 1988).

Basham, A. L., *The Wonder That Was India* (Fontana with Rupa & Co, 1971).

Basham, A.L., *History and Doctrine of the Ajivikas* (London: Luzac & Co., 1951).

Bayley, Susan, *Saints, Goddesses and Kings: Muslims and Christians in South Indian Society, 1700-1900* (Cambridge: Cambridge University Press, 1989).

Bell, Charles, *Tibet Past and Present* (New Delhi: Munshiram Manoharlal, 1990).

Bhandarkar, R.G., *Vaisnavism, Saivism and Minor Religious Systems* (Strassburg, 1913; reprint, New Delhi: Munshiram Manoharlal, 2001).

Bharati, Agehananda, *The Tantric Tradition* (reprint, New Delhi: B.I. Publications, 1983).

Bhargava, Dayanand, *Jaina Ethics* (New Delhi: Motilal Banarsidass, 1968).

Bhatt, Mahesh, *U.G. Krishnamurti: A Life* (New Delhi: Penguin Viking, 1992).

Bhattacharji, Sukumari, *The Indian Theogony: A Comparative Study of Indian Mythology from the Vedas to the Puranas* (Calcutta: Firma KLM, 1978).

Bhattacharya, Deben, trans.,*The Mirror of the Sky: Songs of the Bauls of Bengal* (Prescott, A.Z.: Hohm Press, 1999).

Bhattacharya, N.N., *History of the Tantric Religion* (2nd rev. edn., New Delhi: Manohar, 1999).

Bhattacharya, N.N., *Indian Religious Historiography* (New Delhi: Munshiram Manoharlal, 1996).

Bhattacharya, N.N., *Jain Philosophy: Historical Outline* (2nd rev. edn, New Delhi: Munshiram Manoharlal, 1999).

Bhattacharya, N.N., *Tantrabhidhana: A Tantric Lexicon* (New Delhi: Manohar, 2002).

Bhattacharya, N.N., *The Indian Mother Goddess* (3rd enlarged edn., New Delhi: Manohar, 1999).

Bhatti, Anil and Johannes H. Voigt, ed., *Jewish Exile in India 1933-1945* (New Delhi: Manohar, in association with Max Mueller Bhavan, 1999).

Biswas, S. S., *Bishnupur* (New Delhi: Archaeological Survey of India, 1992).

Blochmann, H., trans., *The Ain-i Akbari* (2nd edn., Delhi: New Imperial Book Depot, 1965).

Bloomfield, Maurice, *A Vedic Concordance* (reprint, Delhi: Motilal Banarsidass, 1996).

Boethlingk, O., and Roth, R., *Sanskrit Worterbuch*, 7 vols (St. Petersberg, 1875, reprint, Delhi: Motilal Banarsidass, 1991).

Booz, Elizabeth B., *Tibet* (Hong Kong, Shangrila Press, 1986).

Bowker, John, ed., *The Concise Oxford Dictionary of World Religions* (Oxford: Oxford University Press, 2000).

Boyce, M., *A History of Zoroastrianism*, 3 vols; (vol , Leiden: Brill, 1975 ,reprint, 1989; vol 2, 1982; vol 3, with F. Grenet, 1991).

Boyce, M., *Textual Sources for the Study of Zoroastrianism* (Manchester: Manchester University Press, 1984).

Boyce, M., *Zoroastrians: Their Religious Beliefs and Practices* (London: Routledge, 1979).

Brantl, George, ed., *Catholicism* (New York: George Braziller, 1962).

Brent, Peter, *Godmen of India* (Harmondsworth: Penguin Books, 1973).

Briggs, George W., *Gorakhnath and the Kanphata Yogis* (reprint, Delhi: Motilal Banarsidass, 1998).

Briggs, John, *History of The Rise of Mahomedan Power in India* (trans. of *Tarikh-i-Firishta*), (1829; reprint, 4 vols, Calcutta : Editions Indian, 1966).

Bromage, Bernard, *Tibetan Yoga* (Wellingborough, Northamptonshire: The Aquarian Press, 1979).

Brooks, Douglas Renfrew, *Auspicious Wisdom: The Text and Traditions of Srividya Sakta Tantrism in South India* (New Delhi: Manohar, 1996).

Brown, C. Mackenzie, *God as Mother: A Feminine Theology of India* (Vermont: Claude Stark & Co., 1974).

Brown, Peter, *The cult of the Saints: Its Rise and Function in Latin Christianity* (Chicago:University of Chicago Press, 1981).

Bryant, Edwin, *The Quest for the Origins of Vedic Culture: The Indo-Aryan Migration Debate* (New Delhi: Oxford University Press, 2001).

Buddhist Shrines in India (1951; reprint, New Delhi: Publications Division, 1994).

Bulfinch, Thomas, *Bulfinch's Mythology* (New York: Grosset & Dunlap, 1913).

Buxi, Lochan Singh, *Prominent Mystic Poets of the Punjab* (New Delhi, Publications Division, 1994).

Carpenter, J. Estlin, *Theism in Medieval India* (1921; reprint, New Delhi: Oriental Books, 1977).

Chadwick, Owen, ed., *The Pelican History of the Church*, 6 vols (New York: Penguin Books, 1960-70).

Chakravarti, S.C., *Philosophical Foundation of Bengal Vaisnavism* (New Delhi: Munshiram Manoharlal, 2004).

Chakravarti, Uma, *The Social Dimensions of Early Buddhism* (New Delhi, Oxford University Press, 1987).

Chandra, Satish, *Mughal Religious Policies, The Rajputs and the Deccan* (New Delhi: Vikas Publishing House, 1993).

Chatterjee, A.K., *A Comprehensive History of Jainism Pt I and II* (Calcutta: Firma KLM, 1978-84).

Chatterjee, A.K., *The Yogacara Idealism* (revised ed., Delhi: Motilal Banarsidass, 1975).

Chatterji, S.K. *Indian Calendric System* (New Delhi: Publications Division, 1998).

Chattopadhyaya, B.D., *Studying Early India* (New Delhi: Permanent Black, 2003).

Chattopadhyaya, D.P., *Lokayata: A Study in Ancient Indian Materialism* (reprint, Delhi: People's Publishing House, 1978).

Chaturvedi, B.K., *Gods and Goddesses of India: Pts 1 – 14*; 1.*Ganesha*; 2. *Brahma*; 3. *Vishnu*; 4. *Shiv*; 5. *Saraswati*; 6. *Lakshmi*; 7. *Durga*; 8. *Hanuman*; 9. *Ram*; 10. *Krishna*; 11.*Ganga*; 12. *Yamuna*; 13. *Agni and Karttikeya*; 14. *Navagrahas* (Delhi: Books For All, 1996-1998); (useful for popular beliefs and legends).

Chawla, Jyotsna, *The Rigvedic Deities and Their Iconic Forms* (New Delhi: Munshiram Manoharlal, 1990).

Chinmayananda, Swami, *Discourses on Kaivalyopanishad* (Bombay: Central Chinmaya Mission Trust, n.d.).

Chinmayananda, Swami, *Discourses on Kathopanishad* (Bombay: Central Chinmaya Mission Trust, n.d.)

Chitre, Dilip, trans., *Says Tuka: Selected Poetry of Tukaram* (New Delhi: Penguin Books, 1991).

Chopra, P.N., ed., *The Gazetteer of India, vol 2, History and Culture* (1973, 5th edn., New Delhi: Publications Division, 1997).

Clothey, Fred W., *The Many Faces of Murukan: The History and Meaning of a South Indian God* (New Delhi: Munshiram Manoharlal, 2005).

Coburn, Thomas B., *Devi-Mahatmaya, The Crystallization of the Goddess Tradition* (Delhi: Motilal Banarsidass, 1984).

Conze, Edward, *Buddhism* (Oxford: Bruno Cassirer, 1951).

Conze, Edward, *Buddhist Thought in India: Three Phases of Buddhist Philosophy* (1967; reprint, Michigan: University of Michigan Press, Ann Arbor Paperbacks, 1983).

Conze, Edward, *The Prajnaparamita Literature* (1958; reprint, New Delhi: Munshiram Manoharlal, 2000).

Coomaraswamy, A. K., and I.B. Horner, *The Living Thoughts of Gotama the Buddha* (London: Cassell, 1948).

Coomaraswamy, A.K., *Elements of Buddhist Iconography* (1935; reprint, New Delhi: Munshiram Manoharlal, 1979).

Coomaraswamy, A.K., *Hinduism and Buddhism* (New York: The Wisdom Library, n.d.).

Coomaraswamy, A.K., *Jain Art* (reprint, New Delhi: Munshiram Manoharlal, 1994).

Coomaraswamy, AK., *Yakshas* (2nd edn., New Delhi: Munshiram Manoharlal, 1980).

Currie, P.M., *The Shrine and Cult of Mu'in al Din Chishti of Ajmer* (New Delhi: Oxford University Press, 1989).

Dadrawala, N.H., *Zarathushtrian Saints* (Mumbai: Dadrawala, 1999).

Dandekar, R.N., *Vedic Mythological Tracts* (Delhi: Ajanta, 1979).

Danielou, Alain, *The Myths and Gods of India* (Rochester, Vermont: Inner Traditions International, 1991).

Danielou, Alain, trans., *Manimekhalai* (New Delhi: Penguin Books, 1993).

Das, R. K., *Temples of Tamil Nadu* (Mumbai: Bharatiya Vidya Bhavan, 2001).

Das, S.K., *The Shadow of the Cross: Christianity and Hinduism in a Colonial Situation* (New Delhi: Munshiram Manoharlal, 1974).

Dasgupta, S., *A History of Indian Philosophy*, 5 vols (1922-55; reprint, Delhi: Motilal Banarsidass, 1975).

Davies, Philip, *The Penguin Guide to the Monuments of India*, vol.II (Harmondsworth: Penguin Books, 1989).

Dawood, N.J., trans., *The Koran* (3rd revised edn, Harmondsworth: Penguin Books, 1968).

Dehejia, V., *Slaves of the Lord: The Path of the Tamil Saints* (New Delhi: Munshiram Manoharlal, 1988).

Desai, P.B., *Jainism in South India and some Jain Epigraphs* (Sholapur: Gulabchand Hirachand Doshi for Jaina Samskrti Samrakshaka Sangha, 1957).

Desai, Ziyaud-din, *Mosques of India* (New Delhi: Publications Division, 1996).

Devotional Poets and Mystics, Pt I and II (reprint, New Delhi: Publications Division, 1991).

Dikshitar, V.R. Ramachandra, *The Purana Index*, 3 vols (reprint, New Delhi: Motilal Banarsidass, 1995).

Dogra, R.C. and Gobind Singh Mansukhani, *Encyclopaedia of Sikh Religion and Culture* (New Delhi: Vikas, 1995).

Dowson, John, *A Classical Dictionary Of Hindu Mythology and Religion* (reprint, New Delhi: D.K. Printworld, 1998).

Duggal, Kartar Singh, *The Sikh Gurus: Their Lives and Teachings* (New Delhi: Vikas, 1980).

Dumont, Louis, *Homo Hierarchicus: The Caste System and Its Implications* (rev. edn., Chicago: University of Chicago, 1980).

Dundas, Paul, *The Jains* (London: Routledge, 1992).

Dunstan, J. Leslie, ed., *Protestantism* (New York: George Braziller, 1962).

Dutt, Sukumar, *The Buddha and Five After-Centuries* (1957; reprint, New Delhi: Munshiram Manoharlal, 1978).

Dutt, Sukumar, *Buddhist Monks and Monasteries of India* (London: George Allen and Unwin, 1962).

Eaton, R. M., *Essays on Islam and Indian History* (New Delhi: Oxford University Press, 2000).

Eliade, M., ed., *The Encyclopedia of Religions*, 16 vols (New York, Macmillan, 1987).

Eliade, Mircea, *The Myth of the Eternal Return* (London: Arkana, 1989).

Elliot, H.M., and Dowson, J., ed. and trans., *The History of India as Told by Its Own Historians*, 8 vols (1867-77; reprint, New Delhi: Low Price Publications,(DK) 1996).

Elwin, Verrier, *Myths of Middle India* (1949; reprint New Delhi: Oxford University Press, 1992).

Elwin, Verrier, *Myths of the North-East Frontier of India* (1958; reprint, New Delhi: Munshiram Manoharlal, 1999).

Embree, Ainslee T., ed., *Sources of Indian Tradition*, vol 1 (2nd edn., New Delhi: Penguin Books, 1992).

Encyclopaedia of Islam, (2nd edn., Leiden: Brill, 1960 etc.).

Erdosy, George, ed., *The Indo-Aryans of Ancient South Asia: Language, Material Culture and Ethnicity* (Indian edn., New Delhi: Munshiram Manoharlal, 1997).

Eschmann, A., et.al., *The Cult of Jagganath and the Regional Tradition of Orissa* (New Delhi: Manohar, 1986).

Fausboll, V. , ed., *Jatakas*, 7 vols., (London, 1877-97); trans. E.B. Cowell (Cambridge, 1895-1913).

Fergusson, J., and James Burgess, *The Cave Temples of India* (reprint, New Delhi: Munshiram Manoharlal, 2000).

Fernando, Leonard and G. Gispert-Sauch, *Christianity in India* (New Delhi, Penguin Viking, 2004).

Festivals of India (New Delhi: National Book Trust, 1982).

Festivals of India (New Delhi: Publications Division, 1992).

Frawley, David, *Tantric Yoga and the Wisdom Goddesses* (Delhi: Motilal Banarsidass, 1996).

Friedmann, Y., ed., *Islam in Asia, vol 1, South Asia* (Jerusalem: The Magnes Press -The Hebrew University, 1984).

Gambhirananda, Swami, *Mandukya Upanishad, with the Karika of Gaudapada and commentary of Sankaracarya* (Calcutta: Advaita Ashram, 1979).

Gard, Richard A., ed., *Buddhism* (New York: George Braziller, 1962).

Getty, Alice, *Ganesa: A Monograph on the Elephant-Faced God* (New Delhi: Munshiram Manoharlal, 1992).

Getty, Alice, *The Gods of Northern Buddhism* (reprint, New Delhi: Munshiram Manoharlal, 2004).

Ghosh, A., ed., *An Encyclopaedia of Indian Archaeology*, 2 vols (New Delhi: Munshiram Mnaoharlal, 1989).

Giles, H.A., trans., *The Travels of Fa –Hsien, 399-414* (Cambridge: Cambridge University Press, 1923).

Gitananda, Swami, *Yoga Samyama* (Pondicherry: Ananda Ashram, n.d.).

Glasenapp, Helmuth von, trans., Shridhar B. Shrotri, *Jainism: An Indian Religion of Salvation* (in German, 1925; Delhi: Lala S.L. Jain Research Series, vol 14, 1999).

Glasse, Cyril, *The Concise Encyclopedia of Islam* (San Francisco: Harper and Row, 1989).

Godman, David, ed., *Be As You Are: The Teachings of Sri Ramana Maharshi* (New Delhi: Penguin Books, 1992).

Gonda, Jan, *Change and Continuity in Indian Religion* (1965; reprint New Delhi: Munshiram Manoharlal, 1997).

Gonda, Jan, *Die Religionen Indiens*, 2 vols (Stuttgart: Kohlhammer,1960-63).

Gonda, Jan, *Medieval Religious Literature in Sanskrit* (Wiesbaden: Harrassowitz,1977).

Gonda, Jan, *Vedic Literature (Samhitas and Brahmanas)* (Wiesbaden: Harrassowitz, 1975).

Goudriaan, Teun, and Sanjukta Gupta, *Hindu Tantric and Sakta Literature* (Wiesbaden: Harrassowitz, 1981).

Goyal, S.R., *A History of Indian Buddhism* (Meerut: Kusumanjali Prakashan, 1987).

Grare, Frederic, *Political Islam in the Indian Subcontinent* (New Delhi: Manohar, 2001).

Grewal, J.S., *The Sikhs of the Punjab* (Cambridge: Cambridge University Press, 1990).

Grewal, J.S., and S.S. Bal, *Guru Gobind Singh: A Biographical Study* (Chandigarh: Panjab University, 1967).

Grewal, J.S., *Contesting Interpretations of Sikh Tradition* (New Delhi: Manohar, 1998).

Grewal, J.S., *From Guru Nanak to Maharaja Ranjit Singh:Essays in Sikh History* (!972; revised ed., Amritsar: GNDU, 1982).

Grewal, J.S., *Guru Nanak in History* (Chandigarh: Panjab University, 1969).

Griffith, R.T.H., trans., *The Hymns of the Rig Veda* (1896; new edn., Delhi: Motilal Banarsidass, 1976).

Griffiths, Bede, *A New Vision of Reality* (New Delhi: Indus, Harper Collins, 1992).

Gupta, Hari Ram, *History of the Sikhs*, 6 vols (New Delhi: Munshiram Manoharlal, 1978-91).

Habib, Irfan, ed., *Akbar and His India* (New Delhi: Oxford University Press, 1997).

Handa, O.C., *Buddhist Monasteries in Himachal Pradesh* (New Delhi: Indus Publishing Company, 1987).

Hanson, Virginia, ed., *H.P.Blavatsky and the Secret Doctrine* (Madras: The Theosophical Publishing House, 1971).

Haq, Anwarul, *The Faith Movement of Mawlana Muhammad Ilyas* (London: George Allen & Unwin, 1972).

Haque, Ishrat, *Glimpses of Mughal Society and Culture – A Study Based on Urdu Literature* (New Delhi: Concept Publishing Company, 1992).

Har Dayal, *The Bodhisattva Doctrine in Buddhist Sanskrit Literature* (reprint, Delhi: Motilal Banarsidass, 1999).

Hardy, Peter, *The Muslims of British India* (Cambridge: Cambridge University Press, 1972).

Hasan, Mushirul, ed., *Islam, Communities and the Nation: Muslim Identities in South Asia and Beyond* (New Delhi: Manohar, 1998).

Hasan, Mushirul, *Legacy of a Divided Nation: India's Muslims Since Independence* (New Delhi: Oxford University Press, 2001).

Hastings, J., ed., *Encyclopaedia of Religion and Ethics*, 13 vols. (Edinburgh: T.& T. Clark, 1908-26; repr. 12 vols, New York: Scribner, 1961).

Hazra, K.L., *Buddhism in India as Described by the Chinese Pilgrims AD 399-689* (New Delhi: Munshiram Manoharlal, 2002).

Hazra, R.C., *Studies in the Puranic Records on Hindu Rites and Customs* (2nd edn., Delhi: Motilal Banarsidass, 1975).

Heehs, Peter, ed., *Indian Religions: The Spiritual Traditions of South Asia – An Anthology* (Delhi: Permanent Black, 2002).

Heesterman, J.C., *The Inner conflict of Tradition: Essays in Indian Ritual, Kingship and Society* (New Delhi: Oxford University Press, 1985).

Hertzberg, Arthur, ed., *Judaism* (New York: George Braziller, 1961).

Hicks, Roger and Ngakpa Chogyam, *Great Ocean: An Authorized Biography, The Dalai Lama* (Harmondsworth: Penguin Books, 1990).

Hinnells, J.R.,ed., *The Penguin Dictionary of Religions* (2nd edn, Harmondsworth: Penguin Books, 1997).

Hinnells, J.R., *Zoroastrianism and the Parsis* (London: Wardlock Educational, 1981).

Hodgson, Marshall G.S., *The Venture of Islam: Conscience and History in a World Civilization*, 3 vols (Chicago: Chicago University Press, 1974).

Holt, P.M., et al., ed., *Cambridge History of Islam* (Cambridge: Cambridge University Press, 1970).

Hopkins, Thomas J. , *The Hindu Religious Tradition* (Belmont, CA: Wadsworth Publishing Company, 1971).

Hopkins, Jeffrey., trans. and ed., *His Holiness the Dalai Lama: How to Practise, the Way to a Meaningful Life* (London: Rider, 2002).

Horstmann, Martha, ed., *Images of Kabir* (New Delhi: Manohar, 2002).

Hourani, George F., ed., *Essays on Islamic Philosophy and Science* (Albany: State University of New York Press, 1975).

Hughes, T.P., *Dictionary of Islam* (1st pub 1885; reprint, New Delhi: Rupa & Co, 1988).

Ilaiah, Kancha, *Why I am not a Hindu* (Kolkata, Samya, 1996).

Islahi, Sadruddin, *Islam at a Glance* (Delhi: Markazi Maktaba Islami, 1978).

Jacobi, H. ed., revised, Muni Shri Punyavijayi, trans into Hindi, Shantilal M. Vora, *Acarya Vimalasuri's Paumcariyam* (2nd ed., Varanasi: Prakrit Text Society, 1962).

Jaffer, Mehru, *The Book of Muhammad* (New Delhi: Penguin Viking, 2003).

Jaffrelot, Christophe, *The Hindu Nationalist Movement and Indian Politics: 1925 - the 1990s* (New Delhi: Penguin Books, 1999).

Jain, J. P., *The Jaina Sources of the History of Ancient India* (New Delhi: Munshiram Manoharlal, 1964).

Jain, J., *Life in Ancient India as Depicted in the Jaina Canon and Commentaries: 6th century BC to 17th century AD* (2nd rev. edn., New Delhi: Munshiram Manoharlal, 1984).

Jain, Nirmal Kumar, *Sikh Religion and Philosophy* (New Delhi: Sterling, 1979).

Jaini, Padmanabha S., *The Jaina Path of Purification* (Delhi: Motilal Banarsidass, 1979).

Jaiswal, Suvira, *The Origin and Development of Vaisnavism* (2nd edn., New Delhi: Munshiram Manoharlal, 1981).

Jayakar, Pupul, *Krishnamurti: A Biography* (San Francisco: Harper & Row, 1986).

Jayakar, Pupul, *The Earth Mother* (New Delhi: Penguin Books, 1989).

Jindal, K.B., *An Epitome of Jainism* (New Delhi: Munshiram Manoharlal, 1987).

Johnson, W.J., *Harmless Souls: Karmic Bondage and Religious Change in Early Jainism with Special Reference to Umasvati and Kundakunda* (Delhi: Motilal Banarsidass, 1995).

Jordens, J.T., *Dayananda Saraswati: Essays on His Life and Ideas* (New Delhi: Manohar, 1998).

Joshi, Lal Mani, *Studies in the Buddhistic Culture of India* (2nd rev edn., Delhi: Motilal Banarsidass, 1977).

Kane, P.V., *History of Dharmasastra*, 5 vols, 2nd ed., (Poona: Bhandarkar Oriental Research Institute, 1968-77).

Katz, Nathan, *Studies of Indian Jewish Identity* (New Delhi: Manohar, 1995).

Khan, Hazrat Inayat, *The Sufi Message*, 14 vols (1st Indian edn., Delhi: Motilal Banarsidass, 1990).

Khanolkar, Savitribai, *Saints of Maharashtra* (Mumbai: Bharatiya Vidya Bhavan, 2000).

Kinsley, David R., *Hinduism: A Cultural Perspective* (London: Prentice Hall, 1982).

Kinsley, David R., *Hindu Goddesses* (Delhi: Motilal Banarsidass, 1987).

Kochhar, Rajesh, *The Vedic People* (New Delhi: Orient Longman, 2000).

Kosambi, D.D., *Myth and Reality: Studies in the Formation of Indian Culture* (Bombay: Popular Prakashan, 1962).

Kramrisch, Stella, *The Hindu Temple*, 2 vols (1946; reprint, Calcutta: University of Calcutta, 1969).

Krishna Deva, *Temples of India*, 2 vols (New Delhi: Aryan Books, 1995).

Kulke, Eckehard, *The Parsees in India* (reprint, New Delhi: Vikas Publishing House, 1993).

Kyt, George, trans., *Sri Jayadeva's Gita Govinda* (Bombay: Kutub Popular, 1940).

Mitra, R., ed., *Lalita Vistara* (1877; reprint, New Delhi: Cosmo, 2004).

Lamotte, Etienne, trans., Sara Webb-Boin, *History of Indian Buddhism From the Origins to the Saka Era* (in French, 1958; Louvain-La- Neuve: Institut Orientalist, 1988,).

Lane, David Christopher, *The Radhasoami Tradition* (New York: Garland Publishing, 1992).

Law, B.C., 'Studies in the Vividha Tirtha Kalpa', *Jaina Antiquary* IV (Arrah, 1938), pp. 109 ff.

Law, B.C., " Studies in the Anguttara Nikaya of the Sutta-pitaka', *Journal of the Ganganath Jha Research Institute*, vol. XX-XXII (Nov 1963 –Aug 1965), pp. 1 ff.

Law, B.C., *History of Pali Literature* (London, 1933; reprint, Varanasi: Bhartiya Publishing House, 1974).

Law, B.C., *Some Jain Canonical Sutras* (1949; Delhi: Indological Book House, 1988).

Lhalungpa, Lobsang P., trans., *The Life of Milarepa* (London: Paladin, 1979).

Ligeti, Louis, ed., *Tibetan and Buddhist Studies*, 2 vols (New Delhi: Munshiram Manoharlal, 2000).

Ling, Trevor O., *Buddhist Revival in India: Aspects of the Sociology of Buddhism* (London: Macmillan, 1980).

Lorenzen, David N., *Bhakti Religion in North India* (New Delhi: Manohar, 1996).

Lutyens, Mary, *Krishnamurti: The Open Door* (New York: Avon Books, 1988).

Lutyens, Mary, *Krishnamurti: The Years of Awakening* (New York: Avon Books, 1976).

Lutyens, Mary, *Krishnamurti: The Years of Fulfilment* (New York: Avon Books, 1983).

Macaulliffe, M.A., *The Sikh Religion: Its Gurus, Sacred Writings and Authors* (1909; reprint Delhi: S.Chand, 1985).

Macdonell, A. A., *The Vedic Mythology* (Varanasi/ Delhi: Indological Book House, 1971).

Macdonell, A.A., *A History of Sanskrit Literature* (1899; reprint, New Delhi: Munshiram Manoharlal, 1972).

Macdonell, A.A., and A.B. Keith, *Vedic Index of Names and Subjects*, 2 vols (reprint, Delhi: Motilal Banarsidass, 1995).

MacHovec, Frank J., trans., *The Tibetan Book of the Dead* (New York: The Peter Pauper Press, 1972).

Madan, T.N., ed., *Religion in India* (New Delhi: Oxford University Press, 1991).

Madhavananda, Swami, trans., *Uddhava Gita* (Calcutta: Advaita Ashram, 1978).

Mahesh Yogi, Maharishi, *Meditation* (Rishikesh: International SRM Publications, 2000).

Majumdar, R.C., ed., *The History and Culture of the Indian People*, 11 vols (Bombay: Bharatiya Vidya Bhavan, 1951-69).

Malalasekera, G.P., *Dictionary of Pali Proper Names* (1937; reprint, London: Luzac & Co, 1960).

Mallory, J.P., *In Search of the Indo-Europeans: Language, Archaeology and Myth* (London: Thames and Hudson, 1991).

Mani, Vettam, *Puranic Encyclopaedia* (reprint, Delhi: Motilal Banarsidass, 2002).

Mascaro, Juan, trans. ,*The Dhammapada* (Harmondsworth: Penguin Books, 1973)

Mascaro, Juan, trans., *The Bhagavad Gita* (Harmondsworth: Penguin Books, 1962).

Mascaro, Juan, trans., *The Upanishads* (reprint, Harmondsworth: Penguin Books, 1971).

Mate, M.S., *Temples and Legends of Maharashtra* (Bombay: Bharatiya Vidya Bhavan, 1988).

Mathur, Y.B., *Muslims and Changing India* (Delhi: Trimurti Publications, 1972).

Matilal, Bimal Krishna, *The Central Philosophy of Jainism* (Ahmedabad: LD Institute of Indology, 1981).

Mcleod, W.H., *Exploring Sikhism: Aspects of Sikh Identity, Culture and Thought* (New Delhi: Oxford University Press, 2000).

McLeod, W.H., *Guru Nanak and the Sikh Religion* (Oxford: Clarendon Press, 1968).

McLeod, W.H., *Historical Dictionary of Sikhism* (New Delhi: Oxford University Press, 1995).

Menachery, G., and Fr. W. Chakkalakal, *Kodungallur—The Cradle of Christianity in India* (Kodungallur: Fr. J.B. Puthur, 2001).

Metcalf, Barbara D., *Islamic Revival in British India: Deoband 1860-1900* (Princeton: Princeton University Press, 1982).

Michell, George, *The Penguin Guide to the Monuments of India*, vol.I (Harmondsworth: Penguin Books, 1990).

Mitchell, A.G., *Hindu Gods and Goddesses* (reprint, New Delhi: UBS Publishers, 1998).

Mitchell, Basil ed., *The Philosophy of Religion* (New York: Oxford University Press, 1971) (mainly on Christianity).

Mitra, Debala, *Ajanta* (New Delhi: Archaeological Survey of India, 1983).

Mitra, Debala, *Buddhist Monuments* (New Delhi: Munshiram Manoharlal, 1980).

Mitra, Debala, *Konarak* (New Delhi: Archaeological Survey of India, 1986).

Mitra, Debala, *Pandrethan, Avantipur and Martand* (New Delhi:ASI, 1993).

Mitra, Debala, *Udayagiri and Khandagiri* (New Delhi: Archaeological Survey of India, 1992).

Modi, J.J., *Religious Ceremonies and Customs of the Parsees* (2nd edn., Bombay: British India Press, 1922).

Monier-Williams, M., *A Sanskrit English Dictionary* (reprint, Delhi: Motilal Banarsidass, 1973).

Morewedge, Parviz, ed., *Islamic Philosophical Theology* (Albany: State University of New York Press, 1979).

Mujeeb, M., *The Indian Muslims* (1967, new edn., New Delhi: Munshiram Manoharlal, 1995).

Mukhia, Harbans, *Perspectives on Medieval History* (New Delhi: Vikas Publishing House, 1993).

Muller, Max, ed., *Sacred Books of the East* (50 vols); [including: vol 1, 15, Max Muller, trans., *The Upanishads*; 2,14, George Buhler, trans., *The Sacred Laws of the Aryas*; 4, 23, 31 J. Darmesteter and L.H. Mills, trans., *The Zend Avesta*; 5,18, 24, 37, 47, E.W. West, trans., *The Pahlavi Texts*; 11, T.W. Rhys Davids, trans., *Buddhist Suttas*; 12, 26, 41, 43, 44, Julius Eggeling, trans.,*The Satapatha Brahmana*; 13, 17, 20, T.W. Rhys Davids and H. Oldenberg, trans., *Vinaya Texts*; 21, H. Kern, trans., *The Saddharma Pundarika*; 22, 45, H. Jacobi, trans., *Jain Sutras*; 25, George Buhler, trans., *Manu Smriti*; 32, 46, Max Muller and H. Oldenberg, trans., *Vedic Hymns*; 49, E.B. Cowell, Max Muller, J.Takakusu, trans., *Buddhist Mahayana Texts*;] (1887; reprinted New Delhi, Low Price Publications, D.K. Publishers, 1995).

Murti, T.R.V., *The Central Philosophy of Buddhism* (London: Allen and Unwin, 1955, reprint, 1980).

Nagaraj, Nalini, *Sravanabelagola* (Bangalore: Art Publishers, 1980).

Nahar, P.C. and K.C. Ghosh, ed., *An Encyclopedia of Jainism* (1916; Delhi: Satguru Publications, 1988).

Nanavutty, Piloo, *Our Sacred Calendar* (Delhi: The Delhi Parsi Anjuman, 1996).

Nanavutty, Piloo, *The Parsis* (reprint, New Delhi: The Delhi Parsi Anjuman, 1992).

Nanavutty, Piloo, trans. and commentary, *The Gathas of Zarathushtra* (Ahmedabad: Mapin Publishing, 1999).

Nanavutty, Piloo, *Zarathushtra* (New Delhi: NCERT, 1968).

Nandakumar, Prema, *Poems of Subramania Bharati* (New Delhi: Sahitya Akademi, 1977).

Nicholson, Reynold A., trans., *The Kashf-al-Mahjub: The Oldest Persian Treatise on Sufism* (1911, reprint, London: Theosophical Publishing House, 1976).

Niyogi, Puspa, *Buddhist Divinities* (New Delhi: Munshiram Manoharlal, 2001).

Nizami, K.A., *Akbar and Religion* (Delhi: DK Printworld, 1989).

Nizami, K.A., *Some Aspects of Religion and Politics in India during the Thirteenth Century* (1961; reprint, Delhi: Idarah-I Adabiyat-I Delli, 1978).

Nizami, K.A., *The Life and Times of Farid-ud-din Ganj- i-Shakar* (1955; reprint, Aligarh: 1973).

O'Flaherty, Wendy Doniger, *Hindu Myths* (Harmondsworth: Penguin Books, 1975).

Oddie, J.A., ed., *Religion in South Asia: Religious Conversion and Revival Movements* (1977; 2nd edn., New Delhi: Manohar, 1991).

Padmanabhan, A., *Story of Eight Saint Reformers* (New Delhi, Publications Division, 1993).

Pagels, Elaine, *The Gnostic Gospels* (New York: Vintage Books, 1989).

Pandey, R., *Hindu Samskaras* (reprint, Delhi: Motilal Banarsidass, 1994).

Pangborn, Cyrus R., *Zoroastrianism: A Beleaguered Faith* (New Delhi: Vikas, 1982).

Pargiter, F.E., trans., *Markandeya Purana* (Calcutta: The Asiatic Society, 1904; reprint, Delhi: Indological Bookhouse, 1969).

Prasad, R.C., ed. and trans., *Tulasidasa's Shriramacharitamanasa* (Delhi: Motilal Banarsidass, 1990).

Qureshi, I.H., *The Muslim Community of the Indo-Pakistan Subcontinent* (The Hague, 1962).

Radhakrishnan, S., *Indian Philosophy*, 2 vols (New Delhi: Oxford University Press, 1999).

Raghavan, V. ed., *Ramayana, Mahabharata and Bhagavata Writers* (reprint, New Delhi: Publications Division, 1990).

Rahman, Fazlur, *Islam* (2nd edn., Chicago: University of Chicago Press, 1979).

Rajagopalan, S., *Old Goa* (New Delhi: Archaeological Survey of India, 1987).

Ramanujan, A.K., trans., *Speaking of Siva* (Harmondsworth: Penguin Books, 1973).

Ramesan, N., *Temples and Legends of Andhra Pradesh* (Bombay: Bharatiya Vidya Bhavan, 1988).

Randhir, G.S., *Sikh Shrines in India* (New Delhi: Publications Division, 1990).

Rao, T.A.G., *Elements of Hindu Iconography*, 2 vols (Madras, 1914, reprint, Delhi: Motilal Banarsidass, 1985).

Ratnagar, S., *Understanding Harappa: Civilization in the Greater Indus Valley* (New Delhi: Tulika, 2001).

Ray, N., *Mauryan and Sunga Art* (2nd edn., Calcutta, 1965).

Raychaudhuri, H., *Political History of Ancient India* (Calcutta: University of Calcutta, 1972).

Renou, Louis, ed., *Hinduism* (New York: George Braziller, 1962).

Renou, Louis, *Religions of Ancient India* (1953; reprint, New York: Schocken Books, 1968).

Rhys Davids, T.W., and C.A F. Rhys Davids, *Dialogues of the Buddha* (1899; reprint, London: Pali Text Society, 1957).

Rhys Davids, T.W., *Buddhism, Its History and Literature* (1909, new edn., 1926; reprint, New Delhi: Vedam Books, 2000).

Rhys Davids, T.W., *Buddhist India* (1903; reprint, Delhi: Motilal Banarsidass, 1997).

Rhys Davids, T.W., trans., *Milinda Panho* (Oxford, 1890-94).

Richards, John F., *The New Cambridge History of India: The Mughal Empire* (New Delhi: Foundation Books, 1993).

Richman, Paula, ed., *Many Ramayanas: The Diversity of a Narrative Tradition in South Asia* (Berkeley: University of California Press, 1991).

Rizvi, S.A.A., *A History of Sufism in India*, 2 vols (New Delhi: Munshiram Manoharlal, 2002).

Rizvi, S.A.A., *Muslim Revivalist Movements in Northern India in the Sixteenth and Seventeenth Centuries* (Agra: Agra University, 1965).

Rizvi, S.A.A., *Religious and Intellectual History of the Muslims in Akbar's Reign* (New Delhi: Munshiram Manoharlal, 1975).

Rizvi, S.A.A., *The Wonder That was India*, vol II (reprint, New Delhi: Rupa & Co, 1993).

Rosenberg, Donna, *World Mythology* (Lincolnwood, Illinois: NTC Publishing Group, 1994).

Rosenfield, J. M., *The Dynastic Arts of the Kushans* (Berkeley/ Los Angeles: University of California, 1967).

Rosenthal, Erwin I.J., *Political Thought in Medieval Islam* (Cambridge: Cambridge University Press, 1962).

Roy Choudhury, P.C., *Temples and Legends of Himachal Pradesh* (Bombay: Bharatiya Vidya Bhavan, 1981).

Roy Choudhury, P.C., *Temples and Legends of Bihar* (Bombay: Bharatiya Vidya Bhavan, 1988).

Roy, Asim, *The Islamic Syncretistic Tradition in Bengal* (Princeton: Princeton University Press, 1983).

Roy, P.C., and K.M. Ganguli, trans., *Mahabharata*, 12 vols (1904-25; reprint, Delhi: Motilal Banarsidass, 1963).

Sankalia, H.D., *Ramayana: Myth or Reality?* (New Delhi: People's Publishing House, 1973).

Sanyal, Usha, *Devotional Islam and Politics in British India: Ahmad Riza Khan Barelwi and his Movement, 1870-1920* (New Delhi: Oxford University Press, 1996).

Sarkar, H., and S.P. Nainar, *Amaravati* (New Delhi: Archaeological Survey of India, 1992).

Sarkar, H., *Monuments of Kerala* (New Delhi: Archaeological Survey of India, 1992).

Sarna, Navtej, *The Book of Nanak* (New Delhi, Penguin Viking, 2003).

Sastri, K.A.N., *A History of South India* (4th edn., Madras: Oxford University Press, 1975).

Sastri, K.A.N., *Development of Religion in South India* (New Delhi: Munshiram Manoharlal, 1992).

Schimmel, Annemarie, *Islam in the Indian Subcontinent* (Leiden: E.J. Brill, 1980).

Scholem, Gershom, trans. Ralph Manheim, *On the Kabbalah and Its Symbolism* (New York: Schocken Books, 1965).

Shah, U.P., 'Beginnings of Jaina Iconography', *Bulletin of Museums and Archaeology*, IX (June 1972), pp. 1 ff.

Shah, U.P., 'Yaksha Worship in Early Jaina Literature', *Journal of Oriental Institute Baroda*, III, Pts I-IV (1954), pp. 94 ff.

Sharif, M.M., ed., *A History of Muslim Philosophy*, 2 vol (Wiesbaden: Harrassowitz, 1963-66); (also available online at www. muslimphilosophy.com).

Sharma, Krishna, *Bhakti and the Bhakti Movement: A New Perspective* (New Delhi: Munshiram Manoharlal, 2000).

Sharma, R.C., 'Pre-Kaniska Buddhist Iconography at Mathura', *Bulletin of Museums and Archaeology*, V-VI (June-Dec 1970), pp. 16 ff.

Sharma, R.S., *India's Ancient Past* (New Delhi: Oxford University Press, 2005).

Shastri, J.L., and G. P. Bhatt, ed., *Ancient Indian Tradition and Mythology*, [Puranas with text and translation; vol 1-4, J.L. Sastri, trans., *Siva Purana*; vol. 5-6, J.L. Shastri, trans., *Linga Purana*; vol 7-11, G.V. Tagore, trans., *Bhagavata Purana*; vols 12-14, J.L. Shastri, trans., *Garuda Purana*; vols 15-19, G.V. Tagore, trans., *Narada Purana*; vols 20-21, trans., G.V. Tagore, *Kurma Purana*; vols 22-26, trans., G.V. Tagore, *Brahmanda Purana*; vols 27-30, trans., N. Gangadharan, *Agni Purana*; vols 31-32, trans. N. Venkitasubramania Iyer, *Varaha Purana*; vols 33-36, trans. J.L. Shastri, *Brahma Purana*; vols 37-38, trans. G.V. Tagore, *Vayu Purana*; vols. 39-48, trans., N.A. Deshpande, *Padma Purana*; vols 49-68, trans., G.V. Tagore, *Skanda Purana*] (Delhi: Motilal Banarsidass, 1999 onwards).

Shivkumar, Muni, *The Doctrine of Liberation in Indian Religion: with special reference to Jainism* (New Delhi: Munshiram Manoharlal, 2000).

Shri Sai Baba, *Focus on the Enlightened Path* (Nagpur: Sai Publications, n.d.).

Shukla, D.N., *Vastu-Sastra*, 2 vols (New Delhi: Munshiram Manoharlal, 1998, 2003)

Shulman, David D., *Tamil Temple Myths: Sacrifice and Divine Marriage in the South Indian Saiva Tradition* (Princeton: Princeton University Press, 1980).

Singh, Dharm Vir, *Hinduism: An Introduction* (Jaipur: Travel Wheels, 1991).

Singh, Gopal, *Guru Gobind Singh* (New Delhi, National Book Trust, 1996).

Singh, Gopal, *History of the Sikh People, 1469-1978* (New Delhi: World Sikh University Press, 1979).

Singh, Gopal, *The Sikhs: Their History, Religion, Culture, Ceremonies and Literature* (Bombay: Popular Prakashan, 1970).

Singh, Gopal, trans., *Guru Granth Sahib*, 4 vols (New Delhi: World Sikh University Press, 1979).

Singh, Harbans, *The Heritage of the Sikhs* (New Delhi: Manohar, 1999).

Singh, Khushwant, *The Sikhs* (1952; reprint, New Delhi. Harper Collins, 2003).

Singh, Mohan , *Kabir and the Bhakti Movement* (Lahore, 1934).

Singh, Trilochan, et. al., trans., *The Sacred Writings of the Sikhs* (Orient Longman and UNESCO, 2000).

Sinh, Pancham, text and trans.,*The Hatha Yoga Pradipika* (New Delhi: Munshiram Manoharlal, 2002).

Sircar, D.C., ed., *The Bharat War and Puranic Genealogies* (Calcutta: University of Calcutta, 1969).

Sivananda, Sri Swami, *Lives of Saints* (Shivananadanagar, Divine Life Society, 2002).

Sivaramamurti, C., *Mahabalipuram* (New Delhi: Archaeological Survey of India, 1992).

Sivaramamurti, C., *The Chola Temples* (New Delhi: Archaeological Survey of India, 1978).

Smith, V.A., *The Jaina Stupa and Other Antiquities of Mathura* (Allahabad, 1901).

Snellgrove, David, *Indo-Tibetan Buddhism: Indian Buddhists and Their Tibetan Successors*, 2 vols (1987; reprint, Boston: Shambhala Publications, 2003).

Sontheimer, Gunther Dietz and Hermann Kulke, ed., *Hinduism Reconsidered* (New Delhi: Manohar, 2001).

Sorensen, S., *Index to the Names in the Mahabharata* (Delhi: Motilal Banarsidass, 1963).

Soundara Rajan, K.V., *Ahmadabad* (New Delhi: Archaeological Survey of India, 1992).

Soundara Rajan, K.V., *Indian Temple Styles* (New Delhi: Munshiram Manoharlal, 1972).

Spencer, Sidney, *Mysticism in World Religion* (Baltimore: Penguin Books, 1963).

Srimad Valmiki Ramayana (with Sanskrit text and Eng trans.) 3 vols (4th edn., Gorakhpur: Gita Press, 1995).

Srinivasan, K.R., *Temples of South India* (New Delhi: National Book Trust, 1972).

Srivastava, V.N., and Misra, S., 'Inventory of Mathura Museum Sculptures Since 1939 up to date', *Bulletin of Museums and Archaeology*, XI–XII (June-Dec 1973), pp. 45 ff.

Stein, R.A., trans., J.E. Stapleton Driver, *Tibetan Civilization* (originally in French, 1962; Stanford: Stanford University Press, 1972).

Stevenson, Sinclair, *The Heart of Jainism* (New Delhi: Munshiram Manoharlal, 1995).

Subhan, J.A., *Sufism, Its Saints and Shrines: An Introduction to Sufism with Special references to India* (1939; 2nd edn, reprint, Lucknow: The Lucknow Publishing House, 1960).

Subramanian, V.K., text and trans., *Saundaryalahari* (Delhi: Motilal Banarsidass, 1977).

Sukthankar, V.S. et al., ed., *Mahabharata* Critical Edition, 18 vols (Poona: Bhandarkar Oriental Research Institute, 1933).

Tagore, Rabindranath, *Gitanjali* (New Delhi: Rupa, 2002).

Takakusu, J., *The Essentials of Buddhist Philosophy*, (Honolulu: University of Hawaii Press, 1947).

Tara Chand, *Influence of Islam on Indian Culture* (1922; reprint, Allhabad: Indian Press, 1946). Taraporewala, I. J.S., *The Religion of Zarathushtra* (Bombay: B.I. Taraporewala, 1979).

Temples of India (reprint, New Delhi: Publications Division, 1990).

Temples of South India (reprint, New Delhi: Publications Division, 1992).

Thapar, R., *Asoka and the Decline of the Mauryas* (2nd revised ed., London: Oxford University Press, 1974).

Thapar, R., ed., *Recent Perspectives of Early Indian History* (Bombay: Popular Prakashan, 1995).

Thapar, R., *The Penguin History of Early India* (New Delhi: Penguin Books India, 2003).

The Brhadaranyaka Upanisad, trans. and commentary (Madras: Sri Ramakrishna Math, 1951).

The Cultural Heritage of India, 5 vols (1937; 2nd edn, Calcutta: The Ramakrishna Mission, 1953-58).

The Greatness of Sringeri (Bombay: Tattvaloka, 1991).

Thomas, P., *Churches in India* (reprint, New Delhi: Publications Division, 1990).

Thompson, Judith and Paul Heelas, *The Way of the Heart: The Rajneesh Movement* (Wellingborough, Northamptonshire: The Aquarian Press, 1986).

Tillich, Paul, *A History of Christian Thought from Its Judaic and Hellenistic Origins to Existentialism* (New York:Touchstone Books, 1972).

Titus, Murray T., *Islam in India and Pakistan* (New Delhi: Munshiram Manoharlal, 2005).

Trimingham, J. Spencer, *The Sufi Orders in Islam* (Oxford: Clarendon Press, 1971).

Troisi, J., *Tribal Religion: Religious Beliefs and Practices Among the Santals* (New Delhi: Manohar, 2000).

Troll, Christian W., ed., *Islam in India, Studies and Commentaries,* vol 1 (New Delhi: Vikas Publishing House, 1982).

Troll, Christian W., ed., *Muslim Shrines in India* (New Delhi: Oxford University Press, 1989).

Troll, Christian W., *Sayyid Ahmad Khan, A Re-interpretation of Muslim Theology* (Delhi: Vikas Publishing House, 1978).

Tucci, G., trans. G. Samuel, *The Religions of Tibet* (in German, 1970; Berkely, California: University of California Press, 1980).

Tuckett, C.M., *Reading the New Testament: Methods of Interpretation* (London: SPCK, 1987).

Vaidya, P.L., *Ramayana* Critical edn. (Baroda: Oriental Institute Baroda, 1962).

Valmiki and Vyasa (New Delhi: Publications Division, 1992).

Varma, Pavan K., *The Book of Krishna* (New Delhi: Penguin Viking, 2001).

Vaudeville, C., *Kabir* (Oxford: Clarendon Press, 1974).

Venkatesananda, Swami, *Yoga Sutras of Patanjali* (2nd edn., Shivanandanagar: The Divine Life Society, 2001).

Vermes, G., *The Dead Sea Scrolls in English* (2nd edn., Harmondsworth: Penguin, 1975).

Vishnudevananda, Swami, *Meditation and Mantras* (Delhi: Motilal Banarsidass, 1978).

Vivekananda, Swami, *Bhakti Yoga* (Calcutta: Advaita Ashram, 1983).

Vivekananda, Swami, *Raja Yoga* (Calcutta: Advaita Ashram, 1978).

Wagle, N.N., *Society at the Time of the Buddha* (Bombay: Popular Prakashan, 1966).

Ward, C.H.S., *Buddhism, vol 1.—Hinayana; vol. 2—Mahayana* (London: The Epworth Press, 1947, 1952).

Warder, A.K., *Indian Buddhism* (2nd rev edn., New Delhi: Motilal Banarsidass, 1980).

Watters, Thomas, *On Yuan Chwang's Travels in India* (2nd Indian edn., New Delhi: Munshiram Manoharlal, 1973).

Wayman, Alex, *The Buddhist Tantras: Light on Indo-Tibetan Esoterism* (1973; reprint, Delhi: Motilal Banarsidass, 1990).

Werner, Karel, ed., *Love Divine: Studies in Bhakti and Devotional Mysticism* (New Delhi: Manohar, 1993).

White, David G., *The Alchemical Body: Siddha Traditions in Medieval India* (New Delhi: Munshiram Manoharlal, 2004).

Williams, J.A., ed., *Islam* (New York: George Braziller, 1962).

Williams, Paul, *Mahayana Buddhism: The Doctrinal Foundation* (London: Routledge, 1989).

Winternitz, Maurice, *History of Indian Literature,* vol 1-2 (3rd edn., New Delhi: Munshiram Manoharlal, 1991).

Woodroffe, John, *The Serpent Power* (3rd edn, reprint, Madras: Ganesh & Co, 1992).

Woodroffe, John, *The Word as Power* (reprint, Madras: Ganesh & Co, 2001).

Yadava, B.N.S., *Society and Culture in Northern India in the Twelfth Century* (Allahabad: Central Book Depot, 1973).

Yarshater, E., ed., *Encyclopaedia Iranica* (Costa Mesa, California: Mazda Publishers, 1982 onwards, online at www.encyclopediairanica.com ; has information on Zoroastrianism and Islam).

Yogananda, Paramahansa, *Autobiography of a Yogi* (Mumbai: Jaico, 1998).

Zaehner, R.C., ed., *The Hutchinson Encyclopedia of Living Faiths* (4th edn., Oxford: Helicon, 1994).

Zaehner, R.C., *Hindu and Muslim Mysticism* (London: University of London, The Athlone Press, 1960).

Zaehner, R.C., *Hinduism* (2nd edn., Oxford: Oxford University Press, 1966).

Zaehner, R.C., *Teachings of the Magi* (London: Allen and Unwin, 1956).

Zaehner, R.C., *The Dawn and Twilight of Zoroastrianism* (London: Weidenfeld, 1961).

Websites

www.akshardham.com (Swaminarayan)

www.al-islam.org (articles on several topics in Islam, online sources).

www.allaboutsikhs.com

www.apsahaj.org (Sahaj Yoga, Nirmala Devi).

www.arabworld.nitle.org (information and Bibliography on Islam and Islamic history)

www.avesta.org (Zoroastrian texts)

www.bahai-library.com (a comprehensive source for books, extracts, and Bahai scriptures)

www.bahai.org

www.banglapedia.org (national encyclopedia of Bangladesh)

www.baptistindia.org

www.beasyouare.info (Ramanna Maharshi)

www.beliefnet.org

www.bishnoi.org

www.buddhist-pilgrimage.com

www.buddhist-temples.com

www.catholocity.com

www.chinmayamission.org

www.earlychristianwritings.com (Gnosticism)

www.fordham.edu/halsall/islam (Internet Islamic history sourcebook: A comprehensive source for Islam on the Internet).

www.indianchristianity.com

www.indianchristianity.org

www.jainism.org

www.jainworld.org

www.jkrishnamurti.org

www.kagyuoffice.org

www.karmapa.org

www.madurai.com (Meenakshi Temple)

www.neepco.com (Meghalaya)

www.newadvent.org/cathen (catholic encyclopedia)

www.questia.com

www.realization.org (Sri Nisargadatta Maharaj)

www.rickross.com (website of Rick A. Ross Institute for the study of destructive cults, controversial groups and movements)

www.sabarimala.org (Sabarimala, Ayyappa)

www.saibaba.org (Shirdi)

www.sakya.org

www.sathysai.org (Sathya Sai Baba)

www.shirdi.org

www.sikhism.com

www.templenet.com (a comprehensive source on temples of India, particularly of south India; includes architecture, rituals, myths and legends, beliefs and practices).

www.tibet.com

www.tibet.net

www.webindia123.com

Personal Communication

Afeefa Banu of Hyderabad University on some aspects of Islam

Simon Porter of Penncroft, England on the House Church movement